THE MODERN ENCYCLOPEDIA
OF BASKETBALL

The Modern Encyclopedia of Basketball

SECOND REVISED EDITION

Edited by Zander Hollander

An Associated Features Book

DOLPHIN BOOKS
DOUBLEDAY & COMPANY, INC.
GARDEN CITY, NEW YORK
1979

Photo Credits: Jim Anderson, 393; Paul Bereswill, 380; Lawrence Berman, 381; Cincinnati Royals, 307; Colorado State University, 134 (bottom right); Dutch Dehnert collection, 273 (right), 277; Detroit Pistons, 318; Duke University, 117; Malcolm Emmons, 69, 72, 78, 80, 81, 88, 90, 94, 96, 97, 99, 102, 111, 113, 120, 122, 126, 130, 137 (bottom), 139 (right), 140 (left and right), 310, 312, 317, 320 (left and right), 324, 326, 328, 330, 344, 348, 373, 385, 395, 396, 397, 407, 409; Eddie Gottlieb collection, 301; Hall of Fame, 4, 6 (top), 7, 270, 278, 434; Indiana University, 138 (upper right); Steve Jenner, 346; George Kaftan collection, 35 (top); George Kalinsky, 323, 342, 410; Kentucky State College, 139 (bottom); Bob Kurland collection, 265; Los Angeles Lakers, 314; Joe Lapchick collection, 273 (right), 274 (left and right), 275, 276; Richard Lee, 227; Madison Square Garden, 14 (bottom), 17, 135 (top), 136 (right), 138 (top left), 325, 414; Marquette University, 138 (bottom right); Herman Masin collection, 134 (top left and bottom left), 135 (bottom right), 137 (right), 221 (right), 413; Eileen Miller, 226; Milwaukee Bucks, 336; National Basketball Association, 316 (right), 337, 349; New York Knickerbockers, 221 (top left); Darryl Norenberg, 415; North Carolina State University, 128; Notre Dame University, 137 (upper left); Ohio University, 22; Oklahoma A&M University, 118; Old Dominion, 228; Philadelphia 76ers, 220 (left), 316 (left); Power Memorial High School, 232; Princeton University, 76; Dick Raphael, 402; Mitchell Reibel, 351, 400; St. Francis University (Pa.), 127; St. Louis Hawks, 221 (bottom left); Seattle SuperSonics, 220 (right); Seton Hall University, 114; Barton Silverman, 327; Stan Stutz collection, 23; UCLA, 19 (bottom), 74, 132; University of Cincinnati, 65 (bottom), 124; University of Kentucky, 105; University of Pittsburgh, 135 (left); University of San Francisco, 141; UPI, 7 (bottom), 8, 13, 14 (top), 16, 18, 19 (top), 21, 25 (top and bottom), 26, 27, 28, 29, 30, 31, 32 (top and bottom), 33, 35 (bottom), 37, 38, 39, 41, 44, 46, 48, 51, 54, 56, 59, 61, 63, 67, 71, 84, 85, 92, 106, 108, 112, 115, 119, 121, 122, 123, 125, 129, 133, 136 (left), 226, 280, 282, 284, 285, 286, 288, 289, 291, 293, 295, 296, 298, 300, 302, 304, 306, 308, 313, 322, 331, 333, 334, 339, 353, 357, 358, 371, 375, 376, 378, 383, 394, 398, 401, 403, 404, 406, 408, 412, 424 (left and right), 429; West Virginia University, 65 (top).

A Dolphin Book
Doubleday & Company, Inc.
ISBN: 0-385-14381-8
Library of Congress Catalog Card Number 78–22636
Copyright © 1969, 1973, 1979 by Associated Features Inc.
All Rights Reserved
Printed in the United States of America

Library of Congress Cataloging in Publication Data

Hollander, Zander.
    The modern encyclopedia of basketball.

    "An Associated features book."
    Includes index.
    1. Basketball—Dictionaries. I. Title.
GV885.H587   1979   796.32'3'0973

To those for whom basketball has meant a way out

Contents

Jerry Lucas • Hank Luisetti • Pete Maravich • Andy Phillip •
Oscar Robertson • Guy Rodgers • Cazzie Russell • Maurice Stokes
• David Thompson • Ernie Vandeweghe • Jimmy Walker •
Bill Walton

APPENDICES

Foreword

At last basketball has a definitive work covering the broad spectrum of one of the world's most popular sports. THE MODERN ENCYCLOPEDIA OF BASKETBALL is exactly what it says it is. Although concentrating on the modern era which began in the mid-1930s with the game's expansion on every level—from college and professional to scholastic and playground—the encyclopedia extends back to the time of Dr. James A. Naismith, founding father of the sport in 1891.

The editor, Zander Hollander, has combined the human story of the game—its players, its teams, its coaches—with an awesome array of vital statistics and dramatic, historic photographs.

Mr. Hollander and his able corps of contributors have produced a unique book that is invaluable to fans and scholars alike. It fills a void that we have long been conscious of in basketball.

WALTER KENNEDY
Commissioner (1963–75)
National Basketball Association

Acknowledgments

Doc Naismith first envisioned basketball as a game in which any number could play. The editor of THE MODERN ENCYCLOPEDIA OF BASKETBALL proceeded along the same lines, although all was not play; many would participate in the challenging task of researching, assembling, writing, rewriting and copyreading the various sections of the manuscript.

The editor wishes to thank Sandy Padwe of *Sports Illustrated,* formerly of the Philadelphia *Inquirer* and *Newsday,* for starting the ball rolling. He suggested the encyclopedia in the first place.

Also a salute of the highest order to David Schulz, who contributed in every way to the original edition and to the first revision, and to two others who were indispensable to the project: Bruce Weber of Scholastic Magazines and David Rosen, formerly of the Columbia *Daily Spectator.*

Also to Original Celtics Dutch Dehnert and the late Joe Lapchick, and Mrs. Everett B. Morris, widow of the *New York Herald Tribune* basketball and yachting expert, for making available their scrapbooks and libraries.

Also to contributing writers Sandy Padwe (The Greatest Pros); Steve Jacobson of Long Island's *Newsday* (The Scandal); Ira Berkow of Newspaper Enterprise Association (The Officials); Phil Pepe of the New York *Daily News* (The Coaches), and Maury Allen of the *New York Post.*

An encyclopedia must depend in part on what has been written before—in newspapers, magazines, books. Among the helpful books were The Cavalcade of Basketball by Alexander M. Weyand, the Converse Basketball Yearbooks, the NCAA's Official Basketball Guides, the official NBA Guides and Ronald's Encyclopedia of Basketball by William G. Mokray.

For their co-operation, the editor also thanks the late Walter Kennedy, Commissioner of the National Basketball Association, and his successor, Lawrence O'Brien; Lee Williams of the Basketball Hall of Fame; Jack Waters and his NCAA staff; Abe Goteiner of the National Association of Intercollegiate Athletics; Brice Durbin and Dave Arnold of the National Federation of State High School Athletic Associations; Martin Weiss of the Amateur Athletic Union; Bob Paul of the United States Olympic Committee; Wallace Lord of the Converse Rubber Company; Eddie Gottlieb, Philadelphia's basketball pioneer; Nick Curran and Haskell Cohen, former NBA publicists, and Mike Recht, former ABA publicist.

Also the late Joe Val, sports editor of the New York *World-Telegram;* John Nucatola, former supervisor of officials for the NBA; Stuart Paxton of the International Association of Approved Basketball Officials; Herman Masin of *Scholastic Coach;* Leonard Koppett, formerly of the *New York Times;* Bus Saidt of the Trenton *Times;* Ray Saul of the Hazleton *Standard-Speaker;* Jim Wergeles of Madison Square Garden; Bill Esposito of St. John's University; Jay Simon, formerly of the University of Kansas, and all of the college sports information directors and pro publicists who supplied and confirmed so much of the material in the encyclopedia.

Also Pete Alfano of *Newsday* and Reid Grosky of the *New York Times,* who wrote much of the new material in the 1979 edition of the encyclopedia; Jim Poris, Lee Stowbridge, Bill Himmelman, Bill Wilson, Sid Borgia, Edward Steitz, Frank Hellriegel, Frank Kelly, Matt Winick, Bill Falk, Steve Guback, Howard Blatt, Seymour Siwoff, George Durham, Clifford Fagan, Norm Drucker, Jules Winn, Steve Boda, Aaron Elson, Eric Compton, Richard Schafer and Gail Torres.

It is impossible to credit everyone who contributed a fact or a suggestion, but three others who cannot be anonymous are Connie Maroselli of the NBA, for help in the bureau of missing persons and missing statistics; Annette Katz Weber, for peerless and tireless typing, and Phyllis Hollander of Associated Features, for faith and all-around performance.

Introduction

Landmarks in basketball, as in anything, often depend on one's point of view. When a New York sportswriter, Ned Irish, ripped his pants climbing through the window of a crowded college gym in the early 1930s, it meant more than just another mending job for Ned's tailor. Irish figured if basketball was so popular that even a working reporter had to worm his way into a game, it deserved a bigger, more glamorous setting. The torn trousers led to Irish's hiring of a hall, Madison Square Garden, and thus inspired the modern era of college basketball.

When World War II ended in 1945, many basketball players—their best years behind them—embarked on new careers. The younger stars were more fortunate. Opportunity beckoned in the form of what was to become the major league in professional basketball—the National Basketball Association.

When City College of New York achieved an unprecedented grand slam of the National Invitation Tournament and the National Collegiate championship in 1950, this was a basketball landmark, indeed. But when players from CCNY's Cinderella team and a number of other colleges were found guilty of "shaving points," the resulting scandal established another type of landmark: the end of the age of innocence.

The modern era of basketball has witnessed such milestones as a 100-point game by Wilt Chamberlain; the signing of the first black head coach in any league, Boston's Bill Russell in the NBA; an estimated $1.4 million contract for Lew Alcindor (who became Kareem Abdul-Jabbar), the UCLA star who signed to play professionally with the Milwaukee Bucks; UCLA's 88-game winning streak and seven consecutive NCAA championships, and the merger of the NBA and ABA.

Call them landmarks, milestones, turning points or simply evolution. They constitute an integral part of the history that Dr. James A. Naismith began with a peach basket and a soccer ball in 1891.

The early years of the game have been covered in an assortment of books. But it has been in the last 45 years—starting with the introduction of intersectional collegiate play at New York's Madison Square Garden and on into the television age—that basketball has experienced its greatest growth.

Fans, players, sportswriters and coaches have expressed the need for a single book that would accent the moderns, yet tell it all from the beginning: A book that would not depend alone on statistics. A book that would have feature stories on the stars, the teams, the coaches, the scandal, the referees. A book that would carry year-by-year roundups of the major colleges and the pros, and all-time records. A book that would also cover women collegians, junior colleges, high schools, the Olympics and the AAU.

A book that would contain a unique section—an all-time pro-player register, comprising the season and career records of every player (more than 1,800) in NBA and ABA history.

To attain these objectives, I enlisted the aid of a number of sportswriters as contributors, and the research took me to such diverse settings as the Basketball Hall of Fame in Springfield, Massachusetts; the Yonkers, New York, attic of Original Celtic and Hall of Fame member Joe Lapchick, and to Trenton, New Jersey, where a police magistrate testified that his uncle played in the first professional game.

More than any other figure in the sport, the late Joe Lapchick provided me with the opinion and guidance that can only come from one who devoted more than a half-century to basketball as player and coach.

My own personal landmarks in basketball are not likely to be found anywhere but here. As a boy in the early 1930s in Edgemere, New York, I used to set local backyard records for consecutive layups on a shaky home-made basket. I earned my high school letter as the center (6-1) at Far Rockaway High and a varsity "Q" at Queens College in Flushing, New York. As a sportswriter for the late *New York World-Telegram,* I broke in by covering high school quintupleheaders at the Fiftieth Street Madison Square Garden. I was there on assignment during basketball's blackest days in the early '50s. The sport came back. I never left it.

As it happened, this was all part of my preparation for THE MODERN ENCYCLOPEDIA OF BASKETBALL.

ZANDER HOLLANDER
Millerton, New York

The Early Years

1

The Invention

The origins of most sports are lost in time. Either they evolved from some everyday activity like running or jumping and needed only to have the rules formalized, or they traced their beginnings to some earlier, less organized game. But not basketball. The birth of this game can be pinpointed with total accuracy.

The time was autumn, 1891, the place was Springfield, Massachusetts, and the inventor was Dr. James Naismith. At the time he was 30 years old. He had been born in Almonte, Ontario, and had attended McGill University in Canada and then spent three years studying for the ministry before deciding that his real interests were in physical education.

He enrolled in the International Young Men's Christian Association Training School (today Springfield College) in Springfield. The school trained general secretaries and physical education instructors for YMCAs throughout the country. Naismith soon joined the faculty as a physical education instructor.

Springfield's physical education program included an hour of daily activity. In the fall the students played football outdoors. And in the spring they went outdoors again to play baseball. But for their exercise between seasons they had to move indoors.

The indoor program for the potential YMCA general secretaries included marching and calisthenics, and the students could see no particular value in those exercises. They protested and were assigned a new instructor, who substituted apparatus work for the calisthenics and marching. But the class grew even more hostile toward physical activity, and this instructor gave up too.

Finally Dr. Luther S. Gulick, the head of the physical education department, assigned Naismith the job of doing something about the incorrigible class.

His first move was to abandon all the exercises and calisthenics and to concentrate on games. But both he and the class found all the popular indoor games both boring and tiring. So Naismith set out to develop some new indoor game. He first thought of adapting one of the popular outdoor games to indoor play.

He tried rugby, but the rough tackling made the game impractical on a hard gym floor. Then he tried soccer, but in the confined area available, many players were bruised and many windows broken by hard

The inventor, Dr. James Naismith, in the early 1890s

shots. Lacrosse also failed as the players frequently beat each other with their sticks.

Naismith soon realized that no existing game was suitable for his purposes and that he would have to invent some sort of new game.

He decided to employ a ball, and settled on a large ball because no intermediate equipment like a bat, stick or racket was necessary to manipulate it. He realized that if the players couldn't run with the ball, there would be no need for rough tackling.

He concluded that by using an elevated goal, he would force the players to shoot on an arc, making accuracy more important than brute strength and eliminating many of the bruises resulting from hard shots.

Then he sat down and wrote out the first set of rules for the new game. He had his secretary type the "Thirteen Rules" and posted them on the bulletin board in the gymnasium.

Because the janitor in the gym did not have the boxes that Naismith envisioned as goals, he was forced to substitute a pair of peach baskets. The height of ten feet for the baskets was established because that was the height of a balcony at each end of the gym to which the baskets were attached.

Naismith announced to the class that if this game was a failure, he was finished with his experiments. But from its first moments of existence, basketball was a success.

Naismith envisioned the new sport as a mass game, in which any number of players could participate. The class had eighteen members, so the first game, played in mid-December, 1891, had nine men on a side. They used an "Association football" (soccer ball).

Over the Christmas vacation of that year, several members of the class introduced the game in their home towns. But none of them had copies of the rules and each played the game as he rather imperfectly remembered it. Not until January, 1892, when the students returned from their vacations, did the school paper publish the rules of the new game.

These were Naismith's original 13 rules:

1. The ball may be thrown in any direction with one or both hands.

2. The ball may be batted in any direction with one or both hands (never with the fist).

3. A player cannot run with the ball. The player must throw it from the spot on which he catches it; allowance to be made for a man who catches the ball when running at a good speed.

4. The ball must be held in or between the hands; the arms or body must not be used for holding it.

5. No shouldering, holding, pushing, tripping or striking, in any way the person of an opponent shall be allowed; the first infringement of this rule by any person shall count as a foul, the second shall disqualify him until the next goal is made; or, if there was evident intent to injure the person for the whole of the game, no substitute shall be allowed.

6. A foul is striking at the ball with the fist, violation of Rules 3, 4, and such as described in Rule 5.

7. If either side makes three consecutive fouls, it shall count a goal for the opponents. (Consecutive means without the opponents in the meantime making a foul.)

8. A goal shall be made when the ball is thrown or batted from the ground into the basket and stays there, providing those defending the goal do not touch or disturb the goal. If the ball rests on the edge and the opponent moves the basket, it shall count as a goal.

9. When the ball goes out of bounds, it shall be thrown into the field and played by the person first touching it. In case of a dispute, the umpire shall throw it straight into the field. The thrower-in is allowed five seconds. If he holds it longer, it shall go to the opponent. If any side persists in delaying the game, the umpire shall call a foul on them.

10. The umpire shall be judge of the men and shall note the fouls and notify the referee when three consecutive fouls have been made. He shall have power to disqualify men according to Rule 5.

11. The referee shall be judge of the ball and shall decide when the ball is in play, in bounds, to which side it belongs, and shall keep the time. He shall decide when a goal has been made, and keep account of the goals, with any other duties that are usually performed by a referee.

12. The time shall be two fifteen minute halves, with five minutes rest between.

13. The side making the most goals in that time shall be declared the winners. In case of a draw, the game may, by agreement of the captains, be continued until another goal is made.

2

The Road to Point-a-minute

The game had its rules, but it had no name. One of Dr. Naismith's students suggested it be called Naismith Ball. The modest inventor vetoed the suggestion and settled on Basketball.

The name and the game caught on immediately. In 1892 Naismith organized the first basketball team with nine members from the International Young Men's Christian Association Training School. The first team went on exhibition tour and performed in Albany, Troy and Schenectady, New York, and Providence and Newport, Rhode Island.

The first game between teams from two different organizations took place in Springfield, Massachusetts, in February, 1892. The teams represented the Central and Armory Hill branches of the YMCA and battled to a 2–2 tie. A month later the two teams met again and the Armory Hill team scored a one goal to zero victory.

Girls got involved in basketball almost at the game's beginning. In March, 1892, a match pitted a team of local Springfield girls against a squad of women teachers. Naismith apparently liked what he saw at the game because he married one of the players, Maude Sherman. Vassar and Smith, both

women's colleges, added basketball to their activities in 1892.

In the same year, Amos Alonzo Stagg, who had been a contemporary of Naismith on the faculty at Springfield, introduced the new game at the University of Chicago. The first college to field a men's team was Vanderbilt University, which defeated the Nash-

The game as played in 1892 (from lecture material of Amos Alonzo Stagg)

6

BASKET BALL OUTFITS.

INDOOR BASKET.

The baskets are strong iron hoops, with braided cord netting, arranged to be secured to a gymnasium gallery or wall for indoor use, or on an upright pipe the bottom of which is spiked to be driven into the ground for outdoor use. By means of a cord the ball is easily discharged after a goal is made.

Indoor Goals, per pair,	$15.00
Outdoor Goals, per pair,	30.00
No 10 Association Foot Ball. each,	3.25
American Rubber Foot Ball,	1.25

Prices for Special Portable Baskets for Exhibitions in Halls or low priced outfits given on application

The basket as it appeared in the Rules Book of 1893

ville, Tennessee, YMCA in March 1893. That same month Hamline College in Minneapolis lost to the Minneapolis YMCA, 13–12.

By 1893 YMCA teams had become widespread enough to be organized into leagues, and various sectional champions emerged. Among the early powerhouse teams were the Brooklyn Central YMCA, which was New York champion in 1893, 1894 and 1895, and Trenton, New Jersey. The Chicago West Side team boasted a 6-4 center, the first of basketball's big men. Trenton's stars, Fred Cooper and Albert Bratton, introduced the use of the short pass to get the ball close to the basket.

A YMCA tournament for the "Championship of America" was staged in Brooklyn on April 24, 1896. All but two of the entrants were from New York. In the final, East District defeated Brooklyn Central, 4–0.

But the spread of basketball among the colleges lagged behind the YMCAs. The first game between two colleges took place on February 9, 1895, when the Minnesota State School of Agriculture crushed Ham-

line College, 9–3. The winners immediately claimed the Minnesota championship. The first eastern intercollegiate game matched Haverford and Temple, with Haverford winning, 6–4, on March 23, 1895.

Interest in basketball began to pick up among the colleges. Yale and Minnesota began playing against club teams. Yale faced the University of Pennsylvania on March 20, 1897, in what is regarded as the first modern intercollegiate game played with five men on a team. The Elis won, 32–10.

Yale, probably the nation's strongest team, went on a western tour in 1900, marking the introduction of intersectional play. Columbia, Cornell, Harvard, Princeton and Yale organized the Eastern League in 1901 and Yale won the first championship. In the same year, Dartmouth, Holy Cross, Williams, Amherst, and Trinity formed the New England League.

By 1908 the focus of basketball power had shifted from the East to the Midwest and little Wabash College of Indiana claimed the world championship. Over a

Maude Sherman, first of the ladies to play the game, became Mrs. James Naismith

The Passaic (N.J.) High School "Wonder Fives" won 159 consecutive games

four-year stretch, Wabash won 66 games and lost only three.

During these years the game, although conceived by Dr. Naismith as a non-contact sport, became so rough that efforts were made to legislate against the violence. In 1915, representatives of the Amateur Athletic Union, the International YMCA, and the National Collegiate Athletic Association attempted to formulate a single uniform code of basketball rules.

Whatever the problems of standardization, basketball continued to grow as an attraction. A game between New York University and City College of New York in 1920 drew a crowd of 10,000 to the 22nd Regiment Armory in New York. This was, at the time, the largest crowd ever to see a basketball game. By then basketball had become firmly established in all sections of the country, and each area had its dominant teams. But except for occasional tours by one of the eastern colleges, there was little intersectional play. All debates about the merits of teams from the various sections and possible national championships had to remain unresolved.

One of the greatest problems the game faced in the 1920s was a reduction in the number of personal fouls. A steady parade of players to the free-throw line interfered severely with the flow of the game. The rules committee in 1923 changed such things as running with the ball or double-dribbling from the designation of fouls, which required free throws, to the category of violations, which merely resulted in loss of possession of the ball.

One of the strongest of the college teams in the late 1920s—at least in the East—was St. John's. Coached by James "Buck" Freeman and known as the "Wonder Five," the team compiled a record of 86 victories and eight defeats over a four-year period. Half the losses came in 1927, the first year they played together, so over the next three years the Wonder Five turned in a record of 70–4. Matty Begovich, a 6-5 center, Mac

Kinsbrunner and Max Posnack, forwards, and Rip Gerson and Allie Schuckman, the guards, made up the team. The Wonder Five prided itself on its defensive abilities, and in its senior year the only team which managed to score as many as 30 points against it was the St. John's alumni.

The five players stayed together after college and played as a touring team for two seasons before moving as a unit into the professional ranks. As the Brooklyn Jewels and later the New York Jewels, the team played for many years in the professional American Basketball League.

(The St. John's quintet was not the only so-called Wonder Five of this era. The Passaic, N.J., High School "Wonder Teams" of 1919–1925 won 159 consecutive games.)

Other great teams of the 1920s and early '30s included Kansas, coached by Phog Allen, and California, which won four straight Pacific Coast Conference titles between 1924 and 1927.

The 1930s also marked the introduction of a new style of play. Frank Keaney, coach of Rhode Island State College, developed a system characterized by fast-breaking, long passes upcourt, and plenty of shooting. His Rhode Islanders became known as "point-a-minute" teams. As other schools adopted

The Jewels, made up mostly of the St. John's "Wonder Five" (l. to r.): Allie Schuckman, Mac Kinsbrunner, Rip Gerson, George Slott, Max Posnack, Jack Poliskin, Honey Russell, and Matty Begovich

this style, the move toward higher-scoring, free-wheeling basketball got underway.

But despite some increase in intersectional play, most teams still played the majority of their games against teams from their own region of the country. Experts found it difficult to compare the merits of the outstanding teams from one section with those of another.

3

The Moderns

College basketball entered the modern era on December 29, 1934. That night 16,188 fans watched NYU defeat Notre Dame, 25–18, and Westminster beat St. John's, 37–33, in the first regularly scheduled doubleheader in New York's Madison Square Garden.

From that night on, the Garden became the showplace of college basketball. Specta-

Ned Irish, the "boy promoter" responsible for big-time basketball

tors in unprecedented numbers came to watch New York's strongest teams take on the best from around the nation.

"Garden basketball" was the brainchild of Ned Irish, a 29-year-old "boy promoter." Irish was a sportswriter on the *New York World-Telegram*. At that time, Columbia and Fordham were the only local schools with gyms that could hold more than 1,200 people. With limited seating capacity, few schools could make basketball pay.

The story, never denied by Irish, or his tailor, was that Ned had a personal reason for moving college basketball into bigger quarters. One night Irish was assigned to cover a basketball game in Manhattan College's tiny gym. Fighting his way into the cramped arena through a window, Irish tore his pants. This convinced him that basketball should be made more accessible to the public.

Irish's theory gained support during the winter of 1931. James J. Walker, the Mayor or New York, had asked a group of sportswriters, including Irish, to arrange a college basketball program to raise money for the relief of the unemployed. On December 31, a capacity crowd watched a tripleheader at the Garden involving six New York City

NYU's Willie Rubinstein (4) vies with Notre Dame's John Jordan at the Garden

NYU vs. Notre Dame in first regular doubleheader at Madison Square Garden, December 29, 1934

colleges. Similar shows in the next two winters did just as well.

Impressed by the drawing power of college basketball, Irish tried to match NYU and CCNY, both unbeaten, in the Garden in March, 1934. NYU had been playing to standing-room-only audiences at almost every game, yet had been losing money (about $3,000) on the season. The Garden couldn't come up with a suitable night for the NYU-CCNY battle. Next, Irish proposed a post-season charity game between NYU and Notre Dame, but the Violets turned it down.

Undaunted, Irish, the following season, worked out a rental arrangement with the Garden, scheduling his first doubleheader for December 29; as an indication of its success he quit his newspaper job and moved full-time into basketball promotion. In his first season, eight Garden doubleheaders (two more than originally planned) drew 99,528 enthusiasts. Its introduction at the Garden put the game on a sound financial footing, made it available to a wider audience, and generated a tremendous upsurge in intersectional play.

The large audiences enabled Irish to bring in the best teams in the country. Previously, prohibitive transportation costs had precluded visits from schools in the hinterlands. All this was changed as New York became the basketball capital of the nation. Playing in the Garden became the dream of every college basketball player.

One of the greatest of the early intersectional games in the Garden occurred in December, 1936. Stanford, led by Hank Luisetti, defeated Long Island University, 45–31, ending the Blackbirds' 43-game winning streak. Luisetti's stunning one-handed shots, new to the East, not only proved too much for LIU but also revolutionized shooting.

With the increase in intersectional play, the fans began to follow the national basketball picture. The idea of a college tournament among the best teams was a natural evolvement. A group of New York sportswriters set it up, and the first National Invitation Tournament was played at Madison Square Garden at the end of the regular 1937–38 season.

YEARLY ROUNDUPS

1937–38

A revolutionary change—the elimination of the center jump after each score—resulted in more playing time, higher scores, and patterned offenses and defenses.

Another trend-setting change was the one-handed "Wild West" style of shooting as practiced by Stanford's Hank Luisetti as he led the Indians past Oregon State in the best-of-three playoff series for the Pacific Coast Conference championship. Luisetti finished a four-year career at Stanford in which he scored 1,596 points, a national collegiate record.

The first big national post-season tournament made its debut in Madison Square Garden as the National Invitation Tournament was started by the Metropolitan Bas-

ketball Writers Association in New York. Six teams competed, with Bradley meeting Temple and LIU playing NYU in first round games. Oklahoma A&M and Colorado were given byes.

Temple, which had finished the season with a 23–2 record, was the Eastern Intercollegiate Conference champion. The Owls won the first NIT by downing Colorado, 60–36, as Ed Boyle of Temple led all scorers with 39 points in three games. Another Owl, Don Shields, was named MVP.

All-American football player Byron "Whizzer" White, a Rhodes scholar who nearly two decades later would be named to the Supreme Court of the United States, led Colorado to a tie with Utah for the first championship in the newly formed Big Seven Conference.

Oklahoma A&M took the Missouri Val-

Colorado's Whizzer White (now U. S. Supreme Court Justice White) is at far left in NIT game against Temple

ley Conference crown with a 13–1 record in league play and 25–3 overall. Purdue won the Big Ten title while Arkansas raced to the Southwest Conference championship. Kentucky captured the regular season title in the Southeastern Conference, but Geor-

gia Tech won the league's post-season tournament.

Kansas, led by Fred Pralle, took the Big Six championship, while Dartmouth won in the Ivy League. Strong independents included Notre Dame, with John Moir and

Paul Nowak, and Loyola (Ill.) with Mike Novak.

Marquette was another strong team in the Midwest; Rhode Island, with a 19–2 mark, was acclaimed No. 1 in New England. Lou Boudreau, a future major league baseball player and manager, was playing for Illinois, and Matt Guokas was leading St. Joseph's to a good season.

Stars included Jewell Young, Purdue; Meyer Bloom, Temple; John Townsend, Michigan; Chuck Chuckovitz, Toledo; Ernie Andres, Indiana; Robert Johnson, Georgia Tech; Jack Robbins, Arkansas; Bonnie Graham, Mississippi; Hubert Kirkpatrick, Baylor; Nat Volpe, Manhattan; John O'Brien, Columbia; Martin Rolek, Minnesota, and Bernard Fliegel, CCNY.

NIT Championship

At New York

Temple (60)	FG	FT	Pts.	Colorado (36)	FG	FT	Pts.
Shields	8	0	16	Schwartz	1	5	7
Usilton	1	0	2	Grove	0	0	0
Alfano	0	0	0	Hendrick	2	1	5
Black	7	0	14	Sidwell	0	0	0
Freiberg	1	0	2	Thruman	0	0	0
Bloom	2	2	6	Harvey	3	5	11
McDermott	1	0	2	Willcoxen	1	1	3
Nicol	1	1	3	White	5	0	10
Henderson	0	1	1				
Boyle	7	0	14				
Busha	0	0	0				
Totals	28	4	60		12	12	36

NIT Scores

Quarterfinals: Temple 53, Bradley 40; NYU 39, LIU 37

Semifinals: Temple 54, Oklahoma A&M 44; Colorado 48, NYU 47

Championship: Temple 60, Colorado 36

Consolation: Oklahoma A&M 37, NYU 24

Stanford's Hank Luisetti

1938–39

College basketball's growing popularity was evidenced by the start of the NCAA postseason championship tournament. Oregon met Ohio State in the final at Patten Gymnasium on the campus of Northwestern University in Evanston, Ill., with Oregon winning, 46–43.

The Webfoots of Oregon, with Laddie Gale, Urgel "Slim" Wintermute, Bob Anet, John Dick, and Wally Johansen, won the Pacific Coast Conference championship by downing California in the traditional North-South playoff. Ohio State, led by James Hull, qualified for the NCAA tourney by winning the Big Ten title, finishing a game ahead of Indiana, led by Ernie Andres.

In the second year of the National Invitation Tournament in New York, undefeated Loyola (Ill.) met unbeaten LIU for the championship. LIU, with Irving Torgoff, extended its winning streak to 26 by beating Loyola, 44–32. The losers were paced by Mike Novak and Wilbert Kautz.

Bill Lloyd of St. John's, who scored 31 points against Roanoke and led the NIT in

Oregon's Bob Anet is in the middle against Ohio State in NCAA final

Colorado took the Big Seven title while New Mexico A&M won its third straight Border Conference championship. Bobby Moers led Texas to the top of the Southwest Conference, and Dartmouth, powered by sophomore guard Gus Broberg, won in the Ivy League.

Alabama finished first in the regular season race in the Southeastern Conference, but Kentucky, with Bernie Opper, won the league's post-season tourney. Banks McFadden led Clemson, eight-place finisher in the season standings, to the championship in the post-season tournament of the Southern Conference. Carnegie Tech and Georgetown shared the crown in the last season of play in the Eastern Intercollegiate Conference.

Chet Jaworski led Rhode Island State, the highest scoring team in the country with its 70-point-per-game average, to the New England Conference title. Other strong teams included Illinois, with Lew Dehner; George Washington, with Bob Faris; and little Roanoke College, which earned an NIT bid on the strength of a 20-game winning streak.

NCAA Championship

At Evanston, Ill.

Oregon (46)	FG	FT	Pts.	Ohio St. (33)	FG	FT	Pts.
Gale	2	4	8	Maag	0	0	0
Dick	5	5	15	Scott	0	1	1
Wintermute	2	0	4	Hull	5	2	12
Anet	4	2	10	Baker	0	0	0
Johansen	4	1	9	Schick	1	0	2
Mullen	0	0	0	Lynch	3	1	7
Pavalunas	0	0	0	Boughner	1	0	2
				Dawson	1	0	2
				Sattler	3	1	7
				Mickelson	0	0	0
				Stafford	0	0	0
Totals	17	12	46		14	5	33

scoring with 50 points in three games, was named MVP although his Redmen lost two of their three games. St. John's had averaged better than 50 points a game during the season.

Marquette, with Irwin "Ike" Graf and Dave Quabius, was strong, as were DePaul, with Bob Neu; Temple, with Howie Black; NYU, with Bob Lewis; Bradley; Villanova; Duquesne, and Notre Dame.

The Midlands teams were evenly matched as Oklahoma, sparked by James McNatt, and Missouri, paced by John Lobsinger, tied for the Big Six Conference title. Drake and Oklahoma A&M shared the Missouri Valley Conference crown.

NCAA SCORES
REGIONALS

East

Semifinals: Villanova 43, Brown 30; Ohio State 64, Wake Forest 52

Championship: Ohio State 53, Villanova 36

West

Semifinals: Oklahoma 50, Utah State 39; Oregon 56, Texas 41

Championship: Oregon 55, Oklahoma 37

FINALS

Championship: Oregon 46, Ohio State 33

St. John's Bill Lloyd (left), who became the MVP of the NIT, accepts congratulations of Roanoke's Gene Studebaker after scoring 31 points in quarterfinal

Two events marked the widespread changes in the development of basketball during this year. Dr. James Naismith, founder of the game nearly 50 years before, died on November 28, 1939. Exactly three months later, Feb. 28, 1940, experimental station W2XBS, forerunner of WNBC in New York, televised college basketball for the first time when it carried the Pitt-Fordham and NYU-Georgetown doubleheader from Madison Square Garden.

Indiana, although finishing second in the Big Ten behind Purdue, won the NCAA tournament by beating Kansas, 60–42. The Hoosiers had a well-balanced team, with any man capable of scoring in double figures, and were selected for NCAA play because they dealt Purdue both of its league losses. Indiana center Marv Huffman was named MVP in the tourney.

NIT Championship

At New York

LIU (44)	FG	FT	Pts.	Loyola (Ill.) (32)	FG	FT	Pts.
Torgoff	5	2	12	Hogan	2	0	4
King	0	0	0	Schell	1	0	2
Kaplowitz	4	1	9	O'Brien	4	1	9
Schwartz	0	2	2	Graham	1	0	2
Scharf	0	0	0	Novak	0	1	1
Sewitch	0	1	1	Kautz	3	0	6
Lobello	0	0	0	Driscoll	0	0	0
Newman	1	1	3	Wenskus	4	0	8
Shelly	1	0	2				
Bromberg	2	1	5				
Shechtman	4	1	9				
Zeitlin	0	1	1				
Totals	17	10	44		15	2	32

NIT SCORES

Quarterfinals: LIU 52, New Mexico A&M 45; St. John's 71, Roanoke 47

Semifinals: LIU 36, Bradley 32; Loyola (Ill.) 51, St. John's 46

Championship: LIU 44, Loyola (Ill.) 32

Consolation: Bradley 40, St. John's 35

UCLA's Jackie Robinson was Pacific Coast scoring champ

Kansas gained its berth in the NCAA tourney after finishing in a three-way tie with Missouri and Oklahoma in the Big Six Conference race. One of the teams the Jayhawks beat en route to the championship was Southern California, considered by many to be the best team in the country. The Trojans, led by Ralph Vaughn, were the Pacific Coast Conference champions and during the season snapped LIU's 34-game winning streak. Jackie Robinson, who would later become the first black to play major league baseball, led the Pacific Coast Conference in scoring at UCLA with 148 points in 12 games.

Big Seven Conference champion Colorado, led by Jack Harvey and Bob Doll, won the NIT by beating DePaul and then Duquesne, 51–40, in the championship game. Doll was named MVP, but scoring honors went to Paul Widowitz of Duquesne.

Rhode Island State and sophomore Stanley "Stutz" Modzelewski set scoring records all over as Modzelewski averaged more than 23 points a game and led the Rams to the New England Conference championship. North Carolina, with George Glamack, took the Southern Conference title by downing Duke in the post-season tournament play, and Alabama finished first in the Southeastern Conference race only to yield to Kentucky in the post-season tournament play.

Oklahoma A&M, with Jesse Renick, won the Missouri Valley Conference championship while other conference champions were Dartmouth, Ivy League; Rice, Southwest; and New Mexico A&M and Arizona, tied, Border.

Among the strong independents were Villanova, 20–2, and NYU, which won its first 18 games only to lose its finale to CCNY. Also strong were DePaul, with Lou Possner and Stan Szukala; LIU; Duquesne; St. John's; and little Springfield (Mass.).

Outstanding players included Bill Hapac, Illinois; Fred Beretta, Purdue; Ed Riska, Notre Dame; Larry Kenny, St. Joseph's; Chet Aubucher, Michigan State; Ralph Giannini, Santa Clara; and Carlisle Towery, Western Kentucky.

NCAA Championship

At Kansas City

Indiana (60)					Kansas (42)		
	FG	FT	Pts.			FG	FT	Pts.
Schafer	4	1	9	Ebling	1	2	4
McCreary	6	0	12	Hunter	0	1	1
Armstrong	4	2	10	Engleman	5	2	12
Gridley	0	0	0	Hogben	2	0	4
Bill Menke	2	1	5	Allen	5	3	13
Bob Menke	0	0	0	Kline	0	0	0
Huffman	5	2	12	Miller	0	2	2
Zimmer	2	1	5	Voran	0	1	1
Dro	3	1	7	Harp	2	1	5
Francis	0	0	0	Sands	0	0	0
				Johnson	0	0	0
Totals	26	8	60		15	12	42

NCAA SCORES
REGIONALS

East

Semifinals: Duquesne 40, Western Kentucky 29; Indiana 48, Springfield 24

Championship: Indiana 39, Duquesne 30

West

Semifinals: Kansas 50, Rice 44; Southern California 38, Colorado 32

Championship: Kansas 43, Southern California 42

FINALS

Championship: Indiana 60, Kansas 42

NIT Championship

At New York

Colorado (51)					Duquesne (40)		
	FG	FT	Pts.			FG	FT	Pts.
Hendricks	3	0	6	Kasperik	3	0	6
Doll	6	3	15	Becker	3	2	8
Harvey	4	6	14	Milkovich	0	2	2
McCloud	1	0	2	Reiber	1	0	2
Hamburg	1	2	4	Lacey	2	3	7
Thurman	4	2	10	Widowitz	7	0	14
				Debnar	0	1	1
Totals	19	13	51		16	8	40

NIT SCORES

Quarterfinals: DePaul 45, LIU 38; Duquesne 38, St. John's 31

Semifinals: Colorado 52, DePaul 37; Duquesne 34, Oklahoma A&M 30

Championship: Colorado 51, Duquesne 40

Consolation: Oklahoma A&M 23, DePaul 22

1940–41

It was 50 years ago this season that the first soccer ball was thrown into a peach basket in that YMCA in Springfield, Mass. The development of the sport had been surprising, and one of the surprises this season was Wisconsin's Badgers.

Wisconsin, ninth-place finisher in the Big Ten in 1939–40, edged defending NCAA champion Indiana for the conference title. The Badgers, led by jumping-jack center Gene Englund and high-scoring sophomore Johnny Kotz, won their last 15 games in a row, including a 39–34 decision over Washington State for the NCAA crown. Kotz was

LIU's Hank Beenders (30) is about to recover rebound against Seton Hall in NIT semifinal that saw the Blackbirds end Seton Hall's winning streak

Ohio University's Frankie Baumholtz was MVP and high scorer in the NIT

Ohio U.'s Frank Baumholtz, a future major league baseball star, was MVP and tournament high scorer with 53 points in three games.

Washington State, led by Paul Lindeman, had won the Pacific Coast Conference championship by beating Stanford in the North-South playoff, and Arkansas, with Johnny Adams, won the Southwest Conference crown. Gus Broberg, the Ivy League MVP, led Dartmouth to its fourth straight title, while Stanley "Stutz" Modzelewski and Fred Conley sparked Rhode Island State to a tie with Connecticut in the New England Conference race.

George Glamack did most of the scoring as North Carolina produced the best record in the Southern Conference. Glamack scored 45 points in one game, only five shy of the national record held by Stanford's Hank Luisetti.

Other conference champions: Creighton, Missouri Valley; Iowa State and Kansas, tied, Big Six; Wyoming, Big Seven; and Kentucky, Southeastern, although Tennessee beat the Wildcats, 36–33, in the post-season conference tournament.

Toledo, with Bob Gerber; Duquesne, with Moe Becker; and Notre Dame, with George Sobek, were strong independents, as were DePaul, with Elmer Gainer; Pitt, Marquette, Bradley, and CCNY.

Among the stars were Bob Kinney, Rice; Howard Engleman, Kansas; Bruce Hale, Santa Clara; Vic Townsend, Oregon; John Barr, Penn State; and Jackie Robinson, UCLA.

named MVP, although Washington State's Kirk Gebert scored 21 points in the NCAA final.

The NIT field was expanded to eight teams, with independents Duquesne and Ohio U. rated as co-favorites. Also entered were high-scoring Rhode Island, averaging better than 73 points a game; Seton Hall, paced by Bob Davies and winner of 42 straight games; Westminster, with a 20–1 record; LIU; Virginia; and CCNY.

LIU, with Oscar Schectman, snapped Seton Hall's victory skein and then downed Ohio U., 56–42, for the championship to become the first team to win the NIT twice.

NCAA Championship

At Kansas City

Wisconsin (39)	FG	FT	Pts.	Washington State (34)	FG	FT	Pts.
Epperson	2	0	4	Gentry	0	1	1
Schrage	0	0	0	Gilberg	1	0	2
Kotz	5	2	12	Butts	1	1	3
Englund	5	3	13	Lindeman	0	3	3
Timmerman	1	0	2	Zimmerman	0	0	0
Rehm	2	0	4	Gebert	10	1	21
Strain	0	2	2	Hunt	0	0	0
Alwin	1	0	2	Sundquist	2	0	4
				Hooper	0	0	0
Totals	16	7	39		14	6	34

NCAA SCORES
REGIONALS
East
Semifinals: Wisconsin 51, Dartmouth 50;
Pittsburgh 26, North Carolina 20

Championship: Wisconsin 36, Pittsburgh 30

West
Semifinals: Washington State 48, Creighton 39;
Arkansas 52, Wyoming 40

Championship: Washington State 64, Arkansas 53

FINALS
Championship: Wisconsin 39, Washington State 34

NIT Championship
At New York

LIU (56)	FG	FT	Pts.	Ohio University (42)	FG	FT	Pts.
Lobello	5	1	11	Baumholtz	8	3	19
Cohen	1	1	3	Snyder	2	0	4
Schneider	0	1	1	Deinzer	0	0	0
Beenders	2	4	8	Bl'k'sd'rf'r	0	0	0
Holub	1	0	2	Lalich	1	2	4
Shechtman	5	2	12	Miller	1	0	2
Schwartz	7	5	19	McSherry	2	2	6
				Wren	0	0	0
				Ott	2	3	7
Totals	21	14	56		16	10	42

NIT SCORES

Quarterfinals: CCNY 64, Virginia 35; Ohio U. 55,
Duquesne 40; Seton Hall 70, Rhode Island 54;
LIU 48, Westminster 36

Semifinals: LIU 49, Seton Hall 26; Ohio U. 45,
CCNY 43

Championship: LIU 56, Ohio U. 42

Consolation: CCNY 47, Seton Hall 27

1941–42

*Stan "Stutz" Modzelewski of Rhode Island
State set all sorts of scoring marks*

The season had just begun when the Japanese attacked Pearl Harbor, and the nation entered World War II. Athletes were soon enlisting in the Armed Forces, some doing so during the season. But play continued, although in some cases on a reduced basis.

Pacific Coast Conference champion Stanford swept to the NCAA title despite the loss of its star, Jim Pollard, who was benched with influenza during the championship game. West Virginia, rated last in the eight-team field, surprised everyone by winning the NIT.

Ivy League kingpin Dartmouth, which had to win its title in a playoff with Princeton, advanced all the way to the NCAA finale before bowing to Stanford, 53–38. Stanford's Pollard had scored 43 points in his first two tournament games, but Don Burness, Ed Voss, Jack Dana and sophomore Howard Dallmar filled in for him in the championship game. Dallmar outplayed Dartmouth's George Munroe, scoring 15 points to earn MVP honors.

West Virginia, compiling a 19–4 record as an independent, started its NIT bid by upsetting top-seeded LIU in overtime. The Mountaineers then leveled Toledo as Rudy Baric held Toledo's Bob Gerber, the tourney's leading scorer, to 14 points. West Virginia won the championship by beating Western Kentucky, 47–45, on free throws in the last 20 seconds by Roger Hicks and

Scotty Hamilton. WVU's Baric was named MVP.

Paced by sophomore Andy Phillip, Illinois took the Big Ten title, while Rice, with center Bob Kinney, shared the Southwest Conference crown with Arkansas. Colorado, with its one-two punch of Leason McCloud and Bob Doll, won the Big Seven competition, and West Texas State, billed as "the world's tallest team" because of its height average of 6-6½ per man, took Border Conference honors.

Other conference champions: Creighton and Oklahoma A&M, tied, Missouri Valley; Kansas and Oklahoma, tied, Big Six; Duke, Southern, and Rhode Island, New England Conference. Tennessee, with Bernie and Dick Mehen, took regular season play in the Southeastern Conference, only to yield to Kentucky in the post-season tournament.

Bob Davies was the workhorse of a strong Seton Hall team. Notre Dame, with Bob Faught, was strong in the Midwest. Other outstanding independents were CCNY, with Red Holzman; LIU; St. John's; Penn State; Duquesne, and Syracuse.

Several scoring records were set, including the four-year career mark by Stanley "Stutz" Modzelewski of Rhode Island. His 1,730 points surpassed the 1,596 accumulated by Hank Luisetti six years earlier at Stanford. West Texas State's Price Brookfield set a single-season mark with 520 points.

Among the outstanding players were Johnny Kotz, Wisconsin; John Mandic, Oregon State; Forest Sprowl, Purdue, and Andy Zimmer, Indiana.

NCAA Championship

At Kansas City

Stanford (53)	FG	FT	Pts.	Dartmouth (38)	FG	FT	Pts.
Dana	7	0	14	Meyers	4	0	8
Eikelman	0	0	0	Parmer	1	0	2
Burness	0	0	0	Munroe	5	2	12
Linari	3	0	6	Shaw	0	0	0
Voss	6	1	13	Olsen	4	0	8
Madden	0	0	0	Pogue	0	0	0
Cowden	2	1	5	Pearson	2	2	6
McCaffery	0	0	0	McKernan	0	0	0
Dallmar	6	3	15	Skaug	1	0	2
Oliver	0	0	0	Briggs	0	0	0
Totals	24	5	53		17	4	38

NCAA SCORES
REGIONALS
East
Semifinals: Dartmouth 44, Penn State 39; Kentucky 46, Illinois 44

Championship: Dartmouth 47, Kentucky 28

West
Semifinals: Stanford 53, Rice 47; Colorado 46, Kansas 44

Championship: Stanford 46, Colorado 35

FINALS
Championship: Stanford 53, Dartmouth 38

NIT Championship
At New York

West Virginia (47)	FG	FT	Pts.	Western Kentucky (45)	FG	FT	Pts.
Hicks	3	3	9	Day	0	0	0
Hamilton	2	1	5	Blevins	4	1	9
Rollins	0	0	0	Shelton	2	1	5
Raese	0	0	0	D. Downing	0	0	0
Kesling	5	4	14	McKinney	4	1	9
Baric	7	3	17	Ray	2	0	4
Kalmar	1	0	2	H. Downing	4	1	9
				Sydnor	4	1	9
Totals	18	11	47		20	5	45

NIT SCORES

Quarterfinals: West Virginia 58, LIU 49; Creighton 59, West Texas State 58; Western Kentucky 49, CCNY 46; Toledo 82, Rhode Island 71

Semifinals: West Virginia 51, Toledo 39; Western Kentucky 49, Creighton 36

Championship: West Virginia 47, Western Kentucky 45

Consolation: Creighton 48, Toledo 46

1942–43

Because of the war many colleges dropped athletics while other schools made freshmen eligible for varsity competition in order to maintain their squads. Players were being drafted in the middle of the season, and in some cases schedules had to be canceled for want of a team.

Wyoming and St. John's won the two big post-season tournaments and then met in a Red Cross benefit game with Wyoming winning, 52–47. The Cowboys from Laramie won the NCAA title with a string of come-from-behind victories over Oklahoma, led by Gerry Tucker, and Texas, with John Hargis, in the Western Regionals. Wyoming then came from behind to beat Georgetown,

Illinois' Whiz Kids: Jack Smiley, Art Mathisen, Ken Menke, Gene Vance, and Andy Phillip

Wyoming's Ken Sailors scoops ball from St. John's Al Moschetti in Red Cross benefit

46–34, in the championship game. Georgetown was led by John Mahnken, but it was Kenny Sailors of Wyoming who won the MVP award. Wyoming's Milo Komenich was tourney high scorer with 48 points in three games.

Harry Boykoff, a 6-9 sophomore, and Andrew "Fuzzy" Levane, the Player of the Year in the New York metropolitan area, teamed to lead St. John's to a 48–27 victory over Toledo, led by Davage Minor, in the NIT final. Boykoff scored 56 points in three games, highest in the tourney, and was named MVP.

Illinois, led by Big Ten MVP Andy Phillip, won all 12 conference games as the team, dubbed the "Whiz Kids," passed up post-season competition in the NCAA and NIT. With Phillip were Art Mathisen, Jack Smiley, Gene Vance and Ken Menke.

Creighton, with Ed Beisser, won 19 straight games, including all 10 of its Missouri Valley Conference encounters, before being beaten in the opening round of the NIT. Rhode Island, scoring a record 80.7 points a game, won in the New England

Conference and Dartmouth, sparked by Stan Skaug, wrapped up its sixth straight Ivy League title.

George Washington, in its second year in the Southern Conference, won the league's post-season tourney after finishing second to Duke in the regular season standings. In the Southeastern Conference, Kentucky finished just ahead of Louisiana State in the regular season race, only to lose to Tennessee in the league's post-season tournament.

West Texas State and Arizona tied for the Border Conference crown after a round-robin league tourney. Rice, with Bill Closs, tied Texas for the Southwest Conference championship; and Kansas, sparked by C. B. Black, won the Big Six title undefeated. William Morris led Washington over Southern California in the North-South playoff for Pacific Coast Conference honors.

Among the leading independents were St. Joseph's with high-scoring George Senesky; NYU, with Jerry Fleishman; Fordham, with Robert Mullen; Manhattan; Villanova; Notre Dame; Marquette; Bowling Green; and DePaul, with a freshman named George Mikan.

Outstanding players included: Gale Bishop, Washington State; Ray Evans, Kansas; Johnny Kotz, Wisconsin; Don Durden, Oregon State; Hal Gensich, Western Michigan; Joe Walthall, West Virginia; Milton Ticco, Kentucky; Clayton Wynne, Arkansas; and footballer Otto Graham, Northwestern.

Though noted as a football player, Northwestern's Otto Graham also was a star in basketball

Championship: Georgetown 53, DePaul 49

West

Semifinals: Texas 59, Washington 55; Wyoming 53, Oklahoma 50

FINALS

Championship; Wyoming 46, Georgetown 34

NIT Championship

At New York

St. John's (48)	FG	FT	Pts.	Toledo (27)	FG	FT	Pts.
Levane	3	0	6	Bolyard	2	1	5
Baxter	3	2	8	Tunnell	0	0	0
Boykoff	5	3	13	Minor	0	0	0
Moschetti	6	1	13	Edwards	0	0	0
Plantamura	1	1	3	Glass	1	0	2
Gotkin	2	1	5	Heiny	0	0	0
				Harmon	2	2	6
				Zuber	3	3	9
				Grove	2	1	5
				Kucer	0	0	0
Totals	20	8	48		10	7	27

NIT SCORES

Quarterfinals: St. John's 51, Rice 49; Fordham 60, Western Kentucky 58; Toledo 54, Manhattan 47; Washington & Jefferson 43, Creighton 42

Semifinals: Toledo 46, Washington & Jefferson 39; St. John's 69, Fordham 43

Championship: St. John's 48, Toledo 27

Consolation: Washington & Jefferson 39, Fordham 34

NCAA Championship

At New York

Wyoming (46)	FG	FT	Pts.	Georgetown (34)	FG	FT	Pts.
Sailors	6	4	16	Reilly	1	0	2
Collins	4	0	8	Potolicchio	1	2	4
Weir	2	1	5	Gabbianelli	1	2	4
Waite	0	0	0	Hyde	0	0	0
Komenich	4	1	9	Mahnken	2	2	6
Volker	2	1	5	Hassett	3	0	6
Roney	0	1	1	Kraus	2	0	4
Reese	1	0	2	Finnerty	0	0	0
				Feeney	4	0	8
				Duffey	0	0	0
Totals	19	8	46		14	6	34

NCAA SCORES
REGIONALS

East

Semifinals: De Paul 45, Dartmouth 35; Georgetown 55, NYU 36

1943–44

Freshmen and the military had a big effect on teams, with teenagers like Arnie Ferrin at Utah, Bob Brannum at Kentucky, and Dick McGuire and Bill Kotsores at St. John's moving their teams into the national spotlight.

The military effect was a two-edged sword, cutting away varsity players and coaches at some schools via the draft, while adding experienced personnel to teams at schools where special Armed Forces training programs were established. McGuire is a case in point. He was named the outstanding player in the New York area while playing at St. John's, but before the season was over he was a military trainee playing in the NCAA tourney for Dartmouth.

The team of the year was Utah, with its "Cinderella Kids" averaging 18½ years of age. Utah was eliminated in the first round of the NIT, but was extended an NCAA bid after Southwest Conference co-champions Arkansas and Rice had to decline invitations.

Utah edged Dartmouth, 42–40, for the NCAA title on a basket by Herb Wilkinson with three seconds left in overtime. Freshman Ferrin was named MVP. The Utes then gained a measure of revenge by beating NIT champion St. John's, 43–36, in a Red Cross fund-raising game.

St. John's won the NIT by beating Bowling Green, Kentucky, and DePaul, 47–39, to become the first team ever to win two consecutive NIT titles. Freshman Kotsores was MVP for the Redmen as DePaul's 6-9 George Mikan led the scoring with 49 points in three games.

Washington and California won the Northern and Southern divisions respectively of the Pacific Coast Conference, but travel restrictions again forced cancellation of the playoff. Ohio State, with Don Grate and Arnie Risen, won in the Big Ten, while Iowa State and Oklahoma, led by Alva Paine, shared the Big Six championship.

Kentucky defeated Tulane, 62–46, for the

Freshman Arnie Ferrin (22) led Utah to victory over St. John's NIT champions

27

championship in the six-team Southeastern Conference tournament. Duke bested North Carolina in the Southern Conference tourney. Yale and Harvard didn't compete, but Dartmouth, led by Aud Brindley, still kept winning in the Ivy League, taking a seventh straight title. Army rolled to a 15–0 record, but didn't participate in the post-season tournaments.

The Big Seven, Border, and New England conferences were among the many which held no regular competition. Missouri Valley Conference coaches voted Oklahoma A&M the title at the end of a 27–6 season.

Other strong teams included Bowling Green, with 6-11 Don Otten; Loyola (La.); Catholic University; and Missouri. Ernie Calverley of Rhode Island led the nation in scoring with a 26.7-point-per-game average as he scored a record 534 points. Rhode Island was the best scoring team in the country, averaging 78.8 points a game while Oklahoma A&M yielded 28.8 points a game.

Bill Kotsores, a freshman, poses with his MVP trophy and teammate Hy Gotkin after NIT triumph

NCAA Championship

At New York

Utah (42)	FG	FT	Pts.	Dartmouth (40)	FG	FT	Pts.
Ferrin	8	6	22	Gale	5	0	10
Smuin	0	0	0	Mercer	0	1	1
Sheffield	1	0	2	Leggat	4	0	8
Misaka	2	0	4	Nordstrom	0	0	0
Wilkinson	3	1	7	Brindley	5	1	11
Lewis	2	3	7	McGuire	3	0	6
				Murphy	0	0	0
				Vancisin	2	0	4
				Goering	0	0	0
Totals	16	10	42		19	2	40

NCAA SCORES
REGIONALS

East

Semifinals: Dartmouth 63, Catholic U. 38; Ohio State 57, Temple 47

Championship: Dartmouth 60, Ohio State 53

West

Semifinals: Utah 45, Missouri 35; Iowa State 44, Pepperdine 39

Championship: Utah 40, Iowa State 31

FINALS

Championship: Utah 42, Dartmouth 40

NIT Championship

At New York

St. John's (47)	FG	FT	Pts.	DePaul (39)	FG	FT	Pts.
Kotsores	3	4	10	Dean	4	0	8
Larkin	0	0	0	Allen	1	0	2
Wertis	6	0	12	Kachan	1	0	2
Summer	4	1	9	DiBenedetto	0	0	0
Wehr	1	1	3	Mikan	4	5	13
Gotkin	2	0	4	Phelan	0	0	0
Duym	3	3	9	Triptow	4	2	10
				Condon	0	0	0
				Stump	1	0	2
				Comerford	1	0	2
				Riordan	0	0	0
Totals	19	9	47		16	7	39

NIT SCORES

Quarterfinals: Oklahoma A&M 43, Canisius 29; Kentucky 46, Utah 38; St. John's 44, Bowling Green 40; DePaul 68, Muhlenberg 45

Semifinals: St. John's 48, Kentucky 45; DePaul 41, Oklahoma A&M 38

Championship: St. John's 47, DePaul 39

Consolation: Kentucky 45, Oklahoma A&M 29

1944–45

In an attempt to take away some of the advantage of extremely tall players like DePaul's 6-10 George Mikan and Oklahoma A&M's 7-foot Bob Kurland, the goal-tending rule was introduced this season. This

Little Lou Goldstein of LIU scurries against 6-10 George Mikan of DePaul

regulation made it illegal for a player to knock away a shot after the ball had begun its downward flight to the basket.

The new rule, though, didn't stop Oklahoma A&M from winning the NCAA tournament or DePaul from capturing the NIT title. Big Ten champion Iowa, led by Dick Ives and former Utah star Dave Wilkinson, was another contender for national honors, but the Hawkeyes didn't compete in either post-season tournament. Iowa lost only one game all year, and that by a single point to Illinois.

Once again, a mixture of freshmen, army rejects, and military trainees formed the backbone of many teams. Oklahoma A&M used the scoring of Cecil Hankin and the 7-foot Kurland to down NYU, 49–45, in the NCAA title game. A&M's tight defense bottled up the Violets' fast break attack and Sid Tannenbaum, who was held to four points. Kurland was named MVP.

DePaul made a shambles of the NIT record book as the Demons set 10 team records and Mikan accounted for 10 individual marks, including a 53-point performance

against Rhode Island. Mikan, the tourney MVP, scored a record 120 points in three games. DePaul held Bowling Green's Wyndol Gray to nine points in beating the Falcons, 71–54, in the championship game.

Oklahoma A&M beat DePaul, 52–44, when they met in the annual Red Cross benefit game at the end of the season. The giant battle between Kurland and Mikan failed to materialize, however, as Mikan fouled out after 14 minutes of play. He had nine points at the time. Kurland finished with 14 points.

Defending NCAA champion Utah won the Big Seven title, but lost Arnie Ferrin and Fred Sheffield to the military just before tournament time. Rice, sparked by pivotman Bill Henry, won the Southwest Conference and lost only one game all season— that to Oklahoma A&M.

Former Stanford ace Howard Dallmar, a Navy trainee at Penn, led the Quakers to the Ivy League crown, ending Dartmouth's seven-year reign. Penn also handed Army its only defeat of the season, ending the Cadets' three-year winning streak at 27. Another Navy trainee, Jim Jordan, led North Carolina to the Southern Conference championship.

Tennessee, the best defensive team in the country, won the regular season competition in the Southeastern Conference, but Kentucky took the league's post-season tourney.

UCLA took the Southern Division and Oregon, playing a 47-game schedule, won the Northern Division in the Pacific Coast Conference. No playoff was held. New Mexico was undefeated in the Border Conference; Iowa State won the Big Six, and Oklahoma A&M was voted the Missouri Valley Conference crown. No championships were decided in the other conferences.

St. John's, with Hy Gotkin and Bill Kotsores, and Notre Dame, with Bill Hassett, were strong independents, as was West Virginia, which brought an all-freshman team to the NIT. Other strong squads included Rhode Island, which scored a record 81.7 points a game; Rensselaer, which won all 13 regular season games before losing in the NIT; Valparaiso; Louisville; Loyola (La.); Tufts; Muhlenberg; and Army.

NCAA Championship

At New York

Oklahoma A&M (49)				NYU (45)			
	FG	FT	Pts.		FG	FT	Pts.
Hankins	6	3	15	Grenert	5	2	12
Parks	0	0	0	Forman	5	1	11
Kern	3	0	6	Goldstein	0	2	2
Wylie	0	0	0	Schayes	2	2	6
Kurland	10	2	22	Walsh	0	0	0
Parrack	2	0	4	Tannenbaum	2	0	4
Williams	1	0	2	Mangiapane	2	2	6
				Most	1	2	4
Totals	22	5	49		17	11	45

NCAA SCORES REGIONALS

East

Semifinals: NYU 59, Tufts 44; Ohio State 45, Kentucky 37

Championship: NYU 70, Ohio State 65

West

Semifinals: Oklahoma A&M 62, Utah 37; Arkansas 79, Oregon 76

Championship: Oklahoma A&M 49, NYU 45

NIT Championship

At New York

DePaul (71)				Bowling Green (54)			
	FG	FT	Pts.		FG	FT	Pts.
Stump	6	3	15	Gray	4	1	9
Phelan	0	0	0	Whitehead	7	3	17
DiBenedetto	1	2	4	Inman	0	1	1
Comerford	0	0	0	Otten	3	1	7
G. Mikan	15	4	34	Rosedale	0	0	0
E. Mikan	0	0	0	Knierim	1	0	2
Allen	2	1	5	Kubiak	1	2	4
LaRochelle	0	0	0	Piel	1	0	2
Furman	0	0	0	Payak	5	2	12
Kachan	6	1	13	Gantt	0	0	0
Niemiera	0	0	0				
Halloran	0	0	0				
Totals	30	11	71		22	10	54

NIT SCORES

Quarterfinals: Rhode Island 51, Tennessee 44; Bowling Green 60, Rensselaer Poly 45; DePaul 76, West Virginia 52; St. John's 34, Muhlenberg 33

Semifinals: DePaul 97, Rhode Island 53; Bowling Green 57, St. John's 44

Championship: DePaul 71, Bowling Green 54

Consolation: St. John's 64, Rhode Island 57

Oklahoma A&M's 7-foot Bob Kurland demonstrates against Temple

Rhode Island's Ernie Calverley lofts one against Bowling Green

1945–46

With World War II over, the veterans returned to find college basketball dominated by 7-foot Bob Kurland and his teammates at Oklahoma A&M. The Aggies became the first team ever to win two NCAA titles, consecutively or otherwise, as they rolled to a 31–2 record.

A&M, the Missouri Valley Conference champion, defeated Baylor and California before beating North Carolina, 43–40, to retain the NCAA crown. The red-headed Kurland, nicknamed "Foothills" because of his height, scored 71 points in three games as he won MVP honors for the second straight year. Kurland, who scored 58 points against St. Louis in the last home game of his collegiate career, finished the season with a record 643 points.

Kentucky, with Jack Parkinson, finished second to Louisiana State, led by Robert Lowther, in the Southeastern Conference. But the Wildcats went on to win the NIT with a 46–45 victory over Rhode Island in the championship game. Freshman Ralph Beard hit a free throw in the final seconds to give Kentucky the victory.

Ernie Calverley, high-scorer and MVP in the NIT, had propelled Rhode Island into the finale when, in an opening-round game against Bowling Green, he hit on a 55-foot shot in the closing seconds of play to send the game into overtime.

New York University, with Sid Tannenbaum, and St. John's battled for supremacy in the New York City area, while West Virginia, using three sophomores and two freshmen, rolled to its best record ever, 24–3, as an independent. Other strong independents included DePaul, with 6-9 George Mikan; Bowling Green, with Don Otten; Syracuse, with Bill Gabor; Navy and Notre Dame, led by Leo Klier and Bill Hassett.

Duke, led by Ed Koffenberger, won the Southern Conference crown with a 13-1 record, but runner-up North Carolina, paced by Jim Jordan and John Dillon, finished with a 12–1 record and received an NCAA bid. Harvard, with former Bowling Green star Wyndol Gray, and Yale, with Tony Lavelli, played as independents, while Dartmouth won the Ivy League competition.

Arizona, with Stewart Udall, who was later to become Secretary of the Interior, won the Border Conference crown. Other conference champions: Ohio State, Big Ten; Kansas, Big Six; Baylor, Southwest; Lafayette, Middle Atlantic; and Wyoming, Big Seven. Idaho won its first Pacific Coast Conference title in 23 years by downing California in the North-South playoff, but California was selected for the NCAA tournament.

Henry Iba, Oklahoma A&M coach, congratulates Bob Kurland after Aggies win second NCAA crown in a row

Ernie Vandeweghe, a 17-year-old freshman at Colgate, was named MVP in the first Fresh Air Fund East-West All-Star game in New York. Among the outstanding players this season were C. B. Black, Kansas; Jack Robinson, Baylor; Herb Wilkinson, Iowa; Jack Goldsmith, LIU; George Kok, Arkansas; Tony Jaros, Minnesota; Paul Hoffman, Purdue; Fred Quinn, Idaho; Andy Wolfe, California; and Kenny Sailors, Wyoming.

One of the largest crowds ever, 28,822, jammed Chicago Stadium to see Ohio State, with Paul Huston, beat Northwestern, led by Max Morris, and DePaul defeat Notre Dame.

NCAA Championship

At New York

Oklahoma A&M (43)	FG	FT	Pts.	North Carolina (40)	FG	FT	Pts.
Aubray	0	1	1	Dillon	5	6	16
Bennett	3	0	6	Anderson	3	2	8
Kern	3	1	7	Paxton	2	0	4
Bradley	1	1	3	McKinney	2	1	5
Kurland	9	5	23	White	0	1	1
Halbert	0	0	0	Thorne	1	0	2
Williams	0	2	2	Jordan	0	4	4
Bell	0	1	1				
Parks	0	0	0				
Totals	16	11	43		13	14	40

Stewart Udall, a future Secretary of the Interior, led his Arizona team to the NIT

Ernie Vandeweghe (11), 17-year-old Colgate freshman, took MVP honors in the East-West All-Star game

NCAA SCORES
REGIONALS

East

Semifinals: Ohio State 46, Harvard 38; North Carolina 57, NYU 49

Championship: North Carolina 60, Ohio State 57

West

Semifinals: Oklahoma A&M 44, Baylor 29; California 50, Colorado 44

Championship: Oklahoma A&M 52, California 35

FINALS

Championship: Oklahoma A&M 43, North Carolina 40

Consolation: Ohio State 63, California 45

NIT Championship

At New York

Kentucky (46)	FG	FT	Pts.	Rhode Island (45)	FG	FT	Pts.
Tingle	2	1	5	Hole	5	2	12
Holland	1	0	2	Nichols	5	1	11
Schu	3	3	9	Palmieri	0	0	0
Jones	3	4	10	Calverley	2	4	8
Campbell	0	2	2	Shea	1	2	4
Parkinson	1	0	2	Allen	3	4	10
Beard	5	3	13	Sclafani	0	0	0
Parker	1	1	3				
Totals	**16**	**14**	**46**		**16**	**13**	**45**

NIT SCORES

Quarterfinals: Rhode Island 82, Bowling Green 79; West Virginia 70, St. John's 58; Kentucky 77, Arizona 53; Muhlenberg 47, Syracuse 41

Semifinals: Rhode Island 59, Muhlenberg 49; Kentucky 59, West Virginia 51

Championship: Kentucky 46, Rhode Island 45

Consolation: West Virginia 65, Muhlenberg 40

1946–47

Fifty years ago this season, on March 20, 1897, Penn visited Yale to play the first intercollegiate game between five-man basketball teams. This season New England again made news as Holy Cross became the first team from that section to win an NCAA championship.

Holy Cross had no gymnasium at its Worcester, Mass., campus and had to play all its games on the road. The Crusaders won 27 of 30, including the last 23 in a row en route to the title. Big Six champion Oklahoma, led by center Gerry Tucker, earned one- and two-point victories in regional games before bowing to Holy Cross, 58–47, in the NCAA finale. Holy Cross' George Kaftan was named MVP for his 18 points and strong rebounding.

Alex Groza was back at Kentucky and Arnie Ferrin returned to Utah after military service. The two teams met for the NIT championship and Utah's deliberate style calmed Kentucky's whirlwind attack, 49–45. Utah's little Wat Misaka bottled up Kentucky's high-scoring Ralph Beard, but it was Ute center Vern Gardner, with 51 points in three games, who won MVP honors.

Texas lost only two games, each by one point, as John Hargis led the Longhorns to the Southwest Conference title. Bob Cook sparked Wisconsin to the top of the Big Ten. St. Louis, with Ed Macauley, won the Missouri Valley Conference crown.

The trio of Lou Beck, Cliff Crandall, and Ephraim "Red" Rocha led Oregon State to the Pacific Coast Conference championship after State downed UCLA, with Don Barksdale and Dave Minor, in the North-South playoff.

Other conference champions: Wyoming, Big Seven; Columbia, Ivy League; Arizona, Border; North Carolina State, Southern; Kentucky, Southeastern; and Montana State, Rocky Mountain. Butler and Cincinnati shared the first title in the Mid-American Conference while the newly formed Yankee Conference produced strong teams in Rhode Island, Connecticut, and Vermont.

West Virginia, paced by Leland Byrd; Notre Dame, with Kevin O'Shea and Johnny Brennan; and St. John's, whose Harry Boykoff scored 54 points in a game against St. Francis, were strong independents. Also powerful were Loyola (Ill.) with Jack Kerris; Navy, with Ken Shugart; LIU; Duquesne; LaSalle; Western Michigan; Georgetown; Santa Clara; and Gonzaga.

George Kaftan (12) paced Holy Cross to 23 straight victories and the NCAA title

Conference also-rans compiling good over-all records included Louisiana State, with future major league baseball player and manager Joe Adcock; Duke; North Carolina; George Washington; Oklahoma A&M; Washington State; and California.

Rhode Island upped the scoring record again, averaging 82.5 points a game while Oklahoma A&M retained its defensive title, yielding 34.8 points per game. Dallas Zuber of Toledo led major college scorers with 441 points.

Some of the better players were Walt Budko, Columbia; James Homer, Alabama; Sid Tannenbaum, NYU; Ralph Hamilton, Indiana; Joe Lord, Villanova; and Jack Smiley and Andy Phillip, both of Illinois.

LSU's Joe Adcock tugs with St. Francis of Brooklyn's Joe Dolan

NCAA Championship

At New York

Holy Cross (58)	FG	FT	Pts.	Oklahoma (47)	FG	FT	Pts.
Kaftan	7	4	18	Reich	3	2	8
Laska	0	0	0	Waters	0	0	0
O'Connell	7	2	16	Day	0	0	0
Curran	0	0	0	Courty	3	2	8
Reilly	0	0	0	Pryor	0	1	1
Oftring	6	2	14	Tucker	6	10	22
Mullaney	0	0	0	Paine	2	2	6
Haggerty	0	0	0	Landon	1	0	2
McMullin	2	4	8	Merchant	0	0	0
Cousy	0	2	2				
Bollinger	0	0	0				
Graver	0	0	0				
Totals	22	14	58		15	17	47

NCAA SCORES
REGIONALS

East

Semifinals: Holy Cross 55, Navy 47; CCNY 70, Wisconsin 56

Championship: Holy Cross 60, CCNY 45

West

Semifinals: Texas 42, Wyoming 40; Oklahoma 56, Oregon State 54

Championship: Oklahoma 55, Texas 54

FINALS

Championship: Holy Cross 58, Oklahoma 47

Consolation: Texas 54, CCNY 50

NIT Championship

At New York

Utah (49)	FG	FT	Pts.	Kentucky (45)	FG	FT	Pts.
Watson	3	7	13	Holland	1	0	2
Misaka	0	2	2	Jones	2	4	8
Gardner	5	5	15	Groza	5	2	12
Ferrin	6	3	15	Tingle	0	0	0
Weidner	1	2	4	Barker	0	0	0
Clark	0	0	0	Rollins	3	0	6
				Line	6	0	12
				Beard	0	1	1
				Jordan	1	2	4
Totals	15	19	49		18	9	45

NIT SCORES

Quarterfinals: Utah 45, Duquesne 44, Kentucky 66, LIU 62; North Carolina State 61, St. John's 55; West Virginia 69, Bradley 60

Semifinals: Utah 64, West Virginia 62; Kentucky 60, North Carolina State 42

Championship: Utah 49, Kentucky 45

Consolation: North Carolina State 64, West Virginia 52

1947–48

Kentucky's three-pronged attack of Alex Groza, Ralph Beard, and Wallace "Wah Wah" Jones brought the Wildcats their first NCAA title in a season that saw them win their fifth consecutive Southeastern Conference championship, lose only two games to collegiate opponents, and finish with a 36–3 record.

Groza, a 6-7 center, was named MVP in the NCAA tourney after the speed, height, and savvy of the Wildcats proved too much for Southwest Conference champion Baylor in a 58–42 rout. The Bears were led by Don Heathington and Jack Robinson.

Another big center, "Easy Ed" Macauley of St. Louis, led the Billikens to the NIT championship as he scored 24 points and outplayed NYU's Dolph Schayes in a 65–52 triumph in the title game. NYU had won 19 straight games before succumbing. The Violets were hampered by the loss of Don Forman who was out with a back injury. Macauley was voted MVP honors ahead of his teammate, D. C. Wilcutt, while scoring honors went to DePaul's Ed Mikan, brother of George, with 64 points in three games.

Holy Cross, with George Kaftan and Bob Cousy, won 18 straight games in an effort to retain its NCAA crown, but the Crusaders were beaten by Kentucky in the NCAA Eastern regional tourney. West Virginia was hurt early in the season when Freddie Schaus sustained a broken ankle, but the Mountaineers finished strong. Larry Foust, at 6-9, led La Salle; sophomore Paul Unruh sparked Bradley; and 6-10 Charlie Share paced Bowling Green to NIT bids.

Notre Dame, with Kevin O'Shea; Loyola, with Jack Kerris; and Colgate, with Ernie Vandeweghe, were strong independents, as were LIU, CCNY, Xavier (O.), Gonzaga, Montana, and Seton Hall.

Washington, led by hook-shot artist Jack Nichols, defeated Oregon State for the Pacific Coast Conference's Northern Division title before beating Southern Division winner California, with Andy Wolfe and

Chuck Hangar, for the league championship.

North Carolina State, sparked by Dick Dickey, retained its Southern Conference crown; Michigan, with Pete Elliott and Bob Harrison, won its first Big Ten title since 1927; and Kansas State jumped from last to first in one season to win the title in the Big Seven (the Big Six before the addition of Colorado).

Other conference champions: Columbia, Ivy League; Connecticut, Yankee; Cincinnati, Mid-American; Oklahoma A&M, Missouri Valley; Arizona, Border; Brigham Young, Skyline Six; Colorado State, Rocky Mountain; and San Jose State, California Collegiate Athletic Association.

Rhode Island, North Carolina State, and Bowling Green averaged more than 70 points a game, led by Rhode Island's 76.3 points a game. Oklahoma A&M and Alabama held opponents to less than 40 points a game. Norm Hankins of Lawrence Tech led scorers with his 22.5 point average.

Among the outstanding players were Murray Weir, Iowa; Tony Lavelli, Yale; George Kok, Arkansas; Leon Watson, Utah; Bob Cook, Wisconsin; Gene Berce, Marquette; and Alex Hannum, Southern California.

NCAA Championship

At New York

Kentucky (58)	FG	FT	Pts.	Baylor (42)	FG	FT	Pts.
Jones	4	1	9	Owen	2	1	5
Line	3	1	7	Pulley	0	1	1
Barker	2	1	5	DeWitt	3	2	8
Groza	6	2	14	Hickman	1	0	2
Holland	1	0	2	Heathington	3	2	8
Beard	4	4	12	Preston	0	0	0
Rollins	3	3	9	Johnson	3	4	10
Barnstable	0	0	0	Srack	0	0	0
				Robinson	3	2	8
Totals	23	12	58		15	12	42

NCAA SCORES
REGIONALS

East

Semifinals: Kentucky 76, Columbia 53; Holy Cross 63, Michigan 45

Championship: Kentucky 60, Holy Cross 52

West

Semifinals: Washington 57, Wyoming 47; Baylor 60, Kansas State 52

Championship: Baylor 64, Washington 62

FINALS

Championship: Kentucky 58, Baylor 42

Consolation: Holy Cross 60, Washington 54

Bob Cousy (17) was the big star at Holy Cross, which won 18 consecutive games

NIT: Dolph Schayes (4) and St. Louis' Lou Lehman (77) and Ed Macauley

NIT Championship

At New York

St. Louis (65)	FG	FT	Pts.	NYU (52)	FG	FT	Pts.
Wilcutt	7	2	16	Kelly	0	1	1
Ossola	1	3	5	Kaufman	6	2	14
Cordia	1	0	2	Lumpp	5	4	14
Schatzmann	1	1	3	Barry	1	1	3
Wrape	0	0	0	Schayes	4	0	8
J. Schmidt	1	1	3	Dolhon	3	1	7
Macauley	11	2	24	DeBonis	1	0	2
B. Schmidt	1	4	6	Benanti	1	0	2
Lehman	0	2	2	Derderian	0	0	0
Cary	0	0	0	Kor	0	0	0
Miller	2	0	4	Quilty	0	1	1
Raymonds	0	0	0				
Totals	**25**	**15**	**65**		**21**	**10**	**52**

NIT SCORES

Quarterfinals: Western Kentucky 68, LaSalle 61; St. Louis 69, Bowling Green 53; NYU 45, Texas 43; DePaul 75, North Carolina State 64

Semifinals: NYU 72, DePaul 59; St. Louis 60, Western Kentucky 53

Championship: St. Louis 65, NYU 52

Consolation: Western Kentucky 61, DePaul 59

All-Americans

AP

Murray Weir, Iowa
Jim McIntyre, Minnesota
Ed Macauley, St. Louis

Ralph Beard, Kentucky
Kevin O'Shea, Notre Dame

1948–49

Kentucky, with the returning trio of Alex Groza, Ralph Beard, and "Wah Wah" Jones, set 22 NCAA team and individual records in repeating as national champion. The Wildcats raced through 13 Southeastern Conference games unbeaten before downing Villanova, Illinois, and Oklahoma A&M to win the NCAA crown. This was the year that a new rule allowing coaches to talk to their teams during a time-out went into effect. But it was Kentucky's Adolph Rupp who obviously knew what to say.

The 6-7 Groza scored a record 82 points in three games and was again named MVP. One of the few jarring notes in the 36–2 season for the Wildcats was a loss to Loyola (Ill.) in the first round of the NIT. Kentucky was rated No. 1 in the country in the Associated Press nationwide poll, taken for the first time this season.

Kentucky, St. Louis, Western Kentucky, and Utah were the top four seeded teams in the NIT and all lost opening round games. St. John's, NYU, CCNY, and Manhattan also lost their opening round NIT games, all on the same day, in what was called the "Manhattan Massacre." San Francisco, with Don Lofgran, Joe McNamee, and Rene Herrerias, defeated Loyola, 48–47, for the championship, Lofgran, who scored 20 points for the Dons and accidentally tapped in a basket for Loyola, was named MVP. Bradley's Paul Unruh was high scorer with 80 points in four games.

Nine major individual scoring records were set, including a single season total of

Ralph Beard (12) vs. Illinois as Wah Wah Jones (27) and Alex Groza (15) look on

39

740 points by William and Mary's Chet Giermak. His 673 field goal attempts and 301 field goals were also records. Paul Arizin of Villanova scored more points, 85, and more field goals, 35, in one game than any other player.

Other records included a career high of 2,199 points by Jim Lacy of Loyola (Md.) while Cornell's Hillary Chollet made a record 19 free throws in one game. Yale's stellar accordion player and scorer, Tony Lavelli, attempted 261 free throws and made 215, both records.

Lavelli led Yale to its first Ivy League championship in 16 years while North Carolina State, with Dick Dickey, Sam Ranzino and Vic Bubas, won its third straight Southern Conference title. Illinois, led by Bill Erickson and Dwight Eddleman, took the Big Ten crown, and Bob Harris powered Oklahoma A&M to the Missouri Valley Conference championship. A&M was pushed by Bradley and St. Louis, with Ed Macauley who made 52.4 per cent of his shots, best in the nation. All three teams were ranked in the top ten.

Other conference champions: Oregon State, Pacific Coast; Wyoming and Utah, tied, Skyline Six; Nebraska and Oklahoma, tied, Big Seven; Arkansas, Baylor, and Rice, tied, Southwest; Western Kentucky, Ohio Valley; Cincinnati, Mid-American; Connecticut, Yankee; Arizona, Border; Colorado State, Rocky Mountain; and San Jose, California Collegiate Athletic Association.

Holy Cross, with Bob Cousy; Colgate, with Ernie Vandeweghe; Bowling Green; Duquesne; Siena; LaSalle; West Virginia; Niagara; Miami (Fla.); and Notre Dame were the best of the non-tournament independents.

Teams that lost conference races but were still noteworthy were Texas, with Slater Martin; Minnesota, led by Meyer "Whitey" Skoog; and Denver, with Vince Boryla. Despite Denver's 18–15 record, the 6-5 Boryla broke virtually every individual shooting record in the Skyline Conference.

NCAA Championship

At Seattle

Kentucky (46)	FG	FT	Pts.	Oklahoma A&M (36)	FG	FT	Pts.
Jones	1	1	3	Yates	1	0	2
Line	2	1	5	Shelton	3	6	12
Groza	9	7	25	Harris	3	1	7
Beard	1	1	3	Bradley	0	3	3
Barker	1	3	5	Parks	2	3	7
Barnstable	1	1	3	Jaquet	0	1	1
Hirsch	1	0	2	McArthur	0	2	2
				Pilgrim	0	2	2
				Smith	0	0	0
Totals	16	14	46		9	18	36

NCAA SCORES
REGIONALS
East

Semifinals: Kentucky 85, Illinois 71; Villanova 72, Yale 67

Championship: Kentucky 76, Illinois 47

West

Semifinals: Oklahoma A&M 40, Wyoming 39; Oregon State 56, Arkansas 38

Championship: Oklahoma A&M 55, Oregon State 30

FINALS

Championship: Kentucky 46, Oklahoma A&M 36

Consolation: Illinois 57, Oregon State 53

Top Ten
AP

Kentucky	Minnesota
Oklahoma A&M	Bradley
St. Louis	San Francisco
Illinois	Tulane
Western Kentucky	Bowling Green

NIT Championship

At New York

San Francisco (48)	FG	FT	Pts.	Loyola (Ill.) (47)	FG	FT	Pts.
Benington	2	1	5	Earle	3	4	10
Hanley	0	0	0	O'Grady	1	0	2
Lofgran	9	2	20	Klaerich	4	2	10
McNamee	1	3	5	Bluitt	4	1	9
Geisen	1	0	2	Kerris	3	1	7
Kuzara	3	1	7	Dawson	1	0	2
Guidance	1	3	5	Nicholl	0	1	1
Herrerias	0	4	4	Hildebrand	1	2	4
				Nagel	0	0	0
Totals	17	14	48		17*	11	45*

*Lofgran scored one goal for Loyola

NIT SCORES

First Round: Bowling Green 77, St. John's 64; San Francisco 68, Manhattan 43; Bradley 89, NYU 67; Loyola 62, CCNY 47

Quarterfinals: Loyola 61, Kentucky 56; Bradley 95, Western Kentucky 86; San Francisco 64, Utah 63; Bowling Green 80, St. Louis 74

All-Americans

AP	UP
Tony Lavelli, Yale	Tony Lavelli, Yale
Vince Boryla, Denver	Ed Macauley, St. Louis
Alex Groza, Kentucky	Wallace Jones, Kentucky
Ed Macauley, St. Louis	Alex Groza, Kentucky
Ralph Beard, Kentucky	Ralph Beard, Kentucky

1949–50

City College of New York became the first team ever to win both the NCAA and NIT championships in the same year. More im-portant, however, was the subsequent reve-lation that CCNY was among the teams in-volved in a point-rigging scandal that shocked the nation.

Starting the season with only one veteran, 6-4 Irwin Dambrot, CCNY had a respect-able, but not outstanding, 17–5 record. The Beavers were unranked nationally and were overlooked in the All-America selections.

The first surprise came in the NIT when CCNY upset Bradley, 69–61, in the cham-pionship game. Later, in the NCAA title game, CCNY again beat Bradley, 71–68. CCNY's Ed Warner was the NIT's leading scorer with 87 points in four games and was named MVP. Dambrot won MVP honors in the NCAA tourney.

Bradley, paced by Paul Unruh and Gene "Squeaky" Melchiorre, won the Missouri Valley Conference, while North Carolina

Villanova's Paul Arizin scores in the East-West game

State, with Dick Dickey and Sam Ranzino, won its fourth straight Southern Conference crown. Dick Schnittker led Ohio State to the Big Ten title, while 6-9 Clyde Lovellette, a sophomore, lifted Kansas into a three-way tie with Nebraska and Kansas State for the Big Seven championship.

Western Kentucky, with Bob Lavoy, went through the Ohio Valley Conference unbeaten, but was upended by Eastern Kentucky in the league's post-season tournament.

UCLA's Ralph Joeckel hit on a shot from more than 50 feet with three seconds remaining to give the Bruins a 60–58 victory over Washington State in the North-South playoff for the Pacific Coast Conference crown. Other conference winners: Kentucky, Southeastern; Cincinnati, Mid-American; Princeton, Ivy; Rhode Island, Yankee; Montana State, Rocky Mountain; Brigham Young, Skyline Six; Muhlenberg, Middle Atlantic; Baylor and Arizona, tied, Southwest; and Arizona, for the fifth year in a row in the Border Conference.

Among the independents, Bob Cousy led Holy Cross while the nation's leading scorer, Paul Arizin, was averaging 25.3 points a game for Villanova. Arizin's 735 points were only five shy of the single-season mark held by William and Mary's Chet Giermak. Other strong independents included Notre Dame, with Kevin O'Shea; LIU, with Sherm White; Duquesne, with Charlie Cooper; Niagara; Syracuse; LaSalle; Toledo; San Francisco; and St. John's, whose Robert "Zeke" Zawoluk scored 65 points in one game.

Led by Arizin, Villanova was the top-scoring team in the country, averaging 72.8 points a game and Oklahoma A&M, as usual, led the defensive ranks, yielding 39.2 points per game.

Among the outstanding players were Bill Sharman, Southern California; Don Rehfeldt, Wisconsin; John Pilch, Wyoming; George Stannich, UCLA; Richard Harmon, Kansas State; Ed Gayda, Washington State; Bob MacKinnon, Canisius; George Yardley, Stanford; and Lou Watson, Indiana.

CCNY's post-season tournament record included victories over defending NIT champion San Francisco and defending

NCAA champion Kentucky in the first two rounds of the NIT. In order to win both the NIT and NCAA tourney, CCNY had to beat the 12th, 6th, 5th, 3rd, and 2nd ranked teams in the country. In each championship game CCNY beat Bradley, rated No. 1 in the nation.

But the triumphs were to be proven hollow as an extensive investigation turned up evidence of the scandal that took the glitter off basketball's shining stars and shook the game to its very foundations.

NCAA Championship

At New York

CCNY (71)	FG	FT	Pts.	Bradley (68)	FG	FT	Pts.
Dambrot	7	1	15	Grover	0	2	2
Roman	6	0	12	Schlictman	0	0	0
Warner	4	6	14	Unruh	4	0	8
Roth	2	1	5	Behnke	3	3	9
Mager	4	6	14	Kelly	0	0	0
Galiber	0	0	0	Mann	2	5	9
Layne	3	5	11	Preece	6	0	12
Nadell	0	0	0	D. M'lch'rre	0	0	0
				G. M'lch'rre	7	2	16
				Chianakas	5	1	11
				Stowell	0	1	1
Totals	26	19	71		27	14	68

NCAA SCORES
REGIONALS

EAST

Semifinals: CCNY 56, Ohio State 55; North Carolina State 87, Holy Cross 74

Championship: CCNY 78, North Carolina State 73

West

Semifinals: Baylor 56, Brigham Young 55; Bradley 73, UCLA 59

Championship: Bradley 68, Baylor 66

FINALS

Championship: CCNY 71, Bradley 68

Consolation: North Carolina State 53, Baylor 41

Top Ten

AP

Bradley	Duquesne
Ohio State	UCLA
Kentucky	Western Kentucky
Holy Cross	St. John's
North Carolina State	LaSalle

NIT Championship

At New York

CCNY (69)	FG	FT	Pts.	Bradley (61)	FG	FT	Pts.
Dambrot	10	3	23	Grover	3	0	6
Warner	6	4	16	Preece	2	0	4
Roman	9	1	19	Unruh	7	1	15
Galiber	0	1	1	Schlictman	1	0	2
Roth	0	0	0	Chianakas	0	0	0
Cohen	0	0	0	Behnke	6	3	15
Mager	2	0	4	Kelly	0	2	2
Layne	2	2	6	Mann	4	0	8
				G. M'lch'rre	2	5	9
Totals	**29**	**11**	**69**		**25**	**11**	**61**

NIT SCORES

First Round: Western Kentucky 79, Niagara 72; CCNY 65, San Francisco 46; Syracuse 80, LIU 52; LaSalle 72, Arizona 66

Quarterfinals: St. John's 69, Western Kentucky 60; Bradley 78, Syracuse 66; Duquesne 49, La Salle 47; CCNY 89, Kentucky 50

Semifinals: CCNY 62, Duquesne 52; Bradley 83, St. John's 72

Championship: CCNY 69, Bradley 61

Consolation: St. John's 69, Duquesne 67

All-Americans

AP	UP
Bob Cousy, Holy Cross	Dick Schnittker,
Dick Schnittker,	Ohio State
Ohio State	Paul Unruh, Bradley
Paul Arizin, Villanova	Paul Arizin, Villanova
Paul Unruh, Bradley	Bob Cousy, Holy Cross
Kevin O'Shea,	Kevin O'Shea,
Notre Dame	Notre Dame

The Scandals

A part of basketball will always turn away its face in shame. A marvelous game played honestly by so many young men will always have, dark in its history, the record of those who played the game not always to win. The fear is never far away that those tragedies may leave their mark again.

The name for basketball's tragedy varies, but each is pronounced with the bite of bitterness and contempt: "Scandal," "Fix," "Dump." There's no trace of dignity to any of them.

The basketball team of City College of New York was returning home by train from Philadelphia on February 19, 1951. CCNY had just scored an impressive victory over Temple, and people were talking about CCNY as the greatest college team of all time. It had won both the National Invitation Tournament and the National Collegiate Athletic Association tournament in 1949–50 with a team composed mostly of sophomores. They and 20,000 undergraduates had made a cheer called "Allagaroo" ring throughout the land. No other team had ever won the NIT and NCAA in the same season, and these young men were still growing, still improving.

"The kids were all gay, having a good time celebrating their big victory. They were terrific against Temple," observed the coach, Nat Holman, who was then known as Mr. Basketball. He was one of the early greats of the game, a player with the Original Celtics, a pioneer, an innovator as coach for generations at CCNY.

"As we neared New Brunswick (N.J.) a gentleman approached me, apologized and said, 'I have some bad news for you, Nat. I've got orders to pick up some of your boys. But I don't want to make a scene.'" The gentleman was from the office of the District Attorney of New York.

"I took the boys aside one at a time and told them I wanted to speak to them when we got to Pennsylvania Station," Holman said. "When we arrived I told them individually, 'When they speak to you, boys, tell them the truth. If your conscience is clear, you have nothing to fear.'"

Tragically, there was so much to fear.

There had been hints of the boil that was building under the skin. In 1945, five Brooklyn College players admitted they had accepted bribes to throw their game with Akron, which was never played. Rumors flowed after that.

In 1949, a George Washington University player reported that he had been approached by gamblers asking that he "do business" with them. There were other signs for everybody to read. They were there in the arenas in the lust of the crowd as it screamed in the last moments of a game. It wasn't only the enthusiastic rooting of the fans for their team to win; some of the fervor was from those to whom the final margin of victory meant winning or losing a bet.

The point spread, as established by bookmakers, is a device to equalize two teams for betting purposes. If one team is considered by the bookmakers to be five points

Coach Nat Holman celebrates CCNY's championship in NCAA tourney

better than the other, then the spread is five points. If a bettor puts his money on the favorite and the team wins by more than the spread, he collects. If the team wins by less than the spread or loses—that difference is inconsequential in gambling terms—the bettor loses. Thus, the margin of victory is actually more important than the outcome of the game. Even if a team is so far behind in the last few minutes of a game that it has no chance of winning, the bettors still can hope that it will manage to beat the spread.

Early in 1951 the rumors or wrongdoing turned into fact. Junius Kellogg, a 6-8 star at Manhattan College, reported that he had been offered $1,000 to control the point spread of a game. Two of his teammates and three gamblers were arrested. Kellogg was far from the best player in the country, but none could have been more honest. The arrests to which Kellogg's testimony led were just a prelude.

The investigation of the 1951 basketball scandal showed that between 1947 and 1950, 86 games had been fixed in 23 cities in 17 states by 32 players from seven colleges: CCNY, LIU, NYU, Manhattan, Kentucky, Bradley, and Toledo. And hardly

anybody was certain that all the guilty parties had been caught.

The collusion did not stop there, however. The lesson was not learned. In 1961 another scandal involved 37 players from 22 colleges. New York District Attorney Frank Hogan was now almost as well known a basketball figure as Dr. Naismith.

Still there was more. In 1965 two Seattle University players were arrested. Each time the sports world hoped it would be the last time.

No sport has ever been so damaged as college basketball. Baseball had a scandal in 1919 that gave the tag "Black Sox" to every dishonest athlete since. But that incident involved only one team and there has been no hint of anything shady since. Professional football has had one significant incident of two players being suspended for a year for betting on games, but there has been no evidence of point fixing. College football has had only a few minor incidents.

Basketball stands apart, perhaps because of the nature of the game. It is a fluid game with both teams scoring repeatedly. It is played with only five on a side, and if one star or two stars on an outstanding team could be controlled, then the margin of victory or even the winning or losing could be altered. One missed layup and two properly-directed bad passes could turn an 11-point margin into a five-point spread. Or the star of the underdog team could make sure that his team lost by more than the bookmakers expected.

The 1951 scandal took a terrible toll of the stars of the game. Most of them have paid for their parts. Professional careers that might have been worth fortunes were wiped out, others never began. Those players who destroyed so much of their lives hardly had a chance to spend the money.

"Tell any others who are tempted to do what I did to look at me," one of the players lamented. "I'm a fine example. I did it because I wanted to be grown up. Sounds funny, doesn't it? I mean I was sick and tired of asking my father for money all the time."

Some of the explanation was simply need. Some of the players were married and had children. Basketball and school didn't leave much time for a man to earn what it took to feed a family. For some others it was easy to blame New York and the environment of Madison Square Garden. In Lexington, University of Kentucky coach Adolph Rupp pontificated that the gamblers couldn't touch his boys "with a 10-foot pole."

Bradley, the team CCNY had beaten in the finals of both tournaments, was implicated. Three of its players were arrested. Then came Kentucky, with the stars of Rupp's two-time NCAA champions.

It was easy for the public, which didn't know the machinery of recruiting and producing big-time basketball, to blame the players. Only days before Kentucky was implicated, Rupp had spoken out for public leniency toward the other players involved. "The Chicago Black Sox threw games," Rupp said, "but these kids shaved only points."

However, among the games the Kentucky players tried to shave was the Loyola of Chicago game in the 1949 NIT. Mighty Kentucky ended up losing, 67–56.

In Madison Square Garden, college basketball doubleheaders had filled the 18,000 seats to the limit of the fire laws. That's where LIU first made itself known to basketball fans in California, Florida, and Illinois.

In 1952 heartbroken Clair Bee, coach of LIU, wrote in the *Saturday Evening Post:*

"'I'm bringing in all these people and playing my heart out for them,' the boys must have said to themselves. 'Clair Bee is getting all the credit and Ned Irish [Madison Square Garden president] and the college are getting all the gravy. Where do I come in?'

". . . The point system enabled fixers to approach players with propositions that seemed to take the curse off dishonesty. 'What's the difference, kid, if you win by eight points instead of 10?' they said. 'You're not letting down the school or the team. We're not asking you to lose the game. Just ease up a little. Everybody's making a good thing out of basketball. Don't be a sucker. There's a thousand bucks in it for you.'

"Boys who fell for that spiel were tragically wrong on two counts. There is no degree of honesty, of course. Shaving points was just as much a criminal offense, morally and legally, as throwing games. That, too, came inevitably when fixers forced players to go all the way by threatening them with exposure."

Judge Saul B. Streit, who presided at the players' trial, had still stronger evidence to uncover in the courtroom. A judge with a famous reputation for austerity, he pointed to the education the basketball players were receiving on their scholarships. Two CCNY players had been admitted through forged entrance papers. The school later admitted that four other players had matriculated the same way.

Judge Streit said that two players were attending college and remaining eligible with IQs in the 80s. In his senior year the academic load of one of the players consisted of public speaking, oil painting, rhythm and dance, and a music seminar.

Still, 10 years later, college basketball had to learn the same lesson again. The names could go on another list, and then another list. The crimes were still the same, just other names at other schools, and sometimes the same school.

When Joe Lapchick returned from the professional Knickerbockers to coach at St. John's University he had assembled a scrapbook to show his players. Before each season they looked at the black pages with their clippings of the scandals, the pictures with the tortured young faces of basketball heroes staring at courtroom floors, surrounded by detectives and unshaven racketeer types. When Lapchick retired, he passed his scrapbook on to his successor, Lou Carnesecca. Pages have been added to keep up with the news: St. Joseph's, Connecticut, Seattle, Seton Hall . . .

How thick the book grows depends on overzealous alumni, unscrupulous coaches, and indifferent college presidents as much as on the players themselves.

1950–51

Revelations of the scandal still had not reached their full extent when the season

Cliff Hagan (6) leads Kentucky against St. John's in NCAA semifinal

began. Kentucky, after a year's absence from the throne, was again crowned NCAA champion and became the first team to win the title three times.

Kentucky was fortunate to make it into the NCAA tourney since one of its two losses of the season came in the championship game of the Southeastern Conference tournament when Vanderbilt beat the Wildcats, 61–57. But in a rule change implemented this season, the NCAA berth went to the team with the best regular-season record and not the conference tournament winner, as in the past.

The NCAA field was expanded to 16 teams, but it made little difference to Kentucky, led by 7-foot Bill Spivey, Frank Ramsey, and sophomore substitute Cliff Hagan. By a 68–58 margin, the Wildcats beat Big Seven champion Kansas State, with Ernie Barrett and Lew Hitch, in the championship

game. Spivey grabbed 55 rebounds and earned the MVP award, although Don Sunderlage of Big Ten champion Illinois, which took third place in the tourney, set four individual records.

Roland "The Cat" Minson and Mel Hutchins paced Brigham Young, Skyline Conference champion, to the NIT crown with a 62–43 victory over Dayton in the final game. Minson was voted MVP while Dayton's Don Meineke, who led the nation with a 51.2 field goal accuracy percentage, scored 85 points in four games for scoring honors.

Duke's Dick Groat, a future major league baseball star, scored 831 points, attempted 338 free throws and made 261 of them, all single season records. Bill Mlkvy of Temple had the highest single season average ever, 29.2 points a game, while taking a record 964 shots.

Lou Rossini was a last minute replacement as coach at Columbia and the Lions, led by John Azary, responded by winning all 22 regular season games and the Ivy League championship. Sam Ranzino, Paul Horvath, and Vic Bubas led North Carolina State to still another Southern Conference title, although the Wolfpack was pushed by West Virginia, with scoring hotshot Mark Workman. Oklahoma A&M, behind Gale McArthur, edged Bradley and St. Louis for the Missouri Valley Conference title. Walter Davis, the 1952 Olympic high jump champion, led Texas A&M to a tie with Texas and Texas Christian in the Southwest Conference.

St. John's, sparked by Bob "Zeke" Zawoluk and Al McGuire, was the leading independent, while Seton Hall, with 6-10 Walter Dukes, was also strong. Larry Hennessy led Villanova and Seattle featured the "Mighty Mites," twins Johnny and Eddie O'Brien, among other independents. Also strong were LaSalle, Holy Cross, Louisville, Toledo, Portland, St. Bonaventure, San Jose, and Lawrence Tech.

Conference champions were Washington, Pacific Coast; Arizona, Border; Montana State, Rocky Mountain; Connecticut, Yankee; Murray State, Ohio Valley; and Pepperdine, California Collegiate Athletic Association. Cincinnati lost its first league game in three years but remained the Mid-American Conference title.

NCAA SCORES
REGIONALS
East

First Round: St John's 63, Connecticut 52; Kentucky 79, Louisville 68; North Carolina State 67, Villanova 62; Illinois 79, Columbia 71

Semifinals: Kentucky 59, St. John's 43; Illinois 84, North Carolina State 70

Championship: Kentucky 76, Illinois 74

West

First Round: Washington 62, Texas A&M 40; Oklahoma A&M 50, Montana State 46; Brigham Young 68, San Jose 61; Kansas State 61, Arizona 59

Semifinals: Oklahoma A&M 61, Washington, 57; Kansas State 64, Brigham Young 54

Championship: Kansas State 68, Oklahoma A&M 44

FINALS

Championship: Kentucky 68, Kansas State 58

Consolation: Illinois 61, Oklahoma A&M 46

Top Ten

AP	UP
Kentucky	Kentucky
Oklahoma A&M	Oklahoma A&M
Columbia	Kansas State
Kansas State	Illinois
Illinois	Columbia
Bradley	Bradley
Indiana	North Carolina State
North Carolina State	Indiana
St. John's	St. John's
St. Louis	Brigham Young

NIT Championship

At New York

Brigham Young (62)	FG	FT	Pts.	Dayton (43)	FG	FT	Pts.
Richey	2	1	5	Boyle	2	1	5
Hillman	3	2	8	Oberst	0	0	0
Craig	0	1	1	Hickey	1	0	2
Minson	11	4	26	Grigsby	0	1	1
Thorne	0	0	0	Joseph	2	0	4
Hutchins	3	0	6	Meineke	1	5	7
Jarman	0	0	0	Taylor	0	0	0
Christensen	4	1	9	Campbell	1	1	3
Heaps	0	0	0	Stein	0	0	0
Jones	0	0	0	Norris	7	6	20
Romney	2	3	7	Flynn	0	1	1
Olson	0	0	0	Hough	0	0	0
Totals	**25**	**12**	**62**		**14**	**15**	**43**

NIT SCORES

First Round: Dayton 77, Lawrence Tech 71; Seton Hall 71, Beloit 57; St. Louis 73, LaSalle 61; St. Bonaventure 70, Cincinnati 67

Quarterfinals: St. John's 60, St. Bonaventure 58; Brigham Young 75, St. Louis 58; Dayton 74, Arizona 68; Seton Hall 71, North Carolina State 59

NCAA Championship

At Minneapolis

Kentucky (68)	FG	FT	Pts.	Kansas State (58)	FG	FT	Pts.
Whitaker	4	1	9	Head	3	2	8
Linville	2	4	8	Stone	3	6	12
Spivey	9	4	22	Hitch	6	1	13
Ramsey	4	1	9	Barrett	2	0	4
Watson	3	2	8	Iverson	3	1	7
Hagan	5	0	10	Rousey	2	0	4
Ts'r'p'lous	1	0	2	Gibson	0	1	1
Newton	0	0	0	Upson	0	0	0
				Knostman	1	1	3
				Peck	2	0	4
				Schuyler	1	0	2
Totals	**28**	**12**	**68**		**23**	**12**	**58**

All-Americans

AP	UP
Bill Mlkvy, Temple	Bill Mlkvy, Temple
Sam Ranzino, N. C. State	Sam Ranzino, N. C. State
Bill Spivey, Kentucky	Bill Spivey, Kentucky
Gene Melchiorre, Bradley	Gene Melchiorre, Bradley
Clyde Lovellette, Kansas	Clyde Lovellette, Kansas

1951–52

With the U.S. involvement in the Korean War, a number of teams faced manpower shortages. As a result, many conferences made freshmen eligible for varsity competition. The freshmen who played didn't have the same effect as freshmen did during World War II, but they did add unpredictability.

St. John's surprised the No. 1 and No. 2 rated teams in the country, Kentucky and Illinois, to gain a berth in the NCAA finale against Kansas. The Jayhawks whipped St. John's 80–63, as "Man Mountain" Clyde Lovellette, at 6-9, scored 33 points and won MVP honors for Kansas. Kansas earned the championship berth by downing upstart Santa Clara, led by Kenny Sears, which had previously upset UCLA and Wyoming.

Lovellette ended his career with a national record of 1,888 points, breaking the old record of 1,886 set two days earlier by Dick Groat of Duke. Lovellette also led the nation in scoring, with a 28.4-point-per-game average, while Groat, who averaged 26.0 points, led the country in assists. Bob Pettit of Louisiana State and Chuck Darling of Iowa each averaged 25.5 points.

Tom Gola, a freshman, and Norm Grekin shared the MVP award as they led LaSalle to a 75–64 victory over Dayton before 18,845 fans to win the NIT championship.

Seattle's Johnny O'Brien set an individual scoring record with this free throw

Dayton, which finished second for the second consecutive year, was led by Don Meineke, who repeated as top scorer with 84 points in four games.

West Virginia, with 6-9 Mark Workman, had the best regular-season record in the Southern Conference, but lost the post-season tournament to North Carolina State, paced by Lee Terrell. Kentucky's one-two punch of Cliff Hagan and Frank Ramsey enabled the Wildcats to easily outdistance the rest of the teams in the Southeastern Conference.

The balanced play of Rod Fletcher, Irv Bemoras, Clive Follmer, and sophomore Johnny Kerr put Illinois at the top of the Big Ten. Wyoming won the Skyline Conference title in the expanded league, now eight teams with the inclusion of Montana and New Mexico. UCLA, with Don Johnson, beat Washington, despite the hook-shot artistry of Bob Houbregs, for the Pacific Coast Conference crown. Western Kentucky's 6-9 Art Spoelstra led the Hilltoppers to the Ohio Valley Conference championship.

Other conference champions: Princeton, Ivy League; Connecticut, Yankee; Texas Christian, Southwest; Colorado State and Montana State, tied, Rocky Mountain; Miami (O.) and Western Michigan, tied, Mid-American; New Mexico A&M and West Texas State, tied, Border; and Pepperdine, California Collegiate Athletic Association.

"Zeke" Zawoluk, Ron MacGilvary, and Jack McMahon led St. John's to preeminence among independents, while other powers included Seton Hall, Holy Cross, DePaul, Oklahoma City, Penn State, and Boston College. Seattle, with 5-9 Johnny O'Brien becoming the first player to score more than 1,000 points (1,051) in one season, ran up a 29–8 record, including an 84–81 triumph over the Harlem Globetrotters. Other strong teams were Louisville, Mississippi Southern, Memphis State, Duke, Indiana, and Marquette.

Among the better players were Bill Stauffer, Missouri; Ab Nicholas, Wisconsin; Ernie Beck, Pennsylvania; Glenn Smith, Utah; Dickie Hemric, Wake Forest; and future professional football star Rick Casares, Florida.

NCAA Championship

At Seattle

Kansas (80)	FG	FT	Pts.	St. John's (63)	FG	FT	Pts.
Kenney	4	4	12	McMahon	6	1	13
Davenport	0	0	0	Davis	1	2	4
Keller	1	0	2	Walsh	3	0	6
Hoag	2	5	9	Zawoluk	7	6	20
Lovellette	12	9	33	Peterson	0	0	0
Born	0	0	0	MacGilvray	3	2	8
D. Kelley	2	3	7	Giancontieri	0	0	0
Smith	0	0	0	Duckett	2	2	6
Lienhard	5	2	12	Walker	0	0	0
Hougland	2	1	5	McMorrow	1	0	2
Heitholt	0	0	0	Sagona	2	0	4
A. Kelley	0	0	0				
Totals	28	24	80		25	13	63

NCAA SCORES
REGIONALS

East

Semifinals: Kentucky 82, Penn State 54; St. John's 60, North Carolina State 49

Championship: St. John's 64, Kentucky 57

Mideast

Semifinals: Illinois 80, Dayton 61; Duquesne 60, Princeton 49

Championship: Illinois 74, Duquesne 68

Midwest

Semifinals: Kansas 68, Texas Christian 64; St. Louis, 62, New Mexico A&M 53

Championship: Kansas 74, St. Louis 55

Far West

Semifinals: Santa Clara 68, UCLA 59; Wyoming 54, Oklahoma City 48

Championship: Santa Clara 56, Wyoming 53

FINALS

Semifinals: Kansas 74, Santa Clara 55; St John's 61, Illinois 59

Championship: Kansas 80, St. John's 63

Consolation: Illinois 67, Santa Clara 64

NIT Championship

At New York

LaSalle (75)	FG	FT	Pts.	Dayton (64)	FG	FT	Pts.
Grekin	5	5	15	Grigsby	8	2	18
Iehle	8	2	18	Meineke	4	5	13
Jones	0	1	1	Paxson	5	5	15
Gilson	0	0	0	Taylor	0	0	0
O'Hara	0	0	0	Donoher	0	0	0
Gola	9	4	22	Horan	3	0	6
Moore	3	2	8	Norris	3	1	7
Donnelly	5	1	11	Boyle	0	0	0
French	0	0	0	Sallee	1	1	3
Altieri	0	0	0	Harris	0	0	0
				Joseph	1	0	2
				Weywood	0	0	0
Totals	30	15	75		25	14	64

NIT SCORES

First Round: Dayton 81, NYU 66; Western Kentucky 62, Louisville 59; LaSalle 80, Seton Hall 76; Holy Cross 77, Seattle 72

Quarterfinals: St. Bonaventure 70, Western Kentucky 69; LaSalle 51, St. John's 45; Duquesne 78, Holy Cross 68; Dayton 68, St. Louis 58

Semifinals: LaSalle 59, Duquesne 46; Dayton 69, St. Bonaventure 62

Championship: LaSalle 75, Dayton 64

Consolation: St. Bonaventure 48, Duquesne 34

AP	UP
Kentucky	Kentucky
Illinois	Illinois
Kansas State	Kansas
Duquesne	Duquesne
St. Louis	Washington
Washington	Kansas State
Iowa	St. Louis
Kansas	Iowa
West Virginia	St. John's
St. John's	Wyoming

All-American

AP	UP
Chuck Darling, Iowa	Chuck Darling, Iowa
Mark Workman, West Virginia	Mark Workman, West Virginia
Clyde Lovellette, Kansas	Clyde Lovellette, Kansas
Dick Groat, Duke	Dick Groat, Duke
Cliff Hagan, Kentucky	Cliff Hagan, Kentucky

1952–53

Indiana and Seton Hall, each with a 6-10 center, were rated one-two in the wire service polls, and went on to win the NCAA and NIT championships, respectively.

Indiana counted on 6-3 Bob Leonard and lanky sophomore pivotman Don Schlundt to win its first Big Ten title ever. The Hoosiers and Kansas' surprising Jayhawks then waded through an expanded 22-team field before meeting for the NCAA crown. Indiana won, 69–68, on a free throw by Leonard with 27 seconds remaining. Kansas' southpaw center, Bertram H. Born, who scored 26 points, was named MVP. This was the first time a player on a non-champion team received the NCAA's MVP award.

Seton Hall used the inside strength of big Walter Dukes and the steady outside play of Richie Regan to cop the NIT. The Pirates downed St. John's, 58–46, as Dukes won MVP honors. He scored 70 points in three games.

Kentucky was barred from Southeastern Conference competition for recruiting violations. In the Wildcats' absence, the Tigers of Louisiana State, led by sophomore Bob Pettit, won the crown. In the Southern Conference tournament, Dickie Hemric led Wake Forest to a 71–70 triumph over regular-season champion North Carolina State. Bob Houbregs led Washington to the Pacific Coast Conference championship.

Other conference champions: Miami (O.), Mid-American; Oklahoma A&M, Missouri Valley; Eastern Kentucky, Ohio Valley; Texas Christian, Southwest; Hardin-Simmons and Arizona, tied, Border; Connecticut, Yankee; Wyoming, Skyline; Idaho State, Rocky Mountain; and Santa Clara and San Francisco shared the crown in the new California Basketball Association.

Among the outstanding independents were LaSalle, with Tom Gola; Duquesne, paced by Dick Ricketts and Jim Tucker; Fordham, with the nation's leading rebounder in Ed Conlin; Notre Dame; DePaul; Louisville; Mississippi Southern; East Tennessee; and Manhattan. Highly regarded Niagara, with set-shot artist Larry Costello, had to go into six overtimes to beat Siena, 88–81.

The one-and-one free throw rule, awarding a bonus shot, sent scoring averages soaring. Furman scored more points, 90.2 per game, and connected on more shots, 44.4 per cent, than any team had before. Leading Furman was Frank Selvy, whose 29.5-point-per-game average was tops in the nation. Villanova's Larry Hennessy was a shade behind, averaging 29.2. Oklahoma A&M, with Bob Mattick at center, won its 14th defensive title in 19 years, allowing a record high 53.8 points per game.

Some of the outstanding players were Togo Palazzi, Holy Cross; Arnie Short, Oklahoma City; Al Bianchi, Bowling Green; Al Ferrari, Michigan State; Gene Shue, Maryland; Dick Knostman, Kansas State; and rebounder Charlie Slack and shooter Walt Walowac at Marshall.

Johnny O'Brien completed three years at Seattle in which he played 99 games, scored 2,537 points on 838 field goals and 861 free throws, all national records.

NCAA Championship

At Kansas City

Indiana (69)	FG	FT	Pts.	Kansas (68)	FG	FT	Pts.
Kraak	5	7	17	Patterson	1	7	9
DeaKyne	0	0	0	A. Kelley	7	6	20
Farley	1	0	2	Davenport	0	0	0
Schlundt	11	8	30	Born	8	10	26
White	1	0	2	Smith	0	1	1
Leonard	5	2	12	Alberts	0	0	0
Poff	0	0	0	D. Kelley	3	2	8
Scott	2	2	6	Reich	2	0	4
Byers	0	0	0				
Totals	25	19	69		21	26	68

Niagara's Larry Costello (69) watches as Seton Hall's Walter Dukes (20) scores

NCAA SCORES
REGIONALS
East
First Round: Lebanon Valley 80, Fordham 67; Holy Cross 87, Navy 74

Semifinals: Louisiana State 89, Lebanon Valley 76; Holy Cross 79, Wake Forest 71

Championship: Louisiana State 81, Holy Cross 73

Mideast
First Round: Notre Dame 72, Eastern Kentucky 57; DePaul 74, Miami (O.) 72

Semifinals: Notre Dame 69, Pennsylvania 57; Indiana 82, DePaul 80

Championship: Indiana 79, Notre Dame 66

Midwest
Semifinals: Oklahoma A&M 71, Texas Christian 54; Kansas 73, Oklahoma City 65

Championship: Kansas 61, Oklahoma A&M 55

Far West
First Round: Seattle 88, Idaho State 77; Santa Clara 81, Hardin-Simmons 56
Semifinals: Washington 92, Seattle 70; Santa Clara 67, Wyoming 52

Championship: Washington 74, Santa Clara 62

FINALS
Semifinals: Indiana 80, Louisiana State 67; Kansas 79, Washington 53

Championship: Indiana 69, Kansas 68

Consolation: Washington 88, Louisiana State 69

Top Ten

AP	UP
Indiana	Indiana
Seton Hall	Washington
Kansas	LaSalle
Washington	Seton Hall
Louisiana State	Kansas
LaSalle	Louisiana State
St. John's	Oklahoma A&M
Oklahoma A&M	North Carolina State
Duquesne	Kansas State
Notre Dame	Illinois

All-Americans

AP	UP
Walter Dukes, Seton Hall	Walter Dukes, Seton Hall
John O'Brien, Seattle	John O'Brien, Seattle
Bob Houbregs, Washington	Bob Houbregs, Washington
Tom Gola, LaSalle	Tom Gola, LaSalle
Ernie Beck, Pennsylvania	Ernie Beck, Pennsylvania

NIT Championship
At New York

Seton Hall (58)	FG	FT	Pts.	St. John's (46)	FG	FT	Pts.
Nathanic	1	2	4	Cunningham	2	0	4
Hannon	1	0	2	Walker	2	0	4
Ring	3	1	7	McMorrow	1	0	2
Dukes	5	11	21	Satalino	3	1	7
Regan	5	3	13	Sagona	0	0	0
Brooks	4	3	11	Davis	5	1	11
O'Hara	0	0	0	Peterson	0	0	0
				Duckett	7	2	16
				Walsh	1	0	2
				Romano	0	0	0
				Nolan	0	0	0
				Giancontieri	0	0	0
Totals	19	20	58		21	4	46

NIT SCORES

First Round: Duquesne 88, Tulsa 69; Louisville 92, Georgetown 79; St. John's 81, St. Louis 66; Niagara 82, Brigham Young 76

Quarterfinals: St. John's 75, LaSalle 74; Manhattan 79, Louisville 66; Seton Hall 79, Niagara 74; Duquesne 69, Western Kentucky 61

Semifinals: Seton Hall 74, Manhattan 56; St. John's 64, Duquesne 55

Championship: Seton Hall 58, St. John's 46

Consolation: Duquesne 81, Manhattan 67

1953–54

Scoring reached new peaks as Furman's Frank Selvy scored 100 points in a single game and broke virtually every major college scoring record on the books. Selvy finished with a 41.7 average for the season. His 100 points came against Newberry. Selvy scored 50 or more points in eight games. Among his career marks were most field goals (922), most points (2,538) and best average (32.5 points a game).

Eastern independents cornered the market on team laurels as LaSalle downed Bradley, 92–76, for the NCAA title, and Holy Cross beat Duquesne, 71–62, for the NIT championship.

Versatile Tom Gola led LaSalle past a first-round scare from Fordham and Eddie Conlin, to sweep past North Carolina State, Navy, Penn State, and Bradley for the NCAA crown in an expanded 24-team field. Gola was MVP and high scorer with 114 points.

Holy Cross, with Togo Palazzi and Tom Heinsohn, beat top-seeded Duquesne, despite the presence of Dick Ricketts, Jim Tucker, and sophomore Sihugo Green. Palazzi was MVP while scoring honors went to Tom Marshall of Western Kentucky's

Ohio Valley Conference champions with 82 points.

Kentucky, led by Cliff Hagan, Frank Ramsey and Lou Tsiropoulos, finished in a 14–0 tie with Bob Pettit-led Louisiana State in the Southeastern Conference. But the Wildcats, with a 25–0 overall record, declined post-season tournament competition when their three graduate student stars were declared ineligible for tournament play.

Led by Selvy, Furman set team marks for highest average, 91.7 points a game, and accuracy, 45.6 per cent from the field. Other new team highs included most free throws attempted, 1,263, and most free throws made, 865, both by Bradley.

Don Schlundt, Bob Leonard, and Dick Farley led Indiana to the Big Ten crown while Bob Mattick paced Oklahoma A&M to the Missouri Valley title. B. H. Born was back to take Kansas to a Big Seven Conference tie with Oklahoma. Southern California, with Roy Irvin, won the Pacific Coast Conference championship in a playoff with Oregon State, featuring 7-3 Wade Halbrook.

Other conference champions: Colorado A&M, Skyline; Cornell, Ivy League; Santa Clara, California Basketball Association; Texas and Rice, tied, Southwest; Texas Tech, Border; and Toledo, Mid-American. North Carolina State won the Southern Conference tournament after George Washington had finished atop the regular season standings.

Among the independents, Notre Dame, with Dick Rosenthal, and Penn State, with Jesse Arnelle, were highly rated. Also strong were Oklahoma City, with Arnie Short; Niagara, with Larry Costello; Navy, with John Clune; and Seattle, which had its 26-game winning streak snapped in the NCAA tourney by Rocky Mountain Conference champion Idaho State.

Other strong teams were Illinois, with Johnny Kerr; Iowa, led by Carl Cain; Maryland, with Gene Shue; Ohio State, with Paul Ebert; Marshall, with Walt Walowac; Wichita, with Cleo Littleton; and St. Francis of Loretto, Pa., with Maurice Stokes.

NCAA Championship

At Kansas City

LaSalle (92)	FG	FT	Pts.	Bradley (76)	FG	FT	
Singley	8	7	23	Petersen	4	2	
Greenberg	2	1	5	Babetch	0	0	
Maples	2	0	4	King	3	6	12
Blatcher	11	1	23	Gower	0	1	1
Gola	7	5	19	Estergard	3	11	17
O'Malley	5	1	11	Carney	3	11	17
Yodsnukis	0	0	0	Utt	0	0	0
O'Hara	2	3	7	Kent	8	0	16
				Riley	1	1	3
Totals	37	18	92		22	32	76

NCAA SCORES REGIONALS

East

First Round: LaSalle 76, Fordham 74; North Carolina State 75, George Washington 73; Navy 85, Connecticut 80

Semifinals: LaSalle 88, North Carolina State 81; Navy 69, Cornell 67

Championship: La Salle 64, Navy 48

Mideast

First Round: Penn State 62, Toledo 50; Notre Dame 80, Loyola (La.) 70

Semifinals: Penn State 78, Louisiana State 70; Notre Dame 65, Indiana 64

Championship: Penn State 71, Notre Dame 63

Midwest

First Round: Bradley 61, Oklahoma City 55

Semifinals: Bradley 76, Colorado 64; Oklahoma A&M 51, Rice 45

Championship: Bradley 71, Oklahoma A&M 57

Far West

First Round: Idaho State 77, Seattle 75; Santa Clara 73, Texas Tech 64

Semifinals: Southern California 73, Idaho State 59; Santa Clara 73, Colorado A&M 50

Championship: Southern California 66, Santa Clara 65

FINALS

Semifinals: LaSalle 69, Penn State 54; Bradley 74, Southern California 72

Championship: LaSalle 92, Bradley 76

Consolation: Penn State 70, Southern California 61

NIT Championship

At New York

Holy Cross (71)	FG	FT	Pts.	Duquesne (62)	FG	FT	Pts.
Palazzi	6	8	20	Ricketts	6	1	13
Liebler	4	2	10	Green	6	4	16
Heinsohn	6	8	20	Fallon	0	0	0
Kasprzak	3	0	6	Iezza	0	0	0
Perry	2	3	7	Tucker	4	3	11
Prothovich	1	3	5	Johnson	0	2	2
Supronowicz	1	0	2	Winograd	4	7	15
Early	0	1	1	Dambrot	2	1	5
Totals	23	25	71		22	18	62

Furman's Frank Selvy set major college scoring records with a 100-point game

NIT SCORES

First Round: St. Francis (N. Y.) 60, Louisville 55; Dayton 90, Manhattan 79; Bowling Green 88, Wichita 84; St. Francis (Pa.) 81, Brigham Young 68

Quarterfinals: Western Kentucky 95, Bowling Green 81; Niagara 77, Dayton 74; Duquesne 69, St. Francis (Pa.) 63; Holy Cross 93, St. Francis (N. Y.) 69

Semifinals: Duquesne 66, Niagara 51; Holy Cross 75, Western Kentucky 69

Championship: Holy Cross 71, Duquesne 62

Consolation: Niagara 71, Western Kentucky 65

Top Ten

AP	UP
Kentucky	Indiana
LaSalle	Kentucky
Holy Cross	Duquesne
Indiana	Oklahoma A&M
Duquesne	Notre Dame
Notre Dame	Western Kentucky
Bradley	Kansas
Western Kentucky	Louisiana State
Penn State	Holy Cross
Oklahoma A&M	Iowa

All-Americans

AP	UP
Frank Selvy, Furman	Frank Selvy, Furman
Don Schlundt, Indiana	Don Schlundt, Indiana
Tom Gola, LaSalle	Tom Gola, LaSalle
Cliff Hagan, Kentucky	Cliff Hagan, Kentucky
Bob Pettit, Louisiana State	Bob Pettit, Louisiana State

1954–55

A lone defeat by UCLA early in the season prevented San Francisco from becoming the first unbeaten team to win an NCAA championship. The Dons, who led the nation in defense by allowing only 52.1 points a game, finished the year by winning 26 straight games, for a 28–1 record.

The NCAA title came on a 77–63 victory over defending champion LaSalle, with Tom Gola. San Francisco center Bill Russell was MVP and tournament high scorer with 118 points in five games. Prior to the finale, the closest call for the Dons, the California Basketball Association champions, was a one-point victory over Pacific Coast Conference champion Oregon State, led by 7-3 Wade Halbrook, in the NCAA quarterfinals.

Si Green and Dick Ricketts combined for 56 of Duquesne's 70 points as the Iron Dukes downed Dayton, 70–58, for the NIT crown. MVP honors went to Maurice Stokes of fourth-place St. Francis of Loretto, Pa. Stokes scored a record 124 points in four games, including 43 against Dayton.

A crowd of 20,176 saw Minnesota, with Chuck Mencel and Dick Garmaker, clinch the Big Ten championship against Iowa, led by Deacon Davis. Kentucky won the Southeastern Conference title even though its 129-game home court winning streak was snapped by lowly Georgia Tech. Princeton beat Columbia and Penn in a playoff for the Ivy League crown, and Jim Krebs led Southern Methodist to Southwest Conference honors. Bob Patterson sparked Tulsa to the top of the Missouri Valley Conference.

Other conference champions: North Carolina, in the newly formed Atlantic Coast; West Texas State and Texas Tech, tied, Border; Connecticut, Yankee; Idaho State, Rocky Mountain; Miami (O.) Mid-American; and Colorado, Big Seven. Western Kentucky won the regular season title in the Ohio Valley Conference, but yielded to Eastern Kentucky in the league's post-season tourney, and Art Bunte led Utah to the Skyline Conference crown.

West Virginia, with sophomore Rod "Hot Rod" Hundley, had the best record in the Southern Conference, but George Washington, with Corky Devlin, won the post-season conference tournament. Other strong teams included UCLA, with Willie Naulls; Santa Clara, with Kenny Sears; Texas Christian, with Richard O'Neal; St. Louis, with Dick Boushka; and Duke and Maryland.

Marquette, led by Terry Rand, won 22 straight games, and Manhattan, whose Ed O'Conner made a record 60.5 per cent of his field goal attempts, were strong independents, as were Cincinnati, with Jack Twyman; Notre Dame, with Jack Stephens; Fordham, with Ed Conlin; Holy Cross, with Tommy Heinsohn; and Canisius, with John McCarthy. Other outstanding teams were Villanova, Penn State, Memphis State, Oklahoma City, Bradley, Seattle, Louisville, Niagara, and Seton Hall.

Marshall's Charlie Slack averaged a record 25.6 rebounds a game, while Darrell Floyd of Furman led all scorers with 35.9 points a game, just ahead of Virginia's Richard "Buzz" Wilkinson, who averaged 32.1. Floyd led Furman to its third straight scoring title, as the Paladins averaged a record 95.3 points a game. Wake Forest' Dickie Hemric finished with a career rec of 2,587 total points.

Duquesne's Si Green (11) and scored 33 in NIT final

NIT Championship

At New York

Duquesne (70)				Dayton (58)			
	FG	FT	Pts.		FG	FT	Pts.
Green	13	7	33	Horan	6	8	20
Dave				Almashy	0	0	0
Ricketts	0	0	0	Parin	0	0	0
Severine	1	2	4	Walsh	0	1	1
Dick				Uhl	10	5	25
Ricketts	7	9	23	Riazzi	0	0	0
Winograd	2	2	6	Sicking	0	0	0
Fallon	1	2	4	Harris	1	2	4
				Sallee	1	0	2
				Jacoby	0	0	0
				Dieringer	0	2	2
				Fiely	2	0	4
Totals	24	22	70		20	18	58

NIT SCORES

First Round: Louisville 91, Manhattan 86; Niagara 83, Lafayette 70; St. Francis (Pa.) 89, Seton Hall 78; St. Louis 110, Connecticut 103

Quarterfinals: Duquesne 74, Louisville 66; Cincinnati 85, Niagara 83; St. Francis (Pa.) 68, Holy Cross 64; Dayton 97, St. Louis 81

Semifinals: Dayton 79, St. Francis (Pa.) 73; Duquesne 65, Cincinnati 51

Championship: Duquesne 70, Dayton 58
Consolation: Cincinnati 96, St. Francis (Pa.) 91

Top Ten

AP	UP
San Francisco	San Francisco
Kentucky	Kentucky
LaSalle	LaSalle
North Carolina State	Utah
Iowa	Iowa
Duquesne	North Carolina State
Utah	Duquesne
Marquette	Oregon State
Dayton	Marquette
Oregon State	Dayton

All-Americans

AP	UP
Tom Gola, LaSalle	Tom Gola, LaSalle
Robin Freeman, Ohio State	Bill Russell, San Francisco
Bill Russell, San Francisco	Dick Garmaker, Minnesota
Dick Ricketts, Duquesne	Si Green, Duquesne
Darrell Floyd, Furman	Dick Ricketts, Duquesne

NCAA Championship

At Kansas City

San Francisco (77)				LaSalle (63)			
	FG	FT	Pts.		FG	FT	Pts.
Mullen	4	2	10	O'Malley	4	2	10
Buchanan	3	2	8	Singley	8	4	20
Russell	9	5	23	Gola	6	4	16
Jones	10	4	24	Lewis	1	4	6
Perry	1	2	4	Greenberg	1	1	3
Wiebusch	2	0	4	Blatcher	4	0	8
Zannini	1	0	2	Maples	0	0	0
Lawless	1	0	2	Fredericks	0	0	0
Kirby	0	0	0				
Totals	31	15	77		24	15	63

NCAA SCORES
REGIONALS

East

First Round: LaSalle 95, West Virginia 61; Canisius 73, Williams 60; Villanova 74, Duke 73

Semifinals: LaSalle 73, Princeton 46; Canisius 73, Villanova 71

Championship: LaSalle 99, Canisius 64

Mideast

First Round: Marquette 90, Miami (O.) 79; Penn State 59, Memphis State 55

Semifinals: Marquette 79, Kentucky 71; Iowa 82, Penn State 53

Championship: Iowa 86, Marquette 81

Midwest

First Round: Bradley 69, Oklahoma City 65

Semifinals: Bradley 81, Southern Methodist 79; Colorado 69, Tulsa 59

Championship: Colorado 93, Bradley 81

Far West

First Round: Seattle 80, Idaho State 63; San Francisco 89, West Texas State 66

Semifinals: Oregon State 83, Seattle 71; San Francisco 78, Utah 59

Championship: San Francisco 57, Oregon State 56

FINAL

Semifinals: LaSalle 76, Iowa 73; San Francisco 62, Colorado 50

Championship: San Francisco 77, La Salle 63

Consolation: Colorado 75, Iowa 54

1955–56

San Francisco, paced by 6-10 Bill Russell, won 29 straight games—stretching its unbeaten string to a record 55 games over two seasons—and successfully defended its NCAA crown.

The Dons were ranked No. 1 by everyone as they swept to the California Basketball Association title and used the best defense in the country to limit opponents to 52.2 points a game. All season long the emphasis lay on the Dons' teamwork, despite the awesome presence of Russell. In the tournament, K. C. Jones was declared ineligible, and reserve Gene Brown filled in to keep the team winning.

The spectre of unbeaten San Francisco probably frightened the two best independents, Louisville and Dayton, into the NIT. In the NCAA tourney, the Dons rolled past UCLA, Utah, and Southern Methodist before beating Big Ten champion Iowa, with Carl Cain and Bill Logan, 83–71, for the NCAA crown. So balanced was San Francisco's team play that MVP honors went to Temple's Hal Lear, who scored a record 160 points in five games in leading the Owls to a third-place finish.

Generally regarded as the No. 2 team in the country was Atlantic Coast Conference champion North Carolina State, led by Ronnie Shavlik and Vic Molodet. The Wolfpack never got a chance to test San Francisco, however, as Canisius, with John McCarthy, scored a first-round upset victory in four overtimes to oust N.C. State from NCAA play.

The NIT finale saw Louisville defeat Dayton, 93–80, for the third time in the season. Charlie Tyra, tournament high scorer and MVP, paced the Cardinals as he outplayed Dayton's 7-foot Bill Uhl. St. Joseph's hit on 31 free throws to take third place from St. Francis (N.Y.).

The free throw lane was expanded this season from six to twelve feet in an effort to neutralize a tall man's height advantage by increasing the three-second area.

Conference champions: Alabama, Southeastern; West Virginia, Southern; Southern Methodist, Southwest; Dartmouth, Ivy League; Marshall, Mid-American; Houston, Missouri Valley; Utah, Skyline; Kansas State, Big Seven; Texas Tech, Border; and Morehead State, Ohio Valley.

Darrell Floyd of Furman and Robin Freeman of Ohio State staged a two-man battle for individual scoring honors, averaging 33.8 and 32.9 points per game, respectively. George Washington's Joe Holup was the top rebounder, grabbing 23 per game, and was the most accurate shooter, making 64.7 per cent of his field goal attempts.

Among the independents, Holy Cross, with Tommy Heinsohn, was tough, as were Duquesne, with Si Green; Notre Dame, with Lloyd Aubrey; Detroit, with Bill Ebben; DePaul, with Ron Sobieszczyk; Oklahoma City; and Seattle.

Stars included Willie Naulls, UCLA; Bob Burrow, Kentucky; Lennie Rosenbluth, North Carolina; Rod Hundley, West Virginia; Norm Stewart, Missouri; Julius McCoy, Michigan State; Jerry Harper, Alabama; Art Bunte, Utah; Paul Judson and Bill Ridley, both Illinois; Joe Capua, Wyoming; James Ray, Toledo; and Temple Tucker, Rice.

NCAA Championship

At Evanston, Ill.

San Francisco (83)	FG	FT	Pts.	Iowa (71)	FG	FT	Pts.
Boldt	7	2	16	Cain	7	3	17
Farmer	0	0	0	Schoof	5	4	14
Preaseau	3	1	7	Logan	5	2	12
Russell	11	4	26	George	0	0	0
Nelson	0	0	0	Scheuerman	4	3	11
Perry	6	2	14	Seaberg	5	7	17
Brown	6	4	16	Martel	0	0	0
Baxter	2	0	4	McConnell	0	0	0
Totals	35	13	83		26	19	71

NCAA SCORES
REGIONAL
East

First Round: Connecticut 84, Manhattan 75; Temple 74, Holy Cross 72; Dartmouth 61, West Virginia 59; Canisius 79, North Carolina State 78

Semifinals: Temple 65, Connecticut 59; Canisius 66, Dartmouth 58

Championship: Temple 60, Canisius 58

Mideast

First Round: Morehead State 107, Marshall 92; Wayne 72, DePaul 63

Semifinals: Kentucky 84, Wayne 64; Iowa 97, Morehead State 83

Championship: Iowa 89, Kentucky 77

Midwest

First Round: Southern Methodist 68, Texas Tech 67; Oklahoma City 91, Memphis State 81

Semifinals: Southern Methodist 89, Houston 74; Oklahoma City 97, Kansas State 93

Championship: Southern Methodist 84, Oklahoma City 63

Far West

First Round: Seattle 68, Idaho State 66

Semifinals: Utah 81, Seattle 72; San Francisco 72, UCLA 61

Championship: San Francisco 92, Utah 77

FINAL

Semifinals: San Francisco 86, Southern Methodist 68; Iowa 83, Temple 76

Championship: San Francisco 83, Iowa 71

Consolation: Temple 90, Southern Methodist 81

San Francisco's Bill Russell after deflecting shot in NCAA final against Iowa

NIT Championship

At New York

Louisville (93)				Dayton (80)			
	FG	FT	Pts.		FG	FT	Pts.
Darragh	4	3	11	Paxson	4	2	10
Harrah	6	0	12	McCarthy	0	0	0
Moreman	0	10	10	Lane	0	2	2
Keffer	0	0	0	Palmer	9	3	21
Tyra	11	5	27	Uhl	6	7	19
Dupont	1	0	2	Sicking	3	2	8
Rollins	6	5	17	Dieringer	2	0	4
Morgan	3	8	14	Riazzi	2	0	4
				Bockhorn	6	0	12
				Almashy	0	0	0
				Bogenrife	0	0	0
Totals	31	31	93		32	16	80

NIT SCORES

First Round: St. Francis (N. Y.) 85, Lafayette 74;
Duquesne 69; Oklahoma A&M 61; Seton
Hall 96, Marquette 78; Xavier (O.) 84,
St. Louis 80

Quarterfinals: Louisville 84, Duquesne 72; St. Francis
(N. Y.) 74, Niagara 72; St. Joseph's 74, Seton
Hall 65; Dayton 72, Xavier (O.) 68

Semifinals: Dayton 89, St. Francis (N. Y.) 58;
Louisville 89, St. Joseph's 79

Championship: Louisville 93, Dayton 80

Consolation: St. Joseph's 93, St. Francis (N. Y.) 82

Top Ten

AP	UP
San Francisco	San Francisco
North Carolina State	North Carolina State
Dayton	Dayton
Iowa	Iowa
Alabama	Alabama
Louisville	Southern Methodist
Southern Methodist	Louisville
UCLA	Illinois
Kentucky	UCLA
Illinois	Vanderbilt

All-American

AP	UP
Bill Russell, San Francisco	Bill Russell, San Francisco
Robin Freeman, Ohio State	Si Green, Duquesne
Si Green, Duquesne	Robin Freeman, Ohio State
Darrell Floyd, Furman	Darrell Floyd, Furman
Tom Heinsohn, Holy Cross	K. C. Jones, San Francisco

1956–57

North Carolina withstood successive triple-overtime challenges from Michigan State and Kansas to capture the NCAA championship at the end of a 32–0 season, best record ever for a tourney winner.

The championship game was set up after

Big Ten ruler Michigan State, led by Johnny Green and Jack Quiggle, pushed North Carolina into three extra periods before succumbing in a semifinal. Kansas breezed through the Western regionals into the final. The Jayhawks were led by a highly publicized sophomore, 7-foot Wilt Chamberlain, who forced the opposition to devise special defenses for him.

Atlantic Coast Conference champion North Carolina, with Lennie Rosenbluth countering Chamberlain, was pushed into three overtimes again in the championship game before downing Kansas, 54–53. Chamberlain outpolled Rosenbluth for MVP, 17–15, as he averaged 30.3 points in four games. Rosenbluth was high scorer, however, with 140 points in five games.

Bradley's one-two punch of Barney Cable and Shelly McMillon led the Braves to an 84–83 victory over Memphis State for the NIT championship. Win Wilfong of the losers was high scorer with 89 points in four games and took MVP honors.

Chamberlain and Seattle's 6-5 Elgin Baylor, also a sophomore, were involved in a hot five-man battle for individual scoring honors, eventually won by South Carolina's Grady Wallace (31.2 points a game). Mississippi's Joe Gibbon, a future major league baseball pitcher, was second with 30.0 points a game, followed by Baylor, Chamberlain, and Columbia's Chet Forte.

Rod "Hot Rod" Hundley, with his Harlem Globetrotter-like antics, ended his collegiate career by leading West Virginia to the Southern Conference crown, while Jim Krebs sparked Southern Methodist to the title in the Southwest Conference. San Francisco, featuring Gene Brown and Mike Farmer, had its three-season winning streak snapped at 60 games, but easily won the California Basketball Association championship.

Morehead, led by another future big league baseball pitcher, Steve Hamilton, was the best rebounding team in the country as it won the Ohio Valley Conference race, and Miami (O.), powered by Wayne Embry, was the Mid-American Conference titlist. Other conference champions were: Yale, Ivy League; California, Pacific Coast; Kentucky, Southeastern; Brigham Young, Skyline; St. Louis, Missouri Valley; Texas Western, Border; Idaho State, Rocky Mountain; and Connecticut, Yankee.

Strong independents included Louisville, with Charlie Tyra; Oklahoma City, with Hub Reed; Niagara, with Alex "Boo" Ellis; Temple, with Guy Rodgers; and St. Bonaventure, led by Brendan McCann. Other prominent teams were Manhattan, which made a record 45.6 per cent of its shots from the floor; Mississippi State, with Bailey Howell; Kansas State, with Jack Parr; Syracuse, with Vince Cohen; Illinois, led by George Bonsalle; and Iowa State, with Gary Thompson.

Several quintets featured players who achieved fame in other sports. They included Ron Kramer (football and track) at Michigan; Frank Howard (football and baseball) at Ohio State; Rafer Johnson (decathlon) at UCLA; Bob Gibson (baseball) at Creighton; and Jimmy Brown (football and lacrosse) at Syracuse.

NCAA Championship
At Kansas City

North Carolina (54)	FG	FT	Pts.	Kansas (53)	FG	FT	Pts.
Rosenbluth	8	4	20	Elstun	4	3	11
Lotz	0	0	0	Loneski	0	2	2
Brennan	4	3	11	L. Johnson	0	2	2
Young	1	0	2	Chamberlain	6	11	23
Quigg	4	2	10	King	3	5	11
Cunningham	0	0	0	Parker	2	0	4
Kearns	4	3	11	Billings	0	0	0
Totals	21	12	54		15	23	53

NCAA SCORES
REGIONALS
East

First Round: Syracuse 82, Connecticut 76; Canisius 64, West Virginia 56; North Carolina 90, Yale 74

Semifinals: Syracuse 75, Lafayette 71; North Carolina 87, Canisius 75

Championship: North Carolina 67, Syracuse 58

Mideast

First Round: Pittsburgh 86, Morehead State 85; Notre Dame 89, Miami (O.) 77

Semifinals: Kentucky 98, Pittsburgh 92; Michigan State 85, Notre Dame 83

Championship: Michigan State 80, Kentucky 68

Midwest

First Round: Oklahoma City 76, Loyola (La.) 55

Semifinals: Oklahoma City 75, St. Louis 66; Kansas 73, Southern Methodist 65

Kansas' Wilt Chamberlain has it as North Carolina's Len Rosenbluth reaches in NCAA final

Championship: Kansas 81, Oklahoma City 61

Far West

First Round: Idaho State 68, Harden-Simmons 57

Semifinals: California 86, Brigham Young 59; San Francisco 50, California 46

FINALS

Semifinals: North Carolina 74, Michigan State 70; Kansas 80, San Francisco 56

Championship: North Carolina 54, Kansas 53

Consolation: San Francisco 67, Michigan State 60

NIT Championship

At New York

Bradley (84)	FG	FT	Pts.	Memphis State (83)	FG	FT	Pts.
Cable	8	1	17	Wilfong	10	11	31
McDade	1	3	5	Ragan	3	4	10
B. Mason	5	12	22	Hockaday	0	2	2
Johnson	0	0	0	Arnold	5	4	14
McMillon	8	2	18	Butcher	7	7	21
Emerson	0	1	1	Swander	2	1	5
Sedgewick	0	0	0	Hays	0	0	0
Myers	1	2	4				
Morse	4	1	9				
Dhabalt	3	2	8				
Totals	30	24	84		27	29	83

NIT SCORES

First Round: Memphis State 77, Utah 75; Xavier (O.) 85, Seton Hall 79; Dayton 79, St. Peter's (N. J.) 71; St. Bonaventure 90, Cincinnati 72

Quarterfinals: Memphis State 80, Manhattan 73; St. Bonaventure 85, Seattle 68; Bradley 116, Xavier (O.) 81; Temple 77, Dayton 66

Semifinals: Memphis State 80, St. Bonaventure 78; Bradley 94, Temple 66

Championship: Bradley 84, Memphis State 83

Consolation: Temple 67, St. Bonaventure 50

Top Ten

AP	UPI
North Carolina	North Carolina
Kansas	Kansas
Kentucky	Kentucky
Southern Methodist	Southern Methodist
Seattle	Seattle
Louisville	California
West Virginia	Michigan State
Vanderbilt	Louisville
Oklahoma City	UCLA
St. Louis	St. Louis

All-Americans

AP	UPI
Wilt Chamberlain, Kansas	Wilt Chamberlain, Kansas
Lennie Rosenbluth, North Carolina	Chet Forte, Columbia
Rod Hundley, West Virginia	Lennie Rosenbluth, North Carolina
Gary Thompson, Iowa State	Grady Wallace, South Carolina
Chet Forte, Columbia	Rod Hundley, West Virginia

1957–58

Oscar Robertson became the first sophomore ever to win a national scoring title as he averaged 35.1 points and teamed with 6-9 Connie Dierking to lead Cincinnati to a 25–3 record and the Missouri Valley Conference title.

A change in the free throw bonus rule, awarding the extra shot only after six team fouls in each half, generally lowered scoring averages. Robertson, Seattle's Elgin Baylor, and Kansas' Wilt Chamberlain were the only players to average more than 30 points a game. Marshall, with Leo Byrd averaging 25.0 points and Hal Greer 23.6 points, led in team scoring with an 88.0 average.

Lightly regarded Kentucky accomplished the unprecedented feat of winning a fourth NCAA championship. The Wildcats, led by Vern Hatton and Adrian Smith, beat Seattle, 84–72, for the NCAA title. Seattle's Baylor won the MVP award as he scored 135 points in tourney play. Southeastern Conference champion Kentucky had the dubious honor of owning the worst record ever for an NCAA champion, 23 victories and six losses.

Another unheralded team, Xavier (O.), took the NIT crown by beating second-seeded Dayton, 78–74, in overtime. Xavier had to overcome a 41-point performance by Niagara's Alex "Boo" Ellis in an early round game in order to advance. Hank Stein of Xavier, with 90 points in four games, won scoring honors and the MVP trophy.

West Virginia, powered by 6-10 Lloyd Sharrar and 6-3 Jerry West, was generally regarded as the top team in the country after winning the Southern Conference title, but the Mountaineers couldn't overcome their NCAA tournament jinx and again lost in the first round. Temple, with Guy Rodgers and Jay Norman, had its 25-game winning streak snapped in the NCAA tourney by Kentucky.

The best defensive team in the country, San Francisco, led by Mike Farmer, won the West Coast Athletic Conference (formerly California Basketball Association) race and Kansas State, paced by Bob Boozer, beat out Chamberlain and Kansas for the Big Eight (formerly Big Seven) title. Rudy LaRusso led Dartmouth to the Ivy League title and Miami (O.), once again powered by Wayne Embry, repeated in the Mid-American Conference. Notre Dame, with Tom Hawkins, was one of the outstanding teams in the Midwest, as was Big Ten champion Indiana, with Archie Dees.

Conference champions: Arkansas and Southern Methodist, tied, Southwest; Tennessee Tech, Ohio Valley; Duke, Atlantic Coast; Connecticut, Yankee; Arizona State, Border; and Idaho State, Rocky Mountain.

Strong teams included Pitt, with little Don Hennon; St. John's with Al Seiden; St. Bonaventure, with Tom Stith; North Carolina, with Pete Brennan; Mississippi State, with Bailey Howell; Washington & Lee, with Dom Flora; Illinois, with Don Ohl; Drake, with Phil Murrell; and Oregon State, with Dave Gambee.

Future major league pitcher Sonny Siebert was the leading scorer for Missouri and Jerry Adair, another big league baseball player, played basketball for Oklahoma State (formerly Oklahoma A&M).

NCAA Championship

At Louisville

Kentucky (84)	FG	FT	Pts.	Seattle (72)	FG	FT	Pts.
Cox	10	4	24	Frizzell	4	8	16
Crigler	5	4	14	Ogorek	4	2	10
Beck	0	0	0	Baylor	9	7	25
Mills	4	1	9	Harney	2	0	4
Hatton	9	12	30	Brown	6	5	17
Smith	2	3	7	Saunders	0	0	0
				Piasecki	0	0	0
Totals	30	24	84		25	22	72

NCAA SCORES
REGIONALS

East

First Round: Maryland 86, Boston College 63; Manhattan 89, West Virginia 84; Dartmouth 75, Connecticut 64

Semifinals: Temple 71, Maryland 67; Dartmouth 79, Manhattan 62

Championship: Temple 69, Dartmouth 50

Mideast

First Round: Miami (O.) 82, Pittsburgh 77; Notre Dame 94, Tennessee Tech 61

Semifinals: Kentucky 94, Miami (O.) 70; Notre Dame 94, Indiana 87

Championship: Kentucky 89, Notre Dame 56

Midwest

First Round: Oklahoma State 59, Loyola (La.) 52

Semifinals: Oklahoma State 65, Arkansas 40; Kansas State 83, Cincinnati 80

Championship: Kansas State 69, Oklahoma State 57

Far West

First Round: Seattle 88, Wyoming 51; Idaho State 72, Arizona State 68

Semifinals: Seattle 69, San Francisco 67; California 54, Idaho State 43

Championship: Seattle 66, California 62

FINALS

Semifinals: Kentucky 61, Temple 60; Seattle 73, Kansas State 51

Championship: Kentucky 84, Seattle 72

Consolation: Temple 67, Kansas State 57

Only a sophomore, Oscar Robertson of Cincinnati won national scoring honors with a 35.1 average

All-Americans

AP	UPI
Wilt Chamberlain, Kansas	Wilt Chamberlain, Kansas
Oscar Robertson, Cincinnati	Oscar Robertson, Cincinnati
Elgin Baylor, Seattle	Elgin Baylor, Seattle
Guy Rogers, Temple	Guy Rodgers, Temple
Don Hennon, Pittsburgh	Don Hennon, Pittsburgh

1958–59

Defense, as executed by its foremost practitioner, California, reigned supreme as the Golden Bears won their last 16 games in a row, including a 71–70 triumph over West Virginia, to gain the NCAA championship.

California, Pacific Coast Conference champion, allowed an average of 51 points a game in compiling a 25–4 record. Leading the Bears were 6-10 Darrall Imhoff and 6-5 defensive specialist Bill McClintock. West Virginia finally made it past the first round of an NCAA tourney as the Mountaineers qualified by winning their fifth consecutive Southern Conference crown. Jerry West and Willie Akers were the mainstays of the West Virginia attack.

St. John's led a New York area resurgence as the Redmen won the NIT, beating Bradley, 76–71, in the championship game. This was the third NIT title for St. John's, the only team to accomplish this feat. Al Seiden of the Redmen set a pair of free throw records and his teammate, Tony Jackson, won MVP honors. Cal Ramsey of third-place NYU was high scorer with 82 points in four games.

The tournament play revealed that ratings meant little, as Kansas State and Kentucky, generally rated one-two in the country, were eliminated in early play. Kansas State, led by Bob Boozer, was the Big Eight champion while Kentucky, with Johnny Cox, played in the NCAA tourney after Southeastern Conference champion Mississippi State withdrew because of the presence of black players in the tournament.

Oscar Robertson retained his individual

NIT Championship

At New York

Xavier (O.) (78)	FG	FT	Pts.	Dayton (74)	FG	FT	Pts.
Viviano	5	0	10	A. Bockhorn	5	0	10
Olberding	2	2	6	Case	10	1	21
Tartaron	6	2	14	McCarthy	9	3	21
Stein	9	5	23	Lane	6	4	16
Castelle	8	3	19	T. Bockhorn	1	4	6
Piontek	3	0	6	H. Bockhorn	0	0	0
				Josefczyk	0	0	0
				Bogenrife	0	0	0
Totals	33	12	78		31	12	74

NIT SCORES

First Round: St. John's 76, Butler 69; St. Joseph's 83, St. Peter's (N. J.) 76; Xavier (O.) 95, Niagara 86; Fordham 83, St. Francis (Pa.) 59

Quarterfinals: St. John's 71, Utah 70; St. Bonaventure 79, St. Joseph's 75; Xavier (O.) 72, Bradley 62; Dayton 74, Fordham 70

Semifinals: Dayton 80, St. John's 56; Xavier (O.) 72, St. Bonaventure 53

Championship: Xavier (O.) 78, Dayton 74

Consolation: St. Bonaventure 84, St. John's 69

Top Ten

AP	UPI
West Virginia	West Virginia
Cincinnati	Cincinnati
Kansas State	San Francisco
San Francisco	Kansas State
Temple	Temple

scoring title, averaging 32.6 points a game, as he took Cincinnati to the Missouri Valley Conference title ahead of strong teams at Bradley, with Bobby Joe Mason, and St. Louis, led by Bob Ferry.

Several conference races ended in ties, including the Ivy League where Dartmouth, with Rudy LaRusso, defeated Princeton in a playoff, and the Atlantic Coast Conference, where North Carolina and North Carolina State were knotted. Bowling Green and Miami (O.) shared the Mid-American Conference honors, and New Mexico State, Arizona State, and Texas Western all tied in the Border Conference.

Tom Meschery led St. Mary's to the West Coast Athletic Conference crown, while other conference champions included Michigan State, Big Ten; Texas Christian, Southwest; St. Joseph's, Middle Atlantic; Idaho State, Rocky Mountain; Eastern Kentucky, Ohio Valley; and Connecticut, Yankee.

Marquette, with Don Kojis and Mike Moran, was strong in the Midwest while Miami (Fla.), with Dick Hickox, was the nation's top scoring team, averaging 87.6 points a game. Other strong teams: Auburn, with Rex Frederick; Denver, with Tim Peay; Marshall, with Leo Byrd; UCLA, with Walt Torrence; Washington, with Doug Smart; Louisville, with Don Goldstein; Tennessee, with Gene Tormohlen; Seattle, with Charlie "Sweet Charlie" Brown; Air Force, with Bob Beckel; Wyoming, with Tony Windis; and Northwestern, with Joe Ruklick.

NCAA SCORES
REGIONALS
East
First Round: West Virginia 82, Dartmouth 68; Boston U. 60, Connecticut 58; Navy 76, North Carolina 63

Semifinals: West Virginia 95, St. Joseph's 92; Boston U. 62, Navy 55

Championship: West Virginia 86, Boston U. 82

Mideast
First Round: Louisville 77, Eastern Kentucky 63; Marquette 89, Bowling Green 79

Semifinals: Louisville 76, Kentucky 61; Michigan State 74, Marquette 69

Championship: Louisville 88, Michigan State 81

Midwest
First Round: DePaul 57, Portland 56

Semifinals: Kansas State 102, DePaul 70; Cincinnati 77, Texas Christian 73

Championship: Cincinnati 85, Kansas State 75

Far West
First Round: Idaho State 62, New Mexico State 61

Semifinals: St Mary's 80, Idaho State 71; California 71, Utah 53

Championship: California 66, St. Mary's 46

FINALS
Semifinals: West Virginia 94, Louisville 79; California 64, Cincinnati 58

Championship: California 71, West Virginia 70

Consolation: Cincinnati 98, Louisville 85

NIT Championship
At New York

	FG	FT	Pts.		FG	FT	Pts.
St. John's (76)				Bradley (71)			
Engert	2	0	4	Smith	4	0	8
Jackson	9	3	21	Morse	6	4	16
Roethel	5	2	12	McDade	6	4	16
Seiden	7	8	22	Mason	7	4	18
Alfieri	5	5	15	Owens	4	2	10
Pedone	0	0	0	Saunders	1	1	3
Ryan	1	0	2	Hewitt	0	0	0
				Voegele	0	0	0
Totals	29	18	76		28	15	71

NIT SCORES
First Round: Butler 94, Fordham 80; NYU 90, Denver 81; Providence 68, Manhattan 66; St. John's 75, Villanova 67

Quarterfinals: Bradley 83, Butler 77; NYU 63, Oklahoma City 48; Providence 75, St. Louis 72; St. John's 82, St. Bonaventure 74

Semifinals: Bradley 59, NYU 57; St. John's 76, Providence 55

Championship: St. John's 76, Bradley 71

Consolation: NYU 71, Providence 57

NCAA Championship
At Louisville

California (71)	FG	FT	Pts.	West Virginia (70)	FG	FT	Pts.
Dalton	6	3	15	West	10	8	28
McClintock	4	0	8	Clousson	4	2	10
Imhoff	4	2	10	Akers	5	0	10
Buch	0	2	2	Bolyard	1	4	6
Fitzpatrick	8	4	20	Smith	2	1	5
Grout	4	2	10	Retton	0	2	2
Simpson	0	0	0	Ritchie	1	2	4
Doughty	3	0	6	Patrone	2	1	5
Totals	29	13	71		25	20	70

Top Ten

AP	UPI
Kansas State	Kansas State
Kentucky	Kentucky
Mississippi State	Michigan State
Bradley	Cincinnati
Cincinnati	North Carolina State
North Carolina State	Tie { North Carolina
Michigan State	{ Mississippi State
Auburn	Bradley
North Carolina	California
West Virginia	Auburn

All-Americans

AP	UPI
Oscar Robertson, Cincinnati	Oscar Robertson, Cincinnati
Jerry West, West Virginia	Bailey Howell, Mississippi State
Bob Boozer, Kansas State	Bob Boozer, Kansas State
Bailey Howell, Mississippi State	Jerry West, West Virginia
Johnny Cox, Kentucky	Don Hennon, Pittsburgh

Jerry West made the headlines as West Virginia won the Southern Conference championship

Cincinnati's Oscar Robertson straddled the world as he took his second scoring title

1959-60

The Big "O," Oscar Robertson, finished a career at Cincinnati that brought innumerable scoring records, including the national scoring title three consecutive years. He led his team to 79 victories in 88 games and three straight Missouri Valley Conference championships. About the only thing that eluded him and his teammates was an NCAA championship.

The NCAA title game this year was a battle between offense and defense, with Pacific Coast Conference champion California yielding 49.5 points a game and Big Ten titlist Ohio State scoring 90.5 points a game. Each team led the nation in its specialty.

California had Darrall Imhoff, Bill McClintock, and Earl Shultz, but Ohio State shot a dazzling 68.4 per cent from the field as 6-8 sophomore Jerry Lucas, John Havlicek, Larry Siegfried, Joe Roberts, and Mel Nowell blended to rout the Golden Bears, 75–55, in the championship game. Lucas was named MVP while Robertson, leading Cincinnati to the consolation title, was the leading scorer with 122 points.

The NIT saw Bradley, runner-up to Cincinnati in the Missouri Valley race, outscore Providence 38–10 in the final ten minutes of the championship game to gain an 88–72 victory. Bradley was led by Chet Walker and Bobby Joe Mason, but it was Providence's Lenny Wilkens who received the MVP award. Tom Stith of St. Bonaventure was the leading scorer with 114 points as the Bonnies scored a record 354 points in their four tourney games.

Billy "The Hill" McGill, a 6-9 sophomore, led Utah to the Skyline Conference title ahead of Utah State, featuring future professional football star Cornell Green. Indiana, with 6-11 Walt Bellamy, was runner-up to Ohio State in the Big Ten, while Wally Frank took Kansas State to a tie in the Big Eight with Kansas, featuring Bill Bridges and Wayne Hightower.

Auburn gained the Southeastern Conference championship ahead of Georgia Tech, with little Roger Kaiser, and Kentucky. West Virginia had its 56-game Southern Conference winning streak snapped as the Mountaineers, led by Jerry West, finished second to Virginia Tech in the regular season standings but won the league's post-season tourney.

Duke emerged as Atlantic Coast Conference titlist after winning the conference post-season tournament, although Wake Forest, with Dave Budd and Len Chappell, and North Carolina, with Lee Shaffer, Doug Moe and York Larese, had better regular season records. Jay Arnett led Texas to the Southwest Conference crown while other conference champions were Ohio U., Mid-American; St. Joseph's, Middle Atlantic; Santa Clara and Loyola (Calif.), tied, West Coast Athletic Conference; Idaho State, Rocky Mountain; Princeton, Ivy League; Connecticut, Yankee; Western Kentucky, Ohio Valley; and New Mexico State, Border.

NYU, with Tom Sanders, was a surprising semifinalist in the NCAA tourney as the Violets vied for independent honors with St. John's, led by Tony Jackson; Holy Cross, with sharp-shooting sophomore Jack "The Shot" Foley, and Detroit, with Dave DeBusschere. Other strong teams were Niagara, with Al Butler; Purdue, with Terry Dischinger; Bowling Green, with Jim Darrow; Villanova; Memphis State; Notre Dame; and DePaul.

NCAA Championship

At San Francisco

Ohio State (75)	FG	FT	Pts.	California (55)	FG	FT	Pts.
Havlicek	4	4	12	McClintock	4	2	10
Roberts	5	0	10	Gillis	4	0	8
Lucas	7	2	16	Imhoff	3	2	8
Nowell	6	3	15	Wendell	0	4	4
Siegfried	5	3	13	Shultz	2	2	6
Gearhart	0	0	0	Mann	3	1	7
Cedargren	0	1	1	Doughty	4	3	11
Furry	2	0	4	Stafford	0	1	1
Hoyt	0	0	0	Morrison	0	0	0
Barker	0	0	0	Averbuck	0	0	0
Knight	0	0	0	Pearson	0	0	0
Nourse	2	0	4	Alexander	0	0	0
Totals	31	13	75		20	15	55

NCAA SCORES
REGIONALS

East

First Round: Duke 84, Princeton 60; West Virginia 94, Navy 86; NYU 78, Connecticut 59

Semifinals: Duke 58, St. Joseph's 56; NYU 82, West Virginia 81

Championship: NYU 74, Duke 59

Mideast

First Round: Ohio U. 74, Notre Dame 66; Western Kentucky 107, Miami (Fla.) 84

Semifinals: Georgia Tech 57, Ohio U. 54; Ohio State 98, Western Kentucky 79

Championship: Ohio State 86, Georgia Tech 69

Midwest

First Round: DePaul 69, Air Force 63

Semifinals: Cincinnati 99, DePaul 59; Kansas 90, Texas 81

Championship: Cincinnati 82, Kansas 71

Far West

First Round: California 71, Idaho State 44; Oregon 68, New Mexico State 60; Utah 80, Southern California 73

Semifinals: California 69, Santa Clara 49; Oregon 65, Utah 54

Championship: California 70, Oregon 49

FINALS

Semifinals: Ohio State 76, NYU 54; California 77, Cincinnati 69

Championship: Ohio State 75, California 55

Consolation: Cincinnati 95, NYU 71

NIT Championship
At New York

Bradley (88)	FG	FT	Pts.	Providence (72)	FG	FT	Pts.
Smith	6	3	15	Whelan	3	0	6
Herndon	11	4	26	Leonard	3	1	7
Walker	4	1	9	Hadnot	5	0	10
Saunders	1	9	11	Egan	5	10	20
Owens	5	3	13	Wilkins	10	5	25
Wodka	3	1	7	Moynahan	2	0	4
Tiemann	1	0	2	Gulmares	0	0	0
Edwards	1	1	3	Folliard	0	0	0
Roecker	1	0	2	Gibson	0	0	0
Granby	0	0	0				
Kissock	0	0	0				
Sash	0	0	0				
Totals	33	22	88		28	16	72

NIT SCORES

First Round: Villanova 88, Detroit 86; Providence 71, Memphis State 70; St. Bonaventure 94, Holy Cross 81; Dayton 72, Temple 51

Quarterfinals: Utah State 73, Villanova 72; Providence 64, St. Louis 53; Bradley 78, Dayton 64; St. Bonaventure 106, St. John's 71

Semifinals: Bradley 82, St. Bonaventure 71; Providence 68, Utah State 62

Championship: Bradley 88, Providence 72

Consolation: Utah State 99, St. Bonaventure 83

MVP of the NCAA tourney: Ohio State sophomore Jerry Lucas

Top Ten

AP	UPI
Cincinnati	California
California	Cincinnati
Ohio State	Ohio State
Bradley	Bradley
West Virginia	Utah
Utah	West Virginia
Indiana	Utah State
Utah State	Georgia Tech
St. Bonaventure	Villanova
Miami (Fla.)	Indiana

All-Americans

AP	UPI
Jerry West, West Virginia	Jerry West, West Virginia
Oscar Robertson, Cincinnati	Oscar Robertson, Cincinnati
Jerry Lucas, Ohio State	Jerry Lucas, Ohio State
Darrall Imhoff, California	Darrall Imhoff, California
Tony Jackson, St. John's	Tom Stith, St. Bonaventure

1960–61

The gamblers and point shavers were once again exposed on college campuses, but the improprieties did not involve as many teams, nor was it as far reaching as the 1951 scandal. Schools acted quickly and decisively, in some cases dismissing freshmen who had never played a game but nevertheless had taken money from gamblers.

On the court, Cincinnati, with Bob Wiesenhahn and Paul Hogue, snapped defending champion Ohio State's 32-game winning streak with a 70–65 overtime victory in the NCAA championship game. Big Ten champion Ohio State was led by Larry Siegfried, John Havlicek and Jerry Lucas, who repeated as MVP. Billy McGill of Utah's Skyline Conference co-champions (with Colorado State) was tournament high scorer with 117 points, including 32 in the consolation playoff with Middle Atlantic Conference champion St. Joseph's. Utah won, 127–120.

St. Bonaventure's 99-game home court winning skein was snapped, but Tom Stith took the Bonnies to the NIT for the third straight year. St. Bonaventure, the highest-scoring team in the nation with an 88.5-point-per-game average, was eliminated early, however, as Providence and St. Louis battled into the championship game. Providence was led by 6-10 Jim Hadnot and 6-0 Johnny Egan, but it was little (5-8) Vinnie Ernst who won MVP honors as the Friars beat St. Louis, 62–59. Jack "The Shot" Foley of Holy Cross was high scorer with 120 points in four games.

North Carolina won the regular season race in the Atlantic Coast Conference, but Wake Forest, with Len Chappell, took the post-season conference tournament.

Mississippi State refused to play in the racially integrated NCAA tourney after winning the Southeastern Conference title and was again replaced by Kentucky, while Southern California, paced by John Rudometkin, won the title in the AAWU (successor to the Pacific Coast Conference). West Virginia, with Lee Patrone and Rod Thorn, finished first in the regular season standings in the Southern Conference, but George Washington, with a 3–9 league record, captured the league's post-season tourney.

Texas Tech, with Del Ray Mounts, swept the Southwest Conference, while other league champions were Kansas State, Big Eight; Loyola (Calif.), West Coast Athletic; Arizona State and New Mexico State,

tied, Border; Ohio U., Mid-American; Princeton, Ivy; Rhode Island, Yankee; and Morehead, Eastern Kentucky, and Western Kentucky, tied, Ohio Valley. Missouri Valley Conference teams turned in outstanding records, with NCAA champion Cincinnati; NIT finalist St. Louis; Bradley, with Chet Walker; Wichita and Drake all winning more than 70 per cent of their non-conference games.

St. John's, with Tony Jackson, was the leading independent in the New York area, while Dayton, with Gary Roggenburk; Seattle, with Eddie Miles; Detroit, with Dave DeBusschere; Marquette, with Don Kojis; and Louisville, with John Turner, were also strong.

Some of the season's better players: Tom Meschery, St. Mary's (Calif.); Terry Dischinger, Purdue; Walt Bellamy, Indiana; Don Nelson, Iowa; Roger Kaiser, Georgia Tech; Gary Phillips, Houston; Bill Bridges and Wayne Hightower, Kansas; Jeff Cohen, William and Mary; Carroll Broussard, Texas A&M; and Howie Carl, DePaul.

NCAA Championship

At Kansas City

Cincinnati (70)				Ohio State (65)			
	FG	FT	Pts.		FG	FT	Pts.
Wiesenhahn	8	1	17	Havlicek	1	2	4
Thacker	7	1	15	Hoyt	3	1	7
Hogue	3	3	9	Lucas	10	7	27
Yates	4	5	13	Nowell	3	3	9
Bouldin	7	2	16	Siegfried	6	2	14
Sizer	0	0	0	Knight	1	0	2
Heidotting	0	0	0	Gearhart	1	0	2
Totals	29	12	70		25	15	65

NCAA SCORES
REGIONALS

East

First Round: Princeton 84, George Washington 67; St. Bonaventure 86, Rhode Island 76; Wake Forest 97, St. John's 74

Semifinals: St. Joseph's 72, Princeton 67; Wake Forest 78, St. Bonaventure 73

Championship: St. Joseph's 96, Wake Forest 86

Mideast

First Round: Louisville 76, Ohio U. 70; Morehead State 71, Xavier (O.) 66

Semifinals: Ohio State 56, Louisville 55; Kentucky 71, Morehead State 64

Championship: Ohio State 87, Kentucky 74

Providence (62)				St. Louis (59)			
	FG	FT	Pts.		FG	FT	Pts.
Zalucki	7	3	17	Reid	3	2	8
Moynahan	3	0	6	Harris	0	0	0
Flynn	3	2	8	Hartwager	0	0	0
Hadnot	6	6	18	Book	2	1	5
Ernst	2	0	4	Nordmann	5	6	16
Egan	4	1	9	Luechtfield	0	0	0
				Kieffer	9	0	18
				Latinovich	0	0	0
				Mankowsky	6	0	12
Totals	25	12	62		25	9	59

NIT SCORES

First Round: St. Louis 58, Miami (Fla.) 56;
Holy Cross 86, Detroit 82; Temple 79,
Army 66; Providence 73, DePaul 67

Quarterfinals: St. Louis 59, Colorado State 53;
Holy Cross 81, Memphis State 69; Dayton 62,
Temple 60; Providence 71, Niagara 68

Semifinals: St. Louis 67, Dayton 60; Providence 90,
Holy Cross 83

Championship: Providence 62, St. Louis 59

Consolation: Holy Cross 85, Dayton 67

Top Ten

AP	UPI
Ohio State	Ohio State
Cincinnati	Cincinnati
St. Bonaventure	St. Bonaventure
Kansas State	Kansas State
North Carolina	Southern California
Bradley	North Carolina
Southern California	Bradley
Iowa	St. John's
West Virginia	Duke
Duke	Wake Forest

All-Americans

AP	UPI
Jerry Lucas, Ohio State	Jerry Lucas, Ohio State
Tom Stith, St. Bonaventure	Tom Stith, St. Bonaventure
Terry Dischinger, Purdue	Terry Dischinger, Purdue
Roger Kaiser, Georgia Tech	Roger Kaiser, Georgia Tech
Chet Walker, Bradley	Chet Walker, Bradley

Cincinnati's Paul Hogue helped snap Ohio State's winning streak despite Jerry Lucas and John Havlicek (5)

Midwest

First Round: Houston 77, Marquette 61

Semifinals: Kansas State 75, Houston 64;
Cincinnati 78, Texas Tech 55

Championship: Cincinnati 69, Kansas State 64

Far West

First Round; Arizona State 72, Seattle 70;
Southern California 81, Oregon 79

Semifinals: Arizona State 86, Southern California 71;
Utah 91, Loyola (Cal.) 75

Championship: Utah 88, Arizona State 80

FINALS

Semifinals: Ohio State 95, St. Joseph's 69;
Cincinnati 82, Utah 67

Championship: Cincinnati 70, Ohio State 65

Consolation: St. Joseph's 127, Utah 120

1961-62

Cincinnati and Ohio State, the only teams from the same state ever to meet in the NCAA championship game, became the only teams ever to play for the championship two years in a row.

Cincinnati barely made it into the finals after being tied by Bradley, with Chet Walker, in the Missouri Valley Conference race. The Bearcats won the playoff and then had to survive an upset bid by UCLA, led by Johnny Green, in a semifinal game.

Ohio State breezed through the Big Ten and the Eastern Regionals, but Jerry Lucas, John Havlicek, Mel Nowell and Co. could not offset the inspired play of the Bearcats, led by Paul Hogue. Cincinnati won, 71–59, with Hogue taking the MVP trophy.

Dayton, after finishing second five times, finally won an NIT crown as the Flyers beat St. John's, 73–67. The title game pitted 6-9 Leroy Ellis of St. John's against 6-10 Bill Chmielewski of Dayton and the big Flyer got the better of it as he won MVP honors and the individual scoring title. It was Bill Green of Colorado State who turned in the outstanding shooting performance, however, as he hit on 14 of 14 shots from the floor in a losing game against Holy Cross.

Billy McGill scored 60 points in one game and topped the nation in scoring with a 38.8 average as he led Utah to the Skyline Conference crown. The Utes were denied an NCAA tourney berth, however, because of a rule infraction. Nate Thurmond and Howie Komives powered Bowling Green to the Mid-American Conference title while Mississippi State, with W. D. Stroud, and Kentucky, led by Cotton Nash, tied in the Southeastern Conference.

Jerry Lucas, with his 20-10 vision, led the nation for the third year in field goal accuracy and for the second time in rebounding. He was one of several Big Ten standouts, which included Purdue's Terry Dischinger; Iowa's Don Nelson; Indiana's Jimmy Rayl; and future professional football flanker Pete Gent of Michigan State.

Loyola (Ill.) was one of the top independents as the Ramblers, sparked by Jerry Harkness, had the highest scoring average in the nation, 90.2 points a game. Sophomores Barry Kramer and Harold "Happy" Hairston led NYU while little Willie Somerset powered Duquesne. Also strong were Creighton, with rebounder Paul Silas; Seattle with John Tresvant and Eddie Miles; Villanova, with Hubie White; Holy Cross; Providence; Memphis State; and Air Force.

Lenny Chappell once again sparked Wake Forest to the Atlantic Coast Conference title after being pushed by Duke, with Art Heyman. Bobby Rascoe and Darel Carrier led Western Kentucky to the Ohio Valley Conference crown while Texas Tech,

with Harold Hudgens, defeated Southern Methodist, led by Jan Loudermilk, for Southwest Conference honors. Other champions: Colorado, Big Eight; West Virginia, Southern; Arizona State, Border; St. Joseph's, Middle Atlantic; Massachusetts, Yankee; Yale, Ivy; and Pepperdine, West Coast Athletic Conference.

NCAA Championship

At Louisville

Cincinnati (71)	FG	FT	Pts.	Ohio State (59)	FG	FT	Pts.
Bonham	3	4	10	Havlicek	5	1	11
Wilson	1	4	6	McDonald	0	3	3
Hogue	11	0	22	Lucas	5	1	11
Thacker	6	9	21	Reasebeck	4	0	8
Yates	4	4	12	Nowell	4	1	9
Sizer	0	0	0	Doughty	0	0	0
				Gearhart	1	0	2
				Bradds	5	5	15
Totals	25	21	71		24	11	59

NCAA SCORES
REGIONALS

East

First Round: Wake Forest 92, Yale 82; NYU 70, Massachusetts 50; Villanova 90, West Virginia 75

Semifinals: Wake Forest 96, St. Joseph's 85, Villanova 79, NYU 76

Championship: Wake Forest 79, Villanova 69

Mideast

First Round: Butler 56, Bowling Green 55; Western Kentucky 90, Detroit 81

Semifinals: Kentucky 81, Butler 60; Ohio State 93, Western Kentucky 73

Championship: Ohio State 74, Kentucky 64

Midwest

First Round: Texas Tech 68, Air Force 66; Creighton 87, Memphis State 83

Semifinals: Colorado 67, Texas Tech 60, Cincinnati 66, Creighton 46

Championship: Cincinnati 73, Colorado 46

Far West

First Round: Oregon State 69, Seattle 65; Utah State 78, Arizona State 73

Semifinals: Oregon State 69, Pepperdine 67; UCLA 73, Utah State 62

Championship: UCLA 88, Oregon State 69

FINALS

Semifinals: Ohio State 84, Wake Forest 68; Cincinnati 72, UCLA 70

Championship: Cincinnati 71, Ohio State 59

Consolation: Wake Forest 82, UCLA 80

Dayton's Bill Chmielewski was NIT MVP

NIT Championship

At New York

Dayton (73)				St. John's (67)		
	FG	FT	Pts.		FG	FT	Pts.
Roggenburk	3	2	8	Hall	2	0	4
Schoen	5	2	12	Loughery	10	6	26
Greenberg	0	0	0	Ellis	5	12	22
Chmielewski	11	2	24	Kovac	2	1	5
G. Hatton	6	6	18	Burks	3	2	8
T. Hatton	4	3	11	O'Hara	0	0	0
				O'Sullivan	1	0	2
Totals	29	15	73		23	21	67

NIT SCORES

First Round: Dayton 79, Wichita 71; Temple 80, Providence 78; Holy Cross 72, Colorado State 71; Duquesne 70, Navy 58

Quarterfinals: Dayton 94, Houston 77; Loyola (III.) 75, Temple 64; Duquesne 88, Bradley 85; St. John's 80, Holy Cross 74

Semifinals: Dayton 98, Loyola (III.) 82; St. John's 75, Duquesne 65

Championship: Dayton 73, St. John's 67

Consolation: Loyola (III.) 95, Duquesne 84

Top Ten

AP	UP
Ohio State	Ohio State
Cincinnati	Cincinnati
Kentucky	Kentucky
Mississippi State	Mississippi State
Bradley	Kansas State
Kansas State	Bradley
Utah	Wake Forest
Bowling Green	Colorado
Colorado	Bowling Green
Duke	Utah

All-Americans

AP	UP
Jerry Lucas, Ohio State	Jerry Lucas, Ohio State
Terry Dischinger, Purdue	Terry Dischinger, Purdue
Billy McGill, Utah	Billy McGill, Utah
Chet Walker, Bradley	Chet Walker, Bradley
Len Chappell, Wake Forest	John Havlicek, Ohio State

1962–63

Loyola (Ill.), the nation's highest scoring team with a 91.8 average, weathered a case of championship jitters to end Cincinnati's bid for a third straight NCAA title.

Loyola, with Jerry Harkness, Les Hunter, Ron Miller, Vic Rouse, and John Egan, opened its NCAA bid by routing Ohio Valley Conference representative Tennessee Tech by 69 points. The Ramblers won the next three games by 10, 15 and 19 points before meeting Missouri Valley Conference champion Cincinnati, the best defensive team in the nation. The Bearcats had yielded 52.9 points a game.

A record crowd of 19,153 in Louisville's Freedom Hall saw Cincinnati dominate the game for 30 minutes before Ron Bonham, Tom Thacker, George Wilson, and Tony Yates got into foul trouble. Loyola then roused itself to earn a 60–58 victory in overtime.

The tourney MVP was Art Heyman of Duke's Atlantic Coast Conference champions, who defeated Oregon State in the consolation game. Oregon State, an independent like Loyola, was led by 7-foot Mel Counts and football Heisman Trophy winner Terry Baker.

Providence, with Ray Flynn, Vinnie Ernst and 6-10 John Thompson, waltzed to the NIT championship with an 81–66 triumph over Canisius, led by Bill O'Connor. Flynn took MVP honors and was high scorer with 83 points in three games.

Juniors Nick Werkman of Seton Hall and Barry Kramer of NYU staged the closest battle ever for the individual scoring crown. Werkman's 29.5-point average was .2 of a

En route to NCAA crown, Loyola's Les Hunter scores on Cincinnati's George Wilson

point better than Kramer's. Creighton's Paul Silas, also a junior, edged Gus Johnson of Idaho for the rebounding title, 20.6 rebounds per game to 20.3.

Arizona State, with Art Becker and Joe Caldwell, won the first title in the newly formed Western Athletic Conference as the Border and Skyline leagues disbanded. Ohio State, with Gary Bradds, tied Illinois, led by Dave Downey, in the Big Ten; while UCLA, sparked by Walt Hazzard, was knotted with Tom Dose-led Stanford in the

AAWU. Sharing the Big Eight title were Colorado, with Ken Charlton, and Kansas State, led by Willie Murrell.

NYU, with Kramer teaming with Harold "Happy" Hairston, was strong among the independents, as were Marquette, with Ron Glaser, Bob Hornack and Dick Nixon; Miami (Fla.) with 7-foot Mike McCoy and Rick Barry, and Seattle, once again powered by Eddie Miles.

Sophomore Bill Bradley made his debut in leading Princeton to the Ivy League title. Other conference champions were San Francisco, West Coast Athletic; Texas, Southwest; Bowling Green, Mid-American; West Virginia, Southern; Mississippi State, Southeastern; St. Joseph's, Middle Atlantic; and Connecticut, Yankee.

Among the stars: Rod Thorn, West Virginia; Fred Hetzel, Davidson; Bud Koper, Oklahoma City; Jeff Mullins, Duke; Ollie Johnson, San Francisco; Billy Cunningham, North Carolina; Bill Buntin, Michigan; Fred Crawford, St. Bonaventure; Nate Thurmond, Bowling Green; Dave Stallworth, Wichita; Cotton Nash, Kentucky; W. D. Stroud, Mississippi State; Wayne Estes, Utah State; and Jimmy Rayl, Indiana.

NCAA Championship

At Louisville

Loyola (III.) (60)	FG	FT	Pts.	Cincinnati (58)	FG	FT	Pts.
Harkness	5	4	14	Bonham	8	6	22
Rouse	6	3	15	Thacker	5	3	13
Hunter	6	4	16	Wilson	4	2	10
Egan	3	3	9	Yates	4	1	9
Miller	3	0	6	Shingleton	1	2	4
				Heidotting	0	0	0
Totals	23	14	60		22	14	58

NCAA SCORES
REGIONALS

East

First Round: NYU 93, Pittsburgh 83; West Virginia 77, Connecticut 71; St. Joseph's 82, Princeton 81

Semifinals: Duke 81, NYU 76; St. Joseph's 97, West Virginia 88

Championship: Duke 73, St. Joseph's 59

Mideast

First Round: Bowling Green 77, Notre Dame 72; Loyola (III.) 111, Tennessee Tech 42

Semifinals: Illinois 70, Bowling Green 67; Loyola (III.) 61, Mississippi State 51

Championship: Loyola (III.) 79, Illinois 64

Midwest

First Round: Oklahoma City 70, Colorado State 67; Texas 67, Texas Western 47

Semifinals: Colorado 78, Oklahoma City 72; Cincinnati 73, Texas 68

Championship: Cincinnati 67, Colorado 60

Far West

First Round: Arizona State 79, Utah State 75; Oregon State 70, Seattle 66

Semifinals: Arizona State 93, UCLA 79; Oregon State 65, San Francisco 61

Championship: Oregon State 83, Arizona State 65

FINALS

Semifinals: Loyola (III.) 94, Duke 75; Cincinnati 80, Oregon State 46

Championship: Loyola (III.) 60, Cincinnati 58

Consolation: Duke 85, Oregon State 63

NIT Championship

At New York

Providence (81)	FG	FT	Pts.	Canisius (66)	FG	FT	Pts.
Kovalski	4	2	10	McClory	0	0	0
Stone	7	9	23	Chester	10	1	21
Thompson	6	3	15	O'Connor	7	8	22
Flynn	9	2	20	Gennari	7	0	14
Ernst	2	5	9	Turtle	0	0	0
Simoni	0	0	0	Swiatek	0	0	0
Spencer	1	2	4	O'Mara	3	1	7
Stein	0	0	0	Kemmer	0	0	0
Nyire	0	0	0	Bossert	0	0	0
Dutton	0	0	0	Harrigan	0	0	0
				Oberding	0	2	2
				Brennan	0	0	0
Totals	29	23	81		27	12	66

NIT SCORES

First Round: Villanova 63, DePaul 51; St. Louis 63, LaSalle 61; Memphis State 70, Fordham 49; Miami (Fla.) 71, St. Francis (N.Y.) 70

Quarterfinals: Villanova 54, Wichita 53; Canisius 76, Memphis State 67; Marquette 84, St. Louis 49; Providence 106, Miami (Fla.) 96

Semifinals: Providence 70, Marquette 64; Canisius 61, Villanova 46

Championship: Providence 81, Canisius 66

Consolation: Marquette 66, Villanova 58

Top Ten

AP	UPI
Cincinnati	Cincinnati
Duke	Duke
Loyola (III.)	Arizona State
Arizona State	Loyola (III.)
Wichita	Illinois
Mississippi State	Wichita
Ohio State	Mississippi State
Illinois	Ohio State
NYU	Colorado
Colorado	Stanford

1963–64

A methodic, balanced UCLA, averaging only 6-5 per man and led by guards Walt Hazzard and Gail Goodrich and forward Kenny Washington, managed to win 30 straight games, including the NCAA championship match against Duke, 98–83.

Although generally rated No. 1 in the country, UCLA was not spectacular as it won the AAWU title and then plodded through three NCAA games, winning none

Gail Goodrich (25) was one of the mainstays of UCLA's 30–0 NCAA champions

by more than six points, before meeting Duke. The Blue Devils, champions of the Atlantic Coast Conference, featured Jay Buckley and Hack Tison, both 6-10, and flashy Jeff Mullins, but it was the steady play of Hazzard that spelled the difference and won MVP honors for the 6-3 Bruin.

Bradley's Braves hit on 62 per cent of their shots to overwhelm New Mexico, 86–54, and win the NIT. Bradley was powered by MVP Levern Tart and Joe Strawder, while New Mexico, Western Athletic Conference co-champion with Arizona State, countered with Ira "Large" Harge. NYU's Harold "Happy" Hairston was tournament high scorer with 91 points.

Bowling Green's Howie Komives won the individual scoring race with a 36.7 average as he was one of seven players to average better than 30 points, the most ever to average that many points in one season. The others were Nick Werkman, Seton Hall; Manny Newsome, Western Michigan; Bill Bradley, Princeton; Rick Barry, Miami (Fla.); Gary Bradds, Ohio State; and Steve Thomas, Xavier (O.). Another Xavier player, Bob Pelkington, edged Creighton's Paul Silas for the rebounding crown, averaging 21.80 rebounds a game to Silas' 21.75.

Michigan, with Bill Buntin and sophomore Cazzie Russell, tied Ohio State for the Big Ten title, while Wichita State, led by Dave Stallworth, and Drake, featuring McCoy McLemore, shared the Missouri Valley Conference crown. Perennial power Cincinnati, with Ron Bonham, finished fourth.

Davidson, sparked by Fred Hetzel, made a record 54.4 per cent of its field goal attempts in winning the Southern Conference crown, although yielding to Virginia Military in the league's post-season tournament. Ollie Johnson and Erwin Mueller led San Francisco to the West Coast Athletic Conference crown as John Beasley took Texas A&M to the top of the Southwest Conference and Cotton Nash sparked Kentucky to the Southeastern Conference title.

Other champions: Kansas State, Big Eight; Ohio U., Mid-American; Temple, Middle Atlantic; Murray State, Ohio Valley; Princeton, Ivy League; Connecticut and

Rhode Island, tied, Yankee; and Montana State in the newly formed Big Sky.

Oregon State, with 7-foot Mel Counts, was strong among the independents, as were Texas Western, with Jim "Bad News" Barnes; Villanova, sparked by little Wally Jones; and Syracuse, with Dave Bing. Also formidable were defending NCAA champion Loyola (Ill.); Army, with Mike Silliman; Providence, with John Thompson; and St. Bonaventure, with Fred Crawford.

Some of the other stars: Billy Cunningham, North Carolina; Wayne Estes, Utah State; Bud Koper, Oklahoma City; Barry Kramer, NYU; Willie Murrell, Kansas State; Dan Schultz, Tennessee; Steve Courtin, St. Joseph's; Mel Northway, Minnesota; and John Tresvant, Seattle.

NCAA Championship
At Kansas City

UCLA (98)	FG	FT	Pts.	Duke (83)	FG	FT	Pts.
Goodrich	9	9	27	Ferguson	2	0	4
Hazzard	4	3	11	Buckley	5	8	18
Hirsch	5	3	13	Tison	3	1	7
Erickson	2	4	8	Harrison	1	0	2
McIntosh	4	0	8	Mullins	9	4	22
Washington	11	4	26	Marin	8	0	16
Darrow	0	3	3	Vacendak	2	3	7
Hoffman	1	0	2	Mann	0	3	3
				Herbster	1	0	2
				Kitching	1	0	2
Totals	36	26	98		32	19	83

NCAA SCORES
REGIONALS

East

First Round: Villanova 77, Providence 66; Connecticut 53, Temple 48; Princeton 86, Virginia Military 60

Semifinals: Duke 87, Villanova 73; Connecticut 52, Princeton 50

Championship: Duke 101, Connecticut 54

Mideast

First Round: Ohio U. 71, Louisville 69; Loyola (Ill.) 101, Murray State 91

Semifinals: Ohio U. 85, Kentucky 69; Michigan 84, Loyola (Ill.) 80

Championship: Michigan 69, Ohio U. 57

Midwest

First Round: Creighton 89, Oklahoma City 78; Texas Western 68, Texas A&M 62

Semifinals: Wichita 84, Creighton 68; Kansas State 64, Texas Western 60

Championship: Kansas State 94, Wichita 86

Far West

First Round: Seattle 61, Oregon 57; Utah State 92, Arizona State 90

Semifinals: UCLA 95, Seattle 90; San Francisco 64, Utah State 58

Championship: UCLA 76, San Francisco 72

FINALS

Semifinals: Duke 91, Michigan 80; UCLA 90, Kansas State 84

Championship: UCLA 98, Duke 83

Consolation: Michigan 100, Kansas State 90

NIT Championship
At New York

Bradley (86)	FG	FT	Pts.	New Mexico (54)	FG	FT	Pts.
R. Patterson	0	0	0	C. Williams	3	1	7
Jackson	7	0	14	Lucero	1	1	3
Strawder	9	3	21	Harge	2	4	8
West	5	2	12	Ellis	7	4	18
Tart	4	5	13	Kruzich	3	1	7
Hall	0	0	0	Zarr	3	0	6
R. Williams	0	1	1	Howard	0	0	0
Thompson	5	1	11	J. Patterson	0	3	3
Martin	3	0	6	Wasson	1	0	2
Frederick	1	2	4	Jordan	0	0	0
Day	2	0	4	Johnstone	0	0	0
Hutchinson	0	0	0	Edsen	0	0	0
Totals	36	14	86		20	14	54

NIT SCORES

First Round: St. Joseph's 86, Miami (Fla.) 76; NYU 77, Syracuse 68; Army 64, St. Bonaventure 62; Drake 87, Pittsburgh 82

Quarterfinals: Bradley 83, St. Joseph's 81; NYU 79, DePaul 66; New Mexico 65, Drake 60; Army 67, Duquesne 65

Semifinals: New Mexico 72, NYU 65; Bradley 67, Army 52

Championship: Bradley 86, New Mexico 54

Consolation: Army 60, NYU 59

Top Ten

AP	UPI
UCLA	UCLA
Michigan	Michigan
Duke	Kentucky
Kentucky	Duke
Wichita	Oregon State
Oregon State	Wichita
Villanova	Villanova
Loyola (Ill.)	Loyola (Ill.)
DePaul	Texas Western
Davidson	Davidson

All-Americans

AP	UPI
Gary Bradds, Ohio State	Gary Bradds, Ohio State
Cotton Nash, Kentucky	Walt Hazzard, UCLA
Walt Hazzard, UCLA	Cotton Nash, Kentucky
Bill Bradley, Princeton	Bill Bradley, Princeton
Dave Stallworth, Wichita	Dave Stallworth, Wichita

1964–65

Joe Lapchick, as a coach, and Bill Bradley, as a player, ended their collegiate careers in spectacular fashion as Lapchick's St. John's team won an unprecedented fourth NIT championship and Bradley, the Player of the Year, led Princeton to the consolation title in the NCAA tournament.

St. John's upset top-seeded Villanova, 55–51, for the NIT title to give Lapchick a victory and NIT crown in his final game as a coach. Villanova was led by Jim Washington, but it was Ken McIntyre of St. John's, scoring 101 points including 16 straight free throws without a miss in one game, who won MVP honors. With an expanded field

Princeton's Bill Bradley was Player of the Year

of 14 teams, a record 114,714 people attended the seven NIT sessions at Madison Square Garden.

Bradley, who refused immediate offers to play professional basketball in order to accept a Rhodes scholarship to study at Oxford, scored a record 58 points in leading Ivy League champion Princeton to a third-place victory over Wichita State, 118–82, in the NCAA tourney. Bradley, who had turned down scholarship offers from schools throughout the country to pay his own way at Princeton, scored a record 177 points during the tourney to win the MVP trophy.

UCLA won its second straight NCAA title with a 91–80 triumph over Big Ten champion Michigan, with Cazzie Russell and Bill Buntin. UCLA was led by Gail Goodrich, who scored 42 points in the championship game, and Keith Erickson.

Rick Barry was the nation's top scorer with a 37.4 average as he led Miami (Fla.) to a record scoring average of 98.4 points a game. Miami made 79.6 per cent of its free throw attempts, also a record high. Runnerup to Barry was Utah State's Wayne Estes, who was accidentally electrocuted midway through the season when his head brushed a live electric power line following a traffic accident.

Fred Hetzel and Dick Snyder combined to lead Davidson to the Southern Conference title while 6-9 Clyde Lee took Vanderbilt to Southeastern Conference honors. Connecticut won the Yankee Conference race behind Toby Kimball, the nation's leading rebounder. Duke, with Bobby Verga and Jack Marin, won the Atlantic Coast Conference title. Wichita State won the Missouri Valley Conference crown on the strength of Kelly Pete and mid-year graduate Dave Stallworth.

St. Joseph's, with Matt Guokas, whose father led the same team 25 years earlier, won the Middle Atlantic Conference crown; and Brigham Young, with John Fairchild, won the Western Athletic Conference race. Other champions: San Francisco, West Coast Athletic; Eastern Kentucky, Ohio Valley; Oklahoma State, Big Eight; Miami (O.) and Ohio U., tied, Mid-American; and Weber State, Big Sky. Texas and Southern Methodist were declared Southwest Conference co-champions after Texas Tech used an ineligible player.

Providence, with sophomore Jimmy Walker, was strong among independents, as were Boston College, with John Austin; Detroit, with Dorrie Murray; Dayton, with Henry Finkel; Duquesne, with Willie Somerset; and Colorado State, with Lonnie Wright. Other quality teams were Minnesota, with Lou Hudson, Archie Clark and Don Yates; New Mexico, with Dick Ellis and Mel Daniels; Kansas, with Walt Wesley; and Oregon State, with Jim Jarvis.

Among the stars: Billy Cunningham, North Carolina; Dave Bing, Syracuse; Tal Brody and Skip Thoren, both Illinois; A. W. Davis, Tennessee; Flynn Robinson, Wyoming; Gary Keller, Florida; Dave Schellhase, Purdue; Dick and Tom Van Arsdale, Indiana; Jim King, Oklahoma State; and Warren Isaac, Iona.

NCAA Championship

At Portland, Oregon

UCLA (91)	FG	FT	Pts.	Michigan (80)	FG	FT	Pts.
Erickson	1	1	3	Darden	8	1	17
Lacey	5	1	11	Pomey	2	0	4
McIntosh	1	1	3	Buntin	6	2	14
Goodrich	12	18	42	Russell	10	8	28
Goss	4	0	8	Tregoning	2	1	5
Washington	7	3	17	Myers	0	0	0
Lynn	2	1	5	Ludwig	1	0	2
Lyons	0	0	0	Clawson	3	0	6
Galbraith	0	0	0	Dill	1	2	4
Hoffman	1	0	2	Brown	0	0	0
Levin	0	0	0	Thompson	0	0	0
Chambers	0	0	0	Bankey	0	0	0
Totals	33	25	91		33	14	80

NCAA SCORES
REGIONALS

East

First Round: Princeton 60, Penn State 58; St. Joseph's 67, Connecticut 61; Providence 91, West Virginia 67

Semifinals: Princeton 66, North Carolina State 48; Providence 81, St. Joseph's 73

Championship: Princeton 109, Providence 69

Mideast

First Round: Dayton 66, Ohio U. 65; DePaul 99, Eastern Kentucky 52

Semifinals: Michigan 98, Dayton 71; Vanderbilt 83, DePaul 79

Championship: Michigan 87, Vanderbilt 85

Midwest

First Round: Houston 99, Notre Dame 98

Semifinals: Oklahoma State 75, Houston 60; Wichita State 86, Southern Methodist 81

Championship: Wichita State 54, Oklahoma State 46

Far West

First Round: Oklahoma City 70, Colorado State 68

Semifinals: San Francisco 91, Oklahoma City 67; UCLA 100, Brigham Young 76

Championship: UCLA 101, San Francisco 93

FINALS

Semifinals: Michigan 93, Princeton 76; UCLA 108, Wichita State 89

Championship: UCLA 91, Michigan 80

Consolation: Princeton 118, Wichita State 82

NIT Championship

At New York

St. John's (55)	FG	FT	Pts.	Villanova (51)	FG	FT	Pts.
B. McIntyre	6	4	16	Soens	2	0	4
Duerr	1	0	2	Erickson	3	0	6
Dove	7	0	14	Washington	6	6	18
Houston	1	3	5	Leftwich	7	1	15
K. McIntyre	8	2	18	Melchionni	2	0	4
Wirell	0	0	0	Schaeffer	2	0	4
Swartz	0	0	0	Kenny	0	0	0
Totals	23	9	55		22	7	51

NIT SCORES

First Round: St. John's 114, Boston College 92; Manhattan 71, Texas Western 53; Western Kentucky 57, Fordham 53; Army 70, St. Louis 66; NYU 71, Bradley 70; Detroit 93, LaSalle 86

Quarterfinals: St. John's 61, New Mexico 54; Villanova 73, Manhattan 71; NYU 87, Detroit 76; Army 58, Western Kentucky 54

Semifinals: Villanova 91, NYU 69; St. John's 67, Army 60

Championship: St. John's 55, Villanova 51

Consolation: Army 75, NYU 74

Top Ten

AP	UPI
Michigan	Michigan
UCLA	UCLA
St. Joseph's	St. Joseph's
Providence	Providence
Vanderbilt	Vanderbilt
Davidson	Brigham Young
Minnesota	Davidson
Villanova	Minnesota
Brigham Young	Duke
Duke	San Francisco

All-Americans

AP	UPI
Bill Bradley, Princeton	Bill Bradley, Princeton
Cazzie Russell, Michigan	Cazzie Russell, Michigan
Rick Barry, Miami (Fla.)	Gail Goodrich, UCLA
Gail Goodrich, UCLA	Fred Hetzel, Davidson
Fred Hetzel, Davidson	Rick Barry, Miami (Fla.)
Wayne Estes, Utah State (posthumously)	

1965–66

Duke's Atlantic Coast Conference champions, with Bobby Verga, Jack Marin and Steve Vacendak, and Southeastern Conference titlist Kentucky, with Louis Dampier, Pat Riley and Larry Conley, were considered the teams to beat.

But unheralded Texas Western came from out of nowhere to capture the NCAA tournament as the Miners upset Kentucky, 72–65, in the championship game. Texas Western, featuring Bobby Joe Hill, Dave Lattin, Willie Cager, Orsten Artis, Neville Shed and Willie Worsley, had lost only one game all season. Duke meanwhile took consolation honors, while the MVP trophy went to Jerry Chambers of Western Athletic Conference champion Utah.

Tall and powerful Brigham Young, with 6-10 Craig Raymond and Steve Kramer leading the way after Dick Nemelka got into

Cazzie Russell led Michigan to the Big Ten title

foul trouble, defeated small but game NYU, 97–84, for the NIT title. NYU was led by 6-1 Mal Graham, 6-4 Stan MacKenzie, 6-3 Rich Dyer and 6-4 Bruce Kaplan. Villanova's Bill Melchionni was named MVP as he led all scorers with 109 points in four games.

Contrasts were recorded in the scores of Houston, led by Joe Hamood and sophomore Elvin Hayes, which beat Texas Wesleyan, 154–67, and Duke, which barely beat North Carolina, 21–20. Syracuse, behind the shooting of Dave Bing, rang up a record 99.0 points a game while making 40.4 field goals per game, also a record. Individual honors went to Purdue's Dave Schellhase, who averaged 32.54 points a game to edge Idaho's Dave Wagnon, averaging 32.50 points.

Rice ended a 27-game losing streak by beating Baylor and Texas A&M used Olympic shotputter Randy Matson, but Southwest conference honors went to Southern Methodist.

The trio of Cliff Anderson, Matt Guokas, and Billy Oakes took St. Joseph's to the top of the Middle Atlantic conference, while the efforts of Cazzie Russell and Oliver Darden retained the Big Ten title for Michigan. Clem Haskins led Western Kentucky to the Ohio Valley Conference crown, and Walt Wesley teamed with sophomore Jo Jo White to win the Big Eight crown at Kansas.

The University of the Pacific, with Keith Swagerty, won the West Coast Athletic Conference race. Dick Snyder sparked Davidson to the Southern Conference crown, and Oregon State, with Loy Peterson, won the AAWU championship. Other champions: Cincinnati, Missouri Valley; Miami (O.), Mid-American; Manhattan, Metropolitan; Penn, Ivy League; Weber State and Gonzaga, tied, Big Sky; and Rhode Island and Connecticut, tied, Yankee.

Jimmy Walker teamed with Dexter Westbrook to make Providence a strong independent, while Loyola (Ill.) with Corky Bell and Jim Coleman, was also powerful. Other independents of note were Boston College, with John Austin; St. John's, with Sonny Dove; DePaul, with Dave Mills; Dayton, with Henry Finkel; and Army, with Mike Silliman.

Among stars of the season: Clyde Lee, Vanderbilt; Don Freeman, Illinois; Lou Hudson, Minnesota; Westley Unseld, Louisville; Bob Lloyd, Rutgers; John Wetzel, Virginia Tech; Dorrie Murray, Detroit; Stan Washington, Michigan State; Joe Allen, Bradley; Warren Armstrong, Wichita State; Clarence McHenry, Hardin-Simmons; George Peeples, Iowa; John Block, Southern California; and Jim Barnett and Nick Jones, both Oregon.

NCAA Championship

At College Park, Maryland

Texas Western (72)	FG	FT	Pts.	Kentucky (65)	FG	FT	Pts.
Hill	7	6	20	Dampier	7	5	19
Artis	5	5	15	Kron	3	0	6
Shed	1	1	3	Conley	4	2	10
Lattin	5	6	16	Riley	8	3	19
Cager	1	6	8	Jaracz	3	1	7
Flournoy	1	0	2	Berger	2	0	4
Worsley	2	4	8	Gamble	0	0	0
				LeMaster	0	0	0
				Tallent	0	0	0
Totals	22	28	72		27	11	65

NCAA SCORES
REGIONALS

East

First Round: St. Joseph's 65, Providence 48; Davidson 95, Rhode Island 65

Semifinals: Syracuse 94, Davidson 79; Duke 76, St. Joseph's 74

Championship: Duke 91, Syracuse 81

Mideast

First Round: Dayton 58, Miami (O.) 51; Western Kentucky 105, Loyola (Ill.) 86

Semifinals: Kentucky 86, Dayton 79; Michigan 80, Western Kentucky 79

Championship: Kentucky 84, Michigan 77

Midwest

First Round: Texas Western 89, Oklahoma City 74

Semifinals: Texas Western 78, Cincinnati 76; Kansas 76, Southern Methodist 70

Championship: Texas Western 81, Kansas 80

Far West

First Round: Houston 82, Colorado State 79

Semifinals: Oregon State 63, Houston 60; Utah 83, University of the Pacific 74

Championship: Utah 70, Oregon State 64

FINALS

Semifinals: Kentucky 83, Duke 79; Texas Western 85, Utah 78

Championship: Texas Western 72, Kentucky 65

Consolation: Duke 79, Utah 77

Willie Cager controls ball as Texas Western beats Kentucky for NCAA crown

NIT Championship

At New York

Brigham Young (97)				NYU (84)			
	FG	FT	Pts.		FG	FT	Pts.
Kramer	9	2	20	MacKenzie	10	7	27
Hill	9	3	21	Kaplan	9	0	18
Raymond	10	1	21	Silen	3	3	9
Nemelka	5	5	15	Graham	8	2	18
Congdon	5	1	11	Dyer	5	2	12
Jimas	2	1	5	Witrock	0	0	0
Ruffner	1	0	2				
Schouten	1	0	2				
Eakins	0	0	0				
James	0	0	0				
Fisher	0	0	0				
Totals	42	13	97		35	14	84

NIT SCORES

First Round: Temple 88, Virginia Tech 73; NYU 68, DePaul 65; San Francisco 89, Penn State 77; Villanova 63, St. John's 61; Army 71, Manhattan 66; Boston College 96, Louisville 90

Quarterfinals: Brigham Young 90, Temple 78; NYU 90, Wichita State 84; Army 80, San Francisco 63; Villanova 86, Boston College 85

Semifinals: Brigham Young 66, Army 60; NYU 69, Villanova 63

Championship: Brigham Young 97, NYU 84

Consolation: Villanova 76, Army 65

Top Ten

AP	UPI
Kentucky	Kentucky
Duke	Duke
Texas Western	Texas Western
Kansas	Kansas
St. Joseph's	Loyola (Ill.)
Loyola (Ill.)	St. Joseph's
Cincinnati	Michigan
Vanderbilt	Vanderbilt
Michigan	Cincinnati
Western Kentucky	Providence

All-Americans

AP	UPI
Cazzie Russell, Michigan	Cazzie Russell, Michigan
Clyde Lee, Vanderbilt	Clyde Lee, Vanderbilt
Dave Schellhase, Purdue	Jimmy Walker, Providence
Louis Dampier, Kentucky	Dave Schellhase, Purdue
Dave Bing, Syracuse	Dave Bing, Syracuse

1966–67

To the surprise of almost no one, UCLA swept past 30 opponents to capture its third NCAA title in four seasons. Led by 7-foot sophomore Lew Alcindor, a unanimous All-America choice, the Bruins had only one close call all season, a 40–35 overtime victory over arch-rival Southern California.

UCLA became only the second team ever to win three NCAA titles in four years. Kentucky turned the trick in 1948, 1949, and 1951. UCLA, dominating the all-tournament team with MVP Alcindor and guards Lucius Allen and Mike Warren, beat the tourney's Cinderella team, Dayton, 79–64, in the final.

The last NIT in the 49th Street Madison

Lew Alcindor's sophomore season at UCLA was capped with an NCAA championship

Square Garden saw the nation's No. 1 small college team, Southern Illinois, surprise St. Peter's of Jersey City, Duke, and Rutgers before downing Marquette, led by Bob Wolfe and George Thompson, 71–56, in the title game. SIU's backcourt whiz Walt Frazier was named MVP while Bob Lloyd of Rutgers tallied 129 points in four games. George Stone collected 46 points as Marshall scored a record total of points in beating Nebraska, 119–88.

North Carolina, with Larry Miller and Bob Lewis, swept to the Atlantic Coast Conference title, while three-sport star Ron Widby sparked Tennessee past Florida and Vanderbilt in the Southeastern Conference. Indiana and Michigan State tied for the championship in one of the closest Big Ten races in years. Peck Hickman closed out a 23-year coaching career at Louisville as the Cardinals, powered by 6-8 Westley Unseld and 6-4 Butch Beard, reigned in the Missouri Valley Conference.

West Virginia, with Ron Williams, Carl Head, and Dave Reaser each averaging 20 points a game, captured both the regular season title and the Southern Conference tournament crown. Other champions: Kansas, Big Eight; Princeton, Ivy League; Temple, Middle Atlantic; Connecticut, Yankee; Western Kentucky, Ohio Valley; Toledo, Mid-American; Southern Methodist, Southwest; University of the Pacific, West Coast Athletic; and Wyoming and Brigham Young, tied, Western Athletic.

UCLA's Alcindor made a record 66.7 per cent of his shots for a 29.0-point-per-game average, second only to the 30.4-point average of Providence's Jimmy Walker. Mal Graham of NYU was third with a 28.7-point-per-game average.

Elvin Hayes led Houston to the top spot among independents, while Dayton, with Don May, was the surprise team in the Midwest. Other strong independents were Boston College, with Terry Driscoll; St. John's, with Sonny Dove; Virginia Tech, with Glen Combs; Oklahoma City, the top-scoring team in the country with a 96.0-point average; Marquette; Providence; Texas Western; New Mexico State, and Seattle.

Some of the outstanding players: Clem Haskins, Western Kentucky; Bob Verga, Duke; Bob Lloyd, Rutgers; Mel Daniels, New Mexico; Chris Thomforde, Princeton; Walt Piatkowski, Bowling Green; Russ Critchfield, California; Tom Kondla, Minnesota; Art Stephenson, Rhode Island; and Dave Lattin, Texas Western.

NCAA Championship

At Louisville

UCLA (79)	FG	FT	Pts.	Dayton (64)	FG	FT	Pts.
Heitz	2	0	4	May	9	3	21
Shackleford	5	0	10	Sadlier	2	1	5
Alcindor	8	4	20	Obrovac	0	0	0
Allen	7	5	19	Klaus	4	0	8
Warren	8	1	17	Hooper	2	2	6
Nielsen	0	0	0	Torain	3	0	6
Sweek	1	0	2	Waterman	4	2	10
Saffer	2	0	4	Sharpenter	2	4	8
Saner	1	0	2	Samanich	0	0	0
Chrisman	0	1	1	Backman	0	0	0
Sutherland	0	0	0	Inderrieden	0	0	0
Lynn	0	0	0	Wannemacher	0	0	0
Totals	**34**	**11**	**79**		**26**	**12**	**64**

NCAA SCORES
REGIONALS

East

First Round: Princeton 68, West Virginia 57; St. John's 57, Temple 53

Semifinals: North Carolina 78, Princeton 70; Boston College 63, St. John's 62

Championship: North Carolina 96, Boston College 80

Mideast

First Round: Dayton 69, Western Kentucky 67; Virginia Tech 82, Toledo 76

Semifinals: Dayton 53, Tennessee 52; Virginia Tech 79, Indiana 70

Championship: Dayton 71, Virginia Tech 66

Midwest

First Round: Houston 59, New Mexico State 58

Semifinals: Houston 66, Kansas 53; Southern Methodist 83, Louisville 81

Championship: Houston 83, Southern Methodist 75

Far West

First Round: Texas Western 62, Seattle 54

Semifinals: Pacific 72, Texas Western 63; UCLA 109, Wyoming 60

Championship: UCLA 80, Pacific 64

FINALS

Semifinals: Dayton 76, North Carolina 62; UCLA 73, Houston 58

Championship: UCLA 79, Dayton 64

Consolation: Houston 84, North Carolina 62

NIT Championship

At New York

Southern Illinois (71)	FG	FT	Pts.	Marquette (56)	FG	FT	Pts.
Garrett	5	2	12	Thompson	4	4	12
C. Smith	3	7	13	Brunkhorst	2	1	5
Johnson	3	1	7	P. Smith	1	2	4
Frazier	8	5	21	Burke	6	3	15
Zastrow	2	0	4	Wolf	7	3	17
Bechtold	3	4	10	Anderson	1	0	2
Griffin	0	0	0	Simmons	0	0	0
Westcott	0	0	0	Luchini	0	1	1
Whitaker	0	0	0	Curran	0	0	0
Taylor	0	0	0	Langenkamp	0	0	0
Benson	2	0	4				
Totals	**26**	**19**	**71**		**21**	**14**	**56**

NIT SCORES

First Round: Marshall 70, Villanova 68; Southern Illinois 103, St. Peter's (N. J.) 58; Providence 77, Memphis State 68; New Mexico 66, Syracuse 64; Marquette 64, Tulsa 60; Rutgers 78, Utah State 76

Quarterfinals: Southern Illinois 72, Duke 63; Marshall 119, Nebraska 88; Rutgers 65, New Mexico 60; Marquette 81, Providence 80

Semifinals: Marquette 83, Marshall 78; Southern Illinois 79, Rutgers 70

Championship: Southern Illinois 71, Marquette 56

Consolation: Rutgers 93, Marshall 76

Top Ten

AP	UPI
UCLA	UCLA
Louisville	Louisville
Kansas	North Carolina
North Carolina	Kansas
Princeton	Princeton
Western Kentucky	Houston
Houston	Western Kentucky
Tennessee	Texas Western
Boston College	Tennessee
Texas Western	Boston College

All-Americans

AP	UPI
Lew Alcindor, UCLA	Lew Alcindor, UCLA
Jimmy Walker, Providence	Jimmy Walker, Providence
Westley Unseld, Louisville	Westley Unseld, Louisville
Elvin Hayes, Houston	Elvin Hayes, Houston
Clem Haskins, Western Kentucky	Bob Lloyd, Rutgers

1967–68

UCLA, with Big A, and Houston, with Big E, were in competition all season for headlines, ratings, and finally, the national championship. Houston's Big E was 6-9 Elvin Hayes, who led the Cougars to a 71–69 victory over UCLA, featuring 7-1 Lew "Big A" Alcindor, before 52,693 people in Houston's Astrodome. The victory, witnessed by the largest crowd ever to watch a basketball game in the United States, snapped UCLA's 47-game winning streak in a season which brought the no-dunk rule aimed at big men like Alcindor and Hayes.

The Bruins, after winning the Pacific Eight title, took revenge against Houston, highest-scoring team in the country with its 97.8-point-per-game average, in the semifinal game of the NCAA tournament. Hayes was held to 10 points, the lowest of his varsity career, as UCLA won, 101–69. The Bruins went on to beat Atlantic Coast Conference champion North Carolina, with Larry Miller and Charlie Scott, to retain the NCAA crown. So overwhelming was UCLA's triumph, 78–55 (the widest spread ever in a championship game), that four Bruins were named to the all-tournament team: MVP Alcindor, Mike Warren, Lucius Allen and Lynn Shackleford, along with North Carolina's Larry Miller.

Dayton used height and strength to overpower Kansas, with Jo Jo White and Roger Bohnenstiehl, 61–48, to win the first NIT in the new Madison Square Garden atop Penn Station in New York. Dayton's Don May was voted MVP after scoring 106 points in the tourney, although Elnardo Webster of St. Peter's scored 51 points against Marshall.

Sophomores Pete Maravich of Louisiana State and Calvin Murphy of Niagara finished one-two in the individual scoring race. Maravich joined Oscar Robertson as the only sophomores ever to lead the nation in scoring as he averaged a record 43.8 points, compared to Murphy's 38.2. Florida's Neal Walk led in rebounding with an average of 19.8.

Army, with Bill Schutsky, was the leading defensive team in the country, yielding 57.9 points a game, and was a strong independent, as were St. Bonaventure, with Bob Lanier and Bill Butler; Marquette, with George "Brute Force" Thompson; Okla-homa City, with Rich Travis; Boston College, with Terry Driscoll; and Notre Dame, with Bob Arnzen and Bob Whitemore.

Louisville, led by Westley Unseld, won the Missouri Valley Conference, while Columbia, powered by 7-foot Dave Newmark and sophomore Jim McMillian, beat Princeton in a playoff for the Ivy League title. New Mexico, led by Ron Nelson, won the Western Athletic Conference honors, and Davidson, featuring Mike Maloy, took the Southern Conference crown. Other champions: Bowling Green, Mid-American; Kansas State, Big Eight; Rhode Island and Massachusetts, tied, Yankee; Texas Christian, Southwest; Kentucky, Southeastern; Santa Clara, West Coast Athletic; and Murray State and East Tennessee, tied, Ohio Valley. Ohio State defeated Iowa for the Big Ten berth in the NCAA tourney.

Among the better teams were Duke, with Mike Lewis; Georgia, with Bob Leinhard; Marshall, with George Stone and Danny D'Antoni; Tennessee, with 7-foot Tom Boerwinkle; and Purdue, with sophomore Rick Mount. There were such outstanding players as: Warren Armstrong, Wichita State; Merv Jackson, Utah; Ron Williams, West Virginia; Joe Franklin, Wisconsin; Shaler Halimon, Utah State; Fred Foster, Miami (O); Joe Allen, Bradley; Harry Hollines, Denver; and Manny Leaks, Niagara.

NCAA Championship

At Los Angeles

UCLA (78)	FG	FT	Pts.	North Carolina (55)	FG	FT	Pts.
Shackleford	3	0	6	Miller	5	4	14
Lynn	1	5	7	Bunting	1	1	3
Alcindor	15	4	34	Clark	4	1	9
Warren	3	1	7	Scott	6	0	12
Allen	3	5	11	Grubar	2	1	5
Nielson	1	0	2	Fogler	1	2	4
Heitz	3	1	7	Brown	2	2	6
Sutherland	1	0	2	Tuttle	0	0	0
Sweek	0	0	0	Frye	1	0	2
Saner	1	0	2	Whitehead	0	0	0
				Delany	0	0	0
				Fletcher	0	0	0
Totals	31	16	78		22	11	55

NCAA SCORES
REGIONALS

East

First Round: Columbia 83, LaSalle 69; Davidson 79, St. John's 70; St. Bonaventure 102, Boston College 93

UCLA's Lew Alcindor (left) and Houston's Elvin Hayes reach for the sky at the Astrodome

Semifinals: Davidson 61, Columbia 59; North Carolina 91, St. Bonaventure 72

Championship: North Carolina 70, Davidson 66

Mideast

First Round: Marquette 72, Bowling Green 71; East Tennessee State 79, Florida State 69

Semifinals: Kentucky 107, Marquette 89; Ohio State 79, East Tennessee State 72

Championship: Ohio State 82, Kentucky 81

Midwest

First Round: Houston 94, Loyola (Ill.) 76

Semifinals: Houston 91, Louisville 75; Texas Christian 77, Kansas State 72

Championship: Houston 103, Texas Christian 68

Far West

First Round: New Mexico State 68, Weber State 57

Semifinals: Santa Clara 86, New Mexico 73; UCLA 58, New Mexico State 49

Championship: UCLA 87, Santa Clara 66

FINALS

Semifinals: North Carolina 80, Ohio State 66; UCLA 101, Houston 69

Championship: UCLA 78, North Carolina 55

Consolation: Ohio State 89, Houston 85

NIT Championship

At New York

	Dayton (61)				Kansas (48)		
	FG	FT	Pts.		FG	FT	Pts.
May	8	6	22	Bohnenstiel	6	0	12
Sadlier	4	1	9	Douglas	3	0	6
Obrovac	0	4	4	Nash	4	2	10
Jim G'ttsch'll	1	6	8	Harmon	1	0	2
Hooper	5	6	16	White	5	0	10
Leffel	0	0	0	Bradshaw	1	0	2
Wannemacher	0	0	0	Sloan	3	0	6
Janky	0	0	0				
Jer. G'ttsch'll	0	2	2				
Torain	0	0	0				
Totals	18	25	61		23	2	48

NIT SCORES

First Round: Duke 97, Oklahoma City 81; St. Peter's (N. J.) 102, Marshall 93; Kansas 82, Temple 76; Villanova 77, Wyoming 66; Dayton 87, West Virginia 68; Fordham 69, Duquesne 60; LIU 80, Bradley 77; Notre Dame 62, Army 58

Quarterfinals: St. Peter's (N. J.) 100, Duke 71; Kansas 55, Villanova 49; Dayton 61, Fordham 60; Notre Dame 62, LIU 60

Semifinals: Kansas 58, St. Peter's (N. J.) 46; Dayton 76, Notre Dame 74

Championship: Dayton 61, Kansas 48

Consolation: Notre Dame 81, St. Peter's (N. J.) 78

Top Ten

AP	UPI
Houston	Houston
UCLA	UCLA
St. Bonaventure	St. Bonaventure
North Carolina	North Carolina
Kentucky	Kentucky
New Mexico	Columbia
Columbia	New Mexico
Davidson	Louisville
Louisville	Davidson
Duke	Marquette

All-Americans

AP	UPI
Elvin Hayes, Houston	Elvin Hayes, Houston
Westley Unseld, Louisville	Lew Alcindor, UCLA
Lew Alcindor, UCLA	Pete Maravich, Louisiana State
Pete Maravich, Louisiana State	Westley Unseld, Louisville
Calvin Murphy, Niagara	Larry Miller, North Carolina

1968-69

The Big A made it all the way again as Lew Alcindor led UCLA to its third straight NCAA championship and in its fifth in six years. Alcindor scored 37 points in the finale and earned MVP honors for the third time as he paced the Bruins to a 92–72 triumph over Big Ten champion Purdue. Rick Mount, the nation's second-leading scorer with a 33-point average and many Big Ten records, had 28 points.

UCLA finished the season with a 29–1 record, losing only to Southern California in the final game of the regular season on a last-minute shot by Ernie Powell.

Drake, with Willie McCarter and Willie Wise, beat Louisville, led by Butch Beard and Mike Grosso, for the Missouri Valley Conference crown and nearly upset UCLA in the semifinals, losing 85–82.

Olympian Spencer Haywood (8) starred as a sophomore at Detroit

The NIT championship was decided between Boston College, where Bob Cousy was closing out his college coaching career, and Temple, which had won the Middle Atlantic Conference title only to lose to St. Joseph's in the post-season playoff. Temple, with John Baum scoring 30 points and Eddie Mast grabbing 22 rebounds, beat Boston College, 89–76, for the title. Tourney MVP Terry Driscoll and soph Jim O'Brien scored 18 points each for the losers.

Louisiana State junior Pete Maravich became the first collegian to score more than 2,000 points in two seasons as he averaged 44.2 points a game and ended his first two varsity seasons with 2,286 points. Detroit sophomore Spencer Haywood, hero of the U. S. Olympic team in Mexico City, was the rebounding leader, averaging 21.5 a game.

Another Olympic hero, 6-5 Charley Scott, led North Carolina to the Atlantic Coast Conference championship, while 6-9 Dan Issel paced Kentucky to Southeastern Conference honors. Davidson, with Mike Maloy, won the Southern; Colorado, led by 6-8 soph Cliff Meely, took the Big Eight, and Santa Clara, featuring Dennis Awtrey and the Ogden brothers, Ralph and Bud, topped the WCAC. St. Peter's and Manhattan tied in the Metropolitan Conference, and Weber State, with Justus Thigpen and Willie Sojourner, swept through the Big Sky undefeated.

John Hummer and Geoff Petrie led Princeton to the Ivy League title; Murray State beat Morehead for the Ohio Valley title and Brigham Young bested Wyoming in the Western Athletic Conference. Other winners: Miami (O.) in the Mid-American; Texas A&M in the Southwest; Massachusetts, Yankee; Long Beach State in the CCAA and little Trinity College of San Antonio, led by Larry Jeffries and Jim Bowles, in the Southland Conference, which earned an NCAA at-large bid.

Topping the ranks of independents were St. Bonaventure, with big Bob Lanier; Marquette, led by George Thompson and sophomore Dean Meminger; St. John's, with Johnny Warren; Niagara, with high-scoring Calvin Murphy; New Mexico State, with Jimmy Collins and Sam Lacey; Duquesne, led by Jarrett Durham; Villanova, with sophomore Howard Porter; Tulsa, sparked by Bobby Smith, and Rutgers, led by Bob Greacen.

Among the standout players were Larry Cannon and Bernie Williams at LaSalle, coached by Tom Gola; Neal Walk, Florida; Dave Scholz, Illinois; Jo Jo White, a mid-year graduate at Kansas; Dave Sorenson, Ohio State; Rudy Tomjanovich, Michigan; Bobby Croft, Tennessee; Simmie Hill, West Texas State; Bob Tallent, George Washington and Rex Morgan, Jacksonville.

NIT Championship

At New York

Temple (89)				Boston College (76)			
	FG	FT	Pts.		FG	FT	Pts.
Baum	10	10	30	Veronneau	6	4	16
Cromer	9	1	19	Fitzgerald	2	0	4
Mast	3	4	10	Driscoll	6	6	18
Strunk	2	0	4	Evans	6	4	16
Brocchi	5	5	15	O'Brien	8	2	18
Wieczerak	2	2	6	LaGace	2	0	4
Snook	0	3	3	Downey	0	0	0
Mulava	0	2	2	Costello	0	0	0
Brooks	0	0	0	Sees	0	0	0
Cassidy	0	0	0	Sollenne	0	0	0
Richardson	0	0	0				
Totals	31	27	89		30	16	76

NIT SCORES

First Round: Temple 82, Florida 66; St. Peter's 75, Tulsa 71; Ohio University 82, West Texas State 80; Tennessee 67, Rutgers 51; Army 51, Wyoming 49; South Carolina 72, Southern Illinois 63; Boston College 78, Kansas 62; Louisville 73, Fordham 70

Quarterfinals: Temple 94, St. Peter's 78; Tennessee 75, Ohio University 64; Army 59, South Carolina 45; Boston College 88, Louisville 83

Semifinals: Temple 63, Tennessee 58; Boston College 73, Army 61

Championship: Temple 89, Boston College 76

Consolation: Tennessee 64, Army 52

Top Ten

AP	UPI
UCLA	UCLA
LaSalle	North Carolina
Santa Clara	Davidson
North Carolina	Santa Clara
Davidson	Kentucky
Purdue	LaSalle
Kentucky	Purdue
St. John's	St. John's
Duquesne	New Mexico State
Villanova	Duquesne

All-Americans

AP	UPI
Lew Alcindor, UCLA	Lew Alcindor, UCLA
Pete Maravich, LSU	Pete Maravich, LSU
Spencer Haywood, Detroit	Rick Mount, Purdue
Rick Mount, Purdue	Spencer Haywood, Detroit
Calvin Murphy, Niagara	Calvin Murphy, Niagara

NCAA Championship

At Louisville

UCLA (92)				Purdue (72)			
	FG	FT	Pts.		FG	FT	Pts.
Shackleford	3	5	11	Gilliam	2	3	7
Rowe	4	4	12	Faerber	1	0	2
Alcindor	15	7	37	Johnson	4	3	11
Heitz	0	0	0	Mount	12	4	28
Vallely	4	7	15	Keller	4	3	11
Sweek	3	0	6	Kaufman	0	2	2
Wicks	0	3	3	Bedford	3	1	7
Schofield	1	0	2	Weatherford	1	2	4
Patterson	1	2	4	Reasoner	0	0	0
Seibert	0	0	0	Taylor	0	0	0
Farmer	0	0	0				
Ecker	1	0	2				
Totals	32	28	92		27	18	72

NCAA SCORES
REGIONALS

East

First Round: Duquesne 74, St. Joseph's 52; Davidson 75, Villanova 61; St. John's 72, Princeton 63

Semifinals: North Carolina 79, Duquesne 78; Davidson 79, St. John's 69

Championship: North Carolina 87, Davidson 85

Mideast

First Round: Marquette 82, Murray State 62; Miami (O.) 63, Notre Dame 60

Semifinals: Marquette 81, Kentucky 74; Purdue 91, Miami (O.) 71

Championship: Purdue 75, Marquette 73

Midwest

First Round: Texas A&M 81, Trinity (Tex.) 66; Colorado State 52, Dayton 50

Semifinals: Drake 81, Texas A&M 63; Colorado State 64, Colorado 56

Championship: Drake 84, Colorado State 77

West

First Round: New Mexico State 74, Brigham Young 62; Weber State 75, Seattle 73

Semifinals: UCLA 53, New Mexico State 38; Santa Clara 63, Weber State 59

Championship: UCLA 90, Santa Clara 52

FINALS

Semifinals: Purdue 92, North Carolina 65; UCLA 85, Drake 82

Championship: UCLA 92, Purdue 72

Consolation: Drake 104, North Carolina 84

1969-70

The polls said Kentucky was No. 1 at the end of the regular season, but when the tournaments were over, UCLA was back in its familiar position atop the NCAA pedestal. With Lew Alcindor gone, the Bruins used a balanced attack built around junior forwards Sidney Wicks and Curtis Rowe and senior guard John Vallely. UCLA took on Jacksonville, which had averaged a record 100.3 points a game, and came away with an 80–69 victory in the title game. The Dolphins' big man was 7-2 Artis Gilmore, the nation's leading rebounder.

UCLA finished with a 28–2 record, marred only by Pacific-Eight Conference losses to Oregon, with 6-9 Stan Love, and Southern California, with flashy Paul Westphal. Perhaps the strongest challenge to UCLA in the tourney would have come from St. Bonaventure, but the Bonnies' 6-11, 260-pound Bob Lanier (29 points, 16 rebounds a game) tore knee ligaments in the Eastern Regional finale.

Another well-balanced team, Marquette, opted for the NIT and went on to win by defeating St. John's, 65–53. The Warriors counted on Jeff Sewell, Ric Cobb, Joe Thomas, Gary Brell and MVP Dean Meminger, while Joe DePre and Billy Paultz were the big guns for St. John's.

The biggest gun of the year was "Pistol Pete" Maravich of LSU, who finished with a dozen scoring records, including 1,381 points in his last season and a 44.5-point-per-game average. Notre Dame's Austin Carr, who scored a record 61 points in an NCAA tourney game, averaged 38.1 points a game, while Purdue's Rick Mount, Kentucky's Dan Issel, Idaho State's Willie Humes, Georgia Tech's Rich Yunkus and Michigan's Rudy Tomjanovich all averaged better than 30 points a game.

Several teams went through their conference schedules unbeaten, including John Roche-led South Carolina, which was upset by North Carolina State, led by Van Williford, in the Atlantic Coast Conference post-season tournament. Davidson, headed by Mike Maloy, prevailed in the Southern Conference, and Jim McDaniels paced Western Kentucky to the Ohio Valley crown. Penn, sparked by guards Dave Wohl and Steve Bilsky, swept through the Ivy League, while Johnny Johnson and Fred Brown guided Iowa past Ohio State, with Dave Sorenson, and Purdue in the Big Ten. John Q. Trapp was the big man for Long Beach State, playing its first year in the university division, as the 49ers went 10–0 in the newly formed Pacific Coast Athletic Association.

Santa Clara, with Dennis Awtrey, repeated in the WCAC, while Nate Archibald gunned Texas-El Paso to the Western Athletic Conference title. Soph Julius Erving helped Massachusetts tie Connecticut in the Yankee and Willie Sojourner led Weber State to another Big Sky championship. Other winners: Ohio U. in the Mid-American; Drake, Missouri Valley; Rice, Southwest; and Temple, which won the Middle Atlantic playoff.

Independents were strong, with three of the four NCAA finalists from the non-conference ranks and unaligned Marquette and St. John's competing for the NIT crown. Among the best were New Mexico State, with little Jimmy Collins; Army, the best defensive team for the third straight year; Niagara, with Calvin Murphy; Utah, led by Mike Newlin; Houston, with Ollie Taylor; Florida State, powered by Dave Cowens; Villanova, with Howard Porter, and Duquesne, led by Jarrett Durham and the 6-10 Nelson twins, Barry and Garry.

Spencer Haywood jumped to the pros after playing only one season, but there were some other super sophs around, like George McGinnis of Indiana and Ralph Simpson of Michigan State.

Some of the other strong clubs were North Carolina, with Charley Scott; Cincinnati, led by Jim Ard; Kansas, with Dave Robisch; Columbia, paced by Jim McMillian; Marshall, with Russell Lee, and Oklahoma, led by Garfield Heard.

Artis Gilmore led Jacksonville to NCAA finals against UCLA

Midwest

First Round: Houston 71, Dayton 64; New Mexico State 101, Rice 77

Semifinals: Drake 92, Houston 87; New Mexico State 70, Kansas State 66

Championship: New Mexico State 87, Drake 78

West

First Round: Long Beach State 92, Weber State 73; Utah State 91, Texas-El Paso 81

Semifinals: UCLA 88, Long Beach State 65; Utah State 69, Santa Clara 68

Championship: UCLA 101, Utah State 79

FINALS

Semifinals: Jacksonville 91, St. Bonaventure 83; UCLA 93, New Mexico State 77

Championship: UCLA 80, Jacksonville 69

Consolation: New Mexico State 79, St. Bonaventure 73

NIT Championship

At New York

Marquette (65)	FG	FT	Pts.	St. John's (53)	FG	FT	Pts.
Brell	4	1	9	Abraham	1	2	4
Thomas	3	5	11	De Pre	0	5	5
Cobb	3	1	7	Paultz	7	1	15
Sewell	8	6	22	Smyth	3	0	6
Meminger	4	8	16	Lyons	1	1	3
McMahon	0	0	0	DeVasto	3	2	8
Burke	0	0	0	Cluess	2	4	8
Lam	0	0	0	Gilkes	1	2	4
				Phillips	0	0	0
Totals	**22**	**21**	**65**		**18**	**17**	**53**

NCAA Championship

At College Park, Maryland

UCLA (80)	FG	FT	Pts.	Jacksonville (69)	FG	FT	Pts.
Rowe	7	5	19	Wedeking	6	0	12
Patterson	8	1	17	Blevins	1	1	3
Wicks	5	7	17	Morgan	5	0	10
Vallely	5	5	15	Burrows	6	0	12
Bibby	2	4	8	Gilmore	9	1	19
Booker	0	2	2	Nelson	3	2	8
Seibert	0	0	0	Dublin	0	2	2
Ecker	1	0	2	Baldwin	0	0	0
Betchley	0	0	0	McIntyre	1	0	2
Chapman	0	0	0	Hawkins	0	1	1
Hill	0	0	0	Selke	0	0	0
Schofield	0	0	0				
Totals	**28**	**24**	**80**		**31**	**7**	**69**

NCAA SCORES
REGIONALS

East

First Round: St. Bonaventure 85, Davidson 72; Niagara 79, Pennsylvania 69; Villanova 77, Temple 69

Semifinals: St. Bonaventure 80, North Carolina State 68; Villanova 98, Niagara 73

Championship: St. Bonaventure 97, Villanova 74

Mideast

First Round: Notre Dame 112, Ohio University 82; Jacksonville 109, Western Kentucky 96

Semifinals: Kentucky 109, Notre Dame 99; Jacksonville 104, Iowa 103

Championship: Jacksonville 106, Kentucky 100

NIT SCORES

First Round: Georgia Tech 78, Duquesne 68; St. John's 70, Miami (O.) 57; Manhattan 95, North Carolina 90; Army 72, Cincinnati 67; Utah 78, Duke 75; Marquette 62, Massachusetts 55; Louisiana State 83, Georgetown 82; Oklahoma 74, Louisville 73

Quarterfinals: Army 77, Manhattan 72; St. John's 56, Georgia Tech 55; Marquette 83, Utah 63; Louisiana State 97, Oklahoma 94

Semifinals: St. John's 60, Army 59; Marquette 101, Louisiana State 79

Championship: Marquette 65, St. John's 53

Consolation: Army 75, Louisiana State 68

Top Ten

AP	UPI
Kentucky	Kentucky
UCLA	UCLA
St. Bonaventure	St. Bonaventure
Jacksonville	New Mexico State
New Mexico State	Jacksonville
South Carolina	South Carolina
Iowa	Iowa
Marquette	Notre Dame
Notre Dame	Drake
North Carolina State	Marquette

AP	UPI
Pete Maravich, LSU	Pete Maravich, LSU
Dan Issel, Kentucky	Bob Lanier,
Bob Lanier,	St. Bonaventure
St. Bonaventure	Rick Mount, Purdue
Rick Mount, Purdue	Calvin Murphy, Niagara
Calvin Murphy, Niagara	Dan Issel, Kentucky

1970–71

It may not have been as easy as it had been in the past, but UCLA extended its NCAA tournament winning streak to 28 games and five straight championships.

The big front line of Sidney Wicks, Curtis Rowe and Steve Patterson, who hit a career high of 29 points in the title game, had to work all the way after an easy opening-round victory over Western Athletic Conference champion Brigham Young, 91–73. In the regional final, UCLA edged Pacific Coast Athletic Association champion Long Beach State, led by Ed Ratleff, 57–55. Then came Big Eight titlist Kansas, with 6-9 Dave Robisch, 68–60. Meanwhile, gutty Villanova, built around 6-8 Howard Porter and 6-6 Hank Siemiontkowski, put away Ohio Valley Conference champion Western Kentucky, led by 7-foot Jim McDaniels, 92–89. In the championship game, UCLA bested Villanova, 68–62, despite brilliant shooting by Siemiontkowski.

UCLA's push to the title was made easier when Marquette, led by Dean Meminger and 6-11 soph Jim Chones, and Ivy League champion Pennsylvania, with Corky Calhoun and Bob Morse, were eliminated in regional play after finishing the regular season with 26–0 records. And Jacksonville, with Artis Gilmore (23.2 rebounds and 21.0 points a game), was knocked off early by Western Kentucky.

North Carolina, which had finished first in the Atlantic Coast Conference race only to yield to South Carolina, with John Roche and Tom Riker, in the post-season tourney, salvaged some glory in the NIT. The Tar Heels, led by tourney MVP Bill Chamberlain, defeated Rich Yunkus-led Georgia Tech, 84–66, for the NIT championship.

UCLA suffered only one defeat all season, 89–82, to Notre Dame, featuring Austin Carr and his 38-point scoring average, second best in the country. Mississippi's 6-6 sophomore, Johnny Neumann, was tops with 40.1 points a game.

In conference races, Drake finished in a three-way tie with Louisville and St. Louis for Missouri Valley honors, while Luke Witte and Allan Hornyak led Ohio State to the Big Ten title. Big John Gianelli powered Pacific to the WCAC crown, while 7-foot Tom Payne, the first black basketball player at Kentucky, paced the Wildcats to the Southeastern Conference title. Other winners were Massachusetts, with Julius Erving, in the Yankee; Texas Christian in the Southwest; Davidson, Southern; Miami (O.), Mid-American, and Weber State, with Willie Sojourner, in the Big Sky.

Hawaii, coached by Red Rocha, was a surprise among independents, while Charlie Yelverton led Fordham to a 23–2 season and an NCAA bid. Duquesne was sparked by Jarrett Durham, and Matt Gantt and Greg Gary were the sparkplugs for St. Bonaventure. Providence was led by Ernie DiGregorio, Syracuse by Greg Kohls and 7-foot Bill Smith, Houston by Dwight Davis, and Utah State by the frontcourt duo of Marv Roberts and Nate Williams.

Some of the better players in the country were Mel Davis, St. John's; Kermit Washington, American U.; Randy Denton, Duke; Charlie Davis, Wake Forest; John Mengelt, Auburn; sophomore Henry Wilmore at Michigan; Rich Rinaldi, St. Peter's; Ken Durrett, LaSalle; Cliff Meely, Colorado, and Gene Phillips, Southern Methodist.

NCAA Championship

At Houston

UCLA (68)	FG	FT	Pts.	Villanova (62)	FG	FT	Pts.
Rowe	2	4	8	Smith	4	1	9
Wicks	3	1	7	Porter	10	5	25
Patterson	13	3	29	S'm'tk'ski	9	1	19
Bibby	6	5	17	Inglesby	3	1	7
Booker	0	0	0	Ford	0	2	2
Schofield	3	0	6	McDowell	0	0	0
Betchley	0	1	1				
Totals	27	14	68		26	10	62

NCAA SCORES
REGIONALS
East

First Round: Pennsylvania 70, Duquesne 65; Villanova 93, St. Joseph's 75; Fordham 105, Furman 74

Semifinals: Pennsylvania 79, South Carolina 64; Villanova 85, Fordham 75

Championship: Villanova 90, Pennsylvania 47

Mideast

First Round: Western Kentucky 74, Jacksonville 72; Marquette 62, Miami (O.) 47

Semifinals: Western Kentucky 107, Kentucky 83; Ohio State 60, Marquette 59

Championship: Western Kentucky 81, Ohio State 78

Midwest

First Round: Notre Dame 102, Texas Christian 94; Houston 72, New Mexico State 69

Semifinals: Drake 79, Notre Dame 72; Kansas 78, Houston 77

Championship: Kansas 73, Drake 71

West

First Round: Brigham Young 91, Utah State 82; Long Beach State 77, Weber State 66

Semifinals: UCLA 91, Brigham Young 73; Long Beach State 78, Pacific 65

Championship: UCLA 57, Long Beach State 55

FINALS

Semifinals: Villanova 92, Western Kentucky 89; UCLA 68, Kansas 60

Championship: UCLA 68, Villanova 62

Consolation: Western Kentucky 77, Kansas 75

NIT Championship

At New York

North Carolina (84)	FG	FT	Pts.	Georgia Tech (66)	FG	FT	Pts.
Chamberlain	13	8	34	Wilson	8	3	19
Chadwick	6	2	14	Murphy	7	5	19
Dedmon	1	1	3	Yunkus	4	2	10
Karl	3	5	11	Samoylo	0	0	0
Previs	1	3	5	Thorne	4	1	9
Gipple	0	0	0	Thompson	0	3	3
Johnston	0	2	2	Hoggle	2	0	4
Huband	4	6	14	Small	0	1	1
Corson	0	1	1	Hyder	0	1	1
Tuttle	0	0	0				
Cox	0	0	0				
Eggleston	0	0	0				
Totals	**28**	**28**	**84**		**25**	**16**	**66**

NIT SCORES

First Round: North Carolina 90, Massachusetts 49; Duke 68, Dayton 60; Providence 64, Louisville 58; Tennessee 84, St. John's 83; Georgia Tech 70, LaSalle 67; Michigan 86, Syracuse 76; St. Bonaventure 94, Purdue 79; Hawaii 87, Oklahoma 86

Quarterfinals: North Carolina 86, Providence 79; Duke 78, Tennessee 64; Georgia Tech 78, Michigan 70; St. Bonaventure 73, Hawaii 64

Semifinals: North Carolina 73, Duke 69; Georgia Tech 76, St. Bonaventure 71

Notre Dame's Austin Carr averaged 38 points a game

Championship: North Carolina 84, Georgia Tech 66

Consolation: St. Bonaventure 92, Duke 88

Top Ten

AP	UPI
UCLA	UCLA
Marquette	Marquette
Pennsylvania	Pennsylvania
Kansas	Kansas
Southern California	Southern California
South Carolina	South Carolina
Western Kentucky	Western Kentucky
Kentucky	Kentucky
Fordham	Fordham
Ohio State	Ohio State

All-Americans

AP	UPI
Austin Carr, Notre Dame	Austin Carr, Notre Dame
Sidney Wicks, UCLA	Sidney Wicks, UCLA
Artis Gilmore, Jacksonville	Artis Gilmore, Jacksonville
Jim McDaniels, Western Kentucky	Dean Meminger, Marquette
Dean Meminger, Marquette	John Roche, South Carolina

1971–72

The names in the box score were different, but the name of the team was still UCLA when the smoke settled after the NCAA tournament. UCLA was the unanimous choice for No. 1 in the polls as it won its sixth straight NCAA title and the eighth in nine years. En route, the Bruins extended their consecutive-game winning streak to 45 and beat opponents by an average of 32.3 points a game, breaking the mark of 27.2 set by the 1953–54 Kentucky squad.

This group of Bruins, dubbed the Walton Gang after its 6-11 center Bill Walton, beat Florida State, led by Ron King and Reggie Royals, 81–76, in the championship game. Senior guard Henry Bibby was the steadying influence for UCLA in the closing minutes.

Maryland, which battled Barry Parkhill-led Virginia and North Carolina, with Bob McAdoo, Bill Chamberlain and Dennis Wuycik, throughout the Atlantic Coast Conference schedule, took the NIT with a 100–69 victory over Niagara, led by Marshall Wingate. Maryland's 6-11 soph, Tom McMillen, and 6-9 center Len Elmore were one, two in the MVP voting.

Professional basketball had a serious effect on the college game. Before the season began, the pros plucked such undergraduates as leading scorer Johnny Neumann of Mississippi, Indiana's George McGinnis, California's Phil Chenier, Kentucky's Tom Payne and Massachusetts' Julius Erving. Before the season was over, Marquette, which was undefeated and battling UCLA in the polls, lost 6-11 Jim Chones.

There were some new names in the major college ranks, such as Southwest Louisiana, with Dwight Lamar, and Oral Roberts University, with Richie Fuqua. Lamar and Fuqua finished one, two for scoring honors with 36.3-point and 35.9-point averages, respectively.

Philadelphia produced a quartet of strong teams, with Pennsylvania, led by Corky Calhoun and Bob Morse, winning the Ivy League, and Temple taking the Middle Atlantic crown. Villanova, with Hank Siemiontkowski, and St. Joseph's, led by Mike Bantom, made it a foursome in post-season play.

In the conference races, Ed Ratleff again led Long Beach State to the PCAA title, while 6-11 Yugoslavian Kresimir Cosic kept Brigham Young at the top of the Western Athletic Conference past defense-minded Texas-El Paso. Louisville, with

league MVP Jim Price, headed the Missouri Valley, and Bob Davis took Weber State to another Big Sky championship. Kansas State won the Big Eight, but not without a fight from Kansas, with Bud Stallworth, and Missouri. Tennessee tied with Kentucky in the Southeastern Conference standings, while Ohio U. beat Toledo for the NCAA bid from the Mid-American Conference. Davidson had the best record in the Southern Conference, but East Carolina won the post-season tourney. Texas beat Southern Methodist in a Southwest Conference playoff, and Eastern Kentucky (which won a playoff) tied with Western Kentucky and Morehead State in the Ohio Valley. Minnesota withstood challenges from Ohio State and Michigan in the Big Ten, San Francisco took the WCAC and Rhode Island was the Yankee Conference champion.

Marquette got good performances from Bob Lackey and Allie McGuire, but wasn't the same without Chones. Tom Riker and Kevin Joyce were the heroes for South Carolina, Hawaii was paced by Bob Nash, Wil Robinson led West Virginia and Greg Kohls was the star for Syracuse. Other strong teams were Houston, with Dwight Davis; Providence, with Ernie DiGregorio; Jacksonville, with Ernie Fleming; Southern California, with Paul Westphal; Princeton, with Brian Taylor; St. John's, led by Mel Davis; American U., with Kermit Washington; Oregon State, with Fred Boyd; Washington, led by Steve Hawes; Lafayette, with Tracy Tripucka, and Loyola of Chicago, with 6-10 LaRue Martin.

NCAA Championship

At Los Angeles

UCLA (81)	FG	FT	Pts.	Florida State (76)	FG	FT	Pts.
Wilkes	11	1	23	Garrett	1	1	3
Farmer	2	0	4	Royals	5	5	15
Walton	9	6	24	McCray	3	2	8
Bibby	8	2	18	King	12	3	27
Lee	0	0	0	Samuel	3	0	6
Hollyfield	1	0	2	Harris	7	2	16
Curtis	4	0	8	Petty	0	1	1
Nater	1	0	2	Cole	0	0	0
Totals	36	9	81		31	14	76

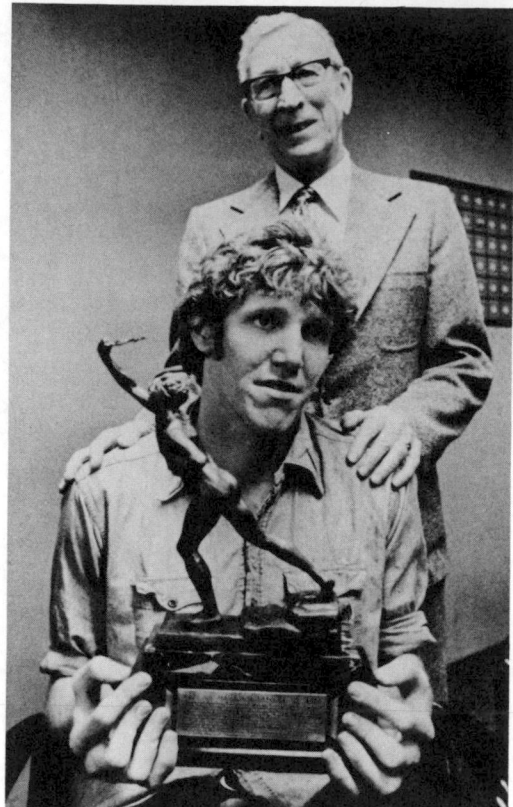

Bill Walton, Sullivan Award winner as best amateur athlete, paced John Wooden's UCLA five to the NCAA championship

NCAA SCORES
REGIONALS
East

First Round: South Carolina 53, Temple 51; Villanova 85, East Carolina 70; Pennsylvania 76, Providence 60

Semifinals: North Carolina 92, South Carolina 69; Pennsylvania 78, Villanova 67

Championship: North Carolina 73, Pennsylvania 59

Mideast

First Round: Marquette 73, Ohio University 49; Florida State 83, Eastern Kentucky 81

Semifinals: Kentucky 85, Marquette 69; Florida State 70, Minnesota 56

Championship: Florida State 73, Kentucky 54

Midwest

First Round: Southwest Louisiana 112, Marshall 101; Texas 85, Houston 74

Semifinals: Louisville 88, Southwest Louisiana 84; Kansas State 66, Texas 55

Championship: Louisville 72, Kansas State 65

West

First Round: Weber State 91, Hawaii 64; Long Beach State 95, Brigham Young 90

Semifinals: UCLA 90, Weber State 58; Long Beach State 75, San Francisco 55

Championship: UCLA 73, Long Beach State 57

FINALS

Semifinals: Florida State 79, North Carolina 75; UCLA 96, Louisville 77

Championship: UCLA 81, Florida State 76

Consolation: North Carolina 105, Louisville 91

NIT Championship

At New York

Maryland (100)	FG	FT	Pts.	Niagara (69)	FG	FT	Pts.
McMillen	7	5	19	Chassar	4	0	8
Brown	3	0	6	Street	2	1	5
Elmore	2	12	16	Royster	4	2	10
White	9	0	18	Williams	6	2	14
Bodell	8	3	19	Wingate	10	10	30
O'Brien	9	0	18	Ellis	1	0	2
Trimble	1	0	2	Hegmann	0	0	0
Neal	0	0	0	Miller	0	0	0
Porac	1	0	2	Whalen	0	0	0
Blank	0	0	0	Farrell	0	0	0
				Reedy	0	0	0
				Taylor	0	0	0
Totals	40	20	100		27	15	69

NIT SCORES

First Round: Lafayette 72, Virginia 71; Jacksonville 94, Fordham 75; Maryland 67, St. Joseph's 55; Syracuse 81, Davidson 77; Oral Roberts 94, Memphis State 74; St. John's 82, Missouri 81; Princeton 68, Indiana 60; Niagara 76, Texas-El Paso 57

Quarterfinals: Jacksonville 87, Lafayette 76; Maryland 71, Syracuse 65; St. John's 94, Oral Roberts 78; Niagara 65, Princeton 60

Semifinals: Maryland 91, Jacksonville 77; Niagara 69, St. John's 67

Championship: Maryland 100, Niagara 69

Consolation: Jacksonville 83, St. John's 80

Top Ten

AP	UPI
UCLA	UCLA
North Carolina	North Carolina
Pennsylvania	Pennsylvania
Louisville	Louisville
Long Beach State	South Carolina
South Carolina	Long Beach State
Marquette	Marquette
Southwest Louisiana	Southwest Louisiana
Brigham Young	Brigham Young
Florida State	Florida State

All-Americans

AP	UPI
Bill Walton, UCLA	Bill Walton, UCLA
Dwight Lamar, Southwest Louisiana	Henry Bibby, UCLA
Ed Ratleff, Long Beach State	Dwight Lamar, Southwest Louisiana
Jim Chones, Marquette	Jim Chones, Marquette
Tom Riker, South Carolina	Ed Ratleff, Long Beach State

UCLA won its seventh successive national title and its seventy-fifth straight game, and Coach John Wooden didn't hesitate when asked the question he'd never liked to answer: "Was this your best team?"

"Yes," replied Wooden, "I'd have to say this one is." Bill Walton, the 6-11 junior, led UCLA to another 30–0 season and dominated the title game against Memphis State. Walton made 21 of 22 shots, scored 44 points, and grabbed 13 rebounds in an 87–66 rout. Keith Wilkes had 16 points, while guards Tommy Curtis and Greg Lee were content to set up Walton with high lob passes. Memphis State was led by 6-9 Larry Kenon and Larry Finch.

UCLA defeated Notre Dame, 82–63, during the season to break the record winning streak of 60 set by San Francisco in the mid-1950s.

The Bruins were not the only unbeaten team in the country. North Carolina State went 27–0 but was barred from tournament action for methods it used in recruiting its star player, David Thompson.

Virginia Tech, snubbed by the NCAA tourney, brought 6-7 Allan Bristow to the NIT and won the title, beating Notre Dame in overtime, 92–91. John Shumate of Notre Dame was the MVP.

Two rule changes of major impact went into effect: Freshmen became eligible for varsity competition, and free throws were prohibited on the first six common fouls of each half. The freshman-eligible rule brought a lot of new and young faces into the college game. Among freshmen players starring on varsity teams were Quinn Buckner of Indiana, Ron Lee of Oregon, Alex English of South Carolina, and Phil Sellers of Rutgers.

William "The Bird" Averitt was the hottest scoring machine in the country, averaging 33.9 points a game for Pepperdine, while Ray Lewis averaged 32.9 for Los Angeles State. Other players with outstanding years included Jim Brewer of Minnesota, Kevin Joyce of South Carolina, Doug Col-

lins of Illinois State, Rich Fuqua of Oral Roberts, John Williamson of New Mexico State, Willie Biles of Tulsa, Kevin Kunnert of Iowa, and Kermit Washington of American.

Providence was the Cinderella team from the East. With Ernie DiGregorio and Marvin Barnes, the 27–4 Friars became the first team from New England in 25 years to reach the NCAA semifinals. But Barnes was injured early in the semifinal game against Memphis State, and Providence lost, 98–85.

Marquette, with Larry McNeill, and Houston, led by Dwight Jones, were two top independent teams, but both were victims of upsets in early rounds of tournament play.

Steve Downing led Indiana to the Big Ten title, while Lon Kruger-led Kansas took the Big Eight. Penn, paced by 6-7 Ron Haigler, won another Ivy League championship, and Mike Bantom sparked St. Joseph's to the top of the Mid-Atlantic. Other conference winners included Southwestern Louisiana, with Bo Lamar, in the Southland; Long Beach State, with Ed Ratleff, in the Pacific Coast; Kentucky, led by sophomore Kevin Grevey, in the Southeast; Austin Peay, with Fly Williams, in the Ohio Valley; and Miami of Ohio, in the Mid-American.

NCAA Championship

At St. Louis

UCLA (87)	FG	FT	Pts.	Memphis State (66)	FG	FT	Pts.
Wilkes	8	0	16	Buford	3	1	7
Farmer	1	0	2	Kenon	8	4	20
Walton	21	2	44	Robinson	3	0	6
Lee	1	3	5	Laurie	0	0	0
Hollyfield	4	0	8	Finch	9	11	29
Curtis	1	2	4	Westfall	0	0	0
Meyers	2	0	4	Cook	1	2	4
Nater	1	0	2	McKinney	0	0	0
Franklin	1	0	2	Jones	0	0	0
Carson	0	0	0	Tetzlaff	0	0	0
Webb	0	0	0	Liss	0	0	0
				Andrews	0	0	0
Totals	40	7	87		24	18	66

NCAA SCORES
REGIONALS

East

First Round: Syracuse 83, Furman 82; Pennsylvania 62, St. John's 61; Providence 89, St. Joseph's 76

Semifinals: Maryland 91, Syracuse 75; Providence 87, Pennsylvania 65

Championship: Providence 103, Maryland 89

Mideast

First Round: Marquette 77, Miami (O.) 62; Austin Peay 77, Jacksonville 75

Semifinals: Indiana 75, Marquette 69; Kentucky 106, Austin Peay 100

Championship: Indiana 72, Kentucky 65

Midwest

First Round: South Carolina 78, Texas Tech 70; Southwest Louisiana 102, Houston 89

Semifinals: Memphis State 90, South Carolina 76; Kansas State 66, Southwest Louisiana 63

Championship: Memphis State 92, Kansas State 72

West

First Round: Long Beach State 88, Weber State 75; Arizona State 103, Oklahoma City 78

Semifinals: San Francisco 77, Long Beach State 67; UCLA 98, Arizona State 81

Championship: UCLA 54, San Francisco 39

FINALS

Semifinals: Memphis State 98, Providence 85; UCLA 70, Indiana 59

Championship: UCLA 87, Memphis State 66

Consolation: Indiana 97, Providence 79

UCLA won its seventh straight NCAA championship as Bill Walton scored 44 points

NIT Championship

At New York

Virginia Tech (92)	FG	FT	Pts.	Notre Dame (91)	FG	FT	Pts.
Frazier	5	1	11	Shumate	10	8	28
Leider	12	2	26	Novak	5	0	10
Bristow	11	2	24	Crotty	4	0	8
Stevens	8	1	17	Clay	8	2	18
Thomas	3	0	6	Brokaw	10	3	23
Wade	2	2	6	Townsend	2	0	4
McKee	0	0	0				
Sensibaugh	1	0	2				
Totals	**42**	**8**	**92**		**39**	**13**	**91**

Top Ten

AP	UPI
UCLA	UCLA
North Carolina State	North Carolina State
Long Beach State	Long Beach State
Providence	Marquette
Marquette	Providence
Indiana	Indiana
Southwest Louisiana	Kansas State*
Maryland	Southwest Louisiana*
Kansas State	Minnesota
Minnesota	Maryland

*Tied for seventh place

All-Americans

AP	UPI
Bill Walton, UCLA	Bill Walton, UCLA
Ed Ratleff, Long Beach State	Ed Ratleff, Long Beach State
David Thompson, North Carolina State	David Thompson, North Carolina State
Ernie DiGregorio, Providence	Doug Collins, Illinois State
Kermit Washington, American	Dwight Lamar, Southwest Louisiana

NIT SCORES

First Round: Notre Dame 69, Southern California 65; Louisville 97, American 84; North Carolina 82, Oral Roberts 65; Massachusetts 78, Missouri 71; Fairfield 80, Marshall 76; Virginia Tech 65, New Mexico 63; Minnesota 68, Rutgers 59; Alabama 87, Manhattan 86

Quarterfinals: North Carolina 73, Massachusetts 63; Notre Dame 79, Louisville 71; Virginia Tech 77, Fairfield 76; Alabama 69, Minnesota 65

Semifinals: Virginia Tech 74, Alabama 73; Notre Dame 78, North Carolina 71

Finals: Virginia Tech 92, Notre Dame 91 (OT)

Consolation: North Carolina 88, Alabama 69

1973–74

David Thompson and North Carolina State ended UCLA's seven-year reign as Thompson became known as "the David Who Slew

Goliath." North Carolina State, which had lost only to UCLA all season, beat the Bruins in double overtime in the NCAA semifinals, 80–77, and then defeated Marquette, 76–64, for the title.

Thompson, a soaring 6-4 guard who could jump like a center, gunned his team to a 30–1 season with a 26-point average. In the semifinal showdown, he scored 28 and combined with 7-4 Tom Burleson and 5-6 Monte Towe to offset UCLA's awesome Bill Walton and Keith Wilkes. Thompson was named MVP after scoring 21 points in the title game against Marquette, with Bo Ellis and Maurice Lucas.

North Carolina State got to the finals with victories over Providence, led by Marvin Barnes, and Pittsburgh, with Billy Knight, and also after surviving a dogfight in the Atlantic Coast Conference against Maryland, with Tom McMillen and Len Elmore, and North Carolina, paced by Bobby Jones.

Hints of UCLA's demise came during the season. The Bruins had their 88-game winning streak snapped by John Shumate-led Notre Dame, 71–70, and also lost twice in one weekend—to Oregon, with Ron Lee, and to Oregon State.

In the NIT, Purdue won the final by defeating Utah, 87–81, although Utes' sophomore Mike Sojourner was named MVP.

Larry Fogle, who transferred to Canisius from probation-plagued Southwestern Louisiana, won the national scoring title with a 33.4 average. Another top gunner was Sam McCants, whose 24-point average powered Oral Roberts to a 23–6 season. Tom Henderson of Hawaii, Brian Winters of South Carolina, and Joe Meriweather of Southern Illinois also shot their teams into the national ratings.

St. John's was strong in the East with Mel Utely, while Manhattan went 18–9 with Bill Campion. In the West, Phil Smith and Kevin Restani powered San Francisco to a 19–9 season and the West Coast Athletic Conference title, while Cliff Pondexter boosted Long Beach State to another Pacific Coast crown. Other top players around the country included Dennis DuVal of Syracuse, Ira Terrell of Southern Methodist, Fly Williams of Austin Peay, Eric Money of Arizona, Len Robinson of Tennessee State, and Mike Robinson of Michigan State.

In the Big Ten, Campy Russell led Michigan to the co-championship and a playoff victory over Indiana, with Kent Benson. Kansas took the Big Eight on the strength of 6-10 Danny Knight, and Louisville won the Missouri Valley with Junior Bridgeman. Jan van Breda Kolff sparked Vanderbilt to a share of first with Leon Douglas-led Alabama in the Southeastern, while Foots Walker helped West Georgia prevail in the South Atlantic. Other winners included Penn in the Ivy and Texas in the Southwest.

NCAA Championship

At Greensboro

N. C. State (76)	FG	FT	Pts.	Marquette (64)	FG	FT	Pts.
Stoddard	3	2	8	Ellis	6	0	12
Thompson	7	7	21	Tatum	2	0	4
Burleson	6	2	14	Lucas	7	7	21
Rivers	4	6	14	Walton	4	0	8
Towe	5	6	16	Washington	3	5	11
Spence	1	1	3	Delsman	0	0	0
Moeller	0	0	0	Daniels	1	1	3
				Campbell	2	0	4
				Homan	0	1	1
				Brennan	0	0	0
Totals	26	24	76		25	14	64

NCAA SCORES

First Round: Providence 84, Pennsylvania 69; Pittsburgh 54, St. Joseph's 42; Furman 75, South Carolina 67; New Mexico 73, Idaho State 65; Dayton 88, Los Angeles State 80; Notre Dame 108, Austin Peay 66; Marquette 85, Ohio University 59; Oral Roberts 86, Syracuse 82; Creighton 77, Texas 61

Second Round: North Carolina State 92, Providence 78; Pittsburgh 81, Furman 78; San Francisco 64, New Mexico 61; UCLA 111, Dayton 100; Michigan 77, Notre Dame 68; Marquette 69, Vanderbilt 61; Oral Roberts 96, Louisville 93; Kansas 55, Creighton 54

Consolations: Providence 95, Furman 83; New Mexico 66, Dayton 61; Notre Dame 118, Vanderbilt 88; Creighton 80, Louisville 71

Regional Championships: North Carolina State 100, Pittsburgh 72; UCLA 83, San Francisco 60; Marquette 72, Michigan 70; Kansas 93, Oral Roberts 90

Semifinals: North Carolina State 80, UCLA 77; Marquette 64, Kansas 51

Championship: North Carolina State 76, Marquette 64

Consolation: UCLA 78, Kansas 61

North Carolina State won NCAA title behind David Thompson

NIT Championship

At New York

Final: Purdue 87, Utah 81

Consolation: Boston College 87, Jacksonville 77

Purdue (87)	FG	FT	Pts.	Utah (81)	FG	FT	Pts.
Rose	5	0	10	Terry	3	0	6
Kendrick	9	7	25	Menatti	4	2	10
Garrett	8	8	24	Sojourner	10	3	23
Parkinson	4	0	8	Burden	11	5	27
Luke	1	0	2	Medley	3	0	6
Scheffler	3	0	6	Whiting	0	0	0
Steele	2	4	8	Jones	1	0	2
Thomas	1	2	4	Jonas	2	3	7
				Bergen	0	0	0
Totals	33	21	87		34	13	81

NIT SCORES

First Round: Maryland (E. Shore) 84, Manhattan 81; Jacksonville 73, Massachusetts 69; Hawaii 66, Fairfield 65; Purdue 82, North Carolina 71; Memphis State 73, Seton Hall 72; Utah 102, Rutgers 89; Connecticut 82, St. John's 70; Boston College 63, Cincinnati 62

Quarterfinals: Jacksonville 85, Maryland (E. Shore) 83; Purdue 82, Hawaii 72; Utah 92, Memphis State 78; Boston College 76, Connecticut 75

Semifinals: Purdue 78, Jacksonville 63; Utah 117, Boston College 93

Top Ten

AP	UPI
North Carolina State	North Carolina State
UCLA	UCLA
Marquette	Notre Dame
Maryland	Maryland
Notre Dame	Marquette
Michigan	Providence
Kansas	Vanderbilt
Providence	North Carolina
Indiana	Indiana
Long Beach State	Kansas

All-Americans

AP	UPI
Bill Walton, UCLA	Bill Walton, UCLA
Keith Wilkes, UCLA	David Thompson, North Carolina State
David Thompson, North Carolina State	John Shumate, Notre Dame
Marvin Barnes, Providence	Keith Wilkes, UCLA
John Shumate, Notre Dame	Marvin Barnes, Providence

1974-75

After 27 years at UCLA, the coach known as the Wizard of Westwood decided to hang up his magic wand. But John Wooden caused some eyebrows to rise by announcing his retirement after the Bruins had reached the national final with a 75–74 semifinal overtime victory over Louisville.

It was suggested, to Wooden's denials, that the announcement was timed to hype the players. If so, it worked, because UCLA downed Kentucky, 92–85, for Wooden's tenth championship in 12 years. He left behind a record of 620–147.

This UCLA team, not considered Wooden's strongest, had lost during the season to Stanford, with 7-0 Rich Kelley, to Notre

UCLA's Richard Washington was NCAA tourney MVP, giving John Wooden his tenth and final title

Dame, and to Washington. But 6-9 Dave Meyers, 7-1 Ralph Drollinger, Pete Trgovich, Andre McCarter, and Richard Washington put it together for the tournament. They defeated Michigan, with C. J. Kupec, and Montana before squeaking by a Louisville squad led by Allen Murphy and Junior Bridgeman. Keven Grevey of Kentucky scored 34 points in the final, but as McCarter said, "There was no way we were going to lose Coach's last game." Washington received the MVP award.

The NIT produced an all-East final in which 6-7 Barnes Hauptfuhrer and Armond Hill led Princeton to an 80–69 title victory over Providence, with Joe Hassett. Oregon's Ron Lee was MVP

In some ways, it was a year of oddities. Maryland recruited 6-11 schoolboy Moses Malone, only to see him skip college altogether and go straight to the pros. Coach Abe Lemons rebuilt Pan American into a 22–2 team behind Marshall Rogers and Gilbert King, but couldn't get into a tournament because the school had been placed on probation. Houston featured a 6-9 guard, Louis Dunbar, while Wisconsin had as its stars a pair of 6-11 twin brothers, Kim and Kerry Hughes.

Also, what was probably the best team in the country failed to make the tournament finals. Indiana, with Kent Benson and Scott May, won its first 31 games and was ranked No. 1 but, with May injured, lost in the regionals to Kentucky, 92–90.

North Carolina State, the defending national champion, also didn't reach the finals, despite David Thompson's 29.9 scoring average. In the usual Atlantic Coast Conference fight to the death, Maryland, led by Mo Howard, came out on top, along with North Carolina, which had Walter Davis, Tom LaGarde, and Mitch Kupchak.

Bob McCurdy of Richmond took national scoring honors with a 32.9 average that included nights of 41, 40, 46, and 53 points in a 17-day span at the end of the season. Other players with outstanding years included Adrian Dantley of Notre Dame, Phil Sellers of Rutgers, Rudy Hackett of Syracuse, 7-1 Marvin Webster of Morgan State, Lloyd Free of Guilford, Gus Williams of USC, Leon Douglas of Ala-

97

bama, Luther Burden of Utah, Bill Robinzine of DePaul, and Alvan Adams of Oklahoma.

LaSalle won the East Coast Conference playoff behind 6-10 Joe Bryant, while Penn took the Ivy League and Massachusetts the Yankee. James McElroy led Central Michigan to the top in the Mid-American, and Kansas took the Big Eight. Among other winners were Arizona State, with Lionel Hollins, in the Western Athletic; Long Beach State, with Bob Gross, in the Pacific Coast; a Nevada-Las Vegas team sparked by Ricky Sobers in the West Coast, and Furman, with Clyde Mayes, in the Southern.

NCAA Championship

At San Diego

UCLA (92)	FG	FT	Pts.	Kentucky (85)	FG	FT	Pts.
Meyers	9	6	24	Grevey	13	8	34
Johnson	3	0	6	Guyette	7	2	16
Washington	12	4	28	Robey	1	0	2
Trgovich	7	2	16	Conner	4	1	9
McCarter	3	2	8	Flynn	3	4	10
Drollinger	4	2	10	Givens	3	2	8
				Phillips	1	2	4
				Johnson	0	0	0
				Hall	1	0	2
				Lee	0	0	0
Totals	38	16	92		33	19	85

NCAA SCORES

First Round: Syracuse 87, LaSalle 83 (OT); North Carolina 93, New Mexico State 69; Boston College 82, Furman 76; Kansas State 69, Pennsylvania 62; Central Michigan 77, Georgetown 75; Kentucky 76, Marquette 54; Indiana 78, Texas-El Paso 53; Oregon State 78, Middle Tennessee 67; Cincinnati 87, Texas A&M 79; Louisville 91, Rutgers 78; Maryland 83, Creighton 79; Notre Dame 77, Kansas 71; Arizona State 97, Alabama 94; Nevada-Las Vegas 90, San Diego State 80; UCLA 103, Michigan 91 (OT); Montana 69, Utah State 63

Second Round: Syracuse 78, North Carolina 76; Kansas State 74, Boston College 65; Kentucky 90, Central Michigan 73; Indiana 81, Oregon State 71; Louisville 78, Cincinnati 63; Maryland 83, Notre Dame 71; Arizona State 84, Nevada-Las Vegas 81; UCLA 67, Montana 64

Consolations: North Carolina 110, Boston College 90; Central Michigan 88, Oregon State 87; Cincinnati 95, Notre Dame 87 (OT); Nevada-Las Vegas 75, Montana 67

Regional Championships: Syracuse 95, Kansas State 87 (OT); Kentucky 92, Indiana 90; Louisville 96, Maryland 82; UCLA 89, Arizona State 75

Semifinals: Kentucky 95, Syracuse 79; UCLA 75, Louisville 74 (OT)

Championship: UCLA 92, Kentucky 85

Consolation: Louisville 96, Syracuse 88

NIT Championship

At New York

Princeton (80)	FG	FT	Pts.	Providence (69)	FG	FT	Pts.
Hauptfuhrer	5	0	10	Eason	2	0	4
Van Blommesteyn	9	5	23	McAndrew	2	5	9
Ramati	5	0	10	Cooper	2	1	5
Hill	2	0	4	Bellow	10	2	22
Steuerer	9	8	26	Hassett	6	1	13
Hartley	0	0	0	Campbell	5	6	16
Malloy	3	1	7	Santos	0	0	0
O'Neill	0	0	0				
Totals	33	14	80		27	15	69

NIT SCORES

First Round: Manhattan 68, Massachusetts 51; Providence 91, Clemson 84; Pittsburgh 70, Southern Illinois 65; St. John's 94, Lafayette 76; South Carolina 71, Connecticut 61; Princeton 84, Holy Cross 63; Oral Roberts 97, Memphis State 95; Oregon 85, St. Peter's 79

Quarterfinals: Providence 101, Pittsburgh 80; St. John's 57, Manhattan 56; Oregon 68, Oral Roberts 59; Princeton 86, South Carolina 67

Semifinals: Providence 85, St. John's 72; Princeton 58, Oregon 57

Final: Princeton 80, Providence 69

Consolation: Oregon 80, St. John's 76 (OT)

Top Ten

AP	UPI
UCLA	Indiana
Kentucky	UCLA
Indiana	Louisville
Louisville	Kentucky
Maryland	Maryland
Syracuse	Marquette
North Carolina State	Arizona State
Arizona State	Alabama
North Carolina	North Carolina State
Alabama	North Carolina

All-Americans

AP	UPI
David Thompson, North Carolina State	David Thompson, North Carolina State
Adrian Dantley, Notre Dame	Adrian Dantley, Notre Dame
David Meyers, UCLA	David Meyers, UCLA
Luther Burden, Utah	John Lucas, Maryland
Scott May, Indiana	Scott May, Indiana

1975–76

Indiana won the national championship, and rarely had there been less doubt about who was No. 1. The big, strong Hoosiers

Kent Benson typified Indiana's physical might as Hoosiers won 32 games and NCAA championship

completed a 32–0 season sweep with consecutive victories over five nationally ranked teams. "They put you through a meat grinder," was what one coach said when his team was ground up by 6-11, 240-pound Kent Benson, 6-7 Scott May, 6-7 Tom Abernethy, 6-6 Bobby Wilkerson, and 6-3 Quinn Buckner.

Benson was voted the MVP after the title game against Big Ten rival Michigan, led by Rickey Green and Phil Hubbard. It was the first time two teams from the same conference had met in the championship game. The final score was 86–68 as May scored 26 points and Benson 25.

Indiana played king of the hill in the tourney, flattening such powers as St. John's, with George Johnson and Frank Alagia, 90–70; Alabama, with Leon Douglas and T. R. Dunn, 74–69; Marquette, with Earl Tatum and Lloyd Walton, 65–56; and UCLA, with Marques Johnson, Richard Washington, and Ralph Drollinger, 65–51.

The safest place for a team to be was a tournament without Indiana, and that's just where Kentucky was. The Wildcats played in the NIT for the first time in 26 years and took the final by defeating North Carolina-Charlotte, 71–67. Cedric "Cornbread" Maxwell, Charlotte's skinny 6-8 forward, was chosen as the MVP.

Rutgers, more noted for playing the nation's first football game, had its finest hour in basketball. Led by Phil Sellers, Mike Dabney, and Ed Jordan, Rutgers won 31 straight games before losing to Michigan in the national semifinals and then to UCLA in the consolation game.

National scoring honors went to 6-2 sharp-shooter Marshall Rogers, who averaged 36.8 points a game for 20–5 Pan American. Freeman Williams, a Portland State sophomore, averaged 30.9, followed closely by Terry Furlow of Michigan State and Adrian Dantley of Notre Dame. Big years were also enjoyed by John Lucas of Maryland, Phil Ford of 25–4 North Carolina, Bernard King of Tennessee, Mel Davis of North Texas State, Wally Walker of Virginia, Hercle Ivy of Iowa State, Bob Carrington of Boston College, and Robert Parish of Centenary.

The top-scoring team was 29–2 Nevada-Las Vegas. The Runnin' Rebels averaged 110.5 points a game behind Ed Owens and Boyd Batts. Princeton, sparked to a 22–5 year by Armond Hill and Barnes Hauptfuhrer, had the best defensive statistics in the nation and ended Penn's six-year domination in the Ivy League.

Among conference champions were Texas A&M, with Sonny Parker, in the Southwest, and Western Michigan, with 6-9 Paul Griffin, in the Mid-American. Hofstra,

led by Rich Laurel, captured the East Coast Conference playoff, while Robert Miller paced Cincinnati to the title in the newly formed Metro. Willie Smith took Missouri all the way in the Big Eight, 6-10 Bob Elliott led Arizona to the top of the Western Athletic, Jim Krovic made VMI the surprise victor in the Southern, and Bob Elmore starred as Wichita State took the Missouri Valley.

NCAA Championship

At Philadelphia

Indiana (86)	FG	FT	Pts.	Michigan (68)	FG	FT	Pts.
Abernethy	4	3	11	Britt	5	1	11
May	10	6	26	Robinson	4	0	8
Benson	11	3	25	Hubbard	4	2	10
Wilkerson	0	0	0	Green	7	4	18
Buckner	5	6	16	Grote	4	4	12
Radford	0	0	0	Bergen	0	0	0
Crews	0	2	2	Slaton	2	3	7
Wisman	0	2	2	Baxter	0	0	0
Valavicius	1	0	2	Thompson	0	0	0
Haymore	1	0	2	Hardy	1	0	2
Bender	0	0	0				
Totals	**32**	**22**	**86**		**27**	**14**	**68**

NCAA SCORES

First Round: DePaul 69, Virginia 60; Virginia Military 81, Tennessee 75; Rutgers 54, Princeton 53; Connecticut 80, Hofstra 78 (OT); Michigan 74, Wichita State 73; Notre Dame 79, Cincinnati 78; Missouri 69, Washington 67; Texas Tech 69, Syracuse 56; Alabama 79, North Carolina 64; Indiana 90, St. John's (N.Y.) 70; Marquette 79, Western Kentucky 60; Western Michigan 77, Virginia Tech 67 (OT); Pepperdine 87, Memphis State 77; UCLA 74, San Diego State 64; Arizona 83, Georgetown 76; Nevada-Las Vegas 103, Boise State 78

Second Round: Virginia Military 71, DePaul 66; Rutgers 93, Connecticut 79; Missouri 86, Texas Tech 75; Michigan 80, Notre Dame 76; Indiana 74, Alabama 69; Marquette 62, Western Michigan 57; UCLA 70, Pepperdine 61; Arizona 114, Nevada-Las Vegas 109 (OT)

Regional Championships: Rutgers 91, Virginia Military 75; Michigan 95, Missouri 88; Indiana 65, Marquette 56; UCLA 82, Arizona 66

Semifinals: Michigan 86, Rutgers 70; Indiana 65, UCLA 51

Championship: Indiana 86, Michigan 68

Consolation: UCLA 106, Rutgers 92

NIT Championship
At New York

Kentucky (71)				North Carolina (Charlotte) (67)			
	FG	FT	Pts.		FG	FT	Pts.
Givens	3	0	6	King	3	3	9
Lee	4	0	8	Massey	5	6	16
Phillips	5	6	16	Maxwell	8	8	24
Johnson	7	2	16	Ball	3	0	6
Warford	7	0	14	Watkins	4	0	8
Casey	3	0	6	Gruber	1	0	2
Haskins	0	0	0	Pearce	0	2	2
Fowler	2	1	5				
Totals	31	9	71		24	19	67

NIT SCORES

First Round: North Carolina (Charlotte) 79, San Francisco 74; Holy Cross 84, St. Peter's 78; Kentucky 67, Niagara 61; Providence 84, North Carolina A&T 68

Quarterfinals: North Carolina (Charlotte) 79, Oregon 72; North Carolina State 78, Holy Cross 68; Kentucky 81, Kansas State 78; Providence 73, Louisville 67

Semifinals: North Carolina (Charlotte) 80, North Carolina State 79; Kentucky 79, Providence 78

Finals: Kentucky 71, North Carolina (Charlotte) 67

Consolation: North Carolina State 74, Providence 69

Top Ten

AP	UPI
Indiana	Indiana
Marquette	Marquette
Nevada-Las Vegas	Rutgers
Rutgers	Nevada-Las Vegas
UCLA	UCLA
Alabama	North Carolina
Notre Dame	Alabama
North Carolina	Notre Dame
Michigan	Michigan
Western Michigan	Washington

All-Americans

AP	UPI
Adrian Dantley, Notre Dame	Scott May, Indiana
Scott May, Indiana	Adrian Dantley, Notre Dame
Kent Benson, Indiana	John Lucas, Maryland
John Lucas, Maryland	Rich Washington, UCLA
Phil Sellers, Rutgers	Kent Benson, Indiana

1976–77

No team had ever won the national championship with as many as seven defeats before Marquette turned the trick as a retirement present for Al McGuire, its flamboyant coach. McGuire's practice of recruiting streetwise players like Butch Lee, Jim Boylan, and Bo Ellis paid off with a 67–59 title victory over North Carolina. Lee ran Marquette's disciplined offense, scored 19 points, and was named MVP.

Marquette's road to a 25–7 season and the championship included tournament triumphs over Cincinnati, Kansas State, and Wake Forest, plus a semifinal victory over upstart North Carolina-Charlotte, with 6-8 Cedric "Cornbread" Maxwell.

One of the surprises in the finals was the absence of Marques Johnson-led UCLA, which was upset in the second round by Idaho State. Run-and-shoot Nevada-Las Vegas, with Glen Gondrezick and Robert Smith, averaged 107.1 points a game but fell short of that in the semifinals as North Carolina's Walter Davis, Phil Ford, Mike O'Koren, and John Kuester proved to be a point stronger, 84–83.

St. Bonaventure took the NIT crown by defeating favored Houston, with Otis Birdsong, 94–91. The Bonnies' Greg Sanders scored 40 points in the final and was named MVP.

The no-dunk rule was rescinded at the start of the season, further opening up the game under the basket. Some of the more dominant big men were James Bailey of Rutgers, Roosevelt Bouie of Syracuse, Bob Elmore of Wichita State, Wayne "Tree" Rollins of Clemson, Wilson Washington of Old Dominion, Jack Sikma of Illinois Wesleyan, and Mychal Thompson of Minnesota.

Another big man, 6-11 Bill Cartwright, keyed San Francisco to 29 straight victories and a No. 1 ranking in the polls. But the Dons lost on the last day of the regular season to Notre Dame, with Toby Knight, and then were beaten in the tournament by Nevada-Las Vegas.

Portland State's Freeman Williams was the country's top gun with a 38.8 average, while Glenn Mosely of Seton Hall led all rebounders with 16.3 a game. Freshman guard Ron Perry stirred memories of Bob Cousy at Holy Cross with flashy ball-handling and a 23-point average, and Rich Laurel brought Hofstra fans to their feet by scoring at a 30.3 clip and leading the team to a 23–7 record. Other stars were Gary Winton of Army, Brad Davis and Steve Sheppard of Maryland, Ricky Marsh of Manhattan, Anthony Roberts of 21-7 Oral Roberts, Bob Carrington of Boston College, Alonzo Bradley of Texas Southern, Tate Armstrong of Duke, Ray Williams of Min-

Butch Lee directed Marquette's streetwise team to the national championship

nesota, Skip Brown of Wake Forest, and Greg Ballard of Oregon.

The Ernie and Bernie Show was a sellout in the Southeastern Conference, where Ernie Grunfeld and Bernard King sparked Tennessee to a share of first place with Jack Givens-led Kentucky. Princeton, with Frank Sowinski, took the Ivy League title; Wesley Cox sparked Louisville to the Metro crown, and Rickey Green put Michigan on top in the Big Ten. Arkansas, paced by Sidney Moncrief, went 26–2 and won in the Southwest; Mike Glenn helped Southern Illinois to cochampion the Missouri Valley with New Mexico State, and Utah was first in the Rocky Mountain. Other winners included Kansas State, with Mike Evans, in the Big Eight, Ron Carter-led VMI and Furman in the Southern, and Long Beach State in the Pacific Coast.

NCAA Championship

At Atlanta

Marquette (67)	FG	FT	Pts.	North Carolina (59)	FG	FT	Pts.
Ellis	5	4	14	Davis	6	8	20
Neary	0	0	0	O'Koren	6	2	14
Whitehead	2	4	8	Yonakor	3	0	6
Lee	6	7	19	Ford	3	0	6
Boylan	5	4	14	Kuester	2	1	5
Rosenberger	1	4	6	Krafcisin	1	0	2
Toone	3	0	6	Zaliagiris	2	0	4
				Bradley	1	0	2
				Buckley	0	0	0
				Wolf	0	0	0
				Colescott	0	0	0
				Coley	0	0	0
				Doughton	0	0	0
				Virgil	0	0	0
Totals	22	23	67		24	11	59

NCAA SCORES

First Round: Virginia Military, 73, Duquesne 66; Kentucky 72, Princeton 58; Notre Dame 90, Hofstra 83; North Carolina 69, Purdue 66; UCLA 87, Louisville 79; Idaho State 83, Long Beach State 72; Utah 72, St. John's (N.Y.) 68; Nevada-Las Vegas 121, San Francisco 95; Michigan 92, Holy Cross 81; Detroit 93, Middle Tennessee State 76; North Carolina-Charlotte 91, Central Michigan 86 (OT); Syracuse 93, Tennessee 88 (OT); Marquette 66, Cincinnati 51; Kansas State 87, Providence 80; Wake Forest 86, Arkansas 80; Southern Illinois 81, Arizona 77

Second Round: Kentucky 93, Virginia Military 78; North Carolina 79, Notre Dame 77; Idaho State 76, UCLA 75; Nevada-Las Vegas 88, Utah 83; Michigan 86, Detroit 81; North Carolina-Charlotte 81, Syracuse 59; Marquette 67, Kansas State 66; Wake Forest 86, Southern Illinois 81

Regional Championships: North Carolina 79, Kentucky 72; Nevada-Las Vegas 107, Idaho State 90; North Carolina-Charlotte 75, Michigan 68; Marquette 82, Wake Forest 68

Semifinals: Marquette 51, North Carolina-Charlotte 49; North Carolina 84, Nevada-Las Vegas 83

Championship: Marquette 67, North Carolina 59

Consolation: Nevada-Las Vegas 106, North Carolina-Charlotte 94

NIT Championship

At New York

St. Bonaventure (94)	FG	FT	Pts.	Houston (91)	FG	FT	Pts.
Hollis	9	6	24	Rose	1	1	3
Sanders	14	12	40	Thompson	6	2	14
Waterman	1	6	8	Schultz	3	3	9
Baron	2	0	4	Birdsong	18	2	38
Hagan	5	4	14	Trammel	2	0	4
Urzetta	0	3	3	Ciolli	0	1	1
Harrod	0	1	1	Kelley	2	0	4
Atkinson	0	0	0	Walker	2	0	4
				Winder	0	0	0
				Williams	1	0	2
				Fears	5	2	12
Totals	31	32	94		40	11	91

NIT SCORES

First Round: Alabama 80, Memphis State 63; Virginia Tech 83, Georgetown 79; Illinois State 65, Creighton 58; Indiana State 83, Houston 82; Villanova 71, Old Dominion 68 (OT); Massachusetts 86, Seton Hall 85; Oregon 90, Oral Roberts 89; St. Bonaventure 79, Rutgers 77

Quarterfinals: Alabama 79, Virginia Tech 72; Houston 91, Illinois State 90; Villanova 81, Massachusetts 71; St. Bonaventure 76, Oregon 73

Semifinals: Houston 82, Alabama 76; St. Bonaventure 86, Villanova 82

Final: St. Bonaventure 94, Houston 91

Consolation: Villanova 102, Alabama 89

Top Ten

AP	UPI
Michigan	Michigan
UCLA	San Francisco
Kentucky	North Carolina
Nevada-Las Vegas	UCLA
North Carolina	Kentucky
Syracuse	Nevada-Las Vegas
Marquette	Arkansas
San Francisco	Tennessee
Wake Forest	Syracuse
Notre Dame	Utah

All-Americans

AP	UPI
Marques Johnson, UCLA	Marques Johnson, UCLA
Rickey Green, Michigan	Rickey Green, Michigan
Phil Ford, North Carolina	Kent Benson, Indiana
Kent Benson, Indiana	Bernard King, Tennessee
Bernard King, Tennessee	Otis Birdsong, Houston

1977–78

The four-corners offense became a fad among teams seeking the best strategy for controlling the ball—but nobody could figure out how to control Kentucky. The Wildcats won their first national title since the days of Adolph Rupp, defeating Duke in the final, 94–88.

Coach Joe Hall called a rare news conference the day before the title game to tell of the pressure he and his No. 1-ranked players had been under. Then Kentucky responded to the ultimate pressure of the final game, especially Jack Givens. The 6-4 forward scored 41 points and took MVP honors as he and Rick Robey, Mike Phillips, Kyle Macy, and James Lee closed the season with a 30–2 record. Young Duke, a surprise finalist, was led by junior Jim Spanarkel, sophomore Mike Gminski, and freshman Eugene Banks.

The tournament was marked by upsets. Highly ranked North Carolina, with Phil Ford, was knocked out in the first round, as were Marquette, with Butch Lee, and Syracuse, with Roosevelt Bouie and Marty Byrnes. California State-Fullerton emerged as the Cinderella team of the first two rounds, beating favored New Mexico, with Marvin Johnson, and then ousting San Francisco, which featured 6-11 Bill Cartwright and Winford Boynes.

Arkansas and Texas proved the Southwest to be more than a football conference. Paced by Sidney Moncrief, Marvin Delph, and Ron Brewer, Arkansas went 32–4 and gained the national semifinals, eliminating along the way UCLA, with David Greenwood and Roy Hamilton.

Texas went to the NIT and won the title with a 101–93 victory over North Carolina State. The Longhorns' Jim Krivacs and Ron Baxter shared MVP honors.

Notre Dame had an excellent team, led by Dave Batton, and gained the semifinals for the first time by beating DePaul, with Dave Corzine, in the regionals.

Freeman Williams of Portland State became the first player since Pete Maravich to lead the country in scoring for two straight years. The 6-4 guard averaged 35.9 points a game and had stunning individual games of 81, 71, and 66 points. Larry Bird of Indiana State was second with a 30.0 average, followed by Purvis Short of Jackson State. Other scoring machines included Michael Brooks of LaSalle, Andrew Toney of Southwestern Louisiana, Reggie King of Alabama, Michael Edwards of 22–4 Pan American, Steve Grant of Manhattan, Gary Winton of Army, Mychal Thompson of Minnesota, Darrell Griffith of Louisville, and John Long of 25–4 Detroit.

In the ECAC, the top teams were Fairfield, with Joe DeSantis; Rutgers, with James Bailey; St. John's, with George Johnson; Virginia Commonwealth, with Gerald Henderson; and Georgetown, with Derrick Jackson. Penn won the Ivy League behind Keven McDonald, and Appalachian State, with Tony Searcy, took the Southern title. Among other conference winners were Kansas, with Darnell Valentine, in the Big Eight; Michigan State, led by freshman Earvin Johnson, in the Big Ten; Creighton, with Rich Apke, in the Missouri Valley; and Harry Davis-led Florida State in the Metro.

NCAA Championship

At St. Louis

Kentucky (94)	FG	FT	Pts.	Duke (88)	FG	FT	Pts.
Givens	18	5	41	Banks	6	10	22
Robey	8	4	20	Dennard	5	0	10
Phillips	1	2	4	Gminski	6	8	20
Macy	3	3	9	Harrell	2	0	4
Claytor	3	2	8	Spanarkel	8	5	21
Lee	4	0	8	Suddath	1	2	4
Shidler	1	0	2	Bender	1	5	7
Williams	1	0	2	Goetsch	0	0	0
Totals	39	16	94		29	30	88

NCAA SCORES

First Round: Duke 63, Rhode Island 62; Penn 92, St. Bonaventure 83; Indiana 63, Furman 62; Villanova 103, LaSalle 97; Utah 86, Missouri 79; Notre Dame 100, Houston 77; DePaul 80, Creighton 78; Louisville 76, St. John's 68; Michigan State 77, Providence 63; Western Kentucky 87, Syracuse 86 (OT); Miami (O.) 84, Marquette 82 (OT); Kentucky 85, Florida State 76; UCLA 83, Kansas 76; Weber State 73, Arkansas 52; San Francisco 68, North Carolina 64; Fullerton State 90, New Mexico 85

Second Round: Duke 84, Penn 80; Villanova 61, Indiana 60; Notre Dame 69, Utah 56; DePaul 90, Louisville 89; Michigan State 90, Western Kentucky 69; Kentucky 91, Miami (O.) 69; Arkansas 74, UCLA 70; Fullerton State 75, San Francisco 72

Regional Championships: Duke 90, Villanova 72; Notre Dame 84, DePaul 64; Kentucky 52, Michigan State 49; Arkansas 61, Fullerton State 58

Semifinals: Duke 90, Notre Dame 86; Kentucky 64, Arkansas 59

Championship: Kentucky 94, Duke 88

Consolation: Arkansas 71, Notre Dame 69

Kentucky's Jack Givens demolished Duke in the NCAA finals

First Round: Nebraska 67, Utah State 66; Texas 72, Temple 58; Rutgers 72, Army 70; Indiana State 73, Illinois State 71; Georgetown 70, Virginia 68 (OT); Dayton 108, Fairfield 93; Detroit 94, Virginia Commonwealth 86; North Carolina State 82, South Carolina 70

Quarterfinals: Texas 67, Nebraska 48; Rutgers 57, Indiana State 56; Georgetown 71, Dayton 62; North Carolina State 84, Detroit 77

Semifinals: Texas 96, Rutgers 76; North Carolina State 86, Georgetown 85

Final: Texas 101, North Carolina State 93

Consolation: Rutgers 85, Georgetown 72

Top Ten

AP	UPI
Kentucky	Kentucky
UCLA	UCLA
DePaul	Marquette
Michigan State	New Mexico
Arkansas	Michigan State
Notre Dame	Arkansas
Duke	DePaul
Marquette	Kansas
Louisville	Duke
Kansas	North Carolina

All-Americans

AP	UPI
Phil Ford, North Carolina	Butch Lee, Marquette
Butch Lee, Marquette	Phil Ford, North Carolina
Mychal Thompson, Minnesota	Mychal Thompson, Minnesota
Larry Bird, Indiana State	Larry Bird, Indiana State
David Greenwood, UCLA	David Greenwood, UCLA

1978–1979

It was the year of the Bird—until a Magic show made him disappear. Indiana State's Larry Bird led the little-known Sycamores to 33 straight victories and a berth in the NCAA championship, where Earvin "Magic" Johnson and his Michigan State teammates ended it all in the 75–64 championship game. It was the Spartans' first national title, and they outscored five opponents by an average of 20.8 points in the tournament.

Bird, a 6-9 center, and Johnson, a 6-7 guard, were easily the two most dominating figures on the college scene. Bird finished second in the country in NCAA Division I scoring with a 28.6 average, and his 14.9 rebound mark placed him fourth in that category. Johnson, while scoring at a 17.1 rate, also averaged eight assists and seven rebounds per game. Magic's showing in the final (24 points) earned him the MVP award and capped off a year in which the Big Ten captured both major tournaments.

Indiana lost 12 games but came through

NIT Championship

At New York

Texas (101)	FG	FT	Pts.	North Carolina State (93)	FG	FT	Pts.
Baxter	11	4	26	Pinder	7	7	21
Branyan	7	0	14	Whitney	11	0	22
Goodner	1	2	4	Sudhop	0	1	1
Krivacs	13	7	33	Austin	6	5	17
Moors	8	6	22	Warren	5	2	12
Stephens	0	0	0	Perkins	2	0	4
Stroud	1	0	2	Matthews	4	0	8
Murphy	0	0	0	Jones	0	0	0
Nichols	0	0	0	Watts	0	0	0
Danks	0	0	0	Davis	4	0	8
Dotson	0	0	0	Montgomery	0	0	0
				Almond	0	0	0
Totals	41	19	101		39	15	93

with the NIT championship, edging another Big Ten representative, Purdue, 53–52. The Hoosiers' Ray Tolbert and Butch Carter shared the MVP award over Purdue's 7-1 Joe Barry Carroll, who burned Alabama for 42 points in a semifinal game.

The NCAA had been a tournament of upsets until the semifinals. The two Atlantic Coast Conference schools, North Carolina (with Mike O'Koren) and Duke (with Jim Spanarkel and Mike Gminski), were ousted in the second round by upstarts St. John's and Penn. Big Ten co-champ Iowa was eliminated by Toledo in the second round and UCLA, with All-American David Greenwood, lost in the West Regional final to DePaul. Coach Ray Meyer's Blue Demons didn't crack the Top 20 until February, but made it to the final four behind freshman star Mark Aguirre.

Notre Dame and Arkansas again fielded strong teams. The Fighting Irish, with Kelly Tripucka, were ranked No. 1 in the country before losses to Maryland, UCLA, and De-Paul dropped them in the rankings. Arkansas upheld the honor of the Southwest Conference when All-American Sidney Moncrief led them to the final of the Midwest Regional.

Penn became the Eastern champion when it followed up its upset of North Carolina with victories over Syracuse and St. John's. The Ivy League champs, led by Tony Price, were the Cinderella team of the tournament until Michigan State blasted the Quakers, 101–67, in the semifinals.

There were some familiar names in the tournament. Perennial contender Marquette, led by Bernard Toone, went 22–7 and was ousted by DePaul. San Francisco, behind 6-11 Bill Cartwright, won 22 games, and Louisville, with high-flying Darrell Griffith, posted another 20-win season for coach Denny Crum.

Lawrence Butler, a 6-3 guard from Idaho State, was the NCAA Division I scoring champion with a 30.1 average to Bird's 28.6. Others in the scoring race, finishing in this order, were Nick Galis of Seton Hall, James Tillman of Eastern Kentucky, Paul Dawkins of Northern Illinois, John Gerdy of Davidson, Ernie Hill of Oklahoma City, and John Stroud of Mississippi. Monti Davis of Tennessee State was the nation's top rebounder and Matt Teahan of Denver had the highest-

scoring game of the year when he poured in 61 points against Nebraska Wesleyan.

In conference races, Villanova captured the Eastern Eight regular-season title, but Rutgers, led by James Bailey, received the NCAA bid for winning the conference tourney. Al Green paced Louisiana State to the Southeastern Conference title and Temple won the East Coast championship. South Alabama took the newly formed Sun Belt Conference, and Mike Olliver sparked Lamar to the Southland title.

Toledo won the Mid-American; Eastern Kentucky, the Ohio Valley; and Oklahoma, the Big Eight in the Midwest. In the Rockies, Weber State was No. 1 in the Big Sky, and Brigham Young triumphed in the Western Athletic Conference. UCLA, San Francisco, and Pacific won NCAA berths with conference championships in the Far West.

Among the other top teams were Rhode Island, with Sly Williams; St. Bonaventure, with Earl Belcher; Maryland, with Albert King, and Georgetown, with Derrick Jackson. Northeast Louisiana, with Calvin Natt, and North Carolina-Charlotte, with Chad Kinch, had good years in the South, as did Alcorn State. Terry Duerod led Detroit to a 22–6 record, and Dayton won 18 games behind forward Jim Paxson. Nevada-Las Vegas topped the nation in scoring (93.1) and recorded another 20-win season, and Southern Cal battled UCLA to the wire in the Pacific 10 race.

Indiana State's Larry Bird was the most exciting player of the collegiate year

NCAA Championship

At Salt Lake City

Michigan State (75)	FG	FT	Pts.	Indiana State (64)	FG	FT	Pts.
Brkovich	1	3	5	Miley	0	0	0
Kelser	7	5	19	Gilbert	2	0	4
Charles	3	1	7	Bird	7	5	19
Donnelly	5	5	15	Nicks	7	3	17
Johnson	8	8	24	Reed	4	0	8
Vincent	2	1	5	Heaton	4	2	10
Gonzalez	0	0	0	Staley	2	0	4
Longaker	0	0	0	Nemcek	1	0	2
Totals	26	23	75		27	10	64

NIT Championship

At New York

Indiana (53)	FG	FT	Pts.	Purdue (52)	FG	FT	Pts.
Turner	6	1	13	Hellman	6	0	12
Woodson	5	0	10	Morris	4	1	9
Tolbert	5	2	12	Carroll	6	2	14
Carter	6	0	12	Sichting	3	0	6
Wittman	2	0	4	B. Walker	1	2	4
Risley	0	2	2	Scearce	2	0	4
Ealls	0	0	0	Edmondson	1	1	3
				Bemenderfer	0	0	0
				S. Walker	0	0	0
Totals	24	5	53		23	6	52

NCAA SCORES
REGIONALS

East

First Round: St. John's 75, Temple 70; Penn 73, Iona 69

Second Round: St. John's 80, Duke 78; Rutgers 64, Georgetown 58; Syracuse 89, Connecticut 81; Penn 72, North Carolina 71

Semifinals: St. John's 67, Rutgers 65; Penn 84, Syracuse 76

Championship: Penn 64, St. John's 62

Mideast

First Round: Lamar 95, Detroit 87; Tennessee 97, Eastern Kentucky 81

Second Round: Michigan State 95, Lamar 64; Louisiana State 71, Appalachian State 57; Toledo 74, Iowa 72; Notre Dame 73, Tennessee 67.

Semifinals: Michigan State 87, Louisiana State 71; Notre Dame 79, Toledo 71

Championship: Michigan State 80, Notre Dame 68

Midwest

First Round: Weber State 81, New Mexico State 78; Virginia Tech 70, Jacksonville 53

Second Round: Arkansas 74, Weber State 63; Louisville 69, South Alabama 66; Oklahoma 90, Texas 76; Indiana State 86, Virginia Tech 69

Semifinals: Arkansas 73, Louisville 62; Indiana State 93, Oklahoma 72

Championship: Indiana State 73, Arkansas 71

West

First Round: Southern California 86, Utah State 67; Pepperdine 92, Utah 88

Second Round: Marquette 73, Pacific 48; DePaul 89, Southern California 78; San Francisco 86, Brigham Young 63; UCLA 76, Pepperdine 71

Semifinals: DePaul 95, UCLA 91

FINALS

Semifinals: Michigan State 101, Penn 67; Indiana State 76, DePaul 74

Championship: Michigan State 75, Indiana State 64

Consolation: DePaul 96, Penn 93

NIT SCORES

First Round: Alabama 98, St. Bonaventure 89; Alcorn State 80, Mississippi State 78; Clemson 68, Kentucky 67; Dayton 105, Holy Cross 81; Indiana 78, Texas Tech 59; Maryland 67, Rhode Island 65; Nevada-Reno 62, Oregon State 61; Ohio State 80, St. Joseph's 66; Old Dominion 83, Wagner 81; Texas A&M 79, New Mexico 68; Virginia 79, Northeast Louisiana 78

Second Round: Alabama 90, Virginia 88; Indiana 73, Alcorn State 69; Ohio State 79, Maryland 72; Old Dominion 61, Clemson 59; Purdue 84, Dayton 70; Texas A&M 67, Nevada-Reno 64

Third Round: Alabama 72, Texas A&M 68; Purdue 67, Old Dominion 59

Semifinals: Purdue 87, Alabama 68; Indiana 64, Ohio State 55

Championship: Indiana 53, Purdue 52.

Consolation: Alabama 96, Ohio State 86

TOP TEN

AP

Indiana State	Indiana State
UCLA	UCLA
Michigan State	North Carolina
Notre Dame	Michigan State
Arkansas	Notre Dame
DePaul	Arkansas
Louisiana State	Duke
Syracuse	DePaul
North Carolina	Louisiana State
Marquette	Syracuse

ALL-AMERICANS

UPI

Larry Bird, Indiana State	Larry Bird, Indiana State
Bill Cartwright, San Francisco	David Greenwood, UCLA
David Greenwood, UCLA	Mike Gminski, Duke
Sidney Moncrief, Arkansas	Earvin Johnson, Michigan State
Earvin Johnson, Michigan State	Jim Spanarkel, Duke

Earvin Johnson (center) leads the cheering after Michigan State beat Indiana State for the 1978–79 NCAA championship

NIT Champions

1938—Temple	1959—St. John's
1939—LIU	1960—Bradley
1940—Colorado	1961—Providence
1941—LIU	1962—Dayton
1942—West Virginia	1963—Providence
1943—St. John's	1964—Bradley
1944—St. John's	1965—St. John's
1945—DePaul	1966—Brigham Young
1946—Kentucky	1967—Southern
	Illinois
1947—Utah	1968—Dayton
1948—St. Louis	1969—Temple
1949—San Francisco	1970—Marquette
1950—CCNY	1971—North Carolina
1951—Brigham Young	1972—Maryland
1952—LaSalle	1973—Virginia Tech
1953—Seton Hall	1974—Purdue
1954—Holy Cross	1975—Princeton
1955—Duquesne	1976—Kentucky
1956—Louisville	1977—St. Bonaventure
1957—Bradley	1978—Texas
1958—Xavier (Ohio)	1979—Indiana

NCAA Champions

Division I

1939—Oregon	1959—California
1940—Indiana	1960—Ohio State
1941—Wisconsin	1961—Cincinnati
1942—Stanford	1962—Cincinnati
1943—Wyoming	1963—Loyola (Ill.)
1944—Utah	1964—UCLA
1945—Oklahoma A&M	1965—UCLA
1946—Oklahoma A&M	1966—Texas Western
1947—Holy Cross	1967—UCLA
1948—Kentucky	1968—UCLA
1949—Kentucky	1969—UCLA
1950—CCNY	1970—UCLA
1951—Kentucky	1971—UCLA
1952—Kansas	1972—UCLA
1953—Indiana	1973—UCLA
1954—LaSalle	1974—North Carolina
	State
1955—San Francisco	1975—UCLA
1956—San Francisco	1976—Indiana
1957—North Carolina	1977—Marquette
1958—Kentucky	1978—Kentucky
	1979—Michigan State

COLLEGIATE PLAYER OF THE YEAR
(Selected by the U. S. Basketball Writers Association)

1959—Oscar Robertson, Cincinnati
1960—Oscar Robertson, Cincinnati
1961—Jerry Lucas, Ohio State
1962—Jerry Lucas, Ohio State
1963—Art Heyman, Duke
1964—Walt Hazzard, UCLA
1965—Bill Bradley, Princeton
1966—Cazzie Russell, Michigan
1967—Lew Alcindor, UCLA
1968—Elvin Hayes, Houston
1969—Lew Alcindor, UCLA
1970—Pete Maravich, Louisiana State
1971—Sidney Wicks, UCLA
1972—Bill Walton, UCLA
1973—Bill Walton, UCLA
1974—Bill Walton, UCLA
1975—David Thompson, North Carolina State
1976—Adrian Dantley, Notre Dame
1977—Marques Johnson, UCLA
1978—Phil Ford, North Carolina
1979—Larry Bird, Indiana State

COLLEGIATE COACH OF THE YEAR
(Selected by the U. S. Basketball Writers Association)

1959—Ed Hickey, Marquette
1960—Pete Newell, California
1961—Fred Taylor, Ohio State
1962—Fred Taylor, Ohio State
1963—Ed Jucker, Cincinnati
1964—John Wooden, UCLA
1965—Bill van Breda Kolff, Princeton
1966—Adolph Rupp, Kentucky
1967—John Wooden, UCLA
1968—Guy Lewis, Houston
1969—John Wooden, UCLA
1970—John Wooden, UCLA
1971—Al McGuire, Marquette
1972—John Wooden, UCLA
1973—John Wooden, UCLA
1974—Norm Sloan, North Carolina State
1975—Bobby Knight, Indiana
1976—Johnny Orr, Michigan
1977—Eddie Sutton, Arkansas
1978—Ray Meyer, DePaul
1979—Dean Smith, North Carolina

ALL-TIME MAJOR COLLEGE RECORDS
(Based on statistics from National Collegiate Sports Services)

INDIVIDUAL

Single Game

Most Points	100	Frank Selvy, Furman, vs Newberry, 1954

Season

Most Points	1,381	Pete Maravich, Louisiana State, 1970
Highest Scoring Average	44.5	Pete Maravich, Louisiana State, 1970
Most F.G. Attempted	1,168	Pete Maravich, Louisiana State, 1970
Most F.G. Made	522	Pete Maravich, Louisiana State, 1970
Highest F.G. Percentage	.699	Joe Senser, West Chester, 1977
Most F.T. Attempted	444	Frank Selvy, Furman, 1954
Most F.T. Made	355	Frank Selvy, Furman, 1954
Highest F.T. Percentage	.944	Carlos Gibson, Marshall, 1978
Most Rebounds	734	Walter Dukes, Seton Hall, 1953
Highest Rebounding Average	25.6	Charlie Slack, Marshall, 1955

Career

Most Points	3,667	Pete Maravich, Louisiana State, 1968—70
Highest Scoring Average	44.2	Pete Maravich, Louisiana State, 1968—70
Most Field Goals	1,387	Pete Maravich, Louisiana State, 1968—70
Most Free Throws	*905	Dickie Hemric, Wake Forest, 1952—55

*Four-year total

TEAM

Single Game

Most Points, one team	164	Nevada-Las Vegas vs. Hawaii-Hilo (111), Feb. 19, 1976
Most Points, two teams	275	Nevada-Las Vegas 164, Hawaii-Hilo 111, Feb. 19, 1976

Season

Most Consecutive Victories	88	UCLA, 1971—74
Most Victories in Perfect Season	32	North Carolina, 1957; Indiana, 1976
Most Points	3,426	Nevada-Las Vegas, 1976, 1977
Highest Scoring Average	110.5	Nevada-Las Vegas, 1976
Highest F.G. Percentage	.547	Maryland, 1975
Highest F.T. Percentage	.809	Ohio State, 1970
Highest Rebound Percentage	.644	Fordham, 1953

4

The Greatest Collegians

Choosing the top players—from the modern era beginning in the mid-1930s and through the late 1970s—is at best a subjective process. One cannot measure greatness on statistics alone. Many intangibles—ranging from desire to often unsung skills such as defense and playmaking—serve as truer yardsticks than scoring average.

All of these were taken into account when Joe Lapchick chose the 20 greatest college players for the first edition of the Encyclopedia in 1969. Lapchick, actively connected with basketball for more than 50 years as an Original Celtic and as a college and pro coach, died in 1970, but his selections remain the nucleus for those players chosen by the editors in the second edition in 1973 and in this new edition.

Lew Alcindor

Not since the Oscar Robertson regime at Cincinnati in 1957–60 did one player dominate the college game the way Lew Alcindor did at UCLA. In three varsity seasons, 7-1⅜ Ferdinand Lewis Alcindor led the Bruins to three consecutive NCAA titles, losing only two games in the process.

Lew could do everything. He moved with surprising grace for a man of his size, picking off rebounds, blocking shots, triggering the fast break with bullet passes, and scoring on short jump shots, hooks, and tip-ins. After his first season, the NCAA rules committee outlawed his favorite, the dunk shot, but it didn't stop Lew. He could score, it seemed, almost anytime he wanted to.

Alcindor scored 30 points in his first frosh scrimmage against the UCLA varsity despite a three-man platoon guarding him, and he scored 56 points in his first varsity game. But no one could ever call him a gunner. "I don't care about points," Alcindor said. "I care about winning. Frank Selvy once scored 100 points in a college game. It's been done before. I don't want them to remember me for scoring records. Bob Cousy doesn't own any scoring records, but I don't think anybody will forget him."

Nobody is likely to forget Alcindor. After one varsity season at UCLA, he was already being compared to the all-time greats.

Alcindor was born large. He was 22½ inches long at birth, weighing 12 pounds, 11 ounces. He was the only child of a 6-2 New York subway policeman and a 6-foot

UCLA's Lew Alcindor

housewife. When he entered St. Jude's school in Manhattan at the age of six, he already towered more than a foot above his classmates.

On the first day of school his teacher spotted the long, lanky figure in the back of the room and yelled, "You, there, please sit down."

Said Alcindor in a soft voice, "But I am sitting down."

Alcindor was a six-footer by the time he was 10 years old. The coach at St. Jude's, Farrell Hopkins, automatically put him on the basketball team. A program of weight-lifting, rope-jumping, and tennis eliminated much of his gawkiness.

At 13, Alcindor stood 6-8 and weighed 200 pounds. A friend, Art Kenny, brought him to the attention of John Donohue, the basketball coach at Power Memorial Academy. Donohue arranged a scholarship for Alcindor, and his fantastic high school career began.

He led Power to 71 straight victories before the Panthers bowed, 46–43, to powerful DeMatha High School of Hyattsville, Maryland. Mr. A, as his teammates called him, scored 2,067 points and collected 2,002 rebounds in his high school career. Both were New York City schoolboy records.

Large Lewie was sought by every college in the country. One coach, deep in the South, said, "Get me Alcindor and I'll integrate. They'll forget his color when he makes us national champions."

Coach Donohue screened all the offers and kept the press, the recruiters, and the public away from his prodigy. The decision narrowed down to New York University, St. John's, Michigan, and UCLA. Ralph Bunche, a UCLA alumnus, left his United Nations post one afternoon to visit Alcindor. Jackie Robinson, another UCLA alumnus, also paid a courtesy call on Alcindor.

On May 3, 1965, in front of television cameras, microphones, his proud mother, and a swarm of reporters in the Power gym, Alcindor announced, "This fall I'll be attending UCLA."

So Alcindor went west. He led the freshmen to an undefeated season, then paced the varsity to an undefeated season and the NCAA title. His shooting, effortless rebounding, ball-handling skill and tenacious defense were beautiful to see. He intimidated the opposition with his height and skills.

UCLA went 45 games without a loss into the middle of his junior year. Then Lew suffered an eye injury in a fight for a rebound and sat out two games which UCLA won.

He returned to action against the No. 2 team in the country, Houston. The largest indoor crowd in the history of basketball, 52,693, augmented by millions of others over television, watched this meeting of the titans in the Astrodome. Alcindor, suffering from double-vision and weak from a hospital stay, was just another man on the court. Houston's Elvin Hayes scored 39 points to 18 for Alcindor, and the UCLA streak was over.

"We'll just have to start another streak," said UCLA coach John Wooden. The Bruins didn't lose again as they went on to win their second straight NCAA title, beating Houston in the semifinals.

In his senior year, Alcindor led UCLA to

an unprecedented third straight NCAA championship, losing only one game en route. For the third time in a row, Lew was named MVP in the tourney. He averaged 26.4 points a game during his three years and made 62.4 per cent of his shots, an NCAA record.

The subject of a bidding war between the National Basketball Association and the fledgling American Basketball Association, Lew signed a contract for more than $1 million with the Milwaukee Bucks of the NBA. It marked the start of a spectacular pro career for the giant who became Kareem Abdul-Jabbar.

Vince Boryla

The most vivid memory of the 1940s for many basketball fans is a picture of the husky figure of Vince Boryla, looking bulkier than his listed 210 pounds and shorter than 6-5, driving to the basket with his left arm in front of his body and his right arm arching for one of the most accurate hook shots ever seen.

Boryla could make a crowd gasp over his soft over-the-head hook. Many times the

Denver's Vince Boryla

ball would float into the basket as Boryla was rolling on the floor from a push. No defense could stop his shot.

The memory is stronger and sharper because Boryla seemed to be around the college scene longer than any other man in history. Indeed, his college career at two different schools was interrupted by military service and a trip to the Olympics. Despite all this, he was only 22 years old when he made most All-America teams in 1949 at the University of Denver.

Boryla was born in East Chicago, Indiana. After an exceptional high school career, he entered Notre Dame in 1945 and was a star from the beginning, since freshmen were eligible for varsity competition because of the war. Basketball had always been No. 2 at Notre Dame, and if Boryla didn't change that, he at least led the Irish to national basketball prominence.

After a season at Notre Dame, Boryla enlisted in the Army Air Corps, where he continued to play basketball at Lowry Air Force Base in Denver, Colorado.

When World War II ended, Boryla stayed on in Denver to play for the AAU Denver Nuggets. In 1948 he performed with the U. S. Olympic team in London. Following the Olympics, Boryla decided to return to college for his degree. He stayed in Denver with his new wife, Cappie, and attended Denver University, where he showed he was still deadly with his patented hook shot.

Boryla broke the Skyline Six Conference scoring record with 624 points in 33 games, including 379 in 20 league games. His top single-game output was 39. Despite a slump in the final week of the season, Vince averaged 18.9 points a game. The Skyline runner-up, Vern Gardner of Utah, averaged 15.1 points. Boryla also was voted the outstanding visiting player in New York after scoring 36 points against St. John's in Madison Square Garden.

Vince's scoring, rebounding, and all-around court sense made him a natural for the professional ranks. He joined the New York Knickerbockers in time for the 1949–50 season and averaged 10 points a game in his rookie year. He improved that to 15 points a game the following season. He lasted three more years as a professional and retired after the 1953–54 season at the age of 27.

Boryla couldn't give up basketball completely, however. He became coach of the AAU Denver Central Bankers. He returned to New York as coach of the Knickerbockers for two-and-a-half seasons through 1957–58.

Vince retired from basketball to devote full time to his insurance and investment business in Denver. He was associated with the Denver Rockets of the American Basketball Association for a time, and later became president and general manager of the Utah Stars. He still played, too, in Saturday morning backyard games with his sons and the neighborhood kids who wanted to see the most uncanny shot in the book come whizzing off a husky old man's ear.

Bill Bradley

Many of college basketball's greatest players have appeared in New York's Madison Square Garden. But none of them ever excited a crowd as Bill Bradley did on December 30, 1964. When Bradley fouled out of the semifinal game of the Holiday Festival that night, 18,499 fans gave him the longest ovation any basketball player had ever received in the history of the Garden.

Play was suspended for more than two minutes as the crowd showered its applause on the 6-5, 200-pound Princeton forward. Singlehandedly, Bradley had led Princeton to the brink of an incredible upset over Michigan, the country's top team. When Bradley fouled out, Princeton led, 75–63, with 4:37 remaining. Of Princeton's 75 points, Bradley had scored 41. He had popped in the Tigers' last 12 points of the first half to put them into the lead. He had nine rebounds, four assists, and on defense had held his man to only one point.

Michigan's Cazzie Russell, along with Bradley the season's most heralded college players, had been completely overshadowed. But without Bradley the Tigers were a different team. Over the next three minutes, Michigan outscored them, 17–1, and went on to an 80–78 victory.

Bradley had a capacity for inspiring his ordinary teammates to extraordinary heights. For many, Bradley, not only that night, but every time he played, was the closest thing to a perfect basketball player that they had ever seen. He moved with such effortless ease, shot with such uncanny perfection, that few realized just how much effort he put into the game.

As a youngster in Crystal City, Missouri, he practiced incessantly. "During the football season, I'd practice for about two hours a day," he recalled. "Then during the basketball season I'd always try to stay after practice for more work. During the summer was the toughest part because many days when it was hot, the perspiration would soak through your shoes and you'd have to quit because you'd start to slip out of your shoes."

At Princeton he continued practicing just as much. "I don't think I've ever seen a harder working boy," said Butch van Breda Kolff, his Princeton coach. After practice

Princeton's Bill Bradley

113

Bradley would stay in the gym for an extra hour, practicing his deadly jump shot.

All the hours of work paid off as Bradley won honor after honor for himself and his Ivy League school. In Bradley's three years the Tigers won three Ivy championships. He averaged 30.1 points a game and was an All-American all three seasons. In 1964, as the only college junior on the team, he paced the United States to the gold medal in basketball at the Tokyo Olympics.

Bradley closed his career with a personal high of 58 points in Princeton's 118–82 victory over Wichita in the consolation finals of the 1965 NCAA championship. This gave him a career total of 2,503 points, making him the fourth most prolific scorer in the history of college basketball.

In 1965 Bradley won the Sullivan Award, given annually by the Amateur Athletic Union to the nation's outstanding amateur athlete. He was the first basketball player ever to win the award.

Bradley was as outstanding academically at Princeton as he was athletically. Because the Ivy League schools do not award athletic scholarships, Bradley paid his own way at Princeton, when he could have had a basketball scholarship at nearly any other school in the country.

In his senior year Bradley was awarded a Rhodes Scholarship for postgraduate study at Oxford University in England. Although the professional New York Knickerbockers made him their first choice in the draft, Bradley turned them down to study abroad for two years.

On his return he reconsidered the professional game and finally signed a four-year contract with the Knicks for an estimated $500,000. This made him basketball's highest-paid rookie. But Bradley, who excelled at almost everything he ever attempted, insisted that it was not the money that had convinced him to sign. "I just wanted to see how I would do against the best players in the world. I just had to know," he said.

He and the basketball world found out soon enough. Bradley became a mainstay of the Knicks during an 11-year career that featured two NBA championships. He retired after the 1976–77 season to pursue a career in politics, and was elected to the U. S. Senate from New Jersey in 1978.

Bob Davies

There was no more spectacular sight on a basketball floor in 1942 than the handsome, blond, tousle-haired youngster from Seton Hall dribbling down the right side of the court, faking his man out of position, switching the ball behind his back and driving to the basket for a left-handed lay-up.

Bob Davies, who stood 6-3 and weighed 180 pounds, was a complete basketball player. He led the New Jersey institution to 43 straight victories and was extolled by all for his tremendous skills. He could shoot, he could pass, he could rebound. The flashy native of Harrisburg, Pennsylvania, earned the nickname "The Harrisburg Houdini" on the strength of his magnificent ball-control, dribbling, and behind-the-back maneuvers.

Davies was considered by many the best all-around basketball player since Stanford's Hank Luisetti, then considered the game's measure of excellence.

"Luisetti was a frontcourt player," said

Seton Hall's Bob Davies

Nat Holman, the coach of City College of New York and one of the early greats of the game, "and Davies is equally as good anywhere on the court. His change of pace dribble is the best and trickiest there is. Davies is a team man, setting up plays and acting as leader. He's got color, coordination, speed, and stamina."

Surprisingly, Davies came to Seton Hall with a reputation as a fine baseball player but unheard of as a basketball player. The Seton Hall coach, Honey Russell, changed Davies' life after he saw him control a ball during one early basketball practice.

Davies said his behind-the-back dribble was just a natural part of his game. "I really never practiced it much," he said. "I found it could throw the opposition off balance and I tried to save it for the right spot."

Davies had a flair for the dramatic, and the right spot would usually be a one-on-one situation with the game hanging on the next basket.

"He had such uncanny control of the ball behind his back," said Russell, "that it never concerned me. He made it look as easy as the conventional dribble."

The exciting maneuver was appreciated by the fans and wherever Seton Hall played, the crowds came to watch Davies and his acrobatic dribbles. The largest crowd ever to see a basketball game up to that time, 18,403, watched Davies and his Seton Hall teammates defeat Rhode Island in the quarterfinals of the National Invitation Tournament at Madison Square Garden on March 19, 1941.

Davies graduated in 1942 and enlisted in the Navy. He led the Great Lakes Naval Training Station team to a 34–3 record. He became an ensign in 1943 and took part in the invasions of Sicily and Normandy as an officer on a sub chaser.

He played professional basketball for ten years and was an all-league selection five times. He also coached Seton Hall to a 24–3 record while playing with the Rochester Royals in the National Basketball Association.

Davies went back to college coaching at Gettysburg for two seasons after he retired as a player. He retired from basketball in 1957 to take a position in sales and promo-

tion with the Converse Rubber Company in Massachusetts.

Bob Davies never averaged more than 11.8 points a game in any of his three college seasons at Seton Hall but no player ever did more to make basketball a show as well as a game. The Harrisburg Houdini was indeed a master of hoop magic.

Tom Gola

The surprising winner of the 1952 National Invitation Tournament in Madison Square Garden was LaSalle College of Philadelphia. Even more surprising was the name of Tom Gola as one of the co-winners of the tourney's Most Valuable Player award with teammate Norm Grekin.

Gola's play in the pressure-packed championships was especially noteworthy since the 6-6, 220-pound forward from Philadelphia was only a freshman. Coach Ken

LaSalle's Tom Gola

Loeffler said of Tom: "I have never seen a youngster with such poise. It is his greatest asset. Nothing rattles him. He can do everything and do it well."

Gola went at his work like a mechanic who is sure of his skills. His play was unspectacular, almost unnoticed, but he always scored the big basket, grabbed the vital rebound, set the tempo and pace of play for his team.

"I have never seen one player control a game by himself as well as Gola does," said Loeffler.

The other players on the LaSalle team didn't take too kindly to the appearance of Gola in the starting line-up as a freshman when the season began. Veteran players tend to downgrade inexperienced players until they can prove themselves. By mid-season, his teammates looked up to Gola as a leader. He scored 504 points in leading LaSalle to a 25–7 season, the NIT championship, and high national ranking.

Tom learned his basketball the hard way, in the three-man playground games in the lower-middle class section of Philadelphia where he grew up. He was one of seven children of a Philadelphia policeman. There was little extra money for recreation so young Tom found his own fun in the basketball games around home.

He scored 2,222 points for LaSalle High School in the Philadelphia Catholic League, was named a first-team high school All-America and led the North to victory in the annual North-South high school all-star game.

After his stunning freshman season, Gola was a marked man. Although every defense was geared to stop him, none succeeded. In each of the next three seasons, the soft-spoken, self-effacing youngster led the Explorers in scoring and improved his average from 17.4 per game as a freshman to 24.1 as a senior.

The handsome, dark-haired Gola excelled off the floor as well as on it. He finished in the upper third of his graduating class with a degree in accounting.

Following military service, Gola became a splendid professional player with the Philadelphia Warriors and the New York Knickerbockers. He retired after the 1965 season to concentrate on his business interests as the owner of a golf driving range, apartment buildings and various other investments, and to run for public office in Pennsylvania.

Dick Groat

Most college athletes who excel in one sport play another just for fun. But few ever make All-America teams in two sports. One notable exception was Dick Groat of Duke, a standout both on the basketball court and the baseball diamond. Groat is probably better remembered as the long-time short-stop of the Pittsburgh Pirates and several other major league baseball teams. But it was as a collegiate basketball player that he first gained national prominence.

In his junior year, 1950–51, Groat led the nation in scoring. The 6-foot, 180-pound guard's 831 points in 31 games, a 25.2 average, set an NCAA single-season scoring record. That season and the following year, when he averaged 26.0 points, Groat earned All-America basketball honors. Besides leading the Blue Devils in scoring, Groat was also the team leader in assists for two years.

"If you tell Dick he's doing something wrong he goes out and practices until he does it perfectly. He's a real team man," said Hal Bradley, the Duke coach. And Gus Tebell, then director of athletics at Virginia, added, "He's the finest basketball player I've seen in the South in my twenty-seven years in the game."

Groat wound up at the North Carolina school even though he grew up in Swissvale, Pennsylvania, and three members of his family attended the nearby University of Pittsburgh. Dick went to Duke because it was a baseball-minded school, and he always considered baseball his best sport.

He received his introduction to basketball at the age of four when Pete Noon, who had been a teammate of two of Groat's brothers at Pitt, gave him a basketball as a present. Although Dick took to the game immediately, he didn't start taking it seriously until his high school days.

Duke's Dick Groat

Army. Both as a collegiate basketball and baseball player, he had been considered extremely quick. But during his Army years he lost a lot of his speed. "I played a great deal of basketball in the Army and the hard floors wore my feet down," he said. Nevertheless, he became an outstanding major league shortstop and in 1960 won the National League Most Valuable Player award and the batting championship.

He retired from baseball after the 1967 season and became manager of a golf course near Pittsburgh.

Bob Kurland

Hank Iba, the coach at Oklahoma A&M, always believed that the key to basketball success was good defense, and his theory paid off when the Aggies won consecutive NCAA championships in 1945 and 1946. The biggest part of the Aggie defense was Bob "Foothills" Kurland, the first of basketball's well-coordinated seven-footers.

Oklahoma A&M (today Oklahoma State University) played a slow, ball-control game and Kurland made that style of play work. He used his height and strength to control the backboards and to frustrate opponents' offensive maneuvers. "Kurland made our type of game go. We knew he would get us the ball so we never had to rush into a bad shot," Iba said.

Kurland had agility for a man of his size, but not much speed. In Iba's style of play it didn't matter. After grabbing a rebound, Kurland would pass the ball to a teammate, and while the big center moved upcourt, the rest of the team would work the ball in a weave. With Kurland in position, the Aggies could either pass into him under the basket, cut off him for a lay-up, or use his huge body for a screen on a shot.

But Bob's greatest contributions came on defense. He was an adept shot-blocker and perfected the goal-tending technique, in which he would knock away a shot just before it reached the basket. Coach Iba disliked this maneuver, though, and rarely allowed Kurland to practice it. By his senior year, the NCAA, influenced by the play of Kurland, George Mikan of DePaul, and

On the basketball court he was an outstanding faker and playmaker as well as a scorer. His favorite shot was a short jumper from the foul line, but he also could go all the way in for a lay-up. He credits Red Auerbach, then an assistant coach at Duke, with teaching him many of his feints. Carl Braun, a professional star with the New York Knicks, said that defense was Groat's only weakness. "But as for offense," Braun added, "I've never seen a better one anywhere."

At Duke, Groat broke most of the school's scoring records. Up until his time no Blue Devil player had ever scored more than 30 points in a game. But in his junior year he exceeded 30 points nine times. His peak single-game output of 48 points came against North Carolina in his senior season. Dick also tallied 46 points against George Washington. He also set a national record by making 261 free throws in 1950–51.

Following his college career, Groat signed a contract with the Pittsburgh Pirates baseball team. Then he spent two years in the

Oklahoma A&M's Bob Kurland

centers was able to establish clear superiority over the other. In the most publicized of their battles, a Red Cross benefit game in Madison Square Garden in March, 1945, Kurland outscored Mikan, 14–9, as Oklahoma A&M won, 52–44.

Kurland passed up large bonus offers from the pros after his graduation and instead went to work for Phillips Petroleum, of Bartlesville, Oklahoma, and played for the famous Phillips 66ers AAU team. During his amateur career, he became the first American to play on two Olympic basketball teams. Kurland was a member of the victorious United States squads in the 1948 Games at London and in 1952 at Helsinki.

After his retirement as a player, he remained with Phillips and went on to become president of Phillips Films Co., a subsidiary of Phillips Petroleum.

Clyde Lovellette

The era of gigantic high-scoring centers dates from the early 1950s, with one player responsible for the trend. He was Clyde Lovellette, the 6-9 center from Kansas University.

Before Lovellette came to Kansas, huge centers were used mainly to get the ball off the backboard for their mates, harass the opposition on defense and use their size to block out opposing players as their teammates drove to the basket.

Coach Phog Allen of Kansas changed all that when he designed an offense around Lovellette and encouraged him to shoot and score. "He is closer to the basket than anyone else on the floor," said Allen, "so I'd rather see him go for it than anyone else."

Lovellette was not a very graceful man and at the end of his college career he weighed nearly 280 pounds. But he was still able to stuff the ball into the basket.

Lovellette was from Terre Haute, Indiana, one of the great hotbeds of high school basketball. He was huge, but his game was only average as a high school player because his great size hampered rather than helped him. Coach Allen knew he could develop the boy after supervising his diet, his practices, and his exercising while Lov-

Harry Boykoff at St. John's, outlawed goaltending.

As a freshman, Kurland was a little-used varsity substitute and averaged only 2.5 points a game. Over the next three seasons he came into his own and in 1945–46 led the nation in scoring with 643 points, a 19.5 average. In his final three college seasons he was an All-America selection and in both 1945 and 1946 was voted the outstanding player in the NCAA tournament.

Usually Kurland was content to concentrate on defense and passing off, but on February 22, 1946, in his last home game, Iba told him to go all-out in scoring. That night he scored 58 points against St. Louis University, the highest single-game total of his career.

The Oklahoma A&M star had a series of classic confrontations with Mikan, DePaul's 6-10 center. The two met several times in their college careers, but neither of the big

Kansas' Clyde Lovellette

and Nebraska for the conference championship, but lost the playoff and an NCAA berth with it.

As a junior, Lovellette was again the leading scorer in the conference, averaging 22.8 points a game as Kansas finished second with a 16–8 record. In his final season Kansas won the NCAA championship with Lovellette scoring 141 points in four games for a tournament record. Forty-four of those points came against St. Louis for a new single-game NCAA tournament record.

His career total of 1,888 points in 1952 was a national record, while his 795 points that season was a conference standard.

The influence of Lovellette made many coaches around the country anxious for large centers of their own who could score more easily than the smaller players. Kansas followed its own tradition when it came up with Wilt Chamberlain several years later.

Lovellette played AAU basketball for a season after graduation and then enjoyed a long career in the National Basketball Association with the Minneapolis Lakers, Cincinnati Royals, St. Louis Hawks, and Boston Celtics. When he retired he was elected sheriff in his home town of Terre Haute.

Jerry Lucas

When Jerry Lucas played high school basketball in Middletown, Ohio, his team won 76 consecutive games and two Ohio state championships. During his three varsity years at Ohio State University, 1959–62, the Buckeyes didn't quite match that record, but nobody complained.

During the Lucas era, Ohio State won three Big Ten championships, one NCAA title, and finished second in the NCAA tournament twice. Overall they won 78 games and lost only six. Playing on a team loaded with outstanding basketball talent— four of his teammates went on to play pro ball—Lucas clearly established himself as the outstanding college player of his time.

Unlike so many point-hungry stars, Lucas, a 6-8, 230-pound pivotman, would just as soon pass the ball to an open teammate as shoot. Over his varsity career he averaged 24.3 points a game, while taking

ellette was a freshman at Kansas. When he joined the Jayhawk varsity in 1949, Lovellette was ready to show the world he could play with the best.

"I knew I had the ability," said Lovellette. "The only thing I was lacking was self-confidence."

Lovellette started his first game at center on the varsity and scored 21 points. From that time on, there was no stopping the husky Hoosier. In his sophomore year Lovellette led Kansas to a 14–11 record and he won the Big Eight scoring title. The Jayhawks finished in a tie with Kansas State

Ohio State's Jerry Lucas

his scholastic career with 2,466 points, breaking Wilt Chamberlain's high school scoring record by more than 200 points.

The only blemish on Lucas' high school record came in his senior year, when Columbus North defeated Middletown, 63–62, in the semifinals of the state tournament. But he couldn't be too bitter about the defeat, since it was there that he met his future wife, Treva Geib, one of the Columbus cheerleaders.

Lucas turned down an estimated 150 scholarship offers—some including such incentives as cars, houses, and even jobs for his father—to accept an academic scholarship at Ohio State. At OSU he excelled as a student as well as an athlete. Lucas was elected to the national honor fraternity for commerce students.

In his first varsity season, the Buckeyes went all the way to the NCAA title, crushing California, 75–55, in the championship game. Lucas held Darrall Imhoff, California's All-American center, to eight points, the lowest total of his career. The next two seasons, Ohio State lost to Cincinnati in the NCAA championship games.

Following his freshman year, Lucas played on the United States Olympic basketball team and led it to the gold medal in Rome. Pete Newell, who coached the Olympic squad, called Lucas "the best player I have ever coached." This was quite a tribute, since the Olympic team also included Oscar Robertson, Jerry West, Walt Bellamy, and Terry Dischinger.

Throughout his career, Lucas insisted he wouldn't play with the pros and after graduation in 1962 he pursued graduate studies for a year at Ohio State. But the Cincinnati Royals persuaded him to turn pro the next season with a long-term contract and bonus, and Lucas became one of the NBA's outstanding forwards. Later he played with the San Francisco Warriors and the New York Knicks.

only about 16 shots a contest. His shooting percentage ranged from an unbelievable .637 as a sophomore to a merely phenomenal .611 as a senior. He led the nation in field goal accuracy all three seasons.

A total team player, Lucas could shoot, rebound, pass, dribble, and play defense. "He has the ideal attitude. He'll play the post and he'll pass off all day. When he has to score, he'll do it. Whenever it looked as though Ohio State needed points, he got them. The rest of the time he passed off," said Frank McGuire, who coached North Carolina to a national championship.

When he had to score points, Lucas frequently used a deadly hook shot, which he could launch with either hand. But he could also score on jumpers from the corner, driving lay-ups or tip-ins of rebounds.

As a schoolboy sensation at Middletown High, Lucas had attracted college offers from schools around the nation. He finished

Hank Luisetti

The fastest gun in the West, Hank Luisetti, came east to Madison Square Garden with his Stanford team in December, 1936, to end Long Island University's 43-game winning streak and leave a lasting imprint on the court game. Luisetti broke up the game and changed basketball forever with his one-handed off-the-ear running shots.

Until Luisetti revolutionized basketball offense, there were two major types of shots, the driving lay-up and the two-handed set shot with feet firmly planted on the ground.

"Two years after Luisetti's appearance in the Garden," wrote his biographer, Dick Friendlich, "every school kid coming to an Eastern college was firing one-handed shots off his ears."

Luisetti's one-handed shot was his most memorable contribution to the game, but his floor play, his playmaking and his court generalship made his name a standard of excellence.

The Stanford star finished second to George Mikan of DePaul as the best basketball player in the first half of the century in an Associated Press poll. This was a notable achievement considering that Luisetti's career ended 15 years before the poll was taken, many voters had never seen him play, and Luisetti's career had been in the era of the center jump.

The dark-haired San Franciscan broke the national scoring record in his four seasons at Stanford with 1,596 points and still holds the school record for most points in a single game with 50 against Duquesne on January 1, 1938.

Angelo "Hank" Luisetti was a lanky 6-2 kid when he was first introduced to the one-handed shot at San Francisco's Galileo High School by his coach, Tommy DeNike.

"Several of my players were using it in practice and in a game once in a while," said DeNike, "but nobody took it like Hank."

Mostly he took the shot from just behind the foul line since he was able to drive past his guarding man and loft it over the last defender's head.

Stanford won three Pacific Coast Conference basketball championships during Luisetti's collegiate career. Despite his brilliant shooting, Luisetti was a team man who constantly looked for the open man on the floor.

Stanford's Hank Luisetti

After graduation from Stanford, Luisetti played and coached club and AAU basketball and became an executive with an automobile and a travel company. He also served three years in the Navy during World War II.

While in service he led St. Mary's Pre-Flight School to several impressive basketball victories over a Coast Guard team led by Jim Pollard, a 1942 Stanford star and later a member of the professional Minneapolis Lakers.

Luisetti's basketball fame in college was such that after graduation he was paid $10,000 to portray a college basketball player in a movie. The picture, called "Campus Confessions," was one of the most forgettable films ever made.

Pete Maravich

Maravich, oh Maravich,
Love to fake, love to score
Love to hear the people roar.
Just a boy of 22,
You made a name at LSU . . .
  —The Ballad of Pete Maravich
  by Woody Jenkins

Press Maravich, when he was coaching at Louisiana State University in the late 1960s, always referred to his son as "Pistol Pete."

A natural reaction. For "Pistol Pete" will be remembered as one of the greatest scorers to play collegiate basketball.

From 1967 through the end of the 1970 season, this skinny backcourtman with the

Louisiana State's Pete Maravich

floppy socks set 11 NCAA records, 16 Southeastern Conference records and 22 LSU marks. All three varsity years, he led the nation in scoring with averages of 43.8, 44.2 and 44.5 points per game. During his varsity career, he scored 3,667 points and had a 44.2 average, breaking the previous collegiate scoring record of Oscar Robertson, who played for the University of Cincinnati.

But Pete Maravich was more than just a scorer. He was one of the game's most brilliant showmen, and this combination led to one of the most lucrative contracts ever given to any athlete. The estimates ranged from $1.5 to $1.9 million when he signed with the Atlanta Hawks. And if one wonders what his worth was to his father, LSU fired the elder Maravich two years later when the team slipped under .500.

When Pete started at LSU, his father was trying to build a team that had finished 3–23 the season before. There were seasons of 14–12 and 13–13 after that and finally, in Pete's senior year, LSU was 22–10 and played in the National Invitation Tournament in Madison Square Garden.

But for years before, everyone knew the thin, scrawny son of Press Maravich was going to be an important figure in basketball. He had set records from the moment he began playing organized ball and by the time he was in prep school he was considered a potential superstar.

He could shoot from outside, drive and handle the ball with the same finesse as Bob Cousy had years before at Holy Cross and with the Boston Celtics.

Pete Maravich wasn't bashful about his talents. He enjoyed stardom and all the publicity. He had a huge mop of brown hair and those baggy sweat socks and the two became as much a part of his game as his jump shot.

Maravich was an extremely affable young man with a quick smile, a pitchman's vocal style and just the right touch of cockiness. And he loved crowds. "If there was no one in the stands," he once said, "I wouldn't suit up. I grew up in a basketball atmosphere. I love fans, the whole scene. The more people, the better I like it. And I don't care what they yell at me either. I never get up tight about someone calling me a hot dog because of what I do on the court."

What he did on the court was score and entertain. His points came on a variety of shots: jumpers, drives, hooks, long one-handers. And his passing and ball-handling, according to his father, were better than Cousy's.

"People," Press Maravich continued, "call him a hot dog because he passes the ball behind his back or between his legs and things like that. They don't realize he's got so many different deliveries and so many different moves on the court. He's done it so much because it's natural. It's his way of playing. He's 10 or 15 years ahead of his time."

Andy Phillip

One or two sophomores on the starting team of any college basketball squad is not considered unusual. The juniors and seniors carry the sophomores until the youngsters mature. Mistakes are the price the coach must pay as his sophomores learn the game.

Illinois coach Doug Mills shocked the Big Ten in the 1941–42 season when he put five sophomores on the starting five. The best of the baby bunch was a 6-2½ scorer from Granite City, Illinois, Andy Phillip. He was the best shooter on the team, a fine dribbler, and an outstanding defensive player who normally drew the other team's biggest and best player. He consistently out-rebounded taller men.

These sophomores blazed through the first season with a 13–2 Big Ten record and an 18–5 overall mark. Their poise surprised all opponents and they soon earned a nickname that was to stay with them throughout their careers, "The Whiz Kids."

The Whiz Kids—Phillip, Gene Vance, Art Mathisen, Jack Smiley, and Ken Menke —opened the season with an easy triumph over Marquette. They lost to Chanute Field at a time when the strongest teams in the country were military teams. They followed that loss with 11 straight victories.

They made it to the NCAA tournament and lost to Kentucky, 46–44, in the first round. Phillip ended the year by being

Illinois' Andy Phillip

selected Illinois' Most Valuable Player and a unanimous All-Big Ten choice.

The 1942–43 season was even better. Illinois won 17 of 18 games, with Phillip showing the way as the leading scorer and playmaker. He set conference season marks for most points (255), most field goals (111), and most points in a single game (40). He ended the season with 305 points in 18 games.

Although Phillip had come to be the best player on the Whiz Kids, it didn't always look as though he would be. "When he joined us as an all-state player from Granite City," Coach Mills said, "he wasn't yet a great player. He had to work as hard as any of the Whiz Kids to reach the point he did."

Phillip was considered a tremendous competitor, playing his best in the toughest games. His face was never expressive on the court. His quick hands were the most noticeable feature of his play, with his long fingers guiding the ball to a teammate or into the basket on a long set shot or driving lay-up.

Phillip was a two-sport athlete at Illinois with three varsity letters in basketball and three more in baseball as a pitcher, first baseman, and outfielder. Following the 1943 season, he was called into active duty with the Marine Corps and served as a lieutenant in the Pacific.

At 24, he returned to college with three other members of the Whiz Kids—Smiley, Vance, and Menke—to team with Fred Green as Illinois finished second in the Big Ten with an 8–4 conference mark and 14–6 overall.

After his college days, Phillip played ten years of professional basketball and was considered one of the finest guards in the game. He retired in 1957 to go into business in California.

Oscar Robertson

Cincinnati's Oscar Robertson

"There's never been one like him. Fabulous! Until this kid came along, I thought Tom Gola was the best soph I'd ever seen. I was wrong," said Joe Lapchick, who had been watching young men play basketball for more than 50 years. "This kid" is Oscar Palmer Robertson, the Big O, and quite possibly the greatest player in the history of college basketball.

In his three varsity seasons at the University of Cincinnati, Robertson scored more points, 2,973, than any major college player had before. When he graduated in 1960, the Big O held 14 NCAA University Division records. A three-time consensus All-American and Player of the Year all three years, Robertson led the Bearcats to records of 25–3, 26–4 and 28–2.

At 6-5 and 215 pounds, Robertson didn't score his points merely by being bigger than everyone else on the court. Instead, he so perfectly mastered the skills of shooting, dribbling, rebounding, and passing, that coach Phog Allen of Kansas was moved to comment, "Oscar Robertson is the greatest player of all time for a fellow of his size."

Early in his sophomore season, Cincinnati came into New York's Madison Square Garden to take on Seton Hall. For many heralded sophomores, the pressure of playing on basketball's most famous court simply proves too much. But not for Oscar. He scored 56 points that night. The entire Seton Hall team scored 54, and Cincinnati won, 118–54. In the history of the Garden, no basketball player—high school, college, or professional—had ever scored more points. He hit on 22 of 32 shots from the floor, made all 12 free throws he attempted, grabbed 15 rebounds, and added six assists.

Robertson went on to have many more big nights, leading the Bearcats in scoring in nearly every game and usually leading them in rebounds and assists as well. He finished his career with a 33.8 scoring average, the highest in collegiate history, and reached a single-game peak of 62 against North Texas State in his senior year.

The first indications of just how good a basketball player the Big O would be came in his junior year at Crispus Attucks High School in Indianapolis, Indiana. As a sophomore he had been good but not great, averaging 12 points a game. But as a junior he led Crispus Attucks to an undefeated season—the first in Indiana high school history—and the state championship. Attucks extended its winning streak to 45 games the next season before finally losing, and again won the state title.

Robertson graduated in the upper tenth of his class and was elected to the National Honor Society. Coupling this with his extraordinary basketball talent, he had his choice of virtually any college in the country. He chose Cincinnati, partly because of a co-op program which allowed students to alternate classroom work with on-the-job training.

Although he was the first black basketball player in the school's history, Robertson insisted that he didn't want to be a crusader for civil rights. "A lot of people thought that I should open doors. But I didn't feel that it was up to me to do it. It's for everybody to do, blacks, whites, everybody," he said. As a black, Robertson frequently found himself singled out for insults. During the Dixie Classic at Raleigh, North Carolina, the fans showered him with racial epithets and Oscar wound up in a wrestling match on the floor with a Wake Forest player.

But none of this could stop Robertson. With some of the quickest reflexes and finest moves ever seen on the court, he completely dominated any game and seemed capable of scoring almost at will. He continued his basketball career with the Cincinnati Royals and became one of the all-time pro stars. Later he was traded to the Milwaukee Bucks where he achieved something he had been pursuing his entire career—an NBA championship—in the 1970–71 season.

Guy Rodgers

Guy Rodgers was one of the fastest, flashiest backcourt operators ever to lace on a pair of basketball shoes. In an era when big men were dominating the game, Rodgers came along, stretched himself fully to reach six feet, and showed the basketball world there was still a place for the small man if he could move the ball like he did, shoot like him or destroy the best defensive plans of the opposition.

Guy learned his basketball in half-court games in South Philadelphia, the spawning ground of many of that city's finest players. "In those games," he later said, "I had to be quick because most of the fellows I played with were taller, tougher and stronger than I was. I knew I couldn't go through them to the basket so I had to learn how to go around them."

After an all-city high school career, Rodgers enrolled at Temple University in Philadelphia, but was still an uncertain prospect because of his size. "All my life I had to prove to coaches that I could play well enough to make their teams. It never bothered me. I always had the confidence," he said.

Coach Harry Litwack of Temple recognized Rodgers' skills almost immediately and gave him the floor leadership of the Owls as a sophomore. Rodgers was on his way. He led the Owls to a record of 27 victories and only four losses in the 1955–56 season and a third-place finish in the NCAA tourney. He was the team leader in assists as well as the high scorer with 573 points. Temple was 20–9 in his second season as Rodgers again led the team in scoring with 591 points. That year the Owls finished third in the NIT.

Temple's Guy Rodgers

In Guy's senior year, Temple won 27 games, lost three, and finished third in the NCAA tournament. The Owls also won the Holiday Festival in New York's Madison Square Garden. Rodgers finished the season with school records for scoring, field goals, and assists. He had 15 assists in a single game against Manhattan College. Rodgers was always a crowd favorite. He could pass a ball behind his back and was a master ball-handler.

Upon graduation from Temple, he led a touring team of college all-stars against the famed Harlem Globetrotters. The Globetrotters tried to get Rodgers to play with them after the tour ended but he decided to try his hand in the National Basketball Association. "I wanted to see if a small man could play in the big league," he said.

Rodgers certainly could. He teamed with another Philadelphian, Wilt Chamberlain, to make the Philadelphia Warriors one of the best teams in the professional game. Guy later played with Chicago, Cincinnati, and Milwaukee.

An extremely personable and witty fellow, Rodgers was successful as a banquet speaker. He also did some part-time teaching and basketball coaching at school clinics during his time off from professional play.

Because he was barely six feet, Guy Rodgers was an inspiring model for all small basketball players.

Cazzie Russell

Football was king at the University of Michigan at Ann Arbor. Talk of the Rose Bowl was everywhere. This was 1963 and only eleven season tickets had been sold for the Wolverines' basketball games. This all changed with the arrival on campus of a burly 6-5 basketball player from Chicago, Cazzie Lee Russell, Jr.

In three seasons at Michigan, Russell elevated the court game to prominence on campus, raised Michigan to the top of the national ratings, and electrified crowds all over the country with his exciting, aggressive style of play.

Russell began his basketball career at Carver High School on Chicago's South Side. His coach, Larry Hawkins, saw the potential in the gangling six-footer and worked for hours to perfect his skills.

"Another thing that helped my career," said Russell, "were some friendly janitors." When Russell was a freshman at the high school he persuaded the janitors to let him into the locked school building, keep the lights on late in the gymnasium and practice for hours on end.

"If it weren't for them letting me practice," Russell claimed, "I might have wound up driving a cab or working in the steel mills or pushing rocks on a construction gang."

Russell became an all-state basketball player at Carver. Soon the college offers poured in. Oscar Robertson advised Cazzie to go to his alma mater, Cincinnati. More than 75 schools put in their bids. Finally the choice narrowed to Cincinnati and Michigan.

"I chose Michigan because I always had some feeling for the underdog. Michigan's basketball team was down and Cincinnati's was up. I thought I just might be only another player at Cincinnati. At Michigan I had a chance to be a star," Russell said.

Michigan's Cazzie Russell

In his first year Cazzie led Michigan to a 23–5 record, the Holiday Festival championship (after a memorable triumph over Princeton in which Bill Bradley had fouled out), the Big Ten title, and third place in the NCAA tournament.

With Cazzie's heroics, basketball interest zoomed on campus. By his fifth game, students were lining up at 1 a.m. to buy tickets that didn't go on sale until 8 a.m.

Russell moved from backcourt to forecourt with ease. He was quick enough to set up the offense, guard the small man on defense and move the team. He was big enough to drive and shoot from the corners, help out with rebounding, and lead the Wolverine offense from in close.

Russell averaged nearly 25 points a game as a sophomore and was named to the All-Big Ten team and several All-America squads. He missed making the 1964 Olympic team when he sustained an ankle injury.

The following season was even better. Cazzie averaged 25.7 points a game, was a unanimous All-Big Ten selection, and made every All-America team. In his senior year, Cazzie averaged 30.8 points a game (the whole team averaged 91), led the Wolverines to a third-place NCAA tourney finish and was named Player of the Year.

The New York Knickerbockers made Cazzie the first choice in the annual pro draft and signed him to a three-year contract for a reported salary and bonus of $200,000. He was on the NBA championship Knick team (1969–70) and later played for the Golden State Warriors, Los Angeles Lakers and Chicago Bulls.

Maurice Stokes

At 6-7 and 240 pounds, Maurice Stokes was a basketball coach's dream. He had the speed and agility of a small man, coupled with the size and strength of a huge center. Maurice the Magnificent, as the newspapers called him, could shoot, drive, and pass off. He could do so much on the basketball court, in fact, that many who saw him play consider him the greatest all-around player of his time.

Certainly nobody who saw Stokes in the

St. Francis' Maurice Stokes

1955 National Invitation Tournament in New York's Madison Square Garden is likely to argue that evaluation. Stokes, the tournament's Most Valuable Player, put on one of the most stunning individual exhibitions ever in the Garden and almost led his school, tiny St. Francis College of Loretto, Pennsylvania, into the finals of the NIT. That the Frankies fell short was no fault of Stokes, who by himself almost outplayed an entire Dayton team.

On the night of March 17, 1955, Stokes in 45 minutes scored 43 points, got 19 rebounds against a Dayton team that had four men taller than he, intercepted numerous passes, and generally frustrated the Flyers on defense. Despite these heroics, Dayton won in overtime, 79–73, but only after Stokes' teammates had missed three unobstructed layups on his perfect lead passes in the last few minutes of the game.

Walter McLaughlin, the St. John's athletic director and chairman of the NIT selection committee, said, "This is the greatest performance I have ever seen. There have been other great players here but what they did pales by comparison." Sportswriters, marveling at Stokes' play, wondered in print how he had previously failed to make the All-America teams.

The answer was obvious. Stokes played for a small school that played many of its games against obscure opponents. As a result he didn't receive much national publicity. Nevertheless, his college statistics were impressive. Because of St. Francis' small size, freshmen were eligible for varsity competition and Stokes didn't waste any time showing what he could do. In his third varsity game, against Villanova, he scored 32 points, and Al Severance, the Villanova coach, commented, "He's the best freshman player I've ever seen."

Stokes finished his freshman season with a 16.7 average. That year the Frankies played 30 games, but after having seen the burly Stokes in action, some opposing schools decided not to reschedule St. Francis—at least not until Stokes graduated. His scoring average increased each season and in his senior year, 1954–55, he averaged 26.6 a game.

The scouts saw Stokes as a natural pro. They were awed by his shooting touch and tremendous strength off the boards. The Rochester Royals made him their first choice in the annual draft, and Stokes, who had turned down an offer from the Harlem Globetrotters, became the NBA's Rookie of the Year. The next season he was even better, making the All-NBA second team.

But the following year, 1957–58, the world that Stokes had built through basketball, collapsed. Encephalitis, a crippling brain disease, turned Stokes into an invalid. For months he was in a coma, but he fought against the illness with the same tenacity that he used to fight for rebounds under the boards. Jack Twyman, his teammate on the Royals, became Stokes' guardian and with his help Maurice began a long and painful period of rehabilitation.

Though Stokes was making progress with his physical rehabilitation, the effort placed too much of a strain on his system and he died following a heart attack in 1970 at the age of 36.

David Thompson

The image resists the blurring of the years that have passed since North Carolina State won its national championship in 1974: little Monte Towe taking the outlet pass from

North Carolina State's David Thompson

huge Tom Burleson and lobbing the ball toward the basket, and David Thompson soaring above the backboard to grab the sphere and stuff it. Alley-oop. Two points, North Carolina State.

David Thompson, only 6-3½ but the possessor of a 42-inch vertical leap that propelled him higher than any player his size had ever gone before, was the main ingredient in the Wolfpack's NCAA title climb.

Thompson, who has earned the nickname "Skywalker" during his pro career with the Denver Nuggets, reached the heights in his sport despite lowly beginnings. He was born in tiny Crest, North Carolina, and his truck-driver father had to work several jobs to provide for his 11 children.

Growing up in a cinder-block house, the youngest Thompson dreamed about playing in the then lily-white Atlantic Coast Conference. "Guess when you're that old, you don't see any colors," he said. He learned his basketball on a dirt court, using a makeshift backboard of wood, a rusted metal rim and, on occasion, the headlights of his father's car for illumination.

When it came time for college, Thompson chose North Carolina State and created a sensation before playing his first varsity game. The school was placed on probation for the 1972–73 season and was ineligible for post-season play because of recruiting violations, supposedly involving Thompson. However, David quickly proved he was worth the trouble, averaging 24.7 points per game and shooting better than 50 per cent from the floor while leading the Wolfpack to a 27–0 record.

The following year, in the Eastern regional final against Pittsburgh, Thompson caught his feet on 6-8 teammate Phil Spence's shoulder and flipped, landing on his head and the back of his neck. "I still can't remember the play," he said. "I remember running downcourt and then there was darkness. The next thing I know I'm in the ambulance with my mother." The injury wasn't as serious as first feared and he returned to the arena, wearing a blood-stained bandage around his head.

Thompson returned for the semifinal triumph over UCLA, which snapped the Bruins' string of seven straight NCAA titles. He scored the crucial points in the closing minute of the second overtime, typical of a college career during which he averaged only a hair under 30 points per game. "David Thompson is the finest athlete I've ever seen in my life and he's even a finer person than he is an athlete," said the North Carolina State coach, Norm Sloan.

David joined his college teammates on a tour of the Philippines, Japan, Taiwan, Thailand, and Hong Kong following the title-winning effort. "Little kids would see him on the street and they would jump up and pretend to be dunking the ball," said Sloan.

Thompson signed with the then-American Basketball Association Denver Nuggets and led the club to a first-place finish in his rookie season in 1975–76. He nearly won the NBA scoring title in 1977–78, tallying 73 points in the season's final to lose out to San Antonio's George Gervin. He was rewarded with a six-year contract of approximately $3 million.

Ernie Vandeweghe

One of the classic all-star basketball games in Madison Square Garden history was the annual East-West encounter for the *Herald Tribune* Fresh Air Fund. The first of the series was played in 1946 and more than 18,000 people jammed the Garden to watch the best college players in the land, led by Bob Kurland, Kenny Sailors, Don Otten, and Charley Black.

When the Garden smoke had cleared, the East was a surprising winner, 60–59, and the Most Valuable Player was a gangling, large-eared 17-year-old Colgate freshman, Ernie Vandeweghe.

Vandeweghe helped double-team the 7-foot Kurland, scored 16 points, set the East's offense, and controlled the pace of the game. Three years later, as a senior,

Colgate's Ernie Vandeweghe

Vandeweghe was again invited to play in the game.

Vandeweghe's career at Colgate spanned 1945–49, the post-World War II seasons when GIs returned to college and dominated the game. Vandeweghe was usually the youngest player on the floor when Colgate met its opposition. Even when he graduated in 1949 at 20, he was still one of the youngest players on his own team, which he had captained in his junior and senior years.

The 6-4 Vandeweghe was born in Montreal, Canada, where his father was a semi-professional basketball player by avocation and a furrier by vocation.

"I was a spoiled little boy," remembers Vandeweghe. "I had everything I wanted, especially when it came to athletic equipment. I had a hockey rink in my backyard, a basketball court, a motorboat, skates, hunting guns, and a horse. That's when I thought I would be a jockey."

He soon grew out of the jockey stage and began concentrating on basketball, soccer, and skating. His family moved to Oceanside, New York, when Ernie was in sixth grade. In the summer he spent his time between games running a lawn-mowing enterprise with a friend.

Vandeweghe earned eight varsity letters in high school in football, basketball, baseball, and track. He entered his father's alma mater, Colgate, in 1945. He gave up football because of a back injury and devoted himself to basketball.

One day he came home from college driving a convertible, a gift from his dad for good grades. A friend asked if the college gave him that car for his basketball playing. "No," said Ernie. "The only thing I get from Colgate is applause."

The applause was loud and clear as Vandeweghe led the Red Raiders in scoring four straight years with a career total of 1,377 for a Colgate record. He made the first team on most All-America squads along with Ed Macauley, Alex Groza and Vince Boryla.

From the time he had written a high school paper on Louis Pasteur, Vandeweghe wanted to be a doctor. He entered medical school upon graduation and played basketball for the New York Athletic Club.

While playing golf one day with coach Joe Lapchick of the New York Knickerbockers, Lapchick suggested the possibility of combining medical studies with professional basketball. For four years Vandeweghe was one of the Knicks' finest guards while he continued his medical studies. When he completed his schooling he retired from basketball to devote full time to his profession.

Vandeweghe married a former Miss America, Colleen Kay Hutchins, sister of Mel Hutchins, who played for the Milwaukee Hawks. The Vandeweghes now make their home in California, where Ernie is a pediatrician.

Jimmy Walker

Some days you never know who you may find in the playground basketball games in the city of Boston. One day it might be a local college hotshot out for some summer fun, or it might be a talented high school senior getting ready for college. It might even be a professional star like Sam Jones of the Boston Celtics.

"I was just out for some exercise," remembers Jones, "and this skinny kid gave me all I could handle."

Jimmy Walker, the skinny kid, grew up to

Providence's Jimmy Walker

be a 6-3, strong-legged 210-pounder who, with the help of his new-found friend, Sam Jones, was to discover a new world, become a college sensation and move into the professional basketball ranks.

"When I first played against Sam in the playground I had no ideas about college," Walker recalled. "I liked basketball and I wanted to go on but I certainly couldn't afford college."

Jones convinced Walker that he could continue both his education and his basketball career if he entered Laurinburg (N.C.) Prep School. Jones arranged for a scholarship and Walker went south from his Boston home to acquire the necessary credits for college admission and, at the same time, smooth out his basketball style.

In the fall of 1963, Walker entered Providence College in Rhode Island on a scholarship. As a freshman basketball player he averaged 22 points a game and gave all signs of being an exceptional star for the school that has a long history of outstanding basketball players, including Len Wilkens, John Egan, and Vinnie Ernst.

As a sophomore, Walker averaged 20.5 points a game and gained many All-America nominations. He was an outstanding scorer, especially in the clutch, and deadly when he got his man in a driving one-on-one situation.

"The thing I liked about Jim most," said his coach, Joe Mullaney, "is he does just what you tell him to help the team win. I remember one game when he scored four points against St. Francis. We used him as a decoy and he took only three shots all night. He was just happy that we won."

As a junior he was selected as the Most Valuable Player in the Holiday Festival at Madison Square Garden and the outstanding player to appear at the Garden all season. He scored 622 points in 27 games and became the first Providence player to score more than 1,000 points before finishing his junior year.

In the final Festival game against Bob Cousy's Boston College team, Walker scored 50 points for the Friars and prompted Cousy to acclaim him as "The nearest thing to Oscar Robertson I've ever seen in college."

Oscar—and Cousy before him—were the standards by which all college backcourt players were measured. Walker was an exciting performer with his aggressive drives to the basket, his uncanny jump-shooting, his ferocious rebounding against taller men, and the amazing way he controlled the tempo of a game.

"He is a tremendous crowd-pleaser," said Joe Lapchick, "and he never lets the crowd down with his performance."

Walker capped his career with unanimous All-America selections, a repeat as MVP in the Holiday Festival, and the scoring leadership of the nation with an average of 30.4 points a game. He tallied 851 points in his final season at Providence.

Jim was named Player of the Year, and was the first choice in the professional basketball draft, being selected by the Detroit Pistons. He played there for five years, averaging 21.3 points in his final year before being traded to Houston, and then to Kansas City.

Bill Walton

Taking turns in the spotlight during the Walton Gang era at UCLA were Bill Walton, superb, intense, 6-11 center laying claim to the title as the best passing pivot the game has ever known, and Bill Walton, child of a politically active campus life, protective of his privacy, suspicious of the publicity attended upon him, sincere and outspoken critic of the American culture and government.

Walton, the freckle-faced redhead whose enormous ability was matched by his enthusiasm for playing basketball, led John Wooden's Bruins to titles in each of Walton's first three seasons at UCLA. He capped his junior season with perhaps his greatest collegiate performance, scoring 44 points in the NCAA final against Memphis State on 21 of 22 shots from the floor. At the same time he pulled down 13 rebounds despite playing in foul trouble much of the contest. "That was the best performance I've ever seen," said the Memphis State coach, Gene Bartow. "I've never seen a player so dominating as Walton."

UCLA's Bill Walton

The son of William Theodore Walton Jr., a district chief of the San Diego Department of Public Works, Bill was raised in suburban San Diego. The accelerated growth that saw him gain six inches during his fifteenth year and that later was suspected to be the cause of a painful tendonitis condition in his knees helped make him a standout at Helix High School.

He averaged 29 points and 22 rebounds a game while helping his school win 49 straight games. Later he was the key figure in UCLA's incredible 88-game winning streak, withstanding the pain in his tender knees to average in the high teens in both scoring and rebounding during each of his college seasons.

After spurning a huge "hardship draft" offer from the Philadelphia 76ers after his junior year, Walton, with some reluctance, accepted a $3 million pact from Portland to turn pro in 1974–75. Injuries severely cut into his playing time and reduced his effectiveness during his first two NBA seasons, and the rumblings concerning his vegetarian diet and anti-establishment lifestyle were joined by whispers that Walton would not play in pain.

He silenced his critics by leading Portland to its first championship in 1976–77 and was named Most Valuable Player. But more injuries and a resulting strained situation with Portland management the following year—he blamed club officials for prematurely putting him back into the lineup—caused him to demand to be traded. His future was uncertain as he sat out 1978–79.

But at his moment of personal triumph, Walton resisted reporters. He said, "I'm not talking because the season is over. You don't see me frowning. You see how happy I am that we won and that it's over. But it's just that I'm no longer No. 32 on the basketball court. I can be Joe Walton now if I want to. And I'm not talking because I don't want to."

Part of his icy reception to the media was because he felt the attention paid to him was attributable to his role as a "Great White Hope." In fact, it seems Walton's career is destined to be surrounded by controversy.

5

The Coaches

They throw towels, they argue, they suffer on the bench. If they win they are lauded. If they lose too frequently, they sometimes find themselves out of a job. But they are the lifeblood of the game. They are the coaches.

Players come and players go, but coaches remain to teach, to improve the game, and to serve as public relations officers and goodwill ambassadors for their beloved sport.

The following is a list of coaches whose contributions have had a vital impact on college basketball. They are not necessarily the coaches with the best won-lost records. They are the coaches who have contributed something of permanent value to the sport, something that has transcended the mere winning of games.

The coaches, such as Pitt's Doc Carlson, pointed to basketball's modern era

Dr. Forrest C. (Phog) Allen

While still a student at the University of Kansas in 1908, Allen took over as coach from Dr. James Naismith, the game's inventor. Almost a half-century later, Allen retired with 771 victories. Only one coach has won more games—Adolph Rupp of Kentucky, who was Allen's pupil. In his 39 seasons at Kansas, Allen's teams won 24 conference championships, climaxed by the NCAA crown in 1952. His teams were always distinguished for outstanding defense and they typified the ball-control style of

Phog Allen

basketball. Allen founded the National Association of Basketball Coaches in 1927 and was later instrumental in having basketball included in the Olympic Games.

Clair Bee

This dynamic, intense little man who stood so tall as coach of Long Island University is a foremost clinician, teacher, strategist, and author of basketball books for boys and coaches. In constant demand at coaching clinics, Bee used to spread his coaching gospel all over the country. As a coach, Bee was a master at capitalizing on opponents' weaknesses. He originated the 1-3-1 zone defense and helped with the development of the 24-second clock, the salvation of the pro game. In 18 seasons at LIU, Bee's teams won 327 games, including winning streaks of 43, 38, 28 and 26, and they lost only 67. Bee is a member of the Hall of Fame.

John Bunn

The most significant change in offensive basketball in the past 50 years was the perfection of one-handed shooting. In 1936 Bunn brought his Stanford five into New York's Madison Square Garden to play LIU, which had won 43 straight games. New York, for the first time, saw one-handed shooting, an art perfectly exemplified by Bunn's prize player, Hank Luisetti. Stanford broke LIU's streak, and soon

Clair Bee

John Bunn

most college players were firing with one hand. Bunn later coached at Springfield and Colorado State, and was elected to the Hall of Fame.

Dr. H. Clifford Carlson

A charter member of the Hall of Fame, Doc Carlson coached Pitt for 31 years, winning 370 games, losing 246. His 1927–28 and 1929–30 teams were acclaimed unofficial national champions. He was the first coach to take an eastern team to the West Coast, in 1931–32. Doc is credited with having

Ed Diddle

Doc Carlson

originated the first patterned offense, the "figure eight." While coaching he maintained a medical practice.

Ed Diddle

Third on the all-time list of winning coaches when he retired in 1964 with 759 victories and 302 defeats at Western Kentucky, Diddle used to delight the audience with his towel act. When unhappy with an official's decision, the performance of his players or anything else, Ed would heave his omnipresent towel to the floor. An advocate of race-horse basketball, Diddle employed the fast break with great success. One of his regrets was that his teams never fared well in New York. But they did very well everywhere else.

Paul (Tony) Hinkle

Although coaching at a small school, Butler, Hinkle rates with the giants. He scheduled the best opponents and beat Big Ten schools with amazing regularity. Through the 1969–70 season, when he retired, he had won 560 games and lost 392 in 41 years. Tony was elected to the Hall of Fame in 1965.

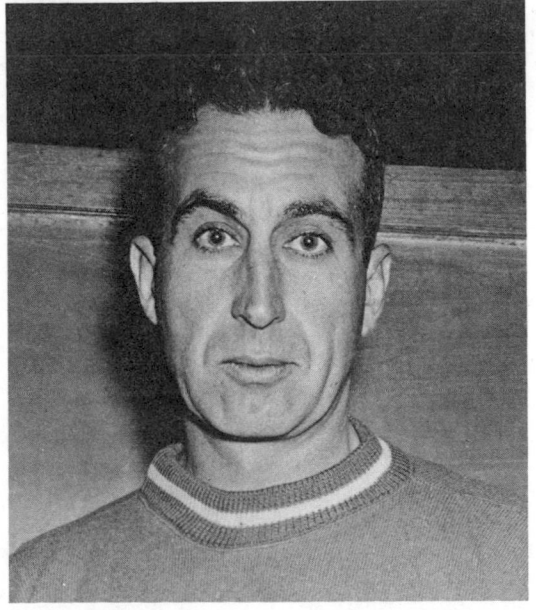

Tony Hinkle

135

Nat Holman

Known as "Mr. Basketball" at City College of New York, Holman was a master teacher and innovator who brought a certain class and sophistication to the game. The erudite Holman was credited with being the brains of the Original Celtics, and he was a natural as a coach. As a player he improvised all sorts of individual moves that eventually became the foundation for "New York basketball," recognized the country over as connoting guile and finesse. Holman, like Clair Bee, was in great demand as a lecturer and wrote several books on basketball techniques. His greatest coaching achievement came in 1949–50, when CCNY's Beavers achieved the Grand Slam of college basketball, winning both major post-season tournaments—the National Invitation Tournament and the NCAA. No other coach accomplished the feat. Holman was elected to the Hall of Fame in 1967.

Hank Iba

Nat Holman

Henry P. (Hank) Iba

Patience is not just a virtue for Hank Iba, it's a way of life. Discipline and ball control are an obsession. Iba's Oklahoma State (formerly Oklahoma A&M) teams shot only when absolutely necessary, when there was nothing else to do with the ball. Iba has made patience an absolute necessity as far as shot-taking. His contributions to the game have been many, one of the most noteworthy being his use of basketball's first good 7-footer, Bob Kurland, who became an All-American, a Hall of Famer, and helped make the word "goon" disappear from the jargon of basketball. Iba's 767 victories when he retired as a college coach in 1970 placed him third on the all-time winning list. He won consecutive NCAA championships in 1944–45 and 1945–46 and he served as U. S. Olympic coach in 1964 at Tokyo, in 1968 at Mexico City and in 1972 at Munich. His Olympians maintained the unbeaten U.S. record that began with the introduction of basketball into the Olympic program in 1936 until the championship game in 1972, when the team lost to the Soviet Union in a controversial contest.

George E. Keogan

From 1923 to 1943, Keogan gave Notre Dame a basketball team that rivaled football at South Bend, if not in prestige and fame, at least in performance. In that span, the Irish won 327 games and lost 96, a fantastic .773 percentage. He studied dentistry, but gave up that career to concentrate on coaching and was elected to the Basketball Hall of Fame in 1961. Keogan is credited with creating the shifting man-to-man defense. A student of the game, he followed professional ball and learned from the pros, particularly the Original Celtics and their pivot man, Dutch Dehnert. From Dehnert, he adopted the successful use of pivots and cuts.

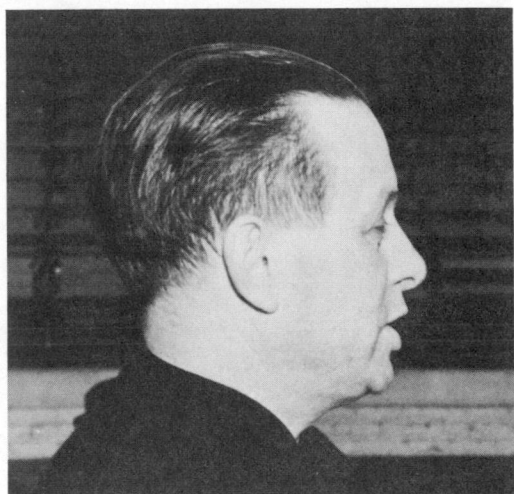

George Keogan

Bobby Knight

In 1975, Knight's Indiana team saw its unbeaten string of 31 consecutive games halted in the NCAA Mid-East regional when the team's star broke his arm late in the regular season. But Knight and the

Bobby Knight

Hoosiers came back to register that elusive unbeaten season and win the national championship in 1976. Knight, who began his coaching career at Army, had a career record of 284–103 through the 1979 campaign. Well known for his demanding style and his short fuse, Knight was the originator of the motion offense, a sophisticated alternative to the traditional patterned attack that gained favor among many of the nation's top coaches.

Ward L. (Piggy) Lambert

He helped put the Big Ten on the basketball map with his powerful Purdue teams, which gained national recognition in the 1920s and '30s. In 29 years as coach, his teams won or shared 11 Big Ten titles and posted

Piggy Lambert

371 victories. He pioneered the fast break style of basketball and his teams were noted for their sustained speed. There was nothing mechanical about their play. "Basketball," he was fond of saying, "is a mental game." Lambert died in 1958. Two years later he was elected to the Hall of Fame.

Joe Lapchick

The game's greatest goodwill ambassador, highly respected as a coach and dedicated

Joe Lapchick

contributor to college basketball, Lapchick viewed more than 50 years of the sport as a player, college coach, professional coach, and college coach again. He was the game's first big man as the 6-5 center of the famed Original Celtics, then helped make St. John's "The Notre Dame of college basketball," according to a rival coach. Lapchick's teams were characterized by their patience, intelligence, ball control, and defense. He was an inspirational coach whose fatherly approach got tremendous mileage out of his players. More than a dozen of his pupils became pro or college coaches themselves. An habitual walker with countless trips to the water cooler during a game, Lapchick was able to adjust and keep pace with the times as the college game changed through the years. He capped a brilliant career in his final game in 1965 by becoming the only coach to win the National Invitation Tournament four times. In 17 seasons Lapchick's Redmen won 291 games, lost 95.

Branch McCracken

The fast break was McCracken's forte, and he employed it successfully to produce some of the highest-scoring teams in collegiate history. His Indiana teams won national championships in 1939–40 and 1952–53, and McCracken was twice selected to conduct clinics for coaches of armed forces

teams overseas, once in Europe, once in Japan. McCracken was voted into the Hall of Fame in 1960. Upon his retirement following the 1964–65 season, he had won 451 games and lost only 277, while competing in the tough and highly competitive Big Ten. His 451 victories place him high on the all-time winning list.

Branch McCracken

Al McGuire

He exited from the coaching ranks with uncharacteristic tears after his Marquette club won the national championship in 1977. McGuire will be remembered for his

Al McGuire

street-fighting style and his smart, opportunistic teams. Beginning his coaching career at little Belmont Abbey College in North Carolina, McGuire moved to Marquette in 1965 and led the Warriors to two NCAA runner-up finishes before winning the tournament during his final season. His 20-year coaching career was highlighted by 404 victories and a lifetime winning percentage of .737. His legendary battles with the referees and his "scrambled eggs" defense were the controversial coach's calling cards.

John McLendon

In more than 20 years of coaching at North Carolina College, Hampton Institute, Tennessee State, Kentucky State, and Cleveland State, McLendon's teams won over 650 games. His winning percentage of nearly .800 is among the highest of all modern coaches. McLendon's Tennessee State teams won three consecutive NAIA championships in 1957–59. Among McLendon's players who have gone on to the pros are NBA stars Sam Jones, Dick Barnett, John Barnhill, and Ben Warley. When he was appointed head coach of the Cleveland Pipers of the short-lived American Basketball League in 1960, McLendon became the first black coach to reach so high a level in professional sports. Later he coached the Denver Rockets in the American Basketball Association.

John McLendon

Adolph (The Baron) Rupp

Kentucky's controversial and outspoken Baron is No. 1 on the all-time list of winning coaches, having been on the winning side 874 times in 1,064 games, an .821 winning percentage through 1972, his 42nd year, when he retired. Rupp was a strong-willed individual who was never afraid to voice his opinion, even if it was a minority and unpopular one. He was a strange mixture of vanity and humility. He developed a mode of operation based on set offenses and made it stand up, never deviating from it regardless of the opposition's style of play.

Adolph Rupp

Much of his success depended on the employment of a stiff man-to-man defense. He produced some of the college game's greatest teams and usually sacrificed height for speed and ruggedness. He once said, "I know I have plenty of enemies, but I'd rather be the most hated winning coach in the country than the most popular losing one." Rupp was Coach of the Year four times, produced 25 All-Americans, won four national championships and made more appearances in the NCAA tournament (20) than any other coach—a record of achievement unmatched in college basketball.

Dean Smith

Since his arrival in North Carolina in 1962, Smith has been one of the college game's most successful coaches, one of its greatest innovators. Through 1979 his Tar Heel teams won 386 games against 127 losses. The only coach in history who made more NCAA Final Four appearances than Smith was UCLA's John Wooden. It was under Smith's guidance that the United States Olympic basketball team won the 1976 gold medal. Smith's trademarks include the run-and-jump defense, the mixing of pressure defenses, the point zone, the free-lance passing game, and the four-corners offense.

John Wooden

Dean Smith

John Wooden

The record acknowledges scholarly and soft-spoken Wooden as a coaching great. He won nine NCAA championships in a 10-year span and added a final title during his last season at UCLA in 1975. During his 29 years of college coaching, Wooden recorded 667 victories and a winning percentage of .806, the third-highest all-time mark. Wooden was an exponent of deliberate basketball. His teams were characterized by conditioning, fundamentals, speed,

quickness, and basketball sense, which Wooden described as "the ability to be in the right place at the right time." Wooden was voted into the Hall of Fame as a player in 1960 and as a coach in 1972, the only man to be so honored.

Phil Woolpert

The measure of Woolpert as a coach is in his 60 consecutive victories at the University of San Francisco in 1954–55 and 1955–56. In those two years he established himself as a genius of defensive basketball. Woolpert had always been violently opposed to fast break, race-horse basketball. "It just isn't good basketball," he once said. "I wouldn't know how to go about coaching it. You can't expect to execute scoring plays when you're racing up and down the court like madmen." Woolpert's teams spent 60 per cent of their practice time on defense, but theory means nothing if you do not have the players to do the execution. In those two years he had the players—rather he made the players. The center was a tall, lanky kid who had been the sixth man on his high school team. Bill Russell was his name. And one guard had been a football player in high school. K. C. Jones was his name. They were the stalwarts on a team that won two successive NCAA titles and lost only one game in two seasons. "The best college team I ever saw," says Joe Lapchick. "They played a defense I never saw before."

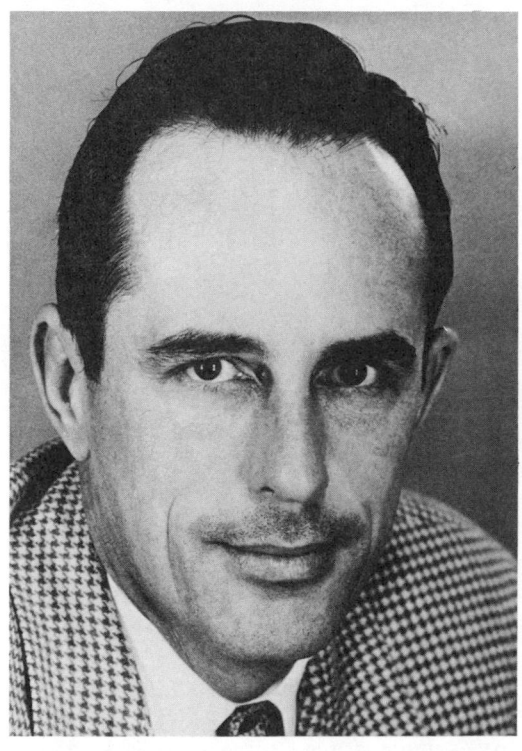

Phil Woolpert

There are many others past and present who can claim a place on the coaching honor roll. They include:

Harold Anderson, Toledo and Bowling Green; **Gene Bartow,** Central Missouri State, Valparaiso, Illinois, Memphis State, UCLA and Alabama at Birmingham; **Tom Blackburn,** Dayton; **Al Brightman,** Seattle; **Vic Bubas,** Duke; **Howard Cann,** NYU; **Lou Carnesecca,** St. John's; **Ben Carnevale,** North Carolina and Navy; **Pete Carril,** Lehigh and Princeton; **Ev Case,** North Carolina State; **Chick Davies,** Duquesne; **Ev Dean,** Carleton, Indiana, and Stanford; **C. G. "Lefty" Driesell,** Davidson and Maryland; **Fred Enke,** Louisville and Arizona; **Bud Foster,** Wisconsin; **Jack Friel,** Washington State; **Zip Gales,** Langston; **John**

"Taps" Gallagher, Niagara; **Jack Gardner,** Kansas State and Utah; **Amory "Slats" Gill,** Oregon State; **Bruce Hale,** Miami (Fla.) and St. Mary's; **Joe Hall,** Regis, Central Missouri, and Kentucky; **Dick Harter,** Rider, Pennsylvania, Oregon, and Penn State; **Jack Hartman,** Southern Illinois and Kansas State; **Ed Hickey,** Creighton, St. Louis, and Marquette; **Bernard "Peck" Hickman,** Louisville; **Fred Hobdy,** Grambling; **Howard Hobson,** Southern Oregon, Oregon, and Yale.

Also **George Ireland,** Loyola (Ill.); **Ed Jucker,** Cincinnati and Rollins; **Alvin "Doggie" Julian,** Muhlenberg, Holy Cross, and Dartmouth; **Bob King,** New Mexico and Indiana State; **Frank Keaney,** Rhode Island; **Jack Kraft,** Villanova and Rhode Island; **Abe Lemons,** Oklahoma City and Texas; **Guy Lewis,** Houston; **Harry Litwack,** Temple; **Ken Loeffler,** Geneva, Yale, LaSalle, and Texas A&M; **Dutch Lonborg,** McPherson, Washburn, and Northwestern; **Arad McCutcheon,** Evansville; **Frank McGuire,** St. John's, North Carolina, and South Carolina; **Ray Mears,** Wittenberg and Tennessee; **Ray Meyer,** DePaul; **Eldon Miller,** Wittenberg, Western Michigan, and Ohio State; **Lucias Mitchell,** Kentucky State; **Donald "Dudey" Moore,** Duquesne and LaSalle; **Joe Mullaney,** Providence and Brown; **Pete Newell,** San Francisco, Michigan State, and California; **C. M. Newton,** Transylvania and Alabama; **John Orr,** Massachusetts and Michigan; **Vadal Peterson,** Utah; **Richard "Digger" Phelps,** Fordham and Notre Dame; **Clarence "Nibs" Price,** California; **Jack Ramsay,** St. Joseph's; **Elmer Ripley,** Georgetown, Yale, Columbia, Notre Dame, Army, and Regis; **Lou Rossini,** Columbia, NYU, and St. Francis; **John "Honey" Russell,** Seton Hall and Manhattan; **Fred Schaus,** West Virginia and Purdue; **Norman Sloan,** Presbyterian, The Citadel, Florida, and North Carolina State; **Jerry Tarkanian,** Long Beach State and Nevada-Las Vegas; **Fred Taylor,** Ohio State; **Bill "Butch" van Breda Kolff,** Lafayette, Hofstra, Princeton, and New Orleans; **Stan Watts,** Bowling Green; **Tex Winter,** Marquette, Kansas State, and Northwestern; **Ned Wulk,** Xavier and Arizona State.

6

The Major Colleges (NCAA Division I)

The following year-by-year records cover the "major colleges" as classified by the National Collegiate Athletic Association. According to the NCAA's Statistics Service, these Division I teams "represent the field of so-called big-time college basketball as judged by the class of competition rather than seasonal records." Some schools listed are no longer in Division I, or have discontinued basketball, but they are included because they are part of modern basketball history.

In keeping with the theme of the "Modern" Encyclopedia, the editors chose the 1937–38 season—which culminated with the first National Invitation Tournament—as the starting point for these annual records.

A variety of circumstances accounts for any omission in a given year. World War II, for example, forced some schools to cancel their schedules. Some records have been destroyed by fire or otherwise lost to the historians. In some cases, schools suspended intercollegiate competition. In a number of instances, records for schools that were at one time college division, junior, or women's colleges, are listed only from the dates when they became four-year or coeducational institutions.

AIR FORCE ACADEMY

Air Force Academy, Colorado

Falcons	W	L	Silver and Blue
1957	11	10	Bob Spear
1958	17	6	Bob Spear
1959	14	9	Bob Spear
1960	12	10	Bob Spear
1961	12	12	Bob Spear
1962	16	7	Bob Spear
1963	10	12	Bob Spear
1964	11	12	Bob Spear
1965	9	14	Bob Spear
1966	14	12	Bob Spear
1967	7	18	Bob Spear
1968	9	15	Bob Spear
1969	11	13	Bob Spear
1970	12	12	Bob Spear
1971	12	14	Bob Spear
1972	12	13	Henry Egan
1973	14	10	Henry Egan
1974	11	13	Henry Egan
1975	13	12	Henry Egan
1976	16	9	Henry Egan
1977	12	15	Henry Egan
1978	15	10	Henry Egan
1979	12	13	Henry Egan

ALABAMA, UNIVERSITY OF

Tuscaloosa, Alabama

Crimson Tide	W	L	Crimson and White
1938	4	13	Henry Crisp
1939	16	5	Henry Crisp
1940	18	6	Henry Crisp
1941	14	8	Henry Crisp
1942	18	6	Henry Crisp
1943	10	10	Paul Burnum
1944	—	—	
1945	10	5	Malcolm Laney
1946	11	5	Henry Crisp
1947	16	6	Floyd Burdette
1948	15	12	Floyd Burdette
1949	13	12	Floyd Burdette
1950	9	12	Floyd Burdette
1951	15	8	Floyd Burdette
1952	13	9	Floyd Burdette
1953	10	9	Johnny Dee
1954	16	8	Johnny Dee
1955	19	5	Johnny Dee
1956	21	3	Johnny Dee
1957	15	11	Dr. Eugene Lambert
1958	17	9	Dr. Eugene Lambert
1959	10	12	Dr. Eugene Lambert
1960	7	17	Dr. Eugene Lambert
1961	7	18	Hayden Riley
1962	11	15	Hayden Riley
1963	14	11	Hayden Riley
1964	14	12	Hayden Riley
1965	17	9	Hayden Riley
1966	16	10	Hayden Riley
1967	13	13	Hayden Riley
1968	10	16	Hayden Riley
1969	4	20	C. M. Newton
1970	8	18	C. M. Newton
1971	10	16	C. M. Newton
1972	18	8	C. M. Newton
1973	22	8	C. M. Newton
1974	22	4	C. M. Newton
1975	22	5	C. M. Newton
1976	23	5	C. M. Newton
1977	25	6	C. M. Newton
1978	17	10	C. M. Newton
1979	22	11	C. M. Newton

ALCORN STATE UNIVERSITY

Lorman, Mississippi

Braves	W	L	Purple and Gold
1945	2	4	H. M. Thompson
1946	—	—	
1947	12	2	L. T. Harris
1948	16	7	L. T. Harris
1949	20	7	Dwight Fisher
1950	22	5	Dwight Fisher
1951	28	3	Dwight Fisher
1952	32	9	Dwight Fisher
1953	34	21	Dwight Fisher
1954	21	22	Dwight Fisher
1955	25	17	Dwight Fisher
1956	8	16	Dwight Fisher
1957	12	12	W. A. Broadus
1958	19	15	W. A. Broadus
1959	18	13	W. A. Broadus
1960	18	13	E. E. Simmons
1961	19	8	E. E. Simmons
1962	25	10	E. E. Simmons
1963	14	12	E. E. Simmons
1964	13	12	E. E. Simmons
1965	13	13	E. E. Simmons
1966	21	8	E. E. Simmons
1967	20	8	Robert Hopkins
1968	24	3	Robert Hopkins
1969	26	1	Robert Hopkins
1970	16	9	Davey Whitney
1971	16	9	Davey Whitney
1972	14	10	Davey Whitney
1973	24	5	Davey Whitney
1974	29	6	Davey Whitney
1975	25	10	Davey Whitney
1976	27	4	Davey Whitney
1977	25	9	Davey Whitney
1978	22	8	Davey Whitney
1979	28	1	Davey Whitney

AMERICAN UNIVERSITY

Washington, D. C.

Eagles	W	L	Red, White, and Blue
1938	8	6	Cassell
1939	10	7	Cassell
1940	10	6	Cassell
1941	8	7	Cassell
1942	9	7	Cassell
1943	7	12	Kalijarvi
1944	6	12	Kalijarvi
1945	15	1	Boyd
1946	16	4	Boyd
1947	15	12	Cassell
1948	17	11	Cassell
1949	17	9	Cassell
1950	22	7	Cassell
1951	18	10	Cassell
1952	18	7	Cassell
1953	15	8	Schulze
1954	12	13	Schulze
1955	8	19	Schulze
1956	11	11	Schulze
1957	10	14	Dave Carrasco
1958	22	6	Dave Carrasco
1959	22	7	Dave Carrasco
1960	23	6	Dave Carrasco
1961	23	6	Dave Carrasco
1962	10	11	Carrasco, J. Williams
1963	10	14	Jim Williams
1964	6	18	Jim Williams
1965	4	19	Jim Williams
1966	8	14	Alan Kyber
1967	16	8	Alan Kyber
1968	14	12	Alan Kyber
1969	4	19	Alan Kyber

Yr.	W	L	Coach
1970	11	12	Tom Young
1971	13	12	Tom Young
1972	16	8	Tom Young
1973	21	5	Tom Young
1974	16	10	Jim Lynam
1975	16	10	Jim Lynam
1976	9	16	Jim Lynam
1977	13	13	Jim Lynam
1978	16	12	Jim Lynam
1979	14	13	Gary Williams

Yr.	W	L	Coach
1951	24	6	Fred Enke
1952	11	16	Fred Enke
1953	13	11	Fred Enke
1954	14	10	Fred Enke
1955	8	17	Fred Enke
1956	11	15	Fred Enke
1957	13	13	Fred Enke
1958	10	16	Fred Enke
1959	4	22	Fred Enke
1960	10	14	Fred Enke
1961	11	15	Fred Enke
1962	12	14	Bruce Larson
1963	13	13	Bruce Larson
1964	15	11	Bruce Larson
1965	17	9	Bruce Larson
1966	15	11	Bruce Larson
1967	8	17	Bruce Larson
1968	11	13	Bruce Larson
1969	17	10	Bruce Larson
1970	12	14	Bruce Larson
1971	10	16	Bruce Larson
1972	6	20	Bruce Larson
1973	16	10	Fred Snowden
1974	19	7	Fred Snowden
1975	22	7	Fred Snowden
1976	24	9	Fred Snowden
1977	21	6	Fred Snowden
1978	15	11	Fred Snowden
1979	16	11	Fred Snowden

APPALACHIAN STATE UNIVERSITY

Boone, North Carolina

Mountaineers			Old Gold and Black
1938	10	6	Flucie Stewart
1939	11	5	Flucie Stewart
1940	19	3	Flucie Stewart
1941	22	3	Clyde Canipe
1942	16	4	Clyde Canipe
1943	13	1	Belus Smawley
1944	0	7	Harold Quincy
1945	6	13	G. P. Eggers
1946	11	7	Francis Hoover
1947	11	2	Flucie Stewart
1948	17	7	Francis Hoover
1949	14	6	Francis Hoover
1950	19	7	Francis Hoover
1951	16	8	Francis Hoover
1952	18	6	Francis Hoover
1953	5	18	Francis Hoover
1954	4	18	Francis Hoover
1955	12	10	Francis Hoover
1956	8	13	Francis Hoover
1957	4	20	Francis Hoover
1958	12	12	Bob Light
1959	15	9	Bob Light
1960	18	8	Bob Light
1961	17	10	Bob Light
1962	11	13	Bob Light
1963	14	12	Bob Light
1964	14	12	Bob Light
1965	14	10	Bob Light
1966	17	10	Bob Light
1967	21	8	Bob Light
1968	14	13	Bob Light
1969	12	15	Bob Light
1970	15	12	Bob Light
1971	8	16	Bob Light
1972	8	18	Bob Light
1973	6	20	Press Maravich
1974	5	21	Press Maravich
1975	3	23	Press Maravich
1976	13	14	Bobby Cremins
1977	17	12	Bobby Cremins
1978	15	13	Bobby Cremins
1979	23	6	Bobby Cremins

ARIZONA, UNIVERSITY OF

Tucson, Arizona

Wildcats			Navy Blue and Cardinal Red
1938	13	8	Fred Enke
1939	12	11	Fred Enke
1940	15	10	Fred Enke
1941	11	7	Fred Enke
1942	9	13	Fred Enke
1943	22	2	Fred Enke
1944	12	2	Fred Enke
1945	7	11	Fred Enke
1946	25	5	Fred Enke
1947	21	3	Fred Enke
1948	19	10	Fred Enke
1949	17	11	Fred Enke
1950	26	5	Fred Enke

ARIZONA STATE UNIVERSITY

Tempe, Arizona

Sun Devils			Maroon and Gold
1938	10	11	Earl Pomeroy
1939	13	13	Earl Pomeroy
1940	9	14	Earl Pomeroy
1941	9	14	Earl Pomeroy
1942	10	6	Rudolph Lavik
1943	9	9	Rudolph Lavik
1944	—	—	
1945	—	—	
1946	12	16	Rudolph Lavik
1947	7	13	Rudolph Lavik
1948	13	11	Rudolph Lavik
1949	12	16	Rudolph Lavik
1950	12	14	Rudolph Lavik
1951	7	17	Bill Kajikawa
1952	8	16	Bill Kajikawa
1953	13	12	Bill Kajikawa
1954	9	21	Bill Kajikawa
1955	10	14	Bill Kajikawa
1956	11	15	Bill Kajikawa
1957	10	15	Bill Kajikawa
1958	13	13	Ned Wulk
1959	17	9	Ned Wulk
1960	18	7	Ned Wulk
1961	23	6	Ned Wulk
1962	23	4	Ned Wulk
1963	26	3	Ned Wulk
1964	16	11	Ned Wulk
1965	13	14	Ned Wulk
1966	12	14	Ned Wulk
1967	5	21	Ned Wulk
1968	11	17	Ned Wulk
1969	11	15	Ned Wulk
1970	4	22	Ned Wulk
1971	16	10	Ned Wulk
1972	18	8	Ned Wulk
1973	19	9	Ned Wulk
1974	18	9	Ned Wulk
1975	25	4	Ned Wulk
1976	17	10	Ned Wulk
1977	15	13	Ned Wulk
1978	13	14	Ned Wulk
1979	16	14	Ned Wulk

Yr.	W	L	Coach

ARKANSAS, UNIVERSITY OF

Fayetteville, Arkansas

Razorbacks			*Cardinal and White*
1938	20	2	Glen Rose
1939	18	5	Glen Rose
1940	12	10	Glen Rose
1941	20	3	Glen Rose
1942	19	4	Glen Rose
1943	19	7	Eugene Lambert
1944	16	7	Eugene Lambert
1945	17	9	Eugene Lambert
1946	16	7	Eugene Lambert
1947	14	10	Eugene Lambert
1948	16	8	Eugene Lambert
1949	15	11	Eugene Lambert
1950	12	12	Presley Askew
1951	13	11	Presley Askew
1952	10	14	Presley Askew
1953	10	11	Glen Rose
1954	13	10	Glen Rose
1955	14	10	Glen Rose
1956	11	13	Glen Rose
1957	11	12	Glen Rose
1958	17	10	Glen Rose
1959	9	14	Glen Rose
1960	12	11	Glen Rose
1961	16	7	Glen Rose
1962	14	10	Glen Rose
1963	13	11	Glen Rose
1964	9	14	Glen Rose
1965	9	14	Glen Rose
1966	13	10	Glen Rose
1967	6	17	P. T. (Duddy) Waller
1968	10	14	P. T. (Duddy) Waller
1969	10	14	P. T. (Duddy) Waller
1970	5	19	P. T. (Duddy) Waller
1971	5	21	Lanny Van Eman
1972	8	18	Lanny Van Eman
1973	16	10	Lanny Van Eman
1974	10	16	Lanny Van Eman
1975	17	9	Eddie Sutton
1976	19	9	Eddie Sutton
1977	26	2	Eddie Sutton
1978	32	4	Eddie Sutton
1979	25	5	Eddie Sutton

ARKANSAS-LITTLE ROCK, UNIVERSITY OF

Little Rock, Arkansas

Trojans			*Cardinal and White*
1938	0	10	Alvin E. Longstreth
1939	1	11	Alvin E. Longstreth
1940	—	—	
1941	—	—	
1942	6	5	—
1943	22	10	—
1944	13	4	—
1945	—	—	—
1946	4	9	Herman Bogan
1947	4	7	George Haynie
1948	11	12	Deno Nichols
1949	7	15	David Sibley
1950	1	20	John Floyd
1951	7	13	Jim Bearden
1952	9	16	John Kincannon
1953	9	15	John Kincannon
1954	12	14	Woody Johnson
1955	10	13	Woody Johnson
1956	3	17	Woody Johnson
1957	—	—	
1958	—	—	
1959	—	—	
1960	—	—	
1961	—	—	

Yr.	W	L	Coach
1962	6	12	Bill Ballard
1963	11	14	Bill Ballard
1964	15	14	Bill Ballard
1965	11	15	Bill Ballard
1966	15	14	Cleve Branscum
1967	8	14	Cleve Branscum
1968	2	23	Happy Mahfouz
1969	6	20	Happy Mahfouz
1970	8	17	Happy Mahfouz
1971	9	14	Happy Mahfouz
1972	16	9	Happy Mahfouz
1973	15	10	Happy Mahfouz
1974	18	6	Happy Mahfouz
1975	15	12	Happy Mahfouz
1976	11	15	Happy Mahfouz
1977	9	17	Happy Mahfouz
1978	9	13	Happy Mahfouz
1979	6	20	Happy Mahfouz

ARKANSAS STATE UNIVERSITY

Jonesboro, Arkansas

Indians			*Scarlet and Black*
1971	15	9	John Rose
1972	13	13	John Rose
1973	9	15	John Rose
1974	17	8	John Rose
1975	13	12	John Rose
1976	10	15	John Rose
1977	15	12	Marvin Adams
1978	9	18	Marvin Adams
1979	15	12	Marvin Adams

ARMY (USMA)

West Point, New York

Cadets			*Black, Gold, and Gray*
1938	12	2	Leo Novak
1939	13	2	Leo Novak
1940	11	4	Valentine Lentz
1941	5	11	Valentine Lentz
1942	10	6	Valentine Lentz
1943	5	10	Valentine Lentz
1944	15	0	Edward A. Kelleher
1945	14	1	Edward A. Kelleher
1946	9	6	Stewart K. Holcomb
1947	9	7	Stewart K. Holcomb
1948	8	9	John W. Mauer
1949	7	10	John W. Mauer
1950	9	8	John W. Mauer
1951	9	8	John W. Mauer
1952	8	9	Elmer Ripley
1953	11	8	Elmer Ripley
1954	15	7	Robert Vanatta
1955	9	9	Orvis Sigler
1956	10	13	Orvis Sigler
1957	7	13	Orvis Sigler
1958	13	12	Orvis Sigler
1959	14	10	George Hunter
1960	14	9	George Hunter
1961	17	7	George Hunter
1962	10	11	George Hunter
1963	8	11	George Hunter
1964	19	7	Taylor (Tates) Locke
1965	21	8	Taylor (Tates) Locke
1966	18	8	Bobby Knight
1967	13	8	Bobby Knight
1968	20	5	Bobby Knight
1969	18	10	Bobby Knight
1970	22	6	Bobby Knight
1971	11	13	Bobby Knight
1972	11	13	Dan Dougherty

Yr.	W	L	Coach
1973	11	13	Dan Dougherty
1974	6	18	Dan Dougherty
1975	3	22	Dan Dougherty
1976	11	14	Mike Krzyzewski
1977	20	8	Mike Krzyzewski
1978	19	9	Mike Krzyzewski
1979	14	11	Mike Krzyzewski

AUBURN UNIVERSITY

Auburn, Alabama

Tigers			Orange and Blue
1938	14	5	Ralph Jordan
1939	14	5	Ralph Jordan
1940	7	9	Ralph Jordan
1941	13	6	Ralph Jordan
1942	11	6	Ralph Jordan
1943	1	14	Robert K. Evans
1944	—	—	
1945	3	14	Robert K. Evans
1946	7	9	Ralph Jordan
1947	3	18	V. J. Edney
1948	12	10	Daniel Doyle
1949	9	15	Daniel Doyle
1950	17	7	Joel Eaves
1951	12	10	Joel Eaves
1952	14	12	Joel Eaves
1953	13	8	Joel Eaves
1954	16	8	Joel Eaves
1955	11	9	Joel Eaves
1956	11	10	Joel Eaves
1957	13	8	Joel Eaves
1958	16	6	Joel Eaves
1959	20	2	Joel Eaves
1960	19	3	Joel Eaves
1961	15	7	Joel Eaves
1962	18	6	Joel Eaves
1963	18	4	Joel Eaves
1964	11	12	Joel Eaves
1965	16	9	Joel Eaves
1966	16	10	Bill Lynn
1967	17	8	Bill Lynn
1968	13	13	Bill Lynn
1969	15	10	Bill Lynn
1970	15	11	Bill Lynn
1971	11	15	Bill Lynn
1972	10	16	Bill Lynn
1973	6	20	Bill Lynn
1974	10	16	Bob Davis
1975	18	8	Bob Davis
1976	16	10	Bob Davis
1977	13	13	Bob Davis
1978	13	14	Paul Lambert
1979	13	16	Sonny Smith

AUSTIN PEAY STATE UNIVERSITY

Clarksville, Tennessee

Governors			Scarlet and White
1938	11	6	Fred Brown
1939	11	7	Fred Brown
1940	19	0	Fred Brown
1941	17	5	Fred Brown
1942	9	10	Fred Brown
1943	1	6	Fred Brown
1944	—	—	
1945	—	—	
1946	2	19	Bee Lowe
1947	23	5	David Aaron
1948	16	9	David Aaron
1949	17	3	David Aaron

Yr.	W	L	Coach
1950	14	11	David Aaron
1951	13	12	David Aaron
1952	11	17	David Aaron
1953	14	12	David Aaron
1954	14	13	David Aaron
1955	7	17	David Aaron
1956	16	11	David Aaron
1957	24	9	David Aaron
1958	17	9	David Aaron
1959	14	10	David Aaron
1960	22	5	David Aaron
1961	22	9	David Aaron
1962	14	12	David Aaron
1963	18	11	George Fisher
1964	14	9	George Fisher
1965	4	17	George Fisher
1966	7	14	George Fisher
1967	14	9	George Fisher
1968	8	16	George Fisher
1969	10	14	George Fisher
1970	5	21	George Fisher
1971	10	14	George Fisher
1972	10	14	Lake Kelly
1973	22	7	Lake Kelly
1974	17	10	Lake Kelly
1975	17	10	Lake Kelly
1976	20	7	Lake Kelly
1977	24	4	Lake Kelly
1978	15	12	Ed Thompson
1979	8	18	Ed Thompson

BALL STATE UNIVERSITY

Muncie, Indiana

Cardinals			Cardinal and White
1939	10	10	Pete Phillips
1940	12	6	Pete Phillips
1941	8	9	Pete Phillips
1942	7	11	Pete Phillips
1943	7	10	Pete Phillips
1944	—	—	
1945	10	3	Pete Phillips
1946	7	9	Pete Phillips
1947	9	8	Pete Phillips
1948	12	5	Pete Phillips
1949	12	6	Dick Stealy
1950	9	9	Dick Stealy
1951	8	12	Dick Stealy
1952	7	15	Dick Stealy
1953	11	11	Robert Primmer
1954	9	12	Robert Primmer
1955	8	12	Jim Hinga
1956	10	14	Jim Hinga
1957	19	8	Jim Hinga
1958	13	11	Jim Hinga
1959	7	15	Jim Hinga
1960	5	17	Jim Hinga
1961	12	11	Jim Hinga
1962	12	10	Jim Hinga
1963	15	9	Jim Hinga
1964	17	8	Jim Hinga
1965	9	13	Jim Hinga
1966	10	15	Jim Hinga
1967	7	14	Jim Hinga
1968	10	12	Jim Hinga
1969	7	16	Bud Getchell
1970	8	16	Bud Getchell
1971	6	20	Bud Getchell
1972	9	15	Bud Getchell
1973	9	15	Jim Holstein
1974	14	12	Jim Holstein
1975	10	15	Jim Holstein
1976	11	14	Jim Holstein
1977	11	14	Jim Holstein
1978	10	15	Steve Yoder
1979	16	11	Steve Yoder

BALTIMORE, UNIVERSITY OF

Baltimore, Maryland

Super Bees			Maroon and Gold
1972	15	13	Frank Szymanski
1973	14	14	Frank Szymanski
1974	18	9	Frank Szymanski
1975	19	11	Frank Szymanski
1976	20	10	Frank Szymanski
1977	24	4	Frank Szymanski
1978	11	16	Frank Szymanski
1979	4	21	Frank Szymanski

BAPTIST COLLEGE

Charleston, South Carolina

Buccaneers			Indigo and Gold
1966	13	7	Howard Bagwell
1967	14	9	Howard Bagwell
1968	11	11	Mel Gibson
1969	15	19	Mel Gibson
1970	18	7	Mel Gibson
1971	13	10	Mel Gibson
1972	10	14	Al Ferner
1973	16	14	Al Ferner
1974	5	22	Billy Henry
1975	4	16	Billy Henry
1976	2	24	Danny Monk
1977	8	19	Danny Monk
1978	8	19	Danny Monk
1979	2	24	David Reese

BAYLOR UNIVERSITY

Waco, Texas

Bears			Green and Gold
1938	8	8	Ralph Wolf
1939	14	7	Ralph Wolf
1940	12	9	Ralph Wolf
1941	10	12	Ralph Wolf
1942	11	9	R. E. "Bill" Henderson
1943	6	14	R. E. "Bill" Henderson
1944	6	12	M. T. "Van" Sweet
1945	0	14	Sweet and Henderson
1946	24	5	R. E. "Bill" Henderson
1947	11	11	R. E. "Bill" Henderson
1948	24	8	R. E. "Bill" Henderson
1949	14	10	R. E. "Bill" Henderson
1950	14	13	R. E. "Bill" Henderson
1951	8	16	R. E. "Bill" Henderson
1952	6	18	R. E. "Bill" Henderson
1953	10	11	R. E. "Bill" Henderson
1954	12	11	R. E. "Bill" Henderson
1955	13	11	R. E. "Bill" Henderson
1956	6	17	R. E. "Bill" Henderson
1957	9	15	R. E. "Bill" Henderson
1958	5	19	R. E. "Bill" Henderson
1959	11	13	R. E. "Bill" Henderson
1960	12	12	R. E. "Bill" Henderson
1961	4	20	R. E. "Bill" Henderson
1962	4	20	Bill Menefee
1963	7	17	Bill Menefee
1964	7	17	Bill Menefee
1965	15	9	Bill Menefee
1966	8	16	Bill Menefee
1967	14	10	Bill Menefee
1968	15	9	Bill Menefee
1969	18	6	Bill Menefee
1970	15	9	Bill Menefee
1971	18	8	Bill Menefee
1972	14	12	Bill Menefee
1973	14	11	Bill Menefee
1974	12	13	Carroll Dawson
1975	10	16	Carroll Dawson
1976	12	15	Carroll Dawson
1977	11	17	C. Dawson, J. Haller
1978	14	13	Jim Haller
1979	16	12	Jim Haller

BOISE STATE UNIVERSITY

Boise, Idaho

Broncos			Orange and Blue
1972	14	12	Murray Satterfield
1973	10	15	M. Satterfield, B. Connor
1974	12	14	Bus Connor
1975	13	13	Bus Connor
1976	18	11	Bus Connor
1977	10	16	Bus Connor
1978	13	14	Bus Connor
1979	11	15	Bus Connor

· BOSTON COLLEGE

Chestnut Hill, Massachusetts

Eagles			Maroon and Gold
1946	3	11	Albert McClellan
1947	11	11	Albert McClellan
1948	13	10	Albert McClellan
1949	9	9	Albert McClellan
1950	11	9	Albert McClellan
1951	17	11	Albert McClellan
1952	22	5	Albert McClellan
1953	7	15	Albert McClellan
1954	11	11	Donald Martin
1955	8	18	Donald Martin
1956	6	17	Donald Martin
1957	13	12	Donald Martin
1958	15	6	Donald Martin
1959	17	9	Donald Martin
1960	11	14	Donald Martin
1961	14	9	Donald Martin
1962	15	7	Donald Martin
1963	10	16	Frank Power
1964	10	11	Bob Cousy
1965	21	7	Bob Cousy
1966	21	5	Bob Cousy
1967	21	3	Bob Cousy
1968	17	8	Bob Cousy
1969	24	4	Bob Cousy
1970	11	13	Chuck Daly
1971	15	11	Chuck Daly
1972	13	13	Bob Zuffelato
1973	11	14	Bob Zuffelato
1974	21	9	Bob Zuffelato
1975	21	9	Bob Zuffelato
1976	9	17	Bob Zuffelato
1977	8	18	Bob Zuffelato
1978	15	11	Tom Davis
1979	21	9	Tom Davis

BOSTON UNIVERSITY

Boston, Massachusetts

Terriers			Scarlet and White
1938	10	6	Merrel Collard
1939	10	4	Merrel Collard
1940	6	6	Merrel Collard
1941	13	3	Merrel Collard

Yr.	W	L	Coach	Yr.	W	L	Coach
1942	8	4	Merrel Collard	1972	4	20	Pat Haley
1943	3	10	Merrel Collard	1973	13	13	Pat Haley
1944	4	5	Russell Peterson	1974	15	11	Pat Haley
1945	—	—		1975	18	10	Pat Haley
1946	11	2	Russell Peterson	1976	12	15	Pat Haley
1947	14	7	Russell Peterson	1977	9	18	John Weinert
1948	10	9	Russell Peterson	1978	12	15	John Weinert
1949	6	12	Charles Cummings	1979	14	13	John Weinert
1950	7	9	Vincent Cronin				
1951	7	11	Vincent Cronin				
1952	9	8	Vincent Cronin				
1953	10	10	Matthew Zunic				
1954	9	11	Matthew Zunic				
1955	13	9	Matthew Zunic				
1956	17	6	Matthew Zunic				
1957	13	10	Matthew Zunic				
1958	15	5	Matthew Zunic				
1959	20	7	Matthew Zunic				
1960	14	10	John Burke				
1961	9	14	John Burke				
1962	5	15	John Burke				
1963	10	9	John Burke				
1964	16	7	John Burke				
1965	10	10	John Burke				
1966	4	19	John Burke				
1967	4	18	Charles Luce				
1968	10	14	Charles Luce				
1969	14	10	Charles Luce				
1970	14	10	Charles Luce				
1971	7	18	Charles Luce				
1972	7	16	Ron Mitchell				
1973	15	10	Ron Mitchell				
1974	9	16	Ron Mitchell				
1975	12	13	Roy Sigler				
1976	7	19	Roy Sigler				
1977	7	19	Roy Sigler				
1978	10	15	Roy Sigler				
1979	17	9	Rick Pitino				

BRADLEY UNIVERSITY

Peoria, Illinois

Braves			*Red and White*
1938	18	2	Alfred Robertson
1939	19	3	Alfred Robertson
1940	14	6	Alfred Robertson
1941	16	4	Alfred Robertson
1942	15	5	Alfred Robertson
1943	8	11	Alfred Robertson
1944	—	—	
1945	—	—	
1946	11	12	Alfred Robertson
1947	25	7	Alfred Robertson
1948	28	3	Alfred Robertson
1949	27	8	Forrest Anderson
1950	32	5	Forrest Anderson
1951	32	6	Forrest Anderson
1952	17	12	Forrest Anderson
1953	15	12	Forrest Anderson
1954	19	13	Forrest Anderson
1955	9	20	Bob Vanatta
1956	13	13	Bob Vanatta
1957	22	7	Chuck Orsborn
1958	20	7	Chuck Orsborn
1959	25	4	Chuck Orsborn
1960	27	2	Chuck Orsborn
1961	21	5	Chuck Orsborn
1962	21	7	Chuck Orsborn
1963	17	9	Chuck Orsborn
1964	23	6	Chuck Orsborn
1965	18	9	Chuck Orsborn
1966	20	6	Joe Stowell
1967	17	9	Joe Stowell
1968	19	9	Joe Stowell
1969	14	12	Joe Stowell
1970	14	12	Joe Stowell
1971	13	12	Joe Stowell
1972	17	9	Joe Stowell
1973	12	14	Joe Stowell
1974	20	8	Joe Stowell
1975	15	11	Joe Stowell
1976	13	13	Joe Stowell
1977	9	18	Joe Stowell
1978	14	14	Joe Stowell
1979	9	17	Dick Versace

BOWLING GREEN STATE UNIVERSITY

Bowling Green, Ohio

Falcons			*Burnt Orange and Seal Brown*
1938	16	4	Paul Landis
1939	12	7	Paul Landis
1940	16	5	Paul Landis
1941	10	12	Paul Landis
1942	8	12	Paul Landis
1943	18	5	Harold Anderson
1944	22	4	Harold Anderson
1945	24	4	Harold Anderson
1946	27	5	Harold Anderson
1947	28	7	Harold Anderson
1948	27	6	Harold Anderson
1949	24	7	Harold Anderson
1950	19	11	Harold Anderson
1951	15	12	Anderson, G. Muellich
1952	17	10	Harold Anderson
1953	12	15	Harold Anderson
1954	17	7	Harold Anderson
1955	6	16	Harold Anderson
1956	4	19	Harold Anderson
1957	14	9	Harold Anderson
1958	15	8	Harold Anderson
1959	18	8	Harold Anderson
1960	10	14	Harold Anderson
1961	10	14	Harold Anderson
1962	21	4	Harold Anderson
1963	19	8	Harold Anderson
1964	14	9	Harold Anderson
1965	9	15	Harold Anderson
1966	9	15	Warren Scholler
1967	11	13	Warren Scholler
1968	18	7	Bill Fitch
1969	9	15	Bob Conibear
1970	15	9	Bob Conibear
1971	7	18	Bob Conibear

BRIGHAM YOUNG UNIVERSITY

Provo, Utah

Cougars			*Royal Blue and White*
1938	8	13	Fred Dixon
1939	12	11	Fred Dixon
1940	15	8	Floyd Millett
1941	12	9	Floyd Millett
1942	17	3	Floyd Millett
1943	15	7	Floyd Millett
1944	3	2	Floyd Millett
1945	11	7	Floyd Millett
1946	13	12	Floyd Millett
1947	9	13	Floyd Millett
1948	16	10	Floyd Millett
1949	22	14	Floyd Millett
1950	22	12	Stan Watts

Yr.	W	L	Coach
1951	26	10	Stan Watts
1952	14	10	Stan Watts
1953	22	8	Stan Watts
1954	18	11	Stan Watts
1955	13	13	Stan Watts
1956	18	8	Stan Watts
1957	19	9	Stan Watts
1958	13	13	Stan Watts
1959	15	11	Stan Watts
1960	8	17	Stan Watts
1961	15	11	Stan Watts
1962	10	16	Stan Watts
1963	12	14	Stan Watts
1964	13	12	Stan Watts
1965	21	7	Stan Watts
1966	20	5	Stan Watts
1967	14	10	Stan Watts
1968	13	12	Stan Watts
1969	17	11	Stan Watts
1970	8	18	Stan Watts
1971	18	11	Stan Watts
1972	21	5	Stan Watts
1973	19	7	Glenn Potter
1974	10	16	Glenn Potter
1975	12	14	Glenn Potter
1976	12	14	Frank Arnold
1977	12	15	Frank Arnold
1978	12	18	Frank Arnold
1979	20	7	Frank Arnold

BROWN UNIVERSITY

Providence, Rhode Island

Yr.	W	L	Coach
Bruins			*Seal Brown and White*
1938	8	11	Arthur Kahler
1939	17	4	George Allen
1940	14	6	George Allen
1941	11	10	George Allen
1942	11	7	William "Tippy" Dye
1943	9	11	Charles "Rip" Engle
1944	10	14	Charles "Rip" Engle
1945	15	4	Charles "Rip" Engle
1946	5	15	Charles "Rip" Engle
1947	8	12	Wilbur "Weeb" Ewbank
1948	6	14	Robert Morris
1949	13	8	Robert Morris
1950	11	14	Robert Morris
1951	8	11	Robert Morris
1952	5	15	Robert Morris
1953	5	14	Robert Morris
1954	13	12	Robert Morris
1955	7	18	L. Stanley Ward
1956	7	18	L. Stanley Ward
1957	8	16	L. Stanley Ward
1958	11	14	L. Stanley Ward
1959	11	13	L. Stanley Ward
1960	13	12	L. Stanley Ward
1961	11	14	L. Stanley Ward
1962	11	14	L. Stanley Ward
1963	11	13	L. Stanley Ward
1964	6	19	L. Stanley Ward
1965	7	17	L. Stanley Ward
1966	9	17	L. Stanley Ward
1967	10	16	L. Stanley Ward
1968	9	16	L. Stanley Ward
1969	3	26	L. Stanley Ward
1970	6	20	J. Gerald Alaimo
1971	10	15	J. Gerald Alaimo
1972	10	16	J. Gerald Alaimo
1973	14	12	J. Gerald Alaimo
1974	17	9	J. Gerald Alaimo
1975	14	12	J. Gerald Alaimo
1976	7	19	J. Gerald Alaimo
1977	6	20	J. Gerald Alaimo
1978	4	22	J. Gerald Alaimo
1979	8	18	Joe Mullaney

BUCKNELL UNIVERSITY

Lewisburg, Pennsylvania

Yr.	W	L	Coach
Bisons			*Orange and Blue*
1938	7	6	Malcolm Musser
1939	8	8	Malcolm Musser
1940	13	7	Malcolm Musser
1941	10	7	Malcolm Musser
1942	9	9	Malcolm Musser
1943	5	8	John Sitarski
1944	9	3	J. Lewood Ludwig
1945	10	7	J. Lewood Ludwig
1946	6	11	J. Lewood Ludwig
1947	11	8	J. Lewood Ludwig
1948	5	17	Jack Guy
1949	2	18	Jack Guy
1950	5	16	Jack Guy
1951	9	13	Jack Guy
1952	8	16	Jack Guy
1953	3	16	Benton Kribbs
1954	4	16	Benton Kribbs
1955	3	18	Benton Kribbs
1956	10	14	Benton Kribbs
1957	16	8	Benton Kribbs
1958	16	8	Benton Kribbs
1959	16	7	Benton Kribbs
1960	10	11	Benton Kribbs
1961	12	11	Benton Kribbs
1962	7	15	Benton Kribbs
1963	7	15	Gene Evans
1964	8	13	Gene Evans
1965	11	13	Gene Evans
1966	15	10	Don Smith
1967	11	11	Don Smith
1968	12	11	Don Smith
1969	13	11	Don Smith
1970	6	17	Don Smith
1971	9	14	Don Smith
1972	5	18	Don Smith
1973	11	14	Jim Valvano
1974	8	16	Jim Valvano
1975	14	12	Jim Valvano
1976	13	13	Charlie Woollum
1977	10	15	Charlie Woollum
1978	13	15	Charlie Woollum
1979	18	9	Charlie Woollum

BUTLER UNIVERSITY

Indianapolis, Indiana

Yr.	W	L	Coach
Bulldogs			*Royal Blue and White*
1938	11	12	Tony Hinkle
1939	14	6	Tony Hinkle
1940	17	6	Tony Hinkle
1941	13	9	Tony Hinkle
1942	13	9	Tony Hinkle
1943	4	9	Frank "Pop" Hedden
1944	—	—	
1945	14	6	Frank "Pop" Hedden
1946	12	8	Tony Hinkle
1947	16	7	Tony Hinkle
1948	14	7	Tony Hinkle
1949	18	5	Tony Hinkle
1950	12	12	Tony Hinkle
1951	5	19	Tony Hinkle
1952	12	12	Tony Hinkle
1953	14	9	Tony Hinkle
1954	13	12	Tony Hinkle
1955	10	14	Tony Hinkle
1956	14	9	Tony Hinkle
1957	11	14	Tony Hinkle
1958	15	10	Tony Hinkle
1959	19	9	Tony Hinkle
1960	15	11	Tony Hinkle
1961	15	11	Tony Hinkle
1962	22	6	Tony Hinkle

Yr.	W	L	Coach	Yr.	W	L	Coach
1963	16	10	Tony Hinkle	1971	16	10	Tim Tift
1964	13	13	Tony Hinkle	1972	16	12	Tim Tift
1965	11	15	Tony Hinkle	1973	15	13	Tim Tift
1966	16	10	Tony Hinkle	1974	14	12	Tim Tift
1967	10	17	Tony Hinkle	1975	17	11	Tim Tift
1968	11	14	Tony Hinkle	1976	14	12	Tim Tift
1969	11	15	Tony Hinkle	1977	10	17	Tim Tift
1970	15	11	Tony Hinkle	1978	8	17	Tim Tift
1971	10	16	George Theofanis	1979	7	19	Tim Tift
1972	6	20	George Theofanis				
1973	14	12	George Theofanis				
1974	14	12	George Theofanis				
1975	10	16	George Theofanis				
1976	12	15	George Theofanis				
1977	13	14	George Theofanis				
1978	15	11	Joe Sexson				
1979	11	16	Joe Sexson				

CALIFORNIA-LOS ANGELES UNIVERSITY OF (UCLA)

Los Angeles, California

Bruins			Navy Blue and Gold
1938	4	20	Caddy Works
1939	7	20	Caddy Works
1940	8	17	Wilbur Johns
1941	6	20	Wilbur Johns
1942	5	18	Wilbur Johns
1943	14	7	Wilbur Johns
1944	10	10	Wilbur Johns
1945	11	12	Wilbur Johns
1946	8	16	Wilbur Johns
1947	18	7	Wilbur Johns
1948	12	13	Wilbur Johns
1949	22	7	John R. Wooden
1950	24	7	John R. Wooden
1951	19	10	John R. Wooden
1952	19	12	John R. Wooden
1953	16	8	John R. Wooden
1954	18	7	John R. Wooden
1955	21	5	John R. Wooden
1956	22	6	John R. Wooden
1957	22	4	John R. Wooden
1958	16	10	John R. Wooden
1959	16	9	John R. Wooden
1960	14	12	John R. Wooden
1961	18	8	John R. Wooden
1962	18	11	John R. Wooden
1963	20	9	John R. Wooden
1964	30	0	John R. Wooden
1965	28	2	John R. Wooden
1966	18	8	John R. Wooden
1967	30	0	John R. Wooden
1968	29	1	John R. Wooden
1969	29	1	John R. Wooden
1970	28	2	John R. Wooden
1971	29	1	John R. Wooden
1972	30	0	John R. Wooden
1973	30	0	John R. Wooden
1974	26	4	John R. Wooden
1975	28	3	John R. Wooden
1976	28	4	Gene Bartow
1977	24	5	Gene Bartow
1978	25	3	Gary Cunningham
1979	25	5	Gary Cunningham

CALIFORNIA, UNIVERSITY OF

Berkeley, California

Golden Bears			Blue and Gold
1938	18	11	Nibs Price
1939	24	8	Nibs Price
1940	15	17	Nibs Price
1941	15	12	Nibs Price
1942	11	19	Nibs Price
1943	9	15	Nibs Price
1944	7	3	Nibs Price
1945	7	8	Nibs Price
1946	30	6	Nibs Price
1947	20	11	Nibs Price
1948	25	9	Nibs Price
1949	14	19	Nibs Price
1950	10	17	Nibs Price
1951	16	16	Nibs Price
1952	17	13	Nibs Price
1953	16	10	Nibs Price
1954	18	9	Nibs Price
1955	9	16	Pete Newell
1956	17	8	Pete Newell
1957	21	5	Pete Newell
1958	19	9	Pete Newell
1959	24	4	Pete Newell
1960	28	2	Pete Newell
1961	13	9	Rene Herrerias
1962	8	17	Rene Herrerias
1963	13	11	Rene Herrerias
1964	11	13	Rene Herrerias
1965	8	15	Rene Herrerias
1966	9	16	Rene Herrerias
1967	15	10	Rene Herrerias
1968	15	9	Rene Herrerias
1969	12	13	Jim Padgett
1970	11	15	Jim Padgett
1971	16	9	Jim Padgett
1972	13	16	Jim Padgett
1973	11	15	Dick Edwards
1974	9	17	Dick Edwards
1975	17	9	Dick Edwards
1976	13	13	Dick Edwards
1977	12	15	Dick Edwards
1978	11	16	Dick Edwards
1979	6	21	Dick Kuchen

CALIFORNIA-SANTA BARBARA, UNIVERSITY OF

Santa Barbara, California

Gauchos			Blue and Gold
1938	7	15	Wilton
1939	10	15	Wilton
1940	21	9	Wilton
1941	23	10	Wilton
1942	10	10	Wilton
1943	10	6	Wilton
1944	—	—	
1945	—	—	
1946	—	—	
1947	20	11	Wilton

CALIFORNIA-IRVINE, UNIVERSITY OF

Irvine, California

Anteaters			Blue and Gold
1966	15	11	Danny Rodgers
1967	15	11	Danny Rodgers
1968	19	7	Dick Davis
1969	18	8	Dick Davis
1970	17	9	Tim Tift

Yr.	W	L	Coach	Yr.	W	L	Coach
1948	17	8	Wilton	1940	8	9	James Wilson
1949	11	9	Wilton	1941	11	9	Allie Seelbach
1950	14	14	Wilton	1942	11	7	Allie Seelbach
1951	14	14	Wilton	1943	11	9	Allie Seelbach
1952	7	20	Findlay	1944	15	6	Allie Seelbach
1953	6	16	Wilton	1945	13	11	Arthur Powell
1954	16	10	Wilton	1946	8	11	Arthur Powell
1955	18	7	Wilton	1947	18	13	Earl Brown
1956	19	7	Wilton	1948	10	15	Brown, J. Niland
1957	7	17	Wilton	1949	16	12	Joseph Niland
1958	13	12	Gallon	1950	17	8	Joseph Niland
1959	4	19	Gallon	1951	15	10	Joseph Niland
1960	17	7	Gallon	1952	15	9	Joseph Niland
1961	20	8	Gallon	1953	9	14	Joseph Niland
1962	12	12	Gallon	1954	9	14	Joseph Curran
1963	16	9	Gallon	1955	18	7	Joseph Curran
1964	18	11	Gallon	1956	19	7	Joseph Curran
1965	12	14	Gallon	1957	22	6	Joseph Curran
1966	10	16	Gallon	1958	2	19	Joseph Curran
1967	10	16	Ralph Barkey	1959	7	16	Curran, R. MacKinnon
1968	9	17	Ralph Barkey	1960	10	13	Robert MacKinnon
1969	17	9	Ralph Barkey	1961	13	10	Robert MacKinnon
1970	12	14	Ralph Barkey	1962	12	9	Robert MacKinnon
1971	20	6	Ralph Barkey	1963	19	7	Robert MacKinnon
1972	17	9	Ralph Barkey	1964	10	14	Robert MacKinnon
1973	17	9	Ralph Barkey	1965	10	12	Robert MacKinnon
1974	16	10	Ralph Barkey	1966	7	15	Robert MacKinnon
1975	18	8	Ralph Barkey	1967	15	10	Robert MacKinnon
1976	17	9	Ralph Barkey	1968	7	17	Robert MacKinnon
1977	8	18	Ralph Barkey	1969	7	16	Robert MacKinnon
1978	8	19	Ralph Barkey	1970	9	13	Robert MacKinnon
1979	12	15	Ed DeLacy	1971	8	13	Robert MacKinnon
				1972	15	11	Robert MacKinnon
				1973	13	11	John Morrison
				1974	14	12	John Morrison
				1975	15	10	John McCarthy
				1976	10	17	John McCarthy
				1977	3	22	John McCarthy
				1978	7	19	Nick Macarchuk
				1979	12	16	Nick Macarchuk

CALIFORNIA STATE-FULLERTON

Fullerton, California

Titans			Blue, Orange, and White
1961	24	6	Alex Omalev
1962	22	7	Alex Omalev
1963	17	6	Alex Omalev
1964	9	16	Alex Omalev
1965	1	25	Alex Omalev
1966	13	10	Alex Omalev
1967	6	19	Alex Omalev
1968	7	18	Alex Omalev
1969	12	13	Alex Omalev
1970	7	17	Alex Omalev
1971	13	13	Alex Omalev
1972	9	17	Alex Omalev
1973	9	17	Moe Radovich
1974	16	10	Bob Dye
1975	13	11	Bob Dye
1976	15	10	Bob Dye
1977	16	10	Bob Dye
1978	23	9	Bob Dye
1979	16	11	Bob Dye

CAMPBELL COLLEGE

Buies Creek, North Carolina

Fighting Camels			Orange and Black
1977	23	10	Danny L. Roberts
1978	9	15	Danny L. Roberts
1979	10	16	Danny L. Roberts

CANISIUS COLLEGE

Buffalo, New York

Griffins			Blue and Gold
1938	8	9	Allie Seelbach
1939	1	13	Allie Seelbach

CATHOLIC UNIVERSITY

Washington, D.C.

Cardinals				Cardinal Red and Black
1938	4	14		Forrest Cotton
1939	3	13		Forrest Cotton
1940	2	14	1 Tie	Forrest Cotton
1941	0	12		Forrest Cotton
1942	10	11		Gus Pirro
1943	8	9		James Hughes
1944	17	7		John Long
1945	—	—		
1946	4	13		Ben Zola
1947	6	18		Ben Zola
1948	8	10		Gene Augustefer
1949	15	5		Abe Rosenfield
1950	7	11		Abe Rosenfield
1951	7	12		Abe Rosenfield
1952	4	15		Abe Rosenfield
1953	4	15		Gene Szklarz
1954	4	18		James Reilly
1955	6	14		James Reilly
1956	11	9		James Reilly
1957	11	8		James Reilly
1958	12	6		James Reilly
1959	15	6		Tom Young
1960	13	11		Tom Young
1961	16	7		Tom Young
1962	16	8		Tom Young
1963	16	11		Tom Young
1964	14	12		Tom Young
1965	14	8		Tom Young
1966	14	13		Tom Young
1967	13	11		Tom Young
1968	12	14		Bill Gardner
1969	10	15		Bill Gardner

Yr.	W	L	Coach
1970	6	18	Bob Reese
1971	16	11	Bob Reese
1972	13	13	Dick Myers
1973	6	20	Dick Myers
1974	4	21	Dick Myers
1975	8	18	Dick Myers
1976	12	14	Jack Kvancz
1977	13	13	Jack Kvancz
1978	12	14	Jack Kvancz
1979	6	20	Jack Kvancz

CENTENARY COLLEGE

Shreveport, Louisiana

Yr.	Gentlemen (W)	L	Cardinal and White (Coach)
1938	13	1	Curtis Parker
1939	10	13	Curtis Parker
1940	15	19	Elmer Smith
1941	8	21	Elmer Smith
1942	1	3	Elmer Smith
1943	—	—	
1944	—	—	
1945	—	—	
1946	2	12	Clayton Cornish
1947	16	7	Jack Clayton
1948	11	21	A. B. Young
1949	21	15	A. B. Young
1950	14	12	F. H. "Buss" Delaney
1951	16	13	F. H. "Buss" Delaney
1952	17	17	F. H. "Buss" Delaney
1953	21	10	F. H. "Buss" Delaney
1954	13	12	F. H. "Buss" Delaney
1955	14	12	F. H. "Buss" Delaney
1956	20	7	Harold Mooty
1957	16	9	Harold Mooty
1958	14	12	Harold Mooty
1959	14	14	Orvis Sigler
1960	12	12	Orvis Sigler
1961	14	12	Orvis Sigler
1962	17	9	Orvis Sigler
1963	12	14	Orvis Sigler
1964	16	8	Orvis Sigler
1965	13	11	Orvis Sigler
1966	12	14	Orvis Sigler
1967	9	17	Orvis Sigler
1968	3	23	Orvis Sigler
1969	9	18	Joe Swank
1970	8	16	Joe Swank
1971	13	13	Joe Swank
1972	13	12	Larry Little
1973	19	8	Larry Little
1974	21	4	Larry Little
1975	25	4	Larry Little
1976	22	5	Larry Little
1977	11	19	Riley Wallace
1978	10	17	R. Wallace, T. Canterbury
1979	9	20	Tom Canterbury

CENTRAL MICHIGAN UNIVERSITY

Mount Pleasant, Michigan

Yr.	Chippewas (W)	L	Maroon and Gold (Coach)
1938	10	6	Rose
1939	14	5	Rose
1940	12	4	Rose
1941	14	3	Rose
1942	10	9	Rose
1943	9	2	Rose
1944	10	6	Finch
1945	11	5	Sweeney
1946	12	6	Sweeney
1947	17	6	Rose
1948	17	3	Rose
1949	15	1	Rose

Yr.	W	L	Coach
1950	11	5	Rose
1951	8	12	Rose
1952	12	10	Rose
1953	10	12	Rose
1954	13	8	Rose
1955	11	10	Kelly
1956	12	11	Kelly
1957	14	11	Kjolhede
1958	11	13	Kjolhede
1959	9	15	Kjolhede
1960	12	14	Kjolhede
1961	3	19	Kjolhede
1962	8	14	Kjolhede
1963	11	11	Kjolhede
1964	18	6	Kjolhede
1965	19	7	Kjolhede
1966	23	6	Kjolhede
1967	23	3	Kjolhede
1968	14	12	Kjolhede
1969	11	12	Kjolhede
1970	22	5	Kjolhede
1971	18	9	Kjolhede
1972	15	11	Dick Parfitt
1973	13	13	Dick Parfitt
1974	14	12	Dick Parfitt
1975	22	6	Dick Parfitt
1976	12	14	Dick Parfitt
1977	18	10	Dick Parfitt
1978	16	10	Dick Parfitt
1979	19	9	Dick Parfitt

CINCINNATI, UNIVERSITY OF

Cincinnati, Ohio

Yr.	Bearcats (W)	L	Red and Black (Coach)
1938	6	11	Walter Van Winkle
1939	12	15	Walter Van Winkle
1940	8	9	Clark Ballard
1941	6	12	Clark Ballard
1942	10	10	Clark Ballard
1943	9	10	Robert Reuss
1944	6	5	Robert Reuss
1945	8	9	Ray Farnham
1946	8	13	Ray Farnham
1947	17	9	John Wiethe
1948	17	7	John Wiethe
1949	23	5	John Wiethe
1950	20	6	John Wiethe
1951	18	4	John Wiethe
1952	11	16	John Wiethe
1953	11	13	George Smith
1954	11	10	George Smith
1955	21	8	George Smith
1956	17	7	George Smith
1957	15	9	George Smith
1958	25	3	George Smith
1959	26	4	George Smith
1960	28	2	George Smith
1961	27	3	Ed Jucker
1962	29	2	Ed Jucker
1963	26	2	Ed Jucker
1964	17	9	Ed Jucker
1965	14	12	Ed Jucker
1966	21	7	Tay Baker
1967	17	9	Tay Baker
1968	18	8	Tay Baker
1969	17	9	Tay Baker
1970	21	6	Tay Baker
1971	14	12	Tay Baker
1972	17	9	Tay Baker
1973	17	9	Gale Catlett
1974	19	8	Gale Catlett
1975	23	6	Gale Catlett
1976	25	6	Gale Catlett
1977	25	5	Gale Catlett
1978	17	10	Gale Catlett
1979	13	14	Ed Badger

CITADEL, THE

Charleston, South Carolina

	Bulldogs		Blue and White
1938	13	4	A. W. Norman
1939	13	6	A. W. Norman
1940	8	8	A. W. Norman
1941	5	13	Benjamin Parker
1942	2	14	Benjamin Parker
1943	9	4	E. H. Sherman
1944	4	3	Benjamin Clemons
1945	16	7	Ernest Wehman
1946	7	12	Eugene Clark
1947	5	11	H. W. Piro
1948	8	9	Bernard S. O'Neil
1949	1	17	Bernard S. O'Neil
1950	4	16	Bernard S. O'Neil
1951	6	11	Bernard S. O'Neil
1952	8	20	Bernard S. O'Neil
1953	4	14	Leo A. Zack
1954	1	18	Leo A. Zack
1955	1	22	Leo A. Zack
1956	2	19	Henry Witt
1957	11	14	Norman Sloan
1958	16	11	Norman Sloan
1959	15	5	Norman Sloan
1960	15	8	Norman Sloan
1961	17	8	Mel Thompson
1962	8	15	Mel Thompson
1963	3	20	Mel Thompson
1964	11	10	Mel Thompson
1965	13	11	Mel Thompson
1966	7	16	Mel Thompson
1967	8	17	Mel Thompson
1968	12	13	Dick Campbell
1969	13	12	Dick Campbell
1970	8	16	Dick Campbell
1971	13	13	Dick Campbell
1972	12	13	George Hill
1973	11	15	George Hill
1974	10	14	George Hill
1975	5	15	Les Robinson
1976	10	17	Les Robinson
1977	8	19	Les Robinson
1978	8	19	Les Robinson
1979	20	7	Les Robinson

CITY COLLEGE OF NEW YORK (CCNY)

New York, New York

	Beavers		Lavender and Black
1938	13	3	Nat Holman
1939	11	6	Nat Holman
1940	8	8	Nat Holman
1941	17	5	Nat Holman
1942	16	3	Nat Holman
1943	8	10	Nat Holman
1944	6	11	Nat Holman
1945	12	14	Nat Holman
1946	14	4	Nat Holman
1947	16	6	Nat Holman
1948	18	3	Nat Holman
1949	17	8	Nat Holman
1950	24	5	Nat Holman
1951	12	7	Nat Holman
1952	8	11	Nat Holman
1953	10	6	Dave Polansky
1954	10	8	Dave Polansky
1955	8	10	Nat Holman
1956	4	14	Nat Holman
1957	11	8	Dave Polansky
1958	9	8	Dave Polansky
1959	6	12	Nat Holman
1960	4	14	Holman, Polanksy
1961	7	10	Dave Polansky
1962	9	9	Dave Polansky
1963	8	10	Dave Polansky
1964	9	9	Dave Polansky
1965	10	8	Dave Polansky
1966	12	6	Dave Polansky
1967	13	6	Dave Polansky
1968	5	13	Dave Polansky
1969	3	17	Jerry Domershick
1970	6	15	Dave Polansky
1971	7	14	Dave Polansky
1972	14	9	Jack Kaminer
1973	6	17	Jack Kaminer
1974	10	12	Floyd Layne
1975	16	14	Floyd Layne
1976	12	15	Floyd Layne
1977	14	11	Floyd Layne
1978	14	11	Floyd Layne
1979	5	19	Floyd Layne

CLEMSON UNIVERSITY

Clemson, South Carolina

	Tigers		Purple and Burnt Orange
1938	16	7	Joe Davis
1939	16	6	Joe Davis
1940	9	12	Joe Davis
1941	8	14	Rock Norman
1942	3	14	Rock Norman
1943	3	13	Rock Norman
1944	2	13	Rock Norman
1945	8	12	Rock Norman
1946	9	11	Rock Norman
1947	7	16	Banks McFadden
1948	6	17	Banks McFadden
1949	10	11	Banks McFadden
1950	10	10	Banks McFadden
1951	11	6	Banks McFadden
1952	17	7	Banks McFadden
1953	8	10	Banks McFadden
1954	5	18	Banks McFadden
1955	2	21	Banks McFadden
1956	9	17	Banks McFadden
1957	7	17	Press Maravich
1958	8	16	Press Maravich
1959	8	16	Press Maravich
1960	10	16	Press Maravich
1961	10	16	Press Maravich
1962	12	15	Press Maravich
1963	12	13	Bobby Roberts
1964	13	12	Bobby Roberts
1965	8	15	Bobby Roberts
1966	15	10	Bobby Roberts
1967	17	8	Bobby Roberts
1968	4	20	Bobby Roberts
1969	6	19	Bobby Roberts
1970	7	19	Bobby Roberts
1971	9	17	Tates Locke
1972	10	16	Tates Locke
1973	12	14	Tates Locke
1974	14	12	Tates Locke
1975	17	11	Tates Locke
1976	18	10	Bill Foster
1977	22	6	Bill Foster
1978	15	12	Bill Foster
1979	19	10	Bill Foster

CLEVELAND STATE UNIVERSITY

Cleveland, Ohio

	Vikings		Forest Green and White
			(as Fenn College)
1938	6	10	Homer E. Woodling
1939	3	13	Homer E. Woodling

Yr.	W	L	Coach
1940	4	11	Homer E. Woodling
1941	4	11	William Bunce
1942	2	12	Bruce T. Brickley
1943	0	13	Aaron L. Andrews
1944	—	—	
1945	—	—	
1946	1	8	George McKinnon
1947	5	10	George McKinnon
1948	10	8	George McKinnon
1949	4	14	George McKinnon
1950	9	8	George Rung
1951	6	11	George Rung
1952	4	12	George Rung
1953	2	15	Homer E. Woodling
1954	1	18	George Rung
1955	2	15	George Rung
1956	3	15	George Rung
1957	3	15	George Rung
1958	6	13	George Rung
1959	7	12	Bill Gallagher
1960	0	19	Jim Rodriguez
1961	4	15	Jim Rodriguez
1962	6	13	Jim Rodriguez
1963	9	9	Jim Rodriguez
1964	10	9	Jim Rodriguez
1965	10	9	Jim Rodriguez

(as Cleveland State)

Yr.	W	L	Coach
1966	4	14	Jim Rodriguez
1967	8	13	John McLendon
1968	7	15	John McLendon
1969	12	14	John McLendon
1970	5	21	Ray Dieringer
1971	5	20	Ray Dieringer
1972	8	18	Ray Dieringer
1973	9	14	Ray Dieringer
1974	6	20	Ray Dieringer
1975	13	11	Ray Dieringer
1976	6	19	Ray Dieringer
1977	10	17	Ray Dieringer
1978	12	13	Ray Dieringer
1979	14	10	Ray Dieringer

COLGATE UNIVERSITY

Hamilton, New York

Yr.	W	L	Coach
Red Raiders			*Maroon and White*
1938	10	9	John E. Galloway
1939	6	13	John E. Galloway
1940	12	6	Paul O. Bixler
1941	9	6	Paul O. Bixler
1942	5	9	Karl J. Lawrence
1943	5	7	Karl J. Lawrence
1944	11	5	Karl J. Lawrence
1945	5	10	Karl J. Lawrence
1946	12	6	Karl J. Lawrence
1947	11	6	Karl J. Lawrence
1948	14	8	Karl J. Lawrence
1949	12	7	Karl J. Lawrence
1950	11	8	Howard Hartman
1951	13	10	Howard Hartman
1952	11	12	Howard Hartman
1953	12	9	Howard Hartman
1954	5	12	Howard Hartman
1955	11	10	Howard Hartman
1956	18	9	Howard Hartman
1957	14	10	Howard Hartman
1958	6	16	Howard Hartman
1959	7	12	Howard Hartman
1960	11	12	Howard Hartman
1961	14	12	Howard Hartman
1962	8	15	Howard Hartman
1963	5	13	Howard Hartman
1964	7	16	Howard Hartman
1965	7	16	Robert Duffy

Yr.	W	L	Coach
1966	8	14	Robert Duffy
1967	10	13	Robert Duffy
1968	11	15	Edward J. Ashnault
1969	10	15	Edward J. Ashnault
1970	14	11	Edward J. Ashnault
1971	15	10	Edward J. Ashnault
1972	16	8	Edward J. Ashnault
1973	11	14	Bill Vesp
1974	15	10	Bill Vesp
1975	8	16	Bill Vesp
1976	13	11	Bill Vesp
1977	13	11	Mike Griffin
1978	7	19	Mike Griffin
1979	12	14	Mike Griffin

COLORADO, UNIVERSITY OF

Boulder, Colorado

Yr.	W	L	Coach
Buffaloes			*Silver and Gold*
1938	15	6	Frosty Cox
1939	14	4	Frosty Cox
1940	17	4	Frosty Cox
1941	10	6	Frosty Cox
1942	16	2	Frosty Cox
1943	—	—	
1944	—	—	
1945	13	3	Frosty Cox
1946	12	6	Frosty Cox
1947	7	11	Frosty Cox
1948	7	14	Frosty Cox
1949	6	12	Frosty Cox
1950	14	8	Frosty Cox
1951	4	20	Horace B. "Bebe" Lee
1952	8	16	Horace B. "Bebe" Lee
1953	10	11	Horace B. "Bebe" Lee
1954	11	11	Horace B. "Bebe" Lee
1955	19	6	Horace B. "Bebe" Lee
1956	11	10	Horace B. "Bebe" Lee
1957	14	9	Russell "Sox" Walseth
1958	8	15	Russell "Sox" Walseth
1959	14	10	Russell "Sox" Walseth
1960	13	11	Russell "Sox" Walseth
1961	19	7	Russell "Sox" Walseth
1962	15	10	Russell "Sox" Walseth
1963	19	7	Russell "Sox" Walseth
1964	15	10	Russell "Sox" Walseth
1965	13	12	Russell "Sox" Walseth
1966	12	13	Russell "Sox" Walseth
1967	17	8	Russell "Sox" Walseth
1968	9	16	Russell "Sox" Walseth
1969	21	7	Russell "Sox" Walseth
1970	14	12	Russell "Sox" Walseth
1971	14	12	Russell "Sox" Walseth
1972	7	19	Russell "Sox" Walseth
1973	13	13	Russell "Sox" Walseth
1974	9	17	Russell "Sox" Walseth
1975	7	19	Russell "Sox" Walseth
1976	7	19	Russell "Sox" Walseth
1977	11	16	Bill Blair
1978	9	18	Bill Blair
1979	14	13	Bill Blair

COLORADO STATE UNIVERSITY

Fort Collins, Colorado

Yr.	W	L	Coach
Rams			*Green and Gold*
1938	7	9	John Davis
1939	2	14	John Davis
1940	6	12	John Davis
1941	10	9	John Davis
1942	3	16	John Davis
1943	7	9	John Davis
1944	—	—	
1945	7	11	John Davis
1946	15	9	E. D. Taylor
1947	3	18	E. D. Taylor

Yr.	W	L	Coach
1948	6	15	E. D. Taylor
1949	14	21	E. D. Taylor
1950	7	23	H. B. Lee
1951	13	20	Bill Strannigan
1952	13	15	Bill Strannigan
1953	12	14	Bill Strannigan
1954	22	7	Bill Strannigan
1955	12	11	Jim Williams
1956	12	13	Jim Williams
1957	9	16	Jim Williams
1958	14	11	Jim Williams
1959	8	14	Jim Williams
1960	13	10	Jim Williams
1961	17	9	Jim Williams
1962	18	9	Jim Williams
1963	18	5	Jim Williams
1964	16	9	Jim Williams
1965	14	8	Jim Williams
1966	16	8	Jim Williams
1967	14	10	Jim Williams
1968	11	13	Jim Williams
1969	18	7	Jim Williams
1970	14	9	Jim Williams
1971	15	10	Jim Williams
1972	15	9	Jim Williams
1973	13	15	Jim Williams
1974	12	14	Jim Williams
1975	14	12	Jim Williams
1976	10	16	Jim Williams
1977	13	12	Jim Williams
1978	18	9	Jim Williams
1979	11	16	Jim Williams

Yr.	W	L	Coach
1976	8	17	Thomas V. Penders
1977	16	10	Thomas V. Penders
1978	15	11	Thomas V. Penders
1979	17	9	Buddy Mahar

COLUMBIA UNIVERSITY

New York, New York

Lions			Light Blue and White
1938	11	8	Paul Mooney
1939	12	5	Paul Mooney
1940	5	13	Paul Mooney
1941	12	5	Paul Mooney
1942	2	13	Paul Mooney
1943	10	8	Cliff Battles
1944	8	10	Elmer Ripley
1945	9	11	Elmer Ripley
1946	11	9	Paul Mooney
1947	15	5	Gordon Ridings
1948	21	3	Gordon Ridings
1949	14	6	Gordon Ridings
1950	22	7	Gordon Ridings
1951	22	1	Lou Rossini
1952	16	10	Lou Rossini
1953	17	6	Lou Rossini
1954	11	13	Lou Rossini
1955	17	8	Lou Rossini
1956	15	9	Lou Rossini
1957	18	6	Lou Rossini
1958	6	18	Lou Rossini
1959	3	21	Archie Oldham
1960	9	14	Archie Oldham
1961	8	15	Oldham, K. Hunter
1962	3	21	John P. Rohan
1963	10	12	John P. Rohan
1964	11	12	John P. Rohan
1965	7	15	John P. Rohan
1966	18	6	John P. Rohan
1967	11	14	John P. Rohan
1968	23	5	John P. Rohan
1969	20	4	John P. Rohan
1970	20	5	John P. Rohan
1971	15	9	John P. Rohan
1972	5	21	John P. Rohan
1973	7	18	John P. Rohan
1974	5	20	John P. Rohan
1975	4	22	Thomas V. Penders

CONNECTICUT, UNIVERSITY OF

Storrs, Connecticut

Huskies			Blue and White
1938	13	5	Donald White
1939	12	6	Donald White
1940	9	7	Donald White
1941	14	2	Donald White
1942	12	5	Donald White
1943	8	7	Donald White
1944	10	9	Donald White
1945	5	11	Donald White
1946	11	6	Blair Gullion
1947	16	2	Gullion, Hugh Greer
1948	17	6	Hugh Greer
1949	19	6	Hugh Greer
1950	17	8	Hugh Greer
1951	22	4	Hugh Greer
1952	20	7	Hugh Greer
1953	17	4	Hugh Greer
1954	23	3	Hugh Greer
1955	20	5	Hugh Greer
1956	17	11	Hugh Greer
1957	17	8	Hugh Greer
1958	17	10	Hugh Greer
1959	17	7	Hugh Greer
1960	17	9	Hugh Greer
1961	11	13	Hugh Greer
1962	16	8	Hugh Greer
1963	18	7	Greer, George Wigton
1964	16	11	Fred Shabel
1965	23	3	Fred Shabel
1966	16	8	Fred Shabel
1967	17	7	Fred Shabel
1968	11	13	Burr Carlson
1969	5	19	Burr Carlson
1970	14	9	Dee Rowe
1971	10	14	Dee Rowe
1972	8	17	Dee Rowe
1973	15	10	Dee Rowe
1974	19	8	Dee Rowe
1975	18	10	Dee Rowe
1976	19	10	Dee Rowe
1977	17	10	Dee Rowe
1978	11	15	Dom Perno
1979	21	8	Dom Perno

CORNELL UNIVERSITY

Ithaca, New York

Big Red			Carnelian and White
1938	11	7	John Rowland
1939	12	12	Blair Gullion
1940	10	13	Blair Gullion
1941	17	6	Blair Gullion
1942	9	12	Blair Gullion
1943	7	15	Emerald Wilson
1944	9	11	Emerald Wilson
1945	12	5	Emerald Wilson
1946	12	5	Emerald Wilson
1947	14	8	Royner Greene
1948	16	9	Royner Greene
1949	11	15	Royner Greene
1950	18	7	Royner Greene
1951	20	5	Royner Greene

Yr.	W	L	Coach
1952	16	9	Royner Greene
1953	10	13	Royner Greene
1954	18	8	Royner Greene
1955	11	13	Royner Greene
1956	11	13	Royner Greene
1957	4	19	Royner Greene
1958	11	11	Royner Greene
1959	8	15	Royner Greene
1960	13	10	Sam MacNeil
1961	14	10	Sam MacNeil
1962	18	7	Sam MacNeil
1963	12	12	Sam MacNeil
1964	15	10	Sam MacNeil
1965	19	5	Sam MacNeil
1966	15	9	Sam MacNeil
1967	19	5	Sam MacNeil
1968	14	11	Sam MacNeil
1969	12	13	Jerry Lace
1970	7	16	Jerry Lace
1971	5	21	Jerry Lace
1972	5	19	Jerry Lace
1973	4	22	Tony Coma
1974	3	23	T. Coma, T. Allen
1975	7	18	Ben Bluitt
1976	8	18	Ben Bluitt
1977	8	18	Ben Bluitt
1978	9	17	Ben Bluitt
1979	8	18	Ben Bluitt

CREIGHTON UNIVERSITY

Omaha, Nebraska

Blue Jays			White and Blue
1938	11	14	Eddie Hickey
1939	11	12	Eddie Hickey
1940	11	9	Eddie Hickey
1941	18	7	Eddie Hickey
1942	19	5	Eddie Hickey
1943	19	2	Eddie Hickey
1944	—	—	
1945	—	—	
1946	9	12	Julius Belford
1947	19	8	Eddie Hickey
1948	10	13	Julius Belford
1949	9	14	Julius Belford
1950	13	14	Julius Belford
1951	9	18	Julius Belford
1952	7	17	Julius Belford
1953	11	14	Sebastian "Subby" Salerno
1954	14	18	Sebastian "Subby" Salerno
1955	5	14	Sebastian "Subby" Salerno
1956	11	12	Theron "Tommy" Thomsen
1957	15	6	Theron "Tommy" Thomsen
1958	10	12	Theron "Tommy" Thomsen
1959	13	9	Theron "Tommy" Thomsen
1960	13	11	John J. "Red" McManus
1961	8	17	John J. "Red" McManus
1962	21	5	John J. "Red" McManus
1963	14	13	John J. "Red" McManus
1964	22	7	John J. "Red" McManus
1965	13	10	John J. "Red" McManus
1966	14	12	John J. "Red" McManus
1967	12	13	John J. "Red" McManus
1968	8	17	John J. "Red" McManus
1969	13	13	John J. "Red" McManus
1970	15	10	Eddie Sutton
1971	14	11	Eddie Sutton
1972	15	11	Eddie Sutton
1973	15	11	Eddie Sutton
1974	23	7	Eddie Sutton
1975	20	7	Tom Apke
1976	19	7	Tom Apke
1977	21	7	Tom Apke
1978	19	9	Tom Apke
1979	14	13	Tom Apke

DARTMOUTH UNIVERSITY

Hanover, New Hampshire

Big Green			Oak Green
1938	20	5	Osborne Cowles
1939	18	5	Osborne Cowles
1940	15	6	Osborne Cowles
1941	19	5	Osborne Cowles
1942	22	4	Osborne Cowles
1943	20	3	Osborne Cowles
1944	19	2	Earl Brown
1945	6	8	Osborne Cowles
1946	13	3	Osborne Cowles
1947	10	15	Elmer Lampe
1948	12	12	Elmer Lampe
1949	15	11	Elmer Lampe
1950	8	17	Elmer Lampe
1951	3	23	Alvin "Doggie" Julian
1952	11	19	Alvin "Doggie" Julian
1953	12	14	Alvin "Doggie" Julian
1954	13	13	Alvin "Doggie" Julian
1955	18	7	Alvin "Doggie" Julian
1956	18	11	Alvin "Doggie" Julian
1957	18	7	Alvin "Doggie" Julian
1958	22	5	Alvin "Doggie" Julian
1959	22	6	Alvin "Doggie" Julian
1960	14	9	Alvin "Doggie" Julian
1961	5	19	Alvin "Doggie" Julian
1962	6	18	Alvin "Doggie" Julian
1963	7	18	Alvin "Doggie" Julian
1964	2	23	Alvin "Doggie" Julian
1965	4	21	Alvin "Doggie" Julian
1966	3	21	Alvin "Doggie" Julian
1967	7	17	Alvin "Doggie" Julian
1968	8	18	Dave Gavitt
1969	10	15	Dave Gavitt
1970	13	12	George Blaney
1971	10	16	George Blaney
1972	14	12	George Blaney
1973	6	20	Tom O'Connor
1974	4	22	Tom O'Connor
1975	8	18	Marcus Jackson
1976	16	10	Gary Walters
1977	4	22	Gary Walters
1978	10	16	Gary Walters
1979	14	12	Gary Walters

DAVIDSON COLLEGE

Davidson, North Carolina

Wildcats			Red and Black
1938	6	9	Red Laird
1939	16	8	Norman Shepard
1940	8	13	Norman Shepard
1941	10	12	Norman Shepard
1942	12	13	Norman Shepard
1943	18	6	Norman Shepard
1944	16	7	Norman Shepard
1945	9	9	Norman Shepard
1946	13	12	Norman Shepard
1947	17	8	Norman Shepard
1948	19	9	Norman Shepard
1949	18	8	Norman Shepard
1950	10	16	Boydson Baird
1951	7	19	Boydson Baird
1952	7	18	Boydson Baird
1953	4	16	Daniel Miller
1954	7	15	Daniel Miller
1955	8	13	Daniel Miller
1956	10	15	Dr. Thomas Scott
1957	7	20	Dr. Thomas Scott
1958	9	15	Dr. Thomas Scott
1959	9	15	Dr. Thomas Scott
1960	5	19	Dr. Thomas Scott
1961	9	14	C. G. "Lefty" Driesell

| --- | --- | --- | --- |
1962	14	11	C. G. "Lefty" Driesell
1963	20	7	C. G. "Lefty" Driesell
1964	22	4	C. G. "Lefty" Driesell
1965	24	2	C. G. "Lefty" Driesell
1966	21	7	C. G. "Lefty" Driesell
1967	15	12	C. G. "Lefty" Driesell
1968	24	5	C. G. "Lefty" Driesell
1969	26	3	C. G. "Lefty" Driesell
1970	22	5	Terry Holland
1971	15	11	Terry Holland
1972	19	9	Terry Holland
1973	18	9	Terry Holland
1974	18	9	Terry Holland
1975	7	19	Robert "Bo" Brickels
1976	5	21	Robert "Bo" Brickels
1977	5	22	Dave Pritchett
1978	9	18	Dave Pritchett
1979	8	19	Eddie Biedenbach

DAYTON, UNIVERSITY OF

Dayton, Ohio

Flyers			Red and Blue
1938	7	10	Joe Holsinger
1939	2	12	Joe Holsinger
1940	4	17	James Carter
1941	9	14	James Carter
1942	12	6	James Carter
1943	9	8	James Carter
1944	—	—	
1945	—	—	
1946	3	13	James Carter
1947	4	17	James Carter
1948	12	14	Tom Blackburn
1949	16	14	Tom Blackburn
1950	24	8	Tom Blackburn
1951	27	5	Tom Blackburn
1952	28	5	Tom Blackburn
1953	16	13	Tom Blackburn
1954	25	7	Tom Blackburn
1955	25	4	Tom Blackburn
1956	25	4	Tom Blackburn
1957	19	9	Tom Blackburn
1958	25	4	Tom Blackburn
1959	14	12	Tom Blackburn
1960	21	7	Tom Blackburn
1961	20	9	Tom Blackburn
1962	24	6	Tom Blackburn
1963	16	10	Tom Blackburn
1964	15	10	Tom Blackburn
1965	22	7	Don Donoher
1966	23	6	Don Donoher
1967	25	6	Don Donoher
1968	21	9	Don Donoher
1969	20	7	Don Donoher
1970	19	8	Don Donoher
1971	18	9	Don Donoher
1972	13	13	Don Donoher
1973	13	13	Don Donoher
1974	20	9	Don Donoher
1975	10	16	Don Donoher
1976	14	13	Don Donoher
1977	16	11	Don Donoher
1978	19	10	Don Donoher
1979	19	10	Don Donoher

DELAWARE, UNIVERSITY OF

Newark, Delaware

Blue Hens			Blue and Gold
1938	6	10	Lyal Clark
1939	9	7	Steven Grenda
1940	4	12	Steven Grenda
1941	7	9	F. L. Stewart

| --- | --- | --- | --- |
1942	7	8	E. Emery Adkins
1943	7	13	E. Emery Adkins
1944	8	9	Edmund Price
1945	4	10	William D. Murray
1946	7	9	D. Kenneth Steers
1947	9	7	Joseph Brunansky
1948	10	8	Joseph Brunansky
1949	6	14	Joseph Brunansky
1950	8	8	Fred Emmerson
1951	13	7	Fred Emmerson
1952	17	6	Fred Emmerson
1953	18	7	Fred Emmerson
1954	9	13	Fred Emmerson
1955	6	16	Irv Wisniewski
1956	8	15	Irv Wisniewski
1957	8	16	Irv Wisniewski
1958	8	12	Irv Wisniewski
1959	9	13	Irv Wisniewski
1960	7	16	Irv Wisniewski
1961	8	11	Irv Wisniewski
1962	17	4	Irv Wisniewski
1963	14	8	Irv Wisniewski
1964	13	10	Irv Wisniewski
1965	3	17	Irv Wisniewski
1966	9	15	Irv Wisniewski
1967	15	9	Dan Peterson
1968	16	7	Dan Peterson
1969	11	10	Dan Peterson
1970	16	9	Dan Peterson
1971	11	14	Dan Peterson
1972	18	7	Don Harnum
1973	14	11	Don Harnum
1974	15	11	Don Harnum
1975	12	13	Don Harnum
1976	10	15	Don Harnum
1977	12	13	Ronald Rainey
1978	16	11	Ronald Rainey
1979	5	22	Ronald Rainey

DELAWARE STATE COLLEGE

Dover, Delaware

Hornets			Red and Blue
1968	10	13	Bennie George
1969	14	11	Bennie George
1970	14	11	Bennie George
1971	10	13	Bennie George
1972	7	15	Ira Mitchell
1973	10	13	Ira Mitchell
1974	18	11	Ira Mitchell
1975	17	9	Ira Mitchell
1976	6	18	Ira Mitchell
1977	2	25	Marshall Emery
1978	10	14	Marshall Emery
1979	18	10	Marshall Emery

DENVER, UNIVERSITY OF

Denver, Colorado

Pioneers			Crimson and Gold
1938	2	16	Clyde Hubbard
1939	5	13	Clyde Hubbard
1940	6	15	Clyde Hubbard
1941	8	9	Ellison Ketchum
1942	4	16	Ellison Ketchum
1943	19	8	Ketchum, Mark Ducan
1944	6	18	Arthur Quinlan
1945	7	16	Clifford Rock
1946	9	15	Ken Loeffler
1947	16	10	Ellison Ketchum
1948	18	11	Ellison Ketchum
1949	18	15	Ketchum, Hoyt Brawner
1950	18	13	Hoyt Brawner

Yr.	W	L	Coach
1951	14	16	Hoyt Brawner
1952	11	15	Hoyt Brawner
1953	9	16	Hoyt Brawner
1954	6	21	Hoyt Brawner
1955	9	14	Hoyt Brawner
1956	13	12	Hoyt Brawner
1957	11	12	Hoyt Brawner
1958	13	12	Hoyt Brawner
1959	14	10	Hoyt Brawner
1960	13	11	Hoyt Brawner
1961	12	14	Hoyt Brawner
1962	8	17	Hoyt Brawner
1963	9	16	Troy Bledsoe
1964	6	20	Troy Bledsoe
1965	11	14	Troy Bledsoe
1966	14	11	Troy Bledsoe
1967	13	12	Troy Bledsoe
1968	11	14	Troy Bledsoe
1969	2	24	Stan Albeck
1970	13	11	Stan Albeck
1971	17	9	Jim Karabetsos
1972	12	14	Jim Karabetsos
1973	17	9	Al Harden
1974	11	15	Al Harden
1975	10	16	Al Harden
1976	12	15	Al Harden
1977	12	15	Al Harden
1978	10	17	Bill Weimar
1979	18	10	Ben Jobe

DE PAUL UNIVERSITY

Chicago, Illinois

Blue Demons			Scarlet and Blue
1938	12	10	Thomas Haggerty
1939	15	7	Thomas Haggerty
1940	22	6	Thomas Haggerty
1941	13	8	William Wendt
1942	10	12	William Wendt
1943	19	5	Ray Meyer
1944	22	4	Ray Meyer
1945	21	3	Ray Meyer
1946	19	5	Ray Meyer
1947	16	9	Ray Meyer
1948	22	8	Ray Meyer
1949	16	9	Ray Meyer
1950	12	13	Ray Meyer
1951	13	12	Ray Meyer
1952	19	8	Ray Meyer
1953	19	9	Ray Meyer
1954	11	10	Ray Meyer
1955	16	6	Ray Meyer
1956	16	8	Ray Meyer
1957	8	14	Ray Meyer
1958	8	12	Ray Meyer
1959	13	11	Ray Meyer
1960	17	7	Ray Meyer
1961	17	8	Ray Meyer
1962	14	9	Ray Meyer
1963	15	8	Ray Meyer
1964	21	4	Ray Meyer
1965	17	10	Ray Meyer
1966	18	8	Ray Meyer
1967	17	8	Ray Meyer
1968	13	12	Ray Meyer
1969	14	11	Ray Meyer
1970	12	13	Ray Meyer
1971	8	17	Ray Meyer
1972	12	11	Ray Meyer
1973	14	11	Ray Meyer
1974	16	9	Ray Meyer
1975	15	10	Ray Meyer
1976	20	9	Ray Meyer
1977	15	12	Ray Meyer
1978	27	3	Ray Meyer
1979	26	6	Ray Meyer

DETROIT, UNIVERSITY OF

Detroit, Michigan

Yr.	W	L	Coach
Titans			*Cardinal and White*
1938	16	4	Lloyd Brazil
1939	15	15	Lloyd Brazil
1940	15	9	Lloyd Brazil
1941	11	10	Lloyd Brazil
1942	13	8	Lloyd Brazil
1943	15	5	Lloyd Brazil
1944	12	6	Lloyd Brazil
1945	9	13	Lloyd Brazil
1946	15	8	Lloyd Brazil
1947	12	13	J. Shada
1948	7	15	J. Shada
1949	13	10	Robert Calihan
1950	20	6	Robert Calihan
1951	15	14	Robert Calihan
1952	14	12	Robert Calihan
1953	11	15	Robert Calihan
1954	11	17	Robert Calihan
1955	15	11	Robert Calihan
1956	13	12	Robert Calihan
1957	11	15	Robert Calihan
1958	13	12	Robert Calihan
1959	11	14	Robert Calihan
1960	20	7	Robert Calihan
1961	18	9	Robert Calihan
1962	15	12	Robert Calihan
1963	14	12	Robert Calihan
1964	14	11	Robert Calihan
1965	20	8	Robert Calihan
1966	17	8	Robert Calihan
1967	10	15	Robert Calihan
1968	13	12	Robert Calihan
1969	16	10	Robert Calihan
1970	7	18	Jim Harding
1971	14	12	Jim Harding
1972	18	6	Jim Harding
1973	16	9	Jim Harding
1974	17	9	Dick Vitale
1975	17	9	Dick Vitale
1976	19	8	Dick Vitale
1977	25	4	Dick Vitale
1978	25	4	Dave Gaines
1979	22	6	Dave Gaines

DRAKE UNIVERSITY

Des Moines, Iowa

Bulldogs			White and Blue
1938	14	6	Bill Williams
1939	14	7	Bill Williams
1940	13	12	Bill Williams
1941	9	11	Bill Williams
1942	2	13	Bill Williams
1943	8	9	Bill Williams
1944	7	13	William Easton
1945	11	13	V. J. Green
1946	10	16	V. J. Green
1947	18	11	Forrest Anderson
1948	14	12	Forrest Anderson
1949	13	13	Jack McClelland
1950	14	12	Jack McClelland
1951	11	14	Jack McClelland
1952	13	12	Jack McClelland
1953	13	12	Jack McClelland
1954	7	16	Jack McClelland
1955	9	12	Jack McClelland
1956	10	14	Jack McClelland
1957	8	16	John Benington
1958	13	12	John Benington
1959	9	15	Maurice John
1960	11	14	Maurice John
1961	19	7	Maurice John
1962	16	8	Maurice John

Yr.	W	L	Coach		Yr.	W	L	Coach
1963	11	14	Maurice John		1943	20	6	Gerry Gerard
1964	21	7	Maurice John		1944	13	13	Gerry Gerard
1965	15	10	Maurice John		1945	13	9	Gerry Gerard
1966	13	12	Maurice John		1946	21	6	Gerry Gerard
1967	9	16	Maurice John		1947	19	8	Gerry Gerard
1968	18	8	Maurice John		1948	17	12	Gerry Gerard
1969	26	5	Maurice John		1949	13	9	Gerry Gerard
1970	22	7	Maurice John		1950	15	15	Gerry Gerard
1971	21	8	Maurice John		1951	20	13	Harold Bradley
1972	7	19	Howard Stacey		1952	24	6	Harold Bradley
1973	14	12	Howard Stacey		1953	18	8	Harold Bradley
1974	13	13	Howard Stacey		1954	22	6	Harold Bradley
1975	19	10	Bob Ortegel		1955	20	8	Harold Bradley
1976	8	19	Bob Ortegel		1956	19	7	Harold Bradley
1977	10	17	Bob Ortegel		1957	13	11	Harold Bradley
1978	6	22	Bob Ortegel		1958	18	7	Harold Bradley
1979	15	12	Bob Ortegel		1959	13	12	Harold Bradley
					1960	17	11	Vic Bubas
					1961	22	6	Vic Bubas

DREXEL UNIVERSITY

Philadelphia, Pennsylvania

Dragons			*Navy Blue and Gold*		Yr.	W	L	Coach
1938	3	12	Ernest Lange		1962	20	5	Vic Bubas
1939	1	13	Ernest Lange		1963	27	3	Vic Bubas
1940	3	13	Ernest Lange		1964	26	5	Vic Bubas
1941	5	9	Lawrence Mains		1965	20	5	Vic Bubas
1942	9	5	Lawrence Mains		1966	26	4	Vic Bubas
1943	12	3	Lawrence Mains		1967	18	9	Vic Bubas
1944	5	6	Maury McMains		1968	22	6	Vic Bubas
1945	2	11	John Marino		1969	15	13	Vic Bubas
1946	2	13	Ralph Chase		1970	17	9	Raymond C. "Bucky" Waters
1947	8	9	Ralph Chase		1971	20	10	Raymond C. "Bucky" Waters
1948	4	14	Ralph Chase		1972	14	12	Raymond C. "Bucky" Waters
1949	12	4	Ralph Chase		1973	12	14	Raymond C. "Bucky" Waters
1950	11	5	Harold Kollar		1974	10	16	Neil McGeachy
1951	5	12	Harold Kollar		1975	13	13	Bill Foster
1952	9	10	Harold Kollar		1976	13	14	Bill Foster
1953	9	8	Sam Cozen		1977	14	13	Bill Foster
1954	15	3	Sam Cozen		1978	27	7	Bill Foster
1955	14	5	Sam Cozen		1979	22	8	Bill Foster
1956	10	8	Sam Cozen					
1957	14	3	Sam Cozen					

DUQUESNE UNIVERSITY

Pittsburgh, Pennsylvania

					Dukes			*Red and Blue*
1958	10	8	Sam Cozen		1938	6	11	Charles "Chick" Davies
1959	10	9	Sam Cozen		1939	14	4	Charles "Chick" Davies
1960	12	7	Sam Cozen		1940	20	3	Charles "Chick" Davies
1961	12	5	Sam Cozen		1941	17	3	Charles "Chick" Davies
1962	11	8	Sam Cozen		1942	15	6	Charles "Chick" Davies
1963	18	5	Sam Cozen		1943	12	7	Charles "Chick" Davies
1964	17	5	Sam Cozen		1944	—	—	
1965	18	4	Sam Cozen		1945	—	—	
1966	20	4	Sam Cozen		1946	—	—	
1967	13	10	Sam Cozen		1947	20	2	Charles "Chick" Davies
1968	12	9	Sam Cozen		1948	17	6	Charles "Chick" Davies
1969	8	11	Bobby Morgan		1949	17	5	Donald "Dudey" Moore
1970	11	11	Frank Szymanski		1950	23	6	Donald "Dudey" Moore
1971	7	17	Frank Szymanski		1951	16	11	Donald "Dudey" Moore
1972	11	14	Frank Szymanski		1952	23	4	Donald "Dudey" Moore
1973	14	7	Ray Haesler		1953	21	8	Donald "Dudey" Moore
1974	15	9	Ray Haesler		1954	26	3	Donald "Dudey" Moore
1975	12	11	Ray Haesler		1955	22	4	Donald "Dudey" Moore
1976	17	6	Ray Haesler		1956	17	10	Donald "Dudey" Moore
1977	11	13	Ray Haesler		1957	16	7	Donald "Dudey" Moore
1978	13	13	Eddie Burke		1958	10	12	Donald "Dudey" Moore
1979	18	9	Eddie Burke		1959	13	11	John "Red" Manning
					1960	8	15	John "Red" Manning
					1961	15	7	John "Red" Manning

DUKE UNIVERSITY

Durham, North Carolina

Blue Devils			*Blue and White*		Yr.	W	L	Coach
					1962	22	7	John "Red" Manning
					1963	13	9	John "Red" Manning
1938	15	9	Eddie Cameron		1964	16	7	John "Red" Manning
1939	10	12	Eddie Cameron		1965	14	10	John "Red" Manning
1940	19	7	Eddie Cameron		1966	14	9	John "Red" Manning
1941	14	8	Eddie Cameron		1967	7	15	John "Red" Manning
1942	22	2	Eddie Cameron		1968	18	7	John "Red" Manning
					1969	21	5	John "Red" Manning
					1970	17	7	John "Red" Manning
					1971	21	4	John "Red" Manning

Yr.	W	L	Coach	Yr.	W	L	Coach
1972	20	5	John "Red" Manning	1960	14	8	Paul McBrayer
1973	16	8	John "Red" Manning	1961	15	9	Paul McBrayer
1974	12	12	John Cinicola	1962	10	6	P. McBrayer, J. Baechtold
1975	14	11	John Cinicola	1963	9	12	Jim Baechtold
1976	12	13	John Cinicola	1964	15	9	Jim Baechtold
1977	15	15	John Cinicola	1965	19	6	Jim Baechtold
1978	11	17	John Cinicola	1966	16	9	Jim Baechtold
1979	13	13	Mike Rice	1967	5	18	Jim Baechtold
				1968	10	14	Guy Strong
				1969	13	9	Guy Strong
				1970	12	10	Guy Strong
				1971	16	8	Guy Strong
				1972	15	11	Guy Strong
				1973	12	13	Guy Strong
				1974	8	15	Bob Mulcahy
				1975	7	18	Bob Mulcahy
				1976	10	15	Bob Mulcahy
				1977	8	16	Ed Byhre
				1978	15	11	Ed Byhre
				1979	21	8	Ed Byhre

EAST CAROLINA UNIVERSITY

Greenville, North Carolina

Pirates			Purple and Gold
1946	14	8	Earl Smith
1947	—	—	
1948	—	—	
1949	—	—	
1950	—	—	
1951	16	6	Howard Porter
1952	11	10	Howard Porter
1953	15	7	Howard Porter
1954	13	8	Howard Porter
1955	21	1	Howard Porter
1956	12	10	Howard Porter
1957	17	11	Howard Porter
1958	15	8	Howard Porter
1959	14	9	Howard Porter
1960	16	8	Earl Smith
1961	12	9	Earl Smith
1962	15	12	Earl Smith
1963	12	10	Earl Smith
1964	9	15	Wendell Carr
1965	12	10	Wendell Carr
1966	11	15	Wendell Carr
1967	7	17	Tom Quinn
1968	9	16	Tom Quinn
1969	17	11	Tom Quinn
1970	16	10	Tom Quinn
1971	13	12	Tom Quinn
1972	15	14	Tom Quinn
1973	13	13	Tom Quinn
1974	13	12	Tom Quinn
1975	19	9	Dave Patton
1976	11	15	Dave Patton
1977	10	18	Dave Patton
1978	9	17	Larry Gillman
1979	12	15	Larry Gillman

EASTERN KENTUCKY STATE UNIVERSITY

Richmond, Kentucky

Maroons			Maroon and White
1938	12	6	Rome Rankin
1939	11	4	Rome Rankin
1940	15	1	Rome Rankin
1941	9	4	Rome Rankin
1942	11	5	Rome Rankin
1943	12	4	
1944	—	—	
1945	20	5	Rome Rankin
1946	21	3	Rome Rankin
1947	21	4	Paul McBrayer
1948	17	7	Paul McBrayer
1949	17	4	Paul McBrayer
1950	16	6	Paul McBrayer
1951	18	8	Paul McBrayer
1952	13	11	Paul McBrayer
1953	16	9	Paul McBrayer
1954	7	16	Paul McBrayer
1955	15	8	Paul McBrayer
1956	9	16	Paul McBrayer
1957	7	15	Paul McBrayer
1958	8	11	Paul McBrayer
1959	16	6	Paul McBrayer

EASTERN MICHIGAN UNIVERSITY

Ypsilanti, Michigan

Hurons			Green and White
1938	9	6	Elton J. Rynearson
1939	6	11	Elton J. Rynearson
1940	6	12	Elton J. Rynearson
1941	4	13	Elton J. Rynearson
1942	11	7	Ray Stites
1943	5	9	Ray Stites
1944	4	7	Ray Stites
1945	0	11	Elton J. Rynearson
1946	9	9	Elton J. Rynearson
1947	9	9	Ray Stites
1948	5	12	William Crouch
1949	8	12	William Crouch
1950	7	12	William Crouch
1951	7	13	William Crouch
1952	9	11	William Crouch
1953	7	12	William Crouch
1954	8	12	Robert Hollway
1955	14	8	James Skala
1956	5	17	James Skala
1957	9	14	James Skala
1958	1	20	James Skala
1959	8	13	James Skala
1960	7	13	James Skala
1961	5	18	J. Richard Adams
1962	8	13	J. Richard Adams
1963	11	9	J. Richard Adams
1964	9	9	J. Richard Adams
1965	11	7	J. Richard Adams
1966	15	3	J. Richard Adams
1967	18	7	James D. Dutcher
1968	20	9	James D. Dutcher
1969	20	9	James D. Dutcher
1970	22	7	James D. Dutcher
1971	22	11	James D. Dutcher
1972	24	7	James D. Dutcher
1973	8	17	Allan Freund
1974	8	18	Allan Freund
1975	12	14	Allan Freund
1976	7	20	Allan Freund
1977	9	18	Ray Scott
1978	11	16	Ray Scott
1979	9	18	Ray Scott

EAST TENNESSEE STATE UNIVERSITY

Johnson City, Tennessee

Buccaneers			Blue and Gold
1945	9	2	Gene McMurray
1946	10	1	Gene McMurray
1947	13	3	Gene McMurray

Yr.	W	L	Coach
1948	11	8	L. T. Roberts
1949	19	6	J. Madison Brooks
1950	17	6	J. Madison Brooks
1951	23	9	J. Madison Brooks
1952	22	9	J. Madison Brooks
1953	23	6	J. Madison Brooks
1954	23	4	J. Madison Brooks
1955	16	7	J. Madison Brooks
1956	19	8	J. Madison Brooks
1957	17	11	J. Madison Brooks
1958	7	17	J. Madison Brooks
1959	13	10	J. Madison Brooks
1960	9	14	J. Madison Brooks
1961	9	15	J. Madison Brooks
1962	11	14	J. Madison Brooks
1963	14	8	J. Madison Brooks
1964	12	10	J. Madison Brooks
1965	6	17	J. Madison Brooks
1966	7	14	J. Madison Brooks
1967	17	9	J. Madison Brooks
1968	19	8	J. Madison Brooks
1969	15	11	J. Madison Brooks
1970	15	11	J. Madison Brooks
1971	12	12	J. Madison Brooks
1972	11	13	J. Madison Brooks
1973	9	17	J. Madison Brooks
1974	8	18	J. Madison Brooks
1975	9	14	J. Madison Brooks
1976	6	20	Leroy Fisher
1977	12	14	Sonny Smith
1978	18	9	Sonny Smith
1979	16	11	Jim Hallihan

Yr.	W	L	Coach
1977	15	12	Arad A. McCutchan
1978	1	3	Bobby Watson
1979	13	16	Dick Walters

FAIRFIELD UNIVERSITY

Fairfield, Connecticut

Stags			Cardinal Red and White
1949	9	14	John Dunn
1950	5	16	Bob Noonan
1951	16	11	Jim Hanrahan
1952	10	9	Jim Hanrahan
1953	9	9	Jim Hanrahan
1954	12	8	Jim Hanrahan
1955	12	8	Jim Hanrahan
1956	6	10	Jim Hanrahan
1957	6	15	Jim.Hanrahan
1958	12	9	Jim Hanrahan
1959	11	11	George Bisacca
1960	17	9	George Bisacca
1961	17	7	George Bisacca
1962	20	5	George Bisacca
1963	11	13	George Bisacca
1964	14	11	George Bisacca
1965	14	7	George Bisacca
1966	19	5	George Bisacca
1967	12	9	George Bisacca
1968	16	10	George Bisacca
1969	10	16	James Lynam
1970	13	13	James Lynam
1971	9	15	Fred Barakat
1972	12	13	Fred Barakat
1973	18	9	Fred Barakat
1974	17	9	Fred Barakat
1975	13	14	Fred Barakat
1976	12	14	Fred Barakat
1977	16	11	Fred Barakat
1978	22	5	Fred Barakat
1979	17	9	Fred Barakat

EVANSVILLE, UNIVERSITY OF

Evansville, Indiana

Purple Aces			Purple and White
1938	4	13	Bill Slyker
1939	9	7	Bill Slyker
1940	10	7	Bill Slyker
1941	13	3	Bill Slyker
1942	12	6	Bill Slyker
1943	13	7	Bill Slyker
1944	3	7	Emerson Henke
1945	10	7	Emerson Henke
1946	16	8	Emerson Henke
1947	7	15	Arad A. McCutchan
1948	8	18	Arad A. McCutchan
1949	14	11	Arad A. McCutchan
1950	14	4	Arad A. McCutchan
1951	23	7	Arad A. McCutchan
1952	7	20	Arad A. McCutchan
1953	10	15	Arad A. McCutchan
1954	12	12	Arad A. McCutchan
1955	20	6	Arad A. McCutchan
1956	16	7	Arad A. McCutchan
1957	18	8	Arad A. McCutchan
1958	23	4	Arad A. McCutchan
1959	21	6	Arad A. McCutchan
1960	25	4	Arad A. McCutchan
1961	11	16	Arad A. McCutchan
1962	14	11	Arad A. McCutchan
1963	21	6	Arad A. McCutchan
1964	26	3	Arad A. McCutchan
1965	29	0	Arad A. McCutchan
1966	18	9	Arad A. McCutchan
1967	8	17	Arad A. McCutchan
1968	20	8	Arad A. McCutchan
1969	12	14	Arad A. McCutchan
1970	12	14	Arad A. McCutchan
1971	22	8	Arad A. McCutchan
1972	22	6	Arad A. McCutchan
1973	14	12	Arad A. McCutchan
1974	19	9	Arad A. McCutchan
1975	13	13	Arad A. McCutchan
1976	20	9	Arad A. McCutchan

FAIRLEIGH DICKINSON UNIVERSITY

Teaneck, New Jersey

Knights			Maroon, Blue and White
1950	10	7	Dick Holub
1951	16	6	Dick Holub
1952	22	4	Dick Holub
1953	20	1	Dick Holub
1954	17	3	Dick Holub
1955	10	14	Dick Holub
1956	9	15	Dick Holub
1957	12	12	Dick Holub
1958	9	15	Dick Holub
1959	17	11	Dick Holub
1960	14	11	Dick Holub
1961	13	10	Dick Holub
1962	12	11	Dick Holub
1963	16	12	Dick Holub
1964	12	10	Dick Holub
1965	9	15	Dick Holub
1966	15	10	Dick Holub
1967	4	19	Jack Devine
1968	10	12	Jack Devine
1969	9	13	Jack Devine
1970	13	10	Al LoBalbo
1971	16	7	Al LoBalbo
1972	15	9	Al LoBalbo
1973	13	13	Al LoBalbo
1974	11	14	Al LoBalbo
1975	11	13	Al LoBalbo
1976	9	13	Al LoBalbo
1977	13	13	Al LoBalbo
1978	6	18	Al LoBalbo
1979	8	18	Al LoBalbo

FLORIDA, UNIVERSITY OF

Gainesville, Florida

Gators			Orange and Blue
1938	11	9	Sam McAllister
1939	9	6	Sam McAllister
1940	13	9	Sam McAllister
1941	15	3	Sam McAllister
1942	8	9	Sam McAllister
1943	8	7	Spurgeon Cherry
1944	—	—	
1945	7	12	Spurgeon Cherry
1946	7	14	Spurgeon Cherry
1947	17	9	Sam McAllister
1948	15	10	Sam McAllister
1949	11	15	Sam McAllister
1950	9	14	Sam McAllister
1951	11	12	Sam McAllister
1952	15	9	John Mauer
1953	13	6	John Mauer
1954	7	15	John Mauer
1955	12	10	John Mauer
1956	11	12	John Mauer
1957	14	10	John Mauer
1958	12	9	John Mauer
1959	8	15	John Mauer
1960	6	16	John Mauer
1961	15	11	Norman Sloan
1962	12	11	Norman Sloan
1963	12	14	Norman Sloan
1964	12	10	Norman Sloan
1965	18	7	Norman Sloan
1966	16	10	Norman Sloan
1967	21	4	Tommy Bartlett
1968	15	10	Tommy Bartlett
1969	18	9	Tommy Bartlett
1970	9	17	Tommy Bartlett
1971	11	15	Tommy Bartlett
1972	10	15	Tommy Bartlett
1973	11	15	Tommy Bartlett
1974	15	11	John Lotz
1975	12	16	John Lotz
1976	12	14	John Lotz
1977	17	9	John Lotz
1978	15	12	John Lotz
1979	8	19	John Lotz

Yr.	W	L	Coach
1970	23	3	Hugh Durham
1971	17	9	Hugh Durham
1972	27	6	Hugh Durham
1973	18	8	Hugh Durham
1974	18	8	Hugh Durham
1975	18	8	Hugh Durham
1976	22	5	Hugh Durham
1977	16	11	Hugh Durham
1978	23	6	Hugh Durham
1979	19	10	Joe Williams

FORDHAM UNIVERSITY

Bronx, New York

Rams			Maroon
1938	10	10	Vincent Cavanaugh
1939	10	8	Edward Kelleher
1940	10	8	Edward Kelleher
1941	12	9	Edward Kelleher
1942	12	7	Edward Kelleher
1943	16	6	Edward Kelleher
1944	—	—	
1945	4	15	Frank Adams
1946	2	17	Frank Adams
1947	18	5	Frank Adams
1948	17	6	Frank Adams
1949	9	16	Frank Adams
1950	15	12	Frank Adams
1951	19	8	John Bach
1952	20	8	John Bach
1953	18	8	John Bach
1954	18	6	John Bach
1955	18	9	John Bach
1956	11	14	John Bach
1957	16	10	John Bach
1958	16	9	John Bach
1959	17	9	John Bach
1960	8	18	John Bach
1961	7	16	John Bach
1962	10	14	John Bach
1963	18	8	John Bach
1964	9	11	John Bach
1965	15	12	John Bach
1966	10	15	John Bach
1967	14	11	John Bach
1968	19	8	John Bach
1969	17	9	Edward Conlin
1970	10	15	Edward Conlin
1971	26	3	Richard "Digger" Phelps
1972	18	9	Hal Wissel
1973	12	16	Hal Wissel
1974	8	17	Hal Wissel
1975	12	13	Hal Wissel
1976	7	19	Hal Wissel
1977	5	21	Dick Stewart
1978	8	18	D. Stewart, T. Tripucka
1979	7	22	Tom Penders

FLORIDA STATE UNIVERSITY

Tallahassee, Florida

Seminoles			Garnet and Gold
1948	5	13	Don Loucks
1949	12	12	J. K. "Bud" Kennedy
1950	15	10	J. K. "Bud" Kennedy
1951	18	9	J. K. "Bud" Kennedy
1952	5	20	J. K. "Bud" Kennedy
1953	11	11	J. K. "Bud" Kennedy
1954	13	7	J. K. "Bud" Kennedy
1955	22	4	J. K. "Bud" Kennedy
1956	16	9	J. K. "Bud" Kennedy
1957	9	17	J. K. "Bud" Kennedy
1958	9	16	J. K. "Bud" Kennedy
1959	8	15	J. K. "Bud" Kennedy
1960	10	15	J. K. "Bud" Kennedy
1961	14	10	J. K. "Bud" Kennedy
1962	15	8	J. K. "Bud" Kennedy
1963	15	10	J. K. "Bud" Kennedy
1964	14	14	J. K. "Bud" Kennedy
1965	16	10	J. K. "Bud" Kennedy
1966	15	11	J. K. "Bud" Kennedy
1967	11	15	Hugh Durham
1968	19	8	Hugh Durham
1969	18	8	Hugh Durham

FRESNO STATE COLLEGE

Fresno, California

Bulldogs			Cardinal and Blue
1971	15	11	Ed Gregory
1972	9	17	Ed Gregory
1973	10	16	Ed Gregory
1974	16	9	Ed Gregory
1975	16	10	Ed Gregory
1976	12	14	Ed Gregory
1977	7	20	Ed Gregory
1978	21	6	Boyd Grant
1979	16	12	Boyd Grant

Yr.	W	L	Coach	Yr.	W	L	Coach

FURMAN UNIVERSITY

Greenville, South Carolina

				1969	12	12	Jack Magee
				1970	18	8	Jack Magee
				1971	12	14	Jack Magee
				1972	3	23	Jack Magee
Paladins			*Purple and White*	1973	12	14	John Thompson
1946	15	4	Lyles Alley	1974	13	13	John Thompson
1947	9	9	Lyles Alley	1975	18	10	John Thompson
1948	11	16	Lyles Alley	1976	21	7	John Thompson
1949	8	14	Lyles Alley	1977	19	9	John Thompson
1950	9	12	Melvin Bell	1978	23	8	John Thompson
1951	3	20	Lyles Alley	1979	24	5	John Thompson
1952	18	6	Lyles Alley				
1953	21	6	Lyles Alley				
1954	20	9	Lyles Alley				
1955	17	10	Lyles Alley				

GEORGE WASHINGTON UNIVERSITY

Washington, D. C.

1956	12	16	Lyles Alley				
1957	10	17	Lyles Alley	*Colonials*			*Buff and Blue*
1958	12	14	Lyles Alley	1938	12	5	Bill Reinhart
1959	14	12	Lyles Alley	1939	13	8	Bill Reinhart
1960	9	16	Lyles Alley	1940	13	6	Bill Reinhart
1961	15	11	Lyles Alley	1941	16	5	Bill Reinhart
1962	15	11	Lyles Alley	1942	10	9	Bill Reinhart
1963	14	14	Lyles Alley	1943	17	6	Otis Zahn
1964	11	15	Lyles Alley	1944	–	–	
1965	6	19	Lyles Alley	1945	–	–	
1966	9	17	Lyles Alley	1946	5	9	Otis Zahn
1967	9	15	Frank Selvy	1947	21	7	Otis Zahn
1968	13	14	Frank Selvy	1948	19	7	Otis Zahn
1969	9	17	Frank Selvy	1949	18	8	Otis Zahn
1970	13	13	Frank Selvy	1950	17	8	Bill Reinhart
1971	15	12	Joe Williams	1951	12	12	Bill Reinhart
1972	17	11	Joe Williams	1952	15	9	Bill Reinhart
1973	20	9	Joe Williams	1953	15	7	Bill Reinhart
1974	22	9	Joe Williams	1954	23	3	Bill Reinhart
1975	22	7	Joe Williams	1955	24	6	Bill Reinhart
1976	9	18	Joe Williams	1956	19	7	Bill Reinhart
1977	18	10	Joe Williams	1957	3	21	Bill Reinhart
1978	19	11	Joe Williams	1958	12	11	Bill Reinhart
1979	20	9	Eddie Holbrook	1959	14	11	Bill Reinhart
				1960	15	11	Bill Reinhart
				1961	9	17	Bill Reinhart
				1962	9	15	Bill Reinhart
				1963	8	15	Bill Reinhart
				1964	11	15	Bill Reinhart

GEORGETOWN UNIVERSITY

Washington, D. C.

Hoyas			*Blue and Gray*	1965	10	13	Bill Reinhart
1938	7	11	Fred Mesmer	1966	3	18	Bill Reinhart
1939	13	9	Elmer Ripley	1967	6	18	James "Babe" McCarthy
1940	8	10	Elmer Ripley	1968	5	19	Wayne Dobbs
1941	16	4	Elmer Ripley	1969	14	11	Wayne Dobbs
1942	9	11	Elmer Ripley	1970	12	15	Wayne Dobbs
1943	22	5	Elmer Ripley	1971	11	14	Carl Slone
1944	–	–		1972	11	14	Carl Slone
1945	–	–		1973	17	9	Carl Slone
1946	11	9	Ken Engles	1974	15	11	Carl Slone
1947	19	7	Elmer Ripley	1975	17	10	Bob Tallent
1948	13	15	Elmer Ripley	1976	20	7	Bob Tallent
1949	9	15	Elmer Ripley	1977	14	12	Bob Tallent
1950	11	12	Buddy O'Grady	1978	15	11	Bob Tallent
1951	8	14	Buddy O'Grady	1979	13	14	Bob Tallent
1952	15	9	Buddy O'Grady				
1953	13	7	Buddy Jeannette				
1954	11	18	Buddy Jeannette				
1955	13	12	Buddy Jeannette				
1956	13	11	Buddy Jeannette				

GEORGIA, UNIVERSITY OF

Athens, Georgia

1957	11	11	Tom Nolan				
1958	10	11	Tom Nolan				
1959	9	14	Tom Nolan	*Bulldogs*			*Red and Black*
1960	11	12	Tom Nolan	1938	12	10	Frank Johnson
1961	11	10	Tom O'Keefe	1939	12	5	Elmer Lampe
1962	14	9	Tom O'Keefe	1940	19	6	Elmer Lampe
1963	13	13	Tom O'Keefe	1941	13	11	Elmer Lampe
1964	15	10	Tom O'Keefe	1942	7	10	Elmer Lampe
1965	13	10	Tom O'Keefe	1943	4	13	Elmer Lampe
1966	16	8	Tom O'Keefe	1944	7	10	Elmer Lampe
1967	12	11	Jack Magee	1945	5	16	Elmer Lampe
1968	11	12	Jack Magee	1946	12	9	Elmer Lampe

Yr.	W	L	Coach
1947	5	14	Ralph Jordan
1948	18	10	Ralph Jordan
1949	17	13	Ralph Jordan
1950	15	9	Jordan, J. Whatley
1951	13	11	James Whatley
1952	3	22	Harbin "Red" Lawson
1953	7	18	Harbin "Red" Lawson
1954	7	18	Harbin "Red" Lawson
1955	9	16	Harbin "Red" Lawson
1956	3	21	Harbin "Red" Lawson
1957	8	16	Harbin "Red" Lawson
1958	7	19	Harbin "Red" Lawson
1959	11	15	Harbin "Red" Lawson
1960	12	13	Harbin "Red" Lawson
1961	8	18	Harbin "Red" Lawson
1962	8	16	Harbin "Red" Lawson
1963	9	17	Harbin "Red" Lawson
1964	12	14	Harbin "Red" Lawson
1965	8	18	Harbin "Red" Lawson
1966	10	15	Ken Rosemond
1967	9	17	Ken Rosemond
1968	17	8	Ken Rosemond
1969	13	12	Ken Rosemond
1970	13	12	Ken Rosemond
1971	6	19	Ken Rosemond
1972	14	12	Ken Rosemond
1973	10	16	Ken Rosemond
1974	6	20	John Guthrie
1975	8	17	John Guthrie
1976	12	15	John Guthrie
1977	9	18	John Guthrie
1978	11	16	John Guthrie
1979	14	14	Hugh Durham

Yr.	W	L	Coach
1943	—	—	
1944	—	—	
1945	—	—	
1946	—	—	
1947	8	12	George Cukro
1948	18	5	J. B. Scearce
1949	21	3	J. B. Scearce
1950	27	3	J. B. Scearce
1951	24	5	J. B. Scearce
1952	22	6	J. B. Scearce
1953	15	14	J. B. Scearce
1954	15	12	J. B. Scearce
1955	20	4	J. B. Scearce
1956	21	7	J. B. Scearce
1957	18	7	J. B. Scearce
1958	12	15	J. B. Scearce
1959	19	12	J. B. Scearce
1960	19	6	J. B. Scearce
1961	11	19	J. B. Scearce
1962	14	13	J. B. Scearce
1963	14	13	J. B. Scearce
1964	20	12	J. B. Scearce
1965	22	5	J. B. Scearce
1966	26	6	J. B. Scearce
1967	17	11	J. B. Scearce
1968	13	11	Frank Radovich
1969	18	7	Frank Radovich
1970	17	6	Frank Radovich
1971	13	12	J. E. Rowe
1972	17	9	J. E. Rowe
1973	8	18	J. E. Rowe
1974	19	7	J. E. Rowe
1975	8	18	Larry Chapman
1976	11	16	Larry Chapman
1977	16	11	Larry Chapman
1978	12	15	J. B. Scearce
1979	9	18	J. B. Scearce

GEORGIA STATE UNIVERSITY

Atlanta, Georgia

Panthers			Royal Blue and Sky Blue
1959	3	9	Herbert Burgess
1960	4	18	Herbert Burgess
1961	10	16	Herbert Burgess
1962	2	24	Herbert Burgess
1963	2	21	Herbert Burgess
1964	1	21	Herbert Burgess
1965	2	19	Richard Wiehr
1966	2	18	Richard Wiehr
1967	4	20	Richard Wiehr
1968	2	20	Jack Waters
1969	6	14	Jack Waters
1970	8	14	Jack Waters
1971	5	16	Frank Davis
1972	5	19	Roger McDowell
1973	5	20	Jack Waters
1974	1	25	Jack Waters
1975	8	18	Jack Waters
1976	12	11	Jack Waters
1977	10	18	Jack Waters
1978	5	21	Roger Couch
1979	7	20	Roger Couch

GEORGIA INSTITUTE OF TECHNOLOGY

Atlanta, Georgia

Yellow Jackets			White and Gold
1938	18	2	Roy Mundorff
1939	6	9	Roy Mundorff
1940	7	8	Roy Mundorff
1941	8	11	Roy Mundorff
1942	8	8	Dwight Keith
1943	11	5	Dwight Keith
1944	14	4	Dwight Keith
1945	11	6	Dwight Keith
1946	10	11	Dwight Keith
1947	12	11	Dwight Keith
1948	12	16	Roy McArthur
1949	11	13	Roy McArthur
1950	14	13	Roy McArthur
1951	8	19	Roy McArthur
1952	7	16	John "Whack" Hyder
1953	5	17	John "Whack" Hyder
1954	2	22	John "Whack" Hyder
1955	12	13	John "Whack" Hyder
1956	12	11	John "Whack" Hyder
1957	18	8	John "Whack" Hyder
1958	15	11	John "Whack" Hyder
1959	17	9	John "Whack" Hyder
1960	22	6	John "Whack" Hyder
1961	13	13	John "Whack" Hyder
1962	10	16	John "Whack" Hyder
1963	21	5	John "Whack" Hyder
1964	17	9	John "Whack" Hyder
1965	14	11	John "Whack" Hyder
1966	13	13	John "Whack" Hyder
1967	17	9	John "Whack" Hyder
1968	12	13	John "Whack" Hyder

GEORGIA SOUTHERN COLLEGE

Statesboro, Georgia

Eagles			Royal Blue and White
1938	10	4	B. L. Smith
1939	7	8	B. L. Smith
1940	10	4	B. L. Smith
1941	7	6	B. L. Smith
1942	4	9	B. L. Smith

Yr.	W	L	Coach
1969	12	13	John "Whack" Hyder
1970	17	10	John "Whack" Hyder
1971	23	9	John "Whack" Hyder
1972	6	20	John "Whack" Hyder
1973	7	18	John "Whack" Hyder
1974	5	21	Dwane Morrison
1975	11	15	Dwane Morrison
1976	13	14	Dwane Morrison
1977	18	10	Dwane Morrison
1978	15	12	Dwane Morrison
1979	17	9	Dwane Morrison

Yr.	W	L	Coach
1975	13	13	Adrian Buoncristiani
1976	13	13	Adrian Buoncristiani
1977	11	16	Adrian Buoncristiani
1978	14	15	Adrian Buoncristiani
1979	16	10	Dan Fitzgerald

GEORGE MASON UNIVERSITY

Fairfax, Virginia

Patriots			Dark Green and Gold
1967	6	12	Raymond Spuhler
1968	5	17	Raymond Spuhler
1969	2	20	Raymond Spuhler
1970	4	23	Raymond Spuhler
1971	9	17	John Linn
1972	12	18	John Linn
1973	15	16	John Linn
1974	19	10	John Linn
1975	19	8	John Linn
1976	16	13	John Linn
1977	9	19	John Linn
1978	9	17	John Linn
1979	17	8	John Linn

GRAMBLING STATE UNIVERSITY

Grambling, Louisiana

Tigers			Black and Gold
1957	28	8	Fred Hobdy
1958	28	4	Fred Hobdy
1959	28	1	Fred Hobdy
1960	26	5	Fred Hobdy
1961	32	4	Fred Hobdy
1962	20	6	Fred Hobdy
1963	30	3	Fred Hobdy
1964	26	4	Fred Hobdy
1965	21	5	Fred Hobdy
1966	27	6	Fred Hobdy
1967	20	7	Fred Hobdy
1968	11	14	Fred Hobdy
1969	20	8	Fred Hobdy
1970	16	8	Fred Hobdy
1971	20	9	Fred Hobdy
1972	19	8	Fred Hobdy
1973	6	18	Fred Hobdy
1974	16	11	Fred Hobdy
1975	16	12	Fred Hobdy
1976	22	6	Fred Hobdy
1977	22	9	Fred Hobdy
1978	11	14	Fred Hobdy
1979	16	11	Fred Hobdy

GONZAGA UNIVERSITY

Spokane, Washington

Bulldogs			Columbia Blue and White
1938	0	2	Claude McGrath
1939	7	10	Claude McGrath
1940	9	15	Claude McGrath
1941	13	14	Claude McGrath
1942	16	13	Claude McGrath
1943	2	9	
1944	22	4	Charles Henry
1945	12	19	Eugene Wozny
1946	6	14	Eugene Wozny
1947	20	9	Claude McGrath
1948	24	11	Claude McGrath
1949	17	12	Claude McGrath
1950	18	11	Bill Underwood
1951	8	22	Bill Underwood
1952	20	17	Hank Anderson
1953	15	14	Hank Anderson
1954	14	13	Hank Anderson
1955	15	11	Hank Anderson
1956	13	15	Hank Anderson
1957	11	16	Hank Anderson
1958	15	10	Hank Anderson
1959	11	15	Hank Anderson
1960	14	12	Hank Anderson
1961	11	15	Hank Anderson
1962	14	12	Hank Anderson
1963	14	12	Hank Anderson
1964	10	15	Hank Anderson
1965	18	6	Hank Anderson
1966	9	15	Hank Anderson
1967	19	6	Hank Anderson
1968	9	17	Hank Anderson
1969	11	15	Hank Anderson
1970	10	16	Hank Anderson
1971	13	13	Hank Anderson
1972	14	12	Hank Anderson
1973	14	12	Adrian Buoncristiani
1974	13	13	Adrian Buoncristiani

HARDIN-SIMMONS UNIVERSITY

Abilene, Texas

Cowboys			Purple and Gold
1938	3	12	Frank Kimbrough
1939	3	12	Frank Kimbrough
1940	2	12	Frank Kimbrough
1941	—	—	
1942	6	10	
1943	1	9	
1944	—	—	
1945	7	23	Warren Woodson
1946	2	11	Warren Woodson
1947	8	26	Westley Bradshaw
1948	7	17	Westley Bradshaw
1949	13	10	Jack Martin
1950	15	10	Jack Martin
1951	13	15	Jack Martin
1952	17	15	Bill Scott
1953	19	12	Bill Scott
1954	7	17	Bill Scott
1955	9	15	Bill Scott
1956	7	18	Bill Scott
1957	17	9	Bill Scott
1958	11	14	Bill Scott
1959	14	12	Bill Scott
1960	8	18	Bill Scott
1961	12	14	Bill Scott
1962	8	17	Bill Scott
1963	10	16	Lou Henson
1964	20	6	Lou Henson
1965	12	8	Lou Henson
1966	20	6	Paul Lambert
1967	17	9	Paul Lambert
1968	10	16	Paul Lambert
1969	13	13	Paul Lambert
1970	17	9	Paul Lambert
1971	9	17	Glen Whitis

Yr.	W	L	Coach
1972	14	12	Glen Whitis
1973	16	9	Russell Berry
1974	11	14	Russell Berry
1975	5	20	Russell Berry
1976	14	13	Berry, Vice
1977	6	21	Preston Vice
1978	10	16	Jim Shuler
1979	7	20	Jim Shuler

HARVARD UNIVERSITY

Cambridge, Massachusetts

Yr.	W	L	Coach
Crimson			*Crimson*
1938	13	5	Wes Fesler
1939	5	14	Wes Fesler
1940	5	14	Wes Fesler
1941	9	10	Wes Fesler
1942	8	16	Earl Brown
1943	12	14	Earl Brown
1944	2	12	Floyd Stahl
1945	2	13	Floyd Stahl
1946	19	3	Floyd Stahl
1947	16	9	William Barclay
1948	5	20	William Barclay
1949	3	20	William Barclay
1950	9	15	Norman Shepard
1951	8	18	Norman Shepard
1952	5	17	Norman Shepard
1953	7	16	Norman Shepard
1954	9	16	Norman Shepard
1955	6	17	Floyd Wilson
1956	8	16	Floyd Wilson
1957	12	9	Floyd Wilson
1958	16	9	Floyd Wilson
1959	10	15	Floyd Wilson
1960	12	11	Floyd Wilson
1961	11	13	Floyd Wilson
1962	10	14	Floyd Wilson
1963	6	15	Floyd Wilson
1964	12	10	Floyd Wilson
1965	11	12	Floyd Wilson
1966	10	14	Floyd Wilson
1967	11	14	Floyd Wilson
1968	7	14	Floyd Wilson
1969	7	18	Bob Harrison
1970	7	19	Bob Harrison
1971	16	10	Bob Harrison
1972	15	11	Bob Harrison
1973	14	12	Bob Harrison
1974	11	13	Tom Sanders
1975	12	13	Tom Sanders
1976	8	18	Tom Sanders
1977	9	16	Tom Sanders
1978	11	15	Frank McLaughlin
1979	8	21	Frank McLaughlin

HAWAII, UNIVERSITY OF

Honolulu, Hawaii

Yr.	W	L	Coach
Rainbows			*Green and White*
1971	23	5	Ephraim "Red" Rocha
1972	24	3	Ephraim "Red" Rocha
1973	16	10	Ephraim "Red" Rocha
1974	19	9	Bruce O'Neil
1975	16	11	Bruce O'Neil
1976	11	16	Bruce O'Neil
1977	9	18	Larry Little
1978	1	26	Larry Little
1979	10	17	Larry Little

HOFSTRA UNIVERSITY

Hempstead, New York

Yr.	W	L	Coach
Flying Dutchmen			*Blue and Gold*
1939	10	8	Jack MacDonald
1940	14	8	Jack MacDonald
1941	13	7	Jack MacDonald
1942	15	6	Jack MacDonald
1943	15	6	Jack MacDonald
1944	14	5	Jack Smith
1945	8	13	Jack Smith
1946	12	7	Jack Smith
1947	18	6	Jack MacDonald
1948	13	6	Jack MacDonald
1949	18	8	Frank Reilly
1950	17	9	Frank Reilly
1951	18	11	Frank Reilly
1952	26	3	Frank Reilly
1953	20	7	Frank Reilly
1954	15	9	Frank Reilly
1955	19	7	Frank Reilly
1956	22	4	Bill van Breda Kolff
1957	11	15	Bill van Breda Kolff
1958	15	8	Bill van Breda Kolff
1959	20	7	Bill van Breda Kolff
1960	23	1	Bill van Breda Kolff
1961	21	4	Bill van Breda Kolff
1962	24	4	Bill van Breda Kolff
1963	23	7	Paul Lynner
1964	23	6	Paul Lynner
1965	11	14	Paul Lynner
1966	16	10	Paul Lynner
1967	12	13	Paul Lynner
1968	13	12	Paul Lynner
1969	12	13	Paul Lynner
1970	13	13	Paul Lynner
1971	16	8	Paul Lynner
1972	11	14	Paul Lynner
1973	8	16	Roger Gaeckler
1974	8	16	Roger Gaeckler
1975	11	13	Roger Gaeckler
1976	18	12	Roger Gaeckler
1977	23	7	Roger Gaeckler
1978	8	19	Roger Gaeckler
1979	8	19	Roger Gaeckler

HOLY CROSS COLLEGE

Worcester, Massachusetts

Yr.	W	L	Coach
Crusaders			*Royal Purple*
1940	2	3	Edward "Moose" Krause
1941	4	7	Edward "Moose" Krause
1942	5	4	Edward "Moose" Krause
1943	1	5	Albert Riopel
1944	6	8	Albert Riopel
1945	4	9	Albert Riopel
1946	12	3	Alvin "Doggie" Julian
1947	27	3	Alvin "Doggie" Julian
1948	26	4	Alvin "Doggie" Julian
1949	19	8	Lester "Buster" Sheary
1950	27	4	Lester "Buster" Sheary
1951	20	5	Lester "Buster" Sheary
1952	24	4	Lester "Buster" Sheary
1953	20	6	Lester "Buster" Sheary
1954	26	2	Lester "Buster" Sheary
1955	19	7	Lester "Buster" Sheary
1956	22	5	Roy Leenig
1957	12	12	Roy Leenig
1958	16	9	Roy Leenig
1959	14	11	Roy Leenig
1960	20	6	Roy Leenig
1961	22	5	Roy Leenig
1962	20	6	Frank A. Oftring

Yr.	W	L	Coach
1963	16	9	Frank A. Oftring
1964	15	8	Frank A. Oftring
1965	13	10	Frank A. Oftring
1966	10	13	Jack Donohue
1967	16	9	Jack Donohue
1968	15	8	Jack Donohue
1969	16	8	Jack Donohue
1970	16	9	Jack Donohue
1971	16	8	Jack Donohue
1972	15	10	Jack Donohue
1973	9	17	George Blaney
1974	8	18	George Blaney
1975	20	8	George Blaney
1976	22	10	George Blaney
1977	23	6	George Blaney
1978	20	8	George Blaney
1979	17	11	George Blaney

Yr.	W	L	Coach
1976	5	21	Bob McKinley
1977	6	23	Bob McKinley
1978	7	19	Gene Iba
1979	11	16	Gene Iba

HOUSTON, UNIVERSITY OF

Houston, Texas

Cougers			Scarlet and White
1946	10	4	Alden Pasche
1947	15	7	Alden Pasche
1948	11	11	Alden Pasche
1949	9	10	Alden Pasche
1950	16	7	Alden Pasche
1951	11	17	Alden Pasche
1952	7	14	Alden Pasche
1953	9	13	Alden Pasche
1954	11	15	Alden Pasche
1955	15	10	Alden Pasche
1956	19	7	Alden Pasche
1957	10	16	Guy V. Lewis
1958	9	16	Guy V. Lewis
1959	12	14	Guy V. Lewis
1960	13	12	Guy V. Lewis
1961	17	11	Guy V. Lewis
1962	21	6	Guy V. Lewis
1963	15	11	Guy V. Lewis
1964	16	10	Guy V. Lewis
1965	19	10	Guy V. Lewis
1966	23	6	Guy V. Lewis
1967	27	4	Guy V. Lewis
1968	31	2	Guy V. Lewis
1969	16	10	Guy V. Lewis
1970	25	5	Guy V. Lewis
1971	22	7	Guy V. Lewis
1972	20	7	Guy V. Lewis
1973	24	3	Guy V. Lewis
1974	17	9	Guy V. Lewis
1975	17	10	Guy V. Lewis
1976	16	10	Guy V. Lewis
1977	29	8	Guy V. Lewis
1978	25	8	Guy V. Lewis
1979	16	15	Guy V. Lewis

HOUSTON BAPTIST UNIVERSITY

Houston, Texas

Huskies			Blue and Orange
(as Houston Baptist College)			
1968	6	20	Gerald Meyers
1969	16	12	Gerald Meyers
1970	10	11	Gerald Meyers
1971	15	11	Lonnie Richards
1972	11	14	Lonnie Richards
1973	11	12	Lonnie Richards
(as Houston Baptist University)			
1974	6	19	Lonnie Richards
1975	9	17	Lonnie Richards

HOWARD UNIVERSITY

Washington, D.C.

Bisons			Blue and White
1958	13	8	Thomas A. Hart
1959	10	12	W. L. Jones
1960	—	—	
1961	—	—	
1962	10	11	James M. Thompson
1963	10	14	James M. Thompson
1964	10	14	James M. Thompson
1965	11	11	James M. Thompson
1966	16	10	James M. Thompson
1967	21	16	Marshall T. Emery
1968	14	10	Marshall T. Emery
1969	5	16	Marshall T. Emery
1970	14	11	Marshall T. Emery
1971	20	7	Marshall T. Emery
1972	18	9	Marshall T. Emery
1973	22	6	Marshall T. Emery
1974	11	15	Marshall T. Emery
1975	13	13	Marshall T. Emery
1976	9	19	A. B. Williamson
1977	18	10	A. B. Williamson
1978	15	9	A. B. Williamson
1979	16	12	A. B. Williamson

IDAHO, UNIVERSITY OF

Moscow, Idaho

Vandals			Silver and Gold
1938	22	11	Forrest Twogood
1939	12	19	Forrest Twogood
1940	13	15	Forrest Twogood
1941	15	14	Forrest Twogood
1942	12	16	Guy Wicks
1943	8	18	Babe Brown
1944	7	16	Babe Brown
1945	11	20	Babe Brown
1946	26	10	Babe Brown
1947	4	24	Guy Wicks
1948	12	18	Charles Finley
1949	17	15	Charles Finley
1950	15	17	Charles Finley
1951	15	14	Charles Finley
1952	19	13	Charles Finley
1953	14	11	Charles Finley
1954	15	8	Charles Finley
1955	8	18	Harlan Hodges
1956	6	19	Harlan Hodges
1957	10	16	Harlan Hodges
1958	17	9	Harlan Hodges
1959	11	15	Harlan Hodges
1960	11	15	Dave Strack
1961	10	16	Joe Cipriano
1962	13	13	Joe Cipriano
1963	20	6	Joe Cipriano
1964	7	19	Jim Goddard
1965	6	19	Jim Goddard
1966	12	14	Jim Goddard
1967	14	11	Wayne Anderson
1968	15	11	Wayne Anderson
1969	11	15	Wayne Anderson
1970	10	15	Wayne Anderson
1971	14	12	Wayne Anderson
1972	4	20	Wayne Anderson
1973	7	19	Wayne Anderson

Yr.	W	L	Coach
1974	12	14	Wayne Anderson
1975	10	16	Jim Jarvis
1976	7	19	Jim Jarvis
1977	5	21	Jim Jarvis
1978	4	22	Jim Jarvis
1979	11	15	Don Monson

IDAHO STATE UNIVERSITY

Pocatello, Idaho

Bengals			Gold and Black
1948	12	16	Walter Carte
1949	11	16	Ed Willett
1950	5	25	Ed Willett
1951	17	12	Steve Belko
1952	16	11	Steve Belko
1953	18	7	Steve Belko
1954	22	5	Steve Belko
1955	18	8	Steve Belko
1956	18	8	Steve Belko
1957	25	4	John Grayson
1958	23	6	John Grayson
1959	21	7	John Grayson
1960	21	5	John Evans
1961	13	12	John Evans
1962	17	9	John Evans
1963	9	15	John Evans
1964	11	13	James L. Nau
1965	7	19	James L. Nau
1966	7	19	Claude Retherford
1967	11	14	Claude Retherford
1968	13	13	Dan Miller
1969	8	18	Dan Miller
1970	13	11	Dan Miller
1971	9	15	Dan Miller
1972	14	12	Jim Killingsworth
1973	18	8	Jim Killingsworth
1974	21	8	Jim Killingsworth
1975	16	10	Jim Killingsworth
1976	16	11	Jim Killingsworth
1977	25	5	Jim Killingsworth
1978	16	10	Lynn Archibald
1979	14	13	Lynn Archibald

ILLINOIS, UNIVERSITY OF

Champaign, Illinois

Illini			Orange and Blue
1938	9	9	Doug Mills
1939	14	5	Doug Mills
1940	14	6	Doug Mills
1941	13	7	Doug Mills
1942	18	5	Doug Mills
1943	17	1	Doug Mills
1944	11	9	Doug Mills
1945	13	7	Doug Mills
1946	14	7	Doug Mills
1947	14	6	Doug Mills
1948	15	5	Harry Combes
1949	21	4	Harry Combes
1950	14	8	Harry Combes
1951	22	5	Harry Combes
1952	22	4	Harry Combes
1953	18	4	Harry Combes
1954	17	5	Harry Combes
1955	17	5	Harry Combes
1956	18	4	Harry Combes
1957	14	8	Harry Combes
1958	11	11	Harry Combes
1959	12	10	Harry Combes
1960	16	7	Harry Combes
1961	9	15	Harry Combes
1962	15	8	Harry Combes
1963	20	6	Harry Combes
1964	13	11	Harry Combes

Yr.	W	L	Coach
1965	18	6	Harry Combes
1966	12	12	Harry Combes
1967	12	12	Harry Combes
1968	11	13	Harvey Schmidt
1969	19	5	Harvey Schmidt
1970	15	9	Harvey Schmidt
1971	11	12	Harvey Schmidt
1972	14	10	Harvey Schmidt
1973	14	10	Harvey Schmidt
1974	5	18	Harvey Schmidt
1975	8	18	Gene Bartow
1976	14	13	Lou Henson
1977	14	16	Lou Henson
1978	13	14	Lou Henson
1979	19	11	Lou Henson

ILLINOIS STATE UNIVERSITY

Normal, Illinois

Redbirds			Red and White
1938	15	4	Joseph Cogdal
1939	17	6	Joseph Cogdal
1940	20	5	Joseph Cogdal
1941	15	4	Joseph Cogdal
1942	17	5	Joseph Cogdal
1943	14	4	Joseph Cogdal
1944	16	7	Joseph Cogdal
1945	7	15	Joseph Cogdal
1946	7	14	Joseph Cogdal
1947	7	13	Joseph Cogdal
1948	7	15	Joseph Cogdal
1949	9	11	Joseph Cogdal
1950	9	15	James Goff
1951	14	12	James Goff
1952	17	7	James Goff
1953	12	12	James Goff
1954	9	12	James Goff
1955	13	12	James Goff
1956	10	14	James Goff
1957	14	13	James Goff
1958	13	14	James Collie
1959	24	5	James Collie
1960	18	8	James Collie
1961	19	7	James Collie
1962	16	11	James Collie
1963	15	10	James Collie
1964	15	10	James Collie
1965	6	18	James Collie
1966	12	14	James Collie
1967	18	13	James Collie
1968	25	3	James Collie
1969	19	10	James Collie
1970	9	16	James Collie
1971	16	10	Will Robinson
1972	16	10	Will Robinson
1973	13	12	Will Robinson
1974	17	9	Will Robinson
1975	16	10	Will Robinson
1976	20	7	Gene Smithson
1977	22	7	Gene Smithson
1978	24	4	Gene Smithson
1979	20	10	Bob Donewald

INDIANA UNIVERSITY

Bloomington, Indiana

Hoosiers			Cream and Crimson
1938	10	10	Everett Dean
1939	17	3	Branch McCracken
1940	20	3	Branch McCracken
1941	16	4	Branch McCracken
1942	15	6	Branch McCracken
1943	18	2	Harry Gold
1944	7	15	Harry Gold

Yr.	W	L	Coach
1945	10	11	Harry Gold
1946	18	3	Branch McCracken
1947	12	8	Branch McCracken
1948	8	12	Branch McCracken
1949	14	8	Branch McCracken
1950	17	5	Branch McCracken
1951	19	3	Branch McCracken
1952	16	6	Branch McCracken
1953	23	3	Branch McCracken
1954	20	4	Branch McCracken
1955	8	14	Branch McCracken
1956	13	9	Branch McCracken
1957	14	8	Branch McCracken
1958	13	11	Branch McCracken
1959	11	11	Branch McCracken
1960	20	4	Branch McCracken
1961	15	9	Branch McCracken
1962	13	11	Branch McCracken
1963	13	11	Branch McCracken
1964	9	15	Branch McCracken
1965	19	5	Branch McCracken
1966	8	16	Lou Watson
1967	18	8	Lou Watson
1968	10	14	Lou Watson
1969	9	15	Lou Watson
1970	7	17	Jerry Oliver
1971	17	7	Lou Watson
1972	17	8	Bob Knight
1973	22	6	Bob Knight
1974	23	5	Bob Knight
1975	31	1	Bob Knight
1976	32	0	Bob Knight
1977	14	13	Bob Knight
1978	21	8	Bob Knight
1979	22	12	Bob Knight

INDIANA STATE UNIVERSITY

Terre Haute, Indiana

Sycamores			Blue and White
1938	1	17	Walter E. Markes
1939	10	9	Glenn M. Curtis
1940	15	3	Glenn M. Curtis
1941	10	9	Glenn M. Curtis
1942	17	4	Glenn M. Curtis
1943	13	4	Glenn M. Curtis
1944	17	4	Glenn M. Curtis
1945	18	6	Glenn M. Curtis
1946	21	7	Glenn M. Curtis
1947	17	8	John R. Wooden
1948	27	7	John R. Wooden
1949	24	8	John L. Longfellow
1950	27	8	John L. Longfellow
1951	15	10	John L. Longfellow
1952	19	10	John L. Longfellow
1953	23	8	John L. Longfellow
1954	12	15	John L. Longfellow
1955	9	15	J. L. Longfellow, P. Stemm, P. Wolf
1956	8	16	Duane Klueh
1957	12	13	Duane Klueh
1958	11	14	Duane Klueh
1959	18	9	Duane Klueh
1960	7	13	Duane Klueh
1961	18	8	Duane Klueh
1962	19	11	Duane Klueh
1963	18	7	Duane Klueh
1964	17	8	Duane Klueh
1965	13	10	Duane Klueh
1966	22	6	Duane Klueh
1967	21	5	Duane Klueh
1968	23	8	Gordon C. Stauffer
1969	13	13	Gordon C. Stauffer
1970	16	10	Gordon C. Stauffer
1971	17	9	Gordon C. Stauffer
1972	12	14	Gordon C. Stauffer

Yr.	W	L	Coach
1973	16	10	Gordon C. Stauffer
1974	12	14	Gordon C. Stauffer
1975	12	14	Gordon C. Stauffer
1976	13	12	Bob King
1977	25	3	Bob King
1978	23	9	Bob King
1979	33	1	Bill Hodges

IONA COLLEGE

New Rochelle, New York

Gaels			Maroon and Gold
1941	14	9	A. A. Loftus
1942	19	4	A. A. Loftus
1943	—	—	
1944	—	—	
1945	—	—	
1946	17	5	A. A. Loftus
1947	15	8	Peter Caruso
1948	12	12	Jim McDermott
1949	18	8	Jim McDermott
1950	22	4	Jim McDermott
1951	20	7	Jim McDermott
1952	16	10	Jim McDermott
1953	18	3	Jim McDermott
1954	11	10	Jim McDermott
1955	10	11	Jim McDermott
1956	8	14	Jim McDermott
1957	13	7	Jim McDermott
1958	18	6	Jim McDermott
1959	14	7	Jim McDermott
1960	13	5	Jim McDermott
1961	10	11	Jim McDermott
1962	8	11	Jim McDermott
1963	12	7	Jim McDermott
1964	15	5	Jim McDermott
1965	12	11	Jim McDermott
1966	5	16	Jim McDermott
1967	11	10	Jim McDermott
1968	13	9	Jim McDermott
1969	11	11	Jim McDermott
1970	12	12	Jim McDermott
1971	10	12	Jim McDermott
1972	6	17	Jim McDermott
1973	6	16	Jim McDermott
1974	12	13	Gene Roberti
1975	4	19	Gene Roberti
1976	10	16	Jim Valvano
1977	15	10	Jim Valvano
1978	17	10	Jim Valvano
1979	23	6	Jim Valvano

IOWA, UNIVERSITY OF

Iowa City, Iowa

Hawkeyes			Gold and Black
1938	11	9	Rollie Williams
1939	8	11	Rollie Williams
1940	9	12	Rollie Williams
1941	12	8	Rollie Williams
1942	12	8	Rollie Williams
1943	7	10	Pops Harrison
1944	14	4	Pops Harrison
1945	17	1	Pops Harrison
1946	14	4	Pops Harrison
1947	12	7	Pops Harrison
1948	15	4	Pops Harrison
1949	10	10	Pops Harrison
1950	15	7	Bucky O'Connor
1951	15	7	Rollie Williams
1952	19	3	Bucky O'Connor
1953	12	10	Bucky O'Connor
1954	17	5	Bucky O'Connor
1955	19	7	Bucky O'Connor
1956	20	6	Bucky O'Connor

Yr.	W	L	Coach
1957	8	14	Bucky O'Connor
1958	13	9	Bucky O'Connor
1959	10	12	Sharm Scheuerman
1960	14	10	Sharm Scheuerman
1961	18	6	Sharm Scheuerman
1962	13	11	Sharm Scheuerman
1963	9	15	Sharm Scheuerman
1964	8	15	Sharm Scheuerman
1965	14	10	Ralph Miller
1966	17	7	Ralph Miller
1967	16	8	Ralph Miller
1968	16	9	Ralph Miller
1969	12	12	Ralph Miller
1970	20	5	Ralph Miller
1971	9	15	Dick Schultz
1972	11	13	Dick Schultz
1973	13	11	Dick Schultz
1974	8	16	Dick Schultz
1975	10	16	Lute Olson
1976	19	10	Lute Olson
1977	18	9	Lute Olson
1978	12	15	Lute Olson
1979	20	8	Lute Olson

IOWA STATE UNIVERSITY

Ames, Iowa

Cyclones			*Cardinal and Gold*
1938	6	9	Louis Menze
1939	8	9	Louis Menze
1940	9	9	Louis Menze
1941	15	4	Louis Menze
1942	11	6	Louis Menze
1943	7	9	Louis Menze
1944	14	4	Louis Menze
1945	11	5	Louis Menze
1946	8	8	Louis Menze
1947	7	14	Louis Menze
1948	15	8	Clayton Sutherland
1949	8	14	Clayton Sutherland
1950	6	17	Clayton Sutherland
1951	10	11	Clayton Sutherland
1952	10	11	Clayton Sutherland
1953	10	11	Clayton Sutherland
1954	6	15	Clayton Sutherland
1955	11	10	Bill Strannigan
1956	18	5	Bill Strannigan
1957	16	7	Bill Strannigan
1958	15	8	Bill Strannigan
1959	9	16	Bill Strannigan
1960	15	9	Glen Anderson
1961	12	13	Glen Anderson
1962	13	12	Glen Anderson
1963	14	11	Glen Anderson
1964	9	16	Glen Anderson
1965	9	16	Glen Anderson
1966	11	14	Glen Anderson
1967	13	12	Glen Anderson
1968	12	13	Glen Anderson
1969	14	12	Glen Anderson
1970	12	14	Glen Anderson
1971	5	21	Glen Anderson
1972	12	14	Maurice John
1973	16	10	Maurice John
1974	15	11	Maurice John
1975	10	16	Ken Trickey
1976	3	24	Ken Trickey
1977	8	19	Lynn Nance
1978	14	13	Lynn Nance
1979	11	16	Lynn Nance

JACKSON STATE UNIVERSITY

Jackson, Mississippi

Tigers			*Blue and White*
1968	24	3	Paul Covington

Yr.	W	L	Coach
1969	15	6	Paul Covington
1970	23	3	Paul Covington
1971	20	6	Paul Covington
1972	15	11	Paul Covington
1973	21	7	Paul Covington
1974	22	6	Paul Covington
1975	25	4	Paul Covington
1976	18	11	Paul Covington
1977	19	8	Paul Covington
1978	21	5	Paul Covington
1979	13	14	Paul Covington

JACKSONVILLE UNIVERSITY

Jacksonville, Florida

Dolphins			*Kelly Green and White*
1959	11	8	Rollie Rourke
1960	11	10	Rollie Rourke
1961	12	11	Dick Kendall
1962	12	13	Dick Kendall
1963	14	12	Dick Kendall
1964	13	13	Dick Kendall
1965	15	11	Joe Williams
1966	12	11	Joe Williams
1967	8	17	Joe Williams
1968	13	13	Joe Williams
1969	17	7	Joe Williams
1970	27	2	Joe Williams
1971	22	4	Tom Wasdin
1972	20	8	Tom Wasdin
1973	21	6	Tom Wasdin
1974	20	10	Bob Gottlieb
1975	15	11	Bob Gottlieb
1976	13	13	Don Beasley
1977	10	19	Don Beasley
1978	14	14	Don Beasley
1979	19	11	Tates Locke

JAMES MADISON UNIVERSITY

Harrisonburg, Virginia

Dukes			*Purple and Gold*
		(as Madison College)	
1970	11	9	Charles Branscom
1971	9	8	Charles Branscom
1972	16	7	Dean Ehlers
1973	16	10	Lou Campanelli
1974	20	6	Lou Campanelli
1975	19	6	Lou Campanelli
1976	18	9	Lou Campanelli
1977	17	9	Lou Campanelli
	(as James Madison University)		
1978	18	8	Lou Campanelli
1979	18	8	Lou Campanelli

KANSAS, UNIVERSITY OF

Lawrence, Kansas

Jayhawks			*Crimson and Blue*
1938	18	2	Dr. Forest "Phog" Allen
1939	13	7	Dr. Forest "Phog" Allen
1940	19	6	Dr. Forest "Phog" Allen
1941	12	6	Dr. Forest "Phog" Allen
1942	17	5	Dr. Forest "Phog" Allen
1943	22	6	Dr. Forest "Phog" Allen
1944	17	9	Dr. Forest "Phog" Allen
1945	12	5	Dr. Forest "Phog" Allen
1946	19	2	Dr. Forest "Phog" Allen
1947	16	11	F. Allen, H. Engleman
1948	9	15	Dr. Forest "Phog" Allen
1949	12	12	Dr. Forest "Phog" Allen
1950	14	11	Dr. Forest "Phog" Allen

Yr.	W	L	Coach
1951	16	8	Dr. Forest "Phog" Allen
1952	28	3	Dr. Forest "Phog" Allen
1953	19	6	Dr. Forest "Phog" Allen
1954	16	5	Dr. Forest "Phog" Allen
1955	11	10	Dr. Forest "Phog" Allen
1956	14	9	Dr. Forest "Phog" Allen
1957	24	3	Dick Harp
1958	18	5	Dick Harp
1959	11	14	Dick Harp
1960	19	9	Dick Harp
1961	17	8	Dick Harp
1962	7	18	Dick Harp
1963	12	13	Dick Harp
1964	13	12	Dick Harp
1965	17	8	Ted Owens
1966	23	4	Ted Owens
1967	23	4	Ted Owens
1968	22	8	Ted Owens
1969	20	7	Ted Owens
1970	17	9	Ted Owens
1971	27	3	Ted Owens
1972	11	15	Ted Owens
1973	8	18	Ted Owens
1974	23	7	Ted Owens
1975	19	8	Ted Owens
1976	13	13	Ted Owens
1977	18	10	Ted Owens
1978	24	5	Ted Owens
1979	18	11	Ted Owens

KANSAS STATE UNIVERSITY

Manhattan, Kansas

Wildcats			Purple and White
1938	7	11	Frank Root
1939	5	13	Frank Root
1940	6	12	Jack Gardner
1941	6	12	Jack Gardner
1942	8	10	Jack Gardner
1943	6	14	Chili Cochrane
1944	7	15	Cliff Rock
1945	10	13	Fritz Knorr
1946	4	20	Fritz Knorr
1947	14	10	Jack Gardner
1948	22	6	Jack Gardner
1949	13	11	Jack Gardner
1950	17	7	Jack Gardner
1951	25	4	Jack Gardner
1952	19	5	Jack Gardner
1953	17	4	Jack Gardner
1954	11	10	Tex Winter
1955	11	10	Tex Winter
1956	17	8	Tex Winter
1957	15	8	Tex Winter
1958	22	5	Tex Winter
1959	25	2	Tex Winter
1960	16	10	Tex Winter
1961	23	4	Tex Winter
1962	22	3	Tex Winter
1963	16	9	Tex Winter
1964	22	7	Tex Winter
1965	12	13	Tex Winter
1966	14	11	Tex Winter
1967	17	8	Tex Winter
1968	19	9	Tex Winter
1969	14	12	Cotton Fitzsimmons
1970	20	8	Cotton Fitzsimmons
1971	11	15	Jack Hartman
1972	19	9	Jack Hartman
1973	23	5	Jack Hartman
1974	19	8	Jack Hartman
1975	20	9	Jack Hartman
1976	20	8	Jack Hartman
1977	23	9	Jack Hartman
1978	18	11	Jack Hartman
1979	16	12	Jack Hartman

KENT STATE UNIVERSITY

Kent, Ohio

Golden Flashes			Blue and Gold
1938	10	13	Donald Starn
1939	12	11	Donald Starn
1940	13	10	Donald Starn
1941	12	10	Donald Starn
1942	14	11	Donald Starn
1943	12	12	Donald Starn
1944	—	—	
1945	3	11	William Satterlee
1946	10	10	William Satterlee
1947	13	11	Harry Adams
1948	15	8	Harry Adams
1949	20	8	David McDowell
1950	18	4	David McDowell
1951	18	8	David McDowell
1952	14	10	Clarence Haerr
1953	7	15	Clarence Haerr
1954	8	13	Clarence Haerr
1955	8	14	Clarence Haerr
1956	10	11	David McDowell
1957	5	18	David McDowell
1958	9	14	William Bertka
1959	11	13	William Bertka
1960	7	16	William Bertka
1961	9	14	William Bertka
1962	2	19	Bob Doll
1963	3	18	Bob Doll
1964	11	13	Bob Doll
1965	9	11	Bob Doll
1966	8	16	Bob Doll
1967	5	18	Frank Truitt
1968	9	15	Frank Truitt
1969	14	10	Frank Truitt
1970	7	17	Frank Truitt
1971	13	11	Frank Truitt
1972	7	17	Frank Truitt
1973	10	16	Frank Truitt
1974	9	17	Frank Truitt
1975	6	20	Rex Hughes
1976	12	14	Rex Hughes
1977	8	19	Rex Hughes
1978	6	21	R. Hughes, M. Boyd
1979	13	14	Ed Douma

KENTUCKY, UNIVERSITY OF

Lexington, Kentucky

Wildcats			Blue and White
1938	13	5	Adolph Rupp
1939	16	4	Adolph Rupp
1940	15	6	Adolph Rupp
1941	17	8	Adolph Rupp
1942	19	6	Adolph Rupp
1943	17	6	Adolph Rupp
1944	19	2	Adolph Rupp
1945	22	4	Adolph Rupp
1946	28	2	Adolph Rupp
1947	34	3	Adolph Rupp
1948	36	3	Adolph Rupp
1949	32	2	Adolph Rupp
1950	25	5	Adolph Rupp
1951	32	2	Adolph Rupp
1952	29	3	Adolph Rupp
1953	—	—	
1954	25	0	Adolph Rupp
1955	23	3	Adolph Rupp
1956	20	6	Adolph Rupp
1957	23	5	Adolph Rupp
1958	23	6	Adolph Rupp
1959	24	3	Adolph Rupp
1960	18	7	Adolph Rupp
1961	19	9	Adolph Rupp

Yr.	W	L	Coach
1962	23	3	Adolph Rupp
1963	16	9	Adolph Rupp
1964	21	6	Adolph Rupp
1965	15	10	Adolph Rupp
1966	27	2	Adolph Rupp
1967	13	13	Adolph Rupp
1968	22	5	Adolph Rupp
1969	23	5	Adolph Rupp
1970	26	2	Adolph Rupp
1971	22	6	Adolph Rupp
1972	21	7	Adolph Rupp
1973	20	8	Joe B. Hall
1974	13	13	Joe B. Hall
1975	26	5	Joe B. Hall
1976	20	10	Joe B. Hall
1977	26	4	Joe B. Hall
1978	30	2	Joe B. Hall
1979	19	12	Joe B. Hall

Yr.	W	L	Coach
1942	12	10	Obie O'Brien
1943	13	10	Obie O'Brien
1944	8	8	Joseph Meehan
1945	11	8	Joseph Meehan
1946	10	13	Joseph Meehan
1947	20	6	Charles McGlone
1948	20	4	Charles McGlone
1949	20	7	Charles McGlone
1950	21	4	Ken Loeffler
1951	22	7	Ken Loeffler
1952	25	7	Ken Loeffler
1953	25	3	Ken Loeffler
1954	26	4	Ken Loeffler
1955	26	5	Ken Loeffler
1956	15	10	Jim Pollard
1957	17	9	Jim Pollard
1958	16	9	Jim Pollard
1959	16	7	Donald "Dudey" Moore
1960	16	6	Donald "Dudey" Moore
1961	15	7	Donald "Dudey" Moore
1962	16	9	Donald "Dudey" Moore
1963	16	8	Donald "Dudey" Moore
1964	16	9	Bob Walters
1965	15	8	Bob Walters
1966	10	15	Joe Heyer
1967	14	12	Joe Heyer
1968	20	8	Jim Harding
1969	23	1	Tom Gola
1970	14	12	Tom Gola
1971	20	7	Paul Westhead
1972	6	19	Paul Westhead
1973	15	10	Paul Westhead
1974	18	10	Paul Westhead
1975	22	7	Paul Westhead
1976	11	15	Paul Westhead
1977	17	12	Paul Westhead
1978	18	12	Paul Westhead
1979	15	13	Paul Westhead

LAFAYETTE COLLEGE

Easton, Pennsylvania

Leopards			Maroon and White
1938	9	8	Michael Michalske
1939	6	11	R. C. Madison
1940	11	8	R. C. Madison
1941	8	10	R. C. Madison
1942	4	12	R. C. Madison
1943	7	6	A. R. Winters
1944	7	3	A. R. Winters
1945	16	2	A. R. Winters
1946	17	3	Ray Stanley
1947	15	7	Ray Stanley
1948	12	9	Ray Stanley
1949	20	9	Ray Stanley
1950	19	6	Ray Stanley
1951	14	11	Ray Stanley
1952	15	9	Bill van Breda Kolff
1953	13	12	Bill van Breda Kolff
1954	17	10	Bill van Breda Kolff
1955	24	3	Bill van Breda Kolff
1956	20	7	George Davidson
1957	22	5	George Davidson
1958	16	10	George Davidson
1959	13	8	George Davidson
1960	12	13	George Davidson
1961	16	8	George Davidson
1962	18	6	George Davidson
1963	13	11	George Davidson
1964	15	8	George Davidson
1965	12	8	George Davidson
1966	9	11	George Davidson
1967	4	21	George Davidson
1968	5	19	Hal Wissel
1969	9	17	Hal Wissel
1970	12	14	Hal Wissel
1971	17	9	Hal Wissel
1972	21	6	Thomas Davis
1973	16	10	Thomas Davis
1974	17	9	Thomas Davis
1975	22	6	Thomas Davis
1976	19	7	Thomas Davis
1977	21	6	Thomas Davis
1978	23	8	Dr. Roy Chipman
1979	16	12	Dr. Roy Chipman

LASALLE COLLEGE

Philadelphia, Pennsylvania

Explorers			Blue and Gold
1938	9	8	Leonard Tanseer
1939	12	6	Leonard Tanseer
1940	12	8	Leonard Tanseer
1941	9	8	Leonard Tanseer

LAMAR UNIVERSITY

Beaumont, Texas

Cardinals			Red and White
1969	20	4	Jack Martin
1970	15	9	Jack Martin
1971	11	13	Jack Martin
1972	12	14	Jack Martin
1973	9	15	Jack Martin
1974	6	19	Jack Martin
1975	7	16	Jack Martin
1976	10	14	Jack Martin
1977	12	17	Billy Tubbs
1978	18	9	Billy Tubbs
1979	23	9	Billy Tubbs

LEHIGH UNIVERSITY

Bethlehem, Pennsylvania

Engineers			Brown and White
1938	7	8	Paul Calvert
1939	10	5	Paul Calvert
1940	5	10	Paul Calvert
1941	5	12	Paul Calvert
1942	7	8	Marty Westerman
1943	5	10	James Gordon
1944	4	12	Leo Prendergast
1945	2	14	Leo Prendergast
1946	3	13	Leo Prendergast
1947	5	13	Daniel Yarbo
1948	2	16	Daniel Yarbo
1949	7	11	Daniel Yarbo
1950	4	14	Daniel Yarbo
1951	6	13	Tony Packer
1952	7	12	Tony Packer
1953	12	8	Tony Packer

Yr.	W	L	Coach	Yr.	W	L	Coach
1954	8	12	Tony Packer	1948	17	4	Clair Bee
1955	10	11	Tony Packer	1949	18	12	Clair Bee
1956	7	11	Tony Packer	1950	20	5	Clair Bee
1957	8	10	Tony Packer	1951	20	4	Clair Bee
1958	8	10	Tony Packer	1952	—	—	
1959	6	16	Tony Packer	1953	—	—	
1960	6	16	Tony Packer	1954	—	—	
1961	5	16	Tony Packer	1955	—	—	
1962	7	12	Tony Packer	1956	—	—	
1963	6	19	Tony Packer	1957	—	—	
1964	5	17	Tony Packer	1958	12	6	Buck Lai
1965	7	13	Tony Packer	1959	7	14	Buck Lai
1966	4	17	Tony Packer	1960	12	9	Buck Lai
1967	11	12	Pete Carrill	1961	13	10	Buck Lai
1968	12	11	Roy Heckman	1962	12	9	Roy Rubin
1969	7	17	Roy Heckman	1963	10	14	Roy Rubin
1970	13	14	Roy Heckman	1964	14	9	Roy Rubin
1971	10	16	Roy Heckman	1965	16	7	Roy Rubin
1972	10	14	Roy Heckman	1966	22	4	Roy Rubin
1973	8	17	Tom Pugliese	1967	22	7	Roy Rubin
1974	3	21	Tom Pugliese	1968	22	2	Roy Rubin
1975	1	23	Tom Pugliese	1969	17	6	Roy Rubin
1976	9	15	Brian Hill	1970	16	9	Roy Rubin
1977	12	15	Brian Hill	1971	10	15	Roy Rubin
1978	8	18	Brian Hill	1972	13	12	Roy Rubin
1979	8	18	Brian Hill	1973	13	12	Ron Smalls
				1974	13	12	Ron Smalls
				1975	13	12	Ron Smalls
				1976	15	12	Paul Lizzo
				1977	9	16	Paul Lizzo
				1978	8	18	Paul Lizzo
				1979	12	13	Paul Lizzo

LONG BEACH STATE

Long Beach, California

49ers			Brown and Gold
1951	3	14	Herm Schwarzkopf
1952	10	13	Herm Schwarzkopf
1953	12	10	Earl Kidd
1954	8	17	Earl Kidd
1955	13	8	Earl Kidd
1956	8	16	Earl Kidd
1957	7	21	Earl Kidd
1958	10	13	Bill Patterson
1959	10	13	Bill Patterson
1960	17	7	Bill Patterson
1961	15	11	Dick Perry
1962	14	12	Dick Perry
1963	10	15	Dick Perry
1964	8	16	Dick Perry
1965	17	9	Dick Perry
1966	8	17	Dick Perry
1967	11	16	Dick Perry
1968	12	13	Randy Sandefur
1969	23	3	Jerry Tarkanian
1970	24	5	Jerry Tarkanian
1971	23	5	Jerry Tarkanian
1972	25	4	Jerry Tarkanian
1973	26	3	Jerry Tarkanian
1974	24	2	Lute Olson
1975	19	7	Dwight Jones
1976	14	12	Dwight Jones
1977	21	8	Dwight Jones
1978	16	13	Tex Winter
1979	16	12	Tex Winter

LONG ISLAND UNIVERSITY

Brooklyn, New York

Blackbirds			Blue and White
1938	23	4	Clair Bee
1939	23	0	Clair Bee
1940	19	4	Clair Bee
1941	25	2	Clair Bee
1942	24	4	Clair Bee
1943	13	6	Clair Bee
1944	12	3	George Wolfe
1945	14	5	George Wolfe
1946	14	9	Clair Bee
1947	17	4	Clair Bee

LOUISIANA STATE UNIVERSITY

Baton Rouge, Louisiana

Tigers			Purple and Gold
1938	10	10	Harry Rabenhorst
1939	13	7	Harry Rabenhorst
1940	10	8	Harry Rabenhorst
1941	9	9	Harry Rabenhorst
1942	8	7	Harry Rabenhorst
1943	18	4	Dale Morey
1944	10	15	Dale Morey
1945	15	9	J. Fatheree, A. L. Swanson
1946	18	3	Harry Rabenhorst
1947	17	4	Harry Rabenhorst
1948	8	18	Harry Rabenhorst
1949	15	10	Harry Rabenhorst
1950	13	12	Harry Rabenhorst
1951	10	14	Harry Rabenhorst
1952	17	7	Harry Rabenhorst
1953	24	3	Harry Rabenhorst
1954	21	5	Harry Rabenhorst
1955	6	18	Harry Rabenhorst
1956	7	17	Harry Rabenhorst
1957	6	19	Harry Rabenhorst
1958	7	18	Jay McCreary
1959	10	15	Jay McCreary
1960	5	18	Jay McCreary
1961	11	14	Jay McCreary
1962	13	11	Jay McCreary
1963	12	12	Jay McCreary
1964	12	13	Jay McCreary
1965	12	14	Jay McCreary
1966	6	20	Frank Truitt
1967	3	23	Press Maravich
1968	14	12	Press Maravich
1969	13	13	Press Maravich
1970	22	10	Press Maravich
1971	14	12	Press Maravich
1972	10	16	Press Maravich
1973	14	10	Dale Brown
1974	12	14	Dale Brown
1975	10	16	Dale Brown
1976	12	14	Dale Brown

Yr.	W	L	Coach	Yr.	W	L	Coach
1977	15	12	Dale Brown	1952	20	6	Bernard "Peck" Hickman
1978	18	9	Dale Brown	1953	22	6	Bernard "Peck" Hickman
1979	23	6	Dale Brown	1954	22	7	Bernard "Peck" Hickman
				1955	19	8	Bernard "Peck" Hickman
				1956	26	3	Bernard "Peck" Hickman
				1957	21	5	Bernard "Peck" Hickman
				1958	13	12	Bernard "Peck" Hickman
				1959	19	12	Bernard "Peck" Hickman
				1960	15	11	Bernard "Peck" Hickman
				1961	21	8	Bernard "Peck" Hickman
				1962	15	10	Bernard "Peck" Hickman
				1963	14	11	Bernard "Peck" Hickman

LOUISIANA TECH

Ruston, Louisiana

Bulldogs			Red and Blue	1964	15	10	Bernard "Peck" Hickman
1938	5	9	Herb Duggins	1965	15	10	Bernard "Peck" Hickman
1939	10	8	Herb Duggins	1966	16	10	Bernard "Peck" Hickman
1940	5	17	Herb Duggins	1967	23	5	Bernard "Peck" Hickman
1941	7	10	Cecil C. Crowley	1968	21	7	John Dromo
1942	13	8	Cecil C. Crowley	1969	21	6	John Dromo
1943	—	—		1970	18	9	John Dromo
1944	—	—		1971	20	9	John Dromo
1945	5	12	Joe Aillet	1972	26	5	Denny Crum
1946	16	8	Cecil C. Crowley	1973	23	7	Denny Crum
1947	12	6	Cecil C. Crowley	1974	21	7	Denny Crum
1948	14	10	Cecil C. Crowley	1975	28	3	Denny Crum
1949	11	11	Cecil C. Crowley	1976	20	8	Denny Crum
1950	11	9	Cecil C. Crowley	1977	21	7	Denny Crum
1951	11	10	Cecil C. Crowley	1978	23	7	Denny Crum
1952	13	11	Cecil C. Crowley	1979	24	8	Denny Crum
1953	18	10	Cecil C. Crowley				
1954	11	14	Cecil C. Crowley				
1955	20	10	Cecil C. Crowley				
1956	11	14	Cecil C. Crowley				
1957	14	11	Cecil C. Crowley				
1958	15	10	Cecil C. Crowley				
1959	21	14	Cecil C. Crowley				
1960	17	9	Cecil C. Crowley				

LOYOLA UNIVERSITY

Chicago, Illinois

1961	7	16	Cecil C. Crowley	Ramblers			Maroon and Gold
1962	6	17	Cecil C. Crowley	1938	12	8	Leonard Sachs
1963	10	13	Cecil C. Crowley	1939	21	1	Leonard Sachs
1964	12	10	Cecil C. Crowley	1940	5	14	Leonard Sachs
1965	11	11	Scotty Robertson	1941	13	8	Leonard Sachs
1966	14	11	Scotty Robertson	1942	17	6	Leonard Sachs
1967	20	8	Scotty Robertson	1943	12	10	John Connelly
1968	16	9	Scotty Robertson	1944	—	—	
1969	12	13	Scotty Robertson	1945	4	8	Alex Wilson
1970	17	5	Scotty Robertson	1946	23	4	Thomas Haggerty
1971	23	5	Scotty Robertson	1947	20	9	Thomas Haggerty
1972	23	3	Scotty Robertson	1948	26	9	Thomas Haggerty
1973	18	8	Scotty Robertson	1949	25	6	Thomas Haggerty
1974	11	13	Scotty Robertson	1950	17	13	Thomas Haggerty
1975	12	13	Emmett Hendricks	1951	15	14	John Jordan
1976	15	11	Emmett Hendricks	1952	17	8	George Ireland
1977	13	13	Emmett Hendricks	1953	8	15	George Ireland
1978	6	21	J. D. Barnett	1954	7	15	George Ireland
1979	17	8	J. D. Barnett	1955	13	11	George Ireland
				1956	10	14	George Ireland
				1957	14	10	George Ireland
				1958	16	8	George Ireland
				1959	11	13	George Ireland
				1960	10	12	George Ireland
				1961	15	8	George Ireland
				1962	23	4	George Ireland
				1963	29	2	George Ireland
				1964	22	6	George Ireland

LOUISVILLE, UNIVERSITY OF

Louisville, Kentucky

Cardinals			Red and Black	1965	11	14	George Ireland
1938	5	11	Lawrence Apitz	1966	22	3	George Ireland
1939	1	16	Lawrence Apitz	1967	14	9	George Ireland
1940	2	18	Lawrence Apitz	1968	16	9	George Ireland
1941	3	14	John Heldman	1969	9	14	George Ireland
1942	8	10	John Heldman	1970	13	11	George Ireland
1943	—	—		1971	4	20	George Ireland
1944	10	10	H. Church, W. Casey	1972	8	14	George Ireland
1945	16	3	Bernard "Peck" Hickman	1973	8	15	George Ireland
1946	22	6	Bernard "Peck" Hickman	1974	12	14	George Ireland
1947	17	6	Bernard "Peck" Hickman	1975	10	15	George Ireland
1948	29	6	Bernard "Peck" Hickman	1976	10	16	Jerry Lyne
1949	23	10	Bernard "Peck" Hickman	1977	13	13	Jerry Lyne
1950	21	11	Bernard "Peck" Hickman	1978	16	11	Jerry Lyne
1951	19	7	Bernard "Peck" Hickman	1979	12	15	Jerry Lyne

Yr.	W	L	Coach

LOYOLA UNIVERSITY*

New Orleans, Louisiana

Wolfpack			Maroon and Gold
1942	14	2	Jack Orsley
1943	21	3	Jack Orsley
1944	25	5	Jack Orsley
1945	22	11	Jack Orsley
1946	15	9	Jack Orsley
1947	20	10	Jack Orsley
1948	11	16	Jack Orsley
1949	7	18	J. Orsley, J. McCafferty
1950	15	12	Tom Haggerty
1951	20	14	Tom Haggerty
1952	14	13	Tom Haggerty
1953	15	9	T. Haggerty, J. McCafferty
1954	13	10	Jim McCafferty
1955	11	14	Jim McCafferty
1956	14	12	Jim McCafferty
1957	16	9	Jim Harding
1958	10	16	Henry Kuzma
1959	12	13	Bill Gardiner
1960	6	18	Bill Gardiner
1961	11	12	Bill Gardiner
1962	11	12	Bill Gardiner
1963	12	11	Bill Gardiner
1964	12	12	Bill Gardiner
1965	8	16	Bill Gardiner
1966	9	17	Bill Gardiner
1967	12	10	Ron Greene
1968	11	14	Ron Greene
1969	5	19	Bob Luksta
1970	12	14	Bob Luksta
1971	16	10	Bob Luksta
1972	14	11	Bob Luksta

*Basketball discontinued in 1973.

LOYOLA MARYMOUNT UNIVERSITY

Los Angeles, California

Lions			Crimson and Gray
			(as Loyola University)
1946	12	15	Scotty McDonald
1947	13	20	Scotty McDonald
1948	22	14	Scotty McDonald
1949	9	17	Scotty McDonald
1950	14	11	Scotty McDonald
1951	12	14	Scotty McDonald
1952	15	14	Edwin Powell
1953	14	16	Bill Donovan
1954	16	9	Bill Donovan
1955	13	12	Bill Donovan
1956	11	16	Bill Donovan
1957	6	18	Bill Donovan
1958	8	15	Bill Donovan
1959	19	8	Bill Donovan
1960	20	7	Bill Donovan
1961	16	8	John Arndt
1962	18	9	John Arndt
1963	9	17	John Arndt
1964	12	13	John Arndt
1965	6	20	John Arndt
1966	11	15	John Arndt
1967	16	10	John Arndt
1968	19	6	John Arndt
1969	6	19	Dick Baker
1970	13	13	Dick Baker
1971	15	10	Dick Baker
1972	11	15	Dick Baker
			(as Loyola Marymount University)
1973	10	16	Dick Baker
1974	15	12	Dave Benaderet
1975	14	12	Dave Benaderet
1976	7	19	Dave Benaderet
1977	11	15	Dave Benaderet
1978	11	15	Dave Benaderet
1979	5	21	Dave Benaderet

MAINE, UNIVERSITY OF

Orono, Maine

Black Bears			Blue and White
1938	4	9	William Kenyon
1939	8	4	H. Woodbury, W. Kenyon
1940	3	9	William Kenyon
1941	4	8	William Kenyon
1942	7	7	William Kenyon
1943	9	6	Samuel Sezak
1944	4	6	Samuel Sezak
1945	4	8	William Kenyon
1946	10	4	Eck Allen
1947	9	8	Eck Allen
1948	11	7	Eck Allen
1949	4	14	Eck Allen
1950	13	6	Rome Rankin
1951	5	13	Rome Rankin
1952	7	12	Rome Rankin
1953	7	10	Rome Rankin
1954	6	12	Rome Rankin
1955	4	13	Russell DeVette
1956	6	12	Harold Woodbury
1957	6	14	Harold Woodbury
1958	8	12	Harold Woodbury
1959	15	7	Brian McCall
1960	19	4	Brian McCall
1961	18	5	Brian McCall
1962	11	13	Brian McCall
1963	8	15	Brian McCall
1964	12	11	Brian McCall
1965	13	10	Brian McCall
1966	9	13	Brian McCall
1967	8	12	Brian McCall
1968	7	17	Brian McCall
1969	10	13	Gilbert Philbrick
1970	7	17	Gilbert Philbrick
1971	8	16	Gilbert Philbrick
1972	15	10	Thomas Chappelle
1973	13	10	Thomas Chappelle
1974	14	10	Thomas Chappelle
1975	11	14	Thomas Chappelle
1976	14	11	Thomas Chappelle
1977	13	13	Thomas Chappelle
1978	17	8	Thomas Chappelle
1979	14	10	Thomas Chappelle

MANHATTAN COLLEGE

Bronx, New York

Jaspers			Green and White
1938	12	6	Neil Cohalan
1939	12	5	Neil Cohalan
1940	14	9	Neil Cohalan
1941	11	7	Neil Cohalan
1942	10	10	Neil Cohalan
1943	18	3	Joseph Daher
1944	—	—	
1945	—	—	
1946	15	8	John "Honey" Russell
1947	13	13	Ken Norton
1948	23	6	Ken Norton
1949	18	8	Ken Norton
1950	13	11	Ken Norton
1951	16	6	Ken Norton
1952	12	9	Ken Norton
1953	20	6	Ken Norton
1954	15	11	Ken Norton

Yr.	W	L	Coach
1955	18	5	Ken Norton
1956	16	8	Ken Norton
1957	15	9	Ken Norton
1958	16	10	Ken Norton
1959	15	6	Ken Norton
1960	13	11	Ken Norton
1961	8	11	Ken Norton
1962	12	10	Ken Norton
1963	9	14	Ken Norton
1964	11	11	Ken Norton
1965	13	9	Ken Norton
1966	13	9	Ken Norton
1967	13	8	Ken Norton
1968	8	14	Ken Norton
1969	13	8	John Powers
1970	18	8	John Powers
1971	13	11	John Powers
1972	11	13	John Powers
1973	18	9	John Powers
1974	14	12	John Powers
1975	14	14	John Powers
1976	13	14	John Powers
1977	12	14	John Powers
1978	12	14	John Powers
1979	6	20	Brian Mahoney

MARQUETTE UNIVERSITY

Milwaukee, Wisconsin

Warriors			Blue and Gold
1938	14	5	William Chandler
1939	12	5	William Chandler
1940	7	9	William Chandler
1941	2	13	William Chandler
1942	6	11	William Chandler
1943	9	10	William Chandler
1944	8	6	William Chandler
1945	7	10	William Chandler
1946	11	7	William Chandler
1947	9	14	William Chandler
1948	9	15	William Chandler
1949	8	13	William Chandler
1950	6	17	William Chandler
1951	8	14	William Chandler
1952	12	14	Tex Winter
1953	13	11	Tex Winter
1954	11	15	Jack Nagle
1955	24	3	Jack Nagle
1956	13	11	Jack Nagle
1957	10	15	Jack Nagle
1958	11	11	Jack Nagle
1959	23	6	Eddie Hickey
1960	13	12	Eddie Hickey
1961	16	11	Eddie Hickey
1962	15	11	Eddie Hickey
1963	20	9	Eddie Hickey
1964	5	21	Eddie Hickey
1965	8	18	Al McGuire
1966	14	12	Al McGuire
1967	21	9	Al McGuire
1968	23	6	Al McGuire
1969	24	5	Al McGuire
1970	26	3	Al McGuire
1971	28	1	Al McGuire
1972	25	4	Al McGuire
1973	25	4	Al McGuire
1974	26	5	Al McGuire
1975	23	4	Al McGuire
1976	27	2	Al McGuire
1977	25	7	Al McGuire
1978	24	4	Hank Raymonds
1979	22	7	Hank Raymonds

MARSHALL UNIVERSITY

Huntington, West Virginia

Yr.	W	L	Coach
Thundering Herd			Green and White
1939	22	5	Cam Henderson
1940	25	4	Cam Henderson
1941	14	9	Cam Henderson
1942	14	9	Cam Henderson
1943	10	6	Cam Henderson
1944	15	7	Cam Henderson
1945	16	9	Cam Henderson
1946	25	9	Cam Henderson
1947	32	5	Cam Henderson
1948	22	11	Cam Henderson
1949	16	12	Cam Henderson
1950	15	9	Cam Henderson
1951	13	13	Cam Henderson
1952	15	11	Cam Henderson
1953	20	4	Cam Henderson
1954	12	9	Cam Henderson
1955	17	4	Cam Henderson
1956	18	5	Jule Rivlin
1957	15	9	Jule Rivlin
1958	17	7	Jule Rivlin
1959	12	12	Jule Rivlin
1960	10	13	Jule Rivlin
1961	11	13	July Rivlin
1962	10	13	July Rivlin
1963	7	16	Jule Rivlin
1964	6	17	Ellis Johnson
1965	4	20	Ellis Johnson
1966	12	12	Ellis Johnson
1967	20	8	Ellis Johnson
1968	17	8	Ellis Johnson
1969	9	15	Ellis Johnson
1970	9	14	Stewart Way
1971	16	10	Stewart Way
1972	23	4	Carl Tacy
1973	20	7	Bob Daniels
1974	17	9	Bob Daniels
1975	13	13	Bob Daniels
1976	13	14	Bob Daniels
1977	8	19	Bob Daniels
1978	14	15	Stu Aberdeen
1979	11	16	Stu Aberdeen

MARYLAND, UNIVERSITY OF

College Park, Maryland

Terrapins, Terps			Red and White
1938	15	9	H. Burton Shipley
1939	15	9	H. Burton Shipley
1940	14	9	H. Burton Shipley
1941	1	21	H. Burton Shipley
1942	7	15	H. Burton Shipley
1943	8	8	H. Burton Shipley
1944	4	14	H. Burton Shipley
1945	2	14	H. Burton Shipley
1946	9	12	H. Burton Shipley
1947	14	10	H. Burton Shipley
1948	11	14	Flucie Stewart
1949	9	18	Flucie Stewart
1950	7	18	Flucie Stewart
1951	16	11	H. A. "Bud" Millikan
1952	13	9	H. A. "Bud" Millikan
1953	15	8	H. A. "Bud" Millikan
1954	23	7	H. A. "Bud" Millikan
1955	17	7	H. A. "Bud" Millikan
1956	14	10	H. A. "Bud" Millikan
1957	15	9	H. A. "Bud" Millikan
1958	22	7	H. A. "Bud" Millikan
1959	10	13	H. A. "Bud" Millikan

Yr.	W	L	Coach
1960	15	8	H. A. "Bud" Millikan
1961	14	12	H. A. "Bud" Millikan
1962	8	17	H. A. "Bud" Millikan
1963	8	13	H. A. "Bud" Millikan
1964	9	17	H. A. "Bud" Millikan
1965	18	8	H. A. "Bud" Millikan
1966	14	11	H. A. "Bud" Millikan
1967	11	14	H. A. "Bud" Millikan
1968	8	16	Frank Fellows
1969	8	16	Frank Fellows
1970	13	13	Charles G. "Lefty" Driesell
1971	14	12	Charles G. "Lefty" Driesell
1972	27	5	Charles G. "Lefty" Driesell
1973	23	7	Charles G. "Lefty" Driesell
1974	23	5	Charles G. "Lefty" Driesell
1975	24	5	Charles G. "Lefty" Driesell
1976	22	6	Charles G. "Lefty" Driesell
1977	19	8	Charles G. "Lefty" Driesell
1978	15	13	Charles G. "Lefty" Driesell
1979	19	11	Charles G. "Lefty" Driesell

Yr.	W	L	Coach
1945	16	5	W. Cusie
1946	15	2	W. Cusie
1947	12	4	W. Cusie
1948	18	5	W. Cusie
1949	11	10	W. Cusie
1950	17	9	W. Cusie
1951	8	10	W. Cusie
1952	16	6	W. Cusie
1953	17	13	Ralph Ward
1954	12	12	Ralph Ward
1955	17	12	Ralph Ward
1956	33	3	Ralph Ward
1957	21	5	Ralph Ward
1958	19	4	Ralph Ward
1959	14	7	Ralph Ward
1960	12	15	Ralph Ward
1961	16	7	Ralph Ward
1962	17	8	Ralph Ward
1963	16	9	Ralph Ward
1964	10	16	Ralph Ward
1965	10	15	Ralph Ward
1966	7	16	Ralph Ward
1967	12	10	Ralph Ward
1968	20	5	Ralph Ward
1969	9	12	Ralph Ward
1970	8	13	Ralph Ward
1971	12	12	Ralph Ward
1972	15	10	Bill Reigel
1973	21	5	Bill Reigel
1974	20	5	Bill Reigel
1975	16	8	E. W. Foy
1976	16	11	E. W. Foy
1977	20	7	E. W. Foy
1978	20	8	Glenn Duhon
1979	10	17	Glenn Duhon

MASSACHUSETTS, UNIVERSITY OF

Amherst, Mass.

Redmen	W	L	Maroon and White
1938	8	6	Wilho Frigard
1939	7	7	Wilho Frigard
1940	1	14	Wilho Frigard
1941	5	9	F. Ellert, L. Bush
1942	8	6	Walter Hargesheimer
1943	5	8	Walter Hargesheimer
1944	—	—	
1945	—	—	
1946	4	8	L. Ball, T. Eck
1947	4	12	Lorin Ball
1948	2	14	Lorin Ball
1949	6	12	Lorin Ball
1950	8	11	Lorin Ball
1951	6	15	Lorin Ball
1952	4	17	Lorin Ball
1953	4	15	Robert Curran
1954	13	9	Robert Curran
1955	10	14	Robert Curran
1956	17	6	Robert Curran
1957	13	11	Robert Curran
1958	13	12	Robert Curran
1959	11	13	Robert Curran
1960	14	10	Matt Zunic
1961	16	10	Matt Zunic
1962	15	9	Matt Zunic
1963	12	12	Matt Zunic
1964	15	9	Johnny Orr
1965	13	11	Johnny Orr
1966	11	13	Johnny Orr
1967	11	14	Jack Leaman
1968	14	11	Jack Leaman
1969	17	7	Jack Leaman
1970	18	7	Jack Leaman
1971	23	4	Jack Leaman
1972	14	12	Jack Leaman
1973	20	7	Jack Leaman
1974	21	5	Jack Leaman
1975	18	8	Jack Leaman
1976	21	6	Jack Leaman
1977	20	11	Jack Leaman
1978	15	12	Jack Leaman
1979	5	22	Jack Leaman

MCNEESE STATE

Lake Charles, Louisiana

Cowboys	W	L	Blue and Gold
1944	12	9	W. Cusie

MEMPHIS STATE UNIVERSITY

Memphis, Tenn.

Tigers	W	L	Blue and Gray
1947	11	7	Zack Curlin
1948	13	10	Zack Curlin
1949	11	11	McCoy Tarry
1950	12	9	McCoy Tarry
1951	13	7	McCoy Tarry
1952	25	10	Eugene Lambert
1953	10	14	Eugene Lambert
1954	15	9	Eugene Lambert
1955	18	4	Eugene Lambert
1956	20	7	Eugene Lambert
1957	24	6	Bob Vanatta
1958	15	7	Bob Vanatta
1959	17	6	Bob Vanatta
1960	18	5	Bob Vanatta
1961	20	3	Bob Vanatta
1962	15	7	Bob Vanatta
1963	19	7	Dean Ehlers
1964	14	11	Dean Ehlers
1965	10	14	Dean Ehlers
1966	10	15	Dean Ehlers
1967	17	9	Moe Iba
1968	8	17	Moe Iba
1969	6	19	Moe Iba
1970	6	20	Moe Iba
1971	18	8	Gene Bartow
1972	21	7	Gene Bartow
1973	24	6	Gene Bartow
1974	19	11	Gene Bartow
1975	20	7	Wayne Yates
1976	21	9	Wayne Yates
1977	20	9	Wayne Yates
1978	19	9	Wayne Yates
1979	13	15	Wayne Yates

MERCER UNIVERSITY

Macon, Georgia

Bears — *Orange and Black*

Yr.	W	L	Coach
1938	10	6	Lake Russell
1939	5	10	Lake Russell
1940	6	13	Joseph Dougherty
1941	15	10	Joseph Dougherty
1942	—	—	
1943	—	—	
1944	—	—	
1945	16	9	Cluff Snow
1946	—	—	
1947	16	9	Jim Cowan
1948	17	5	Jim Cowan
1949	15	7	Jim Cowan
1950	19	7	Jim Cowan
1951	16	9	Jim Cowan
1952	19	10	Dan Nyimicz
1953	21	6	Dan Nyimicz
1954	19	9	Jim Cowan
1955	8	14	Jim Cowan
1956	10	12	Jim Cowan
1957	8	16	Robert Wilder
1958	13	7	Robert Wilder
1959	9	13	Robert Wilder
1960	9	12	Robert Wilder
1961	7	16	Robert Wilder
1962	12	12	Robert Wilder
1963	12	12	Robert Wilder
1964	10	14	Robert Wilder
1965	12	12	Robert Wilder
1966	13	10	Robert Wilder
1967	15	6	Robert Wilder
1968	9	14	Robert Wilder
1969	14	12	Robert Wilder
1970	6	18	Robert Wilder
1971	14	9	Dwayne Morrison
1972	19	7	Dwayne Morrison
1973	15	6	Dwayne Morrison
1974	16	8	Joe Dan Gold
1975	9	17	Bill Bibb
1976	15	10	Bill Bibb
1977	6	19	Bill Bibb
1978	16	11	Bill Bibb
1979	21	6	Bill Bibb

MIAMI, UNIVERSITY OF*

Coral Gables, Florida

Hurricanes — *Orange, Green, and White*

Yr.	W	L	Coach
1939	4	6	Hart Morris
1940	4	12	Hart Morris
1941	10	6	Hart Morris
1942	9	7	Hart Morris
1943	—	—	
1944	—	—	
1945	—	—	
1946	8	5	W. H. Steers
1947	20	7	Hart Morris
1948	11	7	Hart Morris
1949	19	8	Hart Morris
1950	14	9	Hart Morris
1951	10	12	Hart Morris
1952	14	8	Hart Morris
1953	9	12	Hart Morris
1954	5	10	David Wike
1955	9	11	Bruce Hale
1956	14	12	Bruce Hale
1957	13	13	Bruce Hale
1958	14	8	Bruce Hale
1959	18	7	Bruce Hale
1960	23	4	Bruce Hale
1961	20	7	Bruce Hale
1962	14	12	Bruce Hale
1963	23	5	Bruce Hale
1964	20	7	Bruce Hale
1965	22	4	Bruce Hale
1966	15	11	Bruce Hale
1967	15	11	Ron Godfrey
1968	17	11	Ron Godfrey
1969	14	10	Ron Godfrey
1970	9	17	Ron Godfrey
1971	7	19	Ron Godfrey

*Basketball discontinued in 1972.

MIAMI, UNIVERSITY OF

Oxford, Ohio

Redskins — *Red and White*

Yr.	W	L	Coach
1938	11	5	John Mauer
1939	5	13	Wilber "Weeb" Ewbank
1940	12	6	Rip Van Winkle
1941	10	7	Rip Van Winkle
1942	16	9	Rip Van Winkle
1943	11	5	W. J. "Blue" Foster
1944	10	2	W. J. "Blue" Foster
1945	8	7	W. J. "Blue" Foster
1946	10	9	W. J. "Blue" Foster
1947	15	7	W. J. "Blue" Foster
1948	13	15	W. J. "Blue" Foster
1949	8	13	W. J. "Blue" Foster
1950	5	15	John Brickels
1951	10	13	John Brickels
1952	19	6	Bill Rohr
1953	17	6	Bill Rohr
1954	12	10	Bill Rohr
1955	14	9	Bill Rohr
1956	12	8	Bill Rohr
1957	17	8	Bill Rohr
1958	18	9	Dick Shrider
1959	14	11	Dick Shrider
1960	8	16	Dick Shrider
1961	12	12	Dick Shrider
1962	7	17	Dick Shrider
1963	12	12	Dick Shrider
1964	17	7	Dick Shrider
1965	20	5	Dick Shrider
1966	18	7	Dick Shrider
1967	14	10	Taylor "Tates" Locke
1968	11	12	Taylor "Tates" Locke
1969	15	12	Taylor "Tates" Locke
1970	16	8	Taylor "Tates" Locke
1971	20	5	Darrell Hedric
1972	12	12	Darrell Hedric
1973	18	9	Darrell Hedric
1974	13	13	Darrell Hedric
1975	19	7	Darrell Hedric
1976	18	8	Darrell Hedric
1977	20	6	Darrell Hedric
1978	19	9	Darrell Hedric
1979	9	18	Darrell Hedric

MICHIGAN, UNIVERSITY OF

Ann Arbor, Michigan

Wolverines — *Maize and Blue*

Yr.	W	L	Coach
1938	13	7	Franklin Cappon
1939	11	9	Bennie Oosterbaan
1940	13	7	Bennie Oosterbaan
1941	9	10	Bennie Oosterbaan
1942	6	14	Bennie Oosterbaan
1943	10	8	Bennie Oosterbaan
1944	8	10	Bennie Oosterbaan
1945	12	7	Bennie Oosterbaan
1946	12	7	Bennie Oosterbaan
1947	12	8	Osborne Cowles
1948	15	6	Osborne Cowles
1949	16	6	Ernest McCoy
1950	11	11	Ernest McCoy
1951	7	15	Ernest McCoy

Yr.	W	L	Coach
1952	7	15	Ernest McCoy
1953	6	16	William Perigo
1954	9	13	William Perigo
1955	11	11	William Perigo
1956	9	13	William Perigo
1957	13	9	William Perigo
1958	11	11	William Perigo
1959	15	7	William Perigo
1960	4	20	Dave Strack
1961	6	18	Dave Strack
1962	7	17	Dave Strack
1963	16	8	Dave Strack
1964	23	5	Dave Strack
1965	24	4	Dave Strack
1966	18	8	Dave Strack
1967	8	16	Dave Strack
1968	11	13	Dave Strack
1969	13	11	Johnny Orr
1970	11	13	Johnny Orr
1971	19	7	Johnny Orr
1972	14	10	Johnny Orr
1973	13	11	Johnny Orr
1974	22	5	Johnny Orr
1975	19	8	Johnny Orr
1976	25	7	Johnny Orr
1977	26	4	Johnny Orr
1978	16	11	Johnny Orr
1979	15	12	Johnny Orr

MICHIGAN STATE UNIVERSITY

East Lansing, Michigan

Spartans			Green and White
1938	9	8	Benjamin F. Van Alstyne
1939	9	8	Benjamin F. Van Alstyne
1940	14	6	Benjamin F. Van Alstyne
1941	11	6	Benjamin F. Van Alstyne
1942	15	6	Benjamin F. Van Alstyne
1943	2	14	Benjamin F. Van Alstyne
1944	–	–	
1945	10	7	Benjamin F. Van Alstyne
1946	12	9	Benjamin F. Van Alstyne
1947	11	10	Benjamin F. Van Alstyne
1948	12	10	Benjamin F. Van Alstyne
1949	9	12	Benjamin F. Van Alstyne
1950	4	18	Alton S. Kircher
1951	10	11	Peter F. Newell
1952	13	9	Peter F. Newell
1953	13	9	Peter F. Newell
1954	9	13	Peter F. Newell
1955	13	9	Forrest A. Anderson
1956	13	9	Forrest A. Anderson
1957	16	10	Forrest A. Anderson
1958	16	6	Forrest A. Anderson
1959	19	4	Forrest A. Anderson
1960	10	11	Forrest A. Anderson
1961	7	17	Forrest A. Anderson
1962	8	14	Forrest A. Anderson
1963	4	16	Forrest A. Anderson
1964	14	10	Forrest A. Anderson
1965	5	18	Forrest A. Anderson
1966	17	7	John E. Benington
1967	16	7	John E. Benington
1968	12	12	John E. Benington
1969	11	12	John E. Benington
1970	9	15	Gus G. Ganakas
1971	10	14	Gus G. Ganakas
1972	13	11	Gus G. Ganakas
1973	13	11	Gus G. Ganakas
1974	13	11	Gus G. Ganakas
1975	17	9	Gus G. Ganakas
1976	14	13	Gus G. Ganakas
1977	10	17	George M. "Jud" Heathcote
1978	25	5	George M. "Jud" Heathcote
1979	26	6	George M. "Jud" Heathcote

MIDDLE TENNESSEE STATE UNIVERSITY

Murfreesboro, Tennessee

Blue Raiders			Blue and White
1938	6	10	John Floyd
1939	5	8	John Floyd
1940	9	12	Edwin Midgett
1941	7	14	Edwin Midgett
1942	9	9	Edwin Midgett
1943	–	–	
1944	–	–	
1945	–	–	
1946	4	0	Otis Freeman
1947	14	8	Elbert Patty
1948	10	11	Elbert Patty
1949	11	12	Charles Murphy
1950	14	13	Charles Greer
1951	8	14	Charles Greer
1952	19	12	Charles Greer
1953	7	16	Charles Greer
1954	11	17	Charles Greer
1955	11	16	Charles Greer
1956	6	15	Charles Greer
1957	12	13	Edgar Diddle, Jr.
1958	11	10	Edgar Diddle, Jr.
1959	9	17	Edgar Diddle, Jr.
1960	9	14	Edgar Diddle, Jr.
1961	9	14	Edgar Diddle, Jr.
1962	6	12	Edgar Diddle, Jr.
1963	9	15	William M. Stokes
1964	11	10	William M. Stokes
1965	6	18	William M. Stokes
1966	7	17	Ken Trickey
1967	10	15	Ken Trickey
1968	15	9	Ken Trickey
1969	13	13	Ken Trickey
1970	15	11	Jimmy Earle
1971	11	15	Jimmy Earle
1972	15	11	Jimmy Earle
1973	12	13	Jimmy Earle
1974	18	8	Jimmy Earle
1975	23	5	Jimmy Earle
1976	16	12	Jimmy Earle
1977	20	9	Jimmy Earle
1978	18	8	Jimmy Earle
1979	16	11	Jimmy Earle

MINNESOTA, UNIVERSITY OF

Minneapolis, Minnesota

Gophers			Maroon and Gold
1938	16	4	David MacMillan
1939	14	6	David MacMillan
1940	12	8	David MacMillan
1941	11	9	David MacMillan
1942	15	6	David MacMillan
1943	10	9	David MacMillan
1944	7	14	Carl Nordly
1945	8	13	Carl Nordly
1946	14	7	Weston Mitchell
1947	14	7	David MacMillan
1948	10	10	David MacMillan
1949	18	3	Osborne Cowles
1950	13	9	Osborne Cowles
1951	13	9	Osborne Cowles
1952	15	7	Osborne Cowles
1953	14	8	Osborne Cowles
1954	17	5	Osborne Cowles
1955	15	7	Osborne Cowles
1956	11	11	Osborne Cowles
1957	14	8	Osborne Cowles
1958	10	12	Osborne Cowles
1959	8	14	Osborne Cowles
1960	12	12	John Kundla

Yr.	W	L	Coach	Yr.	W	L	Coach
1961	10	14	John Kundla	1941	12	9	Dick Hitt
1962	10	14	John Kundla	1942	13	7	Dick Hitt
1963	12	12	John Kundla	1943	14	8	Dick Hitt
1964	17	7	John Kundla	1944	—	—	
1965	19	5	John Kundla	1945	4	14	Dick Hitt
1966	14	10	John Kundla	1946	5	14	Dick Hitt
1967	9	15	John Kundla	1947	10	11	Dick Hitt
1968	7	17	Bill Fitch	1948	6	12	Paul Gregory
1969	12	12	Bill Fitch	1949	4	13	Paul Gregory
1970	13	11	Bill Fitch	1950	7	11	Paul Gregory
1971	11	13	George Hanson	1951	3	16	Paul Gregory
1972	18	7	Bill Musselman	1952	12	11	Paul Gregory
1973	21	5	Bill Musselman	1953	9	10	Paul Gregory
1974	12	12	Bill Musselman	1954	11	10	Paul Gregory
1975	18	8	Bill Musselman	1955	6	17	Paul Gregory
1976	16	10	Jim Dutcher	1956	12	12	Babe McCarthy
1977	24	3	Jim Dutcher	1957	17	8	Babe McCarthy
1978	17	10	Jim Dutcher	1958	20	5	Babe McCarthy
1979	11	16	Jim Dutcher	1959	24	1	Babe McCarthy
				1960	12	13	Babe McCarthy
				1961	19	6	Babe McCarthy
				1962	24	1	Babe McCarthy
				1963	22	6	Babe McCarthy
				1964	9	17	Babe McCarthy
				1965	10	16	Babe McCarthy

MISSISSIPPI, UNIVERSITY OF

University, Mississippi

Rebels	W	L	Red and Blue	Yr	W	L	Coach
1938	22	12	George "Doc" Bohler	1966	14	11	Joe Dan Gold
1939	10	16	Frank Johnson	1967	14	11	Joe Dan Gold
1940	9	10	Charles Jaskwich	1968	9	17	Joe Dan Gold
1941	2	18	Charles Jaskwich	1969	8	17	Joe Dan Gold
1942	4	15	Charles Jaskwich	1970	6	18	Joe Dan Gold
1943	8	10	E. W. Hale	1971	15	10	Kermit Davis
1944	—	—		1972	13	13	Kermit Davis
1945	14	8	E. W. Hale	1973	11	15	Kermit Davis
1946	8	11	E. W. Hale	1974	16	10	Kermit Davis
1947	7	14	James Whatley	1975	9	17	Kermit Davis
1948	11	12	James Whatley	1976	13	13	Kermit Davis
1949	8	13	James Whatley	1977	14	13	Kermit Davis
1950	8	17	Whatley, Graham	1978	18	9	Ron Greene
1951	12	12	Bonnie Graham	1979	19	9	Jim Hatfield
1952	15	11	Bonnie Graham				
1953	15	11	Bonnie Graham				
1954	12	12	Bonnie Graham				
1955	8	15	Bonnie Graham				
1956	11	13	Bonnie Graham				
1957	9	12	Bonnie Graham				
1958	12	12	Bonnie Graham				
1959	7	17	Bonnie Graham				
1960	15	9	Bonnie Graham				

MISSOURI, UNIVERSITY OF

Columbia, Missouri

Rebels	W	L	Red and Blue	Tigers	W	L	Black and Gold
1961	10	14	Bonnie Graham	1938	9	9	George Edwards
1962	12	13	Bonnie Graham	1939	12	6	George Edwards
1963	7	17	Edward S. Crawford	1940	13	6	George Edwards
1964	10	12	Edward S. Crawford	1941	6	10	George Edwards
1965	4	21	Edward S. Crawford	1942	6	12	George Edwards
1966	5	18	Edward S. Crawford	1943	7	10	George Edwards
1967	13	12	Edward S. Crawford	1944	10	9	George Edwards
1968	7	17	Edward S. Crawford	1945	8	10	George Edwards
1969	10	14	Robert "Cob" Jarvis	1946	6	11	George Edwards
1970	10	15	Robert "Cob" Jarvis	1947	15	10	Wilbur "Sparky" Stalcup
1971	11	15	Robert "Cob" Jarvis	1948	14	10	Wilbur "Sparky" Stalcup
1972	13	12	Robert "Cob" Jarvis	1949	11	13	Wilbur "Sparky" Stalcup
1973	14	12	Robert "Cob" Jarvis	1950	14	10	Wilbur "Sparky" Stalcup
1974	15	10	Robert "Cob" Jarvis	1951	16	8	Wilbur "Sparky" Stalcup
1975	8	18	Robert "Cob" Jarvis	1952	14	10	Wilbur "Sparky" Stalcup
1976	6	21	Robert "Cob" Jarvis	1953	12	9	Wilbur "Sparky" Stalcup
1977	11	16	Bob Weltlich	1954	11	10	Wilbur "Sparky" Stalcup
1978	10	17	Bob Weltlich	1955	16	5	Wilbur "Sparky" Stalcup
1979	11	16	Bob Weltlich	1956	15	7	Wilbur "Sparky" Stalcup
				1957	10	13	Wilbur "Sparky" Stalcup
				1958	9	13	Wilbur "Sparky" Stalcup
				1959	6	19	Wilbur "Sparky" Stalcup
				1960	12	13	Wilbur "Sparky" Stalcup
				1961	9	15	Wilbur "Sparky" Stalcup
				1962	9	16	Wilbur "Sparky" Stalcup
				1963	10	15	Bob Vanatta
				1964	13	11	Bob Vanatta
				1965	13	11	Bob Vanatta
				1966	3	21	Bob Vanatta
				1967	3	22	Bob Vanatta

MISSISSIPPI STATE UNIVERSITY

Mississippi State, Mississippi

Bulldogs	W	L	Maroon and White	Yr	W	L	Coach
1938	9	11	Frank Carideo	1968	10	16	Norm Stewart
1939	8	11	Frank Carideo	1969	14	11	Norm Stewart
1940	9	5	Frank Carideo	1970	15	11	Norm Stewart

Yr.	W	L	Coach	Yr.	W	L	Coach
1971	17	9	Norm Stewart	1950	20	12	John Breeden
1972	21	6	Norm Stewart	1951	24	12	John Breeden
1973	21	6	Norm Stewart	1952	22	14	John Breeden
1974	12	14	Norm Stewart	1953	11	24	John Breeden
1975	18	9	Norm Stewart	1954	18	11	John Breeden
1976	26	5	Norm Stewart	1955	11	16	Wally Lemm
1977	21	8	Norm Stewart	1956	15	14	Keith Lambert
1978	14	16	Norm Stewart	1957	12	13	Keith Lambert
1979	13	15	Norm Stewart	1958	18	8	Keith Lambert

MONTANA, UNIVERSITY OF

Missoula, Montana

Grizzlies			Silver, Copper and Gold
1938	10	19	George Dahlberg
1939	17	13	George Dahlberg
1940	17	8	George Dahlberg
1941	14	14	George Dahlberg
1942	14	10	George Dahlberg
1943	15	9	C. Carpenter, E. Chinske
1944	2	10	Ed Buzzetti
1945	7	23	George Dahlberg
1946	13	16	George Dahlberg
1947	12	16	George Dahlberg
1948	21	11	George Dahlberg
1949	12	13	George Dahlberg
1950	27	4	George Dahlberg
1951	13	18	George Dahlberg
1952	12	14	George Dahlberg
1953	14	11	George Dahlberg
1954	7	20	George Dahlberg
1955	12	14	George Dahlberg
1956	14	12	Frosty Cox
1957	13	9	Frosty Cox
1958	12	10	Frosty Cox
1959	10	14	Frosty Cox
1960	7	17	Frosty Cox
1961	14	9	Frosty Cox
1962	10	14	Frosty Cox
1963	6	18	Ron Nord
1964	6	17	Ron Nord
1965	18	6	Ron Nord
1966	14	10	Ron Nord
1967	6	18	Ron Nord
1968	8	17	Ron Nord
1969	9	17	Bob Cope
1970	8	18	Bob Cope
1971	8	16	Lou Rocheleau
1972	14	12	Jud Heathcote
1973	13	13	Jud Heathcote
1974	19	8	Jud Heathcote
1975	21	8	Jud Heathcote
1976	13	12	Jud Heathcote
1977	18	8	Jim Brandenburg
1978	20	8	Jim Brandenburg
1979	14	13	Mike Montgomery

MONTANA STATE UNIVERSITY

Bozeman, Montana

Bobcats			Blue and Gold
1938	22	5	John Breeden
1939	18	11	John Breeden
1940	10	16	John Breeden
1941	13	12	John Breeden
1942	14	8	John Breeden
1943	17	5	John Breeden
1944	—	—	
1945	10	14	John Breeden
1946	17	10	John Breeden
1947	25	11	John Breeden
1948	18	9	Max Worthington
1949	14	15	John Breeden

Yr.	W	L	Coach
1959	12	13	Keith Lambert
1960	11	14	Keith Lambert
1961	10	15	Keith Lambert
1962	10	13	Keith Lambert
1963	13	13	Roger Craft
1964	16	9	Roger Craft
1965	15	10	Roger Craft
1966	7	17	Roger Craft
1967	14	11	Roger Craft
1968	10	15	Roger Craft
1969	17	8	Roger Craft
1970	4	22	Gary Hulst
1971	12	13	Gary Hulst
1972	10	16	Gary Hulst
1973	17	9	T. H. Anderson
1974	11	15	T. H. Anderson
1975	11	15	Rich Juarez
1976	9	16	Rich Juarez
1977	11	15	Rich Juarez
1978	10	16	Rich Juarez
1979	15	11	Bruce Haroldson

MOREHEAD STATE UNIVERSITY

Morehead, Kentucky

Eagles			Blue and Gold
1938	6	11	Ellis Johnson
1939	16	8	Ellis Johnson
1940	7	14	Ellis Johnson
1941	11	7	Ellis Johnson
1942	12	10	Ellis Johnson
1943	12	7	Ellis Johnson
1944	12	3	Leonard Miller
1945	16	6	Leonard Miller
1946	13	8	Ellis Johnson
1947	11	16	Ellis Johnson
1948	10	17	Ellis Johnson
1949	14	9	Ellis Johnson
1950	12	10	Ellis Johnson
1951	14	12	Ellis Johnson
1952	11	14	Ellis Johnson
1953	13	12	Ellis Johnson
1954	16	8	Robert Laughlin
1955	14	10	Robert Laughlin
1956	19	10	Robert Laughlin
1957	19	8	Robert Laughlin
1958	13	10	Robert Laughlin
1959	11	12	Robert Laughlin
1960	5	14	Robert Laughlin
1961	19	12	Robert Laughlin
1962	14	8	Robert Laughlin
1963	13	7	Robert Laughlin
1964	10	11	Robert Laughlin
1965	13	10	Robert Laughlin
1966	12	12	Bob Wright
1967	16	8	Bob Wright
1968	12	9	Bob Wright
1969	18	9	Bob Wright
1970	13	11	Bill Harrell
1971	8	17	Bill Harrell
1972	16	11	Bill Harrell
1973	14	11	Bill Harrell
1974	17	9	Bill Harrell
1975	13	13	Jack Schalow
1976	13	14	Jack Schalow
1977	15	10	Jack Schalow
1978	4	19	Jack Schalow
1979	14	13	Wayne Martin

Yr.	W	L	Coach		Yr.	W	L	Coach

MURRAY STATE UNIVERSITY

Murray, Kentucky

Thoroughbreds			Blue and Gold
1938	27	4	Carlisle Cutchin
1939	13	8	Carlisle Cutchin
1940	14	9	Carlisle Cutchin
1941	25	5	Carlisle Cutchin
1942	18	4	Rice Mountjoy
1943	23	5	John Miller
1944	5	9	John Miller
1945	12	10	John Miller
1946	10	13	John Miller
1947	14	11	John Miller
1948	13	11	Carlisle Cutchin
1949	13	11	Harlan Hodges
1950	18	13	Harlan Hodges
1951	21	6	Harlan Hodges
1952	24	10	Harlan Hodges
1953	18	9	Harlan Hodges
1954	15	6	Harlan Hodges
1955	11	15	Rex Alexander
1956	15	10	Rex Alexander
1957	11	13	Rex Alexander
1958	8	16	Rex Alexander
1959	10	15	Cal Luther
1960	12	11	Cal Luther
1961	13	10	Cal Luther
1962	13	12	Cal Luther
1963	13	9	Cal Luther
1964	16	9	Cal Luther
1965	19	7	Cal Luther
1966	13	10	Cal Luther
1967	14	9	Cal Luther
1968	16	7	Cal Luther
1969	22	6	Cal Luther
1970	17	9	Cal Luther
1971	19	5	Cal Luther
1972	15	11	Cal Luther
1973	19	8	Cal Luther
1974	12	13	Cal Luther
1975	10	15	Fred Overton
1976	9	17	Fred Overton
1977	17	10	Fred Overton
1978	8	17	Fred Overton
1979	4	22	Ron Greene

NAVY (USNA)

Annapolis, Maryland

Midshipmen			Navy Blue and Gold
1938	11	3	John Wilson
1939	8	6	John Wilson
1940	3	11	John Wilson
1941	9	5	John Wilson
1942	8	6	John Wilson
1943	6	8	John Wilson
1944	10	4	John Wilson
1945	12	2	John Wilson
1946	12	3	John Wilson
1947	16	3	Ben Carnevale
1948	10	7	Ben Carnevale
1949	12	9	Ben Carnevale
1950	14	7	Ben Carnevale
1951	16	6	Ben Carnevale
1952	16	7	Ben Carnevale
1953	16	5	Ben Carnevale
1954	18	8	Ben Carnevale
1955	11	9	Ben Carnevale
1956	10	9	Ben Carnevale
1957	15	8	Ben Carnevale
1958	10	10	Ben Carnevale
1959	18	6	Ben Carnevale
1960	16	6	Ben Carnevale
1961	10	9	Ben Carnevale
1962	13	8	Ben Carnevale
1963	9	9	Ben Carnevale
1964	10	12	Ben Carnevale
1965	10	10	Ben Carnevale
1966	7	12	Ben Carnevale
1967	8	10	Dave Smalley
1968	9	11	Dave Smalley
1969	7	14	Dave Smalley
1970	4	19	Dave Smalley
1971	12	12	Dave Smalley
1972	10	13	Dave Smalley
1973	13	12	Dave Smalley
1974	9	13	Dave Smalley
1975	12	12	Dave Smalley
1976	10	14	Dave Smalley
1977	13	11	Bob Hamilton
1978	14	11	Bob Hamilton
1979	13	12	Bob Hamilton

NEBRASKA, UNIVERSITY OF

Lincoln, Nebraska

Cornhuskers			Scarlet and Cream
1938	9	11	W. H. Browne
1939	7	13	W. H. Browne
1940	6	12	W. H. Browne
1941	8	10	A. J. Lewandowski
1942	6	13	A. J. Lewandowski
1943	6	10	A. J. Lewandowski
1944	2	13	A. J. Lewandowski
1945	2	17	A. J. Lewandowski
1946	7	13	L. F. Klein
1947	10	14	Harry Good
1948	11	13	Harry Good
1949	16	10	Harry Good
1950	16	7	Harry Good
1951	11	14	Harry Good
1952	7	17	Harry Good
1953	9	11	Harry Good
1954	8	13	Harry Good
1955	9	12	Gerard Bush
1956	7	16	Gerard Bush
1957	11	12	Gerard Bush
1958	10	13	Gerard Bush
1959	12	13	Gerard Bush
1960	8	17	Gerard Bush
1961	10	14	Gerard Bush
1962	9	16	Gerard Bush
1963	6	19	Gerard Bush
1964	8	17	Joe Cipriano
1965	10	15	Joe Cipriano
1966	20	5	Joe Cipriano
1967	16	9	Joe Cipriano
1968	15	10	Joe Cipriano
1969	12	14	Joe Cipriano
1970	16	9	Joe Cipriano
1971	18	8	Joe Cipriano
1972	14	12	Joe Cipriano
1973	9	17	Joe Cipriano
1974	14	12	Joe Cipriano
1975	14	12	Joe Cipriano
1976	19	8	Joe Cipriano
1977	15	14	Joe Cipriano
1978	22	8	Joe Cipriano
1979	14	13	Joe Cipriano

NEVADA-LAS VEGAS, UNIVERSITY OF

Las Vegas, Nevada

Rebels			Scarlet and Gray
1959	5	13	Michael Drakulich
1960	13	8	Michael Drakulich
1961	13	12	Michael Drakulich
1962	16	8	Michael Drakulich
1963	21	4	Michael Drakulich

Yr.	W	L	Coach
1964	19	7	Ed Gregory
1965	21	8	Ed Gregory
1966	15	11	Rolland Todd
1967	21	6	Rolland Todd
1968	22	7	Rolland Todd
1969	21	7	Rolland Todd
1970	17	9	Rolland Todd
1971	16	10	John Bayer
1972	14	12	John Bayer
1973	14	14	John Bayer
1974	20	6	Jerry Tarkanian
1975	24	5	Jerry Tarkanian
1976	29	2	Jerry Tarkanian
1977	29	3	Jerry Tarkanian
1978	20	8	Jerry Tarkanian
1979	21	8	Jerry Tarkanian

NEVADA-RENO, UNIVERSITY OF

Reno, Nevada

Wolf Pack			Silver and Blue
1970	5	17	Jack Spencer
1971	3	23	Jack Spencer
1972	2	24	Jack Spencer
1973	10	16	Jim Padgett
1974	11	15	Jim Padgett
1975	10	16	Jim Padgett
1976	12	14	Jim Padgett
1977	15	12	Jim Carey
1978	19	8	Jim Carey
1979	21	7	Jim Carey

NEW HAMPSHIRE, UNIVERSITY OF

Durham, New Hampshire

Wildcats			White and Blue
1938	12	6	Henry Swasey
1939	3	14	Henry Swasey
1940	5	10	Henry Swasey
1941	9	8	Henry Swasey
1942	4	15	Henry Swasey
1943	4	14	Henry Swasey
1944	—	—	
1945	—	—	
1946	3	7	Ed Stanczyk
1947	6	11	Ed Stanczyk
1948	5	12	Ed Stanczyk
1949	7	10	Ed Stanczyk
1950	4	11	Ed Stanczyk
1951	4	12	Andy Morradian
1952	11	9	Dale Hall
1953	8	10	Robert Kerr
1954	8	10	Robert Kerr
1955	4	14	Robert Kerr
1956	2	15	Robert Kerr
1957	2	15	Bill Olson
1958	10	12	Bill Olson
1959	9	14	Bill Olson
1960	9	14	Bill Olson
1961	6	18	Bill Olson
1962	3	20	Bill Olson
1963	7	17	Bill Olson
1964	8	15	Bill Olson
1965	2	19	Bill Olson
1966	3	21	Bill Olson
1967	10	12	F. William Haubrich
1968	1	22	F. William Haubrich
1969	9	15	F. William Haubrich
1970	12	11	Gerry Friel
1971	11	12	Gerry Friel
1972	14	9	Gerry Friel
1973	11	15	Gerry Friel
1974	16	9	Gerry Friel
1975	6	18	Gerry Friel
1976	8	18	Gerry Friel
1977	12	14	Gerry Friel
1978	7	19	Gerry Friel
1979	10	16	Gerry Friel

NEW MEXICO, UNIVERSITY OF

Albuquerque, New Mexico

Lobos			Cherry, Silver & Turquoise
1938	8	12	Roy Johnson
1939	4	19	Roy Johnson
1940	3	22	Roy Johnson
1941	5	18	Roy Johnson
1942	9	13	Willis Barnes
1943	3	11	Willis Barnes
1944	12	2	Willis Barnes
1945	15	2	Woodrow Clements
1946	16	9	Woodrow Clements
1947	11	8	Woodrow Clements
1948	14	15	Woodrow Clements
1949	9	11	Woodrow Clements
1950	5	19	Woodrow Clements
1951	13	11	Woodrow Clements
1952	6	19	Berl Huffman
1953	10	15	Woodrow Clements
1954	11	11	Woodrow Clements
1955	7	17	Woodrow Clements
1956	6	16	William Stockton
1957	5	21	William Stockton
1958	3	21	William Stockton
1959	3	19	Robert Sweeney
1960	6	19	Robert Sweeney
1961	6	17	Robert Sweeney
1962	6	20	Robert Sweeney
1963	16	9	Bob King
1964	23	6	Bob King
1965	19	8	Bob King
1966	16	8	Bob King
1967	19	8	Bob King
1968	23	5	Bob King
1969	17	9	Bob King
1970	13	13	Bob King
1971	14	12	Bob King
1972	15	10	Bob King
1973	21	6	Norm Ellenberger
1974	22	7	Norm Ellenberger
1975	13	13	Norm Ellenberger
1976	16	11	Norm Ellenberger
1977	19	11	Norm Ellenberger
1978	24	4	Norm Ellenberger
1979	19	10	Norm Ellenberger

NEW MEXICO STATE UNIVERSITY

Las Cruces, New Mexico

Aggies			Crimson and White
1938	8	2	Jerry Hines
1939	16	0	Jerry Hines
1940	7	1	Jerry Hines
1941	11	3	Jerry Hines
1942	8	2	Julius Johnson
1943	7	6	Julius Johnson
1944	—	—	
1945	—	—	
1946	—	—	
1947	—	—	
1948	3	12	Raymond Curfman
1949	10	11	Raymond Curfman
1950	15	12	George McCarty
1951	16	11	George McCarty
1952	22	11	George McCarty
1953	7	14	George McCarty
1954	7	12	Presley Askew
1955	6	13	Presley Askew
1956	15	7	Presley Askew

Yr.	W	L	Coach
1957	6	18	Presley Askew
1958	14	9	Presley Askew
1959	17	11	Presley Askew
1960	20	7	Presley Askew
1961	19	5	Presley Askew
1962	10	14	Presley Askew
1963	4	17	Presley Askew
1964	8	15	Presley Askew
1965	8	18	Presley Askew
1966	4	22	Jim McGregor
1967	15	11	Louis Henson
1968	23	6	Louis Henson
1969	24	5	Louis Henson
1970	27	3	Louis Henson
1971	19	8	Louis Henson
1972	19	6	Louis Henson
1973	12	14	Louis Henson
1974	14	11	Louis Henson
1975	20	7	Louis Henson
1976	15	12	Ken Hayes
1977	17	10	Ken Hayes
1978	15	14	Ken Hayes
1979	22	10	Ken Hayes

NEW ORLEANS, UNIVERSITY OF

New Orleans, Louisiana

Privateers			Royal Blue and Silver
1970	18	5	Ronald L. Greene
1971	23	3	Ronald L. Greene
1972	19	9	Ronald L. Greene
1973	10	13	Ronald L. Greene
1974	21	9	Ronald L. Greene
1975	23	7	Ronald L. Greene
1976	18	8	Ronald L. Greene
1977	18	10	Ronald L. Greene
1978	21	6	W. H. van Breda Kolff
1979	11	16	W. H. van Breda Kolff

NEW YORK UNIVERSITY*

New York, New York

Violets			Violet and White
1938	16	8	Howard Cann
1939	11	11	Howard Cann
1940	18	1	Howard Cann
1941	13	6	Howard Cann
1942	12	7	Howard Cann
1943	16	6	Howard Cann
1944	7	7	Howard Cann
1945	14	7	Howard Cann
1946	19	3	Howard Cann
1947	12	9	Howard Cann
1948	22	4	Howard Cann
1949	12	8	Howard Cann
1950	8	11	Howard Cann
1951	12	4	Howard Cann
1952	17	8	Howard Cann
1953	9	11	Howard Cann
1954	9	9	Howard Cann
1955	7	13	Howard Cann
1956	10	8	Howard Cann
1957	8	13	Howard Cann
1958	10	11	Howard Cann
1959	15	8	Lou Rossini
1960	22	5	Lou Rossini
1961	12	11	Lou Rossini
1962	20	5	Lou Rossini
1963	18	5	Lou Rossini
1964	17	10	Lou Rossini
1965	16	10	Lou Rossini
1966	18	10	Lou Rossini
1967	10	16	Lou Rossini
1968	8	16	Lou Rossini
1969	12	9	Lou Rossini
1970	12	12	Lou Rossini
1971	5	20	Lou Rossini

*Basketball discontinued in 1972.

NIAGARA UNIVERSITY

Niagara Falls, N. Y.

Purple Eagles			Purple and White
1938	8	13	Taps Gallagher
1939	11	8	Taps Gallagher
1940	12	7	Taps Gallagher
1941	13	7	Taps Gallagher
1942	16	6	Taps Gallagher
1943	20	6	Taps Gallagher
1944	—	—	
1945	7	6	Edward Flynn
1946	11	8	Edward Flynn
1947	13	8	Taps Gallagher
1948	15	9	Taps Gallagher
1949	24	7	Taps Gallagher
1950	20	7	Taps Gallagher
1951	18	10	Taps Gallagher
1952	8	21	Taps Gallagher
1953	22	6	Taps Gallagher
1954	24	6	Taps Gallagher
1955	20	6	Taps Gallagher
1956	20	7	Taps Gallagher
1957	13	13	Taps Gallagher
1958	19	7	Taps Gallagher
1959	15	8	Taps Gallagher
1960	14	12	Taps Gallagher
1961	16	5	Taps Gallagher
1962	16	8	Taps Gallagher
1963	14	4	Taps Gallagher
1964	8	12	Taps Gallagher
1965	4	17	Taps Gallagher
1966	11	13	Jim Maloney
1967	12	13	Jim Maloney
1968	12	12	Jim Maloney
1969	11	13	Frank Layden
1970	22	7	Frank Layden
1971	14	12	Frank Layden
1972	20	9	Frank Layden
1973	9	16	Frank Layden
1974	12	14	Frank Layden
1975	13	14	Frank Layden
1976	17	12	Frank Layden
1977	13	13	Dan Raskin
1978	14	12	Dan Raskin
1979	6	20	Dan Raskin

NORTH CAROLINA, UNIVERSITY OF

Chapel Hill, North Carolina

Tar Heels			Carolina Blue and White
1938	16	5	Walter Skidmore
1939	10	11	Walter Skidmore
1940	18	3	Bill Lange
1941	15	8	Bill Lange
1942	10	7	Bill Lange
1943	12	10	Bill Lange
1944	15	9	Bill Lange
1945	9	6	Ben Carnevale
1946	29	5	Ben Carnevale
1947	19	8	Tom Scott
1948	20	7	Tom Scott
1949	19	6	Tom Scott
1950	17	12	Tom Scott
1951	12	15	Tom Scott
1952	12	15	Tom Scott
1953	17	10	Frank McGuire
1954	11	10	Frank McGuire
1955	10	11	Frank McGuire
1956	18	5	Frank McGuire

Yr.	W	L	Coach
1957	32	0	Frank McGuire
1958	19	7	Frank McGuire
1959	20	5	Frank McGuire
1960	18	6	Frank McGuire
1961	19	4	Frank McGuire
1962	8	9	Dean Smith
1963	15	6	Dean Smith
1964	12	12	Dean Smith
1965	15	9	Dean Smith
1966	16	11	Dean Smith
1967	26	6	Dean Smith
1968	28	4	Dean Smith
1969	27	5	Dean Smith
1970	18	9	Dean Smith
1971	26	6	Dean Smith
1972	26	5	Dean Smith
1973	25	8	Dean Smith
1974	22	6	Dean Smith
1975	23	8	Dean Smith
1976	25	4	Dean Smith
1977	28	5	Dean Smith
1978	23	8	Dean Smith
1979	23	6	Dean Smith

NORTH CAROLINA-CHARLOTTE, UNIVERSITY OF

Charlotte, North Carolina

Forty-Niners			Green and White
1966	6	17	Harvey Murphy
1967	7	21	Harvey Murphy
1968	5	17	Harvey Murphy
1969	12	10	Harvey Murphy
1970	14	16	Harvey Murphy
1971	15	8	Bill Foster
1972	14	11	Bill Foster
1973	14	12	Bill Foster
1974	22	4	Bill Foster
1975	23	3	Bill Foster
1976	24	6	Lee Rose
1977	28	5	Lee Rose
1978	20	7	Lee Rose
1979	16	11	Mike Pratt

NORTH CAROLINA-WILMINGTON UNIVERSITY OF

Wilmington, North Carolina

Seahawks			Green and Gold
1952	12	4	William J. Brooks
1953	9	5	William J. Brooks
1954	14	9	William J. Brooks
1955	11	8	William J. Brooks
1956	5	12	William J. Brooks
1957	7	12	William J. Brooks
1958	12	9	William J. Brooks
1959	24	5	William J. Brooks
1960	20	6	William J. Brooks
1961	24	6	William J. Brooks
1962	21	6	William J. Brooks
1963	17	10	William J. Brooks
1964	9	8	William J. Brooks
1965	13	10	William J. Brooks
1966	13	11	William J. Brooks
1967	9	19	William J. Brooks
1968	9	16	William J. Brooks
1969	6	23	William J. Brooks
1970	8	16	William J. Brooks
1971	8	18	William J. Brooks
1972	7	16	William J. Brooks
1973	10	14	Mel Gibson
1974	14	10	Mel Gibson
1975	8	17	Mel Gibson
1976	13	15	Mel Gibson

Yr.	W	L	Coach
1977	16	10	Mel Gibson
1978	19	7	Mel Gibson
1979	19	8	Mel Gibson

NORTH CAROLINA STATE UNIVERSITY

Raleigh, North Carolina

Wolfpack			Red and White
1938	13	6	R. R. Sermon
1939	10	7	R. R. Sermon
1940	8	11	R. R. Sermon
1941	6	9	Bob Warren
1942	15	7	Bob Warren
1943	7	9	Leroy Jay
1944	5	13	Leroy Jay
1945	10	11	Leroy Jay
1946	6	12	Leroy Jay
1947	26	5	Everett Case
1948	29	3	Everett Case
1949	25	8	Everett Case
1950	27	6	Everett Case
1951	30	7	Everett Case
1952	24	10	Everett Case
1953	26	6	Everett Case
1954	28	7	Everett Case
1955	28	4	Everett Case
1956	24	4	Everett Case
1957	15	11	Everett Case
1958	18	6	Everett Case
1959	22	4	Everett Case
1960	11	15	Everett Case
1961	16	9	Everett Case
1962	11	6	Everett Case
1963	10	11	Everett Case
1964	8	11	Everett Case
1965	21	5	Press Maravich
1966	18	9	Press Maravich
1967	7	19	Norman Sloan
1968	16	10	Norman Sloan
1969	15	10	Norman Sloan
1970	23	7	Norman Sloan
1971	13	14	Norman Sloan
1972	16	10	Norman Sloan
1973	27	0	Norman Sloan
1974	30	1	Norman Sloan
1975	22	6	Norman Sloan
1976	21	9	Norman Sloan
1977	17	11	Norman Sloan
1978	21	10	Norman Sloan
1979	18	12	Norman Sloan

NORTHEASTERN UNIVERSITY

Boston, Massachusetts

Huskies			Red and Black
1938	7	11	James W. Dunn
1939	6	12	James W. Dunn
1940	4	13	James W. Dunn
1941	3	13	James W. Dunn
1942	6	9	James W. Dunn
1943	7	12	Emmanuel Flumere
1944	8	8	Emmanuel Flumere
1945	7	8	Emmanuel Flumere
1946	4	13	Eugene Pare
1947	6	10	William G. Grinnell
1948	10	8	William G. Grinnell
1949	12	6	Joseph P. Zabilski
1950	6	10	Joseph P. Zabilski
1951	8	9	Joseph P. Zabilski
1952	12	7	Joseph P. Zabilski
1953	7	11	Joseph P. Zabilski
1954	11	8	Joseph P. Zabilski
1955	5	16	Joseph P. Zabilski
1956	10	11	Joseph P. Zabilski
1957	6	17	Joseph P. Zabilski
1958	5	15	Joseph P. Zabilski

Yr.	W	L	Coach	Yr.	W	L	Coach
1959	8	13	Richard E. Dukeshire	1951	8	19	Herb Gregg
1960	10	11	Richard E. Dukeshire	1952	4	23	Herb Gregg
1961	10	10	Richard E. Dukeshire	1953	6	17	Herb Gregg
1962	17	8	Richard E. Dukeshire	1954	20	7	Herb Gregg
1963	21	6	Richard E. Dukeshire	1955	19	3	Herb Gregg
1964	17	8	Richard E. Dukeshire	1956	11	10	Herb Gregg
1965	13	11	Richard E. Dukeshire	1957	14	10	Herb Gregg
1966	18	8	Richard E. Dukeshire	1958	16	7	Herb Gregg
1967	22	4	Richard E. Dukeshire	1959	12	10	Herb Gregg
1968	19	9	Richard E. Dukeshire	1960	14	9	Herb Gregg
1969	16	5	Richard E. Dukeshire	1961	9	13	Herb Gregg
1970	14	8	Richard E. Dukeshire	1962	18	9	Herb Gregg
1971	17	4	Richard E. Dukeshire	1963	11	10	Herb Gregg
1972	12	9	James E. Bowman	1964	12	10	Herb Gregg
1973	19	7	James A. Calhoun	1965	12	10	Herb Gregg
1974	14	11	James A. Calhoun	1966	13	12	Herb Gregg
1975	12	12	James A. Calhoun	1967	16	11	Herb Gregg
1976	12	13	James A. Calhoun	1968	13	12	Herb Gregg
1977	12	14	James A. Calhoun	1969	16	9	Herb Gregg
1978	14	12	James A. Calhoun	1970	18	6	Herb Gregg
1979	13	13	James A. Calhoun	1971	6	19	Herb Gregg
				1972	13	10	Herb Gregg
				1973	6	20	Herb Gregg
				1974	6	20	Herb Gregg
				1975	9	17	John Birkett
				1976	15	12	John Birkett
				1977	12	14	John Birkett
				1978	10	15	John Birkett
				1979	13	14	Joedy Gardner

NORTHEAST LOUISIANA UNIVERSITY

Monroe, Louisiana

Indians			Maroon and Gold
1952	2	15	Cary Phillips
1953	6	18	Cary Phillips
1954	7	16	Arnold Kilpatrick
1955	21	13	Arnold Kilpatrick
1956	16	13	Arnold Kilpatrick
1957	14	10	Arnold Kilpatrick
1958	8	15	Lenny Fant
1959	12	13	Lenny Fant
1960	3	21	Lenny Fant
1961	12	13	Lenny Fant
1962	17	8	Lenny Fant
1963	15	11	Lenny Fant
1964	14	11	Lenny Fant
1965	18	4	Lenny Fant
1966	16	8	Lenny Fant
1967	13	11	Lenny Fant
1968	12	11	Lenny Fant
1969	12	11	Lenny Fant
1970	20	9	Lenny Fant
1971	16	6	Lenny Fant
1972	16	7	Lenny Fant
1973	15	10	Lenny Fant
1974	16	10	Lenny Fant
1975	15	10	Lenny Fant
1976	18	7	Lenny Fant
1977	15	12	Lenny Fant
1978	20	7	Lenny Fant
1979	23	6	Lenny Fant

NORTHERN ARIZONA UNIVERSITY

Flagstaff, Arizona

Lumberjacks, Axers			Blue and Gold
1938	4	15	Aaron McCreary
1939	13	5	Aaron McCreary
1940	8	9	Aaron McCreary
1941	9	9	Frank Brickey
1942	11	10	Frank Brickey
1943	12	8	Frank Brickey
1944	10	9	Frank Brickey
1945	11	8	Frank Brickey
1946	11	9	Frank Brickey
1947	19	7	Frank Brickey
1948	13	9	Nick Ragus
1949	12	9	Nick Ragus
1950	3	15	Ben Reiges

NORTHERN ILLINOIS UNIVERSITY

DeKalb, Illinois

Huskies			Cardinal and Black
1939	12	6	George Evans
1940	12	10	George Evans
1941	16	3	Ralph McKinzie
1942	11	9	Ralph McKinzie
1943	9	8	Ralph McKinzie
1944	7	7	Ralph McKinzie
1945	15	1	Ralph McKinzie
1946	11	8	Ralph McKinzie
1947	11	8	Ralph McKinzie
1948	14	12	Ralph McKinzie
1949	10	10	Gene Fekete
1950	4	17	Gil Wilson
1951	12	7	Gil Hertz
1952	6	16	Gil Hertz
1953	13	7	Gil Hertz
1954	5	14	Gil Hertz
1955	9	10	Bill Healey
1956	5	14	Bill Healey
1957	7	13	Bill Healey
1958	9	11	Bill Healey
1959	11	11	Bill Healey
1960	14	7	Bill Healey
1961	14	8	Bill Healey
1962	11	10	Bill Healey
1963	15	8	Bill Healey
1964	11	11	Ev Cochran
1965	12	10	Ev Cochran
1966	10	13	Ev Cochran
1967	8	12	Tom Jorgensen
1968	10	14	Tom Jorgensen
1969	13	11	Tom Jorgensen
1970	13	12	Tom Jorgensen
1971	13	10	Tom Jorgensen
1972	21	4	Tom Jorgensen
1973	17	8	Tom Jorgensen
1974	8	17	Emory Luck
1975	8	15	Emory Luck
1976	5	21	Emory Luck
1977	13	14	John McDougal
1978	11	16	John McDougal
1979	14	13	John McDougal

NORTH TEXAS STATE UNIVERSITY

Denton, Texas

Eagles			Green and White
1938	15	8	Pete Shands
1939	13	11	Pete Shands
1940	10	16	Pete Shands
1941	6	14	Pete Shands
1942	13	7	Daniel Yarbo
1943	15	15	Lloyd Russell
1944	—	—	
1945	—	—	
1946	—	—	
1947	13	10	Pete Shands
1948	16	9	Pete Shands
1949	10	13	Pete Shands
1950	9	17	Pete Shands
1951	13	13	Pete Shands
1952	15	8	Pete Shands
1953	20	5	Pete Shands
1954	19	9	Pete Shands
1955	8	16	Pete Shands
1956	9	13	Pete Shands
1957	3	20	Pete Shands
1958	3	18	Pete Shands
1959	6	18	Pete Shands
1960	7	19	Charles Johnson
1961	2	22	Charles Johnson
1962	3	23	Charles Johnson
1963	10	14	Charles Johnson
1964	7	17	Charles Johnson
1965	7	19	Charles Johnson
1966	5	20	Dan Spika
1967	12	13	Dan Spika
1968	8	18	Dan Spika
1969	15	10	Dan Spika
1970	18	8	Dan Spika
1971	10	15	Harry Miller
1972	8	18	Gene Robbins
1973	9	16	Gene Robbins
1974	13	13	Gene Robbins
1975	6	20	Gene Robbins
1976	22	4	Bill Blakeley
1977	21	6	Bill Blakeley
1978	22	6	Bill Blakeley
1979	11	16	Bill Blakeley

NORTHWESTERN UNIVERSITY

Evanston, Illinois

Wildcats			Purple and White
1938	10	10	Dutch Lonborg
1939	7	13	Dutch Lonborg
1940	13	7	Dutch Lonborg
1941	7	11	Dutch Lonborg
1942	8	13	Dutch Lonborg
1943	8	9	Dutch Lonborg
1944	12	7	Dutch Lonborg
1945	7	12	Dutch Lonborg
1946	15	5	Dutch Lonborg
1947	15	5	Dutch Lonborg
1948	6	14	Dutch Lonborg
1949	5	16	Dutch Lonborg
1950	10	12	Dutch Lonborg
1951	12	10	Harold Olson
1952	7	15	Harold Olson
1953	6	16	Waldo Fisher
1954	9	13	Waldo Fisher
1955	12	10	Waldo Fisher
1956	2	20	Waldo Fisher
1957	6	16	Waldo Fisher
1958	13	9	William Rohr
1959	15	7	William Rohr
1960	11	12	William Rohr
1961	10	12	William Rohr
1962	8	15	William Rohr

Yr.	W	L	Coach
1963	9	15	William Rohr
1964	8	13	Larry Glass
1965	7	17	Larry Glass
1966	12	12	Larry Glass
1967	11	11	Larry Glass
1968	13	10	Larry Glass
1969	14	10	L. Glass, B. Snyder
1970	9	15	Brad Snyder
1971	7	17	Brad Snyder
1972	5	18	Brad Snyder
1973	5	19	Brad Snyder
1974	9	15	Tex Winter
1975	6	20	Tex Winter
1976	12	15	Tex Winter
1977	7	20	Tex Winter
1978	8	19	Tex Winter
1979	6	21	Rich Falk

NORTHWESTERN STATE UNIVERSITY

Natchitoches, Louisiana

Demons			Purple, Burnt Orange, and White
1938	16	4	H. Lee Prather
1939	16	4	H. Lee Prather
1940	21	3	H. Lee Prather
1941	17	2	H. Lee Prather
1942	5	11	H. Lee Prather
1943	17	3	H. Lee Prather
1944	16	4	H. Lee Prather
1945	13	11	H. Lee Prather
1946	18	9	H. Lee Prather
1947	15	5	H. Lee Prather
1948	19	6	H. Lee Prather
1949	23	5	H. Lee Prather
1950	18	8	H. Lee Prather
1951	15	11	Charles "Red" Thomas
1952	17	14	Charles "Red" Thomas
1953	22	10	Charles "Red" Thomas
1954	23	9	Charles "Red" Thomas
1955	19	10	Charles "Red" Thomas
1956	18	10	Charles "Red" Thomas
1957	14	13	Charles "Red" Thomas
1958	20	7	Huey W. Cranford
1959	18	10	Huey W. Cranford
1960	23	5	Huey W. Cranford
1961	16	11	Huey W. Cranford
1962	10	17	Huey W. Cranford
1963	8	17	Huey W. Cranford
1964	12	14	Huey W. Cranford
1965	9	17	Huey W. Cranford
1966	18	7	Tynes Hildebrand
1967	8	17	Tynes Hildebrand
1968	12	13	Tynes Hildebrand
1969	16	13	Tynes Hildebrand
1970	13	13	Tynes Hildebrand
1971	16	9	Tynes Hildebrand
1972	13	12	Tynes Hildebrand
1973	6	19	Tynes Hildebrand
1974	21	9	Tynes Hildebrand
1975	13	14	Tynes Hildebrand
1976	14	10	Tynes Hildebrand
1977	17	9	Tynes Hildebrand
1978	12	15	Tynes Hildebrand
1979	7	19	Tynes Hildebrand

NOTRE DAME, UNIVERSITY OF

South Bend, Indiana

Fighting Irish			Gold and Blue
1938	20	3	George Keogan
1939	15	6	George Keogan
1940	15	6	George Keogan
1941	17	5	George Keogan
1942	16	6	George Keogan
1943	18	2	Keogan, Ed Krause
1944	10	9	Keogan, Ed Krause

Yr.	W	L	Coach
1945	15	5	Clem Crowe
1946	17	4	Elmer Ripley
1947	20	4	Ed "Moose" Krause
1948	17	7	Ed "Moose" Krause
1949	17	7	Ed "Moose" Krause
1950	15	9	Ed "Moose" Krause
1951	13	11	Ed "Moose" Krause
1952	16	10	John Jordan
1953	19	5	John Jordan
1954	22	3	John Jordan
1955	14	10	John Jordan
1956	9	15	John Jordan
1957	20	8	John Jordan
1958	24	5	John Jordan
1959	12	13	John Jordan
1960	17	9	John Jordan
1961	12	14	John Jordan
1962	8	15	John Jordan
1963	17	9	John Jordan
1964	10	14	John Jordan
1965	15	12	Johnny Dee
1966	5	20	Johnny Dee
1967	14	12	Johnny Dee
1968	21	9	Johnny Dee
1969	20	7	Johnny Dee
1970	21	8	Johnny Dee
1971	20	9	Johnny Dee
1972	6	20	Richard "Digger" Phelps
1973	18	12	Richard "Digger" Phelps
1974	26	3	Richard "Digger" Phelps
1975	19	10	Richard "Digger" Phelps
1976	23	6	Richard "Digger" Phelps
1977	22	7	Richard "Digger" Phelps
1978	23	8	Richard "Digger" Phelps
1979	24	6	Richard "Digger" Phelps

Yr.	W	L	Coach
1975	12	14	Dale Bandy
1976	11	15	Dale Bandy
1977	9	17	Dale Bandy
1978	13	14	Dale Bandy
1979	16	11	Dale Bandy

OHIO STATE UNIVERSITY

Columbus, Ohio

Buckeyes			*Scarlet and Gray*
1938	12	8	Harold Olsen
1939	16	7	Harold Olsen
1940	13	7	Harold Olsen
1941	10	10	Harold Olsen
1942	6	14	Harold Olsen
1943	7	10	Harold Olsen
1944	14	7	Harold Olsen
1945	15	5	Harold Olsen
1946	16	5	Harold Olsen
1947	7	13	Tippy Dye
1948	10	10	Tippy Dye
1949	14	7	Tippy Dye
1950	22	4	Tippy Dye
1951	6	16	Floyd Stahl
1952	8	14	Floyd Stahl
1953	10	12	Floyd Stahl
1954	11	11	Floyd Stahl
1955	10	12	Floyd Stahl
1956	16	6	Floyd Stahl
1957	14	8	Floyd Stahl
1958	9	13	Floyd Stahl
1959	11	11	Fred Taylor
1960	25	3	Fred Taylor
1961	27	1	Fred Taylor
1962	26	2	Fred Taylor
1963	20	4	Fred Taylor
1964	16	8	Fred Taylor
1965	12	12	Fred Taylor
1966	11	13	Fred Taylor
1967	13	11	Fred Taylor
1968	21	8	Fred Taylor
1969	17	7	Fred Taylor
1970	17	7	Fred Taylor
1971	20	6	Fred Taylor
1972	18	6	Fred Taylor
1973	14	10	Fred Taylor
1974	9	15	Fred Taylor
1975	14	14	Fred Taylor
1976	6	20	Fred Taylor
1977	9	18	Eldon Miller
1978	16	11	Eldon Miller
1979	19	12	Eldon Miller

OHIO UNIVERSITY

Athens, Ohio

Bobcats			*Green and White*
1938	12	8	Brandon Grover
1939	12	8	William Trautwein
1940	19	6	William Trautwein
1941	18	4	William Trautwein
1942	12	9	William Trautwein
1943	11	7	William Trautwein
1944	9	7	William Trautwein
1945	10	9	William Trautwein
1946	15	5	William Trautwein
1947	13	10	William Trautwein
1948	10	10	William Trautwein
1949	6	16	William Trautwein
1950	6	14	James Snyder
1951	13	11	James Snyder
1952	12	12	James Snyder
1953	9	13	James Snyder
1954	12	10	James Snyder
1955	16	5	James Snyder
1956	13	11	James Snyder
1957	15	8	James Snyder
1958	16	8	James Snyder
1959	14	10	James Snyder
1960	17	8	James Snyder
1961	17	7	James Snyder
1962	13	10	James Snyder
1963	13	11	James Snyder
1964	21	6	James Snyder
1965	19	7	James Snyder
1966	13	10	James Snyder
1967	8	15	James Snyder
1968	7	16	James Snyder
1969	17	9	James Snyder
1970	20	5	James Snyder
1971	17	7	James Snyder
1972	15	11	James Snyder
1973	16	10	James Snyder
1974	16	11	James Snyder

OKLAHOMA, UNIVERSITY OF

Norman, Oklahoma

Sooners			*Red and White*
1938	14	4	Hugh McDermott
1939	12	9	Bruce Drake
1940	12	7	Bruce Drake
1941	6	12	Bruce Drake
1942	11	7	Bruce Drake
1943	18	9	Bruce Drake
1944	15	8	Bruce Drake
1945	12	13	Bruce Drake
1946	11	10	Bruce Drake
1947	24	7	Bruce Drake
1948	13	9	Bruce Drake
1949	14	9	Bruce Drake
1950	12	10	Bruce Drake
1951	14	10	Bruce Drake
1952	7	17	Bruce Drake
1953	8	13	Bruce Drake
1954	8	13	Bruce Drake
1955	3	18	Bruce Drake
1956	4	19	Doyle Parrack

Yr.	W	L	Coach
1957	8	15	Doyle Parrack
1958	13	10	Doyle Parrack
1959	15	10	Doyle Parrack
1960	14	11	Doyle Parrack
1961	10	15	Doyle Parrack
1962	7	17	Doyle Parrack
1963	12	13	Bob Stevens
1964	7	18	Bob Stevens
1965	8	17	Bob Stevens
1966	11	14	Bob Stevens
1967	8	17	Bob Stevens
1968	13	13	John MacLeod
1969	7	19	John MacLeod
1970	19	9	John MacLeod
1971	19	8	John MacLeod
1972	14	12	John MacLeod
1973	18	8	John MacLeod
1974	18	8	Joe Ramsey
1975	13	13	Joe Ramsey
1976	9	17	Dave Bliss
1977	18	10	Dave Bliss
1978	14	13	Dave Bliss
1979	20	11	Dave Bliss

OKLAHOMA CITY UNIVERSITY

Oklahoma City, Oklahoma

Chiefs	W	L	Blue and White
1938	7	15	Melvin Binford
1939	10	8	Melvin Binford
1940	6	13	Faye Ferguson
1941	7	11	Faye Ferguson
1942	5	11	Merle Rousey
1943	—	—	
1944	—	—	
1945	—	—	
1946	—	—	
1947	7	9	Bo Sherman
1948	18	13	Doyle Parrack
1949	20	6	Doyle Parrack
1950	19	5	Doyle Parrack
1951	16	14	Doyle Parrack
1952	18	9	Doyle Parrack
1953	18	6	Doyle Parrack
1954	18	7	Doyle Parrack
1955	9	18	Doyle Parrack
1956	20	7	Abe Lemons
1957	9	19	Abe Lemons
1958	14	12	Abe Lemons
1959	20	7	Abe Lemons
1960	12	13	Abe Lemons
1961	14	12	Abe Lemons
1962	14	12	Abe Lemons
1963	19	10	Abe Lemons
1964	15	11	Abe Lemons
1965	21	10	Abe Lemons
1966	24	4	Abe Lemons
1967	16	10	Abe Lemons
1968	20	6	Abe Lemons
1969	18	9	Abe Lemons
1970	16	10	Abe Lemons
1971	8	17	Abe Lemons
1972	14	10	Abe Lemons
1973	21	6	Abe Lemons
1974	13	13	Paul Hansen
1975	12	14	Paul Hansen
1976	9	18	Paul Hansen
1977	14	12	Paul Hansen
1978	16	11	Paul Hansen
1979	18	11	Paul Hansen

OKLAHOMA STATE UNIVERSITY

Stillwater, Oklahoma

Cowboys	W	L	Orange and Black
1938	25	3	Henry Iba
1939	19	8	Henry Iba
1940	26	3	Henry Iba
1941	18	7	Henry Iba
1942	20	6	Henry Iba
1943	14	10	Henry Iba
1944	27	6	Henry Iba
1945	27	4	Henry Iba
1946	31	2	Henry Iba
1947	24	8	Henry Iba
1948	27	4	Henry Iba
1949	23	5	Henry Iba
1950	18	9	Henry Iba
1951	29	6	Henry Iba
1952	19	8	Henry Iba
1953	23	7	Henry Iba
1954	24	5	Henry Iba
1955	12	13	Henry Iba
1956	18	9	Henry Iba
1957	17	9	Henry Iba
1958	21	8	Henry Iba
1959	11	14	Henry Iba
1960	10	15	Henry Iba
1961	14	11	Henry Iba
1962	14	11	Henry Iba
1963	16	9	Henry Iba
1964	15	10	Henry Iba
1965	20	7	Henry Iba
1966	4	21	Henry Iba
1967	7	18	Henry Iba
1968	10	16	Henry Iba
1969	12	13	Henry Iba
1970	14	12	Henry Iba
1971	7	19	Sam Aubrey
1972	5	22	Sam Aubrey
1973	7	19	Sam Aubrey
1974	9	17	Guy Strong
1975	10	16	Guy Strong
1976	10	16	Guy Strong
1977	10	17	Guy Strong
1978	10	16	Jim Killingsworth
1979	12	15	Jim Killingsworth

OLD DOMINION UNIVERSITY

Norfolk, Virginia

Monarchs, Big Blue	W	L	Light Blue and White
1938	15	4	Tommy Scott
1939	8	14	Tommy Scott
1940	4	16	Tommy Scott
1941	4	15	George Stirnweiss
1942	0	14	George Stirnweiss
1943	12	10	Scrap Chandler
1944	1	7	Scrap Chandler
1945	6	6	Scrap Chandler
1946	9	8	Scrap Chandler
1947	14	8	Julius Rubin
1948	21	8	Jack Callahan
1949	11	5	Bud Metheny
1950	9	10	Bud Metheny
1951	11	14	Bud Metheny
1952	12	13	Bud Metheny
1953	8	12	Bud Metheny
1954	13	9	Bud Metheny
1955	7	15	Bud Metheny
1956	8	11	Bud Metheny
1957	10	10	Bud Metheny
1958	12	9	Bud Metheny
1959	15	8	Bud Metheny
1960	12	6	Bud Metheny
1961	16	4	Bud Metheny
1962	18	3	Bud Metheny
1963	12	14	Bud Metheny
1964	13	10	Bud Metheny
1965	10	13	Bud Metheny
1966	7	17	Sonny Allen
1967	14	12	Sonny Allen
1968	19	7	Sonny Allen

Yr.	W	L	Coach
1969	21	10	Sonny Allen
1970	21	7	Sonny Allen
1971	21	9	Sonny Allen
1972	14	10	Sonny Allen
1973	19	9	Sonny Allen
1974	20	7	Sonny Allen
1975	25	6	Sonny Allen
1976	19	12	Paul Webb
1977	25	4	Paul Webb
1978	11	15	Paul Webb
1979	23	7	Paul Webb

ORAL ROBERTS UNIVERSITY

Tulsa, Oklahoma

Titans	W	L	Blue, Gold, and White
1972	26	2	Ken Trickey
1973	21	6	Ken Trickey
1974	23	6	Ken Trickey
1975	20	8	Jerry Hale
1976	20	6	Jerry Hale
1977	21	7	Jerry Hale
1978	13	14	Lake Kelly
1979	17	10	Lake Kelly

OREGON, UNIVERSITY OF

Eugene, Oregon

Webfoots	W	L	Yellow and Green
1938	25	8	Howard Hobson
1939	29	5	Howard Hobson
1940	19	12	Howard Hobson
1941	18	18	Howard Hobson
1942	12	15	Howard Hobson
1943	19	10	Howard Hobson
1944	16	10	Howard Hobson
1945	30	13	Howard Hobson
1946	16	17	Howard Hobson
1947	18	9	Howard Hobson
1948	18	11	John Warren
1949	12	18	John Warren
1950	9	19	John Warren
1951	18	13	John Warren
1952	14	16	Bill Borcher
1953	14	14	Bill Borcher
1954	17	10	Bill Borcher
1955	13	13	Bill Borcher
1956	11	15	Bill Borcher
1957	4	21	Steve Belko
1958	13	11	Steve Belko
1959	9	16	Steve Belko
1960	19	10	Steve Belko
1961	15	12	Steve Belko
1962	9	17	Steve Belko
1963	11	15	Steve Belko
1964	14	12	Steve Belko
1965	9	17	Steve Belko
1966	13	13	Steve Belko
1967	9	17	Steve Belko
1968	7	19	Steve Belko
1969	13	13	Steve Belko
1970	17	9	Steve Belko
1971	17	9	Steve Belko
1972	6	20	Dick Harter
1973	16	10	Dick Harter
1974	15	11	Dick Harter
1975	21	9	Dick Harter
1976	20	10	Dick Harter
1977	19	10	Dick Harter
1978	16	11	Dick Harter
1979	12	15	Jim Haney

OREGON STATE UNIVERSITY

Corvallis, Oregon

Beavers	W	L	Orange and Black
1938	17	16	Slats Gill
1939	13	11	Slats Gill
1940	27	11	Slats Gill
1941	19	9	Slats Gill
1942	18	9	Slats Gill
1943	19	9	Slats Gill
1944	8	16	Slats Gill
1945	20	8	Slats Gill
1946	13	11	Slats Gill
1947	28	5	Slats Gill
1948	21	13	Slats Gill
1949	24	12	Slats Gill
1950	13	14	Slats Gill
1951	14	18	Slats Gill
1952	9	19	Slats Gill
1953	11	18	Slats Gill
1954	19	10	Slats Gill
1955	22	8	Slats Gill
1956	8	18	Slats Gill
1957	11	15	Slats Gill
1958	20	6	Slats Gill
1959	13	13	Slats Gill
1960	15	11	Gill, Paul Valenti
1961	14	12	Slats Gill
1962	24	5	Slats Gill
1963	22	9	Slats Gill
1964	25	4	Slats Gill
1965	16	10	Paul Valenti
1966	21	7	Paul Valenti
1967	14	14	Paul Valenti
1968	12	13	Paul Valenti
1969	12	14	Paul Valenti
1970	10	16	Paul Valenti
1971	12	14	Ralph Miller
1972	18	10	Ralph Miller
1973	15	11	Ralph Miller
1974	13	13	Ralph Miller
1975	19	12	Ralph Miller
1976	18	9	Ralph Miller
1977	16	13	Ralph Miller
1978	19	11	Ralph Miller
1979	18	10	Ralph Miller

PACIFIC, UNIVERSITY OF THE

Stockton, California

Tigers	W	L	Orange and Black
1938	5	16	Ralph Francis
1939	5	12	Ralph Francis
1940	6	14	Ralph Francis
1941	16	7	Ralph Francis
1942	13	11	Chris Kjeldsen
1943	11	7	Chris Kjeldsen
1944	13	6	Chris Kjeldsen
1945	12	6	Chris Kjeldsen
1946	12	13	Chris Kjeldsen
1947	16	8	Chris Kjeldsen
1948	11	13	Chris Kjeldsen
1949	14	13	Chris Kjeldsen
1950	7	15	Chris Kjeldsen
1951	19	11	Chris Kjeldsen
1952	10	14	Chris Kjeldsen
1953	3	20	Van Sweet
1954	10	16	Van Sweet
1955	11	15	Van Sweet
1956	15	11	Van Sweet
1957	9	17	Van Sweet
1958	9	15	Van Sweet
1959	12	14	Van Sweet

Yr.	W	L	Coach
1960	9	17	Van Sweet
1961	5	21	Van Sweet
1962	10	16	Van Sweet
1963	4	22	Van Sweet
1964	15	11	Dick Edwards
1965	14	12	Dick Edwards
1966	22	6	Dick Edwards
1967	24	4	Dick Edwards
1968	17	9	Dick Edwards
1969	17	9	Dick Edwards
1970	21	6	Dick Edwards
1971	22	6	Dick Edwards
1972	17	9	Dick Edwards
1973	14	12	Stan Morrison
1974	14	12	Stan Morrison
1975	12	14	Stan Morrison
1976	14	14	Stan Morrison
1977	11	14	Stan Morrison
1978	17	10	Stan Morrison
1979	18	12	Stan Morrison

Yr.	W	L	Coach
1968	9	17	Dick Harter
1969	15	10	Dick Harter
1970	25	2	Dick Harter
1971	28	1	Dick Harter
1972	25	3	Chuck Daly
1973	21	7	Chuck Daly
1974	21	6	Chuck Daly
1975	23	5	Chuck Daly
1976	17	9	Chuck Daly
1977	18	8	Chuck Daly
1978	20	8	Bob Weinhauer
1979	25	7	Bob Weinhauer

PAN AMERICAN UNIVERSITY

Edinburg, Texas

Broncs			Green and White
1969	8	17	Sam Williams
1970	8	16	Sam Williams
1971	13	13	Sam Williams
1972	17	7	Sam Williams
1973	7	19	Sam Williams
1974	13	9	Abe Lemons
1975	22	2	Abe Lemons
1976	20	5	Abe Lemons
1977	17	9	Bill White
1978	22	4	Bill White
1979	13	13	Bill White

PENNSYLVANIA, UNIVERSITY OF

Philadelphia, Pennsylvania

Quakers			Red and Blue
1938	8	10	Lon Jourdet
1939	7	11	Lon Jourdet
1940	5	13	Lon Jourdet
1941	5	12	Lon Jourdet
1942	9	9	Lon Jourdet
1943	14	7	Lon Jourdet
1944	10	4	Don Kellett
1945	12	5	Don Kellett
1946	7	10	Robert Dougherty
1947	14	8	Don Kellett
1948	10	14	Don Kellett
1949	15	8	Howie Dallmar
1950	11	14	Howie Dallmar
1951	19	8	Howie Dallmar
1952	21	8	Howie Dallmar
1953	22	5	Howie Dallmar
1954	17	8	Howie Dallmar
1955	19	6	Ray Stanley
1956	12	13	Ray Stanley
1957	7	19	Jack McCloskey
1958	13	12	Jack McCloskey
1959	12	14	Jack McCloskey
1960	14	11	Jack McCloskey
1961	16	9	Jack McCloskey
1962	17	8	Jack McCloskey
1963	19	6	Jack McCloskey
1964	14	10	Jack McCloskey
1965	15	10	Jack McCloskey
1966	19	6	Jack McCloskey
1967	11	14	Dick Harter

PENNSYLVANIA STATE UNIVERSITY

University Park, Pennsylvania

Nittany Lions			Blue and White
1938	13	5	John Lawther
1939	13	10	John Lawther
1940	15	8	John Lawther
1941	15	5	John Lawther
1942	18	3	John Lawther
1943	15	4	John Lawther
1944	8	7	John Lawther
1945	10	7	John Lawther
1946	7	9	John Lawther
1947	10	8	John Lawther
1948	9	10	John Lawther
1949	7	10	John Lawther
1950	13	10	Elmer Gross
1951	14	9	Elmer Gross
1952	20	6	Elmer Gross
1953	15	9	Elmer Gross
1954	18	6	Elmer Gross
1955	18	10	John Egli
1956	12	14	John Egli
1957	15	10	John Egli
1958	8	11	John Egli
1959	11	9	John Egli
1960	11	11	John Egli
1961	11	13	John Egli
1962	12	11	John Egli
1963	15	5	John Egli
1964	17	8	John Egli
1965	20	4	John Egli
1966	18	6	John Egli
1967	10	14	John Egli
1968	10	10	John Egli
1969	13	9	John Bach
1970	13	11	John Bach
1971	10	12	John Bach
1972	17	8	John Bach
1973	15	8	John Bach
1974	14	12	John Bach
1975	11	12	John Bach
1976	10	15	John Bach
1977	11	15	John Bach
1978	8	19	John Bach
1979	12	18	Dick Harter

PEPPERDINE UNIVERSITY

Los Angeles, California

Waves			Blue and Orange
1939	17	12	Dr. Wade Ruby
1940	14	12	Dr. Wade Ruby
1941	11	13	Dr. Wade Ruby
1942	14	6	Dr. Wade Ruby
1943	23	8	Dr. Wade Ruby
1944	21	13	Dr. Wade Ruby
1945	24	12	Dr. Wade Ruby

Yr.	W	L	Coach
1946	26	9	Dr. Wade Ruby
1947	14	13	Dr. Wade Ruby
1948	22	11	Dr. Wade Ruby
1949	19	11	R. L. "Duck" Dowell
1950	21	12	R. L. "Duck" Dowell
1951	25	8	R. L. "Duck" Dowell
1952	20	5	R. L. "Duck" Dowell
1953	18	8	R. L. "Duck" Dowell
1954	14	10	R. L. "Duck" Dowell
1955	16	9	R. L. "Duck" Dowell
1956	2	24	R. L. "Duck" Dowell
1957	7	18	R. L. "Duck" Dowell
1958	15	11	R. L. "Duck" Dowell
1959	16	8	R. L. "Duck" Dowell
1960	14	11	R. L. "Duck" Dowell
1961	9	16	R. L. "Duck" Dowell
1962	20	7	R. L. "Duck" Dowell
1963	14	11	R. L. "Duck" Dowell
1964	6	19	R. L. "Duck" Dowell
1965	6	19	R. L. "Duck" Dowell
1966	2	24	R. L. "Duck" Dowell
1967	9	17	R. L. "Duck" Dowell
1968	9	17	R. L. "Duck" Dowell
1969	14	12	Gary Colson
1970	14	12	Gary Colson
1971	12	13	Gary Colson
1972	10	15	Gary Colson
1973	14	11	Gary Colson
1974	8	18	Gary Colson
1975	17	8	Gary Colson
1976	22	6	Gary Colson
1977	13	13	Gary Colson
1978	7	19	Gary Colson
1979	22	10	Gary Colson

PITTSBURGH, UNIVERSITY OF

Pittsburgh, Pennsylvania

Panthers			Blue and Gold
1938	9	12	Dr. Harold Carlson
1939	10	8	Dr. Harold Carlson
1940	8	9	Dr. Harold Carlson
1941	13	6	Dr. Harold Carlson
1942	5	10	Dr. Harold Carlson
1943	10	5	Dr. Harold Carlson
1944	7	7	Dr. Harold Carlson
1945	8	4	Dr. Harold Carlson
1946	7	7	Dr. Harold Carlson
1947	8	10	Dr. Harold Carlson
1948	10	11	Dr. Harold Carlson
1949	12	13	Dr. Harold Carlson
1950	4	14	Dr. Harold Carlson
1951	9	17	Dr. Harold Carlson
1952	10	12	Dr. Harold Carlson
1953	12	11	Dr. Harold Carlson
1954	9	14	Bob Timmons
1955	10	16	Bob Timmons
1956	15	10	Bob Timmons
1957	16	11	Bob Timmons
1958	18	7	Bob Timmons
1959	10	14	Bob Timmons
1960	11	14	Bob Timmons
1961	12	11	Bob Timmons
1962	12	11	Bob Timmons
1963	19	6	Bob Timmons
1964	16	7	Bob Timmons
1965	7	16	Bob Timmons
1966	5	17	Bob Timmons
1967	6	19	Bob Timmons
1968	7	15	Bob Timmons
1969	4	20	Charles "Buzz" Ridl
1970	12	12	Charles "Buzz" Ridl
1971	14	10	Charles "Buzz" Ridl
1972	12	12	Charles "Buzz" Ridl
1973	12	14	Charles "Buzz" Ridl
1974	25	4	Charles "Buzz" Ridl
1975	18	11	Charles "Buzz" Ridl

Yr.	W	L	Coach
1976	12	15	Tim Grgurich
1977	6	21	Tim Grgurich
1978	16	11	Tim Grgurich
1979	18	11	Tim Grgurich

PORTLAND, UNIVERSITY OF

Portland, Oregon

Pilots			Purple and White
1938	8	10	Edwin Fitzpatrick
1939	13	9	Edwin Fitzpatrick
1940	16	4	Edwin Fitzpatrick
1941	15	9	Edwin Fitzpatrick
1942	14	7	Edwin Fitzpatrick
1943	16	8	R. Mathews
1944	—	—	
1945	—	—	
1946	8	7	Leonard Yandle
1947	13	18	Mush Torson
1948	15	19	Mush Torson
1949	22	11	Mush Torson
1950	19	12	Mush Torson
1951	23	6	Mush Torson
1952	24	11	Mush Torson
1953	16	14	Mush Torson
1954	9	19	Mush Torson
1955	9	13	A. McLarney, M. Tichy
1956	20	8	Al Negratti
1957	18	12	Al Negratti
1958	18	11	Al Negratti
1959	19	8	Al Negratti
1960	11	15	Al Negratti
1961	16	9	Al Negratti
1962	8	18	Al Negratti
1963	8	18	Al Negratti
1964	17	9	Al Negratti
1965	12	13	Al Negratti
1966	6	19	Al Negratti
1967	10	16	Al Negratti
1968	5	21	Bill Turner
1969	3	23	Bill Turner
1970	4	22	Joe Etzel
1971	5	21	Jack Avina
1972	10	16	Jack Avina
1973	9	19	Jack Avina
1974	15	11	Jack Avina
1975	13	16	Jack Avina
1976	9	18	Jack Avina
1977	12	14	Jack Avina
1978	19	8	Jack Avina
1979	18	10	Jack Avina

PORTLAND STATE UNIVERSITY

Portland, Oregon

Vikings			Green and White
1956	21	8	Sharkey Nelson
1957	11	17	Sharkey Nelson
1958	14	14	Sharkey Nelson
1959	20	8	Sharkey Nelson
1960	14	14	Sharkey Nelson
1961	17	10	Sharkey Nelson
1962	15	13	Sharkey Nelson
1963	7	18	Sharkey Nelson
1964	10	15	Sharkey Nelson
1965	8	18	Sharkey Nelson
1966	6	19	Marion Pericin
1967	19	9	Marion Pericin
1968	16	9	Marion Pericin
1969	10	17	Marion Pericin
1970	12	15	Marion Pericin
1971	18	8	Marion Pericin
1972	19	8	Marion Pericin
1973	12	12	Ken Edwards
1974	16	11	Ken Edwards

Yr.	W	L	Coach
1975	18	8	Ken Edwards
1976	17	10	Ken Edwards
1977	17	10	Ken Edwards
1978	14	13	Ken Edwards
1979	6	21	Glen Kinney

PRINCETON UNIVERSITY

Princeton, New Jersey

Tigers			*Orange and Black*
1938	10	10	Ken Fairman
1939	10	9	Franklin Cappon
1940	14	8	Franklin Cappon
1941	10	13	Franklin Cappon
1942	16	5	Franklin Cappon
1943	14	6	F. Cappon, Wm. Logan
1944	6	12	William Logan
1945	7	12	W. Logan, L. Hettinger
1946	7	12	Wes Fesler
1947	7	16	Franklin Cappon
1948	12	11	Franklin Cappon
1949	13	9	Franklin Cappon
1950	14	9	Franklin Cappon
1951	15	7	Franklin Cappon
1952	16	11	Franklin Cappon
1953	9	14	Franklin Cappon
1954	16	9	Franklin Cappon
1955	13	12	Franklin Cappon
1956	11	13	Franklin Cappon
1957	14	9	Franklin Cappon
1958	15	8	Franklin Cappon
1959	19	5	Franklin Cappon
1960	15	9	Franklin Cappon
1961	18	8	F. Cappon, J. L. McCandless
1962	13	10	J. L. McCandless
1963	19	6	Bill van Breda Kolff
1964	20	9	Bill van Breda Kolff
1965	23	6	Bill van Breda Kolff
1966	16	7	Bill van Breda Kolff
1967	25	3	Bill van Breda Kolff
1968	20	6	Pete Carril
1969	19	7	Pete Carril
1970	16	9	Pete Carril
1971	14	11	Pete Carril
1972	20	7	Pete Carril
1973	16	9	Pete Carril
1974	16	10	Pete Carril
1975	22	8	Pete Carril
1976	22	5	Pete Carril
1977	21	5	Pete Carril
1978	17	9	Pete Carril
1979	14	12	Pete Carril

PROVIDENCE COLLEGE

Providence, Rhode Island

Friars			*Black and White*
1938	7	9	Albert McClellan
1939	4	7	Edward Crotty
1940	5	9	Edward Crotty
1941	11	6	Edward Crotty
1942	13	7	Edward Crotty
1943	15	5	Edward Crotty
1944	—	—	
1945	5	7	Edward Crotty
1946	5	12	Edward Crotty
1947	8	11	Lawrence Drew
1948	10	10	Lawrence Drew
1949	7	19	Lawrence Drew
1950	14	9	James Cuddy
1951	14	10	James Cuddy

Yr.	W	L	Coach
1952	14	9	James Cuddy
1953	11	11	James Cuddy
1954	13	13	James Cuddy
1955	9	12	James Cuddy
1956	14	8	Joe Mullaney
1957	15	9	Joe Mullaney
1958	18	6	Joe Mullaney
1959	20	7	Joe Mullaney
1960	24	5	Joe Mullaney
1961	24	5	Joe Mullaney
1962	20	6	Joe Mullaney
1963	24	4	Joe Mullaney
1964	20	6	Joe Mullaney
1965	24	2	Joe Mullaney
1966	22	5	Joe Mullaney
1967	21	7	Joe Mullaney
1968	11	14	Joe Mullaney
1969	14	10	Joe Mullaney
1970	14	11	Dave Gavitt
1971	20	8	Dave Gavitt
1972	21	6	Dave Gavitt
1973	27	4	Dave Gavitt
1974	28	4	Dave Gavitt
1975	20	11	Dave Gavitt
1976	21	11	Dave Gavitt
1977	24	5	Dave Gavitt
1978	24	8	Dave Gavitt
1979	10	16	Dave Gavitt

PURDUE UNIVERSITY

Lafayette, Indiana

Boilermakers			*Old Gold and Black*
1938	18	2	Ward "Piggy" Lambert
1939	12	7	Ward "Piggy" Lambert
1940	16	4	Ward "Piggy" Lambert
1941	13	7	Ward "Piggy" Lambert
1942	14	7	Ward "Piggy" Lambert
1943	9	11	Ward "Piggy" Lambert
1944	11	10	Ward "Piggy" Lambert
1945	9	11	Ward "Piggy" Lambert
1946	10	11	Lambert, Mel Taube
1947	9	11	Mel Taube
1948	11	9	Mel Taube
1949	13	9	Mel Taube
1950	9	13	Mel Taube
1951	8	14	Ray Eddy
1952	8	14	Ray Eddy
1953	4	18	Ray Eddy
1954	9	13	Ray Eddy
1955	12	10	Ray Eddy
1956	16	6	Ray Eddy
1957	15	7	Ray Eddy
1958	14	8	Ray Eddy
1959	15	7	Ray Eddy
1960	11	12	Ray Eddy
1961	16	7	Ray Eddy
1962	17	7	Ray Eddy
1963	7	17	Ray Eddy
1964	12	12	Ray Eddy
1965	12	12	Ray Eddy
1966	8	16	George King
1967	15	9	George King
1968	15	9	George King
1969	23	5	George King
1970	18	6	George King
1971	18	7	George King
1972	12	12	George King
1973	15	9	Fred Schaus
1974	22	8	Fred Schaus
1975	17	11	Fred Schaus
1976	16	11	Fred Schaus
1977	19	9	Fred Schaus
1978	16	11	Fred Schaus
1979	27	8	Lee Rose

RHODE ISLAND, UNIVERSITY OF

Kingston, Rhode Island

Rams — *Blue and White*

Yr.	W	L	Coach
1938	19	2	Frank Keaney
1939	17	4	Frank Keaney
1940	19	3	Frank Keaney
1941	21	4	Frank Keaney
1942	18	4	Frank Keaney
1943	16	3	Frank Keaney
1944	14	6	Frank Keaney
1945	20	5	Frank Keaney
1946	22	3	Frank Keaney
1947	17	6	Frank Keaney
1948	17	3	Frank Keaney
1949	15	6	Robert Haire
1950	18	8	Robert Haire
1951	13	15	Robert Haire
1952	10	13	Robert Haire
1953	13	10	Jack Guy
1954	8	14	Jack Guy
1955	17	10	Jack Guy
1956	11	14	Jack Guy
1957	11	11	Jack Guy
1958	4	17	Ernie Calverley
1959	8	12	Ernie Calverley
1960	12	14	Ernie Calverley
1961	18	9	Ernie Calverley
1962	14	12	Ernie Calverley
1963	15	11	Ernie Calverley
1964	19	8	Ernie Calverley
1965	15	11	Ernie Calverley
1966	20	8	Ernie Calverley
1967	14	12	Ernie Calverley
1968	15	11	Ernie Calverley
1969	10	15	Tom Carmody
1970	16	10	Tom Carmody
1971	10	17	Tom Carmody
1972	15	11	Tom Carmody
1973	7	18	Tom Carmody
1974	11	14	Jack Kraft
1975	5	20	Jack Kraft
1976	14	12	Jack Kraft
1977	13	13	Jack Kraft
1978	24	7	Jack Kraft
1979	20	9	Jack Kraft
1963	12	11	John Frankie
1964	15	9	George Carlisle
1965	2	22	George Carlisle
1966	1	22	George Carlisle
1967	7	17	Don Knodel
1968	8	16	Don Knodel
1969	10	14	Don Knodel
1970	14	11	Don Knodel
1971	14	12	Don Knodel
1972	6	20	Don Knodel
1973	7	19	Don Knodel
1974	7	19	Don Knodel
1975	5	21	Bob Polk
1976	3	24	Bob Polk
1977	9	18	Bob Polk
1978	4	22	Mike Schuler
1979	7	20	Mike Schuler

RICE UNIVERSITY

Houston, Texas

Owls — *Blue and Gray*

Yr.	W	L	Coach
1938	2	10	James Kitts
1939	12	12	James Kitts
1940	21	3	Buster Brannon
1941	18	6	Buster Brannon
1942	22	5	Buster Brannon
1943	17	9	Joe Davis
1944	15	5	Joe Davis
1945	20	1	Joe Davis
1946	10	11	Buster Brannon
1947	7	17	Joe Davis
1948	10	14	Joe Davis
1949	13	11	Joe Davis
1950	8	15	Don Suman
1951	8	15	Don Suman
1952	9	15	Don Suman
1953	15	6	Don Suman
1954	23	5	Don Suman
1955	10	12	Don Suman
1956	19	5	Don Suman
1957	16	8	Don Suman
1958	13	11	Don Suman
1959	11	13	Don Suman
1960	4	20	John Frankie
1961	11	12	John Frankie
1962	12	11	John Frankie

RICHMOND, UNIVERSITY OF

Richmond, Virginia

Spiders — *Red and Blue*

Yr.	W	L	Coach
1938	15	5	Malcolm U. Pitt
1939	10	10	Malcolm U. Pitt
1940	11	6	Malcolm U. Pitt
1941	11	10	Malcolm U. Pitt
1942	9	9	Malcolm U. Pitt
1943	11	5	Malcolm U. Pitt
1944	7	6	Malcolm U. Pitt
1945	3	4	Malcolm U. Pitt
1946	8	12	Malcolm U. Pitt
1947	17	9	Malcolm U. Pitt
1948	8	14	Malcolm U. Pitt
1949	8	15	Malcolm U. Pitt
1950	8	16	Malcolm U. Pitt
1951	7	14	Malcolm U. Pitt
1952	7	15	Malcolm U. Pitt
1953	20	7	H. Lester Hooker, Jr.
1954	23	8	H. Lester Hooker, Jr.
1955	19	9	H. Lester Hooker, Jr.
1956	16	13	H. Lester Hooker, Jr.
1957	15	11	H. Lester Hooker, Jr.
1958	14	12	H. Lester Hooker, Jr.
1959	11	11	H. Lester Hooker, Jr.
1960	7	18	H. Lester Hooker, Jr.
1961	9	14	H. Lester Hooker, Jr.
1962	6	21	H. Lester Hooker, Jr.
1963	7	18	H. Lester Hooker, Jr.
1964	6	16	Lewis Mills
1965	10	16	Lewis Mills
1966	12	13	Lewis Mills
1967	11	12	Lewis Mills
1968	12	13	Lewis Mills
1969	13	14	Lewis Mills
1970	9	18	Lewis Mills
1971	7	21	Lewis Mills
1972	6	18	Lewis Mills
1973	8	16	Lewis Mills
1974	16	12	Lewis Mills
1975	10	16	Carl J. Slone
1976	14	14	Carl J. Slone
1977	15	11	Carl J. Slone
1978	4	22	Carl J. Slone
1979	10	16	Lou Goetz

RIDER COLLEGE

Lawrenceville, New Jersey

Broncs, Roughriders — *Purple and Gold*

Yr.	W	L	Coach
1938	9	7	Frank Donlon
1939	10	6	Frank Donlon
1940	12	5	Frank Donlon
1941	10	7	Rex Ellis
1942	10	13	Rex Ellis

Yr.	W	L	Coach
1943	13	16	Tom Leyden
1944	3	12	Frank Donlon
1945	5	12	Frank Donlon
1946	11	7	Frank Donlon
1947	13	12	Thomas Leyden
1948	14	6	Thomas Leyden
1949	14	9	Thomas Leyden
1950	11	9	Thomas Leyden
1951	6	13	Thomas Leyden
1952	9	5	Thomas Leyden
1953	9	10	Thomas Leyden
1954	12	12	Thomas Leyden
1955	9	15	Thomas Leyden
1956	16	7	Thomas Leyden
1957	20	7	Thomas Leyden
1958	17	8	Thomas Leyden
1959	12	14	Thomas Leyden
1960	12	14	Thomas Leyden
1961	13	12	Glenn Leach
1962	12	13	Glenn Leach
1963	20	8	Robert Greenwood
1964	15	10	Robert Greenwood
1965	13	11	Robert Greenwood
1966	16	9	Richard Harter
1967	11	12	John Carpenter
1968	9	15	John Carpenter
1969	11	14	John Carpenter
1970	16	10	John Carpenter
1971	20	6	John Carpenter
1972	15	11	John Carpenter
1973	12	14	John Carpenter
1974	13	13	John Carpenter
1975	16	11	John Carpenter
1976	14	13	John Carpenter
1977	8	18	John Carpenter
1978	11	16	John Carpenter
1979	11	15	John Carpenter

RUTGERS UNIVERSITY

New Brunswick, New Jersey

Scarlet Knights			Scarlet
1938	11	4	Frank Hill
1939	8	6	Frank Hill
1940	5	14	Frank Hill
1941	5	14	Frank Hill
1942	8	12	Frank Hill
1943	7	9	Frank Hill
1944	—	—	
1945	10	3	Thomas Kenneally
1946	13	7	Donald White
1947	7	12	Donald White
1948	14	9	Donald White
1949	14	12	Donald White
1950	13	15	Donald White
1951	7	14	Donald White
1952	6	13	Donald White
1953	8	13	Donald White
1954	11	13	Donald White
1955	2	22	Donald White
1956	3	15	Donald White
1957	8	15	Warren Harris
1958	7	15	Warren Harris
1959	9	15	Warren Harris
1960	11	14	Anthony Kuolt
1961	11	10	Anthony Kuolt
1962	10	13	Anthony Kuolt
1963	7	16	Donald White
1964	5	17	William Foster
1965	12	12	William Foster
1966	17	7	William Foster
1967	22	7	William Foster
1968	14	10	William Foster
1969	21	4	William Foster
1970	13	11	William Foster
1971	16	7	William Foster
1972	14	11	Richard Lloyd

Yr.	W	L	Coach
1973	15	11	Richard Lloyd
1974	18	8	Tom Young
1975	22	7	Tom Young
1976	31	2	Tom Young
1977	18	10	Tom Young
1978	24	7	Tom Young
1979	22	9	Tom Young

ST. BONAVENTURE UNIVERSITY

St. Bonaventure, New York

Indians			Brown and White
1938	9	0	Mike Reilly
1939	10	7	Mike Reilly
1940	11	6	Mike Reilly
1941	12	5	Mike Reilly
1942	12	8	Mike Reilly
1943	8	9	Mike Reilly
1944	—	—	
1945	3	7	Rev. Anselm Krieger
1946	12	3	Rev. Anselm Krieger
1947	10	11	Harry Singleton
1948	12	10	Edward Melvin
1949	18	7	Edward Melvin
1950	17	5	Edward Melvin
1951	19	6	Edward Melvin
1952	21	6	Edward Melvin
1953	11	11	Edward Melvin
1954	12	11	Edward Donovan
1955	13	10	Edward Donovan
1956	11	12	Edward Donovan
1957	17	7	Edward Donovan
1958	21	5	Edward Donovan
1959	20	3	Edward Donovan
1960	21	5	Edward Donovan
1961	24	4	Edward Donovan
1962	14	7	Larry Weise
1963	13	12	Larry Weise
1964	16	8	Larry Weise
1965	15	8	Larry Weise
1966	16	7	Larry Weise
1967	13	9	Larry Weise
1968	23	2	Larry Weise
1969	17	7	Larry Weise
1970	25	3	Larry Weise
1971	21	6	Larry Weise
1972	16	8	Larry Weise
1973	13	13	Larry Weise
1974	17	9	Jim Satalin
1975	14	13	Jim Satalin
1976	17	10	Jim Satalin
1977	24	6	Jim Satalin
1978	21	8	Jim Satalin
1979	19	9	Jim Satalin

ST. FRANCIS COLLEGE

Brooklyn, N. Y.

Terriers			Red and Blue
1938	15	8	Rody Cooney
1939	16	7	Rody Cooney
1940	14	5	Rody Cooney
1941	10	9	Rody Cooney
1942	17	2	Joseph Brennan
1943	14	7	Joseph Brennan
1944	11	6	Joseph Brennan
1945	10	9	Joseph Brennan
1946	13	6	Joseph Brennan
1947	15	7	Joseph Brennan
1948	16	9	Joseph Brennan
1949	22	12	Daniel Lynch
1950	9	19	Daniel Lynch
1951	20	11	Daniel Lynch
1952	21	8	Daniel Lynch

Yr.	W	L	Coach		Yr.	W	L			Coach
1953	21	7	Daniel Lynch		1941	11	6			Joe Lapchick
1954	22	5	Daniel Lynch		1942	16	5			Joe Lapchick
1955	21	8	Daniel Lynch		1943	21	3			Joe Lapchick
1956	21	4	Daniel Lynch		1944	18	5			Joe Lapchick
1957	12	14	Daniel Lynch		1945	21	3			Joe Lapchick
1958	14	9	Daniel Lynch		1946	17	6			Joe Lapchick
1959	5	18	Daniel Lynch		1947	16	7			Joe Lapchick
1960	13	8	Daniel Lynch		1948	12	11			Frank McGuire
1961	10	10	Daniel Lynch		1949	16	9			Frank McGuire
1962	8	15	Daniel Lynch		1950	24	5			Frank McGuire
1963	16	7	Daniel Lynch		1951	26	5			Frank McGuire
1964	9	12	Daniel Lynch		1952	25	5			Frank McGuire
1965	11	9	Daniel Lynch		1953	17	6			Alfred DeStefano
1966	5	17	Daniel Lynch		1954	9	11			Alfred DeStefano
1967	14	8	Daniel Lynch		1955	11	9			Alfred DeStefano
1968	7	16	Daniel Lynch		1956	12	12			Alfred DeStefano
1969	7	16	Daniel Lynch		1957	14	9			Joe Lapchick
1970	9	12	Lester Yellin		1958	18	8			Joe Lapchick
1971	8	17	Lester Yellin		1959	20	6			Joe Lapchick
1972	12	14	Lester Yellin		1960	17	8			Joe Lapchick
1973	8	16	Lester Yellin		1961	20	5			Joe Lapchick
1974	12	13	Jack Prenderville		1962	21	5			Joe Lapchick
1975	7	19	Jack Prenderville		1963	9	15			Joe Lapchick
1976	13	13	Lou Rossini		1964	14	11			Joe Lapchick
1977	12	14	Lou Rossini		1965	21	8			Joe Lapchick
1978	16	9	Lou Rossini		1966	18	8			Lou Carnesecca
1979	14	12	Lou Rossini		1967	23	5			Lou Carnesecca
					1968	19	8			Lou Carnesecca
					1969	23	6			Lou Carnesecca
					1970	21	8			Lou Carnesecca
					1971	18	9			Frank Mulzoff
					1972	19	11			Frank Mulzoff
					1973	19	7			Frank Mulzoff
					1974	20	7			Lou Carnesecca
					1975	21	10			Lou Carnesecca
					1976	23	6			Lou Carnesecca
					1977	22	9			Lou Carnesecca
					1978	21	7			Lou Carnesecca
					1979	21	11			Lou Carnesecca

ST. FRANCIS COLLEGE

Loretto, Pennsylvania

Frankies			*Red and White*
1946	1	9	Dr. "Skip" Hughes
1947	11	8	Dr. "Skip" Hughes
1948	15	8	Dr. "Skip" Hughes
1949	16	11	Dr. "Skip" Hughes
1950	17	9	Dr. "Skip" Hughes
1951	19	4	Dr. "Skip" Hughes
1952	23	7	Dr. "Skip" Hughes
1953	13	5	Dr. "Skip" Hughes
1954	21	5	Dr. "Skip" Hughes
1955	21	7	Dr. "Skip" Hughes
1956	10	14	Dr. "Skip" Hughes
1957	12	12	Dr. "Skip" Hughes
1958	20	5	Dr. "Skip" Hughes
1959	20	5	Dr. "Skip" Hughes
1960	14	9	Dr. "Skip" Hughes
1961	6	19	Dr. "Skip" Hughes
1962	14	8	Dr. "Skip" Hughes
1963	10	13	Dr. "Skip" Hughes
1964	10	14	Dr. "Skip" Hughes
1965	10	15	Dr. "Skip" Hughes
1966	8	18	Dr. "Skip" Hughes
1967	20	6	John Clark
1968	19	6	John Clark
1969	16	8	John Clark
1970	13	12	John Hiller
1971	15	10	John Hiller
1972	12	13	Dick Conover
1973	5	21	Dick Conover
1974	15	11	Pete Lonergan
1975	11	14	Pete Lonergan
1976	14	14	Pete Lonergan
1977	15	11	Pete Lonergan
1978	15	11	Pete Lonergan
1979	13	13	Dave Magarity

ST. JOHN'S UNIVERSITY

Jamaica, New York

Redmen			*Red and White*
1938	15	4	Joe Lapchick
1939	18	4	Joe Lapchick
1940	15	4	Joe Lapchick

ST. JOSEPH'S COLLEGE

Philadelphia, Pennsylvania

Hawks			*Crimson and Gray*
1938	13	5	William Ferguson
1939	10	12	William Ferguson
1940	10	5	William Ferguson
1941	12	6	William Ferguson
1942	12	6	William Ferguson
1943	18	4	William Ferguson
1944	18	7	William Ferguson
1945	12	11	William Ferguson
1946	9	11	William Ferguson
1947	16	6	William Ferguson
1948	12	11	William Ferguson
1949	12	11	William Ferguson
1950	10	15	William Ferguson
1951	13	14	William Ferguson
1952	20	7	William Ferguson
1953	14	11	William Ferguson
1954	14	9	John McMenamin
1955	12	14	John McMenamin
1956	23	6	Jack Ramsay
1957	17	7	Jack Ramsay
1958	18	9	Jack Ramsay
1959	22	5	Jack Ramsay
1960	20	7	Jack Ramsay
1961	25	5	Jack Ramsay
1962	18	10	Jack Ramsay
1963	23	5	Jack Ramsay
1964	18	10	Jack Ramsay
1965	26	3	Jack Ramsay
1966	24	5	Jack Ramsay

Yr.	W	L	Coach	Yr.	W	L	Coach
1967	16	10	Jack McKinney	1948	11	13	Benjamin Neff
1968	17	9	Jack McKinney	1949	13	17	Benjamin Neff
1969	17	11	Jack McKinney	1950	3	22	Benjamin Neff
1970	15	12	Jack McKinney	1951	9	11	Thomas Foley
1971	19	9	Jack McKinney	1952	17	10	Thomas Foley
1972	19	9	Jack McKinney	1953	9	11	Thomas Foley
1973	22	6	Jack McKinney	1954	10	14	Thomas Foley
1974	19	11	Jack McKinney	1955	6	19	Thomas Foley
1975	8	17	Harry Booth	1956	16	10	James Weaver
1976	10	16	Harry Booth	1957	17	9	James Weaver
1977	13	13	Harry Booth	1958	11	15	James Weaver
1978	13	15	Harry Booth	1959	19	6	James Weaver
1979	19	11	Jim Lynam	1960	15	11	James Weaver
				1961	19	7	James Weaver
				1962	13	11	James Weaver
				1963	14	11	Mike Cimino
				1964	7	19	Mike Cimino
				1965	8	18	Mike Cimino
				1966	8	17	Mike Cimino
				1967	4	21	Mike Cimino
				1968	4	20	Mike Cimino
				1969	6	19	Mike Cimino
				1970	3	22	Mike Cimino
				1971	10	16	Bruce Hale
				1972	9	17	Bruce Hale
				1973	7	19	Bruce Hale
				1974	16	12	Frank LaPorte
				1975	14	12	Frank LaPorte
				1976	3	23	Frank LaPorte
				1977	11	16	Frank LaPorte
				1978	13	14	Frank LaPorte
				1979	13	15	Frank LaPorte

ST. LOUIS UNIVERSITY

St. Louis, Missouri

Billikens			Blue and White
1938	9	20	Ed Davidson
1939	5	16	Jack Sterrett
1940	4	14	Jack Sterrett
1941	3	14	Robert Klenck
1942	8	12	Robert Klenck
1943	11	10	Robert Klenck
1944	—	—	
1945	10	4	Dukes Duford
1946	13	11	John Flanigan
1947	18	11	John Flanigan
1948	24	3	Eddie Hickey
1949	22	4	Eddie Hickey
1950	17	9	Eddie Hickey
1951	22	8	Eddie Hickey
1952	23	8	Eddie Hickey
1953	16	11	Eddie Hickey
1954	14	12	Eddie Hickey
1955	20	8	Eddie Hickey
1956	18	7	Eddie Hickey
1957	19	9	Eddie Hickey
1958	16	10	Eddie Hickey
1959	20	6	John Benington
1960	19	8	John Benington
1961	21	9	John Benington
1962	11	15	John Benington
1963	16	12	John Benington
1964	13	12	John Benington
1965	18	9	John Benington
1966	15	10	Joe Brehmer
1967	13	13	Joe Brehmer
1968	15	11	Joe Brehmer
1969	6	20	Joe Brehmer
1970	9	17	Bob Polk
1971	12	12	Bob Polk
1972	18	8	Bob Polk
1973	19	7	Randy Albrecht
1974	9	16	Randy Albrecht
1975	12	14	Randy Albrecht
1976	13	14	Randy Albrecht
1977	7	19	Randy Albrecht
1978	7	19	Ron Coleman
1979	10	17	Ron Ekker

ST. MARY'S COLLEGE

St. Mary's, California

Gaels			Red and Blue
1938	24	6	Harlan Dykes
1939	20	11	Harlan Dykes
1940	12	12	Jack Otten
1941	6	11	Louis Conlan
1942	—	—	
1943	12	9	Louis Conlan
1944	—	—	
1945	—	—	
1946	10	5	Clarence Andersen
1947	13	17	Clarence Andersen

ST. PETER'S COLLEGE

Jersey City, New Jersey

Peacocks			Blue and White
1938	6	15	H. M. Sweetman
1939	7	13	H. M. Sweetman
1940	4	10	H. M. Sweetman
1941	9	8	H. M. Sweetman
1942	5	11	H. M. Sweetman
1943	5	7	Thomas O'Brien
1944	—	—	
1945	—	—	
1946	—	—	
1947	5	15	George Babich
1948	16	5	George Babich
1949	18	5	George Babich
1950	13	11	Pete Caruso
1951	11	14	Don Kennedy
1952	14	8	Don Kennedy
1953	18	8	Don Kennedy
1954	17	7	Don Kennedy
1955	12	11	Don Kennedy
1956	14	7	Don Kennedy
1957	18	4	Don Kennedy
1958	20	4	Don Kennedy
1959	15	6	Don Kennedy
1960	15	6	Don Kennedy
1961	16	9	Don Kennedy
1962	13	10	Don Kennedy
1963	12	11	Don Kennedy
1964	13	9	Don Kennedy
1965	10	10	Don Kennedy
1966	11	12	Don Kennedy
1967	18	6	Don Kennedy
1968	24	4	Don Kennedy
1969	21	7	Don Kennedy
1970	13	11	Don Kennedy
1971	11	13	Don Kennedy
1972	13	12	Don Kennedy
1973	8	18	Bernie Ockene
1974	8	18	Bernie Ockene
1975	15	12	Dick McDonald
1976	19	11	Dick McDonald

Yr.	W	L	Coach
1977	13	13	Dick McDonald
1978	8	18	Bob Kelly
1979	10	15	Bob Kelly

SAMFORD UNIVERSITY

Birmingham, Alabama

Bulldogs			Crimson and Blue
1938	15	6	William Bancroft
1939	24	5	Jim Stewart
1940	13	9	Jim Stewart
1941	7	15	Jim Stewart
1942	13	8	Jim Stewart
1943	10	5	Snitz Snider
1944	—	—	
1945	15	3	Bub Walker
1946	10	6	Bub Walker
1947	11	10	Donald Lance
1948	12	14	Herman Roberson
1949	15	12	Herman Roberson
1950	14	11	Herman Roberson
1951	12	11	Earl Gartman
1952	11	15	Earl Gartman
1953	15	11	Earl Gartman
1954	16	18	Earl Gartman
1955	15	14	Earl Gartman
1956	15	13	Virgil Ledbetter
1957	12	15	Virgil Ledbetter
1958	7	16	Virgil Ledbetter
1959	4	10	Virgil Ledbetter
1960	13	21	Walter Barnes
1961	23	1	Walter Barnes
1962	13	9	Walter Barnes
1963	13	9	Walter Barnes
1964	7	19	Virgil Ledbetter
1965	12	11	Virgil Ledbetter
1966	12	14	John Edwards
1967	11	13	John Edwards
1968	9	13	John Edwards
1969	5	21	Van Washer
1970	16	9	Van Washer
1971	16	10	Van Washer
1972	9	15	Van Washer
1973	5	20	Ron Harris
1974	6	20	Ron Harris
1975	9	17	Ron Harris
1976	3	23	Fred Crowell
1977	7	19	Fred Crowell
1978	8	19	Fred Crowell
1979	10	15	Fred Crowell

SAN DIEGO STATE

San Diego, California

Aztecs			Scarlet and Black
1971	12	14	Dick Davis
1972	18	10	Dick Davis
1973	15	11	Dick Davis
1974	7	19	Dick Davis
1975	14	13	Tim Vezie
1976	16	13	Tim Vezie
1977	13	15	Tim Vezie
1978	19	9	Tim Vezie
1979	15	12	Tim Vezie

SAN FRANCISCO, UNIVERSITY OF

San Francisco, California

Dons			Green and Gold
1938	10	12	Scotty Cameron
1939	7	10	Scotty Cameron
1940	9	8	Scotty Cameron
1941	2	13	Scotty Cameron
1942	14	10	Scotty Cameron
1943	13	9	James Needles
1944	8	11	James Needles
1945	—	—	
1946	9	12	William Bussenius
1947	13	14	Pete Newell
1948	13	11	Pete Newell
1949	25	5	Pete Newell
1950	19	7	Pete Newell
1951	9	17	Phil Woolpert
1952	11	13	Phil Woolpert
1953	10	11	Phil Woolpert
1954	14	7	Phil Woolpert
1955	28	1	Phil Woolpert
1956	29	0	Phil Woolpert
1957	21	7	Phil Woolpert
1958	25	2	Phil Woolpert
1959	6	20	Phil Woolpert
1960	8	17	Ross Giudice
1961	17	11	Peter P. Peletta
1962	10	15	Peter P. Peletta
1963	18	9	Peter P. Peletta
1964	23	5	Peter P. Peletta
1965	24	5	Peter P. Peletta
1966	22	6	Peter P. Peletta
1967	13	12	Phil Vukicevich
1968	14	8	Phil Vukicevich
1969	16	10	Phil Vukicevich
1970	15	11	Phil Vukicevich
1971	10	16	B. Gaillard, P. Vukicevich
1972	20	8	Bob Gaillard
1973	23	5	Bob Gaillard
1974	19	7	Bob Gaillard
1975	19	9	Bob Gaillard
1976	22	8	Bob Gaillard
1977	29	2	Bob Gaillard
1978	23	6	Bob Gaillard
1979	22	7	Dan Belluomini

SAN JOSE STATE COLLEGE

San Jose, California

Spartans			Gold and White
1938	19	4	Wilbur Hubbard
1939	12	8	Wilbur Hubbard
1940	14	10	Wilbur Hubbard
1941	19	8	Walter McPherson
1942	4	11	Walter McPherson
1943	11	13	T. E. Blesh
1944	—	—	
1945	8	14	Wilbur Hubbard
1946	17	14	Walter McPherson
1947	19	9	Walter McPherson
1948	23	9	Walter McPherson
1949	22	13	Walter McPherson
1950	21	7	Walter McPherson
1951	18	12	Walter McPherson
1952	15	10	Walter McPherson
1953	15	8	Walter McPherson
1954	12	15	Walter McPherson
1955	16	9	Walter McPherson
1956	15	10	Walter McPherson
1957	13	12	Walter McPherson
1958	13	13	Walter McPherson
1959	5	19	Walter McPherson
1960	6	19	Walter McPherson
1961	11	14	Stu Inman
1962	2	22	Stu Inman
1963	14	14	Stu Inman
1964	14	10	Stu Inman
1965	14	10	Stu Inman
1966	11	13	Stu Inman
1967	9	15	Dan Glines
1968	13	12	Dan Glines
1969	16	8	Dan Glines
1970	3	21	Dan Glines
1971	2	24	Dan Glines

Yr.	W	L	Coach
1972	11	15	Ivan Guevara
1973	11	14	Ivan Guevara
1974	11	15	Ivan Guevara
1975	16	13	Ivan Guevara
1976	17	9	Ivan Guevara
1977	18	11	Ivan Guevara
1978	8	19	Ivan Guevara
1979	7	20	Ivan Guevara

SANTA CLARA, UNIVERSITY OF

Santa Clara, California

Broncos	W	L	Cardinal and White
1938	10	6	George Barsi
1939	15	5	George Barsi
1940	17	3	George Barsi
1941	15	7	George Barsi
1942	10	9	George Barsi
1943	10	9	George Barsi
1944	—	—	
1945	—	—	
1946	9	6	George Barsi
1947	21	4	Ray Pesco
1948	11	11	Ray Pesco
1949	8	15	Ray Pesco
1950	14	8	Ray Pesco
1951	9	15	Bob Feerick
1952	17	12	Bob Feerick
1953	20	7	Bob Feerick
1954	21	7	Bob Feerick
1955	13	11	Bob Feerick
1956	8	16	Bob Feerick
1957	15	7	Bob Feerick
1958	13	11	Bob Feerick
1959	16	9	Bob Feerick
1960	18	9	Bob Feerick
1961	18	9	Bob Feerick
1962	19	6	Bob Feerick
1963	16	9	Dick Garibaldi
1964	6	20	Dick Garibaldi
1965	14	12	Dick Garibaldi
1966	16	11	Dick Garibaldi
1967	13	13	Dick Garibaldi
1968	22	4	Dick Garibaldi
1969	27	2	Dick Garibaldi
1970	23	6	Dick Garibaldi
1971	11	15	Carroll Williams
1972	17	9	Carroll Williams
1973	20	7	Carroll Williams
1974	9	18	Carroll Williams
1975	10	16	Carroll Williams
1976	10	16	Carroll Williams
1977	17	10	Carroll Williams
1978	21	8	Carroll Williams
1979	13	14	Carroll Williams

SEATTLE UNIVERSITY

Seattle, Washington

Chieftains	W	L	Maroon and White
1946	8	22	Joseph Budnick
1947	18	13	Budnick, Fenton, Ryan
1948	10	16	Leonard Yandle
1949	12	14	Al Brightman
1950	12	17	Al Brightman
1951	32	5	Al Brightman
1952	29	8	Al Brightman
1953	29	4	Al Brightman
1954	26	2	Al Brightman
1955	22	7	Al Brightman
1956	18	11	Al Brightman
1957	24	3	John Castellani
1958	24	7	John Castellani
1959	23	6	Vince Cazzetta
1960	16	10	Vince Cazzetta

Yr.	W	L	Coach
1961	19	8	Vince Cazzetta
1962	18	9	Vince Cazzetta
1963	21	6	Cazzetta, Clair Markey
1964	22	6	W. R. "Bob" Boyd
1965	19	7	W. R. "Bob" Boyd
1966	16	10	Lionel Purcell
1967	18	8	Lionel Purcell
1968	15	14	Morris Buckwalter
1969	20	8	Morris Buckwalter
1970	15	10	Morris Buckwalter
1971	12	14	Morris Buckwalter
1972	17	9	Morris Buckwalter
1973	13	13	Bill O'Connor
1974	15	11	Bill O'Connor
1975	8	18	Bill O'Connor
1976	12	15	Bill O'Connor
1977	14	14	Bill O'Connor
1978	11	17	Bill O'Connor
1979	15	11	Jack Schalow

SETON HALL UNIVERSITY

South Orange, New Jersey

Pirates	W	L	Blue and White
1938	10	8	John "Honey" Russell
1939	15	7	John "Honey" Russell
1940	19	0	John "Honey" Russell
1941	20	2	John "Honey" Russell
1942	16	2	John "Honey" Russell
1943	15	3	John "Honey" Russell
1944	—	—	
1945	—	—	
1946	—	—	
1947	24	3	Robert Davies
1948	18	4	John Reitemeier
1949	16	8	John Reitemeier
1950	11	15	John "Honey" Russell
1951	24	7	John "Honey" Russell
1952	25	3	John "Honey" Russell
1953	31	2	John "Honey" Russell
1954	13	10	John "Honey" Russell
1955	17	9	John "Honey" Russell
1956	20	5	John "Honey" Russell
1957	17	10	John "Honey" Russell
1958	7	19	John "Honey" Russell
1959	7	19	John "Honey" Russell
1960	16	7	John "Honey" Russell
1961	15	9	Richie Regan
1962	15	9	Richie Regan
1963	17	6	Richie Regan
1964	13	12	Richie Regan
1965	12	13	Richie Regan
1966	6	18	Richie Regan
1967	7	17	Richie Regan
1968	9	15	Richie Regan
1969	9	15	Richie Regan
1970	10	15	Richie Regan
1971	11	15	William Raftery
1972	10	16	William Raftery
1973	8	17	William Raftery
1974	16	11	William Raftery
1975	16	11	William Raftery
1976	17	10	William Raftery
1977	18	11	William Raftery
1978	16	11	William Raftery
1979	16	11	William Raftery

SIENA COLLEGE

Loudonville, New York

Indians	W	L	Green and Gold
1938	5	5	Jack Carroll
1939	8	2	Jack Carroll
1940	12	7	Henry Bunoski
1941	8	10	Henry Bunoski

Yr.	W	L	Coach	Yr.	W	L	Coach
1942	9	7	Dan Cunha	1949	10	12	Frank Johnson
1943	13	6	Dan Cunha	1950	13	9	Frank Johnson
1944	—	—		1951	13	12	Frank Johnson
1945	—	—		1952	14	10	Frank Johnson
1946	—	—		1953	11	13	Frank Johnson
1947	12	11	Dan Cunha	1954	10	16	Frank Johnson
1948	22	6	Dan Cunha	1955	10	17	Frank Johnson
1949	23	7	Dan Cunha	1956	9	14	Frank Johnson
1950	27	5	Dan Cunha	1957	17	12	Frank Johnson
1951	19	8	Dan Cunha	1958	5	19	Frank Johnson
1952	24	7	Dan Cunha	1959	4	20	Walt Hambrick
1953	10	11	Dan Cunha	1960	10	16	Bob Stevens
1954	7	14	Dan Cunha	1961	9	17	Bob Stevens
1955	3	13	Dan Cunha	1962	15	12	Bob Stevens
1956	7	13	Dan Cunha	1963	9	15	Chuck Noe
1957	5	15	Dan Cunha	1964	10	14	C. Noe, D. Morrison
1958	5	14	Dan Cunha	1965	6	17	Frank McGuire
1959	3	16	Dan Cunha	1966	11	13	Frank McGuire
1960	3	18	Dan Cunha	1967	16	7	Frank McGuire
1961	11	13	Dan Cunha	1968	15	7	Frank McGuire
1962	14	8	Dan Cunha	1969	21	7	Frank McGuire
1963	13	10	Dan Cunha	1970	25	3	Frank McGuire
1964	8	13	Dan Cunha	1971	23	6	Frank McGuire
1965	9	10	Dan Cunha	1972	24	5	Frank McGuire
1966	6	16	Tom Hannon	1973	22	7	Frank McGuire
1967	12	11	Tom Hannon	1974	22	5	Frank McGuire
1968	9	16	Tom Hannon	1975	19	9	Frank McGuire
1969	10	13	Tom Hannon	1976	18	9	Frank McGuire
1970	7	16	Gene Culnan	1977	14	12	Frank McGuire
1971	8	17	Gene Culnan	1978	16	12	Frank McGuire
1972	12	14	G. Culnan, R. Keith	1979	15	12	Frank McGuire
1973	15	8	Bill Kirsch				
1974	18	9	Bill Kirsch				
1975	16	9	Bill Kirsch				
1976	11	11	Bill Kirsch				
1977	9	15	Bill Kirsch				
1978	13	10	Bill Kirsch				
1979	14	12	Bill Kirsch				

SOUTH CAROLINA STATE COLLEGE

Orangeburg, South Carolina

Bulldogs			Garnet Blue
1958	18	5	Ed Martin
1959	10	10	Ed Martin
1960	9	12	Ed Martin
1961	23	4	Ed Martin
1962	22	7	Ed Martin
1963	19	8	Ed Martin
1964	19	8	Ed Martin
1965	16	9	Ed Martin
1966	23	3	Ed Martin
1967	18	5	Ed Martin
1968	12	3	Ed Martin
1969	20	5	Ben Jobe
1970	21	7	Ben Jobe
1971	20	7	Ben Jobe
1972	15	11	Ben Jobe
1973	17	14	Ben Jobe
1974	13	15	Tim Autry
1975	15	11	Tim Autry
1976	17	8	Tim Autry
1977	15	11	Tim Autry
1978	16	12	Tim Autry
1979	8	19	Tim Autry

SOUTH ALABAMA, UNIVERSITY OF

Mobile, Alabama

Jaguars			Red, White, and Blue
1968	10	15	Rex Frederick
1969	11	12	Rex Frederick
1970	8	17	Rex Frederick
1971	14	12	Jim Taylor
1972	8	17	Jim Taylor
1973	14	11	Jim Taylor
1974	22	6	Jim Taylor
1975	19	7	Jim Taylor
1976	18	9	Cliff Ellis
1977	17	10	Cliff Ellis
1978	18	10	Cliff Ellis
1979	20	7	Cliff Ellis

SOUTH CAROLINA, UNIVERSITY OF

Columbia, South Carolina

Gamecocks			Garnet and Black
1938	3	20	Ted Petoskey
1939	5	18	Ted Petoskey
1940	5	13	Ted Petoskey
1941	15	9	Frank Johnson
1942	12	9	Frank Johnson
1943	9	5	Frank Johnson
1944	13	2	Henry Findley
1945	19	3	John McMillan
1946	9	11	Frank Johnson
1947	15	9	Frank Johnson
1948	12	11	Frank Johnson

SOUTH FLORIDA, UNIVERSITY OF

Tampa, Florida

Brahmans, Brahman Bulls			Green and Gold
1972	8	17	Don Williams
1973	14	11	Don Williams
1974	11	14	Don Williams
1975	15	10	Bill Gibson
1976	19	8	Chip Conner
1977	9	18	Chip Conner
1978	13	14	Chip Conner
1979	14	14	Chip Conner

SOUTHERN CALIFORNIA, UNIVERSITY OF

Los Angeles, California

Yr.	W	L	Coach
Trojans			*Cardinal and Gold*
1938	17	9	Sam Barry
1939	20	5	Sam Barry
1940	20	3	Sam Barry
1941	15	10	Sam Barry
1942	12	8	Julie Bescos
1943	23	5	Ernest Holbrook
1944	9	12	E. Holbrook, R. Muth
1945	16	9	Robert Muth
1946	14	9	Sam Barry
1947	10	14	Sam Barry
1948	14	10	Sam Barry
1949	14	10	Sam Barry
1950	16	8	Sam Barry
1951	21	6	Forrest Twogood
1952	16	14	Forrest Twogood
1953	18	6	Forrest Twogood
1954	19	14	Forrest Twogood
1955	15	11	Forrest Twogood
1956	14	12	Forrest Twogood
1957	16	12	Forrest Twogood
1958	12	13	Forrest Twogood
1959	15	11	Forrest Twogood
1960	16	11	Forrest Twogood
1961	21	8	Forrest Twogood
1962	14	11	Forrest Twogood
1963	20	9	Forrest Twogood
1964	10	16	Forrest Twogood
1965	14	12	Forrest Twogood
1966	13	13	Forrest Twogood
1967	13	12	Bob Boyd
1968	18	8	Bob Boyd
1969	15	11	Bob Boyd
1970	18	8	Bob Boyd
1971	24	2	Bob Boyd
1972	16	10	Bob Boyd
1973	18	10	Bob Boyd
1974	24	5	Bob Boyd
1975	18	8	Bob Boyd
1976	12	15	Bob Boyd
1977	6	20	Bob Boyd
1978	14	13	Bob Boyd
1979	20	9	Bob Boyd

SOUTHERN ILLINOIS UNIVERSITY

Carbondale, Illinois

Yr.	W	L	Coach
Salukis			*Maroon and White*
1938	13	4	William McAndrew
1939	11	9	William McAndrew
1940	22	4	William McAndrew
1941	11	12	William McAndrew
1942	8	9	William McAndrew
1943	9	9	William McAndrew
1944	8	7	Abe Martin
1945	15	7	Abe Martin
1946	20	6	Abe Martin
1947	19	10	Lynn Holder
1948	22	4	Lynn Holder
1949	13	11	Lynn Holder
1950	21	6	Lynn Holder
1951	13	13	Lynn Holder
1952	13	11	Lynn Holder
1953	13	11	Lynn Holder
1954	12	11	Lynn Holder
1955	10	13	Lynn Holder
1956	13	11	Lynn Holder
1957	13	11	Lynn Holder
1958	13	11	Lynn Holder
1959	17	10	Harry Gallatin
1960	20	9	Harry Gallatin
1961	21	6	Harry Gallatin
1962	21	10	Harry Gallatin
1963	20	10	Jack Hartman
1964	16	10	Jack Hartman
1965	20	6	Jack Hartman
1966	22	7	Jack Hartman
1967	24	2	Jack Hartman
1968	13	11	Jack Hartman
1969	16	8	Jack Hartman
1970	13	10	Jack Hartman
1971	13	10	Paul Lambert
1972	10	16	Paul Lambert
1973	11	15	Paul Lambert
1974	19	7	Paul Lambert
1975	18	9	Paul Lambert
1976	16	10	Paul Lambert
1977	22	7	Paul Lambert
1978	17	10	Paul Lambert
1979	15	13	Joe Gottfried

SOUTHERN METHODIST UNIVERSITY

Dallas, Texas

Yr.	W	L	Coach
Mustangs			*Cardinal Red and Royal Blue*
1938	9	6	Whitey Baccus
1939	14	8	Whitey Baccus
1940	7	13	Whitey Baccus
1941	10	10	Whitey Baccus
1942	3	16	Whitey Baccus
1943	10	8	James Stewart
1944	8	9	James Stewart
1945	11	10	Roy "Rusty" Baccus
1946	7	16	Whitey Baccus
1947	14	8	Whitey Baccus
1948	13	10	E. O. "Doc" Hayes
1949	11	13	E. O. "Doc" Hayes
1950	10	13	E. O. "Doc" Hayes
1951	14	10	E. O. "Doc" Hayes
1952	11	13	E. O. "Doc" Hayes
1953	8	12	E. O. "Doc" Hayes
1954	13	9	E. O. "Doc" Hayes
1955	15	11	E. O. "Doc" Hayes
1956	25	4	E. O. "Doc" Hayes
1957	22	4	E. O. "Doc" Hayes
1958	15	10	E. O. "Doc" Hayes
1959	16	8	E. O. "Doc" Hayes
1960	17	7	E. O. "Doc" Hayes
1961	12	12	E. O. "Doc" Hayes
1962	18	7	E. O. "Doc" Hayes
1963	9	15	E. O. "Doc" Hayes
1964	12	12	E. O. "Doc" Hayes
1965	17	10	E. O. "Doc" Hayes
1966	17	9	E. O. "Doc" Hayes
1967	20	6	E. O. "Doc" Hayes
1968	6	18	Bob Prewitt
1969	12	12	Bob Prewitt
1970	5	19	Bob Prewitt
1971	16	10	Bob Prewitt
1972	16	11	Bob Prewitt
1973	10	15	Bob Prewitt
1974	15	12	Bob Prewitt
1975	8	18	Bob Prewitt
1976	16	12	Sonny Allen
1977	8	19	Sonny Allen
1978	10	18	Sonny Allen
1979	11	16	Sonny Allen

SOUTHERN MISSISSIPPI, UNIVERSITY OF

Hattiesburg, Mississippi

Yr.	W	L	Coach
Golden Eagles			*Black and Gold*
1950	18	7	Lee Floyd
1951	20	15	Lee Floyd

Yr.	W	L	Coach
1952	29	8	Lee Floyd
1953	27	8	Lee Floyd
1954	23	8	Lee Floyd
1955	11	17	Chuck Finley
1956	16	12	Chuck Finley
1957	12	13	Chuck Finley
1958	18	7	Fred Lewis
1959	12	13	Fred Lewis
1960	20	2	Fred Lewis
1961	23	3	Fred Lewis
1962	13	13	Fred Lewis
1963	12	14	Lee Floyd
1964	16	8	Lee Floyd
1965	15	11	Lee Floyd
1966	12	13	Lee Floyd
1967	16	9	Lee Floyd
1968	19	6	Lee Floyd
1969	15	10	Lee Floyd
1970	15	11	Lee Floyd
1971	7	19	Lee Floyd
1972	0	24	Eugene "Jeep" Clark
1973	8	16	Eugene "Jeep" Clark
1974	11	15	Eugene "Jeep" Clark
1975	11	15	Eugene "Jeep" Clark
1976	11	15	Eugene "Jeep" Clark
1977	11	16	M. K. Turk
1978	13	12	M. K. Turk
1979	13	14	M. K. Turk

SOUTHWESTERN LOUISIANA, UNIVERSITY OF

Lafayette, Louisiana

Yr.	W	L	Coach
	Ragin' Cajuns		*Vermilion and White*
1950	12	13	J. C. Reinhardt
1951	8	10	J. C. Reinhardt
1952	11	16	J. C. Reinhardt
1953	10	16	J. C. Reinhardt
1954	6	13	J. C. Reinhardt
1955	10	14	J. C. Reinhardt
1956	6	13	J. C. Reinhardt
1957	7	19	J. C. Reinhardt
1958	16	11	Beryl Shipley
1959	14	10	Beryl Shipley
1960	20	8	Beryl Shipley
1961	18	5	Beryl Shipley
1962	17	8	Beryl Shipley
1963	12	13	Beryl Shipley
1964	13	10	Beryl Shipley
1965	20	10	Beryl Shipley
1966	17	8	Beryl Shipley
1967	20	11	Beryl Shipley
1968	19	5	Beryl Shipley
1969	20	5	Beryl Shipley
1970	16	10	Beryl Shipley
1971	25	4	Beryl Shipley
1972	25	4	Beryl Shipley
1973	24	5	Beryl Shipley
1974	—	—	
1975	—	—	
1976	7	19	Jim Hatfield
1977	21	8	Jim Hatfield
1978	19	8	Bobby Paschal
1979	16	11	Bobby Paschal

STANFORD UNIVERSITY

Palo Alto, California

Yr.	W	L	Coach
	Cardinals		*Cardinal and White*
1938	21	3	John Bunn
1939	16	9	Everett Dean
1940	14	9	Everett Dean
1941	21	5	Everett Dean
1942	27	4	Everett Dean
1943	10	11	Everett Dean
1944	—	—	
1945	—	—	
1946	6	18	Everett Dean
1947	15	16	Everett Dean
1948	15	11	Everett Dean
1949	19	9	Everett Dean
1950	11	14	Everett Dean
1951	12	14	Everett Dean
1952	19	9	Robert Burnett
1953	7	20	Robert Burnett
1954	15	10	Robert Burnett
1955	17	8	Howard Dallmar
1956	18	6	Howard Dallmar
1957	11	15	Howard Dallmar
1958	12	13	Howard Dallmar
1959	16	9	Howard Dallmar
1960	11	14	Howard Dallmar
1961	7	17	Howard Dallmar
1962	16	6	Howard Dallmar
1963	16	9	Howard Dallmar
1964	15	10	Howard Dallmar
1965	12	13	Howard Dallmar
1966	13	12	Howard Dallmar
1967	15	11	Howard Dallmar
1968	11	15	Howard Dallmar
1969	9	17	Howard Dallmar
1970	5	20	Howard Dallmar
1971	6	20	Howard Dallmar
1972	10	15	Howard Dallmar
1973	14	11	Howard Dallmar
1974	11	14	Howard Dallmar
1975	12	14	Howard Dallmar
1976	11	16	Dick DiBiaso
1977	11	16	Dick DiBiaso
1978	13	14	Dick DiBiaso
1979	12	15	Dick DiBiaso

STETSON UNIVERSITY

DeLand, Florida

Yr.	W	L	Coach
	Hatters		*Green, Gold, and White*
1938	13	4	Chet Freeman
1939	14	7	C. Freeman, B. Cowell
1940	9	11	Ben Clemons
1941	14	6	Ben Clemons
1942	10	3	Brady Cowell
1943	—	—	
1944	—	—	
1945	—	—	
1946	—	—	
1947	11	10	Brady Cowell
1948	7	15	Brady Cowell
1949	2	23	Brady Cowell
1950	8	15	Brady Cowell
1951	13	12	Loren Ellis
1952	16	4	Jay Pattee
1953	14	10	Richard Morland
1954	10	10	Richard Morland
1955	11	10	Richard Morland
1956	17	6	Richard Morland
1957	17	8	Richard Morland
1958	14	11	Glenn Wilkes
1959	17	11	Glenn Wilkes
1960	16	13	Glenn Wilkes
1961	20	7	Glenn Wilkes
1962	16	12	Glenn Wilkes
1963	15	13	Glenn Wilkes
1964	16	9	Glenn Wilkes
1965	16	10	Glenn Wilkes
1966	13	12	Glenn Wilkes
1967	17	10	Glenn Wilkes
1968	8	18	Glenn Wilkes
1969	14	12	Glenn Wilkes
1970	22	7	Glenn Wilkes

Yr.	W	L	Coach
1971	19	9	Glenn Wilkes
1972	6	20	Glenn Wilkes
1973	15	11	Glenn Wilkes
1974	17	9	Glenn Wilkes
1975	22	4	Glenn Wilkes
1976	17	9	Glenn Wilkes
1977	15	12	Glenn Wilkes
1978	14	13	Glenn Wilkes
1979	14	12	Glenn Wilkes

Yr.	W	L	Coach
1950	14	10	Josh Cody
1951	12	13	Josh Cody
1952	9	15	Josh Cody
1953	16	10	Harry Litwack
1954	15	12	Harry Litwack
1955	11	10	Harry Litwack
1956	27	4	Harry Litwack
1957	20	9	Harry Litwack
1958	27	3	Harry Litwack
1959	6	19	Harry Litwack
1960	17	9	Harry Litwack
1961	20	8	Harry Litwack
1962	18	9	Harry Litwack
1963	15	7	Harry Litwack
1964	17	8	Harry Litwack
1965	14	10	Harry Litwack
1966	21	7	Harry Litwack
1967	20	8	Harry Litwack
1968	19	9	Harry Litwack
1969	22	8	Harry Litwack
1970	15	13	Harry Litwack
1971	13	12	Harry Litwack
1972	23	8	Harry Litwack
1973	17	10	Harry Litwack
1974	16	9	Don Casey
1975	7	19	Don Casey
1976	9	18	Don Casey
1977	17	11	Don Casey
1978	24	5	Don Casey
1979	25	4	Don Casey

SYRACUSE UNIVERSITY

Syracuse, New York

Orangemen	W	L	Orange
1938	13	5	Lew Andreas
1939	14	4	Lew Andreas
1940	10	8	Lew Andreas
1941	13	5	Lew Andreas
1942	14	6	Lew Andreas
1943	8	10	Lew Andreas
1944	—	—	
1945	7	12	Lew Andreas
1946	23	4	Lew Andreas
1947	19	6	Lew Andreas
1948	11	13	Lew Andreas
1949	18	7	Lew Andreas
1950	18	9	Lew Andreas
1951	19	9	Marc Guley
1952	14	6	Marc Guley
1953	7	11	Marc Guley
1954	10	9	Marc Guley
1955	10	11	Marc Guley
1956	14	8	Marc Guley
1957	18	7	Marc Guley
1958	11	10	Marc Guley
1959	14	9	Marc Guley
1960	13	8	Marc Guley
1961	4	19	Marc Guley
1962	2	22	Marc Guley
1963	8	13	Fred Lewis
1964	17	8	Fred Lewis
1965	13	10	Fred Lewis
1966	22	6	Fred Lewis
1967	20	6	Fred Lewis
1968	11	14	Fred Lewis
1969	9	16	Roy Danforth
1970	12	12	Roy Danforth
1971	19	7	Roy Danforth
1972	22	6	Roy Danforth
1973	24	5	Roy Danforth
1974	19	7	Roy Danforth
1975	23	9	Roy Danforth
1976	20	9	Jim Boeheim
1977	26	4	Jim Boeheim
1978	22	6	Jim Boeheim
1979	26	4	Jim Boeheim

TEMPLE UNIVERSITY

Philadelphia, Pennsylvania

Owls	W	L	Cherry and White
1938	23	2	James Usilton
1939	10	12	James Usilton
1940	13	10	Ernest Messikomer
1941	12	9	Ernest Messikomer
1942	10	8	Ernest Messikomer
1943	11	11	Josh Cody
1944	14	9	Josh Cody
1945	16	7	Josh Cody
1946	12	8	Josh Cody
1947	8	12	Josh Cody
1948	12	11	Josh Cody
1949	14	9	Josh Cody

TENNESSEE, UNIVERSITY OF

Knoxville, Tennessee

Volunteers	W	L	Orange and White
1938	15	8	Blair Gullion
1939	14	7	John Mauer
1940	14	7	John Mauer
1941	17	5	John Mauer
1942	19	3	John Mauer
1943	14	4	John Mauer
1944	—	—	
1945	18	5	John Mauer
1946	15	5	John Mauer
1947	16	5	John Mauer
1948	20	5	Emmett Lowery
1949	19	7	Emmett Lowery
1950	15	11	Emmett Lowery
1951	10	13	Emmett Lowery
1952	13	9	Emmett Lowery
1953	13	8	Emmett Lowery
1954	11	12	Emmett Lowery
1955	15	7	Emmett Lowery
1956	10	14	Emmett Lowery
1957	13	9	Emmett Lowery
1958	16	7	Emmett Lowery
1959	14	8	Emmett Lowery
1960	12	11	John Sines
1961	10	15	John Sines
1962	4	19	John Sines
1963	13	11	Ray Mears
1964	16	8	Ray Mears
1965	20	5	Ray Mears
1966	18	8	Ray Mears
1967	21	7	Ray Mears
1968	20	6	Ray Mears
1969	21	7	Ray Mears
1970	16	9	Ray Mears
1971	21	7	Ray Mears
1972	19	6	Ray Mears
1973	15	9	Ray Mears
1974	17	9	Ray Mears
1975	18	8	Ray Mears
1976	21	6	Ray Mears

Yr.	W	L	Coach
1977	22	6	Ray Mears
1978	11	16	Cliff Wettig
1979	21	12	Don DeVoe

TENNESSEE-CHATTANOOGA, UNIVERSITY OF

Chattanooga, Tennessee

Moccasins			Navy Blue and Gold
1938	5	16	Pop Keyser
1939	4	16	Pop Keyser
1940	6	12	Perron Shoemaker
1941	4	13	Perron Shoemaker
1942	3	17	Perron Shoemaker
1943	—	—	
1944	—	—	
1945	—	—	
1946	10	5	Bill O'Brien
1947	4	15	Perron Shoemaker
1948	6	12	Bill O'Brien
1949	3	9	Bill O'Brien
1950	5	19	Bill O'Brien
1951	7	7	Bill O'Brien
1952	2	11	Bill O'Brien
1953	9	13	Bill O'Brien
1954	5	8	Bill O'Brien
1955	3	15	Bill O'Brien
1956	3	15	Ben Boulware
1957	6	16	Ben Boulware
1958	4	12	Ben Boulware
1959	11	12	Tommy Bartlett
1960	14	7	Tommy Bartlett
1961	17	7	Tommy Bartlett
1962	15	10	Tommy Bartlett
1963	16	10	Leon Ford
1964	13	13	Leon Ford
1965	16	10	Leon Ford
1966	4	19	Leon Ford
1967	8	18	Leon Ford
1968	12	13	Leon Ford
1969	16	10	Leon Ford
1970	12	12	Leon Ford
1971	18	5	Leon Ford
1972	13	13	Leon Ford
1973	19	9	Ron Shumate
1974	21	5	Ron Shumate
1975	19	9	Ron Shumate
1976	23	9	Ron Shumate
1977	27	5	Ron Shumate
1978	16	11	Ron Shumate
1979	14	13	Ron Shumate

TENNESSEE STATE UNIVERSITY

Nashville, Tennessee

Tigers			Blue and White
1972	26	2	Edward Martin
1973	22	8	Edward Martin
1974	22	6	Edward Martin
1975	19	9	Edward Martin
1976	19	7	Edward Martin
1977	9	16	Edward Martin
1978	13	12	Edward Martin
1979	20	6	Edward Martin

TENNESSEE TECHNOLOGICAL UNIVERSITY

Cookeville, Tennessee

Golden Eagles			Purple and Gold
1938	11	6	P. V. Overall
1939	10	4	P. V. Overall

Yr.	W	L	Coach
1940	9	7	P. V. Overall
1941	6	10	P. V. Overall
1942	9	7	Hooper Eblen
1943	10	9	Hooper Eblen
1944	3	13	Overall, Eblen
1945	6	5	Overall, Eblen
1946	6	8	Overall, Eblen
1947	20	5	Hooper Eblen
1948	18	7	Ray Brown
1949	10	10	Ray Brown
1950	9	12	Ray Brown
1951	12	9	Ray Brown
1952	9	13	Ray Brown
1953	14	11	Ray Brown
1954	12	10	Ray Brown
1955	9	11	Ray Brown
1956	14	7	John Oldham
1957	9	11	John Oldham
1958	17	9	John Oldham
1959	16	9	John Oldham
1960	13	9	John Oldham
1961	6	13	John Oldham
1962	16	6	John Oldham
1963	16	8	John Oldham
1964	11	11	John Oldham
1965	14	11	Kenny Sidwell
1966	17	8	Kenny Sidwell
1967	12	11	Kenny Sidwell
1968	10	16	Kenny Sidwell
1969	13	11	Kenny Sidwell
1970	10	15	Connie Inman
1971	7	17	Connie Inman
1972	14	11	Connie Inman
1973	13	11	Connie Inman
1974	7	18	Connie Inman
1975	13	12	Connie Inman
1976	14	10	Connie Inman
1977	7	19	Cliff Malpass
1978	11	15	Cliff Malpass
1979	11	15	Cliff Malpass

TEXAS, UNIVERSITY OF

Austin, Texas

Longhorns			Orange and White
1938	10	12	Jack Gray
1939	19	6	Jack Gray
1940	18	5	Jack Gray
1941	15	9	Jack Gray
1942	14	9	Jack Gray
1943	19	7	H. C. Gilstrap
1944	14	11	H. C. Gilstrap
1945	10	10	H. C. Gilstrap
1946	16	7	Jack Gray
1947	26	2	Jack Gray
1948	20	5	Jack Gray
1949	17	7	Jack Gray
1950	13	11	Jack Gray
1951	13	14	Jack Gray
1952	16	8	Thurman Hull
1953	12	9	Thurman Hull
1954	16	9	Thurman Hull
1955	4	20	Thurman Hull
1956	12	12	Thurman Hull
1957	11	13	Marshall Hughes
1958	10	13	Marshall Hughes
1959	4	20	Marshall Hughes
1960	18	8	Harold Bradley
1961	14	10	Harold Bradley
1962	16	8	Harold Bradley
1963	20	7	Harold Bradley
1964	15	9	Harold Bradley
1965	16	9	Harold Bradley
1966	12	12	Harold Bradley
1967	14	10	Harold Bradley
1968	11	13	Leon Black
1969	9	15	Leon Black

Yr.	W	L	Coach
1970	11	13	Leon Black
1971	12	12	Leon Black
1972	19	9	Leon Black
1973	13	13	Leon Black
1974	12	15	Leon Black
1975	10	15	Leon Black
1976	9	17	Leon Black
1977	13	13	Abe Lemons
1978	26	5	Abe Lemons
1979	21	8	Abe Lemons

TEXAS A&M UNIVERSITY

College Station, Texas

Aggies			*Maroon and White*
1938	10	8	H. R. McQuillan
1939	7	16	H. R. McQuillan
1940	11	11	H. R. McQuillan
1941	7	13	H. R. McQuillan
1942	8	16	Marty Karow
1943	11	11	Manning Smith
1944	2	15	Manning Smith
1945	3	18	Manning Smith
1946	9	14	Marty Karow
1947	8	17	Marty Karow
1948	7	17	Marty Karow
1949	5	19	Marty Karow
1950	10	14	Marty Karow
1951	17	12	John Floyd
1952	9	15	John Floyd
1953	6	15	John Floyd
1954	2	20	John Floyd
1955	4	20	John Floyd
1956	6	18	Ken Loeffler
1957	7	17	Ken Loeffler
1958	11	13	Bob Rogers
1959	15	9	Bob Rogers
1960	19	5	Bob Rogers
1961	16	8	Bob Rogers
1962	15	9	Bob Rogers
1963	16	8	Bob Rogers
1964	18	7	Shelby Metcalf
1965	14	10	Shelby Metcalf
1966	15	9	Shelby Metcalf
1967	6	18	Shelby Metcalf
1968	14	10	Shelby Metcalf
1969	18	9	Shelby Metcalf
1970	14	10	Shelby Metcalf
1971	9	17	Shelby Metcalf
1972	16	10	Shelby Metcalf
1973	17	9	Shelby Metcalf
1974	15	11	Shelby Metcalf
1975	20	7	Shelby Metcalf
1976	21	6	Shelby Metcalf
1977	14	14	Shelby Metcalf
1978	12	15	Shelby Metcalf
1979	24	9	Shelby Metcalf

TEXAS-ARLINGTON, UNIVERSITY OF

Arlington, Texas

Mavericks			*Royal Blue and White*
1969	8	18	Barry Dowd
1970	8	16	Barry Dowd
1971	8	18	Barry Dowd
1972	14	12	Barry Dowd
1973	13	13	Barry Dowd
1974	7	18	Barry Dowd
1975	6	20	Barry Dowd
1976	6	21	Barry Dowd
1977	3	24	Bob "Snake" LeGrand
1978	10	17	Bob "Snake" LeGrand
1979	11	16	Bob "Snake" LeGrand

TEXAS-EL PASO, UNIVERSITY OF (UTEP)

El Paso, Texas

Miners			*Orange and White*
1938	2	16	Marshall Pennington
1939	3	11	Marshall Pennington
1940	6	12	Marshall Pennington
1941	13	11	Marshall Pennington
1942	11	13	Marshall Pennington
1943	—	—	
1944	—	—	
1945	10	13	Charles L. Finley
1946	13	12	Jack Curtice
1947	12	8	Dale Waters
1948	13	16	Ross Moore
1949	7	11	Dale Waters
1950	17	13	Dale Waters
1951	10	15	Dale Waters
1952	8	17	Dale Waters
1953	4	21	Dale Waters
1954	8	14	George McCarty
1955	13	8	George McCarty
1956	12	10	George McCarty
1957	15	8	George McCarty
1958	14	9	George McCarty
1959	14	9	George McCarty
1960	6	19	Harold Davis
1961	10	12	Harold Davis
1962	18	6	Don Haskins
1963	19	7	Don Haskins
1964	25	3	Don Haskins
1965	17	9	Don Haskins
1966	28	1	Don Haskins
1967	22	6	Don Haskins
1968	14	9	Don Haskins
1969	16	9	Don Haskins
1970	17	8	Don Haskins
1971	15	10	Don Haskins
1972	20	7	Don Haskins
1973	16	10	Don Haskins
1974	18	7	Don Haskins
1975	20	6	Don Haskins
1976	20	7	Don Haskins
1977	11	15	Don Haskins
1978	10	16	Don Haskins
1979	11	15	Don Haskins

TEXAS CHRISTIAN UNIVERSITY

Fort Worth, Texas

Horned Frogs			*Purple and White*
1938	8	15	Mike Brumbelow
1939	2	17	Mike Brumbelow
1940	7	15	Mike Brumbelow
1941	5	17	Mike Brumbelow
1942	13	10	Hub McQuillan
1943	18	9	Hub McQuillan
1944	9	12	Hub McQuillan
1945	9	19	Hub McQuillan
1946	13	11	Hub McQuillan
1947	1	21	Hub McQuillan
1948	3	20	Hub McQuillan
1949	5	19	Buster Brannon
1950	13	11	Buster Brannon
1951	16	9	Buster Brannon
1952	24	4	Buster Brannon
1953	16	8	Buster Brannon
1954	10	14	Buster Brannon
1955	17	7	Buster Brannon
1956	4	20	Buster Brannon
1957	14	10	Buster Brannon
1958	17	7	Buster Brannon
1959	20	6	Buster Brannon
1960	7	17	Buster Brannon
1961	5	19	Buster Brannon

Yr.	W	L	Coach
1962	5	19	Buster Brannon
1963	4	20	Buster Brannon
1964	4	20	Buster Brannon
1965	6	18	Buster Brannon
1966	8	16	Buster Brannon
1967	11	14	Buster Brannon
1968	15	11	Johnny Swaim
1969	12	12	Johnny Swaim
1970	10	14	Johnny Swaim
1971	15	12	Johnny Swaim
1972	15	9	Johnny Swaim
1973	4	21	Johnny Swaim
1974	8	17	Johnny Swaim
1975	9	16	Johnny Swaim
1976	10	17	Johnny Swaim
1977	3	23	Johnny Swaim
1978	4	22	Tim Somerville
1979	6	21	Tim Somerville

Yr.	W	L	Coach
1974	17	9	Gerald Myers
1975	18	8	Gerald Myers
1976	25	6	Gerald Myers
1977	20	9	Gerald Myers
1978	19	10	Gerald Myers
1979	19	11	Gerald Myers

TEXAS SOUTHERN UNIVERSITY

Houston, Texas

Tigers			*Maroon and Gray*
1972	17	11	Lavalius Gordon
1973	14	11	Lavalius Gordon
1974	15	13	Lavalius Gordon
1975	8	16	Kenneth McGowan
1976	23	10	Kenneth McGowan
1977	31	5	Robert Moreland
1978	16	10	Robert Moreland
1979	13	14	Robert Moreland

TEXAS TECH UNIVERSITY

Lubbock, Texas

Red Raiders			*Scarlet and Black*
1938	9	13	Berl Hoffman
1939	13	6	Berl Hoffman
1940	21	7	Berl Hoffman
1941	19	6	Berl Hoffman
1942	17	10	Berl Hoffman
1943	13	11	Polk Robison
1944	5	17	Polk Robison
1945	10	14	Polk Robison
1946	15	10	Polk Robison
1947	10	12	Berl Hoffman
1948	16	12	Polk Robison
1949	21	9	Polk Robison
1950	14	12	Polk Robison
1951	14	14	Polk Robison
1952	13	11	Polk Robison
1953	14	10	Polk Robison
1954	20	5	Polk Robison
1955	18	7	Polk Robison
1956	14	11	Polk Robison
1957	12	11	Polk Robison
1958	15	8	Polk Robison
1959	15	9	Polk Robison
1960	10	14	Polk Robison
1961	15	10	Polk Robison
1962	19	8	Gene Gibson
1963	6	17	Gene Gibson
1964	16	7	Gene Gibson
1965	17	6	Gene Gibson
1966	13	11	Gene Gibson
1967	9	15	Gene Gibson
1968	9	15	Gene Gibson
1969	11	13	Gene Gibson
1970	14	10	Bob Bass
1971	16	10	Gerald Myers
1972	14	12	Gerald Myers
1973	19	8	Gerald Myers

TOLEDO, UNIVERSITY OF

Toledo, Ohio

Rockets			*Midnight Blue and Gold*
1938	14	6	Harold Anderson
1939	17	10	Harold Anderson
1940	24	6	Harold Anderson
1941	21	3	Harold Anderson
1942	23	5	Harold Anderson
1943	22	4	Berle Friddle
1944	5	13	Berle Friddle
1945	9	4	Rollie Boldt
1946	20	7	Rollie Boldt
1947	18	6	Bill Orwig
1948	21	5	Jerry Bush
1949	13	12	Jerry Bush
1950	23	6	Jerry Bush
1951	23	8	Jerry Bush
1952	20	11	Jerry Bush
1953	16	7	Jerry Bush
1954	13	10	Jerry Bush
1955	5	17	Eddie Melvin
1956	9	13	Eddie Melvin
1957	5	19	Eddie Melvin
1958	9	14	Eddie Melvin
1959	11	13	Eddie Melvin
1960	18	6	Eddie Melvin
1961	15	8	Eddie Melvin
1962	14	10	Eddie Melvin
1963	13	11	Eddie Melvin
1964	13	11	Eddie Melvin
1965	13	11	Eddie Melvin
1966	13	11	Bob Nichols
1967	23	2	Bob Nichols
1968	16	8	Bob Nichols
1969	13	11	Bob Nichols
1970	15	9	Bob Nichols
1971	13	11	Bob Nichols
1972	18	7	Bob Nichols
1973	15	11	Bob Nichols
1974	19	9	Bob Nichols
1975	17	9	Bob Nichols
1976	18	7	Bob Nichols
1977	21	6	Bob Nichols
1978	21	6	Bob Nichols
1979	21	8	Bob Nichols

TULANE UNIVERSITY

New Orleans, Louisiana

Green Wave			*Olive and Blue*
1938	8	10	Ray Dauber
1939	5	12	Claude Simons
1940	2	12	Claude Simons
1941	8	5	Claude Simons
1942	4	12	Claude Simons
1943	4	9	Vernon Haynes
1944	16	6	Vernon Haynes
1945	6	10	Vernon Haynes
1946	15	7	Cliff Wells
1947	22	9	Cliff Wells
1948	23	3	Cliff Wells
1949	24	4	Cliff Wells
1950	15	7	Cliff Wells
1951	12	12	Cliff Wells

Yr.	W	L	Coach
1952	12	12	Cliff Wells
1953	12	6	Cliff Wells
1954	15	8	Cliff Wells
1955	14	6	Cliff Wells
1956	12	12	Cliff Wells
1957	15	9	Cliff Wells
1958	8	15	Cliff Wells
1959	13	11	Cliff Wells
1960	13	11	Cliff Wells
1961	11	13	Cliff Wells
1962	12	10	Cliff Wells
1963	6	16	Cliff Wells
1964	1	22	Ted Lenhardt
1965	3	22	Ted Lenhardt
1966	9	16	Ralph Pedersen
1967	14	10	Ralph Pedersen
1968	12	12	Ralph Pedersen
1969	12	14	Ralph Pedersen
1970	5	18	Ralph Pedersen
1971	8	18	Ralph Pedersen
1972	9	17	Dick Longo
1973	12	14	Dick Longo
1974	12	14	Charles Moir
1975	16	10	Charles Moir
1976	18	9	Charles Moir
1977	10	17	Roy Danforth
1978	5	22	Roy Danforth
1979	8	19	Roy Danforth

TULSA, UNIVERSITY OF

Tulsa, Oklahoma

	Golden Hurricane		Blue, Crimson, and Gold
1938	12	10	Chester Benefiel
1939	15	8	Chester Benefiel
1940	12	15	C. Benefiel, "Tex" Ryon
1941	12	9	Jack Sterrett
1942	3	13	"Tex" Ryon
1943	0	10	W. S. Milligan
1944	5	3	W. W. West
1945	4	8	P. J. Alyea
1946	6	12	Don Shields
1947	4	20	Don Shields
1948	7	17	John Garrison
1949	4	20	John Garrison
1950	12	11	Clarence Iba
1951	10	18	Clarence Iba
1952	14	10	Clarence Iba
1953	15	10	Clarence Iba
1954	15	14	Clarence Iba
1955	21	7	Clarence Iba
1956	16	10	Clarence Iba
1957	8	17	Clarence Iba
1958	7	19	Clarence Iba
1959	10	15	Clarence Iba
1960	9	17	Clarence Iba
1961	8	17	Joe Swank
1962	7	19	Joe Swank
1963	17	8	Joe Swank
1964	10	15	Joe Swank
1965	14	11	Joe Swank
1966	16	13	Joe Swank
1967	19	8	Joe Swank
1968	11	12	Joe Swank
1969	19	8	Ken Hayes
1970	15	11	Ken Hayes
1971	17	9	Ken Hayes
1972	15	11	Ken Hayes
1973	18	8	Ken Hayes
1974	18	8	Ken Hayes
1975	15	14	Ken Hayes
1976	9	18	Jim King
1977	6	21	Jim King
1978	9	18	Jim King
1979	13	14	Jim King

UTAH, UNIVERSITY OF

Salt Lake City, Utah

Yr.	W	L	Coach
	Utes		Crimson and White
1938	17	4	Vadal Peterson
1939	12	7	Vadal Peterson
1940	18	4	Vadal Peterson
1941	14	7	Vadal Peterson
1942	13	7	Vadal Peterson
1943	10	12	Vadal Peterson
1944	21	4	Vadal Peterson
1945	17	4	Vadal Peterson
1946	12	8	Vadal Peterson
1947	19	5	Vadal Peterson
1948	11	9	Vadal Peterson
1949	24	8	Vadal Peterson
1950	25	19	Vadal Peterson
1951	23	13	Vadal Peterson
1952	19	9	Vadal Peterson
1953	10	14	Vadal Peterson
1954	12	14	Jack Gardner
1955	24	4	Jack Gardner
1956	22	6	Jack Gardner
1957	19	8	Jack Gardner
1958	20	7	Jack Gardner
1959	21	7	Jack Gardner
1960	26	3	Jack Gardner
1961	23	8	Jack Gardner
1962	23	3	Jack Gardner
1963	12	4	Jack Gardner
1964	19	9	Jack Gardner
1965	17	9	Jack Gardner
1966	23	8	Jack Gardner
1967	15	11	Jack Gardner
1968	14	11	Jack Gardner
1969	13	13	Jack Gardner
1970	18	10	Jack Gardner
1971	15	11	Jack Gardner
1972	13	12	Bill Foster
1973	8	19	Bill Foster
1974	22	8	Bill Foster
1975	17	9	Jerry Pimm
1976	19	8	Jerry Pimm
1977	22	7	Jerry Pimm
1978	23	6	Jerry Pimm
1979	20	10	Jerry Pimm

UTAH STATE UNIVERSITY

Logan, Utah

	Aggies		Blue and White
1938	11	9	Dick Romney
1939	17	7	Dick Romney
1940	11	7	Dick Romney
1941	2	16	Dick Romney
1942	6	10	R. W. Burnett
1943	14	7	Del Young
1944	—	—	
1945	9	10	Del Young
1946	7	12	"Beebe" Lee
1947	14	10	"Beebe" Lee
1948	8	16	Joseph Whitesides
1949	10	21	Joseph Whitesides
1950	18	16	Joseph Whitesides
1951	12	22	Cecil Baker
1952	19	14	Cecil Baker
1953	17	13	Cecil Baker
1954	14	13	Cecil Baker
1955	14	8	Cecil Baker
1956	13	13	Cecil Baker
1957	11	13	Cecil Baker
1958	4	20	Cecil Baker
1959	19	7	Cecil Baker
1960	24	5	Cecil Baker

Yr.	W	L	Coach
1961	12	14	Cecil Baker
1962	22	7	LaDell Andersen
1963	20	7	LaDell Andersen
1964	21	8	LaDell Andersen
1965	13	12	LaDell Andersen
1966	12	14	LaDell Andersen
1967	20	6	LaDell Andersen
1968	14	11	LaDell Andersen
1969	9	17	LaDell Andersen
1970	22	7	LaDell Andersen
1971	20	7	LaDell Andersen
1972	12	14	T. L. Plain
1973	16	10	T. L. Plain
1974	16	10	Dutch Belnap
1975	21	6	Dutch Belnap
1976	14	12	Dutch Belnap
1977	15	12	Dutch Belnap
1978	21	7	Dutch Belnap
1979	19	11	Dutch Belnap

VALPARAISO UNIVERSITY

Valparaiso, Indiana

Crusaders			Brown and Gold
1938	13	6	J. M. Christiansen
1939	5	10	J. M. Christiansen
1940	6	14	J. M. Christiansen
1941	4	12	J. M. Christiansen
1942	4	13	Loren E. Ellis
1943	17	5	Loren E. Ellis
1944	17	8	Loren E. Ellis
1945	21	3	Loren E. Ellis
1946	17	11	Loren E. Ellis
1947	11	20	Loren E. Ellis
1948	8	15	Emory Bauer
1949	8	17	Don Warnke
1950	15	8	Wilbur Allen
1951	12	10	Wilbur Allen
1952	12	12	Kenneth Suesens
1953	9	15	Kenneth Suesens
1954	10	13	Kenneth Suesens
1955	13	11	Kenneth Suesens
1956	12	14	Kenneth Suesens
1957	11	14	Kenneth Suesens
1958	7	14	Kenneth Suesens
1959	12	11	Paul Meadows
1960	12	13	Paul Meadows
1961	7	16	Paul Meadows
1962	17	8	Paul Meadows
1963	7	17	Paul Meadows
1964	9	15	Paul Meadows
1965	13	12	B. Gene Bartow
1966	19	9	B. Gene Bartow
1967	21	8	B. Gene Bartow
1968	11	15	B. Gene Bartow
1969	16	12	B. Gene Bartow
1970	13	13	B. Gene Bartow
1971	13	13	Bill Purden
1972	15	11	Bill Purden
1973	17	11	Bill Purden
1974	15	11	Bill Purden
1975	14	11	Bill Purden
1976	12	14	Bill Purden
1977	13	12	Ken Rochlitz
1978	6	19	Ken Rochlitz
1979	4	21	Ken Rochlitz

VANDERBILT UNIVERSITY

Nashville, Tennessee

Commodores			Gold and Black
1938	9	12	James Buford
1939	14	7	James Buford
1940	10	12	James Buford
1941	8	9	James Buford
1942	7	9	Norman Cooper
1943	10	8	Norman Cooper
1944	11	4	Smokey Harper
1945	6	6	Gus Morrow
1946	3	10	Gus Morrow
1947	7	8	Norman Cooper
1948	8	14	Robert Polk
1949	14	8	Robert Polk
1950	17	8	Robert Polk
1951	19	8	Robert Polk
1952	18	9	Robert Polk
1953	10	9	Robert Polk
1954	12	10	Robert Polk
1955	16	6	Robert Polk
1956	19	4	Robert Polk
1957	17	5	Robert Polk
1958	14	11	Robert Polk
1959	14	10	Roy Skinner
1960	14	9	Robert Polk
1961	19	5	Robert Polk
1962	12	12	Roy Skinner
1963	16	7	Roy Skinner
1964	19	6	Roy Skinner
1965	24	4	Roy Skinner
1966	22	4	Roy Skinner
1967	21	5	Roy Skinner
1968	20	6	Roy Skinner
1969	15	11	Roy Skinner
1970	12	14	Roy Skinner
1971	13	13	Roy Skinner
1972	16	10	Roy Skinner
1973	20	6	Roy Skinner
1974	23	5	Roy Skinner
1975	15	11	Roy Skinner
1976	16	11	Roy Skinner
1977	10	16	Wayne Dobbs
1978	10	17	Wayne Dobbs
1979	18	9	Wayne Dobbs

VERMONT, UNIVERSITY OF

Burlington, Vermont

Catamounts			Green and Gold
1938	10	4	J. P. Sabo
1939	10	5	J. P. Sabo
1940	5	10	J. P. Sabo
1941	10	4	John Evans
1942	10	5	John Evans
1943	10	6	John Evans
1944	—	—	
1945	—	—	
1946	10	4	John Evans
1947	19	3	John Evans
1948	14	6	John Evans
1949	15	5	John Evans
1950	9	11	John Evans
1951	14	6	John Evans
1952	14	6	John Evans
1953	11	10	John Evans
1954	13	7	John Evans
1955	6	15	John Evans
1956	6	12	John Evans
1957	15	5	John Evans
1958	15	10	John Evans
1959	12	10	John Evans
1960	9	11	John Evans
1961	9	11	John Evans
1962	12	12	John Evans
1963	10	13	John Evans
1964	11	10	John Evans
1965	7	13	John Evans
1966	12	8	Art Loche
1967	10	15	Art Loche
1968	12	12	Art Loche
1969	14	11	Art Loche

Yr.	W	L	Coach
1970	8	16	Art Loche
1971	9	15	Art Loche
1972	5	19	Art Loche
1973	9	17	Peter Salzberg
1974	9	17	Peter Salzberg
1975	16	10	Peter Salzberg
1976	15	10	Peter Salzberg
1977	8	17	Peter Salzberg
1978	11	15	Peter Salzberg
1979	8	18	Peter Salzberg

VILLANOVA UNIVERSITY

Villanova, Pennsylvania

Wildcats			Blue and White
1938	25	5	Al Severance
1939	20	5	Al Severance
1940	17	2	Al Severance
1941	13	3	Al Severance
1942	13	9	Al Severance
1943	19	2	Al Severance
1944	9	11	Al Severance
1945	6	11	Al Severance
1946	10	13	Al Severance
1947	17	7	Al Severance
1948	15	9	Al Severance
1949	23	4	Al Severance
1950	25	4	Al Severance
1951	25	7	Al Severance
1952	19	8	Al Severance
1953	22	9	Al Severance
1954	20	11	Al Severance
1955	18	10	Al Severance
1956	14	12	Al Severance
1957	10	15	Al Severance
1958	12	11	Al Severance
1959	18	7	Al Severance
1960	20	6	Al Severance
1961	11	13	Al Severance
1962	21	7	Jack Kraft
1963	19	10	Jack Kraft
1964	24	4	Jack Kraft
1965	23	5	Jack Kraft
1966	18	11	Jack Kraft
1967	17	9	Jack Kraft
1968	19	9	Jack Kraft
1969	21	5	Jack Kraft
1970	22	7	Jack Kraft
1971	23	6	Jack Kraft
1972	20	6	Jack Kraft
1973	11	14	Jack Kraft
1974	7	19	Rollie Massimino
1975	9	18	Rollie Massimino
1976	16	11	Rollie Massimino
1977	23	10	Rollie Massimino
1978	23	9	Rollie Massimino
1979	15	13	Rollie Massimino

VIRGINIA COMMONWEALTH UNIVERSITY

Richmond, Virginia

Rams			Black and Gold
1969	12	11	Benny Dees
1970	13	10	Benny Dees
1971	15	9	Chuck Noe
1972	15	4	Chuck Noe
1973	15	5	Chuck Noe
1974	17	7	Chuck Noe
1975	17	8	Chuck Noe
1976	16	9	Chuck Noe
1977	13	13	Dana Kirk
1978	24	5	Dana Kirk
1979	20	5	Dana Kirk

Yr.	W	L	Coach

VIRGINIA MILITARY INSTITUTE

Lexington, Virginia

Keydets			Red. White, and Yellow
1938	4	11	Pooley Hubert
1939	7	10	James Walker
1940	3	12	James Walker
1941	10	6	James Walker
1942	6	11	James Walker
1943	8	8	Pooley Hubert
1944	0	14	Pooley Hubert
1945	2	10	Joseph Daher
1946	1	10	Jay McWilliams
1947	3	16	Jay McWilliams
1948	3	16	Frank Summers
1949	3	16	Frank Summers
1950	4	17	William O'Hara
1951	3	18	William O'Hara
1952	3	21	William O'Hara
1953	5	19	Chuck Noe
1954	11	12	Chuck Noe
1955	8	15	Chuck Noe
1956	4	19	Jack Null
1957	4	22	Jack Null
1958	4	17	Jack Null
1959	5	13	Weenie Miller
1960	4	16	Weenie Miller
1961	5	17	Weenie Miller
1962	9	11	Weenie Miller
1963	6	15	Weenie Miller
1964	12	12	Weenie Miller
1965	8	13	Gary McPherson
1966	5	18	Gary McPherson
1967	5	16	Gary McPherson
1968	9	12	Gary McPherson
1969	5	18	Gary McPherson
1970	6	19	Mike Schuler
1971	1	25	Mike Schuler
1972	6	19	Mike Schuler
1973	7	19	Bill Blair
1974	6	18	Bill Blair
1975	13	13	Bill Blair
1976	22	9	Bill Blair
1977	26	4	Charlie Schmaus
1978	21	7	Charlie Schmaus
1979	12	15	Charlie Schmaus

VIRGINIA, UNIVERSITY OF

Charlottesville, Virginia

Cavaliers			Orange and Blue
1938	6	10	Gus Tebell
1939	14	5	Gus Tebell
1940	16	5	Gus Tebell
1941	17	5	Gus Tebell
1942	6	10	Gus Tebell
1943	8	13	Gus Tebell
1944	11	8	Gus Tebell
1945	12	5	Gus Tebell
1946	12	5	Gus Tebell
1947	11	11	Gus Tebell
1948	16	10	Gus Tebell
1949	13	10	Gus Tebell
1950	12	13	Gus Tebell
1951	8	14	Gus Tebell
1952	11	13	Evan J. "Bus" Male
1953	10	13	Evan J. "Bus" Male
1954	16	11	Evan J. "Bus" Male
1955	14	15	Evan J. "Bus" Male
1956	10	17	Evan J. "Bus" Male
1957	6	19	Evan J. "Bus" Male
1958	10	13	Billy McCann
1959	11	14	Billy McCann
1960	6	18	Billy McCann
1961	3	23	Billy McCann
1962	5	18	Billy McCann

Yr.	W	L	Coach
1963	5	20	Billy McCann
1964	8	16	Bill Gibson
1965	7	18	Bill Gibson
1966	7	15	Bill Gibson
1967	9	17	Bill Gibson
1968	9	16	Bill Gibson
1969	10	15	Bill Gibson
1970	10	15	Bill Gibson
1971	15	11	Bill Gibson
1972	21	7	Bill Gibson
1973	13	12	Bill Gibson
1974	11	16	Bill Gibson
1975	12	13	Terry Holland
1976	18	12	Terry Holland
1977	12	17	Terry Holland
1978	20	8	Terry Holland
1979	19	10	Terry Holland

VIRGINIA POLYTECHNIC INSTITUTE

Blacksburg, Virginia

Gobblers			Orange and Maroon
1938	6	8	H. M. McEver
1939	3	14	H. M. McEver
1940	4	16	H. M. McEver
1941	7	14	H. M. McEver
1942	10	10	H. M. McEver
1943	7	7	H. M. McEver
1944	11	4	H. M. McEver
1945	6	8	G. S. "Gummy" Proctor
1946	11	8	G. S. "Gummy" Proctor
1947	13	13	G. S. "Gummy" Proctor
1948	14	8	G. F. "Red" Laird
1949	10	13	G. F. "Red" Laird
1950	15	9	G. F. "Red" Laird
1951	19	10	G. F. "Red" Laird
1952	4	16	G. F. "Red" Laird
1953	4	19	G. F. "Red" Laird
1954	3	24	G. F. "Red" Laird
1955	7	20	G. F. "Red" Laird
1956	14	11	Chuck Noe
1957	14	8	Chuck Noe
1958	11	8	Chuck Noe
1959	16	5	Chuck Noe
1960	20	6	Chuck Noe
1961	15	7	Chuck Noe
1962	19	6	Chuck Noe
1963	12	12	Bill Matthews
1964	16	7	Bill Matthews
1965	13	10	Howard Shannon
1966	19	5	Howard Shannon
1967	20	7	Howard Shannon
1968	14	7	Howard Shannon
1969	14	12	Howard Shannon
1970	10	12	Howard Shannon
1971	14	11	Howard Shannon
1972	16	10	Don DeVoe
1973	22	5	Don DeVoe
1974	13	13	Don DeVoe
1975	16	10	Don DeVoe
1976	22	5	Don DeVoe
1977	19	10	Charles Moir
1978	19	8	Charles Moir
1979	21	8	Charles Moir

WAGNER COLLEGE

Staten Island, New York

Seahawks			Green and White
1938	6	12	Herb Sutter
1939	7	6	Herb Sutter
1940	8	11	Herb Sutter
1941	12	6	Herb Sutter
1942	8	11	Herb Sutter

Yr.	W	L	Coach
1943	7	8	Herb Sutter
1944	–	–	
1945	10	7	Herb Sutter
1946	15	7	Herb Sutter
1947	11	14	Herb Sutter
1948	10	10	Herb Sutter
1949	15	7	Herb Sutter
1950	19	5	Herb Sutter
1951	18	7	Herb Sutter
1952	15	12	Herb Sutter
1953	16	11	Herb Sutter
1954	18	6	Herb Sutter
1955	14	7	Herb Sutter
1956	20	3	Herb Sutter
1957	10	16	Herb Sutter
1958	18	9	Herb Sutter
1959	11	13	Herb Sutter
1960	16	8	Herb Sutter
1961	9	15	Herb Sutter
1962	12	14	Herb Sutter
1963	16	6	Herb Sutter
1964	16	8	Herb Sutter
1965	14	12	Herb Sutter
1966	14	12	Chester Sellito
1967	19	9	Chester Sellito
1968	21	8	Chester Sellito
1969	18	10	Chester Sellito
1970	11	14	Chester Sellito
1971	6	19	Chester Sellito
1972	8	17	Chester Sellito
1973	5	20	John Goodwin
1974	6	19	John Goodwin
1975	9	16	John Goodwin
1976	2	23	John Goodwin
1977	3	21	Peter J. Carlesimo
1978	7	19	Peter J. Carlesimo
1979	21	7	Peter J. Carlesimo

WAKE FOREST UNIVERSITY

Winston-Salem, North Carolina

Demon Deacons			Old Gold and Black
1938	7	12	Murray Greason
1939	18	6	Murray Greason
1940	13	9	Murray Greason
1941	9	9	Murray Greason
1942	16	7	Murray Greason
1943	1	10	Murray Greason
1944	–	–	
1945	3	14	Murray Greason
1946	12	6	Murray Greason
1947	11	13	Murray Greason
1948	18	11	Murray Greason
1949	11	13	Murray Greason
1950	14	16	Murray Greason
1951	16	14	Murray Greason
1952	10	19	Murray Greason
1953	22	7	Murray Greason
1954	17	12	Murray Greason
1955	17	10	Murray Greason
1956	19	9	Murray Greason
1957	19	9	Murray Greason
1958	6	17	Horace "Bones" McKinney
1959	10	14	Horace "Bones" McKinney
1960	21	7	Horace "Bones" McKinney
1961	19	11	Horace "Bones" McKinney
1962	22	9	Horace "Bones" McKinney
1963	16	10	Horace "Bones" McKinney
1964	16	11	Horace "Bones" McKinney
1965	12	15	Horace "Bones" McKinney
1966	8	18	Jack Murdock
1967	9	18	Jack McCloskey
1968	5	21	Jack McCloskey
1969	18	9	Jack McCloskey
1970	14	13	Jack McCloskey
1971	16	10	Jack McCloskey

Yr.	W	L	Coach
1972	8	18	Jack McCloskey
1973	12	15	Carl Tacy
1974	13	13	Carl Tacy
1975	13	13	Carl Tacy
1976	17	10	Carl Tacy
1977	22	8	Carl Tacy
1978	19	10	Carl Tacy
1979	12	15	Carl Tacy

WASHINGTON, UNIVERSITY OF

Seattle, Washington

Huskies			Purple and Gold
1938	21	7	Hec Edmundson
1939	20	5	Hec Edmundson
1940	10	15	Hec Edmundson
1941	12	13	Hec Edmundson
1942	18	7	Hec Edmundson
1943	24	7	Hec Edmundson
1944	26	6	Hec Edmundson
1945	22	18	Hec Edmundson
1946	13	14	Hec Edmundson
1947	16	8	Hec Edmundson
1948	23	11	Arthur McLarney
1949	11	15	Arthur McLarney
1950	19	10	Arthur McLarney
1951	24	6	Tippy Dye
1952	25	6	Tippy Dye
1953	30	3	Tippy Dye
1954	8	18	Tippy Dye
1955	13	12	Tippy Dye
1956	15	11	Tippy Dye
1957	17	9	Tippy Dye
1958	8	18	Tippy Dye
1959	18	8	Tippy Dye
1960	15	13	John Grayson
1961	13	13	John Grayson
1962	16	10	John Grayson
1963	13	13	John Grayson
1964	9	17	John Grayson
1965	9	16	John Grayson
1966	10	15	Mac Duckworth
1967	13	12	Mac Duckworth
1968	12	14	Mac Duckworth
1969	13	13	Tex Winter
1970	17	9	Tex Winter
1971	15	13	Tex Winter
1972	20	6	Marv Harshman
1973	18	11	Marv Harshman
1974	16	10	Marv Harshman
1975	16	10	Marv Harshman
1976	23	5	Marv Harshman
1977	17	10	Marv Harshman
1978	14	13	Marv Harshman
1979	11	16	Marv Harshman

WASHINGTON STATE UNIVERSITY

Pullman, Washington

Cougars			Crimson and Gray
1938	19	11	Jack Friel
1939	24	9	Jack Friel
1940	23	10	Jack Friel
1941	26	6	Jack Friel
1942	21	8	Jack Friel
1943	19	11	Jack Friel
1944	8	18	Jack Friel
1945	22	12	Jack Friel
1946	16	13	Jack Friel
1947	23	10	Jack Friel
1948	19	10	Jack Friel
1949	21	9	Jack Friel
1950	19	13	Jack Friel

Yr.	W	L	Coach
1951	17	15	Jack Friel
1952	19	16	Jack Friel
1953	6	27	Jack Friel
1954	10	17	Jack Friel
1955	11	15	Jack Friel
1956	4	22	Jack Friel
1957	8	18	Jack Friel
1958	7	19	Jack Friel
1959	10	16	Marv Harshman
1960	13	13	Marv Harshman
1961	10	16	Marv Harshman
1962	8	18	Marv Harshman
1963	5	20	Marv Harshman
1964	5	21	Marv Harshman
1965	9	17	Marv Harshman
1966	15	11	Marv Harshman
1967	15	11	Marv Harshman
1968	16	9	Marv Harshman
1969	18	8	Marv Harshman
1970	19	7	Marv Harshman
1971	12	14	Marv Harshman
1972	11	15	Bob Greenwood
1973	6	20	George Raveling
1974	8	21	George Raveling
1975	10	16	George Raveling
1976	19	7	George Raveling
1977	19	8	George Raveling
1978	16	11	George Raveling
1979	18	9	George Raveling

WEBER STATE COLLEGE

Ogden, Utah

Wildcats			Purple and White
1963	22	4	Dick Motta
1964	17	8	Dick Motta
1965	22	3	Dick Motta
1966	20	5	Dick Motta
1967	18	7	Dick Motta
1968	21	6	Dick Motta
1969	27	3	Phil Johnson
1970	20	7	Phil Johnson
1971	21	6	Phil Johnson
1972	18	10	Gene Visscher
1973	20	7	Gene Visscher
1974	14	12	Gene Visscher
1975	11	15	Gene Visscher/Neil McCarthy
1976	21	11	Neil McCarthy
1977	20	8	Neil McCarthy
1978	19	10	Neil McCarthy
1979	25	9	Neil McCarthy

WEST CHESTER STATE COLLEGE

West Chester, Pennsylvania

Golden Rams			Purple and Gold
1938	9	8	Glenn Killinger
1939	9	11	Glenn Killinger
1940	15	5	Glenn Killinger
1941	7	14	Lloyd Lux
1942	5	12	Lloyd Lux
1943	6	9	Lloyd Lux
1944	2	12	Graham
1945	3	3	Graham
1946	9	6	Glenn Killinger
1947	12	4	Emil Messikomer
1948	12	7	Emil Messikomer
1949	7	9	Emil Messikomer
1950	17	2	Emil Messikomer
1951	12	5	Emil Messikomer
1952	8	11	Emil Messikomer
1953	9	10	Emil Messikomer
1954	13	6	Emil Messikomer
1955	11	11	Emil Messikomer
1956	7	14	Emil Messikomer

Yr.	W	L	Coach
1957	14	7	Emil Messikomer
1958	14	6	Emil Messikomer
1959	14	7	Emil Messikomer
1960	13	8	Don Swegan
1961	14	9	Tony Hopkins
1962	14	7	Tony Hopkins
1963	9	13	Tony Hopkins
1964	14	12	Tony Hopkins
1965	13	9	Tony Hopkins
1966	5	17	Tony Hopkins
1967	8	15	Walter Funk
1968	6	18	Walter Funk
1969	12	13	Walter Funk
1970	11	15	Walter Funk
1971	7	18	Walter Funk
1972	9	16	Walter Funk
1973	5	21	Walter Funk
1974	11	15	Earl Voss
1975	8	17	Earl Voss
1976	8	17	Earl Voss
1977	11	14	Earl Voss
1978	6	19	Earl Voss
1979	8	18	Earl Voss

WESTERN CAROLINA UNIVERSITY

Cullowee, North Carolina

Catamounts			Purple and Gold
1972	20	16	Jim Hartbarger
1973	12	13	Jim Hartbarger
1974	11	14	Jim Hartbarger
1975	15	11	Fred Conley
1976	13	12	Fred Conley
1977	8	16	Fred Conley
1978	7	19	Steve Cottrell
1979	14	14	Steve Cottrell

WESTERN KENTUCKY UNIVERSITY

Bowling Green, Kentucky

Hilltoppers			Scarlet and White
1938	30	3	Ed Diddle
1939	22	3	Ed Diddle
1940	24	6	Ed Diddle
1941	22	4	Ed Diddle
1942	29	5	Ed Diddle
1943	24	3	Ed Diddle
1944	13	9	Ed Diddle
1945	17	10	Ed Diddle
1946	15	19	Ed Diddle
1947	25	4	Ed Diddle
1948	28	2	Ed Diddle
1949	25	4	Ed Diddle
1950	25	6	Ed Diddle
1951	19	10	Ed Diddle
1952	26	5	Ed Diddle
1953	25	6	Ed Diddle
1954	29	3	Ed Diddle
1955	18	10	Ed Diddle
1956	16	12	Ed Diddle
1957	17	9	Ed Diddle
1958	14	11	Ed Diddle
1959	16	10	Ed Diddle
1960	21	7	Ed Diddle
1961	18	8	Ed Diddle
1962	17	10	Ed Diddle
1963	5	16	Ed Diddle
1964	5	16	Ed Diddle
1965	22	3	John Oldham
1966	25	3	John Oldham
1967	23	3	John Oldham
1968	18	7	John Oldham
1969	16	10	John Oldham
1970	22	3	John Oldham
1971	24	6	John Oldham

Yr.	W	L	Coach
1972	15	11	Jim Richards
1973	10	16	Jim Richards
1974	15	10	Jim Richards
1975	16	8	Jim Richards
1976	20	9	Jim Richards
1977	10	16	Jim Richards
1978	16	14	Jim Richards
1979	17	11	Gene Keady

WESTERN MICHIGAN UNIVERSITY

Kalamazoo, Michigan

Broncos			Brown and Gold
1938	5	13	Buck Read
1939	7	10	Buck Read
1940	10	9	Buck Read
1941	10	8	Buck Read
1942	12	8	Buck Read
1943	15	4	Buck Read
1944	15	4	Buck Read
1945	8	10	Buck Read
1946	15	7	Buck Read
1947	17	7	Buck Read
1948	12	10	Buck Read
1949	12	10	Buck Read
1950	12	10	William Perigo
1951	13	9	William Perigo
1952	16	8	William Perigo
1953	12	9	Joseph Hoy
1954	10	11	Joseph Hoy
1955	12	10	Joseph Hoy
1956	13	9	Joseph Hoy
1957	9	13	Joseph Hoy
1958	5	19	Joseph Hoy
1959	2	20	Donald Boven
1960	13	11	Donald Boven
1961	10	14	Donald Boven
1962	13	11	Donald Boven
1963	12	12	Donald Boven
1964	10	14	Donald Boven
1965	8	16	Donald Boven
1966	8	14	Donald Boven
1967	10	14	Sonny Means
1968	11	13	Sonny Means
1969	11	13	Sonny Means
1970	6	17	Sonny Means
1971	14	10	Eldon Miller
1972	10	14	Eldon Miller
1973	8	18	Eldon Miller
1974	13	13	Eldon Miller
1975	16	10	Eldon Miller
1976	25	3	Eldon Miller
1977	14	13	Dick Shilts
1978	7	20	Dick Shilts
1979	7	23	Dick Shilts

WEST TEXAS STATE COLLEGE

Canyon, Texas

Buffaloes			Maroon and White
1938	27	6	Al Baggett
1939	21	9	Al Baggett
1940	26	8	Al Baggett
1941	29	6	Al Baggett
1942	28	3	Al Baggett
1943	15	7	Gus Miller
1944	—	—	
1945	16	10	Gus Miller
1946	19	8	Gus Miller
1947	13	11	Gus Miller
1948	11	13	Gus Miller
1949	18	6	Gus Miller
1950	19	10	Gus Miller
1951	14	12	Gus Miller

Yr.	W	L	Coach
1952	19	9	Gus Miller
1953	8	13	Gus Miller
1954	13	7	Gus Miller
1955	15	7	Gus Miller
1956	12	10	Gus Miller
1957	6	14	Gus Miller
1958	3	15	Gus Miller
1959	6	16	Borden Price
1960	11	9	Metz LaFollette
1961	7	16	Metz LaFollette
1962	5	18	Metz LaFollette
1963	6	18	James Viramontes
1964	13	9	James Viramontes
1965	16	9	James Viramontes
1966	6	17	James Viramontes
1967	1	18	James Viramontes
1968	10	11	Dennis Walling
1969	18	7	Dennis Walling
1970	12	13	Dennis Walling
1971	19	7	Dennis Walling
1972	14	11	Dennis Walling
1973	9	17	Dennis Walling
1974	11	15	Ron Ekker
1975	9	17	Ron Ekker
1976	17	9	Ron Ekker
1977	18	12	Ron Ekker
1978	9	18	Ron Ekker
1979	8	19	Ken Edwards

WEST VIRGINIA UNIVERSITY

Morgantown, West Virginia

Yr.	W	L	Coach
Mountaineers			*Old Gold and Blue*
1938	6	13	Marshall Glen
1939	10	9	Dyke Raese
1940	13	6	Dyke Raese
1941	13	10	Dyke Raese
1942	19	4	Dyke Raese
1943	14	7	Rudy Baric
1944	8	11	Harry Lothes
1945	12	6	John Brickels
1946	24	3	Lee Patton
1947	19	3	Lee Patton
1948	17	3	Lee Patton
1949	18	6	Lee Patton
1950	13	11	Lee Patton
1951	18	9	Robert N. "Red" Brown
1952	23	4	Robert N. "Red" Brown
1953	19	7	Robert N. "Red" Brown
1954	12	11	Robert N. "Red" Brown
1955	19	11	Fred Schaus
1956	21	9	Fred Schaus
1957	25	5	Fred Schaus
1958	26	2	Fred Schaus
1959	29	5	Fred Schaus
1960	26	5	Fred Schaus
1961	23	4	George King
1962	24	6	George King
1963	23	8	George King
1964	18	10	George King
1965	14	15	George King
1966	19	9	Raymond "Bucky" Waters
1967	19	9	Raymond "Bucky" Waters
1968	19	9	Raymond "Bucky" Waters
1969	12	14	Raymond "Bucky" Waters
1970	11	15	G. E. "Sonny" Moran
1971	13	12	G. E. "Sonny" Moran
1972	13	11	G. E. "Sonny" Moran
1973	10	15	G. E. "Sonny" Moran
1974	11	15	G. E. "Sonny" Moran
1975	14	13	Joedy Gardner
1976	15	13	Joedy Gardner
1977	18	11	Joedy Gardner
1978	12	16	Joedy Gardner
1979	16	12	Joedy Gardner

WICHITA STATE UNIVERSITY

Wichita, Kansas

Yr.	W	L	Coach
Shockers			*Yellow and Black*
1938	10	14	William Hennigh
1939	9	12	William Hennigh
1940	11	7	William Hennigh
1941	9	11	William Hennigh
1942	5	15	Jack Sterrett
1943	12	7	Mel Binford
1944	—	—	
1945	14	4	Mel Binford
1946	14	8	Mel Binford
1947	8	17	Mel Binford
1948	12	13	Mel Binford
1949	10	17	Ken Gunning
1950	7	17	Ken Gunning
1951	9	16	Ken Gunning
1952	11	19	Ralph Miller
1953	16	11	Ralph Miller
1954	27	4	Ralph Miller
1955	17	9	Ralph Miller
1956	14	12	Ralph Miller
1957	15	11	Ralph Miller
1958	14	12	Ralph Miller
1959	14	12	Ralph Miller
1960	14	12	Ralph Miller
1961	18	8	Ralph Miller
1962	18	9	Ralph Miller
1963	19	8	Ralph Miller
1964	23	6	Ralph Miller
1965	21	9	Gary Thompson
1966	17	10	Gary Thompson
1967	14	12	Gary Thompson
1968	12	14	Gary Thompson
1969	11	15	Gary Thompson
1970	8	18	Gary Thompson
1971	10	16	Gary Thompson
1972	16	10	Harry Miller
1973	10	16	Harry Miller
1974	11	15	Harry Miller
1975	11	15	Harry Miller
1976	18	10	Harry Miller
1977	18	10	Harry Miller
1978	13	14	Harry Miller
1979	14	14	Gene Smithson

WILLIAM AND MARY, COLLEGE OF

Williamsburg, Virginia

Yr.	W	L	Coach
Indians			*Green, Gold and Silver*
1938	2	10	J. S. Kellison
1939	10	10	J. S. Kellison
1940	12	11	Dwight Stuessy
1941	16	9	Dwight Stuessy
1942	14	9	Dwight Stuessy
1943	11	10	Dwight Stuessy
1944	10	10	Rube McCray
1945	7	12	Rube McCray
1946	10	10	S. B. Holt
1947	14	12	Richard Gallagher
1948	13	10	Bernard Wilson
1949	24	10	Bernard Wilson
1950	23	9	Bernard Wilson
1951	20	11	Bernard Wilson
1952	15	13	Bernard Wilson
1953	9	13	Les Hooker
1954	9	14	Boydson Baird
1955	11	14	Boydson Baird
1956	12	14	Boydson Baird
1957	9	18	Boydson Baird
1958	15	14	Bill Chambers
1959	13	11	Bill Chambers
1960	15	11	Bill Chambers
1961	14	10	Bill Chambers

Yr.	W	L	Coach
1962	7	17	Bill Chambers
1963	15	9	Bill Chambers
1964	9	13	Bill Chambers
1965	12	13	Bill Chambers
1966	13	12	Bill Chambers
1967	14	11	Warren Mitchell
1968	6	18	Warren Mitchell
1969	6	20	Warren Mitchell
1970	11	16	Warren Mitchell
1971	11	16	Warren Mitchell
1972	10	17	Warren Mitchell
1973	10	17	Ed Ashnault
1974	9	18	E. Ashnault, G. Balanis
1975	16	12	George Balanis
1976	15	13	George Balanis
1977	16	14	George Balanis
1978	16	10	Bruce Parkhill
1979	9	17	Bruce Parkhill

WISCONSIN, UNIVERSITY OF

Madison, Wisconsin

Badgers			*Cardinal and White*
1938	10	10	Bud Foster
1939	10	10	Bud Foster
1940	5	15	Bud Foster
1941	20	3	Bud Foster
1942	14	7	Bud Foster
1943	12	9	Bud Foster
1944	12	9	Bud Foster
1945	10	11	Bud Foster
1946	4	17	Bud Foster
1947	16	6	Bud Foster
1948	12	8	Bud Foster
1949	12	10	Bud Foster
1950	17	5	Bud Foster
1951	10	12	Bud Foster
1952	10	12	Bud Foster
1953	13	9	Bud Foster
1954	12	10	Bud Foster
1955	10	12	Bud Foster
1956	6	16	Bud Foster
1957	5	17	Bud Foster
1958	8	14	Bud Foster
1959	3	19	Bud Foster
1960	8	16	John Erickson
1961	7	17	John Erickson
1962	17	7	John Erickson
1963	14	10	John Erickson
1964	8	16	John Erickson
1965	9	13	John Erickson
1966	11	13	John Erickson
1967	13	11	John Erickson
1968	13	11	John Erickson
1969	11	13	John Powless
1970	10	14	John Powless
1971	9	15	John Powless
1972	13	11	John Powless
1973	11	13	John Powless
1974	16	8	John Powless
1975	8	18	John Powless
1976	10	16	John Powless
1977	9	18	Bill Cofield
1978	8	19	Bill Cofield
1979	12	15	Bill Cofield

WISCONSIN-MILWAUKEE, UNIVERSITY OF

Milwaukee, Wisconsin

Panthers			*Black and Gold*
(as Milwaukee State Teachers College)			
1938	10	6	Guy V. Penwell
1939	10	5	Guy V. Penwell
1940	12	4	Guy V. Penwell

Yr.	W	L	Coach
1941	14	5	Guy V. Penwell
1942	11	3	Guy V. Penwell
1943	8	6	John Tierney
1944	3	10	John Tierney
1945	11	5	John Tierney
1946	12	7	John Tierney
1947	11	8	Guy V. Penwell
1948	14	8	Guy V. Penwell
1949	11	13	Guy V. Penwell
1950	15	12	Guy V. Penwell
1951	10	16	Guy V. Penwell
1952	6	15	Guy V. Penwell
1953	6	15	Russ Rebholz
1954	9	12	Russ Rebholz
1955	11	10	Russ Rebholz
(as Wisconsin-Milwaukee)			
1956	13	8	Russ Rebholz
1957	12	7	Russ Rebholz
1958	13	7	Russ Rebholz
1959	17	4	Russ Rebholz
1960	18	4	Russ Rebholz
1961	8	12	Russ Rebholz
1962	4	17	Russ Rebholz
1963	4	19	Russ Rebholz
1964	3	18	Ray Krzoska
1965	9	14	Ray Krzoska
1966	15	10	Ray Krzoska
1967	14	10	Ray Krzoska
1968	16	11	Ray Krzoska
1969	15	11	Ray Krzoska
1970	14	12	Ray Krzoska
1971	13	10	Charley Parsley
1972	15	11	Charley Parsley
1973	18	8	Charley Parsley
1974	14	12	Bill Klucas
1975	8	18	Bill Klucas
1976	11	15	Bob Gottlieb
1977	19	8	Bob Gottlieb
1978	15	12	Bob Gottlieb
1979	8	18	Bob Gottlieb

WYOMING, UNIVERSITY OF

Laramie, Wyoming

Cowboys			*Brown and Yellow*
1938	12	5	Willard Witte
1939	10	11	Willard Witte
1940	7	10	Everett Shelton
1941	13	6	Everett Shelton
1942	15	5	Everett Shelton
1943	31	2	Everett Shelton
1944	—	—	
1945	10	17	Everett Shelton
1946	22	4	Everett Shelton
1947	22	6	Everett Shelton
1948	18	9	Everett Shelton
1949	25	10	Everett Shelton
1950	25	11	Everett Shelton
1951	26	11	Everett Shelton
1952	28	7	Everett Shelton
1953	20	10	Everett Shelton
1954	19	9	Everett Shelton
1955	17	9	Everett Shelton
1956	7	19	Everett Shelton
1957	6	19	Everett Shelton
1958	13	14	Everett Shelton
1959	4	22	Everett Shelton
1960	5	19	Bill Strannigan
1961	7	18	Bill Strannigan
1962	9	17	Bill Strannigan
1963	11	15	Bill Strannigan
1964	12	14	Bill Strannigan
1965	16	10	Bill Strannigan
1966	17	9	Bill Strannigan
1967	15	14	Bill Strannigan
1968	18	9	Bill Strannigan

Yr.	W	L	Coach		Yr.	W	L	Coach
1969	19	9	Bill Strannigan		1975	11	15	Tay Baker
1970	19	7	Bill Strannigan		1976	14	12	Tay Baker
1971	10	15	Bill Strannigan		1977	10	17	Tay Baker
1972	12	14	Bill Strannigan		1978	13	14	Tay Baker
1973	9	17	Bill Strannigan		1979	14	13	Tay Baker
1974	4	22	Moe Radovich					
1975	10	16	Moe Radovich					
1976	10	17	Moe Radovich					
1977	17	10	Don DeVoe					
1978	12	15	Don DeVoe					
1979	15	12	Jim Brandenburg					

XAVIER UNIVERSITY

Cincinnati, Ohio

Musketeers			Royal Blue and White
1938	10	9	C. Crowe
1939	13	7	C. Crowe
1940	7	16	C. Crowe
1941	13	9	C. Crowe
1942	10	8	C. Crowe
1943	6	10	C. Crowe
1944	—	—	
1945	—	—	
1946	3	16	E. Burns
1947	8	17	L. Hirt
1948	24	8	L. Hirt
1949	16	10	L. Hirt
1950	12	16	L. Hirt
1951	16	10	L. Hirt
1952	10	14	Ned Wulk
1953	11	12	Ned Wulk
1954	18	12	Ned Wulk
1955	13	13	Ned Wulk
1956	17	11	Ned Wulk
1957	20	8	Ned Wulk
1958	19	11	Jim McCafferty
1959	12	13	Jim McCafferty
1960	17	9	Jim McCafferty
1961	17	10	Jim McCafferty
1962	14	12	Jim McCafferty
1963	12	16	Jim McCafferty
1964	16	10	Jim McCafferty
1965	10	15	Jim McCafferty
1966	13	13	Donald Ruberg
1967	13	13	Donald Ruberg
1968	10	16	George Krajack
1969	10	16	George Krajack
1970	5	20	George Krajack
1971	9	17	George Krajack
1972	12	14	Dick Campbell
1973	3	23	Dick Campbell
1974	8	18	Tay Baker

YALE UNIVERSITY

New Haven, Connecticut

Bulldogs			Yale Blue
1938	7	12	Ken Loeffler
1939	4	16	Ken Loeffler
1940	13	6	Ken Loeffler
1941	11	11	Ken Loeffler
1942	7	12	Ken Loeffler
1943	7	17	Robert "Red" Rolfe
1944	14	6	Robert "Red" Rolfe
1945	14	4	Robert "Red" Rolfe
1946	14	1	Robert "Red" Rolfe
1947	7	18	Ivy Williamson
1948	14	13	Howard Hobson
1949	22	8	Howard Hobson
1950	17	9	Howard Hobson
1951	14	13	Howard Hobson
1952	14	14	Howard Hobson
1953	10	15	Howard Hobson
1954	12	14	Howard Hobson
1955	3	21	Howard Hobson
1956	15	11	Howard Hobson
1957	18	8	Joe Vancisin
1958	14	10	Joe Vancisin
1959	10	13	Joe Vancisin
1960	6	17	Joe Vancisin
1961	12	12	Joe Vancisin
1962	18	6	Joe Vancisin
1963	13	10	Joe Vancisin
1964	16	8	Joe Vancisin
1965	10	12	Joe Vancisin
1966	9	12	Joe Vancisin
1967	14	7	Joe Vancisin
1968	15	9	Joe Vancisin
1969	9	16	Joe Vancisin
1970	11	13	Joe Vancisin
1971	4	20	Joe Vancisin
1972	7	17	Joe Vancisin
1973	9	16	Joe Vancisin
1974	8	16	Joe Vancisin
1975	3	20	Joe Vancisin
1976	7	21	Ray Carazo
1977	6	20	Ray Carazo
1978	8	16	Ray Carazo
1979	11	15	Ray Carazo

7

NCAA Divisions II and III

In 1957, in response to the request of smaller NCAA-member institutions for greater opportunity to compete at the national level, the NCAA divided its championship tournament into two divisions, University (for major colleges) and College (for smaller schools). And in 1973 the NCAA set up three divisions—I (roughly 250 "major colleges"), II and III (about 450 of the other NCAA institutions). The caliber of competition and not the size of the college is the determining factor in classification. So it is not unusual for schools with smaller enrollments to be classified "major college" or Division I. Each of the three divisions has its own championship tournament.

DIVISION II CHAMPIONS

YEAR	CHAMPION	SCORE	RUNNER-UP
1957	Wheaton	89-65	Kentucky Wesleyan
1958	South Dakota	75-53	St. Michael's
1959	Evansville	83-67	Southwest Missouri
1960	Evansville	90-69	Chapman
1961	Wittenberg	42-38	Southeast Missouri
1962	Mount St. Mary's	58-57	Sacramento State
1963	South Dakota State	44-42	Wittenberg
1964	Evansville	72-59	Akron
1965	Evansville	85-82	Southern Illinois
1966	Kentucky Wesleyan	54-51	Southern Illinois
1967	Winston-Salem State	54-51	Akron
1968	Kentucky Wesleyan	63-52	Indiana State
1969	Kentucky Wesleyan	75-71	Southwest Missouri
1970	Philadelphia Textile	76-65	Tennessee State
1971	Evansville	97-82	Old Dominion
1972	Roanoke	84-72	Akron
1973	Kentucky Wesleyan	78-76	Tennessee State
1974	Morgan State	67-52	Southwest Missouri
1975	Old Dominion	76-74	New Orleans
1976	Puget Sound	83-74	Tennessee-Chattanooga
1977	Tennessee-Chattanooga	71-62	Randolph-Macon
1978	Cheyney State	47-40	Wisconsin-Green Bay
1979	Northern Alabama	64-50	Wisconsin-Green Bay

DIVISION III CHAMPIONS

YEAR	CHAMPION	SCORE	RUNNER-UP
1975	LeMoyne Owen	57-54	Glassboro State
1976	Scranton	60-57	Wittenberg
1977	Wittenberg	79-66	Oneonta State
1978	North Park	69-57	Widener
1979	North Park	66-62	Potsdam State

NCAA COLLEGE DIVISION RECORDS
(Based on statistics from National Collegiate Statistics Services)

INDIVIDUAL

Single Game

Most Points	113	Clarence "Bevo" Francis, Rio Grande (Ohio) vs. Hillsdale, 1954

Season

Most Points	1,329	Earl Monroe, Winston-Salem, 1967
Highest Average	46.5	Clarence "Bevo" Francis, Rio Grande (Ohio), 1954
Most F. G. Attempted	925	Jim Toombs, Stillman, 1965
Most F. G. Made	539	Travis Grant, Kentucky State, 1972
Highest F. G. Percentage	.733	Edward Phillips, Alabama A&M, 1968 Harold Booker, Cheyney State, 1965

Most F. T. Attempted	510	Clarence "Bevo" Francis, Rio Grande (Ohio), 1954
Most F. T. Made	401	Joe Miller, Alderson-Broaddus, 1957
Highest F. T. Percentage	.933	Jerry Prestier, Baldwin-Wallace, 1978
Most Rebounds	799	Elmore Smith, Kentucky State, 1971
Highest Rebounding Average	29.5	Tom Hart, Middlebury, 1956

Career

Most Points	4,045	Travis Grant, Kentucky State, 1969-72
Highest Average	33.4	Travis Grant, Kentucky State, 1969-72
Most Field Goals	1,760	Travis Grant, Kentucky State, 1969-72
Most Free Throws	1,130	Joe Miller, Alderson-Broaddus, 1955-57

TEAM

Single Season

Most Points, one team	169	Stillman vs. Miles (123), Feb. 17, 1966
Most Points, two teams	306	Livingston 160, Mississippi College 146, Dec. 2, 1969

Season

Most Victories in Perfect Season	30	Central State (Ohio), 1965
Highest Scoring Average	114.2	Mississippi College, 1960
Most Field Goals per game	46.9	Lincoln (Missouri), 1967
Highest F. G. Percentage	.624	Kentucky State, 1976
Most Free Throws per game	36.1	Baltimore, 1955
Highest F. T. Percentage	.815	South Alabama, 1971
Fewest Points Allowed per game	29.1	Mississippi Industrial, 1948

8

NAIA

The National Association of Intercollegiate Athletics (NAIA) basketball tournment is the oldest and largest collegiate championship tournament in the United States. Thirty-two district champions representing more than 500 member institutions throughout the country play each March in Kansas City.

The NAIA, officially organized in 1940, is more than a basketball tournament, however, with a program including 13 national championships ranging from bowling to football. The formation of the organization grew out of a desire by some prominent Kansas City residents to have a championship basketball tournament after the AAU moved its tourney to Denver.

In 1937 these K.C. leaders got together with Dr. James Naismith, inventor of the game who was teaching at the University of Kansas, and Emil S. Liston, athletic director at Baker University in Baldwin, Kansas. The result was an eight-team tournament of Midwest conference champions. The following year saw the first 32-team field entered in what was now the National Intercollegiate Basketball Championship tournament. The National Association of Intercollegiate Basketball (NAIB) was organ-

ized in 1940, changing its name in 1952 to the present NAIA.

The NAIA describes itself as an organization "whose primary and sole purpose is to champion the cause and promote the interests of the college of moderate enrollment and sound athletic philosophy and program."

The basketball tournament has served as a springboard to the professional ranks for a number of stars including Willis Reed of Grambling, Lucious Jackson of Pan American, Zelmo Beaty of Prairie View A&M, Al Tucker of Oklahoma Baptist, Dick Barnett, Ben Warley and John Barnhill of Tennessee A&I, Lloyd Free of Guilford, Foots Walker of West Georgia, Alonzo Bradley of Texas Southern, Joe Pace of Coppin State, Jack Sikma of Illinois Wesleyan and Elmore Smith of Kentucky State.

The tourney also served as the backdrop for the most publicized basketball collegian of the 1950s, Clarence "Bevo" Francis of little (96 students) Rio Grande College in Ohio. In his freshman year, 1954, Francis dominated the pre-tournament talk after averaging 50.1 points in 39 games and scoring 116 points in one outing against Ashland (Kentucky) Junior College. The admiration of the fans for the 6-9 Francis was such that the tournament was sold out the first two nights, until Rio Grande was eliminated. But the coaches did not share the fans' admiration for Francis' exploits and purged the record book of all marks not set in games against schools which granted four-year degrees. Some of the teams Rio Grande played that year were Bliss Business College and Cincinnati Seminary.

Travis Grant and Elmore Smith were the standouts who took Kentucky State to three straight NAIA titles, 1970–72. Grant holds the career points record with 4,045 for a 33.4 average. Smith possesses the season rebound mark with 799 in 1970–71.

Grant won the tournament Most Valuable Player award in 1971 and 1972, the latter on the strength of 60-point and 43-point games. He leads all tournament players with 518 points and a 34.5 average.

Lucious Jackson

Jack Sikma

Willis Reed

Zelmo Beaty

Clarence "Bevo" Francis

The winners, runners-up, and scores of NAIA championships:

YEAR	CHAMPION	SCORE	RUNNER-UP
1937	Central Missouri State	35-24	Morningside
1938	Central Missouri State	45-30	Roanoke
1939	Southwestern (Kansas)	32-31	San Diego State
1940	Tarkio (Missouri)	52-42	San Diego State
1941	San Diego State	36-32	Murray State
1942	Hamline (Minnesota)	33-31	Southeastern Oklahoma
1943	Southeast Missouri State	34-32	Northwest Missouri State
1944	No Tournament		
1945	Loyola (Louisiana)	49-36	Pepperdine
1946	Southern Illinois	49-40	Indiana State
1947	Marshall (West Virginia)	73-59	Mankato State
1948	Louisville (Kentucky)	82-70	Hamline
1949	Hamline (Minnesota)	57-46	Regis
1950	Indiana State	61-47	East Central Oklahoma
1951	Hamline (Minnesota)	69-61	Millikin
1952	Southwest Missouri State	73-64	Murray State
1953	Southwest Missouri State	79-71	Hamline
1954	St. Benedict's (Kansas)	62-56	Western Illinois
1955	East Texas State	71-54	Southeastern Oklahoma
1956	McNeese State (Louisiana)	60-55	Texas Southern
1957	Tennessee State	92-73	Southeastern Oklahoma
1958	Tennessee State	85-73	Western Illinois
1959	Tennessee State	97-87	Pacific Lutheran
1960	Southwest Texas State	66-44	Westminster (Pennsylvania)
1961	Grambling (Louisiana)	95-75	Georgetown (Kentucky)
1962	Prairie View A&M (Texas)	62-53	Westminster (Pennsylvania)
1963	Pan American (Texas)	73-62	Western Carolina
1964	Rockhurst (Missouri)	66-56	Pan American
1965	Central State (Ohio)	85-51	Oklahoma Baptist
1966	Oklahoma Baptist	88-59	Georgia Southern
1967	St. Benedict's (Kansas)	71-65	Oklahoma Baptist
1968	Central State (Ohio)	51-48	Fairmont
1969	Eastern New Mexico	99-76	Maryland State
1970	Kentucky State	79-71	Central Washington State
1971	Kentucky State	102-82	Eastern Michigan
1972	Kentucky State	71-62	Eau Claire State
1973	Guilford	99-96	Maryland-Eastern Shore
1974	West Georgia	97-79	Alcorn State
1975	Grand Canyon	65-54	Midwestern
1976	Coppin State	96-91	Henderson State
1977	Texas Southern	71-44	Campbell
1978	Grand Canyon	79-75	Kearney State
1979	Drury	60-54	Henderson State

NAIA COACH OF THE YEAR

1962—Charles (Buzz) Ridl, Westminster
1963—Fred Hodby, Grambling
1964—Sam Williams, Pan American
1965—Dick Campbell, Carson-Newman
1966—Ted Kjolhede, Central Michigan
1967—Bob Bass, Oklahoma Baptist
1968—Jack Dobbins, Northeastern Oklahoma State
1969—John Retton, Fairmont State
1970—Dean Nicholson, Central Washington State

1971—Lucias Mitchell, Kentucky State
1972—Ken Anderson, Eau Claire State
1973—Archie Porter, Sam Houston State
1974—John Collier, Hanover
1975—Ed Messbarger, St. Mary's
1976—Joe Retton, Fairmont State
1977—Nield Gordon, Newberry
1978—Edsel Matthews, Drury
1979—Lonnie Nichols, Cameron

INDIVIDUAL

Single Game

Most Points	113	Clarence "Bevo" Francis, Rio Grande (Ohio) vs. Hillsdale, 1954
Most Field Goals	38	Clarence "Bevo" Francis, Rio Grande (Ohio) vs. Hillsdale, 1954
Most Free Throws	37	Clarence "Bevo" Francis, Rio Grande (Ohio) vs. Hillsdale, 1954
Highest F.G. Percentage	1.000	(14 of 14) Bob Kauffman, Guilford, vs. Catawba, 1966
Highest F.T. Percentage	1.000	(23 of 23) Carl Hartman, Alderson-Broaddus vs. Salem (W.Va.), 1955
Most Rebounds	44	Bob Ortmyer, Lenoir Rhyne vs. Guilford, 1955
Most Assists	26	Dave Williams, Malone vs. Philadelphia Bible, 1972
		Don Adler, Georgia Southern vs. Jacksonville, 1964

Season

Most Points	1,347	Archie Talley, Salem (W.Va.), 1976
Highest Scoring Average	48.3	Clarence "Bevo" Francis, Rio Grande (Ohio), 1953
Most F.G. Attempted	1,171	Archie Talley, Salem (W.Va.), 1976
Most F.G. Made	577	Archie Talley, Salem (W.Va.), 1976
Highest F.G. Percentage	.778	Robert Thompson, Philander Smith, 1969
Most F.T. Attempted	529	Joe Miller, Alderson-Broaddus, 1957
Most F.T. Made	437	Joe Miller, Alderson-Broaddus, 1957
Highest F.T. Percentage	.938	(75 of 80) Jerry Lewis, Indiana Central, 1959
Most Rebounds	799	Elmore Smith, Kentucky State, 1970
Most Assists	458	Steve Williams, Carson-Newman, 1973

Career

Most Points	4,045	Travis Grant, Kentucky State, 1968-72
Most Field Goals	1,760	Travis Grant, Kentucky State, 1968-72
Scoring Average	33.4	Travis Grant, Kentucky State, 1968-72
Highest F.G. Percentage	.683	(874 of 1,279) David Nelson, Bloomfield (N.J.), 1974-78
Most Free Throws	1,139	Joe Miller, Alderson-Broaddus, 1954-57
Highest F.T. Percentage	.890	Kevin Miller, Spring Hill, 1973-77
Most Rebounds	2,265	Bob Mabry, Rio Grande (Ohio), 1967-70
Most Assists	1,076	Don Trelkeld, Milligan, 1969-73

TEAM

Single Game

Most Points, One Team	169	Stillman vs. Miles, 1966
Most Points, Two Teams	306	Livingston 160, Mississippi College 146, 1970
Most Field Goals	71	Rockford (Ill.) vs. Shimer, 1967
Highest F.G. Percentage	.857	Huntington (Ala.) vs. Troy State, 1963
Most Free Throws	54	Atlantic Christian vs. Lenoir Rhyne, 1954
Highest F.T. Percentage	1.000	Southeastern Louisiana, 1950; Wartburg, 1960; McNeese State, 1961; Kansas Wesleyan, 1965; Morningside, 1966; Culver-Stockton, 1966; Bloomsburg State, 1967; Montevallo, 1967; Alabama College, 1967
Largest Margin of Victory	108	Rockford (Ill.) 154, Shimer 46, 1967
Most Rebounds	126	Bethany, 1957

Season

Best Record	35-0	Newberry, 1977
Worst Record	0-25	Warner Pacific, 1977
Consecutive Victories (one season)	35	Newberry, 1977
Consecutive Victories (two seasons)	36	Central States—30 straight, 1964-65; first six games, 1965-66
Consecutive Losses	29	West Virginia Wesleyan, 1968
Most Points	3,730	Coppin State, 1976
Highest F.G. Percentage	.625	Kentucky State, 1976
Best F.T. Percentage	.827	Fisk, 1965
Most Rebounds	2,447	Coppin State, 1976

9

The Women

The song "I Am Woman" introduced the event—the first women's collegiate basketball game ever played in New York's Madison Square Garden. Nearly 12,000 people attended the game in February 1975, between national champion Immaculata (Pennsylvania) and Queens College (New York), and it was the Garden crowd paying tribute to the women's skill and competitiveness that acknowledged the coming of age of women's basketball.

Women have been playing basketball since 1892, a year after the game's invention. But the game they played differed greatly from the men's. Early rules called for nine women to a side, each confined to an area, with the ball passed from area to area before a shot. This evolved into six-women sides, three guards who stayed at one end of the court for defense, and three forwards at the other end to take shots. In essence, this was a three-on-three halfcourt game.

There was no dribbling in the early women's games, either. Eventually, women were allowed to bounce the ball once before passing or shooting. By the 1950s, they were given two bounces, and in the 1960s, three.

Until five-women teams were generally adopted in 1970, the United States was the only nation using six women a side. Now the differences between the men's and women's games are minimal. Women employ a 30-second clock and have no formal backcourt, so there are no backcourt violations. Quarters are 10 minutes long and there is no three-to-make-two foul-shot procedure.

Despite the liberalized rules, the women's game did not leave the gym class for the big arena until passage of Title IX in the mid-1970s mandated a proportionate allocation of monies for women's athletic programs at federally funded educational institutions. Now women were entitled to uniforms instead of gym suits, coaches instead of phys-ed teachers, cross-state—and in some cases cross-country schedules instead of pickup games, and, most importantly, athletic scholarships.

Attention focused on women's college basketball after Immaculata won three consecutive Association for Intercollegiate Athletics for Women (AIAW) championships. The small, women's Catholic college on Philadelphia's Main Line offered no athletic scholarships, but with experienced players

Montclair State's Carol Blazejowski finished career with 3,119 points

Delta State won three national crowns behind Olympian Lucy Harris

from CYO teams was able to defeat West Chester State in 1972, Queens College in 1973, and Mississippi College in 1974 in the championship games.

Immaculata set the pattern for the first six years of the AIAW tournament: The team with the dominant center would win. In Theresa Shank, the Mighty Macs had a 5-11 pivot who could score. She teamed with Denise Conway and, for two seasons, flashy 5-5 guard Marianne Crawford, to lead the Mighty Macs under coach Cathy Rush to a 64–2 record from 1970 to 1974. In the seven years Rush coached at Immaculata, the Mighty Macs had a 159–15 record.

Immaculata reached the AIAW finals in 1975 and 1976, but each time lost to Mississippi's Delta State and its agile 6-3 center, Lucy Harris. Harris led the Lady Statesmen to a third straight AIAW title in 1977 over LSU. After the season, in an acknowledgment of women's basketball, Harris was chosen by the New Orleans Jazz in the NBA draft.

Until the 1973–74 season, the AIAW had frowned upon athletic scholarships. The AIAW went so far as to ban tiny Wayland Baptist College (Tex.) from its championship because scholarship money was provided by a local fan. All that changed by 1978 when the full effect of Title IX was felt. UCLA, starting five women on scholarship, beat Maryland for the AIAW title, thus signaling the shift in power from the small colleges to the large, well-endowed universities.

The women's game also produced its first national stars. In addition to Shank and Harris, there were Ann Meyers and Nancy Lieberman. The first woman scholarship athlete signed by UCLA and the sister of

Old Dominion's Nancy Lieberman was a teen-age Olympian

Dave Meyers of the NBA Milwaukee Bucks, Ann was a four-time All-American from 1975 to 1978. Carol "The Blaze" Blazejowski of Montclair State (N.J.) set an all-time AIAW career scoring record of 3,119 points and won the first Wade Trophy (named for Delta State coach Margaret Wade) as the nation's best women's college basketball player.

Lieberman was a 1976 U. S. Olympian as a high-school player, and she became one of the most highly regarded women's players at Old Dominion College, which she led to the AIAW championship in 1979.

AIAW Champions

1972—Immaculata (Pa.)	1976—Delta State
1973—Immaculata (Pa.)	1977—Delta State
1974—Immaculata (Pa.)	1978—UCLA
1975—Delta State	1979—Old Dominion

10

Junior Colleges

The National Junior College Athletic Association has been conducting national championships for more than 30 years. Its title competition actually started with an invitational tournament in Compton, California, in 1945. Since 1949, the NJCAA's championship has been held in Hutchinson, Kansas, cosponsored by Rishel Post, American Legion, and Hutchinson Junior College. Hutchinson also serves as NJCAA headquarters.

The NJCAA began women's championship play in 1975 with its Women's Invitational Basketball Tournament, won by Temple (Texas) Junior College.

In 1978, Independence (Kansas) Community College won its second straight national championship, and third overall. Vincennes (Indiana) University Junior College had also won three NJCAA titles through the 1978 season. But Moberly (Missouri) Junior College leads them all with four championships.

A distinguished list of players has gone from the junior-college ranks to four-year schools and on to careers in professional basketball: Bob McAdoo, Artis Gilmore, Lionel Hollins, Ricky Sobers, Larry Kenon, Fred Brown, Spencer Haywood, Mel Dan-

Junior College Champions

1945—Pasadena City College (Calif.)
1946—Sacramento Junior College (Calif.)
1947—Compton College (Calif.)
1948—Marin College (Calif.)
1949—Tyler Junior College (Tex.)
1950—Los Angeles City College (Calif.)
1951—Tyler Junior College (Tex.)
1952—Wharton County Junior College (Tex.)
1953—El Dorado Junior College (Kan.)
1954—Moberly Junior College (Mo.)
1955—Moberly Junior College (Mo.)
1956—Kilgore Junior College (Tex.)
1957—San Angelo College (Tex.)
1958—Kilgore Junior College (Tex.)
1959—Weber College (Utah)
1960—Parsons Junior College (Kan.)
1961—Pueblo Junior College (Kan.)
1962—Coffeyville College (Kan.)
1963—Independence Community College (Kan.)
1964—Dodge City College (Kan.)
1965—Vincennes University Junior College (Ind.)
1966—Moberly Junior College (Mo.)
1967—Moberly Junior College (Mo.)
1968—San Jacinto College (Tex.)
1969—Paducah Junior College (Ken.)
1970—Vincennes University Junior College (Ind.)
1971—Ellsworth Junior College (Iowa)
1972—Vincennes University Junior College (Ind.)
1973—Mercer County Community College (N.J.)
1974—Mercer County Community College (N.J.)
1975—Western Texas College
1976—College of Southern Idaho
1977—Independence Community College (Kan.)
1978—Independence Community College (Kan.)
1979—Three Rivers Community College (Mo.)

Women's Junior College Champions

1975—Temple Junior College (Tex.)
1976—Seminole Junior College (Okla.)
1977—Panola Junior College (Tex.)
1978—Panola Junior College (Tex.)
1979—Northern Oklahoma (Okla.)

iels, Mo Layton, Tom Henderson, Tim Bassett, Jim McElroy, Sonny Parker, Alonzo Bradley, Ray Williams, and Rickey Green.

The NJCAA divides its nearly 600 men's division schools into 23 regions. George Killian is the NJCAA's executive director.

The High Schools

Lew Alcindor was a High-School All-American at New York's Power Memorial Academy

11

Champions and All-Americans

The success of the nation's interscholastic athletic programs can be largely attributed to the efficient and powerful direction provided by the National Federation of State High School Athletic Associations.

Organized in 1920 by administrators from Illinois, Iowa, Michigan, and Wisconsin, the Federation quickly became national in scope and now includes 50-member-state high-school associations as well as affiliated associations in six Canadian provinces.

The growth in size and influence of the state associations as well as the National Federation insures some degree of teamwork on the part of the 20,400 member schools—almost all of which field a varsity basketball team.

The Federation, based in Chicago, was organized primarily to secure adherence to the eligibility rules of the various state associations in interstate contests. Other Federation rules cover sanctioned interstate contests, including distance to be traveled, sponsor, amount of school time involved, and the extent that such interstate events interfere with smaller (local) meets that insure greater participation.

Basketball has been the subject of much of the Federation's legislation. The 1934 rule banning the sanctioning of national championship contests was passed to curb the rash of national tournaments run by various promoters. But this did not close the book on basketball's problems. According to the Federation's Handbook, some promoters attempted to circumvent the rules, and the Federation's National Council voted to refuse to sanction any new interstate basketball tournament except where geographic or topographic conditions make such play practical.

The Federation, whose executive director is Brice B. Durbin, also formulates national policy on high-school bowl and charity games, all-star and out-of-season contests, NCAA all-star regulations (summer games for college-bound seniors), and specialized camps. The Federation is represented on the basketball rules committee.

With more than 764,000 boys and 537,000 girls participating in the sport at member schools, basketball is one of the Federation's major activities. Of the member and affiliated state and provincial associations, all but California, Delaware, Massachusetts, and Ontario conduct post-season state-championship tournaments.

The following lists of state high-school basketball champions since 1938 were furnished by the National Federation and the state associations.

State High-School Champions

1938–39

STATE	CLASS	CHAMPION	STATE	CLASS	CHAMPION
ALABAMA		Scottsboro	NEW HAMPSHIRE	A	Portsmouth
ARIZONA		Duncan	NEW JERSEY		New Brunswick
CONNECTICUT	A	Manchester	NEW MEXICO		House
FLORIDA	A	Jacksonville Jackson	NORTH CAROLINA	A	Durham
GEORGIA	A	Macon Lanier	NORTH DAKOTA	A	Fargo
IDAHO	A	Boise	OHIO		Newark
ILLINOIS		Dundee	OKLAHOMA	A	Ponca City
INDIANA		South Side	OREGON		Baker
IOWA		Diagonal	RHODE ISLAND	A	Pawtucket
KANSAS	A	Kansas City Ward	SOUTH DAKOTA	A	Aberdeen
KENTUCKY		Sharpe	TEXAS		Dallas Wilson
MAINE		Winslow	UTAH		Granite
MICHIGAN	A	Kalamazoo Central	VERMONT	A	Barre Spaulding
MINNESOTA		Thief River Falls	WASHINGTON		Vancouver
MISSOURI		Houston	WEST VIRGINIA		Wheeling
MONTANA	A	Great Falls	WISCONSIN	A	Wausau
NEBRASKA	A	Lincoln	WYOMING		Rock Springs
NEVADA		Carson			

1939–40

STATE	CLASS	CHAMPION	STATE	CLASS	CHAMPION
ALABAMA		Clanton Chilton	NEW HAMPSHIRE		Portsmouth
ARIZONA		Duncan	NEW JERSEY		West New York
ARKANSAS	A	Ash Flat	NEW MEXICO		Lordsburg
COLORADO	A	Denver Manual	NORTH CAROLINA	A	Jamestown
CONNECTICUT	A	Bridgeport Central	OHIO	A	Akron North
FLORIDA	A	Daytona Beach	OKLAHOMA	A	Tulsa (Central)
IDAHO	A	Blackfoot	OREGON		Salem
ILLINOIS		Rockford	RHODE ISLAND	A	Providence Hope
INDIANA		Frankfort	SOUTH CAROLINA	A	Charleston
IOWA		Creston	SOUTH DAKOTA	A	Flandreau Indian
KANSAS	A	Winfield	TENNESSEE		Knoxville City
KENTUCKY		Brooksville	TEXAS		Livingston
LOUISIANA	A	New Orleans Jesuit	UTAH		Vernal (Uintah)
MAINE		Winslow	VERMONT	A	Burlington
MICHIGAN	A	Flint Northern			Cathedral
MINNESOTA		Mountain Lake	VIRGINIA	A	Hampton
MISSISSIPPI		Mossville	WASHINGTON		Hoquiam
MISSOURI	A	Joplin	WEST VIRGINIA		Fairmont West
MONTANA	A	Park County	WISCONSIN	A	Rhinelander
NEBRASKA	A	Falls City	WYOMING		Casper
NEVADA		Panaca Lincoln			

1940–41

STATE	CLASS	CHAMPION	STATE	CLASS	CHAMPION
ALABAMA		Guin Marion	ARKANSAS	A	Jonesboro
ARIZONA		Duncan	COLORADO	A	Pueblo Centennial

STATE	CLASS	CHAMPION	STATE	CLASS	CHAMPION
CONNECTICUT	A	Bridgeport Bassick	NEW MEXICO		Sante Fe St. Michael
FLORIDA	A	Jacksonville R.E. Lee	NORTH CAROLINA	A	Durham
GEORGIA	A	Marion Lanier	OHIO	A	New Philadelphia
IDAHO	A	Emmett	OKLAHOMA	A	Ada
ILLINOIS		Granite City	OREGON		Salem
INDIANA		Hammond Technical	PENNSYLVANIA		Lebanon
IOWA		Mason City	RHODE ISLAND		Pawtucket
KANSAS	A	Winfield	SOUTH CAROLINA	A	Greenville
KENTUCKY		Hazel Green	TENNESSEE		Bradley
LOUISIANA		Shreveport Byrd	TEXAS		San Marcos
MAINE		Portland (Cheverus)	UTAH		Ogden
MICHIGAN	A	Flint Northern	VERMONT	A	Burlington Cathedral
MINNESOTA		Breckenridge	VIRGINIA	A	Lynchburg E.C. Glass
MISSISSIPPI		Runnelstown	WASHINGTON		Everett
MISSOURI	A	St. Louis McBride	WEST VIRGINIA		Wheeling
MONTANA	A	Havre	WISCONSIN		Shawano
NEBRASKA	A	Omaha (Creighton)	WYOMING	A	Casper
NEVADA		Sparks			
NEW HAMPSHIRE	A	Berlin			
NEW JERSEY		East Orange			

1941—42

STATE	CLASS	CHAMPION	STATE	CLASS	CHAMPION
ALABAMA		Clanton Chilton	NEVADA		White Pine
ARIZONA		Miami	NEW JERSEY		Asbury Park
ARKANSAS		Beebe	NEW MEXICO		Las Cruces
COLORADO	A	Fort Collins	NORTH CAROLINA	A	Durham
CONNECTICUT	A	Willimantic Windham	NORTH DAKOTA	A	Wahpeton
FLORIDA	A	Tampa (H.B. Plant)	OHIO	A	Martin's Ferry
GEORGIA	A	Savannah	OKLAHOMA	A	Tulsa Will Rogers
IDAHO	A	Burley	OREGON		Astoria
ILLINOIS		Cicero Morton	PENNSYLVANIA		Lower Merion
INDIANA		Washington	SOUTH DAKOTA	A	Sioux Falls
KANSAS	AA	Wyandotte			Washington
KENTUCKY		Inez	UTAH		Provo
MICHIGAN	A	Benton Harbor	VIRGINIA	A	Roanoke (Jefferson)
MINNESOTA		Buhl	WASHINGTON		Bremerton
MONTANA	A	Butte	WEST VIRGINIA	A	Clarksburg Victory
NEBRASKA	A	Scotts Bluff	WISCONSIN		Two Rivers
			WYOMING	A	Rock Springs

1942—43

STATE	CLASS	CHAMPION	STATE	CLASS	CHAMPION
ALABAMA		Birmingham Woodlawn	MISSOURI		St. Louis Beaumont
			NEBRASKA	A	Lincoln
ARKANSAS	A	No. Little Rock	NEW MEXICO		Capitan
COLORADO	A	Denver (East)	NORTH DAKOTA	A	Fargo
CONNECTICUT	A	Bridgeport (Harding)	OHIO	A	Newark
FLORIDA	A	Ft. Lauderdale (Central)	OKLAHOMA	A	Enid
			OREGON	A	Klamath Falls
GEORGIA	A	Columbus Jordan	PENNSYLVANIA		Ardmore
ILLINOIS		Paris	RHODE ISLAND		Pawtucket St. Raphael
INDIANA		Fort Wayne Central			
IOWA		Mason City	SOUTH DAKOTA	A	Sioux Falls
KANSAS	AA	Shawnee Mission	TENNESSEE		Chattanooga Central
KENTUCKY		Hindman	TEXAS		Houston Jefferson Davis
LOUISIANA	A	New Orleans Holy Cross	WEST VIRGINIA		Wheeling
			WISCONSIN		Racine Washington
MINNESOTA		St. Paul Washington	WYOMING	A	Cheyenne
MISSISSIPPI		Belmont			

1943—44

STATE	CLASS	CHAMPION	STATE	CLASS	CHAMPION
ALABAMA		Scottsboro	GEORGIA	A	Columbus
ARIZONA		Phoenix	ILLINOIS		Taylorville
ARKANSAS		Little Rock	INDIANA		Evansville Bosse
COLORADO	A	Fort Collins	IOWA		Waverly
CONNECTICUT	A	Torrington	KANSAS	AA	Shawnee Mission
FLORIDA	A	Miami Senior	KENTUCKY		Harlan

STATE	CLASS	CHAMPION	STATE	CLASS	CHAMPION
LOUISIANA	A	New Orleans Jesuit	OREGON		Ashland
MICHIGAN	A	Saginaw	PENNSYLVANIA		Duquesne
MINNESOTA		Minneapolis Patrick Henry	RHODE ISLAND		Newport (De LaSalle)
MISSISSIPPI		Macedonia	SOUTH CAROLINA	B	Mullins
MISSOURI		Bismarck	SOUTH DAKOTA		Pierre
MONTANA		Great Falls	TENNESSEE		Nashville West
NEBRASKA	A	Omaha South	TEXAS	AA	Dallas Sunset
NEW HAMPSHIRE		Portsmouth	UTAH	A	Provo
NEW JERSEY	IV	New Brunswick	VERMONT		Montpelier
NEW MEXICO		Virden	WASHINGTON		Spokane Lewis & Clark
NORTH DAKOTA	A	Wahpeton	WEST VIRGINIA		Huntington Central
OHIO	A	Middletown	WISCONSIN		Waukesha
OKLAHOMA	A	Oklahoma City Cap. Hill	WYOMING		Cheyenne

1944—45

STATE	CLASS	CHAMPION	STATE	CLASS	CHAMPION
ALABAMA		Selma Parish	NEW JERSEY	IV	Camden
ARIZONA		Tucson	NEW MEXICO		Las Cruces
ARKANSAS	A	Little Rock	NORTH CAROLINA	A	Greensboro
COLORADO	A	Fort Collins	NORTH DAKOTA	A	Valley City
GEORGIA	A	Macon Lanier	OHIO	A	Bellevue
ILLINOIS		Decatur	OKLAHOMA	A	Norman
INDIANA		Evansville Bosse	OREGON	A	Portland
IOWA		Ames			Washington
KANSAS	AA	Salina	PENNSYLVANIA		Allentown
KENTUCKY		Louisville Male	RHODE ISLAND		East Providence
LOUISIANA	A	New Orleans	SOUTH CAROLINA	A	Greenville
		Holy Cross	SOUTH DAKOTA	A	Huron
MAINE		Waterville	TENNESSEE		Chattanooga Central
MASSACHUSETTS	W	South Hadley	TEXAS	AA	Fort Worth Paschal
MICHIGAN	A	Lansing Sexton	UTAH	A	Provo
MINNESOTA		Minneapolis Henry	VIRGINIA		Alexandria
MISSISSIPPI		New Site			(Washington)
MISSOURI		Conway	WASHINGTON		Seattle Lincoln
MONTANA	A	Helena	WEST VIRGINIA		Normantown
NEBRASKA	A	Omaha Creighton	WISCONSIN		Madison West
NEVADA	A	Las Vegas	WYOMING		Cheyenne
NEW HAMPSHIRE		Manchester Central			

1945—46

STATE	CLASS	CHAMPION	STATE	CLASS	CHAMPION
ALABAMA		Selma	NEBRASKA	A	Lincoln
ARIZONA		Mesa	NEVADA		Boulder City
ARKANSAS	A	Little Rock	NEW HAMPSHIRE	A	Nashua
COLORADO	A	Boulder	NEW JERSEY	IV	Elizabeth Jefferson
CONNECTICUT	A	New Haven Hillhouse	NEW MEXICO		Albuquerque
			NORTH CAROLINA		Durham
FLORIDA	A	Miami Beach	NORTH DAKOTA	A	Grand Forks
GEORGIA	A	Savannah	OHIO	A	Middletown
IDAHO	A	Preston	OKLAHOMA	A	El Reno
ILLINOIS		Champagne	OREGON	A	Eugene
INDIANA		Anderson	PENNSYLVANIA	A	Allentown
IOWA		Iowa City	RHODE ISLAND		Pawtucket East
KANSAS	AA	Newton	SOUTH DAKOTA	A	Brookings
KENTUCKY		Morehead Breckinridge	TENNESSEE		Nashville (West)
			TEXAS	AA	Dallas Crozier
LOUISIANA	AA	New Orleans Jesuit	UTAH	A	North Cache
MAINE	A	Auburn Little	VERMONT	A	Springfield
MASSACHUSETTS	A	New Bedford	VIRGINIA		Richmond Jefferson
MICHIGAN	A	Holland	WASHINGTON	A	Seattle Roosevelt
MINNESOTA		Austin	WEST VIRGINIA		Beckley Wilson
MISSISSIPPI		New Site	WISCONSIN		Reedsville
MISSOURI		St. Louis University	WYOMING	A	Casper Natroua
MONTANA	A	Missoula			

1946—47

STATE	CLASS	CHAMPION	STATE	CLASS	CHAMPION
ALABAMA		Campbell	ARKANSAS	A	Little Rock
ARIZONA		Florence	COLORADO	AA	Denver (South)

STATE	CLASS	CHAMPION	STATE	CLASS	CHAMPION
CONNECTICUT	A	New Haven	NEW JERSEY	IV	Newark Central
FLORIDA	A	Tampa	NEW MEXICO		Carlsbad
		Hillsborough	NEVADA		Henderson Basie
GEORGIA	A	Havana	NORTH DAKOTA	A	Grand Forks
IDAHO	A	Boise	OHIO	A	Middletown
ILLINOIS		Paris	OKLAHOMA	A	Muskogee
INDIANA		Shelbyville	OREGON		Marshfield
IOWA		Davenport	PENNSYLVANIA	A	Allentown
KANSAS	AA	Wellington	RHODE ISLAND		Westerly
KENTUCKY		Maysville	SOUTH CAROLINA		Olympia Boys'
LOUISIANA	AA	New Orleans	SOUTH DAKOTA	A	Sturgis
		St. Aloysius	TENNESSEE		Soddy
MAINE		Bangor	TEXAS	AA	El Paso
MASSACHUSETTS		Worcester South	UTAH	A	Granite
MICHIGAN	A	Fall River Durfee	VERMONT		Rutland
MINNESOTA		Duluth Denfield	VIRGINIA	I	Norfolk Granby
MISSISSIPPI		Belmont	WASHINGTON		Pasco
MISSOURI		St. Louis Beaumont	WEST VIRGINIA		Huntington East
MONTANA	A	Missoula	WISCONSIN		Beloit
NEBRASKA	A	Grand Island	WYOMING	A	Cheyenne
NEW HAMPSHIRE		Portsmouth			

1947—48

STATE	CLASS	CHAMPION	STATE	CLASS	CHAMPION
ALABAMA	A	Attalla Etowah	NEVADA	A	Elko County
ARIZONA		Tucson	NEW HAMPSHIRE	A	Concord
ARKANSAS	A	Fayetteville	NEW JERSEY	IV	Orange
COLORADO	AA	Denver Manual	NEW MEXICO		Portales
CONNECTICUT	A	New Haven	NORTH CAROLINA	AA	High Point
		Hillhouse	NORTH DAKOTA	A	Williston
FLORIDA	A	Miami	OHIO	A	Findlay
GEORGIA	A	Macon Lanier	OKLAHOMA	A	Oklahoma City
IDAHO	A	Lewiston			Classen
ILLINOIS		Pinckneyville	OREGON	A	Corvallis
		Comm.	PENNSYLVANIA	A	Norristown
INDIANA		Lafayette Jefferson	RHODE ISLAND		Westerly
IOWA		Manning	SOUTH CAROLINA	A	North Charleston
KANSAS	AA	Liberty	SOUTH DAKOTA	A	Mitchell
KENTUCKY		Brewers	TENNESSEE		Nashville West End
LOUISIANA	AA	New Orleans Jesuit	TEXAS	AA	Dallas Crozier
MAINE	A	Cheverus	UTAH		Ogden Weber
MASSACHUSETTS		Fall River	VERMONT	A	Burlington
MICHIGAN	A	Jackson	VIRGINIA	I	Richmond Marshall
MINNESOTA		Bemidji	WASHINGTON	A	Spokane
MISSOURI		St. Louis Beaumont			No. Central
MISSISSIPPI		Baldwyn	WEST VIRGINIA		Princeton
MONTANA	A	Anaconda	WISCONSIN		Wauwatosa
NEBRASKA	A	Grand Island	WYOMING	A	Cheyenne

1948—49

STATE	CLASS	CHAMPION	STATE	CLASS	CHAMPION
ALABAMA	A	Lanier	MISSISSIPPI		Booneville
ARIZONA	A	Tucson	MISSOURI		Buffalo
ARKANSAS		No. Little Rock	MONTANA	A	Missoula
COLORADO	AA	La Junta	NEBRASKA	A	Seward
CONNECTICUT	A	New Britain	NEVADA	A	Las Vegas
FLORIDA	A	Miami	NEW HAMPSHIRE	A	Nashua
GEORGIA	A	Roosevelt	NEW JERSEY	IV	West Orange
IDAHO	A	Coeur d'Alene	NEW MEXICO		Lovington
ILLINOIS		Mount Vernon	NORTH CAROLINA	AA	Reynolds
INDIANA		Jasper	NORTH DAKOTA	A	Minot
IOWA	A	Ottumwa	OHIO	A	Hamilton
KANSAS	AA	Newton	OKLAHOMA	A	El Paso
KENTUCKY		Owensboro	OREGON	A	Roosevelt
LOUISIANA	AA	New Orleans	PENNSYLVANIA	A	Aliquippa
		St. Aloysius	RHODE ISLAND		Pawtucket
MAINE	L	Many	SOUTH CAROLINA	A	Gaffney
MARYLAND	A	Cumberland	SOUTH DAKOTA	A	Aberdeen
		Fort Hill	TENNESSEE		Humboldt
MASSACHUSETTS	A	Somerville	TEXAS	AA	Texas City
MICHIGAN	A	Kalamazoo	UTAH	A	Davis
MINNESOTA		St. Paul Humboldt	VERMONT		Montpelier

STATE	CLASS	CHAMPION	STATE	CLASS	CHAMPION
VIRGINIA	II	Radford	WEST VIRGINIA	A	Fairmont West
WASHINGTON	A	Spokane	WISCONSIN		Hurley
		Lewis & Clark	WYOMING	A	Casper

1949—50

STATE	CLASS	CHAMPION	STATE	CLASS	CHAMPION
ALABAMA	AA	Birmingham Ensley	NEVADA	A	Reno
ARIZONA	A	Mesa	NEW HAMPSHIRE	A	Portsmouth
ARKANSAS		Van Buren	NEW JERSEY	IV	Union City
COLORADO	AA	Denver			Emerson
		Manual Arts	NEW MEXICO		Tucumcari
CONNECTICUT	L	New Britain	NORTH CAROLINA	AA	High Point
FLORIDA	A	Tampa Jesuit	NORTH DAKOTA	A	Minot
GEORGIA	AA	Macon Lanier	OHIO	A	Springfield
IDAHO	A	Nampa	OKLAHOMA	A	Oklahoma City
ILLINOIS		Mount Vernon			Classen
INDIANA		Madison	OREGON		Salem
IOWA		Davenport	PENNSYLVANIA	A	Homestead
KANSAS	AA	Salina	SOUTH CAROLINA	A	Lancaster
KENTUCKY		Lexington Lafayette	SOUTH DAKOTA	A	Mitchell
LOUISIANA	AA	Baton Rouge	TENNESSEE		Happy Valley
MAINE	L	Portland	TEXAS	AA	Corpus Christi
MARYLAND	A	Cleveland Alleghany	UTAH	A	Salt Lake City South
MICHIGAN	A	Kalamazoo Central	VIRGINIA		Norfolk Granby
MINNESOTA		Duluth Central	WASHINGTON		South Kitsap
MISSISSIPPI	A	Booneville	WEST VIRGINIA	A	Wheeling
MISSOURI	A	Joplin	WISCONSIN		St. Croix Falls
MONTANA	A	Butte	WYOMING		Rock Springs
		Central Catholic			
NEBRASKA	A	Lincoln Northeast			

1950—51

STATE	CLASS	CHAMPION	STATE	CLASS	CHAMPION
ALABAMA		Florence Coffey	NEBRASKA	A	Fremont
ARIZONA	A	Mesa	NEVADA	A	Ely White Pine
ARKANSAS	A	Fort Smith	NEW HAMPSHIRE	A	Portsmouth
COLORADO	AA	Denver East	NEW JERSEY	IV	Bayonne
CONNECTICUT	L	New London	NEW MEXICO		Clovis
		Bulkeley	NORTH CAROLINA	AAA	Wilmington
FLORIDA	AA	Jacksonville Jackson	NORTH DAKOTA	A	Bismarck St. Mary's
GEORGIA	AA	Macon Lanier	OHIO		Columbus East
IDAHO	A	Idaho Falls	OKLAHOMA	A	Shawnee
ILLINOIS		Freeport	OREGON		Portland Jefferson
INDIANA		Muncie Central	PENNSYLVANIA	A	Allentown
IOWA		Davenport	RHODE ISLAND		Westerly
KANSAS	AA	Wichita East	SOUTH CAROLINA	A	Wellford
KENTUCKY		Clark County	SOUTH DAKOTA	A	Sturgis
LOUISIANA	AA	New Orleans	TENNESSEE		Knoxville
		St. Aloysius	TEXAS	AA	Houston Lamar
MAINE	L	Westbrook	UTAH	A	Jordan
MARYLAND	A	Hagerstown	VERMONT		Barre Spaulding
MASSACHUSETTS	A	Quincy	VIRGINIA	I	Newport News
MICHIGAN	A	Kalamazoo Central	WASHINGTON	A	Highline
MINNESOTA		Gilbert	WEST VIRGINIA	A	Beckley Wilson
MISSISSIPPI	A	Fulton	WISCONSIN		Wisconsin Rapids
MISSOURI	A	Normandy	WYOMING	A	Cheyenne
MONTANA		Kalispell			
		Flathead County			

1951—52

STATE	CLASS	CHAMPION	STATE	CLASS	CHAMPION
ALABAMA	AA	Winfield	ILLINOIS		Hebron
ARIZONA	A	Phoenix West	INDIANA		Muncie
ARKANSAS	A	Pine Bluff	IOWA		Davenport
COLORADO	AA	Denver East	KANSAS		Newton
CONNECTICUT	L	New Haven	KENTUCKY		Cuba
		Hillhouse	LOUISIANA	AA	New Orleans
FLORIDA	AA	Pensacola			St. Aloysius
GEORGIA	AA	Atlanta Brown	MAINE	L	Old Town
IDAHO	A	Idaho Falls	MARYLAND	A	Silver Spring Blair

STATE	CLASS	CHAMPION	STATE	CLASS	CHAMPION
MASSACHUSETTS		Fall River Durfee	OKLAHOMA	A	Enid
MICHIGAN	A	Highland Park	OREGON	A	Portland Lincoln
MINNESOTA		Hopkins	PENNSYLVANIA	A	Farrell
MISSISSIPPI	A	Kossuth	RHODE ISLAND		Newport Rogers
MISSOURI	A	St. Louis University	SOUTH CAROLINA	A	Walhalla
MONTANA	A	Kalispell	SOUTH DAKOTA	A	Brookings
		Flathead County	TENNESSEE		Selmer
NEBRASKA	A	Scottsbluff	TEXAS	I	San Antonio Alamo
NEVADA	A	White Pine	UTAH	A	Salt Lake City
NEW HAMPSHIRE	A	Portsmouth			South
NEW JERSEY	IV	Elizabeth Jefferson	VERMONT	A	Rutland
NEW MEXICO		Roswell	VIRGINIA	I	Newport News
NORTH CAROLINA	AAA	Hendersonville	WASHINGTON	A	Walla Walla
NORTH DAKOTA	A	Grand Forks	WEST VIRGINIA	A	Beckley Wilson
		Central	WISCONSIN		Milwaukee South
OHIO	A	Middletown	WYOMING	AA	Cheyenne

1952–53

STATE	CLASS	CHAMPION	STATE	CLASS	CHAMPION
ALABAMA	AA	Eufula	NEVADA	A	Las Vegas
ARIZONA	A	Phoenix Technical	NEW HAMPSHIRE	A	Portsmouth
ARKANSAS		Clinton	NEW JERSEY	IV	Bloomfield
COLORADO	AA	Denver South	NEW MEXICO		Clovis
CONNECTICUT	L	Waterbury Wilby	NORTH CAROLINA	AAA	Raleigh
FLORIDA	AA	Fort Lauderdale	NORTH DAKOTA	A	Bismarck
GEORGIA	AA	Atlanta No. Fulton	OHIO	A	Middletown
IDAHO	A	Idaho Falls	OKLAHOMA	AA	El Reno
ILLINOIS		LaGrange Lyons	OREGON	A	Coos Bay Marshfield
INDIANA		South Bend Central	PENNSYLVANIA	A	Yeadon
IOWA		Clinton St. Mary's	RHODE ISLAND		Newport
KANSAS	AA	Merriam			De LaSalle Academy
		Shawnee Mission	SOUTH CAROLINA	A	Columbia Olympia
KENTUCKY		Lexington Lafayette	SOUTH DAKOTA	A	Aberdeen
LOUISIANA	AA	New Orleans	TENNESSEE		Old Hickory DuPont
		St. Aloysius	TEXAS	AAAA	Pampa
MAINE	L	Jonesboro Hodge	UTAH	A	Jordan
MARYLAND	A	Ellsworth	VERMONT	A	Burlington
MASSACHUSETTS	A	Boston Mission	VIRGINIA	I	Lynchburg
MICHIGAN	A	Dearborn Fordson			E.C. Glass
MINNESOTA		Hopkins	WASHINGTON	A	Renton
MISSISSIPPI		Hickory	WEST VIRGINIA	A	Beckley Wilson
MISSOURI		St. Louis Cleveland	WISCONSIN		Menasha
MONTANA	A	Helena	WYOMING	AA	Cheyenne
NEBRASKA	A	Boys Town			

1953–54

STATE	CLASS	CHAMPION	STATE	CLASS	CHAMPION
ALABAMA	AA	Dothan	NEVADA	A	Reno
ARIZONA	A	Phoenix West	NEW HAMPSHIRE	A	Nashua
ARKANSAS	A	Jonesboro	NEW JERSEY	IV	Elizabeth Jefferson
COLORADO	A	Brighton	NEW MEXICO	A	Carlsbad
CONNECTICUT	L	Hartford Weaver	NORTH CAROLINA	AAA	Raleigh
FLORIDA	AA	Miami Senior	NORTH DAKOTA	A	Wahpeton
GEORGIA	AA	Columbus Baker	OHIO	A	Hamilton
IDAHO	A	Rexburg Madison	OKLAHOMA	AA	Capitol Hill
ILLINOIS		Mt. Vernon	OREGON		Milwaukie
INDIANA		Milan	PENNSYLVANIA	A	Farrell
IOWA		Muscatine	RHODE ISLAND		East Providence
KANSAS	AA	Wichita North			Senior
KENTUCKY		Inez	SOUTH CAROLINA	A	Orangeburg
LOUISIANA	AA	Baton Rouge	SOUTH DAKOTA	A	Deadwood
MAINE		Ellsworth	TENNESSEE		Nashville West End
MARYLAND	A	Allegheny	TEXAS	AAAA	Pampa
MASSACHUSETTS		Cathedral	UTAH	A	Jordan
MICHIGAN	A	Muskegon Heights	VERMONT		Rutland
MINNESOTA		Brainerd			Mt. St. Joseph
MISSISSIPPI		Walnut	VIRGINIA	I	Richmond Marshall
MISSOURI	A	Cape Giradeau	WASHINGTON	A	Seattle Franklin
		Central	WEST VIRGINIA	A	Beckley Wilson
MONTANA	A	Helena	WISCONSIN		Stevens Point
NEBRASKA	A	Hastings	WYOMING	A	Thermopolis

1954—55

STATE	CLASS	CHAMPION	STATE	CLASS	CHAMPION
ALABAMA	AA	Tuscaloosa	NEBRASKA	AA	Scottsbluff
ARIZONA	AA	Phoenix Union	NEVADA	A	Reno
ARKANSAS	A	Fort Smith	NEW HAMPSHIRE	A	Manchester Central
COLORADO	AA	Denver Man	NEW JERSEY	IV	Union City
CONNECTICUT	L	New Haven			Union Hill
		Hillhouse	NEW MEXICO	A	Carlsbad
FLORIDA	AA	Miami Senior	NORTH CAROLINA	AAA	Asheville
GEORGIA	AA	East Point Russell	NORTH DAKOTA	A	Minot
IDAHO	A	Kellogg	OHIO	A	Zanesville
ILLINOIS		Rockford West	OKLAHOMA	AA	Norman
INDIANA		Indianapolis	OREGON	A	Eugene
		Crispus Attucks	PENNSYLVANIA	A	McKeesport
IOWA		Ames	RHODE ISLAND		Westerly
KANSAS		Kansas City	SOUTH CAROLINA	AA	Spartanburg
		Wyandotte	SOUTH DAKOTA	A	Sioux Falls
KENTUCKY		Hazard			Washington
LOUISIANA	AAA	Lake Charles	TENNESSEE		Linden
MAINE		Bangor	TEXAS	AAAA	Dallas Crozier
MARYLAND	A	Montgomery Blair	UTAH	A	Jordan
MASSACHUSETTS	A	Somerville	VERMONT	A	Burlington
MICHIGAN	A	Jackson	VIRGINIA	I	Roanoke Jefferson
MINNESOTA		Minneapolis	WASHINGTON	A	Seattle (Garfield)
		Washburn	WEST VIRGINIA	A	Mullens
MISSISSIPPI		Wheeler	WISCONSIN		Eau Claire
MISSOURI	A	Joplin	WYOMING	A	Casper
MONTANA	A	Helena			

1955—56

STATE	CLASS	CHAMPION	STATE	CLASS	CHAMPION
ALABAMA	AA	Murphy	MONTANA	A	Butte Central
ARIZONA	AA	Phoenix Union	NEBRASKA		Boys Town
ARKANSAS	A	Jonesboro	NEVADA	A	Henderson Basic
COLORADO	AA	Greeley	NEW HAMPSHIRE	A	Concord
CONNECTICUT		Hartford Weaver	NEW JERSEY	IV	Union City
FLORIDA	AA	Miami Senior			Union Hill
GEORGIA	AA	Columbus Baker	NEW MEXICO	A	Hobbs
IDAHO	A	Kellogg	NORTH CAROLINA	AAA	Wilmington
ILLINOIS		Rockford West Sr.	NORTH DAKOTA	A	Grand Forks
INDIANA		Indianapolis	OHIO	A	Middletown
		Crispus Attucks	OKLAHOMA	AA	Tulsa Will Rogers
IOWA	A	Marshalltown	OREGON	A1	Portland Franklin
KANSAS	AA	Newton	PENNSYLVANIA	A	Farrell
KENTUCKY		Carr Creek	RHODE ISLAND		Westerly
LOUISIANA	AAA	New Orleans	SOUTH CAROLINA	AA	Columbia Dreher
		Fortier	SOUTH DAKOTA	A	Sioux Falls
MAINE	L	Bath (Morse)			Washington
MARYLAND	A	Northwestern	TENNESSEE		Linden
MASSACHUSETTS		West Worcester	UTAH	A	Provo
		Commerce	VERMONT		Springfield
MICHIGAN	A	Muskegon Heights	VIRGINIA	I	Newport News
MINNESOTA		Minneapolis	WASHINGTON	A	Seattle Lincoln
		Roosevelt	WEST VIRGINIA	A	East Bank
MISSISSIPPI		Nantachee	WISCONSIN		Shawano
MISSOURI	L	St. Louis	WYOMING	A	Cheyenne
		Beaumont			

1956—57

STATE	CLASS	CHAMPION	STATE	CLASS	CHAMPION
ALABAMA	AA	Woodlawn	KANSAS	AA	Kansas City
ALASKA		Anchorage			Wyandotte
ARKANSAS	A	Rogers	KENTUCKY		Lafayette
COLORADO	AA	Greeley	LOUISIANA	AAA	New Orleans
CONNECTICUT	L	Hartford Weaver			DeLaSalle
FLORIDA	AA	Lakeland	MAINE	L	Old Town
GEORGIA	AAA	Decatur	MARYLAND	A	Frederick
IDAHO	A	Pocatello	MASSACHUSETTS		Worcester West
ILLINOIS		Herrin	MICHIGAN	A	Muskegon Heights
INDIANA		South Bend Central	MINNESOTA		Minneapolis
IOWA	A	Des Moines			Roosevelt
		Dowling	MISSISSIPPI		Coffeville

STATE	CLASS	CHAMPION	STATE	CLASS	CHAMPION
MISSOURI	L	St. Charles	SOUTH CAROLINA	AA	Columbia Dreher
MONTANA	AA	Butte	SOUTH DAKOTA	A	Belle Fourche
NEBRASKA	AA	Boys Town	TENNESSEE		Linden
NEVADA	A	Fallon	TEXAS	AAAA	Port Arthur
NEW HAMPSHIRE	L	Manchester Central			Thom. Jefferson
NEW JERSEY	IV	Bloomfield	UTAH	A	Salt Lake City
NEW MEXICO	A	Hobbs			(South)
NORTH CAROLINA	AAA	Wilmington	VERMONT	A	Springfield
NORTH DAKOTA	A	Bismarck	VIRGINIA	I	Newport News
OHIO	AA	Middletown	WASHINGTON	A	Seattle Lincoln
OKLAHOMA	AA	Enid	WEST VIRGINIA	A	Beckley Wilson
OREGON	A1	Lincoln	WISCONSIN		Shawano
PENNSYLVANIA	A	Sharon	WYOMING	A	Cody
RHODE ISLAND	A	Providence			

1957—58

STATE	CLASS	CHAMPION	STATE	CLASS	CHAMPION
ALABAMA	AA	Fayette County	MISSISSIPPI		Philadelphia
ALASKA		Juneau	MISSOURI	A	St. Louis University
ARIZONA		Phoenix Union	MONTANA	AA	Butte
ARKANSAS	AA	Fort Smith	NEBRASKA	A	Lincoln
COLORADO	AA	Upper Denver	NEVADA	A	Las Vegas
CONNECTICUT	L	New Haven	NEW HAMPSHIRE	L	Manchester Bradley
		Wilbur Cross	NEW JERSEY	IV	Bloomfield
DISTRICT OF COLUMBIA		Cardozo	NEW MEXICO	A	Hobbs
FLORIDA	AA	Atlanta Murphy	NORTH CAROLINA	AAA	Wilmington
GEORGIA	AAA	Darien			New Hanover
IDAHO	AAA	Moreland	NORTH DAKOTA	A	Bismarck
		Snake River	OHIO	AA	Cleveland
ILLINOIS		Chicago Marshall			East Tech.
INDIANA		Fort Wayne	OKLAHOMA	AA	Tulsa Will Rogers
		(South Side)	OREGON	A1	Klamath Falls
IOWA	A	Davenport	PENNSYLVANIA	A	Haverford
KANSAS	AA	Kansas City	RHODE ISLAND		Westerly
		Wyandotte	S. CAROLINA	AAA	Spartanburg
KENTUCKY		Louisville St. Xavier	SOUTH DAKOTA	A	Huron
LOUISIANA	AAA	New Orleans	TENNESSEE		Lenoir City
		DeLaSalle	TEXAS	AAAA	Pampa
MAINE	A	South Portland	UTAH	A	Springville
MARYLAND	A	Cumberland	VERMONT	L	Rutland
		Fort Hill	VIRGINIA	III	Stuart
MASSACHUSETTS		Somerville East	WASHINGTON	AA	Richland
MICHIGAN	A	Detroit	WEST VIRGINIA	A	Parkersburg
		Austin Cath.	WISCONSIN		Madison East
MINNESOTA		Austin	WYOMING	A	Gillette

1958—59

STATE	CLASS	CHAMPION	STATE	CLASS	CHAMPION
ALABAMA	AA	Pisgah	MISSOURI		St. Louis
ALASKA		Fairbanks			Christian Bros.
ARIZONA		Phoenix Union	MONTANA	AA	Missoula
ARKANSAS	AA	Fort Smith	NEBRASKA	AA	Lincoln
COLORADO	AAA	Greeley	NEVADA	AA	Basic
DISTRICT OF COLUMBIA		Cardozo	NEW HAMPSHIRE	L	Nashua
GEORGIA	AAA	Atlanta Brown	NEW JERSEY	IV	Camden
HAWAII		Farrington	NEW MEXICO	A	Las Cruces
IDAHO	AAA	Kellogg	NORTH CAROLINA	AAA	Greensboro
ILLINOIS		Springfield	NORTH DAKOTA	A	Bismarck
INDIANA		Indianapolis	OHIO	AA	Cleveland
		Crispus Attucks			East Tech.
IOWA	A	Sioux Center	OKLAHOMA	AA	Norman
KANSAS	AA	Kansas City	OREGON	A-1	Portland (Franklin)
		Wyandotte	PENNSYLVANIA	A	Farrell
KENTUCKY		Calvert City	RHODE ISLAND		Providence Hope
		N. Marshall	SOUTH CAROLINA	AAA	Greenville Parker
LOUISIANA	AAA	New Orleans	SOUTH DAKOTA	A	Watertown
		DeLaSalle	TENNESSEE		Alcoa
MAINE		Bangor	UTAH	A	Bear River
MARYLAND	A	Bethesda	VERMONT	L	St. Albans
		Chevy Chase			Bellows Free
MICHIGAN	A	Lansing Sexton	VIRGINIA	I	Lynchburg
MINNESOTA		Wayzata			E. C. Glass
MISSISSIPPI		Wheeler	WASHINGTON	AA	Tacoma Stadium

STATE	CLASS	CHAMPION	STATE	CLASS	CHAMPION
WEST VIRGINIA	AAA	South Charleston	WYOMING	A	Sheridan
WISCONSIN		Milwaukee Lincoln			

1959–60

STATE	CLASS	CHAMPION	STATE	CLASS	CHAMPION
ALABAMA	AA	Tuscaloosa	MISSOURI		St. Louis (Christian Bros.)
ALASKA		Juneau	MONTANA	AA	Billings
ARIZONA	AA	Phoenix Union	NEBRASKA	A	Omaha South
ARKANSAS	AAA	Leachville	NEVADA	AA	Las Vegas
COLORADO	AAA	Greeley	NEW HAMPSHIRE	L	Nashua
CONNECTICUT	L	New Haven	NEW JERSEY	A	Camden
		Wilbur Cross	NEW MEXICO	A	Las Cruces
FLORIDA	AA	North Miami	NORTH CAROLINA		Wilmington
GEORGIA	AAA	Atlanta Sylvan	NORTH DAKOTA	A	Valley City
HAWAII		Honolulu	OHIO		Dayton Roosevelt
		Farrington	OKLAHOMA	AA	Enid
IDAHO	AAA	Idaho Falls	OREGON		Medford
ILLINOIS		Chicago Marshall	PENNSYLVANIA	A	Farrell
INDIANA		East Chicago	RHODE ISLAND		Westerly
		Washington	SOUTH CAROLINA	AAA	Anderson Boys'
IOWA	A	Marshalltown	SOUTH DAKOTA	A	Rapid City
KANSAS	AA	Kansas City	TENNESSEE		Hampton
		Wyandotte	TEXAS	AAAA	Beaumont S. Park.
KENTUCKY		Flaget	UTAH	A	Bingham
LOUISIANA	AAA	Bossier	VIRGINIA	I	Highland Springs
MAINE		Lewiston	WASHINGTON	AA	Renton
MARYLAND	A	Bladensburg	WEST VIRGINIA	AAA	Parkersburg
MICHIGAN	A	Lansing Sexton	WISCONSIN		Wausau
MINNESOTA		Edgerton	WYOMING	A	Rock Springs
MISSISSIPPI		Pass Christian N. Central			

1960–61

STATE	CLASS	CHAMPION	STATE	CLASS	CHAMPION
ALABAMA	AA	Tuscaloosa	MONTANA	AA	Missoula County
ALASKA		Juneau Douglas	NEBRASKA	A	Fremont
ARIZONA	AA	Phoenix Union	NEVADA	AA	Rancho
ARKANSAS	AA	Helena	NEW HAMPSHIRE	L	Portsmouth
COLORADO	AAA	Denver	NEW JERSEY	IV	Trenton
		Washington	NEW MEXICO	A	Las Cruces
CONNECTICUT	L	New Haven	NORTH CAROLINA	AAAA	Wilmington
		Wilbur Cross	NORTH DAKOTA	A	Minot
DISTRICT OF COLUMBIA		Spingarn	OHIO	AA	Portsmouth
FLORIDA	AA	St. Petersburg	OKLAHOMA	AA	Norman
		D. Hollins	OREGON	AI	Klamath Falls
GEORGIA	AAA	Atlanta Sylvan	PENNSYLVANIA	A	Nanticoke
IDAHO	AAA	Idaho Falls	RHODE ISLAND		Providence Hope
ILLINOIS		Collinsville	SOUTH CAROLINA	AAA	Columbia (Dreher)
INDIANA		Kokomo	SOUTH DAKOTA	A	Aberdeen Central
IOWA		Marshalltown	TENNESSEE		Oak Ridge
KANSAS	AA	Kansas City	TEXAS	AAAA	Houston Austin
		Wyandotte	UTAH	A	Davis
KENTUCKY		Ashland	VERMONT	L	Barre (Spaulding)
LOUISIANA	AAA	Baton Rouge	VIRGINIA	IA	Arlington Wakefield
MAINE	L	Portland Cheverus	WASHINGTON	AA	Seattle Garfield
MICHIGAN	A	Detroit Cath. Central	WEST VIRGINIA	AAA	Huntington
MINNESOTA		Duluth Central	WISCONSIN		Milwaukee Lincoln
MISSISSIPPI		Potts Camp	WYOMING	A	Cheyenne Central
MISSOURI	A	St. Louis University			

1961–62

STATE	CLASS	CHAMPION	STATE	CLASS	CHAMPION
ALABAMA	AA	Montgomery Lanier	FLORIDA	AA	St. Petersburg
ALASKA	A	Ketchikan			Hollins
ARIZONA	AA	Tucson	GEORGIA	AAA	Columbus
ARKANSAS	AAA	Jonesboro	HAWAII		Kamehameha
COLORADO	AAA	Greeley	IDAHO	AAA	Pocatello
CONNECTICUT	L	Hartford	ILLINOIS		Decatur
DISTRICT OF COLUMBIA		Eastern	INDIANA		Evansville Bosee

STATE	CLASS	CHAMPION	STATE	CLASS	CHAMPION
IOWA		Cedar Rapids Regis	NORTH DAKOTA	A	Rugby
KANSAS	AA	Wichita East	OHIO	AA	Hamilton Taft
KENTUCKY		Louisville St. Xavier	OKLAHOMA	AA	Lawton
LOUISIANA	AAA	New Orleans DeLaSalle	OREGON	A-1	Grants Press
			PENNSYLVANIA	A	Uniontown
MAINE	LL	Bath Morse	RHODE ISLAND		East Providence
MARYLAND	AA	Montgomery Blair	SOUTH CAROLINA	AAA	Greenville
MICHIGAN	A	Saginaw	SOUTH DAKOTA	A	Brookings
MINNESOTA		St. Louis Park	TENNESSEE		Cleveland
MISSISSIPPI		McComb	TEXAS	AAAA	Dallas Jefferson
MISSOURI	L	Columbia Hickman	UTAH	A	Jordan
MONTANA	AA	Great Falls	VERMONT	L	Barre Spaulding
NEBRASKA	A	Lincoln Northeast	VIRGINIA	L-A	Arlington Wash.-Lee
NEVADA	AA	Western			
NEW HAMPSHIRE	L	Concord	WASHINGTON	AA	Seattle Garfield
NEW JERSEY	IV	Newark Weequahic	WEST VIRGINIA		Beckley Wilson
NEW MEXICO	A	Albuquerque Sandia	WISCONSIN	A	Milwaukee Lincoln
NORTH CAROLINA	AAAA	Wilmington New Hanover	WYOMING		Cheyenne

1962–63

STATE	CLASS	CHAMPION	STATE	CLASS	CHAMPION
ALABAMA	AA	Montgomery Lanier	NEBRASKA	A	Omaha Technical
ALASKA	A	Juneau Douglas	NEVADA	AA	Reno
ARIZONA	AA	Tucson Catalina	NEW HAMPSHIRE	L	Manchester Bradley
ARKANSAS	AAA	Paragould	NEW JERSEY	IV	Newark Catholic
COLORADO	AAA	Wheat Ridge	NEW MEXICO	A	Roswell
CONNECTICUT	L	New Haven Hillhouse	NEW YORK	AA	Oneonta
			NORTH CAROLINA	AAAA	Rocky Mount
DISTRICT OF COLUMBIA		Eastern	NORTH DAKOTA	A	Williston
FLORIDA	AA	Pompano	OHIO	AA	Columbus East
GEORGIA	AAA	LaGrange	OKLAHOMA	A	Norman
HAWAII		Kamehameha	OREGON	A-1	North Eugene
IDAHO	AAA	Couer d'Alene	PENNSYLVANIA	A	Plymouth Meet. Whitemarsh
ILLINOIS		Chicago Carver			
INDIANA		Muncie Central	RHODE ISLAND		Newport Rogers
IOWA		Newton	SOUTH CAROLINA	AAA	Columbia Dreher
KANSAS	AA	Salina	SOUTH DAKOTA	A	Sisserton
KENTUCKY		Louisville Seneca	TENNESSEE		Oak Ridge
LOUISIANA	AAA	Fair Park	TEXAS	AAAA	San Angelo Central
MAINE	LL	Bath Morse	VERMONT	L	Barre (Spaulding)
MARYLAND	AA	Towson	VIRGINIA	IA	Arlington Wash.-Lee
MICHIGAN	A	Ferndale			
MINNESOTA		Marshall	WASHINGTON	AA	Seattle Blanchet
MISSISSIPPI		Bonneville	WEST VIRGINIA	AAA	Weirton
MISSOURI		St. Louis Christian Bros.	WISCONSIN		Manitowoc
			WYOMING	AA	Cheyenne Central
MONTANA	AA	Billings West			

1963–64

STATE	CLASS	CHAMPION	STATE	CLASS	CHAMPION
ALABAMA	AAAA	Tuscaloosa	MARYLAND	AA	Allegheny
ALASKA		Fairbanks Lathrop	MICHIGAN	A	Benton Harbor
ARIZONA	AA	Phoenix Camelback	MINNESOTA		Luverne
ARKANSAS	AA	N. Little Rock	MISSISSIPPI		Baldwin
COLORADO	AAA	Denver East	MISSOURI	L	St. Louis Bishop Dubourg
CONNECTICUT	L	New Haven Hillhouse			
			MONTANA	A	Missoula
DISTRICT OF COLUMBIA		Cardozo	NEBRASKA	A	Omaha Creighton
FLORIDA	AA	Pensacola	NEVADA	AA	Western
GEORGIA	AAA	Marietta Osborne	NEW HAMPSHIRE	L	Manchester Bradley
HAWAII		Hilo	NEW JERSEY	IV	Newark Central
IDAHO	A-1	Kellogg	NEW MEXICO	AA	Roswell
ILLINOIS		Pekin	NORTH CAROLINA	AAAA	Grimsley
INDIANA		Lafayette Jefferson	NORTH DAKOTA	A	Grafton
IOWA		Newton	OHIO	AA	Dayton Belmont
KANSAS	AA	Kansas City Wyandotte	OKLAHOMA	AA	Oklahoma City Classen
KENTUCKY		Louisville Seneca	OREGON		Portland Parkrose
LOUISIANA	AAA	New Orleans Jesuit	PENNSYLVANIA		Uniontown
MAINE	A	Millinocket Stearns	RHODE ISLAND		Pawtucket Tolman

STATE	CLASS	CHAMPION	STATE	CLASS	CHAMPION
SOUTH CAROLINA	AAA	Greenville	VIRGINIA	1-A	Newport News
SOUTH DAKOTA	A	Mitchell	WASHINGTON	AA	Vancouver
TENNESSEE		Donelson			Hudson's Bay
TEXAS	AAAA	Houston Austin	WEST VIRGINIA	AAA	Logan
UTAH	A	East	WISCONSIN		Dodgeville
VERMONT	L	Barre Spaulding	WYOMING	AA	Laramie

1964–65

STATE	CLASS	CHAMPION	STATE	CLASS	CHAMPION
ALABAMA	AAAA	Montgomery Lanier	MISSOURI	L	Springfield Parkview
ALASKA		Ketchikan	MONTANA	A	Great Falls
ARIZONA	AA	Tucson Rincon	NEBRASKA	A	Boys Town
ARKANSAS	AAA	Fort Smith	NEVADA	AA	Las Vegas
COLORADO	AAA	Denver East	NEW HAMPSHIRE	L	Portsmouth
CONNECTICUT	L	New Haven Hillhouse	NEW JERSEY	IV	Bridgewater-Raritan
			NEW MEXICO	AA	Albuquerque Valley
DISTRICT OF COLUMBIA		Cardozo	NORTH CAROLINA	AAAA	Fayetteville
FLORIDA	AA	Jacksonville Paxon	NORTH DAKOTA	A	Minot
GEORGIA	AAA	LaGrange	OHIO	AA	Columbus South
HAWAII	A	Kamehameha	OKLAHOMA	AA	Oklahoma City Northwest
IDAHO	A-1	Boise Borah	OREGON	A-1	Klamath Falls
ILLINOIS		Collinsville	PENNSYLVANIA	A	Midland
INDIANA		Indianapolis Washington	RHODE ISLAND		South Kingston
IOWA		Des Moines Roosevelt	SOUTH CAROLINA	AAA	Greenville
KANSAS	AA	Kansas City Wyandotte	SOUTH DAKOTA	A	Sioux Falls Washington
KENTUCKY		Breckinridge	TENNESSEE		Murfreesboro Central
LOUISIANA	AAA	Jesuit	TEXAS	AAAA	Houston Jones
MAINE	A	Millinocket Stearns	UTAH	A	Highland
MARYLAND	AA	Surrattsville	VERMONT	L	Bennington Catholic
MASSACHUSETTS		West Roxbury Cath. Memorial	VIRGINIA	I-A	Portsmouth Wilson
MICHIGAN	A	Benton Harbor	WASHINGTON	AA	Yakima Davis
MINNESOTA		Minnetonka	WEST VIRGINIA	AAA	Beckley Wilson
MISSISSIPPI	AA	Tupelo	WISCONSIN		Monroe
			WYOMING	AA	Laramie

1965–66

STATE	CLASS	CHAMPION	STATE	CLASS	CHAMPION
ALABAMA	AAAA	Huntsville Butler	MISSOURI	L	Kansas City Central
ALASKA		Ketchikan	MONTANA	A	Libby
ARIZONA	AA	Phoenix Camelback	NEBRASKA	A	Boys Town
ARKANSAS	AAA	Little Rock Central	NEVADA	AAA	Las Vegas
COLORADO	AAA	Denver Manual	NEW HAMPSHIRE	L	Winnacunnet
CONNECTICUT	LL	New Haven Wilbur Cross	NEW JERSEY	IV	Newark Weequahic
			NEW MEXICO	AA	Hobbs
DISTRICT OF COLUMBIA		McKinley	NORTH CAROLINA	AAAA	Fayetteville
FLORIDA	AA	Pensacola	NORTH DAKOTA	A	Mandan
GEORGIA	AAA	Augusta Butler	OHIO	AA	Dayton Chaminade
HAWAII	A	St. Louis	OKLAHOMA	AA	Tulsa Webster
IDAHO	A-1	Boise Borah	OREGON	A-1	Eugene North
ILLINOIS		Harvey Thornton Twp.	PENNSYLVANIA	A	Pittsburgh Schenley
INDIANA		Michigan City Elston	RHODE ISLAND		South Kingston
IOWA		Marshalltown	SOUTH CAROLINA	AAA	Anderson
KANSAS	AA	Garden City	SOUTH DAKOTA	A	Webster
KENTUCKY		Shelby County	TENNESSEE		Nashville Pearl
LOUISIANA	AA	North Caddo	TEXAS	AAAA	Houston Memorial
MAINE		Augusta Cony	UTAH	A	Highland
MARYLAND	AA	Richard Montgomery	VERMONT	L	Bennington Catholic
MASSACHUSETTS		Fall River	VIRGINIA	IA	Arlington Washington-Lee
MICHIGAN	A	Ferndale	WASHINGTON	AA	Renton
MINNESOTA		Edina	WEST VIRGINIA	AAA	Dunbar
MISSISSIPPI		Tupelo	WISCONSIN		Milwaukee Lincoln
			WYOMING	AA	Powell

1966–67

STATE	CLASS	CHAMPION	STATE	CLASS	CHAMPION
ALABAMA	AAAA	Sidney Lanier	ARIZONA	AA	Phoenix Union
ALASKA	A	Ketchikan	ARKANSAS	AAA	N. Little Rock

STATE	CLASS	CHAMPION	STATE	CLASS	CHAMPION
COLORADO	AAA	Denver Jefferson	MONTANA	A	Billings
CONNECTICUT	LL	New Haven	NEBRASKA	A	Lincoln Northeast
		Wilbur Cross	NEVADA	AAA	Las Vegas
DELAWARE		Mt. Pleasant	NEW HAMPSHIRE	L	Manchester Central
DISTRICT OF COLUMBIA		Cardozo	NEW JERSEY	IV	Newark Weequahic
FLORIDA	AA	St. Petersburg	NEW MEXICO	AA	Albuquerque Sandia
		Gibbs	NORTH CAROLINA	AAAA	Gastonia Ashley
GEORGIA	AAA	Savannah Beach	NORTH DAKOTA	A	Mandan
HAWAII		St. Louis	OHIO	AA	Columbus
IDAHO	A-1	Caldwell			McKinley
ILLINOIS		Pekin	OKLAHOMA	AAA	Bartlesville College
INDIANA		Evansville North	OREGON	A-1	David Douglas
IOWA	AA	Cedar Rapids	PENNSYLVANIA	A	Ambridge
		Jefferson	RHODE ISLAND	A	South Kingston
KANSAS	AA	Kansas City	SOUTH CAROLINA	AAA	Hanna
KENTUCKY	1-A	Earlington	SOUTH DAKOTA	A	Milbank
LOUISIANA	AAA	LaGrange	TENNESSEE		Alcoa
MAINE		Old Town	UTAH	A	Clearfield
MARYLAND	AA	Northwestern	VERMONT	L	Rutland
MASSACHUSETTS		Melrose	VIRGINIA	L-A	Lynchburg Glass
MICHIGAN	A	Detroit Pershing	WASHINGTON	AA	Renton
MINNESOTA		Edina	WEST VIRGINIA	AAA	Beckley Wilson
MISSISSIPPI		Forest Hill	WISCONSIN		Milwaukee Lincoln
MISSOURI	L	Joplin	WYOMING	AA	Cheyenne Central

1967–68

STATE	CLASS	CHAMPION	STATE	CLASS	CHAMPION
ALABAMA	AAAA	Lee	MONTANA	A	Wolf Point
ALASKA		Ketchikan	NEBRASKA	A	Lincoln Northeast
ARIZONA	AA	Phoenix Union	NEVADA	AA	Clark
ARKANSAS	AAA	Fort Smith	NEW HAMPSHIRE	L	Dover
		Northside	NEW JERSEY	IV	Perth Amboy
COLORADO	AAA	Wheat Ridge	NEW MEXICO	AA	Hobbs
CONNECTICUT	LL	New Haven	NORTH CAROLINA	AAAA	New Hanover
		Wilbur Cross	NORTH DAKOTA	A	Williston
DELAWARE		Wilmington	OHIO	AA	Columbus East
		P. S. DuPont	OKLAHOMA	AAA	Oklahoma City Northwest
DISTRICT OF COLUMBIA		McKinley			
FLORIDA	AA	Key West	OREGON	A-1	McNary
GEORGIA	AAA	Savannah Johnson	PENNSYLVANIA	A	Laurel Highlands
HAWAII		St. Louis	RHODE ISLAND	A	Sacred Heart Academy
IDAHO	A-1	Boise Capital			
ILLINOIS		Evanston Twp.	SOUTH CAROLINA	AAA	Spartanburg
INDIANA		Gary Roosevelt	SOUTH DAKOTA	A	Brookings
IOWA	AA	Storm Lake	TENNESSEE		Chattanooga Riverside
KANSAS	AA	Kansas City			
		Wyandotte	TEXAS	AAAA	Houston Wheatley
KENTUCKY		Glasgow	UTAH	A	Hillcrest
LOUISIANA	AAA	Baton Rouge	VERMONT	L	Rice Memorial
MAINE	LL	Millinockett Stearns	VIRGINIA	L-A	Salem Andrew Lewis
MARYLAND	AA	Northwestern			
MASSACHUSETTS		Boston English	WASHINGTON	AA	Spokane Central Valley
MICHIGAN	A	Grand Rapids Ottawa Hills	WEST VIRGINIA	AAA	Charleston
MINNESOTA		Edina	WISCONSIN		Manitowoc
MISSISSIPPI		Tupelo	WYOMING	AA	Lander Fremont Vocational
MISSOURI	L	St. Louis O'Fallon			

1968–69

STATE	CLASS	CHAMPION	STATE	CLASS	CHAMPION
ALABAMA	AAAA	Birmingham Parker	ILLINOIS		Proviso East
ALASKA	AA	Juneau Douglas	INDIANA		Indianapolis Washington
ARIZONA	AAA	Tucson			
ARKANSAS	AAA	North Little Rock	IOWA	AA	Washington
COLORADO	AAA	Denver South	KANSAS	AAAAA	Kansas City Wyandotte
CONNECTICUT	LL	Hillhouse			
DELAWARE		De La Warr	KENTUCKY		Louisville Central
DISTRICT OF COLUMBIA		McKinley	LOUISIANA	AAA	Shreveport Woodlawn
FLORIDA	AA	Gainesville	MAINE	LL	Caribou
GEORGIA	AAA	Mark Smith	MARYLAND	AA	Montgomery Blair
HAWAII		Radford	MASSACHUSETTS		Catholic Memorial
IDAHO	A-1	Pocatello			

STATE	CLASS	CHAMPION	STATE	CLASS	CHAMPION
MICHIGAN	A	Grand Rapids Ottawa Hills	OKLAHOMA	AAA	Tulsa Central
MINNESOTA		Rochester John Marshall	OREGON	A-1	Grant
			PENNSYLVANIA	A	Farrell
MISSISSIPPI		New Site	RHODE ISLAND	A	Central
MISSOURI	L	St. Louis Sumner	SOUTH CAROLINA	AAAA	A. C. Flora
MONTANA	A	Laurel	SOUTH DAKOTA	A	Rapid City
NEBRASKA	A	Omaha Creighton	TENNESSEE		Chattanooga Riverside
NEVADA	AA	Clark	TEXAS	AAAA	Houston Wheatley
NEW HAMPSHIRE	L	Nashua	UTAH	A	Bountiful
NEW JERSEY	IV	East Orange	VERMONT	L	Burlington
NEW MEXICO	AA	Hobbs	VIRGINIA	1-A	Hampton
NORTH CAROLINA	AAAA	Atkins	WASHINGTON	AAA	Ingraham
NORTH DAKOTA	A	Grand Forks Red River	WEST VIRGINIA	AAA	Huntington
			WISCONSIN		Beloit Memorial
OHIO	AA	Columbus East	WYOMING	AA	Laramie

1969–70

STATE	CLASS	CHAMPION	STATE	CLASS	CHAMPION
ALABAMA	AAAA	Decatur	MISSOURI	L	Raytown South
ALASKA	AA	East Anchorage	MONTANA	AA	Kalispell
ARIZONA	AAA	Tucson Sahuaro	NEBRASKA	A	Lincoln Northeast
ARKANSAS	AAAA	Little Rock Central	NEVADA	AA	Clark
COLORADO	AAA	Denver South	NEW HAMPSHIRE	L	Manchester Memorial
CONNECTICUT	LL	Hillhouse			
DELAWARE		Delaware	NEW JERSEY	IV	Woodrow Wilson
DISTRICT OF COLUMBIA		Eastern	NEW MEXICO	AAAA	Hobbs
FLORIDA	AA	Pensacola Washington	NORTH CAROLINA	AAAA	South Mecklenberg
			NORTH DAKOTA	A	Grand Forks Central
GEORGIA	AAA	Decatur			
HAWAII	A	Punahou	OHIO	AA	Dayton Chaminade
IDAHO	A-4	Oakley	OKLAHOMA	AAAA	Norman
ILLINOIS		LaGrange Lyons Twp.	OREGON	A-1	Corvalis
			PENNSYLVANIA	A	Beaver Falls
INDIANA		East Chicago Roosevelt	RHODE ISLAND	A	Central
			SOUTH CAROLINA	AAAA	Wade Hampton
IOWA	AA	Davenport Central	SOUTH DAKOTA	A	Sioux Falls Lincoln
KANSAS	AAAAA	Kansas City Wyandotte	TENNESSEE		Nashville Cameron
			TEXAS	AAAA	Wheatley
KENTUCKY		Louisville Male	UTAH	AA	East
LOUISIANA	AAA	Brother Martin	VERMONT	L	Rice Memorial
MAINE	LL	Stearns	VIRGINIA	1-A	Jefferson Senior
MARYLAND	AA	Duvall	WASHINGTON	AAA	Snohomish
MASSACHUSETTS	A	Boston English	WEST VIRGINIA	AAA	Parkersburg
MICHIGAN	A	Detroit Pershing	WISCONSIN		Appleton West
MINNESOTA		Sherburn	WYOMING	AA	Casper
MISSISSIPPI	AA	Gulfport			

1970–71

STATE	CLASS	CHAMPION	STATE	CLASS	CHAMPION
ALABAMA	AAAA	Birmingham Parker	MAINE	A	South Portland
ALASKA		Anchorage Dimond	MARYLAND	AA	College Park Parkdale
ARIZONA	AAA	Phoenix East			
ARKANSAS	AAAA	North Little Rock	MASSACHUSETTS	Large	Lexington
COLORADO	AAA	Colorado Springs Gen. Mitchell	MICHIGAN	A	Flint Northern
			MINNESOTA	AA	Duluth Central
CONNECTICUT	LL	Hartford Weaver	MISSISSIPPI	AA	Greenville
DELAWARE		Milford	MISSOURI	L	St. Louis Vashon
DISTRICT OF COLUMBIA		McKinley	MONTANA	AA	Helena Senior
FLORIDA	AA	West Palm Beach Twin Lakes	NEBRASKA	A	Lincoln East
			NEVADA	AAA	Las Vegas Western
GEORGIA	AAA	Columbus Carver	NEW HAMPSHIRE	L	Manchester Memorial
HAWAII	A	Kahuku			
IDAHO	AAAA	Oakley	NEW JERSEY	IV	Bloomfield
ILLINOIS		Dolton Thornridge	NEW MEXICO	AAAA	Albuquerque
INDIANA		East Chicago Washington	NORTH CAROLINA	AAAA	Charlotte South Mecklenberg
IOWA	AA	Davenport West	NORTH DAKOTA	A	Minot Central
KANSAS	AAAA	Wichita Southeast	OHIO	AAA	Columbus Walnut Ridge
KENTUCKY		Louisville Male			
LOUISIANA	AAAA	New Orleans Brother Martin	OKLAHOMA	AAAA	Tulsa Central
			OREGON	AAA	Portland Benson

STATE	CLASS	CHAMPION	STATE	CLASS	CHAMPION
PENNSYLVANIA	A	Pittsburgh Schenley	UTAH	AA	Ogden Weber
RHODE ISLAND	A	Providence Central	VERMONT	L	South Burlington Rice Memorial
SOUTH CAROLINA	AAAA	Greenville Wade Hampton	VIRGINIA	AAA	Richmond Maggie Walker
SOUTH DAKOTA	A	Sioux Falls Washington	WASHINGTON	AAA	Puyallup
TENNESSEE		Nashville Cameron	WEST VIRGINIA	AAA	Charleston George Washington
TEXAS	AAAA	Houston Cy-Fair	WYOMING	AA	Rock Springs

1971—72

STATE	CLASS	CHAMPION	STATE	CLASS	CHAMPION
ALABAMA	AAAA	Birmingham West End	NEVADA	AAA	Las Vegas
			NEW HAMPSHIRE	L	Milford
ARIZONA	AAA	Phoenix Maryvale	NEW JERSEY	IV	Westfield
ARKANSAS	AAAA	Little Rock Central	NEW MEXICO	AAAA	Albuquerque
COLORADO	AAA	Denver Manual			Highland
CONNECTICUT	LL	New Haven Wilbur Cross	NORTH CAROLINA	AAAA	Charlotte S. Mecklenburg
DELAWARE		Wilmington		(girls)	Bethel North Pitt
DISTRICT OF COLUMBIA		Eastern	NORTH DAKOTA	A	Bismarck St. Mary's
FLORIDA	AAAA	Miami Carol City Opa-Locka	OHIO	AAA	Cleveland East Tech
			OKLAHOMA	AAAA	Oklahoma City Putnam City
GEORGIA	AAA	Savannah		AA (girls)	Mangum
HAWAII	AA	Honolulu Kailua			
IDAHO	A	Moscow	OREGON	AAA	Portland Jefferson
ILLINOIS	AA	Dolton Thornridge	PENNSYLVANIA	A	Farrell
INDIANA		Connersville	RHODE ISLAND		Providence Central
IOWA	AA	Cedar Rapids Kennedy	SOUTH CAROLINA	AAAA	Charleston Middleton
				AAAA (girls)	Beaufort
KANSAS	AAAAA	Wichita East	SOUTH DAKOTA	A	Miller
KENTUCKY		Owensboro	TENNESSEE		Chattanooga Riverside
LOUISIANA	AAAA	Shreveport Woodlawn		(girls)	Lewisburg Marshall County
MAINE	A	Westbrook			
MARYLAND	AA	Springbrook	TEXAS	AAAA	Dallas Roosevelt
MASSACHUSETTS	I	Lexington	UTAH	AAA	Kearns
MICHIGAN	A	Flint Northern	VERMONT	L	Burlington
MINNESOTA	AA	St. Paul Mount View	VIRGINIA	AAA	Hopewell
			WASHINGTON	AAA	Richland Columbia
MISSISSIPPI	AA	Hattiesburg	WEST VIRGINIA	AAA	Fairlea Greenbrier East
	AA (girls)	South Panola			
MISSOURI	L	Raytown South	WISCONSIN	A	Milwaukee Hamilton
MONTANA	AA	Missoula Sentinel			
NEBRASKA	A	Columbus	WYOMING	AA	Rock Springs

1972—73

STATE	CLASS	CHAMPION	STATE	CLASS	CHAMPION
ALABAMA	AAAA	Decatur Austin	MICHIGAN	A	Detroit Southwestern
ALASKA		Juneau	MINNESOTA	AA	Anoka
ARIZONA	AAA	Phoenix East	MISSISSIPPI	AA	Callaway
ARKANSAS	AAAA	L. R. Central		AA (girls)	Louisville
COLORADO	AAA	Colorado Spgs. Gen. Mitchell	MISSOURI	M	St. Louis Lutheran South
CONNECTICUT	LL	New Haven Wilbur Cross		(girls)	Ravenwood N. E. Nodaway
DELAWARE		Wilmington Howard	MONTANA	AA	Missoula Sentinel
FLORIDA	AAAA	Winter Haven	NEBRASKA	A	Lincoln Northeast
GEORGIA	AAA	Macon Southwest	NEVADA	AAA	N. Las Vegas Rancho
	AAA (girls)	Canton Cherokee	NEW HAMPSHIRE	L	Manchester West
HAWAII	AA	Wahiawa Leilehua	NEW JERSEY	IV	Newark Weequahic
IDAHO	AAAA	Murtaugh	NEW MEXICO	AAAA	Albuquerque Manzana
ILLINOIS	AA	Chicago Hirsch		(girls)	San Jon High
INDIANA		New Albany			
IOWA	AA	Ames	NORTH CAROLINA	AAAA	Reidsville
KANSAS	AAAAA	Topeka		(girls)	Denver East Lincoln
KENTUCKY		Louisville Shawnee	NORTH DAKOTA	A	Fort Yates
LOUISIANA	AAAA	N. O. Booker T. Washington	OHIO	AAA	Cincinnati Elder
			OKLAHOMA	AAAA	Oklahoma City Capitol Hill
MAINE	A	Augusta Cony		(girls)	Elk City
MARYLAND	AA	Bladensburg			
MASSACHUSETTS	I	Worcester Holy Name	OREGON	AAA	Portland Benson

STATE	CLASS	CHAMPION	STATE	CLASS	CHAMPION
PENNSYLVANIA	A	Braddock	TEXAS	AAAA	Houston Wheatley
(girls)		Allentown Central	UTAH	AAAA	Provo
		Catholic	VERMONT	L	Burlington
RHODE ISLAND		Providence Central	VIRGINIA	AAA	Petersburg
SOUTH CAROLINA	AAAA	Columbia Eau Claire	WASHINGTON	AAA	Seattle Roosevelt
	AAAA (girls)	Easley	WEST VIRGINIA	AAA	Charleston
SOUTH DAKOTA	A	Huron	WISCONSIN	A	Beloit Memorial
TENNESSEE	L	Gallatin	WYOMING	AA	Rock Springs
	L (girls)	Cleveland Bradley County			

1973–74

STATE	CLASS	CHAMPION	STATE	CLASS	CHAMPION
ALABAMA	AAAA	Birmingham Hayes	MONTANA	AA	Billings West
ALASKA		Ketchikan		(girls)	Anaconda
	(girls)	Anchorage Service	NEBRASKA	A	Omaha Central
ARIZONA	AAA	Phoenix Alhambra	NEVADA	AAA	Las Vegas
ARKANSAS	AAAA	Fort Smith Northside	NEW HAMPSHIRE	L	Manchester Central
	(girls)	Wilson Rivercrest	NEW JERSEY	IV	East Orange
COLORADO	AAA	Denver Bear Creek		(girls)	Gloucester Catholic
CONNECTICUT	LL	New Haven W. Cross	NEW MEXICO	AAAA	Albuquerque
	L (girls)	Trumbull			Manzana
DISTRICT OF COLUMBIA		A. B. Williamson		(girls)	Amistad
DELAWARE		Wilmington	NORTH CAROLINA	AAAA	Henderson Vance
	(girls)	Wilmington Ursuline		(girls)	Four Oaks
FLORIDA	AAAA	Miami Jackson			South Johnston
GEORGIA	AAA	Savannah	NORTH DAKOTA	A	Grand Forks Central
	AAA (girls)	Waycross	OHIO	AAA	Cincinnati Elder
HAWAII	AA	Punahou	OKLAHOMA	AAAA	Tulsa Memorial
IDAHO	AAAA	Fairfield Camas		AA (girls)	Fairview
		County	OREGON	AAA	Portland Benson
ILLINOIS	AA	Maywood Proviso	PENNSYLVANIA	A	Abington
		East		(girls)	Lancaster Catholic
INDIANA		Fort Wayne	RHODE ISLAND		Providence Central
IOWA	AA	Waterloo East	SOUTH CAROLINA	AAAA	Charleston
KANSAS	AAAAA	Hutchinson			Middleton
	AAAAA			AAAA	
	(girls)	Wichita South		(girls)	Easley
KENTUCKY		Louisville Central	SOUTH DAKOTA	A	Yankton
LOUISIANA	AAAA	New Orleans	TENNESSEE	L	Memphis Melrose
		Bro. Martin		L (girls)	Shelbyville Central
	AAAA		TEXAS	AAAA	Houston Kashmere
	(girls)	DeRidder		AAA (girls)	Canyon
MAINE	A	Rumford	UTAH	AAAA	Provo
MARYLAND	AA	Annapolis	VERMONT	L	Mt. Anthony
	(girls)	Sherwood			Bennington
MASSACHUSETTS	I	Boston English		L (girls)	Hinesburg Champlain
MICHIGAN	A	Birmingham Rice	VIRGINIA	AAA	Petersburg
	A (girls)	Detroit Dominican	WASHINGTON	AAA	Seattle Garfield
MINNESOTA	AA	Bemidji	WISCONSIN	A	Superior
MISSISSIPPI		Hattiesburg	WEST VIRGINIA	AAA	Charleston
	(girls)	Amory Hatley	WYOMING	AA	Casper Kelly Walsh
MISSOURI	AAAA	Florissant McCluer			
	(girls)	Shelbina South			
		Shelby			

1974–75

STATE	CLASS	CHAMPION	STATE	CLASS	CHAMPION
ALABAMA	AAAA	Birmingham A. H. Parker	FLORIDA	AAAA	Orlando Maynard Evans
ALASKA		Anchorage East	GEORGIA	AAA	Macon Southwest
	(girls)	Valdez		AAA	
ARIZONA	AAA	Phoenix East		(girls)	Macon Northeast
	(girls)	Valley Union	HAWAII	AA	Honolulu Punahou
ARKANSAS	AAAA	Little Rock Central	IDAHO	AAAA	Deary
	A (girls)	Stephens	ILLINOIS	AA	Chicago
COLORADO	AAA	Westminster			Wendell Phillips
CONNECTICUT	LL	Bridgeport Central	INDIANA		Marion
	L (girls)	New Haven Lee	IOWA	AAA	Des Moines Lincoln
DELAWARE		Lewes Cape Henlcpen	KANSAS	AAAAA	Hutchinson
	(girls)	Wilmington Ursuline		AAAA	
DISTRICT OF COLUMBIA		Dunbar		(girls)	Wichita North

248

STATE	CLASS	CHAMPION	STATE	CLASS	CHAMPION
KENTUCKY		Louisville Male		(girls)	Newton Foard
	(girls)	Louisville Butler	NORTH DAKOTA	A	Williston
LOUISIANA	AAAA	Bastrop		A (girls)	Jamestown
	AAAA		OHIO	AAA	Columbus Linden McKinley
	(girls)	DeRidder	OKLAHOMA	AAAA	Muskogee
MAINE	A	Westbrook		AAA	
	A (girls)	Gardiner		(girls)	Choctaw
MARYLAND	AA	Silver Spring Montgomery	OREGON	AAA	Beaverton Sunset
	(girls)	Bladensburg	PENNSYLVANIA	A	Pittsburgh Schenley
MASSACHUSETTS	I	Boston English		(girls)	Allentown Dieruff
	(girls)	West Hampton Hampshire	RHODE ISLAND		Providence Central
MICHIGAN	A	Highland Park	SOUTH CAROLINA	AAAA	Columbia Keenas
	A (girls)	Detroit Dominican		AAAA	
MINNESOTA	AA	Little Falls		(girls)	Aiken
MISSISSIPPI		Gulfport	SOUTH DAKOTA	A	Aberdeen Roncalli
	(girls)	Houlka	TENNESSEE	L	Memphis Northside
MISSOURI	AAAA	Florissant McCluer		L (girls)	Cleveland Bradley Central
	AA (girls)	St. Louis, St. Joseph Acad.	TEXAS	AAAA	Houston Kashmere Gardens
MONTANA	AA	Billings West		AAA (girls)	Waco Midway
	A (girls)	Great Falls	UTAH	AAAA	West
NEBRASKA	A	Omaha Central	VERMONT	L	Bennington Mt. Anthony
NEVADA	AAA	Carson City		L (girls)	Burlington
NEW HAMPSHIRE	L	Manchester Trinity	VIRGINIA	AAA	Richmond Thomas Jefferson
	AA (girls)	Concord	WASHINGTON	AAA	Tacoma Lincoln
NEW JERSEY	I	East Orange Clifford Scott		(girls)	Bellevue
	(girls)	Asbury Park	WEST VIRGINIA	AAA	Barboursville
NEW MEXICO	AAAA	Las Cruces	WISCONSIN	A	Neenah
	AA (girls)	Albuquerque Eldorado	WYOMING	AA	Casper Kelly Walsh
NORTH CAROLINA	AAAA	Winston-Salem R. J. Reynolds			

1975—76

STATE	CLASS	CHAMPION	STATE	CLASS	CHAMPION
ALABAMA	AAAA	Florence Bradshaw		AAAA	
ALASKA	A	Anchorage Dimond		(girls)	DeRidder
	(girls)	Fairbanks East Lathrop	MAINE	A	Rumford
ARIZONA	AAA	Chandler		A (girls)	Hampden Academy
	AAA (girls)	Tuba City	MARYLAND	AA	Riverdale Parkdale
ARKANSAS	AAAA	ElDorado		AA (girls)	Bladensburg
	AA (girls)	Alma	MASSACHUSETTS	I	Don Bosco
COLORADO	AAA	Denver Manual		I (girls)	Brockton
CONNECTICUT	LL	New Haven Lee	MICHIGAN	A	Detroit Catholic Center
	LL (girls)	Shelton		A (girls)	Detroit Northeastern
DELAWARE		Lewes Cape Henlopen	MINNESOTA	AA	Bloomington Jefferson
	(girls)	New Castle Wm. Penn		AA (girls)	St. Paul Central
DISTRICT OF COLUMBIA		Dunbar	MISSISSIPPI	AA	Gulfport
FLORIDA	AAAA	Edgewater		AA (girls)	Lucedale George County
	AAAA		MISSOURI	AAAA	Kansas City Center
	(girls)	Fletcher		AA (girls)	Edina Knox County
GEORGIA	AAA	Savannah	MONTANA	AA	Great Falls
	AAA (girls)	Canton Cherokee		A (girls)	Great Falls C. M. Russell
HAWAII	AA	Honolulu	NEBRASKA	A	Omaha Creighton Prep.
IDAHO	A-1	Boise Capital	NEVADA	AAA	Las Vegas
	A (girls)	Pocatello	NEW HAMPSHIRE	L	Manchester Trinity
ILLINOIS	AA	Chicago Morgan Park		AA (girls)	Milford
INDIANA		Marion	NEW JERSEY	IV	Plainfield
	(girls)	Warsaw		IV (girls)	Martinsville Bridgewater-Raritan
IOWA	AAA	Ames	NEW MEXICO	AAAA	Las Cruces
KANSAS	AAAAA	Kansas City Wyandotte		AA (girls)	Albuquerque Eldorado
	AAAAA		NORTH CAROLINA	AAAA	Charlotte South Mecklenburg
	(girls)	Hutchinson		(girls)	Cameron Union Pines
KENTUCKY		Brownsville Edmonson County			
	(girls)	Louisville Sacred Heart			
LOUISIANA	AAAA	New Orleans L. B. Landry			

STATE	CLASS	CHAMPION	STATE	CLASS	CHAMPION
NORTH DAKOTA	A	Jamestown	TEXAS	AAAA	El Paso Eastwood
	A (girls)	Williston		AAAA	
OHIO	AAA	Barberton		(girls)	Duncanville
	AAA (girls)	Toledo Woodward	UTAH	AAAA	Salt Lake Skyline
OKLAHOMA	AAAA	Spencer		AAAA	
		Star-Spencer		(girls)	Midvale Hillcrest
	AAA (girls)	Woodward	VERMONT	L	Bennington
OREGON	AAA	North Eugene			Mt. Anthony
	AAA (girls)	South Salem		L (girls)	Burlington
PENNSYLVANIA	AAA	Pittsburgh	VIRGINIA	AAA	Maggie Walker-
		Fifth Avenue			Richmond
	AAA (girls)	Allentown Dieruff		AAA (girls)	Woodbridge Garfield
RHODE ISLAND		Providence East	WASHINGTON	AAA	Seattle Cleveland
SOUTH CAROLINA	AAAA	Charleston Burke		AAA (girls)	Bellevue Sammanish
	AAAA		WEST VIRGINIA	AAA	Wheeling
	(girls)	West Florence	WISCONSIN	A	South Milwaukee
SOUTH DAKOTA	A	Sioux Falls Lincoln		A (girls)	Madison West
	A (girls)	Yankton	WYOMING	AA	Rock Springs
TENNESSEE	AAA	Nashville McGavock		AA (girls)	Cheyenne East
	AAA (girls)	Cleveland Bradley			
		Central			

1976–77

STATE	CLASS	CHAMPION	STATE	CLASS	CHAMPION
ALABAMA	AAAA	Selma	MINNESOTA	AA	Prior Lake
ALASKA	A	Anchorage		AA (girls)	Burnsville
		East Fairbanks	MISSISSIPPI	AA	Florence
	(girls)	Anchorage Bartlett		AA (girls)	Gulfport
ARIZONA	AAA	Tucson Pueblo			Harrison Central
	AA (girls)	Snowflake	MISSOURI	AAAA	Raytown
ARKANSAS	AAAA	Pine Bluff		AAA (girls)	Hickman Mills
	AA (girls)	Lonoke	MONTANA	AA	Great Falls
COLORADO	AAA	Boulder			Charles M. Russell
	AAA (girls)	Wheat Ridge		A (girls)	Havre
CONNECTICUT	LL	Norwalk	NEBRASKA	A	Omaha Burke
		Brien McMahon		A (girls)	Lincoln
	LL (girls)	New Haven Lee	NEVADA	AAA	Las Vegas Rancho
DELAWARE		Wilmington		AAA (girls)	Las Vegas Rancho
		Brandywine	NEW HAMPSHIRE	L	Dover
	(girls)	Greenville		AA (girls)	Dover
		Alexis I. DuPont	NEW JERSEY	IV	North Bergen
DISTRICT OF COLUMBIA		McKinley		IV (girls)	Nutley
	(girls)	Eastern	NEW MEXICO	AAAA	Albuquerque
FLORIDA	AAAA	Orlando Boone		AAAA	
	AAAA			(girls)	Clovis
	(girls)	Plantation	NORTH CAROLINA	AAAA	Gastonia Hunter Huss
GEORGIA	AAA	Lagrange		AAAA	
	AAA (girls)	Valdosta Lowndes		(girls)	Southern Pines
HAWAII	AA	Honolulu			Pinecrest
IDAHO	A-1	Boise Capital	NORTH DAKOTA	A	Fargo North
	A-1 (girls)	Boise Capital		A (girls)	Williston
ILLINOIS	AA	Peoria	OHIO	AAA	Columbus
	(girls)	Sterling			Linden-McKinley
INDIANA		Carmel		AAA (girls)	Springfield North
IOWA	AAA	Iowa City West	OKLAHOMA	AAAA	Spencer
KANSAS	AAAAA	Wichita-Heights			Star-Spencer
	AAAAA			AAA (girls)	Woodward
	(girls)	Wichita North	OREGON	AAA	Eugene North
KENTUCKY		Louisville		AAA (girls)	Portland Wilson
		Ballard	PENNSYLVANIA	AAA	Pittsburgh
	(girls)	London Laurel			Fox Chapel
		County		AAA (girls)	Norristown
LOUISIANA	AAAA	New Orleans Rummel	RHODE ISLAND		Providence Our Lady
	AAAA				of Providence
	(girls)	Hammond		(girls)	Pawtucket Tolman
MAINE	A	Rumford	SOUTH CAROLINA	AAAA	Charleston
	A (girls)	South Portland			Middleton
MARYLAND	AA	Silver Spring		AAAA	Mt. Pleasant
		Montgomery-Blair		(girls)	Wando
	AA (girls)	Lanham DuVal	SOUTH DAKOTA	A	Aberdeen Central
MASSACHUSETTS	I	Fall River Durfee		A (girls)	Watertown
	I (girls)	Chicopee	TENNESSEE	AAA	Knoxville
		Comprehensive			Austin-East
MICHIGAN	A	Lansing Everett		AAA (girls)	Mt. Juliet
	A (girls)	Marquette			

STATE	CLASS	CHAMPION	STATE	CLASS	CHAMPION
TEXAS	AAAA	Dallas S. Oak Cliff		AAA (girls)	Hampton Phoebus
	AAAA (girls)	Dallas S. Oak Cliff	WASHINGTON	AAA	Mountlake Terrace
UTAH	AAAA	Salt Lake Skyline		AAA (girls)	Bellevue Sammanish
	AAAA (girls)	Clearfield	WEST VIRGINIA	AAA	Logan
VERMONT	L	Burlington		AAA (girls)	Dunbar
	L (girls)	Bellows Falls	WISCONSIN	A	Madison LaFollette
VIRGINIA	AAA	Alexandria T. C. Williams		A (girls)	Watertown
			WYOMING	AA	Sheridan

1977—78

STATE	CLASS	CHAMPION	STATE	CLASS	CHAMPION
ALABAMA	AAAA	Carver Birmingham	MISSOURI	AAAA	DeSmet Jesuit St. Louis
	AAAA (girls)	Jeff Davis		AAA (girls)	Lee's Summit
ALASKA		East Anchorage	MONTANA	AA	Bozeman Senior
	(girls)	Bartlett		AA (girls)	C. M. Russell Great Falls
ARIZONA	AAA	Pueblo	NEBRASKA	A	Lincoln East
	AAA (girls)	Chaparral		A (girls)	Omaha Burke
ARKANSAS	Overall	Parkview	NEVADA	AAA	Bishop Gorman
	Overall (girls)	Stephens		AAA (girls)	Eldorado
COLORADO	AAA	Colorado Springs Wasson	NEW HAMPSHIRE	L	Nashua
	AAA (girls)	Arvada West		L (girls)	Manchester Central
CONNECTICUT	LL	Hillhouse New Haven	NEW JERSEY	IV	Snyder Jersey City
	LL (girls)	Richard C. Lee New Haven		IV (girls)	Passaic Valley Little Falls
DELAWARE	Open	Wilmington	NEW YORK	AAA	Mt. Vernon
	Open (girls)	John Dickinson Wilmington	NORTH CAROLINA	AAAA	Rocky Mount
DISTRICT OF COLUMBIA		Dunbar		AAAA (girls)	Garner
	(girls)	Eastern	NORTH DAKOTA	A	Jamestown
FLORIDA	AAAA	Miami Central Miami		A (girls)	Williston
	AAAA (girls)	Boone Orlando	OHIO	A	Mansfield St. Peters
GEORGIA	AAA	Southwest Macon		A (girls)	Ada
	AAA (girls)	Lowndes Valdosta	OKLAHOMA	AAAA	John Marshall Oklahoma City
HAWAII	AA	University Maryknoll		AAAA (girls)	Moore
ILLINOIS	A	Nashville	OREGON	AAA	Parkrose
	(girls)	Joliet West		AAA (girls)	Crescent Valley
INDIANA		Muncie	PENNSYLVANIA	AAA	Fox Chapel
	(girls)	Warsaw		AAA (girls)	Norristown
IOWA	AAA	Roosevelt Des Moines	RHODE ISLAND		Central Providence
KANSAS	AAAAA	Wichita South		(girls)	St. Xavier's Providence
	AAAAA (girls)	Wichita South	SOUTH CAROLINA	AAAA	Orangeburg Wilkinson
KENTUCKY		Shelby County Shelbyville		AAAA (girls)	Spring Valley
	(girls)	Laurel County London	SOUTH DAKOTA	A	Yankton
LOUISIANA	AAAA	Rummel New Orleans		A (girls)	Yankton
	AAAA (girls)	Hammond Hammond	TENNESSEE	AAA	Memphis Melrose
MAINE	A	Cony Augusta		AAA (girls)	Bolivar Central
	A (girls)	Westbrook	TEXAS	AAAA	Wheatley Houston
MARYLAND	AA	Winston Churchill Potomac		AAAA (girls)	S. Oak Cliff Dallas
	AA (girls)	Parkdale Riverdale	UTAH	AAAA	Bingham
MASSACHUSETTS	Div. I	Lexington		AAAA (girls)	Viewmont
	Div. I (girls)	Chicopee	VERMONT	L	Windsor
MICHIGAN	A	Flint Northern		L (girls)	South Burlington
	A (girls)	Our Lady of Mercy Farmington	VIRGINIA	AAA	Homer Ferguson
MINNESOTA	AA	Prior Lake		AAA (girls)	Heritage
	AA (girls)	Bloomington Jefferson	WASHINGTON	AAA	Garfield
MISSISSIPPI		Ingomar		AAA (girls)	Clover Park
	(girls)	Harrison Central	WEST VIRGINIA	AAA	Logan
				AAA (girls)	Morgantown
			WISCONSIN	A	Neenah
				A (girls)	Neenah
			WYOMING	AA	Cheyenne Central
				AA (girls)	Lander

All-American High-School Squad

Selection to a bona-fide All-American team is the ultimate individual achievement of every high-school basketball player. Most of the greatest basketball names first became known to the public when they appeared on an All-American list.

One of the most reliable A-A lists is annually prepared by *Scholastic Magazine*'s All-American selection board under the direction of Bob Lapidus. Over the years, *Scholastic*'s squads have included such illustrious names, among others, as Oscar Robertson, Dave Bing, Dave DeBusschere, Bill Cunningham, Lew Alcindor, Jerry Lucas, Rod Thorn, Cazzie Russell, Bill Bradley, Dick and Tom Van Arsdale, Calvin Murphy, Gail Goodrich, Rick Mount, Alvan Adams, Moses Malone, Otis Birdsong, Phil Ford and Butch Lee.

1955—56

Name and School	Ht.
Al Attar (Durfee) Fall River, Mass.	6-2
Dennis Boone (Manual) Denver, Colo.	5-11
George Burkel (Cleveland) St. Louis, Mo.	6-7
Kelly Coleman (Wayland) Ky.	6-3
Albert Ellison (Linden) Tenn.	6-4
Nolden Gentry (West Rockford) Ill.	6-7
Earl Irvine (Lincoln) Seattle, Wash.	6-4
Tony Jackson (Jefferson) Brooklyn, N.Y.	6-3½
Bjarne Jensen (Franklin) Portland, Ore.	6-9
Ron Johnson (New Prague) Minn.	6-7
Fred LaCour (St. Ignatius) San Francisco	6-4½
Art Lambiotte (Warwick) Hilton Village, Va.	6-4
Jerry Lucas (Middletown) Ohio	6-7
Walt Mangham (New Castle) Pa.	6-3
Douglas Moe (Erasmus) Brooklyn, N.Y.	6-4
Lance Olson (Green Bay West) Wis.	6-3
Mel Peterson (Stephenson) Mich.	6-5
Jerry Pimm (Montebello) Calif.	5-11
Jack Pirrie (Maplewood) Mo.	6-6
George Ramming (Union Hill) Union City, N.J.	6-5
Oscar Robertson (Attucks) Indianapolis, Ind.	6-4
Barry Shetrone (Southern) Baltimore, Md.	6-3
Tom Stith (St. Francis) Brooklyn, N.Y.	6-5
Larry Swift (Keokuk) Iowa	6-6
Mike Tipton (Natrona County) Casper, Wyo.	6-2
Horace Walker (Chester) Pa.	6-3
Jerry West (East Bank) W. Va.	6-3
Max Williams (Avoca) Tex.	5-10
Rollie Williams (Kellogg) Idaho	6-6
Corky Withrow (Central City) Ky.	6-4

1956—57

Name and School	Ht.
Jim Altenhofen (Cent. Cath.) Portland, Oreg.	6-5
Terry Bethel (Collinsville) Ill.	6-7
Norris Brown (Richland) Wash.	6-0
Ed Burton (Muskegon Heights) Mich.	6-6
Al Butler (East) Rochester, N.Y.	6-2
Jerry Cobb (Sunset) Dallas, Tex.	6-3
Julie Cohen (Erasmus) Brooklyn, N.Y.	5-11
Larry Conley (Wyandotte) Kansas City, Kan.	6-5
Ray Cronk (Bemidji) Minn.	6-4
Dick Cullers (High Point) N.C.	5-11
Howard Dardeen (Gersimeyer) Terre Haute, Ind.	6-4
John Egan (Weaver) Hartford, Conn.	5-11

Name and School	Ht.
Edmond Gary (Forest Hill) Miss.	6-3
Jerry Graves (Lexington) Tenn.	6-5
Bob Heffner (Allentown) Pa.	6-4
Dave Jackson (Central) Pueblo, Colo.	6-3
Tony Jackson (Jefferson) Brooklyn, N.Y.	6-4
Bill Kilmer (Citrus) Azusa, Calif.	6-0
Billy Ray Lickert (Lafayette) Lexington, Ky.	6-3
Jerry Lucas (Middletown) Ohio	6-8
Billy McGill (Jefferson) Los Angeles, Calif.	6-11
Bob McLeod (Markel) Tex.	6-4
Tom Meschery (Lowell) San Francisco, Calif.	6-4½
Bob Mikvy (Polmerton) Pa.	6-4½
George Ramming (Union Hill) Union City, N.J.	6-6
Wayne Richards (Richmond Acad.) Augusta, Ga.	6-7
Lee Sager (East Orange) N.J.	6-5
Tom Stith (St. Francis) Brooklyn, N.Y.	6-5
Loren Wolf (Shawano) Wis.	6-4½
Dave Woolery (Rosedale) Kansas City, Kan.	5-11

1957—58

Name and School	Ht.
Ernie Cage (DeMatha) Hyattsville, Md.	6-3
Ernie Davis (Elmira Free Academy) N.Y.	6-2
Dave DeBusschere (Austin) Detroit, Mich.	6-5½
Jack Foley (Assumption) Worcester, Mass.	6-5
Norman Grow (Foley) Minn.	6-5
Willie Hall (Malloy) Queens, N.Y.	6-4
Phil Hart (El Cerrito) Calif.	6-3
Wayne Hightower (Overbrook) Phila., Pa.	6-8
Herman Keller (Newport News) Va.	6-4
Gene Kunz (Ogden) Utah	6-3
Jerry Lucas (Middletown) Ohio	6-9½
Mike McCoy (South Side) Fort Wayne, Ind.	7-0
Bill McGill (Jefferson) Los Angeles, Calif.	6-11
Sandy Pomerantz (University City) Mo.	6-5½
John Rudometkin (Santa Maria) Calif.	6-5½
Rod Thorn (Princeton) W. Va.	6-4
Harry Todd (Earlington) Ky.	6-8
Charles Vaughn (Alexander) Tamms, Ill.	6-2
Charles Warren (South) Eugene, Oreg.	6-4
Gary White (Midwest City) Okla.	6-5

1958—59

Name and School	Ht.
Tom Hoover (Carroll) Washington, D.C.	6-9
Tom McGrann (Watertown) S.D.	6-8

Name and School	Ht.
Al Santio (Hope) Providence, R.I.	6-7
Ken Glenn (East Tech) Cleveland, Ohio	6-6
Tommy Boyer (Fort Smith) Ark	6-6
Pat Richter (Madison East) Wis.	6-6
Dave Downey (Canton) Ill.	6-5
Bill Galantai (James Madison) Brooklyn, N.Y.	6-5
Rod Thorn (Princeton) W. Va.	6-5
Steve Gray (Washington) San Francisco, Calif.	6-4½
Tom Bolyard (South Side) Fort Wayne, Ind.	6-4
Bob Cozby (Olympus) Holladay, Utah	6-4
Art Heyman (Oceanside) N.Y.	6-4
Rich Porter (Kellogg) Idaho	6-4
Jim Smith (Santa Cruz) Calif.	6-4
Bill Raftery (St. Cecilia's) Kearny, N.J.	6-3½
Steve Pauly (Beaverton) Oreg.	6-3½
Ralph Heyward (Overbrook) Philadelphia, Pa.	6-3
Tom Kezar (Austin) Minn.	6-3
Darrell Sutherland (Glendale) Calif.	6-3
Ed Thomas (McClymonds) Oakland, Calif.	6-3
Pat Doyle (North Marshall County) Ky.	6-2
Nolan Ellison (Wyandotte) Kansas City, Kan.	6-2
Bill Small (West Aurora) Ill.	6-2
Dom Perno (Wilbur Cross) New Haven, Conn.	6-1
Jim Rayl (Kokomo) Ind.	6-1
Granny Lash (Chester) Pa.	6-½
Donnie Burks (Molloy) Queens, N.Y.	5-11
Ernie Moore (Sumner) Kansas City, Kan.	5-10
Vinnio Ernst (St. Aloysius) Jersey City, N.J.	5-8

1959—60

Name and School	Ht.
John Thompson (Carroll) Washington, D.C.	6-11
Jay Buckley (Bladensburg) Md.	6-10
Mel Counts (Marshfield) Coos Bay, Oreg.	6-10
James Barnes (Stillwater) Okla.	6-8
Gene Lane (East Tech) Cleveland, Ohio	6-8
Bill Vincent (South) Omaha, Neb.	6-8
George Wilson (Marshall) Chicago, Ill.	6-8
Tom Dose (Glendale) Calif.	6-7
Garry Garrison (Christian Bros.) Clayton, Mo.	6-7
Bernie Mills (Dunbar) Chicago, Ill.	6-7
Paul Silas (McClymonds) Oakland, Calif.	6-6½
Ray Brown (Roosevelt) Dayton, Ohio	6-6
Connie Hawkins (Boys) Brooklyn, N.Y.	6-6
Bill Bradley (Crystal City) Mo.	6-5
Roger Brown (Wingate) Brooklyn, N.Y.	6-5
Dennis Dairman (North Phoenix) Ariz.	6-5
Dave Hicks (Wilbur Cross) New Haven, Conn.	6-5
Barry Kramer (Linton) Schenectady, N.Y.	6-5
Charles Nash (Lake Charles) La.	6-5
Ron Bonham (Central) Muncie, Ind.	6-4
Joe Caldwell (Fremont) Los Angeles, Calif.	6-4
Don Frye (Monticello) Ky.	6-4
Bill Maphis (Romney) W. Va.	6-4
Walt Hazzard (Overbrook) Philadelphia, Pa.	6-3
Jeff Mullins (Lafayette) Lexington, Ky.	6-3
Jim McKay (Greeley) Colo.	6-2
Ron Smith (Camden) N.J.	6-1
Donnie Kessinger (Forrest City) Ark.	6-0
George Leftwich (Carroll) Washington, D.C.	6-0
Doug Hutton (Clinton) Miss.	5-10½

1960—61

Name and School	Ht.
Reggie Harding (Eastern) Detroit, Mich.	6-11
Haskell Tison (Geneva) Ill.	6-11
Ron Krick (West Reading) Pa.	6-9
Gary Cook (Idaho Falls) Ida.	6-8
Fred Hetzel (Landon) Bethesda, Md.	6-8
A.W. Davis (Rutledge) Tenn.	6-7
Bogie Redmon (Collinsville) Ill.	6-7
Bill Bradley (Crystal City) Mo.	6-5
Carlos Gripado (Pawhuska) Okla.	6-6
Marty Lentz (Mount Vernon) Va.	6-6

Name and School	Ht.
Harry Hammonds (Tuscaloosa) Ala.	6-5
Dave Hicks (W. Cross) West Haven, Conn.	6-5
Don Nelson (Marshalltown) Ia.	6-5
Jerry Rook (Nettletown) Ark.	6-5
Bill Cunningham (Erasmus) Brooklyn, N.Y.	6-4½
Emerson Baynard (Chester) Pa.	6-4
George Lee (Central) Trenton, N.J.	6-4
Dick VanArsdale (Manual) Indianapolis	6-4
Tom VanArsdale (Manual) Indianapolis	6-4
Keith Allred (Pleasant Grove) Utah	6-3½
Fred Goss (Compton) Calif.	6-1½
Luther Harper (Phoenix Union) Ariz.	6-1½
Roy Birk (Waukesha) Wis.	6-1
Lloyd Hinchey (Norwich) Conn.	6-1
Ken Cunningham (East Liverpool) Ohio	6-0
Jim Jarvis (Roseburg) Oreg.	6-0
Gail Goodrich (Poly) Los Angeles.	5-11
Bill Lawrence (Molloy) Queens, N.Y.	5-11
Ricky Ray (Huntington) W. Va.	5-11
Randy Embry (Owensboro) Ky.	5-10½

1961—62

Name and School	Ht.
Ray Kosanke (Tucson) Ariz.	6-9
Gary Keller (Hollins) St. Petersburg, Fla.	6-9
Bob Bedell (Bell Gardens) Calif.	6-7
Jim Ligon (Kokomo) Ind.	6-7
Henry Burlong (Roosevelt) Dayton, Ohio	6-6
David Lattin (Worthing) Houston, Tex.	6-6
Ed Bastian (Washington) Cedar Rapids, Iowa	6-6
Barrie Haynie (Ringgold) Ga.	6-5
Mike Silliman (St. Xavier) Louisville, Ky.	6-5
Bob McIntyre (Holy Cross) Queens, N.Y.	6-5
Cazzie Russell (Carver) Chicago, Ill.	6-5
Paul Presthus (Rugby) N.D.	6-5
Dick Sherman (Central) Cheyenne, Wyo.	6-4
Rich Calmus (Webster) Tulsa, Okla.	6-4
Albie Grant (Columbus) Bronx, N.Y.	6-4
Larry Humes (Madison) Ind.	6-4
Louis Hudson (Dudley) Greensboro, N.C.	6-4
Dave Fearheller (Hickman) Columbia, Mo.	6-4
Larry Conley (Ashland) Ky.	6-4
Ernie Thompson (Saginaw) Mich.	6-3
David Bing (Spingarn) Washington, D.C.	6-2
Don Yates (Uniontown) Pa.	6-2
Tony Horton (University) Los Angeles, Calif.	6-2
Ron Paradis (Washburn) Bethel, Kan.	6-2
Bob Bruggers (Danube) Minn.	6-2
Max Walker (Lincoln) Milwaukee, Wis.	6-1
Lon Wright (Southside) Newark, N.J.	6-1
John Austin (DeMatha) Hyattsville, Md.	6-0
Ed Griffin (Hartford) Conn.	5-11
Dan Homan (Ingraham) Seattle, Wash.	5-10

1962—63

Name and School	Ht.
Lewis Alcindor (Power) New York City	7-¼
Nick Pino (St. Michael's) Santa Fe, N.Mex.	7-0
Frank Hollendoner (St. Patrick) Chicago, Ill.	6-11
Craig Dill (Arthur Hill) Saginaw, Mich.	6-10
Rich Mason (Washington) E. Chicago, Ind.	6-8
Lloyd Dove (St. Francis) Brooklyn, N.Y.	6-7
Jim Gardner (Harding) Warren, Ohio	6-7
Edgar Lacey (Jefferson) Los Angeles, Calif.	6-7
David Lattin (Worthing) Houston, Tex.	6-7
Randy Mahaffey (LaGrange) Ga.	6-7
Ed Hummer (Washington-Lee) Arlington, Va.	6-6
Henry Watkins (Pearl) Nashville, Tenn.	6-5½
Dick Harrington (Morse) Bath, Me.	6-5
Bob Krulish (El Camino) Sacramento, Calif.	6-5
Paul Presthus (Rugby) N. Dak.	6-5
Tom Workman (Blanchet) Seattle, Wash.	6-5
Terry Campbell (Pocatello) Ida.	6-4
James Cummins (Regis) Cedar Rapids, Iowa	6-4
Clem Haskins (Taylor) Campbellsville, Ky.	6-4

Name and School	Ht.
Doug Hice (Cathedral) Trenton, N.J.	6-4
Don Kaull (Rogers) Newport, R.I.	6-4
Larry Miller (Catasauqua) Pa.	6-4
Pat Riley (Linton) Schenectady, N.Y.	6-4
Gary Hill (Gunnison) Utah.	6-3
Bob Lewis (St. John's) Washington, D.C.	6-3
Cliff Williams (Southwestern) Detroit, Mich.	6-3
Mike Redd (Seneca) Louisville, Ky.	6-2½
Jay Cole (South) Knoxville, Tenn.	6-2
Ian Morrison (St. Petersburg) Fla.	6-2
Ron Williams (Weirton) W.Va.	6-2
Fred Hare (Omaha Tech) Neb.	6-1
Pat Frink (Wheat Ridge) Colo.	6-1
Steve Sarantopoulos (Brockton) Mass.	6-1
Ron Coleman (Jefferson City) Mo.	6-0
Rick Jones (Central) Muncie, Ind.	5-11

1963—64

Name and School	Ht.
Lewis Alcindor (Power) New York, N.Y.	7-¼
David Newmark (Lincoln) Brooklyn, N.Y.	6-11
Rich Nieman (DuBourg) St. Louis, Mo.	6-10
Ron Teixeira (Cath. Memorial) Roxbury, Mass.	6-8
Westley Unseld (Seneca) Louisville, Ky.	6-8
Wally Anderzunas (Creighton) Omaha, Neb.	6-7
Richard Jones (Lester) Memphis, Tenn.	6-7
Mike Lewis (Missoula) Mont.	6-7
John Pinkstaff (South Eugene) Oreg.	6-7
Steve Vandenberg (Allegheny) Cumberl'd, Md.	6-7
Bill Hosket (Belmont) Dayton, Ohio.	6-6
Jerry Newsom (Columbus) Ind.	6-6
Mike Weaver (Huntington) Ind.	6-6
Richard Baldwin (North Little Rock) Ark.	6-5
Willie Betts (River Rouge) Mich.	6-5
Rodger Bohnenstiehl (Collinsville) Ill.	6-5
Tim Kolodziej (Amsterdam) N.Y.	6-5
Don Chaney (McKinley) Baton Rouge, La.	6-4
Chris Ellis (Newport News) Va.	6-4
Richard Hanson (Blaine) Wash.	6-4
Bobby Lane (Newman) New Orleans, La.	6-4
Larry Miller (Catasauqua) Pa.	6-4
Mike Butler (Kingsbury) Memphis, Tenn.	6-3
Bryan Grohnke (Edina-Morningside) Minn.	6-3
James McBride (Dunbar) Washington, D.C.	6-3
Alan Robinson (Emporia) Kan.	6-3
Doug Timmer (Hanford) Calif.	6-3
Warren Armstrong (Central) Kansas City, Mo.	6-2
Dennis Brady (Jefferson) Lafayette, Ind.	6-2
Jim Davidson (Logan) W. Va.	6-2
David Lawyer (Oxnard) Calif.	6-2
Jerry Sharman (Charter Oak) Covina, Calif.	6-2
Walter Simon (Roosevelt) Los Angeles, Calif.	6-2
Ron Williams (Weirton) W. Va.	6-2
Bill Schutsky (Hillside) N.J.	6-1
Eldridge Webb (Boys) Brooklyn, N.Y.	6-0
Doug Wardlaw (W. Cross) New Haven, Conn.	5-11
Willie Worsley (DeWitt Clinton) Bronx, N.Y.	5-9

1964—65

Name and School	Ht.
Lewis Alcindor (Power) New York, N.Y.	7-1
Rusty Clark (Fayetteville) N.C.	6-11
Chris Thomforde (Lutheran) Brookville, N.Y.	6-10
Mike Davis (Hinkley) Aurora, Colo.	6-9
Joe Bergman (St. Mary's) Clinton, Iowa	6-9
Ron Teixeira (Memorial) Roxbury, Mass.	6-8½
Ted Wierman (Davis) Yakima, Wash.	6-8¼
Mike Grosso (Bridgewater-Raritan) N.J.	6-8
Bob Bundy (Manchester) Richmond, Va.	6-8
Don Ross (East) Waterloo, Iowa	6-8
Howard Arndt (Republic) Mo.	6-8

Name and School	Ht.
Fred Lind (Highland Park) Ill.	6-7
Isiah King (St. Augustine) New Orleans	6-7
Melvin Bell (Clinton) Okla.	6-7
Sam Robinson (Jefferson) Los Angeles, Cal.	6-7
Steve Vandenberg (Allegheny) C'berland, Md.	6-7
Sim Hill (Midland) Pa.	6-6
Andy Owens (Hillsborough) Tampa, Fla.	6-6
Dick Haucke (LaSalle) Cincinnati, Ohio	6-6
Roger Leitner (McCook) Neb.	6-6
Bob Portman (St. Ignatius) San Francisco	6-5
Lee Lafayette (South) Grand Rapids, Mich.	6-5
Bob Smith (Melrose) Memphis, Tenn.	6-5
Walt Esdaille (Hillhouse) New Haven, Conn.	6-5
Larry Cannon (Lincoln) Philadelphia, Pa.	6-4
L. C. Bowen (Benton Harbor) Mich.	6-4
Bob Sullivan (Manitowoc) Wis.	6-4
Lynn Parsons (South Sevier) Monroe, Utah	6-4
Lynn Shackelford (Burroughs) Burbank, Calif.	6-4
Rick Mount (Lebanon) Ind.	6-3
Bernard Williams (DeMatha) Hyattsville, Md.	6-3
Al Beard (Breckenridge) Hardinsburg, Ky.	6-3
Dave Golden (Pekin) Ill.	6-2½
Lucius Allen (Wyandotte) Kansas City, Kans.	6-2
Jon MacDonald (Stearns) Millinocket, Me.	6-1
Larry Hisle (Portsmouth) Ohio	6-0

1965—66

Name and School	Ht.
Chuck Bavis (Garrett) Ind.	7-0
Bob Lienhard (Rice) New York, N.Y.	6-11
Dan Issel (Batavia) Ill.	6-9
Gary Freeman (Borah) Boise, Idaho	6-9
Dennis Awtrey (Blackford) San Jose, Calif.	6-9
Mike Mardy (Memorial) West New York, N.J.	6-8½
Greg Douglas (Keokuk) Iowa	6-8
John Hummer (Wash.-Lee) Arlington, Va.	6-7
Elvin Ivory (C. W. Hayes) Birmingham, Ala.	6-7
Rudy Tomjanovich (Hamtramck) Mich.	6-7
Sam Robinson (Jefferson) Los Angeles, Calif.	6-7
Ken Durrett (Schenley) Pittsburgh, Pa.	6-6
Dave Sorenson (Findlay) Ohio	6-6
Doug Cook (Ridgewood) N.J.	6-6
Jim McMillian (Jefferson) Brooklyn, N.Y.	6-5
Perry Wallace (Pearl) Nashville, Tenn.	6-5
Doug Jackson (West) Shawnee Mission, Kan.	6-5
Ralph Ogden (Lincoln) San Jose, Calif.	6-5
Mike Casey (Shelby Co.) Shelbyville, Ky.	6-4½
Jeff Petrie (Springfield) Delaware Co., Pa.	6-4
Charlie Scott (Laurinberg Institute) N.C.	6-4
Rick Tannenberger (Little Rock Central) Ark.	6-4
Fabien Mang (Jesuit) New Orleans, La.	6-4
Jerry Kroll (Memorial) Spring Branch, Texas	6-4
Chuck Moore (Polytechnic) Long Beach, Cal.	6-4
Ron White (Boys Town) Neb.	6-3½
Bob Dukiet (Livingston) N.J.	6-3½
Marshall Lewis (Technical) Boston, Mass.	6-3
Roosevelt Philips (Troy) N.Y.	6-3
Rick Mount (Lebanon) Ind.	6-3
Rich Bradshaw (Marshall) Chicago, Ill.	6-3
Bob Hummell (Moundsville) W. Va.	6-2
Jerry Francis (West) Columbus, Ohio.	6-2
Frank Price (River Rouge) Mich.	6-1
Tom Little (Mackin) Washington, D. C.	6-0
Dean Meminger (Rice) New York, N.Y.	6-0
Trent Gaines (Polytechnic) Long Beach, Calif.	6-0
Don Crosby (Cony) Augusta, Maine	5-11
Calvin Murphy (Norwalk) Conn.	5-10
Billy Nickleberry (Jefferson) Portland, Oreg.	5-8

1966—67

Name and School	Ht.
Artis Gilmore (Carver) Dothan, Ala.	7-2

Name and School	Ht.
Jim McDaniels (Allen Cty.) Scottsville, Ky.	7-½
Greg Northington (Wood) Indianapolis, Ind.	6-11½
Steve Niles (Lee) San Antonio, Texas	6-11
Dana Lewis (Weequahic) Newark, N.J.	6-10
Randy Denton (Enloe) Raleigh, N.C.	6-10
Dave Robisch (Springfield) Ill.	6-9
Tom Masterson (Walnut Grove) Minn.	6-9
Harold Porter (Booker) Sarasota, Fla.	6-8
Levi Wyatt (Liddell) Fayette, Miss.	6-8
Spencer Haywood (Pershing) Detroit, Mich.	6-8
Oscar Foster (San Diego) Calif.	6-7
Dean Kratovil (West) Billings, Mont.	6-7
Willie Long (South Side) Fort Wayne, Ind.	6-7
Rich Yunkus (Benton) Ill.	6-7
Thorpe Weber (Joplin) Mo.	6-7
Ken Durrett (Schenley) Pittsburgh, Pa.	6-6
Curtis Rowe (Fremont) Los Angeles, Calif.	6-6
Ernie Fleming (Durfee) Fall River, Mass.	6-5
Mike Garman (Caldwell) Idaho	6-4
Ray Russell (Northeast) Oklahoma City, Okla.	6-4
James Mayberry (Thompson) Natchez, Miss.	6-4
Art Roberts (Washington) Montgomery, Ala.	6-4
Rudy Benjamin (Roosevelt) Dayton, Ohio.	6-3
Austin Carr (Mackin) Washington, D.C.	6-3
Jim Rose (Hazard) Ky.	6-3
Curry Todd (Treadwell) Memphis, Tenn.	6-3
Pierre Russell (Wyandotte) Kansas City, Kan.	6-3
Jack Ridgle (Martin) Altheimer, Ark.	6-3
Greg Starrick (Marion) Ill.	6-3
James Welch (LaGrange) Lake Charles, La.	6-2
Dana Pagett (El Segundo) Calif.	6-1
Charlie Davis (Bklyn Tech) Brooklyn, N.Y.	6-1
Dean Meminger (Rice) New York, N.Y.	6-0
Lanny Taylor (Hana) Anderson, S.C.	6-0
Jim Harris (Adm. King) Lorain, Ohio.	5-11½
Mel Knight (Seton Hall) South Orange, N.J.	5-11
Chas. Johnson (Sequoia) Redwood City, Cal.	5-11
Dwight Tolliver (Public) Hartford, Conn.	5-10
Dick DeVenzio (Ambridge) Pa.	5-10

1967—68

Name and School	Ht.
Steve Turner (Bartlett) Memphis, Tenn.	7-2
Charles Jura (Schuyler) Neb.	6-10
Ansley Truitt (Wilson) San Francisco, Calif.	6-9½
Tom Riker (St. Dominic's) Oyster Bay, N.Y.	6-9
Cyril Baptiste (Curley) Miami, Fla.	6-8
Ken Grabinski (Clear Lake) Iowa	6-7
Randy Noll (Catholic) Covington, Ky.	6-7
Joby Wright (Johnson) Savannah, Ga.	6-7
Dennis Wuycik (Ambridge) Pa.	6-7
Bob Ford (North) Evansville, Ind.	6-7
Bob Zender (Edina) Minn.	6-7
Clyde Baker (Bonneville) Utah	6-7
Roland Garrett (Rogers) Canton, Miss.	6-7
Steve Berg (Shorewood) Wis.	6-6
Al Sanders (Baton Rouge) La.	6-6
Tom Parker (Collinsville) Ill.	6-6
William Franklin (B. T. Washington) Norfolk, Va.	6-6
Bill Chamberlain (Lutheran) Brookville, N.Y.	6-6
Greg Davis (Schlarman) Danville, Ill.	6-5
John Fraley (Middletown) Ohio.	6-5
Joe Mackey (Coronado) Scottsdale, Ariz.	6-5
Russell Lee (Hyde Park) Mass.	6-5
Jeff Hickman (Central) Lockport, Ill.	6-5
Kent Hollenbeck (Bearden) Knoxville, Tenn.	6-4
Chris Ford (Holy Spirit) Absecon, N.J.	6-4
Ralph Simpson (Pershing) Detroit, Mich.	6-4
Pat Taylor (Leavenworth) Kans.	6-4
Jerry Bonney (Wheatley) Houston, Tex.	6-3
Henry Bacon (Male) Louisville, Ky.	6-3
Alex Scott (Wilbur Cross) New Haven, Conn.	6-2
Aubrey Nash (DeMatha) Hyattsville, Md.	6-2
Wilbert Robinson (Highlands) Uniontown, Pa.	6-2

Name and School	Ht.
Henry Harris (Greene Co.) Boligee, Ala.	6-2
Phil Westphal (Aviation) Redondo Beach, Calif.	6-2
Henry Bibby (Person-Albion) Franklinton, N.C.	6-2
Harold Fox (Northwestern) Hyattsville, Md.	6-1
Almer Lee (Northside) Ft. Smith, Ark.	6-0
Ron Johnson (Van Buren) Queens, N.Y.	5-11
John Somogyi (St. Peter's) New Brunswick, N.J.	5-11
Billy Shepherd (Carmel) Ind.	5-10

1968—69

Name and School	Ht.
Tom Payne (Shawnee) Louisville, Ky.	7-1
Luke Witte (Marlington) Ohio.	7-0
Tom McMillen (Mansfield) Pa.	6-11
Alan Shaw (Millville) N.J.	6-11
Jim Chones (St. Catherine) Racine, Wis.	6-11
Randy Canfield (Southeast) Wichita, Kan.	6-11
Mike Fink (Central Valley) Redding, Calif.	6-10
Reggie Royals (Whiteville) N.C.	6-9
Mike Carson (Sistersville) W. Va.	6-9
Ken Brady (Flint Central) Mich.	6-9
Steve Downing (Washington) Indianapolis, Ind.	6-9
Dwight Jones (Wheatley) Houston, Texas	6-9
Leonard Gray (Sumner) Kansas City, Kan.	6-8
Bill Daake (Priory) St. Louis, Mo.	6-8
Floyd Lewis (Western) Washington, D.C.	6-7
George McGinnis (Washington) Indianapolis, Ind.	6-7
Nick Weatherspoon (McKinley) Canton, Ohio.	6-7
Jim O'Brien (J. E. B. Stuart) Falls Church, Va.	6-7
Mel Davis (Boys) Brooklyn, N.Y.	6-6
Phil Hankinson (North) Great Neck, N.Y.	6-6
Jim Brewer (Proviso East) Maywood, Ill.	6-6
Eddie Ratleff (East) Columbus, Ohio.	6-6
Bob Lauriski (Logan) Utah	6-6
James Brown (DeMatha) Hyattsville, Md.	6-5½
Jesse Leonard (Thompson) Natchez, Miss.	6-5
Rick Holdt (Paramus) N.J.	6-5
John Neumann (Overton) Memphis, Tenn.	6-5
Larry Hollyfield (Compton) Calif.	6-5
Ron King (Central) Louisville, Ky.	6-4
Dan Kirkland (Columbus) Ga.	6-4
Richie O'Connor (St. Michael) Union City, N.J.	6-3½
Kevin Joyce (Achbshp. Molloy) Jamaica, N.Y.	6-3
Tom Ingelsby (Card. O'Hara) Springfield, Pa.	6-3
Warren Morse (Hayward) Cal.	6-3
John Williamson (W. Cross) New Haven, Conn.	6-2
Brian Taylor (Perth Amboy) N.J.	6-2
Allan Hornyak (St. John's) Bellaire, Ohio	6-2
Mike D'Antoni (Mullens) W. Va.	6-2
James Brown (Long Island City) N.Y.	6-1
Jeff Dawson (North) Downers Grove, Ill.	6-1

1969—70

Name and School	Ht.
Tom Burleson (Avery County) Newland, N.C.	7-3
Tom McMillen (Mansfield) Pa.	6-11
Brent Wilson (Flathead) Kalispell, Mont.	6-11
Bill Walton (Helix) LaMesa, Calif.	6-10
Les Cason (East Rutherford) N.J.	6-10
Steve Ericksen (Beaverton) Ore.	6-10
Mark Cartwright (Niles West) Ill.	6-10
Dwight Jones (Wheatley) Houston, Texas	6-10
Roy Ebron (B. T. Washington) Norfolk, Va.	6-9
Bill Morris (Beaumont) St. Louis, Mo.	6-9
Keith Bowman (Savannah) Ga.	6-8
Jim Bradley (Roosevelt) East Chicago, Ind.	6-8

Name and School	Ht.
Carl Meier (East Bakersfield) Calif.	6-8
John Shumate (Jefferson) Elizabeth, N.J.	6-7½
Harold Sullinger (Wilson) Camden, N.J.	6-7½
Neil Fegebank (Paullina) Iowa.	6-7
Campanella Russell (Pontiac Central) Mich.	6-7
Don Washington (St. Anthony's) Washington, D.C.	6-7
Wardell Jackson (Macomber) Toledo, Ohio	6-7
Keith Wilkes (Santa Barbara) Calif.	6-6
Ed Searcy (Power Memorial) New York, N.Y.	6-6
Sam Hervey (Crozier Tech) Dallas, Texas	6-6
Charles Cleveland (Bibb County) Centerville, Ala.	6-5
Kris Berymon (Harper) Chicago, Ill.	6-5
Ronnie Brown (Columbia Gram.) New York, N.Y.	6-4
Brian Winters (Molloy) Queens, N.Y.	6-4
Greg Lee (Reseda) Calif.	6-4
Tony Byers (Bessemer City) N.C.	6-3
Lloyd Batts (Thornton) Ill.	6-3
Tom Kivisto (Aurora East) Ill.	6-3
Andre McCarter (Overbrook) Philadelphia, Pa.	6-3
Gary Erickson (West) Salt Lake City, Utah	6-3
John Williamson (Wilbur Cross) New Haven, Conn.	6-2
Henry Kinsey (Boys) Brooklyn, N.Y.	6-2
Tom Gilbert (Speedway) Ind.	6-2
Lamont Weaver (Memorial) Beloit, Wis.	6-1
Donald Smith (Roth) Dayton, Ohio	6-0
James Outlaw (Ballard-Hudson) Macon, Ga.	5-11
Ronnie Lyons (Mason County) Maysville, Ky.	5-10
Dave Shepherd (Carmel) Ind.	5-10

1970—71

Name and School	Ht.
Fessor Leonard (Carver) Columbus, Ga.	7-1
David Vaughn (Cameron) Nashville, Tenn.	6-11
John Lambert (Berkeley) Calif.	6-11
Les Cason (East Rutherford) N.J.	6-10
Ed Stahl (Walnut Ridge) Columbus, Ohio	6-10
John Garrett (Peru) Ind.	6-10
Maurice Presley (Jeff. Davis) Houston, Texas	6-10
Tom Roy (South Windsor) Conn.	6-9
Bob Guyette (Marquette) Ottawa, Ill.	6-9
Lindsey Hairston (Kettering) Detroit, Mich.	6-9
Larry Haralson (Male) Louisville, Ky.	6-9
Owen Brown (Lyons) LaGrange, Ill.	6-8
Joe Fisher (Central Catholic) Lima, Ohio	6-8
Campy Russell (Pontiac Central) Mich.	6-7
Don Washington (St. Anthony's) Washington, D.C.	6-7
Maurice Lucas (Schenley) Pittsburgh, Pa.	6-7
Louis Dunbar (Webster) Minden, La.	6-7
Jim Baker (Olney) Philadelphia, Pa.	6-7
Clyde Mayes (Wade Hampton) Greenville, S.C.	6-7
Ron Haigler (Madison) Brooklyn, N.Y.	6-7
Otho Tucker (Paris) Ill.	6-6
Bob Iverson (Webster) Tulsa, Okla.	6-6
Pete Trgovich (Washington) East Chicago, Ind.	6-6
Roscoe Pondexter (S. J. Memorial) Fresno, Calif.	6-6
Charles Cleveland (Bibb County) Centerville, Ala.	6-5
Henry Williams (Eisenhower) Norristown, Pa.	6-5
Kevin Grevey (Taft) Hamilton, Ohio	6-5
Mel Montgomery (Kensington) Buffalo, N.Y.	6-5
Andre McCarter (Overbrook) Philadelphia, Pa.	6-4
Jim Dan Conner (Anderson County) Lawrenceburg, Ky.	6-4
Sam McCants (Catholic) Pensacola, Fla.	6-4
Ernie Douse (Boys) Brooklyn, N.Y.	6-4
Mel Utley (Far Rockaway) N.Y.	6-4
Gary Brokaw (New Brunswick) N.J.	6-3
Jerome McDaniel (Fairmont Heights) Md.	6-3

Name and School	Ht.
Ricky Coleman (Schenley) Pittsburgh, Pa.	6-2
Mike Flynn (Jeffersonville) Ind.	6-2
Ray Lewis (Verbum Dei) Los Angeles, Calif.	6-0
Gus Williams (Mt. Vernon) N.Y.	5-11
Lloyd Walton (Mt. Carmel) Chicago, Ill.	5-10

1971—72

Name and School	Ht.
Robert Parish (Woodlawn) Shreveport, La.	7-0
Richard Washington (Benson) Portland, Oreg.	6-11
Leon Douglas (Colbert County) Leighton, Ala.	6-10
Edmond Lawrence (Boston) Lake Charles, La.	6-10
Alvan Adams (Putnam City) Okla.	6-10
Mitch Kupchak (Brentwood) N.Y.	6-9
Lewis Brown (Verbum Dei) Los Angeles, Calif.	6-9
Major Jones (Desha Central) Rohwer, Ark.	6-8
Cliff Pondexter (San Joaquin Memorial) Fresno, Calif.	6-8
Al Fleming (Elston) Michigan City, Ind.	6-8
Charles Jordan (Shortridge) Indianapolis, Ind.	6-8
John Engels (St. Peter's) Staten Island, N.Y.	6-8
Greg Grady (Eastern District) Brooklyn, N.Y.	6-8
Joe Bryant (Bartram) Philadelphia, Pa.	6-8
Jerry Thruston (Owensboro) Ky.	6-7
Lamont Turner (Vashon) St. Louis, Mo.	6-7
Ira Terrell (Roosevelt) Dallas, Texas	6-7
Warren Baker (Greenbrier East) Fairlea, W. Va.	6-7
John Drew (Shields) Beatrice, Ala.	6-6
Eugene Short (Blair) Hattiesburg, Miss.	6-6
Craig Lynch (Start) Toledo, Ohio	6-6
Wally Walker (Penn Manor) Millersville, Pa.	6-6
Bill Cook (White Station) Memphis, Tenn.	6-6
Walt Luckett (Kolbe) Bridgeport, Conn.	6-5
Al Smith (Albany) Ga.	6-5
Jim Crews (University) Normal, Ill.	6-5
Nino Samuel (Salina Central) Kansas	6-5
Larry Fogle (Cooley) Detroit, Mich.	6-5
Phil Sellers (Jefferson) Brooklyn, N.Y.	6-5
Walter Davis (South Mecklenburg) Pineville, N.C.	6-5
Scott May (Sandusky) Ohio	6-5
Mickey Heard (Wilbur Cross) New Haven, Conn.	6-4
Earl Tatum (Mt. Vernon) N.Y.	6-4
Quinn Buckner (Thornridge) Dolton, Ill.	6-3
Ronald Lee (Lexington) Mass.	6-3
Mike Dunleavy (Nazareth) New York, N.Y.	6-2
Bob Hawkins (Pershing) Detroit, Mich.	6-2
John McKnight (Battle Ground) Wash.	6-2
Maurice Howard (St. Joseph's) Philadelphia, Pa.	6-1
Mark Haddon (Alisal) Salinas, Calif.	5-11

1972—73

Name and School	Ht.
Richard Washington (Benson) Portland, Oreg.	7-0
Kent Benson (New Castle) Ind.	6-11
Moses Malone (Petersburg) Va.	6-11
Tom LaGarde (C. Catholic) Detroit, Mich.	6-10
Paul Berwanger (Central) Cornwall, N.Y.	6-10
Lewis Brown (Verbum Dei) Los Angeles, Calif.	6-9
Bo Ellis (Parker) Chicago, Ill.	6-9
Mike Patterson (Mitchell) Colorado Springs, Colo.	6-8
Cliff Pondexter (Memorial) Fresno, Calif.	6-8
Steve Burgason (Ames) Iowa	6-7
Walter Actwood (Greenwood) Miss.	6-7
Eddie Owens (Wheatley) Houston, Texas	6-7
Melvin Baker (Gallup) N. M.	6-6

Name and School	Ht.
Marques Johnson (Crenshaw) Los Angeles Calif.	6-6
Jess Randell (Castlemont) Oakland, Calif.	6-6
Bob Siegel (Fairbury) Neb.	6-6
Gavin Smith (Van Nuys) Calif.	6-6
Wesley Cos (Male) Louisville, Ky.	6-5
Adrian Dantley (DeMatha) Hyattsville, Md.	6-5
Bill Paterno (C. B. A.) Lincroft, N.J.	6-5
Anthony Roberts (Riverside) Chattanooga, Tenn.	6-5
Brian Williams (South) Columbus, Ohio	6-5
Archie Aldridge (Middletown) Ohio	6-4
T. R. Dunn (West End) Birmingham, Ala.	6-4
Wayne Golden (Shawnee) Louisville, Ky.	6-4
Ernie Grunfeld (Forest Hills) N.Y.	6-4
Joe Hassett (LaSalle) Providence, R.I.	6-4
Ernie Kent (West) Rockford, Ill.	6-4
Steve Sheppard (Clinton) Bronx, N.Y.	6-4
Otis Birdsong (Winter Haven) Fla.	6-3
Jeep Kelley (Schenley) Pittsburgh, Pa.	6-3
Mark Lonetto (Eustace) Pennsauken, N.J.	6-3
Jim Webb (Adams) South Bend, Ind.	6-3
Bill Langloh (DeMatha) Hyattsville, Md.	6-2
Dexter Reed (Parkview) Little Rock, Ark.	6-2
Johnny Davis (Murray-Wright) Detroit, Mich.	6-1
Marty Giovacchini (Memorial) S. L. City, Utah	6-1
Wayne Smalls (Camden) N.J.	6-1
Larry Wright (Western) Washington , D.C.	6-1
Jim Spillane (Palos Verdes) Calif.	5-11

1973—74

Name and School	Ht.
Bill Cartwright (Elk Grove) Calif.	7-0
Brett Vroman (Provo) Utah	6-11
Moses Malone (Petersburg) Va.	6-11
Steve Malovic (Alhambra) Phoenix, Ariz.	6-10
Mike Phillips (Manchester) Akron, Ohio	6-10
Bruce Campbell (Wilbur Cross) New Haven, Conn.	6-9½
Rick Robey (Bro. Martin) New Orleans, La.	6-9
Cyrus Mann (Southeastern) Detroit, Mich.	6-9
John Gunn (Melrose) Memphis, Tenn.	6-9
Jackie Dorsey (Archer) Atlanta, Ga.	6-8
Larry Boston (Kennedy) Cleveland, Ohio	6-8
Marvin Thomas (Jordan) Los Angeles, Calif.	6-7
Mark Olberding (Melrose) Minn.	6-7
George Johnson (New Utrecht) Brooklyn, N.Y.	6-7
Kim Stewart (Ballard) Seattle, Wash.	6-7
Keith Herron (Mackin) Washington, D.C.	6-6
Ron Anthony (Fletcher) Neptune Beach, Fla.	6-6
Billy Lewis (Farragut) Chicago, Ill.	6-6
Wayne Walls (Jeffersonville) Ind.	6-6
Ken Carr (DeMatha) Hyattsville, Md.	6-6
Larry Harris (Clearview) Lorain, Ohio	6-6
Charlie Floyd (Malvern) Pa.	6-6
Earl Evans (Lincoln) Port Arthur, Tex.	6-6
Mike Jones (Charleston) W. Va.	6-5½
Audie Matthews (Bloom) Chicago Hts., Ill.	6-4
Jack Givens (Bryan Sta.) Lexington, Ky.	6-4
Skip Wise (Dunbar) Baltimore, Md.	6-4
James Jackson (Crane) Chicago, Ill.	6-3
Tony Smith (Saginaw) Mich.	6-3
Brad Davis (Monaca) Pa.	6-3
Jim Krivacs (Southport) Indianapolis, Ind.	6-2
Al Green (Me. Central Prep) Pittsfield, Me.	6-2
Jack Gilloon (Memorial) W. New York, N.J.	6-2
Alex Eldridge (Taft) Bronx, N.Y.	6-2
Tom Hicks (St. Anthony) Smithtown, N.Y.	6-2
Phil Ford (Rocky Mount) N.C.	6-2
Mark Wulfemeyer (Troy) Fullerton, Calif.	6-1
Milt Gibson (Goddard) Roswell, N.M.	6-1
Butch Lee (Clinton) Bronx, N.Y.	6-0
Gary Rosenberger (Marquette) Wauwatosa, Wis.	6-0

1974—75

Name and School	Ht.
Bill Cartwright (Elk Grove) Calif.	7-0
Bill Laimbeer (Palos Verdes) Calif.	6-11
Mark Hoisington (Benson) Portland, Ore.	6-10
Larry Gibson (Dunbar) Baltimore, Md.	6-10
Darryl Dawkins (Evans) Orlando, Fla.	6-10
Glen Grunwald (E. Leyden) Franklin Pk., Ill.	6-9
Bernard Toone (Gorton) Yonkers, N.Y.	6-9
Dave Greenwood (Verbum Dei) Los Angeles	6-9
Bob Roma (C.B.A.) Lincroft, N.J.	6-9
James Hardy (Jordan) Long Beach, Calif.	6-9
Wayne McKoy (Lutheran) Brookville, N.Y.	6-9
Bruce Flowers (Berkley) Mich.	6-8½
Bill Willoughby (Morrow) Englewood, N.J.	6-8½
Jim Graziano (Farmingdale) N.Y.	6-8
Cedric Hordges (Lee) Montgomery, Ala.	6-8
Albert King (Ft. Hamilton) Brooklyn, N.Y.	6-7
Phil Hubbard (McKinley) Canton, Ohio	6-7
Eugene Banks (West) Philadelphia, Pa.	6-6
Anthony Price (Taft) Bronx, N.Y.	6-6
Winford Boynes (Capitol Hill) Oklahoma City	6-6
Reggie King (Jackson-Olin) Birmingham, Ala.	6-6
Loren Lutz (Alamosa) Colo.	6-5
Sam Drummer (Northside) Muncie, Ind.	6-5
Lynbert Johnson (Haaren) New York, N.Y.	6-5
Larry Wilson (LaFourche) Mathews, La.	6-5
Alan Hardy (Northwestern) Detroit, Mich.	6-5
Pat Foschi (Virginia) Minn.	6-4½
Jim Tillman (Eastern) Washington, D.C.	6-4
Karl Godine (Kashmere) Houston, Texas	6-4
Darrell Griffith (Male) Louisville, Ky.	6-3½
Bob Bender (Bloomington) Ill.	6-3
Clint Richardson (O'Dea) Seattle, Wash.	6-3
Reggie Carter (Lutheran) Brookville, N.Y.	6-2½
Brad Holland (Cres. Valley) La Crescenta, Calif.	6-2½
Bernard Rencher (Mater Christi) Astoria, N.Y.	6-2
Kyle Macy (Peru) Ind.	6-2
Stacy Robinson (Dunbar) Washington, D.C.	6-2
Roy Hamilton (Verbum Dei) Los Angeles, Calif.	6-1½
Ron Perry (Cath. Mem.) W. Roxbury, Mass.	6-1
Richie Wright (Abington) Pa.	5-8½

1975—76

Name and School	Ht.
Jawann Oldham (Cleveland) Seattle, Wash.	6-11½
Stuart House (Denby) Detroit, Mich.	6-11
Mike Gminski (Masuk) Monroe, Conn.	6-11
Ricky Brown (West Fulton) Atlanta, Ga.	6-10
Derek Holcomb (Richwoods) Peoria, Ill.	6-10
Jim Graziano (Farmingdale) N.Y.	6-9
Glen Grunwald (East Leyden) Franklin Park, Ill.	6-9
Wayne McKoy (Lutheran) Brookville, N.Y.	6-9
Albert Jones (Worthing) Houston, Texas.	6-8
Jonathan Moore (Burke) Charleston, S.C.	6-8
James Ratiff (Eastern) Washington, D.C.	6-8
James Wilkes (Dorsey) Los Angeles, Calif.	6-8
Albert King (Ft. Hamilton) Brooklyn, N.Y.	6-7
LaVon Williams (Manual) Denver, Colo.	6-7
Sylvester Williams (Lee) New Haven, Conn.	6-7
Johnny Nash (Poly) Long Beach, Calif.	6-6½
Francois Wise (Balboa) San Francisco, Calif.	6-6½
Gene Banks (W. Philadelphia) Philadelphia, Pa.	6-6
Bill Bryant (Carroll) Washington, D.C.	6-6
Earvin Jonnson (Everett) Lansing, Mich.	6-6
Greg Johnson (Lockland) Cincinnati, Ohio	6-6
Mike O'Koren (Hudson Cath.) Jersey City, N.J.	6-6
Craig Shelton (Dunbar) Washington, D.C.	6-6

Name and School	Ht.
Curtis Redding (Canarsie) Brooklyn, N.Y. . . .	6-5
Butch Carter (Middletown) Ohio	6-5
Stan Walker (Sunset) Beaverton, Oreg.	6-5
Charles Whitney (DeMatha) Hyattsville, Md. .	6-5
Mike Woodson (Broad Ripple) Indianapolis, Ind.	6-5
Darrell Griffith (Male) Louisville, Ky.	6-4
John Virgil (Elm City) N.C.	6-4
Rich Branning (Marina) Huntington Beach, Calif.	6-3½
Jo Jo Hunter (Mackin) Washington, D.C. . . .	6-2½
Clyde Austin (Maggie Walker) Richmond, Va.	6-2
Hasan Houston (University City) Mo.	6-2
Jay Shidler (Lawrenceville) III.	6-2
Brian Walker (Lebanon) Ind.	6-2
Tyrone Ladson (Canarsie) Brooklyn, N.Y. . . .	6-1
Lowes Moore (Mt. Vernon) N.Y.	6-1
Ron Perry (Cath. Memorial) W. Roxbury, Mass.	6-1
Dave Colescott (Marion) Ind.	6-0

1976—77

Name and School	Ht.
Herb Williams (Marion-Franklin) Columbus, Ohio	6-10
Gil Salinas (Burbank) San Antonio, Texas . . .	6-10
Norm Anchrum (Jones Valley) Birmingham, Ala.	6-10
Wayne McKoy (Lutheran) Brookville, N.Y. . . .	6-9
Jeff Ruland (Sachem) Lake Ronkonkoma, N.Y.	6-9
Ray Tolbert (Madison) Anderson, Ind.	6-9
Dave Netherton (East) Pueblo, Colo.	6-9
James Ratiff (Eastern) Washington, D.C. . . .	6-9
Pete Budko (Loyola) Towson, Md.	6-9
Steve Risley (Central) Lawtence, Ind.	6-8
Brian Allsmiller (Buffalo Grove) III.	6-8
Earvin Johnson (Everett) Lansing, Mich.	6-8
Orlando Woolridge (Mansfield) La.	6-8
Reggie Hannah (Titusville) Fla.	6-8
Cliff Robinson (Castlemont) Oakland, Calif.	6-8
Gene Banks (West) Philadelphia, Pa.	6-7
Purvis Miller (Compton) Calif.	6-7
Albert King (Fort Hamilton) Brooklyn, N.Y. .	6-7
Danny Vranes (Skyline) Salt Lake City, Utah	6-7
Art Jones (Hampton) Va.	6-7
Cornelius Thompson (Middletown) Conn. . . .	6-7
Eddie Johnson (Westinghouse) Chicago, III. . .	6-7
Andra Griffin (Central) Minneapolis, Minn. . .	6-7
Al Wood (Jones County) Gray, Ga.	6-6
Oliver Lee (DeLand) Fla.	6-6
Barry Brooks (Pasadena) Calif.	6-6
Drake Morris (Washington) E. Chicago, Ind. . .	6-6
Sam Clancy (Brashear) Pittsburgh, Pa.	6-6
Kelly Tripucka (Bloomfield) N.J.	6-6
Mike McGee (North) Omaha, Neb.	6-5
Alex Bradley (Long Branch) N. J.	6-5

Name and School	Ht.
Jeff Lamp (Ballard) Louisville, Ky.	6-5
Tracy Jackson (Paint Branch) Burtonsville, Md.	6-5
Felton Sealey (Don Bosco) Boston, Mass. . . .	6-4
Dan Ainge (North) Eugene, Oreg.	6-4
Kenny Page (McKee) Staten Island, N.Y. . . .	6-3
Wes Matthews (Harding) Bridgeport, Conn. . .	6-2
Kenny Matthews (Dunbar) Washington, D.C. .	6-2
Kevin Smith (Bro. Rice) Birmingham, Mich. . .	6-1½
Darnell Valentine (Wichita Hts.) Wichita, Kan.	6-1

1977—78

Name and School	Ht.
Wallace Bryant (Emerson) Gary, Ind.	7-0
Sam Bowie (Lebanon) Pa.	6-11½
Bill Ross (Lake Placid) Fla.	6-10
Earl Jones (Mt. Hope) W. Va.	6-10
James Griffin (Dunbar) Ft. Worth, Tex. . . .	6-10
Landon Turner (Arsenal) Indianapolis, Ind. .	6-9½
Micah Blunt (E. Jefferson) Metairie, La.	6-9
Carlton McCray (Mt. Vernon) N.Y.	6-9
Guy Williams (Bishop O'Dowd) Oakland, Cal.	6-8
James Worthy (Ashbrook) Gastonia, N.C. . . .	6-8
Charles Williams (Rocky Mount) N.C.	6-8
Clark Kellogg (St. Joseph) Cleveland, Ohio . .	6-8
John Garris (Bassick) Bridgeport, Conn. . . .	6-8
Leonel Marquetti (Verbum Dei) Los Angeles, Calif.	6-7
Cornelius Thompson (Middletown) Conn. . .	6-7
Derrick Hord (Tennessee) Bristol, Tenn. . . .	6-7
Clarence Tillman (West) Philadelphia, Pa. . .	6-7
Guy Morgan (First Colonial) Va. Beach, Va. .	6-7
Mark Aguirre (Westinghouse) Chicago, III. . .	6-6
Chuck Verderber (Lincoln) III.	6-6
Kevin Boyle (St. Laurence) Burbank, III. . . .	6-6
Tony Guy (Loyola) Towson, Md.	6-6
Alvis Rogers (Washington) N.C.	6-6
Devin Durrant (Provo) Utah	6-6
Mike McKay (Harding) Bridgeport, Conn. . .	6-5½
Dave Crosby (Morris) Bronx, N.Y.	6-5
Vince Taylor (Tates Creek) Lexington, Ky. . .	6-4½
Walker Russell (Central) Pontiac, Mich.	6-4
Tyren Naulls (Lynwood) Calif.	6-4
Darryl Mitchell (N. Shore) W. Palm Beach, Fla.	6-4
Jerry Eaves (Ballard) Louisville, Ky.	6-4
Rick Harmon (Middle Twp.) Cape May CH, N.J.	6-4
Reggie Jackson (Roman Cath.) Phil., Pa. . . .	6-4
Quintin Dailey (Gibbons) Baltimore, Md. . .	6-3½
Lewis Card (Auburn) Ala.	6-3
Dwight Anderson (Roth) Dayton, Ohio	6-3
Mike Mitchell (Capuchino) San Bruno, Calif.	6-2
Greg Goorjian (Crescenta) LaCrescenta, Calif.	6-2
Mark Hall (Commerce) Springfield, Calif. . .	6-2
Dan Callandrillo (North Bergen) N.J.	6-2

The Amateurs

12

Olympic Games and AAU

Olympics

Until the last game in Munich, Germany, in 1972, when an official's error caused Olympian confusion, the history of Olympic basketball was marked by an unbroken string of United States victories.

U.S. teams played exhibition games in the 1904, 1924, and 1928 Olympics, but these games were officially classified as demonstrations and no medals were awarded.

But by 1936 basketball had become sufficiently popular around the world to be included on the Olympic program. The U.S. set the pattern for its future appearances that year, winning all five of its games in Berlin by lopsided scores. In the final, the U.S. crushed Canada, 19–8, in a game played outdoors in a driving rain.

When Olympic competition resumed in 1948 after a twelve-year break forced by World War II, the United States picked up in London right where it had left off in Berlin. Led by collegiate stars Alex Groza of Kentucky and 7-1 Bob Kurland of Oklahoma A&M, the U.S. swept through seven opponents to win its second gold medal. France finished second and Brazil third.

Four years later in Helsinki, with Clyde Lovellette and Kurland leading the way, the U.S. won again. The United States played the Soviet Union for the first time ever in the final game and overcame the Russians' stalling, ball-control tactics to score a 36–25 triumph.

At the Melbourne Olympics in 1956, the U.S. again completely outclassed its opponents, winning all eight of its games by at least 30 points. Bill Russell and K. C. Jones, who had led the University of San Francisco to two consecutive national championships, starred as the U.S. crushed the USSR, 89–55, in the final. Uruguay won its second consecutive bronze medal.

The 1960 U.S. team is generally considered to have been the strongest ever to represent this country in the Olympics. It boasted such collegiate stars as Jerry Lucas, Oscar Robertson, Jerry West, Walt Bellamy and Terry Dischinger, all of whom went on to star in professional basketball. With this pool of talent, the U.S. had no trouble with any of its eight opponents, winning four of the games by more than 40-point margins.

In the 1964 Olympics at Tokyo, the U.S. again swept through all eight foes on the way to its sixth basketball gold medal. The

USSR's Aleksander Belov makes the shot that ends the U. S. Olympic winning streak in 1972

had passed up the Olympic trials, leaving the squad without big-name stars.

Coach Henry Iba, though, stressing defense and team play, molded his players into a powerful, cohesive unit that crushed Yugoslavia, 65–60, in the championship game. The outstanding players included Spencer Haywood, a 6-8, 19-year-old center with amazing defensive talents, and Jo Jo White, a sharp-shooting guard.

The 1972 finale was more frustration than finesse. The U.S. which had won 62 straight games in Olympic competition, and Soviet Union were matched in the championship game. Russia led throughout the game, but with three seconds left, the U.S. took the lead, 50–49. The USSR had three chances to play the final seconds—through various misunderstandings among the referees, coaches, timers and other officials— and finally won, 51–50. The U.S. team members refused to accept silver medals, symbolic of second place.

Despite some forecasts of doom, the United States regained its Olympian throne in 1976 at Montreal. The team put together by North Carolina coach Dean Smith included Phil Ford, Mitch Kupchak, Adrian Dantley, Walter Davis, and Scott May. After surviving a 95–94 scare by a Puerto Rican team led by Marquette standout Butch Lee, the American squad twice defeated an experienced Yugoslavian quintet to capture the gold medal without a loss.

For the first time a women's championship was held. The United States sent a team whose nucleus had been together for the world championships and Pan American Games in 1975. The team reached the finals, surviving a loss to Japan, but was no match for the Soviet Union. Led by their towering center, Semenova, estimated to be at least 7-4, the Soviets easily beat the Americans, 112–77, for the gold medal.

playmaking talents of Princeton's Bill Bradley kept the team together. The squad also included Luke Jackson, Walt Hazzard and 7-0 Mel Counts. In the final, the U.S. again trounced the USSR, 73–59.

The 1968 team continued the nation's unbeaten streak through nine more games and another gold medal. For the first time, though, the U.S. had entered Olympic competition as an underdog. Many of the nation's top collegiate players, including Lew Alcindor, Elvin Hayes and Westley Unseld,

OLYMPIC BASKETBALL RESULTS

1936—Berlin

United States 2, Spain 0 (forfeit)
United States 52, Estonia 28
United States 56, Philippines 23
United States 25, Mexico 10
United States 19, Canada 8 (final)

1948—London

United States 86, Switzerland 21
United States 53, Czechoslovakia 28
United States 59, Argentina 57
United States 66, Egypt 28
United States 61, Peru 33
United States 63, Uruguay 28
United States 71, Mexico 40
United States 65, France 21 (final)

1952—Helsinki

United States 66, Hungary 48
United States 72, Czechoslovakia 47
United States 57, Uruguay 44
United States 86, USSR 58
United States 103, Chile 55
United States 57, Brazil 53
United States 85, Argentina 76
United States 36, USSR 25 (final)

1956—Melbourne

United States 98, Japan 40
United States 101, Thailand 29
United States 121, Philippines 53
United States 85, USSR 55
United States 113, Brazil 51
United States 101, Uruguay 38
United States 89, USSR 55 (final)

1960—Rome

United States 88, Italy 54
United States 125, Japan 66
United States 107, Hungary 63
United States 104, Yugoslavia 42
United States 108, Uruguay 50
United States 81, USSR 57
United States 112, Italy 81
United States 90, Brazil 63 (final)

1964—Tokyo

United States 78, Australia 45
United States 77, Finland 51
United States 60, Peru 45
United States 83, Uruguay 28
United States 69, Yugoslavia 61
United States 86, Brazil 53
United States 116, Korea 50
United States 62, Puerto Rico 42
United States 73, USSR 59 (final)

1968—Mexico City

United States 81, Spain 46
United States 93, Senegal 36
United States 96, Philippines 75
United States 95, Panama 60
United States 100, Italy 61
United States 73, Yugoslavia 58
United States 61, Puerto Rico 56
United States 75, Brazil 63
United States 65, Yugoslavia 50 (final)

1972—Munich

United States 66, Czechoslovakia 35
United States 81, Australia 55
United States 67, Cuba 48
United States 61, Brazil 54
United States 96, Egypt 31
United States 72, Spain 56
United States 99, Japan 33
United States 68, Italy 38
USSR 51, United States 50 (final)

1976—Montreal

United States, Egypt (U.S. won by forfeit)
United States 106, Italy 86
United States 95, Puerto Rico 94
United States 81, Czechoslovakia 76
United States 112, Yugoslavia 93
United States 95, Yugoslavia 74 (final)

(Women)

United States 95, Bulgaria 79
United States 89, Canada 75
Japan 84, United States 71
United States 83, Czechoslovakia 67
USSR, 112, United States 77

Amateur Athletic Union

The Amateur Athletic Union conducts the oldest basketball championship in the United States, dating back to 1897. That year the first "national" championship, little more than a sectional series of games, was held in New York City under the auspices of the Metropolitan Association of the AAU. The winner was New York's 23rd St. YMCA.

Two of the early champions were the Ravenswood YMCA of Chicago, 1901, and the Buffalo Germans, 1904 (no national championships were held in 1902 or '03). The Germans' victory came in a tournament that was held in conjunction with the Olympic Games in St. Louis. It was the first AAU tourney that was truly national in scope. In addition to Buffalo, there were the Xavier AA of New York, Chicago Central YMCA, the Turner Tigers of Los Angeles and the Missouri AA.

From 1905 through 1912 no AAU championships were held, paving the way for many unofficial claims to the crown. The first came in 1905 when the Kansas City AC, whose player-manager, Forrest "Phog" Allen, was later to become a famous college coach at Kansas, whipped the Buffalo Germans. Allen's club was "dethroned" the following year by the Wachter brothers' Company E team from Schenectady, N.Y. They subsequently were declared professionals. This development caused many member clubs to defect from the AAU and to form the Protective Basketball Association. The PBA lasted only a couple of years.

The AAU tournament bounced around a number of cities after its New York debut, and included Buffalo, St. Louis, Kansas City, Chicago, San Francisco, Los Angeles and Atlanta before it was housed in Kansas City's Convention Hall in 1921 for 14 years.

The tourney was moved to Denver in 1935 and remained there through 1968, except for one year, 1949, when Oklahoma City was host. Since 1968 the tournament site has been rotated with host cities including Macon, Georgia; Columbia, South Carolina; and London, Kentucky.

The 1920 staging at Atlanta was hailed as the move that triggered a basketball boom throughout the South. The final was all-collegiate, with New York University beating Rutgers. A forward on NYU was Howard Cann, who was to coach at his alma mater for many years.

The NYU triumph was one of only four fashioned by the colleges over the years. The others were by Utah, 1916; Butler, 1924; and Washburn, 1925.

The most successful of all teams in the AAU festival has been the Phillips 66ers. They won their first crown in 1940 and 10 more have followed (including six in a row, 1943–48).

The tournament is replete with great names, many of whom went on to play in professional basketball. They include Bob Boozer, Don Ohl, Hank Luisetti, Bob Doll, Kenny Sailors, Andy Phillip, Bob Kurland, Vince Boryla, Don Barksdale, George Yardley, Cazzie Russell, Ken Sears and Richie Guerin.

The list of AAU champions, runners-up and scores of the final game for all years in which an official tournament was held:

1897—New York 23rd Street YMCA (Round Robin)
1899—New York Knickerbocker YMCA (Round Robin)
1900—New York Knickerbocker YMCA (Round Robin)
1901—Chicago Ravenswood YMCA 16, Fond du Lac, Wis., 15
1904—Buffalo Germans (Round Robin)
1910—Company F, Portage, Wis., 36, Premiere Lodge 14.
1913—Chicago Cornell-Armour (Round Robin)
1914—Chicago Cornell-Armour 83, Young Men's Fellowship 26
1915—San Francisco Olympic Club 29, Whittier College 16
1916—Utah University 28, Illinois Athletic Club 27
1917—Illinois Athletic Club 27, Brigham Young 14
1919—Los Angeles Athletic Club 23, San Francisco Olympic Club 22

1920—New York University 49, Rutgers University 24

1921—Kansas City Athletic Club 42, SW Kansas College 36

1922—Kansas City Lowe-Campbell 42, Kansas City Athletic Club 28

1923—Kansas City Athletic Club 31, Kansas City Hillyards, 18

1924—Butler University 30, Kansas City Athletic Club 26

1925—Washburn College 42, Kansas City Hillyards 30

Phillips 66er Bob Kurland scores in 1947 AAU game at Bartlesville, Oklahoma

1926—Kansas City Hillyards 25, Kansas City Athletic Club 20

1927—Kansas City Hillyards 29, Ke-Nash-A 10

1928—Kansas City Cooks 25, Kansas City Athletic Club 23

1929—Kansas City Cooks 51, Wichita Henrys 35

1930—Wichita Henrys 29, San Francisco Olympic Club 16

1931—Wichita Henrys 38, Kansas City Athletic Club 14

1932—Wichita Henrys 15, NW Missouri State College 14

1933—Tulsa Diamond Oilers 25, Chicago Rosenberg-Arveys 23

1934—Tulsa Diamond Oilers 29, Wyoming University 19.

1935—Kansas City Stage Lines 45, McPherson Globe Refiners 26

1937—Denver Safeways 43, Phillips 66ers 38

1938—Kansas City Healeys 40, Denver Safeways 38

1939—Denver Nuggets 25, Phillips 66ers 22

1940—Phillips 66ers 39, Denver Nuggets 36

1941—20th Century-Fox 47, San Francisco Olympic Club 34

1942—Denver Legion 45, Phillips 66ers 32

1943—Phillips 66ers 57, Denver Legion 40

1944—Phillips 66ers 50, Denver Legion 43

1945—Phillips 66ers 47, Denver Ambrose 46

1946—Phillips 66ers 45, San Diego Dons 34

1947—Phillips 66ers 62, Oakland Bittners 41

1948—Phillips 66ers 62, Denver Nuggets 48

1949—Oakland Bittners 55, Phillips 66ers 51

1950—Phillips 66ers 65, Oakland Blue-Gold Nuggets 42

1951—San Francisco Stewarts 76, Poudre Valley Creamery 55

1952—Peoria Cats 66, Phillips 66ers 53

1953—Peoria Cats 73, Los Alamitos Navy 62

1954—Peoria Cats 63, San Diego Grihalva Buicks 55

1955—Phillips 66ers 66, Boulder Luckett-Nix Clippers 64

1956—Seattle Buchan Bakers 59, Phillips 66ers 57

1957—Air Force All-Stars 87, San Francisco Olympic Club 74

1958—Peoria Cats 74, Denver D-C Truckers 71 (4 overtimes)

1959—Wichita Vickers 105, Phillips 66ers 83

1960—Peoria Cats 87, Akron Goodyear Wingfoots 73

1961—Cleveland Pipers 107, Denver D-C Truckers 96

1962—Phillips 66ers 70, Denver D-C Truckers 59

1963—Phillips 66ers 100, Denver D-C Truckers 70

1964—Akron Goodyears 86, Phillips 66ers 78

1965—Armed Forces All-Stars 77, Denver Capitol Federal 75

1966—Ford Mustangs 71, Phillips 66ers 67

1967—Akron Goodyear Tires 77, Phillips 66ers 62

1968—Armed Forces All-Stars 73, Spokane Vaughn Realty 69

1969—Armed Forces All-Stars 62, Akron Goodyears 45

1970—Armed Forces All-Stars 68, Columbia Sertoma 67

1971—Armed Forces All-Stars 90, Lexington Marathon Oil 77

1972—Armed Forces All-Stars 92, Lexington Marathon Oil 80

1973—Lexington Marathon Oil 89, Cincinnati Schlitz 84

1974—Jacksonville Buccaneers 98, Ranco Hawks 97

1975—Capitol Insulation 105, California Jr. College All-Stars 91

1976—Athletes-in-Action 94, Armed Forces All-Stars 80

1977—Armed Forces All-Stars 101, Reliable Lumber 100

1978—Christian Youth Center 108, Carver YMCA 106

1979—Christian Youth Center 110, Armed Forces All-Stars 100

AAU Women

The first National AAU championship for women, in 1926, was staged at Pasadena, California. Champion of the six-team field, which played under men's rules, was the Pasadena Athletic and Country Club. Later they played under women's rules, but now it's all the same. As with the men's AAU, the girls' tournament tried many locations before it found a permanent home. After 11 years at Wichita, Kansas, the tourney was moved to St. Joseph, Missouri, in 1940, to Dallas in 1951, returned to Wichita for the next two years and then on once again to St. Joseph, where it stayed until 1967. Since then it has been held in such places as Council Bluffs, Iowa, and Gallup, New Mexico.

The greatest name ever to grace AAU Women's Basketball was that of Mildred "Babe" Didrikson. Although she went on to her biggest fame in track and field and in golf, she was outstanding enough on the court to lead her Dallas Golden Cyclones to the crown in Dallas in 1931. Babe scored 106 points in five tournament games. She was named captain of the All-American team. The phenomenal Texan, voted by the nation's sports writers in 1950 the greatest female athlete of the first half of the 20th century, died of cancer in 1956. She was 42.

The AAU women's champions:

1926—Pasadena A. and C.C., Pasadena, California
1929—Schepps Aces, Dallas, Texas
1930—Sunoco Oilers, Dallas, Texas
1931—Golden Cyclones, Dallas, Texas
1932—Durant Cardinals, Oklahoma
1933—Durant Cardinals, Oklahoma
1934—Tulsa Business College, Oklahoma
1935—Tulsa Business College, Oklahoma
1936—Tulsa Business College, Oklahoma
1937—Little Rock Flyers, Arkansas
1938—Galveston, Texas, Anicos
1939—Galveston, Texas, Anicos
1940—Lewis-Norwood Flyers, Little Rock, Arkansas
1941—Lewis-Norwood Flyers, Little Rock, Arkansas
1942—A.I.C., Davenport, Iowa
1943—A.I.C., Davenport, Iowa
1944—Vultee Aircraft, Nashville, Tennessee
1945—Vultee Aircraft, Nashville, Tennessee
1946—Nashville Goldblumes, Tennessee
1947—Atlanta, Georgia, Sports Arenas
1948—Nashville Goldblumes, Tennessee
1949—Nashville Goldblumes, Tennessee
1950—Nashville Business College, Tennessee
1951—Hanes Hosiery Mills, Winston-Salem, North Carolina
1952—Hanes Hosiery Mills, Winston-Salem, North Carolina
1953—Hanes Hosiery Mills, Winston-Salem, North Carolina
1954—Wayland College, Plainview, Texas
1955—Wayland College, Plainview, Texas
1956—Wayland College, Plainview, Texas
1957—Wayland College, Plainview, Texas
1958—Nashville Business College, Tennessee
1959—Wayland College, Plainview, Texas
1960—Nashville Business College, Tennessee
1961—Wayland College, Plainview, Texas
1962—Nashville Business College, Tennessee
1963—Nashville Business College, Tennessee
1964—Nashville Business College, Tennessee
1965—Nashville Business College, Tennessee
1966—Nashville Business College, Tennessee
1967—Nashville Business College, Tennessee
1968—Nashville Business College, Tennessee
1969—Nashville Business College, Tennessee
1970—Wayland-Hutcherson Flying Queens, Texas
1971—Wayland-Hutcherson Flying Queens, Texas
1972—J. F. Kennedy College, Nebraska
1973—J. F. Kennedy College, Nebraska

1974—Wayland-Hutcherson Queens, Texas   Flying

1975—Wayland-Hutcherson Queens, Texas   Flying

1976—National General West, California

1977—Anna's Bananas, California

1978—Anna's Bananas, California

1979—Anna's Bananas, California

The Professionals

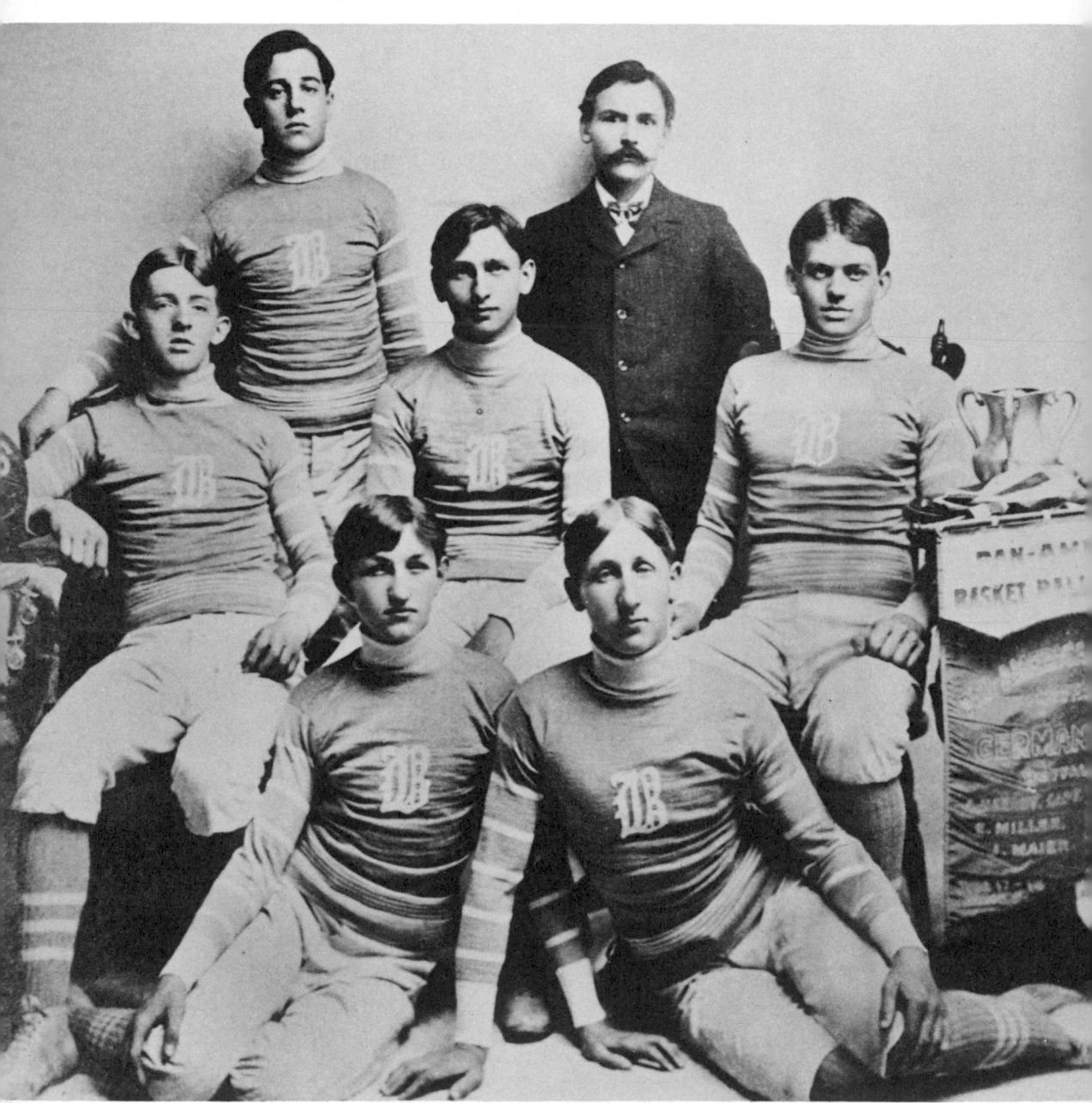

The 1902 Buffalo Germans (l. to r.): rear row, Maier and Burkhardt; middle row, Faust, Captain Heerdt, and Miller; front row, Redlein and Rohde

13

The Pivotal Era

Professional basketball was born in the eastern United States just before the turn of the 20th century more as an economic necessity than as a profit-making venture.

When the young men at the various YMCAs along the eastern seaboard became converts to the sport invented by James Naismith in 1891, they played with such abandon that the Ys decided to drop basketball because of its growing roughness. That left the players no other choice than to rent halls in which to continue playing the sport. And to meet the rentals—and the guarantees for the visiting teams—admission charges had to be instituted.

Uncertainty surrounds the date and location of the first professional game. The strongest claim is for Trenton, New Jersey, in 1896. Attendance for a game at the Masonic Hall there was large enough so that after meeting expenses, the Trenton club had enough extra money to pay each player $15. Fred Cooper, the captain, received an extra dollar. A less substantiated claim has it that the first game was played in Herkimer, New York, in 1893. A group of local players supposedly rented the Fox Opera House in Herkimer and brought in a team from Utica. After paying the visiting team's expenses, there was only change left over for the Herkimer players.

The first professional league, the National Basketball League, was organized in 1898 in Philadelphia. The league disbanded after the 1902–03 season.

As the NBL broke up, the Philadelphia League came into being and welcomed a number of players from the original circuit. The Philadelphia League expanded in 1909 into the Eastern League and embraced teams from New Jersey and New York as well as Pennsylvania.

Professional leagues soon began to spring up elsewhere. The Central League got started in western Pennsylvania in 1906. The Hudson River League was formed in New York three years later. Other leagues established about that time were the New York State League, 1911; Western Pennsylvania League, 1912; Pennsylvania State League, 1914; Inter-State League, 1915; and the Metropolitan Basketball League, 1921. The American Basketball League was formed in 1926.

The Hudson River League and the New York State League were the showcases for the finest professional team of the era, Ed Wachter's Troy (New York) Trojans. Originally formed to challenge the famous Buffalo Germans, who claimed the national championship by virtue of their triumph at the Buffalo Exposition of 1901, the Trojans swept to two consecutive Hudson River League crowns before that league collapsed. The Trojans then became charter members of the New York State League and won three titles in four years before that circuit also failed. Wachter took his team on tour after that and it won 38 straight games before he broke it up.

It was during the Trojans' second season in the Hudson River League that they were able to experiment with some of Wachter's new ideas for the game. Up to that time, passing consisted of short tosses caught on the fly by the receivers.

Wachter had his players adopt the bounce pass, which was much harder to intercept. Another of his innovations was the fast break. The fashion had been for everyone to scramble after the ball. But Wachter set his men in strategic places, with two pursuing the ball, prepared to throw it over the defense to an unguarded teammate in scoring position.

Wachter and the Trojans also anticipated the foul shot rule. All the Trojans were so good at shooting free throws that they encouraged a rule requiring the player to take the shot himself. Until then, each team used a specialist who shot all its free throws. The new rule, though, was not generally accepted for many years.

Early professional basketball was a rugged sport, with anything short of complete mayhem allowed. The rules depended mainly on what court the teams played on and who refereed the game. And there were other shortcomings as well. For example, the games were merely a sideshow for the dances usually held in conjunction with them. There would be dancing before the game, during halftime and after. The highly-waxed floors, excellent for dancing, were hardly conducive to quick starts and stops by the basketball players.

There was no such thing as an out-of-bounds ball because the courts, usually of $60' \times 40'$ bandbox dimensions, were enclosed with chicken wire fences. Because the teams appeared caged in by the fences, the players soon received the nickname "cagers." Later the courts were enclosed with a netting of rope. The more adroit players used the ropes to their advantage, ricocheting in one direction or another.

Then, too, there was little stability among the professionals. Players sold their services to the highest bidder. They jumped from one club to another with impunity. A man would play with Troy one night and against them the next. The better players often played in several leagues at the same time. Under these conditions, team play didn't exist and coaching was almost nonexistent as well. Players relied on trial and error and sought advice from teammates on how to play a particular opponent.

Under these chaotic conditions the New York Celtics were organized in 1914 as a settlement house team in a tough neighborhood on the city's West Side. Among the best players on the club were John Whitty and Pete Barry. The Celtics played together for three seasons and broke up with the United States' entrance into the World War in 1917.

After the Armistice in 1918, Jim Furey, a New York promoter, and his brother Tom decided to reorganize the Celtics. However, Frank McCormack, who had been the founder of the first New York Celtics team, refused to give up the rights to the name. So the Fureys settled for the Original Celtics as the name of their new team. Whitty and Barry from the New York Celtics, and Ernie Reich, Joe Trippe, Eddie White and Mike Smolick made up the team. They were good, but far from the dominant team of their time.

The next season, Jim Furey turned the Celtics into a powerhouse by adding Swede Grimstead, Henry "Dutch" Dehnert and Johnny Beckman. Grimstead was a veteran and Dehnert and Beckman were two of the best young players. Beckman was considered the best foul shooter of the era and because of him the Celtics were unwilling to adopt the Troy Trojans' innovation requiring the player fouled to take the foul shot.

The other outstanding team of this time was the New York Whirlwinds, organized by Tex Rickard. The Whirlwinds included Barney Sedran, Nat Holman and Chris

Leonard. The public naturally wanted to see the two teams meet. Neither the Celtics nor the Whirlwinds willingly recognized the other's existence, but a three-game series was finally arranged in 1921. The teams played in New York's 71st Regiment Armory. The Whirlwinds won the opening

Dutch Dehnert

game, 40–27, before a crowd of 11,000, but the Celtics came back to win, 26–24, the following night. The third game was never played for fear of violence among the wrought-up partisans of the two teams.

At the end of the season, Furey persuaded Holman and Chris Leonard to jump from the Whirlwinds to the Celtics. In addition he signed all the Celtics to exclusive contracts with guaranteed salaries. With this move, wildcat basketball was on the way out. Furey wasn't content to stand pat and

Nat Holman

273

Because the same players were together almost every night, the Celtics developed an almost uncanny sense of teamwork. Out of this came several of the great innovations in basketball strategy, including the pivot play, the switching defense and the give-and-go offense. The Celtics were so superior to most of the teams they played that they were able to perfect their new theories under actual game conditions without much fear of losing.

One night the Celtics ran up an early lead of 30–1 over a team in Miami, Florida. The

Chris Leonard

Pete Barry

continually added the best players he could find. These included Joe Lapchick, Davey Banks, Horace "Horse" Haggerty, and Nat Hickey.

Beginning at the time Furey signed the Celtics to exclusive contracts for the 1922–23 season, the club totally dominated the game through the 1920s. The Celtics would travel anywhere and take on any opponent. They were paid comparatively well for the time, but money was never the most important thing to them. The Celtics had tremendous pride and always tried to win, although they seldom went out of their way to run up the score. At the same time they usually tried to have some fun, too.

Davey Banks was smallest Original Celtic

ball up. This was the pivot play but we didn't even know it at the time."

Before the coming of the Celtics, basketball was strictly an individual game. Each player considered himself personally responsible for the player who lined up opposite him at the center jump. But the Celtics played as a team, and each player guarded the nearest man, regardless of whose personal opponent he was. Joe Lapchick, at 6-5 one of the big men of his time, had trouble adjusting to these defensive switches when he first joined the Celtics. Finally Johnny Whitty took him aside and explained the essential element of the Celtics' philosophy. "It isn't how many goals you get, Joe, or how often you get the tap. We know what you can do with the ball. It's how you are without the ball that determines how good a basketball player you are," Whitty said.

The Celtics were a confident bunch and were convinced that wherever they went they were the best. Always they knew that they were a marked team, that opponents and fans alike were out to get them. The players had to ignore such indignities as hatpins jabbed into their posteriors by courtside spectators. Holman, one of the smallest of the Celtics, was frequently a target. He was a brilliant passer and faker, and sometimes opposing players would vent their frustrations on Nat after being embarrassed by one of his clever moves. "Horse Haggerty was my personal bodyguard. Any time I got hit, and I got hit a lot in those early days, Haggerty would go over to the fellow who fouled me, give him a robust nudge in the ribs and say 'Now we're even.' They always knew what he meant, too," Nat recalled.

Haggerty, at 6-4 and 225 pounds, was truly a giant of a man and was quite capable of meeting any roughness on the court in kind. One night he was riled by a fan who had been continually insulting Holman. Horse beckoned the fan over and then knocked him cold with one punch. Another time he knocked out a referee when Horse thought his decisions too obviously favored the other team. Before Haggerty could get out of town that night, he was jumped by a

Celts took the opportunity to practice their passing and set plays, but the other team's standing guard continually got in the way. The standing guard, common at the time, stood at the foul line and never moved downcourt, even when his own team had the ball.

Then an idea occurred to Dutch Dehnert. "I volunteered to stand in front of him with my back to the basket, so that instead of the guard breaking up our passes, they could pass to me and I could give it back to them. We tried this, and in an effort to bat the ball out of my hands, the standing guard moved around to my right side. All I had to do was pivot to my left, take one step and lay the

The Celtics, reborn for one last fling in the 1930s (l. to r.); rear, Pat Herlihy, Dutch Dehnert, Joe Lapchick; front, Paul Birch, Davey Banks, Nat Hickey

gang of toughs, one of the few times he lost a fight.

As the Celtics were rolling over all opposition, winning about 90 per cent of their games, George Preston Marshall, a Washington laundry tycoon, decided to organize a big-time professional league. His idea was sound but the independent Celtics refused to cooperate. They were too busy making money on their barnstorming tours to have any part of Marshall's American Basketball League. The Celtics added further insults by routing the league's teams in exhibition games.

Finally the ABL blacklisted the Celtics, forbidding any of the league's teams to play games against the Celtics. With their revenue sharply curtailed, the Celtics had no choice but to join the league, which they did midway through the 1926–27 season. The Celtics ran away with the second-half title, winning 19 of 20 games. The following year the Celtics easily won both halves of the ABL championship and then beat Fort Wayne in a playoff series.

Marshall, the owner of the Washington Palace Five, spent more than $65,000 in salaries trying to hire players good enough to beat the Celtics. But the spending didn't do his team any good. "We'll break you yet, George," Dehnert would yell to Marshall as the Celtics rolled over the Palace Five. The

Celtics were so good, in fact, that fans around the league began to lose interest and attendance dropped. In a desperate attempt to restore competitive balance, the league decided to break up the Celtics and parcel out their players to the other teams.

Lapchick, Holman and Barry found their way to the Cleveland Rosenblums and stamped that team with the Celtics' mold. The Rosenblums made a shambles of the league opposition, winning the championship outright in 1928–29 and taking the first-half crown and the playoff against Rochester the following season before the ABL had to cease operations during the latter part of the 1930–31 season. The Cleveland Rosenblums had withdrawn from the league after playing only 12 games, and the circuit fell victim to an attendance drop brought about by the Depression.

Another possible contributor to the league's demise was the rookie rule in-

Cleveland Rosenblums (l. to r.): Red Skurnick, Carl "Sox" Husta, Pete Barry, Ray Dickerson, Dutch Dehnert, George "Dink" Irwin, Dave Kerr, and Joe Lapchick

stituted by ABL Commissioner Joe Carr. It required that three of the eight players on each team's roster have less than a year's experience in the ABL and that two rookies be in the game at all times. The ruling had a profound, negative effect on the quality of play in the league.

The Renaissance Big Five, an independent all-black team from New York, succeeded the Celtics as rulers of the basketball world. The Rens, as they were popularly known, took on all comers and from 1932 until 1936 unquestionably proved themselves the best team in the nation. The Rens would go on the road for about four months, playing one-night stands. They traveled in their own bus and often ended up sleeping in it since most hotels refused to offer them accommodations.

The Rens had been organized by Bob Douglas in New York's Harlem in 1922. Not until the 1925–26 season, though, did they capture the public's eye. That year Douglas acquired James "Pappy" Ricks, Clarence "Fat" Jenkins and Eyre "Bruiser" Saitch. Jenkins was also an outstanding outfielder in the Negro National Baseball League, but discrimination against blacks prevented him from ever reaching the major leagues.

Douglas next added Charles "Tarzan" Cooper, Bill Yancey and John "Casey" Holt. In 1932 Douglas signed the seventh Ren, Wee Willie Smith, and the great years began. Over the next four seasons, the Rens compiled a record of 473–49. In their best year, 1933–34, they were 127–7, including an 88-game winning streak. In the four years the seven stars played together, the Rens claimed the world's championship each year without any serious dispute. In 1963 the team was elected to the Hall of Fame.

The American Basketball League, which the Celtics had put out of business, resumed play for the 1933–34 season after a lapse of

The Rens (l. to r.): Clarence "Fat" Jenkins, Bill Yancey, John "Casey" Holt, James "Pappy" Ricks, Eyre "Bruiser" Saitch, Charles "Tarzan" Cooper, Wee Willie Smith. Inset: owner Bob Douglas

two years. The Philadelphia Sphas, from the South Philadelphia Hebrew Association and coached by Eddie Gottlieb, emerged as the top team in the revived ABL. The Sphas won seven titles in 13 years. The New York Jewels, another of the league's good teams, were made up of the same men who had played for the St. John's "Wonder Five" during their college days.

In its later years, though, the ABL declined in stature and with the founding of the Basketball Association of America in 1946 lost recognition as a major league.

The National Basketball League began play in 1937. The NBL was organized by Lonnie Darling, who had formed the Oshkosh All-Stars a few years before. The Akron Goodyears won the first NBL title. The league had most of its franchises in smaller Midwestern cities. Among the teams at one time or another were Oshkosh, Anderson, Tri-Cities, Flint, Youngstown, Toledo, Fort Wayne, Dayton, Waterloo and Hammond, as well as such larger cities as Detroit, Chicago, Denver, Minneapolis and Syracuse. With this assortment of franchises and few of its teams in the nation's largest cities, the NBL had difficulty achieving recognition as a truly major league.

Minneapolis' George Mikan (99) was the biggest man in the early NBA years

14

Big League

In the summer of 1946 owners of some of the nation's largest sports arenas became convinced that the time was right to bring major league professional basketball to the biggest cities. With the conclusion of World War II, many fine collegiate players were discharged from the Armed Forces and became available to the pro teams. In addition, the lifting of wartime restrictions on the economy left Americans with more money for entertainment.

The group of arena owners, led by Walter Brown, president of the Boston Garden, and Al Sutphin, owner of the Cleveland Arena, all had successfully promoted such events as ice hockey, ice shows, boxing, rodeos and other sporting attractions. Encouraged by the drawing power of college basketball, they felt that a large potential audience for the professional game existed as well.

On June 6, 1946, these men met in New York City to organize a new major professional league, the Basketball Association of America. The owners chose Maurice Podoloff, a New Haven, Connecticut, lawyer, as president of the league. At the time Podoloff was president of the American Hockey League. Podoloff is given credit for

holding the league together through its difficult early years. The BAA began play with teams in 11 cities: Boston, New York, Philadelphia, Providence, Toronto, Washington, Chicago, St. Louis, Cleveland, Detroit and Pittsburgh.

To encourage an offense-minded game, the new league outlawed all varieties of zone defense. Only man-to-man defenses were permitted.

The National Basketball League, with most of its franchises in smaller Midwestern cities, had been in operation since the 1937–38 season, and the two leagues immediately embarked on a struggle for supremacy in professional basketball. The BAA and NBL competed for the services of the best graduating college players each season. For 1947–48, Minneapolis of the NBL signed George Mikan, the 6-10 giant from DePaul who was basketball's greatest drawing card.

But before the 1948–49 season the BAA dealt the older league a crushing blow by picking up four of its best franchises, including Minneapolis with Mikan. A year later the war was over. The two leagues merged to form a new 17-team circuit called the National Basketball Association. Podoloff was elected president of the NBA and Ike W. Duffey, who had headed the NBL, became chairman of the new league's Executive Board.

A detailed year-by-year history of the modern era in professional basketball, dating from the establishment of the Basketball Association of America in the 1946–47 season, follows:

YEARLY ROUNDUPS

1946–47

The established National Basketball League and the brand-new Basketball Association of America each unveiled a high-powered scorer this season. And each of these stars led his team to victory in the playoffs.

The Philadelphia Warriors, paced by Joe Fulks, won the first championship in the BAA, and the Chicago American Gears, with 6-10 George Mikan, won the NBL playoffs, although Rochester emerged as the NBL champion.

The BAA began play with 11 teams, divided into two divisions, In the East, the Washington Capitols, coached by Arnold "Red" Auerbach, finished the regular sea-

Washington's Bones McKinney made the BAA's first All-Star team

son 14 games ahead of Eddie Gottlieb's Philadelphia Warriors. The New York Knickerbockers, Providence Steamrollers, Toronto Huskies and Boston Celtics followed.

The Western Division race was much closer, with the Chicago Stags finishing just one game ahead of the St. Louis Bombers. The Cleveland Rebels, Detroit Falcons and Pittsburgh Ironmen trailed. In the final series for the league championship, the Warriors crushed Chicago, four games to one. The crowd numbered 8,221 for the final playoff game in Philadelphia.

Fulks, a 6-6 ex-marine, was the BAA's top individual performer. He earned 23.1 points a game and consistently outleaped taller opponents. Jumpin' Joe scored 41 points against Toronto, the highest individual total in the BAA's first season.

Fulks shot more times (1,557)—and scored more baskets (475)—than anyone else in the league. He finished with a lead of more than 400 points over his nearest rival, Bob Feerick of Washington.

Other top players included little 5-10 Ernie Calverley of Providence and Max Zaslofsky of Chicago. Calverley, who had played on the famous "point-a-minute" teams at Rhode Island State, led the league in assists and also finished sixth in scoring with a 14.3 average. Zaslofsky, who ignored the jump shot in favor of a two-hand set, was the fifth-leading scorer with a 14.4 average. Many of his points came on shots from beyond the 30-foot mark.

The first BAA All-Star team included Fulks, who was a unanimous selection; Feerick, Zaslofsky, Stan Miasek of Detroit and Bones McKinney of Washington.

While Fulks was burning up the BAA, George Mikan, the giant from DePaul University, was making his pro debut with the NBL's Chicago Gears. The Gears, with player-coach Bobby McDermott and Mikan, who averaged 16.5 points, won the playoffs after finishing the regular season tied for third in the Western Division. A new league rule, however, gave the championship to the team with the best record for the entire season, and on this basis Rochester was declared the champion.

The NBL's All-Star team included Mikan, McDermott, Fred Lewis of Sheboygan, and Al Cervi and Bob Davies of the Rochester Royals. Cervi, one of the few pros in the league who didn't go to college, was the NBL's leading scorer with a 14.4 average.

STANDINGS

Eastern Division	W.	L.	Pct.	Western Division	W.	L.	Pct.
Washington	49	11	.817	Chicago	39	22	.639
Philadelphia	35	25	.583	St. Louis	38	23	.623
New York	33	27	.550	Cleveland	30	30	.500
Providence	28	32	.467	Detroit	20	40	.333
Toronto	22	38	.367	Pittsburgh	15	45	.250
Boston	22	38	.367				

PLAYOFFS

First Round

Chicago defeated Washington 4 games to 2
Philadelphia defeated St. Louis 2 games to 1

New York defeated Cleveland 2 games to 1
Philadelphia defeated New York 2 games to 1

Championship

Philadelphia defeated Chicago 4 games to 1

TOP SCORERS

	Pts.	Ave.
Joe Fulks, Philadelphia	1389	23.2
Bob Feerick, Washington	926	16.8
Stan Miasek, Detroit	895	14.9
Ed Sadowski, Toronto-Cleveland	877	16.5
Max Zaslofsky, Chicago	877	14.4

LEADERS IN ASSISTS

	No.	Ave.
Ernie Calverley, Providence	202	3.4
Ken Sailors, Cleveland	134	2.3
Ossie Schectman, New York	109	2.0
Howie Dallmar, Philadelphia	104	1.7
Marv Rottner, Chicago	93	1.7

1947–48

The Basketball Association of America lost four of its original franchises and added one new team for its second season. And it was the Baltimore Bullets, the new team, which provided the biggest surprise by winning the league championship.

The entire Western Division finished in almost a dead heat. St. Louis was first, with a 29–19 record, and the other three teams, Baltimore, Chicago and Washington, finished in a three-way tie for second place, one game back. A special series of games had to be held to settle the final standings before the playoffs could get under way.

The Eastern Division race was close too, with the Philadelphia Warriors, the defending champions, finishing one game ahead of the New York Knicks. Toronto, Cleveland, Pittsburgh and Detroit, all BAA members in the league's first season, had folded before the second campaign began, making it an eight-team circuit.

Baltimore came on in the playoffs and beat Philadelphia, four games to two, to win the league championship. Baltimore's player-coach, Buddy Jeanette, led the Bullets to the title with slick floor play and a 10.7 scoring average.

Philadelphia's Joe Fulks had the highest scoring average for the season, 22.1, but Chicago's Max Zaslofsky, with his long-range set shot, scored the most points, 1,009.

New York's Carl Braun, a 6-5 rookie from Colgate University, showed that he was a quick learner and one fine marksman when he shattered Fulks' single-game scoring mark of 41 points. Braun, a deadly outside shot, collected 47 points against Providence on December 6. Braun finished the season as the BAA's sixth-leading scorer with a 14.2 average.

Fulks, Zaslofsky and Bob Feerick of Washington all repeated as All-BAA selec-

New York rookie Carl Braun scored 47 points in one game

tions. They were joined by Howie Dallmar of Philadelphia, the league leader in assists, and Ed Sadowski of Boston.

In the National Basketball League, Minneapolis, with George Mikan, won the playoff for the league title. The Lakers had taken over the franchise of Detroit, which had won only four games the previous season, but the addition of Mikan and Jim Pollard converted them into champions. Mikan, the NBL's Most Valuable Player,

broke virtually all the league's scoring records as he averaged 21.3 points a game and reached a peak of 42 points against Syracuse. In the final playoff series, Minneapolis defeated Rochester, the defending champion, three games to one.

The All-NBL team included Mikan and Pollard of Minneapolis, Rookie of the Year Marko Todorovich of Sheboygan and Al Cervi and Red Holzman of Rochester.

Philadelphia's Howie Dallmar drives on New York's Dick Holub

STANDINGS

Eastern Division

	W.	L.	Pct.
Phildadelphia	27	21	.563
New York	26	22	.542
Boston	20	28	.417
Providence	6	42	.104

Western Division

	W.	L.	Pct.
St. Louis	29	19	.604
Baltimore	28	20	.583
Chicago	28	20	.583
Washington	28	20	.583

PLAYOFFS

FIRST ROUND

Philadelphia defeated St. Louis 4 games to 3
Baltimore defeated New York 2 games to 1

Chicago defeated Boston 2 games to 1
Baltimore defeated Chicago 2 games to 0

Championship

Baltimore defeated Philadelphia 4 games to 2

TOP SCORERS

	Pts.	Ave.
Max Zaslofsky, Chicago	1007	21.0
Joe Fulks, Philadelphia	949	22.1
Ed Sadowski, Boston	910	19.4
Bob Feerick, Washington	775	16.1
Stan Miasek, Chicago	716	14.9

LEADERS IN ASSISTS

	No.	Ave.
Howie Dallmar, Philadelphia	120	2.5
Ernie Calverley, Providence	119	2.5
Jim Seminoff, Chicago	89	1.8
Chuck Gilmur, Chicago	77	1.6
Ed Sadowski, Boston	74	1.6

1948–49

Disaster struck the old National Basketball League in midsummer as four of its best franchises switched to the Basketball Association of America. The NBL lost the Minneapolis Lakers and George Mikan, their great 6-10 center; Rochester, the defending league champions; Fort Wayne and Indianapolis. These switches just about killed the NBL's chances for survival and left the

Minneapolis, with Mikan (99), won the title in its first year in the BAA

pro basketball field virtually clear for the BAA.

Minneapolis and Mikan burst on the BAA scene with a vengeance. The Lakers won the league championship in their first season and Mikan used his tremendous strength and 240 pounds to great advantage. He dethroned Philadelphia's Joe Fulks, the BAA's resident scoring whiz, as the scoring champion. Mikan poured in an average of 28.3 points a game, comfortably ahead of Fulks' 26.0.

The Rochester Royals, with Arnie Risen and Bob Davies, finished a game ahead of the Lakers in the Western Division. But in the playoffs, Minneapolis eliminated Rochester in two straight games and went on to defeat Red Auerbach's Washington Capitols in six games for the BAA title. The Capitols had finished the season six games ahead of the New York Knicks and then eliminated the Knicks, two games to one, in the playoffs.

Old NBL players dominated the All-BAA selections as Mikan and Jim Pollard of Minneapolis and Rochester's Davies, who had led the league in assists and averaged 15.1 points, all made the team. Mikan was a unanimous pick. Joining them were two familiar faces, Fulks, and Max Zaslofsky of Chicago, each making the all-league squad for the third consecutive year.

Fulks turned in the outstanding individual performance of the season by scoring 63 points against the Indianapolis Jets. His outburst totally eclipsed the league's old scoring high of 47 points, set by Carl Braun of New York the season before.

The Lakers played the famed Harlem Globetrotters twice and split the two games. One of the contests attracted a crowd of 20,046. The BAA's Philadelphia Warriors also took a game from the Globetrotters, winning 58–54.

The NBL, breathing its last, added Denver, Dayton, Hammond and Waterloo to make up for the loss of the four teams that jumped to the BAA and the disbanding of the Toledo and Flint franchises. The Anderson Duffey Packers finished first in the East and defeated the Oshkosh All-Stars, Western champions, in the playoffs. Don Otten of the Tri-Cities Blackhawks topped the NBL's scorers.

Otten, along with Dick Mehen of Waterloo, Al Cervi of Syracuse, Frank Brian of Anderson and Gene Englund of Oshkosh, made the All-NBL team.

STANDINGS

Eastern Division	W.	L.	Pct.	Western Division	W.	L.	Pct.
Washington	38	22	.633	Rochester	45	15	.750
New York	32	28	.533	Minneapolis	44	16	.733
Baltimore	29	31	.483	Chicago	38	22	.633
Philadelphia	28	32	.467	St. Louis	29	31	.483
Boston	25	35	.417	Fort Wayne	22	38	.367
Providence	12	48	.200	Indianapolis	18	42	.300

PLAYOFFS

First Round

Washington defeated Philadelphia 2 games to 0
New York defeated Baltimore 2 games to 1

Rochester defeated St. Louis 2 games to 0
Minneapolis defeated Chicago 2 games to 0

Semifinals

Minneapolis defeated Rochester 2 games to 0

Washington defeated New York 2 games to 1

Championship

Minneapolis defeated Washington 4 games to 2

TOP SCORERS

	Pts.	Ave.
George Mikan, Minneapolis	1698	28.3
Joe Fulks, Philadelphia	1560	26.0
Max Zaslofsky, Chicago	1197	20.6
Arnie Risen, Rochester	995	16.6
Ed Sadowski, Philadelphia	920	15.3

LEADERS IN ASSISTS

	No.	Ave.
Bob Davies, Rochester	321	5.4
Andy Phillip, Chicago	319	5.3
John Logan, St. Louis	276	4.8
Ernie Calverley, Providence	251	4.3
George Senesky, Philadelphia	233	3.9

1949–50

The war between the leagues came to an end as the BAA and the NBL merged to form the new National Basketball Association. The merger left an unwieldy 17-team league, divided into three divisions.

The Central Division included Minneapolis, Rochester, Fort Wayne, Chicago, and St. Louis, BAA teams the year before. New York, Washington, Philadelphia, Boston, and Baltimore from the BAA and Syracuse of the NBL were in the Eastern Division. The West contained six former NBL teams, Indianapolis, Anderson, Tri-Cities, Sheboygan, Waterloo, and Denver.

But despite all the teams and new alignments, the league still had a familiar look as George Mikan and the Minneapolis Lakers won the championship. Mikan set all sorts of individual records, including the highest scoring average, 27.4 points a game; most field goals, 649, and most foul shots, 567 of 728 attempts. He rolled up the highest one-game scoring total of the season with 51 points against Rochester.

Even with Mikan, Jim Pollard, Vern Mikklesen, Arnie Ferrin and Slater Martin, the Lakers still had to beat Rochester in a

The little man in the middle is Maurice Podoloff, first commissioner of the NBA

Chicago's Andy Phillip, second in NBA in assists, tries to stop New York's Paul Noel

special playoff after the two teams had tied for the Central title.

In the championship round of the playoffs, Minneapolis defeated Anderson, which had surprised Western champion Indianapolis, in two straight games and Syracuse, the Eastern champions, in a hard-fought six-game series.

Two outstanding rookies, Ed Macauley with St. Louis and Alex Groza with Indianapolis, came into the league. Groza, who played his college ball at Kentucky, finished second to Mikan with a 23.4 scoring average and led the NBA in field-goal accuracy with a 47.8 mark. Macauley, a two-time All-American at St. Louis University, was fifth with a 16.1 average. Another rookie, Dick McGuire of the New York Knicks, topped the league in assists.

Mikan came within one vote of being a unanimous all-league pick for the second straight year. Joining him on the team were his teammate Jim Pollard; Max Zaslofsky of Chicago; Bobby Davies of Rochester and Groza.

The Lakers played the Harlem Globetrotters twice, winning both games. One of the games, in Chicago, attracted a crowd of 21,666.

STANDINGS

Eastern Division

	W.	L.	Pct.
Syracuse	51	13	.797
New York	40	28	.588
Washington	32	36	.471
Philadelphia	26	42	.382
Baltimore	25	43	.368
Boston	22	46	.324

Western Division

	W.	L.	Pct.
Indianapolis	39	25	.609
Anderson	37	27	.578
Tri-Cities	29	35	.453
Sheboygan	22	40	.355
Waterloo	19	43	.306
Denver	11	51	.177

Central Division

	W.	L.	Pct.
Minneapolis*	51	17	.750
Rochester	51	17	.750
Fort Wayne*	40	28	.588
Chicago	40	28	.588
St. Louis	26	42	.382

*Won playoff to break tie

PLAYOFFS

First Round

Syracuse defeated Philadelphia 2 games to 0
New York defeated Washington 2 games to 0

Minneapolis defeated Chicago 2 games to 0
Fort Wayne defeated Rochester 2 games to 0

Indianapolis defeated Sheboygan 2 games to 2
Anderson defeated Tri-Cities 2 games to 1

Second Round

Syracuse defeated New York 2 games to 1
Minneapolis defeated Fort Wayne 2 games to 1
Anderson defeated Indianapolis 2 games to 1

Third Round

Minneapolis defeated Anderson 2 games to 0

Championship

Minneapolis defeated Syracuse 4 games to 2

TOP SCORERS

	Pts.	Ave.
George Mikan, Minneapolis	1865	27.4
Alex Groza, Indianapolis	1496	23.4
Frank Brian, Anderson	1138	17.8
Max Zaslofsky, Chicago	1115	16.4
Ed Macauley, St. Louis	1081	16.1

LEADERS IN ASSISTS

	No.	Ave.
Dick McGuire, New York	386	5.7
Andy Phillip, Chicago	377	5.8
Bob Davies, Rochester	294	4.6
George Senesky, Philadelphia	264	3.9
Al Cervi, Syracuse	264	4.7

1950–51

When the Chicago franchise disbanded after the 1949–50 season, the remaining teams divided up the Stags' players. The Boston Celtics came up with Bob Cousy, a 6-1 guard who many other teams considered too small for the NBA. But this season, and for many seasons to come, Cousy would prove just how wrong were the skeptics. He averaged 15.6 points a game, ninth best in the league, and was named Rookie of the Year.

For the first time blacks played in the NBA. The New York Knicks obtained Nat "Sweetwater" Clifton from the Harlem Globetrotters, and the Boston Celtics drafted Chuck Cooper of Duquesne. In general, though, rookies had trouble making the teams, with only 12 first-year men in the league.

The NBA got down to a more manageable size when six franchises—Chicago, St. Louis, Anderson, Waterloo, Sheboygan, and Denver—dropped out. The remaining 11 teams were organized into two divisions. The collapse of the Washington Capitols on

New York's Sweetwater Clifton, ex-Globetrotter, was one of the first blacks in the NBA

January 9, though, left the league with 10 teams for most of the season.

The Rochester Royals, with Arnie Risen, Bob Davies, and Bob Wanzer, ended the Minneapolis Lakers' three-year reign as world champions. The Royals eliminated the Lakers, three games to one, in the playoff semifinals after having finished three games behind Minneapolis in the West. In the East, Philadelphia finished two-and-a-half games ahead of Boston, coached by Red Auerbach, and four games ahead of New York. But the Knicks won the Eastern playoffs before losing to Rochester, four games to three, for the championship.

Two highlights of the campaign were a 19–18 victory by Fort Wayne over Minneapolis in a stalling battle and a 75–73 triumph by Indianapolis over Rochester in six overtimes.

As he had every season since entering the league, George Mikan won the scoring title with a 28.4 average, Alex Groza of the Indianapolis Jets was second with a 21.7 mark, and "Easy Ed" Macauley of Boston was third with 20.4. For the second year in a row Groza was the NBA's most accurate shooter, connecting on 47.0 percent of his shots from the floor. Andy Phillip of Philadelphia led in assists and the Syracuse Nationals' Dolph Schayes topped the NBA in rebounding.

The league played its first All-Star Game in the Boston Garden on March 2 and 10,094 fans turned out to see the East down the West, 111–94. The winners' Macauley, MVP, led the scorers with 20 points and held Mikan to four field goals.

The All-NBA team included Mikan, a unanimous selection; Groza and Macauley, each in his second NBA season; Bob Davies of the champion Rochester Royals, and Ralph Beard of Indianapolis, who had been a college teammate of Groza at Kentucky.

STANDINGS

Eastern Division

	W.	L.	Pct.
Philadelphia	40	26	.606
Boston	39	30	.565
New York	36	30	.545
Syracuse	32	34	.485
Baltimore	24	42	.364
Washington*	10	25	.286

*Disbanded Jan. 10, 1951

Western Division

	W.	L.	Pct.
Minneapolis	44	24	.647
Rochester	41	27	.603
Fort Wayne	32	36	.471
Indianapolis	31	37	.456
Tri-Cities	25	43	.368

PLAYOFFS

First Round

New York defeated Boston 2 games to 0
Syracuse defeated Philadelphia 2 games to 0
Rochester defeated Fort Wayne 2 games to 1
Minneapolis defeated Indianapolis 2 games to 1

Semifinals

New York defeated Syracuse 3 games to 2
Rochester defeated Minneapolis 3 games to 1

Championship

Rochester defeated New York 4 games to 3

TOP SCORERS

	Pts.	Ave.
George Mikan, Minneapolis	1932	28.4
Alex Groza, Indianapolis	1429	21.7
Ed Macauley, Boston	1384	20.4
Joe Fulks, PHiladelphia	1236	18.7
Frank Brian, Tri-Cities	1144	16.8

TOP REBOUNDERS

	No.	Ave.
Dolph Schayes, Syracuse	1080	16.4
George Mikan, Minneapolis	958	14.1
Harry Gallatin, New York	800	12.1
Arnie Risen, Rochester	795	12.0
Alex Groza, Indianapolis	709	10.7

LEADERS IN ASSISTS

	No.	Ave.
Andy Phillip, Philadelphia	414	6.3
Dick McGuire, New York	400	6.3
George Senesky, Philadelphia	342	5.3
Bob Cousy, Boston	341	4.9
Ralph Beard, Indianapolis	318	4.8

1951-52

Minneapolis regained the league championship, its second since the merger of the BAA and the NBL. The Lakers did it with big, strong scorers and rebounders in 6-10 George Mikan, 6-8 Vern Mikkelsen, and 6-3 Jim Pollard. The Laker stars weren't hampered by the wider free-throw lanes, increased from six to twelve feet, designed to keep pivot men further from the basket by enlarging the three-second area.

For the first time in his NBA career, though, Mikan failed to lead the league in scoring. Instead the honors went to Paul Arizin, a 6-4 forward in his second pro season with the Philadelphia Warriors. Arizin finished with a 25.4 average, and Mikan was second with 23.8. Arizin led the NBA in field-goal accuracy with 44.8 per cent,

Knicks' Vince Boryla has Celtics' Ed Macauley up in the air

and also hit on 17 successive free throws, the longest streak of the season.

Mikan had the best single game of the year, scoring 61 points against Rochester on January 20. This was only two less than the NBA record set by Joe Fulks. Larry Foust of Fort Wayne and Mel Hutchins of Milwaukee tied for the rebounding lead.

The divisional races were the closest in the NBA's short history. Syracuse won by a single game over New York in the East, and Rochester, the defending NBA champion, by the same margin in the West. Neither of the first-place finishers made it to the playoff finals, however. The Knicks ousted Syracuse and Minneapolis eliminated Rochester. In the playoff finals, the Lakers beat the Knicks in a seven-game series for the title.

The league showed signs of increasing stability, with only one franchise shift. The Tri-Cities Blackhawks, one of the old NBL teams, moved to Milwaukee and became the Milwaukee Hawks. The change of scenery didn't help, though, as the team finished last in the West for the second straight year.

As usual Mikan headed the selections for the All-NBA team. The other members were Arizin; Boston's Bob Cousy, the third-leading scorer with a 21.7 average; Ed Macauley, Cousy's teammate and the NBA's fourth scorer with a 19.2 average; Bob Davies of Rochester, fifth with 16.2, and Dolph Schayes of Syracuse. Davies and Schayes shared the fifth spot on the team.

For the second consecutive year the All-Star Game was held in Boston and for the second time the East scored a convincing victory. Arizin led the East to a 108–91 triumph with 26 points and was named the game's Most Valuable Player. Mikan scored 26 for the West.

STANDINGS

Eastern Division

	W.	L.	Pct.
Syracuse	40	26	.606
Boston	39	27	.591
New York	37	29	.561
Philadelphia	33	33	.500
Baltimore	20	46	.303

Western Division

	W.	L.	Pct.
Rochester	41	25	.621
Minneapolis	40	26	.606
Indianapolis	34	32	.515
Fort Wayne	29	37	.439
Milwaukee	17	49	.258

PLAYOFFS

First Round

Syracuse defeated Philadelphia 2 games to 1
New York defeated Boston 2 games to 1
Minneapolis defeated Indianapolis 2 games to 0
Rochester defeated Fort Wayne 2 games to 0

Semifinals

New York defeated Syracuse 3 games to 1
Minneapolis defeated Rochester 3 games to 1

Championship

Minneapolis defeated New York 4 games to 3

TOP SCORERS

	Pts.	Ave.
Paul Arizin, Philadelphia	1674	25.4
George Mikan, Minneapolis	1523	23.8
Bob Cousy, Boston	1433	21.7
Ed Macauley, Boston	1264	19.2
Bob Davies, Rochester	1052	16.2

TOP REBOUNDERS

	No.	Ave.
Mel Hutchins, Milwaukee	880	13.3
Larry Foust, Fort Wayne	880	13.3
George Mikan, Minneapolis	866	13.5
Arnie Risen, Rochester	841	12.7
Dolph Schayes, Syracuse	773	12.3

LEADERS IN ASSISTS

	No.	Ave.
Andy Phillip, Philadelphia	539	8.2
Bob Cousy, Boston	441	6.7
Bob Davies, Rochester	390	6.0
Dick McGuire, New York	388	6.1
Fred Scolari, Baltimore	303	4.7

1952–53

Bob Cousy, Boston's incredible guard, turned in the outstanding performance of the year when he scored 50 points against Syracuse in a playoff game on March 21. The game went into four overtimes before the Celtics finally won, 111–105. Cousy made good on 10 of 22 field-goal attempts, most of them from long range, and added a phenomenal 30 of 32 free throws. His 50 points were the most ever scored in a playoff game.

Despite Cousy's heroics, the playoffs had a familiar look as Minneapolis defeated New York for its second straight title and fourth in five seasons. The Knicks battled into the playoff finals for the third straight time and lost for the third consecutive year.

For the first time in its history the NBA opened the season with the same teams that had finished the year before. The Eastern division race was particularly close, with New York finishing half-a-game ahead of Syracuse and a game-and-a-half in front of the Celtics. In the West, Minneapolis wound up four games ahead of second-place Rochester.

Neil Johnston, Philadelphia's 6-8 center, won the scoring title with a 22.3 average. The Lakers' George Mikan, with a 20.6 mark, was second. Johnston was also the NBA's most accurate shooter, hitting on 45.2 per cent of his shots. Mikan led in rebounds with a 14.4 average.

Seventeen individual and team records fell during the season. Boston's Cousy set new game (18) and season (547) records for assists and also tied the league record by making 15 of 15 free throws in a game.

Bill Sharman, Cousy's backcourt partner on the Celtics, made his first 11 shots from

Playmaker Bob Cousy showed he could score . . . with a 50-point game

the floor against Philadelphia for a single-game mark. Another Celtic, Ed Macauley, and Mikan each scored 46 points in a game, high for the season. Mikan's performance was in a game against Baltimore in which he scored 32 points in the first half, 19 in the second quarter.

The West won its first All-Star Game in three tries, defeating the East, 79–75, before 10,322 fans in Fort Wayne. Mikan was the leading scorer with 22 points and was chosen MVP, but it was Bobby Davies of Rochester who broke the game open by scoring eight straight points for the West in the final five minutes of play.

Syracuse's Dolph Schayes was named to the All-NBA team with Mikan, Johnston, Cousy and Macauley.

STANDINGS

Eastern Division

	W.	L.	Pct.
New York	47	23	.671
Syracuse	47	24	.662
Boston	46	25	.648
Baltimore	16	54	.229
Philadelphia	12	57	.174

Western Division

	W.	L.	Pct.
Minneapolis	48	22	.686
Rochester	44	26	.629
Fort Wayne	36	33	.522
Indianapolis	28	43	.394
Milwaukee	27	44	.380

PLAYOFFS

First Round

New York defeated Baltimore 2 games to 0
Boston defeated Syracuse 2 games to 0
Fort Wayne defeated Rochester 2 games to 1
Minneapolis defeated Indianapolis 2 games to 0

Semifinals

New York defeated Boston 3 games to 1
Minneapolis defeated Fort Wayne 3 games to 2

Championship

Minneapolis defeated New York 4 games to 1

TOP SCORERS

	Pts.	Ave.
Neil Johnston, Philadelphia	1564	22.3
George Mikan, Minneapolis	1442	20.6
Bob Cousy, Boston	1407	19.8
Ed Macauley, Boston	1402	20.3
Dolph Schayes, Syracuse	1262	17.8

TOP REBOUNDERS

	No.	Ave.
George Mikan, Minneapolis	1007	14.4
Neil Johnston, Philadelphia	976	13.9
Dolph Schayes, Syracuse	920	13.0
Harry Gallatin, New York	916	13.1
Mel Hutchins, Milwaukee	793	11.2

LEADERS IN ASSISTS

	No.	Ave.
Bob Cousy, Boston	547	7.7
Andy Phillip, Fort Wayne	397	5.7
George King, Syracuse	364	5.1
Dick McGuire, New York	296	4.9
Paul Seymour, Syracuse	294	4.4

1953–54

George Mikan, the magnificent 6-10 center, played his last season as a pro and led the Minneapolis Lakers to their third straight championship and fifth in six years in three leagues. Mikan, later named the greatest basketball player of the first half of the century in an Associated Press poll, averaged 18.4 points a game, fourth-best in the league. He also was the all-league center, as he was in every year of his pro career.

Indianapolis dropped out of the league, leaving five teams in the East and four in the West. Both divisional races were close, with New York taking the Eastern crown by two games over Syracuse and Boston, and Minneapolis winning by two over Rochester in the West. Syracuse made it to the playoff finals but bowed to Minneapolis in a seven-game series for the championship.

The Philadelphia Warriors' Neil Johnston retained the scoring title with a 24.4 average. Bob Cousy of Boston was second with a 19.2 mark and his teammate Ed Macauley was third.

Macauley was the NBA's most accurate shooter from the floor with a .486 percentage, and Boston's Bill Sharman was tops from the free-throw line, making 84.4 per

Warriors' Neil Johnston set a Madison Square Garden pro scoring mark with 50 points

cent of his shots. New York's Harry "The Horse" Gallatin hauled in a record-setting total of 1,098 rebounds, an average of 15.3 a game. What made his feat more remarkable was that, at 6-6, Gallatin was usually battling against taller men.

The East scored a 98–93 overtime victory in the annual All-Star Game, staged before a crowd of 16,478 in Madison Square Garden. Mikan tied the score at 84-all by hitting two free throws with no time left in regulation play. But Cousy, the game's MVP, scored 10 of the East's 14 points in the overtime period for the East's third victory in four games. Jim Pollard of Minneapolis led the West with 23 points.

The All-NBA team included Cousy, who was a unanimous pick; Johnston, Mikan, Dolph Schayes of Syracuse, and Gallatin. Ray Felix, a skinny 6-11 center from Long Island University, averaged 17.6 points a game for Baltimore and won Rookie of the Year honors.

STANDINGS

Eastern Division

	W.	L.	Pct.
New York	44	28	.611
Boston	42	30	.583
Syracuse	42	30	.583
Philadelphia	29	43	.403
Baltimore	16	56	.222

Western Division

	W.	L.	Pct.
Minneapolis	46	26	.639
Rochester	44	28	.611
Fort Wayne	40	32	.556
Milwaukee	21	51	.292

PLAYOFFS

First Round

Boston defeated New York 2 games to 0
Syracuse defeated New York 2 games to 0
Syracuse defeated Boston 2 games to 0
Rochester defeated Fort Wayne 2 games to 0
Minneapolis defeated Fort Wayne 2 games to 0
Minneapolis defeated Rochester 1 game to 0

Semifinals

Syracuse defeated Boston 2 games to 0
Minneapolis defeated Rochester 2 games to 1

Championship

Minneapolis defeated Syracuse 4 games to 3

TOP SCORERS

	Pts.	Ave.
Neil Johnston, Philadelphia	1759	24.4
Bob Cousy, Boston	1383	19.2
Ed Macauley, Boston	1344	18.9
George Mikan, Minneapolis	1306	18.1
Ray Felix, Baltimore	1269	17.6

TOP REBOUNDERS

	No.	Ave.
Harry Gallatin, New York	1098	15.3
George Mikan, Minneapolis	1028	14.3
Larry Foust, Fort Wayne	967	13.4
Ray Felix, Baltimore	958	13.3
Dolph Schayes, Syracuse	879	12.1

LEADERS IN ASSISTS

	No.	Ave.
Bob Cousy, Boston	578	7.2
Andy Phillip, Fort Wayne	449	6.3
Paul Seymour, Syracuse	364	5.1
Dick McGuire, New York	354	5.2
Bob Davies, Rochester	323	4.5

1954–55

The NBA made several important rules changes in an attempt to speed up play and eliminate excessive fouling. The most important was the introduction of the 24-second rule, requiring a team to shoot within 24 seconds of gaining possession of the ball. The league also decided to limit teams to six personal fouls a quarter. Any additional personals would be punished by a bonus foul shot.

The Syracuse Nationals won the league championship, defeating the Fort Wayne Pistons in the final playoff series. The Nats

Minneapolis' Jim Pollard captures rebound in face of Fort Wayne's Paul Walther

won the title when George King tossed in a foul shot with ten seconds remaining in the decisive seventh game to break a 91–91 deadlock.

Syracuse had won the Eastern Division title by five games over New York and Fort Wayne had finished three games ahead of the defending NBA champion, Minneapolis, in the West. The Lakers, champions in five of the last six seasons, had to get used to

playing without George Mikan, their great center who had retired to attend law school.

The Baltimore Bullets disbanded early in the season after having played 14 games and their players were divided among the eight remaining teams.

Neil Johnston of Philadelphia continued his domination as the league's top point-maker, winning the scoring title for the third consecutive year. He averaged 22.7

points a game, beating out teammate Paul Arizin and Bob Cousy of Boston. Johnston also led in rebounding with a 15.1 average. Cousy was the league leader in assists, but Rochester's Bob Davies, playing his last season, set a single-game assist record of 20.

Several other outstanding individual performances highlighted the year. Johnston scored 45 points in a game against Rochester, and grabbed 39 rebounds against Syracuse. Boston's Bill Sharman, the league's best foul shooter, converted a record 50 consecutive free throws over a 10-game stretch.

The season's outstanding rookie was Bob Pettit, Milwaukee's 6-9 forward. Pettit, from Louisiana State, finished fourth in scoring with a 20.4 average. The Hawks also came up with another good rookie in

Frank Selvy. Selvy came to Milwaukee after the collapse of the Baltimore franchise and wound up as the NBA's fifth-leading scorer with a 19.0 average. He reached a single-game peak of 42 against Minneapolis.

The East scored a 100–91 victory in the annual All-Star Game, played before 13,138 in Madison Square Garden. The Boston backcourt combination of Cousy and Sharman led the East, with Sharman picked as the game's MVP. He scored 15 points, Cousy 20.

Pettit, Johnston and Cousy made the All-NBA team, along with Dolph Schayes of Syracuse and Larry Foust of Fort Wayne. Schayes had averaged 18.8 points and 12.3 rebounds in leading the Nationals to the championship and Foust, a 6-9 center, was the NBA's leader in field-goal accuracy with a .487 percentage.

STANDINGS

Eastern Division

	W.	L.	Pct.
Syracuse	43	29	.597
New York	38	34	.528
Boston	36	36	.500
Philadelphia	33	39	.458

Western Division

	W.	L.	Pct.
Fort Wayne	43	29	.597
Minneapolis	40	32	.556
Rochester	29	43	.403
Milwaukee	29	46	.361

PLAYOFFS

First Round

Boston defeated New York 2 games to 1
Minneapolis defeated Rochester 2 games to 1

Semifinals

Syracuse defeated Boston 3 games to 1
Fort Wayne defeated Minneapolis 3 games to 1

Championship

Syracuse defeated Fort Wayne 4 games to 3

TOP SCORERS

	Pts.	Ave.
Neil Johnston, Philadelphia	1631	22.7
Paul Arizin, Philadelphia	1512	21.0
Bob Cousy, Boston	1504	21.2
Bob Pettit, Milwaukee	1466	20.4
Frank Selvy, Milwaukee	1348	19.0

TOP REBOUNDERS

	No.	Ave.
Neil Johnston, Philadelphia	1085	15.1
Harry Gallatin, New York	995	13.8
Bob Pettit, Milwaukee	994	13.8
Dolph Schayes, Syracuse	887	12.3
Ray Felix, New York	818	11.4

LEADERS IN ASSISTS

	No.	Ave.
Bob Cousy, Boston	558	7.8
Dick McGuire, New York	542	7.6
Andy Phillip, Fort Wayne	491	7.7
Paul Seymour, Syracuse	483	6.7
Slater Martin, Minneapolis	427	5.9

1955–56

Bob Pettit, the NBA's Rookie of the Year a season ago, proved totally immune to the sophomore jinx. The 6-9 forward swept just about all the league's individual honors. He led the league in scoring, with a 25.7 average; in rebounding with a 16.2 average; won the Podoloff Cup as the NBA's Most Valuable Player, and was the outstanding player in the All-Star Game.

But despite Pettit's individual feats, for the well-traveled Hawks, now in St. Louis, Philadelphia won the NBA championship, its first since the league's initial season. The Warriors won by six games over Boston in the East and Fort Wayne took the Western title by four games over Minneapolis. Both teams made it to the playoff finals, with Philadelphia defeating Fort Wayne, four games to one. Paul Arizin and Neil Johnston, the NBA's second- and third-leading scorers, led the Warriors to victory.

The Hawks, who had started out as the Tri-Cities Blackhawks in the old NBL, moved from Milwaukee to St. Louis in the only franchise shift of the season. Another link to the past was broken when the Pistons' Max Zaslofsky, who had been on four all-league teams, was waived out of the circuit. This left Connie Simmons of Rochester as the only player who had been in the league since its founding as the Basketball Association of America a decade earlier.

Joe Lapchick, who had coached the New York Knickerbockers for nine seasons, retired in February and was succeeded by Vince Boryla, one of his former players.

The West, behind Pettit's brilliant all-around play, defeated the East, 108–94, in the annual All-Star Game at Rochester. Pettit scored 20 points and grabbed 24 rebounds on his way to MVP honors in the game. Philadelphia's Johnston scored 17 to pace the losers.

The All-NBA team included Pettit, the Warriors' Arizin and Johnston, and Cousy and Bill Sharman of Boston, who were the league's outstanding backcourt duo. Cousy broke his own record with 642 assists dur-ing the season and Sharman led the league in foul-shooting for the fourth consecutive year with an .867 percentage. Johnston, with a .457 percentage, was the best shooter from the floor.

The Rochester Royals came up with two outstanding rookies, Maurice Stokes and Jack Twyman. Stokes, the NBA Rookie of the Year from tiny St. Francis of Loretto (Pa.) College, averaged 16.8 points a game and was second to Pettit in rebounding. Twyman averaged 14.4 points a game.

St. Louis Hawk Bob Pettit (9) was MVP, and a lot else

300

Joe Graboski · Neil Johnston · Paul Arizin · Jin E. George · George Senesky · Edward Gottlieb · Tom Gola · Walter F. Davis · George P. Dempsey · Ernest J. Beck · Lawrence C. Hennessy · John T. Moore

PHILADELPHIA WARRIORS
NATIONAL BASKETBALL ASSOCIATION
and
WORLD CHAMPIONS
1955-56

STANDINGS

Eastern Division	W.	L.	Pct.	Western Division	W.	L.	Pct.
Philadelphia	45	27	.625	Fort Wayne	37	35	.514
Boston	39	33	.542	Minneapolis*	33	39	.458
Syracuse*	35	37	.486	St. Louis	33	39	.458
New York	35	37	.486	Rochester	31	41	.431

*Won playoff to break tie

PLAYOFFS

First Round

Syracuse defeated Boston 2 games to 1
St. Louis defeated Minneapolis 2 games to 1

Semifinals

Philadelphia defeated Syracuse 3 games to 2
Fort Wayne defeated St. Louis 3 games to 2

Championship

Philadelphia defeated Fort Wayne 4 games to 1

TOP SCORERS

	Pts.	Ave.
Bob Pettit, St. Louis	1849	25.7
Paul Arizin, Philadelphia	1741	24.2
Neil Johnston, Philadelphia	1547	22.1
Clyde Lovellette, Minneapolis	1526	21.5
Dolph Schayes, Syracuse	1472	20.4

TOP REBOUNDERS	No.	Ave.	LEADERS IN ASSISTS	No.	Ave.
Bob Pettit, St. Louis	1164	16.2	Bob Cousy, Boston	642	8.9
Maurice Stokes, Rochester	1094	16.3	Jack George, Philadelphia	457	6.3
Clyde Lovellette, Minneapolis	992	14.0	Slater Martin, Minneapolis	445	6.2
Neil Johnston, Philadelphia	872	12.5	Andy Phillip, Fort Wayne	410	5.9
Dolph Schayes, Syracuse	872	12.4	George King, Syracuse	410	5.7

1956–57

Bill Russell came to the Boston Celtics and brought the key to the NBA championship with him. Russell, a lanky 6-10 rookie from the University of San Francisco, joined the Celtics in December after having led the United States to victory in the 1956 Olympic Games.

With his tremendous rebounding and defensive skills, Russell provided the missing

Rookie Bill Russell (6) led ascension of Boston to its first NBA title

ingredient in the Celtics' championship blend. On offense he made Boston's fast break work, getting the ball to Bob Cousy and Bill Sharman. And on defense his amazing shot-blocking talent intimidated opposing shooters.

Even with Russell, though, the Celtics had to struggle to win their first NBA title. The final playoff series with the St. Louis Hawks went the full seven games. Four of the games were decided by a single basket and two went into double overtime. In the decisive seventh game the lead changed hands 20 times before Frank Ramsey's 20-foot jump shot in the second overtime put Boston ahead, 124–122. The Celtics held on to win, 125–123.

Boston won the Eastern title by a comfortable six-game margin over Syracuse, but in the West three teams tied for first. St. Louis, Minneapolis and Fort Wayne all finished with identical 34–38 marks. In special playoff games to sort out the Western teams, St. Louis beat the Lakers and Pistons.

Paul Arizin of Philadelphia, with a 25.6 average, dethroned St. Louis' Bob Pettit as the scoring champion. Pettit seemed headed for a second straight title until he broke his wrist in mid-February and had to play the rest of the season in a cast. He wound up second with a 24.7 average.

Neil Johnston of Philadelphia, the fourth-leading scorer, was the NBA's most accurate shooter with a .447 percentage from the floor. Bill Sharman, as usual, led in free-throw accuracy. Rochester's Maurice Stokes was the leading rebounder, although Russell, who missed a third of the season because of the Olympics, had the highest rebound average.

The East defeated the West, 109–97, in the All-Star Game at Boston. Cousy won the game MVP award for the second time with his brilliant floor play and Sharman stunned the crowd with a 70-foot field goal.

Cousy was the NBA's Most Valuable Player and was joined on the All-NBA team by Sharman, Arizin, Dolph Schayes of Syracuse and Pettit. Another Boston player, Tom Heinsohn, won Rookie of the Year honors, averaging 16.2 points a game.

STANDINGS

Eastern Division

	W.	L.	Pct.
Boston	44	28	.611
Syracuse	38	34	.528
Philadelphia	37	35	.514
New York	36	36	.500

Western Division

	W.	L.	Pct.
St. Louis*	34	38	.472
Minneapolis	34	38	.472
Fort Wayne	34	38	.472
Rochester	31	41	.431

*Won playoff with Minneapolis and Fort Wayne to break tie

PLAYOFFS

First Round

Syracuse defeated Philadelphia 2 games to 0
Minneapolis defeated Fort Wayne 2 games to 0

Semifinals

Boston defeated Syracuse 3 games to 0
St. Louis defeated Minneapolis 3 games to 0

Championship

Boston defeated St. Louis 4 games to 3

TOP SCORERS

	Pcts.	Ave.
Paul Arizin, Philadelphia	1817	25.6
Bob Pettit, St. Louis	1755	24.7
Dolph Schayes, Syracuse	1617	22.5
Neil Johnston, Philadelphia	1575	22.8
George Yardley, Fort Wayne	1547	21.5

TOP REBOUNDERS

	No.	Ave.
Maurice Stokes, Rochester	1256	17.4
Bob Pettit, St. Louis	1037	14.6
Dolph Schayes, Syracuse	1008	14.0
Bill Russell, Boston	943	19.6
Clyde Lovellette, Minneapolis	932	13.5

LEADERS IN ASSISTS

	No.	Ave.
Bob Cousy, Boston	478	7.4
Jack McMahon, St. Louis	367	5.1
Maurice Stokes, Rochester	331	4.6
Jack George, Philadelphia	307	4.6
Slater Martin, St. Louis	269	4.1

1957–58

The St. Louis Hawks, behind the magnificent shooting of Bob Pettit, dethroned Boston in the playoffs and won their first NBA championship. The Hawks and Celtics met in the playoff finals for the second straight year, with St. Louis winning, four games to two. The Hawks' four triumphs came by a total of eight points.

In the decisive sixth playoff game, Pettit scored 50 points, including 19 of the Hawks' last 21. The Hawks' victory gave the NBA its fifth different champion in five seasons.

Boston won by eight games over Syracuse in the East and St. Louis took the Western crown by the same margin over Detroit. The Celtics' hopes of repeating as league champions, though, were crushed when Bill Russell, their outstanding center, sprained his ankle in the third playoff game against St. Louis and had to miss the remainder of the series.

As part of the NBA's shift away from the smaller cities, the Rochester franchise moved to Cincinnati and the Fort Wayne Pistons relocated in Detroit.

George Yardley of Detroit captured the scoring title with a 27.8 average. His total of 2,001 points was a record, eclipsing the old mark of 1,932 set by George Mikan in the 1951–52 season. Yardley scored more than 50 points in a game twice, getting 51 against Boston on January 15 and topping that with 52 against Syracuse on February 4.

Dolph Schayes of Syracuse was second in scoring with a 24.9 average, followed by Pettit with 24.6. Jack Twyman of Cincinnati led the circuit in field-goal accuracy with a .452 percentage and Schayes, with a

.904 percentage, dethroned perennial leader Bill Sharman of Boston as the best free-throw shooter. Russell topped the rebounders with a 22.7 average, and Cousy, averaging 7.1 assists a game, led in that department for the seventh straight season.

Harry Gallatin of Detroit, who played in his 682nd regular season game and 65th consecutive playoff contest, retired after ten years in the NBA.

The Hawks' Cliff Hagan and the Minne-

George Yardley was top NBA scorer when Pistons moved to Detroit

apolis Lakers' Dick Garmaker each scored 26 points in a single quarter, a league record.

In the All-Star Game at St. Louis, Cousy broke the game open with seven consecutive points to lead the East to a 130–118 victory. But Pettit, with 28 points and 26 rebounds, was the MVP.

Bill Russell won the Most Valuable Player award for the season in a vote of the players, but the annual poll of sportswriters only put him on the All-NBA second team. The first team included Schayes, Yardley, Pettit, Cousy and Sharman. Woody Sauldsberry of Philadelphia was the Rookie of the Year.

In a tragic development, Maurice Stokes, the 6-7 Cincinnati forward who had been the 1955–56 Rookie of the Year, was stricken with encephalitis. The crippling brain disease ended his career and put him in the hospital for extensive treatment.

STANDINGS

Eastern Division

	W.	L.	Pct.
Boston	49	23	.681
Syracuse	41	31	.569
Philadelphia	37	35	.514
New York	35	37	.486

Western Division

	W.	L.	Pct.
St. Louis	41	31	.569
Detroit	33	39	.458
Cincinnati	33	39	.458
Minneapolis	19	53	.264

PLAYOFFS

First Round

Philadelphia defeated Syracuse 2 games to 1
Detroit defeated Cincinnati 2 games to 0

Semifinals

Boston defeated Philadelphia 4 games to 1
St. Louis defeated Detroit 4 games to 1

Championship

St. Louis defeated Boston 4 games to 2

TOP SCORERS

	Pts.	Ave.
George Yardley, Detroit	2001	27.8
Dolph Schayes, Syracuse	1791	24.9
Bob Pettit, St. Louis	1719	24.6
Clyde Lovellette, Cincinnati	1659	23.4
Paul Arizin, Philadelphia	1406	20.7

TOP REBOUNDERS

	No.	Ave.
Bill Russell, Boston	1564	22.7
Bob Pettit, St. Louis	1216	17.4
Maurice Stokes, Cincinnati	1142	18.1
Dolph Schayes, Syracuse	1022	14.2
John Kerr, Syracuse	963	13.4

LEADERS IN ASSISTS

	No.	Ave.
Bob Cousy, Boston	463	7.1
Dick McGuire, Detroit	454	6.6
Maurice Stokes, Cincinnati	403	6.4
Carl Braun, New York	393	5.5
George King, Cincinnati	337	5.3

1958–59

Elgin Baylor, a 6-5 forward from Seattle University, made his pro debut with the Minneapolis Lakers and immediately became one of the NBA's brightest stars. He finished fourth in the individual scoring race with a 24.9 average and became only the third rookie in the history of the league to make the All-NBA team.

Alex Groza in 1949–50 and Bob Pettit in 1954–55 were the others to make the all-league squad in their first seasons.

Baylor boasted tremendous body control, some of the best inside moves ever seen in the league and an amazing capacity for seemingly hanging suspended in mid-air. His best scoring effort came against Cincinnati on February 25, when he tallied 55 points.

But it was Boston, with Bill Russell in the middle and Bob Cousy and Bill Sharman in backcourt, which won the NBA title, its sec-

Detroit's Dick McGuire battles Boston's Bill Sharman

December 25, and bettered that with a crowd of 18,496 on February 3. These were the two largest crowds in the history of the NBA.

Several individual records were set as well. The St. Louis Hawks' Bob Pettit won the scoring crown with a 29.2 average, the highest ever. His total of 2,105 points was also a new mark. Russell set a new standard with 1,612 rebounds for a 23.0 average. Cousy set a new record of 28 assists in a game against Minneapolis, with 19 in one half and 12 in one quarter. The Celtics set a scoring record in that game, bombing the Lakers, 173–139.

Kenny Sears of New York was the most accurate shooter with a .490 percentage from the floor and Sharman recaptured the foul-shooting title from Dolph Schayes with a phenomenal 92.9 percent. Cousy led in assists for the eighth straight year.

The West upset the East, 124–108, in the All-Star Game at Detroit. Elgin Baylor had 24 points and Bob Pettit 25 for the winners. The two were named co-winners of the MVP award.

Neil Johnston and Paul Arizin of Philadelphia, Sharman and Vern Mikklesen of Minneapolis all pushed their career scoring totals above 10,000 points during the season.

Pettit, the league's Most Valuable Player, headed the selections for the All-NBA team. He set a record by scoring over 50 points three times during the year. Joining him on the team were Baylor of the Lakers and Cousy, Sharman and Russell, the three leaders of the Celtics. Baylor, of course, won Rookie of the Year honors. But another rookie, Hal Greer of Syracuse, put on a phenomenal shooting exhibition by scoring 39 points in the first half, including 18 field goals, against Boston on February 14. He finished the game with 45 points.

ond in three years. The Celtics coasted to a 12-game spread over New York in the East, Boston's 52 victories setting an NBA record. St. Louis, defending NBA champion, finished 16 games in front of Minneapolis in the West. But the Lakers, led by Baylor, eliminated the Hawks, four games to two in the playoffs. In the playoff finals Boston scored an unprecedented four-game sweep over the Lakers.

Financially, the league had its best season. Despite the runaways in the two divisional races, attendance reached an all-time high of over 1,449,000. The Knicks drew 18,376 fans in Madison Square Garden on

STANDINGS

Eastern Division	W.	L.	Pct.	Western Division	W.	L.	Pct.
Boston	52	20	.722	St. Louis	49	23	.681
New York	40	32	.556	Minneapolis	33	39	.458
Syracuse	35	37	.486	Detroit	28	44	.389
Philadelphia	32	40	.444	Cincinnati	19	53	.264

PLAYOFFS

First Round

Syracuse defeated New York 2 games to 0
Minneapolis defeated Detroit 2 games to 1

Semifinals

Boston defeated Syracuse 4 games to 3
Minneapolis defeated St. Louis 4 games to 2

Championship

Boston defeated Minneapolis 4 games to 0

TOP SCORERS

	Pts.	Ave.
Bob Pettit, St. Louis	2105	29.2
Jack Twyman, Cincinnati	1857	25.8
Paul Arizin, Philadelphia	1851	26.4
Elgin Baylor, Minneapolis	1742	24.9
Cliff Hagan, St. Louis	1707	23.7

TOP REBOUNDERS

	No.	Ave.
Bill Russell, Boston	1612	23.0
Bob Pettit, St. Louis	1182	16.4
Elgin Baylor, Minneapolis	1050	15.0
John Kerr, Syracuse	1008	13.4
Dolph Schayes, Syracuse	962	13.4

LEADERS IN ASSISTS

	No.	Ave.
Bob Cousy, Boston	557	8.6
Dick McGuire, Detroit	443	6.2
Larry Costello, Syracuse	379	5.4
Richie Guerin, New York	364	5.1
Carl Braun, New York	349	4.8

1959–60

Wilt Chamberlain, the 7-1 center who had played two seasons of college basketball at Kansas and then toured for a year with the Harlem Globetrotters, signed with the Philadelphia Warriors. The Big Dipper had an unparalleled rookie season and quickly proved that he was the greatest offensive force in the league.

The Warrior star set numerous records, including most points, 2,707; highest scoring average, 37.6; most field goals attempted, 2,311; most field goals scored, 1,065; most rebounds, 1,941; highest rebound average, 26.9, and most games with 50 or more points, five.

But Wilt wasn't the only NBA performer to set records. Elgin Baylor, in his second season with Minneapolis, scored 64 points against Boston on November 8, breaking Joe Fulks' 11-year-old record of 63 points. Boston's Bill Russell set a record with 51 rebounds against Syracuse, and Dolph Schayes of Syracuse became the first player to score more than 15,000 points in his career. He finished the season with 15,798 points to move past George Mikan as the all-time scoring leader.

Boston became the first team in six seasons to repeat as league champion. The Cel-

tics edged St. Louis, four games to three, in the playoff finals. Despite the scoring feats of Philadelphia's Chamberlain, Boston had won the Eastern title by 10 games over the second-place Warriors. Boston won 59

Cincinnati's Jack Twyman averaged 31.2 points, second only to Wilt Chamberlain

games, the most in the NBA's history, and tied a league record with 17 consecutive victories. In the West, St. Louis had an even easier time, breezing to a 16-game margin over the Detroit Pistons.

In the scoring race Cincinnati's Jack Twyman averaged 31.2 points a game. Although no other player had ever averaged over 30 points, Twyman's feat was com- pletely overshadowed by Chamberlain's domination of the scoring statistics.

The Knicks' Kenny Sears led the league in field-goal accuracy with a .477 percentage and Schayes regained the free-throw title from Boston's Bill Sharman with an .892 percentage. The Celtics' Bob Cousy continued as the NBA's top playmaker, setting a season record with 715 assists and

Philadelphia's Wilt Chamberlain has the ball, but Bill Russell's Celtics won title again

becoming the first to get more than 5,000 assists in his career.

The East trounced the West, 125–115, in the All-Star Game at Philadelphia, with Chamberlain scoring 23 points and winning the MVP award. Twyman had 26 for the West.

Chamberlain, the Rookie and Most Valu-able Player of the Year headed the All-NBA team. He was joined by Baylor, Cousy, Gene Shue of Detroit and Bob Pettit of St. Louis. Pettit, along with New York's Carl Braun and St. Louis' Larry Foust, went over the 10,000-point mark for his career.

STANDINGS

Eastern Division	W.	L.	Pct.
Boston	59	16	.787
Philadelphia	49	26	.653
Syracuse	45	30	.600
New York	27	48	.360

Western Division	W.	L.	Pct.
St. Louis	46	29	.613
Detroit	30	45	.400
Minneapolis	25	50	.333
Cincinnati	19	56	.253

PLAYOFFS

First Round

Philadelphia defeated Syracuse 2 games to 1
Minneapolis defeated Detroit 2 games to 0

Semifinals

Boston defeated Philadelphia 4 games to 2
St. Louis defeated Minneapolis 4 games to 3

Championship

Boston defeated St. Louis 4 games to 3

TOP SCORERS

	Pts.	Ave.
Wilt Chamberlain, Philadelphia	2707	37.6
Jack Twyman, Cincinnati	2338	31.2
Elgin Baylor, Minneapolis	2074	29.6
Bob Pettit, St. Louis	1882	26.1
Cliff Hagan, St. Louis	1858	24.8

TOP REBOUNDERS

	No.	Ave.
Wilt Chamberlain, Philadelphia	1941	26.9
Bill Russell, Boston	1778	24.0
Bob Pettit, St. Louis	1221	16.9
Elgin Baylor, Minneapolis	1150	16.4
Dolph Schayes, Syracuse	959	12.8

LEADERS IN ASSISTS

	No.	Ave.
Bob Cousy, Boston	715	9.5
Guy Rodgers, Philadelphia	482	7.1
Richie Guerin, New York	468	6.3
Larry Costello, Syracuse	446	6.3
Tom Gola, Philadelphia	409	5.4

1960–61

The NBA became truly a national league when the Minneapolis Lakers moved to Los Angeles and brought professional basketball to the West Coast. The Lakers came up with an outstanding rookie, Jerry West of West Virginia University, to team with Elgin Baylor, their All-NBA forward.

But the most exciting rookie of the year was Oscar Robertson of the Cincinnati Royals. Robertson had led the nation in scoring for three years as a collegian at Cin-cinnati and quickly showed that he could score with equal ease in the pro game. The Big O averaged 30.5 points a game, fourth-best in the NBA, to become the highest-scoring guard in the league's history. Robertson excelled as a playmaker as well, taking over from Boston's Bob Cousy as the leader in assists. Robertson averaged 9.7 assists, the highest in history, and attendance in Cincinnati more than tripled.

Philadelphia's Wilt Chamberlain, who had set a basket of new scoring and re-bounding records as a rookie, broke all of his own marks in his second season. He averaged 38.4 points a game and became the first player to score more than 3,000 points in a season, finishing with 3,033. He also set a record for rebounds with an average of 27.2 a game and led in field-goal accuracy with a .505 percentage.

The Lakers' sensational Baylor erased his own NBA record by scoring 71 points against New York on November 15. He hit on 28 of 48 attempts and 15 of 19 free throws. In addition he grabbed 25 rebounds. Chamberlain produced the most impressive rebounding feat, though, hauling down a record 55 against Boston. Bill Sharman of Boston recaptured the free-throw title with a .921 percentage.

The Celtics established themselves as one of the finest teams in history by winning their third consecutive championship and fourth in five seasons. Boston won the Eastern title with ease, finishing 11 games ahead of the Chamberlain-led Philadelphia Warriors. St. Louis beat the Lakers by 15 games in the West. Boston crushed the Hawks, four games to one, in the playoff finals.

The West bombed the East, 153–131, in the All-Star Game at Syracuse. Bob Pettit of St. Louis, the league's second-highest scorer, posted 29 points for the West, but Oscar Robertson won the MVP award. The Big O had 23 points and 14 assists for the winners.

Bill Russell of Boston won his second Podoloff Cup as the NBA's Most Valuable Player in a vote of the players. But the sportswriters relegated him to the second All-NBA team in their poll. The All-NBA team included Pettit, Chamberlain, Baylor, Cousy and Robertson, the Rookie of the Year.

New York had the rather dubious distinction of losing a game by 62 points, the greatest margin of defeat in the league's history. The Knicks, who finished last in the East, absorbed a 162–100 beating at the hands of Syracuse on Christmas Day.

Rookie Oscar Robertson of Cincinnati keeps Boston's K. C. Jones at arm's length

STANDINGS

Eastern Division

	W.	L.	Pct.
Boston	57	22	.722
Philadelphia	46	33	.582
Syracuse	38	41	.481
New York	21	58	.266

Western Division

	W.	L.	Pct.
St. Louis	51	28	.646
Los Angeles	36	43	.456
Detroit	34	45	.430
Cincinnati	33	46	.418

PLAYOFFS

First Round

Syracuse defeated Philadelphia 3 games to 0
Los Angeles defeated Detroit 3 games to 2

Semifinals

Boston defeated Syracuse 4 games to 1
St. Louis defeated Los Angeles 4 games to 3

Championship

Boston defeated St. Louis 4 games to 1

TOP SCORERS

	Pts.	Ave.
Wilt Chamberlain, Philadelphia	3033	38.4
Elgin Baylor, Los Angeles	2538	34.8
Oscar Robertson, Cincinnati	2165	30.5
Bob Pettit, St. Louis	2120	27.9
Jack Twyman, Cincinnati	1997	25.3

TOP REBOUNDERS

	No.	Ave.
Wilt Chamberlain, Philadelphia	2149	27.2
Bob Pettit, St. Louis	1540	20.3
Elgin Baylor, Los Angeles	1447	19.8
Bailey Howell, Detroit	1111	14.4
Willie Naulls, New York	1055	13.4

LEADERS IN ASSISTS

	No.	Ave.
Oscar Robertson, Cincinnati	690	9.7
Guy Rodgers, Philadelphia	677	8.9
Bob Cousy, Boston	591	7.8
Gene Shue, Detroit	530	6.8
Richie Guerin, New York	503	6.4

1961–62

Wilt Chamberlain, Philadelphia's mighty 7-1 center, dwarfed all past scoring feats by recording 100 points in a single game. Wilt's incredible performance came in the Warriors' 169–147 victory over New York in Hershey, Pennsylvania, on March 2. The 316 points the two teams scored also set an NBA record.

Chamberlain hit on 36 of 63 field-goal attempts and belied his reputation as the NBA's worst foul shooter by connecting on 28 of 32 shots from the free-throw line.

Wilt again obliterated all season scoring records. He averaged a phenomenal 50.4 points a game, nearly 19 points ahead of Chicago's Walt Bellamy, his nearest rival. In the 80 regular season games, Wilt scored 60 or more points 15 times and over 50 points 44 times. Los Angeles' Elgin Baylor and Jerry West each had 63-point games and Baylor also scored 61 points.

But all this scoring couldn't stop Boston, with a beautifully balanced attack and Bill Russell at center, from winning its fourth consecutive title and fifth in six seasons. The Celtics again made a shambles of the Eastern Division race, finishing 11 games ahead of Philadelphia. Tommy Heinsohn, Boston's best scorer, was no better than 11th in the league with a 22.3 average.

The NBA added a ninth team, the Chicago Packers, which joined the West and finished last. The division winner, Los Angeles, beat Cincinnati by 11 games as St. Louis, Western champions since 1957, dropped to fourth place. The final playoff series between the Lakers and Celtics went the full seven games, with Boston's Sam Jones scoring the winning basket with two seconds left in the deciding game.

Chamberlain won the rebounding title with a 25.6 average. Bellamy, a 6-11 rookie center from Indiana, was the most accurate shooter from the floor with a .513 percentage and Dolph Schayes of Syracuse was

Bob Cousy, a 15,000-point man, shoots against Royals' Arlen Bockhorn and Oscar Robertson

tops from the free-throw line with an .896 mark. Cincinnati's Oscar Robertson set a new record, averaging 11.4 assists a game. But Boston's Bob Cousy, who dropped to third in assists, became the first player to go over the 6,000 mark for his career.

Schayes broke Harry Gallatin's consecutive-game record of 682 but saw his own streak snapped at 706 when he suffered a fractured cheekbone on December 26.

Cousy, Bob Pettit of St. Louis and Paul Arizin of Philadelphia all passed the 15,000-point plateau for their careers.

The West scored a convincing 150–130 victory in the All-Star Game at St. Louis as Bob Pettit, with 27 rebounds and 25 points, took MVP honors for the third time. Wilt Chamberlain set an All-Star scoring record with 42 points for the losers.

Russell, the hub of the Celtics, won his second consecutive Most Valuable Player award but again did not make the All-NBA first team. The All-NBA team included Pettit, Baylor, Chamberlain, West and Robertson, with Chicago's Bellamy the Rookie of the Year.

Syracuse's Dolph Schayes slips past St. Louis' Cliff Hagan (16)

STANDINGS

Eastern Division	W.	L.	Pct.	Western Division	W.	L.	Pct.
Boston	60	20	.750	Los Angeles	54	26	.675
Philadelphia	49	31	.613	Cincinnati	43	37	.538
Syracuse	41	39	.513	Detroit	37	43	.463
New York	29	51	.363	St. Louis	29	51	.363
				Chicago	18	62	.225

PLAYOFFS

First Round

Philadelphia defeated Syracuse 3 games to 2
Detroit defeated Cincinnati 3 games to 1

Semifinals

Boston defeated Philadelphia 4 games to 3
Los Angeles defeated Detroit 4 games to 2

Championship

Boston defeated Los Angeles 4 games to 3

TOP SCORERS

	Pts.	Ave.
Wilt Chamberlain, Philadelphia	4029	50.4
Walt Bellamy, Chicago	2495	31.6
Oscar Robertson, Cincinnati	2432	30.3
Bob Pettit, St. Louis	2429	31.1
Jerry West, Los Angeles	2310	30.8

TOP REBOUNDERS

	No.	Ave.
Wilt Chamberlain, Philadelphia	2052	25.6
Bill Russell, Boston	1891	24.9
Walt Bellamy, Chicago	1500	19.0
Bob Pettit, St. Louis	1457	18.7
John Kerr, Syracuse	1176	14.7

LEADERS IN ASSISTS

	No.	Ave.
Oscar Robertson, Cincinnati	899	11.4
Guy Rodgers, Philadelphia	663	7.9
Bob Cousy, Boston	584	7.8
Richie Guerin, New York	539	6.9
Gene Shue, Detroit	465	5.8

1962–63

The NBA continued its march to the West as Eddie Gottlieb, a pioneer professional owner and former coach, sold the Philadelphia Warriors to a San Francisco group. Gottlieb, who was frequently said to have carried his office around in his hat, reportedly received $850,000 for the Warriors.

Western champions Elgin Baylor, left, and Jerry West with their Laker coach, Fred Schaus

The Boston Celtics won their fifth consecutive title and sixth in seven years behind their incomparable team of Bob Cousy and Bill Russell. Cousy, generally regarded as the greatest guard in the history of the game, announced his retirement after 13 seasons. The only player to appear in all 13 All-Star Games, Cousy made the All-NBA first team 10 times and the second team twice.

Russell, the league's top defensive player, won his third straight Most Valuable Player award and returned to the All-NBA team after a two year absence.

As usual, Boston made a runaway of the Eastern Division race. The Celts finished 10 games ahead of Syracuse. In the West, Los Angeles, with Elgin Baylor and Jerry West, successfully defended its divisional title, finishing five games ahead of St. Louis. Both division champions made it into the playoff finals, where Boston defeated the Lakers, four games to two.

San Francisco's Wilt Chamberlain won his fourth scoring title in four seasons in the NBA with a 44.8 average. Baylor finished second with a 34.0 average and Cincinnati's Oscar Robertson was third with 28.3. Chamberlain also led in rebounding with a 24.3 average and in field-goal accuracy, making 52.8 percent of his shots. San Francisco's Guy Rodgers led the league with

10.8 assists a game, most of them coming on passes to Chamberlain. Larry Costello of Syracuse was tops in free-throw accuracy with an .881 percentage.

Syracuse's Dolph Schayes, in his 15th professional season, played in his 1,000th game and scored his 19,000th point during the year. Bob Pettit of St. Louis broke the 17,000 barrier, and Richie Guerin of New York, Cliff Hagan of St. Louis, Tom Heinsohn of Boston, Chamberlain and Baylor all went over 10,000 points for their careers. Russell, who finished second to Chamberlain in rebounding, became the all-time rebound leader with 11,499.

The East won the All-Star Game at Los Angeles, 115–108, with Robertson scoring 21 points for the East and Pettit 25 for the West. But Russell, who dominated the backboards, won the game MVP award for the second consecutive year.

Baylor, Pettit, Robertson, Russell and West made the All-NBA team as Chamberlain was relegated to the second team for the first time in his career. Terry Dischinger, who two years before had played on the U. S. Olympic team as a college sophomore, won Rookie of the Year honors with Chicago. He averaged 25.5 points a game.

STANDINGS

Eastern Division

	W.	L.	Pct.
Boston	58	22	.725
Syracuse	48	32	.600
Cincinnati	42	38	.525
New York	21	59	.263

Western Division

	W.	L.	Pct.
Los Angeles	53	27	.663
St. Louis	48	32	.600
Detroit	34	46	.425
San Francisco	31	49	.388
Chicago	25	55	.313

PLAYOFFS

First Round

Cincinnati defeated Syracuse 3 games to 2
St. Louis defeated Detroit 3 games to 1

Semifinals

Boston defeated Cincinnati 4 games to 3
Los Angeles defeated St. Louis 4 games to 3

Championship

Boston defeated Los Angeles 4 games to 2

TOP SCORERS

	Pts.	Ave.
Wilt Chamberlain, San Francisco	3586	44.8
Elgin Baylor, Los Angeles	2719	34.0
Oscar Robertson, Cincinnati	2264	28.3
Bob Pettit, St. Louis	2241	28.4
Walt Bellamy, Chicago	2233	27.9

TOP REBOUNDERS

	No.	Ave.
Wilt Chamberlain, San Francisco	1946	24.3
Bill Russell, Boston	1843	23.6
Walt Bellamy, Chicago	1310	16.4
Bob Pettit, St. Louis	1195	15.1
Elgin Baylor, Los Angeles	1146	14.3

LEADERS IN ASSISTS

	No.	Ave.
Guy Rodgers, San Francisco	825	10.6
Oscar Robertson, Cincinnati	758	9.5
Bob Cousy, Boston	515	6.8
Sihugo Green, Chicago	422	5.8
Elgin Baylor, Los Angeles	386	4.8

1963–64

The Boston Celtics, playing without Bob Cousy who had retired to coach at Boston College, won their sixth consecutive NBA title and seventh in eight seasons. The Celtics dynasty, which began when Bill Russell joined the team in 1956–57, reached a new peak in the history of American sports.

The New York Yankees in baseball and the Montreal Canadiens in hockey had each won championships in five straight years, but never before had any major-league professional team won six consecutive titles.

Both divisional races were close. Boston

Philadelphia's Johnny Kerr played in his 745th straight game

Commissioner Walter Kennedy

won by five games over Cincinnati, which had Oscar Robertson and rookie sensation Jerry Lucas, and San Francisco, coached by Alex Hannum, held off St. Louis by two games in the West. The Celtics blasted San Francisco, four games to one, in the final playoff series.

Maurice Podoloff, who had served as president of the NBA since its founding 17 years before, retired at the close of the previous season. He was succeeded by Walter Kennedy, the original publicist of the NBA and a former mayor of Stamford, Connecticut. Financially the NBA enjoyed its best season, as attendance climbed above 2,000,000 for the first time. The Chicago franchise, after finishing last in the West for its two seasons of existence, moved to Baltimore. The team revived the nickname of Bullets, which had been used by an earlier Baltimore franchise in the league, and escaped the cellar with a fourth-place finish.

Bob Pettit of St. Louis closed the season with 19,756 career points, making him the most productive scorer ever in the NBA. Dolph Schayes, the first man to score more than 19,000 points, had retired to coach the Philadelphia 76ers. The 76ers, actually the transplanted Syracuse Nationals, brought professional basketball back to Philadelphia after a two-year absence.

Philadelphia's Johnny Kerr played in his 745th consecutive regular season game and 62nd straight playoff contest. Kerr's 707th game in a row broke Schayes' record. An early-season eye injury halted Cincinnati's

Cincinnati's Jerry Lucas was Rookie of the Year

Jack Twyman's consecutive-game streak at 609.

Wilt Chamberlain won his fifth straight scoring title with a 36.5 average and scored 59 points three times during the year. Oscar Robertson of Cincinnati was second. Robertson also led the league in assists and free-throw accuracy. Cincinnati's Lucas, the Rookie of the Year, beat out Chamberlain as the leader in field-goal accuracy with a .527 percentage and Boston's Russell took the rebounding title.

In the All-Star Game at Boston, Robertson led the East to a 111–107 triumph. The Big O, the MVP both in the game and for the season, scored 26 points. Robertson was a unanimous choice for the All-NBA team, and was joined by Pettit, Chamberlain, and Elgin Baylor and Jerry West of the Lakers.

After the season, the State Department sponsored an NBA All-Star team on a tour of Europe and the Middle East. The NBA stars swept all 21 games against teams in Poland, Rumania, Yugoslavia and Egypt.

STANDINGS

Eastern Division

	W.	L.	Pct.
Boston	59	21	.738
Cincinnati	55	25	.688
Philadelphia	34	46	.425
New York	22	58	.275

Western Division

	W.	L.	Pct.
San Francisco	48	32	.600
St. Louis	46	34	.575
Los Angeles	42	38	.525
Baltimore	31	49	.388
Detroit	23	57	.288

PLAYOFFS

First Round

Cincinnati defeated Philadelphia 3 games to 2
St. Louis defeated Los Angeles 3 games to 2

Semifinals

Boston defeated Cincinnati 4 games to 1
San Francisco defeated St. Louis 4 games to 3

Championship

Boston defeated San Francisco 4 games to 1

TOP SCORERS

	Pts.	Ave.
Wilt Chamberlain, San Francisco	2948	36.5
Oscar Robertson, Cincinnati	2480	31.4
Bob Pettit, St. Louis	2190	27.4
Walt Bellamy, Baltimore	2159	27.0
Jerry West, Los Angeles	2064	27.0

TOP REBOUNDERS

	No.	Ave.
Bill Russell, Boston	1930	24.7
Wilt Chamberlain, San Francisco	1687	21.1
Jerry Lucas, Cincinnati	1375	17.4
Walt Bellamy, Baltimore	1361	17.0
Bob Pettit, St. Louis	1224	15.3

LEADERS IN ASSISTS

	No.	Ave.
Oscar Robertson, Cincinnati	868	11.0
Guy Rodgers, San Francisco	556	7.0
K. C. Jones, Boston	407	5.1
Jerry West, Los Angeles	403	5.6
Wilt Chamberlain, San Francisco	403	5.0

1964–65

News of basketball's biggest trade rocked the NBA world on January 15, the night of the annual All-Star Game in St. Louis. At a post-midnight press conference, San Francisco owner Franklin Mieuli announced that he had traded Wilt Chamberlain, his 7-1 scoring machine, to the Philadelphia 76ers.

Detroit player-coach Dave DeBusschere goes against Boston's Bill Russell

In return the Warriors received three journeyman players, Connie Dierking, Paul Neumann, and Lee Shaffer, and an undisclosed amount of cash.

Neither the change in locale nor the change to a wider free throw lane (16 feet instead of 12) prevented Wilt from winning his sixth consecutive scoring title with a 34.7 average. Los Angeles' Jerry West was second with 31.0, and Cincinnati's Oscar Robertson was third with 30.4.

The seemingly invincible Boston Celtics won their seventh NBA title in a row and eighth in nine seasons. The Celtics, who won a record 62 games, finished 14 games ahead of Cincinnati in the East. Along the way, the Celtics posted winning streaks of 11 and 16 games.

But it was Philadelphia, which had acquired Wilt in mid-season and finished third in the East, which gave Boston the greatest trouble. The 76ers extended Boston to the full seven games in the Eastern playoff finals. In the decisive final game, Boston's John Havlicek intercepted an in-bounds pass under the Philadelphia basket with five seconds remaining to preserve Boston's 110–109 victory.

The final playoff series came as something of an anticlimax, with Boston whipping Western champion Los Angeles in five games. The Lakers had won in the West by four games over St. Louis. Los Angeles' brilliant Elgin Baylor injured his ankle in the opening game of the Western playoff finals against Baltimore and missed the remainder of the playoffs. Even the fantastic play of the Lakers' Jerry West, who averaged 40.6 points a game during the playoffs, could not overcome Boston's balanced attack.

The Detroit Pistons made NBA history by naming Dave DeBusschere, their outstanding 24-year-old forward, as player-coach. He became the youngest coach in league annals. St. Louis also selected veteran guard Richie Guerin as player-coach.

Chamberlain led the league in field-goal accuracy with a .510 percentage and his Philadelphia teammate, Larry Costello, led in free-throw accuracy with an .877 mark. The Big O was the top playmaker, averaging a record-shattering 11.5 assists a game, and Boston's Bill Russell was the top rebounder.

The East scored a 124–123 victory in the All-Star Game at St. Louis. Robertson scored 28 for the East and Gus Johnson of Baltimore had 25 for the West, but Cincinnati's Jerry Lucas won the MVP award for his outstanding rebounding and 25 points.

Bob Pettit of St. Louis, the most prolific scorer in NBA history, passed the 20,000-point mark for his career and later announced his retirement. Cincinnati's Jack Twyman went over the 15,000 mark, and Robertson, Russell and Los Angeles' Willie Naulls all topped 10,000 career points.

Russell, the NBA's MVP for the fifth time; Baylor, West, Lucas and Robertson made the All-NBA team. New York's Willis Reed was Rookie of the Year.

Walter Brown, the owner of the Boston Celtics, one of the founders of the NBA and the originator of the All-Star Game, died shortly before the start of the season. The Celtics wore a black strip of cloth on their uniforms in his memory throughout the campaign.

STANDINGS

Eastern Division

	W.	L.	Pct.
Boston	62	18	.715
Cincinnati	48	32	.600
Philadelphia	40	40	.500
New York	31	49	.388

Western Division

	W.	L.	Pct.
Los Angeles	49	31	.613
St. Louis	45	35	.563
Baltimore	37	43	.463
Detroit	31	49	.388
San Francisco	17	63	.213

PLAYOFFS

First Round

Philadelphia defeated Cincinnati 3 games to 1
Baltimore defeated St. Louis 3 games to 1

Semifinals

Boston defeated Philadelphia 4 games to 3
Los Angeles defeated Baltimore 4 games to 2

Championship

Boston defeated Los Angeles 4 games to 1

TOP SCORERS

	Pts.	Ave.
Wilt Chamberlain, San Francisco—Philadelphia	2534	34.7
Jerry West, Los Angeles	2292	31.0
Oscar Robertson, Cincinnati	2279	30.4
Sam Jones, Boston	2070	25.9
Elgin Baylor, Los Angeles	2009	27.1

TOP REBOUNDERS

	No.	Ave.
Bill Russell, Boston	1879	24.1
Wilt Chamberlain, San Francisco—Philadelphia	1673	22.9
Nate Thurmond, San Francisco	1395	18.1
Jerry Lucas, Cincinnati	1321	20.0
Willis Reed, New York	1175	14.7

LEADERS IN ASSISTS

	No.	Ave.
Oscar Robertson, Cincinnati	861	11.5
Guy Rodgers, San Francisco	565	7.3
K. C. Jones, Boston	437	5.6
Len Wilkens, St. Louis	431	5.5
Bill Russell, Boston	410	5.3

1965-66

For the first time in a decade, Boston failed to win the Eastern Division title. But the Celtics came back in the playoffs to win their eighth consecutive title and ninth in ten seasons.

The Philadelphia 76ers, with Wilt Chamberlain, Hal Greer and Chet Walker, won their last 11 games to finish a game ahead of Boston. But Boston easily ousted Philadelphia, four games to one in the Eastern playoff finals.

Los Angeles, with Elgin Baylor and Jerry West, won by seven games over Baltimore in the West and was the only team in the division to win more than half its games. In the playoff finals, Boston, despite the retirement of Tom Heinsohn, the high-scoring forward, beat the Lakers, four games to two.

Chamberlain won his seventh consecutive scoring title with a 33.5 average and also passed Bob Pettit as the all-time high scorer with a career total of 21,486 points in his seven NBA seasons. In addition, Wilt led in field-goal accuracy with a .540 percentage and rebounding with a 24.6 average. Chamberlain also won the Podoloff Cup as the league's Most Valuable Player and contin-

ued his streak of never having fouled out in his seven pro seasons.

San Francisco's Rick Barry, a 6-7 forward from Miami (Fla.), was the season's outstanding rookie. He averaged 25.7 points, fourth-best in the league, and reached a single-game high of 57 against New York. Barry joined Chamberlain, Chicago's Walt Bellamy and Cincinnati's Oscar Robertson as the only players to score more than 2,000 points in their first seasons.

Robertson retained his playmaking title with an average of 11.1 assists a game, and Boston's Larry Siegfried was the leading foul shooter with an .881 percentage.

Boston coach Red Auerbach with the man who would succeed him, Bill Russell

San Francisco's Rick Barry (24) scored more than 2,000 points in his rookie season

Several all-time stars played their last season. They included Cincinnati's Jack Twyman, New York's Tom Gola, Los Angeles' Willie Naulls and Baltimore's John Kerr. Kerr had played in 844 consecutive games since entering the NBA in 1954 until an injury snapped his streak on November 5.

The East won its 11th All-Star Game in 16 tries, smashing the West, 137–94, at Cincinnati. Cincinnati's Adrian Smith, the last man selected for the game, led the East with 24 points and won MVP honors.

Chamberlain, Lucas, Robertson, Barry and West made the All-NBA team, with Boston's Bill Russell again back on the second five.

During the season West, Philadelphia's Hall Greer, Baltimore's Bailey Howell and Boston's Sam Jones all entered the exclusive 10,000-career-point club.

STANDINGS

Eastern Division

	W.	L.	Pct.
Philadelphia	55	25	.688
Boston	54	26	.675
Cincinnati	45	35	.563
New York	30	50	.375

Western Division

	W.	L.	Pct.
Los Angeles	45	35	.563
Baltimore	38	42	.475
St. Louis	36	44	.450
San Francisco	35	45	.438
Detroit	22	58	.275

PLAYOFFS

First Round

Boston defeated Cincinnati 3 games to 2
St. Louis defeated Baltimore 3 games to 0

Semifinals

Boston defeated Philadelphia 4 games to 1
Los Angeles defeated St. Louis 4 games to 3

Championship

Boston defeated Los Angeles 4 games to 3

TOP SCORERS

	Pts.	Ave.
Wilt Chamberlain, Philadelphia	2649	33.5
Jerry West, Los Angeles	2476	31.4
Oscar Robertson, Cincinnati	2378	31.3
Rick Barry, San Francisco	2059	25.7
Walt Bellamy, New York	1820	22.8

TOP REBOUNDERS

	No.	Ave.
Wilt Chamberlain, Philadelphia	1943	24.6
Bill Russell, Boston	1779	22.8
Jerry Lucas, Cincinnati	1668	21.8
Nate Thurmond, San Francisco	1312	18.0
Walt Bellamy, New York	1254	15.7

LEADERS IN ASSISTS

	No.	Ave.
Oscar Robertson, Cincinnati	847	11.1
Guy Rodgers, San Francisco	846	10.7
K. C. Jones, Boston	503	6.3
Jerry West, Los Angeles	480	6.1
Howard Komives, New York	426	5.3

1966–67

Sports' greatest success story ended when the Boston Celtics, NBA champions for the past eight seasons, yielded the league championship to Wilt Chamberlain and the Philadelphia 76ers. The 76ers won the most games (68), had the highest winning percentage (.840) in the history of the league and finished eight games ahead of the Celtics in the Eastern Division.

Before the season, Red Auerbach, the mastermind of Boston's phenomenal success, had retired and turned the coaching job over to Bill Russell. Russell, who continued as a player, became the first black head coach of a major-league team in America. Auerbach closed out a 20-year coaching career with a record of 1,037 vic-

Wilt Chamberlain and 76er teammates celebrate title defeat of Celtics

tories and 548 losses and nine NBA championships.

For the first time since coming into the league, Chamberlain failed to win the scoring title. But under the coaching of Alex Hannum, Chamberlain played the best all-around basketball of his career and excelled on defense and as a playmaker. San Francisco's Rick Barry, in his second pro season, took over as the scoring leader. Barry averaged 35.6 points a game and Chamberlain dropped to third behind Cincinnati's Oscar Robertson. Barry scored 50 or more points six times during the season.

Chamberlain won the Most Valuable Player award for the second straight year and established a record by hitting on 68.3 percent of his field-goal attempts. He also led in rebounding with a 24.2 average.

Cincinnati's Adrian Smith led in foul-shooting with a .903 percentage, and Guy Rodgers of Chicago won his second assist title with an average of 11.1 a game.

The NBA returned to Chicago after a three-year absence and the new Chicago Bulls surprised everyone by making the playoffs in their very first season. Much of the credit went to John Kerr, who won Coach of the Year honors. Detroit finished below the Bulls in the West, and Dave

The Knicks, with Cazzie Russell, made the playoffs

Detroit's Dave Bing was top rookie

DeBusschere, their player-coach, resigned as coach late in the season. He was replaced by Donnis Butcher.

San Francisco, with Barry and Nate Thurmond, won the Western title by five games over the St. Louis Hawks. Philadelphia ousted Boston, four games to one, in the Eastern finals and then downed the Warriors, four games to two, for the NBA championship.

The West, behind Barry, scored a 135–120 triumph in the All-Star Game at San Francisco. Barry scored 40 points on his way to MVP honors.

Barry, Chamberlain, Robertson, and Los Angeles' Elgin Baylor and Jerry West made the All-NBA team and Dave Bing of Detroit was named Rookie of the Year. Bing finished tenth in scoring with a 20.0 average.

New York, after seven years of failure, finally made it into the playoffs. But the Knicks' success was short-lived, as Boston eliminated them, three games to one, in the opening round.

After the season, the NBA, under pressure from the players, agreed to establish a major medical health insurance program and to institute a pension plan that would pay 10-year veterans of the league $600 a month when they reach age 65.

STANDINGS

Eastern Division	W.	L.	Pct.	Western Division	W.	L.	Pct.
Philadelphia	68	13	.840	San Francisco	44	37	.543
Boston	60	21	.741	St. Louis	39	42	.481
Cincinnati	39	42	.481	Los Angeles	36	45	.444
New York	36	45	.444	Chicago	33	48	.470
Baltimore	20	61	.247	Detroit	30	51	.370

PLAYOFFS

First Round

Philadelphia defeated Cincinnati 3 games to 1
Boston defeated New York 3 games to 1
San Francisco defeated Los Angeles 3 games to 0
St. Louis defeated Chicago 3 games to 0

Semifinals

Philadelphia defeated Boston 4 games to 1
San Francisco defeated St. Louis 4 games to 2

Championship

Philadelphia defeated San Francisco 4 games to 2

TOP SCORERS

	Pts.	Ave.
Rick Barry, San Francisco	2775	35.6
Oscar Robertson, Cincinnati	2412	30.5
Wilt Chamberlain, Philadelphia	1956	24.1
Jerry West, Los Angeles	1892	28.7
Elgin Baylor, Los Angeles	1862	26.6

TOP REBOUNDERS

	No.	Ave.
Wilt Chamberlain, Philadelphia	1957	24.2
Bill Russell, Boston	1700	21.0
Jerry Lucas, Cincinnati	1547	19.1
Nate Thurmond, San Francisco	1382	21.3
Bill Bridges, St. Louis	1190	15.1

LEADERS IN ASSISTS

	No.	Ave.
Guy Rodgers, Chicago	908	11.2
Oscar Robertson, Cincinnati	845	10.7
Wilt Chamberlain, Philadelphia	630	7.8
Bill Russell, Boston	472	5.8
Jerry West, Los Angeles	447	6.8

1967–68

Boston's tired old men battled back to recapture the NBA championship they had held for so long. The Celtics finished second in the East, eight games behind Philadelphia, the defending champion, and then fell behind the 76ers, three games to one, in the Eastern playoff finals.

But with Bill Russell, the 34-year-old player-coach, 35-year-old Sam Jones, 31-year-old Bailey Howell, and John Havlicek, a relative youngster at 28, Boston swept the next three games. The Celtics then went on to crush Los Angeles, four games to two, for their tenth championship in twelve seasons. Los Angeles had finished four games behind St. Louis in the West, but had eliminated the Hawks in four straight games to reach the playoff finals.

Rick Barry, the NBA's leading scorer a year ago, attempted to sign with Oakland of the new American Basketball Association. Bruce Hale, Barry's father-in-law, was the Oakland coach. But San Francisco brought legal action to stop Barry, and the former Warrior star was forced to sit out the season.

Dave Bing, the Rookie of the Year at Detroit in 1966–67, took over from Barry as the scoring leader. The Pistons' flashy guard averaged 27.1 points a game. Los Angeles' Elgin Baylor, who made an amazing recovery from a knee injury, was second.

Rhodes scholar Bill Bradley graduated from Oxford to the Knicks

Baltimore's Earl "The Pearl" Monroe, Rookie of the Year, ponders Royals' Oscar Robertson

Wilt Chamberlain soars in new Madison Square Garden

Wilt Chamberlain, the NBA's leader in field-goal percentage with a .595 mark, also became the first center ever to lead the league in assists, averaging 8.6 a game. Wilt finished third in the scoring race, but did become the first player to reach a career mark of 25,000 points. Cincinnati's Oscar Robertson led in free-throw accuracy with an .873 percentage and Chamberlain, as usual, was the top rebounder, averaging 23.8 a game.

Bill Bradley, a three-time All-American at Princeton, finally made his pro debut with the New York Knickerbockers after spending two years at England's Oxford University as a Rhodes Scholar. Bradley joined the Knicks in mid-season and averaged only 8.0 points a game. The Knicks showed tremendous progress, though, and finished third in the East, their best showing in 10 years. Much of the improvement came after Red Holzman replaced Dick McGuire as coach in mid-season.

The NBA added two new franchises, San Diego and Seattle, to the Western Division, creating a 12-team league. The San Diego Rockets had the somewhat dubious distinction of losing 67 games, erasing a record of 63 losses set by San Francisco in 1964–65.

The East scored a 144–124 victory in the All-Star Game at New York, with Hal Greer of Philadelphia winning the MVP award. Greer tallied 21 points and Havlicek had 26 for the winners.

Chamberlain, the Most Valuable Player for the third consecutive year, headed the All-NBA team. He was joined by Russell, Bing, Robertson and Cincinnati's Jerry Lucas. Earl "The Pearl" Monroe, Baltimore's outstanding 6-3 guard, was Rookie of the Year. Monroe averaged 24.3 points a game, fourth in the league, and proved an exciting playmaker and dribbler.

The league announced plans to expand to 14 teams for the 1968–69 season. The

Boston's John Havlicek rose from supersub to superstar

owners voted to locate new franchises in Phoenix and Milwaukee. The Phoenix team would be the first major-league professional team ever in Arizona.

The NBA owners agreed that beginning with the 1968–69 season, rookies would be paid a minimum of $10,000 a year. This figure would be raised to a minimum of $13,000 for the 1970–71 season. The NBA also agreed to pay veteran players a minimum of $12,500 for 1968–69 and $13,500 the following year. The minimum pay scale was adopted at the urging of the NBA Players Association, whose president was Oscar Robertson.

STANDINGS

Eastern Division

	W.	L.	Pct.
Philadelphia	62	20	.756
Boston	54	28	.659
New York	43	39	.524
Detroit	40	42	.488
Cincinnati	39	43	.476
Baltimore	36	46	.439

Western Division

	W.	L.	Pct.
St. Louis	56	26	.683
Los Angeles	52	30	.634
San Francisco	43	39	.524
Chicago	29	53	.354
Seattle	23	59	.280
San Diego	15	67	.183

PLAYOFFS

First Round

Philadelphia defeated New York 4 games to 2
Boston defeated Detroit 4 games to 2
Los Angeles defeated Chicago 4 games to 1
San Francisco defeated St. Louis 4 games to 2

Semifinals

Boston defeated Philadelphia 4 games to 3
Los Angeles defeated San Francisco 4 games to 0

Championship

Boston defeated Los Angeles 4 games to 2

TOP SCORERS

	Pts.	Ave.
Dave Bing, Detroit	2142	27.1
Elgin Baylor, Los Angeles	2002	26.0
Wilt Chamberlain, Philadelphia	1992	24.3
Earl Monroe, Baltimore	1991	24.3
Hal Greer, Philadelphia	1976	24.1

TOP REBOUNDERS

	No.	Ave.
Wilt Chamberlain, Philadelphia	1952	23.8
Jerry Lucas, Cincinnati	1560	19.0
Bill Russell, Boston	1451	18.6
Clyde Lee, San Francisco	1141	13.9
Nate Thurmond, San Francisco	1121	22.0

LEADERS IN ASSISTS

	No.	Ave.
Wilt Chamberlain, Philadelphia	702	8.6
Len Wilkens, St. Louis	679	8.3
Oscar Robertson, Cincinnati	633	9.7
Dave Bing, Detroit	509	6.4
Walt Hazzard, Seattle	493	6.2

1968–69

New names, new faces and new teams were in unfamiliar places during the season, but when all the shooting was over, the Boston Celtics were champions once again, for the 11th time in 13 seasons.

Boston, with its worst record in 13 years, finished fourth in the Eastern Division behind surprising Baltimore, Philadelphia and New York. But like the champions they were, the Celtics rose to the occasion in the playoffs and once again defeated Los Angeles in the seventh game of the championship series, 108–106, on the Lakers' home court. It was the final game for Bill Russell, both as a player and a coach, and also marked the end of the line for Sam Jones, the greatest scorer in Celtic history with 15,380 points.

Baltimore, with guards Earl Monroe and Kevin Loughery complementing the pivot play of rookie Westley Unseld, leaped from last place last season to win the divisional title, a move that earned Gene Shue Coach of the Year honors. Unseld was named Rookie of the Year and the league's Most Valuable Player, the first man to win both awards since Wilt Chamberlain did it in 1960.

Even more surprising than Baltimore's rise to the top, however, was New York's four-game sweep of the Bullets in the opening round of the playoffs. Dave DeBusschere came to the Knicks in a mid-season trade with Detroit and he joined forces with Willis Reed, Walt Frazier, Dick Barnett and Bill Bradley to take the Knicks past the first playoff round for the first time in 16 years.

There were big changes in the West, too, where Wilt Chamberlain was now en-

Rookie of the Year and league MVP Wes Unseld (41) vies with Boston's John Havlicek

sconced—with a million-dollar-plus contract —with the Los Angeles Lakers and where rookie Elvin Hayes led San Diego into the playoffs in only its second year of existence. Hayes topped the league scorers with 28.4 points a game and was fourth in rebounds, averaging 17.1. Hayes, a two-time All-American at the University of Houston, was

the main attraction as a record 41,163 fans saw an NBA doubleheader in Houston's Astrodome.

With Chamberlain joining superstars Elgin Baylor and Jerry West, Los Angeles again topped the Western Division and found the going easy in the playoffs until it ran into Boston. The Hawks, now playing

Bill Russell closes out his career with another championship at the expense of Los Angeles

in Atlanta after inception in Tri-Cities and stays in Milwaukee and St. Louis, finished second to the Lakers and far ahead of San Francisco, where Jeff Mullins and Nate Thurmond still hadn't adjusted to the loss of Rick Barry.

For the first time since their respective rookie seasons, Bill Russell and Wilt Chamberlain failed to make either the first or second units of the all-league team. Unseld headed the first team, while New York's Reed was on the second team. Joining Unseld were his Baltimore teammate Earl Monroe, Baylor, Philadelphia's Billy Cunningham and Cincinnati's Oscar Robertson, who again led the league in assists with a

9.8 per game average. And for the third time in his career, Robertson was named MVP in the All-Star Game as the East beat the West, 123–112, at Baltimore.

Among those finishing their careers were Wayne Embry, who passed the 10,000-career-point mark with the first-year Milwaukee Bucks; Rudy LaRusso, who finished the season at San Francisco with a career 11,507 points, and Tom Hawkins, who started with the Lakers in Minneapolis, went to Cincinnati, and wrapped it up in Los Angeles.

STANDINGS

Eastern Division

	W.	L.	Pct.
Baltimore	57	25	.695
Philadelphia	55	27	.671
New York	54	28	.659
Boston	48	34	.585
Cincinnati	41	41	.500
Detroit	32	50	.390
Milwaukee	27	55	.329

Western Division

	W.	L.	Pct.
Los Angeles	55	27	.671
Atlanta	48	34	.585
San Francisco	41	41	.500
San Diego	37	45	.451
Chicago	33	49	.402
Seattle	30	52	.366
Phoenix	16	66	.195

PLAYOFFS

First Round

New York defeated Baltimore 4 games to 0
Boston defeated Philadelphia 4 games to 1
Los Angeles defeated San Francisco 4 games to 2
Atlanta defeated San Diego 4 games to 2

Semifinals

Boston defeated New York 4 games to 2
Los Angeles defeated Atlanta 4 games to 1

Championship

Boston defeated Los Angeles 4 games to 3

TOP SCORERS

	Pts.	Ave.
Elvin Hayes, San Diego	2327	28.4
Earl Monroe, Baltimore	2065	24.8
Billy Cunningham, Philadelphia	2034	24.8
Bob Rule, Seattle	1965	24.0
Oscar Robertson, Cincinnati	1955	24.7

TOP REBOUNDERS

	No.	Ave.
Wilt Chamberlain, Los Angeles	1712	21.1
Wes Unseld, Baltimore	1491	18.2
Bill Russell, Boston	1484	19.3
Elvin Hayes, San Diego	1406	17.1
Nate Thurmond, San Francisco	1402	19.7

LEADERS IN ASSISTS

	No.	Ave.
Oscar Robertson, Cincinnati	772	9.8
Lenny Wilkens, Seattle	674	8.2
Walt Frazier, New York	635	7.9
Guy Rodgers, Milwaukee	561	6.9
Dave Bing, Detroit	546	7.1

1969–70

The New York Knickerbockers won 23 of their first 24 games, including a record 18 in a row, and kept right on rolling throughout the regular season and playoffs to win their first championship in the 24-year history of the league.

There was a lot of history being made by other teams as well. Boston, with former Celtic star Tom Heinsohn taking over the coaching reins, missed making the playoffs for the first time since 1950. Milwaukee, which had won a coin toss with Phoenix and a bidding war with the American Basketball Association, landed UCLA's 7-2 Lew Alcindor and finished second in the East with the best record ever achieved by a second-year expansion club. Phoenix also made the playoffs in its second year, mainly through the efforts of Connie Hawkins, the ABA's Most Valuable Player, who jumped into the older league this season.

But the biggest happening was in New York, where for virtually every home game 19,000 fans were on hand screaming "dee-fense, dee-fense" to one of the most balanced teams ever to win the NBA crown. Center Willis Reed was the team's top scorer, but ranked only 15th among league shooters. Reed, the league MVP, was supported by forwards Dave DeBusschere and Bill Bradley, guards Dick Barnett and Walt Frazier, and frequently-used reserves Dave Stallworth, Cazzie Russell and Mike Riordan.

Alcindor, who scored more points than anyone else in the league, received support from rookie forward Bob Dandridge and backcourtmen Flynn Robinson and Jon McGlocklin in taking the Bucks to the runner-up spot behind the Knicks, only four games out of first. Milwaukee scored a rec-

New York's Walt Frazier drives past Lakers' Jerry West on way to NBA title

MVP Willis Reed shoots against Kareem Abdul-Jabbar

ord 156 points in routing Philadelphia in their opening round playoff series. The 76ers had finished fourth behind New York, Milwaukee and Baltimore in the Eastern Division.

In the West, Atlanta lost Zelmo Beaty, who was sitting out a year after signing with the ABA a la Rick Barry. But the Hawks acquired Walt Bellamy from Detroit midway through the season and he worked well with Lou Hudson, Joe Caldwell, Walt Hazzard and Bill Bridges to bring Atlanta the divisional title by two games over Los Angeles.

The Lakers lost Wilt Chamberlain after the ninth game of the season and Elgin Baylor was able to play in only 54 games. Jerry West did what he could, averaging a league-leading 31.2 points a game, and received help from journeymen Happy Hairston and John Tresvant at forward and Johnny Egan at guard. Chicago, with Chet Walker, Bob Love and Clem Haskins all averaging over 20 points a game, finished third ahead of Phoenix.

Los Angeles stumbled in the playoffs against Phoenix before winning, four games to three, as Chamberlain played himself back into shape. The Lakers then swept Atlanta in five games. New York, surprisingly, had to go to seven games to oust Baltimore, then handled Milwaukee in five games.

The championship series went to seven games with the Knicks taking the deciding contest at home. Willis Reed had sustained a crippling knee injury but played the last game shot full of drugs and he was as inspirational as he was ineffective.

Reed, who was the All-Star Game MVP in the East's 142–135 victory over the West in Philadelphia, headed the all-league team. With him were New York teammate Walt Frazier, Jerry West, Connie Hawkins and Philadelphia's Billy Cunningham.

Lenny Wilkens, who won the league assist title for the first time in his career, was the player-coach at Seattle, while Bob Cousy, coaching at Cincinnati, and Richie Guerin at Atlanta unretired themselves to play briefly for their teams. Among those playing their final NBA games were Guy Rodgers at Milwaukee, Don Ohl at Atlanta and Dave Gambee at San Francisco.

STANDINGS

Eastern Division

	W.	L.	Pct.
New York	60	22	.732
Milwaukee	56	26	.683
Baltimore	59	32	.610
Philadelphia	42	40	.512
Cincinnati	36	46	.439
Boston	34	48	.415
Detroit	31	51	.378

Western Division

	W.	L.	Pct.
Atlanta	48	34	.585
Los Angeles	46	36	.561
Chicago	39	43	.476
Phoenix	39	43	.476
Seattle	36	46	.439
San Francisco	30	52	.366
San Diego	27	55	.329

PLAYOFFS

First Round

Milwaukee defeated Philadelphia 4 games to 1
New York defeated Baltimore 4 games to 3
Atlanta defeated Chicago 4 games to 1
Los Angeles defeated Phoenix 4 games to 3

Semifinals

New York defeated Milwaukee 4 games to 1
Los Angeles defeated Atlanta 4 games to 0

Championship

New York defeated Los Angeles 4 games to 3

TOP SCORERS

	Pts.	Ave.
Jerry West, Los Angeles	2309	31.2
Lew Alcindor, Milwaukee	2361	28.8
Elvin Hayes, San Diego	2256	27.5
Billy Cunningham, Philadelphia	2114	26.1
Lou Hudson, Atlanta	2031	25.4

TOP REBOUNDERS

	No.	Ave.
Elvin Hayes, San Diego	1386	16.9
Wes Unseld, Baltimore	1370	16.7
Lew Alcindor, Milwaukee	1190	14.5
Bill Bridges, Atlanta	1181	14.4
Gus Johnson, Baltimore	1086	13.9

LEADERS IN ASSISTS

	No.	Ave.
Lenny Wilkens, Seattle	683	9.1
Walt Frazier, New York	629	8.2
Clem Haskins, Chicago	624	7.6
Gail Goodrich, Phoenix	605	7.5
Jerry West, Los Angeles	554	7.5

1970–71

Before the NBA's silver anniversary season got under way, many players shifted allegiance as new teams were added in Buffalo, Cleveland and Portland. The league was realigned with three four-team divisions (Atlantic and Central in the Eastern Conference; Midwest in the Western Conference) and a five-team division, the Pacific, rounding out the West.

The single most important shift, though, was Oscar Robertson's when Cincinnati traded him to Milwaukee. All the great things the Big O had done for Cincinnati were overshadowed by the fact that he had never been on a championship team. At Milwaukee, he became the steadying force, the playmaker and the outside shooter that Lew Alcindor needed as the Bucks became the first expansion team ever to win an NBA title. En route they snapped New York's year-old record by winning 20 straight games and set five other team records. Alcindor and Robertson added five individual marks between them and big Lew

Oscar Robertson teamed with Kareem Abdul-Jabbar to lead Milwaukee to the NBA championship

was the league's Most Valuable Player and scoring champion with a 31.7-point-per-game average.

The Bucks played in the Midwest Division with Chicago, Phoenix and Detroit. Without any of the new expansion teams, it was a most competitive division as all four teams played better than .500 and won more games than any other four teams. The new clubs, the Buffalo Braves, Cleveland Cavaliers and Portland Trail Blazers, were assigned to the Atlantic, Central and Pacific divisions, respectively, and each finished last.

New York, with its championship unit intact, finished atop the Atlantic, five games ahead of Philadelphia, while Baltimore won the Central Division, six games ahead of Atlanta. Chicago, with Chet Walker and Bob Love holding forth, was runner-up to Milwaukee and earned Coach of the Year honors for Dick Motta. Los Angeles took the Pacific Division by seven games over

San Francisco, where Al Attles was the player-coach directing Nate Thurmond, Jerry Lucas and Jeff Mullins.

In the new playoff setup, the first-place team in one division played the second-place finisher in the other division in its conference. The Milwaukee Bucks defeated San Francisco in five games while Los Angeles beat Chicago in seven. In the East, defending champion New York defeated Atlanta in five games while it took Baltimore seven games to eliminate Philadelphia. Baltimore then exacted a measure of revenge, beating New York four games to three as the Bucks took the Lakers in five games. The championship round was no contest as Milwaukee won four straight. The Bucks, who had shot at a record 50.9 per cent from the field during the season, earned $212,000 in playoff money—the highest ever. The Bullets earned $152,000, a record for losers.

The bidding war with the ABA was heat-

The Silver Anniversary Team (l. to r.): Paul Arizin, Bill Russell, Joe Fulks, George Mikan, Bob Davies, Dolph Schayes, Bob Cousy, Bob Pettit, Bill Sharman, and Sam Jones

ing up as 1968 Olympic hero Spencer Haywood jumped from Denver in the new league to Seattle, and premier rookies Pete Maravich (Atlanta), Dave Cowens (Boston), Geoff Petrie (Portland), Calvin Murphy (San Diego), and Bob Lanier (Detroit) were landed by the NBA. Lost to the ABA were All-Americans Dan Issel of Kentucky and North Carolina star Charlie Scott.

Jerry West and Hal Greer of Philadelphia, both West Virginia natives, joined the 20,000-career-point club. Veteran forwards Bailey Howell, now at Philadelphia, and Tom Meschery, playing for Seattle, were ending their careers. Seattle player-coach Lenny Wilkens earned MVP honors in the All-Star Game at San Diego as the revamped West beat the East, 108–107.

The all-league team had Alcindor at center, Jerry West and Detroit's Dave Bing at guards and Philadelphia's Billy Cunningham and Boston's John Havlicek at forwards. This was Havlicek's initial first-team selection after five consecutive seasons on the second unit.

The league selected a silver anniversary team of the ten best retired players in league history. They were Bob Pettit, Dolph Schayes, Paul Arizin, Joe Fulks, Bill Russell, George Mikan, Bob Cousy, Bill Sharman, Bob Davies and Sam Jones.

STANDINGS

Eastern Conference

Atlantic Division

	W.	L.	Pct.
New York	52	30	.634
Philadelphia	47	35	.573
Boston	44	38	.537
Buffalo	22	60	.268

Central Division

	W.	L.	Pct.
Baltimore	42	40	.512
Atlanta	36	46	.439
Cincinnati	33	49	.402
Cleveland	15	67	.183

Western Conference

Midwest Division

	W.	L.	Pct.
Milwaukee	66	16	.805
Chicago	51	31	.622
Phoenix	48	34	.585
Detroit	45	37	.549

Pacific Division

	W.	L.	Pct.
Los Angeles	48	34	.585
San Francisco	41	41	.500
San Diego	40	42	.488
Seattle	38	44	.463
Portland	29	53	.354

PLAYOFFS

First Round

New York defeated Atlanta 4 games to 1
Baltimore defeated Philadelphia 4 games to 3
Milwaukee defeated San Francisco 4 games to 1
Los Angeles defeated Chicago 4 games to 3

Semifinals

Baltimore defeated New York 4 games to 3
Milwaukee defeated Los Angeles 4 games to 1

Championship

Milwaukee defeated Baltimore 4 games to 0

TOP SCORERS

	Pts.	Ave.
Lew Alcindor, Milwaukee	2596	31.7
John Havlicek, Boston	2338	28.9
Elvin Hayes, San Diego	2350	28.7
Dave Bing, Detroit	2213	27.0
Lou Hudson, Atlanta	2039	26.8

TOP REBOUNDERS

	No.	Ave.
Wilt Chamberlain, Los Angeles	1493	18.2
Wes Unseld, Baltimore	1253	16.9
Elvin Hayes, San Diego	1362	16.6
Lew Alcindor, Milwaukee	1311	16.0
Jerry Lucas, San Francisco	1265	15.8

LEADERS IN ASSISTS

	No.	Ave.
Norm Van Lier, Cincinnati	832	10.1
Len Wilkens, Seattle	654	9.2
Oscar Robertson, Milwaukee	668	8.2
John Havlicek, Boston	607	7.5
Walt Frazier, New York	536	6.7

1971–72

After years of frustration, Los Angeles finally won an NBA championship, its first since the move west from Minneapolis a dozen years earlier. The Lakers did it in convincing style, setting eight records along the way including 33 straight victories, 69 triumphs in 82 games and the best winning percentage ever, .841.

Bill Sharman, the former Celtic star, was the head coach. He had previously won championships with the Los Angeles entry in the old American Basketball League and with the Utah Stars in the American Basketball Association. After Elgin Baylor retired early in the season, Sharman, who earned Coach of the Year honors, settled on a regular unit of Jerry West and Gail Goodrich at guards, Wilt Chamberlain at center, and Happy Hairston and Jim McMillian at forwards. The team scored more than 100 points in 81 of the 82 games and beat the Warriors in one game 162–99, the largest margin of victory in league history.

Chamberlain won the rebounding title, averaging 19.2 a game, and West took his first assist title, averaging 9.7. In the process, Chamberlain became the first man to score more than 30,000 points in an NBA career and West was the All-Star Game's Most Valuable Player as his last-second shot gave the West a 112–110 victory over the East in the classic at Los Angeles.

The Lakers won the Pacific Division by 18 games over the Warriors, now called Golden State because they were playing home games in Oakland and San Diego. The Rockets vacated San Diego for a home in Houston.

The Milwaukee Bucks finished six games ahead of Chicago in the Midwest. Lew Alcindor, who changed his name to Kareem

It was Wilt Chamberlain and the Lakers in a 4–1 laugher over the Knicks

Abdul-Jabbar, won the scoring title with a 34.8-point-per-game average. He also won the Podoloff Trophy, given to the league's outstanding player based on a poll of the players.

Boston, with Jo Jo White, John Havlicek, Dave Cowens, and Don Nelson working well together, won its first divisional title in seven years, finishing eight games ahead of New York in the Atlantic. The Knicks lost center Willis Reed early in the year and were forced to go with Jerry Lucas, obtained from the Warriors as a forward, in the pivot. Baltimore and Atlanta finished one-two in the Central Division, where every team lost more games than it won.

The first round of the playoffs provided few surprises as Los Angeles defeated Chicago and Milwaukee beat Golden State in the West and Boston and New York defeated their Central opponents, Atlanta and Baltimore, respectively. Oscar Robertson was ailing and played only sparingly for the Bucks against Los Angeles. The Lakers couldn't stop Kareem Abdul-Jabbar but held the rest of the team in check and ousted the defending champions in six games. New York handled Boston with surprising ease, winning in five games.

The championship series began as a repeat of 1970, with Los Angeles versus New York. The outcome was different this time, as the Lakers settled the issue in five games and won $225,500 in bonus money for their season's work.

Among the individual milestones reached during the season was one by Philadelphia's Hal Greer, who finished the season with 1,084 games played in a career which began 14 years earlier in Syracuse. For the second consecutive year, Portland had the top rookie, Sidney Wicks, who became the eighth first-year man to score more than 2,000 points in a season.

Abdul-Jabbar headed the all-league team, with Havlicek and Seattle's Spencer Haywood at forwards, and West and New York's Walt Frazier at guards.

The bidding for players continued with the ABA as 7-foot rookies Artis Gilmore and Jim McDaniels signed with the new league, while Curtis Rowe and Sidney Wicks of UCLA's national champions, and Notre Dame's scoring whiz Austin Carr signed with the NBA. Before the season was over, though, McDaniels and Charlie Scott jumped to the NBA.

Court action was in prospect after the season ended with judges considering competing claims from the Warriors and the New York Nets for Rick Barry's services, and between Philadelphia and the Carolina Cougars for Billy Cunningham. And there was the matter of a merger between the two leagues, a topic that was being considered more and more as the rivalry for players increased and cost of their services continued to rise.

Meanwhile, in the only franchise shift, the Royals left Cincinnati and became the Kansas City-Omaha Kings, effective in the 1972–73 season.

STANDINGS

Eastern Conference

Atlantic Division

	W.	L.	Pct.
Boston	56	26	.683
New York	48	34	.585
Philadelphia	30	52	.366
Buffalo	22	60	.268

Central Division

	W.	L.	Pct.
Baltimore	38	44	.463
Atlanta	36	46	.439
Cincinnati	30	52	.366
Cleveland	23	59	.280

Western Conference

Midwest Division

	W.	L.	Pct.
Milwaukee	63	19	.768
Chicago	57	25	.695
Phoenix	49	33	.598
Detroit	26	56	.317

Pacific Division

	W.	L.	Pct.
Los Angeles	69	13	.841
Golden State	51	31	.622
Seattle	47	35	.573
Houston	34	48	.415
Portland	18	64	.220

PLAYOFFS

First Round

Boston defeated Atlanta 4 games to 2
New York defeated Baltimore 4 games to 2
Milwaukee defeated Golden State 4 games to 1
Los Angeles defeated Chicago 4 games to 0

Semifinals

New York defeated Boston 4 games to 1
Los Angeles defeated Milwaukee 4 games to 2

Championship

Los Angeles defeated New York 4 games to 1

TOP SCORERS

	Pts.	Ave.
Kareem Abdul Jabbar, Milwaukee	2822	34.8
Nate Archibald, Cincinnati	2145	28.2
John Havlicek, Boston	2252	27.5
Spencer Haywood, Seattle	1914	26.2
Gail Goodrich, Los Angeles	2127	25.9

TOP REBOUNDERS

	No.	Ave.
Wilt Chamberlain, Los Angeles	1572	19.2
Wes Unseld, Baltimore	1336	17.6
Kareem Abdul-Jabbar, Milwaukee	1346	16.6
Nate Thurmond, Golden State	1252	16.1
Dave Cowens, Boston	1203	15.2

LEADERS IN ASSISTS

	No.	Ave.
Jerry West, Los Angeles	747	9.7
Lenny Wilkens, Seattle	766	9.6
Nate Archibald, Cincinnati	701	9.2
Archie Clark, Phila.-Balt.	613	8.0
John Havlicek, Boston	614	7.5

1972–73

It was not quite as dramatic as in the spring of 1970, when Willis Reed limped onto the Madison Square Garden court for the seventh game of the NBA final, but it was his presence for most of the season and in the playoffs that enabled the New York Knicks to win their second championship in four years.

Reed, the forceful captain of the team, had never regained the form that made him a perennial all-star following that agonizing hip injury in the fifth game of the 1970 final. A succession of knee troubles had slowed him down, but he returned this season to play in 69 games. In the playoffs, he was as close to being the old Willis Reed as he ever would be as he and teammate Jerry Lucas held their own against Wes Unseld, Dave Cowens, and Wilt Chamberlain.

The Knicks finished 11 games behind the more youthful Boston Celtics in the Atlantic Division, but the Knicks were an experienced team that chose to coast to a playoff berth rather than challenge the rambunctious Celtics. The teams met in the Eastern Conference final. It was a dramatic series, filled with unexpected turns. John Havlicek

of the Celtics suffered a shoulder injury in the third game, seemingly opening the way for an easy series for the Knicks. They led 3–1 at one point, but Dave Cowens brought Boston back as even Havlicek tried to help, playing virtually with one arm.

In a dramatic upset at Madison Square Garden, Cowens helped Boston even the series. But in Boston two days later, the Knicks put on one of the best defensive performances in playoff history as they held the Celtics to 78 points.

Reed's outside touch kept Chamberlain chasing him throughout the final as the Knicks defeated the Lakers in five games. The Knicks' cause was aided when the Lakers' Jerry West was injured in the second game and was mostly ineffective for the remainder of the series.

As the veteran Knicks celebrated in the locker room following the clinching of the title, Reed was told he was named the series' Most Valuable Player.

Boston, Baltimore, Milwaukee, and Los Angeles won the division titles. The Celtics lost just 14 games during the regular season; the Lakers lost only 22 times. The Milwaukee Bucks won 60 games, including the last 14 in succession. It marked the third consecutive year the Bucks—led by Kareem Abdul-Jabbar—had won 60 or more games.

Playoff MVP Willis Reed took the Knicks to their second championship

It was a little man who made the biggest impression in the scoring race, however. Nate Archibald of the Kansas City Kings became the shortest player in league history to win a scoring title. The 6-foot Archibald, nicknamed "Tiny," averaged 34.9 points. The Kings moved to Kansas City from Cincinnati, where they were known as the Royals.

Chamberlain led the NBA in rebounding, averaging 18.6 per game. Archibald also was the assists leader with an 11.4 average. The Knicks were the best defensive team in the league. They held opponents to just 98.2 points a game. Milwaukee was second with a 99-point average.

The East won the All-Star Game played in Chicago, defeating the West, 104–84, in what customarily is a high-scoring game. Cowens led the way with 15 points and 13 rebounds. Tom Heinsohn of the Celtics was named Coach of the Year; Bob McAdoo of Buffalo was the Rookie of the Year, and Cowens was named the Most Valuable Player. Havlicek and Spencer Haywood of Seattle were the forwards on the all-league team, with Abdul-Jabbar at center and Archibald and West at guard.

STANDINGS

Eastern Conference

Atlantic Division

	W.	L.	Pct.
Boston	68	14	.829
New York	57	25	.695
Buffalo	21	61	.256
Philadelphia	9	73	.110

Central Division

	W.	L.	Pct.
Baltimore	52	30	.634
Atlanta	46	36	.561
Houston	33	49	.402
Cleveland	32	50	.390

Western Conference

Midwest Division

	W.	L.	Pct.
Milwaukee	60	22	.732
Chicago	51	31	.622
Detroit	40	42	.488
KC-Omaha	36	46	.439

Pacific Division

	W.	L.	Pct.
Los Angeles	60	22	.732
Golden State	47	35	.573
Phoenix	38	44	.463
Seattle	26	56	.317
Portland	21	61	.256

PLAYOFFS

First Round

Boston defeated Atlanta 4 games to 2
New York defeated Baltimore 4 games to 1
Golden State defeated Milwaukee 4 games to 2
Los Angeles defeated Chicago 4 games to 3

Semifinals

New York defeated Boston 4 games to 3
Los Angeles defeated Golden State 4 games to 1

Championship

New York defeated Los Angeles 4 games to 1

TOP SCORERS

	Pts.	Ave.
Nate Archibald, KC-Omaha	2719	34.9
Kareem Abdul-Jabbar, Milwaukee	2292	30.2
Spencer Haywood, Seattle	2251	29.2
Lou Hudson, Atlanta	2029	27.1
Pete Maravich, Atlanta	2063	26.1

TOP REBOUNDERS

	No.	Ave.
Wilt Chamberlain, Los Angeles	1526	18.6
Nate Thurmond, Golden State	1349	17.1
Dave Cowens, Boston	1329	16.2
Kareem Abdul-Jabbar, Milwaukee	1224	16.1
Wes Unseld, Baltimore	1260	15.9

LEADERS IN ASSISTS

	No.	Ave.
Nate Archibald, KC-Omaha	910	11.4
Lenny Wilkens, Cleveland	628	8.4
Dave Bing, Detroit	637	7.8
Oscar Robertson, Milwaukee	551	7.5
Norm Van Lier, Chicago	567	7.1

1973-74

He helped lead the Boston Celtics to nine championships and now he was back. Fortunately for the teams in the NBA, however, Bill Russell returned as a coach and general manager, this time for the Seattle SuperSonics. As a player-coach he led the Celtics to a championship in 1969, but it was quite a bit different in Seattle. The Sonics won only 36 games, and Russell discovered the secret of his coaching success in Boston—he had Bill Russell playing center there.

Perhaps it was a coincidence, but the return of Russell also marked the year when the Celtics regained what seemed to be their rightful place at the top of the NBA. Dave Cowens and Jo Jo White had matured, and John Havlicek and Paul Silas were at the height of their game as the Celtics won the Atlantic Division by seven games over the Knicks, then eliminated their nemesis in five games in the Eastern final.

The Knicks felt their age during the sea-

Dave Cowens came of age and put the Celtics back on top

son. Following it, Dave DeBusschere and Jerry Lucas retired. And Willis Reed once again was plagued by knee woes. He played in just 19 games. Still, the Celtics were wary. They had won the previous two division championships only to be ambushed by New York in the playoffs. This time it was no contest. Cowens, Havlicek, White, and Silas paced the Celtics' attack and keyed their defense. Cowens humbled Reed and Lucas, while Silas outmuscled the Knicks' forwards. It was over quickly.

The Celtics had had a more difficult time in the opening round, defeating a youthful Buffalo team in six games. The Braves were led by Bob McAdoo, who emerged as the league's most prolific scorer. He was not exciting to watch, but he seemed programmed as he methodically sank jump shot after jump shot from 15 feet away. McAdoo, a 6-9 center-forward, already was being called by some observers the best shooting big man in the game.

The Celtics survived Buffalo, winning the final two games of the series by a total of five points. In the West, Kareem Abdul-Jabbar once again was showing the way for the Milwaukee Bucks, an average team that rode his coattails to another division title. An aging Oscar Robertson added his guidance in the backcourt. The Bucks defeated Los Angeles in five games, then swept the Chicago Bulls to reach the final.

It was an unusual final, too, as the series went seven games. But it did not go according to form. The Celtics won three times in Milwaukee while the Bucks won twice in Boston, including the exciting sixth game, which Abdul-Jabbar won with a sky hook at the buzzer.

The Celtics, however, dominated the seventh game, winning handily, 102–87. Havlicek made the rounds of the locker room following the championship, shaking hands and kissing teammates. And it seemed as if the Celtics had always been champions.

Abdul-Jabbar was named the Most Valuable Player, although he did not lead in any individual category. In winning the scoring championship McAdoo hit an uncanny 54 per cent of his shots. Elvin Hayes was the top rebounder with an 18.1 average per game. Ernie DiGregorio, a fireplug guard, broke into the pros with Buffalo and won the assists title with an 8.2 average per game. Ernie D. was named the best rookie, although some of his behind-the-back passes landed in the loge seats.

Ray Scott took over the sagging Detroit Pistons and guided them to a playoff berth. The Pistons finished third in the tough Midwest Division but won 52 games. Milwaukee, Boston, Los Angeles, and the Capital Bullets were the division champs.

The Bullets had moved from Baltimore and while awaiting completion of a new arena in surburban Landover, Maryland, they played at the University of Maryland field house.

At Seattle, the West defeated the East, 134–123, in the All-Star Game. Havlicek, Rick Barry of Golden State, Abdul-Jabbar, Walt Frazier of the Knicks, and the Lakers' Gail Goodrich were named to the all-league team.

STANDINGS

Eastern Conference

Atlantic Division

	W.	L.	Pct.
Boston	56	26	.683
New York	49	33	.598
Buffalo	42	40	.512
Philadelphia	25	57	.305

Central Division

	W.	L.	Pct.
Capital	47	35	.573
Atlanta	35	47	.427
Houston	32	50	.390
Cleveland	29	53	.354

Western Conference

Midwest Division

	W.	L.	Pct.
Milwaukee	59	23	.720
Chicago	54	28	.659
Detroit	52	30	.604
KC-Omaha	33	49	.402

Pacific Division

	W.	L.	Pct.
Los Angeles	47	35	.573
Golden State	44	38	.537
Seattle	36	46	.439
Phoenix	30	52	.366
Portland	27	55	.329

PLAYOFFS

First Round

Boston defeated Buffalo 4 games to 2
New York defeated Capital 4 games to 3
Milwaukee defeated Los Angeles 4 games to 1
Chicago defeated Detroit 4 games to 3

Semifinals

Boston defeated New York 4 games to 1
Milwaukee defeated Chicago 4 games to 0

Championship

Boston defeated Milwaukee 4 games to 3

TOP SCORERS

	Pts.	Ave.
Bob McAdoo, Buffalo	2261	30.6
Pete Maravich, Atlanta	2107	27.7
Kareem Abdul-Jabbar, Milwaukee	2191	27.0
Gail Goodrich, Los Angeles	2076	25.3
Rick Barry, Golden State	2009	25.1

TOP REBOUNDERS

	No.	Ave.
Elvin Hayes, Capital	1463	18.1
Dave Cowens, Boston	1257	15.7
Bob McAdoo, Buffalo	1117	15.1
Kareem Abdul-Jabbar, Milwaukee	1178	14.5
Nate Thurmond, Golden State	878	14.2

LEADERS IN ASSISTS

	No.	Ave.
Ernie DiGregorio, Buffalo	663	8.2
Calvin Murphy, Houston	603	7.4
Lenny Wilkens, Cleveland	522	7.1
Walt Frazier, New York	551	6.9
Dave Bing, Detroit	555	6.9

1974–75

The staid old East produced no changes. There were the Celtics on top in the Atlantic Division once again. In the Central, the Bullets, changing identities for the third straight season, won the division title by a resounding 19 games. They had changed their first name from Baltimore to Capital to Washington, but, alas, by any name they dominated. If there was to be an infusion of new blood, surely it would have to come from the West, where Jerry West had retired from the Lakers and Oscar Robertson had called it quits with Milwaukee.

Bill Walton was the heralded rookie, and the tall redhead was a dominant center in the Russell-Chamberlain-Abdul-Jabbar mold. Walton was expected to lead the Portland Trail Blazers from obscurity to a playoff berth, at least.

Instead, Walton's first year was filled with controversy. The player who dominated collegiate basketball at UCLA became brittle and spent most of the season on crutches

Itinerant Rick Barry led Warriors to a sweep of the Bullets in the finals

and in a cast. He played in just 35 games. Portland finished third in the Pacific Division. The West looked weak and ripe for the taking.

Then there was the biggest surprise of all. The Golden State Warriors, the best team in a weak Pacific Division, got stronger and stronger and stronger as the playoffs progressed, and shocked pro basketball fans by winning the championship—in four games, no less. And against the Bullets.

Rick Barry, the rebellious golden boy who had returned to the Warriors two years earlier following a successful stay in the rival ABA, was the catalyst on a team of relatively unknown players. Al Attles, the coach and a former guard, was better known than any of his backcourt players.

The Warriors won by using a liberal substitution system that helped make up for their lack of superstar players. Barry was the only player who regularly saw action for more than 40 minutes a game. Attles employed the shuttle to keep players fresh and happy and performing at their optimum.

Golden State opened the playoffs by taking Seattle in six games. It was forced to seven by the Chicago Bulls, a team that thought it was ready to step out of the shadow of Milwaukee and Los Angeles to win in the West. But Barry and Clifford Ray, and talented rookies such as Keith (now Jamaal) Wilkes and Phil Smith provided a blend that was not to be beat.

The Bullets—no longer victims of the Knicks in early playoff confrontations—beat Buffalo in seven games, then cleared what they expected to be their highest hurdle when they defeated defending champion Boston in six games.

In the first game of the final, the Bullets moved to a big early lead against the Warriors. It looked simple. By game's end, however, the Warriors had fought back to win by six. The next two games were played in the Bay Area, and the Warriors won both. Back in Landover, Maryland, they clinched the championship in Barry's finest hour.

The Bullets were left with individual achievements. Wes Unseld led the NBA in rebounding with a 14.8 average per game. Kevin Porter led in assists, averaging 8. And Elvin Hayes was named to an all-league team that included Barry, Bob McAdoo of Buffalo, Nate Archibald of Kansas City, and Walt Frazier of New York.

McAdoo again won the scoring title, with a 34.5 average. Phil Johnson, previously an assistant to Dick Motta in Chicago, was named Coach of the Year, leading Kansas City to 44 victories and second place in the Midwest Division.

Willis Reed of the Knicks joined West and Robertson in retirement, one month before the start of training camp. But Frazier provided the All-Star Game with a familiar hero, as he scored 30 points to lead the East to a 108–102 victory over the West in Phoenix.

STANDINGS

Eastern Conference

Atlantic Division

	W.	L.	Pct.
Boston	60	22	.732
Buffalo	49	33	.598
New York	40	42	.488
Philadelphia	34	48	.415

Central Division

	W.	L.	Pct.
Washington	60	22	.732
Houston	41	41	.500
Cleveland	40	42	.488
Atlanta	31	51	.378
New Orleans	23	59	.280

Western Conference

Midwest Division

	W.	L.	Pct.
Chicago	47	35	.573
KC-Omaha	44	38	.537
Detroit	40	42	.488
Milwaukee	38	44	.463

Pacific Division

	W.	L.	Pct.
Golden State	48	34	.585
Seattle	43	39	.524
Portland	38	44	.463
Phoenix	32	50	.390
Los Angeles	30	52	.366

PLAYOFFS

Qualifying Round

Houston defeated New York 2 games to 1
Seattle defeated Detroit 2 games to 1

First Round

Boston defeated Houston 4 games to 1
Washington defeated Buffalo 4 games to 3
Golden State defeated Seattle 4 games to 2
Chicago defeated Kansas City 4 games to 2

Semifinals

Washington defeated Boston 4 games to 2
Golden State defeated Chicago 4 games to 3

Championship

Golden State defeated Washington 4 games to 0

TOP SCORERS

	Pts.	Ave.
Bob McAdoo, Buffalo	2831	34.5
Rick Barry, Golden State	2450	30.6
Kareem Abdul-Jabbar, Milwaukee	1949	30.0
Nate Archibald, KC-Omaha	2170	26.5
Charlie Scott, Phoenix	1680	24.3

TOP REBOUNDERS

	No.	Ave.
Wes Unseld, Washington	1077	14.8
Dave Cowens, Boston	958	14.7
Sam Lacey, KC-Omaha	1149	14.2
Bob McAdoo, Buffalo	1155	14.1
Kareem Abdul-Jabbar, Milwaukee	912	14.0

LEADERS IN ASSISTS

	No.	Ave.
Kevin Porter, Washington	650	8.0
Dave Bing, Detroit	610	7.7
Nate Archibald, KC-Omaha	557	6.8
Randy Smith, Buffalo	534	6.5
Pete Maravich, New Orleans	488	6.2

1975–76

It was an eventful season, with as much happening off the court as on it. With the addition of more franchises over the years and the competitive balance it helped bring to the league, the age of dynasties had passed. The Boston Celtics, however, showed that if they could no longer win the championship every year, then every other year wasn't so bad.

The Celtics, again led by John Havlicek, Dave Cowens, Jo Jo White, and Paul Silas, won the Atlantic Division title and went on to win their thirteenth championship. There were more surprises in the West, where Golden State, the defending champion, posted the best record in the league during the regular season, but was upset by the Phoenix Suns in the conference final.

The Suns had a mediocre won-lost record during the season, finishing two games above .500. They had an impressive rookie in center Alvan Adams, and former Celtic Paul Westphal had emerged as a star, how-

John Havlicek and Company showed their Celtic lineage by achieving a thirteenth NBA championship for Boston

348

ever, so the Suns were to be reckoned with in the playoffs. They defeated the Warriors in seven games before losing to the Celtics in a six-game final. And they might have been champions too had they won the fifth game, a three-overtime classic in Boston. The Celtics prevailed, 128–126, before a capacity crowd that became unruly as the game progressed.

The Celtics, Warriors, Milwaukee Bucks, and Cleveland Cavaliers captured the divisional titles. The Cavaliers, under coach Bill Fitch, unseated Washington in the Central Division, relying on the stingiest defense in the league. Fitch was named Coach of the Year.

Bob McAdoo scored the triple in the scoring race, leading the league in this department for the third consecutive season. He averaged 31.1 points per game.

There were a couple of familiar faces in new places, and one new face who made a lot of news. Kareem Abdul-Jabbar asked the Bucks to trade him either to the Lakers or New York Knicks. Abdul-Jabbar preferred the Knicks, but their offer did not match the one made by Los Angeles, which sent Brian Winters and several excellent No. 1 draft choices to the Bucks. Kareem was the leading rebounder with a 16.9 average, but he had little help. The Lakers finished fourth in the Pacific Division.

The Knicks acquired high-scoring Spencer Haywood from Seattle on the opening day of the season. Prior to the season, they illegally signed ABA star George McGinnis to a multi-year contract. McGinnis, an all-star forward with the Indiana Pacers, had been drafted by the Philadelphia 76ers in the NBA. The 76ers threatened legal action against the Knicks, but it was not necessary. Lawrence O'Brien, the new commissioner who had succeeded Walter Kennedy, voided the Knicks' contract with McGinnis. He penalized them their top choice for the 1976 draft and fined them.

McGinnis eventually signed a six-year, $3.2 million contract with the 76ers and led them to a second-place finish in the Atlantic Division. He was named to the all-league team and was joined by Rick Barry of the

Warriors, Abdul-Jabbar, Nate Archibald of Kansas City, and Pete Maravich of New Orleans.

O'Brien, former Democratic National Party chairman who had worked for two Presidents (Kennedy and Johnson), helped negotiate a settlement to the class-action lawsuit filed in 1970 by Oscar Robertson on

Lawrence O'Brien, adviser to two Presidents (Kennedy and Johnson), succeeded Walter Kennedy as NBA commissioner

behalf of the NBA players. As a result, the option clause was eliminated (effective the following season), the college draft was revised so teams no longer would hold lifetime rights to the players chosen, and a compensation clause for free agents who had signed with new teams would remain in effect until 1980–81. Then the league would adopt a policy of right of first refusal.

Back on the court, the East defeated the West, 123–109, in the All-Star Game in Philadelphia.

STANDINGS

Eastern Conference

Atlantic Division

	W.	L.	Pct.
Boston	54	28	.659
Buffalo	46	36	.561
Philadelphia	46	36	.561
New York	38	44	.463

Central Division

	W.	L.	Pct.
Cleveland	49	33	.598
Washington	48	34	.585
Houston	40	42	.488
New Orleans	38	44	.463
Atlanta	29	53	.354

Western Conference

Midwest Division

	W.	L.	Pct.
Milwaukee	38	44	.463
Detroit	36	46	.439
Kansas City	31	51	.378
Chicago	24	58	.293

Pacific Division

	W.	L.	Pct.
Golden State	59	23	.720
Seattle	43	39	.524
Phoenix	42	40	.512
Los Angeles	40	42	.488
Portland	37	45	.451

PLAYOFFS

Qualifying Round

Buffalo defeated Philadelphia 2 games to 1
Detroit defeated Milwaukee 2 games to 1

First Round

Boston defeated Buffalo 4 games to 2
Cleveland defeated Washington 4 games to 3
Golden State defeated Detroit 4 games to 2
Phoenix defeated Seattle 4 games to 2

Semifinals

Boston defeated Cleveland 4 games to 2
Phoenix defeated Golden State 4 games to 3

Championship

Boston defeated Phoenix 4 games to 2

TOP SCORERS

	Pts.	Ave.
Bob McAdoo, Buffalo	2427	31.1
Kareem Abdul-Jabbar, Los Angeles	2275	27.7
Pete Maravich, New Orleans	1604	25.9
Nate Archibald, Kansas City	1935	24.8
Fred Brown, Seattle	1757	23.1

TOP REBOUNDERS

	No.	Ave.
Kareem Abdul-Jabbar, Los Angeles	1383	16.9
Dave Cowens, Boston	1246	16.0
Wes Unseld, Washington	1036	13.3
Paul Silas, Boston	1025	12.7
Sam Lacey, Kansas City	1024	12.6

LEADERS IN ASSISTS

	No.	Ave.
Slick Watts, Seattle	661	8.1
Nate Archibald, Kansas City	615	7.9
Calvin Murphy, Houston	596	7.3
Norm Van Lier, Chicago	500	6.6
Rick Barry, Golden State	496	6.1

1976–77

For nine years the leagues had competed for players, sending salaries soaring and resulting in lawsuits, raids, and unethical acts committed by players and owners alike. But no more. Prior to the start of the season the NBA absorbed four ABA franchises, terminating the existence of the rival league and bringing relative peace to professional basketball.

For an entry fee of $3.2 million each, the Denver Nuggets, Indiana Pacers, San Antonio Spurs, and New York Nets gained admittance to the NBA. The price was steep —so steep that Nets' owner Roy Boe refused to renegotiate the contract of Julius

The past was forgotten as Bill Walton guided the Trail Blazers to the title

Erving, considered by many to be the most exciting player in the game. Erving, who helped the Nets win two ABA titles, was sold to the Philadelphia 76ers, giving that team a star-studded lineup and leaving the Nets depleted.

In Philadelphia, Erving teamed with George McGinnis, Doug Collins, Lloyd Free and Henry Bibby to give the league one of its most colorful teams ever. But the 76ers were not widely applauded. They bickered among themselves and played the type of one-on-one game that made purists shudder. But they were good, so good, and they made it to the final against the Portland Trail Blazers.

In his third season, with his injuries kept to a minimum, Bill Walton became the force everyone expected him to be. He led a well-schooled Trail Blazer team to a third-place finish during the regular season and then on to the championship.

The Blazers were coached by Jack Ramsay, who had had minimal success in Philadelphia and Buffalo before realizing his dream in Portland, a frontier city of backpackers and seemingly endless rain. Walton was the key. He scored, rebounded, played defense, and orchestrated the passing game that made the Blazers' attack impressive.

After defeating Chicago in an opening-round series, the Blazers swept Los Angeles in the Western semifinal. Jerry West had returned to coach the Lakers, and Kareem Abdul-Jabbar had one of his finest seasons, leading a group of lesser-known players to first place in the Pacific Division.

After Portland defeated Denver, a merger team that won the Midwest title, it faced the 76ers, winners against Boston and Houston in the East. Basketball fans perceived it as a morality play—the Blazers' team style against the free-lance Sixers. Philadelphia won the first two games before Portland showed remarkable poise and confidence by sweeping the next four to wrap it all up.

Walton had vindicated himself and became a folk hero in Portland. One superstar who did not fare as well was Bob McAdoo. At odds with Buffalo owner Paul Snyder, he was traded to the New York Knicks. McAdoo averaged 25 points but failed to lead the Knicks to the playoffs. Pete Maravich unseated him as scoring champion, averaging 31.1 points per game.

Tom Nissalke, who guided the Houston Rockets to the Central Division championship, was named Coach of the Year. Moses Malone, who skipped college to turn pro with Utah of the ABA, was acquired by the Rockets from Buffalo early in the season, and he gave them the big man that made them formidable.

Adrian Dantley of Buffalo was the top rookie, while Elvin Hayes of Washington, David Thompson of Denver, Abdul-Jabbar, Pete Maravich and Paul Westphal of Phoenix were named to the all-league team.

In the All-Star Game in Milwaukee, the West defeated the East, 125–124. The league set an all-time attendance record by drawing 9,898,521 fans.

351

STANDINGS

Eastern Conference

Atlantic Division

	W.	L.	Pct.
Philadelphia	50	32	.610
Boston	44	38	.537
New York Knicks	40	42	.486
Buffalo	30	52	.366
New York Nets	22	60	.288

Central Division

	W.	L.	Pct.
Houston	49	33	.598
Washington	48	34	.585
San Antonio	44	38	.537
Cleveland	43	39	.524
New Orleans	35	47	.427
Atlanta	31	51	.378

Western Conference

Midwest Division

	W.	L.	Pct.
Denver	50	32	.610
Detroit	44	38	.537
Chicago	44	38	.537
Kansas City	40	42	.488
Indiana	36	46	.439
Milwaukee	30	52	.366

Pacific Division

	W.	L.	Pct.
Los Angeles	53	29	.646
Portland	49	33	.598
Golden State	46	36	.561
Seattle	40	42	.488
Phoenix	34	48	.415

PLAYOFFS

Qualifying Round

Boston defeated San Antonio 2 games to 0
Washington defeated Cleveland 2 games to 1
Golden State defeated Detroit 2 games to 1
Portland defeated Chicago 2 games to 1

First Round

Philadelphia defeated Boston 4 games to 3
Houston defeated Washington 4 games to 2
Los Angeles defeated Golden State 4 games to 3
Portland defeated Denver 4 games to 2

Semifinals

Philadelphia defeated Houston 4 games to 2
Portland defeated Los Angeles 4 games to 0

Championship

Portland defeated Philadelphia 4 games to 2

TOP SCORERS

	Pts.	Ave.
Pete Maravich, New Orleans	2273	31.1
Billy Knight, Indiana	2075	26.6
Kareem Abdul-Jabbar, Los Angeles	2152	26.2
David Thompson, Denver	2125	25.9
Bob McAdoo, New York Knicks	1861	25.8

TOP REBOUNDERS

	No.	Ave.
Bill Walton, Portland	934	14.4
Kareem Abdul-Jabbar, Los Angeles	1090	13.3
Moses Malone, Houston	1072	13.1
Artis Gilmore, Chicago	1070	13.0
Bob McAdoo, New York Knicks	926	12.9

LEADERS IN ASSISTS

	No.	Ave.
Don Buse, Indiana	685	8.5
Slick Watts, Seattle	630	8.0
Norm Van Lier, Chicago	636	7.8
Kevin Porter, Detroit	592	7.3
Tom Henderson, Washington	598	6.9

1977–78

They made two previous trips to the final, and on both occasions they were given a good chance to win the championship. Twice, however, the Washington Bullets failed to win a game as they were swept by Milwaukee and Golden State. Now, when no one, not even the players, anticipated it, the Bullets were in the final again. Seven games later, they were the champions.

At the start of the season it appeared that Portland would have little difficulty winning the Pacific Division and advancing to the final to defend its championship. After a

Elvin Hayes buried his choke image in taking the Bullets to the crown

stormy start, in which coach Gene Shue was fired and replaced by folk hero Billy Cunningham, Philadelphia righted itself and appeared headed for a rematch with the Trail Blazers.

It was not to be. The Blazers were struck down by injuries to their six best players—including Bill Walton—and what looked like a record-setting year ended in disappointment. They limped to the division title, but were beaten by the Seattle SuperSonics in the Western semifinals. The Sonics then defeated the Denver Nuggets and were even a bigger surprise than the Bullets.

Bill Russell had retired as the Sonics' coach before the season started, and his assistant, Bob Hopkins, succeeded him. The Sonics lost 15 of their first 22 games, however, and owner Sam Schulman fired Hopkins. Lenny Wilkens, a favorite of the Seattle fans before Schulman traded him four years earlier, took over the team. It was an amazing turnabout.

Back in the East, the 76ers rolled past the

Knicks in four games in the first round of the playoffs. Feeling a bit overconfident, the 76ers lost to the Bullets in the first game of the Eastern final and never recovered. Playing unselfishly, the Bullets won the series in six.

The Sonics won three of the first five games in the championship round and were only one victory away from a remarkable season. Marvin Webster, the 7-foot center who was acquired from Denver, was the difference. He supplied the rebounding and shot-blocking the team needed. The Bullets did not give in, though. They trounced the Sonics in the sixth game in Landover, Maryland, then stunned the Sonics' fans by winning the championship in Seattle. After 10 years in the pros, coach Dick Motta had reached his goal. After 10 years, Wes Unseld and Elvin Hayes were vindicated.

The Bullets-Sonics series showed that finishing first in the division may not be terribly important after all. The 76ers, Blazers, Nuggets, and San Antonio Spurs would attest to that. Despite being sidelined for the last two months, Walton was named the Most Valuable Player. When healthy, he led the Blazers to 50 victories in 60 games. George Gervin of the Spurs won the scoring title with a 27.2 average per game.

Hubie Brown, who guided a group of discards to a .500 record and a playoff berth in Atlanta, was named as the top coach. Walter Davis of Phoenix was Rookie of the Year in a season that produced a number of excellent first-year players such as Bernard King of the New Jersey Nets, Marques Johnson of the Milwaukee Bucks, Norm Nixon of the Los Angeles Lakers, and Jack Sikma of the Sonics.

But Milwaukee's Kent Benson, the top pick in the collegiate draft, was a flop. He began the season by elbowing Kareem Abdul-Jabbar in the midsection, then being knocked down by a right hand thrown by Kareem. When the season ended, Benson was on the bench.

Embattled owner Roy Boe moved the Nets from Long Island to New Jersey, where they played at the new Rutgers arena before sparse crowds.

The biggest news of the season was made by John Havlicek, the seemingly tireless Celtic who announced his retirement effective at the end of the season. Havlicek was given sentimental farewells in each franchise city. The Knicks' Bill Bradley had retired prior to the start of the season to run for the U. S. Senate from New Jersey. Walt Frazier, another well-known Knick, was traded at the start of the season to the Cleveland Cavaliers. Willis Reed, a third member of the Knicks' championship teams, completed his first year as the team's coach.

In the All-Star Game in Atlanta, the East defeated the West, 133–125, as Buffalo's Randy Smith scored 27 points.

STANDINGS

Eastern Conference

Atlantic Division

	W.	L.	Pct.
Philadelphia	55	27	.671
New York	43	39	.524
Boston	32	50	.390
Buffalo	27	55	.329
New Jersey	24	58	.293

Central Division

	W.	L.	Pct.
San Antonio	52	30	.634
Washington	44	38	.537
Cleveland	43	39	.524
Atlanta	41	41	.500
New Orleans	39	43	.476
Houston	28	54	.341

Western Conference

Midwest Division

	W.	L.	Pct.
Denver	48	34	.585
Milwaukee	44	38	.537
Chicago	40	42	.488
Detroit	38	44	.463
Indiana	31	51	.378
Kansas City	31	51	.378

Pacific Division

	W.	L.	Pct.
Portland	58	24	.707
Phoenix	49	33	.598
Seattle	47	35	.573
Los Angeles	45	37	.549
Golden State	43	39	.524

PLAYOFFS

Qualifying Round

New York defeated Cleveland 2 games to 0
Washington defeated Atlanta 2 games to 0
Milwaukee defeated Phoenix 2 games to 0
Seattle defeated Los Angeles 2 games to 1

First Round

Philadelphia defeated New York 4 games to 0
Washington defeated San Antonio 4 games to 2
Seattle defeated Portland 4 games to 2
Denver defeated Milwaukee 4 games to 3

Semifinals

Washington defeated Philadelphia 4 games to 2
Seattle defeated Denver 4 games to 2

Championship

Washington defeated Seattle 4 games to 3

TOP SCORERS

	Pts.	Ave.
George Gervin, San Antonio	2232	27.21
David Thompson, Denver	2172	27.15
Bob McAdoo, New York	2097	26.5
Kareem Abdul-Jabbar, Los Angeles	1600	25.8
Calvin Murphy, Houston	1949	25.6

TOP REBOUNDERS

	No.	Ave.
Truck Robinson, New Orleans	1288	15.7
Moses Malone, Houston	886	15.0
Dave Cowens, Boston	1078	14.0
Elvin Hayes, Washington	1075	13.3
Swen Nater, Buffalo	1029	13.2

LEADERS IN ASSISTS

	No.	Ave.
Kevin Porter, New Jersey	837	10.2
John Lucas, Houston	768	9.4
Ricky Sobers, Indiana	584	7.4
Norm Nixon, Los Angeles	553	6.8
Norm Van Lier, Chicago	531	6.8

1978–79

It was one of the most difficult seasons for supporters of the NBA as critics seemed to take more shots at the league than the players took during games. Many felt that the games were too high scoring, that high-salaried players did not perform to their capabilities every night, and that perhaps audiences could not identify with predominantly black teams.

There were others who said interest had not waned despite poor television ratings. The problem? Well, it seems the big-city teams in New York, Chicago, Boston, and Los Angeles were not contenders. In fact, the Knicks, Bulls, and Celtics finished a combined 74 games below .500. The Lakers finished third in the Pacific Division, but attendance in Los Angeles dropped anyway.

The big-city teams faltered, but in some of the smaller towns, basketball flourished. The Seattle SuperSonics overcame losing center Marvin Webster to free agency and his replacement, Tom LaGarde, to injury, to finish first in the Pacific Division. The Sonics played in a division in which five of the six teams finished above .500. The com-petition primed them for the playoffs.

The Sonics overcame a 3–2 deficit to win the Western Conference final against Phoenix. In the East, the defending champion Washington Bullets became only the third team in league history to overcome a 3–1 disadvantage in the playoffs. The Bullets outlasted the San Antonio Spurs to set up a rematch against the Sonics in the final.

This time it was the Sonics' turn. They reversed last year's final and defeated the Bullets in five games to win the NBA championship. Thus for the eleventh consecutive year no team in the NBA could repeat as champion.

The Sonics relied on guards Dennis Johnson and Gus Williams to carry their offense. The front line of John Johnson, Jack Sikma and Lonnie Shelton used their muscle to battle the Bullets on the boards. Washington —led by Elvin Hayes and Wes Unseld—led the league in rebounding. Seattle was fourth.

A disciplined fast-break offense and a stingy defense enabled the Sonics to make up for any lack of depth. Coach Lenny Wilkens' poise on the bench was reflected in his team's play.

While the Sonics overcame adversity, they

were not the biggest surprise in the NBA. The Kansas City Kings staged a complete reversal as they climbed to first place in the Midwest Division, beating out Denver by one game. The Kings added two important ingredients to account for their success. Cotton Fitzsimmons became their coach, while rookie Phil Ford put aside his reservations about playing in Kansas City to spark the team as its playmaker.

When Ford was drafted by the Kings in June 1978, he said he did not want to play for a loser. He thought of going to Europe. He relented, however, and helped make the Kings a winner, teaming with second-year guard Otis Birdsong. Ford was named the NBA Rookie of the Year, winning handily. He finished fourth in assists, averaging 8.6. He was fifth in steals, and he added 15.9 points a game. Fitzsimmons was Coach of the Year.

Washington won easily in the Atlantic Division, while San Antonio beat out Houston by one game in the Central.

Moses Malone of Houston was named Most Valuable Player. He averaged 24.8 points and led the NBA in rebounding with a 17.6 average.

Malone had 587 offensive rebounds, establishing himself as the best offensive rebounder of this decade. Rich Kelley of New Orleans finished second in rebounding with a 12.8 average. Kareem Abdul-Jabbar of the Lakers finished with the same average as Kelley but one less rebound.

George "Iceman" Gervin won the scoring championship for the second consecutive season. The lanky 6-8 guard averaged 29.6 points. Lloyd Free, who could not succeed as a third guard in Philadelphia, was traded to San Diego, where he started, and averaged 28.8 points.

As always, Rick Barry and Calvin Murphy were at the top of the free-throw shooting list. This time they were teammates on the Houston Rockets. Barry won the title, hitting .949 of his free throws. Murphy made .928 of his. Kevin Porter of the Detroit Pistons set an NBA record for career assists, accumulating 1,099, a 13.4 average. M. L. Carr of the Pistons led in steals with a 2.46 average. Abdul-Jabbar averaged 3.95 blocked shots to lead in that category.

News was made off the court too. Bill Walton, the Portland center who sat out the season with injuries, became a free agent and signed a seven-year, $7-million contract with San Diego. Walton then underwent surgery for the removal of bone spurs on both ankles. If healthy, he could make the Clippers a challenger for the championship immediately.

Bill Fitch, the only coach the Cleveland Cavaliers ever had, quit to become coach of the Celtics in 1979–80.

STANDINGS

Eastern Conference

Atlantic Division

	W.	L.	Pct.
Washington	54	28	.659
Philadelphia	47	35	.573
New Jersey	37	45	.451
New York	31	51	.378
Boston	29	53	.354

Central Division

	W.	L.	Pct.
San Antonio	48	34	.585
Houston	47	35	.573
Atlanta	46	36	.661
Cleveland	30	52	.366
Detroit	30	52	.366
New Orleans	26	56	.317

Western Conference

Midwest Division

	W.	L.	Pct.
Kansas City	48	34	.585
Denver	47	35	.573
Indiana	38	44	.463
Milwaukee	38	44	.463
Chicago	31	51	.378

Pacific Division

	W.	L.	Pct.
Seattle	52	30	.634
Phoenix	50	32	.610
Los Angeles	47	35	.573
Portland	45	37	.549
San Diego	43	39	.524
Golden State	38	44	.463

PLAYOFFS

Qualifying Round

Philadelphia defeated New Jersey 2 games to 0
Atlanta defeated Houston 2 games to 0
Phoenix defeated Portland 2 games to 1
Los Angeles defeated Denver 2 games to 1

First Round

Washington defeated Atlanta 4 games to 3
San Antonio defeated Philadelphia 4 games to 3
Seattle defeated Los Angeles 4 games to 1
Phoenix defeated Kansas City 4 games to 1

Semifinals

Washington defeated San Antonio 4 games to 3
Seattle defeated Phoenix 4 games to 3

Championship

Seattle defeated Washington 4 games to 1

TOP SCORERS

	Pts.	Ave.
George Gervin, San Antonio	2365	29.6
Lloyd Free, San Diego	2244	28.8
Marques Johnson, Milwaukee	1972	25.6
Bob McAdoo, Boston	1487	24.8
Moses Malone, Houston	2031	24.8

TOP REBOUNDERS

	No.	Ave.
Moses Malone, Houston	1444	17.6
Rich Kelley, New Orleans	1026	12.8
Kareem Abdul-Jabbar, Los Angeles	1025	12.8
Artis Gilmore, Chicago	1043	12.7
Jack Sikma, Seattle	1013	12.4

LEADERS IN ASSISTS

	No.	Ave.
Kevin Porter, Detroit	1099	13.4
John Lucas, Golden State	762	9.3
Norm Nixon, Los Angeles	737	9.0
Phil Ford, Kansas City	681	8.6
Paul Westphal, Phoenix	529	6.5

Seattle's Jack Sikma beats Washington's Wes Unseld to the rebound as the Super-Sonics roll to the NBA crown in fifth and final game

Houston's Moses Malone was the NBA's MVP

ALL-TIME NBA RECORDS
INDIVIDUAL
Single Game

Most Points	100	Wilt Chamberlain, Philadelphia, vs N.Y. at Hershey, Pa., March 2, 1962
Most F. G. Attempted	63	Wilt Chamberlain, Philadelphia, vs N.Y. at Hershey, Pa., March 2, 1962
Most F. G. Made	36	Wilt Chamberlain, Philadelphia, vs N.Y. at Hershey, Pa., March 2, 1962
Most F. T. Attempted	34	Wilt Chamberlain, Philadelphia, vs St. Louis at Philadelphia, Feb. 22, 1962
Most F. T. Made	28	Wilt Chamberlain, Philadelphia, vs N.Y. at Hershey, Pa., March 2, 1962
Most Rebounds	55	Wilt Chamberlain, Philadelphia, vs Boston at Philadelphia, Nov. 24, 1960
Most Assists	28	Bob Cousy, Boston, vs Minneapolis at Boston Feb. 27, 1959
	28	Guy Rodgers, San Francisco, vs St. Louis at San Francisco, March 14, 1963
Most Personal Fouls	8	Don Otten, Tri-Cities, at Sheboygan, Nov. 24, 1949
Most Free Throws Missed	22	Wilt Chamberlain, Philadelphia, vs Seattle, Dec. 1, 1967
Most Consecutive Points	32	Larry Costello, Syracuse vs Boston at Boston Dec. 8, 1961
Most Consecutive Free Throws	19	Bob Pettit, St. Louis, vs Boston Nov. 22, 1961

Season

Most Points	4,029	Wilt Chamberlain, Philadelphia, 1961-62
Highest Average	50.4	Wilt Chamberlain, Philadelphia, 1961-62
Most F. G. Attempted	3,159	Wilt Chamberlain, Philadelphia, 1961-62
Most F. G. Made	1,597	Wilt Chamberlain, Philadelphia, 1961-62
Highest F. G. Percentage	.727	Wilt Chamberlain, Los Angeles, 1972-73
Most F. T. Attempted	1,363	Wilt Chamberlain, Philadelphia, 1961-62
Most F. T. Made	840	Jerry West, Los Angeles, 1965-66
Highest F. T. Percentage	.945	Ernie DiGregorio, Buffalo, 1976-77
Most Rebounds	2,149	Wilt Chamberlain, Philadelphia, 1960-61
Most Assists	1,099	Kevin Porter, Detroit, 1978-79
Most Personal Fouls	366	Bill Bridges, St. Louis, 1967-68
Most Disqualifications	26	Don Meineke, Fort Wayne, 1952-53

Career

Most Points Scored	31,419	Wilt Chamberlain, Philadelphia Warriors, San Francisco Warriors, Philadelphia 76ers, and Los Angeles Lakers, 1960-73
Highest Scoring Average	30.1	Wilt Chamberlain, 1960-73
Most F. G. Attempted	23,930	John Havlicek, Boston, 1963-78
Most F. G. Made	12,681	Wilt Chamberlain, 1960-73
Highest F. G. Percentage	.557	Kareem Abdul-Jabbar, Milwaukee and Los Angeles, 1970-79
Most F. T. Attempted	11,862	Wilt Chamberlain, 1960-73

Most F. T. Made	7,694	Oscar Robertson, Cincinnati and Milwaukee, 1961-74
Highest F. T. Percentage	.902	Rick Barry, San Francisco and Golden State Warriors, 1965-67, 1972-78
Most Rebounds	23,924	Wilt Chamberlain, 1960-73
Most Assists	9,887	Oscar Robertson, 1961-74
Most Minutes	46,471	John Havlicek, 1963-78
Most Games	1,270	John Havlicek, 1963-78
Most Personal Fouls	3,885	Hal Greer, Syracuse and Philadelphia, 1959-72
Most Times Disqualified	127	Vern Mikkelsen, Minneapolis, 1950-59

TEAM RECORDS

Single Game

Most Points, One Team	173	Boston vs Minneapolis at Boston, Feb. 27, 1959
Most Points, Two Teams	316	Philadelphia 169, New York 147 at Hershey, Pa., March 2, 1962
	316	Cincinnati 165, San Diego 151 at Cincinnati, March 2, 1970
Most F. G. Attempted, One Team	153	Philadelphia vs Los Angeles at Philadelphia, Dec. 8, 1961
Most F. G. Attempted, Two Teams	291	Philadelphia 153, Los Angeles 138 at Philadelphia, Dec. 8, 1961
Most F. G. Made, One Team	72	Boston vs Minneapolis at Boston, Feb. 27, 1959
Most F. G. Made, Two Teams	134	Cincinnati 67, San Diego 67 at Cincinnati, March 12, 1970
Most F. T. Attempted, One Team	86	Syracuse vs Anderson at Syracuse (In 5 overtimes), Nov. 14, 1949
Most F. T. Attempted, Two Teams	160	Syracuse 86, Anderson 74 at Syracuse (In 5 overtimes), Nov. 24, 1949
Most F. T. Made, One Team	59	Syracuse vs Anderson at Syracuse (In 5 overtimes), Nov. 24, 1949
Most F. T. Made, Two Teams	116	Syracuse 59, Anderson 57 at Syracuse (In 5 overtimes), Nov. 24, 1949
Most Rebounds, One Team	112	Philadelphia vs Cincinnati at Philadelphia, Nov. 8, 1959
	112	Boston vs Detroit at Boston, Dec. 24, 1960
Most Rebounds, Two Teams	215	Philadelphia 110, Los Angeles 105 at Philadelphia (In 3 overtimes), Dec. 8, 1961
Most Assists, One Team	60	Boston at Baltimore (In 1 overtime), Nov. 15, 1952
Most Assists, Two Teams	88	Phoenix 47, San Diego 41 at Tucson, Ariz., March 15, 1969
Most Personal Fouls, One Team	66	Anderson at Syracuse (In 5 overtimes), Nov. 24, 1949
Most Personal Fouls, Two Teams	122	Anderson 66, Syracuse 56 at Syracuse (In 5 overtimes), Nov. 24, 1949
Most Disqualifications, One Team	8	Syracuse vs Baltimore at Syracuse (In 1 overtime), Nov. 15, 1952
Most Disqualifications, Two Teams	13	Syracuse 8, Baltimore 5 at Syracuse (In 1 overtime), Nov. 15, 1962
Most Points in a Losing Game	151	San Diego at Cincinnati, March 12, 1970

Widest Point Spread	63	Los Angeles 162, Golden State 99, March 19, 1972
Most Consecutive Points in a Game	24	Philadelphia vs Baltimore, March 20, 1966

Season

Most Games Won	69	Los Angeles, 1971-72
Most Games Lost	73	Philadelphia, 1972-73
Longest Winning Streak	33	Los Angeles, Nov. 5, 1971 to Jan. 7, 1972
Longest Losing Streak	20	Philadelphia, Jan. 9, 1972 to Feb. 11, 1973
Most Points Scored	10,143	Philadelphia, 1966-67
Most Points Allowed	10,261	Seattle, 1967-68
Highest Scoring Average	125.4	Philadelphia, 1961-62
Highest Average, Points Allowed	125.1	Seattle, 1967-68
Most F. G. Attempted	9,295	Boston, 1960-61
Most F. G. Made	3,972	Milwaukee, 1970-71
Highest F. G. Percentage	.509	Milwaukee, 1970-71
Most F. T. Attempted	3,411	Philadelphia, 1966-67
Most F. T. Made	2,434	Phoenix, 1969-70
Highest F. T. Percentage	.821	KC-Omaha, 1974-75
Most Rebounds	6,131	Boston, 1960-61
Most Assists	2,320	Boston, 1972-73

All-NBA Teams

1946-47

First	Second
Joe Fulks, Philadelphia	Ernie Calverley, Providence
Bob Feerick, Washington	Frank Baumholtz, Cleveland
Stan Miasek, Detroit	John Logan, St. Louis
Bones McKinney, Washington	Chuck Halbert, Chicago
Max Zaslofsky, Chicago	Fred Scolari, Washington

1947-48

Joe Fulks, Philadelphia	John Logan, St. Louis
Max Zaslofsky, Chicago	Carl Braun, New York
Ed Sadowski, Boston	Stan Miasek, Chicago
Howie Dallmar, Philadelphia	Fred Scolari, Washington
Bob Feerick, Washington	Buddy Jeannette, Baltimore

1948-49

George Mikan, Minneapolis	Arnie Risen, Rochester
Joe Fulks, Philadelphia	Bob Feerick, Washington
Bob Davies, Rochester	Bones McKinney, Washington
Max Zaslofsky, Chicago	Ken Sailors, Providence
Jim Pollard, Minneapolis	John Logan, St. Louis

First

George Mikan, Minneapolis
Jim Pollard, Minneapolis
Alex Groza, Indianapolis
Bob Davies, Rochester
Max Zaslofsky, Chicago

Second

Frank Brian, Anderson
Fred Schaus, Fort Wayne
Dolph Schayes, Syracuse
Al Cervi, Syracuse
Ralph Beard, Indianapolis

1950-51

George Mikan, Minneapolis
Alex Groza, Indianapolis
Ed Macauley, Boston
Bob Davies, Rochester
Ralph Beard, Indianapolis

Dolph Schayes, Syracuse
Frank Brian, Tri-Cities
Vern Mikkelsen, Minneapolis
Joe Fulks, Philadelphia
Dick McGuire, New York

1951-52

George Mikan, Minneapolis
Ed Macauley, Boston
Paul Arizin, Philadelphia
Bob Cousy, Boston
Bob Davies, Rochester
Dolph Schayes, Syracuse

Larry Foust, Fort Wayne
Vern Mikkelsen, Minneapolis
Jim Pollard, Minneapolis
Bob Wanzer, Rochester
Andy Phillip, Philadelphia

1952-53

George Mikan, Minneapolis
Bob Cousy, Boston
Neil Johnston, Philadelphia
Ed Macauley, Boston
Dolph Schayes, Syracuse

Bill Sharman, Boston
Vern Mikkelsen, Minneapolis
Bob Wanzer, Rochester
Bob Davies, Rochester
Andy Phillip, Philadelphia

1953-54

Bob Cousy, Boston
Neil Johnston, Philadelphia
George Mikan, Minneapolis
Dolph Schayes, Syracuse
Harry Gallatin, New York

Ed Macauley, Boston
Jim Pollard, Minneapolis
Carl Braun, New York
Bob Wanzer, Rochester
Paul Seymour, Syracuse

1954-55

Neil Johnston, Philadelphia
Bob Cousy, Boston
Dolph Schayes, Syracuse
Bob Pettit, Milwaukee
Larry Foust, Fort Wayne

Vern Mikkelsen, Minneapolis
Harry Gallatin, New York
Paul Seymour, Syracuse
Slater Martin, Minneapolis
Bill Sharman, Boston

First

Bob Pettit, St. Louis
Paul Arizin, Philadelphia
Neil Johnston, Philadelphia
Bob Cousy, Boston
Bill Sharman, Boston

Second

Dolph Schayes, Syracuse
Maurice Stokes, Rochester
Clyde Lovellette, Minneapolis
Slater Martin, Minneapolis
Jack George, Philadelphia

1956-57

Paul Arizin, Philadelphia
Dolph Schayes, Syracuse
Bob Pettit, St. Louis
Bob Cousy, Boston
Bill Sharman, Boston

George Yardley, Fort Wayne
Maurice Stokes, Rochester
Neil Johnston, Philadelphia
Dick Garmaker, Minneapolis
Slater Martin, St Louis

1957-58

Dolph Schayes, Syracuse
George Yardley, Detroit
Bob Pettit, St. Louis
Bob Cousy, Boston
Bill Sharman, Boston

Cliff Hagan, St. Louis
Maurice Stokes, Cincinnati
Bill Russell, Boston
Tom Gola, Philadelphia
Slater Martin, St. Louis

1958-59

Bob Pettit, St. Louis
Elgin Baylor, Minnesota
Bill Russell, Boston
Bob Cousy, Boston
Bill Sharman, Boston

Paul Arizin, Philadelphia
Cliff Hagan, St. Paul
Dolph Schayes, Syracuse
Slater Martin, St. Louis
Richie Guerin, New York

1959-60

Bob Pettit, St. Louis
Elgin Baylor, Minneapolis
Wilt Chamberlain, Philadelphia
Bob Cousy, Boston
Gene Shue, Detroit

Jack Twyman, Cincinnati
Dolph Schayes, Syracuse
Bill Russell, Boston
Richie Guerin, New York
Bill Sharman, Boston

1960-61

Elgin Baylor, Los Angeles
Bob Pettit, St. Louis
Wilt Chamberlain, Philadelphia
Bob Cousy, Boston
Oscar Robertson, Cincinnati

Dolph Schayes, Syracuse
Tom Heinsohn, Boston
Bill Russell, Boston
Larry Costello, Syracuse
Gene Shue, Detroit

1961-62

First
Bob Pettit, St. Louis
Elgin Baylor, Los Angeles
Wilt Chamberlain, Philadelphia
Jerry West, Los Angeles
Oscar Robertson, Cincinnati

Second
Tom Heinsohn, Boston
Jack Twyman, Cincinnati
Bill Russell, Boston
Richie Guerin, New York
Bob Cousy, Boston

1962-63

Elgin Baylor, Los Angeles
Bob Pettit, St. Louis
Bill Russell, Boston
Oscar Robertson, Cincinnati
Jerry West, Los Angeles

Tom Heinsohn, Boston
Bailey Howell, Detroit
Wilt Chamberlain, San Francisco
Bob Cousy, Boston
Hal Greer, Syracuse

1963-64

Bob Pettit, St. Louis
Elgin Baylor, Los Angeles
Wilt Chamberlain, San Francisco
Oscar Robertson, Cincinnati
Jerry West, Los Angeles

Tom Heinsohn, Boston
Jerry Lucas, Cincinnati
Bill Russell, Boston
John Havlicek, Boston
Hal Greer, Philadelphia

1964-65

Elgin Baylor, Los Angeles
Jerry Lucas, Cincinnati
Bill Russell, Boston
Oscar Robertson, Cincinnati
Jerry West, Los Angeles

Bob Pettit, St. Louis
Gus Johnson, Baltimore
Wilt Chamberlain, S. F.-Phila.
Sam Jones, Boston
Hal Greer, Philadelphia

1965-66

Rick Barry, San Francisco
Jerry Lucas, Cincinnati
Wilt Chamberlain, Philadelphia
Oscar Robertson, Cincinnati
Jerry West, Los Angeles

John Havlicek, Boston
Gus Johnson, Baltimore
Bill Russell, Boston
Sam Jones, Boston
Hal Greer, Philadelphia

1966-67

Rick Barry, San Francisco
Elgin Baylor, Los Angeles
Wilt Chamberlain, Philadelphia
Jerry West, Los Angeles
Oscar Robertson, Cincinnati

Willis Reed, New York
Jerry Lucas, Cincinnati
Bill Russell, Boston
Hal Greer, Philadelphia
Sam Jones, Boston

1967-68

First
Elgin Baylor, Los Angeles
Jerry Lucas, Cincinnati
Wilt Chamberlain, Philadelphia
Dave Bing, Detroit
Oscar Robertson, Cincinnati

Second
Willis Reed, New York
John Havlicek, Boston
Bill Russell, Boston
Hal Greer, Philadelphia
Jerry West, Los Angeles

1968-69

Billy Cunningham, Philadelphia
Elgin Baylor, Los Angeles
Wes Unseld, Baltimore
Earl Monroe, Baltimore
Oscar Robertson, Cincinnati

John Havlicek, Boston
Dave DeBusschere, Det.-N.Y.
Willis Reed, New York
Hal Greer, Philadelphia
Jerry West, Los Angeles

1969-70

Billy Cunningham, Philadelphia
Connie Hawkins, Phoenix
Willis Reed, New York
Jerry West, Los Angeles
Walt Frazier, New York

John Havlicek, Boston
Gus Johnson, Baltimore
Lew Alcindor, Milwaukee
Lou Hudson, Atlanta
Oscar Robertson, Cincinnati

1970-71

John Havlicek, Boston
Billy Cunningham, Philadelphia
Lew Alcindor, Milwaukee
Jerry West, Los Angeles
Dave Bing, Detroit

Gus Johnson, Baltimore
Bob Love, Chicago
Willis Reed, New York
Walt Frazier, New York
Oscar Robertson, Milwaukee

1971-72

John Havlicek, Boston
Spencer Haywood, Seattle
Kareem Abdul-Jabbar, Milwaukee
Jerry West, Los Angeles
Walt Frazier, New York

Bob Love, Chicago
Billy Cunningham, Philadelphia
Wilt Chamberlain, Los Angeles
Nate Archibald, Cincinnati
Archie Clark, Phila.-Balt.

1972-73

John Havlicek, Boston
Spencer Haywood, Seattle
Kareem-Abdul-Jabbar, Milwaukee
Nate Archibald, KC-Omaha
Jerry West, Los Angeles

Elvin Hayes, Baltimore
Rick Barry, Golden State
Dave Cowens, Boston
Walt Frazier, New York
Pete Maravich, Atlanta

1973-74

John Havlicek, Boston
Rick Barry, Golden State
Kareem Abdul-Jabbar, Milwaukee
Walt Frazier, New York
Gail Goodrich, Los Angeles

Elvin Hayes, Capital
Spencer Haywood, Seattle
Bob McAdoo, Buffalo
Dave Bing, Detroit
Norm Van Lier, Chicago

1974-75

Rick Barry, Golden State
Elvin Hayes, Washington
Bob McAdoo, Buffalo
Nate Archibald, KC-Omaha
Walt Frazier, New York

John Havlicek, Boston
Spencer Haywood, Seattle
Dave Cowens, Boston
Phil Chenier, Washington
Jo Jo White, Boston

1975-76

Rick Barry, Golden State
George McGinnis, Philadelphia
Kareem Abdul-Jabbar, Los Angeles
Nate Archibald, Kansas City
Pete Maravich, New Orleans

Elvin Hayes, Washington
John Havlicek, Boston
Dave Cowens, Boston
Randy Smith, Buffalo
Phil Smith, Golden State

1976-77

Kareem Abdul-Jabbar, Los Angeles
Pete Maravich, New Orleans
Paul Westphal, Phoenix
Elvin Hayes, Washington
David Thompson, Denver

Bill Walton, Portland
George Gervin, San Antonio
Jo Jo White, Boston
Julius Erving, Philadelphia
George McGinnis, Philadelphia

1977-78

Truck Robinson, New Orleans
Julius Erving, Philadelphia
Bill Walton, Portland
George Gervin, San Antonio
David Thompson, Denver

Walter Davis, Phoenix
Maurice Lucas, Portland
Kareem Abdul-Jabbar, Los Angeles
Paul Westphal, Phoenix
Pete Maravich, New Orleans

1978-79

Marques Johnson, Milwaukee
Elvin Hayes, Washington
Moses Malone, Houston
George Gervin, San Antonio
Paul Westphal, Phoenix

Walter Davis, Phoenix
Bob Dandridge, Washington
Kareem Abdul-Jabbar, Los Angeles
Lloyd Free, San Diego
Phil Ford, Kansas City

NBA Champions

Season	Champion	Eastern Conference			Western Conference		
		W.	L.		W.	L.	
1946-47	Philadelphia	49	11	Washington	39	22	Chicago
1947-48	Baltimore	27	21	Philadelphia	29	19	St. Louis
1948-49	Minneapolis	38	22	Washington	45	15	Rochester
1949-50	Minneapolis	51	13	Syracuse	39	25	Indianap.*
1950-51	Rochester	40	26	Philadelphia	44	24	Minneapolis
1951-52	Minneapolis	40	26	Syracuse	41	25	Rochester
1952-53	Minneapolis	47	23	New York	48	22	Minneapolis
1953-54	Minneapolis	44	28	New York	46	26	Minneapolis
1954-55	Syracuse	43	29	Syracuse	43	29	Ft. Wayne
1955-56	Philadelphia	45	27	Philadelphia	37	35	Ft. Wayne
1956-57	Boston	44	28	Boston	34	38	StL-Mpl-FtW
1957-58	St. Louis	49	23	Boston	41	31	St. Louis
1958-59	Boston	52	20	Boston	49	23	St. Louis
1959-60	Boston	59	16	Boston	46	29	St. Louis
1960-61	Boston	57	22	Boston	51	28	St. Louis
1961-62	Boston	60	20	Boston	54	26	Los Angeles
1962-63	Boston	58	22	Boston	53	27	Los Angeles
1963-64	Boston	59	21	Boston	48	32	San Fran.
1964-65	Boston	62	18	Boston	49	31	Los Angeles
1965-66	Boston	55	25	Philadelphia	45	35	Los Angeles
1966-67	Philadelphia	68	13	Philadelphia	44	37	San Fran.
1967-68	Boston	62	20	Philadelphia	56	26	St. Louis
1968-69	Boston	57	25	Baltimore	55	27	Los Angeles
1969-70	New York	60	22	New York	48	34	Atlanta
1970-71	Milwaukee	42	40	Baltimore	66	16	Milwaukee
1971-72	Los Angeles	48	34	New York	69	13	Los Angeles
1972-73	New York	57	25	New York	60	22	Los Angeles
1973-74	Boston	56	26	Boston	59	23	Milwaukee
1974-75	Golden State	60	22	Washington	48	34	Golden State
1975-76	Boston	54	28	Boston	42	40	Phoenix
1976-77	Portland	50	32	Philadelphia	49	33	Portland
1977-78	Washington	44	38	Washington	47	35	Seattle
1978-79	Seattle	54	28	Washington	52	30	Seattle

*1949-50 Central Division Champ: Minneapolis and Rochester tied 51-17.

Rookie of the Year

Year	Player	Team
1952-53	Don Meineke	Fort Wayne
1953-54	Ray Felix	Baltimore
1954-55	Bob Pettit	Milwaukee
1955-56	Maurice Stokes	Rochester
1956-57	Tom Heinsohn	Boston
1957-58	Woody Sauldsberry	Philadelphia
1958-59	Elgin Baylor	Minneapolis
1959-60	Wilt Chamberlain	Philadelphia
1960-61	Oscar Robertson	Cincinnati
1961-62	Walt Bellamy	Chicago
1962-63	Terry Dischinger	Chicago
1963-64	Jerry Lucas	Cincinnati
1964-65	Willis Reed	New York
1965-66	Rick Barry	San Francisco
1966-67	Dave Bing	Detroit
1967-68	Earl Monroe	Baltimore
1968-69	Wes Unseld	Baltimore
1969-70	Lew Alcindor	Milwaukee
1970-71	Dave Cowens	Boston
	Geoff Petrie	Portland
1971-72	Sidney Wicks	Portland
1972-73	Bob McAdoo	Buffalo
1973-74	Ernie DiGregorio	Buffalo
1974-75	Keith Wilkes	Golden State
1975-76	Alvan Adams	Phoenix
1976-77	Adrian Dantley	Buffalo
1977-78	Walter Davis	Phoenix
1978-79	Phil Ford	Kansas City

Most Valuable Player
Podoloff Cup

(By vote of players)

Year	Player	Team
1955-56	Bob Pettit	St. Louis
1956-57	Bob Cousy	Boston
1957-58	Bill Russell	Boston
1958-59	Bob Pettit	St. Louis
1959-60	Wilt Chamberlain	Philadelphia
1960-61	Bill Russell	Boston
1961-62	Bill Russell	Boston
1962-63	Bill Russell	Boston
1963-64	Oscar Robertson	Cincinnati
1964-65	Bill Russell	Boston
1965-66	Wilt Chamberlain	Philadelphia
1966-67	Wilt Chamberlain	Philadelphia
1967-68	Wilt Chamberlain	Philadelphia
1968-69	Wes Unseld	Baltimore
1969-70	Willis Reed	New York
1970-71	Lew Alcindor	Milwaukee
1971-72	Kareem Abdul-Jabbar	Milwaukee
1972-73	Dave Cowens	Boston
1973-74	Kareem Abdul-Jabbar	Milwaukee
1974-75	Bob McAdoo	Buffalo
1975-76	Kareem Abdul-Jabbar	Los Angeles
1976-77	Kareem Abdul-Jabbar	Los Angeles
1977-78	Bill Walton	Portland
1978-79	Moses Malone	Houston

Coach of the Year

1963	Harry Gallatin	St. Louis
1964	Alex Hannum	San Francisco
1965	Red Auerbach	Boston
1966	Dolph Schayes	Philadelphia
1967	Johnny Kerr	Chicago
1968	Richie Guerin	St. Louis
1969	Gene Shue	Baltimore
1970	Red Holzman	New York
1971	Dick Motta	Chicago
1972	Bill Sharman	Los Angeles
1973	Tom Heinsohn	Boston
1974	Ray Scott	Detroit
1975	Phil Johnson	Kansas City-Omaha
1976	Bill Fitch	Cleveland
1977	Tom Nissalke	Houston
1978	Hubie Brown	Atlanta
1979	Cotton Fitzsimmons	Kansas City

All-Rookie Teams

1963-64

Jerry Lucas, Cincinnati
Gus Johnson, Baltimore
Nate Thurmond, San Francisco
Art Heyman, New York
Rod Thorn, Baltimore

1964-65

Willis Reed, New York
Jim Barnes, New York
Howie Komives, New York
Luke Jackson, Philadelphia
Wally Jones, Baltimore
Joe Caldwell, Detroit

1965-66

Rick Barry, San Francisco
Bill Cunningham, Philadelphia
Tom Van Arsdale, Detroit
Dick Van Arsdale, New York
Fred Hetzel, San Francisco

1966-67

Lou Hudson, St. Louis
Jack Marin, Baltimore
Erwin Mueller, Chicago
Cazzie Russell, New York
Dave Bing, Detroit

1967-68

Earl Monroe, Baltimore
Bob Rule, Seattle
Al Tucker, Seattle
Walt Frazier, New York
Phil Jackson, New York

1968-69

Wes Unseld, Baltimore
Elvin Hayes, San Diego
Bill Hewitt, Los Angeles
Art Harris, Seattle
Gary Gregor, Phoenix

1969-70

Lew Alcindor, Milwaukee
Bob Dandridge, Milwaukee
Jo Jo White, Boston
Mike Davis, Baltimore
Dick Garrett, Los Angeles

1970-71

Geoff Petrie, Portland
Dave Cowens, Boston
Pete Maravich, Atlanta
Calvin Murphy, San Diego
Bob Lanier, Detroit

1970-71

Geoff Petrie, Portland
Dave Cowens, Boston
Pete Maravich, Atlanta
Calvin Murphy, San Diego
Bob Lanier, Detroit

1971-72

Elmore Smith, Buffalo
Phil Chenier, Baltimore
Sidney Wicks, Portland
Austin Carr, Cleveland
Clifford Ray, Chicago

1972-73

Bob McAdoo, Buffalo
Lloyd Neal, Portland
Fred Boyd, Philadelphia
Dwight Davis, Cleveland
Jim Price, Los Angeles

1973-74

Ernie DiGregorio, Buffalo
Ron Behagen, KC-Omaha
Mike Bantom, Phoenix
John Brown, Atlanta
Nick Weatherspoon, Capital

1974-75

Keith Wilkes, Golden State
John Drew, Atlanta
Scott Wedman, KC-Omaha
Tom Burleson, Seattle
Brian Winters, Los Angeles

1975-76

Alvan Adams, Phoenix
Gus Williams, Golden State
Joe Meriweather, Houston
John Shumate, Phoenix-Buffalo
Lionel Hollins, Portland

1976-77

Adrian Dantley, Buffalo
Scott May, Chicago
Mitch Kupchak, Washington
John Lucas, Houston
Ron Lee, Phoenix

1977-78

Walter Davis, Phoenix
Marques Johnson, Milwaukee
Jack Sikma, Seattle
Bernard King, New Jersey
Norm Nixon, Los Angeles

1978-79

Phil Ford, Kansas City
Mychal Thompson, Portland
Ron Brewer, Portland
Reggie Theus, Chicago
Terry Tyler, Detroit

15

American Basketball Association

1967–68

With one eye toward the rapid growth of pro basketball and the other eye seeing the many untapped areas ripe for the sport, a group of promoters got together in New York on February 2, 1967, and formed the American Basketball Association.

There were 11 original franchises—Pittsburgh, Minnesota, Indiana, Kentucky, New Jersey, New Orleans, Dallas, Denver, Houston, Anaheim and Oakland—and George Mikan, the former great center with the Minneapolis Lakers, was named commissioner.

It was Mikan's idea to use a red, white, and blue basketball, which became synonymous with the ABA, and the league adopted the three-point field goal for shots from 25 feet or more.

Several former standout pros became coaches in the new league, such as Cliff Hagan at Dallas, Slater Martin at Houston, Max Zaslofsky at New Jersey and Jim Pollard at Minnesota.

One of the biggest boosts for the new league was Rick Barry, the scoring leader in the rival National Basketball Association,

Pittsburgh's Connie Hawkins, who was the MVP and led Pipers to first ABA championship, drives on New Orleans' Doug Moe

who was persuaded to jump from the San Francisco Warriors to the ABA's Oakland club.

The ABA also opened the bidding war for collegians by making Mel Daniels, an All-American from New Mexico, its first draft choice and outbidding the NBA for him.

Connie Hawkins was the other "name" player in the league that first season. Banned from the NBA because of his alleged connection with gamblers as a college freshman, Hawkins got his chance in the ABA and led the Pittsburgh Pipers to the Eastern Division title with a 26.8-point

scoring average, best in the league. He also was voted the Most Valuable Player.

Minnesota, with Daniels averaging 15.6 rebounds a game, finished second to Pittsburgh.

New Orleans, led by Doug Moe, won the Western Division crown under coach Babe McCarthy while Oakland finished last as Barry had to sit out that first season during court action by the NBA to get back his services.

Pittsburgh, coached by Vince Cazzetta, won the first ABA title by beating New Orleans in the final playoff series, four games to three.

STANDINGS

Eastern Division

	W.	L.	Pct.
Pittsburgh	54	24	.692
Minnesota	50	28	.641
Indiana	38	40	.487
Kentucky	36	42	.462
New Jersey	36	42	.462

Western Division

	W.	L.	Pct.
New Orleans	48	30	.615
Dallas	46	32	.590
Denver	45	33	.577
Houston	29	49	.372
Anaheim	25	53	.321
Oakland	22	56	.282

PLAYOFFS

First Round

Pittsburgh defeated Indiana 3 games to 0
Minnesota defeated Kentucky 3 games to 2
Dallas defeated Houston 3 games to 0
New Orleans defeated Denver 3 games to 2

Semifinals

Pittsburgh defeated Minnesota 4 games to 1
New Orleans defeated Dallas 4 games to 1

Championship

Pittsburgh defeated New Orleans 4 games to 3

TOP SCORERS

	Pts.	Ave.
Connie Hawkins, Pittsburgh	1875	26.8
Doug Moe, New Orleans	1884	24.2
Levern Tart, Oakland-New Jersey	1718	23.5
Darel Carrier, Kentucky	1765	22.9
Larry Jones, Denver	1742	22.9

TOP REBOUNDERS

	No.	Ave.
Mel Daniels, Minnesota	1213	15.6
Connie Hawkins, Pittsburgh	945	13.5
John Beasley, Dallas	982	12.8
Ira Harge, Pittsburgh-Oakland	1038	12.7
Red Robbins, New Orleans	894	12.2

LEADERS IN ASSISTS

	No.	Ave.
Larry Brown, New Orleans	506	6.5
Cliff Hagan, Dallas	276	4.9
Steve Chubin, Anaheim	364	4.7
Connie Hawkins, Pittsburgh	320	4.6
Roger Brown, Indiana	327	4.3

1968-69

The ABA began its second season with numerous changes on and off the court—new cities, new coaches, new players.

Minnesota moved to Miami and was replaced in Minnesota by the Pittsburgh franchise, New Jersey moved onto Long Island as the New York Nets and Anaheim moved to Los Angeles.

Rick Barry finally got to play for Oakland and led Oaks to title

On the sidelines, Alex Hannum and Bill Sharman jumped from the NBA, Hannum to coach Oakland and Sharman to handle Los Angeles, and Bob Leonard took over the Indiana Pacers shortly after the season began.

In the draft the new league missed out on the two top college graduates—Elvin Hayes and Wes Unseld. However, it was signing a number of lesser known college stars and NBA rejects who blossomed when given the chance they never could have gotten in the more established league. Those players included Roger Brown, Don Freeman, Larry Jones, Jim Jones, Bob Netolicky, Red Robbins, Steve Jones, Cincy Powell and Louie Dampier.

But most important was the first appearance of Rick Barry in an ABA uniform. Although he played only 35 games because of injury, Barry led the league in scoring average with 34 points a game.

Bolstered by Barry and a trade that brought Doug Moe and Larry Brown, the ABA assists leader, from New Orleans, Oakland ran off with the Western Division title by 14 games over New Orleans, posing a 60–18 record. The Oaks also had the Rookie of the Year in Warren Armstrong and set a league mark of 16 consecutive victories.

In the East, Mel Daniels had been traded to Indiana and his 16.5 rebounds, tops in the league, and 24 points a game led the Pacers to the Eastern Division title by one game over Miami and earned him MVP honors.

Oakland, with Armstrong taking up the slack in the absence of Barry, scored two overtime victories over Indiana in the championship series and won the crown in five games.

STANDINGS

Eastern Division	W.	L.	Pct.	Western Division	W.	L.	Pct.
Indiana	44	34	.564	Oakland	60	18	.769
Miami	43	35	.551	New Orleans	46	32	.590
Kentucky	42	36	.538	Denver	44	34	.564
Minnesota	36	42	.462	Dallas	41	37	.526
New York	17	61	.218	Los Angeles	33	45	.423
				Houston	23	55	.295

PLAYOFFS

First Round

	Pts.	Ave.

Indiana defeated Kentucky 4 games to 3
Miami defeated Minnesota 4 games to 3
Oakland defeated Denver 4 games to 3
New Orleans defeated Dallas 4 games to 3

	Pts.	Ave.
Rick Barry, Oakland	1190	34.0
Connie Hawkins, Minnesota	1420	30.2
Larry Jones, Denver	2133	28.4
Jim Jones, New Orleans	2050	26.6
Louie Dampier, Kentucky	1933	24.8

Semifinals

Indiana defeated Miami 4 games to 1
Oakland defeated New Orleans 4 games to 0

Championship

Oakland defeated Indiana 4 games to 1

TOP REBOUNDERS

	No.	Ave.
Mel Daniels, Indiana	1256	16.5
Red Robbins, New Orleans	1024	13.5
Skip Thoren, Miami	1046	13.4
Tom Washington, Minnesota	868	12.6
Connie Hawkins, Minnesota	534	11.4

LEADERS IN ASSISTS

	No.	Ave.
Larry Brown, Oakland	544	7.1
Don Freeman, Miami	501	6.4
Louie Dampier, Kentucky	456	5.8
Jim Jones, New Orleans	437	5.7
Roger Brown, Indiana	345	4.6
Steve Chubin, New York	354	4.6

1969–70

Lew Alcindor, who had led UCLA to three consecutive NCAA titles, was the man of the hour in the spring of 1969 and when the ABA lost him to the NBA in the signing war, it seemed as if time might have run out on the new league.

And things got worse when Connie Hawkins decided to switch leagues and join the NBA.

They were crushing blows, but by the end of the 1969–70 season the ABA not only still was around, it appeared to be on the upswing.

First, the ABA partially offset the loss of Alcindor and Hawkins by first signing NBA star Zelmo Beaty and then young Spencer Haywood, All-American and Olympic hero, who came off the Detroit campus as a hardship case after his sophomore year.

Haywood, 6-8, immediately proved his worth by leading Denver to the Western Division title, topping the league in scoring and rebounding and winning Rookie of the Year and Most Valuable Player honors.

Haywood also won the MVP award in the All-Star Game at Indianapolis, a milestone affair. It was the ABA's first nationally televised contest, carried over CBS. CBS also televised several playoff games and much of the credit for that went to Jack Dolph, the former CBS executive who had been named commissioner at the beginning of the season.

The ABA gained status by signing away four top referees from the NBA. It was during the same period that the first merger talks between the leagues were started and broken off.

Meanwhile, the Houston team moved to Carolina as the first regional franchise, Oakland moved to Washington, D.C., and Minnesota returned to Pittsburgh.

While Denver was winning the West, Indiana won the East by 14 games over Kentucky.

Denver was upset in the playoffs by the fourth-place Los Angeles Stars, who played without Beaty, sitting out the season by court order. Indiana, however, ended the Stars' Cinderella dream by winning the title in six games behind Mel Daniels and Roger Brown.

Roger Brown (35) helped power Indiana to the ABA's best record and the championship

STANDINGS

Eastern Division	W.	L.	Pct.
Indiana	59	25	.702
Kentucky	45	39	.536
Carolina	42	42	.500
New York	39	45	.464
Pittsburgh	29	55	.345
Miami	23	61	.274

Western Division	W.	L.	Pct.
Denver	51	33	.607
Dallas	45	39	.536
Washington	44	40	.524
Los Angeles	43	41	.512
New Orleans	42	42	.500

PLAYOFFS

First Round

Indiana defeated Carolina 4 games to 0
Kentucky defeated New York 4 games to 3
Denver defeated Washington 4 games to 3
Los Angeles defeated Dallas 4 games to 2

Semifinals

Indiana defeated Kentucky 4 games to 1
Los Angeles defeated Denver 4 games to 1

Championship

Indiana defeated Los Angeles 4 games to 2

TOP SCORERS

	Pts.	Ave.
Spencer Haywood, Denver	2519	30.0
Rick Barry, Washington	1442	27.7
Bob Verga, Carolina	2258	27.5
Don Freeman, Miami	2163	27.4
Louis Dampier, Kentucky	2125	25.9

TOP REBOUNDERS

	No.	Ave.
Spencer Haywood, Denver	1637	19.5
Mel Daniels, Indiana	1462	17.6
Red Robbins, New Orleans	1332	16.2
Gerald Govan, New Orleans	1217	14.5
Ira Harge, Washington	1177	14.0

LEADERS IN ASSISTS

	No.	Ave.
Larry Brown, Washington	580	7.1
Bill Melchionni, New York	457	5.7
Mack Calvin, Los Angeles	478	5.7
Larry Jones, Denver	426	5.7
Louie Dampier, Kentucky	447	5.5

1970–71

The battle for collegians and established stars continued to dominate the action involving the two pro basketball leagues, and the ABA won a few, lost a few.

Lost were Spencer Haywood, lured away by Seattle of the NBA, and multi-million dollar collegians Pete Maravich and Bob Lanier.

But Zelmo Beaty and Joe Caldwell, both stars with the NBA's Atlanta Hawks, played their first games in the new league after jumping, and the ABA also outbid the NBA for college stars Dan Issel, Charlie Scott, and Rick Mount. Issel of Kentucky and Scott of Virginia made it immediately, sharing Rookie of the Year honors.

Beaty, upgrading the all-important center position, was the key to Utah's championship under Bill Sharman in its first season in Salt Lake after moving from Los Angeles.

Indiana, which had switched to the Western Division while Virginia (formerly Washington) moved to the East, beat out Utah by one game for the division title behind MVP Mel Daniels. But the Pacers lost to the Stars in seven games in the division playoff finals.

Virginia, the Eastern champ, was upset

Dan Issel (44) won scoring title, but Kentucky lost to Utah in the finals

by Kentucky in the division final and then Beaty and Willie Wise led the Utah Stars past Kentucky in six games for the title.

Issel won the scoring crown with an average of 29.9 points a game, just a half-point a game more than Rick Barry, who had been traded by Virginia to New York.

Meanwhile, merger talks continued on and off and CBS televised the ABA All-Star Game and playoff contests. With that kind of exposure the league went over the 2,500,000 mark in attendance as the season ended on a hopeful note.

STANDINGS

Eastern Division

	W.	L.	Pct.
Virginia	55	29	.655
Kentucky	44	40	.524
New York	40	44	.476
Floridians	37	47	.440
Pittsburgh	36	48	.429
Carolina	34	50	.405

Western Division

	W.	L.	Pct.
Indiana	58	26	.690
Utah	57	27	.679
Memphis	41	43	.488
Texas	30	54	.357
Denver	30	54	.357

PLAYOFFS

First Round

Kentucky defeated Floridians 4 games to 2
Virginia defeated New York 4 games to 2
Indiana defeated Memphis 4 games to 0
Utah defeated Texas 4 games to 0

Semifinals

Kentucky defeated Virginia 4 games to 2
Utah defeated Indiana 4 games to 3

Championship

Utah defeated Kentucky 4 games to 3

TOP SCORERS

	Pts.	Ave.
Dan Issel, Kentucky	2480	29.9
Rick Barry, New York	1734	29.4
John Brisker, Pittsburgh	2315	29.3
Mack Calvin, Floridians	2201	27.2
Charlie Scott, Virginia	2276	27.1

TOP REBOUNDERS

	No.	Ave.
Mel Daniels, Indiana	1475	18.0
Julius Keye, Denver	1454	17.5
Zelmo Beaty, Utah	1190	15.7
Mike Lewis, Pittsburgh	1213	14.6
Gerald Govan, Memphis	1138	13.6

LEADERS IN ASSISTS

	No.	Ave.
Bill Melchionni, New York	672	8.3
Mack Calvin, Floridians	619	7.6
Jim Jones, Memphis	468	5.9
Charlie Scott, Virginia	472	5.6
George Lehmann, Carolina	464	5.6

1971–72

The ABA's fifth season proved to be a stunner on the court and in court as lawsuits ran neck and neck with ball games for public attention.

The season began on an upswing when Kentucky signed All-American Artis Gilmore of Jacksonville, a 7-2 center being compared to Bill Russell, and Carolina landed 7-foot Jim McDaniels, another All-American, from Western Kentucky.

The growing league also continued the signing of select undergraduates as Virginia got Julius Erving, Indiana signed George McGinnis and Memphis lured Johnny Neumann.

For the first time, all 11 clubs opened in the same cities in which they finished the previous season. There were, however, numerous coaching changes. The 1970–71 finalists had new mentors, LaDell Anderson at Utah and Joe Mullaney at Kentucky.

There was new interest on the court from the opening tipoff of the exhibition season

New York's Rick Barry wins rebound from Indiana's Mel Daniels, but Pacers took the title

games ahead of Virginia. Utah easily won the West by 13 games over Indiana.

Virginia's Charlie Scott, 34.6, won the scoring title and Gilmore, 17.6, the rebound crown. Gilmore also was honored as the Most Valuable Player and Rookie of the Year.

In between these happenings, merger remained stalled in a Congressional subcommittee and the battle between the leagues still was going strong.

First, Seattle of the NBA stole away McDaniels and then Phoenix grabbed Scott, precipitating a basket full of court suits. Then Erving signed a 1975 pact with Atlanta. The ABA, however, got a boost when the courts ruled that NBA star Billy Cunningham had to play the 1972–73 season with Carolina after signing a previous contract.

The playoffs proved to be the biggest shocker as New York, playing in its new Nassau Coliseum to record crowds, ousted Kentucky in six games and then bested Virginia in seven to land in the final series for the first time. The Nets were sparked by the scoring of Barry and rookie John Roche and the play of Bill Melchionni, Ollie Taylor, Tom Washington and Billy Paultz. In the West, Indiana had difficulty getting past Denver in the first round, then ousted defending champion Utah in seven games. The Pacers, led by little Freddie Lewis, then became the first team to win two ABA championships by defeating the Nets in six games. Attendance, including the playoffs, increased to 2,800,000.

After the season was over, and with merger talk heating up, the ABA eliminated the financially weak franchises in Pittsburgh and Miami, distributing the players among the nine remaining teams. Charles O. Finley, who made a name for himself as owner of baseball's Oakland A's and hockey's California Golden Seals, bought the Memphis franchise, which was also losing money, but promised to keep the team in Memphis.

when Dallas played the first inter-league game against NBA champion Milwaukee on September 21 and lost by three points. After 23 inter-league games, the NBA showed a 15–8 edge.

In regular-season play, Kentucky, with Gilmore at center and Dan Issel switching to forward, raced away to a record 68 victories for the Eastern Division title, 23

STANDINGS

Eastern Division

	W.	L.	Pct.
Kentucky	68	16	.810
Virginia	45	39	.536
New York	44	40	.524
Floridians	36	48	.429
Carolina	35	49	.417
Pittsburgh	25	59	.298

Western Division

	W.	L.	Pct.
Utah	60	24	.714
Indiana	47	37	.560
Dallas	42	42	.500
Denver	34	50	.405
Memphis	26	58	.310

PLAYOFFS

First Round

New York defeated Kentucky 4 games to 2
Virginia defeated Floridians 4 games to 0
Utah defeated Dallas 4 games to 0
Indiana defeated Denver 4 games to 3

Semifinals

New York defeated Virginia 4 games to 3
Indiana defeated Utah 4 games to 3

Championship

Indiana defeated New York 4 games to 2

TOP SCORERS

	Pts.	Ave.
Charlie Scott, Virginia	2524	34.6
Rick Barry, New York	2518	31.5
Dan Issel, Kentucky	2538	30.6
John Brisker, Pittsburgh	1417	28.9
Ralph Simpson, Denver	2300	27.4

TOP REBOUNDERS

	No.	Ave.
Artis Gilmore, Kentucky	1491	17.6
Mel Daniels, Indiana	1297	16.4
Julius Erving, Virginia	1319	15.7
Gerald Govan, Memphis	1182	14.2
Jim McDaniels, Carolina	814	14.0

LEADERS IN ASSISTS

	No.	Ave.
Bill Melchionni, New York	669	8.4
George Lehmann, Memphis	411	7.8
Larry Brown, Denver	549	7.2
Jim Jones, Utah	485	6.2
Louie Dampier, Kentucky	515	6.2

1972–73

It was just like in the good old days at the University of North Carolina. Billy Cunningham played there. So did Larry Brown. Now together again, they helped the Carolina Cougars rise from fifth place to win the Eastern Division and post the best record in the league.

Brown's liberal use of substitutions and his enthusiastic college-style approach helped inspire the remarkable turnabout for this regional franchise, which played its home games at three different cities in North Carolina. Cunningham was an inspiration, too. He left the Philadelphia 76ers of the NBA to sign with the Cougars and was named the ABA's Most Valuable Player. He averaged 24 points and was among the league leaders in rebounds and assists. He led in steals with 216.

After they defeated the New York Nets in five games in the opening round of the playoffs, the Cougars' surprising season came to an end. The Kentucky Colonels, who had finished a game behind, eliminated them in a seven-game series. The Colonels won the division title a year earlier and always seemed to be in contention. They were led by Dan Issel and Artis Gilmore.

In the West, the Utah Stars repeated as champion. They also failed to reach the final. Indiana, with George McGinnis, ousted the Stars in six games.

The Pacers then won their second consecutive championship. They needed seven games to defeat the Colonels and did it the hard way by winning three times in Kentucky.

Julius Erving of the Virginia Squires won the scoring championship, averaging 31.9 points. Gilmore was the top rebounder with a 17.4 average. Brown was named Coach of the Year, while Brian Taylor, New York's flashy guard, was acclaimed the best rookie. In the All-Star Game in Salt Lake City, the West defeated the East, 123–111.

As in most seasons, there were some departures and addition as the league continued its struggle to survive. With the Floridians and Pittsburgh Condors gone, the San Diego Conquistadors were a new entry.

Cunningham and Erving were named to the all-league team with Gilmore, James Jones of Utah and Warren Jabali of Denver.

Billy Cunningham (32) jumped from NBA 76ers to become ABA MVP with the Cougars

STANDINGS

Eastern Division	W.	L.	Pct.	Western Division	W.	L.	Pct.
Carolina	57	27	.679	Utah	55	29	.655
Kentucky	56	28	.667	Indiana	51	33	.607
Virginia	42	42	.500	Denver	47	27	.560
New York	30	54	.357	San Diego	30	54	.357
Memphis	24	60	.286	Dallas	28	56	.333

PLAYOFFS

First Round

Carolina defeated New York 4 games to 1
Kentucky defeated Virginia 4 games to 1
Utah defeated San Diego 4 games to 0
Indiana defeated Denver 4 games to 1

Semifinals

Kentucky defeated Carolina 4 games to 3
Indiana defeated Utah 4 games to 2

Championship

Indiana defeated Kentucky 4 games to 3

TOP SCORERS

	Pts.	Ave.
Julius Erving, Virginia	2268	31.9
George McGinnis, Indiana	2261	27.6
Dan Issel, Kentucky	2292	27.3
Billy Cunningham, Carolina	2028	24.1
Ralph Simpson, Denver	1890	23.3

TOP REBOUNDERS

	No.	Ave.
Artis Gilmore, Kentucky	1476	17.5
Mel Daniels, Indiana	1247	15.4
Billy Paultz, New York	1015	12.5
George McGinnis, Indiana	1022	12.4
Randy Denton, Memphis	820	12.4

LEADERS IN ASSISTS

	No.	Ave.
Bill Melchionni, New York	453	7.5
Chuck Williams, San Diego	582	7.0
Warren Jabali, Denver	539	6.6
Louie Dampier, Kentucky	521	6.5
Billy Cunningham, Carolina	530	6.3

1973–74

The spirit of co-operation and the resolve to continue were reinforced as the ABA embarked upon its seventh season. Mike Storen, who as general manager of the Kentucky Colonels acquired Dan Issel and Artis Gilmore at the expense of the NBA, was named the league's commissioner. He was expected to deal with a strong hand.

A strong team in New York, most observers felt, would also help the league solidify its footing. All the ABA owners helped finance the Nets' acquisition of Julius Erving from the Virginia Squires. Erving, who grew up on Long Island, was regarded as the most exciting and salable player in the ABA. He had bolted Virginia for the Atlanta Hawks of the NBA but was ordered back to the Squires by a federal court judge.

Nets' owner Roy Boe purchased more than a crowd-pleasing player. He also bought a championship. Erving was the catalyst on a team of great offensive potential. It included Larry Kenon, Brian Taylor, John Williamson and Billy Paultz. Coach Kevin Loughery was the beneficiary. Just a year earlier, Loughery finished out the season as coach of the Philadelphia 76ers, who lost 73 games.

Erving was named the Most Valuable Player and led the scorers with a 27-point average. The Nets won the Eastern Division title and defeated Virginia in five games in the first round of the playoffs. In what was expected to be their toughest series, they swept Kentucky in the Eastern final.

In the West, Utah once again finished first, and this time went to the final by defeating San Diego and Indiana. The Stars

were no match for the Nets, though, who won the title in a five-game series. The Conquistadors had qualified for the playoffs even though they finished 10 games under .500 and in a tie for fourth place. The Q's beat Denver in a one-game playoff to earn a playoff berth.

Their coach was Wilt Chamberlain, who left the Los Angeles Lakers with one year remaining on his contract. A federal court

ABA owners financed Nets' acquisition of Julius Erving and saw Dr. J dissect league

judge prohibited him from playing with the Q's, but he was allowed to coach them.

Swen Nater, Bill Walton's backup at UCLA, was Rookie of the Year. He played for San Antonio. Babe McCarthy of Kentucky and Joe Mullaney of Utah shared

Coach of the Year honors. In the All-Star Game in Norfolk, Virginia, the East defeated the West, 128–112. And the all-league team included Erving, George McGinnis of Indiana, Gilmore, James Jones of Utah and Mack Calvin of Carolina.

STANDINGS

Eastern Division

	W.	L.	Pct.
New York	55	29	.655
Kentucky	53	31	.631
Carolina	47	37	.560
Virginia	28	56	.333
Memphis	21	63	.250

Western Division

	W.	L.	Pct.
Utah	51	33	.607
Indiana	46	38	.548
San Antonio	45	39	.536
Denver	37	47	.440
San Diego	37	47	.440

PLAYOFFS

First Round

New York defeated Virginia 4 games to 1
Kentucky defeated Carolina 4 games to 2
Utah defeated San Diego 4 games to 2
Indiana defeated San Antonio 4 games to 3

Semifinals

New York defeated Kentucky 4 games to 0
Utah defeated Indiana 4 games to 3

Championship

New York defeated Utah 4 games to 1

TOP SCORERS

	Pts.	Ave.
Julius Erving, New York	2299	27.4
George McGinnis, Indiana	2071	25.9
Dan Issel, Kentucky	2118	25.5
George Gervin, San Antonio	1730	23.4
Willie Wise, Utah	1826	22.3

TOP REBOUNDERS

	No.	Ave.
Artis Gilmore, Kentucky	1538	18.3
George McGinnis, Indiana	1187	15.0
Caldwell Jones, San Diego	1095	13.9
Swen Nater, San Antonio	998	12.6
Mel Daniels, Indiana	885	11.6

LEADERS IN ASSISTS

	No.	Ave.
Al Smith, Denver	619	8.2
Chuck Williams, Kentucky	557	6.2
Louie Dampier, Kentucky	473	5.6
Roland Taylor, Virginia	416	5.2
James Jones, Utah	429	5.2

1974–75

Hubie Brown was the third coach of the Kentucky Colonels in as many years. This despite the fact that the Colonels were a competitive team always on the verge of winning the championship. They took the final step this season and won the title.

They finished in a tie for first in the Eastern Division with the New York Nets. The teams met in a one-game playoff, and the Colonels won. But they were spared the

task of having to face the Nets again in the playoffs. The Spirits of St. Louis took care of that.

The Spirits upset the Nets in five games in the opening round, while the Colonels disposed of Memphis. Kentucky then had little difficulty getting into the final as it breezed past St. Louis.

Larry Brown once again was making news, this time out West in Denver. On a team with no superstars, he coached and cajoled it to 65 victories, tops in the league. Denver finished first, but after an easy first-round triumph against Utah, it was upset by

ABA Commissioner Dave DeBusschere gives Kentucky Colonels championship trophy

Indiana. Brown's teams were earning a reputation of collapsing in the playoffs.

The Pacers were only an average team after having won three championships in eight years. They provided little competition for Kentucky, which won its long-awaited title in five games.

The ABA made its biggest waves at the beginning of the season when Utah signed Moses Malone right out of high school. Malone had signed a letter of intent with the University of Maryland but chose the money instead. The ABA attracted several excellent college players, too, including Marvin Barnes, who signed with St. Louis; Bobby Jones, who went to Denver; and Billy Knight, who signed with Indiana.

Barnes was named Rookie of the Year. He averaged 24 points. Malone was an impressive teen-ager, averaging 18.7 points. Larry Brown again was named Coach of the Year. Julius Erving of New York and George McGinnis of Indiana tied for the Most Valuable Player award.

Erving, McGinnis, Artis Gilmore of Kentucky, Mack Calvin of Denver, and Ron Boone of Utah were named to the all-league team. In the All-Star Game in San Antonio, the East trounced the West, 151–124.

The league had a typical turnover. There were three new owners, six new coaches and thirty new players.

STANDINGS

Eastern Division	W.	L.	Pct.	Western Division	W.	L.	Pct.
Kentucky	58	26	.690	Denver	65	19	.774
New York	58	26	.690	San Antonio	51	33	.607
St. Louis	32	52	.381	Indiana	45	39	.536
Memphis	27	57	.321	Utah	38	46	.452
Virginia	15	69	.179	San Diego	31	53	.369

383

PLAYOFFS

First Round

Kentucky defeated Memphis 4 games to 1
St. Louis defeated New York 4 games to 1
Indiana defeated San Antonio 4 games to 2
Denver defeated Utah 4 games to 2

Semifinals

Kentucky defeated St. Louis 4 games to 1
Indiana defeated Denver 4 games to 3

Championship

Kentucky defeated Indiana 4 games to 1

TOP SCORERS

	Pts.	Ave.
George McGinnis, Indiana	2353	29.8
Julius Erving, New York	2343	27.9
Ron Boone, Utah	2117	25.2
Travis Grant, San Diego	1335	25.2
Marvin Barnes, St. Louis	1849	24.0

TOP REBOUNDERS

	No.	Ave.
Swen Nater, San Antonio	1279	16.4
Artis Gilmore, Kentucky	1361	16.2
Marvin Barnes, St. Louis	1202	15.6
Moses Malone, Utah	1209	14.6
George McGinnis, Indiana	1126	14.3

LEADERS IN ASSISTS

	No.	Ave.
Mack Calvin, Denver	570	7.7
Chuck Williams, Memphis	576	7.1
George McGinnis, Indiana	495	6.3
Jim O'Brien, San Diego	443	5.6
Warren Jabali, San Diego	358	5.7

1975–76

There was no way to know that this would be the last time. There was no way to be sure that the red, white and blue basketball would not keep bouncing indefinitely. After all, previous reports of the ABA's demise had been premature.

In fact, the league was polishing its image. Dave DeBusschere, the popular former forward of the New York Knicks and the general manager of the New York Nets the previous season, was hired as the league's commissioner. Playing forward, he discovered, was an easier job.

The ABA attempted to introduce a new franchise in the Baltimore Claws. The Claws, however, were undercapitalized, and DeBusschere would not allow them to begin the season on shaky grounds. The franchise was terminated and the players dispersed.

But other franchises tottered, too. Usually they were able to survive the season, but not this time. Utah and San Diego were disbanded, and the East and West divisions were merged into a single, seven-team league.

The Denver Nuggets finished on top with 60 victories. The New York Nets were sec-ond. The Nuggets under coach Larry Brown were favored to win the championship. They got to the final this time, but the Nets had Julius Erving and, by now, he had become a one-man show. History will note that the Nets won the last ABA title.

The Nets had more difficulty in the semifinal round against San Antonio than they did in the final against the Nuggets. Controversy and emotion were the passwords as the Nets and Spurs traded insults off the court and interrupted the well-played games with unfortunate brawls. The fans were also in on it.

The Nets eventually won in seven games as Erving was dazzling. He carried twice the burden that he did when the Nets won their first championship two years before. They were more of a defensive team now, with players who were acquired to fill specific needs. Mostly, it was to get the ball to Dr. J.

Erving captured individual honors during the season as well. He won his third scoring title with a 29.3 average. He also was named the Most Valuable Player for the third consecutive year.

Larry Brown was named the top coach, and it was the third time he had won the award. Artis Gilmore was the top rebounder with a 15.5 average.

Denver's David Thompson lends excitement to ABA in its last season

David Thompson, who helped Denver to finish first, proved to be just as exciting a professional player as he was a college one at North Carolina State. He was named Rookie of the Year and also made the all-league team with Erving, Billy Knight of Indiana, Gilmore, James Silas of San Antonio and Ralph Simpson of Denver.

Just a month after the season ended, the league was disbanded as San Antonio, New York, Denver, and Indiana were absorbed into the NBA.

STANDINGS

	W.	L.	Pct.
Denver	60	24	.714
New York	55	29	.665
San Antonio	50	34	.595
Kentucky	46	38	.548
Indiana	39	45	.464
St. Louis	35	49	.417
Virginia	15	68	.181

PLAYOFFS

First Round

Kentucky defeated Indiana 2 games to 1

Semifinals

New York defeated San Antonio 4 games to 3
Denver defeated Kentucky 4 games to 3

Championship

New York defeated Denver 4 games to 2

TOP SCORERS

	Pts.	Ave.
Julius Erving, New York	2462	29.3
Billy Knight, Indiana	1969	28.1
David Thompson, Denver	2158	26.0
Artis Gilmore, Kentucky	2067	24.6
Marvin Barnes, St. Louis	1616	24.1

TOP REBOUNDERS

	No.	Ave.
Artis Gilmore, Kentucky	1303	15.5
Maurice Lucas, St. Louis-Kentucky	970	11.3
Caldwell Jones, St. Louis	853	11.2
Larry Kenon, San Antonio	897	11.1
Julius Erving, New York	925	11.0

LEADERS IN ASSISTS

	No.	Ave.
Don Buse, Indiana	689	8.2
Ralph Simpson, Denver	597	7.1
Mack Calvin, Virginia	271	6.0
Louie Dampier, Kentucky	467	5.7
Jim Silas, San Antonio	452	5.4

ALL-TIME ABA RECORDS

Champions

1968	Pittsburgh		1973	Indiana
1969	Oakland		1974	New York
1970	Indiana		1975	Kentucky
1971	Utah		1976	New York
1972	Indiana			

INDIVIDUAL

Single Game

Most Points	67	Larry Miller, Carolina; vs Memphis at Greensboro, N.C., Mar. 18, 1972
Most 2-Point F. G. Attempted	46	Julius Erving, New York, vs San Diego at San Diego, Feb. 14, 1975 (4 OT)
Most 2-Point F. G. Made	25	Mel Daniels, Indiana, vs New York at Indianapolis, April 18, 1969
	25	Larry Miller, Carolina, vs Memphis at Greensboro, N.C., Mar. 18, 1972
	25	Julius Erving, New York, vs San Diego at San Diego, Feb. 14, 1975 (4 OT)
	25	Marvin Barnes, St. Louis, vs Memphis at St. Louis, Mar. 16, 1975 (OT)

Most 3-Point F. G. Attempted	26	Les Selvage, Anaheim, vs Denver at Denver, Feb. 15, 1968
Most 3-Point F. G. Made	10	Les Selvage, Anaheim, vs Denver at Denver, Feb. 15, 1968
Most F. T. Attempted	30	George Thompson, Memphis, vs San Diego at San Diego, Oct. 14, 1972
Most F. T. Made	24	Tony Jackson, New Jersey, vs Kentucky at Louisville, Nov. 27, 1967
Most Rebounds	40	Artis Gilmore, Kentucky, vs New York at New York, Feb. 3, 1974
Most Assists	23	Larry Brown, Denver, vs Pittsburgh at Denver, Feb. 20, 1972
Most Consecutive F. T.	23	Rick Barry, Oakland, vs Kentucky at Louisville, Feb. 7, 1969

Season

Most Points	2,538	Dan Issel, Kentucky, 1971-72
Highest Average	34.58	Charlie Scott, Virginia, 1971-72
Most 2-Point F. G. Attempted	2,082	Charlie Scott, Virginia, 1971-72
Most 2-Point F. G. Made	986	Spencer Haywood, Denver, 1969-70
Highest 2-Point F. G. Percentage	.605	Bobby Jones, Denver, 1974-75
Most 3-Point F. G. Attempted	552	Louie Dampier, Kentucky, 1968-69
Most 3-Point F. G. Made	199	Louie Dampier, Kentucky, 1968-69
Highest 3-Point F. G. Percentage	.420	Billy Shepherd, Memphis, 1974-75
Most F. T. Attempted	805	Mack Calvin, Floridians, 1970-71
Most F. T. Made	696	Mack Calvin, Floridians, 1970-71
Highest F. T. Percentage	.896	Mack Calvin, Denver, 1974-75
Most Rebounds	1,637	Spencer Haywood, Denver, 1969-70
Most Assists	689	Don Buse, Indiana, 1975-76
Most Personal Fouls	382	Gene Moore, Kentucky, 1969-70
Most Times Disqualified	25	Gene Moore, Kentucky, 1969-70

Career

Most Points Scored	13,726	Louie Dampier, Kentucky, 1968-76
Highest Scoring Average (Minimum 250 Games)	28.7	Julius Erving, Virginia and New York, 1971-76
Most 2-Point F. G. Attempted	9,886	Mel Daniels, Minnesota, Indiana and Memphis, 1967-75
Most 2-Point F. G. Made	4,692	Mel Daniels, Minnesota, Indiana and Memphis, 1967-75
Most 3-Point F. G. Attempted	2,217	Louie Dampier, Kentucky, 1968-76
Most 3-Point F. G. Made	794	Louie Dampier, Kentucky, 1968-76
Most F. T. Attempted	4,105	Mack Calvin, Los Angeles, Miami, Carolina, Denver and Virginia, 1969-76
Most F. T. Made	3,554	Mack Calvin, Los Angeles, Miami, Carolina, Denver and Virginia, 1969-76
Most Rebounds	9,494	Mel Daniels, Minnesota, Indiana and Memphis, 1967-75
Most Assists	4,084	Louie Dampier, Kentucky, 1968-76
Most Minutes Played	27,770	Louie Dampier, Kentucky, 1968-76
Most Personal Fouls	1,689	Jim Ligon, Kentucky, Pittsburgh and Virginia, 1967-74

| Most Times Disqualified | 43 | Gene Moore, Kentucky, Texas, Dallas, New York, San Diego and St. Louis, 1968-74 |
| Most Games Played | 728 | Louie Dampier, Kentucky, 1968-76 |

TEAM
Single Game

Most Points, One Team	177	Indiana vs Pittsburgh at Indianapolis, April 12, 1970
Most Points, Two Teams	342	San Diego (176) vs New York (166) at San Diego, Feb. 14, 1975 (4 OT)
Fewest Points, One Team	66	Indiana vs San Antonio at San Antonio, Oct. 20, 1973
Largest Winning Margin	57	Utah 150, Carolina 93 at Salt Lake City, Oct. 19, 1971
Most 2-Point F. G. Attempted	131	Minnesota vs New Orleans at New Orleans (overtime) Dec. 6, 1967
	131	Miami vs Dallas at Dallas, Feb. 10, 1970
Most 2-Point F. G. Made	66	San Diego vs New York at San Diego, Feb. 14, 1975 (4 OT)
Most 3-Point F. G. Attempted	32	Anaheim vs Denver at Denver, Feb. 15, 1968
Most 3-Point F. G. Made	12	Kentucky vs Miami at Louisville, March 1, 1969
Most F. T. Attempted	73	Miami vs New York at Miami Beach, Fla., Nov. 20, 1968
Most F. T. Made	60	Indiana vs Los Angeles at Indianapolis, Feb. 1, 1969
Most Rebounds	93	Denver vs Dallas at Denver, April 8, 1970
Most Assists	51	Virginia vs Memphis at Virginia, Feb. 3, 1973
Most Personal Fouls	46	New York vs Washington at West Hempstead, N.Y., Dec. 26, 1969
		Carolina vs Indiana at Greensboro, N.C., Dec. 11, 1970

Season

Most Games Won	68	Kentucky, 1971-72
Most Games Lost	69	Virginia, 1974-75
Highest Winning Percentage	.810	Kentucky, 1971-72
Most Points	10,355	Virginia, 1970-71
Highest Scoring Average	126.49	Oakland, 1968-69
Most 2-Point F. G. Attempted	8,375	Denver, 1970-71
Most 2-Point F. G. Made	3,960	Virginia, 1970-71
Most 3-Point F. G. Attempted	1,024	Indiana, 1970-71
Most 3-Point F. G. Made	335	Kentucky, 1968-69
Most F. T. Attempted	3,434	Oakland, 1968-69
Most F. T. Made	2,607	Oakland, 1968-69
Most Rebounds	4,866	Utah, 1970-71
Most Assists	2,231	Virginia, 1970-71

All-ABA Teams

1967-68

First
Connie Hawkins, Pittsburgh
Doug Moe, New Orleans
Mel Daniels, Minnesota
Larry Jones, Denver
Charlie Williams, Pittsburgh

Second
Roger Brown, Indiana
Cincy Powell, Dallas
John Beasley, Dallas
Larry Brown, New Orleans
Louie Dampier, Kentucky

1968-69

Connie Hawkins, Minnesota
Rick Barry, Oakland
Mel Daniels, Indiana
James Jones, New Orleans
Larry Jones, Denver

John Beasley, Dallas
Doug Moe, Oakland
Red Robbins, New Orleans
Don Freeman, Miami
Louie Dampier, Kentucky

1969-70

Rick Barry, Washington
Spencer Haywood, Denver
Mel Daniels, Indiana
Bob Verga, Carolina
Larry Jones, Denver

Roger Brown, Indiana
Bob Netolicky, Indiana
Red Robbins, New Orleans
Louie Dampier, Kentucky
Don Freeman, Miami

1970-71

Roger Brown, Indiana
Rick Barry, New York
Mel Daniels, Indiana
Mack Calvin, Floridians
Charlie Scott, Virginia

John Brisker, Pittsburgh
Joe Caldwell, Carolina
Zelmo Beaty, Utah
Dan Issel, Kentucky
Don Freeman, Texas
Larry Cannon, Denver

1971-72

Rick Barry, New York
Dan Issel, Kentucky
Artis Gilmore, Kentucky
Don Freeman, Dallas
Bill Melchionni, New York

Willie Wise, Utah
Julius Erving, Virginia
Zelmo Beaty, Utah
Ralph Simpson, Denver
Charlie Scott, Virginia

1972-73

Billy Cunningham, Carolina
Julius Erving, Virginia
Artis Gilmore, Kentucky
James Jones, Utah
Warren Jabali, Denver

George McGinnis, Indiana
Dan Issel, Kentucky
Mel Daniels, Indiana
Ralph Simpson, Denver
Mack Calvin, Carolina

1973-74

Julius Erving, New York
George McGinnis, Indiana
Artis Gilmore, Kentucky
James Jones, Utah
Mack Calvin, Carolina

Dan Issel, Kentucky
Willie Wise, Utah
Swen Nater, San Antonio
Ron Boone, Utah
Louie Dampier, Kentucky

1974-75

Julius Erving, New York
George McGinnis, Indiana
Artis Gilmore, Kentucky
Mack Calvin, Denver
Ron Boone, Utah

Marvin Barnes, St. Louis
George Gervin, San Antonio
Swen Nater, San Antonio
Brian Taylor, New York
James Silas, San Antonio

1975-76

Julius Erving, New York
Billy Knight, Indiana
Artis Gilmore, Kentucky
James Silas, San Antonio
Ralph Simpson, Denver

David Thompson, Denver
Bobby Jones, Denver
Dan Issel, Denver
Don Buse, Indiana
George Gervin, San Antonio

Most Valuable Player

1968	Connie Hawkins	Pittsburgh
1969	Mel Daniels	Indiana
1970	Spencer Haywood	Denver
1971	Mel Daniels	Indiana
1972	Artis Gilmore	Kentucky
1973	Billy Cunningham	Carolina
1974	Julius Erving	New York
1975	{ Julius Erving	New York
	{ George McGinnis	Indiana
1976	Julius Erving	New York

Rookie of the Year

1968	Mel Daniels	Minnesota
1969	Warren Armstrong	Oakland
1970	Spencer Haywood	Denver
1971	{ Charlie Scott	Virginia
	{ Dan Issel	Kentucky
1972	Artis Gilmore	Kentucky
1973	Brian Taylor	New York
1974	Swen Nater	San Antonio
1975	Marvin Barnes	St. Louis
1976	David Thompson	Denver

Coach of the Year

1967-68	Vince Cazetta	Pittsburgh
1968-69	Alex Hannum	Oakland
1969-70	{ Bill Sharman	Los Angeles
	{ Joe Belmont	Denver
1970-71	Al Bianchi	Virginia
1971-72	Tom Nissalke	Dallas
1972-73	Larry Brown	Carolina
1973-74	{ Babe McCarthy	Kentucky
	{ Joe Mullaney	Utah
1974-75	Larry Brown	Denver
1975-76	Larry Brown	Denver

All-Rookie Teams

1968

Tom Washington, Pittsburgh
Bob Netolicky, Indiana
Mel Daniels, Minnesota
Louie Dampier, Kentucky
James Jones, New Orleans

1969

Larry Miller, Los Angeles
Walt Piatkowski, Denver
Gene Moore, Kentucky
Warren Armstrong, Oakland
Ron Boone, Dallas

1970

Willie Wise, Los Angeles
John Brisker, Pittsburgh
Spencer Haywood, Denver
Mike Barrett, Washington
Mack Calvin, Los Angeles

1971

Wendell Ladner, Memphis
Sam Robinson, Floridians
Dan Issel, Kentucky
Charlie Scott, Virginia
Joe Hamilton, Texas

1972

Julius Erving, Virginia
George McGinnis, Indiana
Artis Gilmore, Kentucky
John Roche, New York
Johnny Neumann, Memphis

1973

George Gervin, Virginia
Dennis Wuycik, Carolina
Jim Chones, New York
Brian Taylor, New York
James Silas, Dallas

1974

Larry Kenon, New York
Mike Green, Denver
Swen Nater, San Antonio
Dwight Lamar, San Antonio
John Williamson, New York

1975

Bobby Jones, Denver
Marvin Barnes, St. Louis
Moses Malone, Utah
Billy Knight, Indiana
Gus Gerard, St. Louis

1976

David Thompson, Denver
Mark Olberding, San Antonio
Kim Hughes, New York
M. L. Carr, St. Louis
Ticky Burden, Virginia

16

The Greatest Pros

Joe Lapchick was intimately involved with professional basketball throughout his long and productive career. He starred for the Original Celtics, the greatest professional team in basketball's early years. Later he coached the New York Knickerbockers of the NBA. During his half-century in the game, Lapchick gained respect as one of the keenest observers of basketball talent. His rating of the professionals of the modern era (since World War II), which appeared in the first edition of the Encyclopedia, was the basis for the twenty greatest pros chosen in the first revised edition, and it figures in the selection by the editors in this second revised edition.

Kareem Abdul-Jabbar

During the National Basketball Association playoffs of 1972, Bill Russell, the former Boston Celtics star, found himself working as a broadcaster for the American Broadcasting Company, which televised the NBA games.

Now there are many who claim that either Russell or Wilt Chamberlain, then playing for the Los Angeles Lakers, were

the greatest players in the history of basketball.

Bill Russell, however, had a different opinion. "Kareem Abdul-Jabbar," he said during one telecast, "is the greatest player to play this game."

Jabbar—known as Lew Alcindor before he took the Muslim name in 1971—had been a high-school great at Power Memorial in New York and then a three-time All-American center for UCLA.

And when he joined the Milwaukee Bucks as their first draft choice in 1969, he transformed a drab expansion basketball team into a world champion after two seasons.

Actually, the Bucks had won the rights to Jabbar in a coin toss with the Phoenix Suns. That coin made the Milwaukee Bucks' management richer than it had ever hoped because the Milwaukee Arena became the center of professional basketball in the United States. And this happened in a city where pro basketball had failed several years earlier.

That first year, Jabbar had something of a slow start. Though he was scoring, his aggressiveness on the boards was being questioned around the league. But by mid-

Kareem Abdul-Jabbar topped NBA centers

Jabbar led the Bucks to the playoffs three times after the 1971 championship season, gaining the finals against the Boston Celtics in 1974, only to lose in seven games. He also won his third MVP award that year, finishing third in scoring and fourth in rebounding.

Dissatisfied with the coaching style of Larry Costello and simply unhappy in the city of Milwaukee, Jabbar asked the Bucks to trade him when his contract expired after the 1974–75 season. The Bucks accommodated him. He was traded to the Los Angeles Lakers prior to the 1975–76 season.

His first season there brought Jabbar a fourth MVP award, but the Lakers failed to make the playoffs for the second straight year. His 16.9 rebound average enabled him to lead the league for the first time.

Jabbar had the Lakers in contention with the best record in the NBA in 1976–77. But not even a fifth MVP award could help him and the Lakers against the Bill Walton-led Portland Trail Blazers in the Western Conference final. The Lakers lost in four straight.

In the first game of the 1977–78 season, Jabbar punched Milwaukee rookie Kent Benson, incurring a $5,000 fine and a broken wrist that kept him sidelined for 20 games. He played unenthusiastically after returning to the lineup, and expressed thoughts of quitting. But after a long talk with Laker coach Jerry West, Jabbar returned to form during the second half of the season.

Jabbar's enormous basketball skills and his off-court life as a member of a strict Islamic sect often seem to clash on the court, where many have sensed in him an indifference to the game. His religion had made him a target of death threats from publicity-seeking fanatics. But while others have debated his commitment to basketball, Jabbar has remained outwardly calm. Few dispute that when his mind is on the game, no one plays basketball better.

Paul Arizin

It was like a Renoir or a Rembrandt. Paul Arizin's jump shot was perfection. The best

season that criticism had begun to fade as the 7-footer adjusted to the professional game.

Jabbar finished as Rookie of the Year. His 28.8 scoring average was second only to Jerry West's and he was third in rebounding with 1,190.

The next season the Bucks won the NBA crown after Jabbar led them to a 66–16 regular-season record. Any Jabbar skeptics vanished when he won the scoring championship (2,596 points, 31.7 average) and finished fourth in rebounding (1,311 rebounds, 16.0 average). He followed his MVP season with another in 1971–72. Again, Jabbar led the league in scoring with 2,822 points for a 34.8 average, and finished third in rebounding with 1,346 for a 16.6 average.

description was this one in a Philadelphia newspaper: ". . . flicking the ball on the crest of his leap like a man riding an invisible surf, this is Arizin's moment of expression."

Arizin played 10 years in the National Basketball Association for the Philadelphia Warriors. During those 10 years, he averaged 22.8 points per game and won scoring championships in 1951–52 with a 25.4 average and in 1956–57 with 25.6.

There is no telling how much a two-year marine hitch hurt Arizin right after he won his first scoring championship. Certainly, it claimed what might have been two of his most productive years, but even though he missed them, he still had a remarkable career.

Arizin came to the Warriors after making All-American at Villanova University. Even in college, the jump shot was his trademark. "The truth is," Arizin said, "that it came by

Paul Arizin is en route to one of his leaping shots

accident. I was playing in the Catholic Club League in Philadelphia and our games were on a slick dance floor. When I tried to hook, my feet would go out from under me. So I jumped. The ceiling was low and I had to throw line drives. I just never changed."

It's a good thing he didn't. The 6-4, 210-pounder played forward for the Warriors and the jump shot enabled him to get the ball away despite defensive counterparts who stood 6-7 and 6-8. Theoretically, big, agile professionals should have been able to stop Arizin. But he possessed marvelous timing and an important intangible called anticipation. Of course, he had natural spring in his legs, but it was the timing and anticipation which often meant the difference between scoring and not scoring.

Arizin was the fifth man in NBA history to reach the 10,000-point mark, and his career high in a single game was 44 points. At times one wondered how Arizin even made it up and down the court because he was constantly wheezing and seemingly trying to regain his breath. Arizin laughed when people suggested he was not in shape. "That panting and coughing is a sinus condition I've always had. It doesn't hurt my endurance," he said.

And so he would run down the court, gulping for air, an unruly cowlick on the back of his head flopping up and down. He would head for the corner, take a pass, then fake and jump, hanging in the air for a split second before firing his line-drive shot. A second later the ball would nestle in the basket.

Rick Barry

For seven straight years, Wilt Chamberlain dominated the NBA scoring statistics. It was during the 1965–66 season that a rookie named Rick Barry appeared in a San Francisco uniform. That was the year Wilt made it seven in a row. But the following season Rick Barry stunned the basketball world by taking the title away from Chamberlain.

Only in his second year, Barry was magnificent, leading the Warriors into the championship finals against the Philadelphia

76ers. As a second-year man, Barry scored 2,775 points in 78 games for a 35.6 points per game average. "In his second year as a pro," said Los Angeles coach Fred Schaus, "he's ahead of Bob Pettit at the same stage. Rick's a better shooter and a little quicker than Bob."

Schaus made the comparison with Pettit because when Rick first entered the league after starring at the University of Miami (Fla.), he was a rather skinny, 6-7, 200 pounds. Just like Pettit, who went on to become one of the game's greats. And, like Pettit, a lot of people doubted if Barry had the physical assets to take the punishment in the NBA. They found out quickly. As a rookie, he scored 2,059 points for a 25.7 average and he grabbed 850 rebounds. For that performance he was named Rookie of the Year.

During college, Barry, a native of Roselle Park, N.J., was a controversial basketball player. He had a quick temper that often got him into trouble on the court. When he turned professional, he remained just as controversial. That first year was a tough one. Barry took much punishment. The second year wasn't quite as bad. By then, he was recognized as one of the game's superstars. His game improved, too. Not just in scoring, but playmaking also. "He and Elgin Baylor are the greatest passing forwards in the game," San Francisco coach Bill Sharman said. Center Nate Thurmond also praised Barry: "Nobody on the team got the ball into me better than Rick."

With his future ahead, Barry gambled and lost during the 1967 off-season. He had been persuaded to sign a contract with the Oakland Oaks of the newly-formed American Basketball Association. The three-year contract called for $75,000 a year, plus a 15 per cent interest in the team, plus five per cent of any home gate which exceeded $600,000. Barry's father-in-law (and college coach), Bruce Hale, was the general manager of the Oaks. Barry signed the contract and the Warriors contested it in court. Due to a court order, he had to miss the whole 1967–68 season, thus interrupting his sensational career.

But Barry came back strong, leading the Oakland Oaks to the ABA championship in

Rick Barry as a young Warrior

1968–69, and taking the New York Nets to the championship round for the first time in their history in 1972. At the end of the 1971–72 season, Rick was named to the All-ABA team for the fourth consecutive year and had compiled the highest career scoring average in the league, 30.46 points a game.

However, Barry's career in the ABA appeared at an end when, in the summer of 1972, a federal judge ruled that Rick would have to honor a contract previously signed with his old San Francisco team (now Golden State Warriors) in the NBA. Thus a new chapter in the odyssey of Rick Barry.

Although his hair was thinner and he had added several pounds since he first left the NBA, Barry displayed the same marvelous talent upon his return. In the 1974–75 season he achieved his greatest accomplishment as a professional when he led a group of relatively unknown Warriors to the NBA title. The euphoria did not last long, however. After two more years with the

Warriors—years in which the outspoken Barry often incurred the wrath of his teammates—the nomadic forward was on the move again. In the summer of 1978, now 34, he played out his contract with Golden State and signed with the Houston Rockets.

Elgin Baylor

It was during a playoff game against the Baltimore Bullets in 1965. Elgin Baylor took a nasty spill. His teammates had to help him from the floor as 16,000 fans in the Los Angeles Sports Arena looked on in stunned silence. Nobody knew it then, but Elgin Baylor had just ripped off part of his kneecap.

The next year was the toughest of Baylor's career. The old, graceful moves didn't

Elgin Baylor does it all in the air

seem to be there any more. No more of those twisting driving layups, those unbelievable jump shots. Around the league, they were saying Elgin Baylor—the greatest forward for his size—was through.

For seven years, the 6-5 Seattle graduate had been one of the leading scorers in the league and together with guard Jerry West gave the Lakers the greatest one-two scoring punch ever seen in professional basketball. Despite the pain and the problems brought on by calcium deposits in his knees, Baylor continued to work to strengthen his weak legs. And then finally on February 2, 1966, he scored 29 points and grabbed 21 rebounds in a game against Cincinnati. The obituary notices were discarded.

Baylor did pretty well the next two seasons, averaging 26 points a game both years and in 1967–68 he and West steered the Lakers into the NBA finals against the Boston Celtics.

When Elgin retired shortly after the start of the 1971–72 season, he was the all-time leading scorer for the Lakers with 23,149 points and ranked third in the league overall.

His best scoring year came in 1961–62 when he averaged 38.2 in 48 games. Baylor will be remembered for his sure touch with the ball. At times one wondered how he cleared opposition defenses. The answer was a combination of agility and muscle. This agility and tremendous spring and strength enabled him to outrebound forwards much bigger than he was.

When Baylor signed with the Lakers out of Seattle University, he actually saved a faltering franchise. At the time, the Lakers were still playing in Minneapolis. "If he had turned me down then," Laker president Bob Short said at the time, "I'd have been out of business. The club would have gone bankrupt."

Well, Baylor did sign and the Lakers slowly began to regain their old form. However, the team moved to Los Angeles and Baylor became one of the biggest stars in a town which had its share. His presence turned the Lakers' franchise into one of the most rewarding in sports.

He was all-pro first team on nine different occasions and played in eight consecutive

All-Star games. In a game against New York in 1960 he scored 71 points. And in a game against Boston in 1959, he scored 64 points. The 71 points stood as a league record until Wilt Chamberlain broke it in 1962.

After a four-year absence from the game, Baylor returned during the 1976–77 season as an assistant to coach Butch van Breda Kolff in New Orleans. When van Breda Kolff was fired midway through the season, Baylor was named coach. Unfortunately, there were no forwards named Elgin Baylor to make the job easier for him.

Wilt Chamberlain

The greatest offensive player in the history of basketball. It is as simple as that. From the moment the 7-1 center entered the National Basketball Association for the 1959–60 season, he was an awesome, powerful figure on offense.

He will be remembered most for his scoring ability, but in the latter years of his career his game changed and as his proficiency on defense increased (and his proficiency at playmaking) so did the records of the teams he played for.

Chamberlain led the Philadelphia 76ers to the NBA championship in 1966–67. That ended—for a while—comments about Chamberlain being a great scorer, but not being very valuable when it came to helping his teams win championships. That tag went as far back as his collegiate days at the University of Kansas. The criticism became meaningless in 1971–72 when, as a member of the Los Angeles Lakers, Wilt led them to 33 consecutive victories during the regular season and was named Most Valuable Player as he paced the Lakers to their first championship in 12 years in Los Angeles.

Chamberlain was one of the most publicized high-school basketball players in history. He went from Philadelphia's Overbrook High School to Kansas where he played only two varsity years before dropping out to play for Abe Saperstein's Harlem Globetrotters. He joined the NBA the following season.

In his rookie season with the old Phila-

Wilt Chamberlain wrote the record book

delphia Warriors, Chamberlain averaged 37.6 points per game. He increased that the next season to 38.4. But it was in 1961–62 that he was at his best as a scorer, finishing with 4,029 points in 80 games, an average of 50.4 points per game. On March 2, 1962, in a game against the New York Knickerbockers at Hershey, Pa., he scored an incredible 100 points on 36 field goals and 28 foul shots.

Chamberlain led the league in scoring for seven straight years until Rick Barry of San Francisco broke his string in 1966–67. He also led the league five times in rebounding, his highest figure being 2,149 in 1960–61. On November 24, 1960, in a game against the Boston Celtics, Chamberlain set an NBA record with 55 rebounds.

He also won seven field goal percentage titles and was a constant leader in the minutes played department. And in the latter part of his career, he added to his all-time NBA scoring record every time he stepped on the floor. But despite all his records and all his feats, Chamberlain also will be remembered as one of the most controversial figures in the game. A moody, introspective individual, Chamberlain often missed practice sessions, creating friction not only with his coaches, but among his teammates, too. He needed the practice, too, because he was one of the poorest foul shooters in the history of the game. His lifetime average hovered around the 50 per cent mark. He set a number of records for foul shooting which he would like to forget: Most foul tries missed in one game (18); most foul tries missed in a season (528); and most foul tries missed in a playoff game (17). Opposing teams often considered it good strategy to foul Chamberlain rather than allow him to attempt a field goal.

Chamberlain, however, established some fantastic individual shooting records. At one point in the 1966–67 season he made 35 straight shots from the field. And he also finished that season with a 68.3 shooting percentage, another record.

A perennial all-league selection, Chamberlain was named the league's Most Valuable Player four times. His place in basketball history can not be disputed. He was considered such a valuable property that he was paid $250,000 for the 1967–68 season by the 76ers.

Before the start of the 1968–69 season, Chamberlain was traded to the Los Angeles Lakers for three players. The 76ers had been unable to reach salary terms with Chamberlain, but Jack Kent Cooke, owner of the Lakers, agreed to pay Chamberlain a reported $3,000,000 for five seasons. And before the contract had run its course, Wilt owned a matching pair of championship rings and Cooke had a return on his investment.

Bob Cousy

It was Joe Fulks and George Mikan who first focused the public's attention on modern-day professional basketball. It was Bob Cousy, however, who made the game fun and attracted the crowds.

Cousy was the best ballhandler and backcourtman in the history of basketball. Writers all over the country constantly thought up new nicknames for him. "The

Bob Cousy demonstrates his artistry to Sweetwater Clifton

Mobile Magician" was one; "The Houdini of the Hardwood" another. Though the nicknames may have been a little corny, they were accurate. His forte was playmaking, though he was an excellent scorer, too. Cousy's playmaking abilities were due to superb reflexes, a fine knowledge of the game and peripheral vision which enabled him to command a 180-degree angle of the action on the court.

For eight consecutive years (1953–60), Cousy led the NBA in assists. "Cousy," said Red Auerbach, who coached him in Boston, "was one of the greatest all-around basketball players in the game, and undoubtedly he was the best backcourt player."

Put a ball in Cousy's hands and one could not anticipate the next move. It might go behind his back, between his legs, nobody knew. And frequently this led to a basket for Cousy or the Celtics. Of course, a lot of people thought Cousy was showboating, but they were wrong. "Actually," he said, "I don't use the behind-the-back pass as often as people think I do. When I use it, I have a good reason for it. When a situation develops where I can help the club with a certain maneuver, I go ahead with it."

Cousy came to the Celtics in 1950 after a brilliant college career at Holy Cross. Thirteen seasons later, he retired and when he did, he left behind a set of statistics which serves as a standard for a backcourtman. For example, he once held the all-time record for most minutes played (30,230) and he held the NBA record for most assists (6,949). When he retired, he was the fourth-leading scorer in NBA history (16,955 points) and was second in total games played (917). He also was named to the all-league team for 10 successive seasons. And he was the only player to participate in 13 All-Star Games. In 1962, a poll of sports editors of 100 major daily papers named Cousy the NBA's all-time number one player.

It is hard to pick Cousy's greatest feat. He once scored 50 points in a game, but some of his other contributions were even greater, though the amount of points was not as high. There was a game in Madison Square Garden in 1954 when the New York Knickerbockers were leading, 93–89, with 30 seconds remaining. Cousy stole the ball twice within the 30 seconds and the Celtics forced an overtime. Then another. Finally they won, Cousy having scored 12 of the 20 points in overtime.

Or there was another time in New York —in 1960—when he dribbled the ball so cunningly and killed the clock for the last 23 seconds of the game. Nobody could stop him. The next day, Jimmy Cannon of the New York *Journal-American* wrote, "If Cousy never put the ball in the basket, he'd still be the most respected man in the league. At the finish, Boston had a one-point lead with 23 seconds to play. It was then that Bob proved his greatness. He held onto the ball . . . dribbling it among the Knicks, scampering among them in a wild solo. He ran in a lunging crouch, his body bent to protect the ball from their hands, a thrilling dwarf among the frustrated giants."

Julius Erving

He is at his best, it seems, while in mid-air, where he displays more agility than most players do when their feet are planted on the ground. Dunking is a form of self-expression in professional basketball, but Julius Erving has made it an art form. That split second he is airborne evokes a response from audiences that is worth more than the accumulated applause from a lifetime of making jump shots.

He is Dr. J, perhaps the most emulated player in the NBA. He is, with little doubt, the most exciting player of his or any generation, yet he remains outwardly a soft-spoken man with a deep baritone voice and a whimsical explanation for his flamboyant style.

"It's easy," Erving says of dunking, "once you learn how to fly."

Erving was born in Hempstead, Long Island, New York, where at the Salvation Army Youth Center, one youngster on the basketball team now is rewarded with the opportunity to wear No. 32 and is called "the Doctor."

Another tribute to Dr. J can be found in Roosevelt, Long Island, where he spent his childhood. At Roosevelt Park, one of the places he honed his talent, a sign reads: "This is where Julius Erving learned the game of basketball."

But while he was a fine high-school player and a better one in college at the University of Massachusetts, there was no reason to suspect that he would become the force he did at the professional level. He first gained national prominence on April 5, 1971, when he left Massachusetts after his junior year to sign a four-year, $500,000 contract with the Virginia Squires of the American Basketball Association.

"Basically, I felt I was ready to play pro ball. I have my college degree in basketball," he said.

Erving was a standout with the Squires, but the team was sinking in red ink and the ABA as a whole suffered from a lack of media attention. Erving attempted to break

three times the Most Valuable Player in the ABA and twice the catalyst on Nets' championship teams, was sent to the Philadelphia 76ers, a team already overstocked with stars.

Although he was in the NBA at last, Erving showed only glimpses of his form in his first two years with the Sixers. He had to share the limelight; he had to wait his turn. But when frontcourt mate George McGinnis was traded to Denver before the start of the 1978–79 season, it led to speculation that Erving would once again be able to play to the maximum of his ability. Fans would be treated to the real Dr. J.

"I do want to be the greatest," Erving said. "I realize all the potential that is there. I have talents. I have a job because of those talents."

Joe Fulks

Julius Erving operates as Dr. J

his contract, and a year later signed with the Atlanta Hawks. He played in three exhibition games before a federal court judge ordered him back to Virginia.

After another season there, owner Earl Foreman traded Erving to the New York Nets, who played their home games on Long Island, not far from where Erving grew up. It was a natural, and Erving began receiving the attention he deserved. Who was this marvelous player who exhausted a reporter's storehouse of adjectives with his moves on the court? At 6-7 and 205 pounds, Dr. J combines the size and strength of a big man with the grace and fluidity of a guard. Even those in the NBA took notice. He was a crowd-pleaser, a showman who could fill the house.

Many believe that when the NBA absorbed the four ABA teams and ended the war between the leagues, it was really Erving it was after. Then, in a stunning development, Erving and Nets' owner Roy Boe reached an impasse in the renegotiation of his contract, resulting in a trade. Dr. J,

Joe Fulks was the man who focused the attention of the world on professional basketball. For when he was at his best, the game was still developing and basketball was not considered a high-scoring game. But Joe Fulks changed that and he changed many other things, too. He was the link between the prewar days and the modern era of professional basketball.

When Eddie Gottlieb, the coach and owner of the Philadelphia Warriors, signed him to a contract in 1946, he told the press: "We have a fellow by the name of Joe Fulks. You've probably never heard of him but I believe he has the potentialities of a great scorer."

Even Gottlieb did not realize how deep that potential was. In his first year, Fulks led the league in scoring with what then was considered an astounding average of 23.2 points per game (1,389 points in 60 contests). The Warriors won the championship that season and the name Joe Fulks became synonymous with professional basketball.

Fulks had been a high-school star in Kuttawa, Kentucky. From there he went to nearby Murray State College where he set scoring records with amazing alacrity. World War II ended any immediate hopes for a college degree as Joe joined the Ma-

Joe Fulks was the first of the great scorers

Despite his great scoring ability—when he retired, only George Mikan had scored more points—Fulks was often criticized. But even the critics had to admit his value to the Warriors. John "Honey" Russell, then coach of the Boston Celtics, once said: "Fulks is slow and he's not a great defensive player. And how can he be a great team player when he takes so many shots? But I wish I had him. I'd sure build my team around him."

Fulks viewed all the publicity and acclaim quite realistically. "They give me the ball and I shoot. That's all there is to it." That's an oversimplification, of course. Joe Fulks was a great basketball player and the game owes much of its early success to him.

John Havlicek

rine Corps. He saw service on Iwo Jima and Guam while on duty in the Pacific. Before signing with the Warriors, Fulks played on a Marine Corps team with Andy Phillip from Illinois and Kenny Sailors of Wyoming.

Fulks was a slim 6-5, 190 pounds when he joined the Warriors as a 24-year-old rookie. His twisting pivot shots were the forerunner of the jump shot. He finished his career at the end of the 1953–54 season, after eight years of playing, with 8,003 points. But Joe's greatest feat came against the Indianapolis Jets at the Philadelphia Arena on February 10, 1949, when he electrified the sports world by scoring a record 63 points in one game. At that time, many teams did not score 63 points in a whole ball game.

That night, he shot spinning one-handers, running shots with either hand and his soft, looping set shots. They all worked. Only 10 players have scored 63 points or higher in a major-league professional game: Fulks, Wilt Chamberlain, Elgin Baylor, Jerry West, Zelmo Beaty, Larry Miller, Julius Erving, Pete Maravich, David Thompson and George Gervin.

It was not necessary to refer to him by his first name or his last name or both. He was simply Hondo, and for 16 seasons he was an unrelenting basketball player. John Havlicek joined the Boston Celtics in 1962–63, a defensive-minded player from Ohio State who did not have the natural talent to guarantee himself a spot on the Celtics' roster.

Havlicek possessed a quality, though, that would endear him to the fans and enable him to become one of the greatest players in NBA history. Whether playing guard or forward—and he played either extremely well—Hondo was a man on the run. He began his career in the famous role of the Celtics' sixth man and eventually moved into the starting lineup. He made their fast break nearly perfect. All because of his ability to run and run and run after others had tired of the chase.

"It started in high school," Havlicek once said. "I was always able to run. In college I never got tired. It was freakish for a while. One season I spent three quarters of it not drinking a Coke because I was afraid it would affect my wind."

It was this ability to run that enabled Havlicek to more than compensate for any lack of natural ability. Let no one, however, underestimate his ability to score. At the peak of his career, he averaged more than

Boston's John Havlicek was a marvel of endurance

20 points per game in eight consecutive seasons.

As a reserve on the great Celtics' teams that included Bill Russell, Bob Cousy, Tom Heinsohn, and Sam Jones, and as captain of the Celtic teams that won a pair of titles, Havlicek always remained a soft-spoken, modest individual who led by example.

"John is the guts of the team," former coach and later Celtics' president Red Auerbach said.

Havlicek hastened the era of the small forward. This occurred in 1966–67 after four years as the sixth man. He moved into the starting lineup and drove taller, slower forwards to the bench with his persistent running. "All the forwards then were 6-8 and big. It was easy for me on offense," he said. "On defense, I got help from Russell."

When he moved into the backcourt, he took advantage of his height. "The guards mostly were small," he said. "Me and Oscar Robertson and Tom Gola were the only ones as big as 6-5."

As good a basketball player as he was, Havlicek was considered to be football material as well. The Cleveland Browns invited him to a tryout and thought he could be their starting tight end. But he was to make his impact in basketball, remaining an unspoiled player even when the salaries doubled and tripled seemingly overnight. He could not understand complacency in others. "Untested players are signing for a million," he said. "The money has made it easy to lose."

He was 38 years old when he retired in 1978. There are many observers who feel he could have played another year or two without embarrassing himself. Three years earlier, Havlicek said as much himself. "I'll be retired and I'll still be able to run as well as most guys who will still be playing," he said.

Neil Johnston

Neil Johnston was another victim of the George Mikan era. And though he was a three-time scoring champion, he could never break through and win the national acceptance that Mikan had. Eddie Gottlieb, who coached Johnston in Philadelphia, said, "I doubt if Johnston will ever receive the recognition that Mikan got because Neil didn't come into the league with the fanfare and blowing of trumpets that accompanied Mikan."

Johnston was an Ohio State graduate and a 6-8 center whose hook shot was a work of art. He also was accurate with a one-hander from the outside. In eight seasons, from 1952 through 1959, he scored 10,023 points and had an average of 19.4 points per game. He won the scoring title in successive seasons. In 1951–52 he scored 1,564 points for a 22.3 average; in 1953–54

he scored 1,759 for a 24.4 average; and in 1954–55 he had 1,631 points for 22.7.

He was just as adept at shooting and rebounding, winning the shooting percentage title three times (.452, .457 and .447). He won the rebounding title in 1954–55 with 1,085. For two seasons—1952–53, 1953–54—he led the league in most minutes played.

He might have been even greater, but a knee injury cut his career short when he was only 30 years old and still had some good years left. Despite the knee trouble, he tried to play. "On one good leg," said Al Cervi, one of his coaches with the Warriors, "he's better than some of the other men in this league. When he's out of the lineup it just kills us."

Finally, the knee no longer could stand the pain and the rigors of the rugged NBA schedule. Johnston had to end his outstanding career in 1959. He had made the NBA All-Star first team four times. When he retired, he was named coach of the Warriors just when another pretty good cen-

Neil Johnston: man with a hook

ter, Wilt Chamberlain, was breaking in. Johnston remained as Warrior coach for two years. He was a frustrated man who had to watch from the bench instead of being out on the court playing.

Ed Macauley

Some called him Easy Ed because of his modest, easy-going temperament. But he really earned the nickname on the basketball court, where he made his driving layups and virtually unstoppable hook shot look as easy as pushing a button.

Actually Ed Macauley had to develop his graceful smoothness almost out of necessity. At 6-8 and only 190 pounds, he just wasn't strong enough to battle some of the beefier NBA players. So Macauley concentrated on playmaking and shooting and it paid off. In nine and a fraction seasons in the league, Macauley made the All-NBA first team three times and the second team once and

Easy Ed Macauley (22) made it look easy

established himself as one of the all-time great NBA centers.

He graduated from St. Louis University in 1949 as a two-time All-American and signed a two-year contract for a reported $30,000 with the hometown St. Louis Bombers, who were struggling to stay in business. Macauley had a good rookie year, averaging 16.1 points a game, fifth-best in the league, but the Bombers folded after the season ended.

The New York Knicks thought so much of Easy Ed that they offered to buy the entire St. Louis franchise just to obtain Macauley. But the NBA vetoed the transaction and the next season Macauley wound up with the Boston Celtics. Along with Bob Cousy and Bill Sharman, Macauley helped make the pro game a success in Boston.

Macauley played in the All-Star Game seven times and always did well. He was, in fact, the outstanding player in the very first All-Star Game in 1951. Three years later, in 1954, he was the only unanimous selection for the All-Star Game.

Macauley played six seasons for the Celtics and always finished among the league leaders in scoring. Over that span, he never averaged less than 17.5 points a game. More than merely a gunner, he usually finished among the leaders in field-goal accuracy, too.

On March 6, 1953, he had the greatest scoring night of his career, riddling the Minneapolis Lakers with their great center, George Mikan, for 46 points.

For the 1956–57 season, Easy Ed moved back to St. Louis, his hometown. Ben Kerner, the owner of the St. Louis Hawks, had the draft rights to Bill Russell. But he felt that Russell, who had been a great college star at San Francisco, would probably sign with the Harlem Globetrotters after returning from the Olympic Games. So Kerner traded the rights to Russell to the Celtics in return for Macauley and Cliff Hagan.

Macauley, Bob Pettit and Hagan led the Hawks to two consecutive Western Division titles and in 1957–58 the Hawks beat Boston for the NBA championship. Early in the next season Easy Ed retired as a player and took over as coach and general manager of the Hawks. In the two seasons he coached the Hawks, they won two Western titles. But he resigned in 1962 in order to devote more time to outside business interests.

In his years in the NBA, Macauley proved that a player didn't have to be a brute to be a good NBA center. He showed that agility and coordination were at least as important as sheer strength. Macauley made the game look easy—for himself and the fans who watched him, but never for the opponents who had to stop him.

George Mikan

When analyzing George Mikan's position in the history of basketball, you must consider only the era he played: the late 1940s and early 1950s. This was before Wilt Chamberlain and Bill Russell.

Until the emergence of Chamberlain and Russell, Mikan had been considered the greatest big man in the game's history. But it is unfair to compare him with Chamberlain and Russell because they were different types completely.

George Mikan did much to revolutionize the game. And he did a lot to make the NBA a major-league attraction because he was the main reason the Minneapolis Lakers won five world's championships. Mikan was so good during his time that when every other possible defense against him, fair or foul, had been tried and found wanting, the NBA was forced to widen the lanes under the basket from six to 12 feet.

During Mikan's heyday—and that of the Lakers—he dominated the record book. The 6-10 center from DePaul University scored 44 points or more in nine different games. His best effort was 61 points against the Rochester Royals in 1952. At one point, he held the all-time seasonal scoring average of 28.4 points per game. In his six big seasons with the Lakers—from 1948 to 1954—he led the league in scoring three times, was second twice and fourth in his last and worst year. He made the league All-Star first team each of the six years.

Mikan's size (245 pounds) also made him a target for the opposition. Each of his legs was broken once. His right foot, the

Perhaps the greatest tribute paid Mikan was in New York at Madison Square Garden. It was not the size of the crowd nor was it a special night where he received a number of gifts. It was just a simple message on the marquee outside the Garden. All it said was:

Tonite
George Mikan
vs.
Knicks

Bob Pettit

George Mikan vs. the All-Stars

arch of his left foot, his right wrist, his nose and one thumb also were broken at one time or another. Three of his fingers were broken, too. His nose was ripped open by swinging elbows. He received a total of 166 stitches.

When Mikan first announced his retirement after the 1954 season, the basketball community was stunned and saddened. Of course, they realized he could not go on forever. Johnny Kundla, the Lakers' coach, was glum when he heard Mikan's plans. But later Kundla confessed to the press: "This should even up our league."

He was right. Mikan had dominated the game. Nobody was able to handle No. 99 during those years. Mikan stuck to his retirement for a year, but in the middle of the 1955–56 season he decided to try a comeback. It was not a success. He scored only 390 points in 37 games and when he retired for good at the end of the year, he left the NBA with 11,764 points and a 22.6 average.

They said he was too skinny. Too light. He would not hold up as a corner man in the National Basketball Association. Bob Pettit listened politely to the evaluation. And he smiled. He had just been graduated from Louisiana State and had been drafted by the Milwaukee Hawks.

The 6-9, 215-pound Pettit reported to the Hawks in 1954 and that first year scored 1,466 points for a 20.4 average. That ended the doubt and the speculation. The following year, Bob Pettit was even more sensational. The Hawks had moved to St. Louis and Pettit made the game a success there by winning the scoring title (1,849 points) and rebounding title (1,164). He also won the Most Valuable Player award and was selected as the MVP in the All-Star Game. You can go on and on listing Bob Pettit's records and achievements.

It would not be an overstatement to say he may have been the best frontcourtman ever to play professional basketball. He won the MVP award twice, the scoring title twice and the rebounding title once. Four times he was selected as the outstanding performer in the All-Star Game, and he was named to the All-NBA team 10 years in a row. He was a pleasure to watch: a smooth shooter with an exceedingly accurate jump shot, a deceptive rebounder who used finesse to outwit and out-rebound stronger men.

Pettit ranks as the second-leading scorer in the history of the NBA. He played 11 years, scoring 20,880 points in 792 games for a lifetime average of 26.4. That scoring average was the fifth-best in the league's history. He also ranked second in minutes played until Chamberlain overtook him. And he was the league's third-leading rebounder (12,851). He had six games in which he scored more than 50 points including a career high of 57 in 1961. Until Elgin Baylor broke the record, Pettit also was the leading scorer in playoff history.

Off the court, Pettit was all class. The same as he was in uniform. He had an inordinate amount of pride. "What it is with me, I guess," he said, "is that as you go along in life and work hard, you reach new plateaus of accomplishment. With each plateau you reach, the demands upon you become greater. And your pride increases to meet the demands. You drive yourself harder than before. You can't afford negative thinking, so you always believe you'll win. You build an image of yourself that has nothing to do with ego—but it has to be satisfied. When I fall below what I know I can do, my belly growls and growls. Anytime I'm not playing up to my very best I can count on a jolt of indigestion."

Bob Pettit: 20,880 points

Bob Pettit had a unique barometer. But judging from the record, he could not have suffered too badly.

Jim Pollard

In 1952, the players who had been in the National Basketball Association since its inception in 1946 voted in a special poll to determine who was the best player of the period. The winner was Jim Pollard, the frontcourtman for the Minneapolis Lakers. To win the poll, Pollard finished ahead of such greats as teammate George Mikan and Joe Fulks.

It was a wonderful tribute to a player who contributed as much to the success of the Lakers as the high-scoring Mikan. Of course, Pollard never received the publicity Mikan did. Pollard was not a high scorer like Mikan. He averaged 13.1 points per game during his eight-year career and scored 6,522 points. But he was the classic team player. "You can get a lot of points in a game," he once said, "and still be dissatisfied with yourself. After all, it isn't an individual record you're after, but a victory."

Pollard's best weapon was his jump shot. Together with Vern Mikkelsen and Mikan he helped the Lakers dominate the game in those early years. Mikkelsen, Mikan and Pollard were the best one-two-three punch the game had seen.

You can get a better picture of Pollard when you listen to the comments some of his fellow pros made when the poll was taken. Said Fred Scolari of the Fort Wayne Pistons: "Pollard can do more things than anyone. He is better than most big men and decidedly better than the little men. He's been in the shade of Mikan. He is a basketball player's player all the way."

Bones McKinney, another Pollard opponent, had tremendous respect for him, too. "Pollard," McKinney said, "was the greatest cornerman ever. On another club no one would touch him. He can do everything on a basketball floor and do it with finesse."

Finesse is important when you speak of Jim Pollard. He seldom made the wrong move. And he was consistent. His playoff scoring average was 13.4, three tenths of a point above his career average.

Another interesting statistic: Pollard was considered one of the cleanest players in basketball and in one three-year stretch committed only 194 personal fouls. He was a graduate of Stanford University. Later he coached the Lakers for a brief period before becoming a college coach.

Oscar Robertson

There is a story Tom Meschery, the former NBA forward, enjoyed telling when asked about Oscar Robertson's myriad talents. "We were playing Cincinnati and Earl Strom was one of the officials. Somehow I wound up guarding Oscar after a switch. Well, Oscar throws that ball behind his back, heads for the basket and leaves me behind. It was a fantastic move, split second like always with him. Just as the ball goes

Jim Pollard: cleanest team player

The Big O

in, Strom calls walking. Oscar gets real excited and starts screaming at him, 'How can you call that walking, you never saw that move before.' "

Oscar probably was right, but the official prevailed. Some of the moves he has made throughout his career have been unbelievable. As they said in the NBA: "Never turn your head on Oscar, there is no telling what he might show you next. His body control is even more amazing than his shooting touch."

Red Auerbach, the former Boston coach, was one of Robertson's greatest admirers. "There is nothing he can't do," Auerbach said. "No one comes close to him or has the ability to break open a game as Oscar. He's so great he scares me. He can beat you all by himself and usually does."

Robertson, 6-5 and weighing 205 pounds, was an All-American at the University of Cincinnati before joining the Cincinnati Royals in 1960–61, when he promptly showed his greatness with a 30.5 scoring average. The second-leading scorer in NBA history, Robertson averaged better than 27 points a game.

He is also one of the greatest playmakers in history and holds the league record for assists in a career (9,887). He led the league in assists six times, and his per-game assist average of 11.5 (in 1964–65) is the second-highest in history. Oscar also led the NBA in free-throw accuracy in 1963–64 (.853) and 1964–65 (.873).

One thing that had eluded Oscar in his years at Cincinnati was an NBA championship. But at the start of the 1970–71 season he was traded to Milwaukee where Kareem Abdul-Jabbar, then known as Lew Alcindor, was fast maturing as a pro. Robertson became Mr. Outside, Abdul-Jabbar was Mr. Inside and the Bucks won the championship in only their third season.

Robertson will be remembered best for his versatility. There was nothing beyond his talent—or imagination—on the basketball floor. Three times (1961, 1964 and 1969) he was named Most Valuable Player in the NBA All-Star Game and he played in the game each year he was in the league.

Robertson also was a leader off the court, where he spent a term as president of the NBA Players' Association. In 1970, he filed a class-action suit on the behalf of all the players which, in part, prevented merger talks between the NBA and the ABA without the players' approval. The Robertson suit was resolved in 1976. As a result, the college draft laws were revised, and players gained more freedom to move from team to team.

Following his retirement, Robertson spent a year as a television basketball analyst.

In a poll of sports editors of the nation's 100 largest newspapers, the Academy of Sports selected Robertson on the all-time NBA team. He received 51 per cent of the voting points, only two points behind Wilt Chamberlain.

Bill Russell

If a player's value is measured by the number of championships he helps his team win, then Bill Russell must be considered the greatest player in the history of basketball.

Certainly no one will quarrel with the statement that he is the best defensive player in the game's history. In fact, he completely revolutionized professional basketball and brought back the emphasis on defense. And in doing so, he led the Boston Celtics to 11 world championships in 13 years.

Standing 6-10 and weighing 220 pounds, Russell entered the NBA during the 1956–57 season following a sensational college career at the University of San Francisco where he led his team to a pair of national championships.

He didn't change his winning habits when

Bill Russell set the standards for defense

he turned professional. His forte was rebounding. Until Wilt Chamberlain broke it, Russell held the individual game rebounding record with 51. On two other occasions Russell gathered in 49 rebounds in a game. He led the league in rebounding four different times, and was named Most Valuable Player five times.

Russell never was a great scorer—his lifetime average being 15 points per game. Nor was he an outstanding shooter from the field or foul line. It was on defense where he caused the opposition so much trouble. And he was well-paid for it, reaching the $100,000 class and approaching the $200,000 class.

Too bad the NBA did not keep statistics for shots blocked or broken plays. Russell would have led in both departments. Opposing centers often could not sleep the night before they had to face Russell in the pivot. Some of Russell's greatest duels were against Chamberlain, and Chamberlain provides the final commentary on that rivalry with the statement: "I've been in seven playoffs with Boston where it came down to the final game and Boston won six."

It is also interesting to note that Russell scored at a somewhat accelerated pace (17.2) throughout his playoff career and his rebounding also was better during this period. He will be remembered as one of the game's greatest "money" players. During the 1965–66 playoffs, for example, he grabbed 428 rebounds in 17 games for an average of 25.1 rebounds per game.

The only years during his career when the Celtics did not win the championship were 1957–58 and 1966–67. His finest year, however, may have been 1967–68. The Celtics finished second that year in the season's standings behind Philadelphia. In the opening round of the playoffs, they had a tough time against the Detroit Pistons. Their age, the experts claimed, was beginning to show. They were heavy underdogs when they met the 76ers for the Eastern Division championship.

Down 3 games to 1 in the best-of-seven series, Russell took command and 'led the Celtics to a stunning comeback. He mastered Chamberlain completely in the sev-

enth game, holding him to a mere two shots in the second half.

In 1966, Russell took over as player-coach of the Celtics following Red Auerbach's retirement. When the Celtics failed to win the title that first year, Russell's job was considered in jeopardy. But when Boston won the next season, nobody complained.

Russell's Celtics made it two straight in 1969, and then Bill retired as player and coach. He now had other goals beyond basketball.

For a while he was a TV analyst for NBA games, but then he returned as general manager and coach of the Seattle SuperSonics in 1973. He was there for four years before deciding again to look for other goals.

Dolph Schayes

There once was a team, a wonderful team, that night after night gave the simplest, most exciting display of pure basketball ever seen in the National Basketball Association. It wasn't a big team and it did not have a roster full of All-Americans or towering frontcourtmen. What the Syracuse Nationals did have was a distinct spirit and a forward named Dolph Schayes.

Schayes personified the spirit of the Nats. Each time he scored a goal, he would run to the opposite end of the court, fist clenched triumphantly above his head. From the start, when he made Rookie of the Year in 1949, Schayes was one of the league's class players. When ne retired at the end of the 1964 season, he was the all-time leading scorer with 19,240 points (18.2). He has since been passed, but it hardly matters because Schayes' place in NBA history is secure. Schayes was 6-8 and a forward but he was such a versatile performer that he was one of the last of the deadly two-hand set shooters. This helped make him great. He could score from the outside as easily as he could drive underneath for a layup.

One got a complete picture of Dolph Schayes the competitor when listening to him speak following his 29th birthday: "I

Dolph Schayes: wherever the action was

Schayes' hustle has become legendary when people speak of and write about NBA history. He played with broken wrists, he played with other injuries, and he played when he was sick because he had to—for all those years—carry the burden of the Syracuse offense. Watching the Nationals play was a treat. They believed in the team game and patterned, but exciting, offense. And the most exciting, most dramatic individual on that team was Dolph Schayes.

Bill Sharman

When listing basketball's best shooters, Bill Sharman must be included. "Sharman," said Red Auerbach, his coach with the Celtics, "is the greatest shooter from the backcourt the game has ever seen." Eddie Gottlieb, the former owner and coach of the Philadelphia Warriors, watched Sharman destroy his team on many a cold winter night. "Sharman," he said, "must be listed with the all-time greats if only for his shooting ability."

Sharman and Bob Cousy formed the most potent backcourt in the history of basketball. If the defense let up on Sharman, Cousy would explode. If the defense was tough on Cousy, Bill Sharman—with his sure, deft touch—would start pumping those one-handers which made him famous. Sharman played 11 seasons for the Celtics, joining them for the 1950–51 season and retiring at the end of the 1961 season. He ranks among the top scorers in league history with 12,665 points in 710 games, a 17.8 average.

Oddly, Sharman never was considered an exceptional "long" shooter. His best scoring range was from 20 feet. Rarely did he attempt a shot from beyond that distance. Inside it, he was a sure bet. His career field-goal percentage was .423, making him the best shooting guard of his time. Writer Dick Kaplan once said: "What made Sharman's shooting remarkable was its purity. He shot with almost robot-like precision, his style so polished and precise that it seemed like an illustration for a book on how to play basketball." Appropriately, Sharman did write

feel I can still improve. Where? Defensively for one thing. And you can always become a better shot, can't you?"

Schayes was a rugged rebounder, winning the individual title in 1951 and finishing his career in fourth place on the all-time list. He was not afraid to become involved in the rough play under the boards and long held the NBA record for most personal fouls in a career. He also held, however, the record for most free throws made (6,979) which stood until 1972 and that tells even more about Schayes' competitive nature. He was a tireless performer, too, playing 29,800 minutes in 1,059 games.

It was hard to move Schayes out of the lineup. In 1952, he broke his right wrist. A cast was applied and Schayes continued to play. "The cast," he said in a typical Schayes statement, "made me work on my left-handed shots, which soon improved. Later, when the left wrist was cracked, my right-handed shots improved."

Though the Nats won only one world's championship during Schayes' career, they never missed the playoffs and Schayes holds the league record for most playoff series (15). During that time he played in 103 playoff games.

and can discuss it for hours. "I aim for the back rim," he said. "I've found that most shots are missed 'short' because players get tired. Their shots start bouncing off that front rim. But if you shoot for the back rim, you get three factors working for you. First, most players shoot with backspin. If a backspinning ball hits the front rim, it skids away. But if it hits the back rim, the 'English' practically forces it into the basket. Second, if you overshoot and miss the back rim, you still have a chance for a cheap basket. The ball can bank in off the backboard. Third, the rim of the basket has an eighteen-inch diameter; the basketball about nine inches. So if you shoot for the rear rim, you have a nine-inch margin for error."

Sound like a science? It is. And Bill Sharman earned his doctorate.

Bill Sharman was sharpest-shooting Celtic

a book on shooting, titled *Sharman on Shooting*.

Sharman and Cousy were with the Celtics when the Boston team was ripping off championship after championship. Though Cousy received most of the publicity, the NBA players recognized Sharman's abilities and voted him to the All-Star first team four different years. Sharman was recognized as the game's finest foul shooter and is the all-time league leader in this department. During his career, he made 3,143 of 3,557 attempts for an .883 percentage. He won the foul shooting title seven different times.

A great natural athlete from the University of Southern California, Sharman almost had a major league baseball career. He was an outfielder in the Brooklyn Dodgers' system and was with the team at the end of the 1951 season when Bobby Thomson of the New York Giants hit the celebrated home run to give the Giants the pennant.

Luckily for Auerbach and the Celtics, Sharman chose basketball. There will be few to match him. He made shooting an art

Jack Twyman

Red Auerbach, as Boston coach, had the best description of Jack Twyman. "Show him a little daylight," Auerbach said, "and it's up and in." Twyman was one of the great shooting forwards in the NBA and ranked eighth in the all-time scoring derby with a 19.2 average and 15,840 points during an 11-year career with the Rochester Royals and then the Cincinnati Royals.

From the very start, Twyman, an All-American at the University of Cincinnati, impressed people around the NBA. Bobby Wanzer, his coach at Rochester where he broke in, claimed that "Twyman has more determination than any player I've seen. He's the kind of guy who can key himself into things."

One can understand Twyman's dedication to shooting on hearing him explain his workout routine during the off-season. "I usually work out four days a week and during every session I shoot 100 fouls, 200 jump shots and between 100 and 150 set shots." He had some fantastic scoring years for the Royals but he never won a scoring championship. In 1958–59 he finished second to Bob Pettit in the scoring race and the following season, his best as a scorer, he averaged 31.2 points and finished second to Wilt Chamberlain.

Jack Twyman (31) will be remembered for more than his playing

For a cornerman, Twyman had some outstanding shooting percentages. In 1960–61, he had a .488 average, in 1961–62 it was .479 and the year after that .480. "You can feel it when you're hot," Twyman used to say. "You feel like everything you throw up there at the basket is going to drop through." In the case of Twyman, the shots fell through.

When Twyman retired he ranked in the top ten of the all-time list in number of games played (823), most field goals scored (6,237) and most minutes played (26,055). Jack couldn't stay away from the court, however, and for several seasons he did color commentary on nationally televised NBA games.

But Twyman will be remembered for more than just his basketball talent. He was one of the great humanitarians—not just in sports—but in all walks of life. When his teammate Maurice Stokes was paralyzed with a brain ailment at the end of the 1958 season, Twyman became his legal guardian and raised funds for Maurice's rehabilitation. Each year Twyman assembled pro stars at Kutsher's Country Club in Monticello, N.Y., to play a benefit game for the

Maurice Stokes Fund. But Twyman's concern and dedication were not enough. Stokes died of a heart attack in 1970.

Jerry West

Fred Schaus, who coached Jerry West at West Virginia University and later with the Los Angeles Lakers, has nothing but admiration for one of the finest guards ever to set foot on a basketball court.

Said Schaus: "If you sat down to build a 6-foot-3-inch basketball player you would come up with a Jerry West. He is the man that has everything—a fine shooting touch, speed, quickness, all the physical assets, including a tremendous dedication to the game." It was the perfect summation, and perhaps the last part of Schaus' statement was the most important. Jerry West's dedication made him great. Throughout his college career he had been compared with Oscar Robertson. Both broke into the NBA together. Oscar, however, got off to a sensational professional start, averaging 30.5 points per game as a rookie. West didn't do nearly as well, averaging 17.6. Immediately the doubters were saying "I told you so."

There was a lot of pressure, but the next season, Jerry West—through sheer determination—wound up with a 30.8 scoring average and from that point he was considered to be on the same level with Robertson. West is the fourth-leading scorer in NBA history, a goal achieved despite the fact that he missed many games due to injuries.

"Jerry," said former Laker general manager Lou Mohs, "gets hurt a lot because he plays recklessly and doesn't spare himself." One of the oddities of sport is that West has suffered a broken nose eight times during his career, which says something for his gameness and willingness to mix it up under the boards despite his lack of size.

He has had some fine scoring seasons including 31.0 in 1964–65 and a career high of 31.4 during the 1965–66 season. He has had some fantastic playoff series including the 1964–65 season when he averaged 40.6 points for 11 games. The next season he averaged 34.2 in 14 games. Red Auerbach,

the Boston Celtics coach, often became exasperated with West's performances against his teams. "You really can't stop West," Auerbach said. "You can try in a number of ways: play him close, loose, keep him away from the ball. Still he'll find a way to get his 25 to 30 points."

West's most effective weapon was a graceful jump shot from any spot on the floor. He was also an extremely good driver and an excellent playmaker. He was a perennial all-league selection and an annual performer in the All-Star Game. The high point of his career, by his own evaluation, came in 1972 when, after 11 years of frustration, the Lakers finally won an NBA championship. It was a fitting climax to a season in which West spearheaded a record 33-game winning streak, led the league in assists and earned Most Valuable Player honors in the All-Star Game.

West retired following the 1974 season as age and nagging injuries finally took their toll. He also did not have the best relationship possible with the Lakers' owner, Jack Kent Cooke. Still, these adversaries were to be paired again at the start of the 1976 season. West became coach of the Lakers then, and in his first year he led them to the Pacific Division title.

Jerry West: greatest in the clutch

17

The Teams

All-Time Club Records

(National Basketball Association teams unless otherwise noted)

ANAHEIM AMIGOS (ABA)

See Utah Stars, 1967-68

Season	Coach	W.	L.
ANDERSON PACKERS			
1949-50	Howard Schultz (21-14)		
	Ike Duffey (1-2)		
	Doxie Moore (15-11)	37	27
	Totals	37	27

ATLANTA HAWKS

Season	Coach	W.	L.
1949-50	Roger Potter (1-6)		
	Arnold Auerbach (28-29)	29	35
1950-51	Dave McMillan (9-14)		
	John Logan (2-1)		
	Marko Todorovich (14-28)	25	43
1951-52*	Doxie Moore	17	49
1952-53	Andrew Levane	27	44
1953-54	Andrew Levane (11-35)		
	William Holzman (10-16)	21	51
1954-55	William Holzman	26	46
1955-56**	William Holzman	33	39
1956-57	William Holzman (14-19)		
	Slater Martin (5-3)		
	Alex Hannum (15-16)	34	38
1957-58	Alex Hannum	41	31
1958-59	Andy Phillip (6-4)		
	Ed Macauley (43-19)	49	23
1959-60	Ed Macauley	46	29
1960-61	Paul Seymour	51	28
1961-62	Paul Seymour (5-9)		
	Andrew Levane (20-40)		
	Bob Pettit (4-2)	29	51

Season	Coach	W.	L.
1962-63	Harry Gallatin	48	32
1963-64	Harry Gallatin	46	34
1964-65	Harry Gallatin (17-16)		
	Richie Guerin (28-19)	45	35
1965-66	Richie Guerin	36	44
1966-67	Richie Guerin	39	42
1967-68	Richie Guerin	56	26
1968-69***	Richie Guerin	48	34
1969-70	Richie Guerin	48	34
1970-71	Richie Guerin	36	46
1971-72	Richie Guerin	36	46
1972-73	Lowell Fitzsimmons	46	36
1973-74	Lowell Fitzsimmons	35	47
1974-75	Lowell Fitzsimmons	31	51
1975-76	Lowell Fitzsimmons (28-46)		
	Gene Tormohlen (1-7)	29	53
1976-77	Hubert Brown	31	51
1977-78	Hubert Brown	41	41
1978-79	Hubert Brown	46	36
	Totals	1125	1195

*Team moved from Tri-Cities to Milwaukee
**Team moved from Milwaukee to St. Louis
***Team moved from St. Louis to Atlanta

BALTIMORE BULLETS

Season	Coach	W.	L.
1947-48	Buddy Jeannette	28	20
1948-49	Buddy Jeannette	29	31
1949-50	Buddy Jeannette	25	43
1950-51	Buddy Jeannette (14-23)		
	Walt Budko (10-19)	24	42
1951-52	Fred Scolari (12-27)		
	John Reiser (8-19)	20	46
1952-53	John Reiser (0-3)		
	Clair Bee (16-51)	16	54
1953-54	Clair Bee	16	56
1954-55*	Clair Bee (2-9)		
	Al Barthelme (1-2)	3	11
	Totals	161	303

* Team disbanded Nov. 27, 1954

BALTIMORE BULLETS
See Washington Bullets, 1972-73

BOSTON CELTICS

Season	Coach	W.	L.
1946-47	John Russell	22	38
1947-48	John Russell	20	28
1948-49	Alvin Julian	25	35
1949-50	Alvin Julian	22	46
1950-51	Arnold Auerbach	39	30
1951-52	Arnold Auerbach	39	27
1952-53	Arnold Auerbach	46	25
1953-54	Arnold Auerbach	42	30
1954-55	Arnold Auerbach	36	36
1955-56	Arnold Auerbach	39	33
1956-57	Arnold Auerbach	44	28
1957-58	Arnold Auerbach	49	23
1958-59	Arnold Auerbach	52	20
1959-60	Arnold Auerbach	59	16
1960-61	Arnold Auerbach	57	22
1961-62	Arnold Auerbach	60	20
1962-63	Arnold Auerbach	58	22
1963-64	Arnold Auerbach	59	21
1964-65	Arnold Auerbach	62	18
1965-66	Arnold Auerbach	54	26
1966-67	Bill Russell	60	21
1967-68	Bill Russell	54	28
1968-69	Bill Russell	48	34
1969-70	Tom Heinsohn	34	48
1970-71	Tom Heinsohn	44	38
1971-72	Tom Heinsohn	56	26
1972-73	Tom Heinsohn	68	14
1973-74	Tom Heinsohn	56	26
1974-75	Tom Heinsohn	60	22
1975-76	Tom Heinsohn	54	28
1976-77	Tom Heinsohn	44	38
1977-78	Tom Heinsohn (11-23)		
	Tom Sanders (21-27)	32	50
1978-79	Tom Sanders (2-12)		
	Dave Cowens (27-41)	29	53
	Totals	1523	970

BUFFALO BRAVES
See San Diego Clippers, 1978-79

CAPITAL BULLETS
See Washington Bullets, 1973-74

CAROLINA COUGARS (ABA)
See St. Louis Spirits, 1969-74

CHICAGO BULLS

Season	Coach	W.	L.
1966-67	John Kerr	33	48
1967-68	John Kerr	29	53
1968-69	Dick Motta	33	49
1969-70	Dick Motta	39	43
1970-71	Dick Motta	51	31
1971-72	Dick Motta	57	25
1972-73	Dick Motta	51	31
1973-74	Dick Motta	54	28
1974-75	Dick Motta	47	35
1975-76	Dick Motta	24	58
1976-77	Ed Badger	44	38
1977-78	Ed Badger	40	42
1978-79	Larry Costello (20-36)		
	Scotty Robertson (11-15)	31	51
	Totals	533	532

CHICAGO PACKERS
See Baltimore Bullets, 1961-62

CHICAGO STAGS

Season	Coach	W.	L.
1946-47	Harold Olsen	39	22
1947-48	Harold Olsen	28	20
1948-49	Harold Olsen (28-21)		
	Philip Brownstein (10-1)	38	22
1949-50	Philip Brownstein	40	28
	Totals	145	92

CHICAGO ZEPHYRS
See Baltimore Bullets, 1962-63

CINCINNATI ROYALS
See Kansas City Kings, 1971-72

CLEVELAND CAVALIERS

Season	Coach	W.	L.
1970-71	Bill Fitch	15	67
1971-72	Bill Fitch	23	59
1972-73	Bill Fitch	32	50
1973-74	Bill Fitch	29	53
1974-75	Bill Fitch	40	42
1975-76	Bill Fitch	49	33
1976-77	Bill Fitch	43	39
1977-78	Bill Fitch	43	39
1978-79	Bill Fitch	30	52
	Totals	304	434

CLEVELAND REBELS

Season	Coach	W.	L.
1946-47	Dutch Dehnert (17-20)		
	Roy Clifford (13-10)	30	30
	Totals	30	30

DALLAS CHAPARRALS (ABA)
See San Antonio Spurs, 1972-73

DENVER ROCKETS (ABA)
See Denver Nuggets 1974-75

DENVER NUGGETS

Season	Coach	W.	L.
1949-50	James Darden	11	51

DENVER NUGGETS (ABA-NBA)

Season	Coach	W.	L.
1967-68	Bob Bass	45	33
1968-69	Bob Bass	44	34
1969-70	John McLendon (9-19)		
	Joe Belmont (42-14)	51	33
1970-71	Joe Belmont (3-10)		
	Stan Albeck (27-44)	30	54
1971-72	Alex Hannum	34	50
1972-73	Alex Hannum	47	37
1973-74	Alex Hannum	37	47
1974-75*	Larry Brown	65	19
1975-76	Larry Brown	60	24
1976-77**	Larry Brown	50	32
1977-78	Larry Brown	48	34
1978-79	Larry Brown (28-25)		
	Donny Walsh (19-10)	47	35
	Totals	558	432

*Changed name from Rockets to Nuggets
**Joined NBA

DETROIT FALCONS

Season	Coach	W.	L.
1946-47	Glenn Curtis (12-22)		
	Philip Sachs (8-18)	20	40
	Totals	20	40

Season	Coach	W.	L.
DETROIT PISTONS			
1948-49	Carl Bennett (0-6)		
	Paul Armstrong (22-32)	22	38
1949-50	Murray Mendenhall	40	28
1950-51	Murray Mendenhall	32	36
1951-52	Paul Birch	29	37
1952-53	Paul Birch	36	33
1953-54	Paul Birch	40	32
1954-55	Charles Eckman	43	29
1955-56	Charles Eckman	37	35
1956-57	Charles Eckman	34	38
1957-58*	Charles Eckman (9-16)		
	Ephraim Rocha (24-23)	33	39
1958-59	Ephraim Rocha	28	44
1959-60	Ephraim Rocha (13-21)		
	Dick McGuire (17-24)	30	45
1960-61	Dick McGuire	34	45
1961-62	Dick McGuire	37	43
1962-63	Dick McGuire	34	46
1963-64	Charles Wolf	23	57
1964-65	Charles Wolf (2-9)		
	Dave DeBusschere (29-40)	31	49
1965-66	Dave DeBusschere	22	58
1966-67	Dave DeBusschere (28-45)		
	Donnis Butcher (2-6)	30	51
1967-68	Donnis Butcher	40	42
1968-69	Donnis Butcher (10-12)		
	Paul Seymour (22-38)	32	50
1969-70	Bill van Breda Kolff	31	51
1970-71	Bill van Breda Kolff	45	37
1971-72	Bill van Breda Kolff (6-6)		
	Terry Dischinger (0-2)		
	Earl Lloyd (20-50)	26	58
1972-73	Earl Lloyd (2-5)		
	Ray Scott (38-37)	40	42
1973-74	Ray Scott	52	30
1974-75	Ray Scott	40	42
1975-76	Ray Scott (17-25)		
	Herb Brown (19-21)	36	46
1976-77	Herb Brown	44	38
1977-78	Herb Brown (9-15)		
	Bob Kauffman (29-29)	38	44
1978-79	Dick Vitale	30	52
	Totals	1069	1313

*Team moved from Fort Wayne to Detroit

FORT WAYNE PISTONS

See Detroit Pistons, 1957-58

GOLDEN STATE WARRIORS

Season	Coach	W.	L.
1946-47	Edward Gottlieb	35	25
1947-48	Edward Gottlieb	27	21
1948-49	Edward Gottlieb	28	32
1949-50	Edward Gottlieb	26	42
1950-51	Edward Gottlieb	40	26
1951-52	Edward Gottlieb	33	33
1952-53	Edward Gottlieb	12	57
1953-54	Edward Gottlieb	29	43
1954-55	Edward Gottlieb	33	39
1955-56	George Senesky	45	27
1956-57	George Senesky	37	35
1957-58	George Senesky	37	35
1958-59	Al Cervi	32	40
1959-60	Neil Johnston	49	26
1960-61	Neil Johnston	46	33
1961-62	Frank McGuire	49	31
1962-63*	Bob Feerick	31	49
1963-64	Alex Hannum	48	32
1964-65	Alex Hannum	17	63
1965-66	Alex Hannum	35	45
1966-67	Bill Sharman	44	37
1967-68	Bill Sharman	43	39
1968-69	George Lee	41	41
1969-70	George Lee (22-30)		
	Al Attles (8-22)	30	52
1970-71	Al Attles	41	41
1971-72**	Al Attles	51	31
1972-73	Al Attles	51	31
1973-74	Al Attles	44	38
1974-75	Al Attles	48	34
1975-76	Al Attles	59	23
1976-77	Al Attles	46	36
1977-78	Al Attles	43	39
1978-79	Al Attles	38	44
	Totals	1264	1224

*Team moved from Philadelphia to San Francisco
**Became Golden State Warriors

HOUSTON MAVERICKS (ABA)

See St. Louis Spirits, 1967-69

HOUSTON ROCKETS

Season	Coach	W.	L.
1967-68	Jack McMahon	15	67
1968-69	Jack McMahon	37	45
1969-70	Jack McMahon (9-17)		
	Alex Hannum (18-38)	27	55
1970-71	Alex Hannum	40	42
1971-72*	Tex Winter	34	48
1972-73	Tex Winter (17-30)		
	John Egan (16-19)	33	49
1973-74	John Egan	32	50
1974-75	John Egan	41	41
1975-76	John Egan	40	42
1976-77	Tom Nissalke	49	33
1977-78	Tom Nissalke	28	54
1978-79	Tom Nissalke	47	35
	Totals	423	561

*Team moved from San Diego to Houston

INDIANA PACERS (ABA-NBA)

Season	Coach	W.	L.
1967-68	Larry Staverman	38	40
1968-69	Larry Staverman (2-7)		
	Bob Leonard (42-27)	44	34
1969-70	Bob Leonard	59	25
1970-71	Bob Leonard	58	26
1971-72	Bob Leonard	47	37
1972-73	Bob Leonard	51	33
1973-74	Bob Leonard	46	38
1974-75	Bob Leonard	45	39
1975-76	Bob Leonard	39	45
1976-77*	Bob Leonard	36	46
1977-78	Bob Leonard	31	51
1978-79	Bob Leonard	38	44
	Totals	532	458

*Joined NBA

INDIANAPOLIS JETS

Season	Coach	W.	L.
1948-49	Bruce Hale (4-13)		
	Burl Friddle (14-29)	18	42

INDIANAPOLIS OLYMPIANS

Season	Coach	W.	L.
1949-50	Clifford Barker	39	25
1950-51	Clifford Barker (24-32)		
	Wallace Jones (7-5)	31	37
1951-52	Herman Schaefer	34	32
1952-53	Herman Schaefer	28	43
	Totals	132	137

KANSAS CITY KINGS

Season	Coach	W.	L.
1948-49	Les Harrison	45	15
1949-50	Les Harrison	51	17
1950-51	Les Harrison	41	27
1951-52	Les Harrison	41	25
1952-53	Les Harrison	44	26

Season	Coach	W.	L.
1953-54	Les Harrison	44	28
1954-55	Les Harrison	29	43
1955-56	Bob Wanzer	31	41
1956-57	Bob Wanzer	31	41
1957-58*	Bob Wanzer	33	39
1958-59	Bob Wanzer (3-15)		
	Tom Marshall (16-38)	19	53
1959-60	Tom Marshall	19	56
1960-61	Charles Wolf	33	46
1961-62	Charles Wolf	43	37
1962-63	Charles Wolf	42	38
1963-64	Jack McMahon	55	25
1964-65	Jack McMahon	48	32
1965-66	Jack McMahon	45	35
1966-67	Jack McMahon	39	42
1967-68	Ed Jucker	39	43
1968-69	Ed Jucker	41	41
1969-70	Bob Cousy	36	46
1970-71	Bob Cousy	33	49
1971-72**	Bob Cousy	30	52
1972-73	Bob Cousy	36	46
1973-74	Bob Cousy (6-14)		
	Draff Young (0-4)		
	Phil Johnson (27-31)	33	49
1974-75	Phil Johnson	44	38
1975-76	Phil Johnson	31	51
1976-77	Phil Johnson	40	42
1977-78	Phil Johnson (13-24)		
	Larry Staverman (18-27)	31	51
1978-79	Lowell Fitzsimmons	48	34
	Totals	**1135**	**1166**

*Team moved from Rochester to Cincinnati
**Team moved from Cincinnati to Kansas City at end of season and changed name to Kings

KENTUCKY COLONELS (ABA)

Season	Coach	W.	L.
1967-68	John Givens (5-12)		
	Gene Rhodes (31-30)	36	42
1968-69	Gene Rhodes	42	36
1969-70	Gene Rhodes	45	39
1970-71	Gene Rhodes (10-5)		
	Alex Groza (2-0)		
	Frank Ramsey (32-35)	44	40
1971-72	Joe Mullaney	68	16
1972-73	Joe Mullaney	56	28
1973-74	Babe McCarthy	53	31
1974-75	Hubert Brown	58	26
1975-76*	Hubert Brown	46	38
	Totals	**448**	**296**

*Franchise folded, 1976

LOS ANGELES LAKERS

Season	Coach	W.	L.
1948-49	John Kundla	44	16
1949-50	John Kundla	51	17
1950-51	John Kundla	44	24
1951-52	John Kundla	46	26
1952-53	John Kundla	48	22
1953-54	John Kundla	40	26
1954-55	John Kundla	40	32
1955-56	John Kundla	33	39
1956-57	John Kundla	34	38
1957-58	George Mikan (9-30)		
	John Kundla (10-23)	19	53
1958-59	John Kundla	33	39
1959-60	John Castellani (11-25)		
	Jim Pollard (14-25)	25	50
1960-61*	Fred Schaus	36	43
1961-62	Fred Schaus	54	26
1962-63	Fred Schaus	53	27
1963-64	Fred Schaus	42	38
1964-65	Fred Schaus	49	31
1965-66	Fred Schaus	45	35
1966-67	Fred Schaus	36	45
1967-68	Bill van Breda Kolff	52	30

Season	Coach	W.	L.
1968-69	Bill van Breda Kolff	55	27
1969-70	Joe Mullaney	46	36
1970-71	Joe Mullaney	48	34
1971-72	Bill Sharman	69	13
1972-73	Bill Sharman	60	22
1973-74	Bill Sharman	47	35
1974-75	Bill Sharman	30	52
1975-76	Bill Sharman	40	42
1976-77	Jerry West	53	29
1977-78	Jerry West	45	37
1978-79	Jerry West	47	35
	Totals	**1364**	**1019**

*Team moved from Minneapolis to Los Angeles

LOS ANGELES STARS (ABA)
See Utah Stars, 1968-69

MEMPHIS PROS (ABA)
See Memphis Sounds, 1970-71

MEMPHIS SOUNDS (ABA)

Season	Coach	W.	L.
1967-68	James (Babe) McCarthy	48	30
1968-69	James (Babe) McCarthy	46	32
1969-70	James (Babe) McCarthy	42	42
1970-71*	James (Babe) McCarthy	41	43
1971-72	James (Babe) McCarthy	26	58
1972-73**	Bob Bass	24	60
1973-74	Butch van Breda Kolff	21	63
1974-75***	Joe Mullaney	27	57
	Totals	**275**	**385**

*Team moved from New Orleans to Memphis changed name to Pros
**Changed name to Tams
***Changed name to Sounds; folded, 1975

MEMPHIS TAMS (ABA)
See Memphis Sounds, 1972-73

MIAMI FLORIDIANS (ABA)

Season	Coach	W.	L.
1967-68	Jim Pollard	50	28
1968-69*	Jim Pollard	43	35
1969-70	Jim Pollard (5-15)		
	Hal Blitman (18-46)	23	61
1970-71	Hal Blitman (18-30)		
	Bob Bass (19-17)	37	47
1971-72**	Bob Bass	36	48
	Totals	**189**	**219**

*Team moved from Minnesota to Miami, changed name to Floridians
**Team folded, 1972

MILWAUKEE HAWKS
See Atlanta Hawks, 1951-52

MILWAUKEE BUCKS

Season	Coach	W.	L.
1968-69	Larry Costello	27	55
1969-70	Larry Costello	56	26
1970-71	Larry Costello	66	16
1971-72	Larry Costello	63	19
1972-73	Larry Costello	60	22
1973-74	Larry Costello	59	23
1974-75	Larry Costello	38	44
1975-76	Larry Costello	38	44
1976-77	Larry Costello (3-15)		
	Don Nelson (27-37)	30	52
1977-78	Don Nelson	44	38
1978-79	Don Nelson	38	44
	Totals	**519**	**383**

Season	Coach	W.	L.

MINNEAPOLIS LAKERS
See Los Angeles Lakers, 1960-61

MINNESOTA MUSKIES (ABA)
See Miami Floridians, 1968-69

MINNESOTA PIPERS (ABA)
See Pittsburgh Condors, 1968-69

NEW JERSEY AMERICANS (ABA)
See New York Nets, 1967-68

NEW ORLEANS BUCCANEERS (ABA)
See Memphis Sounds, 1970-71

NEW ORLEANS JAZZ

Season	Coach	W.	L.
1974-75	Scotty Robertson (1-15)		
	Bill van Breda Kolff (22-44)	23	59
1975-76	Bill van Breda Kolff	38	44
1976-77	Bill van Breda Kolff (14-12)		
	Elgin Baylor (21-35)	35	47
1977-78	Elgin Baylor	39	43
1978-79	Elgin Baylor	26	56
	Totals	161	249

NEW YORK KNICKERBOCKERS

Season	Coach	W.	L.
1946-47	Neil Cohalan	33	27
1947-48	Joe Lapchick	26	22
1948-49	Joe Lapchick	32	28
1949-50	Joe Lapchick	40	28
1950-51	Joe Lapchick	36	30
1951-52	Joe Lapchick	37	29
1952-53	Joe Lapchick	47	23
1953-54	Joe Lapchick	44	28
1954-55	Joe Lapchick	34	38
1955-56	Joe Lapchick (26-25)		
	Vince Boryla (9-12)	35	37
1956-57	Vince Boryla	36	36
1957-58	Vince Boryla	35	37
1958-59	Andrew Levane	40	32
1959-60	Andrew Levane (8-19)		
	Carl Braun (19-29)	27	48
1960-61	Carl Braun	21	58
1961-62	Eddie Donovan	29	51
1962-63	Eddie Donovan	21	59
1963-64	Eddie Donovan	22	58
1964-65	Eddie Donovan (12-26)		
	Harry Gallatin (19-23)	31	49
1965-66	Harry Gallatin (6-15)		
	Dick McGuire (24-35)	30	50
1966-67	Dick McGuire	36	45
1967-68	Dick McGuire (15-22)		
	William Holzman (28-17)	43	39
1968-69	William Holzman	54	28
1969-70	William Holzman	60	22
1970-71	William Holzman	52	30
1971-72	William Holzman	48	34
1972-73	William Holzman	57	25
1973-74	William Holzman	49	33
1974-75	William Holzman	40	42
1975-76	William Holzman	38	44
1976-77	William Holzman	40	42
1977-78	Willis Reed	43	39
1978-79	Willis Reed (6-8)		
	William Holzman (25-43)	31	51
	Totals	1121	1164

NEW JERSEY NETS (ABA-NBA)

Season	Coach	W.	L.
1967-68	Max Zaslofsky	36	42
1968-69*	Max Zaslofsky	17	61
1969-70	York Larese	39	45
1970-71	Lou Carnesecca	40	44
1971-72	Lou Carnesecca	44	40
1972-73	Lou Carnesecca	30	54
1973-74	Kevin Loughery	55	29
1974-75	Kevin Loughery	58	26
1975-76	Kevin Loughery	55	29
1976-77**	Kevin Loughery	22	60
1977-78	Kevin Loughery	24	58
1978-79	Kevin Loughery	37	45
	Totals	457	533

*Moved from New Jersey to New York, changed name to Nets
**Joined NBA, changed name from New York to New Jersey Nets

OAKLAND OAKS (ABA)
See Virginia Squires, 1968-69

PHILADELPHIA WARRIORS
See Golden State Warriors, 1962-63

PHILADELPHIA 76ERS

Season	Coach	W.	L.
1949-50	Al Cervi	51	13
1950-51	Al Cervi	32	34
1951-52	Al Cervi	40	26
1952-53	Al Cervi	47	24
1953-54	Al Cervi	42	30
1954-55	Al Cervi	43	29
1955-56	Al Cervi	35	37
1956-57	Al Cervi (4-8)		
	Paul Seymour (34-26)	38	34
1957-58	Paul Seymour	41	31
1958-59	Paul Seymour	35	37
1959-60	Paul Seymour	45	30
1960-61	Alex Hannum	38	41
1961-62	Alex Hannum	41	39
1962-63	Alex Hannum	48	32
1963-64*	Dolph Schayes	34	46
1964-65	Dolph Schayes	40	40
1965-66	Dolph Schayes	55	25
1966-67	Alex Hannum	68	13
1967-68	Alex Hannum	62	20
1968-69	Jack Ramsay	55	27
1969-70	Jack Ramsay	42	40
1970-71	Jack Ramsay	47	35
1971-72	Jack Ramsay	30	52
1972-73	Roy Rubin (4-47)		
	Kevin Loughery (5-26)	9	73
1973-74	Gene Shue	25	57
1974-75	Gene Shue	34	48
1975-76	Gene Shue	46	36
1976-77	Gene Shue	50	32
1977-78	Gene Shue (2-4)		
	Billy Cunningham (53-23)	55	27
1978-79	Billy Cunningham	47	35
	Totals	1214	1046

*Team moved from Syracuse to Philadelphia, changed name to 76ers

PHOENIX SUNS

Season	Coach	W.	L.
1968-69	Johnny Kerr	16	66
1969-70	Johnny Kerr (15-23)		
	Jerry Colangelo (24-20)	39	43
1970-71	Lowell Fitzsimmons	48	34
1971-72	Lowell Fitzsimmons	49	33
1972-73	Bill van Breda Kolff (3-4)		
	Jerry Colangelo (35-40)	38	44
1973-74	John MacLeod	30	52
1974-75	John MacLeod	32	50
1975-76	John MacLeod	42	40
1976-77	John MacLeod	34	48

Season	Coach	W.	L.
1977-78	John MacLeod	49	33
1978-79	John MacLeod	50	32
	Totals	427	475

PITTSBURGH CONDORS (ABA)

Season	Coach	W.	L.
1967-68*	Vince Cazetta	54	24
1968-69**	Jim Harding (20-12)		
	Vern Mikkelsen (6-7)		
	Verl Young (10-23)	36	42
1969-70***	John Clark (14-25)		
	Buddy Jeannette (15-30)	29	55
1970-71****	Jack McMahon	36	48
1971-72*****	Jack McMahon (4-6)		
	Mark Binstein (21-53)	25	59
	Totals	180	228

*Played in Pittsburgh as Pittsburgh Pipers
**Team moved from Pittsburgh to Minnesota
***Team returned from Minnesota to Pittsburgh
****Changed name from Pipers to Condors
*****Team folded, 1972

PITTSBURGH IRONMEN

Season	Coach	W.	L.
1946-47	Paul Birch	15	45

PITTSBURGH PIPERS (ABA)

See Pittsburgh Condors, 1967-68, 1969-70

PORTLAND TRAIL BLAZERS

Season	Coach	W.	L.
1970-71	Rolland Todd	29	53
1971-72	Rolland Todd (12-44)		
	Stu Inman (6-20)	18	64
1972-73	Jack McCloskey	21	61
1973-74	Jack McCloskey	27	55
1974-75	Lenny Wilkens	38	44
1975-76	Lenny Wilkens	37	45
1976-77	Jack Ramsay	49	33
1977-78	Jack Ramsay	58	24
1978-79	Jack Ramsay	45	37
	Totals	322	416

PROVIDENCE STEAMROLLERS

Season	Coach	W.	L.
1946-47	Robert Morris	28	32
1947-48	Albert Soar (2-17)		
	Nat Hickey (4-25)	6	42
1948-49	Ken Loeffler	12	48
	Totals	46	122

ST. LOUIS BOMBERS

Season	Coach	W.	L.
1946-47	Ken Loeffler	38	33
1947-48	Ken Loeffler	29	19
1948-49	Grady Lewis	29	31
1949-50	Grady Lewis	26	42
	Totals	122	125

ST. LOUIS HAWKS

See Atlanta Hawks, 1967-68

ST. LOUIS SPIRITS (ABA)

Season	Coach	W.	L.
1967-68	Slater Martin	29	49
1968-69	Slater Martin (3-9)		
	Jim Weaver (20-46)	23	55
1969-70*	Bones McKinney	42	42
1970-71	Bones McKinney (17-25)		
	Jerry Steele (17-25)	34	50
1971-72	Tom Meschery	35	49
1972-73	Larry Brown	57	27
1973-74**	Larry Brown	47	37

Season	Coach	W.	L.
1974-75	Bob MacKinnon	32	52
1975-76***	Rod Thorn	35	49
	Totals	334	410

*Team moved from Houston to Carolina, changed name to Cougers
**Team moved from Carolina to St. Louis, changed name to Spirits
***Team folded in 1976

SAN ANTONIO SPURS (ABA-NBA)

Season	Coach	W.	L.
1967-68	Cliff Hagan	46	32
1968-69	Cliff Hagan	41	37
1969-70	Cliff Hagan (22-21)		
	Max Williams (23-18)	45	39
1970-71*	Max Williams (5-14)		
	Bill Blakely (25-40)	30	54
1971-72	Tom Nissalke	42	42
1972-73	Babe McCarthy (24-48)		
	Dave Brown (4-8)	28	56
1973-74**	Tom Nissalke	45	39
1974-75	Tom Nissalke (13-10)		
	Bob Bass (38-23)	51	33
1975-76	Bob Bass	50	34
1976-77***	Doug Moe	44	38
1977-78	Doug Moe	52	30
1978-79	Doug Moe	48	34
	Totals	518	468

*Played season as Texas Chaparrals
**Francise moved to San Antonio, changed name to Spurs
***Joined NBA

SAN DIEGO CLIPPERS

Season	Coach	W.	L.
1970-71	Dolph Schayes	22	60
1971-72	Dolph Schayes (0-1)		
	John McCarthy (22-59)	22	60
1972-73	Jack Ramsay	21	61
1973-74	Jack Ramsay	42	40
1974-75	Jack Ramsay	49	33
1975-76	Jack Ramsay	46	36
1976-77	Tates Locke (16-30)		
	Bob MacKinnon (3-4)		
	Joe Mullaney (11-18)	30	52
1977-78	Cotton Fitzsimmons	27	55
1978-79	Gene Shue	43	39
	Totals	302	436

SAN DIEGO CONQUISTADORS (ABA)

Season	Coach	W.	L.
1972-73	K. C. Jones	30	54
1973-74	Wilt Chamberlain	37	47
1974-75	Alex Groza (15-23)		
	Beryl Shipley (16-30)	31	53
1975-76*	Bill Musselman	3	8
	Totals	101	162

*Team changed name to Sails, folded 1976

SAN DIEGO ROCKETS

See Houston Rockets, 1971-72

SAN DIEGO SAILS (ABA)

See San Diego Conquistadors, 1975-76

SEATTLE SUPERSONICS

Season	Coach	W.	L.
1967-68	Al Bianchi	23	59
1968-69	Al Bianchi	30	52
1969-70	Len Wilkens	36	46
1970-71	Len Wilkens	38	44
1971-72	Len Wilkens	47	35
1972-73	Tom Nissalke (13-32)		
	Morris Buckwalter (13-24)	26	56
1973-74	Bill Russell	36	46

Season	Coach	W.	L.
1974-75	Bill Russell	43	39
1975-76	Bill Russell	43	39
1976-77	Bill Russell	40	42
1977-78	Bob Hopkins (5-17)		
	Lenny Wilkens (42-18)	47	35
1978-79	Lenny Wilkens	52	30
	Totals	461	523

SHEBOYGAN REDSKINS

1949-50	Ken Suesens	22	40

SYRACUSE NATIONALS

See Philadelphia 76ers, 1963-64

TEXAS CHAPARRALS (ABA)

See Dallas Chaparrals, 1970-71

TORONTO HUSKIES

1946-47	Ed Sadowski (3-9)		
	Lew Hayman (0-1)		
	Dick Fitzgerald (2-1)		
	Robert Rolfe (17-27)	22	38

TRI-CITIES BLACKHAWKS

See Atlanta Hawks, 1951-52

UTAH STARS (ABA)

1967-68*	Al Brightman (12-24)		
	Harry Dinnell (13-29)	25	53
1968-69**	Bill Sharman	33	45
1969-70	Bill Sharman	43	41
1970-71***	Bill Sharman	57	27
1971-72	LaDell Anderson	60	24
1972-73	LaDell Anderson	55	29
1973-74	Joe Mullaney	51	33
1974-75	Morris Buckwalter (24-32)		
	Tom Nissalke (14-14)	38	46
1975-76****	Tom Nissalke	4	12
	Totals	366	310

 *Played in Anaheim as Anaheim Amigos
 **Team moved to Los Angeles, changed name to
  Stars
 ***Team moved from Los Angeles to Utah
****Team folded, 1976

VIRGINIA SQUIRES (ABA)

1967-68*	Bruce Hale	22	56
1968-69	Alex Hannum	60	18
1969-70**	Al Bianchi	44	40
1970-71***	Al Bianchi	55	29
1971-72	Al Bianchi	45	39
1972-73	Al Bianchi	42	42
1973-74	Al Bianchi	28	56

Season	Coach	W.	L.
1974-75	Al Bianchi	15	69
1975-76****	Al Bianchi (1-5)		
	Bill Musselman (4-26)		
	Mack Calvin (0-5)		
	Jim Ankerson (1-0)		
	Zelmo Beaty (9-32)	15	68
	Totals	326	417

  *Played in Oakland as Oakland Oaks
 **Team moved from Oakland to Washington,
   changed name to Capitols
***Team moved from Washington to Virginia,
   changed name to Squires
****Team folded, 1976

WASHINGTON BULLETS

1961-62*	Jim Pollard	18	62
1962-63**	Jack McMahon (12-26)		
	Bob Leonard (13-29)	25	55
1963-64***	Bob Leonard	31	49
1964-65	Buddy Jeannette	37	43
1965-66	Paul Seymour	38	42
1966-67	Mike Farmer (1-8)		
	Buddy Jeannette (3-13)		
	Gene Shue (16-40)	20	61
1967-68	Gene Shue	36	46
1968-69	Gene Shue	57	25
1969-70	Gene Shue	50	32
1970-71	Gene Shue	42	40
1971-72	Gene Shue	38	44
1972-73	Gene Shue	52	30
1973-74****	K. C. Jones	47	35
1974-75*****	K. C. Jones	60	22
1975-76	K. C. Jones	48	34
1976-77	Dick Motta	48	34
1977-78	Dick Motta	44	38
1978-79	Dick Motta	54	38
	Totals	745	720

    *Played in Chicago as Chicago Packers
   **Played in Chicago as Chicago Zephyrs
  ***Moved to Baltimore, changed name to Bullets
 ****Played in Washington, D.C., as Capital Bullets
*****Changed name to Washington Bullets

WASHINGTON CAPITOLS

1946-47	Arnold Auerbach	49	11
1947-48	Arnold Auerbach	28	20
1948-49	Arnold Auerbach	38	22
1949-50	Bob Feerick	32	36
1950-51*	Horace McKinney	10	25
	Totals	157	114

*Team disbanded January 9, 1951

WASHINGTON CAPITOLS (ABA)

See Virginia Squires, 1969-70

WATERLOO HAWKS

1949-50	Charles Shipp (8-27)		
	Jack Smile (11-16)	19	43

18

The Globetrotters

Basketball fans around the world will attest that the Harlem Globetrotters are the game's greatest show. Their hilarious blend of comedy and outstanding basketball talent has captivated millions of fans in more than 90 countries. They've played before kings, princes and Popes and have drawn the biggest crowds in basketball's history, including 75,000 in Berlin's Olympic Stadium in 1951.

Everywhere the Trotters go, their show is the same. Numerous television appearances have made their routines familiar to all, but the exposure has never hurt the Trotters' drawing power. From their opening warm-up drill—always performed to the musical accompaniment of "Sweet Georgia Brown" —to their last trick shot, the Trotters provoke a torrent of laughter no matter where they appear.

Today the Globbetrotters are strictly a show; they make little effort to play serious basketball. Both the opponents and the officials are part of the act and they fully realize that the fans are more interested in seeing the Trotters' antics than in watching an authentic game. The final score is really an incidental matter and Red Klotz, the perennial coach of the touring opposition team,

can't remember when he last beat the Trotters.

But it wasn't always this way. When Abe Saperstein founded the team in 1926, the Trotters were strictly a serious barnstorming team. The humorous side of their play didn't appear immediately. Saperstein had organized a team that played in Chicago's Savoy Ballroom. When the dance hall failed and was turned into a skating rink, Saperstein's team was left without a place to play.

Saperstein saw no alternative but to take the team on the road. Since he reached that decision, the Globetrotters have never had a home court. Basketball at that time had not caught on generally and an unknown team from Chicago didn't seem like much of an attraction, the players were all black, as they still are today. Although none were from New York, Saperstein decided to call the team the Harlem Globetrotters. "'Harlem' because I wanted people to know the team was black and 'Globetrotters' because I wanted them to know we'd been around," Saperstein said.

The Trotters traveled around the country, playing any team anywhere they could schedule a game. The early years, especially during the Depression, were bleak, but Sa-

Founder Abe Saperstein made the Globetrotters a familiar sight around the world

as one of the best ball-handlers in the history of the game. He could dribble from every conceivable position—sitting down, lying on his back, his stomach, or on his knees, in addition to the conventional running style. He would frequently dribble around his opponents for minutes at a time, faking them off their feet. Like Tatum, Haynes left to tour with his own team.

Lemon filled Tatum's role as the premier comedian and to many fans around the world he became the clown prince of basketball. Meadowlark played the pivot and masterminded the Trotter's offense, which is just as likely to kick the ball into the basket as shoot it.

To call the Globetrotters a team is inaccurate, since they are in fact several teams. Saperstein divided his players into several units because he couldn't possibly meet all the requests for bookings with just one

perstein hung on. He found the best black players he could and the team soon became so good that nobody wanted to play them. To stimulate interest, Saperstein began to add the clowning routines that were to become the team's trademark. Fans liked the act but real success didn't come until the Globetrotters won the world professional tournament in Chicago in 1940.

Although it has been the style of play rather than the individual players that has made the team famous, several outstanding stars have emerged. Among the most famous have been Reece "Goose" Tatum, Marques Haynes and Meadowlark Lemon. Tatum, probably the team's greatest clown, was an amazing physical specimen. Although only 6-3, he had a reach of 84 inches, which the Trotters billed as the longest in pro sports. A lanky, loose-jointed man, the Goose drew laughs with his antics. When he chose to, though, he could also play extraordinary basketball. He had an amazingly accurate hook shot, which he would casually launch seemingly without paying any attention to the location of the basket. Tatum eventually left the Trotters to form a touring team of his own.

Haynes excelled as a dribbler and ranks

The great clown of the Globetrotters: Goose Tatum

team. Today the various Globetrotter units will frequently appear simultaneously in different parts of the United States and overseas.

Regardless of which team plays, the show never varies much. Tricky ball-handling has always been the Globetrotters' hallmark and all the players are adept at this. One of their favorite maneuvers is a weave pattern around the foul circle. The Trotters spread themselves out and pass the ball back and forth at lightning speed, behind the back, between their legs, up one arm down the other. They'll frequently take time out to spin the ball on a fingertip or hide it in someone's jersey. The overall effect is of the entire team moving at breakneck speed in an intricate pattern. Because the team has to be fresh enough to play nearly every night, the key to all their routines is to keep the ball moving quickly while the players remain relatively stationary and have a chance to rest.

Through the years the Globetrotters have signed several famous college players to tour with them. The most prominent of these was Wilt Chamberlain, who appeared with the Trotters for a season. A few other Globetrotters, such as Nat "Sweetwater" Clifton and Connie Hawkins, went on to play in the National Basketball Association. Today virtually all of the good black collegians choose to play in the professional leagues, but the Trotters still manage to come up with enough new talent to keep the show going.

Saperstein died in 1966, and his heirs sold the team for more than $3,000,000. The new owners decided not to tamper with success, and the Trotters continued to operate as they had under their founder.

19

The Other Pros

AMERICAN BASKETBALL LEAGUE

The American Basketball League, planned as a rival to the NBA, began play in the 1961–62 season and collapsed midway through the following campaign. Abe Saperstein, the owner of the Harlem Globetrotters, organized the ABL and served as its commissioner.

The league opened play with Cleveland, Pittsburgh, Chicago, and Washington in the Eastern Division and Kansas City, Los Angeles, San Francisco, and Hawaii in the West. Before the end of the season, Washington moved to New York (Long Island) and Los Angeles disbanded.

The ABL season was divided into halves, with Kansas City winning both halves of the Western title. Cleveland won the first-half Eastern title and tied Chicago in the second half of the schedule. Cleveland defeated Kansas City for the ABL championship.

Connie Hawkins of Pittsburgh won the scoring title with a 27.5 average. Several NBA players, the most prominent of whom were Dick Barnett, Ken Sears, and Mike Farmer, jumped to the ABL.

On December 31, 1963, the ABL folded, with losses to the owners estimated at $2,000,000. In its brief history the ABL introduced one interesting feature, awarding three points for field goals scored from 25 or more feet from the basket.

EASTERN LEAGUE

The Continental Basketball Association, previously known as the Eastern League, has served since 1947 as a training ground for professional basketball players and officials. As professional basketball's lone surviving minor league, the circuit has served as a farm for the NBA and other major leagues as they have appeared on the scene. In addition, a number of NBA officials began their pro careers in the Eastern League.

The Eastern League was organized on April 23, 1946 in Hazleton, Pennsylvania, with William Morgan, a local newspaper-man, as its first president. The six charter members included Binghamton (N.Y.) and Hazleton, Reading, Wilkes-Barre, Lancaster, and Allentown, all in Pennsylvania. James Drucker became the league commissioner in May 1978.

*EASTERN LEAGUE CHAMPIONS

Year	Pennant Winner	Playoff Winner
1946-47	Wilkes-Barre Barons	Wilkes-Barre Barons
1947-48	Pottsville Packers	Reading Keys
1948-49	Williamsport Billies	Pottsville Packers
1949-50	Williamsport Billies	Williamsport Billies
1950-51	Sunbury Mercuries	Sunbury Mercuries
1951-52	Pottsville Packers	Pottsville Packers
1952-53	Sunbury Mercuries	Williamsport Billies
1953-54	Sunbury Mercuries	Williamsport Billies
1954-55	Williamsport Billies	Wilkes-Barre Barons
1955-56	Williamsport Billies	Wilkes-Barre Barons
1956-57	Scranton Miners	Scranton Miners
1957-58	Wilkes-Barre Barons	Wilkes-Barre Barons
1958-59	Scranton Miners	Wilkes-Barre Barons
1959-60	Easton Madisons	Easton Madisons
1960-61	Allentown Jets	Baltimore Bullets
1961-62	Allentown Jets	Allentown Jets
1962-63	Allentown Jets	Allentown Jets
1963-64	Allentown Jets	Camden Bullets
1964-65	Camden Bullets	Allentown Jets
1965-66	Wilmington Blue Bombers (East. Div.) Wilkes-Barre Barons (West. Div.)	Wilmington Blue Bombers
1966-67	Wilmington Blue Bombers (East. Div.) Scranton Miners (West. Div.)	Wilmington Blue Bombers
1967-68	Allentown Jets	Allentown Jets
1968-69	Wilmington Blue Bombers (East. Div.) Wilkes-Barre Barons (West. Div.)	Wilkes-Barre Barons
1969-70	Allentown Jets	Allentown Jets
1970-71	Hamden Bics (Northern Div.) Scranton Apollos (Southern Div.)	Scranton Apollos
1971-72	Allentown Jets	Allentown Jets
1972-73	Hartford Capitols	Wilkes-Barre Barons
1973-74	Hartford Capitols	Hartford Capitols
1974-75	Hazleton Bullets	Allentown Jets
1975-76	Allentown Jets	Allentown Jets
1976-77	Allentown Jets	Scranton Apollos
1977-78	Jersey Shore Bullets (East Div.) Anchorage Northern Knights (West Div.)	Wilkes-Barre Barons
1978-79	Wilkes-Barre (Southern Div.) Rochester (Northern Div.)	Rochester Zeniths

*Now known as the continental Basketball Association

20

The Officials

A basketball official has never appeared on any list of Ten Most Popular Men. It was so from the beginning of basketball in 1891. It is so today.

Regardless of his degree of popularity, the official has always played a vital role in the game. Dr. James Naismith, inventor of basketball, described the function of officials in his original thirteen rules:

"RULE 10: The umpire shall be judge of the men and shall note the fouls and notify the referee when three consecutive fouls have been made. He shall have power to disqualify men. . . .

"RULE 11: The referee shall be judge of the ball and shall decide when the ball is in play, in bounds, to which side it belongs, and shall keep the time. He shall decide when a goal has been made, and keep account of the goals, with any other duties that are usually performed by a referee."

Two major rules changes affecting officials occurred in 1895. The referee was given authority to call fouls. Also, timers and scorers were instituted, relieving the referee of those duties. The use of only one official on the playing floor was commonplace, and remained so until 1929, when the double-floor-official system became standard. Starting with the 1978–79 season, the pros and a number of colleges initiated the use of three officials—one referee and two umpires.

Today, the distinction between a referee (or crew chief in the pros) and an umpire is slight. The referee or crew chief is usually the senior official, in age and experience. Also, he has the job of tossing up the ball at the beginning of a period; has the sole power to forfeit the game; decides matters upon which the timers and scorers disagree; decides whether a goal should count in the event of a disagreement between officials; makes decisions on any points not covered in the rules; and approves the final score.

The game was devised by Dr. Naismith to be an entertaining, noncontact form of wintertime physical recreation. However, games often resembled tribal warfare. Walls and pillars in the small gyms would form part of the boundaries, and tactics called for balls and opponents to be bounced off the woodwork. The official had the thankless job of arbiter. One early official told Dr. Naismith that he always checked to see which window in his dressing room was unlocked, in case a hasty exit was imperative. Fans and players alike treated the official with deep derision. It was in these early years that the Philadelphia YMCA dropped basketball because of the "rowdy element" it attracted. At one point the Trenton YMCA discontinued play because it was "unfit for Christians." In 1908 Charles W. Eliot, Harvard president, called the game "more brutal than football." Two years later many college athletic administrators felt the game was getting uncontrollable, and some began using two officials.

George Hepbron, the first to author a book on basketball, *How to Play Basketball,* in 1904, was also the first outstanding referee in the game's history. He approached officiating with a seriousness and

dedication that was uncommon. George Hoyt, another widely respected official of the early years, founded in 1920 the Eastern Massachusetts Officials Board, the first officiating organization. Hepbron and Hoyt were instrumental in elevating the standards of their profession. Former editors of the Basketball Rules, Oswald Tower (1915–59) and John Bunn (1959–67), and present editor and national interpreter, Dr. Edward S. Steitz, have also contributed to the game through their writings and interpretations of the rules. And referees Pat Kennedy, David Walsh, David Tobey, and John Nucatola were so highly regarded that they gained admittance to the Naismith Memorial Basketball Hall of Fame.

"Distinctive attire" for officials was rec-

With typical histrionics, Pat Kennedy blows hard at a DePaul-LIU game

ommended by college basketball boards in 1917. Before that an official would wear anything that pleased him. The late Adolph Rupp, University of Kentucky coach, refereed games in those early years. "I'd just grab an old pair of pants and a shirt, usually white or blue," said Rupp. "Sometimes my shirt was the same color as a team's jersey. And I'd be ducking a lot of passes."

A basic requirement of a good official is to have complete knowledge of the rules. This criterion presented a problem in the early years. There were as many as five sets of rules, with many variations designed to fit local conditions.

Not until 1934 were basketball rules standardized. Disparities, however, did not disappear overnight. Rupp recalled when sectional difference of rules emphasis cost his team a game. In January 1935, at Madison Square Garden, Kentucky lost to New York University in the last six seconds of play. Kentucky had the ball and a foul was called on the Wildcats on a "pickoff" play. "NYU sank the free throw," said Rupp, "and we lost, 23–22. This created quite a furor because that kind of foul was never called in our area. Now it is established throughout the country."

The Big Ten, for example, with its "no harm, no foul" concept, permitted more contact than most college conferences. UCLA Coach John Wooden noted that East and Midwest refs gave an advantage to the offense. "In those areas," said Wooden, "the man with the ball could do no harm. In the West, charging and other offensive infractions were called much closer by officials."

Today, as a result of the many rules clinics, distributed written materials, movies, and lectures, there is a high degree of national consistency and uniformity of interpretation. The NCAA and high-school rules leaders have conformed to a "one rule, one interpretation" philosophy, especially on provocative calls such as charging, screening, blocking, traveling, and fouling.

No two officials see the same game precisely the same way. A division is made by basketball people between the literal referee and the practical referee. The practical referee is preferred by the overwhelming ma-

jority. He allows the game to flow easily, though exercising his authority in a respectable manner. He is, as one coach termed it, "inconspicuous but always there." He understands the spirit and intent of the rules. The literal referee has a stringent grasp of the rules, but he often inhibits play and does not have the good rapport with players and coaches that a practical ref enjoys. A West Coast coach described the difference this way: "If a foul shooter has his foot a thirty-second of an inch over the line, and makes the shot, the literal ref will call it no shot. A practical ref gives more leeway. He believes the infraction was too slight to bother with."

Dr. Edward S. Steitz, the rules editor, interpreter and consultant, has set some basic guidelines for a well-officiated game. They are: (1) The official must be on top of the play or as close as possible in order to make accurate judgment. (2) All officials should make decisions on any play, especially if one colleague does not see the play or is screened out. For an official to say, "It wasn't my call," defeats the spirit and intent of moving to a three-man officiating team. (3) The good official does not anticipate a foul but rules on the act that has been committed. With today's talented player, anticipation of a call and a too-quick whistle deprive a talented player of a fine maneuver. (4) For a play to be called correctly the official must see the entire scene. (5) It is not a question of who is right, but what is right. There is one interpretation that officials must abide by and that is the interpretation that has been passed by the official Rules Committee under which the game is being played. It is his responsibility to call the rules in accordance with the official rules and interpretations. (6) A thorough knowledge of the rules and mechanics are also necessary.

The United States has more registered amateur officials than the rest of the world combined. There are an estimated 100,000 registered basketball officials for high school, college, and professional levels of play.

Amateur officials must pass written and practical examinations to qualify for high-school or collegiate assignments. Collegiate conferences also have their own registered and approved officials.

The International Association of Approved Basketball Officials (IAABO) has approximately 15,000 registered officials. The Collegiate Basketball Officials Association (CBOA), with over 650 members from 12 northeastern states, is the largest collegiate officials' organization.

Though there are no specific requirements in age, experience, or physical stature to become a professional referee, candidates have an average of three to seven years of officiating experience on a club, amateur, semipro, or minor-league level, according to Norm Drucker, the NBA's supervisor of officials.

Surprisingly, few pro referees gained experience in collegiate circles, a notable exception being Mendy Rudolph, who worked big-time college basketball games for two years before embarking on his pro career. Many officials get their training in the Continental Basketball Association (formerly the Eastern League), an NBA-subsidized minor-league affiliate.

The league first solicits recommendations of aspiring officials and then sends its observers around the country to scout applicants. The field of candidates is reduced at annual summer camps, and those who display the greatest potential are then subjected to physical and psychological testing and an examination of their knowledge of the rules. "But the most important thing is whether they can do the job on the court during the game," says Drucker.

The qualities Drucker considers prerequisites are: integrity, conscientiousness, even temperament, intestinal fortitude, good judgment, good reactions to changing situations, knowledge of the rules, and excellent physical condition.

NBA referees were given contracts for the first time at the start of the 1967–68 season. Before then, they were paid on a game-to-game basis. "We felt that our officials deserved security," said Walter Kennedy, NBA commissioner at the time.

Twenty-four of 26 NBA officials joined in a strike prior to the start of the 1977 playoffs. Minor-league officials were utilized until a settlement was reached after a 15-day walkout. The National Association of Basketball Referees achieved recognition as a bargaining agent, and the officials received a pay increase of $150 a game for the playoffs.

Now membership in the union is mandatory. Regular-season pay scales have been raised significantly. New officials begin at $20,000 a year and salaries range as high as $42,500 annually. The rates for playoff games escalate from first round to championship round. By 1980, officials are scheduled to receive a minimum of approximately $1,000 a game in the playoffs.

At one time, basketball officiating was not the sole means of income for pro referees. For instance, Rudolph was eastern sales manager of WGN-TV in Chicago and Earl Strom was a real-estate salesman. The same was true of college referees. Jim Enright, for example, was a Chicago sportswriter who also officiated games. Many referees officiated in other sports. Two of the best-known referees in the 1920s and 1930s were Bill Grieve and Ernie Quigley, both major-league baseball umpires.

Few NBA referees have other jobs now, the result of higher pay scales, more demanding travel schedules, and a season that extends from September exhibitions to playoffs ending as late as June.

The NBA adopted a three-referee setup prior to the 1978–79 season. "Basketball has developed so through the years that refereeing with two men had become very difficult, especially in the pros, where players know all the tricks," Drucker says.

The job will continue to be quite demanding. "Basketball referees have the toughest of all officiating jobs," maintains Drucker. "No other sport demands such attention, with plays happening every eight or nine seconds. In hockey and baseball the confrontations are usually between two men. In basketball the action takes place in a small area and six men might be going for the same rebound."

The late Joe Lapchick, who coached in the college and pro ranks, once explained why an outstanding college official may not be successful in the pros: "The abuse of officials by players, coaches, and fans is much greater than in college basketball. It takes a different breed of cat to make it in pro ball. I'll never forget the undoing of a rookie pro referee who had a distinguished college career. The game was at Syracuse, which was one of the roughest towns on the pro circuit. Syracuse was losing by three points with only seconds left. Dolph Schayes, the Syracuse star, had the ball and went head-hunting—that is, he drove to the hoop and tried to make contact while making the basket. He was trying for a three-point play to tie the game. But this rookie referee called Schayes for charging. Well, all hell broke loose. The ref was so unhappy with this degradation of a person he soon left the pro ranks."

Rudolph, whose pro officiating career began in 1953 and spanned 23 years and a record 2,113 games, was philosophical about such vilification. "I don't let it bother me," he said. "That comes only with experience, but you eventually learn to shut out criticism during a game. You hear it, but you ignore it. Rabbit ears in this business can be fatal for an official."

A pro official will work several games involving the same team during a season. The players and coaches come to learn his characteristics. "There are some officials," said one NBA player, "who we know we can get to if we crab enough. In close situations, he might give us the edge on a call. So the complaining sometimes pays off."

The good officials, of course, are not swayed or intimidated. The classic example of a fearless official was Chuck Solodare. He won respect by solid work, but he was a fine showman. In a game at Fort Wayne, Indiana, in the early years of the NBA, Solodare was under a barrage of jeers by the fans. Late in the game he suddenly stopped play. He opened his shirt, withdrew a steak, and flung it into the stands. "Here, you wolves," he shouted. "Chew on that."

Pat Kennedy was another official known for his skill and dramatic style. He was described as "sometimes appearing on the verge of apoplexy, so fervently does he throw himself into his job." Besides working top college and pro games (he was supervisor of NBA officials from 1946 to 1950), Kennedy became widely known through his tours with the Harlem Globetrotters.

Why do men become basketball officials? Rudolph quipped: "Don't ask me. Just ask a psychiatrist."

Sid Borgia, former NBA official, said officiating presents a great challenge, "especially when refereeing under pressure. It either brings out the best in a man or the worst. But it is satisfying to know that you are part of a spectacle that interests all those people in the stands. And that you contribute to keeping the game moving. Most important, I think, is that you just plain love the game."

Pro referees have come in varying sizes, but it is a curious fact that most officials are relatively short. Various reasons are given. One is that smaller men have greater maneuverability; they can get into good position easier. Another is that smaller men are more temperamentally suited to control a game. It is, ventured a prominent basketball executive, the Napoleonic complex of the small man making himself known.

Physical deformity has not been a deterrent, either. John Catalano had one hand. Joe Burns had an arm shriveled by polio. Dominic Cuccinello worked, amazingly, with an artifical leg.

Good physical condition is a key factor in maneuverability. Referees often go through rigorous training programs to prepare for the season. Borgia, for example, said that even during the early part of a season he would run two miles after some games. "When I could run two miles without getting tired," he said, "then I knew I was in condition."

Some referees are known as "homers"—that is, they have a reputation for giving the advantage to the local team. In basketball's early years, this was expected of an official. The athletic director or coach hired the official, often his friend. The official knew if he wanted to work a game for that team again, he must meet certain expectations. "Homers" still exist, but to a much lesser extent. Officials' organizations have elevated the profession by achieving pay increases and insisting on probity and good work.

Basketball experts agree that most modern-day officials are superior to those of the past. For one thing, officials have had to keep up with the fantastic improvements in the game. The players now are bigger, faster, and better, thus demanding more from an official. Changes in the game, like the elimination of the center jump after a basket, and the introduction of the three-second and ten-second rules also have necessitated a more alert and competent official.

Another factor in improving the work of officials has been the construction of newer and better basketball facilities. Officials are less troubled by rabid fans. Once it was common for spectators to sit alongside the court, where they sometimes tripped and shoved officials. It is rarer now for officials to have to fight their way out of gymnasiums. But precautions are still being employed. Highway patrolmen or local policemen often escort officials to the game, on and off the court, and away from the gymnasium.

It is apparent that, despite the growth of the game, officials are as beloved now as they were in 1891. They just have more protection today.

JAMES NAISMITH, M.D. 1861–1939
ELECTED 1959—CONTRIBUTOR
Graduated from McGill (1887), Presbyterian
(1890), and Springfield (1893). Minister,
Doctor, Teacher, Leader of Men. Founded
Game of Basketball in December 1891.

21

The Hall of Fame

The opening of the Naismith Memorial Basketball Hall of Fame in February, 1968, climaxed more than 30 years of planning, fund-raising, and many setbacks. The Hall of Fame, named after the founder of basketball, and located on the Springfield College campus where Dr. James Naismith invented the game in 1891, honors the sport's outstanding individuals and teams.

Dr. Naismith himself first suggested in 1936 that a Hall of Fame be built. After his death in 1939, Springfield College alumni began a fund-raising campaign that came to a standstill during World War II. In 1946, Ed Hickox retired as Springfield College coach, and as the first Executive Secretary he began working toward the establishment of the Hall of Fame. In 1948 the National Association of Basketball Coaches (NABC) set up a Hall of Fame Committee, headed by John Bunn, a former student of Dr. Naismith's and later the coach at Stanford and Springfield.

Since then the NABC spearheaded the building drive. It paid the operating costs of the Hall of Fame, thus allowing every dollar contributed by outsiders to be used for construction of the building itself.

Among the features of the Hall of Fame facility are a museum with souvenirs and mementos from basketball's earliest days, a library and an Honors Court.

Election is in the hands of a 13-member Honors Committee. The members represent every level of the game: college, professional, high school, the Amateur Athletic Union and news media. Players must be retired five years and officials ten years before they can be considered for election.

The first group of 15 individuals and two teams was elected in 1959. Since then elections have been held every year and a total of 82 individuals and four teams have been enshrined. Individuals gain election in one of four categories: Contributions to the Game, College Player, Pro Player, Coach.

Lee Williams, former basketball coach and director of athletics at Colby College, has been Executive Director of the Hall of Fame since 1964. He succeeded Clifford Wells.

Colored reproductions of each of the Hall of Fame members appear on glass in the Honors Court. The names of the members with inscriptions are as follows:

OSWALD TOWER 1883–1968
ELECTED 1959—CONTRIBUTOR
Graduated from Drury (Mass.) H.S. '01 and Williams '07. Player, Official 35 years. Member Rules Committee, 49 years. Editor and Rules Interpreter, 44 years.

RALPH MORGAN 1884–1965
ELECTED 1959—CONTRIBUTOR
Graduated from Friends (Pa.) School '02 and Pennsylvania '06. Founder of Collegiate Rules Committee 1905, now National B.B. Rules Committee; Member 26 years. Organized Eastern Intercollegiate Basketball League in 1910, now Ivy League.

JOHN J. SCHOMMER 1884–1960
ELECTED 1959—COLLEGE PLAYER
Graduated from Chicago '09. First "C" man to win 12 letters. Led Big Ten scorers 1907–08–09. Captain 1909 National Champions. Recognized as first great Western player. Taught at Illinois Tech 47 years. Leading football and basketball official.

FORREST C. ALLEN 1885–1974
ELECTED 1959—CONTRIBUTOR
Graduated from Independence (Mo.) H.S. 1905 and Kansas, 1909. Great Player. UK Athletic Director 19 years. Basketball coach 39 years. NCAA Champion 1952. Founded Coaches Association 1927; President 1927 and 1928. Helped organize basketball in Olympics 1936 and NCAA Tournament 1939. Teams won 771 games and 31 championships.

H. CLIFFORD CARLSON, M.D.
1894–1964
ELECTED 1959—COACH
Graduated from Bellefonte (Pa.) Academy '14 and Pittsburgh '18. M.D. Degree '20 from Pitt. Coached Pitt teams 31 years, won National Championships 1928 and 1930. Invented "Figure 8" offense. President, Coaches Association 1937. Practiced medicine since 1921 at Carnegie Steel and Pitt.

DR. LUTHER H. GULICK 1865–1918
ELECTED 1959—CONTRIBUTOR
Graduated from Oberlin (O.) Prep '85 and M.D. Degree from NYU '89. Leading authority on Physical Training. Originated the Triangle of the YMCA. Organized the Public School League of N.Y.C., the Playground Assoc., the National Recreation Assoc., the Camp Fire Girls and assisted with the Boy Scouts. Asked James Naismith to create "an indoor game"

while Physical Training Chairman at Springfield College.

EDWARD J. HICKOX 1878–1966
ELECTED 1959—CONTRIBUTOR
Edward J. Hickox, Coach for forty years, was elected in 1959 and was our first Executive Secretary. His honors included Presidency of NABC 1944–46, membership of the Rules Committee 18 years and Historian 20 years. He received a purple heart in WWI. In 1961 he was awarded a Doctorate in Humanics by Springfield College.

CHARLES D. HYATT 1908–1978
ELECTED 1959—COLLEGE PLAYER
Graduated from Uniontown (Pa.) H.S. '26 and Pittsburgh '30. All-State 1925, '26. H.S. All-American 1926. All-American 1928–29–30. Nation's leading scorer 1930. Led Pitt to Nat'l. Championship 1928 and 1930. Teams won 60 lost 7 in 3 years. A.A.U. All-American 9 years. Known as "Chuck."

MATTHEW P. KENNEDY 1908–1957
ELECTED 1959—REFEREE
Graduated from Hoboken (N.J.) Demarest H.S. '26 and Montclair (N.J.) State '28. Began refereeing at age 20 to become nation's best known official. Many of the great games demonstrated his dramatic manner. After legendary college career he became supervisor of NBA officials 4 years before working as a truly great attraction with Harlem Globetrotters 7 years. Known as "Pat."

ANGELO LUISETTI 1916–
ELECTED 1959—COLLEGE PLAYER
Graduated from San Francisco (Calif.) Galileo H.S. 1934 and Stanford 1938. All-City 3 years, All-American 1937 and 1938. Led team to 3 Conference Titles, all-time All Pacific Coast. First player to score 50 points in a regular game, scored 1,596 in 4 years. Nearly 3,000 in career. Began one-hand shot. Known as "Hank."

WALTER E. MEANWELL, M.D.
1884–1953
ELECTED 1959—COACH
Graduated from Rochester (N.Y.) H.S. and Maryland 1909. Born in England, never played basketball, yet coached Wisconsin 20 years, and Missouri 2 years to 290 wins. Won 2 titles at Missouri and 4 Big Ten Titles and 4 ties at Wisconsin. Writer, member Rules Committee, charter member Coaches Association, Athletic

Director and Doctor. Developed criss-cross system of offense. Known as "Little Doctor."

GEORGE L. MIKAN 1924–
ELECTED 1959—COLLEGE PLAYER

Graduated from Chicago (Ill.) Quigley Prep 1941 and DePaul 1946. All-American 1944–45–46, scored 1,870 points including high of 53 at Madison Square Garden. Player of Year 1945 and 1946. Led Minneapolis Lakers to 5 titles, All-League 9 years with 11,764 points scored. Voted top player of First-Half Century.

HAROLD G. OLSEN 1895–1953
ELECTED 1959—CONTRIBUTOR

Graduated from Rice Lake (Wis.) H.S. 1913 and Wisconsin 1917. Three-sport H.S. player, 2 years All-Conference for Wisconsin Big Ten Champions. Coached Ripon, Ohio State, Northwestern, and Chicago Stags. Won 5 titles at O.S.U. Helped found NCAA Tournament; Committee Chairman 8 years. President of Coaches Association 1933. Chairman NCAA Rules Committee, member 1948 Olympic Committee. Helped initiate 10-second rule.

AMOS ALONZO STAGG 1862–1965
ELECTED 1959—CONTRIBUTOR

Graduated from Exeter (Mass.) Academy 1884, Yale 1890, and Springfield 1892. Star pitcher and All-American End at Yale. Played in first public basketball game March 11, 1892. Became athletic head at Chicago, coached 7 basketball champions and football 40 years. He awarded first varsity letter for basketball 1908. Organized Big Ten Conference, conducted National High School Tournament 1917–1930 which did much to standardize rules. Member football Hall of Fame.

JOHN R. WOODEN 1910–
ELECTED 1959—COLLEGE PLAYER

Graduated from Martinsville (Ind.) H.S. 1928 and Purdue 1932. High School All-State 1926–27–28. All-Big Ten 1930–31–32. All-American 1930–31–32. Captain 1931, 1932; set Conference scoring record 1932. Led Nat'l. Champions 1932. Star in semi-pro basketball. Made 138 consecutive free throws in competition. Member all-time All-American Team. Became outstanding high school and university coach.

ERNEST A. BLOOD 1872–1955
ELECTED 1960—COACH

First played game in 1892, began coaching in 1897. Never lost to high school opponent, at Potsdam (N.Y.) H.S., 1906–1915. Won 200, lost 1, including 159 straight wins at Passaic (N.J.) H.S., 1915–1924. Won 421 at St. Benedict's Prep (Newark) 1925–1949. Won 56, lost 7 at West Point and Clarkson. "Prof" won 5 State Prep titles at St. Benedict's and 7 State H.S. titles with the immortal Passaic "Wonder Team."

VICTOR A. HANSON 1903–
ELECTED 1960—COLLEGE PLAYER

Graduated from Syracuse, N.Y. (Central H.S.) 1922, Manlius Acad. 1923 and Syracuse U. 1927. Four-sport H.S. star, led Central to N.Y. State title 1921. At Syracuse "Vic" was a nine-letter man, three-sport captain 1926–27, Basketball All-American 1925–26–27. Led 1926 team to Nat'l. title, teams won 48, lost 7 in 3 years. Player of Year 1927, named all-time All-American in 1952. New York State's greatest amateur player. Great pro with Cleveland Rosenblums, played baseball with N.Y. Yankees, coached football at Syracuse 1930–36.

GEORGE T. HEPBRON 1863–1946
ELECTED 1960—REFEREE

As friend of Naismith and Gulick was a pioneer authority on Basketball. As YMCA Director, saw need to curb roughness in game. First official referee at Brooklyn YMCA. Refereed first AAU Tournament at Bay Ridge A.C. Helped with first Guide in 1896. Secretary Olympic Basketball Committee 1903. Secretary AAU Committee 1896–1915, Sec'y Joint Rules Committee 1915–1936. (Made Life Member 1936.) Conducted First Nat'l. Rules Questionnaire. Served on many committees which organized early basketball.

FRANK W. KEANEY 1886–1967
ELECTED 1960—COACH

Graduated from Boston, Mass. (Cambridge Latin) 1906 and Bates 1911. Four-sport college star with flair for speed. Stole 38 bases in 1910, college record. Coached Putnam, Conn., Woonsocket, R.I., & Everett, Mass. 1911–1920. Coached all sports Rhode Island, Basketball 28 yrs. and A.D. 36 yrs. Changed slow-break pattern basketball to fast-break, high scoring "Point a Minute." Won 401, lost 124, took

"Little Rhody" 4 times to NIT. Awarded NABC Metropolitan Award 1957.

WARD L. LAMBERT 1888–1958
ELECTED 1960—COACH

Graduated from Crawfordsville, Ind. H.S. and Wabash College 1911. Trained in chemistry, "Piggy" played and coached basketball through all its rules changes from groups to 5-man game. Led Lebanon, Ind. H.S. to great records 1912–1916. Coached Purdue to 11 Big Ten titles, 371 victories and several All-American players in 29 years. Pioneered fast-break style of offense. Wrote "Practical Basketball." Honored as nation's outstanding coach in 1945. Awarded NABC Metropolitan Award in 1954.

EDWARD C. MACAULEY 1928–
ELECTED 1960—COLLEGE PLAYER

Graduated from St. Louis, Mo. (University) H.S. 1945 and St. Louis U. 1949. After 6.8 points average in 81 high school games, "Easy Ed" became one of Billikens' great players. During yrs. 1946–49, was named to every All-American team selected. Was All-Conference 4 years, was MVP in NIT Tournament in 1948, and AP Player-of-the-Year 1949. Led nation with .524 shooting in 1947. Was All-NBA 1950 through 1954, played in 8 NBA All-Star Games. Scored over 11,000 points in 9 NBA seasons.

BRANCH McCRACKEN 1908–1970
ELECTED 1960—COLLEGE PLAYER

Graduated from Monrovia, Ind. H.S. 1926 and Indiana U. 1930. Led his H.S. team to Tri-State titles 1925 and 1926, was MVP both years. Led college team in scoring 3 years, was All Big Ten 3 years. Was Conference MVP 1928. Set Big Ten scoring record in senior year when he was named on every All-American team elected. In playing career scored 32% of all points scored by his team and twice won Indiana Balfour Award. Became great coach at Indiana to win 4 Conference titles and 2 NCAA Championships in 1940 and 1953.

CHARLES C. MURPHY 1907–
ELECTED 1960—COLLEGE PLAYER

Graduated from Marion, Ind. H.S. 1926 and Purdue 1930. All-State in 1926 as team won Indiana State title. "Stretch" was one of first great "Big Men" in game. Big Ten's foremost offensive threat. Led team to Co-Championship in 1928. Set Big Ten scoring record in 1929, was captain in 1930 as undefeated team won Conference title. Named All-American 1929

and 1930. Named to all-time All-American Team.

HENRY V. PORTER 1891–1975
ELECTED 1960—CONTRIBUTOR

Graduated from Illinois State Normal 1918 and M.A., U. of Illinois 1925. After winning a letter in baseball and coaching basketball at Mt. Zion, Keithsburg, Delavan, and Athens, Ill. 1913–28, "H.V." turned to administration. As State Assoc. Executive and Executive Director of Nat'l. Federation he pioneered the invention of the "Molded" Basketball, the fan-shaped backboard and $29\frac{1}{2}''$ ball. With Mr. Tower he codified the Basketball Rules and started nationwide system of rules analysis. Was first high school representative on Rules Committee, a member 30 years and Secretary 18 years. Wrote basketball handbook and developed use of films.

FORREST S. DeBERNARDI 1889–1970
ELECTED 1961—A.A.U. PLAYER

Graduated from Iola, Kan. and Kansas City (North East) H.S. 1919 and Westminster Coll. 1923. After selection as Kansas All-State and All Kansas City, "De" was 2 years All Conference. Considered one of greatest players in Mid-West. He was an A.A.U. All-American 1921–22–23. Led Hillyards to A.A.U. title in 1926 and 1927 and Cook Painters in 1928 and 1929. In 11 A.A.U. Tournaments, "De" was All Tournament 7 times and All-American in 3 positions. Elected all-time All-American in 1938.

GEORGE H. HOYT 1883–1962
ELECTED 1961—REFEREE

An early pioneer of the game concerned with Sportsmanship and Fair Play, he traveled throughout New England to help players and officials. Living in South Boston, Mass., he organized first Officials' Board in Eastern Mass. and was admitted to the Collegiate Officials Directory in 1911. Coached many teams and for 34 years was associated with Eastern Mass. H.S. Tournament as an official and Honorary Chief Official. Considered "Mr. Basketball" in New England.

GEORGE E. KEOGAN 1890–1943
ELECTED 1961—COACH

Graduated from Detroit Lakes, Minn. H.S. 1909. Began great coaching career in high schools at Lockport and Riverside, Ill. and Superior State, St. Louis U., St. Thomas, Allegheny and Valparaiso before reaching Notre

Dame in 1923. Led "Fighting Irish" to 327 wins in 20 years to win 77% of games played. During 1925–28 teams won 56, lost 5 while the 1935–36 and 1936–37 teams won 42, lost 5 for a strong claim to national title. Created "shifting man-to-man" defense and coached many All-Americans in career suddenly shortened by death during 1943 season.

ROBERT A. KURLAND 1924–
ELECTED 1961—COLLEGE PLAYER

Graduated from St. Louis, Mo. (Jennings) H.S. 1942 and Oklahoma State 1946. The first of the truly great "7 Footers," Bob wrote basketball history of his time. Four years a college regular, he led his team to NCAA titles in 1945 and 1946 when he was the nat'l. scoring leader and in 1945–46 the NCAA-MVP winner. Elected to every All-American team, he joined A.A.U. Phillips "Oilers" to become selected All League and All A.A.U. for 6 years. Was a member of U. S. Olympic Teams in 1948 and 1952. Selected by Grantland Rice on all-time All-American Team.

ERNEST C. QUIGLEY 1880–1960
ELECTED 1961—REFEREE

Graduated from Concordia, Kansas, H.S. 1900 and Kansas U. 1904. An outstanding four-sport star at Kansas, "Quig" had thoughts of Law, but coached St. Mary's (Kansas) from 1903–12. Turned to officiating football and baseball in spare time to become National League umpire in 1913. Became one of greatest year-round officials as he handled all top games in football and basketball and 5 World Series. Traveled 100,000 miles a year before retiring in 1944 to become Athletic Director at Kansas. One of basketball's most colorful and respected officials, relying on his shrill voice rather than the whistle.

JOHN S. ROOSMA 1900–
ELECTED 1961—COLLEGE PLAYER

Graduated from Passaic, N.J. H.S. 1921 and U. S. Military Academy 1926. All-State 1918–1921 and State Tournament high scorer all 3 years. Johnny was a key part of the "Wonder Team" as his team won 41 straight games in the string of 159. Coach Blood called him Passaic's Greatest. A 10-letter winner at West Point, he led his team to 73 wins and 13 losses, scoring 44% of his team's points, 354 in one season and over 1,100 overall. Won coveted Army Athletic Sabre as outstanding athlete as he scored game high of 28 points sev-

eral times while starring as a defensive player. Served in Army 1926–56, retiring as Colonel.

LEONARD D. SACHS 1897–1942
ELECTED 1961—COACH

Graduated from Chicago, Ill. (Carl Schurz H.S.) in 1914, Am. College of Phys. Educ. 1923, and Loyola (Chicago) 1935. Won 11 H.S. letters and became star of Illinois A.C. which won AAU title in 1918. Coached at Wendell Phillips and Marshall H.S. before taking over Loyola in 1924. Lennie's great 2-2-1 zone defense with goal tender created great new interest in "big" man and new rule in basketball, prohibiting goal tending. In 1927–29 teams won 32 straight and 20 straight in 1938–39 before losing NIT title to undefeated LIU. With 3 City titles, won great recognition with use of meager material to win 224 games in 19 years.

ARTHUR A. SCHABINGER 1889–1972
ELECTED 1961—CONTRIBUTOR

Graduated from Emporia, Kansas, H.S. 1908, Coll. of Emporia 1913 and Springfield Coll. 1915. Four-letter man in H.S. and college, "Schabie" had an 80% winning mark in 20 years of coaching at Ottawa U., Emporia State, and Creighton U., where he won 9 Conference titles. Pioneered Intersectional games, conducted clinics, and helped organize NABC. Held many offices and was President 1932. Directed Olympic Basketball Tournament 1936, member Rules Committee, helped research molded ball, founder and director of Official Sports Film Service 1946–56, a great aid to uniform rules interpretation. Awarded NABC Metropolitan Award in 1955.

CHRISTIAN STEINMETZ 1882–1963
ELECTED 1961—COLLEGE PLAYER

Graduated from Milwaukee, Wis. (South Division) H.S. 1902 and Wisconsin 1905. Great two-sport captain in H.S. "Chris" organized first team at Alma Mater. The "Father of Wisconsin Basketball" scored 462 points in 1905—50 points, 20 field goals in one game and with 238 free-throws averaged 25.7 points per game, all long-standing records. As captain in 1905, he was elected All-Western Conference as he became first player ever to score over 1,000 points in college career. For 19 years selected the All-Western Conference Teams as he gained fame as one of his State's all-time Athletic Greats.

DAVID TOBEY 1898–
ELECTED 1961—REFEREE

Graduated from New York City (DeWitt Clinton H.S.), Savage School 1918, and New York U. 1935 and 1940. In a life devoted entirely to Youth and Physical Training, Dave enjoyed every outlet. He played on many great pro teams with and against all great players of his time. Enjoyed great coaching success in H.S. with 367 wins and in colleges with 348 wins including 35 straight wins at Savage School 1924–27. From 1918 to 1925 he refereed all important pro games and in 1926 was assigned vital West Point-Syracuse game (Hanson vs. Roosma). Until 1946 he was leading E.I.A. official working most important Eastern games. Wrote first officiating book, "Basketball Officiating" in 1943.

ARTHUR L. TRESTER 1878–1944
ELECTED 1961—CONTRIBUTOR

Graduated from Plainfield, Ind. Academy 1897 and Earlham Coll. 1904, Columbia U. 1913. First a teacher then a coach, a H.S. Principal and Superintendent, "A.L." became Secretary of the struggling Indiana H.S. Athletic Assoc. in 1913. He led its growth to more than 800 schools and in 1922 became Commissioner of the now financially sound, politically devoid organization which became the model for many states. His administrative ability, unquestioned integrity, and warm good humor enabled Indiana's Basketball Tournament to be universally recognized as a model of efficiency.

EDWARD A. WACHTER 1883–1966
ELECTED 1961—PRO PLAYER

Began basketball in 1895 and in '96–97 joined Troy YMCA team to begin a career that was to include perhaps 1,800 games and over 20 years of coaching. Nearly all towns and leagues in the East enjoyed Ed's talent which saw him chosen All-League regularly and which was culminated when he led Schenectady, N.Y. Co. "E" to the World's title win over Kansas City Blue Diamonds in 1905. In 1922 called "the greatest Center Man in Basketball." He led scoring in every league he played. Selected all-time Center in 1928. Worked for common rules and conditions, as he led discussion at first Officials' meeting in Boston. A Basketball Legend who played on more championship teams than anyone in his generation.

DAVID H. WALSH 1889–1975
ELECTED 1961—REFEREE

Graduated from Hoboken, N.J. H.S. 1907 and Montclair State 1911. Began teaching and coaching at Hoboken 1911 and combined basketball officiating in Pro, H.S. and College. About 1914 concentrated on college game to become one of East's leading referees while he enjoyed great coaching success. Appointed Assoc. Director Collegiate Officials Bureau 1941–1956, conducting clinics, supervising and assigning officials. From 1922 very active with group forerunner of I.A.A.B.O. and in 1948 elected Secretary of I.A.A.B.O. Did much for rules uniformity and improving officials. Considered one of six best Eastern officials of his era.

BERNHARD BORGMANN 1899–
ELECTED 1961—PRO PLAYER

Graduated from Clifton, N.J. H.S. 1917. As a brilliant H.S. scorer and continuing through 2,500 Pro games, Benny was recognized as an all-time all-pro playing in the American, National, Metropolitan, Eastern, New York State, and Western Mass. Leagues. He was always one of the highest scorers, frequently scoring 10 or more points when the team scored 20. At 5-8, he was a brilliant offensive performer. He was in demand by many teams and cities wherever pro ball was played. Upon his retirement as a great performer, he enjoyed a successful coaching career with 7 years with pro teams and 6 years at St. Michael's and Muhlenberg Colleges.

JOHN J. O'BRIEN 1888–1967
ELECTED 1961—CONTRIBUTOR

Graduated from Brooklyn, N.Y. (Commercial H.S.) 1907. Played three sports in H.S. and continued basketball activity by playing YMCA and pro ball 1908–19 and refereeing 1910–30. From 1920–30 "Jack" was a senior Intercollegiate Basketball League official. Administration was his real hobby as he helped organize the Interstate Pro League 1914 and served as President 1915-16-17. He organized the Metropolitan Basketball League in 1921 as well as the Brooklyn Arcadians who were to defeat the Celtics. Served as President and Treasurer of the League 1922–28 before reorganizing the American Basketball League as its President until 1953. New dignity and integrity were brought to owners, players, officials, and the game under his leadership.

ANDY PHILLIP 1922–
ELECTED 1961—COLLEGE PLAYER

Graduated from Granite City, Ill. H.S. 1940 and Illinois U. 1947. First team All State 1940 while his team won coveted State Title, Andy became one of nation's greatest players as vital member of the Illini "Whiz Kids." Set Big Ten scoring records in 1941–42 and 1942–43 as his team won 2 Conference titles. He led them to 14 straight wins and 25 of 27 in Soph. and Jr. years. Scored 40 pts. and 16 goals for Conference record in 1943. MVP of team as a Soph., Conference MVP, and member of every All-American team as Jr. He was elected captain of 1944 before serving 3 years in Marines. Regained outstanding class in delayed senior year to again become All-American before embarking on very successful NBA career.

JACK McCRACKEN 1911–1958
ELECTED 1962—A.A.U. PLAYER

Graduated from Oklahoma City, Okla. (Classen) H.S. 1929, and Northwest Missouri State, 1933. All-State 1928, 1929; All-American, 1929. College All-American, 1931, 1932, as one of nation's great all-round players. A.A.U.-All American 7 times, with Denver Pigs and Denver Nuggets. Considered an All-Time Great of his time.

FRANK MORGENWECK 1875–1941
ELECTED 1962—CONTRIBUTOR

A great veteran of Pro Basketball, "Pop" wielded much influence among players, coaches, and owners. Starting 1901–92 as a Manager in the National League, "Morgie" was a successful leader of basketball through 1931. Introducing many young players destined for greatness, he led teams to various championships from 1912 to 1931. His 30 years' contribution served to raise the standards of the game and players.

HARLAN O. PAGE 1887–1965
ELECTED 1962—COLLEGE PLAYER

Graduated from Chicago (Lewis Institute), 1906, and U. Chicago, 1910. Led high school to a midwest Championship. Was a great three-sport star at the University. A stellar defensive player, his team won Western Conference titles 1907, 1909, and 1910; the A.A.U. Title, 1907. They defeated Penn for National Title in 1908 and were undefeated 1909. "Pat" was Player-of-Year, 1910, before embarking on successful coaching career at Chicago, Butler, College of Idaho, and Indiana.

BARNEY SEDRAN 1891–1969
ELECTED 1962—PRO PLAYER

Graduated from DeWitt Clinton (NYC) H.S. 1907, and C.C.N.Y., 1911. At 5-4, adjudged too small for H.S. team, played independent ball before starring for C.C.N.Y. Leading scorer for 3 years, Captain 1910. Selected on many All-Star teams. Beginning in 1911 in 15 years played on 10 Championship teams. In 1913 scored 17 goals from 25–30 feet on court with no backboards. Played with all major Eastern pro teams including Carbondale when team won 35 straight, 1914–15. Led great Ft. Wayne "K of C" in 1923–24 and finished playing with Cleveland Rosenblums 1924–26. Later coached Pro Basketball for 20 years.

LYNN W. ST. JOHN 1876–1950
ELECTED 1962—CONTRIBUTOR

Graduated from Monroe, Ohio, H.S. 1896, Ohio State, 1900, College of Wooster, 1906. Played 4 sports in high school and football in college. Successful basketball coach at College of Wooster and Ohio Wesleyan before Ohio State, 1912–19. OSU Athletic Director, 1915–1947. Member NCAA Rules Committee, 25 years; Chairman, 18 years. Chairman, Joint Committee, 5 years. Instrumental in formation of National Basketball Committee of U.S. and Canada. Chairman, 1933–37. Member Olympic Basketball Committee, 1936.

JOHN A. THOMPSON 1906–
ELECTED 1962—COLLEGE PLAYER

Graduated from St. George, Utah (Dixie) H.S. 1926, and Montana State, 1930. Led H.S. to Utah State Title and consolation Championship at National Tournament in Chicago in 1925. At Montana State, led Golden Bobcats to their greatest record. Team won 72, lost 4 in 1928 and 1929. Were selected Helms National Champions in 1929 when "Cat" was Player-of-Year. Captain in 1930, All-Rocky Mountain Conference, 1928–29–30. He scored 1,539 points in 3 years of play. Played one year AAU before a 14-year coaching career.

ROBERT F. GRUENIG 1913–1958
ELECTED 1963—A.A.U. PLAYER

Graduated from Chicago, Ill. (Crane Tech.) H.S. 1931. All-City 3 years, All-State 3 years, led his team to a State Championship. All 3 years he was League High Scorer, with a single game high of 35 points. An A.A.U. Immortal, the 6-8 Center was first team All-Tournament 10 times from 1937 through 1948 and led the Denver Safeways, in 1937, and Denver Legion, in 1942, to A.A.U. Championships. Awarded the Los Angeles Sports Award Medallion as nation's greatest player, 1943. "Ace" became a high school coach after retiring as a great player.

WILLIAM A. REID 1893–1955
ELECTED 1963—CONTRIBUTOR

Graduated from Adrian, Mich. H.S. 1912 and Colgate, 1918. Captain and All-State Center of 1912, Michigan State Champions. Led Colgate teams to three-year, won 40 lost 12, record and A.E.F. Tours Team to service title, 1919. Coached Colgate to 151 wins in 10 years. Graduate Manager and Athletic Director at Colgate, 36 years. President, E.C.A.C., 1944–45. Vice President, N.C.A.A., 1942–46. Honorary LL.D., Colgate, 1946, as distinguished Coach and Administrator.

JOHN W. BUNN 1898–
ELECTED 1964—CONTRIBUTOR

Graduated from Humboldt, Kan. H.S. 1916, and Kansas 1921 (B.S.) and 1936 (M.S.). A 12-letter man in high school, became the first UK athlete to earn 10 varsity letters. Assisted his coach "Phog" Allen 9 years at UK before 25 successful years as head coach at Stanford, Springfield, and Colorado State (Greeley) for 321 wins and 3 Pacific Coast Titles, 1936–37–38. Wrote 6 textbooks on Basketball. Chairman Basketball Hall of Fame Committee, 1949–64; Editor of Basketball Guide and Official Rules Interpreter, 1959–67. Became first Executive Director of Basketball Federation, 1965. NABC President, 1949–50. NABC Metropolitan Award winner 1961.

HAROLD E. FOSTER 1906–
ELECTED 1964—COLLEGE PLAYER

Graduated from Mason City, Iowa, H.S. 1924, and Wisconsin, 1930. Led the high school to a third in State Tournament in 1924 and Mason City Jr. College to 21 wins in 1925. "Bud" was a 3-year star at Wisconsin in 1928–29–30. Team was Western Conference Champion in 1929 as he was named to several All-Conference and All-Western Teams in 1929 and 1930. All-American, 1930. Played pro ball with Oshkosh, Chicago, and Milwaukee before coaching 25 years at Wisconsin, winning 3 Big Ten Titles in 1935, 1941, and 1947, with NCAA Championship in 1941. NABC President, 1955–56. NABC Metropolitan Award winner, 1964.

NAT HOLMAN 1896–
ELECTED 1964—PRO PLAYER

Graduated from New York City (Commerce) H.S. 1916 and attended Savage School and N.Y.U. Played 4 sports in high school. In 1916, as a "young kid," was picked to play for Hoboken, N.J., and scored 23 of team's 28 to 25 win. Until 1920 starred for Bridgeport, Scranton, Germantown, and N.Y. Whirlwinds. In 1920–28 he led fabulous Original Celtics era as a great shooter, fine team player, and exceptional ball handler and passer. Team never lost a series. Later starred for Syracuse and Chicago. Retired from playing in 1933 to concentrate on 41-year coaching career at CCNY which saw his team win NIT and NCAA Titles in 1950, a feat never before accomplished. NABC President, 1940–41. NABC Metropolitan Award winner, 1941.

EDWARD S. IRISH 1905–
ELECTED 1964—CONTRIBUTOR

Graduated from New York City (Erasmus Hall) H.S., and Penn, 1928. While in high school launched an extensive newspaper career and throughout college covered sports for three NYC and Philadelphia papers. Returned to NYC upon graduation, to continue newspaper work. In 1934 became Basketball Director of Madison Square Garden and immediately began Collegiate double-header programs. Basketball enjoyed instant popularity, as great crowds could attend the games. When "Ned" began intersectional play, the game became truly national; helped standardize rules and coaching; helped to build larger facilities and became Number One in fan interest. He helped organize the NBA and formed the N.Y. Knickerbockers in 1946. Received NABC Metropolitan Award in 1942.

R. WILLIAM JONES 1906–
ELECTED 1964—CONTRIBUTOR

British born in Rome, Italy. Graduated from high school in Rome, 1923, and Springfield College, 1928. Attended colleges in Denmark, Germany, and Switzerland, 1929–32. Introduced basketball in Switzerland, 1929. Cofounder International Amateur Basketball Federation (FIBA) 1932. In June 1932 became Secretary General of FIBA which controls all international competition, including the Olympics, which he supervised each 4 years since 1936. Through this, helped spread basketball to 130 nations. Director, UNESCO Youth Institute, 1956, and appointed Secretary-General

International Council of Sport and Physical Education, 1958. Honorary Doctor of Humanics, Springfield 1963.

KENNETH D. LOEFFLER 1902–1974
ELECTED 1964—COACH

Graduated from Beaver Falls, Pa., H.S. 1920, and Penn State, 1924, plus Law degree from Pitt. Starred in 3 sports in high school. Played 3 years at Penn State, 1921–24. Captain, 1924. Played pro ball, 1924–29, before a coaching career of 22 years in colleges and 3 years in NBA. At Geneva, Yale, LaSalle, and Texas A&M, he won 310 games. At LaSalle he won the NIT Title in 1952 and was runner-up, 1953; also won the NCAA Title in 1954 and was second in 1955. His St. Louis Bombers won NBA Division Title in 1948. Coached East All-Stars in 1955.

JOHN D. RUSSELL 1903–1973
ELECTED 1964—PRO PLAYER

Graduated from Brooklyn, N.Y. (Alexander Hamilton) H.S. 1919; Seton Hall, B.S., and NYU, M.A. In high school "Honey" began a pro career that in 28 years saw him playing in every major Pro League and gaining acclaim as the top Defensive Player of his era. In over 3,200 games, he played the game's great individual opponents and led many teams to championships, including 5 straight titles, 1925–29, with Cleveland Rosenblums. As Player-Coach for 20 years, "Honey" was selected All-League, 1926–27–28–29. He coached Seton Hall to 294 wins, including 44 straight, and the NIT Title. Was the first coach of the NBA Boston Celtics, 1947.

WALTER A. BROWN 1905–1964
ELECTED 1965—CONTRIBUTOR

Graduated from Hopkinton, Mass. H.S. 1922, Boston Latin, 1923, and Exeter, N.H., Academy, 1926. Served apprenticeship in Sports Promotion under his father, George, General Manager of Boston Arena. Succeeded in 1937 as President of Boston Garden Arena Corp. Made Boston the Sports Center of New England. In 1946 was the driving force to organize the NBA and the Boston Celtics were his great basketball gift. Walter brought College Doubleheaders and the State and New England H.S. Tournaments to the Garden. Tireless worker for many charities and athletic projects. Was an Olympic official. Was Chairman of the Board of Trustees of the Basketball Hall of Fame, 1961–64. He helped all sports, all groups, and persons.

PAUL D. HINKLE 1899–
ELECTED 1965—CONTRIBUTOR

Graduated from Chicago, Ill., (Calumet) H.S. 1916, and Chicago, 1921. A 3-sport star in H.S. and College. One of the only two to win 3 letters at Chicago. All-Conference 2 years, Captain 2 years, and All-American in 1920. Arriving at Butler in 1921, "Tony" took his only job as he coached three sports and was Athletic Director continuously to become dean of Indiana coaches. At one time had 55 proteges coaching in Indiana. Led his teams to over 500 wins with a National Title in 1929. Coached Great Lakes N.T.S. to 98 wins, 1942–44, and National Service Title, 1942–43. Member of National Basketball Rules Committee, 1937–38, '42–48; Chairman, 1948–50. "Tony" was NABC President, 1954–55, and received the NABC Metropolitan Award, 1962.

HOWARD A. HOBSON 1903–
ELECTED 1965—COACH

Graduated from Portland, Ore. (Franklin) H.S. 1922, Oregon (B.A.) 1926 and Columbia (M.A. and EDD) 1929 and 1947. Won 12 letters and was All-State in H.S. Brilliant two-sport record at Oregon; two years Captain of Baseball and Basketball. Three-sport coaching career of about 1,100 games in 28 years with 725 wins. In basketball won 495 games at Southern Oregon, U. of Oregon, and Yale. At Oregon he won the first NCAA Title in 1939 along with 3 Conference Titles in 1937–38–39. His teams pioneered intersectional play. At Yale won or tied 5 Big Three crowns. He was the first coach to win major titles on both coasts. "Hobby" was a member of the Olympic Committee 12 years; Rules Committee 4 years. Contributed much to basketball through his extensive studies and writings. NABC President, 1947–48.

WILLIAM G. MOKRAY 1907–1974
ELECTED 1965—CONTRIBUTOR

Graduated from Passaic, N.J., H.S. 1925, and Rhode Island, 1929. Seeing most of the 159 straight wins of the Passaic "Wonder Teams" gave Bill early ideas on basketball and statistics. Helping URI exploit its "2 points-a-minute" Rams led to his prolific contributions as basketball Director at Boston Garden. Since 1946 has provided statistics for Converse Yearbook. He was editor of the NBA Guide. Wrote history of the game for *Encyclopaedia Britannica* in 1957. Helped organize several basketball tournaments. Bill is an honorary Life Member of NABC and the IAABO. He was first Chairman of Hall of Fame Honors Committee, 1959–64.

EVERETT S. DEAN 1898–
ELECTED 1966—COACH

Graduated from Salem, Ind., H.S. 1917, and Indiana 1921 (A.B.) and 1936 (M.A.). Four-year star in H.S., three-year regular at Indiana U. In 1921 Everett was All-Conference Center, All-American, and won the Western Conference Medal for Proficiency in Scholarship and Athletics. After winning 48 of 52 games at Carleton College, 1921–24, he returned to Indiana to coach 14 years to win 163 games and tie for Big Ten Titles in 1926–28–36. In 1938 he joined Stanford to lead them to an NCAA crown in 1942. In 1955 completed 34 years of coaching with the universal recognition of being one of finest gentlemen in the game. He wrote two important books, was a member of the All-American Selection Committee, 1949, and a member of the National Sports Committee, 1948.

JOE LAPCHICK 1900–1970
ELECTED 1966—PRO PLAYER

As immigrant parents needed his support, Joe began playing at 17 without a H.S. education. Attracted by his agility and 6-5 frame, great teams sought him and for 19 years, 1917–36, he was the best center of his time. Holyoke (Western Mass. League), Brooklyn Visitations (Metropolitan League), Troy (N.Y. State League), 1919–23. He became the center for the immortal Original Celtics, 1923–27. They never lost a series and were broken up, with Joe going to Cleveland Rosenblums. In 1927–30 they won 2 world titles. Reorganized the Celtics for a tour, 1930–36, before becoming one of America's great coaches in 20 years at St. John's U. and 9 years with the N.Y. Knickerbockers in NBA. Won NABC Metropolitan Award, 1965.

CLAIR F. BEE 1900–
ELECTED 1967—CONTRIBUTOR

Graduated from Grafton, West Virginia, H.S. 1917, B.A. from Waynesburg College 1925, and M.A. from Rutgers 1932. Coach 29 years. Lost 7 games in 5 years at Rider; won 95% of games at Long Island University 1931–1952, including 43 straight. Undefeated teams 1936 and 1939. NIT Champions in 1939 and 1941. Baltimore "Bullets" 1952–54. Member All-American Selection Board. Traveled and lectured extensively abroad. Rules innovator including "3 Second" and "24 Second" Rules. Prolific writer including 5 "Clair Bee" books in 1935 and many books and articles that remain valuable references. Received many coaching awards around the world.

HOWARD G. CANN 1895–
ELECTED 1967—COACH

Graduated from New York (Commerce) H.S. 1913 and New York University 1920. Great three sport athlete in high school and college. Member 1920 Olympic team. Led N.Y.U. to National AAU Title 1920 as its "Greatest All-Around Athlete." Coached at N.Y.U. 35 years. Teams won 409, lost 232. Coach of Year 1947. East Coach 1948. Received N.Y. Writers Distinguished Service Award. NABC Merit Award 1967. Coached many great players in outstanding coaching career.

AMORY T. GILL 1901–1966
ELECTED 1967—COACH

Graduated from Salem, Oregon, H.S. 1920 and Oregon State University 1924. Captain and twice All-State 1919 and 1920. All Conference and All American 1924. Coached 2 years at Oakland, California, H.S.; 36 years at Oregon State where he won 599 games. Won Pacific Coast Title 5 years, Far West Classic 8 years. Fourth in NCAA Tourney 1949 and 1963. Olympic Trials Coach 1964. NABC West Coach 1964. "Slats" was NABC President, 1957–58.

ALVIN F. JULIAN 1901–1967
ELECTED 1967—COACH

Graduated from Reading, Pennsylvania, H.S. 1919 and Bucknell University 1923. Won 12 letters in high school and 10 in college. After playing pro football and baseball, began 41 years' coaching 3 sports at various times. In basketball won 381 games at Albright, Muhlenberg, Holy Cross, Dartmouth, and the Boston Celtics. Teams were in 5 NCAA Tourneys and 2 NIT Tourneys, won NCAA Title for Holy Cross in 1947. Won 3 Ivy Titles at Dartmouth 1956, 1958, 1959. Boston Writers Coach of Year, 1947; Philadelphia Writers Award, 1966. Coach NABC West Team, 1965. NABC Merit Award 1967. "Doggie" was NABC President, 1966–67. NABC Metropolitan Award 1967.

ARNOLD J. AUERBACH 1917–
ELECTED 1968—COACH

Graduated Eastern District H.S. (Brooklyn) 1935; George Washington U. 1940. Captain and 3-year regular in H.S. and College. Coach at St. Albans Prep and Roosevelt H.S. (D.C.) 1940–43. Joined newly formed NBA in 1946. Led Washington Caps and Tri-Cities to 143 wins. "Red" took over Boston Celtics in 1950 to lead them to 9 Division Championships and 8 straight World Titles. Coached 11 straight NBA East Teams; won 99 Play-off games. NBA Coach of the Year 1965 en route to 1,037 pro victories. Only coach to win over 1,000 games, leading Boston Celtics to World Professional dominance 1956–66. Washington, D.C. Touchdown Club, Coach of Decade. Wrote outstanding book; traveled internationally for clinics and game promotion. Recipient of several civic awards in career which developed many great players and led Pro Basketball to its greatest recognition and acclaim.

HENRY G. DEHNERT 1898–1979
ELECTED 1968—PLAYER
Without high school or collegiate training, "Dutch" began memorable basketball career playing in Eastern, Penn State, New York State, and New England Leagues before joining immortal Original Celtics in 1920. While dominating Eastern Basketball for 8 years and to make an easy game interesting, "Dutch" went to foul line to receive passes from famous Celtic teammates. The Pivot Play was born. He became famous for its execution and success. Played with Cleveland Rosenblums for American League titles 1928, 1929, 1930, and New York Celtics for 1,900 wins until 1939. As Coach, led Detroit Eagles to World Titles 1940 and 1941; Sheboygan, Wisconsin, Indians to Western Titles 1945 and 1946. Though he discovered the Pivot Play by chance, he played and coached it so well that the 3-Second Rule was adopted.

HENRY P. IBA 1904–
ELECTED 1968—COACH
Graduated from Easton, Missouri, H.S. 1923; Westminster and Maryville, Missouri, 1929. Played 4 years H.S.; 2 years All-Conference at Westminster; AAU Sterling Milk (Oklahoma City) and Hillyards. Coached Classen (Oklahoma City) H.S. to 51 wins in 3 years; moved to Maryville for 61 wins. After 1 year at U-Colorado joined Oklahoma State U. in 1934. Memorable coaching career of nearly 800 wins included a National AAU Runner-up, 1932 (Maryville); 14 Missouri Valley Titles, and 1965 Big 8 Championship at OSU. Won consecutive NCAA Titles 1945 and 1946 which won him two Coach of Year Awards. NCAA Runner-up 1949. Led Championship USA Team in 1964 Olympics at Tokyo.

Chosen unprecedented 2nd time, 1968, and led USA to Championship in Olympics at Mexico City. NABC President 1968, NABC Metropolitan Award 1947.

ADOLPH F. RUPP 1901–1977
ELECTED 1968—COACH
Graduated from Halstead, Kansas, H.S. 1919; U-Kansas 1923. Member 1923 Kansas National Champions, coached by Forrest C. Allen who won 771 games. Coach Allen saw his protege win over 800 games to become the winningest college coach. Coached 5 years at Marshalltown, Iowa, and Freeport, Illinois, H.S. and since 1930 at U-Kentucky. Adolph won 24 Southeast Conference Titles; 4 NCAA Titles in 1948, 1949, 1951, 1958; NIT Title in 1946; NCAA Runner-up, 1966. Was Co-Coach of 1948 USA Olympic Team at London. Won every important award including Coach of the Year, 4 times, and Columbus, Ohio, Touchdown Club Coach of the Century, 1967. Coached 24 All-Americans, 7 Olympic Team players, and 26 Professional Players. Took 11 overseas clinic trips. Won many civic awards. Member Basketball Rules Committee, 1964–68. NABC Metropolitan Award 1966.

CHARLES H. TAYLOR 1901–1969
ELECTED 1968—CONTRIBUTOR
Graduated from Columbus, Indiana, H.S. 1918. Two years All-State in outstanding 4 years of high-school play. Played 11 years of pro ball. In 1921 "Chuck" became interested in developing a shoe designed for the growing game. What began as a business promotion developed into a career of selling Basketball. In 1922 at North Carolina State he did a public demonstration which became first "Basketball Clinic." A lifetime of building players, coaches and spectator interest through clinics and demonstrations took him to every major American city as well as Puerto Rico, Hawaii, Canada, Mexico, South America, Africa, and Europe. Began Converse Yearbook of Basketball in 1922; designed "Chuck" Taylor Basketball shoe in 1931; selected All-American Teams since 1932. Coached Air Force Basketball Team in World War II, won award for outstanding services in Air Force as he conducted clinics at many bases in USA and Overseas. Truly an Ambassador of Basketball.

BERNARD L. CARNEVALE 1915–
ELECTED 1969—COACH
Graduated from Somerville (N.J.) H.S., 1934; N.Y.U., 1938. All District, Captain, and MVP

in 1938, Ben played two years pro with Jersey City Reds, 1938–40. Coached Cranford, N.J., H.S. to 75 wins 1939–42; North Carolina, 51 wins 1944–46; and U. S. Naval Academy to 257 wins in 20 years. His teams won two Southern Conference titles and Eastern NCAA Title 1946 at UNC. Played in 5 NCAA Tourneys and 1 NIT at Navy. Collegiate Coach-of-Year, 1947. Considered a master coach of average material and a classic clinician teaching fellow coaches. Member NCAA Tournament Committee, 1964; Chairman, 1968. Member NIT and ECAC Holiday Festival selection committee since 1966. Ben was manager of 1968 Olympic champions at Mexico City and in 1969 was appointed Chairman of International Basketball Board. NABC President, 1966.

ROBERT E. DAVIES 1920–
ELECTED 1969—PLAYER
Graduated from John Harris (Harrisburg, Pa.) H.S., 1937; Seton Hall, 1942. In brilliant college career was captain 2 years; MVP, 3 years; All-American, 2 years. Led Seton Hall to record 43 straight wins. Selected MVP in 1942 College All-Star Game in Chicago. After leading Great Lakes N.T.S. to Service Title in 1943, joined Rochester Royals in 1945 for a great 10-year Pro career in BAA and NBA Seven years, All-League; MVP in 1947; led Royals to World Titles in 1946, 1947, 1951. League leading assist man for 6 straight years including record 20 in a game. Bob starred in 67 play-off games; scored 7,771 points as a pro. His original and famous behind-the-back dribble was a crowd pleaser in a great collegiate and pro career which saw him selected as the sixth Greatest Player of the First Half Century of Basketball and considered first superstar of modern pro basketball.

ABRAHAM M. SAPERSTEIN 1902–1966
ELECTED 1970—CONTRIBUTOR
Graduated from Lakeview High School in Chicago in 1919. Born in London, England, on July 4. Abe arrived in Chicago where sports became his life. Accepted job coaching Negro American Legion team in 1925. Became the Savoy Big 5 and then the Harlem Globetrotters to play first game at Hinckley, Ill., on Jan. 7, 1927. Forty years later Abe had added a new dimension to the game. His Globetrotters had played before 55 million fans in 87 countries including 75,000 in Berlin in 1951. Won world pro title in 1940; International Cup in 1943, 1944. Only sports unit the subject of

two full-length movies. The tireless founder, coach and owner, Abe was a man of great integrity who made basketball truly international. A respected citizen of the world, welcomed wherever he went, he assembled a most unique sports team which created a new art of playing the game.

ROBERT L. PETTIT 1932–
ELECTED 1970—PLAYER
Graduated from Baton Rouge (La.) H.S. in 1950 and L.S.U. in 1954. High school All-State and All-American 1950. All-Southeastern Conference 1952, 1953, 1954 and MVP all three years. All-American 1952–53, consensus All-American 1954, averaging 27.4 points a game for three years. NBA Rookie of Year 1955 to begin celebrated 11-year pro career. Bob was 11 years All-League and MVP in 1956, 1959; on 11 All-Star teams and MVP in 1956, 1958, 1959, 1962. An NBA superstar, retired in 1965 as highest scorer in NBA history with 20,880 points; fifth best scoring average, 26.4 per game; second leading All-Star Game scorer, 224 points; third most rebounds in NBA history and third most free throws. Led St. Louis Hawks to NBA title in 1958 and runners-up 1957, 1959, 1960, 1961. Selected to All NBA 25-year team in 1971.

ROBERT J. COUSY 1928–
ELECTED 1970—PLAYER
Graduated from Andrew Jackson (Queens, N.Y.) H.S. 1946, Holy Cross 1950. High School All-N.Y. City 1946. College MVP 1949, 1950; captain 1950; All-American 1948, 1949, consensus All-American 1950. Joined Boston Celtics 1950, led them to five straight NBA titles 1959–63. As "Mr. Basketball," helped lift pro game to major status in his incomparable career: All-NBA first team 10 years in a row; a star in all 13 All-Star Games; league MVP 1957; All-Star MVP 1954, 1957. Bob held 13 playoff records, 6 All-Star marks, most of league assist records. Had 6,959 lifetime assists and scored 16,960 points. At 6-1 perhaps the most spectacular performer in history of game. Coached Boston College to five tournaments 1963–69. Became coach of Cincinnati Royals 1969–70. Selected to All-NBA 25-year team in 1971.

EDGAR A. DIDDLE 1895–1970
ELECTED 1971—COACH
Graduated Adair County H.S. Columbia, Ky., 1915; Centre College 1920. Captain and All-Southern selection in 1920. Coached Monticello H.S. to state finals in 1921 and Green-

ville H.S. to regional in 1922. One of the first to use all five players on offense, Ed went to Western Kentucky U. in 1922 for 42 years of record-breaking coaching career. His Hilltoppers used flashy fast-break to play in every national collegiate event; won or shared in 32 conference titles including 13 Kentucky Intercollegiate, 8 Southern and 11 Ohio Valley in first 16 years of the conference; participated in 3 NCAA and 8 NIT tournaments. Ed was first coach to guide a team in 1,000 games at same college and at time of election was 4th winningest collegiate coach with 759 wins for a winning percentage of .720. Had 18 seasons with 20 or more victories including 10 straight years, 1934–43. His immortal tradition inspired the dedication of Edgar A. Diddle Arena at Western Kentucky University.

ROBERT L. DOUGLAS 1884–
ELECTED 1971—CONTRIBUTOR

Born in St. Kitts, British West Indies, and brought to America at age of 4. Bob was soon attracted to athletics. With no high school or college background, he did learn well the qualities of loyalty and integrity. Gathering the best black players and requiring excellence in performance, Bob organized the Renaissance Five in 1922. Largely a road club, faced with the well-known "road problems" the Rens won 88 consecutive games; won 128 games in 1934; in 1939 won the world's pro title in Chicago, en route to a record which made Bob winningest coach ever, during an era when basketball needed his memorable contributions and leadership. His word was his contract; his players were legendary in their performance. The impact of this highminded and enlightened man made basketball a more influential and better game.

PAUL ENDACOTT 1902–
ELECTED 1971—PLAYER

Graduated Lawrence (Kan.) H.S. 1919; Kansas University 1923. After selection as All-State guard in 1919, Paul began storied career at Kansas to become the "greatest player ever coached" by the fabled "Phog" Allen. Selected All-Conference second team in 1921, first team in 1922 and 1923, led Jayhawks to mythical national title in 1923, including first-ever undefeated in conference games. Endy was selected by Helms Foundation as national Player-of-the-Year in 1923; selected in 1924 as All-Time Kansas by Dr. James Naismith and in 1943 was selected by Helms on the All-Time All-American second team. In 1951 was selected by Dr. Allen as member of National

All-Time College team and 1969 was recipient of the Sportsmen's World Award in basketball as "an athlete whose championship performances have stood the test of time and whose exemplary personal conduct has made him an outstanding inspiration for youth to emulate."

MAX FRIEDMAN 1889–
ELECTED 1971—PLAYER

Graduated Hebrew Tech Institute N.Y.C. 1908. Played with University Settlement House Metropolitan A.A.U. champions 1906–08 before turning pro with New York Roosevelts in 1909 to begin a career of playing in every pro league in East. Acknowledged as one of the great defensive stars and leader of each team including Newburgh in 1911–1912, Hudson in 1913 in Hudson River League; Utica in 1914 in New York State League; Carbondale 1915 in Pennsylvania League; Philadelphia Jaspers in 1916–17 Eastern League; Albany in 1920 in N.Y. State League; Easthampton, Mass., in 1921–22 in Interstate League. Marty finished a starry career as captain and coach of the Cleveland Rosenblums from 1923 through 1927. Won championships with nearly every team; won 35 straight games with Carbondale, Pa., in 1915 and won American League championships in 1926 and 1927. As captain of Tours team, A.E.F. champions, won Inter-Allied Games in 1919; followed by brilliant play with independent New York Whirlwinds fulfilling a basketball record widely acclaimed as most remarkable for a player 5-8. Marty and his pal, Barney Sedran, were called the "Heavenly Twins."

EDWARD GOTTLIEB 1898–
ELECTED 1971—CONTRIBUTOR

Graduated South Philadelphia H.S. 1916; Philadelphia School of Pedagogy, 1918. Captain in 1918. Gotty organized the team representing South Philadelphia Hebrew Association in 1918. Playing 75–80 games annually, the Sphas peaked in 1925–26 season to defeat the Original Celtics and Original Rens in a special series before rebuilding in the 1930s to dominate the Eastern and American leagues with 11 championships. Constantly promoting basketball, Eddie helped pull the pro game through difficult times. He helped organize the BAA in 1946, later to become the NBA. His Philadelphia Warriors won the first championship in 1946–47. Clearly basketball's super salesman, he helped organize the overseas tours of the Harlem Globetrotters; promoted pro doubleheaders; suggested ideas and rules that appealed to rapidly increasing fan interest. As chairman of the NBA Rules Committee for 25 years when elected, as NBA schedule-maker, successful coach, owner of Philadelphia Warriors, great promoter of honor and integrity, truly Eddie is "the mogul" of basketball.

W. R. CLIFFORD WELLS 1896–1977
ELECTED 1971—CONTRIBUTOR

Graduated Bloomington (Ind.) H.S. 1916; Indiana University 1920. Began 29-year Indiana coaching career with 5 years at Bloomington, followed by 1 at Columbus and 23 years at Logansport. As dean of Indiana H.S. coaches, won 617 games for 71 per cent including 50 district, regional and invitational tourneys and state championships at Bloomington in 1919 and at Logansport in 1934. Moved to Tulane University in 1945 until 1963. Cliff won 885 and lost 418, completing 47 years of coaching, coaching teams in 1,303 games. Was the first president of the Indiana H.S. Coaches Association; directed the Indiana Coaching School 1935–64; conducted more than 100 clinics across the nation and overseas; has written over 50 articles on basketball; was a member of National Rules Committee 1952–56. Cliff held every NABC office including president in 1959 and was appointed executive secretary in 1960. He was executive director of Basketball Hall of Fame 1963–66. Was elected to the Helms Hall of Fame in 1962 and the Indiana Hall of Fame in 1965. Received Metropolitan Award 1963.

JOHN R. WOODEN 1910–
REHONORED 1972—COACH

After two years at Dayton (Ky.) H.S. and nine years at Central of South Bend (Ind.) H.S. winning 83 per cent with 218 wins and 42 losses, John won 47 and lost 14 at Indiana State 1946–48 before arriving at UCLA in 1948–49, there to establish the greatest coaching record in college basketball history. Maintaining a winning percentage of 79 per cent (four wins in five games), John led the Bruins to absolute domination of college basketball beginning in 1962 winning eight of nine Pacific-8 titles; eight of nine NCAA titles including six straight in 1967, 1968, 1969, 1970, 1971, 1972, losing only five games. Elected Coach of the Year in 1964–67–69, he swept four coach of year awards (NABC, USBWA, AP, UPI) in 1970.

JOHN BECKMAN 1895–1968
ELECTED 1972—PLAYER

Known in the 1920s and part of the 1930s as the "Babe Ruth of Basketball" for his play with the Original Celtics. Born in New York City, captained the Celtics. Played in a number of professional leagues with many teams, beginning in 1910 with St. Gabriel's of New York. Pro clubs included Kingston, N.Y., Paterson, N.J., Nanticoke, Pa., Philadelphia, and Baltimore, in addition to the Celtics. One of the reasons the Celtics were elected to the Hall of Fame as a team.

BRUCE DRAKE 1905–
ELECTED 1972—COACH

Though much of his fame came through coaching, he also made the Helms All-America team in 1929, when he was captain at the University of Oklahoma. Born in Gentry, Tex., became head coach at Oklahoma for 17 seasons and invented the "Drake Shuffle." His teams won 200 games and captured or tied for the conference championship 6 times. Oklahoma lost the national championship game to Holy Cross in 1947. Former president of the National Collegiate Coaches' Association. Assistant coach of 1956 U. S. Olympic team.

ARTHUR C. LONBORG 1898–
ELECTED 1972—COACH

Born in Gardner, Ill., spent 29 years coaching college basketball teams. Started with McPherson College, moved to Washburn University, and then had 23 seasons at Northwestern. In 1925, his Washburn team won the AAU championship, the last time a college won the crown. In 1931, he coached Northwestern to its first Big Ten championship. Served as president of the Coaches' Association in 1935 and as manager of the U. S. Olympic team in 1960.

ELMER H. RIPLEY 1891–
ELECTED 1972—CONTRIBUTOR

Career spanned 20 years with a number of championship teams. Pro career started with Carbondale, Pa., team. Also played for Scranton, the Original Celtics, Fort Wayne K. of C., Brooklyn, and Cleveland. Later turned to coaching at Georgetown, Yale, Columbia, Notre Dame, Army, and Regis. Conducted many clinics and toured Israel for the U. S. State Department. Coached the 1960 Canadian Olympic team. Had a three-year stint as coach of the Harlem Globetrotters. Born in Staten Island, New York.

ADOLPH SCHAYES 1928–
ELECTED 1972—PLAYER

Born in New York City, entered NYU when only 16, and finished college career as an All-American. Joined the Syracuse Nationals in

1948 and for the next decade was one of the top scorers in professional basketball, while the Nats were one of the best teams. A member of the NBA All-Star team 12 times as a forward with an exciting outside touch. Scored 19,249 points and played in a one-time record 1,059 games. Later coached the Philadelphia 76ers—formerly the Nats—and Buffalo Braves. Was Coach of the Year with 76ers in 1965–66. Also served as supervisor of NBA officials.

HARRY A. FISHER 1882–1967
ELECTED 1973—CONTRIBUTOR

Born in New York City, scoring leader at Columbia 1902–5. Lions won 2 Ivy League titles in that time. Established school record of 13 field goals in one game that stood for 48 years. Member of committee that rewrote collegiate basketball rules. First full-time coach at Columbia in 1906. Led school to 3 Ivy crowns and 101–39 record during 10-year stay. Columbia graduate manager of athletics 1911–17. Editor of *Collegiate Guide* until 1915.

MAURICE PODOLOFF 1890–
ELECTED 1973—CONTRIBUTOR

Born in Elizabethgrad, Russia, graduated from Yale in 1913 and from Yale Law School two years later. Because of legal and administrative background, was asked to assume leadership of Basketball Association of America. Led BAA into merger with NBA in 1949. Guided NBA through early years and secured first TV contract in 1954. Did much to bring NBA into national prominence before retiring in 1963 after 17 years as commissioner.

ERNEST J. SCHMIDT 1911–
ELECTED 1973—PLAYER

Born in Nashville, Kans., led Winfield (Kans.) H.S. to 3 state championships. Continued winning ways at Kansas State by leading Wildcats to a record 47 straight wins and 4 conference titles. Conference high scorer 3 times before graduating in 1933. Won All-American recognition in 1932. Voted Greatest College Player in Missouri Valley same year. All-Central Conference center 4 years.

JOSEPH R. BRENNAN 1900–
ELECTED 1974—PLAYER

Graduated from St. Augustine's Academy, Brooklyn, 1919, "Poison Joe" went directly from high school to a brilliant professional career. After serving as high-school captain, he joined the famous Brooklyn Visitations in 1919 and became the team leader in their rise to basketball prominence. As the league scoring leader, led the Visitation Triangles to the "Met" League championship and the unofficial world championship in 1931. In pro career of 17 years, played with the Brooklyn Jewels, Whirlwinds, Dodgers, the Union City Reds, Troy, N.Y., and served as captain with nearly every team. In 1950 was voted by the New York Basketball Old-Timers second only to Johnny Beckman as the greatest pro player of his era.

EMIL S. LISTON 1890–1949
ELECTED 1974—CONTRIBUTOR

Graduated from Baker Academy, Baldwin, Kans., in 1909 and Baker University in 1913. While a student at Baker, won Kansas State title in 1912 coaching at Baldwin H.S. Coached at Ft. Scott, Kansas, Kemper Military, Michigan College, Wesleyan of Connecticut, and 25 years at Baker. Organized the Kansas Coaches Association and in 1936 was the Missouri Valley AAU representative. While at the Denver meeting, "Liz" got the idea for a small college national tournament and organized the NAIB in 1937. Beginning with an 8-team field, that first National College Tournament played at Kansas City grew to 32 teams in 1938. Was first executive director of NAIB from 1940 until his death in 1949, founding this small college organization, which has grown to over 500 members and is now the NAIA.

WILLIAM F. RUSSELL 1934–
ELECTED 1974—PLAYER

Graduated from McClymonds H.S., Oakland, Calif., 1952, and from University of San Francisco, 1956. High-school All-State; a two-year All-American in college. Was college Player of Year in 1956 while his team was en route to a 55-game winning streak. Led the 1956 U. S. Olympic team to the championship at Melbourne. Joined the Boston Celtics in 1956 as the highest-paid rookie ever. Revolutionized the game with his defensive wizardry and outstanding "team" concept, which enabled the Celtics to win 8 straight NBA titles and 11 in 13 seasons. Grabbed 21,721 rebounds (49 in one game) and averaged 15.1 points per game. Was on 11 All-Star teams and was league MVP 5 times. As player-coach for 3 years, he led the Celtics to NBA championships in 1968 and 1969. Was named Sportsman of the Year in 1968 by *Sports Illustrated,* Athlete of the Decade in 1970 by *Sporting News,* and to the NBA Silver Anniversary Team in 1971.

ROBERT P. VANDIVIER 1903–
ELECTED 1974—PLAYER

Graduated from Franklin, Ind., H.S., 1922, and Franklin College, 1926. A four-year regular, "Fuzzy" became one of the greatest high-school players in the history of Indiana basketball. As a freshman, his team barely lost the state championship, but in each of his last 3 years, Franklin won in 1920, 1921, and 1922. The captain of the "Franklin Wonder Five" was selected All-State all 3 years, the only player ever so honored. He and his teammates entered Franklin College to create its greatest basketball record, 1922–26. Became All-Midwest guard in 1925 while serving as captain for 2 years. An Indiana legend and a member of the All-Time All-Star Five of Indiana.

THOMAS J. GOLA 1933–
ELECTED 1975—PLAYER

Graduated from LaSalle H.S. in Philadelphia, 1951, LaSalle University, 1955. Considered one of finest all-around schoolboy stars in Philadelphia history, scoring 2,222 points. The second four-year college All-American was recognized as one of the game's most versatile players. Twice captain, averaged 21 points and 20 rebounds; selected MVP in 1952 NIT and 1954 NCAA, he led LaSalle to both titles. Scored 2,461 points and had 2,201 rebounds in four years. During outstanding 10-year pro career with Philadelphia and San Francisco Warriors, scored 7,871 points and was a leader in rebounds and assists. Led league in steals and was an outstanding defensive player. All-NBA in 1958. Inch for inch, considered one of basketball's greatest all-around players. Was selected to *Sport* magazine's all-time All-American team in 1960.

HARRY LITWACK 1907–
ELECTED 1975—COACH

Graduated from South Philadelphia H.S., 1925, and Temple, 1930. High-school All-Star, college captain 2 years. In 7 years with Philadelphia Sphas, in Eastern and American leagues, was always a leader. Won 15, lost 2 at Gratz H.S. in 1930 and was 181–32 as Temple frosh coach while doubling as assistant coach of Philadelphia Warriors before amassing 373 wins and 193 losses in 21 years as head coach at Temple. Led the Owls to 13 post-season tournaments, including NIT championship in 1969 and third place in NCAA in 1956 and 1958. Widely acclaimed as a fine gentleman of basketball. It is written that he

did more with less than any coach in basketball history.

EDWARD W. KRAUSE 1913–
ELECTED 1975—PLAYER

Graduated from De LaSalle, Chicago, H.S., 1930, and Notre Dame, 1934. All-City three-sport star in high school. Concentrated on 2 sports in college to become All-American 3 years in both sports. At 6-3, 215 pounds, and considered to be the first agile, rebounding pivot man, "Moose" established all-time scoring records for one game, one season, and for three seasons. A fine passer whose awesome center play led Notre Dame to a three-year record of 54–12. Was All-American in 1932, 1933, and 1934, team captain under coach George Keogan in 1934. Widely acclaimed star on Midwest, New England pro teams. Coach and athletic director at St. Mary's in Minnesota, 1934–39; coached basketball at Notre Dame, 1946–51, and became athletic director in 1949.

WILLIAM W. SHARMAN 1926–
ELECTED 1975—PLAYER

Graduated from Porterville, Calif., H.S., 1944, and University of Southern California, 1950. Scoring star and captain 3 years in high school. Two years All-Pacific Coast, 2 years conference MVP. Set conference scoring record in 1950 and was All-American in 1949 and 1950. Was All-NBA 7 years as member of the Washington Caps in 1951 and the Boston Celtics for 10 years. Was MVP in 1955 All-Star Game. A fierce competitor who scored 12,665 points, was NBA's greatest foul shooter with record 56 straight in 1956, record 93 per cent one season, 1959, and 89 per cent lifetime. Considered one of the greatest shooting guards ever, was selected to the NBA Silver Anniversary Team in 1971. After playing career, became coach, winning titles in ABL, ABA, and NBA.

ELGIN BAYLOR 1934–
ELECTED 1976—PLAYER

Graduated from Spingarn H.S. in Washington, D.C., 1954, and from Seattle University, 1958. High-school All-American; All-West Coast 1957, 1958; All-American 1958. Scored 60 points in one game, averaged 31.5 points, and had 590 rebounds in leading Seattle to 1958 NCAA runner-up. NBA Rookie of the Year 1959, All-Star MVP 1959, first-team All-Star 10 years. Scored record 71 points in one game for 1960 L.A. Lakers, averaged 38.2 points in 1962, and scored 2,719 points in 1973. Scored

23,149 points in only 846 NBA games, scored 3,623 in 134 playoff games, and averaged 27.4 points per game in career. Scored record 61 points in 1962 playoff game. Third leading rebounder in playoffs, fifth in All-Star Games, and seventh career regular season with 11,463. Widely thought to be greatest forward in basketball. Elected to NBA Silver Anniversary Team in 1971.

CHARLES T. COOPER 1907–
ELECTED 1976—PLAYER

Graduated from Central H.S. in Philadelphia 1925. Began 20-year pro career with Philadelphia Panther Pros in 1925 and then with Philadelphia Giants, 1926–29. At 6-4, 215 pounds, joined New York Renaissance for brilliant 11-year career during which Rens won 1,303 games, lost 203, and in 1932–33 won 88 straight. "Tarzan" was a superb center, considered team MVP and leader of Rens that won world pro championship tournament in 1939. Acclaimed to be greatest center of his era, he later led Washington Bears to "world pro title" in 1943.

LAUREN GALE 1917–
ELECTED 1976—PLAYER

Graduated from Oakridge, Oregon, H.S., 1935, and University of Oregon, 1939. Four-year regular and All-State in 1935. A clever 6-5 forward, as a junior and senior scored 815 points and in 1939 led Oregon to the Pacific Coast title and the first NCAA tournament championship. "Laddie" was selected All-Pacific Coast Conference first team in 1938 and 1939 and made All-American in 1939. Played pro basketball with Detroit Eagles and Salt Lake City. Coached Salt Lake City team to Olympic tournament finals in 1948, losing to Phillips 66 team by one point. Selected to the All-Time Pacific Coast Northern Division team and to the Oregon Hall of Fame in 1964, the first year he was eligible. A star player on the "Tall Firs," who brought national recognition to Pacific Northwest basketball.

WILLIAM C. JOHNSON 1911–
ELECTED 1976—PLAYER

Graduated from Central, Oklahoma, H.S., 1929, University of Kansas, 1933. All-City and All-State 1928, 1929, All-American 1929. "Skinny" was a three-year star center at Kansas, leading team to a 42–11 record and 3 Big Six titles. Was All-Big Six in 1932, 1933; conference MVP and All-American in 1933. Became a third category (AAU) All-American in 1934 with Southern Kansas Stage Line as Mis-

souri Valley leading scorer. While only 6-4, he dominated most games with his jumping ability in the era of the crucial center tap. Selected as all-time great in Oklahoma in 1975.

FRANK J. McGUIRE 1916–
ELECTED 1976—COACH

Graduated from St. Xavier, New York, H.S., 1932, and St. John's University, 1936. Star player in high school, college, and in American League. Coached 11 years at St. Xavier H.S. (126–39). Only coach to win 100 or more games at each of three colleges: 103 at St. John's, 164 at North Carolina, and over 235 at South Carolina. Only coach with NCAA finalists at two colleges: St. John's and North Carolina. In 1957, won NCAA title undefeated (32–0) at North Carolina; overall, led teams to 8 NCAA and 6 NIT tournaments. Three-time Coach of the Year. Won over 500 college games and had at least 11 20-victory seasons, including 3 at St. John's, 2 at North Carolina, and 6 straight at South Carolina. In 1962, won 49, lost 31 with NBA Philadelphia Warriors. When elected, had won over 675 games in a high-school, college, and pro coaching career in which he won over 70 per cent of his games.

PAUL J. ARIZIN 1928–
ELECTED 1977—PLAYER

Graduated from LaSalle, Philadelphia, H.S., 1946, and from Villanova, 1950. Averaged 25 and 26 points per game 1949, 1950, was unanimous All-American and College Player of the Year 1950. "Pitchin' Paul" was drafted No. 1 by Philadelphia Warriors. Averaged 17 points as a rookie and over 20 points for last nine seasons, with high of 28 in 1956. Retired as third greatest NBA scorer with 16,266 points. In 10 NBA All-Star Games, and was All-Star MVP in 1952. Was league-leading scorer in 1952, 1957, led Warriors to title in 1956. The 6-6 forward with deadly jump shot hit 42 per cent and grabbed 6,546 rebounds in pro career. Was selected to NBA Silver Anniversary Team in 1971.

JOSEPH E. FULKS 1921–1976
ELECTED 1977—PLAYER

Graduated from Kuttawa, Kentucky, H.S., 1940; left Murray State in 1943 to join Marines. With great jump shot, either hand or two hands, was college and Service All-Star and joined Philadelphia Warriors 1946. "Jumpin' Joe" amazed basketball world, scoring 1,560 points (26 average). Scored astounding 63 points in February 1949 for record that stood 10 years. Scored 30 points 12 times and 41 once as first superstar of BAA and NBA. Led Warriors to BAA title in 1947, twice scored on 49 consecutive free throws. Was unanimous All-League first team 3 years during 8-year career. Was selected to NBA Silver Anniversary team in 1971.

CLIFFORD O. HAGAN 1931–
ELECTED 1977—PLAYER

Graduated from Owensboro, Kentucky, H.S., 1949, and from University of Kentucky, 1954. Led Owensboro to state title in 1949, when he was All-State and All-American schoolboy. Kentucky All-American 1952 and 1954. Teams won 86 of 91 games; won NCAA title 1951 and were undefeated in 25 games in 1954. Had NCAA record 528 rebounds, averaged 29 points, and scored UK record 51 points in one game in 1954. Ten-year NBA career with St. Louis Hawks, for whom he scored 12,433 points (18.5 average). Played in 5 NBA All-Star Games and was MVP in 1958. Helped lead Hawks to six Western Division titles and NBA championship in 1958. Scored 44 points in 1960 playoffs. Completed 13-year pro career as player-coach of ABA Dallas Chaparrals, with career scoring total of 14,908 points. Selected to all-time Southeastern Conference team in 1974 and was named all-time top Kentucky collegiate player. One of the greatest hook shooters.

JOHN P. NUCATOLA 1907–
ELECTED 1977—REFEREE

Graduated from Newtown, New York, H.S., 1926 and from Jamaica (N.Y.) Teachers College, 1930. After 10-year pro playing career and during a 12-year high-school coaching career at Newtown, he began an outstanding officiating career of over 2,000 games. Member of IAABO since 1935, he officiated for top games in ECAC, Atlantic Coast, Southern, Big 8, and for most great All-Star games and college tournaments, including NCAA and NIT. He refereed in the ABL, BAA, and NBA before retiring in 1959 to concentrate on an administrative supervisor's career. Was supervisor of officials for Ivy League, ECAC (helped found CBOA), and retired in 1977 as supervisor for NBA. Conducted over 1,200 basketball clinics around the world, wrote *Officiating Basketball*. Was an original proponent of 3-man officiating in a career devoted to the game of basketball.

JAMES C. POLLARD 1922–
ELECTED 1977—PLAYER

Graduated from Oakland Tech, California, H.S., 1940 and attended Stanford. High-school All-State 1940; Stanford All-American as sophomore when team won NCAA championship in 1942. Three-year All-Service All-Star, followed by two-year AAU All-Star and MVP in 1947, 1948. Joined Minneapolis Lakers for brilliant NBA career, 1949–1955. Selected three times as first-team All-Star forward and twice on second team; starter in four All-Star Games, 1951, 1952, 1954, 1955. Was considered one of the greatest all-around players. Smooth and with great finesse. Jump shot and passing enabled him to total 6,522 points, 1,417 assists, and 2,487 rebounds in seven pro years during which Lakers won two NBL titles and five NBA championships. Chosen in 1955 as all-time Pacific Coast forward and in 1963 as member of all-time NBA team in vote of Academy of Sports editors.

WILTON N. CHAMBERLAIN 1936–
ELECTED 1978—PLAYER

Graduated Overbrook (Philadelphia) H.S., 1955 and Kansas University, 1958. Joined Harlem Globetrotters in 1958 and Philadelphia Warriors in 1959. Dominated professional basketball during 14-year career with Philadelphia, Golden State and Los Angeles. Scoring records include 31,419 points and 30.1 average for career, 4,029 for one season, 100 for one game, and 50.4 average for one season. Rebounding records include 23,924 for career, 2,149 for one season, and 55 for one game. "Wilt the Stilt" played 47,859 minutes in 1,045 NBA games without ever fouling out. Played in 13 All-Star Games; was Rookie of the Year 1960 and NBA MVP in 1960, 1966, 1967, 1968.

JUSTIN M. BARRY 1892–1950
ELECTED 1978—COACH

Graduated Madison, (Wis.) H.S., 1911; attended Lawrence College, graduated Wisconsin University, 1914. Coached Knox College 1918–22, winning Illinois Conference 1919–20. Won Big 10 in 1923 and was co-champion in 1926 during seven years at Iowa University. At USC 17 years, "Sam" won Pacific Coast Conference in 1930, 1935, 1940. Received NABC Metropolitan Award in 1951.

JAMES E. ENRIGHT 1910–
ELECTED 1978—REFEREE

Graduated Eau Clair (Mich.) H.S., 1928. "Drafted" for a grade school game in 1930, Jim embarked on officiating career that would include championship H.S., college, A.A.U. and pro games. Particularly respected by "road" teams, he was a key official of Big 10, Big 8, and Missouri Valley conferences. At the same time he was a sportswriter. In 1967 he was president of the U. S. Basketball Writers Assn.

EDGAR S. HICKEY 1902–
ELECTED 1978—COACH

Graduated Trinity Prep (Sioux City, Ia.), 1922 and Creighton University, 1927. Began 35-year coaching career at Creighton Prep (nine years) before 26 memorable years at Creighton University, St. Louis University, and Marquette. Won seven Missouri Valley Titles and led the three schools to NCAA tournament five times and NIT nine times. Won 436 games in career. Coach of the Year in 1959, NABC president in 1954, and recipient of Metropolitan Award in 1970.

JOHN B. McLENDON, Jr. 1915–
ELECTED 1978—CONTRIBUTOR

Graduated Sumner (Kansas City, Kan.) H.S., 1932 and Kansas University, 1936. While an advisee of Dr. Naismith at UK, he began eminent coaching career at Lawrence (Kan.)

Memorial H.S. Went on to win 522 and 76% of games as H.S., college, A.A.U., and pro coach. First coach to win three consecutive national (NAIA) titles with Tennessee State, 1957–58–59. Was acknowledged leader of emergence of black colleges into varied national programs. Received Metropolitan Award in 1977.

RAY MEYER 1913–
ELECTED 1978—COACH

Graduated St. Patrick's (Chicago) H.S., 1933 and Notre Dame, 1938. Was ND assistant coach two years before assuming, in 1942, only head coaching job he has ever had, at DePaul University. When elected, Ray was nation's winningest active coach with 619 wins, 7 trips to NCAA and NIT tournaments, and NIT title in 1945. Widely respected as one of America's coaching leaders.

PETER F. NEWELL 1915–
ELECTED 1978—CONTRIBUTOR

Graduated St. Agnes (Los Angeles) H.S., 1933 and Loyola University (L.A.), 1939. After Navy service coached San Francisco University, 1946–50, Michigan State, 1950–54, and UC-Berkeley, 1954–60. Won unprecedented triple as head coach: NIT 1949, NCAA 1959, and Olympic title 1960. Won four consecutive Pac-8 titles and was Coach of the Year 1960. Widely respected as college administrator, pro general manager and for his expertise in clinics. Won Metropolitan Award in 1968.

TEAMS

Teams in the Hall of Fame and year of election:

THE FIRST TEAM, 1959
ORIGINAL CELTICS, 1959
BUFFALO GERMANS, 1961
THE RENAISSANCE (THE RENS), 1963

22

All-Time Player Register

ACTIVE PLAYERS

This section of the All-Time Player Register includes the season-by-season records and lifetime totals of every player who appeared in an NBA game during the 1977–78 season. The records of those who played in the ABA prior to the NBA are included.

Each player's individual record lists his team, games played (G), field goals made (FG), free throws made (FT), total points

(TP), and average (Avg.). The number in parentheses following field goals for ABA players indicates the number of three-point field goals scored. Wherever available, each player's date of birth, height, weight, and college are listed.

(For those players whose careers ended prior to 1977–78, see *Retired Players* section.)

Yr	Team	G	FG	FT	TP	Avg.
ABDUL-JABBAR, KAREEM (Lew Alcindor)						
b. April 16, 1947 Ht. 7-2 Wt. 225 College—UCLA						
1969-70	Milwaukee	82	938	485	2361	28.8
1970-71	Milwaukee	82	1063	470	2596	31.7
1971-72	Milwaukee	81	1159	504	2822	34.8
1972-73	Milwaukee	76	982	328	2292	30.2
1973-74	Milwaukee	81	948	295	2191	27.0
1974-75	Milwaukee	65	812	325	1949	30.0
1975-76	Los Angeles	82	914	447	2275	27.7
1976-77	Los Angeles	82	888	376	2152	26.2
1977-78	Los Angeles	62	663	274	1600	25.8
1978-79	Los Angeles	80	777	349	1903	23.8
	Totals	773	9144	3853	22141	28.6

Yr	Team	G	FG	FT	TP	Avg.
ABERNETHY, TOM						
b. May 6, 1954 Ht. 6-7 Wt. 220 College—Indiana						
1976-77	Los Angeles	70	169	101	439	6.3
1977-78	Los Angeles	73	201	91	493	6.8
1978-79	Gold. St.	70	176	70	422	6.0
	Totals	213	546	262	1354	6.4

Yr	Team	G	FG	FT	TP	Avg.
ADAMS, ALVAN						
b. July 19, 1954 Ht. 6-9 Wt. 220 College—Oklahoma						
1975-76	Phoenix	80	629	261	1519	19.0
1976-77	Phoenix	72	522	252	1296	18.0
1977-78	Phoenix	70	434	214	1082	15.5
1978-79	Phoenix	77	569	231	1369	17.8
	Totals	299	2154	958	5266	17.6

Yr	Team	G	FG	FT	TP	Avg.
ALLEN, LUCIUS						
b. Sept. 26, 1947 Ht. 6-2 Wt. 175 College—UCLA						
1969-70	Seattle	81	306	182	794	9.8
1970-71	Milwaukee	61	178	77	433	7.1
1971-72	Milwaukee	80	441	198	1080	13.5
1972-73	Milwaukee	80	547	143	1237	15.5
1973-74	Milwaukee	72	526	216	1268	17.6
1974-75	Mil.-L.A.	66	511	238	1260	19.1
1975-76	Los Angeles	76	461	197	1119	14.7
1976-77	Los Angeles	78	472	195	1139	14.6
1977-78	Kansas City	77	373	174	920	11.9
1978-79	Kansas City	31	69	19	157	5.1
	Totals	702	3884	1639	9407	13.4

Yr	Team	G	FG	FT	TP	Avg.

ANDERSON, KIM

b. May 12, 1955 Ht. 6-7 Wt. 200 College—Missouri

Yr	Team	G	FG	FT	TP	Avg.
1978-79	Portland	21	24	15	63	3.0

ARCHIBALD, NATE

b. April 18, 1948 Ht. 6-1 Wt. 160 College—Texas-El Paso

Yr	Team	G	FG	FT	TP	Avg.
1970-71	Cincinnati	82	486	336	1308	16.0
1972-72	Cincinnati	76	734	677	2145	28.2
1972-73	K.C.-Omaha	80	1028	663	2719	34.0
1973-74	K.C.-Omaha	35	222	173	617	17.6
1974-75	K.C.-Omaha	82	759	652	2170	26.5
1975-76	Kansas City	78	717	501	1935	24.8
1976-77	N.Y. Nets	34	250	197	697	20.5
1977-78	Buffalo			[Injured]		
1978-79	Boston	69	259	242	760	11.0
	Totals	545	4455	3441	12351	22.7

ARMSTRONG, TATE

b. Oct. 5, 1955 Ht. 6-3 Wt. 175 College—Duke

Yr	Team	G	FG	FT	TP	Avg.
1977-78	Chicago	66	131	22	284	4.3
1978-79	Chicago	26	28	10	66	2.5
	Totals	92	159	32	350	3.8

AWTREY, DENNIS

b. Feb. 22, 1948 Ht. 6-10 Wt. 250 College—Santa Clara

Yr	Team	G	FG	FT	TP	Avg.
1970-71	Philadelphia	70	200	104	504	7.2
1971-72	Philadelphia	58	98	49	245	4.2
1972-73	Phila.-Chi.	82	146	86	378	4.6
1973-74	Chicago	68	65	54	184	2.7
1974-75	Phoenix	82	339	132	810	9.9
1975-76	Phoenix	74	142	75	359	4.9
1976-77	Phoenix	72	160	91	411	5.7
1977-78	Phoenix	81	112	69	293	3.6
1978-79	Bost.-Seattle	63	44	41	129	2.0
	Totals	650	1306	701	3313	5.1

BAILEY, GUS

b. Feb. 18, 1951 Ht. 6-5 Wt. 185 Coll.—Texas-El Paso

Yr	Team	G	FG	FT	TP	Avg.
1974-75	Houston	47	51	20	122	2.6
1975-76	Houston	30	28	14	70	2.3
1977-78	New Orleans	48	59	37	155	3.2
1978-79	New Orleans	2	2	0	4	2.0
	Totals	127	140	71	351	2.8

BALLARD, GREG

b. Jan. 19, 1955 Ht. 6-7 Wt. 215 College—Oregon St.

Yr	Team	G	FG	FT	TP	Avg.
1977-78	Washington	76	142	88	372	4.9
1978-79	Washington	82	260	119	639	7.8
	Totals	158	402	207	1011	6.4

BANTOM, MIKE

b. Dec. 3, 1951 Ht. 6-9 Wt. 220 Coll.—St. Joseph's (Pa.)

Yr	Team	G	FG	FT	TP	Avg.
1973-74	Phoenix	76	314	141	769	10.1
1974-75	Phoenix	82	418	185	1021	12.5
1975-76	Pho.-Sea.	73	220	136	576	7.9
1976-77	Sea.-N.Y.Nets	77	361	224	946	12.3
1977-78	Indiana	82	502	254	1258	15.3
1978-79	Indiana	81	482	227	1191	14.7
	Totals	471	2297	1167	5761	12.2

BARKER, TOM

b. March 11, 1955 Ht. 6-11 Wt. 230 College—Hawaii

Yr	Team	G	FG	FT	TP	Avg.
1976-77	Atlanta	59	182	112	476	8.1
1978-79	Hou.-Bost.-N.Y.	39	68	27	163	4.2
	Totals	98	250	139	639	6.5

BARNES, MARVIN

b. July 27, 1952 Ht. 6-9 Wt. 225 College—Providence

Yr	Team	G	FG	FT	TP	Avg.
1974-75	St. Louis ABA	77	777 (0)	295	1849	24.0
1975-76	St. Louis ABA	67	678 (3)	251	1616	24.1
1976-77	Detroit	53	202	106	510	9.6
1977-78	Det.-Buff.	60	279	128	686	11.4
1978-79	Boston	38	133	43	309	8.1
	Totals	295	2069 (3)	823	4970	16.8

BARRY, RICHARD (Rick)

b. March 28, 1944 Ht. 6-7 Wt. 205 College—Miami (Fl.)

Yr	Team	G	FG	FT	TP	Avg.
1965-66	San. Fran.	80	745	569	2059	25.7
1966-67	San Fran.	78	1011	753	2775	35.6
1968-69	Oakland ABA	35	389 (3)	403	1190	34.0
1969-70	Wash. ABA	52	509 (8)	400	1442	27.7
1970-71	N.Y. ABA	59	613 (19)	451	1734	29.4
1971-72	N.Y. ABA	80	829 (73)	641	2518	31.5
1972-73	Gold. St.	82	737	358	1832	22.3
1973-74	Gold. St.	80	796	417	2009	25.1
1974-75	Gold. St.	80	1028	394	2450	30.6
1975-76	Gold. St.	81	707	287	1701	21.0
1976-77	Gold. St.	79	682	359	1723	21.8
1977-78	Gold. St.	82	760	378	1898	23.1
1978-79	Houston	80	461	160	1082	13.5
	Totals	948	9267 (103)	5570	24413	25.8

BASSETT, TIM

b. April 1, 1951 Ht. 6-8 Wt. 225 College—Georgia

Yr	Team	G	FG	FT	TP	Avg.
1973-74	San D. ABA	82	233 (0)	99	565	6.9
1974-75	San D. ABA	72	241 (3)	82	573	8.0
1975-76	N.Y. ABA	84	172 (1)	58	405	4.8
1976-77	N.Y. Nets	76	293	101	687	9.0
1977-78	New Jersey	65	149	50	348	5.4
1978-79	New Jersey	82	116	89	321	3.9
	Totals	461	1204 (4)	479	2899	6.3

BEARD, AL (Butch)

b. May 4, 1947 Ht. 6-3 Wt. 185 College—Louisville

Yr	Team	G	FG	FT	TP	Avg.
1969-70	Atlanta	72	183	135	501	7.0
1970-71	Cleveland		In Military Service			
1971-72	Cleveland	68	394	260	1048	15.4
1972-73	Seattle	73	191	100	482	6.6
1973-74	Golden State	79	316	173	805	10.2
1974-75	Golden State	82	408	232	1048	12.8
1975-76	Cleve.-N.Y.	75	228	144	600	8.0
1976-77	N.Y. Knicks	70	148	75	371	5.3
1977-78	New York	79	308	129	745	9.4
1978-79	New York	7	11	0	22	3.1
	Totals	605	2187	1248	5622	9.3

Yr	Team	G	FG	FT	TP	Avg.

BEHAGEN, RON

b. Jan. 19, 1951 Ht. 6-9 Wt. 185 College—Minnesota

Yr	Team	G	FG	FT	TP	Avg.
1973-74	Kansas City	80	357	162	876	11.0
1974-75	Kansas City	81	333	199	865	10.7
1975-76	New Orleans	66	308	144	760	11.5
1976-77	New Orleans	60	213	90	516	8.6
1977-78	Hou.-Art.-Ind.	80	346	179	871	10.9
1978-79	Det.-N.Y.-K.C.	15	28	10	66	4.4
	Totals	382	1585	784	3954	10.4

BENSON, KENT

b. Dec. 27, 1954 Ht. 6-11 Wt. 245 College—Indiana

Yr	Team	G	FG	FT	TP	Avg.
1977-78	Milwaukee	69	220	92	532	7.7
1978-79	Milwaukee	82	413	180	1006	12.3
	Totals	151	633	272	1538	10.2

BESHORE, DELMAR

b. Nov. 29, 1956 Ht. 6-1 Wt. 165 College—Calif. (Pa.)

Yr	Team	G	FG	FT	TP	Avg.
1978-79	Milwaukee	1	0	0	0	0.0

BIBBY, HENRY

b. Nov. 24, 1949 Ht. 6-1 Wt. 185 College—UCLA

Yr	Team	G	FG	FT	TP	Avg.
1972-73	New York	55	78	73	229	4.2
1973-74	New York	66	210	73	493	7.5
1974-75	N.Y.-N.O.	75	270	137	677	9.0
1975-76	New Orleans	79	266	200	732	9.3
1976-77	Philadelphia	81	302	221	825	10.2
1977-78	Philadelphia	82	286	171	743	9.1
1978-79	Philadelphia	82	368	266	1002	12.2
	Totals	520	1780	1141	4701	9.0

BIGELOW, BOB

b. Dec. 26, 1953 Ht. 6-7 Wt. 215 College—Pennsylvania

Yr	Team	G	FG	FT	TP	Avg.
1975-76	Kansas City	31	16	24	56	1.8
1976-77	Kansas City	29	35	15	85	2.9
1977-78	KC-Bost.	5	4	0	8	1.6
1978-79	San Diego	29	36	13	85	2.9
	Totals	94	91	52	234	2.5

BIRDSONG, OTIS

b. Dec. 9, 1955 Ht. 6-4 Wt. 190 College—Houston

Yr	Team	G	FG	FT	TP	Avg.
1977-78	Kansas City	73	470	216	1156	15.8
1978-79	Kansas City	82	741	296	1778	21.7
	Totals	155	1211	512	2934	18.9

BOONE, RON

b. Sept. 6, 1946 Ht. 6-2 Wt. 200 College—Idaho State

Yr	Team	G	FG	FT	TP	Avg.
1968-69	Dallas ABA	78	518 (2)	436	1478	18.9
1969-70	Dallas ABA	84	406 (17)	300	1163	13.9
1970-71	Dallas-Utah ABA	86	561 (49)	278	1547	18.0
1971-72	Utah ABA	84	391 (13)	271	1092	13.0
1972-73	Utah ABA	84	556 (10)	415	1557	18.5
1973-74	Utah ABA	84	581 (6)	300	1480	17.6

Yr	Team	G	FG	FT	TP	Avg.
1974-75	Utah ABA	84	862 (10)	363	2117	25.2
1975-76	Utah-St. L. ABA	78	697 (16)	277	1719	22.0
1976-77	Kansas City	82	747	324	1818	22.2
1977-78	Kansas City	82	563	322	1448	17.7
1978-79	Los Angeles	82	259	90	608	7.4
	Totals	908	6141 (123)	3376	16027	17.7

BOSWELL, TOM

b. Oct. 2, 1953 Ht. 6-8 Wt. 215 College—South Carolina State and South Carolina

Yr	Team	G	FG	FT	TP	Avg.
1975-76	Boston	35	41	14	96	2.7
1976-77	Boston	70	175	96	446	6.4
1977-78	Boston	65	185	93	463	7.1
1978-79	Denver	79	321	198	840	10.6
	Totals	249	722	401	1845	7.4

BOYD, FRED

b. June 13, 1950 Ht. 6-2 Wt. 180 College—Oregon State

Yr	Team	G	FG	FT	TP	Avg.
1972-73	Philadelphia	82	362	136	860	10.5
1973-74	Philadelphia	73	286	141	713	9.5
1974-75	Philadelphia	66	205	55	465	7.0
1975-76	Phila.-N.O.	36	74	29	177	4.9
1976-77	New Orleans	47	194	79	467	9.9
1977-78	New Orleans	21	44	14	102	4.9
1978-79	Detroit	5	3	0	6	1.2
	Totals	330	1168	454	279	8.5

BOYNES, WINFORD

b. May 17, 1957 Ht. 6-6½ Wt. 186 Coll.—San Francisco

Yr	Team	G	FG	FT	TP	Avg.
1978-79	New Jersey	69	256	133	645	9.3

BRADLEY, ALONZO

b. Oct. 16, 1953 Ht. 6-7 Wt. 195 College—Texas Southern

Yr	Team	G	FG	FT	TP	Avg.
1977-78	Houston	43	130	43	303	7.0
1978-79	Houston	34	37	22	96	2.8
	Totals	77	167	65	399	5.2

BRATZ, MIKE

b. Oct. 17, 1955 Ht. 6-2 Wt. 185 College—Stanford

Yr	Team	G	FG	FT	TP	Avg.
1977-78	Phoenix	80	159	56	374	4.7
1978-79	Phoenix	77	242	139	623	8.1
	Totals	157	401	195	997	6.4

BREWER, JIM

b. Dec. 3, 1951 Ht. 6-9 Wt. 220 College—Minnesota

Yr	Team	G	FG	FT	TP	Avg.
1973-74	Cleveland	82	210	80	500	3.1
1974-75	Cleveland	82	291	103	685	8.4
1975-76	Cleveland	82	400	140	940	11.5
1976-77	Cleveland	81	296	97	689	8.5
1977-78	Cleveland	80	175	46	396	5.0
1978-79	Cleve.-Det.	80	141	26	308	3.9
	Totals	487	1513	492	3518	7.2

Yr	Team	G	FG	FT	TP	Avg.

BREWER, RON

b. Sept. 16, 1955 Ht. 6-4 Wt. 180 College—Arkansas

Yr	Team	G	FG	FT	TP	Avg.
1978-79	Portland	81	434	210	1078	13.3

BRIDGEMAN, JUNIOR

b. Sept. 17, 1953 Ht. 6-5 Wt. 210 College—Louisville

Yr	Team	G	FG	FT	TP	Avg.
1975-76	Milwaukee	81	286	128	700	8.6
1976-77	Milwaukee	82	491	197	1179	14.4
1977-78	Milwaukee	82	476	166	1118	13.6
1978-79	Milwaukee	82	540	189	1269	15.5
	Totals	327	1793	680	4266	13.0

BRISTOW, ALLAN

b. Aug. 23, 1951 Ht. 6-7 Wt. 227 College—Toledo

Yr	Team	G	FG	FT	TP	Avg.
1973-74	Philadelphia	55	108	42	258	4.7
1974-75	Philadelphia	72	163	121	447	6.2
1975-76	San Antonio ABA	47	125 (0)	78	328	6.0
1976-77	San Antonio	82	365	206	936	11.4
1977-78	San Antonio	82	257	152	666	8.1
1978-79	San Antonio	74	174	124	472	6.4
	Totals	412	1192 (0)	723	3107	7.5

BROWN, FRED

b. July 7, 1948 Ht. 6-3 Wt. 185 College—Iowa

Yr	Team	G	FG	FT	TP	Avg.
1971-72	Seattle	33	59	22	140	4.2
1972-73	Seattle	79	471	121	1063	13.5
1973-74	Seattle	82	578	195	1351	16.5
1974-75	Seattle	81	737	226	1700	21.0
1975-76	Seattle	76	742	273	1757	23.1
1976-77	Seattle	72	534	168	1236	17.2
1977-78	Seattle	72	508	176	1192	16.6
1978-79	Seattle	77	446	183	1075	14.0
	Totals	572	4075	1364	9514	16.6

BROWN, JOHN

b. Dec. 14, 1951 Ht. 6-7 Wt. 220 College—Missouri

Yr	Team	G	FG	FT	TP	Avg.
1973-74	Atlanta	77	277	163	717	9.3
1974-75	Atlanta	73	315	185	815	11.2
1975-76	Atlanta	75	215	162	592	7.9
1976-77	Atlanta	77	160	121	441	5.7
1977-78	Atlanta	75	192	165	549	7.3
1978-79	Chicago	77	152	84	388	5.0
	Totals	454	1311	880	3502	7.7

BRYANT, JOE

b. Oct. 19, 1954 Ht. 6-9 Wt. 215 College—La Salle

Yr	Team	G	FG	FT	TP	Avg.
1975-76	Philadelphia	75	233	92	558	7.4
1976-77	Philadelphia	61	107	53	267	4.4
1977-78	Philadelphia	81	190	111	491	6.1
1978-79	Philadelphia	70	205	123	533	7.6
	Totals	287	735	379	1849	6.4

BUCKNER, QUINN

b. Aug. 20, 1954 Ht. 6-3 Wt. 205 College—Indiana

Yr	Team	G	FG	FT	TP	Avg.
1976-77	Milwaukee	79	299	83	681	8.6
1977-78	Milwaukee	82	314	131	759	9.3
1978-79	Milwaukee	81	251	79	581	7.2
	Totals	242	864	293	2021	8.4

BUNCH, GREG

b. May 15, 1956 Ht. 6-6 Wt. 190 College—Cal. St.-Fullerton

Yr	Team	G	FG	FT	TP	Avg.
1978-79	New York	12	9	10	28	2.3

BURLESON, TOM

b. Feb. 24, 1952 Ht. 7-2 Wt. 228 College—North Carolina State

Yr	Team	G	FG	FT	TP	Avg.
1974-75	Seattle	82	322	182	826	10.1
1975-76	Seattle	82	496	291	1283	15.6
1976-77	Seattle	82	288	220	796	9.7
1977-78	Kansas City	76	228	197	653	8.6
1978-79	Kansas City	56	157	121	435	7.8
	Totals	378	1491	1011	3993	10.6

BUSE, DON

b. Aug. 10, 1950 Ht. 6-4 Wt. 195 College—Evansville

Yr	Team	G	FG	FT	TP	Avg.
1972-73	Indiana ABA	77	158 (5)	82	413	5.4
1973-74	Indiana ABA	77	134 (36)	48	424	5.5
1974-75	Indiana ABA	80	178 (38)	47	517	6.5
1975-76	Indiana ABA	84	328 (72)	179	1051	12.5
1976-77	Indiana	81	266	114	646	8.0
1977-78	Phoenix	82	287	112	686	8.4
1978-79	Phoenix	82	285	70	640	7.8
	Totals	563	1636 (151)	652	4377	7.8

BYRNES, MARTY

b. April 30, 1956 Ht. 6-7 Wt. 218 College—Syracuse

Yr	Team	G	FG	FT	TP	Avg.
1978-79	Phoenix-N.O.	79	187	106	480	6.1

CALHOUN, CORKY

b. Nov. 1, 1950 Ht. 6-7 Wt. 210 College—Pennsylvania

Yr	Team	G	FG	FT	TP	Avg.
1972-73	Phoenix	82	211	71	493	6.0
1973-74	Phoenix	77	268	98	634	8.2
1974-75	Pho.-L.A.	70	132	58	322	4.6
1975-76	Los Angeles	76	172	65	409	5.4
1976-77	Portland	70	85	66	236	3.4
1977-78	Portland	79	175	66	416	5.3
1978-79	Indiana	81	153	72	378	4.7
	Totals	535	1196	496	2888	5.4

CARR, AUSTIN

b. March 10, 1948 Ht. 6-4 Wt. 200 College—Notre Dame

Yr	Team	G	FG	FT	TP	Avg.
1971-72	Cleveland	43	381	149	911	21.2
1972-73	Cleveland	82	702	281	1685	20.5
1973-74	Cleveland	81	748	279	1775	21.9
1974-75	Cleveland	41	252	89	593	14.5
1975-76	Cleveland	65	276	106	658	10.1
1976-77	Cleveland	82	558	213	1329	16.2
1977-78	Cleveland	82	414	183	1011	12.3
1978-79	Cleveland	82	551	292	1394	17.0
	Totals	558	3882	1592	9356	16.8

CARR, KEN

b. Aug. 15, 1955 Ht. 6-7 Wt. 215 College—North Carolina State

Yr	Team	G	FG	FT	TP	Avg.
1977-78	Los Angeles	52	134	55	323	6.2
1978-79	Los Angeles	72	225	83	533	7.4
	Totals	124	359	138	856	6.9

Yr	Team	G	FG	FT	TP	Avg.

CARR, MICHAEL LEON (M.L.)

b. Jan. 9, 1951 Ht. 6-6 Wt. 205 College—Guilford

Yr	Team	G	FG	FT	TP	Avg.
1975-76	St. Louis ABA	74	371 (9)	137	906	12.2
1976-77	Detroit	82	443	205	1091	13.3
1977-78	Detroit	79	390	200	980	12.4
1978-79	Detroit	80	587	323	1497	18.7
	Totals	315	1791 (9)	865	4474	14.2

CARTER, RON

b. Aug. 31, 1956 Ht. 6-5 Wt. 190 College—VMI

Yr	Team	G	FG	FT	TP	Avg.
1978-79	Los Angeles	46	54	36	144	3.1

CATCHINGS, HARVEY

b. Sept. 2, 1951 Ht. 6-9 Wt. 218 College—Hardin-Simmons

Yr	Team	G	FG	FT	TP	Avg.
1974-75	Philadelphia	37	41	16	98	2.6
1975-76	Philadelphia	75	103	58	264	3.5
1976-77	Philadelphia	53	62	33	157	3.0
1977-78	Philadelphia	61	70	34	174	2.9
1978-79	Phila.-N.J.	56	102	60	264	4.7
	Totals	282	378	201	957	3.4

CHANEY, DON (Duck)

b. March 22, 1946 Ht. 6-5½ Wt. 210 College—Houston

Yr	Team	G	FG	FT	TP	Avg.
1968-69	Boston	20	36	8	80	4.0
1969-70	Boston	63	115	82	312	5.0
1970-71	Boston	81	348	234	930	11.5
1971-72	Boston	79	373	197	943	11.9
1972-73	Boston	79	414	210	1038	13.1
1973-74	Boston	81	348	149	845	10.4
1974-75	Boston	82	321	133	775	9.5
1976-77	Los Angeles	81	213	70	496	6.1
1977-78	L.A.-Bos.	51	104	38	246	4.8
1978-79	Boston	65	174	36	384	5.9
	Totals	682	2446	1157	6049	8.9

CHEEKS, MAURICE

b. Sept. 8, 1956 Ht. 6-1 Wt. 180 Coll.—W. Texas St.

Yr	Team	G	FG	FT	TP	Avg.
1978-79	Philadelphia	82	292	101	685	8.4

CHENIER, PHIL

b. Oct. 30, 1950 Ht. 6-3 Wt. 180 College—California

Yr	Team	G	FG	FT	TP	Avg.
1971-72	Baltimore	81	407	182	996	12.3
1972-73	Baltimore	71	602	194	1398	19.7
1973-74	Capital	76	697	274	1668	21.9
1974-75	Washington	77	690	301	1681	21.8
1975-76	Washington	80	654	282	1590	19.9
1976-77	Washington	78	654	270	1578	20.2
1977-78	Washington	36	200	109	509	14.1
1978-79	Washington	27	69	18	156	5.8
	Totals	526	3973	1630	9576	18.2

CHONES, JIM

b. Nov. 30, 1949 Ht. 6-11 Wt. 220 College—Marquette

Yr	Team	G	FG	FT	TP	Avg.
1972-73	New York ABA	82	395 (0)	142	932	11.4
1973-74	Carolina ABA	83	535 (0)	155	1225	14.7
1974-75	Cleveland	76	446	152	1044	14.5
1975-76	Cleveland	82	563	172	1298	15.8
1976-77	Cleveland	82	450	155	1055	12.9
1977-78	Cleveland	82	525	180	1230	15.0
1978-79	Cleveland	82	472	158	1102	13.4
	Totals	569	3386 (6)	1114	7886	13.9

CLEAMONS, JIM

b. Sept. 13, 1949 Ht. 6-3½ Wt. 185 College—Ohio State

Yr	Team	G	FG	FT	TP	Avg.
1971-72	Los Angeles	38	35	28	98	2.6
1972-73	Cleveland	80	192	75	459	5.7
1973-74	Cleveland	81	236	93	565	7.0
1974-75	Cleveland	74	369	144	882	11.9
1975-76	Cleveland	82	413	174	1000	12.2
1976-77	Cleveland	60	257	112	626	10.4
1977-78	New York	79	215	81	511	6.5
1978-79	New York	79	311	130	752	9.5
	Totals	573	2028	837	4893	8.5

COLEMAN, E. C.

b. Sept. 25, 1950 Ht. 6-8 Wt. 225 College—Houston Baptist

Yr	Team	G	FG	FT	TP	Avg.
1973-74	Houston	58	128	47	303	5.2
1974-75	New Orleans	77	253	116	622	8.1
1975-76	New Orleans	67	216	59	491	7.3
1976-77	New Orleans	77	290	82	662	8.6
1977-78	Golden State	72	212	40	464	6.4
1978-79	Houston	6	5	1	11	1.8
	Totals	357	1104	345	2553	7.2

COLLINS, DOUG

b. July 28, 1951 Ht. 6-6 Wt. 180 College—Illinois State

Yr	Team	G	FG	FT	TP	Avg.
1973-74	Philadelphia	25	72	55	199	8.0
1974-75	Philadelphia	81	561	331	1453	17.9
1975-76	Philadelphia	77	614	372	1600	20.8
1976-77	Philadelphia	58	426	210	1062	18.3
1977-78	Philadelphia	79	643	267	1553	19.7
1978-79	Philadelphia	47	358	201	914	19.5
	Totals	367	2674	1436	6784	18.5

COOPER, MIKE

b. April 15, 1956 Ht. 6-5 Wt. 170 College—New Mexico

Yr	Team	G	FG	FT	TP	Avg.
1978-79	Los Angeles	3	3	0	6	2.0

COOPER, WAYNE

b. Nov. 16, 1956 Ht. 6-10 Wt. 220 College—N.O.

Yr	Team	G	FG	FT	TP	Avg.
1978-79	Golden State	65	128	41	297	4.6

CORZINE, DAVE

b. April 25, 1956 Ht. 6-11 Wt. 250 College—DePaul

Yr	Team	G	FG	FT	TP	Avg.
1978-79	Washington	59	63	49	175	3.0

COWENS, DAVE

b. Oct. 25, 1948 Ht. 6-9 Wt. 230 College—Florida State

Yr	Team	G	FG	FT	TP	Avg.
1970-71	Boston	81	550	273	1373	17.0
1971-72	Boston	79	657	175	1489	18.8
1972-73	Boston	82	740	204	1684	20.5
1973-74	Boston	80	645	226	1518	19.0
1974-75	Boston	65	569	191	1329	20.4
1975-76	Boston	78	611	157	1379	17.7
1976-77	Boston	50	328	162	818	16.4
1977-78	Boston	77	598	239	1435	18.6
1978-79	Boston	68	488	151	1127	16.6
	Totals	660	5186	1780	12152	18.4

Yr	Team	G	FG	FT	TP	Avg.

COX, WESLEY
b. Jan. 27, 1955 Ht. 6-6 Wt. 215 College—Louisville

Yr	Team	G	FG	FT	TP	Avg.
1977-78	Golden State	43	69	58	196	4.6
1978-79	Golden State	31	53	40	146	4.7
	Totals	74	122	98	342	4.6

CRISS, CHARLES
b. Nov. 6, 1949 Ht. 5-8 Wt. 165 College—New Mexico St.

Yr	Team	G	FG	FT	TP	Avg.
1977-78	Atlanta	77	319	236	874	11.4
1978-79	Atlanta	54	109	67	285	5.3
	Totals	131	428	303	1159	8.8

CROMPTON, GEFF
b. July 4, 1955 Ht. 6-11 Wt. 270 College—No. Car.

Yr	Team	G	FG	FT	TP	Avg.
1978-79	Denver	20	10	6	26	1.3

DAMPIER, LOUIE
b. Nov. 20, 1944 Ht. 6-0 Wt. 170 College—Kentucky

Yr	Team	G	FG	FT	TP	Avg.
1967-68	Kentucky ABA	72	582 (38)	209	1487	20.7
1968-69	Kentucky ABA	78	514 (199)	308	1933	24.8
1969-70	Kentucky ABA	82	545 (198)	447	2131	25.9
1970-71	Kentucky ABA	84	463 (103)	320	1555	18.5
1971-72	Kentucky ABA	83	393 (84)	281	1319	15.9
1972-73	Kentucky ABA	80	461 (54)	262	1346	16.8
1973-74	Kentucky ABA	84	555 (48)	238	1492	17.8
1974-75	Kentucky ABA	83	560 (38)	161	1395	16.8
1975-76	Kentucky ABA	82	423 (32)	126	1068	13.0
1976-77	San Antonio	80	233	64	530	6.6
1977-78	San Antonio	82	336	76	748	9.1
1978-79	San Antonio	70	123	29	275	3.9
	Totals	960	5188 (794)	2521	15279	15.9

DANDRIDGE, BOB
b. Nov. 15, 1947 Ht. 6-6 Wt. 195 College—Norfolk State

Yr	Team	G	FG	FT	TP	Avg.
1969-70	Milwaukee	81	434	199	1067	13.2
1970-71	Milwaukee	79	594	264	1452	18.4
1971-72	Milwaukee	80	630	215	1475	18.4
1972-73	Milwaukee	73	638	198	1474	20.2
1973-74	Milwaukee	71	583	175	1341	18.9
1974-75	Milwaukee	80	691	211	1593	19.9
1975-76	Milwaukee	73	650	271	1571	21.5
1976-77	Milwaukee	70	585	283	1453	20.8
1977-78	Washington	75	560	330	1450	19.3
1978-79	Washington	78	629	331	1589	20.4
	Totals	760	5994	2477	14465	19.0

DANTLEY, ADRIAN
b. Feb. 26, 1956 Ht. 6-5 Wt. 208 College—Notre Dame

Yr	Team	G	FG	FT	TP	Avg.
1976-77	Buffalo	77	544	476	1564	20.3
1977-78	Ind.-L.A.	79	578	541	1697	21.5
1978-79	Los Angeles	60	374	292	1040	17.3
	Totals	216	1496	1309	4301	19.9

DAVIS, BRAD
b. Dec. 17, 1955 Ht. 6-3 Wt. 180 College—Maryland

Yr	Team	G	FG	FT	TP	Avg.
1977-78	Los Angeles	33	30	22	82	2.5
1978-79	L.A.-Ind.	27	31	16	78	2.9
	Totals	60	61	38	160	2.7

DAVIS, HARRY
b. Jan. 27, 1956 Ht. 6-7 Wt. 220 College—Florida St.

Yr	Team	G	FG	FT	TP	Avg.
1978-79	Cleveland	40	66	30	162	4.1

DAVIS, JOHNNY
b. Oct. 21, 1955 Ht. 6-1 Wt. 170 College—Dayton

Yr	Team	G	FG	FT	TP	Avg.
1976-77	Portland	79	234	166	634	8.0
1977-78	Portland	82	343	188	874	10.7
1978-79	Indiana	79	565	314	1444	18.3
	Totals	240	1142	668	2952	12.3

DAVIS, WALTER
b. Sept. 9, 1954 Ht. 6-6 Wt. 193 College—North Carolina

Yr	Team	G	FG	FT	TP	Avg.
1977-78	Phoenix	81	786	387	1959	24.2
1978-79	Phoenix	79	764	340	1868	23.6
	Totals	160	1550	727	3827	23.9

DAWKINS, DARRYL
b. Jan. 11, 1957 Ht. 6-11 Wt. 252 College—None

Yr	Team	G	FG	FT	TP	Avg.
1975-76	Philadelphia	37	41	8	90	2.4
1976-77	Philadelphia	59	135	40	310	5.3
1977-78	Philadelphia	70	332	156	820	11.7
1978-79	Philadelphia	78	430	158	1018	13.1
	Totals	244	938	362	2238	9.2

DIETRICK, COBY
b. July 23, 1948 Ht. 6-10½ Wt. 230 Coll.—San Jose St.

Yr	Team	G	FG	FT	TP	Avg.
1970-71	Memphis ABA	37	61 (0)	21	143	3.8
1971-72	Memphis ABA	1	1 (0)	0	2	2.0
1972-73	Dallas ABA	77	205 (0)	96	506	6.6
1973-74	San Antonio ABA	84	251 (0)	81	583	6.9
1974-75	San Antonio ABA	82	220 (2)	76	522	6.4
1975-76	San Antonio ABA	81	199 (1)	68	469	5.8
1976-77	San Antonio	82	285	119	689	8.4
1977-78	San Antonio	79	250	89	589	7.5
1978-79	San Antonio	76	209	79	497	6.5
	Totals	599	1681 (3)	629	4000	6.7

DORSEY, JACKY
b. Dec. 18, 1954 Ht. 6-7 Wt. 230 College—Georgia

Yr	Team	G	FG	FT	TP	Avg.
1977-78	Denver	7	3	3	9	1.3
1978-79	Houston	20	24	8	56	2.8
	Totals	27	27	11	65	2.4

DOUGLAS, LEON
b. Aug. 26, 1954 Ht. 6-10 Wt. 230 College—Alabama

Yr	Team	G	FG	FT	TP	Avg.
1976-77	Detroit	82	245	127	617	7.5
1977-78	Detroit	79	321	221	863	10.9
1978-79	Detroit	78	342	208	892	11.4
	Totals	239	908	556	2372	9.9

Yr	Team	G	FG	FT	TP	Avg.

DREW, JOHN

b. Sept. 30, 1954 Ht. 6-6 Wt. 205 College—Gardner-Webb

Yr	Team	G	FG	FT	TP	Avg.
1974-75	Atlanta	78	527	388	1442	18.5
1975-76	Atlanta	77	586	488	1660	21.6
1976-77	Atlanta	74	689	412	1790	24.2
1977-78	Atlanta	70	593	437	1623	23.2
1978-79	Atlanta	79	650	495	1795	22.7
	Totals	378	3045	2220	8310	22.0

DUDLEY, CHARLES

b. March 5, 1950 Ht. 6-2 Wt. 180 College—Washington

Yr	Team	G	FG	FT	TP	Avg.
1972-73	Seattle	12	10	14	34	2.8
1974-75	Golden State	67	102	70	274	4.1
1975-76	Golden State	82	182	157	521	6.4
1976-77	Golden State	79	220	129	569	7.2
1977-78	Golden State	78	127	138	392	5.0
1978-79	Chicago	43	45	28	118	2.7
	Totals	361	686	536	1908	5.3

DUNLEAVY, MIKE

b. March 21, 1954 Ht. 6-3 Wt. 180 College—South Carolina

Yr	Team	G	FG	FT	TP	Avg.
1976-77	Philadelphia	32	60	34	154	4.8
1977-78	Phil.-Hou.	15	20	13	53	3.5
1978-79	Houston	74	215	159	589	8.0
	Totals	121	295	206	796	6.6

DUNN, T. R.

b. Feb. 1, 1955 Ht. 6-4 Wt. 192 College—Alabama

Yr	Team	G	FG	FT	TP	Avg.
1977-78	Portland	63	100	37	237	3.8
1978-79	Portland	80	246	122	614	7.7
	Totals	143	346	159	851	6.0

EDWARDS, JAMES

b. Nov. 22, 1955 Ht. 7-0 Wt. 225 College—Washington

Yr	Team	G	FG	FT	TP	Avg.
1977-78	L.A.-Ind.	83	495	272	1262	15.2
1978-79	Indiana	82	534	298	1366	16.7
	Totals	165	1029	570	2628	15.9

ELLIOTT, BOB

b. Aug. 18, 1955 Ht. 6-9½ Wt. 225 College—Arizona

Yr	Team	G	FG	FT	TP	Avg.
1978-79	New Jersey	14	41	41	123	8.8

ELLIS, BO

b. Aug. 8, 1954 Ht. 6-9 Wt. 195 College—Marquette

Yr	Team	G	FG	FT	TP	Avg.
1977-78	Denver	78	133	72	338	4.3
1978-79	Denver	42	42	29	113	2.7
	Totals	120	175	101	451	3.8

ELMORE, LEN

b. March 28, 1952 Ht. 6-10 Wt. 230 Coll.—Maryland

Yr	Team	G	FG	FT	TP	Avg.
1974-75	Indiana ABA	77	217 (1)	72	509	6.6
1975-76	Indiana ABA	76	480 (0)	152	1112	14.6
1976-77	Indiana	6	7	4	18	3.0
1977-78	Indiana	69	142	88	372	5.4
1978-79	Indiana	80	139	56	334	4.2
	Totals	308	985 (1)	372	2345	7.6

ENGLISH, ALEX

b. Jan. 5, 1954 Ht. 6-7 Wt. 190 College—South Carolina

Yr	Team	G	FG	FT	TP	Avg.
1976-77	Milwaukee	60	132	46	310	5.2
1977-78	Milwaukee	82	343	104	790	9.6
1978-79	Indiana	81	563	173	1299	16.0
	Totals	223	1038	323	2399	10.8

EPPS, RAY

b. Aug. 20, 1956 Ht. 6-6 Wt. 195 College—Norfolk St.

Yr	Team	G	FG	FT	TP	Avg.
1978-79	Golden State	13	10	6	26	2.0

ERVING, JULIUS

b. Feb. 22, 1950 Ht. 6-6 Wt. 200 Coll.—Massachusetts

Yr	Team	G	FG	FT	TP	Avg.
1971-72	Virginia ABA	84	907 (3)	467	2290	27.3
1972-73	Virginia ABA	71	889 (5)	475	2268	31.9
1973-74	New York ABA	84	897 (17)	454	2299	27.4
1974-75	New York ABA	84	885 (29)	486	2343	27.9
1975-76	New York ABA	84	915 (34)	530	2462	29.3
1976-77	Philadelphia	82	685	400	1770	21.6
1977-78	Philadelphia	74	611	306	1528	20.6
1978-79	Philadelphia	78	715	373	1803	23.1
	Totals	641	6504 (88)	3491	16763	26.2

FORD, CHRIS

b. Jan. 11, 1949 Ht. 6-5 Wt. 190 College—Villanova

Yr	Team	G	FG	FT	TP	Avg.
1972-73	Detroit	74	208	60	476	6.4
1973-74	Detroit	82	264	57	585	7.1
1974-75	Detroit	80	206	63	475	5.9
1975-76	Detroit	82	301	83	685	8.4
1976-77	Detroit	82	437	131	1005	12.3
1977-78	Detroit	82	374	113	861	10.5
1978-79	Det.-Bost.	81	538	172	1248	15.4
	Totals	563	2328	679	5335	9.5

FORD, DON

b. Dec. 31, 1952 Ht. 6-8 Wt. 215 College—Santa Barbara

Yr	Team	G	FG	FT	TP	Avg.
1975-76	Los Angeles	76	311	104	726	9.6
1976-77	Los Angeles	82	262	73	597	7.3
1977-78	Los Angeles	79	272	68	612	7.7
1978-79	Los Angeles	79	228	72	528	6.7
	Totals	316	1073	317	2463	7.8

FORD, PHIL

b. Feb. 9, 1956 Ht. 6-2 Wt. 176 Coll.—North Carolina

Yr	Team	G	FG	FT	TP	Avg.
1978-79	Kansas City	79	467	326	1260	15.9

FORREST, BAYARD

b. July 8, 1954 Ht. 6-10 Wt. 235 College—Grand Canyon

Yr	Team	G	FG	FT	TP	Avg.
1977-78	Phoenix	64	111	49	271	4.2
1978-79	Phoenix	75	118	62	298	4.0
	Totals	139	229	111	569	4.1

Yr	Team	G	FG	FT	TP	Avg.

FRAZIER, WALT

b. Mar. 29, 1945 Ht. 6-4 Wt. 202 College—Southern Illinois

Yr	Team	G	FG	FT	TP	Avg.
1967-68	New York	74	256	154	666	9.0
1968-69	New York	80	531	341	1403	17.5
1969-70	New York	77	600	409	1609	20.9
1970-71	New York	80	651	434	1736	21.7
1971-72	New York	77	669	450	1788	23.2
1972-73	New York	78	681	286	1648	21.1
1973-74	New York	80	674	295	1643	20.5
1974-75	New York	78	672	331	1675	21.5
1975-76	New York	59	470	186	1126	19.1
1976-77	N.Y. Knicks	76	532	259	1323	17.4
1977-78	Cleveland	51	336	153	825	16.2
1978-79	Cleveland	12	54	21	129	10.8
	Totals	822	6126	3319	15571	18.9

FREE, LLOYD

b. Dec. 9, 1953 Ht. 6-1 Wt. 185 College—Guilford

Yr	Team	G	FG	FT	TP	Avg.
1975-76	Philadelphia	71	239	112	590	8.3
1976-77	Philadelphia	78	467	334	1268	16.3
1977-78	Philadelphia	76	390	411	1191	15.7
1978-79	San Diego	78	795	654	2244	28.8
	Totals	303	1891	1511	5293	17.5

FURLOW, TERRY

b. Oct. 8, 1954 Ht. 6-5 Wt. 200 College—Michigan State

Yr	Team	G	FG	FT	TP	Avg.
1976-77	Philadelphia	32	34	16	84	2.6
1977-78	Cleveland	53	192	88	472	8.9
1978-79	Cleve.-Atl.	78	388	163	939	12.0
	Totals	163	614	267	1495	9.2

GALE, MIKE

b. July 18, 1950 Ht. 6-1 Wt. 190 Coll.—Elizabeth City

Yr	Team	G	FG	FT	TP	Avg.
1971-72	Kentucky ABA	78	201 (0)	95	497	6.4
1972-73	Kentucky ABA	81	217 (1)	100	537	6.6
1973-74	Ken.-N.Y. ABA	80	312 (2)	105	735	9.2
1974-75	New York ABA	72	221 (7)	72	535	7.4
1975-76	San Antonio ABA	78	227 (3)	64	527	6.8
1976-77	San Antonio	82	353	137	843	10.3
1977-78	San Antonio	70	275	87	637	9.1
1978-79	San Antonio	82	284	91	659	8.0
	Totals	623	2090 (13)	751	4970	8.0

GERARD, GUS

b. July 27, 1953 Ht. 6-8 Wt. 200 College—Virginia

Yr	Team	G	FG	FT	TP	Avg.
1974-75	St. Louis ABA	84	553 (1)	206	1315	15.7
1975-76	St. L.-Den. ABA	82	328 (4)	175	843	10.3
1976-77	Den.-Buf.	65	201	78	480	7.4
1977-78	Buf.-Det.	57	170	75	415	7.3
1978-79	Det.-K.C.	58	84	50	218	3.8
	Totals	346	1336 (5)	584	3271	9.5

GERVIN, GEORGE

b. April 27, 1952 Ht. 6-7 Wt. 185 Coll.—E. Michigan

Yr	Team	G	FG	FT	TP	Avg.
1972-73	Virginia ABA	30	155 (6)	96	424	14.1
1973-74	Vir.-S.A. ABA	74	664 (8)	378	1730	23.4
1974-75	San Antonio ABA	84	767 (17)	380	1965	23.4
1975-76	San Antonio ABA	81	692 (14)	342	1768	21.8
1976-77	San Antonio	82	726	443	1895	23.1
1977-78	San Antonio	82	864	504	2232	27.2
1978-79	San Antonio	80	947	471	2365	29.6
	Totals	513	4815 (45)	2614	12379	24.1

GIANELLI, JOHN

b. June 10, 1950 Ht. 6-10 Wt. 220 College—Pacific

Yr	Team	G	FG	FT	TP	Avg.
1972-73	New York	52	79	23	181	3.5
1973-74	New York	70	208	92	508	7.3
1974-75	New York	80	343	135	821	10.3
1975-76	New York	82	325	114	764	9.3
1976-77	NYK-Buf.	76	257	90	604	7.9
1977-78	Milwaukee	82	307	79	693	8.5
1978-79	Milwaukee	82	256	72	584	7.1
	Totals	524	1775	605	4155	7.9

GILMORE, ARTIS

b. Aug. 21, 1948 Ht. 7-2 Wt. 240 Coll.—Jacksonville

Yr	Team	G	FG	FT	TP	Avg.
1971-72	Kentucky ABA	84	806 (0)	391	2003	23.9
1972-73	Kentucky ABA	84	686 (1)	368	1743	20.9
1973-74	Kentucky ABA	84	621 (0)	326	1568	18.7
1974-75	Kentucky ABA	84	783 (1)	412	1981	23.6
1975-76	Kentucky ABA	84	773 (0)	521	2067	24.6
1976-77	Chicago	82	570	387	1527	18.6
1977-78	Chicago	82	704	471	1879	22.9
1978-79	Chicago	82	753	434	1940	23.7
	Totals	666	5696 (2)	3310	14708	22.1

GIVENS, JACK

b. Sept. 21, 1956 Ht. 6-5 Wt. 205 College—Kentucky

Yr	Team	G	FG	FT	TP	Avg.
1978-79	Atlanta	74	234	102	570	7.7

GLENN, MIKE

b. Sept. 10, 1955 Ht. 6-3 Wt. 175 College—Southern Illinois

Yr	Team	G	FG	FT	TP	Avg.
1977-78	Buffalo	56	195	51	441	7.9
1978-79	New York	75	263	57	583	7.8
	Totals	131	458	108	1024	7.8

GOODRICH, GAIL

b. April 23, 1943 Ht. 6-1 Wt. 170 College—UCLA

Yr	Team	G	FG	FT	TP	Avg.
1965-66	Los Angeles	65	203	103	509	7.8
1966-67	Los Angeles	77	352	253	957	12.4
1967-68	Los Angeles	79	395	302	1092	13.8
1968-69	Phoenix	81	718	495	1931	23.8
1969-70	Phoenix	81	568	488	1624	20.0
1970-71	Los Angeles	79	558	264	1380	17.5
1971-72	Los Angeles	82	826	475	2127	25.9
1972-73	Los Angeles	76	750	314	1814	23.9
1973-74	Los Angeles	82	784	508	2076	25.3
1974-75	Los Angeles	72	656	318	1630	22.6
1975-76	Los Angeles	75	583	293	1459	19.5
1976-77	New Orleans	27	136	68	340	12.6
1977-78	New Orleans	81	520	264	1304	16.1
1978-79	New Orleans	74	382	174	938	12.7
	Totals	1031	7431	4319	19181	18.6

Yr	Team	G	FG	FT	TP	Avg.

GONDREZICK, GLEN

b. Aug. 30, 1955 Ht. 6-6 Wt. 218 Coll.—NV Las Vegas

Yr	Team	G	FG	FT	TP	Avg.
1977-78	New York	72	131	83	345	4.8
1978-79	New York	75	161	55	377	5.0
	Totals	147	292	138	722	4.9

GREEN, MIKE

b. Aug. 6, 1951 Ht. 6-10 Wt. 200 Coll.—LA Tech

Yr	Team	G	FG	FT	TP	Avg.
1973-74	Denver ABA	79	366 (1)	169	904	11.4
1974-75	Denver ABA	81	593 (0)	225	1411	17.4
1975-76	Virginia ABA	54	385 (0)	154	924	17.1
1976-77	Seattle	76	290	166	746	9.8
1977-78	Sea.-S.A.	72	238	107	583	8.1
1978-79	San Antonio	76	235	101	571	7.5
	Totals	438	2107	922	5139	11.7

GREEN, RICKEY

b. Aug. 18, 1954 Ht. 6-2 Wt. 170 College—Michigan

Yr	Team	G	FG	FT	TP	Avg.
1977-78	Golden State	76	143	54	340	4.5
1978-79	Detroit	27	67	45	179	6.6
	Totals	103	210	99	519	5.0

GREEN, STEVE

b. Oct. 4, 1953 Ht. 6-7 Wt. 220 College—Indiana

Yr	Team	G	FG	FT	TP	Avg.
1975-76	Utah-St. L. ABA	52	195 (0)	84	474	9.1
1976-77	Indiana	70	183	84	450	6.4
1977-78	Indiana	44	56	39	151	3.4
1978-79	Indiana	39	42	20	104	2.7
	Totals	205	476 (0)	227	1179	5.8

GREEN, TOMMY

b. April 8, 1956 Ht. 6-2 Wt. 185 College—Southern

Yr	Team	G	FG	FT	TP	Avg.
1978-79	New Orleans	59	92	48	232	3.9

GREVEY, KEVIN

b. May 12, 1953 Ht. 6-5 Wt. 210 College—Kentucky

Yr	Team	G	FG	FT	TP	Avg.
1975-76	Washington	56	79	52	210	3.8
1976-77	Washington	76	224	79	527	6.9
1977-78	Washington	81	505	243	1253	15.5
1978-79	Washington	65	418	173	1009	15.5
	Totals	278	1226	547	2999	10.8

GRIFFIN, PAUL

b. Jan. 1, 1954 Ht. 6-9 Wt. 205 College—W. Michigan

Yr	Team	G	FG	FT	TP	Avg.
1976-77	New Orleans	81	140	145	425	5.2
1977-78	New Orleans	82	160	112	432	5.3
1978-79	New Orleans	77	106	91	303	3.9
	Totals	240	406	348	1160	4.8

GROSS, BOB

b. Aug. 3, 1953 Ht. 6-6 Wt. 200 College—Long Beach St.

Yr	Team	G	FG	FT	TP	Avg.
1975-76	Portland	76	209	97	515	6.8
1976-77	Portland	82	376	183	935	11.4
1977-78	Portland	72	381	152	914	12.7
1978-79	Portland	53	209	96	514	9.7
	Totals	283	1175	528	2878	10.2

GRUNFELD, ERNIE

b. April 24, 1955 Ht. 6-6 Wt. 215 College—Tennessee

Yr	Team	G	FG	FT	TP	Avg.
1977-78	Milwaukee	73	204	94	502	6.9
1978-79	Milwaukee	82	326	191	843	10.3
	Totals	155	530	285	1345	8.7

HANSEN, GLENN

b. April 21, 1952 Ht. 6-4 Wt. 205 College—Ut. S. & LSU

Yr	Team	G	FG	FT	TP	Avg.
1975-76	Kansas City	66	173	85	431	6.5
1976-77	Kansas City	41	67	23	157	3.8
1977-78	Chi.-K.C.	5	0	0	0	0.0
1978-79	Seattle	15	29	18	76	5.1
	Totals	127	269	126	664	5.2

HARDY, JAMES

b. Dec. 1, 1956 Ht. 6-8 Wt. 220 College—San Fran.

Yr	Team	G	FG	FT	TP	Avg.
1978-79	New Orleans	68	196	61	453	6.7

HASSETT, JOE

b. Sept. 11, 1955 Ht. 6-5 Wt. 180 College—Providence

Yr	Team	G	FG	FT	TP	Avg.
1977-78	Seattle	48	91	10	192	4.0
1978-79	Seattle	55	100	23	223	4.1
	Totals	103	191	33	415	4.0

HAWES, STEVE

b. May 26, 1950 Ht. 6-9 Wt. 220 College—Washington

Yr	Team	G	FG	FT	TP	Avg.
1974-75	Houston	55	140	45	325	5.9
1975-76	Hou.-Port.	72	199	87	485	6.7
1976-77	Atlanta	44	147	67	361	8.2
1977-78	Atlanta	75	387	175	949	12.7
1978-79	Atlanta	81	372	108	852	10.5
	Totals	327	1245	482	2972	9.1

HAWKINS, ROBERT (Bubbles)

b. June 30, 1954 Ht. 6-4 Wt. 190 College—Illinois St.

Yr	Team	G	FG	FT	TP	Avg.
1975-76	Golden State	32	53	20	126	3.9
1976-77	N.Y. Nets	52	406	194	1006	19.3
1977-78	New Jersey	15	69	25	163	10.9
1978-79	Detroit	4	6	6	18	4.5
	Totals	103	534	245	1313	12.7

HAYES, ELVIN

b. Nov. 17, 1945 Ht. 6-9 Wt. 235 College—Houston

Yr	Team	G	FG	FT	TP	Avg.
1968-69	San Diego	82	930	467	2327	28.4
1969-70	San Diego	82	914	428	2256	27.5
1970-71	San Diego	82	948	454	2350	28.7
1971-72	Houston	82	832	399	2063	25.2
1972-73	Baltimore	81	713	291	1717	21.2
1973-74	Capital	81	689	357	1735	21.4
1974-75	Washington	82	739	409	1887	23.0
1975-76	Washington	80	649	287	1585	19.8
1976-77	Washington	82	760	422	1942	23.7
1977-78	Washington	81	636	326	1598	19.7
1978-79	Washington	82	720	349	1789	21.8
	Totals	897	8530	4189	21249	23.7

Yr	Team	G	FG	FT	TP	Avg.

HAYWOOD, SPENCER

b. April 22, 1949 Ht. 6-8 Wt. 225 Coll.—Detroit

Yr	Team	G	FG	FT	TP	Avg.
1969-70	Denver ABA	84	986 (0)	547	2519	30.0
1970-71	Seattle	33	260	160	680	20.6
1971-72	Seattle	73	717	480	1914	26.2
1972-73	Seattle	77	889	473	2251	29.2
1973-74	Seattle	75	694	373	1761	23.5
1974-75	Seattle	68	608	309	1525	22.4
1975-76	New York	78	605	339	1549	19.9
1976-77	N.Y. Knicks	31	202	109	513	16.5
1977-78	New York	67	412	96	920	13.7
1978-79	N.Y.-N.O.	68	595	231	1421	20.9
Totals		654	5968	3117	15053	23.0

HEARD, GARFIELD

b. May 3, 1948 Ht. 6-8 Wt. 220 College—Oklahoma

Yr	Team	G	FG	FT	TP	Avg.
1970-71	Seattle	65	152	82	386	5.9
1971-72	Seattle	58	190	79	459	7.9
1972-73	Sea.-Chi.	81	350	116	816	10.1
1973-74	Buffalo	81	524	191	1239	15.3
1974-75	Buffalo	67	318	106	742	11.1
1975-76	Phoenix	86	392	158	942	11.0
1976-77	Phoenix	46	173	100	446	9.7
1977-78	Phoenix	80	265	90	620	7.8
1978-79	Phoenix	63	162	71	395	6.3
Totals		627	2526	993	6045	9.6

HENDERSON, TOM

b. Jan. 26, 1952 Ht. 6-3 Wt. 190 College—Hawaii

Yr	Team	G	FG	FT	TP	Avg.
1974-75	Atlanta	79	367	168	902	11.4
1975-76	Atlanta	81	469	216	1154	14.2
1976-77	Atl.-Wash.	87	371	233	975	11.2
1977-78	Washington	75	339	179	857	11.4
1978-79	Washington	70	299	156	754	10.8
Totals		392	1845	952	4642	11.8

HERRON, KEITH

b. June 14, 1956 Ht. 6-6 Wt. 195 College—Villanova

Yr	Team	G	FG	FT	TP	Avg.
1978-79	Atlanta	14	14	12	40	2.9

HICKS, PHIL

b. Jan. 31, 1953 Ht. 6-7 Wt. 205 College—Tulane

Yr	Team	G	FG	FT	TP	Avg.
1976-77	Hou.-Chi.	37	41	11	93	2.5
1978-79	Denver	20	18	3	39	2.0
Totals		57	59	14	132	2.3

HIGGS, KEN

b. Jan. 31, 1955 Ht. 6-0 Wt. 185 College—Louisiana St.

Yr	Team	G	FG	FT	TP	Avg.
1978-79	Cleveland	68	127	85	339	5.0

HILL, ARMOND

b. March 31, 1953 Ht. 6-4 Wt. 190 College—Princeton

Yr	Team	G	FG	FT	TP	Avg.
1976-77	Atlanta	81	175	139	489	6.0
1977-78	Atlanta	82	304	189	797	9.7
1978-79	Atlanta	82	296	246	838	10.2
Totals		245	775	574	2124	8.7

HILLMAN, DARNELL

b. Aug. 29, 1949 Ht. 6-9 Wt. 215 Coll.—San Jose St.

Yr	Team	G	FG	FT	TP	Avg.
1971-72	Indiana ABA	73	199 (1)	114	515	7.1
1972-73	Indiana ABA	84	328 (0)	148	804	9.6
1973-74	Indiana ABA	83	325 (3)	99	758	9.1
1974-75	Indiana ABA	81	486 (0)	152	1124	13.9
1975-76	Indiana ABA	74	374 (1)	243	994	13.4
1976-77	Indiana	82	359	161	879	10.7
1977-78	N.J.-Den.	78	340	167	847	10.9
1978-79	Kansas City	78	211	125	547	7.0
Totals		633	2622 (5)	1209	6468	10.2

HOLLAND, WILBUR

b. Nov. 8, 1951 Ht. 6-0 Wt. 175 College—New Orleans

Yr	Team	G	FG	FT	TP	Avg.
1975-76	Atlanta	33	85	22	192	5.8
1976-77	Chicago	79	509	158	1176	14.9
1977-78	Chicago	82	569	223	1361	16.6
1978-79	Chicago	82	445	141	1031	12.6
Totals		276	1608	544	3760	13.6

HOLLINS, LIONEL

b. Oct. 19, 1953 Ht. 6-3 Wt. 185 College—Arizona St.

Yr	Team	G	FG	FT	TP	Avg.
1975-76	Portland	74	311	178	800	10.8
1976-77	Portland	76	452	215	1119	14.7
1977-78	Portland	81	531	223	1285	15.9
1978-79	Portland	64	402	172	976	15.3
Totals		295	1696	788	4180	14.2

HOLLIS, ESSIE

b. May 16, 1955 Ht. 6-6 Wt. 195 College—St. Bonaventure

Yr	Team	G	FG	FT	TP	Avg.
1978-79	Detroit	25	30	9	69	2.8

HOWARD, OTIS

b. Nov. 6, 1956 Ht. 6-7 Wt. 220 College—Austin Peay

Yr	Team	G	FG	FT	TP	Avg.
1978-79	Milw.-Detr.	14	24	11	59	4.2

HUDSON, LOU

b. July 11, 1944 Ht. 6-5 Wt. 220 College—Minnesota

Yr	Team	G	FG	FT	TP	Avg.
1966-67	St. Louis	80	620	231	1471	18.4
1967-68	St. Louis	46	227	120	574	12.5
1968-69	Atlanta	81	716	338	1770	21.9
1969-70	Atlanta	80	830	371	2031	25.4
1970-71	Atlanta	76	829	381	2039	26.8
1971-72	Atlanta	77	775	349	1899	24.7
1972-73	Atlanta	75	816	397	2029	27.1
1973-74	Atlanta	65	678	295	1651	25.4
1974-75	Atlanta	11	97	48	242	22.0
1975-76	Atlanta	81	569	237	1375	17.0
1976-77	Atlanta	58	413	142	968	16.7
1977-78	Los Angeles	82	493	137	1123	13.7
1978-79	Los Angeles	78	329	110	768	9.8
Totals		890	7392	3156	17940	20.2

HUGHES, KIM

b. June 4, 1952 Ht. 6-11 Wt. 220 College—Wisconsin

Yr	Team	G	FG	FT	TP	Avg.
1975-76	New York ABA	84	300 (0)	92	692	8.2
1976-77	N.Y. Nets	81	151	19	321	4.0
1977-78	New Jersey	56	57	9	123	2.2
1978-79	Denver	81	98	18	214	2.6
Totals		302	606 (0)	138	1350	4.5

Yr	Team	G	FG	FT	TP	Avg.

ISSEL, DAN

b. Oct. 25, 1948 Ht. 6-9 Wt. 240 College—Kentucky

Yr	Team	G	FG	FT	TP	Avg.
1970-71	Kentucky ABA	83	938 (0)	604	2480	29.9
1971-72	Kentucky ABA	83	969 (3)	591	2538	30.6
1972-73	Kentucky ABA	84	899 (3)	485	2292	27.3
1973-74	Kentucky ABA	83	826 (3)	457	2118	25.5
1974-75	Kentucky ABA	83	614 (0)	237	1465	17.7
1975-76	Denver ABA	84	751 (1)	425	1930	23.0
1976-77	Denver	79	660	445	1765	22.3
1977-78	Denver	82	659	428	1746	21.3
1978-79	Denver	81	532	316	1380	17.0
	Totals	742	6848 (10)	3988	17714	23.9

JACKSON, PHIL

b. Sept. 17, 1945 Ht. 6-8 Wt. 220 College—No. Dakota

Yr	Team	G	FG	FT	TP	Avg.
1967-68	New York	75	182	99	463	6.2
1968-69	New York	47	126	80	332	7.1
1970-71	New York	71	118	95	331	4.7
1971-72	New York	80	205	167	577	7.2
1972-73	New York	80	245	154	644	8.1
1973-74	New York	82	361	191	913	11.1
1974-75	New York	78	324	193	841	10.8
1975-76	New York	80	185	110	480	6.0
1976-77	N.Y. Knicks	76	102	51	255	3.4
1977-78	New York	63	55	43	153	2.4
1978-79	New Jersey	59	144	86	374	6.3
	Totals	791	2047	1269	5363	6.8

JAMES, AARON

b. Oct. 5, 1952 Ht. 6-8 Wt. 210 College—Grambling

Yr	Team	G	FG	FT	TP	Avg.
1974-75	New Orleans	76	370	147	887	11.7
1975-76	New Orleans	75	262	153	677	9.0
1976-77	New Orleans	52	238	89	565	10.9
1977-78	New Orleans	80	428	117	973	12.2
1978-79	New Orleans	73	311	105	727	10.0
	Totals	356	1609	611	3829	10.8

JOHNSON, CHARLES

b. March 31, 1949 Ht. 6-0 Wt. 170 College—California

Yr	Team	G	FG	FT	TP	Avg.
1972-73	Gold. St.	70	171	33	375	5.4
1973-74	Gold. St.	59	194	38	426	7.2
1974-75	Gold. St.	79	394	75	863	10.9
1975-76	Gold. St.	81	342	60	744	9.2
1976-77	Gold. St.	79	255	49	559	7.1
1977-78	Gold. St.	71	237	49	523	7.4
1978-79	Washington	82	342	67	751	9.2
	Totals	521	1935	371	4241	8.1

JOHNSON, CLEMON

b. Sept. 12, 1956 Ht. 6-10 Wt. 240 College—Fla. A&M

Yr	Team	G	FG	FT	TP	Avg.
1978-79	Portland	74	102	36	240	3.2

JOHNSON, DENNIS

b. Sept. 18, 1954 Ht. 6-4 Wt. 210 College—Pepperdine

Yr	Team	G	FG	FT	TP	Avg.
1976-77	Seattle	81	285	179	749	9.2
1977-78	Seattle	81	367	297	1031	12.7
1978-79	Seattle	80	482	306	1270	15.9
	Totals	242	1134	782	3050	12.6

JOHNSON, EDDIE

b. Feb. 24, 1955 Ht. 6-2 Wt. 175 College—Auburn

Yr	Team	G	FG	FT	TP	Avg.
1977-78	Atlanta	79	332	164	828	10.5
1978-79	Atlanta	78	501	243	1245	16.0
	Totals	157	833	407	2073	13.2

JOHNSON, GEORGE

b. Dec. 18, 1948 Ht. 6-11 Wt. 205 College—Dillard

Yr	Team	G	FG	FT	TP	Avg.
1972-73	Golden State	56	41	7	89	1.6
1973-74	Golden State	66	173	59	405	6.1
1974-75	Golden State	82	152	60	364	4.4
1975-76	Golden State	82	165	70	400	4.9
1976-77	G.S.-Buf.	78	198	71	467	6.0
1977-78	New Jersey	81	285	133	703	8.7
1978-79	New Jersey	78	206	105	517	6.6
	Totals	523	1220	505	2945	5.6

JOHNSON, GEORGE

b. Dec. 8, 1956 Ht. 6-7 Wt. 205 Coll.—St. John's (NY)

Yr	Team	G	FG	FT	TP	Avg.
1978-79	Milwaukee	67	165	84	414	6.2

JOHNSON, JOHN

b. Oct. 18, 1947 Ht. 6-7 Wt. 200 College—Iowa

Yr	Team	G	FG	FT	TP	Avg.
1970-71	Cleveland	67	435	240	1110	16.6
1971-72	Cleveland	82	557	277	1391	17.0
1972-73	Cleveland	82	492	199	1183	14.4
1973-74	Portland	69	459	212	1130	16.4
1974-75	Portland	80	527	236	1290	16.1
1975-76	Port.-Hou.	76	316	120	752	9.9
1976-77	Houston	79	319	94	732	9.3
1977-78	Hou.-Sea.	77	342	133	817	10.6
1978-79	Seattle	82	356	190	902	11.0
	Totals	694	3803	1701	9307	13.4

JOHNSON, MARQUES

b. Feb. 8, 1956 Ht. 6-7 Wt. 218 College—UCLA

Yr	Team	G	FG	FT	TP	Avg.
1977-78	Milwaukee	80	628	301	1557	19.5
1978-79	Milwaukee	77	820	332	1972	25.6
	Totals	157	1448	633	3529	22.5

JOHNSON, OLLIE

b. May 11, 1949 Ht. 6-6 Wt. 200 College—Temple

Yr	Team	G	FG	FT	TP	Avg.
1972-73	Portland	78	308	156	772	9.9
1973-74	Portland	79	209	77	495	6.3
1974-75	N.O.-K.C.-O.	73	203	95	501	6.9
1975-76	Kansas City	81	348	125	821	10.1
1976-77	Kansas City	81	218	101	537	6.6
1977-78	Atlanta	82	292	111	695	8.5
1978-79	Chicago	71	281	88	650	9.2
	Totals	545	1859	753	4471	8.2

JOHNSON, WALLACE (Mickey)

b. Aug. 31, 1952 Ht. 6-10 Wt. 190 College—Aurora

Yr	Team	G	FG	FT	TP	Avg.
1974-75	Chicago	38	53	37	143	3.8
1975-76	Chicago	81	478	283	1239	15.3
1976-77	Chicago	81	538	324	1400	17.3
1977-78	Chicago	81	561	362	1484	18.3
1978-79	Chicago	82	496	273	1265	15.4
	Totals	363	2126	1279	5531	15.2

Yr	Team	G	FG	FT	TP	Avg.

JONES, BOBBY

b. Dec. 18, 1951 Ht. 6-9 Wt. 210 Coll.—No. Carolina

Yr	Team	G	FG	FT	TP	Avg.
1974-75	Denver ABA	84	529 (0)	187	1245	14.8
1975-76	Denver ABA	83	510 (0)	215	1235	14.9
1976-77	Denver	82	501	236	1238	15.1
1977-78	Denver	75	440	208	1088	14.5
1978-79	Philadelphia	80	378	209	965	12.1
	Totals	404	2358 (0)	1055	5771	14.3

JONES, CALDWELL

b. Aug. 4, 1950 Ht. 6-11 Wt. 213 Coll.—Albany St. (Ga.)

Yr	Team	G	FG	FT	TP	Avg.
1973-74	San Diego ABA	79	505 (2)	171	1187	15.0
1974-75	San Diego ABA	76	603 (3)	264	1479	19.5
1975-76	S.D.-Ken.- St. L. ABA	76	423 (0)	140	986	13.0
1976-77	Philadelphia	82	215	64	494	6.0
1977-78	Philadelphia	81	169	96	434	5.4
1978-79	Philadelphia	78	302	121	725	9.3
	Totals	472	2217	856	5305	11.2

JONES, DWIGHT

b. Feb. 27, 1952 Ht. 6-10 Wt. 210 College—Houston

Yr	Team	G	FG	FT	TP	Avg.
1973-74	Atlanta	74	238	116	592	8.0
1974-75	Atlanta	75	323	132	778	10.4
1975-76	Atlanta	66	251	163	665	10.1
1976-77	Houston	74	167	101	435	5.9
1977-78	Houston	82	346	181	873	10.6
1978-79	Houston	81	181	96	458	5.7
	Totals	452	1506	789	3801	8.4

JORDAN, ED

b. Jan. 19, 1955 Ht. 6-1 Wt. 170 College—Rutgers

Yr	Team	G	FG	FT	TP	Avg.
1977-78	Cleve.-N.J.	73	215	131	561	7.7
1978-79	New Jersey	82	401	213	1015	12.4
	Totals	155	616	344	1576	10.2

JUDKINS, JEFF

b. March 23, 1956 Ht. 6-6 Wt. 185 College—Utah

Yr	Team	G	FG	FT	TP	Avg.
1978-79	Boston	81	295	119	709	8.8

KELLEY, RICH

b. March 23, 1953 Ht. 7-0 Wt. 230 College—Stanford

Yr	Team	G	FG	FT	TP	Avg.
1975-76	New Orleans	75	184	159	527	7.0
1976-77	New Orleans	76	184	156	524	6.9
1977-78	New Orleans	82	304	225	833	10.2
1978-79	New Orleans	80	440	373	1253	15.7
	Totals	313	1112	913	3137	10.0

KENON, LARRY

b. Dec. 13, 1952 Ht. 6-9 Wt. 205 Coll.—Memphis St.

Yr	Team	G	FG	FT	TP	Avg.
1973-74	New York ABA	84	589 (0)	156	1334	15.9
1974-75	New York ABA	84	675 (1)	217	1570	18.7
1975-76	San Antonio ABA	81	647 (0)	221	1515	18.7
1976-77	San Antonio	78	706	293	1705	21.9
1977-78	San Antonio	81	698	276	1672	20.6
1978-79	San Antonio	81	748	295	1791	22.1
	Totals	489	4063	1458	9587	19.6

KING, BERNARD

b. Dec. 4, 1956 Ht. 6-7 Wt. 205 College—Tennessee

Yr	Team	G	FG	FT	TP	Avg.
1977-78	New Jersey	79	798	313	1909	24.2
1978-79	New Jersey	82	710	349	1769	21.6
	Totals	161	1508	662	3678	22.8

KNIGHT, BILLY

b. June 9, 1952 Ht. 6-7 Wt. 200 College—Pittsburgh

Yr	Team	G	FG	FT	TP	Avg.
1974-75	Indiana ABA	80	576 (4)	207	1371	17.1
1975-76	Indiana ABA	70	768 (6)	415	1969	28.1
1976-77	Indiana	78	831	413	2075	26.6
1977-78	Buffalo	53	457	301	1215	22.9
1978-79	Indiana	79	441	249	1131	14.3
	Totals	360	3073	1585	7761	21.6

KNIGHT, TOBY

b. April 3, 1955 Ht. 6-9 Wt. 210 College—Notre Dame

Yr	Team	G	FG	FT	TP	Avg.
1977-78	New York	80	222	63	507	6.3
1978-79	New York	82	609	145	1363	16.6
	Totals	162	831	208	1870	11.5

KRAMER, JOEL

b. Oct. 30, 1955 Ht. 6-7 Wt. 203 Coll.—San Diego St.

Yr	Team	G	FG	FT	TP	Avg.
1978-79	Phoenix	82	181	125	487	5.9

KUESTER, JOHN

b. Feb. 6, 1955 Ht. 6-3 Wt. 182 College—North Car.

Yr	Team	G	FG	FT	TP	Avg.
1977-78	K.C.	78	145	87	377	4.8
1978-79	Denver	33	16	13	45	1.4
	Totals	111	161	100	422	3.8

KUNNERT, KEVIN

b. Nov. 11, 1951 Ht. 7-0 Wt. 231 College—Iowa

Yr	Team	G	FG	FT	TP	Avg.
1973-74	Buf.-Hou.	64	105	21	231	3.6
1974-75	Houston	75	346	116	808	10.8
1975-76	Houston	80	465	102	1032	12.9
1976-77	Houston	81	333	93	759	9.4
1977-78	Houston	80	368	93	829	10.4
1978-79	San Diego	81	234	56	524	6.5
	Totals	461	1851	481	4183	9.1

KUPCHAK, MITCH

b. May 24, 1954 Ht. 6-10 Wt. 230 College—North Car.

Yr	Team	G	FG	FT	TP	Avg.
1976-77	Wash.	82	341	170	852	10.4
1977-78	Wash.	67	393	280	1066	15.9
1978-79	Wash.	66	369	223	961	14.6
	Totals	215	1103	673	2879	13.4

LACEY, SAM

b. March 28, 1948 Ht. 6-10 Wt. 235 College—N.Mex.St.

Yr	Team	G	FG	FT	TP	Avg.
1970-71	Cincinnati	81	467	156	1090	13.5
1971-72	Cincinnati	81	410	119	939	11.6
1972-73	K.C.-Omaha	79	471	126	1068	13.5
1973-74	K.C.-Omaha	79	467	185	1119	14.2
1974-75	K.C.-Omaha	81	392	144	928	11.5
1975-76	Kansas City	81	409	217	1035	12.8
1976-77	Kansas City	82	327	215	869	10.6
1977-78	Kansas City	77	265	134	664	8.6
1978-79	Kansas City	82	350	167	867	10.6
	Totals	723	3558	1463	8579	11.9

Yr	Team	G	FG	FT	TP	Avg.
LAGARDE, TOM						
b. Feb. 10, 1955 Ht. 6-10 Wt. 220 College—No. Car.						
1977-78	Denver	77	96	114	306	4.0
1978-79	Seattle	23	98	57	253	11.0
	Totals	100	194	171	559	5.6
LAMBERT, JOHN						
b. Jan. 14, 1953 Ht. 6-10 Wt. 225 College—USC						
1975-76	Cleveland	54	49	25	123	2.3
1976-77	Cleveland	63	67	25	159	2.5
1977-78	Cleveland	76	142	27	311	4.1
1978-79	Cleveland	70	148	35	331	4.7
	Totals	263	406	112	924	3.5
LANDSBERGER, MARK						
b. May 21, 1955 Ht. 6-8 Wt. 215 College—Arizona St.						
1977-78	Chicago	62	127	91	345	5.6
1978-79	Chicago	80	278	91	647	8.1
	Totals	142	405	182	992	7.0
LANIER, BOB						
b. Sept. 10, 1948 Ht. 6-11 Wt. 265 Coll.—St. Bonaventure						
1970-71	Detroit	82	504	273	1281	15.6
1971-72	Detroit	80	834	388	2056	25.7
1972-73	Detroit	81	810	307	1927	23.8
1973-74	Detroit	81	748	326	1822	22.5
1974-75	Detroit	76	731	361	1823	24.0
1975-76	Detroit	64	541	284	1366	21.3
1976-77	Detroit	64	678	260	1616	25.3
1977-78	Detroit	63	622	298	1542	24.5
1978-79	Detroit	53	489	275	1253	23.6
	Totals	644	5957	2772	14686	22.8
LEE, ALFRED "BUTCH"						
b. Dec. 5, 1956 Ht. 6-0 Wt. 185 College—Marquette						
1978-79	Atl.-Cleve.	82	290	175	755	9.2
LEE, RON						
b. Nov. 2, 1952 Ht. 6-3 Wt. 193 College-Oregon						
1976-77	Phoenix	82	347	142	836	10.2
1977-78	Phoenix	82	417	170	1004	12.2
1978-79	Phoenix-N.O.	60	218	98	534	8.9
	Totals	224	982	410	2374	10.6
LLOYD, SCOTT						
b. Dec. 19, 1952 Ht. 6-10 Wt. 230 Coll.—Arizona St.						
1976-77	Milwaukee	69	153	95	401	5.8
1977-78	Mil.-Buff.	70	80	49	209	3.0
1978-79	S.D.-Chi.	72	42	27	111	1.5
	Totals	211	275	171	721	3.4
LONG, JOHN						
b. Aug, 28, 1956 Ht. 6-5 Wt. 210 College—Detroit						
1978-79	Detroit	82	581	157	1319	16.1
LUCAS, JOHN						
b. Oct. 31, 1953 Ht. 6-2 Wt. 180 College—Maryland						
1976-77	Houston	82	388	135	911	11.1
1977-78	Houston	82	412	193	1017	12.4
1978-79	Golden State	82	530	264	1324	16.1
	Totals	246	1330	592	3252	13.2

Yr	Team	G	FG	FT	TP	Avg.
LUCAS, MAURICE						
b. Feb. 18, 1952 Ht. 6-9 Wt. 215 College—Marquette						
1974-75	St. Louis ABA	83	591 (0)	375	1557	18.8
1975-76	St. L.-Ken. ABA	86	617 (3)	217	1460	17.0
1976-77	Portland	79	632	335	1599	20.2
1977-78	Portland	68	453	207	1113	16.4
1978-79	Portland	69	568	270	1406	20.4
	Totals	385	2861 (3)	1404	7135	18.5
MALONE, MOSES						
b. March 23, 1954 Ht. 6-10 Wt. 215 College—None						
1974-75	Utah ABA	83	591 (0)	375	1557	18.8
1975-76	St. Louis ABA	43	251 (0)	112	614	14.3
1976-77	Buf.-Hou.	82	389	305	1083	13.5
1977-78	Houston	59	413	318	1144	19.4
1978-79	Houston	82	716	599	2031	24.8
	Totals	349	2360 (0)	1709	6429	18.4
MARAVICH, PETE						
b. June 22, 1948 Ht. 6-5 Wt. 200 College—Louisiana St.						
1970-71	Atlanta	81	738	404	1880	23.2
1971-72	Atlanta	66	460	355	1275	19.3
1972-73	Atlanta	79	789	485	2063	26.1
1973-74	Atlanta	76	819	469	2107	27.7
1974-75	New Orleans	79	655	390	1700	21.5
1975-76	New Orleans	62	604	396	1604	25.9
1976-77	New Orleans	73	886	501	2273	31.1
1977-78	New Orleans	50	556	240	1352	27.0
1978-79	New Orleans	49	436	233	1105	22.6
	Totals	615	5943	3473	15359	25.0
MAXWELL, CEDRIC (Cornbread)						
b. Nov. 21, 1955 Ht. 6-8 Wt. 205 Coll.—N.C. Charlotte						
1977-78	Boston	72	170	188	528	7.3
1978-79	Boston	80	472	574	1518	19.0
	Totals	152	642	762	2046	13.5
MAY, SCOTT						
b. March 19, 1954 Ht. 6-7 Wt. 215 College—Indiana						
1976-77	Chicago	72	431	188	1050	14.6
1977-78	Chicago	55	280	175	735	13.4
1978-79	Chicago	37	59	30	148	4.0
	Totals	164	770	393	1933	11.8
McADOO, BOB						
b. Sept. 25, 1951 Ht. 6-9 Wt. 210 College—North Car.						
1972-73	Buffalo	80	585	271	1441	18.0
1973-74	Buffalo	74	901	459	2261	30.6
1974-75	Buffalo	82	1095	641	2831	34.5
1975-76	Buffalo	78	934	559	2427	31.1
1976-77	Buf.-NYK	72	740	381	1861	25.8
1977-78	New York	79	814	469	2097	26.5
1978-79	N.Y.-Bos.	60	596	295	1487	24.8
	Totals	525	5665	3075	14405	27.4
McCLAIN, TED						
b. Aug. 30, 1947 Ht. 6-3 Wt. 190 Coll.—Tenn. State						
1971-72	Carolina ABA	64	135 (13)	110	419	6.6
1972-73	Carolina ABA	84	317 (8)	145	803	9.6

Yr	Team	G	FG	FT	TP	Avg.
1973-74	Carolina ABA	84	421 (2)	251	1099	13.1
1974-75	Kentucky ABA	72	255 (1)	104	617	8.6
1975-76	Ken.-N.Y. ABA	73	264 (3)	136	673	9.2
1976-77	Denver	72	245	99	589	8.2
1977-78	Buff.-Phil.	70	123	57	303	4.3
1978-79	Phoenix	36	62	42	166	4.6
Totals		555	1822 (27)	944	4669	8.4

McELROY, JIM

b. Oct. 4, 1953 Ht. 6-3 Wt. 190 College—Central Mich.

Yr	Team	G	FG	FT	TP	Avg.
1975-76	New Orleans	51	151	81	383	7.5
1976-77	New Orleans	73	301	169	771	10.6
1977-78	New Orleans	74	287	123	697	9.4
1978-79	New Orleans	79	539	259	1337	16.9
Totals		277	1278	632	3188	11.5

McGINNIS, GEORGE

b. Aug. 12, 1950 Ht. 6-8 Wt. 235 College—Indiana

Yr	Team	G	FG	FT	TP	Avg.
1971-72	Indiana ABA	73	459 (6)	298	1234	16.9
1972-73	Indiana ABA	82	860 (8)	517	2261	27.6
1973-74	Indiana ABA	80	784 (5)	488	2071	25.9
1974-75	Indiana ABA	79	811 (62)	545	2353	29.8
1975-76	Philadelphia	77	647	475	1769	23.0
1976-77	Philadelphia	79	659	372	1690	21.4
1977-78	Philadelphia	78	588	411	1587	20.3
1978-79	Denver	76	603	509	1715	22.6
Totals		624	5411 (81)	3615	14680	23.5

McKINNEY, BILLY

b. June 5, 1955 Ht. 6-0 Wt. 162 College—Northwestern

Yr	Team	G	FG	FT	TP	Avg.
1978-79	Kansas City	78	240	129	609	7.8

McMILLEN, TOM

b. May 26, 1952 Ht. 6-11 Wt. 215 College—Maryland

Yr	Team	G	FG	FT	TP	Avg.
1975-76	Buffalo	50	96	41	233	4.7
1976-77	Buf.-NYK	76	274	96	644	8.5
1977-78	Atlanta	68	280	116	676	9.9
1978-79	Atlanta	82	232	106	570	7.0
Totals		276	882	359	2123	7.7

McMILLIAN, JIM

b. March 11, 1948 Ht. 6-5 Wt. 225 College—Columbia

Yr	Team	G	FG	FT	TP	Avg.
1970-71	Los Angeles	81	289	100	678	8.4
1971-72	Los Angeles	80	642	219	1503	18.8
1972-73	Los Angeles	81	655	223	1533	18.9
1973-74	Buffalo	82	600	325	1525	18.6
1974-75	Buffalo	62	347	194	888	14.3
1975-76	Buffalo	74	492	188	1172	15.8
1976-77	N.Y. Knicks	67	298	67	663	9.9
1977-78	New York	81	288	115	691	8.5
1978-79	Portland	23	33	17	83	3.6
Totals		631	3644	1448	8736	13.8

McNEILL, LARRY

b. Jan. 31, 1951 Ht. 6-9 Wt. 195 College—Marquette

Yr	Team	G	FG	FT	TP	Avg.
1973-74	K.C. Omaha	54	106	99	311	5.8
1974-75	K.C. Omaha	80	296	189	781	9.8
1975-76	K.C. Omaha	82	295	207	797	9.7
1976-77	NYN-G.S.	24	47	52	146	6.1
1977-78	G.S.-Buff.	46	162	145	469	10.2
1978-79	Detroit	11	9	11	29	2.6
Totals		297	915	703	2533	8.5

MENGELT, JOHN

b. Oct. 11, 1949 Ht. 6-2½ Wt. 195 College—Auburn

Yr	Team	G	FG	FT	TP	Avg.
1971-72	Cincinnati	78	287	208	782	10.0
1972-73	K.C.-O.-Det.	79	320	127	767	9.7
1973-74	Detroit	77	249	182	680	8.8
1974-75	Detroit	80	336	211	883	11.0
1975-76	Detroit	67	264	192	720	10.7
1976-77	Chicago	61	209	89	507	8.3
1977-78	Chicago	81	325	184	834	10.3
1978-79	Chicago	75	338	150	826	11.0
Totals		598	2328	1343	5999	10.0

MERIWEATHER, JOE

b. Oct. 26, 1953 Ht. 6-10 Wt. 215 College—So. Illinois

Yr	Team	G	FG	FT	TP	Avg.
1975-76	Houston	81	338	154	830	10.2
1976-77	Atlanta	74	319	182	820	11.1
1977-78	New Orleans	54	194	87	475	8.8
1978-79	N.O.-NYK	77	242	126	610	7.9
Totals		286	1093	549	2735	9.6

MEYERS, DAVID

b. April 21, 1953 Ht. 6-8 Wt. 215 College—UCLA

Yr	Team	G	FG	FT	TP	Avg.
1975-76	Milwaukee	72	198	135	531	7.4
1976-77	Milwaukee	50	179	127	485	9.7
1977-78	Milwaukee	80	432	314	1178	14.7
1978-79	Milwaukee			[injured]		
Totals		202	809	576	2194	10.9

MITCHELL, MIKE

b. Jan. 1, 1956 Ht. 6-7½ Wt. 215 College—Auburn

Yr	Team	G	FG	FT	TP	Avg.
1978-79	Cleveland	80	362	131	855	10.7

MIX, STEVE

b. Dec. 30, 1947 Ht. 6-7 Wt. 215 College—Toledo

Yr	Team	G	FG	FT	TP	Avg.
1969-70	Detroit	18	48	23	119	6.6
1970-71	Detroit	35	111	68	290	8.3
1971-72	Detroit	8	15	7	37	4.6
1971-72	Denver ABA	1	1 (0)	0	2	2.0
1973-74	Philadelphia	82	495	228	1218	14.9
1974-75	Philadelphia	46	280	159	719	15.6
1975-76	Philadelphia	81	421	287	1129	13.9
1976-77	Philadelphia	75	288	215	791	10.5
1977-78	Philadelphia	82	291	175	757	9.2
1978-79	Philadelphia	74	265	161	691	9.3
Totals		502	2215 (0)	1323	5753	11.5

MONEY, ERIC

b. Feb. 6, 1956 Ht. 6-0 Wt. 170 College—Arizona

Yr	Team	G	FG	FT	TP	Avg.
1974-75	Detroit	66	144	31	319	4.8
1975-76	Detroit	80	449	145	1043	13.0
1976-77	Detroit	73	329	90	748	10.2
1977-78	Detroit	76	600	214	1414	18.6
1978-79	N.J.-Phil.	69	444	170	1058	15.3
Totals		364	1966	650	4582	12.6

Yr	Team	G	FG	FT	TP	Avg.

MONROE, EARL (The Pearl)

b. Nov. 21, 1944 Ht. 6-3 Wt. 180 Coll.—Winston-Salem

Yr	Team	G	FG	FT	TP	Avg.
1967-68	Baltimore	82	742	507	1991	24.3
1968-69	Baltimore	80	809	447	2065	25.8
1969-70	Baltimore	82	695	532	1922	23.4
1970-71	Baltimore	81	663	406	1732	21.4
1971-72	Balti.-N.Y.	63	287	175	749	11.9
1972-73	New York	75	496	171	1163	15.5
1973-74	New York	41	240	93	573	14.0
1974-75	New York	78	668	297	1633	20.9
1975-76	New York	76	647	280	1574	20.7
1976-77	N.Y. Knicks	77	613	307	1533	19.9
1977-78	New York	76	556	242	1354	17.8
1978-79	New York	64	329	129	787	12.3
	Totals	875	6745	3586	17076	19.5

MOSLEY, GLENN

b. Dec. 26, 1955 Ht. 6-8 Wt. 195 College—Seton Hall

Yr	Team	G	FG	FT	TP	Avg.
1977-78	Philadelphia	6	5	3	13	2.2
1978-79	San Antonio	26	31	23	85	3.3
	Totals	32	36	26	98	3.1

MURPHY, CALVIN

b. May 9, 1948 Ht. 5-9 Wt. 165 College—Niagara

Yr	Team	G	FG	FT	TP	Avg.
1970-71	San Diego	82	471	356	1298	15.8
1971-72	Houston	82	571	349	1491	18.2
1972-73	Houston	77	381	239	1001	13.0
1973-74	Houston	81	671	310	1652	20.4
1974-75	Houston	78	557	341	1455	18.7
1975-76	Houston	82	675	372	1722	21.0
1976-77	Houston	82	596	272	1464	17.9
1977-78	Houston	76	852	245	1949	25.6
1978-79	Houston	82	707	246	1660	20.2
	Totals	722	5481	2730	13692	18.9

NASH, BOB

b. Aug. 24, 1950 Ht. 6-8 Wt. 204 College—Hawaii

Yr	Team	G	FG	FT	TP	Avg.
1972-73	Detroit	36	16	11	43	1.2
1973-74	Detroit	35	41	24	106	3.0
1974-75	San Diego ABA	17	27 (0)	13	67	3.9
1977-78	Kansas City	66	157	50	364	5.5
1978-79	Kansas City	82	227	69	523	6.4
	Totals	236	468	167	1103	4.0

NATER, SWEN

b. Jan. 14, 1950 Ht. 6-11 Wt. 250 College—UCLA

Yr	Team	G	FG	FT	TP	Avg.
1973-74	Vir.-S.A. ABA	79	467 (0)	180	1114	14.1
1974-75	San Antonio ABA	78	495 (0)	185	1175	15.1
1975-76	N.Y.-Vir. ABA	76	320 (0)	108	748	9.8
1976-77	Milwaukee	72	383	172	938	13.0
1977-78	Buffalo	78	501	208	1210	15.5
1978-79	San Diego	79	357	132	846	10.7
	Totals	462	2523 (0)	985	6031	13.1

NEAL, LLOYD

b. Dec. 10, 1950 Ht. 6-7 Wt. 225 College—Tenn. State

Yr	Team	G	FG	FT	TP	Avg.
1972-73	Portland	82	455	187	1097	13.4
1973-74	Portland	80	246	117	609	7.6
1974-75	Portland	82	409	189	1007	12.3
1975-76	Portland	68	435	186	1056	15.5
1976-77	Portland	58	160	77	397	6.8
1977-78	Portland	61	272	127	671	11.0
1978-79	Portland	4	4	1	9	2.3
	Totals	435	1981	884	4846	11.1

NEWLIN, MIKE

b. Jan. 2, 1949 Ht. 6-4 Wt. 200 College—Utah

Yr	Team	G	FG	FT	TP	Avg.
1971-72	Houston	82	256	108	620	7.6
1972-73	Houston	82	534	327	1395	17.0
1973-74	Houston	76	510	380	1400	18.4
1974-75	Houston	79	436	265	1137	14.4
1975-76	Houston	82	569	385	1523	18.6
1976-77	Houston	82	387	269	1043	12.7
1977-78	Houston	45	216	152	584	13.0
1978-79	Houston	76	283	212	778	10.2
	Totals	604	3191	2098	8480	14.0

NIXON NORM

b. Oct. 10, 1955 Ht. 6-2 Wt. 175 College—Duquesne

Yr	Team	G	FG	FT	TP	Avg.
1977-78	Los Angeles	81	496	115	1107	13.7
1978-79	Los Angeles	82	623	158	1404	17.1
	Totals	163	1119	273	2511	15.4

NORMAN, CONIEL

b. Sept. 24, 1953 Ht. 6-3 Wt. 176 College—Arizona

Yr	Team	G	FG	FT	TP	Avg.
1974-75	Philadelphia	12	23	2	48	4.0
1975-76	Philadelphia	65	183	20	386	5.9
1978-79	San Diego	22	71	19	161	7.3
	Totals	99	277	41	595	6.0

OLBERDING, MARK

b. April 21, 1956 Ht. 6-8 Wt. 230 College—Minnesota

Yr	Team	G	FG	FT	TP	Avg.
1975-76	S.D.-S.A. ABA	81	302 (0)	191	795	9.8
1976-77	San Antonio	82	301	251	853	10.4
1977-78	San Antonio	79	231	184	646	8.2
1978-79	San Antonio	80	261	233	755	9.4
	Totals	322	1095 (0)	859	3049	9.5

OLIVE, JOHN

b. March 1, 1955 Ht. 6-7 Wt. 225 College—Villanova

Yr	Team	G	FG	FT	TP	Avg.
1978-79	San Diego	34	13	18	44	1.3

OWENS, TOM

b. June 28, 1949 Ht. 6-10 Wt. 223 Coll.—So. Carolina

Yr	Team	G	FG	FT	TP	Avg.
1971-72	Mem.-Carolina ABA	69	196 (1)	109	504	7.3
1972-73	Carolina ABA	83	393 (0)	193	979	11.8
1973-74	Carolina ABA	81	442 (2)	226	1116	13.8
1974-75	St.L.-Mem. ABA	82	511 (0)	217	1239	15.1
1975-76	Ken.-S.A. ABA	74	178 (0)	92	448	6.1
1976-77	Houston	46	68	52	188	4.1
1977-78	Portland	82	313	206	832	10.1
1978-79	Portland	82	600	320	1520	18.5
	Totals	599	2701	1415	6826	11.4

PARISH, ROBERT

b. Aug. 30, 1953 Ht. 7-0 Wt. 235 College—Centenary

Yr	Team	G	FG	FT	TP	Avg.
1976-77	Gold. St.	77	288	121	697	9.1
1977-78	Gold. St.	82	430	165	1025	12.5
1978-79	Gold. St.	76	554	196	1304	17.2
	Totals	235	1272	482	3026	12.9

Yr	Team	G	FG	FT	TP	Avg.

PARKER, SONNY

b. March 22, 1955 Ht. 6-7 Wt. 215 Coll.—Texas A & M

Yr	Team	G	FG	FT	TP	Avg.
1976-77	Gold. St.	65	154	71	379	5.8
1977-78	Gold. St.	82	406	122	934	11.4
1978-79	Gold. St.	79	512	175	1199	15.2
	Totals	226	1072	368	2512	11.1

PAULTZ, BILLY (The Whopper)

b. July 30, 1948 Ht. 6-11 Wt. 240 Coll.—Cameron and St. John's

Yr	Team	G	FG	FT	TP	Avg.
1970-71	New York ABA	83	510 (0)	201	1221	14.7
1971-72	New York ABA	83	498 (0)	207	1203	14.5
1972-73	New York ABA	81	532 (0)	287	1351	16.7
1973-74	New York ABA	77	519 (0)	222	1260	16.4
1974-75	New York ABA	80	524 (0)	214	1262	15.8
1975-76	San Antonio ABA	83	566 (0)	238	1370	16.5
1976-77	San Antonio	82	521	238	1280	15.6
1977-78	San Antonio	80	518	230	1266	15.8
1978-79	San Antonio	79	399	114	912	11.5
	Totals	728	4587 (0)	1951	11125	15.3

PHEGLEY, ROGER

b. Oct. 16, 1956 Ht. 6-6 Wt. 205 College—Bradley

Yr	Team	G	FG	FT	TP	Avg.
1978-79	Washington	29	28	24	80	2.8

PIETKIEWICZ, STAN

b. July 14, 1956 Ht. 6-5 Wt. 200 College—Auburn

Yr	Team	G	FG	FT	TP	Avg.
1978-79	San Diego	4	1	2	4	1.0

POQUETTE, BEN

b. May 7, 1955 Ht. 6-9 Wt. 235 College—Central Mich.

Yr	Team	G	FG	FT	TP	Avg.
1977-78	Detroit	52	95	42	232	4.5
1978-79	Detroit	76	198	111	507	6.7
	Totals	128	293	153	739	5.8

PORTER, KEVIN

b. April 17, 1950 Ht. 6-0 Wt. 175 Coll.—St. Francis (Pa.)

Yr	Team	G	FG	FT	TP	Avg.
1972-73	Baltimore	71	205	62	472	6.6
1973-74	Capital	81	477	180	1134	14.0
1974-75	Washington	81	406	131	943	11.6
1975-76	Detroit	19	99	42	240	12.6
1976-77	Detroit	81	310	97	717	8.9
1977-78	Det.-N.J.	82	495	244	1234	15.0
1978-79	Detroit	82	534	192	1260	15.4
	Totals	497	2526	948	6000	12.1

PRICE, JIM

b. Nov. 27, 1949 Ht. 6-3 Wt. 195 College—Louisville

Yr	Team	G	FG	FT	TP	Avg.
1972-73	Los Angeles	59	158	60	376	6.4
1973-74	Los Angeles	82	538	187	1263	15.4
1974-75	L.A.-Mil.	50	317	169	803	16.1
1975-76	Milwaukee	80	398	141	937	11.7
1976-77	Mil.-Buf.-Den.	81	253	83	589	7.3
1977-78	Den.-Detroit	83	294	135	723	8.7
1978-79	Los Angeles	75	171	55	397	5.3
	Totals	510	2129	830	5088	9.9

RADFORD, WAYNE

b. May 29, 1956 Ht. 6-3 Wt. 205 College—Indiana

Yr	Team	G	FG	FT	TP	Avg.
1978-79	Indiana	52	83	36	202	3.9

RAY, CLIFFORD

b. Jan. 21, 1949 Ht. 6-9 Wt. 235 College—Oklahoma

Yr	Team	G	FG	FT	TP	Avg.
1971-72	Chicago	82	222	134	578	7.0
1972-73	Chicago	73	254	117	625	8.6
1973-74	Chicago	80	313	121	747	9.3
1974-75	Gold. St.	82	299	171	769	9.4
1975-76	Gold. St.	82	212	140	564	6.9
1976-77	Gold. St.	77	263	105	631	8.2
1977-78	Gold. St.	79	272	148	692	8.8
1978-79	Gold. St.	82	231	106	568	6.9
	Totals	637	2066	1042	5174	8.1

REDMOND, MARLON

b. April 15, 1955 Ht. 6-6 Wt. 188 College—San Fran.

Yr	Team	G	FG	FT	TP	Avg.
1978-79	K.C.-Phil.	53	163	31	357	6.7

REID, ROBERT

b. Aug. 30, 1955 Ht. 6-8 Wt. 205 Coll.—St. Mary's Tex.

Yr	Team	G	FG	FT	TP	Avg.
1977-78	Houston	80	261	63	585	7.3
1978-79	Houston	82	382	131	895	10.9
	Totals	162	643	194	1480	9.1

RESTANI, KEVIN

b. Dec. 23, 1951 Ht. 6-9 Wt. 225 College—San Fran.

Yr	Team	G	FG	FT	TP	Avg.
1974-75	Milwaukee	76	188	35	411	5.4
1975-76	Milwaukee	82	234	24	492	6.0
1976-77	Milwaukee	64	173	12	358	5.6
1977-78	Mil.-K.C.	54	72	9	153	2.8
1978-79	Milwaukee	81	262	51	575	7.1
	Totals	357	929	131	1989	5.6

RICHARDSON, MICHAEL RAY

b. April 11, 1955 Ht. 6-5 Wt. 189 College—Montana

Yr	Team	G	FG	FT	TP	Avg.
1978-79	New York	72	200	69	469	6.5

ROBERTS, ANTHONY

b. April 15, 1955 Ht. 6-5 Wt. 185 Coll.—Oral Roberts U.

Yr	Team	G	FG	FT	TP	Avg.
1977-78	Denver	82	311	153	775	9.5
1978-79	Denver	63	211	76	498	7.9
	Totals	145	522	229	1273	8.8

ROBERTSON, TONY

b. Jan. 1, 1956 Ht. 6-4 Wt. 195 College—West Virginia

Yr	Team	G	FG	FT	TP	Avg.
1977-78	Atlanta	63	168	37	373	5.9
1978-79	Golden State	12	15	6	36	3.0
	Totals	75	183	43	409	5.5

ROBEY, RICK

b. Jan. 30, 1956 Ht. 6-11 Wt. 230 College—Kentucky

Yr	Team	G	FG	FT	TP	Avg.
1978-79	Ind.-Boston	79	322	174	818	10.4

ROBINSON, JACKIE

b. May 20, 1955 Ht. 6-6 Wt. 206 Coll.—Nev.-Las Vegas

Yr	Team	G	FG	FT	TP	Avg.
1978-79	Seattle	12	19	8	46	3.8

ROBINSON, LEN (Truck)

b. Oct. 4, 1951 Ht. 6-7 Wt. 225 College—Tenn. State

Yr	Team	G	FG	FT	TP	Avg.
1974-75	Washington	76	191	60	442	5.8
1975-76	Washington	82	354	211	919	11.2
1976-77	Wash.-Atl.	77	574	314	1462	19.0
1977-78	New Orleans	82	748	366	1862	22.7
1978-79	N.O.-Phoe.	69	566	324	1456	21.1
	Totals	386	2433	1275	6141	15.9

Yr	Team	G	FG	FT	TP	Avg.

ROBINZINE, BILL

b. Jan. 20, 1953 Ht. 6-7 Wt. 230 College—DePaul

Yr	Team	G	FG	FT	TP	Avg.
1975-76	Kansas City	75	229	145	603	8.0
1976-77	Kansas City	75	307	159	773	10.3
1977-78	Kansas City	82	305	206	816	10.0
1978-79	Kansas City	82	459	180	1098	13.4
	Totals	314	550	690	3290	10.5

ROBISCH, DAVE

b. Dec. 22, 1949 Ht. 6-10 Wt. 235 College—Kansas

Yr	Team	G	FG	FT	TP	Avg.
1971-72	Denver ABA	84	505 (0)	294	1304	15.5
1972-73	Denver ABA	83	521 (0)	309	1351	16.3
1973-74	Denver ABA	84	449 (0)	318	1216	14.5
1974-75	Denver ABA	84	392 (0)	304	1088	13.0
1975-76	S.D.-Ind. ABA	87	436 (0)	324	1196	13.7
1976-77	Indiana	80	369	213	951	11.9
1977-78	Ind.-L.A.	78	177	100	454	5.8
1978-79	Los Angeles	80	150	86	386	4.8
	Totals	660	2999 (0)	1948	7946	12.0

ROLLINS, WAYNE

b. June 16, 1955 Ht. 7-1 Wt. 235 College—Clemson

Yr	Team	G	FG	FT	TP	Avg.
1977-78	Atlanta	80	253	104	610	7.6
1978-79	Atlanta	81	297	89	683	8.4
	Totals	161	550	193	1293	8.0

ROUNDFIELD, DAN

b. May 26, 1953 Ht. 6-8 Wt. 205 Coll.—Cent. Michigan

Yr	Team	G	FG	FT	TP	Avg.
1975-76	Indiana ABA	67	131 (0)	77	339	5.1
1976-77	Indiana	61	342	164	848	13.9
1977-78	Indiana	79	421	218	1060	13.4
1978-79	Atlanta	80	462	300	1224	15.3
	Total	287	1356	759	3471	12.1

ROWE, CURTIS

b. July 2, 1949 Ht. 6-7 Wt. 225 College—UCLA

Yr	Team	G	FG	FT	TP	Avg.
1971-72	Detroit	82	369	192	930	11.2
1972-73	Detroit	81	547	210	1304	16.1
1973-74	Detroit	82	380	118	878	10.7
1974-75	Detroit	82	422	171	1015	12.4
1975-76	Detroit	80	514	252	1280	16.0
1976-77	Boston	79	315	170	800	10.1
1977-78	Boston	51	123	66	312	6.1
1978-79	Boston	53	151	52	354	6.7
	Totals	590	2821	1231	6873	11.6

RUDD, JOHN

b. Aug. 7, 1955 Ht. 6-7 Wt. 230 College—McNeese St.

Yr	Team	G	FG	FT	TP	Avg.
1978-79	New York	58	59	66	184	3.2

RUSSELL, CAMPY

b. Jan. 12, 1952 Ht. 6-8 Wt. 215 College—Michigan

Yr	Team	G	FG	FT	TP	Avg.
1974-75	Cleveland	68	150	124	424	6.2
1975-76	Cleveland	82	483	266	1232	15.0
1976-77	Cleveland	70	435	288	1158	16.5
1977-78	Cleveland	72	523	352	1398	19.4
1978-79	Cleveland	74	603	417	1623	21.9
	Totals	366	2194	1447	5835	15.9

SANDERS, FRANK

b. Jan. 23, 1957 Ht. 6-6 Wt. 200 College—Southern

Yr	Team	G	FG	FT	TP	Avg.
1978-79	S.A.-Boston	46	105	54	264	5.7

SCOTT, ALVIN

b. Sept. 14, 1955 Ht. 6-7 Wt. 185 Col.—Oral Roberts

Yr	Team	G	FG	FT	TP	Avg.
1977-78	Phoenix	81	180	132	492	6.1
1978-79	Phoenix	81	212	120	544	6.7
	Totals	162	392	252	1036	6.4

SCOTT, CHARLIE

b. Dec. 15, 1948 Ht. 6-5 Wt. 175 Coll.—No. Carolina

Yr	Team	G	FG	FT	TP	Avg.
1970-71	Virginia ABA	84	836 (16)	456	2276	27.1
1971-72	Virginia ABA	73	956 (29)	525	2524	34.6
1971-72	Phoenix	6	48	17	113	18.8
1972-73	Phoenix	81	806	436	2048	25.3
1973-74	Phoenix	52	538	246	1322	25.4
1974-75	Phoenix	69	703	274	1680	24.3
1975-76	Boston	82	588	267	1443	17.6
1976-77	Boston	43	326	129	781	18.2
1977-78	Bos.-L.A.	79	435	194	1064	13.5
1978-79	Denver	79	393	161	947	12.0
	Totals	648	5679 (45)	2705	14198	21.9

SHELTON, LONNIE

b. Oct. 19, 1955 Ht. 6-9 Wt. 235 College—Oregon St.

Yr	Team	G	FG	FT	TP	Avg.
1976-77	N.Y. Knicks	82	398	159	955	11.6
1977-78	New York	82	508	203	1219	14.9
1978-79	Seattle	76	446	131	1023	13.5
	Totals	240	1352	493	3197	13.3

SHEPPARD, STEVE

b. March 21, 1954 Ht. 6-6 Wt. 220 College—Maryland

Yr	Team	G	FG	FT	TP	Avg.
1977-78	Chicago	64	119	37	275	4.3
1978-79	Chi.-Det.	42	36	20	92	2.2
	Totals	106	155	57	367	3.5

SHORT, PURVIS

b. July 2, 1957 Ht. 6-7 Wt. 210 College—Jackson St.

Yr	Team	G	FG	FT	TP	Avg.
1978-79	Golden State	75	369	57	795	10.6

SHUMATE, JOHN

b. April 6, 1952 Ht. 6-9 Wt. 235 College—Notre Dame

Yr	Team	G	FG	FT	TP	Avg.
1975-76	Pho.-Buf.	75	332	212	876	11.7
1976-77	Buffalo	74	407	302	1116	15.1
1977-78	Buf.-Det.	80	391	400	1182	14.8
1978-79	Detroit			[injured]		
	Totals	229	1130	914	3174	13.9

SIKMA, JACK

b. Nov. 14, 1955 Ht. 6-11 Wt. 230 Coll.—Ill. Wesleyan

Yr	Team	G	FG	FT	TP	Avg.
1977-78	Seattle	82	342	192	865	10.7
1978-79	Seattle	82	476	329	1281	15.6
	Totals	164	818	521	2157	13.2

SILAS, JAMES

b. Feb. 11, 1949 Ht. 6-1 Wt. 185 College—S.F. Austin

Yr	Team	G	FG	FT	TP	Avg.
1972-73	Dallas ABA	78	341 (0)	389	1071	13.7
1973-74	San Antonio ABA	84	486 (0)	349	1321	15.7
1974-75	San Antonio ABA	82	578 (0)	430	1586	19.3

Yr	Team	G	FG	FT	TP	Avg.
1975-76	San Antonio ABA	84	718 (0)	564	2000	23.8
1976-77	San Antonio	22	61	87	209	9.5
1977-78	San Antonio	37	43	60	146	3.9
1978-79	San Antonio	79	466	334	1266	16.0
	Totals	466	2693 (0)	2213	7599	16.3

SILAS, PAUL

b. July 12, 1943 Ht. 6-7 Wt. 235 College—Creighton

1964-65	St. Louis	79	140	83	363	4.6
1965-66	St. Louis	46	70	35	175	3.8
1966-67	St. Louis	76	207	113	527	6.9
1967-68	St. Louis	82	399	299	1097	13.4
1968-69	Atlanta	79	241	204	686	8.7
1969-70	Phoenix	78	373	250	996	12.8
1970-71	Phoenix	81	338	285	961	11.9
1971-72	Phoenix	80	485	433	1403	17.5
1972-73	Boston	80	400	266	1066	13.3
1973-74	Boston	82	340	264	944	11.5
1974-75	Boston	82	312	244	868	10.6
1975-76	Boston	81	315	236	866	10.7
1976-77	Denver	81	206	170	582	7.2
1977-78	Seattle	82	184	109	477	5.8
1978-79	Seattle	82	170	116	456	5.6
	Totals	1171	4180	3107	11467	9.8

SIMPSON, RALPH

b. Aug. 10, 1949 Ht. 6-5 Wt. 200 Coll.— Michigan St.

1970-71	Denver ABA	81	443 (17)	215	1152	14.2
1971-72	Denver ABA	84	917 (3)	457	2300	27.4
1972-73	Denver ABA	81	727 (5)	421	1890	23.3
1973-74	Denver ABA	75	595 (2)	208	1404	18.7
1974-75	Denver ABA	82	693 (1)	303	1692	20.6
1975-76	Denver ABA	84	615 (4)	273	1515	18.0
1976-77	Detroit	77	356	138	850	11.0
1977-78	Det.-Den.	64	216	85	517	8.1
1978-79	Phil.-N.J.	69	174	76	424	6.2
	Totals	697	4736 (32)	2176	11744	16.8

SKINNER, AL

b. June 16, 1952 Ht. 6-4 Wt. 195 Coll.—Massachusetts

1974-75	New York ABA	51	129 (1)	72	333	6.5
1975-76	New York ABA	83	328 (2)	203	865	10.4
1976-77	N.Y. Nets	79	382	231	995	12.6
1977-78	N.J.-Det.	77	222	162	606	7.9
1978-79	N.J.-Phil.	45	91	99	281	6.2
	Totals	335	1152 (3)	767	3080	9.2

SMITH, BOBBY

b. Feb. 26, 1946 Ht. 6-5 Wt. 212 College—Tulsa

1969-70	San Diego	75	242	66	550	7.3
1970-71	Cleveland	77	495	178	1168	15.2
1971-72	Cleveland	82	527	178	1232	15.0
1972-73	Cleveland	73	268	64	600	8.2
1973-74	Cleveland	82	536	139	1211	14.8
1974-75	Cleveland	82	585	132	1302	15.9
1975-76	Cleveland	81	495	111	1101	13.6
1976-77	Cleveland	81	513	148	1174	14.5
1977-78	Cleveland	82	369	108	846	10.3
1978-79	Cleveland	72	361	83	805	11.2
	Totals	787	4391	1207	9989	12.7

SMITH, ELMORE

b. May 9, 1949 Ht. 7-1 Wt. 250 Coll.—Kentucky State

Yr	Team	G	FG	FT	TP	Avg.
1971-72	Buffalo	78	579	194	1352	17.3
1972-73	Buffalo	76	600	188	1388	18.3
1973-74	Los Angeles	81	434	147	1015	12.5
1974-75	Los Angeles	74	346	112	804	10.9
1975-76	Milwaukee	78	498	222	1218	15.6
1976-77	Mil.-Cleve	70	241	117	599	8.6
1977-78	Cleveland	81	402	205	1009	12.5
1078-79	Cleveland	24	69	18	156	6.5
	Totals	562	3169	1203	7541	13.4

SMITH, PHIL

b. April 22, 1952 Ht. 6-4 Wt. 187 College—San Fran.

1974-75	Golden State	74	221	127	569	7.7
1975-76	Golden State	82	659	323	1641	20.0
1976-77	Golden State	82	631	295	1557	19.0
1977-78	Golden State	82	648	316	1612	19.7
1978-79	Golden State	59	489	194	1172	19.9
	Totals	379	2648	1258	6551	17.3

SMITH, RANDY

b. Dec. 12, 1948 Ht. 6-3 Wt. 180 College—Buffalo St.

1971-72	Buffalo	76	432	158	1022	13.4
1972-73	Buffalo	82	511	192	1214	14.8
1973-74	Buffalo	82	531	205	1267	15.5
1974-75	Buffalo	82	610	236	1456	17.8
1975-76	Buffalo	82	702	383	1787	21.8
1976-77	Buffalo	82	702	294	1698	20.7
1977-78	Buffalo	82	789	443	2021	24.6
1978-79	San Diego	82	693	292	1678	20.5
	Totals	650	5538	2203	12143	18.7

SMITH, ROBERT

b. March 10, 1955 Ht. 5-11 Wt. 165 Coll.—NV.-Ls Vgs.

1977-78	Denver	45	50	21	121	2.7
1978-79	Denver	82	184	159	527	6.4
	Totals	127	234	180	648	5.1

SMITH, SAM

b. Jan. 8, 1955 Ht. 6-4 Wt. 200 College—NV.-Ls Vgs.

1978-79	Milwaukee	16	19	18	56	3.5

SMITH, WILLIE

b. Oct. 26, 1953 Ht. 6-3 Wt. 210 College—Missouri

1976-77	Chicago	2	0	0	0	0.0
1977-78	Indiana	1	0	0	0	0.0
1978-79	Portland	13	23	12	58	4.5
	Totals	16	23	12	58	3.6

SNYDER, DICK

b. Feb. 1, 1944 Ht. 6-5 Wt. 210 College—Davidson

1966-67	St. Louis	54	144	46	334	6.2
1967-68	St. Louis	75	257	129	643	8.6
1968-69	Phoenix	81	399	185	983	12.1
1969-70	Pho.-Sea.	82	456	169	1081	13.2
1970-71	Seattle	82	645	302	1592	19.4
1971-72	Seattle	73	496	218	1210	16.6
1972-73	Seattle	82	473	186	1132	13.8
1973-74	Seattle	74	572	194	1338	18.1
1974-75	Cleveland	82	498	165	1161	14.2
1975-76	Cleveland	82	441	155	1037	12.6
1976-77	Cleveland	82	316	127	759	9.3
1977-78	Cleveland	58	112	56	280	4.8
1978-79	Seattle	56	81	43	205	3.7
	Totals	963	4890	1975	11755	12.2

Yr	Team	G	FG	FT	TP	Avg.

SOBERS, RICKY

b. Jan. 15, 1953 Ht. 6-3 Wt. 198 Coll.—Nev.-Las Vegas

Yr	Team	G	FG	FT	TP	Avg.
1975-76	Phoenix	78	280	158	718	9.2
1976-77	Phoenix	79	414	243	1071	13.6
1977-78	Indiana	79	553	330	1436	18.2
1978-79	Indiana	81	553	298	1404	17.3
	Totals	317	1800	1029	4629	14.6

STACOM, KEVIN

b. Sept. 4, 1951 Ht. 6-3 Wt. 185 College—Providence

Yr	Team	G	FG	FT	TP	Avg.
1974-75	Boston	61	72	29	173	2.8
1975-76	Boston	77	170	68	408	5.3
1976-77	Boston	79	179	46	404	5.1
1977-78	Boston	55	206	54	466	8.5
1978-79	Ind.-Bos.	68	128	44	300	4.4
	Totals	340	755	241	1751	5.2

STEELE, LARRY

b. May 5, 1949 Ht. 6-5 Wt. 180 College—Kentucky

Yr	Team	G	FG	FT	TP	Avg.
1971-72	Portland	72	148	70	366	5.1
1972-73	Portland	66	159	71	389	5.9
1973-74	Portland	81	325	135	785	9.7
1974-75	Portland	76	265	122	652	8.6
1975-76	Portland	81	322	154	798	9.9
1976-77	Portland	81	326	183	835	10.3
1977-78	Portland	65	210	100	520	8.0
1978-79	Portland	72	203	112	518	7.2
	Totals	594	1958	947	4863	8.2

TATUM, EARL

b. July 26, 1953 Ht. 6-4½ Wt. 185 College-Marquette

Yr	Team	G	FG	FT	TP	Avg.
1976-77	Los Angeles	68	283	72	638	9.4
1977-78	L.A.-Ind.	82	510	153	1173	14.3
1978-79	Bos.-Det.	79	280	52	612	7.7
	Totals	229	1073	277	2423	10.6

TAYLOR, BRIAN

b. June 9, 1951 Ht. 6-2 Wt. 185 College—Princeton

Yr	Team	G	FG	FT	TP	Avg.
1972-73	New York ABA	63	391 (4)	168	962	15.3
1973-74	New York ABA	75	355 (8)	100	834	11.1
1974-75	New York ABA	79	462 (10)	150	1104	14.0
1975-76	New York ABA	54	322 (32)	164	904	16.7
1976-77	Kansas City	72	501	225	1227	17.0
1977-78	Denver	39	182	88	452	11.6
1978-79	San Diego	20	30	16	76	3.8
	Totals	402	2243 (54)	911	5559	13.8

TERRELL, IRA

b. June 19, 1954 Ht. 6-8 Wt. 205 College—SMU

Yr	Team	G	FG	FT	TP	Avg.
1976-77	Phoenix	78	277	111	665	8.5
1978-79	N.O.-Port.	49	93	35	221	4.5
	Totals	127	370	146	886	7.0

THEUS, REGGIE

b. Oct. 13, 1957 Ht. 6-7 Wt. 205 College—NV.-Ls. Vgs.

Yr	Team	G	FG	FT	TP	Avg.
1978-79	Chicago	82	537	264	1338	16.3

THOMPSON, DAVID

b. July 13, 1954 Ht. 6-5 Wt. 195 College—N.C.

Yr	Team	G	FG	FT	TP	Avg.
1975-76	Denver ABA	83	804 (3)	541	2158	26.0
1976-77	Denver	82	824	477	2125	25.9
1977-78	Denver	80	826	520	2172	27.2
1978-79	Denver	76	693	439	1825	24.0
	Totals	321	3147 (3)	1977	8280	25.8

THOMPSON, MYCHAL

b. Jan. 30, 1955 Ht. 6-10 Wt. 226 College—Minnesota

Yr	Team	G	FG	FT	TP	Avg.
1978-79	Portland	73	460	154	1074	14.7

TOMJANOVICH, RUDY

b. Nov. 24, 1948 Ht. 6-8 Wt. 218 College—Michigan

Yr	Team	G	FG	FT	TP	Avg.
1970-71	San Diego	77	168	73	409	5.3
1971-72	Houston	78	500	172	1172	15.0
1972-73	Houston	81	655	250	1560	19.3
1973-74	Houston	80	788	385	1961	24.5
1974-75	Houston	81	694	289	1677	20.7
1975-76	Houston	79	622	221	1465	18.5
1976-77	Houston	81	733	287	1753	21.6
1977-78	Houston	23	217	61	495	21.5
1978-79	Houston	74	620	168	1408	19.0
	Totals	654	3897	1906	11900	18.2

TOWNSEND, RAYMOND

b. Dec. 20, 1955 Ht. 6-3 Wt. 175 College—UCLA

Yr	Team	G	FG	FT	TP	Avg.
1978-79	Golden St.	65	127	50	304	4.7

TWARDZIK, DAVE

b. Sept. 20, 1950 Ht. 6-1 Wt. 180 Coll.—Old Dominion

Yr	Team	G	FG	FT	TP	Avg.
1972-73	Virginia ABA	80	139 (2)	178	462	5.8
1973-74	Virginia ABA	57	160 (3)	168	497	8.7
1974-75	Virginia ABA	76	358 (1)	317	1036	13.6
1975-76	Virginia ABA	43	97 (3)	113	316	7.4
1976-77	Portland	74	263	239	765	10.3
1977-78	Portland	75	242	183	667	8.9
1978-79	Portland	64	203	261	667	10.4
	Totals	469	1462 (9)	1459	4410	9.4

TYLER, TERRY

b. Oct. 30, 1956 Ht. 6-7 Wt. 215 College—Detroit

Yr	Team	G	FG	FT	TP	Avg.
1978-79	Detroit	82	456	144	1056	12.9

UNSELD, WESTLEY

b. March 14, 1946 Ht. 6-8 Wt. 245 College—Louisville

Yr	Team	G	FG	FT	TP	Avg.
1968-69	Baltimore	82	427	277	1131	13.8
1969-70	Baltimore	82	526	273	1325	16.2
1970-71	Baltimore	74	424	199	1647	14.1
1971-72	Baltimore	76	409	171	989	13.0
1972-73	Baltimore	79	421	149	991	12.5
1973-74	Capital	56	146	36	328	5.9
1974-75	Washington	73	273	126	672	9.2
1975-76	Washington	78	318	114	750	9.6
1976-77	Washington	82	270	100	640	7.8
1977-78	Washington	80	257	93	607	7.6
1978-79	Washington	77	346	151	843	10.9
	Totals	839	3817	1689	9323	11.1

VAN BREDA KOLFF, JAN

b. Dec. 16, 1951 Ht. 6-7 Wt. 200 College—Vanderbilt

Yr	Team	G	FG	FT	TP	Avg.
1974-75	Denver ABA	84	155 (0)	177	487	5.8
1975-76	Vir.-Ken. ABA	80	221 (2)	165	613	7.7

Yr	Team	G	FG	FT	TP	Avg.
1976-77	N.Y. Nets	72	271	195	737	10.2
1977-78	New Jersey	68	107	87	301	4.4
1978-79	New Jersey	80	196	146	538	6.7
	Totals	384	950 (2)	770	2676	6.9

VAN LIER, NORM

b. Apr. 1, 1947 Ht. 6-2 Wt. 175 College—St. Fran. (Pa.)

Yr	Team	G	FG	FT	TP	Avg.
1969-70	Cincinnati	81	302	166	770	9.5
1970-71	Cincinnati	82	478	359	1315	16.0
1971-72	Cin.-Chi.	79	334	237	905	11.5
1972-73	Chicago	80	474	166	1114	13.9
1973-74	Chicago	80	427	288	1142	14.3
1974-75	Chicago	70	407	236	1050	15.0
1975-76	Chicago	76	361	235	957	12.6
1976-77	Chicago	82	300	238	838	10.2
1977-78	Chicago	78	200	172	572	7.3
1978-79	Milwaukee	38	30	47	107	2.8
	Totals	746	3313	2144	8770	11.8

WAKEFIELD, ANDRE

b. Jan. 11, 1955 Ht. 6-3 Wt. 176 College—Loyola (Chi.)

Yr	Team	G	FG	FT	TP	Avg.
1978-79	Chic.-Detr.	73	62	48	172	2.4

WALKER, CLARENCE (Foots)

b. May 21, 1951 Ht. 6-1 Wt. 172 College—W. Georgia

Yr	Team	G	FG	FT	TP	Avg.
1974-75	Cleveland	72	111	80	302	4.2
1975-76	Cleveland	81	143	84	370	4.6
1976-77	Cleveland	62	157	89	403	6.5
1977-78	Cleveland	81	287	159	733	9.0
1978-79	Cleveland	55	208	137	553	10.1
	Totals	351	906	549	2361	6.7

WALKER, WALLY

b. July 18, 1854 Ht. 6-6 Wt. 200 College—Virginia

Yr	Team	G	FG	FT	TP	Avg.
1976-77	Portland	66	137	67	341	5.2
1977-78	Port.-Sea.	77	204	75	483	6.3
1978-79	Seattle	60	168	58	394	6.6
	Totals	203	509	200	1218	6.0

WALTON, BILL

b. Nov. 5, 1952 Ht. 6-11 Wt. 225 College—UCLA

Yr	Team	G	FG	FT	TP	Avg.
1974-75	Portland	35	177	94	448	12.8
1975-76	Portland	51	345	133	823	16.1
1976-77	Portland	65	491	228	1210	18.6
1977-78	Portland	58	460	177	1097	18.9
1978-79	Portland			[injured]		
	Totals	209	1473	632	3578	17.1

WALTON, LLOYD

b. Nov. 23, 1953 Ht. 6-1 Wt. 160 College—Marquette

Yr	Team	G	FG	FT	TP	Avg.
1976-77	Milwaukee	53	88	53	229	4.3
1977-78	Milwaukee	76	154	54	362	4.8
1978-79	Milwaukee	75	157	61	375	5.0
	Totals	204	399	168	966	4.7

WASHINGTON, KERMIT

b. Sept. 17, 1951 Ht. 6-8 Wt. 230 College—American

Yr	Team	G	FG	FT	TP	Avg.
1973-74	Los Angeles	45	73	26	172	3.8
1974-75	Los Angeles	55	87	72	246	4.5
1975-76	Los Angeles	36	39	45	123	3.4
1976-77	Los Angeles	53	191	132	514	9.7
1977-78	L.A.-Bos.	57	247	170	664	11.6
1978-79	San Diego	82	350	227	927	11.3
	Totals	328	987	672	2646	8.1

WASHINGTON, RICHARD

b. July 15, 1955 Ht. 6-10 Wt. 220 College—UCLA

Yr	Team	G	FG	FT	TP	Avg.
1976-77	Kansas City	82	446	177	1069	13.0
1977-78	Kansas City	78	425	150	1000	12.8
1978-79	Kansas City	18	14	10	38	2.1
	Totals	178	885	337	2107	11.8

WASHINGTON, WILSON

b. Aug. 3, 1955 Ht. 6-9 Wt. 227 Coll.—Old Dominion

Yr	Team	G	FG	FT	TP	Avg.
1977-78	Phil.-N.J.	38	100	29	229	6.0
1978-79	New Jersey	62	218	66	502	8.1
	Totals	100	318	95	731	7.3

WATTS, DON (Slick)

b. July 21, 1951 Ht. 6-1 Wt. 175 College—Xavier

Yr	Team	G	FG	FT	TP	Avg.
1973-74	Seattle	62	198	100	496	8.0
1974-75	Seattle	82	232	93	557	6.8
1975-76	Seattle	82	433	199	1065	13.0
1976-77	Seattle	79	428	172	1028	13.0
1977-78	Sea.-N.O.	71	219	92	530	7.5
1978-79	Houston	61	92	41	225	3.7
	Totals	437	1602	697	3901	8.9

WEATHERSPOON, NICK

b. July 20, 1950 Ht. 6-7 Wt. 197 College—Illinois

Yr	Team	G	FG	FT	TP	Avg.
1973-74	Capital	65	199	96	494	7.6
1974-75	Washington	82	256	103	615	7.5
1975-76	Washington	64	218	96	532	8.3
1976-77	Wash.-Sea.	62	310	91	711	11.5
1977-78	Chicago	41	86	37	209	5.1
1978-79	San Diego	82	479	176	1134·	13.8
	Totals	396	1548	599	3695	9.3

WEBSTER, MARVIN

b. April 13, 1952 Ht. 7-1 Wt. 230 College—Morgan St.

Yr	Team	G	FG	FT	TP	Avg.
1975-76	Denver ABA	38	55 (0)	55	165	4.3
1976-77	Denver	80	198	143	539	6.7
1977-78	Seattle	82	427	290	1144	14.0
1978-79	New York	60	264	150	678	11.3
	Totals	260	944 (0)	638	2526	9.7

WEDMAN, SCOTT

b. July 29, 1952 Ht. 6-7 Wt. 215 College—Colorado

Yr	Team	G	FG	FT	TP	Avg.
1974-75	K.C.-O.	80	375	139	889	11.1
1975-76	Kansas City	82	538	191	1267	15.5
1976-77	Kansas City	81	521	206	1248	15.4
1977-78	Kansas City	81	607	221	1435	17.7
1978-79	Kansas City	73	561	216	1338	18.3
	Totals	397	2602	973	6177	15.6

WESTPHAL, PAUL

b. Nov. 30, 1950 Ht. 6-4 Wt. 195 College—USC

Yr	Team	G	FG	FT	TP	Avg.
1972-73	Boston	60	89	67	245	4.1
1973-74	Boston	82	238	112	588	7.2
1974-75	Boston	82	342	119	803	9.8
1975-76	Phoenix	82	657	365	1679	20.5
1976-77	Phoenix	81	682	362	1726	21.3
1977-78	Phoenix	80	809	396	2014	25.2
1978-79	Phoenix	81	801	339	1941	24.0
	Totals	548	3618	1760	8996	16.4

Yr	Team	G	FG	FT	TP	Avg.
WHITE, JOSEPH (Jo Jo)						
b. Nov. 16, 1946 Ht. 6-3 Wt. 190 College—Kansas						
1969-70	Boston	60	309	111	729	12.2
1970-71	Boston	75	693	215	1601	21.3
1971-72	Boston	79	770	285	1825	23.1
1972-73	Boston	82	717	178	1612	19.7
1973-74	Boston	82	649	190	1488	18.1
1974-75	Boston	82	658	186	1502	18.3
1975-76	Boston	82	670	212	1552	18.9
1976-77	Boston	82	638	333	1609	19.6
1977-78	Boston	46	289	103	681	14.8
1978-79	Bost.-G.S.	76	404	139	947	12.5
	Totals	746	5797	1952	13546	18.2

Yr	Team	G	FG	FT	TP	Avg.
WHITE, RUDY						
b. June 23, 1953 Ht. 6-2 Wt. 195 College—Arizona St.						
1975-76	Houston	32	42	18	102	3.2
1976-77	Houston	46	47	15	109	2.4
1977-78	Houston	21	31	14	76	3.6
1978-79	Houston			[injured]		
	Totals	99	120	47	287	2.9

Yr	Team	G	FG	FT	TP	Avg.
WHITEHEAD, JEROME						
b. Sept. 30, 1956 Ht. 6-10 Wt. 220 College—Marquette						
1978-79	San Diego	31	15	8	38	1.2

Yr	Team	G	FG	FT	TP	Avg.
WICKS, SIDNEY						
b. Sept. 19, 1949 Ht. 6-9 Wt. 225 College—UCLA						
1971-72	Portland	82	784	441	2009	24.5
1972-73	Portland	80	761	384	1906	23.8
1973-74	Portland	75	685	314	1684	22.5
1974-75	Portland	82	692	394	1778	21.7
1975-76	Portland	79	580	345	1505	19.7
1976-77	Boston	82	464	310	1238	15.1
1977-78	Boston	81	433	217	1083	13.4
1978-79	San Diego	79	312	147	771	9.8
	Totals	640	4711	2552	11974	18.7

Yr	Team	G	FG	FT	TP	Avg.
WILKERSON, BOB						
b. Aug. 15, 1954 Ht. 6-7 Wt. 195 College—Indiana						
1976-77	Seattle	78	221	84	526	6.7
1977-78	Denver	81	382	157	921	11.4
1978-79	Denver	80	396	119	911	11.4
	Totals	239	999	360	2358	9.9

Yr	Team	G	FG	FT	TP	Avg.
WILKES, JAMAAL						
b. May 2, 1953 Ht. 6-7 Wt. 190 College—UCLA						
1974-75	Golden State	82	502	160	1164	14.2
1975-76	Golden State	82	617	227	1461	17.8
1976-77	Golden State	76	548	247	1343	17.7
1977-78	Los Angeles	51	277	106	660	12.9
1978-79	Los Angeles	82	626	272	1524	18.6
	Totals	373	2570	1012	6152	16.5

Yr	Team	G	FG	FT	TP	Avg.
WILLIAMS, EARL						
b. March 24, 1951 Ht. 6-7 Wt. 230 Coll.—Winston-Salem						
1974-75	Phoenix	79	163	45	371	4.7
1975-76	Detroit	46	73	22	168	3.7
1976-77	N.Y. Nets	1	0	3	3	3.0
1978-79	Boston	20	54	14	122	6.1
	Totals	146	290	84	664	4.5

Yr	Team	G	FG	FT	TP	Avg.
WILLIAMS, FREEMAN						
b. May 15, 1956 Ht. 6-4 Wt. 195 College—Portland St.						
1978-79	San Diego	72	335	76	746	10.4

Yr	Team	G	FG	FT	TP	Avg.
WILLIAMS, GUS						
b. Oct. 10, 1953 Ht. 6-2 Wt. 175 College—USC						
1975-76	Golden State	77	365	173	903	11.7
1976-77	Golden State	82	325	112	762	9.3
1977-78	Seattle	79	602	227	1431	18.1
1978-79	Seattle	76	606	245	1457	19.2
	Totals	314	1898	757	4553	14.5

Yr	Team	G	FG	FT	TP	Avg.
WILLIAMS, NATE						
b. May 2, 1950 Ht. 6-5 Wt. 225 College—Utah State						
1971-72	Cincinnati	81	418	127	963	11.9
1972-73	K.C.-O.	80	417	106	940	11.8
1973-74	K.C.-O.	82	538	193	1269	15.5
1974-75	K.C.-O.-N.O.	85	474	181	1129	13.3
1975-76	New Orleans	81	421	197	1039	12.8
1976-77	New Orleans	79	414	146	974	12.3
1977-78	N.O.-G. State	73	312	101	725	9.9
1978-79	Golden State	81	284	102	670	8.3
	Totals	642	3278	1153	7709	12.0

Yr	Team	G	FG	FT	TP	Avg.
WILLIAMS, RAY						
b. Oct. 14, 1954 Ht. 6-2 Wt. 188 College—Minnesota						
1977-78	New York	81	305	146	756	9.3
1978-79	New York	81	575	251	1401	17.3
	Totals	162	880	397	2157	13.3

Yr	Team	G	FG	FT	TP	Avg.
WILLIAMSON, JOHN						
b. Nov. 10, 1952 Ht. 6-2 Wt. 185 Coll.—N. Mex. St.						
1973-74	New York ABA	77	480 (2)	150	1116	14.5
1974-75	New York ABA	75	367 (3)	123	866	11.5
1975-76	New York ABA	76	511 (8)	187	1233	16.2
1976-77	NYN-Ind.	72	618	259	1495	20.8
1977-78	Ind.N.J.	75	723	331	1777	23.7
1978-79	New Jersey	74	635	373	1643	22.5
	Totals	449	3334 (13)	1423	8130	18.1

Yr	Team	G	FG	FT	TP	Avg.
WILSON, RICK						
b. Feb. 7, 1956 Ht. 6-5 Wt. 200 College—Louisville						
1978-79	Atlanta	61	81	24	186	3.0

Yr	Team	G	FG	FT	TP	Avg.
WINTERS, BRIAN						
b. March 1, 1952 Ht. 6-4 Wt. 185 College—S. Carolina						
1974-75	Los Angeles	68	359	76	794	11.7
1975-76	Milwaukee	78	618	180	1416	18.2
1976-77	Milwaukee	78	652	205	1509	19.3
1977-78	Milwaukee	80	674	246	1594	19.9
1978-79	Milwaukee	79	662	237	1561	19.8
	Totals	383	2965	944	6874	17.9

Yr	Team	G	FG	FT	TP	Avg.
WRIGHT, LARRY						
b. Nov. 23, 1954 Ht. 6-0 Wt. 175 College—Grambling						
1976-77	Washington	78	262	88	612	7.8
1977-78	Washington	70	283	76	642	9.2
1978-79	Washington	73	276	125	677	9.3
	Totals	221	821	289	1931	8.7

Contained in this section are the year-by-year records and lifetime totals of every man who played in the Basketball Association of America (BAA), National Basketball Association (NBA), and the American Basketball Association (ABA), and retired prior to the 1978–79 season. Included as well are the records of all National Basketball League (NBL) players who later appeared in BAA or NBA games.

Each player's individual record lists his team, games played (G), field goals made (FG), free throws made (FT), total points (TP), and average (Avg.). The number in parentheses following field-goal totals for ABA players indicates the number of three-point field goals scored. Wherever available, each player's date of birth, height, weight, and college are listed.

Yr	Team	G	FG	FT	TP	Avg.

ABDUL-AZIZ, ZAID (Don Smith)
b. April 7, 1946 Ht. 6-9 Wt. 235 College—Iowa

Yr	Team	G	FG	FT	TP	Avg.
1968-69	Cin.-Mil.	49	144	70	352	7.3
1969-70	Milwaukee	80	237	119	593	7.4
1970-71	Seattle	61	263	139	665	10.9
1971-72	Seattle	58	322	154	798	13.8
1972-73	Houston	48	149	119	413	8.7
1973-74	Houston	79	336	193	865	10.9
1974-75	Houston	65	235	159	629	9.7
1975-76	Seattle	27	35	16	96	3.2
1976-77	Buffalo	22	25	33	83	3.8
1977-78	Bos.-Hou.	16	23	17	63	3.9
	Totals	505	1769	1019	4557	9.0

ABDUL-RAHMAD, MAHDI (Walt Hazzard)
b. April 15, 1942 Ht. 6-2 Wt. 190 College—UCLA

Yr	Team	G	FG	FT	TP	Avg.
1964-65	Los Angeles	66	117	46	280	4.2
1965-66	Los Angeles	80	458	182	1098	13.7
1966-67	Los Angeles	79	301	129	731	9.3
1967-68	Seattle	79	733	428	1894	23.9
1968-69	Atlanta	80	345	208	898	11.2
1969-70	Atlanta	82	493	267	1253	15.3
1970-71	Atlanta	82	517	315	1349	16.5
1971-72	Buffalo	72	450	237	1137	15.8
1972-73	Buf.-G.S.	55	107	47	261	4.7
1973-74	Seattle	49	76	34	186	3.8
	Totals	724	3597	1893	9087	12.6

ABLE, FOREST
b. July 27, 1932 Ht. 6-3 Wt. 180 College—Western Ky.

Yr	Team	G	FG	FT	TP	Avg.
1956-57	Syracuse	1	0	0	0	0.0

ABRAMOVIC, JOHN (Brooms)
b. Feb. 9, 1919 Ht. 6-3 Wt. 196 College—Salem

Yr	Team	G	FG	FT	TP	Avg.
1946-47	Pittsburgh	47	202	123	527	11.2
1947-48	St. L.-Balt.	9	1	4	6	0.7
1947-48	Syracuse NL	35	72	42	186	5.3
	Totals	91	275	169	719	7.9

ACKERMAN, DONALD (Buddy)
b. Sept. 4, 1930 Ht. 6-0 Wt. 183 Coll.—Lg. Island Univ.

Yr	Team	G	FG	FT	TP	Avg.
1953-54	New York	28	14	15	43	1.5

ACTON, CHARLES (Bud)
Ht. 6-6 Wt. 210 College—Alma and Hillsdale

Yr	Team	G	FG	FT	TP	Avg.
1967-68	San Diego	23	29	19	77	3.3

ADAMS, DON
b. Nov. 27, 1947 Ht. 6-7 Wt. 210 Coll.—Northwestern

Yr	Team	G	FG	FT	TP	Avg.
1970-71	San Diego	82	391	155	937	11.4
1971-72	Houston-At.	73	313	205	831	11.4
1972-73	Atl.-Det.	74	265	145	675	9.1
1973-74	Detroit	74	303	153	759	10.3
1974-75	Detroit	51	127	45	299	5.9
1974-75	St. Louis ABA	16	42 (0)	17	101	6.3
1975-76	St. Louis ABA	20	99 (0)	63	261	13.1
1975-76	Buffalo	56	67	40	174	3.1
1976-77	Buffalo	77	216	129	561	7.3
	Totals	523	1823 (0)	952	4598	8.8

ADAMS, GEORGE
b. May 15, 1949 Ht. 6-6 Wt. 210 Coll.—Gardner-Webb

Yr	Team	G	FG	FT	TP	Avg.
1972-73	San Diego ABA	60	151 (2)	65	373	6.2
1973-74	San Diego ABA	80	252 (1)	78	585	7.3
1974-75	San Diego ABA	75	309 (1)	73	694	9.3
	Totals	215	712 (4)	216	1652	7.7

ADELMAN, RICK
b. June 16, 1946 Ht. 6-1 Wt. 178 Coll.—Loyola (Calif.)

Yr	Team	G	FG	FT	TP	Avg.
1968-69	San Diego	77	177	131	485	6.3
1969-70	San Diego	35	96	68	260	7.4
1970-71	Portland	81	378	267	1023	12.6
1971-72	Portland	80	329	151	809	10.1
1972-73	Portland	76	214	73	501	6.6
1973-74	Chicago	55	64	54	182	3.3
1974-75	Chi.-N.O.-K.C.-O.	58	123	73	319	5.5
	Totals	462	1381	817	3579	7.7

Yr	Team	G	FG	FT	TP	Avg.

AITCH, MATT
b. 1945 Ht. 6-7 Wt. 230 College—Michigan State

Yr	Team	G	FG	FT	TP	Avg.
1967-68	Indiana ABA	45	100 (0)	52	252	5.6

AKIN, HENRY
b. July 31, 1944 Ht. 6-10 Wt. 235 Coll.—Morehead St.

Yr	Team	G	FG	FT	TP	Avg.
1966-67	New York	50	83	26	192	3.8
1967-68	Seattle	36	46	20	112	3.1
1968-69	Kentucky ABA	2	1 (0)	2	4	2.0
	Totals	68	130 (0)	48	308	3.5

ALCORN, GARY
b. Oct. 8, 1936 Ht. 6-9 Wt. 225 College—Fresno State

Yr	Team	G	FG	FT	TP	Avg.
1960-61	Los Angeles	19	12	7	31	1.6

ALLEN, BILL

Yr	Team	G	FG	FT	TP	Avg.
1967-68	Anaheim ABA	38	118 (2)	58	300	7.9

ALLEN, BOB
b. July 17, 1946 Ht. 6-9 Wt. 205 College—Marshall

Yr	Team	G	FG	FT	TP	Avg.
1968-69	San Fran.	27	14	20	48	1.8

ALLEN, WILLIE
Ht. 6-6 Wt. 230 College—Miami (Fla.)

Yr	Team	G	FG	FT	TP	Avg.
1971-72	Floridians ABA	7	4 (0)	5	13	1.9

ALLISON, ODIS
b. Oct. 2, 1949 Ht. 6-6 Wt. 195 College—Nev.-Las V.

Yr	Team	G	FG	FT	TP	Avg.
1971-72	Gold. St.	36	17	33	67	1.9

ANDEREGG, ROBERT
b. Aug. 24, 1937 Ht. 6-3 Wt. 200 College—Mich. State

Yr	Team	G	FG	FT	TP	Avg.
1959-60	New York	33	55	23	133	4.0

ANDERSON, ANDY
b. Feb. 6, 1945 Ht. 6-2 Wt. 185 College—Canisius

Yr	Team	G	FG	FT	TP	Avg.
1967-68	Oakland ABA	77	270 (9)	163	730	9.5
1968-69	Oak.-Miami ABA	36	123 (0)	98	344	9.6
	Totals	113	393 (9)	261	1074	9.5

ANDERSON, CLIFF
b. Sept. 7, 1944 Ht. 6-4 Wt. 200 College—St. Joseph's (Pa.)

Yr	Team	G	FG	FT	TP	Avg.
1967-68	Los Angeles	18	7	12	26	1.4
1968-69	Los Angeles	35	44	47	135	3.9
1969-70	Denver ABA	3	2 (0)	2	6	2.0
1970-71	Cleve.-Phila.	28	20	46	86	3.1
	Totals	84	73 (0)	107	253	3.0

ANDERSON, DAN
b. Feb. 15, 1943 Ht. 6-10 Wt. 230 College—Augsburg

Yr	Team	G	FG	FT	TP	Avg.
1967-68	New Jersey ABA	78	463 (0)	223	1149	14.7
1968-69	N.Y.-Ky.-Minn. ABA	62	220 (0)	118	558	9.0
	Totals	140	683 (0)	341	1707	12.2

ANDERSON, DAN
b. Jan. 1, 1951 Ht. 6-2 Wt. 185 College—USC

Yr	Team	G	FG	FT	TP	Avg.
1974-75	Portland	43	47	26	120	2.8
1975-76	Portland	52	88	51	227	4.4
	Totals	95	135	77	347	3.7

ANDERSON, JEROME
b. October 9, 1953 Ht. 6-5 Wt. 195 College—W. Va.

Yr	Team	G	FG	FT	TP	Avg.
1975-76	Boston	22	25	11	61	2.8
1976-77	Indiana	27	26	14	66	2.4
	Totals	49	51	25	127	2.6

ANDERZUNAS, WALLY
b. Jan. 11, 1946 Ht. 6-7 Wt. 220 College—Creighton

Yr	Team	G	FG	FT	TP	Avg.
1969-70	Cincinnati	44	65	29	159	3.6

ANIELAK, DON
b. 1932 Ht. 6-7½ Wt. 192 College—Southwest Missouri

Yr	Team	G	FG	FT	TP	Avg.
1954-55	New York	1	0	3	3	3.0

ARCENEAUX, STACEY (Robert L. Stacey)
b. Feb. 17, 1936 Ht. 6-4½ Wt. 220 College—Iowa St.

Yr	Team	G	FG	FT	TP	Avg.
1961-62	St. Louis	7	22	6	50	7.1

ARD, JIM
b. Sept. 19, 1948 Ht. 6-9 Wt. 215 College—Cincinnati

Yr	Team		G	FG	FT	TP	Avg.
1970-71	N.Y.	ABA	73	174(0)	79	427	5.9
1971-72	N.Y.	ABA	71	157(2)	77	397	5.6
1972-73	N.Y.	ABA	42	53(0)	34	140	3.3
1973-74	Memphis	ABA	27	64(2)	40	174	6.4
1974-75	Boston		59	89	48	226	3.8
1975-76	Boston		81	107	71	285	3.5
1976-77	Boston		63	96	49	241	3.8
1977-78	Bos.-Chi.		15	8	3	19	1.3
	Totals		431	748(4)	401	1909	4.4

ARIZIN, PAUL
b. April 9, 1928 Ht. 6-4 Wt. 200 College—Villanova

Yr	Team	G	FG	FT	TP	Avg.
1950-51	Philadelphia	65	352	417	1121	17.2
1951-52	Philadelphia	66	548	578	1674	25.4
1954-55	Philadelphia	72	529	454	1512	21.0
1955-56	Philadelphia	72	617	507	1741	24.2
1956-57	Philadelphia	71	613	591	1817	25.6
1957-58	Philadelphia	68	483	440	1406	20.7
1958-59	Philadelphia	70	632	587	1851	26.4
1959-60	Philadelphia	72	593	420	1606	22.3
1960-61	Philadelphia	79	650	532	1832	23.2
1961-62	Philadelphia	78	611	484	1706	21.9
	Totals	713	5628	5010	16266	22.8

Yr	Team	G	FG	FT	TP	Avg.

ARMSTRONG, PAUL (Curly)

Ht. 5-11 Wt. 170 College—Indiana

Yr	Team	G	FG	FT	TP	Avg.
1941-42	Ft. Wayne NL	24	69	60	198	8.3
1942-43	Ft. Wayne NL	23	67	49	183	8.0
1943-45	Ft. Wayne NL		In Military Service			
1945-46	Ft. Wayne NL	6	3	1	7	1.2
1946-47	Ft. Wayne NL	44	127	134	388	8.8
1947-48	Ft. Wayne NL	53	148	139	435	8.2
1948-49	Ft. Wayne	52	131	118	380	7.3
1949-50	Ft. Wayne	·63	144	170	458	7.3
1950-51	Ft. Wayne	38	72	58	202	5.3
	Totals	303	761	729	2251	7.1

ARMSTRONG, ROBERT

b. June 17, 1933 Ht. 6-8 Wt. 230 College—Mich. State

Yr	Team	G	FG	FT	TP	Avg.
1956-57	Philadelphia	19	11	6	28	1.5

ARMSTRONG, WARREN

See Jabali, Warren

ARNELLE, JESSE

b. Dec. 30, 1933 Ht. 6-5 Wt. 220 College—Penn State

Yr	Team	G	FG	FT	TP	Avg.
1955-56	Ft. Wayne	31	52	43	147	4.7

ARNETTE, JAY

b. Dec. 19, 1938 Ht. 6-2 Wt. 175 College—Texas

Yr	Team	G	FG	FT	TP	Avg.
1963-64	Cincinnati	48	71	42	184	3.8
1964-65	Cincinnati	63	91	56	238	3.8
1965-66	Cincinnati	3	1	0	2	0.7
	Totals	114	163	98	424	3.7

ARNZEN, BOB

b. Nov. 3, 1947 Ht. 6-6 Wt. 215 College—Notre Dame

Yr	Team	G	FG	FT	TP	Avg.
1969-70	New York ABA	13	19 (0)	2	40	3.1
1970-71	Cincinnati	55	128	45	301	5.5
1972-73	Indiana ABA	23	20 (0)	6	46	2.0
1973-74	Indiana ABA	20	23 (1)	7	56	2.8
	Totals	111	190 (1)	60	443	4.0

ARTHURS, JOHN

b. Aug. 15, 1947 Ht. 6-4 Wt. 185 College—Tulane

Yr	Team	G	FG	FT	TP	Avg.
1969-70	Milwaukee	11	12	11	35	3.2

ASMONGA, DON

Ht. 6-2 Wt. 185 College—Geneva

Yr	Team	G	FG	FT	TP	Avg.
1953-54	Baltimore	7	2	1	5	0.7

ATHA, RICHARD

b. Sept. 21, 1931 Ht. 6-2 Wt. 195 College—Indiana St.

Yr	Team	G	FG	FT	TP	Avg.
1955-56	New York	25	36	21	93	3.7
1957-58	Detroit	18	17	10	44	2.4
	Totals	43	53	31	137	3.2

ATTLES, ALVIN

b. Nov. 7, 1936 Ht. 6-2 Wt. 175 Coll.—No. Car. A&T

Yr	Team	G	FG	FT	TP	Avg.
1960-61	Philadelphia	77	222	97	541	7.0
1961-62	Philadelphia	75	343	158	844	11.2
1962-63	San Fran.	71	301	133	735	10.4
1963-64	San Fran.	70	289	185	763	10.9
1964-65	San Fran.	73	254	171	679	9.3
1965-66	San Fran.	79	364	154	882	11.2
1966-67	San Fran.	70	212	88	512	7.3
1967-68	San Fran.	67	252	150	654	9.8
1968-69	San Fran.	51	162	95	419	8.2
˙969-70	San Fran.	45	78	75	231	5.1
970-71	San Fran.	34	22	24	68	2.0
	Totals	712	2499	1330	6328	8.9

AUBUCHON, CHET (Aubie)

b. May 8, 1916 Ht. 5-10 Wt. 145 College—Mich. State

Yr	Team	G	FG	FT	TP	Avg.
1946-47	Detroit	30	23	19	65	2.2

AUSTIN, JOHN

b. Aug. 31, 1944 Ht. 6-0 Wt. 175 College—Boston Coll.

Yr	Team	G	FG	FT	TP	Avg.
1966-67	Baltimore	4	5	13	23	5.9
1967-68	New Jersey ABA	41	108 (0)	101	317	7.7
	Totals	45	113 (0)	114	340	7.6

AVERITT, WILLIAM (BIRD)

b. July 22, 1952 Ht. 6-2 Wt. 175 College—Pepperdine

Yr	Team	G	FG	FT	TP	Avg.
1973-74	San Ant. ABA	74	334 (9)	156	851	11.5
1974-75	Kentucky ABA	84	415 (7)	249	1100	13.1
1975-76	Kentucky ABA	78	506 (40)	266	1398	17.9
1976-77	Buffalo	75	234	121	589	7.9
1977-78	NJ-Buf	55	198	100	496	9.0
	Totals	366	1687 (56)	892	4434	12.1

BACH, JOHN

b. July 10, 1924 Ht. 6-2 Wt. 180 Coll.—Rochstr. & Ford.

Yr	Team	G	FG	FT	TP	Avg.
1948-49	Boston	34	34	51	119	3.5

BACON, HENRY

Ht. 6-3 Wt. 205 College—Louisville

Yr	Team	G	FG	FT	TP	Avg.
1972-73	San Diego ABA	47	58 (2)	44	166	3.5

BAECHTOLD, JIM

b. Dec. 9, 1927 Ht. 6-4 Wt. 205 College—Eastern Ky.

Yr	Team	G	FG	FT	TP	Avg.
1952-53	Baltimore	64	242	177	661	10.3
1953-54	New York	70	170	134	474	6.8
1954-55	New York	72	362	279	1003	13.9
1955-56	New York	70	268	233	769	11.0
1956-57	New York	45	75	66	216	4.8
	Totals	321	1117	889	3123	9.7

Yr	Team	G	FG	FT	TP	Avg.
BAKER, JIMMIE						
b. Dec. 25, 1953 Ht. 6-9 Wt. 220 College—Hawaii						
1975-76	Kentucky ABA	5	3 (0)	0	6	1.2
BAKER, NORMAN						
Ht. 6-0 College—McGill						
1946-47	Chicago	4	0	0	0	0.0
BALTIMORE, HERSCHEL						
b. June 21, 1921 Ht. 6-4 Wt. 195 College—Penn St.						
1946-47	St. Louis	58	53	32	138	2.4
BANKS, WALKER						
Ht. 6-10 Wt. 205 College—Western Kentucky						
1970-71	Pittsburgh ABA	16	17 (0)	7	41	2.6
BARBER, JOHN						
b. June 27, 1927 Ht. 6-6 Wt. 210 College—L.A. State						
1956-57	St. Louis	5	2	3	7	1.4
BARKER, CLIFF						
b. Jan. 15, 1921 Ht. 6-2 Wt. 185 College—Kentucky						
1949-50	Indianapolis	49	102	75	279	5.7
1950-51	Indianapolis	56	51	50	152	2.7
1951-52	Indianapolis	44	48	30	126	2.9
	Totals	149	201	155	557	3.7
BARKSDALE, DON						
b. March 31, 1923 Ht. 6-6 Wt. 200 College—UCLA						
1951-52	Baltimore	62	272	237	781	12.6
1952-53	Baltimore	65	321	257	899	13.8
1953-54	Boston	63	156	149	461	7.3
1954-55	Boston	72	267	220	754	10.5
	Totals	262	1016	863	2895	11.0
BARNES, HARRY						
b. July 25, 1945 Ht. 6-3 Wt. 205 College—Northeastern						
1968-69	San Diego	22	18	7	43	2.0
BARNES, JIM (Bad News)						
b. April 13, 1941 Ht. 6-8 Wt. 240 College—Tex. West.						
1964-65	New York	75	454	251	1159	15.5
1965-66	N.Y.-Balt.	73	348	212	908	12.4
1966-67	Los Angeles	80	217	128	562	7.0
1967-68	L.A.-Chicago	79	221	133	575	7.3
1968-69	Chi.-Bos.	59	115	75	305	5.2
1969-70	Boston	77	178	95	451	5.9
1970-71	Baltimore	11	15	7	37	3.4
	Totals	454	1548	901	3997	8.8
BARNETT, JIM						
b. July 7, 1944 Ht. 6-4 Wt. 180 College—Oregon						
1966-67	Boston	48	78	42	198	4.1
1967-68	San Diego	47	179	84	442	9.4
1968-69	San Diego	80	465	233	1163	14.5
1969-70	San Diego	80	450	289	1189	14.9
1970-71	Portland	78	559	326	1444	18.5
1971-72	Gold. St.	80	374	244	992	12.4
1972-73	Gold. St.	82	394	183	971	11.8
1973-74	Gold. St.	77	350	184	884	11.5
1974-75	N.O.-N.Y.	73	285	199	769	10.5
1975-76	New York	71	164	90	418	5.9
1976-77	Philadelphia	16	28	10	66	4.1
	Totals	732	3326	1884	8536	11.7
BARNETT, NATE						
b. Jan. 29, 1953 Ht. 6-4 Wt. 180 College—Akron						
1975-76	Indiana ABA	12	12 (0)	3	27	2.3
BARNETT, RICHARD (Dick)						
b. Oct. 2, 1936 Ht. 6-4 Wt. 190 College—Tenn. State						
1959-60	Syracuse	57	289	128	706	12.4
1960-61	Syracuse	78	540	240	1320	16.9
1962-63	Los Angeles	80	547	343	1437	18.0
1963-64	Los Angeles	78	541	351	1433	18.4
1964-65	Los Angeles	74	375	270	1020	13.8
1965-66	New York	75	631	467	1729	23.1
1966-67	New York	67	454	231	1139	17.0
1967-68	New York	81	559	343	1461	18.0
1968-69	New York	82	565	312	1442	17.6
1969-70	New York	82	494	232	1220	14.9
1970-71	New York	82	540	193	1273	15.5
1971-72	New York	79	401	162	964	12.2
1972-73	New York	51	88	16	192	3.8
1973-74	New York	5	10	2	22	4.4
	Totals	971	6034	3290	15358	15.8
BARNHILL, JOHN (Rabbit)						
b. March 30, 1938 Ht. 6-1 Wt. 180 Coll.—Tenn. State						
1962-63	St. Louis	77	360	181	901	11.7
1963-64	St. Louis	74	208	70	486	6.6
1964-65	St. Louis	41	121	45	287	7.0
1965-66	St. L.-Det.	76	243	113	599	7.9
1966-67	Baltimore	53	187	66	440	8.3
1967-68	San Diego	75	295	154	744	9.9
1968-69	Baltimore	30	76	39	191	6.4
1969-70	Indiana ABA	77	254 (71)	158	879	11.4
1970-71	Ind.-Den. ABA	67	149 (32)	96	490	7.3
1971-72	Indiana ABA	19	24 (4)	8	68	3.6
	Totals	589	1917 (107)	930	5085	8.6
BARNHILL, NORTON						
b. July 15, 1953 Ht. 6-4 Wt. 205 College—Wash. St.						
1976-77	Seattle	4	2	0	4	1.0
BARNHORST, LEO						
b. May 17, 1924 Ht. 6-4 Wt. 195 College—Notre Dame						
1949-50	Chicago	67	174	90	438	6.5
1950-51	Ind.	68	232	82	546	8.0
1951-52	Ind.	66	349	122	820	12.4
1952-53	Ind.	71	402	163	967	13.6
1953-54	Balt.-Ft. Wayne	72	199	63	461	6.4
	Totals	344	1356	520	3232	9.4
BARR, JOHN E.						
b. Aug. 18, 1918 Ht. 6-3 Wt. 205 College—Penn State						
1946-47	St. Louis	58	124	47	295	5.1

Yr	Team	G	FG	FT	TP	Avg.

BARR, MIKE

b. Oct. 9, 1950 Ht. 6-3 Wt. 180 College—Duquesne

Yr	Team	G	FG	FT	TP	Avg.
1972-73	Virginia ABA	79	288 (1)	141	720	9.1
1973-74	Virginia ABA	45	80 (2)	33	199	4.4
1974-75	St. Louis ABA	54	136 (0)	28	300	5.6
1975-76	St. Louis ABA	56	118 (6)	46	300	5.4
1976-77	Kansas City	73	122	41	285	3.9
	Totals	307	744 (9)	289	1804	5.9

BARR, MOE

b. June 19, 1944 Ht. 6-4 Wt. 195 College—Duquesne

Yr	Team	G	FG	FT	TP	Avg.
1970-71	Cincinnati	31	25	11	61	2.0

BARRETT, ERNIE

b. Dec. 27, 1929 Ht. 6-3 Wt. 180 College—Kan. State

Yr	Team	G	FG	FT	TP	Avg.
1953-54	Boston	59	60	14	134	2.3
1955-56	Boston	72	207	93	507	7.0
	Totals	131	267	107	641	4.9

BARRETT, MICHAEL

b. Sept. 5. 1943 Ht. 6-2 Wt. 160 Coll.—W. Va. Tech.

Yr	Team	G	FG	FT	TP	Avg.
1969-70	Washington ABA	84	417 (62)	232	1252	14.9
1970-71	Virginia ABA	84	430 (28)	208	1152	13.7
1972-73	San Diego ABA	19	33 (4)	18	96	5.1
	Totals	187	880 (94)	458	2500	13.4

BARTELS, ED

b. Oct. 8, 1925 Ht. 6-5 Wt. 195 College—No. Car. St.

Yr	Team	G	FG	FT	TP	Avg.
1949-50	Den.-N.Y.	15	22	19	63	4.2
1950-51	Washington	17	24	24	72	4.2
	Totals	32	46	43	135	4.2

BARTOLOME, VIC

b. Sept. 29, 1948 Ht. 7-0 Wt. 230 College—Oreg. State

Yr	Team	G	FG	FT	TP	Avg.
1971-72	Gold. St.	38	15	4	34	0.9

BASKERVILLE, JERRY

b. Nov. 10, 1951 Ht. 6-7 Wt. 190 College—Temple

Yr	Team	G	FG	FT	TP	Avg.
1975-76	Philadelphia	21	8	10	26	1.2

BATTS, LLOYD

b. May 9, 1951 Ht. 6-4 Wt. 185 College—Cincinnati

Yr	Team	G	FG	FT	TP	Avg.
1974-75	Virginia ABA	58	247 (42)	58	598	10.3

BAUM, JOHN

b. June 19, 1946 Ht. 6-5 Wt. 200 College—Temple

Yr	Team	G	FG	FT	TP	Avg.
1969-70	Chicago	3	3	0	6	2.0
1970-71	Chicago	62	123	40	286	4.6
1971-72	New York ABA	44	103 (0)	41	247	5.6
1972-73	New York ABA	75	221 (0)	107	549	7.3
1973-74	Mem.-Ind. ABA	60	180 (0)	50	410	6.8
	Totals	244	630 (0)	238	1498	6.1

BAUMHOLTZ, FRANK

b. Oct. 7, 1919 Ht. 5-10 Wt. 170 College—Oh. Univ.

Yr	Team	G	FG	FT	TP	Avg.
1945-46	Youngstown NL	26	99	76	274	10.5
1946-47	Cleveland	45	255	121	631	14.0
	Totals	71	354	197	905	12.7

BAYLOR, ELGIN

b. Sept. 16, 1934 Ht. 6-5 Wt.225 College—Seattle

Yr	Team	G	FG	FT	TP	Avg.
1958-59	Minneapolis	70	605	532	1742	24.9
1959-60	Minneapolis	70	755	564	2074	29.6
1960-61	Los Angeles	73	931	676	2538	34.8
1961-62	Los Angeles	48	680	476	1836	38.2
1962-63	Los Angeles	80	1029	661	2719	34.0
1963-64	Los Angeles	78	756	471	1983	25.4
1964-65	Los Angeles	74	763	483	2009	27.1
1965-66	Los Angeles	65	415	249	1079	16.6
1966-67	Los Angeles	70	711	440	1862	26.6
1967-68	Los Angeles	77	757	488	2002	26.0
1968-69	Los Angeles	76	730	421	1881	24.8
1969-70	Los Angeles	54	511	276	1298	24.0
1970-71	Los Angeles	2	8	4	20	10.0
1971-72	Los Angeles	9	42	22	106	11.8
	Totals	846	8693	5763	23149	27.4

BAYNE, HOWARD

Ht. 6-6 Wt. 235 College—Tennessee

Yr	Team	G	FG	FT	TP	Avg.
1967-68	Kentucky ABA	69	129 (1)	77	338	4.9

BEACH, ED

b. Jan. 25, 1929 Ht. 6-3 Wt. 200 College—West Va.

Yr	Team	G	FG	FT	TP	Avg.
1950-51	Minn.-Tri-Cit.	12	8	6	22	1.8

BEARD, AL

Ht. 6-9½ College—Norfolk State

Yr	Team	G	FG	FT	TP	Avg.
1967-68	New Jersey ABA	12	12 (0)	6	30	2.5

BEARD, RALPH

b. Dec. 2, 1927 Ht. 5-10 Wt. 176 College—Kentucky

Yr	Team	G	FG	FT	TP	Avg.
1949-50	Indianapolis	60	340	215	895	14.9
1950-51	Indianapolis	66	409	293	1111	16.8
	Totals	126	749	508	2006	15.9

BEASLEY, CHARLES

b. Sept. 23, 1945 Ht. 6-5 Wt. 190 College—Southern Methodist

Yr	Team	G	FG	FT	TP	Avg.
1967-68	Dallas ABA	78	371 (3)	285	1036	13.3
1968-69	Dallas ABA	75	219 (1)	161	602	8.0
1969-70	Dallas ABA	80	273 (19)	231	834	10.4
1970-71	Fla.-Tex. ABA	48	50 (7)	43	164	3.4
	Totals	281	913 (30)	720	2636	9.4

BEASLEY, JOHN MICHAEL

b. Feb. 5, 1944 Ht. 6-9 Wt. 225 College—Texas A&M

Yr	Team	G	FG	FT	TP	Avg.
1967-68	Dallas ABA	77	622 (0)	271	1515	19.7
1968-69	Dallas ABA	78	582 (3)	332	1505	19.3

Yr	Team	G	FG	FT	TP	Avg.
1969-70	Dallas ABA	84	623 (3)	284	1539	18.3
1970-71	Texas ABA	83	516 (16)	236	1316	15.8
1971-72	Dallas-Utah ABA	70	124 (8)	61	333	4.8
1972-73	Utah ABA	71	185 (29)	62	519	7.3
1973-74	Utah ABA	43	53 (22)	10	182	4.2
	Totals	506	2705 (81)	1256	6909	13.7

BEATY, ZELMO (Big Z)

b. Oct. 25, 1939 Ht. 6-9 Wt. 235 College—Prairie View

Yr	Team	G	FG	FT	TP	Avg.
1962-63	St. Louis	80	297	220	814	10.2
1963-64	St. Louis	59	287	200	774	13.1
1964-65	St. Louis	80	505	341	1351	16.9
1965-66	St. Louis	80	616	424	1656	20.7
1966-67	St. Louis	48	328	197	853	17.8
1967-68	St. Louis	82	639	455	1733	21.1
1968-69	Atlanta	72	588	370	1546	21.5
1969-70			Did Not Play			
1970-71	Utah ABA	76	659 (2)	418	1742	22.9
1971-72	Utah ABA	84	729 (0)	522	1980	23.6
1972-73	Utah ABA	82	521 (0)	306	1348	16.4
1973-74	Utah ABA	77	417 (0)	194	1028	13.4
1974-75	Los Angeles	69	136	108	380	5.5
	Totals	889	5722 (2)	3755	15205	17.1

BECK, BYRON

b. Jan. 25, 1945 Ht. 6-9 Wt. 240 College—Denver

Yr	Team	G	FG	FT	TP	Avg.
1967-68	Denver ABA	71	275 (0)	119	669	9.4
1968-69	Denver ABA	71	421 (2)	182	1030	14.5
1969-70	Denver ABA	79	440 (0)	137	1017	12.9
1970-71	Denver ABA	84	486 (4)	158	1142	13.6
1971-72	Denver ABA	66	337 (0)	140	814	12.3
1972-73	Denver ABA	77	464 (2)	158	1092	14.2
1973-74	Denver ABA	82	425 (0)	120	970	11.8
1974-75	Denver ABA	84	384 (0)	81	849	10.1
1975-76	Denver ABA	80	329 (5)	97	770	9.6
1976-77	Denver	53	107	36	250	4.7
	Totals	747	3668 (13)	1228	8603	11.5

BECK, ERNEST

b. Dec. 11, 1931 Ht. 6-4 Wt. 190 College—Pennsylvania

Yr	Team	G	FG	FT	TP	Avg.
1953-54	Philadelphia	15	39	34	112	7.5
1954-55	Philadelphia		In Military Service			
1955-56	Philadelphia	67	136	76	348	5.2
1956-57	Philadelphia	72	195	111	501	7.0
1957-58	Philadelphia	71	272	170	714	10.1
1958-59	Philadelphia	70	163	43	369	5.3
1959-60	Philadelphia	66	114	27	255	3.9
	Totals	361	919	461	2299	6.4

BECKER, ARTHUR C.

b. Jan. 12, 1942 Ht. 6-8 Wt. 210 College—Arizona St.

Yr	Team	G	FG	FT	TP	Avg.
1967-68	Houston ABA	76	559 (4)	297	1427	18.8
1968-69	Houston ABA	78	423 (0)	200	1046	13.4
1969-70	Indiana ABA	82	309 (0)	111	729	8.9
1970-71	Ind.-Den. ABA	80	365 (5)	135	880	11.0
1971-72	Denver ABA	84	435 (0)	165	1035	12.3
1972-73	N.Y.-Dal. ABA	14	16 (0)	11	43	3.1
	Totals	414	2107 (9)	919	5160	12.5

BECKER, MORRIS (Moe)

b. Feb. 24, 1917 Ht. 6-1 Wt. 185 College—Duquesne

Yr	Team	G	FG	FT	TP	Avg.
1944-45	Cleveland NL	1	0	0	0	0.0
1945-46	Youngstown NL	30	115	40	270	9.0
1946-47	Pitt.-Bos.-Det.	43	70	22	162	3.8
	Totals	74	185	62	432	5.8

BEDELL, ROBERT GEORGE

b. June 26, 1944 Ht. 6-8 Wt. 205 College—Stanford

Yr	Team	G	FG	FT	TP	Avg.
1967-68	Anaheim ABA	76	325 (0)	142	792	10.4
1968-69	Dallas ABA	42	92 (0)	48	232	5.5
1969-70	Dallas ABA	80	283 (2)	207	779	9.7
1970-71	Texas	71	167 (9)	93	454	6.4
	Totals	269	867 (11)	490	2257	8.4

BEENDERS, HENRY (Hank)

b. June 2, 1916 Ht. 6-6 Wt. 185 Coll.—Lg. Island U.

Yr	Team	G	FG	FT	TP	Avg.
1946-47	Providence	58	266	181	713	12.3
1947-48	Prov.-Phila.	45	76	51	203	4.5
1948-49	Boston	8	6	7	19	2.4
	Totals	111	348	239	935	8.4

BEHNKE, ELMER

b. Feb. 3, 1929 Ht. 6-7 Wt. 210 College—Bradley

Yr	Team	G	FG	FT	TP	Avg.
1951-52	Milwaukee	4	6	4	16	4.0

BELL, DENNIS

b. June 2, 1951 Ht. 6-5 Wt. 225 College—Drake

Yr	Team	G	FG	FT	TP	Avg.
1973-74	New York	1	0	0	0	0.0
1974-75	New York	52	68	20	156	3.0
1975-76	New York	10	8	3	19	1.9
	Totals	63	76	23	175	2.5

BELL, WILLIAM H. (Whitey)

b. Sept. 13, 1932 Ht. 6-0 Wt. 181 Coll.—N.C. State

Yr	Team	G	FG	FT	TP	Avg.
1959-60	New York	31	70	28	168	5.4
1960-61	New York	5	7	1	15	3.0
	Totals	36	77	29	183	5.1

Yr	Team	G	FG	FT	TP	Avg.

BELLAMY, WALTER (Bells)

b. July 24, 1939 Ht. 6-10½ Wt. 245 College—Indiana

Yr	Team	G	FG	FT	TP	Avg.
1961-62	Chicago	79	973	549	2495	31.6
1962-63	Chicago	80	840	553	2233	27.9
1963-64	Baltimore	80	811	537	2159	27.0
1964-65	Baltimore	80	733	515	1981	24.8
1965-66	Balt.-N.Y.	80	695	430	1820	22.8
1966-67	New York	79	565	369	1499	19.0
1967-68	New York	82	511	350	1372	16.7
1968-69	N.Y.-Detroit	88	563	401	1527	17.4
1969-70	Det.-Atlanta	79	351	215	917	11.6
1970-71	Atlanta	82	433	336	1202	14.7
1971-72	Atlanta	82	593	340	1526	18.6
1972-73	Atlanta	74	455	283	1193	16.1
1973-74	Atlanta	77	389	233	1011	13.1
1974-75	New Orleans	1	2	2	6	6.0
	Totals	1043	7914	5113	20941	20.1

BEMORAS, IRV

b. Nov. 18, 1930 Ht. 6-3 Wt. 187 College—Illinois

Yr	Team	G	FG	FT	TP	Avg.
1953-54	Milwaukee	69	185	139	509	7.4
1956-57	St. Louis	62	124	70	318	5.1
	Totals	131	309	209	827	6.3

BENBOW, LEON

b. July 23, 1952 Ht. 6-4 Wt. 185 College—Jacksonville

Yr	Team	G	FG	FT	TP	Avg.
1974-75	Chicago	39	35	15	85	2.2
1975-76	Chicago	76	219	105	543	7.1
	Totals	115	254	120	628	5.4

BENNETT, MEL

b. Jan. 4, 1955 Ht. 6-7 Wt. 220 College—Pittsburgh

Yr	Team	G	FG	FT	TP	Avg.
1975-76	Virginia ABA	75	329	246	904	12.1
1976-77	Indiana	67	101	112	314	4.7
1977-78	Indiana	31	23	28	74	2.4
	Totals	173	453	386	1292	7.5

BENNETT, WILLIS (Spider)

b. Aug. 4, 1943 Ht. 6-3 Wt. 190 College—Winston-Salem

Yr	Team	G	FG	FT	TP	Avg.
1968-69	Dallas-Hou. ABA	59	141 (6)	140	440	7.5

BERCE, EUGENE

b. Nov. 22, 1926 Ht. 5-11 Wt. 175 College—Marquette

Yr	Team	G	FG	FT	TP	Avg.
1948-49	Oshkosh NL	58	120	101	341	5.9
1949-50	Tri-Cities	3	5	0	10	3.3
	Totals	61	125	101	351	5.8

BERGEN, GARY

b. 1933 Ht. 6-8 Wt. 212 College—Utah

Yr	Team	G	FG	FT	TP	Avg.
1956-57	New York	6	3	2	8	1.3

BERGH, LARRY

b. April 2, 1945 Ht. 6-8 Wt. 215 College—Tuskegee

Yr	Team	G	FG	FT	TP	Avg.
1969-70	Pittsburgh ABA	20	49 (0)	23	121	6.1

BIALOSUKNIA, WES

b. June 8, 1945 Ht. 6-2 Wt. 185 College—Connecticut

Yr	Team	G	FG	FT	TP	Avg.
1967-68	Oakland ABA	70	209 (29)	103	608	8.7

BIANCHI, ALFRED (Al)

b. March 26, 1932 Ht. 6-3 Wt. 185 Coll.—Bowling Green

Yr	Team	G	FG	FT	TP	Avg.
1956-57	Syracuse	68	199	165	563	8.3
1957-58	Syracuse	69	215	140	570	8.3
1958-59	Syracuse	72	285	149	719	10.0
1959-60	Syracuse	69	215	112	542	7.8
1960-61	Syracuse	52	118	60	296	5.7
1961-62	Syracuse	80	336	154	826	10.3
1962-63	Syracuse	61	202	120	524	8.6
1963-64	Philadelphia	78	257	109	623	8.0
1964-65	Philadelphia	60	175	54	404	6.7
1965-66	Philadelphia	78	214	66	494	6.3
	Totals	687	2216	1129	5561	8.1

BIASETTI, HENRY

b. Jan. 14, 1925 Ht. 6-0 Wt. 180 Coll.—Assump. (Ont.)

Yr	Team	G	FG	FT	TP	Avg.
1946-47	Toronto	6	2	2	6	1.0

BIEDENBACH, EDWARD

b. Aug. 12, 1945 Ht. 6-1 Wt. 175 Coll.—N. C. State

Yr	Team	G	FG	FT	TP	Avg.
1968-69	Phoenix	7	0	4	4	0.6

BIELKE, DON

Ht. 6-8 Wt. 240 College—Valparaiso

Yr	Team	G	FG	FT	TP	Avg.
1955-56	Ft. Wayne	7	5	4	14	2.0

BILLINGLY, LIONEL

Ht. 6-9 Wt. 215 College—Duquesne

Yr	Team	G	FG	FT	TP	Avg.
1974-75	Virginia ABA	46	150 (0)	93	393	8.5

BING, DAVE

b. Nov. 24, 1943 Ht. 6-3 Wt. 180 College—Syracuse

Yr	Team	G	FG	FT	TP	Avg.
1966-67	Detroit	80	664	273	1601	20.0
1967-68	Detroit	79	835	472	2142	27.1
1968-69	Detroit	77	678	444	1800	23.4
1969-70	Detroit	70	575	454	1604	22.9
1970-71	Detroit	82	799	615	2213	27.0
1971-72	Detroit	45	369	278	1016	22.6
1972-73	Detroit	82	692	456	1840	22.4
1973-74	Detroit	81	582	356	1520	18.0
1974-75	Detroit	79	578	343	1499	19.0
1975-76	Washington	82	497	332	1326	16.2
1976-77	Washington	64	271	136	678	10.6
1977-78	Boston	80	422	244	1088	13.6
	Totals	901	6962	4403	18327	20.3

BIRD, JERRY

b. 1934 Ht. 6-6 Wt. 215 College—Kentucky

Yr	Team	G	FG	FT	TP	Avg.
1958-59	New York	11	12	1	25	2.3

BISHOP, GALE

b. June 9, 1922 Ht. 6-3 Wt. 195 College—Wash. State

Yr	Team	G	FG	FT	TP	Avg.
1948-49	Philadelphia	56	170	127	467	8.3

BLACK, CHARLES (Hawk)

b. June 15, 1921 Ht. 6-5 Wt. 200 College—Kansas

Yr	Team	G	FG	FT	TP	Avg.
1947-48	Anderson NL	58	148	149	445	7.7
1948-49	Ft. W.-Ind.	58	203	161	567	9.8
1949-50	Ft. W.-Andsn.	65	226	209	661	10.2
1951-52	Milwaukee	13	6	5	17	1.3
	Totals	194	583	524	1690	8.7

Yr	Team	G	FG	FT	TP	Avg.

BLACK, TOM

b. July 9, 1941 Ht. 6-10½ Wt. 234 Coll.—S. Dakota St.

1970-71	Sea.-Cin.	71	121	57	299	4.2

BLANEY, GEORGE

b. Nov. 12, 1939 Ht. 6-1 Wt. 175 College—Holy-Cross

1961-62	New York	36	54	9	117	3.3

BLEVINS, LEON

b. June 25, 1926 Ht. 6-2 Wt. 160 College—Arizona

1950-51	Indianapolis	3	1	0	2	0.7

BLOCK, JOHN

b. April 16, 1944 Ht. 6-9 Wt. 207 College—USC

1966-67	Los Angeles	22	20	24	64	2.9
1967-68	San Diego	52	366	316	1048	20.2
1968-69	San Diego	78	448	299	1195	15.3
1969-70	San Diego	82	453	287	1193	14.5
1970-71	San Diego	73	245	212	702	9.6
1971-72	Milwaukee	79	233	206	672	8.5
1972-73	Phila.-K.C.-O.	73	391	300	1082	14.8
1973-74	K.C.-Omaha	82	275	164	714	8.7
1974-75	N.O.-Chi.	54	159	114	432	8.0
1975-76	Chi.	2	2	0	4	2.0
	Totals	597	2592	1922	7106	11.9

BLOOM, MEYER (Mike)

b. Jan. 14, 1915 Ht. 6-6 Wt. 190 College—Temple

1947-48	Balt.-Boston	48	174	160	508	10.6
1948-49	Minn.-Chic.	45	35	56	126	2.8
	Totals	93	209	216	634	6.8

BOBB, NELSON

b. Feb. 25, 1924 Ht. 6-0 Wt. 170 College—Temple

1949-50	Philadelphia	57	80	82	242	4.2
1950-51	Philadelphia	53	52	44	148	2.8
1951-52	Philadelphia	62	110	99	319	5.1
1952-53	Philadelphia	55	119	105	343	6.2
	Totals	227	361	330	1052	4.6

BOCKHORN, ARLEN (Bucky)

b. July 8, 1933 Ht. 6-4 Wt. 200 College—Dayton

1958-59	Cincinnati	71	294	138	726	10.2
1959-60	Cincinnati	75	323	145	791	10.5
1960-61	Cincinnati	79	420	152	992	12.6
1961-62	Cincinnati	80	531	198	1260	15.7
1962-63	Cincinnati	80	375	183	933	11.7
1963-64	Cincinnati	70	242	96	580	8.3
1964-65	Cincinnati	19	60	28	148	7.8
	Totals	474	2245	940	5430	11.5

BOERWINKLE, THOMAS

b. Aug. 23, 1945 Ht. 7-0 Wt. 265 College—Tennessee

1968-69	Chicago	80	318	145	781	9.8
1969-70	Chicago	81	348	150	846	10.4
1970-71	Chicago	82	357	168	882	10.8
1971-72	Chicago	80	219	118	556	7.0
1972-73	Chicago	8	9	12	30	3.8
1973-74	Chicago	46	58	42	158	3.4
1974-75	Chicago	80	132	73	337	4.2
1975-76	Chicago	74	265	118	648	8.8
1976-77	Chicago	82	134	34	302	3.7
1977-78	Chicago	22	23	10	56	2.5
	Totals	635	1863	870	4596	7.2

Yr	Team	G	FG	FT	TP	Avg.

BOLGER, BILL

b. Aug. 21, 1931 Ht. 6-5 Wt. 205 College—Georgetown

1953-54	Baltimore	20	24	8	56	2.8

BOLSTORFF, DOUG

b. Oct. 29, 1931 Ht. 6-4 Wt. 195 College—Minnesota

1957-58	Detroit	3	2	0	4	1.3

BOND, PHIL

b. July 27, 1954 Ht. 6-2 Wt. 175 College—Louisville

1977-78	Houston	7	2	0	4	0.6

BONHAM, RON

b. May 31, 1942 Ht. 6-5 Wt. 200 College—Cincinnati

1964-65	Boston	37	91	92	274	7.4
1965-66	Boston	39	76	52	204	5.2
1967-68	Indiana ABA	42	80 (0)	85	245	5.8
	Totals	118	247 (0)	229	723	6.1

BON SALLE, GEORGE

b. July 1, 1935 Ht. 6-8 Wt. 220 College—Illinois

1961-62	Chicago	3	2	0	4	1.3

BOOKER, HAL (Butch)

Ht. 6-10 Wt. 230 College—Cheyney State

1969-70	Miami ABA	12	30 (0)	10	70	5.8

BOOZER, ROBERT (Bullet Bob)

b. April 26, 1937 Ht. 6-8 Wt. 215 College—Kan. State

1960-61	Cincinnati	79	250	166	666	8.4
1961-62	Cincinnati	79	410	263	1083	13.7
1962-63	Cincinnati	79	440	252	1132	14.3
1963-64	Cinn. N.Y.	81	468	272	1208	14.9
1964-65	New York	80	424	288	1136	14.2
1965-66	Los Angeles	78	365	225	955	12.2
1966-67	Chicago	80	538	360	1436	18.0
1967-68	Chicago	77	622	411	1655	21.5
1968-69	Chicago	79	661	394	1716	21.7
1969-70	Seattle	82	493	263	1249	15.2
1970-71	Milwaukee	80	290	148	728	9.1
	Totals	874	4961	3042	12964	14.8

BORNHEIMER, DAVE

Ht. 6-5 Wt. 205 College—Muhlenberg

1948-49	Philadelphia	15	34	20	88	5.9
1949-50	Philadelphia	60	88	78	254	4.2
	Totals	75	122	98	342	4.6

BORSAVAGE, COSTIC (Ike)

b. July 25, 1924 Ht. 6-8 Wt. 220 College—Temple

1950-51	Philadelphia	24	26	12	64	2.7

BORYLA, VINCE

b. March 11, 1927 Ht. 6-5 Wt. 210 Coll.—Notre Dame & Denver

1949-50	New York	59	204	204	612	10.4
1950-51	New York	66	352	278	982	14.9
1951-52	New York	42	202	96	500	11.9
1952-53	New York	66	254	165	673	10.2
1953-54	New York	52	175	70	420	8.1
	Totals	285	1187	813	3187	11.2

Yr	Team	G	FG	FT	TP	Avg.

BOSTIC, JIM

b. Jan. 28, 1953 Ht. 6-7 Wt. 225 College—New Mexico State

1977-78	Detroit	4	12	2	26	6.5

BOVEN, DON

b. March 6, 1925 Ht. 6-4 Wt. 210 Coll.—West. Mich.

1949-50	Waterloo	62	208	240	656	10.6
1951-52	Milwaukee	66	200	256	656	9.9
1952-53	Milw.- Ft. Wayne	67	153	145	451	6.7
	Totals	195	561	641	1763	9.0

BOWENS, TOM

b. July 7, 1940 Ht. 6-8 Wt. 220 College—Grambling

1967-68	Denver ABA	67	176 (1)	55	410	6.1
1968-69	New York ABA	76	186 (0)	83	455	6.0
1969-70	New Orleans ABA	68	110 (0)	47	267	3.9
	Totals	211	472 (1)	185	1132	5.4

BOWLING, ORB

Ht. 6-10 Wt. 215 College—Tennessee

1967-68	Kentucky ABA	11	9 (0)	3	21	1.9

BOWMAN, NATE

b. March 19, 1943 Ht. 6-10 Wt. 230 Coll.—Wichita St.

1966-67	Chicago	9	8	6	22	2.4
1967-68	New York	42	52	10	114	2.7
1968-69	New York	67	82	29	193	2.9
1969-70	New York	81	98	41	237	2.9
1970-71	Buffalo	44	58	20	136	3.1
1971-72	Pittsburgh ABA	18	19 (0)	5	43	2.4
	Totals	261	317 (0)	111	745	2.9

BOYD, KEN

b. March 25, 1952 Ht. 6-5 Wt. 195 College—Bos. Univ.

1974-75	New Orleans	6	7	5	19	3.2

BOYKOFF, HARRY (Big Hesh)

b. July 24, 1922 Ht. 6-10 Wt. 227 College—St. John's (N.Y.)

1947-48	Toledo NL	59	225	124	574	9.7
1948-49	Waterloo NL	61	293	191	777	12.7
1949-50	Waterloo	61	288	203	779	12.8
1950-51	Boston-Tri. Cit.	48	126	74	326	6.8
	Totals	229	932	592	2456	10.7

BRACEY, STEVE

b. August 1, 1950 Ht. 6-1 Wt. 185 College—Tulsa

1972-73	Atlanta	70	192	73	457	6.5
1973-74	Atlanta	75	241	69	551	7.3
1974-75	Golden State	42	54	25	133	3.2
	Totals	187	487	167	1141	6.1

Yr	Team	G	FG	FT	TP	Avg.

BRADDS, GARY (Tex)

b. July 26, 1942 Ht. 6-8 Wt. 210 College—Ohio State

1964-65	Baltimore	41	46	45	137	3.3
1965-66	Baltimore	3	2	3	7	2.3
1967-68	Oakland ABA	49	199 (0)	221	619	12.6
1968-69	Oakland ABA	75	516 (1)	364	1399	18.7
1969-70	Washington ABA	60	292 (0)	217	801	13.4
1970-71	Carolina- Dallas ABA	26	52 (0)	39	143	5.5
	Totals	254	1107 (1)	889	3106	12.2

BRADLEY, BILL

b. July 28, 1943 Ht. 6-5 Wt. 205 College—Princeton

1967-68	New York	45	142	76	360	8.0
1968-69	New York	82	407	206	1020	12.4
1969-70	New York	67	413	145	971	14.5
1970-71	New York	78	413	144	970	12.4
1971-72	New York	78	504	169	1177	15.1
1972-73	New York	82	575	169	1319	16.1
1973-74	New York	82	502	146	1150	14.0
1974-75	New York	79	452	144	1048	13.3
1975-76	New York	82	392	130	914	11.1
1976-77	N.Y. Knicks	67	127	34	288	4.3
	Totals	742	3927	1363	9217	12.4

BRADLEY, BILL

Ht. 5-11 Wt. 167 College—Tennessee

1967-68	Kentucky ABA	58	79 (3)	51	218	3.8

BRADLEY, JIM

b. March 16, 1952 Ht. 6-8 Wt. 215 Coll.—Northern Ill.

1973-74	Kentucky ABA	35	130 (0)	31	291	8.3
1974-75	Kentucky ABA	56	144 (0)	76	364	6.5
1975-76	Denver ABA	7	15 (0)	2	32	4.6
	Totals	98	289 (0)	109	687	6.5

BRADLEY, JOE

b. 1928 Ht. 6-3 Wt. 175 College—Oklahoma State

1949-50	Chicago	46	36	15	87	1.9

BRANNUM, ROBERT (Beeb)

b. May 28, 1925 Ht. 6-5½ Wt. 215 Coll.—Ky. & Mi.St.

1948-49	Sheboygan NL	64	169	169	507	7.9
1949-50	Sheboygan	59	234	245	713	12.1
1951-52	Boston	66	149	107	405	6.1
1952-53	Boston	71	188	110	486	6.8
1953-54	Boston	71	140	129	409	5.8
1954-55	Boston	71	176	90	442	6.2
	Totals	402	1056	850	2962	7.4

BRANSON, JESSEE

b. Jan. 7, 1942 Ht. 6-7 Wt. 200 College—Elon

1965-66	Philadelphia	5	1	3	5	1.0
1967-68	New Orleans ABA	78	374 (2)	332	1086	13.9
	Totals	83	375 (2)	335	1091	13.1

Yr	Team	G	FG	FT	TP	Avg.

BRASCO, JIM

b. Feb. 3, 1931 Ht. 6-1 Wt. 170 College—N.Y.U.

Yr	Team	G	FG	FT	TP	Avg.
1952-53	Syr.-Milw.	30	36	38	110	3.7

BRAUN, CARL

b. Sept. 25, 1927 Ht. 6-5 Wt. 180 College—Colgate

Yr	Team	G	FG	FT	TP	Avg.
1947-48	New York	47	276	119	671	14.3
1948-49	New York	57	299	212	810	14.2
1949-50	New York	67	373	285	1031	15.4
1952-53	New York	70	323	331	977	14.0
1953-54	New York	72	354	354	1062	14.8
1954-55	New York	71	400	274	1074	15.1
1955-56	New York	72	396	320	1112	15.4
1956-57	New York	72	378	245	1001	13.9
1957-58	New York	71	426	321	1173	16.5
1958-59	New York	72	287	180	754	10.5
1959-60	New York	54	285	129	699	12.9
1960-61	New York	15	37	11	85	5.7
1961-62	Boston	48	78	20	176	3.6
	Totals	788	3912	2801	10625	13.5

BRENNAN, PETER

b. Sept. 23, 1936 Ht. 6-6 Wt. 205 College—N. Carolina

Yr	Team	G	FG	FT	TP	Avg.
1958-59	New York	16	13	14	40	2.5

BRENNAN, THOMAS

Ht. 6-4 Wt. 200 College—Villanova

Yr	Team	G	FG	FT	TP	Avg.
1954-55	Philadelphia	11	5	0	10	0.9

BRIAN, FRANK (Flash)

b. May 1, 1923 Ht. 6-1½ Wt. 180 College—La. State

Yr	Team	G	FG	FT	TP	Avg.
1947-48	Anderson NL	59	248	155	651	11.0
1948-49	Anderson	64	216	201	633	9.9
1949-50	Anderson	64	368	402	1138	17.8
1950-51	Tri-Cities	68	363	418	1144	16.8
1951-52	Ft. Wayne	66	342	367	1051	15.9
1952-53	Ft. Wayne	68	245	236	726	10.7
1953-54	Ft. Wayne	64	132	137	401	6.3
1954-55	Ft. Wayne	71	237	217	691	9.7
1955-56	Ft. Wayne	37	78	72	228	6.2
	Totals	561	2229	2205	6663	11.9

BRIDGES, BILL

b. April 4, 1939 Ht. 6-6½ Wt. 228 College—Kansas

Yr	Team	G	FG	FT	TP	Avg.
1962-63	St. Louis	27	66	32	164	6.1
1963-64	St. Louis	80	268	146	682	8.5
1964-65	St. Louis	79	362	186	910	11.5
1965-66	St. Louis	78	377	257	1011	13.0
1966-67	St. Louis	79	503	367	1373	17.4
1967-68	St. Louis	82	466	347	1279	15.6
1968-69	Atlanta	80	351	239	941	11.8
1969-70	Atlanta	82	443	331	1217	14.8
1970-71	Atlanta	82	382	211	975	11.9
1971-72	Atl.-Phila.	78	379	222	980	12.6
1972-73	Phil.-L.A.	82	333	179	845	10.3
1973-74	Los Angeles	65	216	116	548	8.4
1974-75	L.A.-G.S.	32	35	17	87	2.7
	Totals	926	4181	2650	11012	11.9

BRIGHTMAN, ALBERT

b. 1922 Ht. 6-2 Wt. 195 College—Morris Harvey

Yr	Team	G	FG	FT	TP	Avg.
1946-47	Boston	58	223	121	567	9.8

BRINDLEY, AUDLEY

b. Dec. 31, 1923 Ht. 6-4 Wt. 175 College—Dartmouth
d. Nov. 19, 1958

Yr	Team	G	FG	FT	TP	Avg.
1946-47	New York	12	14	6	34	2.8

BRISKER, JOHN

b. June 15, 1947 Ht. 6-5 Wt. 210 College—Toledo

Yr	Team	G	FG	FT	TP	Avg.
1969-70	Pittsburgh ABA	77	593 (34)	329	1617	21.0
1970-71	Pittsburgh ABA	79	809 (89)	430	2315	29.3
1971-72	Pittsburgh ABA	49	520 (43)	248	1417	28.9
1972-73	Seattle	70	352	194	898	12.8
1973-74	Seattle	35	178	82	438	12.5
1974-75	Seattle	21	60	42	162	7.7
	Totals	331	2512 (166)	1325	6847	20.7

BRITT, TYRONE

Ht. 6-4 Wt. 190 College—North Carolina College

Yr	Team	G	FG	FT	TP	Avg.
1967-68	San Diego	11	13	2	28	2.5

BRITT, WAYMAN

b. Aug. 31, 1952 Ht. 6-2 Wt. 185 College—Michigan

Yr	Team	G	FG	FT	TP	Avg.
1977-78	Detroit	7	3	3	9	1.3

BROKAW, GARY

b. Jan. 11, 1954 Ht. 6-4 Wt. 180 College—Notre Dame

Yr	Team	G	FG	FT	TP	Avg.
1974-75	Milwaukee	73	234	126	594	8.1
1975-76	Milwaukee	75	237	159	633	8.4
1976-77	Milw.-Cleve.	80	242	163	647	8.1
1977-78	Buffalo	13	18	18	54	4.2
	Totals	241	731	466	1928	8.0

BROOKFIELD, PRICE

b. May 11, 1920 Ht. 6-4½ Wt. 185 College—West Texas State and Iowa State

Yr	Team	G	FG	FT	TP	Avg.
1946-47	Chicago NL	42	82	24	188	4.5
1947-48	Anderson NL	49	82	27	191	3.9
1948-49	Indianapolis	54	176	90	442	8.2
1949-50	Rochester	7	11	12	34	4.9
	Totals	152	351	153	855	5.6

BROOKINS, CLARENCE

b. 1946 Ht. 6-4 Wt. 190 College—Temple

Yr	Team	G	FG	FT	TP	Avg.
1970-71	Miami ABA	8	8 (0)	5	21	2.6

BROWN, BOB

b. 1925 Ht. 6-4½ Wt. 205 College—Miami (Ohio)

Yr	Team	G	FG	FT	TP	Avg.
1948-49	Providence	20	37	34	108	5.4
1949-50	Denver	62	276	172	724	11.7
	Totals	82	313	206	832	10.1

BROWN, DARRELL

b. Mar. 14, 1923 Ht. 6-2 Wt. 175 Coll.—Humboldt St.

Yr	Team	G	FG	FT	TP	Avg.
1948-49	Baltimore	3	2	0	4	1.3

BROWN, GEORGE

b. Oct. 30, 1935 Ht. 6-6 Wt. 190 College—Wayne (Mi.)

Yr	Team	G	FG	FT	TP	Avg.
1957-58	Minneapolis	1	0	1	1	1.0

BROWN, HAROLD (Brownie)

b. Oct. 2, 1923 Ht. 6-0 Wt. 155 College—Evansville

Yr	Team	G	FG	FT	TP	Avg.
1946-47	Detroit	54	95	74	264	4.9

Yr	Team	G	FG	FT	TP	Avg.

BROWN, LARRY

b. Sept. 14, 1940 Ht. 5-9 Wt. 160 College—N.C.

Yr	Team	G	FG	FT	TP	Avg.
1967-68	New Orleans ABA	78	311 (19)	366	1045	13.4
1968-69	Oakland ABA	77	300 (8)	301	925	12.0
1969-70	Washington ABA	82	366 (10)	362	1124	13.7
1970-71	Vir.-Den. ABA	63	121 (6)	186	446	7.1
1971-72	Denver ABA	76	238 (5)	198	689	9.1
	Totals	376	1336 (48)	1413	4229	11.2

BROWN, LEON (Stretch)

b. Oct. 12, 1919 Ht. 6-3 Wt. 190 College—Wyoming

Yr	Team	G	FG	FT	TP	Avg.
1946-47	Cleveland	5	3	0	6	0.8

BROWN, ROGER

b. May 22, 1942 Ht. 6-5 Wt. 207 College—Dayton

Yr	Team	G	FG	FT	TP	Avg.
1967-68	Indiana ABA	76	530 (14)	390	1492	19.6
1968-69	Indiana ABA	75	558 (5)	442	1573	21.0
1969-70	Indiana ABA	84	679 (40)	457	1935	23.1
1970-71	Indiana ABA	82	547 (63)	407	1690	20.6
1971-72	Indiana ABA	78	475 (57)	323	1444	18.5
1972-73	Indiana ABA	72	290 (42)	203	909	12.6
1973-74	Indiana ABA	82	323 (56)	155	969	11.8
1974-75	Mem.-Ut.-Ind. ABA	56	146 (35)	89	486	8.7
1975-76	Denver ABA	37	26 (2)	16	74	2.0
	Totals	642	3574 (314)	2482	10572	16.5

BROWN, ROGER

b. Feb. 23, 1950 Ht. 6-11 Wt. 230 College—Kansas

Yr	Team	G	FG	FT	TP	Avg.
1972-73	Los Angeles	1	0	1	1	1.0
1972-73	Carolina ABA	62	59 (0)	28	146	2.4
1973-74	S.A.-Vir. ABA	63	98 (0)	34	230	3.7
1975-76	Detroit	29	29	14	72	2.5
1976-77	Detroit	43	21	18	60	1.4
	Totals	198	207 (0)	95	509	2.6

BROWN, STANLEY

b. 1929 Ht. 6-3 Wt. 200

Yr	Team	G	FG	FT	TP	Avg.
1947-48	Philadelphia	19	19	12	50	2.6
1951-52	Philadelphia	15	22	10	54	3.6
	Totals	34	41	22	104	3.1

BROWNE, JAMES

b. 1930 Ht. 6-10 Wt. 235

Yr	Team	G	FG	FT	TP	Avg.
1948-49	Chicago	4	1	1	3	0.8
1949-50	Denver	31	17	13	47	1.5
	Totals	35	18	14	50	1.4

BRUNKHORST, BRIAN (Bronk)

b. June 12, 1945 Ht. 6-6 Wt. 210 College—Marquette

Yr	Team	G	FG	FT	TP	Avg.
1968-69	Los Angeles ABA	3	6 (0)	13	25	8.3

BRUNS, GEORGE

b. Aug. 30, 1946 Ht. 6-0 Wt. 160 College—Manhattan

Yr	Team	G	FG	FT	TP	Avg.
1972-73	New York ABA	13	29 (2)	22	86	6.6

BRYANT, EMMETTE

b. Nov. 4, 1938 Ht. 6-1 Wt. 175 College—DePaul

Yr	Team	G	FG	FT	TP	Avg.
1964-65	New York	77	145	87	377	4.9
1965-66	New York	71	212	74	498	7.0
1966-67	New York	63	236	74	546	8.7
1967-68	New York	77	112	59	283	3.7
1968-69	Boston	80	197	65	459	5.7
1969-70	Boston	71	210	135	555	7.8
1970-71	Buffalo	73	228	151	727	10.0
1971-72	Buffalo	54	101	75	277	5.1
	Totals	566	1501	720	3722	6.6

BUCCI, GEORGE

b. July 9, 1953 Ht. 6-3 Wt. 202 College—Manhattan

Yr	Team	G	FG	FT	TP	Avg.
1975-76	New York ABA	33	50 (0)	28	128	3.9

BUCKHALTER, JOSEPH

b. Aug. 1, 1937 Ht. 6-7 Wt. 210 College—Manhattan

Yr	Team	G	FG	FT	TP	Avg.
1961-62	Cincinnati	63	153	67	373	5.9
1962-63	Cincinnati	2	0	2	2	1.0
	Totals	65	153	69	375	5.8

BUCKNER, CLEVELAND

b. Aug. 17, 1938 Ht. 6-9 Wt. 210 College—Jackson St.

Yr	Team	G	FG	FT	TP	Avg.
1961-62	New York	62	158	83	399	6.4
1962-63	New York	6	5	2	12	2.0
	Totals	68	163	85	411	6.0

BUDD, DAVID

b. Oct. 28, 1938 Ht. 6-6 Wt. 210 College—Wake Forest

Yr	Team	G	FG	FT	TP	Avg.
1960-61	New York	61	156	87	399	6.5
1961-62	New York	79	188	138	514	6.5
1962-63	New York	78	294	151	739	9.5
1963-64	New York	73	128	84	340	4.7
1964-65	New York	62	196	121	513	8.3
	Totals	353	962	581	2505	7.1

BUDKO, WALTER

Ht. 6-5 Wt. 220 College—Columbia

Yr	Team	G	FG	FT	TP	Avg.
1948-49	Baltimore	60	224	244	692	11.5
1949-50	Baltimore	66	198	199	595	9.0
1950-51	Baltimore	64	165	166	496	7.8
1951-52	Philadelphia	63	97	60	254	4.0
	Totals	253	684	669	2037	8.1

BUNCE, LARRY

b. July 29, 1945 Ht. 7-0 Wt. 245 College—Utah State

Yr	Team	G	FG	FT	TP	Avg.
1967-68	Anaheim ABA	71	300 (0)	256	856	12.1
1968-69	Den.-Dal. Hou. ABA	58	86 (0)	114	286	4.9
	Totals	129	386 (0)	370	1142	8.9

Yr	Team	G	FG	FT	TP	Avg.

BUNT, DICK

b. July 13, 1930 Ht. 6-0 Wt. 170 College—N.Y.U.

Yr	Team	G	FG	FT	TP	Avg.
1952-53	N.Y.-Balt.	26	29	34	92	3.5

BUNTIN, WILLIAM

b. May 5, 1942 Ht. 6-7 Wt. 250 College—Michigan
d. May 9, 1968

Yr	Team	G	FG	FT	TP	Avg.
1965-66	Detroit	42	118	88	324	7.7

BUNTING, BILL

b. Aug. 26, 1947 Ht. 6-8 Wt. 200 College—N.C.

Yr	Team	G	FG	FT	TP	Avg.
1969-70	Carolina ABA	57	96 (0)	79	271	4.8
1970-71	N.Y.-Vir. ABA	72	114 (0)	104	332	4.6
1971-72	Virginia ABA	16	4 (0)	12	20	1.3
	Totals	145	214 (0)	195	623	4.3

BURDEN, TICKY

b. Feb. 28, 1953 Ht. 6-2 Wt. 190 College—Utah

Yr	Team	G	FG	FT	TP	Avg.
1975-76	Virginia ABA	71	553 (8)	283	1413	19.9
1976-77	N. Y. Knicks	61	148	51	347	5.7
1977-78	New York	2	1	0	2	1.0
	Totals	134	702 (8)	334	1762	13.1

BURMASTER, JACK

b. Dec. 23, 1926 Ht. 6-3 Wt. 190 College—Illinois

Yr	Team	G	FG	FT	TP	Avg.
1948-49	Oshkosh NL	64	140	80	360	5.6
1949-50	Sheboygan	61	237	124	598	9.8
	Totals	125	377	204	958	7.7

BURNS, JIM

b. Sept. 21, 1945 Ht. 6-3½ Wt. 195 College—Northwestern

Yr	Team	G	FG	FT	TP	Avg.
1967-68	Chicago	3	2	0	4	1.3
1967-68	Dallas ABA	33	52 (0)	51	155	4.7
	Totals	36	54 (0)	51	159	4.4

BURRIS, ART

b. 1927 Ht. 6-5 Wt. 220 College—Tennessee

Yr	Team	G	FG	FT	TP	Avg.
1950-51	Ft. Wayne	3	28	21	77	2.3
1951-52	Ft. W.-Milw.	41	42	26	110	2.7
	Totals	74	70	47	187	2.5

BURROW, ROBERT

b. June 29, 1934 Ht. 6-7 Wt. 230 College—Kentucky

Yr	Team	G	FG	FT	TP	Avg.
1956-57	Rochester	67	137	130	404	6.0
1957-58	Minnesota	14	22	11	55	3.9
	Totals	81	159	141	459	5.7

BURTON, ED

b. Aug. 13, 1939 Ht. 6-6½ Wt. 225 Coll.—Michigan St.

Yr	Team	G	FG	FT	TP	Avg.
1961-62	New York	8	7	1	15	1.9
1964-65	St. Louis	7	7	4	18	2.6
	Totals	15	14	5	33	2.2

BUSTION, DAVE

b. Aug. 30, 1949 Ht. 6-8 Wt. 215 College—Denver

Yr	Team	G	FG	FT	TP	Avg.
1972-73	Denver ABA	47	58 (0)	42	158	3.4

BUTCHER, DONNIS (Donnie)

b. Feb. 8, 1936 Ht. 6-3 Wt. 200 College—Pikeville

Yr	Team	G	FG	FT	TP	Avg.
1961-62	New York	47	48	42	138	2.9
1962-63	New York	68	172	131	475	7.0
1963-64	N.Y.-Det.	78	202	159	563	7.2
1964-65	Detroit	71	143	126	412	5.8
1965-66	Detroit	15	45	18	108	7.2
	Totals	279	610	476	1696	6.1

BUTLER, ELBERT (Al)

b. July 9, 1938 Ht. 6-2 Wt. 175 College—Niagara

Yr	Team	G	FG	FT	TP	Avg.
1961-62	Boston-N.Y.	59	350	131	831	14.1
1962-63	New York	74	297	144	738	10.0
1963-64	New York	76	260	138	658	8.7
1964-65	Baltimore	25	24	11	59	2.4
	Totals	234	931	424	2286	9.8

BUTLER, MIKE

b. Oct. 22, 1946 Ht. 6-2 Wt. 175 Coll.—Memphis St.

Yr	Team	G	FG	FT	TP	Avg.
1968-69	New Orleans ABA	77	157 (50)	112	576	7.5
1969-70	New Orleans ABA	83	211 (87)	135	818	9.9
1970-71	Utah ABA	71	239 (32)	153	727	10.2
1971-72	Utah ABA	14	11 (3)	6	37	2.6
	Totals	245	618 (172)	406	2158	8.8

BYRD, WALT

Ht. 6-7 Wt. 205 College—Temple

Yr	Team	G	FG	FT	TP	Avg.
1969-70	Miami ABA	22	14 (0)	5	33	1.5

BYRNES, THOMAS

b. Feb. 19, 1923 Ht. 6-3 Wt. 175 College—Seton Hall

Yr	Team	G	FG	FT	TP	Avg.
1946-47	New York	60	175	103	453	7.6
1947-48	New York	47	117	65	299	6.4
1948-49	N.Y.-Indiana	57	160	92	412	7.2
1949-50	Baltimore	53	120	87	327	6.2
1950-51	Balt.-Wash.-Tri.-C.	48	83	55	221	4.6
	Totals	265	655	402	1712	6.5

BYTZURA, MICHAEL

b. June 18, 1922 Ht. 6-3 Wt. 175 College—Duquesne & LIU

Yr	Team	G	FG	FT	TP	Avg.
1944-45	Cleveland NL	30	113	35	261	8.7
1945-46	Cleveland NL	33	78	35	191	5.8
1946-47	Pittsburgh	60	87	36	210	3.5
	Totals	123	278	106	662	5.4

CABLE, BARNEY

b. July 29, 1935 Ht. 6-7 Wt. 200 College—Bradley

Yr	Team	G	FG	FT	TP	Avg.
1958-59	Detroit	31	43	23	109	3.5
1959-60	Syracuse	57	109	44	262	4.6
1960-61	Syracuse	75	266	73	605	8.1
1961-62	Chi.-St. Louis	67	305	118	728	10.9
1962-63	St. Louis-Chi.	62	173	62	408	6.6
1963-64	Baltimore	71	116	28	260	3.7
	Totals	363	1012	348	2372	6.5

Yr	Team	G	FG	FT	TP	Avg.

CALABRESE, GERRY

b. Feb. 4, 1925 Ht. 6-1 Wt. 175 College—St. John's

Yr	Team	G	FG	FT	TP	Avg.
1950-51	Syracuse	46	70	61	201	4.4
1951-52	Syracuse	58	109	73	291	5.0
	Totals	104	179	134	492	4.7

CALDWELL, JIM

b. Jan. 28, 1943 Ht. 6-10 Wt. 240 Coll.—Georgia Tech.

Yr	Team	G	FG	FT	TP	Avg.
1967-68	New York	2	0	0	0	0.0
1967-68	N.J.-Ky. ABA	70	222 (1)	99	546	7.8
1968-69	Kentucky ABA	65	166 (1)	87	422	6.5
	Totals	137	388 (2)	186	968	7.1

CALDWELL, JOE (Pogo)

b. Nov. 1, 1941 Ht. 6-5 Wt. 195 College—Ariz. State

Yr	Team	G	FG	FT	TP	Avg.
1964-65	Detroit	66	290	129	709	10.7
1965-66	Det.-St. Louis	79	411	179	1001	12.7
1966-67	St. Louis	81	458	200	1116	13.8
1967-68	St. Louis	79	564	165	1293	16.4
1968-69	Atlanta	81	561	159	1281	15.8
1969-70	Atlanta	82	674	379	1727	21.1
1970-71	Carolina ABA	72	679 (6)	302	1678	23.3
1971-72	Carolina ABA	61	429 (5)	159	1032	16.9
1972-73	Carolina ABA	77	554 (1)	172	1283	14.4
1973-74	Carolina ABA	79	499 (3)	128	1135	14.6
1974-75	St. Louis ABA	25	158 (3)	39	364	17.5
	Totals	782	5297 (18)	2011	12619	16.1

CALHOUN, WILLIAM

b. 1927 Ht. 6-3 Wt. 180

Yr	Team	G	FG	FT	TP	Avg.
1947-48	Rochester NL	43	31	18	80	1.9
1948-49	Rochester	56	146	75	367	6.6
1949-50	Rochester	62	207	146	560	9.0
1950-51	Rochester	66	175	161	511	7.7
1951-52	Baltimore	55	129	125	383	7.0
1952-53	Syra.-Milw.	62	180	211	571	9.2
1953-54	Milwaukee	72	190	214	594	8.3
1954-55	Milwaukee	69	144	166	454	6.6
	Totals	485	1202	1116	3520	7.3

CALLAHAN, THOMAS

b. 1921 Ht. 6-1 Wt. 180 College—Not. Dam. / Rockh.

Yr	Team	G	FG	FT	TP	Avg.
1946-47	Providence	13	6	5	17	1.3

CALVERLEY, ERNEST

b. Jan. 30, 1924 Ht. 5-10 Wt. 155 College—Rhode Is.

Yr	Team	G	FG	FT	TP	Avg.
1946-47	Providence	59	323	199	845	14.3
1947-48	Providence	47	226	107	559	11.9
1948-49	Providence	59	218	121	557	9.4
	Totals	165	767	427	1961	11.9

CALVIN, MACK

b. July 27, 1949 Ht. 6-0 Wt. 165 Coll.—So. California

Yr	Team	G	FG	FT	TP	Avg.
1969-70	Los Angeles ABA	84	438 (3)	529	1414	16.8
1970-71	Floridians ABA	81	727 (17)	696	2201	27.2
1971-72	Floridians ABA	82	541 (11)	611	1726	21.1
1972-73	Carolina ABA	84	467 (11)	500	1467	17.5
1973-74	Carolina ABA	83	488 (10)	490	1496	18.0
1974-75	Denver ABA	74	480 (3)	475	1444	19.5
1975-76	Virginia ABA	45	299 (7)	253	872	19.4
1976-77	L.A.-S.A.-Den.	76	220	287	727	9.6
1977-78	Denver	77	147	173	467	6.1
	Totals	686	3807 (62)	4014	11814	17.2

CANNON, LARRY

b. April 12, 1947 Ht. 6-5 Wt. 195 College—LaSalle

Yr	Team	G	FG	FT	TP	Avg.
1969-70	Miami ABA	57	245 (8)	158	672	11.8
1970-71	Denver ABA	80	733 (18)	606	2126	26.6
1971-72	Memphis-Ind. ABA	54	225 (3)	164	623	11.5
1973-74	Indiana ABA	3	3 (0)	1	7	2.3
1973-74	Philadelphia	19	49	19	117	6.2
	Totals	213	1255 (29)	948	3545	16.6

CARD, FRANK

b. Dec. 28, 1944 Ht. 6-7 Wt. 195 College—S.C. State

Yr	Team	G	FG	FT	TP	Avg.
1968-69	Minnesota ABA	76	221 (1)	146	591	7.8
1969-70	Washington ABA	74	350 (1)	178	881	11.9
1970-71	Virginia-Car. ABA	70	302 (1)	196	803	11.5
1971-72	Car.-Den. ABA	82	235 (0)	130	600	7.3
1972-73	Denver ABA	4	6 (0)	9	21	5.3
	Totals	306	1114 (3)	659	2896	9.5

CARL, HOWARD

b. June 7, 1938 Ht. 5-9½ Wt. 160 Coll.—Ill. & DePaul

Yr	Team	G	FG	FT	TP	Avg.
1961-62	Chicago	31	67	36	170	5.5

CARLISLE, CHESTER

b. Nov. 2; 1916 Ht. 6-5 Wt. 195 College—California

Yr	Team	G	FG	FT	TP	Avg.
1946-47	Chicago	51	100	56	256	5.0

CARLOS, DON

b. March 3, 1944 Ht. 6-4½ Wt. 210 College—Otterbein

Yr	Team	G	FG	FT	TP	Avg.
1968-69	Houston ABA	56	207 (0)	214	628	11.2

CARLSON, AL

b. Sept. 17, 1951 Ht. 6-11 Wt. 235 Coll.—S. California

Yr	Team	G	FG	FT	TP	Avg.
1975-76	Seattle	28	27	18	72	2.6

CARLSON, DON (Swede)

b. March 20, 1920 Ht. 6-0 Wt. 170 College—Minnesota

Yr	Team	G	FG	FT	TP	Avg.
1946-47	Chicago	59	272	86	630	10.7
1947-48	Minneapolis NL	58	205	65	475	8.2
1948-49	Minneapolis	55	211	86	508	9.2
1949-50	Minneapolis	57	99	69	267	4.7
1950-51	Washington	9	17	8	42	4.7
	Totals	238	804	314	1922	8.1

Yr	Team	G	FG	FT	TP	Avg.

CARNEY, BOB
b. Aug. 3, 1932 Ht. 6-3 Wt. 172 College—Bradley

Yr	Team	G	FG	FT	TP	Avg.
1954-55	Minneapolis	19	24	21	69	3.6

CARPENTER, ROBERT
b. Nov. 6, 1917 Ht. 6-5 Wt. 200 College—East Texas

Yr	Team	G	FG	FT	TP	Avg.
1940-41	Oshkosh NL	24	40	41	121	5.0
1945-46	Oshkosh NL	34	186	101	473	13.9
1946-47	Oshkosh NL	44	199	115	513	11.7
1947-48	Oshkosh NL	60	211	160	582	9.7
1948-49	Ham.-Osh. NL	47	160	131	451	9.6
1949-50	Ft. Wayne	66	212	190	614	9.3
1950-51	F.W.-Tri.-C.	56	109	105	323	5.8
	Totals	331	1117	843	3077	9.3

CARRIER, DAREL
b. Oct. 26, 1940 Ht. 6-3 Wt. 185 College—Western Ky.

Yr	Team	G	FG	FT	TP	Avg.
1967-68	Kentucky ABA	77	559 (84)	395	1765	22.0
1968-69	Kentucky ABA	73	434 (125)	447	1690	23.2
1969-70	Kentucky ABA	77	503 (107)	454	1781	23.1
1970-71	Kentucky ABA	84	442 (63)	327	1380	16.4
1971-72	Ken.-Mem. ABA	23	101 (16)	76	326	14.2
	Totals	334	2039 (395)	1699	6942	20.8

CARRINGTON, BOB
b. July 3, 1953 Ht. 6-6 Wt. 195 College—Boston College

Yr	Team	G	FG	FT	TP	Avg.
1977-78	N.J.-Ind.	72	253	130	636	8.8

CARTER, FRED
b. Feb. 14, 1945 Ht. 6-3 Wt. 185 Coll.—Mt. St. Mary's

Yr	Team	G	FG	FT	TP	Avg.
1969-70	Baltimore	76	157	80	394	5.2
1970-71	Baltimore	77	340	119	799	10.4
1971-72	Balt.-Phila.	79	446	182	1074	13.6
1972-73	Philadelphia	81	679	259	1617	20.0
1973-74	Philadelphia	78	706	254	1666	21.4
1974-75	Philadelphia	77	715	256	1686	21.9
1975-76	Philadelphia	82	665	219	1549	18.9
1976-77	Phila.-Milw.	61	209	68	486	8.0
	Totals	611	3917	1437	9271	15.2

CARTER, GEORGE
b. Jan. 18, 1944 Ht. 6-5 Wt. 218 Coll.—St. Bonaventure

Yr	Team	G	FG	FT	TP	Avg.
1967-68	Detroit	1	1	1	3	3.0
1969-70	Washington ABA	67	390 (7)	167	968	14.4
1970-71	Virginia ABA	81	594 (0)	346	1534	18.9
1971-72	Pitt.-Car. ABA	75	538 (0)	388	1464	19.5
1972-73	New York ABA	83	569 (0)	440	1578	19.3
1973-74	Virginia ABA	80	529 (32)	392	1546	18.4
1974-75	Memphis ABA	82	580 (10)	318	1508	18.4
1975-76	Utah ABA	10	25 (0)	32	82	8.2
	Totals	479	3226 (49)	2084	8683	18.0

CARTER, JOHN (Jake)
b. July 25, 1924 Ht. 6-5 Wt. 195 College—East Texas

Yr	Team	G	FG	FT	TP	Avg.
1948-49	Hammond NL	62	133	188	454	7.3
1949-50	Den.-Anderson	24	23	36	82	3.4
	Totals	86	156	224	536	6.2

CARTY, JAY
b. July 4, 1941 Ht. 6-8 Wt. 230 College—Oregon St.

Yr	Team	G	FG	FT	TP	Avg.
1968-69	Los Angeles	28	34	8	76	2.7

CASH, CORNELIUS
b. March 3, 1952 Ht. 6-8 Wt. 220 Coll.—Bowling Green

Yr	Team	G	FG	FT	TP	Avg.
1976-77	Detroit	6	9	3	21	3.5

CASH, SAM
b. 1950 Ht. 6-8 Wt. 230 College—Riverside

Yr	Team	G	FG	FT	TP	Avg.
1972-73	Memphis ABA	7	4 (0)	12	20	2.9

CATLETT, SID
b. April 8, 1948 Ht. 6-8 Wt. 230 College—Notre Dame

Yr	Team	G	FG	FT	TP	Avg.
1971-72	Cincinnati	9	2	2	6	0.7

CERVI, ALFRED (Digger)
b. Feb. 12, 1917 Ht. 5-11½ Wt. 185

Yr	Team	G	FG	FT	TP	Avg.
1937-38	Buffalo NL	9	19	6	44	4.9
1945-46	Rochester NL	28	112	76	300	10.7
1946-47	Rochester NL	44	228	176	632	14.4
1947-48	Rochester NL	49	234	187	655	13.4
1948-49	Syracuse NL	57	204	287	695	12.2
1949-50	Syracuse	56	143	287	573	10.2
1950-51	Syracuse	53	132	194	458	8.6
1951-52	Syracuse	55	99	219	417	7.6
1952-53	Syracuse	38	31	81	143	3.8
	Totals	389	1202	1513	3917	10.1

CHAMBERLAIN, BILL
b. Dec. 16, 1949 Ht. 6-6 Wt. 205 College—N.C.

Yr	Team	G	FG	FT	TP	Avg.
1972-73	Ken.-Mem. ABA	50	110 (2)	36	262	5.2
1973-74	Phoenix	28	57	39	153	5.5
	Totals	78	167 (2)	75	415	5.3

CHAMBERLAIN, WILT
b. Aug. 21, 1936 Ht. 7-1 Wt. 275 College—Kansas

Yr	Team	G	FG	FT	TP	Avg.
1959-60	Philadelphia	72	1065	577	2707	37.6
1960-61	Philadelphia	79	1251	531	3033	38.4
1961-62	Philadelphia	80	1597	835	4029	50.4
1962-63	San Francisco	80	1463	660	3586	44.8
1963-64	San Francisco	80	1204	540	2948	36.9
1964-65	S.F.-Phila.	73	1063	408	2534	34.7
1965-66	Philadelphia	79	1074	501	2649	33.5
1966-67	Philadelphia	81	785	386	1956	24.1
1967-68	Philadelphia	82	819	354	1992	24.3
1968-69	Los Angeles	81	641	382	1664	20.5
1969-70	Los Angeles	12	129	70	328	27.3
1970-71	Los Angeles	82	668	360	1696	20.7
1971-72	Los Angeles	82	496	221	1213	14.8
1972-73	Los Angeles	82	426	232	1084	13.2
	Totals	1045	12681	6057	31419	30.1

Yr	Team	G	FG	FT	TP	Avg.

CHAMBERS, JERRY

b. July 18, 1943 Ht. 6-5 Wt. 186 College—Utah

Yr	Team	G	FG	FT	TP	Avg.
1966-67	Los Angeles	69	224	68	516	7.5
1969-70	Phoenix	79	283	91	657	8.3
1970-71	Atlanta	65	237	106	580	8.9
1971-72	Buffalo	26	78	22	178	6.8
	Totals	239	822	287	1931	8.1

CHANEY, JOHN

b. Feb. 29, 1920 Ht. 6-3 Wt. 190 College—La. State

Yr	Team	G	FG	FT	TP	Avg.
1946-47	Syracuse NL	42	138	86	362	8.6
1947-48	Syracuse NL	40	107	80	294	7.4
1948-49	Syracuse NL	57	79	65	223	3.9
1949-50	Tri.-Cities-She.	16	25	20	70	4.4
	Totals	155	349	251	949	6.1

CHAPMAN, WAYNE

b. June 15, 1945 Ht. 6-6 Wt. 190 College—Western Ky.

Yr	Team	G	FG	FT	TP	Avg.
1968-69	Kentucky ABA	48	64 (4)	54	194	4.0
1969-70	Kentucky ABA	82	253 (8)	134	664	8.1
1970-71	Den.-Ind. ABA	69	199 (15)	113	556	8.1
1971-72	Indiana ABA	7	6 (1)	3	18	2.6
	Totals	206	522 (28)	304	1432	7.0

CHAPPELL, LEONARD

b. Jan. 31, 1941 Ht. 6-8 Wt. 240 College—Wake Forest

Yr	Team	G	FG	FT	TP	Avg.
1962-63	Syracuse	80	281	148	710	8.9
1963-64	Phila.-N.Y.	79	531	288	1350	17.1
1964-65	New York	43	145	68	358	8.3
1965-66	New York	46	100	46	246	5.3
1966-67	Chicago-Cinn.	73	132	53	317	4.3
1967-68	Cinn.-Detroit	68	235	138	608	8.9
1968-69	Milwaukee	80	459	250	1168	14.6
1969-70	Milwaukee	75	243	135	621	8.3
1970-71	Cleve.-Atl.	48	86	71	243	5.1
1971-72	Dallas ABA	79	231 (0)	144	606	7.7
	Totals	671	2443 (0)	1341	6227	9.3

CHARLES, KEN

b. July 10, 1951 Ht. 6-3 Wt. 180 College—Fordham

Yr	Team	G	FG	FT	TP	Avg.
1973-74	Buffalo	59	88	53	229	3.9
1974-75	Buffalo	79	240	120	600	7.6
1975-76	Buffalo	81	328	161	817	10.1
1976-77	Atlanta	82	354	205	913	11.1
1977-78	Atlanta	21	73	42	188	9.0
	Totals	322	1083	581	2747	8.5

CHOLLET, LEROY

b. March 5, 1925 Ht. 6-2 Wt. 190 College—Canisius

Yr	Team	G	FG	FT	TP	Avg.
1949-50	Syracuse	49	61	35	157	3.2
1950-51	Syracuse	14	6	12	24	1.7
	Totals	63	67	47	181	2.9

CHRIST, FRED

b. 1930 Ht. 6-4 Wt. 210 College—Fordham

Yr	Team	G	FG	FT	TP	Avg.
1954-55	New York	6	5	10	20	3.3

CHRISTENSEN, CAL

b. June 6, 1927 Ht. 6-5 Wt. 210 College—Toledo

Yr	Team	G	FG	FT	TP	Avg.
1950-51	Tri-Cities	67	134	175	443	6.6
1951-52	Milwaukee	24	29	30	88	3.7
1952-53	Rochester	59	72	68	212	3.6
1953-54	Rochester	70	137	138	412	5.9
1954-55	Rochester	71	114	124	352	5.0
	Totals	291	486	535	1507	5.2

CHRISTIAN, BOB

b. May 11, 1944 Ht. 7-0 Wt. 245 College—Grambling

Yr	Team	G	FG	FT	TP	Avg.
1969-70	N.Y.-Dallas ABA	2	1 (0)	0	2	1.0
1970-71	Atlanta	54	55	40	150	2.8
1971-72	Atlanta	56	66	44	176	3.1
1972-73	Atlanta	55	85	60	230	4.2
1973-74	Phoenix	81	140	106	386	4.8
	Totals	248	347	250	944	318

CHUBIN, STEVE (Chube)

b. Feb. 8, 1944 Ht. 6-2 Wt. 200 College—Rhode Island

Yr	Team	G	FG	FT	TP	Avg.
1967-68	Anaheim ABA	77	437 (2)	518	1398	18.2
1968-69	L.A.-Minn.-Ind. N.Y. ABA	77	341 (3)	386	1077	14.0
1969-70	Pittsburgh ABA	72	122 (5)	170	429	6.0
	Totals	226	900 (10)	1074	2904	12.8

CLARK, ARCHIE

b. July 15, 1941 Ht. 6-2 Wt. 175 College—Minnesota

Yr	Team	G	FG	FT	TP	Avg.
1966-67	Los Angeles	76	331	136	798	10.5
1967-68	Los Angeles	81	628	356	1612	19.9
1968-69	Philadelphia	82	444	219	1107	13.5
1969-70	Philadelphia	76	594	311	1499	19.7
1970-71	Philadelphia	82	662	422	1746	21.3
1971-72	Phila.-Balt.	77	712	514	1938	25.2
1972-73	Baltimore	39	302	111	715	18.3
1973-74	Capital	56	315	103	733	13.1
1974-75	Seattle	77	455	161	1071	13.9
1975-76	Detroit	79	250	100	600	7.6
	Totals	725	4693	2433	11819	16.3

CLARK, DICK

b. Jan. 5, 1944 Ht. 6-4 Wt. 195 College—Eastern Ky.

Yr	Team	G	FG	FT	TP	Avg.
1967-68	Minnesota ABA	26	46 (0)	48	140	5.4
1968-69	Houston ABA	32	63 (1)	89	218	6.8
	Totals	58	109 (1)	137	358	6.2

CLAWSON, JOHN

b. May 15, 1944 Ht. 6-4 Wt. 200 College—Michigan

Yr	Team	G	FG	FT	TP	Avg.
1968-69	Oakland ABA	70	147 (0)	37	331	4.7

CLEMENS, BARRY

b. May 1, 1942 Ht. 6-7 Wt. 210 College—Ohio Wesleyan

Yr	Team	G	FG	FT	TP	Avg.
1965-66	New York	70	161	54	376	5.4
1966-67	Chicago	60	186	68	440	7.3
1967-68	Chicago	78	301	123	725	9.3
1968-69	Chicago	75	235	82	552	7.4
1969-70	Seattle	78	270	111	651	8.3
1970-71	Seattle	78	247	83	577	7.4

Yr	Team	G	FG	FT	TP	Avg.
1971-72	Seattle	82	252	76	580	7.1
1972-73	Cleveland	72	209	53	471	6.5
1973-74	Cleveland	71	163	62	388	5.5
1974-75	Portland	77	168	45	381	4.9
1975-76	Portland	49	70	31	171	3.5
	Totals	790	2262	788	5312	6.7

CLIFTON, NATHANIEL (Sweetwater)

b. Oct. 13 1922 Ht. 6-7 Wt. 225 College—Xavier (La.)

Yr	Team	G	FG	FT	TP	Avg.
1950-51	New York	65	211	140	562	8.6
1951-52	New York	62	244	170	658	10.6
1952-53	New York	70	272	200	744	10.6
1953-54	New York	72	257	174	688	9.6
1954-55	New York	72	360	224	944	13.1
1955-56	New York	64	213	135	561	8.8
1956-57	New York	71	308	146	762	10.7
1957-58	Detroit	68	217	91	525	7.7
	Totals	544	2082	1280	5444	10.0

CLOSS, WILLIAM

b. Jan. 8, 1922 Ht. 6-6 Wt. 205 College—Rice

Yr	Team	G	FG	FT	TP	Avg.
1946-47	Indianapolis NL	44	119	34	272	6.2
1947-48	Indianapolis NL	55	162	72	396	7.2
1948-49	Anderson NL	64	203	110	516	8.1
1949-50	Anderson NL	64	283	186	752	11.8
1950-51	Philadelphia	65	202	166	570	8.8
1951-52	Ft. Wayne	57	120	107	347	6.1
	Totals	349	1089	675	2853	8.2

CLOYD, PAUL

b. June 13, 1920 Ht. 6-2 Wt. 180 College—Wisconsin

Yr	Team	G	FG	FT	TP	Avg.
1947-48	Sheboygan NL	60	213	129	555	9.3
1948-49	Sheboygan NL	56	119	98	336	6.0
1949-50	Balt.-Waterloo	7	7	5	19	2.7
	Totals	123	339	232	910	7.3

CLUGGISH, ROBERT

b. 1918 Ht. 6-10 Wt. 235 College—Kentucky

Yr	Team	G	FG	FT	TP	Avg.
1946-47	New York	54	93	52	238	6.3

CLYDE, BEN

b. June 10, 1951 Ht. 6-7 Wt. 198 Coll.—Florida State

Yr	Team	G	FG	FT	TP	Avg.
1974-75	Boston	25	31	7	69	2.8

COLEMAN, JACK

b. May 23, 1924 Ht. 6-7 Wt. 230 College—Louisville

Yr	Team	G	FG	FT	TP	Avg.
1949-50	Rochester	68	250	90	590	8.7
1950-51	Rochester	67	315	134	764	11.4
1951-52	Rochester	66	308	120	736	11.2
1952-53	Rochester	70	314	135	763	10.9
1953-54	Rochester	71	289	108	686	9.7
1954-55	Rochester	72	400	124	924	12.8
1955-56	Roch.-St. Lo.	75	390	177	957	12.8
1956-57	St. Louis	72	316	123	755	10.5
1957-58	St. Louis	72	231	84	546	7.6
	Totals	633	2813	1095	6721	10.6

COLLINS, JIMMY

b. Nov. 24, 1946 Ht. 6-2 Wt. 175 Coll.—N. Mex. St.

Yr	Team	G	FG	FT	TP	Avg.
1970-71	Chicago	55	92	35	219	4.0
1971-72	Chicago	19	26	10	62	3.3
	Totals	74	118	45	281	3.8

COLONE, JOE (Bells)

b. Jan. 23, 1926 Ht. 6-5 Wt. 210

Yr	Team	G	FG	FT	TP	Avg.
1948-49	New York	15	35	13	83	5.5

COMBS, GLEN COURTNEY

b. Oct. 30, 1946 Ht. 6-2 Wt. 185 College—Virginia Tech.

Yr	Team	G	FG	FT	TP	Avg.
1968-69	Dallas ABA	72	280 (84)	300	1112	15.4
1969-70	Dallas ABA	84	510 (130)	458	1868	22.2
1970-71	Tex.-Utah ABA	86	533 (77)	448	1745	20.3
1971-72	Utah ABA	84	380 (103)	319	1388	16.5
1972-73	Utah ABA	50	177 (51)	154	661	13.2
1973-74	Ut.-Mem. ABA	76	252 (52)	156	816	10.7
1974-75	Virginia ABA	13	17 (6)	24	76	5.9
	Totals	465	2149 (503)	1859	7666	16.5

COMEAUX, JOHN

b. Sept. 5, 1943 Ht. 6-5 Wt. 193 College—Grambling

Yr	Team	G	FG	FT	TP	Avg.
1967-68	New Orleans ABA	23	27 (0)	23	77	3.3

COMLEY, LARRY

b. Aug. 17, 1939 Ht. 6-5½ Wt. 210 Coll.—Kansas State

Yr	Team	G	FG	FT	TP	Avg.
1963-64	Baltimore	11	8	9	25	2.3

CONGDON, JEFF

b. Oct. 17, 1943 Ht. 6-2 Wt. 180 College—Brigham Young

Yr	Team	G	FG	FT	TP	Avg.
1967-68	Ana.-Denver ABA	64	137 (13)	49	362	5.7
1968-69	Denver ABA	59	102 (5)	69	288	4.9
1969-70	Denver ABA	83	236 (63)	151	812	9.8
1970-71	Utah-N.Y. ABA	80	160 (18)	79	453	5.7
1971-72	Dallas ABA	20	27 (3)	17	80	4.0
	Totals	306	622 (102)	365	1995	6.5

CONLEY, GENE

b. Nov. 10, 1930 Ht. 6-8 Wt. 255 Coll.—Washington St.

Yr	Team	G	FG	FT	TP	Avg.
1952-53	Boston	39	35	18	88	2.3
1958-59	Boston	50	86	37	209	4.2
1959-60	Boston	71	201	76	478	6.7
1960-61	Boston	75	183	106	472	6.3
1962-63	New York	70	254	122	630	9.0
1963-64	New York	46	74	44	192	4.2
	Totals	351	833	403	2069	5.9

CONLEY, LARRY

Ht. 6-3 Wt. 175 College—Kentucky

Yr	Team	G	FG	FT	TP	Avg.
1967-68	Kentucky ABA	1	1 (0)	0	2	2.0

CONLIN, EDWARD

b. Sept. 2, 1933 Ht. 6-6 Wt. 200 College—Fordham

Yr	Team	G	FG	FT	TP	Avg.
1955-56	Syracuse	66	211	121	543	8.2
1956-57	Syracuse	71	335	283	953	13.4
1957-58	Syracuse	60	343	215	901	15.0
1958-59	Syr.-Detroit	72	329	197	855	11.9

Yr	Team	G	FG	FT	TP	Avg.
1959-60	Detroit	70	300	181	781	11.2
1960-61	Philadelphia	76	216	104	536	7.1
1961-62	Philadelphia	70	128	66	322	4.6
	Totals	485	1862	1167	4891	10.1

CONNORS, Kevin (Chuck)

b. April 10, 1921 Ht. 6-7 Wt. 205 College—Seton Hall

Yr	Team	G	FG	FT	TP	Avg.
1945-46	Rochester NL	14	11	6	28	2.0
1946-47	Boston	49	94	39	227	4.6
1947-48	Boston	4	5	2	12	3.0
	Totals	67	110	47	267	4.0

COOK, BERT

b. April 26, 1929 Ht. 6-3 Wt. 186 College—Utah State

Yr	Team	G	FG	FT	TP	Avg.
1954-55	New York	37	42	34	118	3.2

COOK, NORM

b. March 21, 1955 Ht. 6-8 Wt. 210 College—Kansas

Yr	Team	G	FG	FT	TP	Avg.
1976-77	Boston	25	27	9	63	2.5
1977-78	Denver	2	1	0	2	1.0
	Totals	27	28	9	65	2.4

COOK, ROBERT (Cookie)

b. 1923 Ht. 5-10½ Wt. 155 College—Wisconsin

Yr	Team	G	FG	FT	TP	Avg.
1948-49	Sheboygan NL	64	172	98	442	6.9
1949-50	Sheboygan	51	222	143	587	11.5
	Totals	115	394	241	1029	8.9

COOKE, JOE

b. Aug. 14, 1948 Ht. 6-3 Wt. 175 College—Indiana

Yr	Team	G	FG	FT	TP	Avg.
1970-71	Cleveland	73	134	48	316	4.3

COOPER, CHARLES (Chuck)

b. 1927 Ht. 6-5 Wt. 215 College—Duquesne

Yr	Team	G	FG	FT	TP	Avg.
1950-51	Boston	66	207	201	615	9.3
1951-52	Boston	66	197	149	543	8.2
1952-53	Boston	70	157	144	458	6.5
1953-54	Boston	70	78	78	234	3.3
1954-55	Milwaukee	70	193	187	573	8.2
1955-56	St. L.-Ft. W.	67	101	100	302	4.5
	Totals	409	933	859	2725	6.7

CORLEY, KENNETH

Ht. 6-8 Wt. 220 College—Georgetown

Yr	Team	G	FG	FT	TP	Avg.
1946-47	Cleveland	3	0	0	0	0.0

CORLEY, RAY

b. Jan. 1, 1928 Ht. 6-0 Wt. 180 College—Notre Dame & Georgetown

Yr	Team	G	FG	FT	TP	Avg.
1949-50	Syracuse	60	117	75	309	5.2
1950-51	Balt.-Tri.-C.	18	29	16	74	4.1
1952-53	Ft. Wayne	8	3	5	11	1.4
	Totals	86	149	96	394	4.6

COSTELLO, LARRY

b. July 2, 1931 Ht. 6-1 Wt. 188 College—Niagara

Yr	Team	G	FG	FT	TP	Avg.
1954-55	Philadelphia	19	46	26	118	6.2
1956-57	Philadelphia	72	186	175	547	7.6
1957-58	Syracuse	72	378	320	1076	14.9
1958-59	Syracuse	70	414	280	1108	15.8
1959-60	Syracuse	71	372	249	993	14.0
1960-61	Syracuse	75	407	270	1084	14.5
1961-62	Syracuse	63	310	247	867	13.7
1962-63	Syracuse	78	285	288	858	11.0
1963-64	Philadelphia	45	191	147	529	11.8
1964-65	Philadelphia	64	309	243	861	13.5
1966-67	Philadelphia	49	130	120	380	7.8
1967-68	Philadelphia	28	67	67	201	7.2
	Totals	706	3095	2432	8622	12.2

COTTON, JOHN

b. Oct. 15, 1924 Ht. 6-7 Wt. 205 College—Wyoming

Yr	Team	G	FG	FT	TP	Avg.
1946-47	Chicago NL	3	1	2	4	1.3
1948-49	Denver NL	57	71	67	209	3.7
1949-50	Denver	54	97	82	276	5.1
	Totals	114	169	151	489	4.3

COUNTS, MEL

b. Oct. 16, 1941 Ht. 7-0 Wt. 230 College—Oregon St.

Yr	Team	G	FG	FT	TP	Avg.
1964-65	Boston	54	100	58	258	4.7
1965-66	Boston	67	221	120	562	8.4
1966-67	Balt.-L.A.	56	177	69	423	7.6
1967-68	Los Angeles	82	384	190	958	11.7
1968-69	Los Angeles	77	390	178	958	12.4
1969-70	Los Angeles	81	434	156	1024	12.6
1970-71	Phoenix	80	365	149	879	11.0
1971-72	Phoenix	76	147	101	395	5.2
1972-73	Phil.-L.A.	66	132	39	303	4.6
1973-74	Los Angeles	45	61	24	146	3.2
1974-75	New Orleans	75	217	86	520	6.9
1975-76	New Orleans	30	37	16	90	3.0
	Totals	789	2665	1186	6516	8.3

COURTIN, STEVE

b. Sept. 21, 1942 Ht. 6-1 Wt. 188 Coll.—St. Jo. (Pa.)

Yr	Team	G	FG	FT	TP	Avg.
1964-65	Philadelphia	24	42	17	101	4.2

COUSY, BOB

b. Aug. 9, 1928 Ht. 6-1 Wt. 175 College—Holy Cross

Yr	Team	G	FG	FT	TP	Avg.
1950-51	Boston	69	401	276	1078	15.6
1951-52	Boston	66	512	409	1433	21.7
1952-53	Boston	71	464	479	1407	19.8
1953-54	Boston	72	486	411	1383	19.2
1954-55	Boston	71	522	460	1504	21.2
1955-56	Boston	72	440	476	1356	18.8
1956-57	Boston	64	478	363	1319	20.6
1957-58	Boston	65	445	277	1167	18.0
1958-59	Boston	65	484	329	1297	20.0
1959-60	Boston	75	568	319	1455	19.4
1960-61	Boston	76	513	352	1378	18.1
1961-62	Boston	75	462	251	1175	15.7
1962-63	Boston	76	392	219	1003	13.2
1969-70	Cincinnati	7	1	3	5	0.7
	Totals	924	6168	4624	16960	18.4

COX, JOHN

b. Nov. 1, 1936 Ht. 6-4 Wt. 180 College—Kentucky

Yr	Team	G	FG	FT	TP	Avg.
1962-63	Chicago	73	239	95	573	7.8

CRAWFORD, FRED

b. Dec. 23, 1941 Ht. 6-4 Wt. 190 Coll.—St. Bonaventure

Yr	Team	G	FG	FT	TP	Avg.
1966-67	New York	19	44	24	112	5.9
1967-68	N.Y.-L.A.	69	224	111	559	8.1
1968-69	Los Angeles	81	211	83	505	6.2
1969-70	Milwaukee	77	243	101	587	7.6
1970-71	Buffalo-Phila.	51	110	48	268	5.3
	Totals	297	832	367	2031	6.8

CREIGHTON, JIM

b. April 18, 1950 Ht. 6-8 Wt. 200 College—Colorado

Yr	Team	G	FG	FT	TP	Avg.
1975-76	Atlanta	32	12	7	31	1.0

Yr	Team	G	FG	FT	TP	Avg.
CRISLER, HERBERT						
Ht. 6-3 Wt. 215						
1946-47	Boston	4	2	2	6	1.5

CRITCHFIELD, RUSS

b. June 27, 1946 Ht. 5-10 Wt. 150 College—California

Yr	Team	G	FG	FT	TP	Avg.
1968-69	Oakland ABA	47	53 (0)	55	161	3.4

CROCKER, DILLARD

b. 1925 Ht. 6-4 Wt. 205 College—Western Michigan

Yr	Team	G	FG	FT	TP	Avg.
1948-49	Det.-And. NL	51	101	95	297	5.8
1948-49	Ft. Wayne	2	1	4	6	3.0
1949-50	Denver	53	245	233	723	13.6
1951-52	Ind.-Milw.	38	98	97	293	7.7
1952-53	Milwaukee	61	100	130	330	5.4
	Totals	205	545	559	1649	8.0

CROFT, BOBBY

Ht. 6-10 Wt. 200 College—Tennessee

Yr	Team	G	FG	FT	TP	Avg.
1970-71	Ky.-Texas ABA	62	126 (0)	73	325	5.2

CROSS, PETE

b. March 28, 1948 Ht. 6-9 Wt. 231 Coll.—San Francisco
d. Jan. 2, 1977

Yr	Team	G	FG	FT	TP	Avg.
1970-71	Seattle	79	245	140	630	8.0
1971-72	Seattle	74	152	103	407	5.5
1972-73	K.C.-O.-Sea.	29	6	8	20	0.7
	Totals	182	403	251	1057	5.8

CROSSIN, FRANCIS (Chink)

b. June 4, 1924 Ht. 6-1 Wt. 165 College—Pennsylvania

Yr	Team	G	FG	FT	TP	Avg.
1947-48	Philadelphia	39	29	13	71	1.8
1948-49	Philadelphia	44	74	26	174	3.0
1949-50	Philadelphia	64	185	79	449	7.0
	Totals	147	288	118	694	4.7

CROW, BILL

Yr	Team	G	FG	FT	TP	Avg.
1967-68	Anaheim ABA	1	1 (0)	1	3	3.0

CROW, MARK

b. Oct. 22, 1954 Ht. 6-7 Wt. 210 College—Duke

Yr	Team	G	FG	FT	TP	Avg.
1977-78	New Jersey	15	35	14	84	5.6

CUETO, AL

b. Aug. 2, 1946 Ht. 6-8 Wt. 230 College—Tulsa

Yr	Team	G	FG	FT	TP	Avg.
1969-70	Miami ABA	78	177 (5)	102	471	6.0
1970-71	Memphis ABA	71	134 (0)	55	323	4.6
	Totals	149	311 (5)	157	794	5.3

CUNNINGHAM, BILLY

b. June 3, 1943 Ht. 6-6 Wt. 220 College—N.C.

Yr	Team	G	FG	FT	TP	Avg.
1965-66	Philadelphia	80	431	281	1143	14.3
1966-67	Philadelphia	81	556	383	1495	18.5
1967-68	Philadelphia	74	516	368	1400	19.0
1968-69	Philadelphia	82	739	556	2034	24.8
1969-70	Philadelphia	81	802	510	2114	26.1
1970-71	Philadelphia	81	702	455	1859	23.0
1971-72	Philadelphia	75	658	428	1744	23.3
1972-73	Carolina ABA	84	757 (14)	472	2028	24.1

Yr	Team	G	FG	FT	TP	Avg.
1973-74	Carolina ABA	32	252 (1)	149	656	20.5
1974-75	Philadelphia	80	609	345	1563	19.5
1975-76	Philadelphia	20	103	68	274	13.7
	Totals	770	6125 (15)	4015	16310	21.2

CUNNINGHAM, DICK

b. July 11, 1946 Ht. 6-10 Wt. 240 Coll.—Murray State

Yr	Team	G	FG	FT	TP	Avg.
1968-69	Milwaukee	77	141	69	351	4.6
1969-70	Milwaukee	60	52	22	126	2.1
1970-71	Milwaukee	76	81	39	201	2.6
1971-72	Houston	63	67	37	171	2.7
1972-73	Milwaukee	74	64	29	157	2.1
1973-74	Milwaukee	8	3	0	6	0.8
1974-75	Milwaukee	2	0	0	0	0.0
	Totals	360	408	196	1012	2.8

CURE, ARMAND

b. Aug. 7, 1919 Ht. 6-1 Wt. 198 Coll.—Rhode Island

Yr	Team	G	FG	FT	TP	Avg.
1946-47	Providence	12	4	2	10	0.8

CURRAN, FRANCIS

b. Sept. 19, 1925 Ht. 6-0 Wt. 175 College—Notre Dame

Yr	Team	G	FG	FT	TP	Avg.
1947-48	Toledo NL	58	129	119	377	6.5
1948-49	Rochester	57	61	85	207	3.6
1949-50	Rochester	66	98	199	395	6.0
	Totals	181	288	403	979	5.4

DABICH, MIKE (Dabbo)

b. Dec. 27, 1942 Ht. 7-0 Wt. 255 College—N.M. State

Yr	Team	G	FG	FT	TP	Avg.
1967-68	Oakland-Dal. ABA	10	8 (0)	4	20	2.0

DAHLER, ED

b. Jan. 31, 1926 Ht. 6-5 Wt. 190 College—Duquesne

Yr	Team	G	FG	FT	TP	Avg.
1951-52	Philadelphia	14	14	7	35	2.5

DALLMAR, HOWARD

b. May 24, 1922 Ht. 6-4 Wt. 202 Coll.—Stan. & Pa.

Yr	Team	G	FG	FT	TP	Avg.
1946-47	Philadelphia	60	199	130	528	8.8
1947-48	Philadelphia	48	215	157	587	12.2
1948-49	Philadelphia	38	105	83	293	7.7
	Totals	146	519	370	1408	9.6

DANIELS, MEL

b. July 20, 1944 Ht. 6-9 Wt. 220 College—N.M.

Yr	Team	G	FG	FT	TP	Avg.
1967-68	Minnesota ABA	78	668 (1)	390	1729	22.3
1968-69	Indiana ABA	76	712 (0)	400	1824	24.0
1969-70	Indiana ABA	83	613 (0)	330	1556	18.8
1970-71	Indiana ABA	82	697 (1)	326	1723	21.0
1971-72	Indiana ABA	79	598 (0)	317	1513	19.2
1972-73	Indiana ABA	81	586 (1)	322	1497	18.5
1973-74	Indiana ABA	76	478 (0)	211	1167	15.4
1974-75	Memphis ABA	71	290 (0)	116	696	9.8
1976-77	N.Y. Nets	11	13	13	39	3.5
	Totals	637	4655 (3)	2425	11744	18.4

Yr	Team	G	FG	FT	TP	Avg.

D'ANTONI, MIKE

b. May 8, 1951 Ht. 6-3 Wt. 190 College—Marshall

Yr	Team	G	FG	FT	TP	Avg.
1973-74	K.C.-O.	52	107	33	247	4.8
1974-75	K.C.-O	67	69	28	166	2.5
1975-76	Kansas City	9	7	2	16	1.8
1975-76	St. Louis ABA	50	77 (0)	19	173	3.5
1976-77	San Antonio	2	1	1	3	1.5
	Totals	180	261 (0)	83	605	3.4

DARCEY, PETER

b. March 3, 1930 Ht. 6-7 Wt. 235 Coll.—Okla. A&M

Yr	Team	G	FG	FT	TP	Avg.
1952-53	Milwaukee	12	3	5	11	0.9

DARDEN, JAMES

b. June 19, 1922 Ht. 6-1 Wt. 170 Coll.—W.Y. & Denver

Yr	Team	G	FG	FT	TP	Avg.
1948-49	Denver NL	57	197	193	587	10.3
1949-50	Denver	26	78	55	211	4.3
	Totals	83	275	248	798	9.6

DARDEN, OLIVER

b. July 28, 1944 Ht. 6-7 Wt. 240 College—Michigan

Yr	Team	G	FG	FT	TP	Avg.
1967-68	Indiana ABA	77	371 (0)	180	922	12.0
1968-69	N.Y.-Ky. ABA	77	317 (1)	178	815	10.6
1969-70	Ky.-Ind. ABA	69	125 (1)	57	310	4.5
	Totals	223	813 (2)	415	2047	9.2

DARK, JESSE

b. Sept. 2, 1951 Ht. 6-5 Wt. 210 Coll.—Va. Com.

Yr	Team	G	FG	FT	TP	Avg.
1974-75	New York	47	74	22	170	3.6

DARNELL, RICK

b. 1953 Ht. 6-10 Wt. 215 College—San Jose State

Yr	Team	G	FG	FT	TP	Avg.
1975-76	Virginia ABA	11	11 (0)	4	26	2.4

DARROW, JAMES

b. Sept. 25, 1937 Ht. 5-10¾ Wt. 170 Coll.—Bowl. Gr.

Yr	Team	G	FG	FT	TP	Avg.
1961-62	St. Louis	5	3	6	12	2.4

DAUGHTRY, MACK

Ht. 6-3 Wt. 175 College—Albany State (Ga.)

Yr	Team	G	FG	FT	TP	Avg.
1970-71	Carolina ABA	4	4 (0)	5	13	3.3

DAVIES, BOB

b. Jan. 15, 1920 Ht. 6-1 Wt. 175 College—Seton Hall

Yr	Team	G	FG	FT	TP	Avg.
1945-46	Rochester NL	27	86	70	242	9.0
1946-47	Rochester NL	32	166	130	462	14.4
1947-48	Rochester NL	48	176	120	472	9.8
1948-49	Rochester	60	317	270	904	15.1
1949-50	Rochester	64	317	261	895	14.0
1950-51	Rochester	63	326	303	955	15.2
1951-52	Rochester	65	379	294	1052	16.2
1952-53	Rochester	66	339	351	1029	15.6
1953-54	Rochester	72	288	311	887	12.3
1954-55	Rochester	72	326	220	872	12.1
	Totals	569	2720	2330	7770	13.7

DAVIS, AUBREY

b. 1923 Ht. 6-2 Wt. 175 College—Oklahoma Baptist

Yr	Team	G	FG	FT	TP	Avg.
1946-47	St. Louis	59	107	73	287	4.9
1948-49	Hammond NL	8	3	3	9	1.1
	Totals	67	110	76	296	4.4

DAVIS, BOB

b. April 2, 1950 Ht. 6-7 Wt. 215 Coll.—Weber State

Yr	Team	G	FG	FT	TP	Avg.
1972-73	Portland	9	6	4	16	1.8

DAVIS, CHARLIE

b. Sept. 7, 1949 Ht. 6-2 Wt. 160 Coll.—Wake Forest

Yr	Team	G	FG	FT	TP	Avg.
1971-72	Cleveland	61	229	142	600	9.8
1972-73	Cleve.-Port.	75	263	130	656	8.7
1973-74	Portland	8	14	3	31	3.9
	Totals	144	506	275	1287	8.9

DAVIS, DWIGHT

b. Oct. 28, 1949 Ht. 6-8 Wt. 220 College—Houston

Yr	Team	G	FG	FT	TP	Avg.
1972-73	Cleveland	81	293	176	762	9.4
1973-74	Cleveland	76	376	197	949	12.5
1974-75	Cleveland	78	295	176	766	9.8
1975-76	Golden State	72	111	78	300	4.2
1976-77	Golden State	33	55	49	159	4.8
	Totals	340	1130	676	2936	8.6

DAVIS, JAMES

b. 1933 Ht. 6-7 Wt. 220 Coll.—St. John's (N.Y.)

Yr	Team	G	FG	FT	TP	Avg.
1955-56	Rochester	3	0	2	2	0.7

DAVIS, JIM

b. Dec. 18, 1941 Ht. 6-9½ Wt. 235 College—Colorado

Yr	Team	G	FG	FT	TP	Avg.
1967-68	St. Louis	50	61	25	147	2.9
1968-69	Atlanta	78	265	154	684	8.8
1969-70	Atlanta	82	438	240	1116	13.6
1970-71	Atlanta	82	241	195	677	8.3
1971-72	Atl.-Hou.-Det.	75	147	100	394	5.3
1972-73	Detroit	73	131	72	334	4.6
1973-74	Detroit	78	117	90	324	4.2
1974-75	Detroit	79	118	85	321	4.1
	Totals	597	1518	961	3997	6.7

DAVIS, LEE

b. Oct. 11, 1945 Ht. 6-8 Wt. 240 College—N.C. College

Yr	Team	G	FG	FT	TP	Avg.
1968-69	New Orleans ABA	65	87 (1)	45	222	3.4
1969-70	New Orleans ABA	16	16 (0)	8	40	2.5
1970-71	Memphis ABA	75	197 (0)	63	457	6.1
1971-72	Memphis ABA	58	100 (1)	25	228	3.9
1972-73	Memphis ABA	78	453 (0)	131	1037	13.3
1973-74	Memphis ABA	79	265 (1)	98	631	8.0
1974-75	San Diego ABA	75	383 (4)	113	891	11.9
1975-76	San Diego ABA	7	2 (0)	1	5	0.7
	Totals	453	1503 (7)	484	3511	7.8

Yr	Team	G	FG	FT	TP	Avg.

DAVIS, MEL

b. Oct. 28, 1949 Ht. 6-8 Wt. 220 College—St. John's

Yr	Team	G	FG	FT	TP	Avg.
1973-74	New York	30	33	12	78	2.6
1974-75	New York	62	154	48	356	5.7
1975-76	New York	42	76	22	174	4.1
1976-77	NYK-NYN	56	168	64	400	7.1
	Totals	190	431	146	1008	5.3

DAVIS, MICKEY

b. June 15, 1950 Ht. 6-7 Wt. 215 College—Duquesne

Yr	Team	G	FG	FT	TP	Avg.
1971-72	Pittsburgh ABA	23	25 (0)	14	64	2.8
1972-73	Milwaukee	74	152	76	380	5.1
1973-74	Milwaukee	73	169	93	431	5.9
1974-75	Milwaukee	75	174	78	426	5.7
1975-76	Milwaukee	45	55	50	160	3.6
1976-77	Milwaukee	19	29	23	81	4.3
	Totals	309	604 (0)	334	1542	5.0

DAVIS, MIKE

b. July 26, 1946 Ht. 6-3 Wt. 185 College—VA. Union

Yr	Team	G	FG	FT	TP	Avg.
1969-70	Baltimore	56	260	149	669	11.9
1970-71	Buffalo	73	317	199	833	11.4
1971-72	Buffalo	62	213	138	564	9.1
1972-73	Baltimore	13	50	23	123	9.5
1972-73	Memphis ABA	38	87 (6)	62	254	6.7
	Totals	242	927 (6)	571	2443	10.1

DAVIS, RALPH

b. Sept. 7, 1938 Ht. 6-4 Wt. 180 College—Cincinnati

Yr	Team	G	FG	FT	TP	Avg.
1960-61	Cincinnati	73	181	34	396	5.4
1961-62	Chicato	77	364	71	799	10.4
	Totals	150	545	105	1195	8.0

DAVIS, RON

b. May 1, 1954 Ht. 6-6 Wt. 195 Coll.—Washington St.

Yr	Team	G	FG	FT	TP	Avg.
1976-77	Atlanta	7	8	4	20	2.9

DAVIS, WALTER (Buddy)

b. Jan. 5, 1931 Ht. 6-8 Wt. 205 College—Texas A&M

Yr	Team	G	FG	FT	TP	Avg.
1953-54	Philadelphia	68	167	65	399	5.9
1954-55	Philadelphia	61	70	35	175	2.9
1955-56	Philadelphia	70	123	77	323	4.6
1956-57	Philadelphia	65	178	74	430	6.6
1957-58	Phila.-St. L.	61	85	61	231	3.8
	Totals	325	623	312	1558	4.8

DAVIS, WARREN

b. June 30, 1943 Ht. 6-6 Wt. 213 College—N.C. A&T

Yr	Team	G	FG	FT	TP	Avg.
1967-68	Anaheim ABA	54	342 (1)	229	916	17.0
1968-69	Los Angeles ABA	78	356 (0)	282	994	12.7
1969-70	L.A.-Pitt. ABA	80	427 (1)	304	1161	14.5
1970-71	Florida ABA	76	308 (0)	209	825	10.9
1971-72	Car.-Mem. ABA	86	337 (0)	207	881	10.2
1972-73	Memphis ABA	73	250 (0)	172	672	9.2
	Totals	447	2020 (2)	1403	5449	12.2

DAVIS, WILLIAM

b. Oct. 3, 1921 Ht. 6-3 Wt. 215 College—Notre Dame

Yr	Team	G	FG	FT	TP	Avg.
1946-47	Chicago	47	35	14	84	1.8

DAVIS, WILLIE

b. 1946 Ht. 6-8½ Wt. 234 College—North Texas State

Yr	Team	G	FG	FT	TP	Avg.
1970-71	Dallas ABA	8	7 (0)	4	18	2.3

DAWSON, JAMES

Ht. 6-0 College—Illinois

Yr	Team	G	FG	FT	TP	Avg.
1967-68	Indiana ABA	21	45 (1)	25	118	5.6

DEANGELIS, BILLY

b. 1946 Ht. 6-1 Wt. 180 College—St. Joseph's

Yr	Team	G	FG	FT	TP	Avg.
1970-71	New York ABA	8	3 (0)	4	10	1.3

DeBUSSCHERE, DAVE

b. Oct. 16, 1940 Ht. 6-6 Wt. 220 College—Detroit

Yr	Team	G	FG	FT	TP	Avg.
1962-63	Detroit	80	406	206	1018	12.7
1963-64	Detroit	15	52	25	129	8.6
1964-65	Detroit	79	508	306	1322	16.7
1965-66	Detroit	79	524	249	1297	16.4
1966-67	Detroit	78	531	361	1423	18.2
1967-68	Detroit	80	573	289	1435	17.9
1968-69	Det.-N.Y.	76	506	229	1241	16.3
1969-70	New York	79	488	176	1152	14.6
1970-71	New York	81	523	217	1263	15.6
1971-72	New York	80	520	193	1233	15.4
1972-73	New York	77	532	194	1258	16.3
1973-74	New York	71	559	164	1282	18.1
	Totals	875	5722	2609	14053	16.1

DEE, DON

Ht. 6-8 Wt. 210 College—St. Louis and St. Mary of the Plains

Yr	Team	G	FG	FT	TP	Avg.
1968-69	Indiana ABA	58	138 (0)	56	332	5.7

DEES, ARCHIE

b. Feb. 22, 1936 Ht. 6-8 Wt. 205 College—Indiana

Yr	Team	G	FG	FT	TP	Avg.
1958-59	Cincinnati	68	200	159	559	8.2
1959-60	Detroit	73	271	165	707	9.7
1960-61	Detroit	28	53	39	145	5.2
1961-62	Chi.-St. Louis	21	51	35	137	6.5
	Totals	190	575	398	1548	8.1

DEHNERT, ROBERT (Red)

b. 1924 Ht. 6-3 Wt. 178 College—St. John's

Yr	Team	G	FG	FT	TP	Avg.
1946-47	Providence	10	6	2	14	1.4

DeLONG, NATE

b. 1928 Ht. 6-6½ Wt. 220 College—River Falls

Yr	Team	G	FG	FT	TP	Avg.
1951-52	Milwaukee	17	20	24	64	3.8

DEMPSEY, GEORGE

b. July 19, 1929 Ht. 6-3 Wt. 192 College—King's (N.Y.)

Yr	Team	G	FG	FT	TP	Avg.
1954-55	Philadelphia	48	127	98	352	7.3
1955-56	Philadelphia	72	126	88	340	4.7
1956-57	Philadelphia	71	134	55	323	4.5
1957-58	Philadelphia	67	112	70	294	5.1
	Totals	258	499	311	1309	5.1

Yr	Team	G	FG	FT	TP	Avg.

DENNING, BLAINE

Ht. 6-2 Wt. 175 College—Lawrence Tech

Yr	Team	G	FG	FT	TP	Avg.
1952-53	Baltimore	1	2	1	5	5.0

DENTON, RANDY

b. Feb. 18, 1949 Ht. 6-10 Wt. 245 College—Duke

Yr	Team	G	FG	FT	TP	Avg.
1971-72	Car.-Mem. ABA	81	430 (0)	135	995	12.3
1972-73	Memphis ABA	66	469 (3)	177	1124	17.0
1973-74	Memphis ABA	79	447 (0)	156	1050	13.3
1974-75	Utah ABA	75	300 (0)	92	692	9.2
1975-76	Utah-St.L. ABA	67	283 (0)	83	649	9.7
1976-77	Atlanta	45	103	33	239	5.3
	Totals	413	2032 (3)	676	4749	11.5

DePRE, JOE

b. Dec. 19, 1947 Ht. 6-3½ Wt. 185 College—St. John's

Yr	Team	G	FG	FT	TP	Avg.
1970-71	New York ABA	72	250 (0)	132	632	8.8
1971-72	New York ABA	46	77 (2)	34	194	4.3
	Totals	118	327 (2)	166	826	7.0

DERLINE, ROD

b. March 11, 1952 Ht. 6-4 Wt. 175 College—Seattle

Yr	Team	G	FG	FT	TP	Avg.
1974-75	Seattle	58	142	43	327	5.6
1975-76	Seattle	49	73	45	191	3.9
	Totals	107	215	88	518	4.8

DEUTSCH, DAVE

b. May 13, 1945 Ht. 6-1 Wt. 170 College—Rochester

Yr	Team	G	FG	FT	TP	Avg.
1966-67	New York	19	6	9	21	1.1

DEVLIN, WALTER (Corky)

b. Dec. 21, 1931 Ht. 6-5 Wt. 195 Coll.—G. Washington

Yr	Team	G	FG	FT	TP	Avg.
1955-56	Fort Wayne	69	200	146	546	7.9
1956-57	Fort Wayne	71	190	97	477	6.7
1957-58	Minneapolis	70	170	133	473	6.8
	Totals	210	560	376	1496	7.1

DeZONIE, HANK

Ht. 6-6 Wt. 215 College—Clark (Ga.)

Yr	Team	G	FG	FT	TP	Avg.
1948-49	Dayton NL	18	90	44	224	12.4
1950-51	Tri-Cities	5	6	5	17	3.4
	Totals	23	96	49	241	10.5

DICKERSON, HENRY

b. Nov. 27, 1951 Ht. 6-4 Wt. 190 Coll.—Morris-Harvey

Yr	Team	G	FG	FT	TP	Avg.
1975-76	Detroit	17	9	10	28	1.6
1976-77	Atlanta	6	6	5	17	2.9
	Totals	23	15	15	45	2.0

DICKEY, CLYDE

b. Dec. 14, 1951 Ht. 6-3 Wt. 185 College—Boston Coll.

Yr	Team	G	FG	FT	TP	Avg.
1974-75	Utah ABA	57	64 (2)	16	150	2.6

DICKEY, DERRICK

b. March 20, 1951 Ht. 6-7 Wt. 218 College—Cincinnati

Yr	Team	G	FG	FT	TP	Avg.
1973-74	Golden State	66	115	51	281	4.3
1974-75	Golden State	80	274	66	614	7.7
1975-76	Golden State	79	220	62	502	6.4
1976-77	Golden State	49	158	45	361	7.4
1977-78	G.S.-Chi.	47	87	30	204	4.3
	Totals	321	854	254	1962	6.1

DICKEY, DICK

b. Oct. 26, 1926 Ht. 6-1 Wt. 175 Coll.—N. Carolina St.

Yr	Team	G	FG	FT	TP	Avg.
1951-52	Boston	45	40	47	127	2.8

DICKSON, JOHN

b. Nov. 18, 1945 Ht. 6-10 Wt. 240 College—Ariz. State

Yr	Team	G	FG	FT	TP	Avg.
1967-68	New Orleans ABA	21	14 (0)	8	36	1.7

DIERKING, CONNIE

b. Oct. 2, 1936 Ht. 6-10 Wt. 222 College—Cincinnati

Yr	Team	G	FG	FT	TP	Avg.
1958-59	Syracuse	64	105	83	293	3.6
1959-60	Syracuse	71	192	108	492	6.9
1963-64	Philadelphia	76	191	114	496	6.5
1964-65	Phil.-San. Fr.	68	218	100	536	7.9
1965-66	Cincinnati	57	134	50	318	5.6
1966-67	Cincinnati	77	291	134	716	9.3
1967-68	Cincinnati	81	544	237	1325	16.4
1968-69	Cincinnati	82	546	243	1335	16.3
1969-70	Cincinnati	76	521	230	1272	16.7
1970-71	Cin.-Phila.	54	125	61	311	5.8
	Totals	706	2867	1360	7094	10.0

DI GREGORIO, ERNIE

b. Jan. 15, 1951 Ht. 6-0 Wt. 180 College—Providence

Yr	Team	G	FG	FT	TP	Avg.
1973-74	Buffalo	81	530	174	1234	15.2
1974-75	Buffalo	31	103	35	241	7.8
1975-76	Buffalo	67	182	86	450	6.7
1976-77	Buffalo	81	365	138	868	10.7
1977-78	L.A.-Bos.	52	88	28	204	3.9
	Totals	312	1268	461	2997	9.6

DILL, CRAIG

b. 1945 Ht. 6-11 Wt. 220 College—Michigan

Yr	Team	G	FG	FT	TP	Avg.
1967-68	Pittsburgh ABA	65	187 (0)	71	445	6.8

DILLARD, DAVE

Yr	Team	G	FG	FT	TP	Avg.
1975-76	Utah ABA	3	1	2	4	1.3

DILLE, ROBERT (Oscar)

b. July 2, 1917 Ht. 6-3 Wt. 200 College—Valparaiso

Yr	Team	G	FG	FT	TP	Avg.
1940-41	Hammond NL	3	8	3	19	6.3
1946-47	Detroit	57	111	74	296	5.2
	Totals	60	119	77	315	5.3

DILLON, JOHN (Hooks)

b. Jan. 8, 1924 Ht. 6-3 Wt. 180 Coll.—Ken. & N.C.

Yr	Team	G	FG	FT	TP	Avg.
1949-50	Washington	22	10	16	36	1.6

DINKINS, JACKIE

b. Jan. 22, 1950 Ht. 6-5 Wt. 210 College—Voorhees

Yr	Team	G	FG	FT	TP	Avg.
1971-72	Chicago	18	17	11	45	2.5

Yr	Team	G	FG	FT	TP	Avg.
DINNELL, HARRY						
Ht. 6-4 Wt. 200 College—Pepperdine						
1967-68	Anaheim ABA	11	6 (0)	7	19	1.7
DINWIDDIE, BILL						
b. 1943 Ht. 6-7 Wt. 220 Coll.—New Mexico Highlands						
1967-68	Cincinnati	67	141	62	344	5.1
1968-69	Cincinnati	69	124	45	293	4.2
1970-71	Boston	61	123	54	300	4.9
1971-72	Milwaukee	23	16	5	37	1.6
	Totals	220	404	166	974	4.4
DISCHINGER, TERRY						
b. Nov. 21, 1940 Ht. 6-7 Wt. 189 College—Purdue						
1962-63	Chicago	57	525	402	1452	25.5
1963-64	Baltimore	80	604	454	1662	20.8
1964-65	Detroit	80	568	320	1456	18.2
1967-68	Detroit	78	394	237	1025	13.1
1968-69	Detroit	75	264	130	658	8.8
1969-70	Detroit	75	342	174	858	11.4
1970-71	Detroit	65	304	161	769	11.8
1971-72	Detroit	79	295	156	746	9.4
1972-73	Portland	63	161	64	386	6.1
	Totals	652	3457	2098	9012	13.8
DIUTE, FRED						
Ht. 6-3 Wt. 210 College—St. Bonaventure						
1954-55	Milwaukee	7	2	7	11	1.6
DODD, EARL						
Ht. 6-5 College—Northeast Missouri						
1949-59	Denver	9	6	3	15	1.7
DOLHON, JOE						
b. 1928 Ht. 6-0 Wt. 175 College—New York University						
1949-50	Baltimore	64	143	157	443	6.9
1950-51	Baltimore	11	15	9	39	3.5
	Totals	75	158	166	482	6.4
DOLL, ROBERT						
b. Aug. 10, 1919 Ht. 6-5 Wt. 195 College—Colorado d. Sept. 18, 1959						
1946-47	St. Louis	60	194	134	522	8.7
1947-48	St. Louis	42	174	98	446	10.6
1948-49	Denver NL	9	16	13	45	5.0
1948-49	Boston	47	145	80	370	7.9
1949-50	Boston	47	120	75	315	6.7
	Totals	205	649	400	1698	8.3
DONHAM, BOB						
b. Oct. 11, 1926 Ht. 6-2 Wt. 190 College—Ohio State						
1950-51	Boston	68	151	114	416	6.1
1951-52	Boston	66	201	149	551	8.3
1952-53	Boston	71	169	113	451	6.4
1953-54	Boston	68	141	118	400	5.9
	Totals	273	662	494	1818	6.7
DONOVAN, HARRY						
b. Sept. 10, 1926 Ht. 6-2 Wt. 190 College—Muhlenberg						
1949-50	New York	45	90	73	253	5.6

Yr	Team	G	FG	FT	TP	Avg.
DORSEY, RON						
b. Oct. 10, 1948 Ht. 6-4 Wt. 200 College—Tenn. State						
1971-72	Carolina ABA	1	2 (0)	0	4	4.0
DOVE, LLOYD (Sonny)						
b. Aug. 16, 1945 Ht. 6-8 Wt. 198 College—St. John's (N.Y.)						
1967-68	Detroit	28	22	12	56	2.0
1968-69	Detroit	29	47	24	118	4.1
1969-70	New York ABA	80	454 (2)	140	1154	14.4
1970-71	New York ABA	83	463 (4)	186	1124	13.5
1971-72	New York ABA	2	2 (0)	2	6	3.0
	Totals	222	988 (6)	264	2458	11.1
DOVER, JERRY						
b. Oct. 16, 1949 Ht. 5-7 Wt. 155 College—LeMoyne						
1971-72	Memphis ABA	4	1 (2)	0	8	2.0
DOWNEY, BILL						
b. 1923 Ht. 6-6 Wt. 210 College—Marquette						
1947-48	Providence	3	0	0	0	0.0
DOWNING, STEVE						
b. Sept. 9, 1950 Ht. 6-8 Wt. 225 College—Indiana						
1973-74	Boston	24	21	22	64	2.7
1974-75	Boston	3	0	0	0	0.0
	Totals	27	21	22	64	2.4
DOYLE, DANIEL						
b. Feb. 6, 1940 Ht. 6-8 Wt. 200 Coll.—Belmont Abbey						
1962-63	Detroit	4	6	4	16	4.0
DRISCOLL, TERRY						
b. Aug. 28, 1947 Ht. 6-7 Wt. 215 Coll.—Boston College						
1970-71	Detroit	69	132	108	372	5.4
1971-72	Baltimore	40	40	27	107	2.7
1972-73	Balt.-Milw.	60	140	43	323	5.4
1973-74	Milwaukee	64	88	30	206	4.3
1974-75	Milwaukee	11	3	1	7	0.6
1974-75	St. Louis ABA	30	46 (0)	20	112	3.7
	Totals	274	449 (0)	229	1127	4.1
DUCKETT, RICHARD						
b. March 25, 1933 Ht. 6-1 Wt. 185 College—St. John's (N.Y.)						
1957-58	Cincinnati	34	54	24	132	3.9
DUFFY, ROBERT						
b. July 5, 1922 Ht. 6-4 Wt. 175 College—Tulane						
1946-47	Chic.-Bost.	17	7	5	19	1.1
DUFFY, ROBERT						
b. Sept. 26, 1940 Ht. 6-3 Wt. 185 College—Colgate						
1962-63	St. Louis	42	66	22	154	3.7
1963-64	St. L.-N.Y.-Det.	48	94	44	232	4.8
1964-65	Detroit	4	4	6	14	3.5
	Totals	94	164	72	400	4.3

Yr	Team	G	FG	FT	TP	Avg.

DUKES, WALTER

b. June 23, 1930 Ht. 7-0 Wt. 220 College—Seton Hall

Yr	Team	G	FG	FT	TP	Avg.
1955-56	New York	60	149	167	465	7.8
1956-57	Minneapolis	71	228	264	720	10.1
1957-58	Detroit	72	278	247	803	11.2
1958-59	Detroit	72	318	297	933	13.0
1959-60	Detroit	66	314	376	1004	15.2
1960-61	Detroit	73	286	281	853	11.7
1961-62	Detroit	77	256	208	720	9.3
1962-63	Detroit	62	83	101	267	4.3
	Totals	553	1912	1941	5765	10.4

DUMAS, RICH

College—Northeastern Oklahoma

Yr	Team	G	FG	FT	TP	Avg.
1968-69	Houston ABA	1	1 (0)	0	2	2.0

DUNCAN, ANDREW

b. 1923 Ht. 6-6 Wt. 195 College—Kentucky and William & Mary

Yr	Team	G	FG	FT	TP	Avg.
1947-48	Rochester NL	60	200	119	519	8.7
1948-49	Rochester	55	162	83	407	7.4
1949-50	Rochester	67	125	60	310	4.6
1950-51	Boston	14	7	15	29	2.1
	Totals	196	494	277	1265	6.5

DUNN, PAT

b. March 17, 1931 Ht. 6-2 Wt. 170 College—Utah State

Yr	Team	G	FG	FT	TP	Avg.
1957-58	Philadelphia	28	28	14	70	2.5

DURHAM, JARRETT

Ht. 6-5 Wt. 188 College—Duquesne

Yr	Team	G	FG	FT	TP	Avg.
1971-72	New York ABA	1	0 (0)	0	0	0.0

DURRETT, KEN

b. Dec. 8, 1948 Ht. 6-8 Wt. 190 College—LaSalle

Yr	Team	G	FG	FT	TP	Avg.
1971-72	Cincinnati	19	31	21	83	4.4
1972-73	K.C.-Omaha	8	8	6	22	2.8
1973-74	K.C.-Omaha	45	86	42	214	4.8
1974-75	K.C.-O.-Phila.	48	67	31	165	3.4
	Totals	120	192	100	484	4.0

DUVAL, DENNIS

b. March 31, 1952 Ht. 6-3 Wt. 175 College—Syracuse

Yr	Team	G	FG	FT	TP	Avg.
1974-75	Washington	5	3	1	7	1.4
1975-76	Atlanta	13	15	6	36	2.8
	Totals	18	18	7	43	2.4

DWAN, JACK

b. May 3, 1921 Ht. 6-4 Wt. 200 College—Loyola (III.)

Yr	Team	G	FG	FT	TP	Avg.
1947-48	Minneapolis NL	55	128	50	306	5.5
1948-49	Minneapolis	60	121	34	276	4.6
	Totals	115	249	84	582	5.1

DYKER, GENE

b. Feb. 17, 1930 Ht. 6-6 Wt. 225 College—DePaul

Yr	Team	G	FG	FT	TP	Avg.
1953-54	Milwaukee	11	6	4	16	1.5

EAKINS, JIM

b. May 24, 1946 Ht. 6-11 Wt. 215 Coll.—Brig. Young

Yr	Team	G	FG	FT	TP	Avg.
1968-69	Oakland ABA	78	351 (0)	309	1011	13.0
1969-70	Washington ABA	82	181 (0)	166	528	6.4
1970-71	Virginia ABA	84	332 (0)	242	906	10.8
1971-72	Virginia ABA	84	371 (0)	288	1030	12.3
1973-74	Virginia ABA	84	445 (0)	339	1229	14.6
1974-75	Utah ABA	84	380 (0)	291	1051	12.5
1975-76	Utah-Va.-NY ABA	73	215 (0)	198	628	8.6
1976-77	Kansas City	82	151	188	490	6.0
1977-78	S.A.-Mil.	33	44	50	138	4.2
	Totals	684	2470 (0)	2071	7011	10.3

EARLE, EDWIN (Ed)

b. April 28, 1927 Ht. 6-3 Wt. 190 College—Loyola (III.)

Yr	Team	G	FG	FT	TP	Avg.
1953-54	Syracuse	2	1	2	4	2.0

EBBEN, WILLIAM

b. Oct. 7, 1935 Ht. 6-4 Wt. 200 College—Detroit

Yr	Team	G	FG	FT	TP	Avg.
1957-58	Detroit	8	6	3	15	1.9

EBERHARD, AL

b. May 10, 1952 Ht. 6-6 Wt. 225 College—Missouri

Yr	Team	G	FG	FT	TP	Avg.
1974-75	Detroit	34	31	17	79	2.3
1975-76	Detroit	81	283	191	757	9.3
1976-77	Detroit	68	181	109	471	6.9
1977-78	Detroit	37	71	41	183	4.9
	Totals	220	566	358	1490	6.8

EBRON, ROY

b. Aug. 31, 1951 Ht. 6-9 Wt. 225 College—Southwest Louisiana

Yr	Team	G	FG	FT	TP	Avg.
1973-74	Utah ABA	40	103 (0)	43	249	6.2

EDDLEMAN, DWIGHT (Dike)

b. Dec. 27, 1922 Ht. 6-3 Wt. 189 College—Illinois

Yr	Team	G	FG	FT	TP	Avg.
1949-50	Tri-Cities	64	332	162	826	12.9
1950-51	Tri-Cities	68	398	244	1040	15.3
1951-52	Milwaukee-Ft. Wayne	65	269	202	740	11.4
1952-53	Ft. Wayne	69	241	134	616	8.9
	Totals	266	1240	742	3222	12.1

EDGE, CHARLIE

b. Feb. 27, 1950 Ht. 6-6 Wt. 210 Coll.—Lemoyne-Owen

Yr	Team	G	FG	FT	TP	Avg.
1973-74	Memphis ABA	78	312 (12)	124	784	9.6
1974-75	Indiana ABA	77	195 (0)	63	453	5.9
	Totals	155	507 (12)	187	1237	8.0

EDMONDS, BOBBY JOE

b. March 8, 1941 Ht. 6-7 Wt. 220 College—Tenn. St.

Yr	Team	G	FG	FT	TP	Avg.
1967-68	Indiana ABA	72	212 (1)	150	577	8.0
1969-70	Indiana ABA	3	1 (0)	1	3	1.0
	Totals	75	213 (1)	151	580	7.7

Yr	Team	G	FG	FT	TP	Avg.

EGAN, JOHN

b. Jan. 31, 1939 Ht. 6-0 Wt. 180 College—Providence

Yr	Team	G	FG	FT	TP	Avg.
1961-62	Detroit	58	128	64	320	5.5
1962-63	Detroit	46	110	53	273	5.9
1963-64	Det.-N.Y.	66	334	193	861	13.0
1964-65	New York	74	258	162	678	9.2
1965-66	N.Y.-Balt.	76	259	173	691	9.1
1966-67	Baltimore	71	267	185	719	10.1
1967-68	Baltimore	67	163	142	468	7.0
1968-69	Los Angeles	82	246	204	696	8.5
1969-70	Los Angeles	72	215	99	529	7.3
1970-71	Cleve.-S.D.	62	67	42	176	2.8
1971-72	Houston	38	42	26	110	2.9
	Totals	712	2089	1343	5521	7.8

EGGLESTON, LONNIE

b. June 8, 1918 Ht. 6-0½ Wt. 170 College—Okla. A&M

Yr	Team	G	FG	FT	TP	Avg.
1948-49	St. Louis	2	1	2	4	2.0

EHLERS, EDWIN (Bulbs)

b. 1924 Ht. 6-3 Wt. 198 College—Purdue

Yr	Team	G	FG	FT	TP	Avg.
1947-48	Boston	40	104	78	286	7.2
1948-49	Boston	59	182	150	514	8.7
	Totals	99	286	228	800	8.1

EICHHORST, RICHARD

b. Oct. 21, 1933 Ht. 6-3 Wt. 200 Coll.—Southeast Mi.

Yr	Team	G	FG	FT	TP	Avg.
1961-62	St. Louis	1	1	0	2	2.0

ELIASON, ROBERT

Ht. 6-2 College—Hamline

Yr	Team	G	FG	FT	TP	Avg.
1946-47	Boston	1	0	0	0	0.0

ELLEFSON, RAY

b. Nov. 18, 1922, Ht. 6-8 Wt. 230 College—Oklahoma A&M and Colorado

Yr	Team	G	FG	FT	TP	Avg.
1948-49	Minneapolis	3	1	0	2	0.7
1948-49	Waterloo NL	7	4	8	16	2.3
1950-51	N.Y.-Balt.	3	0	4	4	1.3
	Totals	13	5	12	22	1.7

ELLIS, ALEX (Boo)

b. Feb. 11, 1936 Ht. 6-5 Wt. 185 College—Niagara

Yr	Team	G	FG	FT	TP	Avg.
1958-59	Minneapolis	72	163	102	428	5.9
1959-60	Minneapolis	46	64	51	179	3.9
	Totals	118	227	153	607	5.1

ELLIS, JOSEPH

b. May 3, 1944 Ht. 6-6 Wt. 175 College—San Francisco

Yr	Team	G	FG	FT	TP	Avg.
1966-67	San Francisco	41	67	19	153	3.7
1967-68	San Francisco	51	111	32	254	5.0
1968-69	San Francisco	74	371	147	889	12.0
1969-70	San Francisco	76	501	200	1202	15.8
1970-71	San Francisco	80	356	151	863	10.8
1971-72	Golden State	78	280	95	655	8.4
1972-73	Golden State	74	199	69	467	6.3
1973-74	Golden State	50	61	18	140	2.8
	Totals	524	1946	731	4623	8.8

ELLIS, LEROY

b. March 10, 1940 Ht. 6-10 Wt. 210 College—St. John's (N.Y.)

Yr	Team	G	FG	FT	TP	Avg.
1962-63	Los Angeles	80	222	133	577	7.2
1963-64	Los Angeles	78	200	112	512	6.6
1964-65	Los Angeles	80	311	198	820	10.3
1965-66	Los Angeles	80	393	186	972	12.2
1966-67	Baltimore	81	496	211	1203	14.9
1967-68	Baltimore	78	380	207	967	12.4
1968-69	Baltimore	80	229	117	575	7.2
1969-70	Baltimore	72	194	86	474	6.6
1970-71	Portland	74	485	209	1179	15.9
1971-72	Los Angeles	74	138	66	342	4.6
1972-73	L.A.-Phil.	79	421	129	971	12.3
1973-74	Philadelphia	81	326	147	799	9.9
1974-75	Philadelphia	82	287	72	646	7.9
1975-76	Philadelphia	29	61	17	139	4.8
	Totals	1048	4143	1890	10176	9.7

ELSTON, DARRELL

b. Aug. 15, 1952 Ht. 6-4 Wt. 205 College—N.C.

Yr	Team	G	FG	FT	TP	Avg.
1974-75	Virginia ABA	72	247 (3)	93	596	8.3
1976-77	Indiana	5	2	1	5	1.0
	Totals	77	249 (3)	94	601	7.8

EMBRY, WAYNE (Goose)

b. March 26, 1937 Ht. 6-8 Wt. 255 Coll.—Miami (Ohio)

Yr	Team	G	FG	FT	TP	Avg.
1958-59	Cincinnati	66	272	206	750	11.4
1959-60	Cincinnati	73	303	167	773	10.6
1960-61	Cincinnati	79	458	221	1137	14.4
1961-62	Cincinnati	75	564	356	1484	19.8
1962-63	Cincinnati	76	534	343	1411	18.6
1963-64	Cincinnati	80	556	271	1383	17.3
1964-65	Cincinnati	74	352	239	943	12.7
1965-66	Cincinnati	80	232	141	605	7.6
1966-67	Boston	72	147	82	376	5.2
1967-68	Boston	78	193	109	495	6.3
1968-69	Milwaukee	78	382	259	1023	13.1
	Totals	831	3993	2394	10380	12.5

ENDRESS, NED

b. March 2, 1918 Ht. 6-2 Wt. 200 College—Akron

Yr	Team	G	FG	FT	TP	Avg.
1943-44	Cleveland NL	16	25	15	65	4.1
1944-45	Cleveland NL	29	62	46	170	5.9
1945-46	Cleveland NL	22	58	36	152	6.9
1946-47	Cleveland	16	3	8	14	0.9
	Totals	83	148	105	401	4.8

ENGLISH, CLAUDE

b. Dec. 26, 1946 Ht. 6-4 Wt. 190 Coll.—Rhode Island

Yr	Team	G	FG	FT	TP	Avg.
1970-71	Portland	18	11	5	27	1.5

ENGLISH, SCOTT

b. Oct. 20, 1950 Ht. 6-6 Wt. 205 College—N.C.

Yr	Team	G	FG	FT	TP	Avg.
1972-73	Phoenix	29	36	21	93	3.2
1973-74	Virginia ABA	5	3 (0)	4	10	2.0
1974-75	San Diego ABA	71	209 (1)	69	490	6.9
	Totals	105	248 (1)	94	593	5.6

ENGLUND, GENE

b. Oct. 21, 1917 Ht. 6-5 Wt. 205 College—Wisconsin

Yr	Team	G	FG	FT	TP	Avg.
1941-42	Oshkosh NL	22	61	42	164	7.5
1942-43	Oshkosh NL	17	41	48	130	7.6
1943-44	Oshkosh NL	2	9	5	23	11.5

Yr	Team	G	FG	FT	TP	Avg.
1945-46	Oshkosh NL	33	78	64	220	6.7
1946-47	Oshkosh NL	43	187	105	479	11.1
1947-48	Oshkosh NL	58	246	242	734	12.7
1948-49	Oshkosh NL	63	284	282	850	13.5
1949-50	Boston-Tri-Cities	46	104	152	360	7.8
	Totals	284	1010	940	2960	10.4

ERIAS, BALTICO (Bo)
b. July 30, 1932 Ht. 6-3½ Wt. 220 College—Niagara

Yr	Team	G	FG	FT	TP	Avg.
1957-58	Minneapolis	18	59	30	148	8.2

ERICKSON, KEITH
b. April 19, 1944 Ht. 6-5 Wt. 195 College—UCLA

Yr	Team	G	FG	FT	TP	Avg.
1965-66	San Francisco	65	95	43	233	3.6
1966-67	Chicago	76	235	117	587	7.7
1967-68	Chicago	78	377	194	948	12.2
1968-69	Los Angeles	77	264	120	648	8.4
1969-70	Los Angeles	68	258	91	607	8.9
1970-71	Los Angeles	73	369	85	823	11.3
1971-72	Los Angeles	15	40	6	86	5.7
1972-73	Los Angeles	76	299	89	687	9.0
1973-74	Phoenix	66	393	177	963	14.6
1974-75	Phoenix	49	237	130	604	12.3
1975-76	Phoenix	74	305	134	744	10.1
1976-77	Phoenix	50	142	37	321	6.4
	Totals	767	3014	1223	7251	9.5

ESKRIDGE, JACK
b. Jan. 21, 1924 Ht. 6-5 Wt. 200 College—Kansas

Yr	Team	G	FG	FT	TP	Avg.
1948-49	Chi.-Ind.	23	25	14	64	2.8

EVANS, BILL
Ht. 6-0 Wt. 170 College—Boston College

Yr	Team	G	FG	FT	TP	Avg.
1969-70	New York ABA	53	32 (0)	38	102	1.9

EVANS, BOB
b. May 31, 1925 Ht. 6-2 Wt. 175 Coll.—Ind. & Butler

Yr	Team	G	FG	FT	TP	Avg.
1949-50	Indianapolis	47	56	30	142	3.0

EZERSKY, JOHN
b. 1921 Ht. 6-3 Wt. 175 College—St. John's

Yr	Team	G	FG	FT	TP	Avg.
1947-48	Tri-Cities NL	5	9	5	23	4.6
1947-48	Providence	25	95	63	253	10.1
1948-49	Prov.-Bos.-Balt.	56	128	109	365	6.5
1949-50	Balt.-Boston	54	143	127	413	7.6
	Totals	140	375	304	1054	7.5

FABEL, JOSEPH
Ht. 6-1 Wt. 190 College—Pittsburgh

Yr	Team	G	FG	FT	TP	Avg.
1938-39	Pittsburgh NL	1	3	0	6	6.0
1946-47	Pittsburgh	30	25	13	63	2.1
	Totals	31	28	13	69	2.2

FAIRCHILD, JOHN
b. April 28, 1943 Ht. 6-7½ Wt. 205 College—Brigham Young

Yr	Team	G	FG	FT	TP	Avg.
1965-66	Los Angeles	30	23	14	60	2.0

Yr	Team	G	FG	FT	TP	Avg.
1967-68	Anaheim ABA	62	270 (1)	135	678	10.9
1968-69	Den.-Ind. ABA	63	103 (10)	89	325	5.2
1969-70	Ind.-Ky. ABA	10	4 (3)	5	22	2.2
	Totals	165	400 (14)	243	1085	6.6

FARBMAN, PHILIP
b. 1924 Ht. 6-4 Wt. 185 College—CCNY

Yr	Team	G	FG	FT	TP	Avg.
1948-49	Phil.-Bos.	48	50	55	155	3.2

FARLEY, RICHARD
b. April 13, 1932 Ht. 6-4 Wt. 190 College—Indiana
d. Oct. 1, 1969

Yr	Team	G	FG	FT	TP	Avg.
1954-55	Syracuse	69	136	136	408	5.9
1955-56	Syracuse	72	168	143	479	6.6
	Totals	141	304	279	887	6.1

FARMER, MIKE
b. Sept. 26, 1936 Ht. 6-7 Wt. 210 Coll.—San Francisco

Yr	Team	G	FG	FT	TP	Avg.
1958-59	New York	72	176	83	435	6.0
1959-60	New York	67	212	70	494	7.4
1960-61	N.Y.-Cinn.	59	180	69	429	7.3
1962-63	St. Louis	80	239	117	595	7.4
1963-64	St. Louis	76	178	68	424	5.6
1964-65	St. Louis	60	167	75	409	6.8
	Totals	414	1152	482	2786	6.7

FAUGHT, ROBERT
b. Sept. 2, 1921 Ht. 6-5 Wt. 185 College—Notre Dame

Yr	Team	G	FG	FT	TP	Avg.
1946-47	Cleveland	51	141	61	343	6.7

FEDOR, DAVID
b. Dec. 10, 1940 Ht. 6-6 Wt. 192 College—Florida State

Yr	Team	G	FG	FT	TP	Avg.
1962-63	San Francisco	7	3	0	6	0.9

FEERICK, BOB
b. Jan. 2, 1920 Ht. 6-3 Wt. 190 College—Santa Clara
d. June 8, 1976

Yr	Team	G	FG	FT	TP	Avg.
1945-46	Oshkosh NL	21	81	36	198	9.4
1946-47	Washington	55	364	198	926	16.8
1947-48	Washington	48	293	189	775	16.1
1948-49	Washington	58	248	256	752	13.0
1949-50	Washington	60	172	139	483	8.1
	Totals	242	1158	818	3134	13.0

FEHER, BUTCH
b. May 19, 1954 Ht. 6-4 Wt. 185 College—Vanderbilt

Yr	Team	G	FG	FT	TP	Avg.
1976-77	Phoenix	48	86	76	248	5.2

FEIEREISEL, RON
b. Aug. 6, 1931 Ht. 6-3 Wt. 185 College—DePaul

Yr	Team	G	FG	FT	TP	Avg.
1955-56	Minneapolis	10	8	14	30	3.0

FEIGENBAUM, GEORGE
b. July 2, 1929 Ht. 6-1 Wt. 185 Coll.—LIU & Kentucky

Yr	Team	G	FG	FT	TP	Avg.
1949-50	Baltimore	12	14	8	36	3.0
1952-53	Milwaukee	5	4	8	16	3.2
	Totals	17	18	16	52	3.1

Yr	Team	G	FG	FT	TP	Avg.

FELIX, RAY

b. Dec. 10, 1930 Ht. 6-11 Wt. 220 College—LIU

Yr	Team	G	FG	FT	TP	Avg.
1953-54	Baltimore	72	410	449	1269	17.6
1954-55	New York	72	364	310	1038	14.4
1955-56	New York	72	277	331	885	12.3
1956-57	New York	72	295	277	867	12.0
1957-58	New York	72	304	271	879	12.2
1958-59	New York	72	260	229	749	10.4
1959-60	N.Y.-Minn.	47	136	70	342	7.3
1960-61	Los Angeles	78	189	135	513	6.6
1961-62	Los Angeles	80	171	90	432	5.4
	Totals	637	2406	2162	6974	10.9

FENDLEY, JAKE

b. June 12, 1929 Ht. 6-1 Wt. 180 Coll.—Northwestern

Yr	Team	G	FG	FT	TP	Avg.
1951-52	Ft. Wayne	58	54	75	183	3.2
1952-53	Ft. Wayne	45	32	40	104	2.3
	Totals	103	86	115	287	2.8

FENLEY, WILLIAM

b. Feb. 8, 1922 Ht. 6-3½ Wt. 190 College—Manhattan

Yr	Team	G	FG	FT	TP	Avg.
1946-47	Boston	23	31	23	85	3.7

FERNSTEN, ERIC

b. Nov. 1, 1953 Ht. 6-8 Wt. 215 Coll.—San Francisco

Yr	Team	G	FG	FT	TP	Avg.
1975-76	Cleve.-Chi.	37	33	26	92	2.5
1976-77	Chicago	5	3	8	14	2.8
	Totals	42	36	34	106	2.5

FERRARI, ALBERT

b. July 6, 1933 Ht. 6-4 Wt. 190 Coll.—Michigan State

Yr	Team	G	FG	FT	TP	Avg.
1955-56	St. Louis	68	191	164	546	8.0
1958-59	St. Louis	72	134	145	413	5.7
1959-60	St. Louis	71	216	176	608	8.6
1960-61	St. Louis	63	117	95	329	5.2
1961-62	St. Louis	79	208	175	591	7.5
1962-63	Chicago	18	12	14	38	2.1
	Totals	371	878	769	2525	6.8

FERRIN, ARNOLD

b. July 29, 1925 Ht. 6-4 Wt. 180 College—Utah

Yr	Team	G	FG	FT	TP	Avg.
1948-49	Minneapolis	47	130	85	345	7.3
1949-50	Minneapolis	63	132	76	340	5.4
1950-51	Minneapolis	68	119	114	352	5.2
	Totals	178	381	275	1037	5.8

FERRY, ROBERT

b. May 31, 1937 Ht. 6-8 Wt. 230 College—St. Louis

Yr	Team	G	FG	FT	TP	Avg.
1959-60	St. Louis	62	144	76	364	5.9
1960-61	Detroit	79	350	189	889	11.3
1961-62	Detroit	80	411	286	1108	13.8
1962-63	Detroit	79	426	220	1072	13.6
1963-64	Detroit	74	298	186	782	10.6
1964-65	Baltimore	77	143	122	408	5.3
1965-66	Baltimore	66	188	105	481	7.3
1966-67	Baltimore	51	132	70	334	6.5
1967-68	Baltimore	59	128	73	329	5.6
1968-69	Baltimore	7	5	3	13	1.0
	Totals	634	2225	1330	5780	9.1

FEUTSCH, HERMAN (Dutch)

b. July 6, 1921 Ht. 6-0 Wt. 170 College—UCLA

Yr	Team	G	FG	FT	TP	Avg.
1945-46	Cleveland NL	27	82	61	225	8.3
1947-48	Baltimore	42	42	25	109	2.6
	Totals	69	124	86	334	4.8

FIELDS, BOBBY

b. Oct. 20, 1949 Ht. 6-3 Wt. 175 College—LaSalle

Yr	Team	G	FG	FT	TP	Avg.
1971-72	Utah ABA	22	20 (2)	8	54	2.5

FILIPEK, RON

b. Feb. 5, 1944 Ht. 6-5 Wt. 210 Coll.—Tennessee Tech

Yr	Team	G	FG	FT	TP	Avg.
1967-68	Philadelphia	19	18	7	43	2.3

FILLMORE, GREG

b. March 7, 1947 Ht. 7-1 Wt. 250 Coll.—Cheyney State

Yr	Team	G	FG	FT	TP	Avg.
1970-71	New York	39	45	13	103	2.6
1971-72	New York	10	7	1	15	1.5
	Totals	49	52	14	118	2.4

FINCH, LARRY

b. Feb. 16, 1951 Ht. 6-2 Wt. 195 College—Memphis St.

Yr	Team	G	FG	FT	TP	Avg.
1973-74	Memphis ABA	65	157 (7)	108	443	6.8
1974-75	Memphis ABA	64	264 (20)	115	663	10.5
	Totals	128	421 (27)	223	1106	8.6

FINKEL, HENRY

b. April 20, 1942 Ht. 7-0 Wt. 240 College—Dayton

Yr	Team	G	FG	FT	TP	Avg.
1966-67	Los Angeles	27	17	7	41	1.5
1967-68	San Diego	53	242	131	615	11.6
1968-69	San Diego	35	49	31	129	3.7
1969-70	Boston	80	310	156	776	9.7
1970-71	Boston	80	214	93	521	6.5
1971-72	Boston	78	103	43	249	3.2
1972-73	Boston	76	78	28	184	2.4
1973-74	Boston	60	60	28	148	2.5
1974-75	Boston	62	52	23	127	2.0
	Totals	551	1125	540	2790	5.1

FINN, DANIEL

b. May 27, 1928 Ht. 6-1 Wt. 185 Coll.—St. John's (NY)

Yr	Team	G	FG	FT	TP	Avg.
1952-53	Philadelphia	31	135	99	369	11.9
1953-54	Philadelphia	68	170	126	466	6.9
1954-55	Philadelphia	43	77	53	207	4.8
	Totals	142	382	278	1042	7.3

FISHER, RICK

b. Oct. 27, 1948 Ht. 6-5 Wt. 220 College—Colorado St.

Yr	Team	G	FG	FT	TP	Avg.
1971-72	Utah-Fla. ABA	12	18 (0)	1	37	3.1

FITZGERALD, RICHARD

b. 1921 Ht. 6-5 Wt. 175

Yr	Team	G	FG	FT	TP	Avg.
1946-47	Toronto	60	118	41	277	4.6
1947-48	Providence	1	0	0	0	0.0
	Totals	61	118	41	277	4.5

FITZGERALD, ROBERT

b. March 14, 1923 Ht. 6-5 Wt. 190 College—Seton Hall and Fordham

Yr	Team	G	FG	FT	TP	Avg.
1945-46	Rochester NL	10	9	15	33	3.3
1946-47	Tor.-N.Y.	50	70	81	221	4.4
1947-48	Syracuse NL	1	0	0	0	0.0
1948-49	Rochester	18	6	7	19	1.1
	Totals	79	85	103	273	3.5

Yr	Team	G	FG	FT	TP	Avg.

FLEISHMAN, JERRY

b. Feb. 14, 1922 Ht. 6-2 Wt. 190 Coll.—N.Y.U.

1946-47	Philadelphia	59	97	69	263	4.5
1947-48	Philadelphia	46	119	95	333	7.2
1948-49	Philadelphia	59	123	77	323	5.5
1949-50	Philadelphia	65	102	93	297	4.6
1952-53	Phila.-N.Y.	33	100	96	296	9.0
	Totals	262	541	430	1512	5.8

FLEMING, AL

b. April 5, 1954 Ht. 6-7 Wt. 215 College—Arizona

1977-78	Seattle	20	15	10	40	2.0

FLEMING, EDWARD

b. July 25, 1933 Ht. 6-3 Wt. 190 College—Niagara

1955-56	Rochester	71	306	277	889	12.5
1956-57	Rochester	51	109	139	357	7.0
1957-58	Minneapolis	72	226	181	633	8.8
1958-59	Minneapolis	71	162	137	461	6.5
1959-60	Minneapolis	27	59	53	171	6.3
	Totals	292	862	787	2511	8.6

FLYNN, MIKE

b. July 3, 1953 Ht. 6-3 Wt. 190 College—Kentucky

1975-76	Indiana ABA	67	141 (25)	64	421	6.3
1976-77	Indiana	73	250	101	601	8.2
1977-78	Indiana	71	120	55	295	4.2
	Totals	211	511 (25)	220	1317	6.2

FOGLE, LARRY

b. March 19, 1953 Ht. 6-5 Wt. 210 College—Canisius

1975-76	New York	2	1	0	2	1.0

FOLEY, JACK (The Shot)

b. Nov. 17, 1940 Ht. 6-5 Wt. 185 College—Holy Cross

1962-63	Boston-N.Y.	11	20	13	53	4.8

FONTAINE, LEVI

b. Nov. 1, 1948 Ht. 6-4 Wt. 190 Coll.—Maryland State

1970-71	San Francisco	35	53	28	134	3.8

FORD, BOB

b. 1950 Ht. 6-7 Wt. 228 College—Purdue

1972-73	Memphis ABA	9	5 (0)	4	14	1.6

FORD, JAKE

b. April 29, 1946 Ht. 6-3 Wt. 181 Coll.—Maryland St.

1970-71	Seattle	5	9	16	34	6.8
1971-72	Seattle	26	33	26	92	3.5
	Totals	31	42	42	126	4.1

FORMAN, DON

b. Jan. 17, 1926 Ht. 6-1 Wt. 175 College—N.Y.U.

1948-49	Minneapolis	44	68	43	179	4.1

FOSTER, FRED

b. March 18, 1946 Ht. 6-5 Wt. 210 Coll.—Miami (Ohio)

1968-69	Cincinnati	56	74	43	191	3.4
1969-70	Cincinnati	73	461	176	1098	15.0
1970-71	Cincinnati	67	148	73	369	5.5
1971-72	Philadelphia	74	347	185	879	11.9

Yr	Team	G	FG	FT	TP	Avg.
1972-73	Detroit	63	243	61	547	8.7
1973-74	Cleveland	58	112	54	278	4.8
1974-75	Cleveland	73	217	69	503	6.9
1975-76	Buffalo	59	99	30	228	3.9
	Totals	523	1701	691	4093	7.8

FOSTER, JIMMY

b. Dec. 16, 1951 Ht. 6-1 Wt. 175 College—Connecticut

1974-75	St. Louis ABA	41	78 (0)	27	183	4.5
1975-76	Denver ABA	48	53 (1)	39	148	3.1
	Totals	89	131 (1)	66	331	3.7

FOUST, LARRY

b. June 24, 1928 Ht. 6-9 Wt. 250 College—LaSalle

1950-51	Ft. Wayne	68	327	261	915	13.5
1951-52	Ft. Wayne	66	390	267	1047	15.9
1952-53	Ft. Wayne	67	311	336	958	14.3
1953-54	Ft. Wayne	72	376	338	1090	15.1
1954-55	Ft. Wayne	70	398	393	1189	17.0
1955-56	Ft. Wayne	72	367	432	1166	16.2
1956-57	Ft. Wayne	61	243	273	759	12.4
1957-58	Minneapolis	72	391	428	1210	16.8
1958-59	Minneapolis	72	301	280	882	12.3
1959-60	Minneapolis-St. Louis	72	312	253	877	12.2
1960-61	St. Louis	68	194	164	552	8.1
1961-62	St. Louis	57	204	145	553	9.7
	Totals	817	3814	3570	11198	13.7

FOWLER, CALVIN

b. 1940 Ht. 6-0½ Wt. 175 College—St. Francis (Pa.)

1969-70	Carolina ABA	78	124 (7)	74	343	4.4

FOWLER, JERRY

b. 1926 Ht. 6-8 Wt. 236 College—Missouri

1951-52	Milwaukee	6	4	1	9	1.5

FOX, HAROLD

b. Aug. 29, 1949 Ht. 6-2 Wt. 175 College—Jacksonville

1972-73	Buffalo	10	12	7	31	3.1

FOX, JIM

b. May 7, 1943 Ht. 6-10 Wt. 230 Coll.—S. Carolina

1967-68	Cin.-Detroit	55	66	66	198	3.6
1968-69	Det.-Phoenix	76	318	191	827	10.9
1969-70	Phoenix	81	413	218	1044	12.9
1970-71	Chicago	82	280	239	799	9.7
1971-72	Chi.-Cin.	81	354	227	935	11.5
1972-73	Seattle	74	316	214	846	11.4
1973-74	Seattle	78	322	241	885	11.3
1974-75	Seattle	75	253	170	676	9.0
1975-76	Milwaukee	70	105	62	272	3.9
1976-77	N.Y. Nets	71	184	95	463	6.5
	Totals	743	2611	1723	6945	9.3

FRANKEL, NAT

b. 1914 Ht. 6-2 Wt. 195

1939-40	Detroit NL	27	73	55	201	7.4
1946-47	Pittsburgh	6	4	8	16	2.7
	Totals	33	77	63	217	6.6

Yr	Team	G	FG	FT	TP	Avg.

FRANKLIN, BILL

b. Oct. 19, 1949 Ht. 6-7 Wt. 225 College—Purdue

Yr	Team	G	FG	FT	TP	Avg.
1973-74	Virginia ABA	73	216 (2)	107	545	7.5
1974-75	San Antonio ABA	24	32 (0)	15	79	3.3
1975-76	San Antonio ABA	10	12 (0)	9	33	3.3
	Totals	107	260 (2)	131	657	6.1

FRANZ, RON

b. Oct. 20, 1945 Ht. 6-7 Wt. 207 College—Kansas

Yr	Team	G	FG	FT	TP	Avg.
1967-68	Oakland ABA	74	329 (25)	197	930	12.6
1968-69	New Orleans ABA	73	370 (11)	286	1059	14.5
1969-70	New Orleans ABA	55	224 (7)	163	632	11.5
1970-71	Floridians ABA	67	302 (7)	188	813	12.1
1971-72	Floridians ABA	74	340 (2)	171	857	11.6
1972-73	Mem.-Dal. ABA	60	147 (1)	145	442	7.4
	Totals	403	1712 (53)	1150	4733	11.7

FRAZIER, WILBERT

b. Aug. 24, 1942 Ht. 6-7 Wt. 210 College—Grambling

Yr	Team	G	FG	FT	TP	Avg.
1965-66	San Francisco	2	0	1	1	0.5
1967-68	Houston ABA	76	357 (1)	228	945	12.4
1968-69	New York ABA	75	217 (0)	120	554	7.4
	Totals	153	574 (1)	349	1500	9.8

FREEMAN, DON

b. July 18, 1944 Ht. 6-3 Wt. 185 College—Illinois

Yr	Team	G	FG	FT	TP	Avg.
1967-68	Minnesota ABA	69	414 (0)	296	1124	16.3
1968-69	Miami ABA	78	649 (2)	420	1724	22.1
1969-70	Miami ABA	79	761 (5)	626	2173	27.4
1970-71	Utah-Tex. ABA	66	596 (0)	367	1559	23.6
1971-72	Dallas ABA	72	626 (2)	475	1733	24.1
1972-73	Indiana ABA	77	410 (2)	277	1103	14.3
1973-74	Indiana ABA	66	383 (0)	177	943	14.3
1974-75	San Antonio ABA	77	453 (0)	289	1195	15.5
1975-76	Los Angeles	64	263	163	689	10.8
	Totals	648	4555 (11)	3090	12233	18.9

FREEMAN, GARY

b. July 25, 1948 Ht. 6-9 Wt. 208 Coll.—Oregon State

Yr	Team	G	FG	FT	TP	Avg.
1970-71	Milw.-Cleve.	52	69	29	167	3.2

FREEMAN, ROD

b. May 11, 1950 Ht. 6-7 Wt. 225 College—Vanderbilt

Yr	Team	G	FG	FT	TP	Avg.
1973-74	Philadelphia	35	39	28	106	3.0

FREY, FRIDO

b. Oct. 26, 1921 Ht. 6-2 Wt. 195 College—St. John's and Long Island U.

Yr	Team	G	FG	FT	TP	Avg.
1946-47	New York	23	28	32	88	3.8

FRIEND, LARRY

b. April 14, 1935 Ht. 6-4 Wt. 186 College—California

Yr	Team	G	FG	FT	TP	Avg.
1957-58	New York	44	74	27	175	4.0

FRINK, PAT

b. Feb. 18, 1945 Ht. 6-4 Wt. 195 College—Colorado

Yr	Team	G	FG	FT	TP	Avg.
1968-69	Cincinnati	48	50	23	123	2.6

FRITSCHE, JAMES

b. Dec. 10, 1931 Ht. 6-8 Wt. 210 College—Hamline

Yr	Team	G	FG	FT	TP	Avg.
1953-54	Minn.-Balt.	68	116	49	281	4.1
1954-55	Ft. Wayne	16	16	13	45	2.8
	Totals	84	132	62	326	3.9

FRYER, BERNIE

b. Dec. 25, 1949 Ht. 6-3 Wt. 185 College—Brigham Young

Yr	Team	G	FG	FT	TP	Avg.
1973-74	Portland	80	226	107	559	7.0
1974-75	New Orleans	31	47	33	127	4.1
1974-75	St. Louis ABA	9	24 (0)	22	70	7.8
	Totals	120	297 (0)	162	756	6.3

FUCARINO, FRANK

b. July 24, 1920 Ht. 6-2 Wt. 175 College—L.I.U.

Yr	Team	G	FG	FT	TP	Avg.
1946-47	Toronto	28	53	34	140	5.0

FULKS, JOSEPH (Jumpin' Joe)

b. 1921 Ht. 6-5 Wt. 190 College—Murray State
d. March 21, 1976

Yr	Team	G	FG	FT	TP	Avg.
1946-47	Philadelphia	60	475	439	1389	23.2
1947-48	Philadelphia	43	326	297	949	22.1
1948-49	Philadelphia	60	529	502	1560	26.0
1949-50	Philadelphia	68	336	293	965	14.2
1950-51	Philadelphia	66	429	378	1236	18.7
1951-52	Philadelphia	61	336	250	922	15.1
1952-53	Philadelphia	70	332	168	832	11.9
1953-54	Philadelphia	61	61	28	150	2.5
	Totals	489	2824	2355	8003	16.4

FULLER, CARL

b. Jan. 10, 1946 Ht. 6-9 Wt. 225 College—Bethune-Cookman

Yr	Team	G	FG	FT	TP	Avg.
1970-71	Floridians ABA	70	170 (0)	72	412	5.9
1971-72	Fla.-Mem. ABA	6	6 (0)	9	21	2.5
	Totals	76	176 (0)	81	433	5.7

GABOR, WILLIAM (Bullet)

b. May 13, 1922 Ht. 5-11½ Wt. 180 College—Syracuse

Yr	Team	G	FG	FT	TP	Avg.
1948-49	Syracuse NL	55	113	124	350	6.4
1949-50	Syracuse	56	226	157	609	10.9
1950-51	Syracuse	61	255	179	689	11.3
1951-52	Syracuse	57	173	142	488	8.6
1952-53	Syracuse	69	215	217	647	9.4
1953-54	Syracuse	61	204	139	547	9.0
1954-55	Syracuse	3	7	3	17	5.7
	Totals	362	1193	961	3347	9.2

Yr	Team	G	FG	FT	TP	Avg.

GAINER, ELMER

b. 1919 Ht. 6-6 Wt. 195 College—DePaul

Yr	Team	G	FG	FT	TP	Avg.
1941-42	Fort Wayne NL	24	36	28	100	4.2
1943-44	Sheboygan NL	22	15	20	50	2.3
1944-45	Chicago NL	29	44	38	126	4.3
1945-46	Chicago NL	5	2	2	6	1.2
1946-47	Anderson	43	77	59	213	5.0
1947-48	Baltimore	5	1	3	5	1.0
1948-49	Waterloo NL	36	33	30	96	2.7
1949-50	Waterloo NL	15	9	6	24	1.6
	Totals	179	217	186	620	3.5

GAINES, BILL

College—East Texas State

1968-69	Houston ABA	1	1 (0)	0	2	2.0

GAINES, DAVE

Ht. 6-1 Wt. 170 College—LeMoyne

1967-68	Kentucky ABA	3	3 (1)	1	10	3.3

GALLATIN, HARRY (The Horse)

b. April 26, 1928 Ht. 6-6 Wt. 215 Coll.—Northeast Mo.

1948-49	New York	52	157	120	434	8.3
1949-50	New York	68	263	277	803	11.8
1950-51	New York	66	293	259	845	12.8
1951-52	New York	66	233	275	741	11.2
1952-53	New York	70	282	301	865	12.4
1953-54	New York	72	258	433	949	13.2
1954-55	New York	72	330	393	1053	14.6
1955-56	New York	72	322	358	1002	13.9
1956-57	New York	72	332	415	1079	15.0
1957-58	Detroit	72	340	392	1072	14.9
	Totals	682	2810	3223	8843	13.0

GAMBEE, DAVE

b. April 16, 1937 Ht. 6-6 Wt. 215 Coll.—Oregon State

1958-59	St. Louis	2	1	0	2	1.0
1959-60	St. L.-Cin.	61	117	69	303	5.0
1960-61	Syracuse	79	397	291	1085	13.7
1961-62	Syracuse	80	477	384	1338	16.7
1962-63	Syracuse	60	235	199	669	11.2
1963-64	Philadelphia	41	149	151	449	11.0
1964-65	Philadelphia	80	356	299	1011	12.6
1965-66	Philadelphia	72	168	159	495	6.9
1966-67	Philadelphia	63	150	107	407	6.5
1967-68	San Diego	80	375	321	1071	13.4
1968-69	Milw.-Det.	59	210	159	579	9.8
1969-70	San Francisco	73	185	156	526	7.2
	Totals	750	2820	2295	7935	10.6

GANTT, ROBERT

b. 1923 Ht. 6-4 Wt. 205 College—Duke

1946-47	Washington	23	29	13	71	3.1
1947-48	Sheboygan NL	6	4	3	11	1.8
	Totals	29	33	16	82	2.8

GARDNER, CHARLES

Ht. 6-8 Wt. 205 College—Colorado

1967-68	Denver ABA	42	71 (0)	55	197	4.7

GARDNER, EARL

b. 1926 Ht. 6-3 Wt. 200 College—DePaul

1948-49	Minneapolis	50	38	13	89	1.8

GARDNER, KEN

b. 1950 Ht. 6-5 Wt. 205 College—Utah

1975-76	Utah ABA	9	6 (0)	2	14	1.6

GARDNER, VERN

b. May 14, 1925 Ht. 6-5 Wt. 200 College—Utah

1949-50	Philadelphia	63	313	227	853	13.5
1950-51	Philadelphia	61	129	69	327	5.4
1951-52	Philadelphia	27	72	15	159	5.9
	Totals	151	514	311	1339	8.9

GARFINKEL, JACK (Dutch)

b. June 13, 1918 Ht. 6-0 Wt. 190 College—St. John's

1945-46	Rochester NL	18	14	6	34	1.9
1946-47	Rochester NL	10	5	3	13	1.3
1946-47	Boston	40	81	17	179	4.5
1947-48	Boston	43	114	35	263	6.1
1948-49	Boston	9	12	10	34	3.8
	Totals	120	226	71	523	4.4

GARMAKER, DICK

b. Oct. 29, 1932 Ht. 6-3½ Wt. 206 College—Minnesota

1955-56	Minneapolis	68	138	112	388	5.7
1956-57	Minneapolis	72	406	365	1177	16.3
1957-58	Minneapolis	68	390	314	1094	16.1
1958-59	Minneapolis	72	350	284	984	13.7
1959-60	Minn.-N.Y.	70	323	203	849	12.1
1960-61	New York	71	415	275	1105	15.6
	Totals	421	2022	1553	5597	13.3

GARNER, BILL

Ht. 6-10 Wt. 220 College—Portland

1967-68	Anaheim ABA	53	28 (0)	25	81	1.5

GARRETT, ELDO (Dick)

b. Jan. 31, 1947 Ht. 6-3 Wt. 185 Coll.—Southern Ill.

1969-70	Los Angeles	73	354	138	846	11.6
1970-71	Buffalo	75	373	218	964	12.9
1971-72	Buffalo	73	325	136	786	10.8
1972-73	Buffalo	78	341	96	778	10.0
1973-74	N.Y.-Mil.	40	43	15	101	2.5
	Totals	339	1436	603	3475	10.3

GARRETT, ROWLAND

b. July 16, 1950 Ht. 6-6 Wt. 212 Coll.—Florida State

1972-73	Chicago	35	52	21	125	3.6
1973-74	Chicago	41	68	21	157	3.8
1974-75	Chicago	70	228	77	533	7.6
1975-76	Chi.-Cleve.	55	108	53	269	4.9
1976-77	Cleve.-Milw.	62	106	41	253	4.1
	Totals	263	562	213	1337	5.1

GARVIN, JIM

b. Feb. 5, 1950 Ht. 6-7 Wt. 200 College—Boston U.

1973-74	Boston	6	1	0	2	0.3

Yr	Team	G	FG	FT	TP	Avg.

GATES, FRANK (Needle)

b. April 12, 1920 Ht. 6-0 Wt. 167 Coll.—S. Houston St.

Yr	Team	G	FG	FT	TP	Avg.
1946-47	And.-Ft. W. NL	32	68	30	166	5.2
1948-49	Anderson NL	64	150	78	378	5.9
1949-50	Anderson	64	113	61	287	4.5
	Totals	160	331	169	831	5.2

GAYDA, EDWARD

b. May 11, 1927 Ht. 6-4 Wt. 210 Coll.—Washington St.

Yr	Team	G	FG	FT	TP	Avg.
1950-51	Tri-Cities	14	18	18	54	3.9

GEORGE, JACK

b. Nov. 13, 1928 Ht. 6-3 Wt. 190 College—La Salle

Yr	Team	G	FG	FT	TP	Avg.
1953-54	Philadelphia	71	259	157	675	9.5
1954-55	Philadelphia	68	291	192	774	11.4
1955-56	Philadelphia	72	352	296	1000	13.9
1956-57	Philadelphia	67	253	200	706	10.5
1957-58	Philadelphia	72	232	178	642	8.9
1958-59	Phil.-N.Y.	71	233	153	619	8.7
1959-60	New York	69	250	155	655	9.5
1960-61	New York	16	31	20	82	5.1
	Totals	506	1901	1351	5153	10.2

GETCHELL, GORHAM

b. Aug. 14, 1920 Ht. 6-6 Wt. 215 College—Temple

Yr	Team	G	FG	FT	TP	Avg.
1946-47	Pittsburgh	16	0	5	5	0.3

GIBBS, DICK

b. Dec. 20, 1948 Ht. 6-5 Wt. 210 Coll.—Texas El Paso

Yr	Team	G	FG	FT	TP	Avg.
1971-72	Houston	64	90	55	235	3.7
1972-73	Hou.-K.C.-O.	67	80	47	207	3.1
1973-74	Seattle	71	302	162	766	10.8
1974-75	Washington	59	74	48	196	3.3
1975-76	Buffalo	72	129	77	335	4.7
	Totals	333	675	389	1739	5.2

GIBSON, DEE (Gibby)

b. 1923 Ht. 5-11 Wt. 175 College—Western Kentucky

Yr	Team	G	FG	FT	TP	Avg.
1948-49	Tri-Cities NL	64	94	113	301	4.7
1949-50	Tri-Cities	44	77	127	281	6.4
	Totals	108	171	240	582	5.4

GIBSON, MEL

b. Dec. 30, 1940 Ht. 6-3 Wt. 180 College—W. Carolina

Yr	Team	G	FG	FT	TP	Avg.
1963-64	Los Angeles	9	6	1	13	1.4

GIBSON, WARD (Hoot)

b. Dec. 6, 1921 Ht. 6-5 Wt. 215 College—Creighton

Yr	Team	G	FG	FT	TP	Avg.
1948-49	Den.-Tri-C. NL	62	291	223	805	12.8
1949-50	Bos.-Wat.	32	67	42	176	5.5
	Totals	94	358	265	981	10.4

GILLESPIE, JACK

College—Montana State

Yr	Team	G	FG	FT	TP	Avg.
1969-70	New York ABA	2	0 (0)	2	2	1.0

GILLETTE, GENE

b. 1922 Ht. 6-2 Wt. 201 College—St. Mary's (Calif.)

Yr	Team	G	FG	FT	TP	Avg.
1946-47	Washington	14	1	6	8	0.6

GILLIAM, HERM

b. May 5, 1946 Ht. 6-3 Wt. 190 College—Purdue

Yr	Team	G	FG	FT	TP	Avg.
1969-70	Cincinnati	57	179	68	426	7.5
1970-71	Buffalo	80	378	142	898	11.2
1971-72	Atlanta	82	345	145	835	10.2
1972-73	Atlanta	76	471	123	1065	14.0
1973-74	Atlanta	62	384	106	874	14.1
1974-75	Atlanta	60	314	94	722	12.0
1975-76	Seattle	81	299	90	688	8.5
1976-77	Portland	80	326	92	744	9.3
	Totals	578	2696	860	6252	10.8

GILMORE, WALT

b. Feb. 27, 1947 Ht. 6-6 Wt. 235 Coll.—Fort Valley St.

Yr	Team	G	FG	FT	TP	Avg.
1970-71	Portland	27	23	12	58	2.1

GILMUR, CHARLES

b. Aug. 13, 1922 Ht. 6-4 Wt. 225 College—Washington

Yr	Team	G	FG	FT	TP	Avg.
1946-47	Chicago	51	76	26	178	3.5
1947-48	Chicago	48	181	97	459	9.6
1948-49	Chicago	56	110	66	286	5.1
1949-50	Chi.-Wash.	68	127	164	418	6.1
1950-51	Washington	16	17	17	51	3.2
	Totals	239	511	370	1392	5.8

GLAMACK, GEORGE (Blind Bomber)

b. June 17, 1919 Ht. 6-9 Wt. 230 College—N. Carolina

Yr	Team	G	FG	FT	TP	Avg.
1941-42	Akron NL	24	87	82	256	10.7
1945-46	Rochester NL	34	151	115	417	12.3
1946-47	Rochester	44	141	90	372	8.5
1947-48	Indianapolis NL	57	215	162	592	10.4
1948-49	Indianapolis	11	30	42	102	9.3
1948-49	Hammond NL	43	169	163	501	11.7
	Totals	213	793	654	2240	10.5

GLICK, NORMIE

b. Nov. 10, 1927 Ht. 6-7 Wt. 190 Coll.—Loyola (Calif.)

Yr	Team	G	FG	FT	TP	Avg.
1949-50	Minneapolis	1	1	0	2	2.0

GLOVER, CLARENCE

b. Nov. 1, 1947 Ht. 6-8 Wt. 210 College—W. Kentucky

Yr	Team	G	FG	FT	TP	Avg.
1971-72	Boston	25	25	15	65	2.6

GOLA, TOM

b. Jan. 13, 1933 Ht. 6-6 Wt. 205 College—LaSalle

Yr	Team	G	FG	FT	TP	Avg.
1955-56	Philadelphia	68	244	244	732	10.8
1957-58	Philadelphia	59	295	223	813	13.8
1958-59	Philadelphia	64	310	281	901	14.1
1959-60	Philadelphia	75	426	270	1122	15.0
1960-61	Philadelphia	74	420	210	1050	14.2
1961-62	Philadelphia	60	322	176	820	13.7
1962-63	S.F.-N.Y.	73	363	170	896	12.3
1963-64	New York	74	258	154	670	9.1
1964-65	New York	77	204	133	541	7.0
1965-66	New York	74	122	82	326	4.4
	Totals	698	2964	1943	7871	11.3

GOLDFADEN, BEN

b. Sept. 6, 1913 Ht. 6-3 Wt. 185 Coll.—G. Washington

Yr	Team	G	FG	FT	TP	Avg.
1946-47	Washington	2	0	2	2	1.0

Yr	Team	G	FG	FT	TP	Avg.

GOODWIN, WILFRED (Pop)

b. 1921 Ht. 6-2 Wt. 203

Yr	Team	G	FG	FT	TP	Avg.
1945-46	Sheboygan NL	2	1	1	3	1.5
1946-47	Providence	55	98	60	256	4.7
1947-48	Providence	24	36	19	91	3.8
	Totals	81	135	80	350	4.3

GORDON, PAUL

b. April 8, 1927 Ht. 6-3 Wt. 195 College—Notre Dame

Yr	Team	G	FG	FT	TP	Avg.
1949-50	Baltimore	4	0	3	3	0.8

GOTTLIEB, LEO

b. 1920 Ht. 5-11 Wt. 180

Yr	Team	G	FG	FT	TP	Avg.
1946-47	New York	57	149	36	334	5.9
1947-48	New York	27	59	13	131	4.9
	Totals	84	208	49	465	5.5

GOVAN, GERALD

b. Jan. 2, 1942 Ht. 6-10 Wt. 220 College—St. Mary of Plains

Yr	Team	G	FG	FT	TP	Avg.
1967-68	New Orleans ABA	78	155 (1)	79	392	5.0
1968-69	New Orleans ABA	77	210 (1)	134	567	7.2
1969-70	New Orleans ABA	84	421 (1)	208	1053	12.5
1970-71	Memphis ABA	84	295 (1)	119	712	8.6
1971-72	Memphis ABA	83	277 (0)	162	716	8.6
1972-73	Utah ABA	84	229 (0)	81	539	6.4
1973-74	Utah ABA	83	255 (0)	73	583	7.0
1974-75	Utah ABA	84	238 (1)	83	562	6.7
1975-76	Virginia ABA	24	57 (0)	23	137	5.7
	Totals	681	2137 (5)	962	5251	7.7

GOVEDARICA, BATO

b. 1928 Ht. 5-11 Wt. 185 College—DePaul

Yr	Team	G	FG	FT	TP	Avg.
1953-54	Syracuse	23	25	25	75	3.3

GRABOSKI, JOE (Grabbo)

b. Jan. 15, 1930 Ht. 6-8 Wt. 230

Yr	Team	G	FG	FT	TP	Avg.
1948-49	Chicago	45	54	17	125	2.8
1949-50	Chicago	57	75	53	203	3.6
1951-52	Indianapolis	66	320	264	904	13.7
1952-53	Indianapolis	69	272	350	894	13.0
1953-54	Philadelphia	71	354	236	944	13.3
1954-55	Philadelphia	70	373	208	954	13.6
1955-56	Philadelphia	72	397	240	1034	14.4
1956-57	Philadelphia	72	390	252	1032	14.3
1957-58	Philadelphia	72	341	227	909	12.6
1958-59	Philadelphia	72	394	270	1058	14.7
1959-60	Philadelphia	73	217	131	565	7.7
1960-61	Philadelphia	68	169	127	465	6.8
1961-62	St. Louis-Chicago-Syracuse	38	77	39	193	5.1
	Totals	845	3433	2414	9280	11.0

GRAHAM, CAL

Ht. 6-2½ Wt. 195 College—Gannon

Yr	Team	G	FG	FT	TP	Avg.
1967-68	Pittsburgh ABA	8	4 (0)	5	13	1.6

GRAHAM, MAL

b. Feb. 23, 1945 Ht. 6-1 Wt. 185 College—N.Y.U.

Yr	Team	G	FG	FT	TP	Avg.
1967-68	Boston	48	117	56	290	6.0
1968-69	Boston	22	13	11	37	1.7
	Totals	70	130	67	327	4.7

GRANT, HARRY (Bud)

b. May 20, 1927 Ht. 6-3 Wt. 193 College—Minnesota

Yr	Team	G	FG	FT	TP	Avg.
1949-50	Minneapolis	35	42	7	91	2.6
1950-51	Minneapolis	61	53	52	158	2.6
	Totals	96	95	59	249	2.6

GRANT, TRAVIS

b. Jan. 1, 1950 Ht. 6-7 Wt. 215 Coll.—Kentucky State

Yr	Team	G	FG	FT	TP	Avg.
1972-73	Los Angeles	33	51	23	125	3.8
1973-74	Los Angeles	3	1	1	3	1.0
1973-74	San Diego ABA	56	356 (1)	141	856	15.3
1974-75	San Diego ABA	53	575 (1)	182	1335	25.2
1975-76	Ken.-Ind. ABA	56	198 (0)	52	448	8.0
	Totals	201	1181 (2)	399	2767	13.8

GRATE, DON

b. Aug. 27, 1922 Ht. 6-2½ Wt. 185 College—Ohio State

Yr	Team	G	FG	FT	TP	Avg.
1947-48	Indianapolis NL	11	14	3	31	2.8
1949-50	Sheboygan	2	1	2	4	2.0
	Totals	13	15	5	35	2.7

GRAY, GARY

b. 1945 Ht. 6-1 Wt. 185 College—Oklahoma City

Yr	Team	G	FG	FT	TP	Avg.
1967-68	Cincinnati	44	49	7	105	2.4

GRAY, LEONARD

b. Dec. 19, 1951 Ht. 6-8 Wt. 240 Coll.—Long Beach St.

Yr	Team	G	FG	FT	TP	Avg.
1974-75	Seattle	75	378	104	860	11.5
1975-76	Seattle	66	394	126	914	13.8
1976-77	Sea.-Wash.	83	258	118	634	7.6
	Totals	224	1030	348	2408	10.8

GRAY, WYNDOL

b. March 20, 1922 Ht. 6-1 Wt. 175 College—Harvard and Bowling Green

Yr	Team	G	FG	FT	TP	Avg.
1946-47	Boston	55	139	72	350	6.4
1947-48	Prov.-St. L.	12	6	1	13	1.1
	Totals	67	145	73	363	5.4

GREACEN, BOB

b. Sept. 15, 1947 Ht. 6-7 Wt. 210 College—Rutgers

Yr	Team	G	FG	FT	TP	Avg.
1969-70	Milwaukee	41	44	18	106	2.6
1970-71	Milwaukee	2	1	3	5	2.5
1971-72	New York ABA	4	1 (0)	0	2	0.5
	Totals	47	46 (0)	21	113	2.4

GREEN, JOHN

b. Dec. 8, 1933 Ht. 6-5 Wt. 200 Coll.—Michigan State

Yr	Team	G	FG	FT	TP	Avg.
1959-60	New York	69	209	63	481	7.0
1960-61	New York	78	326	145	797	10.2
1961-62	New York	80	507	261	1275	16.1

Yr	Team	G	FG	FT	TP	Avg.
1962-63	New York	80	582	280	1444	18.1
1963-64	New York	80	482	195	1159	14.5
1964-65	New York	78	346	165	857	11.0
1965-66	N.Y.-Balt.	79	358	202	918	11.6
1966-67	Baltimore	61	203	96	502	8.2
1967-68	San Diego-Philadelphia	77	310	139	759	10.0
1968-69	Philadelphia	74	146	57	349	4.7
1969-70	Cincinnati	78	481	254	1216	15.6
1970-71	Cincinnati	75	502	248	1252	16.7
1971-72	Cincinnati	82	331	141	803	9.8
1972-73	K.C.-Omaha	66	190	89	469	7.1
	Totals	1057	4973	2335	12281	11.6

GREEN, LAMAR

b. March 22, 1947 Ht. 6-7 Wt. 210 Coll.—Morehead St.

Yr	Team	G	FG	FT	TP	Avg.
1969-70	Phoenix	58	101	41	243	4.2
1970-71	Phoenix	68	167	64	398	5.9
1971-72	Phoenix	67	133	66	332	5.0
1972-73	Phoenix	80	224	89	537	6.7
1973-74	Phoenix	72	129	38	296	4.1
1974-75	Virginia ABA	51	115 (0)	40	270	5.3
	Totals	447	869	338	2076	4.6

GREEN, LUTHER

b. Nov. 13, 1946 Ht. 6-7 Wt. 190 Coll.—L.I.U.

Yr	Team	G	FG	FT	TP	Avg.
1969-70	New York ABA	59	114 (0)	55	283	4.8
1970-71	New York ABA	26	40 (0)	18	98	3.8
	Totals	85	154 (0)	73	381	4.5

GREEN, SIHUGO

b. Aug. 20, 1934 Ht. 6-2 Wt. 185 College—Duquesne

Yr	Team	G	FG	FT	TP	Avg.
1956-57	Rochester	13	50	49	149	11.5
1957-58	Cincinnati	In Military Service				
1958-59	Cincinnati-St. Louis	46	146	104	396	8.6
1959-60	St. Louis	70	159	111	429	6.1
1960-61	St. Louis	76	263	174	700	9.2
1961-62	St. L.-Chi.	71	341	218	900	12.7
1962-63	Chicago	73	322	209	853	11.7
1963-64	Baltimore	75	287	198	772	10.3
1964-65	Baltimore	70	152	101	405	5.8
1965-66	Boston	10	12	8	32	3.2
	Totals	504	1732	1172	4636	9.2

GREENSPAN, GERALD (Jerry)

b. Nov. 22, 1941 Ht. 6-5 Wt. 195 College—Maryland

Yr	Team	G	FG	FT	TP	Avg.
1963-64	Philadelphia	20	32	34	98	4.9
1964-65	Philadelphia	5	8	8	24	4.8
	Totals	25	40	42	122	4.9

GREER, HAL

b. June 26, 1936 Ht. 6-2 Wt. 176 College—Marshall

Yr	Team	G	FG	FT	TP	Avg.
1958-59	Syracuse	68	308	137	753	11.1
1959-60	Syracuse	70	388	148	924	13.2
1960-61	Syracuse	79	623	305	1551	19.6
1961-62	Syracuse	71	644	331	1619	22.8
1962-63	Syracuse	80	600	362	1562	19.5
1963-64	Philadelphia	80	715	435	1865	23.3
1964-65	Philadelphia	70	539	335	1413	20.2
1965-66	Philadelphia	80	703	413	1819	22.7
1966-67	Philadelphia	80	699	367	1765	22.1
1967-68	Philadelphia	82	777	422	1976	24.1
1968-69	Philadelphia	82	732	432	1896	23.1
1969-70	Philadelphia	80	705	352	1762	22.0
1970-71	Philadelphia	81	591	326	1508	18.6
1971-72	Philadelphia	81	389	181	959	11.8
1972-73	Philadelphia	38	91	32	214	5.6
	Totals	1122	8504	4578	21586	19.2

GREGOR, GARY

b. Aug. 13, 1945 Ht. 6-7 Wt. 235 Coll.—South Carolina

Yr	Team	G	FG	FT	TP	Avg.
1968-69	Phoenix	80	400	85	885	11.1
1969-70	Atlanta	81	286	88	660	8.1
1970-71	Portland	44	181	59	421	9.6
1971-72	Portland	82	399	114	912	11.1
1972-73	Milwaukee	9	11	5	27	3.0
1972-73	New York ABA	40	98 (1)	32	231	5.8
1973-74	New York ABA	25	38 (2)	9	91	3.6
	Totals	361	1413 (3)	392	3227	8.9

GREKIN, NORMAN

b. June 22, 1930 Ht. 6-5 Wt. 180 College—LaSalle

Yr	Team	G	FG	FT	TP	Avg.
1953-54	Philadelphia	1	0	0	0	0.0

GREY, DENNIS

b. Aug. 26, 1947 Ht. 6-8 Wt. 215 Coll.—Calif. Western

Yr	Team	G	FG	FT	TP	Avg.
1968-69	Los Angeles ABA	58	184 (0)	157	525	9.1
1969-70	New York ABA	4	6 (0)	6	18	4.5
	Totals	62	190 (0)	163	543	8.8

GRIFFIN, GREG

b. Sept. 6, 1952 Ht. 6-7 Wt. 190 College—Idaho St.

Yr	Team	G	FG	FT	TP	Avg.
1977-78	Phoenix	36	61	23	145	4.0

GRIGSBY, CHUCK

b. 1930 Ht. 6-5 Wt. 190 College—Dayton

Yr	Team	G	FG	FT	TP	Avg.
1954-55	New York	7	7	2	16	2.3

GRIMSHAW, GEORGE (Woodie)

b. Sept. 24, 1919 Ht. 6-1 Wt. 185 College—Brown

Yr	Team	G	FG	FT	TP	Avg.
1946-47	Providence	21	20	21	61	2.9

GROAT, DICK

b. Nov. 4, 1930 Ht. 6-1 Wt. 185 College—Duke

Yr	Team	G	FG	FT	TP	Avg.
1952-53	Ft. Wayne	26	100	109	309	11.9

GROSSO, MIKE

b. Sept. 7, 1947 Ht. 6-9 Wt. 232 College—Louisville

Yr	Team	G	FG	FT	TP	Avg.
1971-72	Pittsburgh ABA	25	45 (0)	13	103	4.1

GROTE, JERRY

b. Dec. 28, 1940 Ht. 6-4 Wt. 216 Coll.—Loyola (Calif.)

Yr	Team	G	FG	FT	TP	Avg.
1964-65	Los Angeles	11	6	2	14	1.3

GROZA, ALEX

b. Oct. 7, 1926 Ht. 6-7 Wt. 218 College—Kentucky

Yr	Team	G	FG	FT	TP	Avg.
1949-50	Indianapolis	64	521	454	1496	23.4
1950-51	Indianapolis	66	492	445	1429	21.7
	Totals	130	1013	899	2925	22.5

GRUBAR, DICK

Ht. 6-4 Wt. 184 College—North Carolina

Yr	Team	G	FG	FT	TP	Avg.
1969-70	Indiana ABA	2	2 (0)	0	4	2.0

Yr	Team	G	FG	FT	TP	Avg.

GUARILIA, GENE

b. Sept. 13, 1927 Ht. 6-5 Wt. 220 Coll.—Potomac State and George Washington

Yr	Team	G	FG	FT	TP	Avg.
1959-60	Boston	48	58	29	145	3.0
1960-61	Boston	25	38	3	79	3.2
1961-62	Boston	46	61	41	163	3.5
1962-63	Boston	11	11	4	26	2.4
	Totals	130	168	77	413	3.2

GUERIN, RICHIE

b. May 29, 1932 Ht. 6-4 Wt. 210 College—Iona

Yr	Team	G	FG	FT	TP	Avg.
1956-57	New York	72	257	181	695	9.7
1957-58	New York	63	344	353	1041	16.5
1958-59	New York	71	443	405	1291	18.2
1959-60	New York	74	579	457	1615	21.8
1960-61	New York	79	612	496	1720	21.8
1961-62	New York	78	839	625	2303	29.5
1962-63	New York	79	596	509	1701	21.5
1963-64	N.Y.-St. L.	80	351	347	1049	13.1
1964-65	St. Louis	57	295	231	821	14.4
1965-66	St. Louis	80	414	362	1190	14.9
1966-67	St. Louis	79	394	304	1092	13.8
1968-69	Atlanta	27	47	57	151	5.6
1969-70	Atlanta	8	3	1	7	0.9
	Totals	847	5174	4328	14676	17.3

GUNTHER, COULBY

b. Feb. 5, 1924 Ht. 6-4 Wt. 190 College—Brown

Yr	Team	G	FG	FT	TP	Avg.
1946-47	Pittsburgh	52	254	226	734	14.1
1948-49	St. Louis	32	57	45	159	5.0
	Totals	84	311	271	893	10.6

GUNTHER, DAVID

b. July 22, 1937 Ht. 6-7 Wt. 220 College—Iowa

Yr	Team	G	FG	FT	TP	Avg.
1962-63	San Francisco	1	1	0	2	2.0

GUOKAS, ALBERT (Gook)

b. Aug. 7, 1925 Ht. 6-5½ Wt. 200 College—St. Joseph's (Pa.)

Yr	Team	G	FG	FT	TP	Avg.
1948-49	Denver NL	60	146	81	373	6.2
1949-50	Den.-Phil.	57	93	28	214	3.8
	Totals	117	239	109	587	5.0

GUOKAS, JR., MATT

b. Feb. 25, 1944 Ht. 6-5 Wt. 175 College—St. Joseph's (Pa.)

Yr	Team	G	FG	FT	TP	Avg.
1966-67	Philadelphia	69	79	49	207	3.0
1967-68	Philadelphia	82	190	118	498	6.1
1968-69	Philadelphia	72	92	54	238	3.3
1969-70	Philadelphia	80	189	106	484	6.1
1970-71	Phila.-Chi.	79	206	101	513	6.5
1971-72	Cincinnati	61	191	64	446	7.3
1972-73	K.C.-Omaha	79	322	74	718	9.1
1973-74	K.C.-O.-Hou.-Buffalo	75	195	39	429	5.7
1974-75	Chicago	82	255	78	588	7.2
1975-76	Chi.-K.C.	56	73	18	164	2.9
	Totals	735	1792	701	4285	5.8

GUOKAS, SR., MATT

b. Nov. 11, 1915 Ht. 6-3 Wt. 195 College—St. Joseph's (Pa.)

Yr	Team	G	FG	FT	TP	Avg.
1946-47	Philadelphia	47	28	26	82	1.7

HACKETT, RUDY

b. May 10, 1953 Ht. 6-9 Wt. 215 College—Syracuse

Yr	Team	G	FG	FT	TP	Avg.
1975-76	St. Louis ABA	22	55 (0)	31	141	6.4
1976-77	N.Y. Nets-Ind.	6	3	8	14	2.3
	Totals	28	58 (0)	39	155	5.5

HADNOT, JIM

b. Jan. 15, 1940 Ht. 6-10 Wt. 237 College—Providence

Yr	Team	G	FG	FT	TP	Avg.
1967-68	Oakland ABA	77	488 (0)	368	1344	17.5

HAGAN, CLIFF

b. Dec. 9, 1931 Ht. 6-4 Wt. 215 College—Kentucky

Yr	Team	G	FG	FT	TP	Avg.
1956-57	St. Louis	67	134	100	368	5.5
1957-58	St. Louis	70	503	385	1391	19.9
1958-59	St. Louis	72	646	415	1707	23.7
1959-60	St. Louis	75	719	421	1859	24.8
1960-61	St. Louis	78	661	383	1705	21.9
1961-62	St. Louis	77	701	362	1764	22.9
1962-63	St. Louis	79	491	244	1226	15.5
1963-64	St. Louis	77	572	269	1413	18.4
1964-65	St. Louis	77	393	214	1000	13.0
1965-66	St. Louis	74	419	176	1014	13.7
1967-68	Dallas ABA	56	371 (0)	277	1019	18.2
1968-69	Dallas ABA	35	132 (0)	123	387	11.1
1969-70	Dallas ABA	3	8 (0)	1	17	5.7
	Totals	840	5750 (0)	3370	14870	17.7

HAGAN, THOMAS MEDARD

b. Jan. 29, 1947 Ht. 6-4 Wt. 185 College—Vanderbilt

Yr	Team	G	FG	FT	TP	Avg.
1969-70	Dallas ABA	24	30 (7)	22	103	4.3
1970-71	Texas ABA	45	86 (12)	43	251	5.6
	Totals	69	116 (19)	65	354	5.1

HAHN, BOB

b. Aug. 25, 1925 Ht. 6-10 Wt. 240 Coll.—N. Carolina St.

Yr	Team	G	FG	FT	TP	Avg.
1949-50	Chicago	10	4	2	10	1.0

HAIRSTON, AL

b. Dec. 11, 1945 Ht. 6-1 Wt. 170 Coll.—Bowling Green

Yr	Team	G	FG	FT	TP	Avg.
1968-69	Seattle	39	38	8	84	2.2
1969-70	Seattle	3	3	1	7	2.3
	Totals	42	41	9	91	2.2

HAIRSTON, HAROLD (Happy)

b. May 31, 1942 Ht. 6-7 Wt. 225 College—N.Y.U.

Yr	Team	G	FG	FT	TP	Avg.
1964-65	Cincinnati	61	131	110	372	6.1
1965-66	Cincinnati	72	398	220	1016	14.1
1966-67	Cincinnati	79	461	252	1174	14.9
1967-68	Cinn.-Detroit	74	481	365	1327	17.9
1968-69	Detroit	81	530	404	1464	18.1
1969-70	Det.-L.A.	70	483	326	1292	18.5
1970-71	Los Angeles	80	574	337	1485	18.6
1971-72	Los Angeles	80	368	311	1047	13.1
1972-73	Los Angeles	28	158	140	456	16.3
1973-74	Los Angeles	77	385	343	1113	14.5
1974-75	Los Angeles	74	271	217	759	10.3
	Totals	776	4240	3025	11505	14.8

Yr	Team	G	FG	FT	TP	Avg.
HAIRSTON, LINDSAY						

b. Dec. 8, 1951 Ht. 6-8 Wt. 190 Coll.—Michigan St.

Yr	Team	G	FG	FT	TP	Avg.
1975-76	Detroit	47	104	65	273	5.8

HALBERT, CHARLES (Chick)

b. Feb. 27, 1919 Ht. 6-9½ Wt. 225 Coll.—West Texas

Yr	Team	G	FG	FT	TP	Avg.
1946-47	Chicago	61	280	213	773	12.7
1947-48	Chi.-Phila.	46	156	140	452	9.8
1948-49	Bos.-Prov.	60	202	214	618	10.3
1949-50	Washington	68	108	112	328	4.8
1950-51	Wash.-Balt.	68	164	172	500	7.4
	Totals	303	910	851	2671	8.8

HALBROOK, HARVEY WADE (Swede)

b. Jan. 30, 1933 Ht. 7-3 Wt. 235 College—Oregon State

Yr	Team	G	FG	FT	TP	Avg.
1960-61	Syracuse	79	155	76	386	4.9
1961-62	Syracuse	64	152	96	400	6.2
	Totals	143	307	172	786	5.5

HALE, BRUCE

b. Aug. 31, 1918 Ht. 6-1 Wt. 170 College—Santa Clara

Yr	Team	G	FG	FT	TP	Avg.
1946-47	Chicago NL	41	156	116	428	10.4
1947-48	Indianapolis NL	48	196	155	547	11.4
1948-49	Ind.-Ft. W.	52	187	172	546	10.5
1949-50	Indianapolis	64	217	223	657	10.3
1950-51	Indianapolis	26	40	14	94	3.6
	Totals	231	796	680	2272	9.8

HALE, HAL

Ht. 6-1 College—Utah State

Yr	Team	G	FG	FT	TP	Avg.
1967-68	Houston ABA	72	98 (35)	60	361	5.0

HALIMON, SHALER

b. March 30, 1945 Ht. 6-6 Wt. 199 Coll.—Utah State

Yr	Team	G	FG	FT	TP	Avg.
1968-69	Philadelphia	50	88	10	186	3.7
1969-70	Chicago	38	96	49	241	6.3
1970-71	Chi.-Port.	81	301	107	709	8.8
1971-72	Atlanta	1	0	0	0	0.0
1971-72	Dallas ABA	55	123 (0)	62	308	5.6
1972-73	Dallas ABA	29	58 (1)	23	142	4.9
	Totals	254	666 (1)	251	1586	6.2

HALLIBURTON, JEFF

b. July 3, 1949 Ht. 6-5 Wt. 199 College—Drake

Yr	Team	G	FG	FT	TP	Avg.
1971-72	Atlanta	37	61	25	147	4.0
1972-73	Atl.-Phil.	55	172	71	415	7.5
	Totals	92	233	96	562	6.1

HAMILTON, DALE

b. Aug. 16, 1919 Ht. 6-1 Wt. 198 College—Franklin

Yr	Team	G	FG	FT	TP	Avg.
1939-40	Hammond NL	7	5	1	11	1.6
1941-42	Ft. Wayne NL	16	10	16	36	2.3
1942-43	Ft. Wayne NL	18	8	1	17	0.9
1943-44	Ft. Wayne NL	11	2	0	4	0.4
1944-45	Ft. Wayne NL	2	0	0	0	0.0
1946-47	Toledo NL	44	114	67	295	6.7

Yr	Team	G	FG	FT	TP	Avg.
1947-48	Toledo NL	53	93	62	248	4.7
1948-49	Waterloo NL	62	78	94	250	4.0
1949-50	Waterloo	14	8	9	25	1.8
	Totals	227	318	250	886	3.9

HAMILTON, DENNIS

b. May 8, 1944 Ht. 6-8 Wt. 210 College—Arizona State

Yr	Team	G	FG	FT	TP	Avg.
1967-68	Los Angeles	44	54	13	121	2.8
1968-69	Atlanta	25	37	2	76	3.0
	Totals	69	91	15	197	2.9

HAMILTON, JOE

b. July 5, 1948 Ht. 5-10 Wt. 175 Coll.—N. Texas State

Yr	Team	G	FG	FT	TP	Avg.
1970-71	Texas ABA	84	415 (85)	233	1318	15.7
1971-72	Dallas ABA	82	271 (46)	201	881	10.7
1972-73	Dallas ABA	83	304 (66)	209	1015	12.2
1973-74	S.A.-Ken. ABA	73	294 (37)	117	816	11.2
1974-75	Kentucky ABA	9	12 (3)	5	38	4.2
	Totals	331	1296 (237)	765	4068	12.3

HAMILTON, RALPH (Ham)

b. June 10, 1921 Ht. 6-1 Wt. 188 College—Indiana

Yr	Team	G	FG	FT	TP	Avg.
1947-48	Ft. Wayne NL	49	143	101	387	7.9
1948-49	Ft. W.-Ind.	48	114	61	289	6.0
	Totals	97	257	162	676	7.0

HAMILTON, STEVE

b. Nov. 30, 1934 Ht. 6-7 Wt. 190 Coll.—Morehead St.

Yr	Team	G	FG	FT	TP	Avg.
1958-59	Minneapolis	67	109	74	292	4.4
1959-60	Minneapolis	15	29	18	76	5.1
	Totals	82	138	92	368	4.5

HAMMOND, JULIAN

b. May 7, 1943 Ht. 6-5 Wt. 205 College—Tulsa

Yr	Team	G	FG	FT	TP	Avg.
1967-68	Denver ABA	74	224 (0)	143	591	8.0
1968-69	Denver ABA	78	329 (0)	165	823	10.6
1969-70	Denver ABA	69	329 (0)	169	827	12.0
1970-71	Denver ABA	83	435 (0)	273	1143	13.8
1971-72	Denver ABA	25	66 (0)	31	163	6.5
	Totals	329	1383 (0)	781	3547	10.8

HAMOOD, JOE

Ht. 6-0 College—Houston

Yr	Team	G	FG	FT	TP	Avg.
1967-68	Houston ABA	76	258 (16)	186	750	9.9

HANKINS, CECIL

b. Jan 6, 1922 Ht. 6-1 Wt. 175 Coll.—Oklahoma A&M

Yr	Team	G	FG	FT	TP	Avg.
1946-47	St. Louis	55	117	90	324	5.9
1947-48	Boston	25	23	24	70	2.8
1947-48	Sheboygan NL	1	0	1	1	1.0
	Totals	81	140	115	395	4.9

Yr	Team	G	FG	FT	TP	Avg.
HANKINSON, PHIL						
b. July 26, 1951 Ht. 6-8 Wt. 195 College—Pennsylvania						
1973-74	Boston	28	50	10	110	3.9
1974-75	Boston	3	6	0	12	4.0
	Totals	31	56	10	122	3.0
HANNUM, ALEX						
b. July 19, 1923 Ht. 6-7 Wt. 225 Coll.—So. California						
1948-49	Oshkosh NL	64	126	113	365	5.7
1949-50	Syracuse	64	177	128	482	7.5
1950-51	Syracuse	63	182	107	471	7.5
1951-52	Balt.-Roch.	66	170	98	438	6.6
1952-53	Rochester	68	129	88	346	5.1
1953-54	Rochester	72	175	102	452	6.3
1954-55	Milwaukee	53	126	61	313	5.9
1955-56	St. Louis	71	146	93	385	5.4
1956-57	Ft. W.-St. Lo.	59	77	37	191	3.2
	Totals	580	1308	827	3443	5.9
HANRAHAN, DON						
b. Feb. 6, 1929 Ht. 6-7 Wt. 200 College—Loyola (III.)						
1952-53	Indianapolis	18	11	11	33	1.8
HANS, ROLLEN						
b. 1930 Ht. 6-2 Wt. 210 College—Long Island U.						
1953-54	Baltimore	67	191	101	483	7.2
1954-55	Baltimore	13	30	13	73	5.6
	Totals	80	221	114	556	7.0
HARDING, REGGIE						
b. May 4, 1942 Ht. 7-0 Wt. 255						
1963-64	Detroit	39	184	61	429	11.0
1964-65	Detroit	78	405	128	938	12.0
1966-67	Detroit	74	172	63	407	5.5
1967-68	Chicago	14	24	17	65	4.6
1967-68	Indiana ABA	25	142 (0)	52	336	13.4
	Totals	230	927 (0)	321	2175	9.5
HARDNETT, CHARLES						
b. Sept. 13, 1938 Ht. 6-8 Wt. 225 College—Grambling						
1962-63	Chicago	78	301	225	827	10.6
1963-64	Baltimore	67	107	84	298	4.4
1964-65	Baltimore	20	25	23	73	3.7
	Totals	165	433	332	1198	7.3
HARDY, DARRELL						
Ht. 6-7 College—Baylor						
1967-68	Houston ABA	17	32 (0)	25	89	5.2
HARGE, IRA						
b. March 14, 1941 Ht. 6-9 Wt. 225 Coll.—New Mexico						
1967-68	Pitt.-Oak. ABA	82	311 (0)	202	824	10.0
1968-69	Oakland ABA	78	269 (0)	123	661	8.5
1969-70	Washington ABA	84	415 (0)	196	1026	12.2
1970-71	Car.-Fla. ABA	82	458 (2)	197	1119	13.7
1971-72	Fla.-Utah ABA	84	314 (0)	104	732	8.7
1972-73	Utah-Car. ABA	17	14 (0)	6	34	2.0
	Totals	427	1781 (2)	828	4396	10.3

Yr	Team	G	FG	FT	TP	Avg.
HARGIS, JOHN (Shotgun)						
b. Aug. 20, 1920 Ht. 6-2 Wt. 185 College—Texas						
1947-48	Anderson NL	59	235	172	642	10.9
1948-49	Anderson NL	57	169	106	444	7.8
1949-50	Anderson	60	223	197	643	10.7
1950-51	Ft.W.-Tri.-C.	14	25	17	67	4.8
	Totals	190	652	492	1796	9.5
HARKNESS, JERRY						
b. May 7, 1940 Ht. 6-2 Wt. 175 College—Loyola (III.)						
1963-64	New York	5	13	3	29	5.8
1967-68	Indiana ABA	71	171 (1)	152	497	7.0
1968-69	Indiana ABA	10	31 (0)	30	92	9.2
	Totals	86	215 (1)	185	618	7.2
HARLICKA, JULES (Skip)						
b. Oct. 14, 1946 Ht. 6-1½ Wt. 185 Col.—S. Carolina						
1968-69	Atlanta	26	41	24	106	4.1
HARRIS, ART						
b. Jan. 13, 1947 Ht. 6-4 Wt. 186 College—Stanford						
1968-69	Seattle	80	416	161	993	12.4
1969-70	Seattle-Phoe.	81	285	86	656	8.1
1970-71	Phoenix	56	199	69	467	8.3
1971-72	Phoenix	21	23	9	55	2.6
	Totals	238	923	325	2171	9.1
HARRIS, BERNIE						
b. Nov. 26, 1950 Ht. 6-10 Wt. 200 Coll.—Va. Com.						
1974-75	Buffalo	11	2	1	5	0.5
HARRIS, BILLY						
b. Nov. 12, 1951 Ht. 6-2 Wt. 190 Coll.—No. Illinois						
1974-75	San Diego ABA	76	248 (16)	65	609	8.0
HARRIS, BOB						
b. Mar. 16, 1927 Ht. 6-7 Wt. 195 Coll.—Murray St. & Oklahoma State						
1949-50	Ft. Wayne	62	168	140	476	7.7
1950-51	Ft. W.-Boston	56	98	86	282	5.0
1951-52	Boston	66	190	134	514	7.8
1952-53	Boston	70	192	133	517	7.4
1953-54	Boston	71	156	108	420	5.9
	Totals	325	804	601	2209	6.8
HARRIS, CHRIS						
b. Aug. 11, 1933 Ht. 6-3 Wt. 190 College—Dayton						
1955-56	St. L.-Roch.	41	37	27	101	2.5
HARRISON, BOB						
b. Aug. 12, 1927 Ht. 6-1 Wt. 190 College—Michigan						
1949-50	Minneapolis	66	125	50	300	4.6
1950-51	Minneapolis	68	150	101	401	5.9
1951-52	Minneapolis	65	156	89	401	6.2
1952-53	Minneapolis	70	195	107	497	7.1
1953-54	Minn.-Milw.	64	144	94	382	6.0
1954-55	Milwaukee	72	299	126	724	10.1
1955-56	St. Louis	72	260	97	617	8.6
1956-57	Syracuse	66	243	93	579	8.8
1957-58	Syracuse	72	210	97	517	7.2
	Totals	615	1782	854	4418	7.2

Yr	Team	G	FG	FT	TP	Avg.
HASKINS, CLEM						

b. Aug. 11, 1944 Ht. 6-2 Wt. 195 Coll.—W. Kentucky

Yr	Team	G	FG	FT	TP	Avg.
1967-68	Chicago	76	273	133	679	8.9
1968-69	Chicago	79	537	282	1356	17.2
1969-70	Chicago	82	668	332	1668	20.3
1970-71	Phoenix	82	562	338	1462	17.8
1971-72	Phoenix	79	509	220	1238	15.7
1972-73	Phoenix	77	339	130	808	10.5
1973-74	Phoenix	81	364	171	899	11.1
1974-75	Washington	70	115	53	283	4.0
1975-76	Washington	55	148	54	350	6.4
	Totals	681	3515	1713	8743	12.8

HASSETT, WILLIAM

b. Oct. 21, 1921 Ht. 6-1 Wt. 180 Coll.—Georgetown and Notre Dame

Yr	Team	G	FG	FT	TP	Avg.
1946-47	Tri-Cities NL	27	73	66	212	7.9
1947-48	Tri-Cities NL	56	199	203	601	10.7
1948-49	Tri-Cities NL	64	125	106	356	5.6
1949-50	Tri-C.-Minn.	60	84	104	272	4.5
1950-51	Baltimore	30	45	40	130	4.3
	Totals	237	526	519	1571	6.6

HATTON, VERNON

b. Jan. 13, 1936 Ht. 6-3 Wt. 195 College—Kentucky

Yr	Team	G	FG	FT	TP	Avg.
1958-59	Cin.-Phila.	64	149	77	375	5.9
1959-60	Philadelphia	67	127	53	307	4.6
1960-61	Philadelphia	54	97	46	240	4.4
1961-62	Ch.-St. Louis	40	112	98	322	8.1
	Totals	225	485	274	1244	5.5

HAVLICEK, JOHN (Hondo)

b. April 8, 1940 Ht. 6-5 Wt. 205 College—Ohio State

Yr	Team	G	FG	FT	TP	Avg.
1962-63	Boston	80	483	174	1140	14.3
1963-64	Boston	80	640	315	1595	19.9
1964-65	Boston	75	570	235	1375	18.3
1965-66	Boston	71	530	274	1334	18.8
1966-67	Boston	81	684	365	1733	21.4
1967-68	Boston	82	666	368	1700	20.7
1968-69	Boston	82	692	387	1771	21.6
1969-70	Boston	81	736	488	1960	24.2
1970-71	Boston	81	892	554	2338	28.9
1971-72	Boston	82	897	458	2252	27.5
1972-73	Boston	80	766	370	1902	23.8
1973-74	Boston	76	685	346	1716	22.6
1974-75	Boston	82	642	289	1573	19.2
1975-76	Boston	76	504	281	1289	17.0
1976-77	Boston	79	580	235	1395	17.7
1977-78	Boston	82	546	230	1322	16.1
	Totals	1270	10513	5369	26395	20.8

HAWKINS, CONNIE

b. July 17, 1942 Ht. 6-8 Wt. 215 College—Iowa

Yr	Team	G	FG	FT	TP	Avg.
1967-68	Pittsburgh ABA	70	633 (2)	603	1875	26.8
1968-69	Minnesota ABA	47	493 (3)	425	1420	30.2
1969-70	Phoenix	81	709	577	1995	24.6
1970-71	Phoenix	71	512	457	1481	20.9
1971-72	Phoenix	76	571	456	1598	21.0
1972-73	Phoenix	75	441	322	1204	16.1
1973-74	Phoe.-L.A.	79	404	191	999	12.6
1974-75	Los Angeles	43	139	68	346	8.0
1975-76	Atlanta	74	237	136	610	8.2
	Totals	616	4139 (5)	3235	11528	18.7

Yr	Team	G	FG	FT	TP	Avg.
HAWKINS, MARSHALL						

b. Aug. 3, 1924 Ht. 6-3 Wt. 210 College—Tennessee

Yr	Team	G	FG	FT	TP	Avg.
1948-49	Oshkosh NL	64	200	116	516	8.1
1949-50	Indianapolis	39	55	42	152	3.9
	Totals	103	255	158	668	6.5

HAWKINS, THOMAS (Hawk)

b. Dec. 22, 1936 Ht. 6-5 Wt. 210 College—Notre Dame

Yr	Team	G	FG	FT	TP	Avg.
1959-60	Minneapolis	69	220	106	546	7.9
1960-61	Los Angeles	78	310	140	760	9.7
1961-62	Los Angeles	79	289	143	721	9.1
1962-63	Cincinnati	79	299	147	745	9.4
1963-64	Cincinnati	73	256	113	625	8.6
1964-65	Cincinnati	79	220	116	556	7.0
1965-66	Cincinnati	79	273	116	662	8.4
1966-67	Los Angeles	76	275	82	632	8.3
1967-68	Los Angeles	78	389	125	903	11.6
1968-69	Los Angeles	74	230	62	522	7.1
	Totals	764	2761	1150	6672	8.7

HAWTHORNE, NATE

b. Jan. 15, 1950 Ht. 6-4 Wt. 190 College—S. Illinois

Yr	Team	G	FG	FT	TP	Avg.
1973-74	Los Angeles	33	38	30	106	3.2
1974-75	Phoenix	50	118	61	297	5.9
1975-76	Phoenix	79	182	115	479	6.1
	Totals	162	338	206	882	5.4

HAYES, JIM

b. Feb. 18, 1948 Ht. 6-3 Wt. 200 Coll.—Boston Univ.

Yr	Team	G	FG	FT	TP	Avg.
1970-71	New York ABA	47	46 (0)	52	144	3.1

HAZEN, JOHN

b. 1927 Ht. 6-2 Wt. 172 College—Indiana State

Yr	Team	G	FG	FT	TP	Avg.
1948-49	Boston	6	6	6	18	3.0

HAZZARD, WALT

(See Abdul-Rahmad, Mahdi)

HEANEY, BRIAN

b. Sept. 3, 1946 Ht. 6-2 Wt. 180 College—Acadia

Yr	Team	G	FG	FT	TP	Avg.
1969-70	Baltimore	14	13	2	28	2.0

HEDDERICK, HERMAN

b. Jan. 1, 1930 Ht. 6-5 Wt. 170 College—Canisius

Yr	Team	G	FG	FT	TP	Avg.
1954-55	New York	5	2	0	4	0.8

HEINSOHN, TOM

b. Aug. 26, 1934 Ht. 6-7 Wt. 218 College—Holy Cross

Yr	Team	G	FG	FT	TP	Avg.
1956-57	Boston	72	446	271	1163	16.2
1957-58	Boston	69	468	294	1230	17.8
1958-59	Boston	66	465	312	1242	18.8
1959-60	Boston	75	673	283	1629	21.7
1960-61	Boston	74	627	325	1579	21.3
1961-62	Boston	78	692	358	1742	22.3
1962-63	Boston	77	550	340	1440	18.7
1963-64	Boston	76	487	283	1257	16.5
1964-65	Boston	67	365	182	912	13.6
	Totals	654	4773	2648	12194	18.6

Yr	Team	G	FG	FT	TP	Avg.

HEMRIC, DIXON (Dick)

b. Aug. 29, 1933 Ht. 6-6 Wt. 220 College—Wake Forest

Yr	Team	G	FG	FT	TP	Avg.
1955-56	Boston	71	161	177	499	7.0
1956-57	Boston	67	109	146	364	5.4
	Totals	138	270	323	863	6.3

HENRIKSEN, DON

b. Oct. 10, 1929 Ht. 6-7 Wt. 225 College—California

1952-53	Baltimore	68	199	176	574	8.4
1954-55	Rochester	70	139	137	415	5.9
	Totals	138	338	313	989	7.2

HENRY, AL

b. Feb. 9, 1949 Ht. 6-9 Wt. 190 College—Wisconsin

1970-71	Philadelphia	6	1	5	7	1.2
1971-72	Philadelphia	43	68	51	187	4.3
	Totals	49	69	56	194	4.0

HENRY, WILLIAM (Big Bill)

b. Dec. 27, 1924 Ht. 6-9 Wt. 215 College—Rice

1948-49	Ft. Wayne	32	96	125	317	9.9
1949-50	Ft. Wayne-Tri-Cities	63	89	118	296	4.7
	Totals	95	185	243	613	6.5

HENTZ, CHARLIE

b. Sept. 13, 1947 Ht. 6-6 Wt. 235 Coll.—Ark. A.M.&N.

1970-71	Pittsburgh ABA	57	142 (0)	57	341	6.0

HERMAN, BILL

b. May 17, 1924 Ht. 6-3 Wt. 170 College—Mt. Union

1949-50	Denver	13	25	6	56	4.3

HERMSEN, CLARENCE (Kleggie)

b. March 12, 1923 Ht. 6-9 Wt. 235 Coll.—Minnesota

1943-44	Sheboygan NL	12	3	5	11	0.9
1945-46	Sheboygan NL	21	19	17	55	2.6
1946-47	Cleve.-Tor.	32	113	71	297	9.3
1947-48	Baltimore	48	212	151	575	12.0
1948-49	Washington	60	248	212	708	11.8
1949-50	Chicago	67	196	153	545	8.1
1950-51	Tri-Cities-Bos.	71	189	155	533	7.5
1952-53	Bos.-Ind.	10	4	3	11	1.1
	Totals	321	984	767	2735	8.5

HERN, BEN

1967-68	Denver ABA	1	0 (0)	2	2	2.0

HERTZBERG, SIDNEY (Sonny)

b. July 29, 1922 Ht. 5-10 Wt. 195 College—CCNY

1946-47	New York	59	201	113	515	8.7
1947-48	N.Y.-Wash.	41	110	58	278	6.8
1948-49	Washington	60	154	134	442	7.4
1949-50	Boston	68	275	143	693	10.2
1950-51	Boston	65	206	223	635	9.8
	Totals	293	946	671	2563	8.7

HESTER, DAN

Ht. 6-8 Wt. 210 College—Louisiana State

1970-71	Denver-Ky. ABA	42	92 (5)	49	248	5.9

HETZEL, FRED

b. July 21, 1942 Ht. 6-8 Wt. 230 College—Davidson

1965-66	San Francisco	56	160	63	383	6.8
1966-67	San Francisco	77	373	192	938	12.2
1967-68	San Francisco	77	533	395	1461	19.0
1968-69	Milw.-Cin.	84	456	299	1211	14.4
1969-70	Philadelphia	63	156	71	383	6.1
1970-71	Los Angeles	59	111	60	282	4.8
	Totals	416	1789	1080	4658	11.2

HEWITT, BILL

b. Aug. 8, 1944 Ht. 6-7 Wt. 210 Coll.—S. California

1968-69	Los Angeles	75	239	61	539	7.2
1969-70	L.A.-Det.	65	110	54	274	4.2
1970-71	Detroit	62	203	69	475	7.7
1971-72	Detroit	68	131	41	303	4.5
1972-73	Buffalo	73	152	41	345	4.7
1974-75	Chicago	18	56	14	126	7.0
	Totals	361	891	280	2062	5.7

HEWSON, JACK

b. Sept. 7, 1924 Ht. 6-6 Wt. 195 College—Temple

1947-48	Boston	24	22	21	65	2.7

HEYMAN, ARTHUR

b. June 24, 1941 Ht. 6-5 Wt. 205 College—Duke

1963-64	New York	75	432	289	1153	15.4
1964-65	New York	55	114	88	316	5.7
1965-66	Cinn.-Phila.	17	18	14	50	2.9
1967-68	N.J.-Pitt. ABA	73	422 (35)	400	1349	18.5
1968-69	Minnesota ABA	71	313 (37)	285	1022	14.4
1969-70	Pitt.-Miami ABA	19	47 (0)	46	140	7.4
	Totals	310	1346 (72)	1122	4030	13.0

HICKEY, MATTHEW (Nat)

b. Jan. 30, 1902 Ht. 5-11½ Wt. 180

1944-45	Pittsburgh NL	2	3	2	8	4.0
1945-46	Indianapolis NL	13	30	13	73	5.6
1946-47	Buf.-Tri-C. NL	8	9	6	24	3.0
1947-48	Tri-Cities NL	3	1	1	3	1.0
1947-48	Providence	1	0	0	0	0.0
	Totals	27	43	22	108	4.0

HIGGINS, BILL

b. Nov. 12, 1951 Ht. 6-2 Wt. 185 Coll.—Northern Ill.

1974-75	Virginia ABA	15	60 (1)	15	138	9.2

HIGGINS, EARLE

Ht. 6-8 Wt. 200 College—Eastern Michigan

1970-71	Indiana ABA	53	101 (3)	20	231	4.4
1971-72	Indiana ABA	0	0 (0)	0	0	0.0
	Totals	53	101 (3)	20	231	4.4

HIGHTOWER, WAYNE

b. Jan. 14, 1940 Ht. 6-8½ Wt. 192 College—Kansas

1962-63	San Francisco	66	192	105	489	7.4
1963-64	San Francisco	79	393	260	1046	13.2

Yr	Team	G	FG	FT	TP	Avg.
1964-65	San Francisco-Baltimore	75	196	195	587	7.8
1965-66	Baltimore	24	63	57	183	7.6
1966-67	Balt.-Detroit	72	195	153	543	7.5
1967-68	Denver ABA	74	431 (0)	420	1282	17.3
1968-69	Denver ABA	67	311 (0)	311	933	13.9
1969-70	Los Angeles ABA	27	180 (0)	129	489	18.1
1970-71	Utah-Tex. ABA	68	339 (0)	268	946	13.9
1971-72	Carolina ABA	13	20 (0)	30	70	5.4
	Totals	565	2320 (0)	1928	6568	11.6

HILL, CLEO

b. May 24, 1938 Ht. 6-1 Wt. 185 College—Winston-Salem State

Yr	Team	G	FG	FT	TP	Avg.
1961-62	St. Louis	58	110	106	326	5.6

HILL, GARY

b. Oct. 7, 1941 Ht. 6-4 Wt. 185 College—Ok. City

Yr	Team	G	FG	FT	TP	Avg.
1963-64	San Francisco	66	145	51	341	5.2
1964-65	S.F.-Balt.	12	10	7	27	2.3
	Totals	78	155	58	368	4.7

HILL, SIMMIE

Ht. 6-7 Wt. 235 College—West Texas State

Yr	Team	G	FG	FT	TP	Avg.
1969-70	L.A.-Miami ABA	53	292 (5)	126	725	13.7
1971-72	Dallas ABA	70	277 (4)	129	695	9.9
1972-73	San Diego ABA	69	288 (27)	103	760	11.0
1973-74	San Antonio ABA	60	112 (0)	45	269	4.5
	Totals	252	969 (36)	403	2449	9.7

HILLHOUSE, ARTHUR

b. June 12, 1916 Ht. 6-7 Wt. 220 College—L.I. Univ.

Yr	Team	G	FG	FT	TP	Avg.
1946-47	Philadelphia	60	120	120	360	6.0
1947-48	Philadelphia	11	14	30	58	5.3
	Totals	71	134	150	418	5.9

HILTON, FRED

b. Jan. 15, 1948 Ht. 6-3 Wt. 185 College—Grambling

Yr	Team	G	FG	FT	TP	Avg.
1971-72	Buffalo	61	309	90	708	11.6
1972-73	Buffalo	59	191	41	423	7.2
	Totals	120	400	131	1131	9.4

HIRSCH, MEL

b. July 31, 1921 Ht. 5-8 Wt. 165 College—Bklyn Coll.

Yr	Team	G	FG	FT	TP	Avg.
1946-47	Boston	13	9	1	19	1.5

HITCH, LEW

b. July 16, 1929 Ht. 6-8 Wt. 200 College—Kansas St.

Yr	Team	G	FG	FT	TP	Avg.
1951-52	Minneapolis	61	77	63	217	3.6
1952-53	Minneapolis	70	89	83	261	3.7
1953-54	Milwaukee	72	221	133	575	8.0
1954-55	Milwaukee	74	167	115	449	6.1
1955-56	Milw.-Minn.	69	94	100	288	4.2
1956-57	Minn.-Phila.	68	111	63	285	4.2
	Totals	414	759	557	2075	5.0

HOEFER, CHARLES (Dutch)

b. 1922 Ht. 5-9 Wt. 158 College—Queens

Yr	Team	G	FG	FT	TP	Avg.
1946-47	Tor.-Bos.	58	130	91	351	6.1
1947-48	Boston	7	3	4	10	1.4
	Totals	65	133	95	361	5.6

HOFFMAN, PAUL (Bear)

b. April 12, 1922 Ht. 6-2 Wt. 205 College—Purdue

Yr	Team	G	FG	FT	TP	Avg.
1947-48	Baltimore	37	142	104	388	10.5
1949-50	Baltimore	60	312	242	866	14.4
1950-51	Baltimore	41	127	105	359	8.8
1952-53	Baltimore	69	240	224	704	10.2
1953-54	Baltimore	72	253	217	723	10.0
1954-55	Balt.-N.Y.-Phila.	38	65	64	194	5.1
	Totals	317	1139	956	3234	10.2

HOGSETT, BOB

b. Jan. 29, 1941 Ht. 6-7½ Wt. 230 College—Tennessee

Yr	Team	G	FG	FT	TP	Avg.
1966-67	Detroit	7	5	6	16	2.3
1968-69	Pittsburgh ABA	13	7 (0)	7	21	1.6
	Totals	20	12 (0)	13	37	1.9

HOGUE, PAUL (Duke)

b. April 28, 1940 Ht. 6-9 Wt. 240 College—Cincinnati

Yr	Team	G	FG	FT	TP	Avg.
1962-63	New York	50	152	79	383	7.7
1963-64	N.Y.-Balt.	15	12	2	26	1.7
	Totals	65	164	81	409	6.3

HOLCOMB, DOUGLAS

b. Feb. 9, 1925 Ht. 6-4 Wt. 200 College—Wisconsin

Yr	Team	G	FG	FT	TP	Avg.
1948-49	Baltimore	3	3	9	15	5.0

HOLLAND, JOE

b. Sept. 26, 1925 Ht. 6-4 Wt. 185 Coll.—Berea & Ken.

Yr	Team	G	FG	FT	TP	Avg.
1949-50	Indianapolis	64	145	98	388	6.1
1950-51	Indianapolis	67	196	78	470	7.0
1951-52	Indianapolis	55	93	40	226	4.1
	Totals	186	434	216	1084	5.8

HOLMAN, DENNY

Ht. 6-3 Wt. 175 College—Southern Methodist

Yr	Team	G	FG	FT	TP	Avg.
1967-68	Dallas ABA	46	51 (4)	62	176	3.8

HOLSTEIN, JIM

b. Sept. 24, 1930 Ht. 6-3 Wt. 180 College—Cincinnati

Yr	Team	G	FG	FT	TP	Avg.
1952-53	Minneapolis	66	98	70	266	4.0
1953-54	Minneapolis	70	88	64	240	3.4
1954-55	Minneapolis	62	107	67	281	4.5
1955-56	Ft. Wayne	27	24	24	72	2.7
	Totals	225	317	225	859	3.3

HOLT, A. W.

b. Aug. 26, 1946 Ht. 6-7½ Wt. 210 Coll.—Jackson St.

Yr	Team	G	FG	FT	TP	Avg.
1970-71	Chicago	6	1	2	4	0.7

HOLUB, RICHARD

b. Oct. 29, 1921 Ht. 6-6 Wt. 205 Coll.—L.I. Univ.

Yr	Team	G	FG	FT	TP	Avg.
1947-48	New York	48	195	114	504	10.5

Yr	Team	G	FG	FT	TP	Avg.
HOLUP, JOSEPH						
b. Feb. 26, 1934 Ht. 6-6 Wt. 215 Coll.—G. Washington						
1956-57	Syracuse	71	160	204	524	7.4
1957-58	Syr.-Det.	53	91	71	253	4.8
	Totals	124	251	275	777	6.3
HOLZMAN, WILLIAM (Red)						
b. Aug. 10, 1920 Ht. 5-10 Wt. 175 Coll.—Balt. & CCNY						
1945-46	Rochester NL	34	143	77	363	10.7
1946-47	Rochester NL	44	227	74	528	12.0
1947-48	Rochester NL	60	246	117	609	10.2
1948-49	Rochester	60	225	96	546	9.1
1949-50	Rochester	68	206	144	556	8.2
1950-51	Rochester	68	183	130	496	7.3
1951-52	Rochester	65	104	61	269	4.1
1952-53	Rochester	46	38	27	103	2.2
1953-54	Milwaukee	51	74	48	196	3.8
	Totals	496	1446	774	3666	7.4
HOOPER, BOBBY						
b. Dec. 22, 1946 Ht. 6-0 Wt. 180 College—Dayton						
1968-69	Indiana ABA	54	103 (4)	53	271	5.0
HOOSER, CARROLL						
Ht. 6-7 Wt. 230 College—Southern Methodist						
1967-68	Dallas ABA	56	127 (1)	59	316	5.6
HOOVER, THOMAS						
b. Jan. 23, 1941 Ht. 6-10 Wt. 240 College—Villanova						
1963-64	New York	59	102	81	285	4.8
1964-65	New York	24	13	8	34	1.4
1966-67	St. Louis	17	13	5	31	1.8
1967-68	Denver ABA	70	157 (4)	128	454	6.5
1968-69	Hou.-Minn.-New York ABA	53	191 (0)	125	507	9.6
	Totals	223	476 (4)	347	1311	5.9
HOPKINS, ROBERT						
b. Nov. 3, 1934 Ht. 6-8 Wt. 205 College—Grambling						
1956-57	Syracuse	62	130	94	354	5.7
1957-58	Syracuse	69	221	123	565	8.2
1958-59	Syracuse	67	246	176	668	10.0
1959-60	Syracuse	75	257	136	650	8.7
	Totals	273	854	529	2237	8.2
HORAN, JOHN						
b. Nov. 24, 1932 Ht. 6-8 Wt. 190 College—Dayton						
1955-56	Minneapolis	19	12	10	34	1.8
HORN, RON						
b. May 24, 1938 Ht. 6-7 Wt. 225 College—Indiana						
1961-62	St. Louis	3	1	1	3	1.0
1962-63	Los Angeles	28	27	20	74	2.6
	Totals	31	28	21	77	2.5

Yr	Team	G	FG	FT	TP	Avg.
HOSKET, BILL						
b. Dec. 20, 1946 Ht. 6-8 Wt. 225 College—Ohio State						
1968-69	New York	50	53	24	130	2.6
1969-70	New York	36	46	26	118	3.3
1970-71	Buffalo	13	47	11	105	8.1
1971-72	Buffalo	44	89	42	220	5.0
	Totals	143	235	103	573	4.0
HOUBREGS, BOB (Houby)						
b. March 12, 1932 Ht. 6-8 Wt. 225 College—Washington						
1953-54	Milw.-Balt.	70	209	190	608	8.7
1954-55	Balt.-Bos.-Ft. W.	64	148	129	425	6.6
1955-56	Ft. Wayne	70	247	283	777	11.1
1956-57	Ft. Wayne	60	253	167	673	11.2
1957-58	Detroit	17	49	30	128	7.5
	Totals	281	906	799	2611	9.3
HOWARD, GREGG						
b. Jan. 8, 1948 Ht. 6-9 Wt. 215 College—New Mexico						
1970-71	Phoenix	44	68	37	173	3.9
1971-72	Cleveland	48	50	39	139	2.9
	Totals	92	118	76	312	3.4
HOWARD, MO						
b. Aug. 25, 1954 Ht. 6-2 Wt. 175 College—Maryland						
1976-77	Clev.-N.O.	32	64	24	152	4.8
HOWELL, BAILEY						
b. Jan. 20, 1937 Ht. 6-7 Wt. 220 College—Miss. State						
1959-60	Detroit	75	510	312	1332	17.8
1960-61	Detroit	77	607	601	1815	23.4
1961-62	Detroit	79	553	470	1576	19.9
1962-63	Detroit	79	637	519	1793	22.7
1963-64	Detroit	77	598	470	1666	21.6
1964-65	Baltimore	80	515	504	1534	19.2
1965-66	Baltimore	79	481	402	1364	17.3
1966-67	Boston	81	636	349	1621	20.0
1967-68	Boston	82	643	335	1621	19.8
1968-69	Boston	78	612	313	1537	19.7
1969-70	Boston	82	399	235	1033	12.6
1970-71	Philadelphia	82	324	230	878	10.7
	Totals	951	6515	4740	17770	18.7
HUBBARD, ROBERT						
b. Dec. 27, 1922 Ht. 6-6 Wt. 215 College—Springfield						
1947-48	Tri-Cities NL	20	27	22	76	3.8
1947-48	Providence	28	58	36	152	5.4
1948-49	Providence	34	25	22	72	2.1
	Totals	82	110	80	300	3.7
HUMMER, JOHN						
b. May 4, 1948 Ht. 6-9 Wt. 230 College—Princeton						
1970-71	Buffalo	81	339	225	913	11.3
1971-72	Buffalo	55	113	58	284	5.2
1972-73	Buffalo	66	206	115	527	8.0
1973-74	Chi.-Sea.	53	144	59	347	6.5
1974-75	Seattle	43	41	14	96	2.2
1975-76	Seattle	29	32	17	81	2.8
	Totals	327	875	488	2248	6.9

Yr	Team	G	FG	FT	TP	Avg.
HUNDLEY, RODNEY (Hot Rod)						
b. Oct. 26, 1934 Ht. 6-4 Wt. 185 College—West Virginia						
1957-58	Minneapolis	65	174	104	452	7.0
1958-59	Minneapolis	71	259	164	682	9.6
1959-60	Minneapolis	73	365	203	933	12.8
1960-61	Los Angeles	79	323	223	869	11.0
1961-62	Los Angeles	79	173	83	429	5.4
1962-63	Los Angeles	65	88	84	250	4.0
	Totals	432	1382	861	3625	8.4
HUNTER, LESLIE (Big Game)						
b. Aug. 16, 1942 Ht. 6-7 Wt. 212 College—Loyola (Ill.)						
1964-65	Baltimore	24	18	6	42	1.8
1967-68	Minnesota ABA	75	511 (2)	290	1318	17.6
1968-69	Miami ABA	77	476 (0)	335	1287	16.7
1969-70	New York ABA	79	480 (6)	317	1295	16.0
1970-71	Kentucky ABA	80	278 (10)	159	745	9.3
1971-72	Kentucky ABA	70	178 (5)	101	472	6.7
	Totals	405	1941 (23)	1208	5159	12.7
HURLEY, ROY						
b. 1922 Ht. 6-2½ Wt. 170 Coll.—Ind. & Murray St.						
1945-46	Indianapolis NL	30	76	24	176	5.9
1946-47	Toronto	46	100	39	239	5.2
1947-48	Tri.-C.-Syra. NL	16	19	13	51	3.2
	Totals	92	195	76	466	5.1
HUSTON, PAUL						
b. June 2, 1925 Ht. 6-3 Wt. 175 Coll.—Ohio State						
1947-48	Chicago	46	51	62	164	3.6
HUTCHINS, MEL (Hutch)						
b. Nov. 22, 1928 Ht. 6-6 Wt. 205 Coll.—Brigham Young						
1951-52	Milwaukee	66	231	145	607	9.2
1952-53	Milwaukee	71	319	193	831	11.7
1953-54	Ft. Wayne	72	295	151	741	10.3
1954-55	Ft. Wayne	72	341	182	864	12.0
1955-56	Ft. Wayne	66	325	142	792	12.0
1956-57	Ft. Wayne	72	369	152	890	12.4
1957-58	New York	18	51	24	126	7.0
	Totals	437	1931	989	4851	11.1
HUTTON, JOE						
b. Oct. 6, 1928 Ht. 6-1 Wt. 170 College—Hamline						
1950-51	Minneapolis	60	59	29	147	2.5
1951-52	Minneapolis	60	53	49	155	2.6
	Totals	120	112	78	302	2.5
HYDER, GREG						
b. June 21, 1948 Ht. 6-6 Wt. 215 Coll.—East. N.M.						
1970-71	Cincinnati	77	183	51	417	5.4
IMHOFF, DARRALL						
b. Oct. 11, 1938 Ht. 6-10 Wt. 220 College—California						
1960-61	New York	62	122	49	293	4.7
1961-62	New York	76	186	80	452	5.9
1962-63	Detroit	45	48	24	120	2.7

Yr	Team	G	FG	FT	TP	Avg.
1963-64	Detroit	58	104	69	277	4.8
1964-65	Los Angeles	76	145	88	378	4.8
1965-66	Los Angeles	77	151	77	379	4.9
1966-67	Los Angeles	81	370	127	867	10.7
1967-68	Los Angeles	82	293	177	763	9.3
1968-69	Philadelphia	82	279	194	752	9.2
1969-70	Philadelphia	79	430	215	1075	13.6
1970-71	Cincinnati	34	119	37	275	8.1
1971-72	Cin.-Port.	49	52	24	128	2.6
	Totals	801	2299	1161	5759 `	7.2
INGLESBY, TOM						
b. Feb. 12, 1951 Ht. 6-3 Wt. 185 College—Villanova						
1973-74	Atlanta	48	50	29	129	2.7
1974-75	St. Louis ABA	22	40 (3)	20	109	5.0
	Totals	70	90 (3)	49	238	3.4
INGRAM, McCOY						
b. Aug. 31, 1931 Ht. 6-0 Wt. 210 Coll.—Jackson State						
1957-58	Minneapolis	24	27	13	67	2.8
INNIGER, ERV						
b. Jan. 16, 1945 Ht. 6-4 Wt. 190 College—Indiana						
1967-68	Minnesota ABA	75	340 (5)	99	794	10.6
1968-69	Miami ABA	34	70 (3)	21	170	5.0
	Totals	109	410 (8)	120	964	8.8
IRVINE, GEORGE						
b. Feb. 1, 1948 Ht. 6-6 Wt. 200 College—Washington						
1970-71	Virginia ABA	34	81 (2)	26	194	5.7
1971-72	Virginia ABA	75	197 (3)	54	457	6.1
1972-73	Virginia ABA	79	417 (7)	169	1024	13.0
1973-74	Virginia ABA	75	242 (12)	120	640	8.5
1974-75	Virginia ABA	59	298 (13)	139	774	13.1
1975-76	Denver ABA	3	2 (0)	0	4	1.3
	Totals	325	1237 (37)	508	3093	9.5
IVERSON, WILLIE						
b. Oct. 8, 1945 Ht. 6-0 Wt. 180 Coll.—Central Michigan						
1968-69	Miami ABA	28	50 (0)	36	136	4.9
IVORY, ELVIN						
b. July 2, 1948 Ht. 6-8 Wt. 215 Coll.—S. Louisiana						
1968-69	Los Angeles ABA	20	37 (1)	11	88	4.4
JABALI, WARREN (Warren Armstrong)						
b. Aug. 29, 1946 Ht. 6-2 Wt. 200 Coll.—Wichita State						
1968-69	Oakland ABA	71	562 (11)	373	1520	21.5
1969-70	Washington ABA	40	323 (19)	210	913	22.8
1970-71	Indiana ABA	62	180 (47)	180	681	11.0
1971-72	Floridians ABA	81	467 (102)	375	1615	19.9
1972-73	Denver ABA	82	405 (36)	480	1398	17.1

Yr	Team	G	FG	FT	TP	Avg.
1973-74	Denver ABA	49	212 (45)	220	779	15.9
1974-75	San Diego ABA	62	192 (62)	179	749	12.1
	Totals	447	2341 (322)	2017	7665	17.1

JACKSON, AL
b. July 29, 1943 Ht 6-1½ Wt. 185 Coll. —Wilberforce

Yr	Team	G	FG	FT	TP	Avg.
1967-68	Cincinnati	2	0	0	0	0.0

JACKSON, GREG
b. Aug. 2, 1952 Ht. 6-0 Wt. 185 College—Guilford

Yr	Team	G	FG	FT	TP	Avg.
1974-75	N.Y.-Phoe.	49	73	36	182	3.7

JACKSON, LUCIOUS (Luke)
b. Oct. 31, 1941 Ht. 6-9 Wt. 240 Coll.—Pan American

Yr	Team	G	FG	FT	TP	Avg.
1964-65	Philadelphia	76	419	288	1126	14.8
1965-66	Philadelphia	79	246	158	650	8.2
1966-67	Philadelphia	81	386	198	970	12.0
1967-68	Philadelphia	82	401	166	968	11.8
1968-69	Philadelphia	25	145	69	359	14.4
1969-70	Philadelphia	37	71	60	202	5.5
1970-71	Philadelphia	79	199	131	529	6.7
1971-72	Philadelphia	63	137	92	366	5.8
	Totals	522	2004	1162	5170	9.9

JACKSON, MERV
b. Aug. 15, 1946 Ht. 6-3 Wt. 175 College—Utah

Yr	Team	G	FG	FT	TP	Avg.
1968-69	Los Angeles ABA	71	404 (19)	249	1114	15.7
1969-70	Los Angeles ABA	52	153 (16)	92	446	8.6
1970-71	Utah ABA	65	344 (7)	192	901	13.8
1971-72	Utah ABA	52	180 (5)	92	467	9.0
1972-73	Memphis ABA	22	30 (4)	28	100	4.5
	Totals	262	1111 (51)	653	3028	11.5

JACKSON, MIKE
b. July 31, 1949 Ht. 6-7 Wt. 230 Coll.—California State

Yr	Team	G	FG	FT	TP	Avg.
1972-73	Utah ABA	30	36 (0)	28	100	3.3
1973-74	Utah-Mem. ABA	72	244 (3)	110	607	8.4
1974-75	Virginia ABA	82	381 (1)	232	997	12.2
1975-76	Virginia ABA	80	390 (0)	199	979	12.2
	Totals	264	1051 (4)	569	2683	10.2

JACKSON, TONY
b. Nov. 7, 1940 Ht. 6-4 Wt. 200 College—St. John's

Yr	Team	G	FG	FT	TP	Avg.
1967-68	New Jersey ABA	74	358 (91)	450	1439	19.5
1968-69	N.Y.-Minn.-Hou. ABA	64	178 (32)	299	751	11.7
	Totals	138	536 (123)	749	2190	15.9

JACKSON, WARDELL
b. July 18, 1951 Ht. 6-7 Wt. 200 College—Ohio State

Yr	Team	G	FG	FT	TP	Avg.
1974-75	Seattle	56	96	51	243	4.3

JACOBS, FRED
b. Dec. 2, 1922 Ht. 6-3 Wt. 175 College—Denver

Yr	Team	G	FG	FT	TP	Avg.
1946-47	St. Louis	18	19	12	50	2.8

JAMES, BILLY
b. 1951 Ht. 6-3 Wt. 185 College—Marshall

Yr	Team	G	FG	FT	TP	Avg.
1973-74	Kentucky ABA	1	1 (0)	0	2	2.0

JAMES, GENE (Goose)
b. Feb. 15, 1925 Ht. 6-4½ Wt. 180 College—Marshall

Yr	Team	G	FG	FT	TP	Avg.
1948-49	New York	11	18	6	42	3.8
1949-50	New York	29	19	14	52	1.8
1950-51	N.Y.-Balt.	48	79	44	202	4.2
	Totals	88	116	64	296	3.4

JANISCH, JOHN
b. March 15, 1920 Ht. 6-3 Wt. 200 College—Valparaiso

Yr	Team	G	FG	FT	TP	Avg.
1946-47	Detroit	60	283	131	697	11.6
1947-48	Boston-Prov.	10	14	9	37	3.7
1947-48	Flint NL	36	36	21	93	2.6
	Totals	106	333	161	827	7.8

JANOTTA, HOWARD
b. Oct. 19, 1924 Ht. 6-3 Wt. 185 College—Seton Hall

Yr	Team	G	FG	FT	TP	Avg.
1949-50	Baltimore	9	9	13	31	3.4

JAROS, ANTHONY
b. Feb. 22, 1920 Ht. 6-3 Wt. 185 College—Minnesota

Yr	Team	G	FG	FT	TP	Avg.
1946-47	Chicago	59	177	128	482	8.2
1947-48	Minneapolis NL	58	95	83	273	4.7
1948-49	Minneapolis	59	132	79	343	5.8
1949-50	Minneapolis	61	84	72	240	3.9
1950-51	Minneapolis	63	88	65	241	3.8
	Totals	300	576	427	1579	5.3

JARVIS, JIM
b. March 3, 1943 Ht. 6-1 Wt. 175 Coll.—Oregon State

Yr	Team	G	FG	FT	TP	Avg.
1967-68	Pittsburgh ABA	63	120 (12)	53	329	5.2
1968-69	Minn.-L.A. ABA	62	128 (19)	86	399	6.4
	Totals	125	248 (31)	139	728	5.8

JEANNETTE, HARRY (Buddy)
b. Sept. 15, 1917 Ht. 5-11 Wt. 175 Coll.—Washington and Jefferson

Yr	Team	G	FG	FT	TP	Avg.
1938-39	War.-Cleve. NL	26	54	65	173	6.7
1939-40	Detroit NL	25	45	52	142	5.7
1940-41	Detroit NL	23	75	54	204	8.9
1942-43	Sheboygan NL	4	24	14	62	15.5
1943-44	Fort Wayne NL	22	68	48	184	8.4
1944-45	Fort Wayne NL	27	85	82	252	9.3

Yr	Team	G	FG	FT	TP	Avg.
1945-46	Fort Wayne NL	34	99	105	303	8.9
1947-48	Baltimore	46	150	191	491	10.7
1948-49	Baltimore	56	73	167	313	5.6
1949-50	Baltimore	37	42	109	193	5.2
	Totals	300	715	887	2317	7.7

JETER, HAL

College—Drake

Yr	Team	G	FG	FT	TP	Avg.
1969-70	Washington ABA	5	1 (0)	0	2	0.4

JOHNSON, ANDY

b. Nov. 3, 1931 Ht. 6-5 Wt. 215 College—Portland

Yr	Team	G	FG	FT	TP	Avg.
1958-59	Philadelphia	67	174	115	463	6.9
1959-60	Philadelphia	75	245	125	615	8.2
1960-61	Philadelphia·	79	299	157	755	9.6
1961-62	Chicago	71	365	284	1014	14.3
	Totals	292	1083	681	2847	9.8

JOHNSON, ARNITZ (Arnie)

b. May 17, 1920 Ht. 6-5 Wt. 240 Coll.—Bemidji State

Yr	Team	G	FG	FT	TP	Avg.
1946-47	Rochester NL	32	68	68	204	6.4
1947-48	Rochester NL	57	101	97	299	5.2
1948-49	Rochester	60	156	199	511	8.5
1949-50	Rochester	68	149	200	498	7.3
1950-51	Rochester	68	185	269	639	9.4
1951-52	Rochester	66	178	301	657	10.0
1952-53	Rochester	70	140	303	583	8.3
	Totals	421	977	1437	3391	8.1

JOHNSON, ED

b. June 17, 1944 Ht. 6-9 Wt. 205 Coll.—Tennessee St.

Yr	Team	G	FG	FT	TP	Avg.
1968-69	Los Angeles ABA	58	263 (0)	156	682	11.8
1969-70	New York ABA	74	404 (1)	226	1037	14.0
1970-71	N.Y.-Tex. ABA	34	119 (0)	82	320	9.4
	Totals	166	786 (1)	464	2039	12.3

JOHNSON, GEORGE

b. June 19, 1947 Ht. 6-11 Wt. 255 College—Stephen F. Austin

Yr	Team	G	FG	FT	TP	Avg.
1970-71	Baltimore	24	41	11	93	3.9
1971-72	Dallas ABA	67	128 (0)	61	317	4.7
	Totals	91	169 (0)	72	410	4.5

JOHNSON, GUS (Honeycomb)

b. Dec. 13, 1938 Ht. 6-6 Wt. 235 College—Idaho

Yr	Team	G	FG	FT	TP	Avg.
1963-64	Baltimore	78	571	210	1352	17.3
1964-65	Baltimore	76	577	261	1415	18.6
1965-66	Baltimore	42	273	131	677	16.1
1966-67	Baltimore	73	620	271	1511	20.7
1967-68	Baltimore	60	482	180	1144	19.0
1968-69	Baltimore	49	359	160	878	17.9
1969-70	Baltimore	78	578	197	1353	17.3
1970-71	Baltimore	66	494	214	1202	18.2
1971-72	Baltimore	39	103	43	249	6.4
1972-73	Phoenix	20	69	25	163	8.2
1972-73	Indiana ABA	50	128 (4)	31	299	6.0
	Totals	631	4254 (4)	1723	10243	16.2

JOHNSON, HAROLD

b. Jan. 20, 1920 Ht. 6-6 Wt. 240 Coll.—Indiana State

Yr	Team	G	FG	FT	TP	Avg.
1946-47	Detroit	27	4	7	15	0.6

JOHNSON, LARRY

b. Nov. 28, 1954 Ht. 6-3 Wt. 205 College—Kentucky

Yr	Team	G	FG	FT	TP	Avg.
1977-78	Buffalo	4	3	0	6	1.5

JOHNSON, NEIL

b. April 14, 1943 Ht. 6-7 Wt. 220 College—Creighton

Yr	Team	G	FG	FT	TP	Avg.
1966-67	New York	51	59	57	175	3.4
1967-68	New York	43	44	23	111	2.6
1968-69	Phoenix	80	177	110	464	5.8
1969-70	Phoenix	28	20	8	48	1.4
1970-71	Virginia ABA	78	398 (0)	194	990	12.7
1971-72	Virginia ABA	31	127 (1)	65	322	10.4
1972-73	Virginia ABA	69	210 (0)	103	523	7.6
	Totals	380	1035 (1)	560	2633	6.9

JOHNSON, RALPH (Boag)

b. Dec. 6, 1921 Ht. 5-11 Wt. 170 College—Huntington

Yr	Team	G	FG	FT	TP	Avg.
1947-48	Anderson NL	57	84	31	199	3.5
1948-49	Anderson NL	64	218	85	521	8.1
1949-50	And.-Ft. W.	67	243	104	590	8.8
1950-51	Ft. Wayne	68	235	114	584	8.6
1951-52	Ft. Wayne	66	211	101	523	7.9
1952-53	Ft. Wayne	3	3	2	8	2.7
	Totals	325	994	437	2425	7.5

JOHNSON, RICH

b. Dec. 18, 1946 Ht. 6-9 Wt. 210 College—Grambling

Yr	Team	G	FG	FT	TP	Avg.
1968-69	Boston	31	29	11	69	2.2
1969-70	Boston	65	167	46	380	5.8
1970-71	Boston	1	4	0	8	8.0
	Totals	97	200	57	457	4.7

JOHNSON, RONALD

b. July 20, 1938 Ht. 6-8 Wt. 215 College—Minnesota

Yr	Team	G	FG	FT	TP	Avg.
1960-61	Detroit-L.A.	14	13	11	37	2.6

JOHNSON, STEWART

b. Aug. 19, 1944 Ht. 6-9 Wt. 225 Coll.—Murray State

Yr	Team	G	FG	FT	TP	Avg.
1967-68	Ky.-N.J. ABA	72	230 (25)	69	604	8.4
1968-69	N.Y.-Hous. ABA	78	552 (64)	199	1495	19.2
1969-70	Pittsburgh ABA	81	529 (15)	137	1240	15.3
1970-71	Pittsburgh ABA	84	581 (12)	144	1342	15.9
1971-72	Pitt.-Car. ABA	67	352 (16)	73	825	12.3
1972-73	San Diego ABA	80	732 (37)	195	1770	22.1
1973-74	San Diego ABA	84	657 (59)	199	1690	20.1
1974-75	S.D.-Mem. ABA	81	624 (40)	63	1431	17.7
1975-76	S.D.-S.A. ABA	20	60 (1)	18	141	7.1
	Totals	647	4317 (269)	1097	10538	16.3

Yr	Team	G	FG	FT	TP	Avg.

JOHNSTON, NEIL

b. Feb. 4, 1929 Ht. 6-8 Wt. 215 College—Ohio State

Yr	Team	G	FG	FT	TP	Avg.
1951-52	Philadelphia	64	141	100	382	6.0
1952-53	Philadelphia	70	504	556	1564	22.3
1953-54	Philadelphia	72	591	577	1759	24.4
1954-55	Philadelphia	72	521	589	1631	22.7
1955-56	Philadelphia	70	499	549	1547	22.1
1956-57	Philadelphia	69	520	535	1575	22.8
1957-58	Philadelphia	71	473	442	1388	19.5
1958-59	Philadelphia	28	54	69	177	6.3
Totals		516	3303	3417	10023	19.4

JOLLIFF, HOWARD

b. July 20, 1938 Ht. 6-7 Wt. 218 Coll.—Ohio Univ.

Yr	Team	G	FG	FT	TP	Avg.
1960-61	Los Angeles	46	46	11	103	2.2
1961-62	Los Angeles	64	104	41	249	3.9
1962-63	Los Angeles	28	15	6	36	1.3
Totals		138	165	58	388	2.8

JONES, JAKE

b. May 9, 1949 Ht. 6-3 Wt. 180 College—Assumption

Yr	Team	G	FG	FT	TP	Avg.
1971-72	Philadelphia	6	6	7	19	3.2

JONES, JAMES

b. Jan. 1, 1945 Ht. 6-4 Wt. 188 College—Grambling

Yr	Team	G	FG	FT	TP	Avg.
1967-68	New Orleans	78	549	360	1464	18.8
	ABA		(2)			
1968-69	New Orleans	77	763	521	2050	26.6
	ABA		(1)			
1969-70	New Orleans	70	531	380	1448	20.7
	ABA		(2)			
1970-71	Memphis	80	589	374	1564	19.5
	ABA		(4)			
1971-72	Utah	78	461	282	1207	15.5
	ABA		(1)			
1972-73	Utah	80	496	345	1337	16.7
	ABA		(0)			
1973-74	Utah	83	583	229	1395	16.8
	ABA		(0)			
1974-75	Washington	73	237	103	577	7.1
1975-76	Washington	64	153	72	378	5.9
1976-77	Washington	3	2	2	6	2.0
Totals		686	4364	2668	11426	16.7
			(10)			

JONES, J. COLLIS

b. July 3, 1949 Ht. 6-7 Wt. 205 College—Notre Dame

Yr	Team	G	FG	FT	TP	Avg.
1971-72	Dallas	78	162	98	425	5.5
	ABA		(1)			
1972-73	Dallas	81	357	227	941	11.6
	ABA		(0)			
1973-74	Kentucky	58	102	51	255	4.4
	ABA		(0)			
1974-75	Memphis	81	328	134	805	9.9
	ABA		(5)			
1975-76	Ken.-St. L.	76	423	140	986	13.0
	ABA		(0)			
Totals		374	1372	650	3412	9.1
			(6)			

JONES, JOHN

b. March 12, 1943 Ht. 6-7½ Wt. 205 Coll.—L.A. St.

Yr	Team	G	FG	FT	TP	Avg.
1967-68	Boston	51	86	42	214	4.2
1968-69	Kentucky	29	81	41	203	7.0
	ABA		(0)			
Totals		80	167	83	417	5.2
			(0)			

JONES, K. C.

b. May 25, 1932 Ht. 6-1 Wt. 202 Coll.—San Francisco

Yr	Team	G	FG	FT	TP	Avg.
1958-59	Boston	49	65	41	171	3.5
1959-60	Boston	74	169	128	466	6.3
1960-61	Boston	78	203	186	592	7.6
1961-62	Boston	79	289	145	723	9.1
1962-63	Boston	79	230	112	572	7.2
1963-64	Boston	80	283	88	654	8.2
1964-65	Boston	78	253	143	649	8.3
1965-66	Boston	80	240	209	689	8.6
1966-67	Boston	78	182	119	483	6.2
Totals		675	1914	1171	4999	7.4

JONES, RICH WESLEY

b. Dec. 27, 1946 Ht. 6-8 Wt. 230 Coll.—Memphis State

Yr	Team	G	FG	FT	TP	Avg.
1969-70	Dallas	2	9	10	28	14.0
	ABA		(0)			
1970-71	Texas	79	338	175	950	12.0
	ABA		(33)			
1971-72	Dallas	82	461	212	1176	14.3
	ABA		(14)			
1972-73	Dallas	67	521	324	1495	22.3
	ABA		(43)			
1973-74	San Antonio	78	497	186	1219	15.6
	ABA		(13)			
1974-75	San Antonio	83	636	287	1598	19.3
	ABA		(13)			
1975-76	New York	83	426	199	1096	13.2
	ABA		(15)			
1976-77	N.Y. Nets	34	134	92	360	10.6
Totals		508	3022	1485	7922	15.6
			(131)			

JONES, ROBIN (Major)

b. Feb. 2, 1954 Ht. 6-9 Wt. 215 Coll.—Albany St. (Ga.)

Yr	Team	G	FG	FT	TP	Avg.
1976-77	Portland	63	139	66	344	5.5
1977-78	Houston	12	11	4	26	2.2
Totals		75	150	70	370	4.9

JONES, RYAN (Nick)

b. March 28, 1945 Ht. 6-2 Wt. 191 College—Oregon

Yr	Team	G	FG	FT	TP	Avg.
1967-68	San Diego	42	86	55	227	5.4
1968-69	Dallas-Miami	7	9	2	20	2.9
	ABA		(0)			
1970-71	San Francisco	81	225	111	561	6.9
1971-72	Golden State	65	82	51	215	3.3
1972-73	Dallas	3	3	2	8	2.7
	ABA		(0)			
Totals		198	405	221	1031	5.2
			(0)			

JONES, SAM

b. June 24, 1933 Ht. 6-4 Wt. 205 Coll.—N. Car. Col.

Yr	Team	G	FG	FT	TP	Avg.
1957-58	Boston	56	100	60	260	4.6
1958-59	Boston	71	305	151	761	10.7
1959-60	Boston	74	355	168	878	11.9
1960-61	Boston	78	474	210	1158	14.8
1961-62	Boston	78	589	239	1417	18.2
1962-63	Boston	76	621	257	1499	19.7
1963-64	Boston	76	612	249	1473	19.4
1964-65	Boston	80	821	428	2070	25.9
1965-66	Boston	68	626	325	1577	23.2
1966-67	Boston	72	638	318	1594	22.1
1967-68	Boston	73	621	311	1553	21.3
1968-69	Boston	70	496	148	1140	16.3
Totals		872	6258	2864	15380	17.6

Yr	Team	G	FG	FT	TP	Avg.

JONES, STEVE

b. Oct. 17, 1942 Ht. 6-5 Wt. 205 College—Oregon

Yr	Team	G	FG	FT	TP	Avg.
1967-68	Oakland ABA	76	255 (23)	186	765	10.1
1968-69	New Orleans ABA	78	524 (52)	348	1552	19.9
1969-70	New Orleans ABA	84	674 (15)	412	1805	21.5
1970-71	Memphis ABA	83	692 (40)	332	1836	22.1
1971-72	Dallas ABA	84	546 (26)	367	1537	18.3
1972-73	Dal.-Car. ABA	80	417 (13)	200	1073	13.4
1973-74	Car.-Den. ABA	86	387 (13)	128	941	10.9
1974-75	St. Louis ABA	69	283 (4)	171	749	10.9
1975-76	Portland	64	168	78	414	6.5
	Totals	704	3946 (186)	2222	10672	15.2

JONES, WALI

b. Feb. 14, 1942 Ht. 6-2 Wt. 180 College—Villanova

Yr	Team	G	FG	FT	TP	Avg.
1964-65	Baltimore	77	154	99	407	5.3
1965-66	Philadelphia	80	296	128	720	9.0
1966-67	Philadelphia	81	423	223	1069	13.2
1967-68	Philadelphia	77	413	159	985	12.8
1968-69	Philadelphia	81	432	207	1071	13.2
1969-70	Philadelphia	78	366	190	922	11.8
1970-71	Philadelphia	41	168	79	415	10.1
1971-72	Milwaukee	48	144	74	362	7.5
1972-73	Milwaukee	27	59	16	134	5.0
1974-75	Utah ABA	71	206 (6)	102	532	7.5
1975-76	Det.-Phil.	17	23	9	55	3.2
	Totals	678	2684 (6)	1286	6672	9.8

JONES, WALLACE (Wah Wah)

b. July 14, 1926 Ht. 6-4 Wt. 225 College—Kentucky

Yr	Team	G	FG	FT	TP	Avg.
1949-50	Indianapolis	60	264	223	751	12.5
1950-51	Indianapolis	22	93	61	247	11.2
1951-52	Indianapolis	58	164	102	430	7.4
	Totals	140	521	386	1428	10.2

JONES, WALTER (Larry)

b. Sept. 22, 1941 Ht. 6-2½ Wt. 180 College—Toledo

Yr	Team	G	FG	FT	TP	Avg.
1964-65	Philadelphia	23	47	37	131	5.7
1967-68	Denver ABA	76	594 (8)	530	1742	22.9
1968-69	Denver ABA	75	735 (24)	591	2133	28.4
1969-70	Denver ABA	75	584 (41)	579	1870	24.9
1970-71	Floridians ABA	84	719 (45)	471	2044	24.3
1971-72	Floridians ABA	66	405 (18)	300	1164	17.6
1972-73	Utah-Dal. ABA	80	224 (16)	202	698	8.7
	Totals	479	3308 (152)	2710	9782	20.4

JONES, WILBERT

b. Feb. 27, 1947 Ht. 6-8 Wt. 205 Coll.—Albany St. (Ga.)

Yr	Team	G	FG	FT	TP	Avg.
1969-70	Miami ABA	74	241 (2)	118	606	8.2
1970-71	Memphis ABA	84	390 (1)	174	957	11.4
1971-72	Memphis ABA	84	504 (2)	240	1254	14.9
1972-73	Memphis ABA	76	343 (1)	146	835	11.0
1973-74	Memphis ABA	81	450 (3)	163	1072	13.2
1974-75	Kentucky ABA	84	458 (0)	139	1055	12.6
1975-76	Kentucky ABA	83	480 (3)	158	1127	13.6
1976-77	Indiana	80	438	166	1042	13.0
1977-78	Buffalo	79	226	84	536	6.8
	Totals	725	3530 (12)	1388	8484	11.7

JONES, WILLIE (The Bird)

b. June 29, 1936 Ht. 6-3½ Wt. 185 Coll.—Northwestern

Yr	Team	G	FG	FT	TP	Avg.
1960-61	Detroit	35	78	40	196	5.6
1961-62	Detroit	69	177	64	418	6.0
1962-63	Detroit	79	305	118	728	9.2
1963-64	Detroit	77	265	100	630	8.2
1964-65	Detroit	12	21	2	44	3.7
	Totals	272	846	324	2016	7.4

JORDAN, CHARLES

b. Jan. 31, 1954 Ht. 6-8 Wt. 220 College—Canisius

Yr	Team	G	FG	FT	TP	Avg.
1975-76	Indiana ABA	71	160 (2)	43	369	5.2

JORDON, PHIL

b. Sept. 12, 1933 Ht. 6-10 Wt. 205 College—Whitworth
d. June 7, 1965

Yr	Team	G	FG	FT	TP	Avg.
1956-57	New York	9	18	8	44	4.9
1957-58	Detroit	58	193	64	450	7.8
1958-59	Detroit	72	399	231	1029	14.3
1959-60	Cincinnati	75	381	242	1004	13.4
1960-61	Cin.-N.Y.	79	360	208	928	11.7
1961-62	New York	76	403	96	902	11.9
1962-63	St. Louis	73	211	56	478	6.5
	Totals	442	1965	905	4835	10.9

JORGENSEN, JOHN

b. Dec. 28 1921 Ht. 6-2 Wt. 185 College—DePaul
d. Jan. 19, 1973

Yr	Team	G	FG	FT	TP	Avg.
1947-48	Chicago-Balt.	3	4	1	9	3.0
1947-48	Minneapolis NL	38	37	27	101	2.7
1948-49	Minneapolis	48	41	24	106	2.2
	Totals	89	82	52	216	2.4

JORGENSEN, NOBLE (Jorgy)

b. May 18, 1925 Ht. 6-9 Wt. 230 College—Iowa and Westminster (Pa.)

Yr	Team	G	FG	FT	TP	Avg.
1946-47	Pittsburgh	15	25	16	66	4.4
1948-49	Sheboygan NL	63	218	194	630	10.0
1949-50	Sheboygan	54	218	268	704	13.0
1950-51	Tri-Cities-Syr.	63	223	182	628	10.0
1951-52	Syracuse	66	190	149	529	8.0
1952-53	Syracuse	70	145	146	436	6.2
	Totals	331	1019	955	2993	9.0

JORGENSEN, ROGER

b. Sept. 2, 1920 Ht. 6-5 Wt. 200 College—Ohio State

Yr	Team	G	FG	FT	TP	Avg.
1946-47	Pittsburgh	28	14	13	41	1.5

Yr	Team	G	FG	FT	TP	Avg.

JOYCE, KEVIN

b. June 27, 1951 Ht. 6-3 Wt. 190 Coll.—South Carolina

Yr	Team	G	FG	FT	TP	Avg.
1973-74	Indiana ABA	56	166 (5)	64	411	7.3
1974-75	Indiana ABA	81	522 (8)	142	1210	14.9
1975-76	S.D.-Ken. ABA	43	112 (2)	55	285	6.6
	Totals	180	800 (15)	261	1906	10.6

JOYNER, HARRY (Butch)

College—Indiana

Yr	Team	G	FG	FT	TP	Avg.
1968-69	Indiana ABA	2	0 (0)	0	0	0.0

KACHAN, ED

b. Sept. 15, 1925 Ht. 6-2 Wt. 175 College—DePaul

Yr	Team	G	FG	FT	TP	Avg.
1948-49	Chi.-Minn.	52	38	36	112	2 2

KAFTAN, GEORGE

b. Feb. 22, 1928 Ht. 6-3 Wt. 190 College—Holy Cross

Yr	Team	G	FG	FT	TP	Avg.
1948-49	Boston	21	116	72	304	14.5
1949-50	Boston	55	199	136	534	9.7
1950-51	New York	61	111	78	300	4.9
1951-52	New York	52	115	92	322	6.2
1952-53	Baltimore	23	45	44	134	5.8
	Totals	212	586	422	1594	7.5

KALAFAT, ED

b. Oct. 13, 1932 Ht. 6-6 Wt. 245 College—Minnesota

Yr	Team	G	FG	FT	TP	Avg.
1954-55	Minneapolis	72	118	111	347	4.8
1955-56	Minneapolis	72	194	186	574	8.0
1956-57	Minneapolis	65	178	197	553	8.5
	Totals	209	490	494	1474	7.1

KAPLOWITZ, RALPH (Kappy)

b. May 18, 1919 Ht. 6-2 Wt. 170 College—N.Y.U.

Yr	Team	G	FG	FT	TP	Avg.
1946-47	N.Y.-Phila.	57	146	111	403	7.1
1947-48	Philadelphia	48	71	47	189	3.9
	Totals	105	217	158	592	5.6

KAPPEN, ANTHONY

b. April 13, 1919 Ht. 5-10 Wt. 165

Yr	Team	G	FG	FT	TP	Avg.
1946-47	Pitt.—Boston	59	128	128	384	6.5

KARL, GEORGE

b. May 12, 1951 Ht. 6-2 Wt. 185 Coll.—No. Carolina

Yr	Team	G	FG	FT	TP	Avg.
1973-74	San Antonio ABA	74	228 (8)	94	574	7.7
1974-75	San Antonio ABA	82	257 (4)	137	663	8.1
1975-76	San Antonio ABA	75	150 (0)	81	381	5.1
1976-77	San Antonio	29	25	29	79	2.7
1977-78	San Antonio	4	2	2	6	1.5
	Totals	264	662 (12)	343	1703	6.5

KASID, EDWARD

b. Aug. 13, 1923 Ht. 5-11 Wt. 185

Yr	Team	G	FG	FT	TP	Avg.
1946-47	Toronto	8	6	0	12	1.5

KATKAVECK, LEO

b. April 17, 1923 Ht. 6-0 Wt. 185 Coll.—N. Caro. St.

Yr	Team	G	FG	FT	TP	Avg.
1948-49	Washington	53	84	53	221	4.2
1949-50	Balt.-Wash.	54	101	34	236	4.4
	Totals	107	185	87	457	4.3

KAUFFMAN, BOB

b. July 13, 1946 Ht. 6-8 Wt. 240 College—Guilford

Yr	Team	G	FG	FT	TP	Avg.
1968-69	Seattle	82	219	203	641	7.8
1969-70	Chicago	64	94	88	276	4.3
1970-71	Buffalo	78	616	359	1591	20.4
1971-72	Buffalo	77	558	341	1457	18.9
1972-73	Buffalo	77	535	280	1350	17.5
1973-74	Buffalo	74	171	107	449	6.1
1974-75	Atlanta	73	113	59	285	3.9
	Totals	525	2306	1437	6049	11.5

KAUTZ, WILBERT (Wibs)

b. Sept. 7, 1915 Ht. 6-0 Wt. 180 Coll.—Loyola (Ill.)

Yr	Team	G	FG	FT	TP	Avg.
1939-40	Chicago NL	28	105	63	273	9.8
1940-41	Chicago NL	21	94	39	227	10.8
1941-42	Chicago NL	20	85	40	210	10.5
1946-47	Chicago	50	107	39	253	5.1
	Totals	119	391	181	963	8.1

KEARNS, MICHAEL

Ht. 6-2 Wt. 178 College—Princeton

Yr	Team	G	FG	FT	TP	Avg.
1954-55	Philadelphia	6	0	1	1	0.2

KEARNS, THOMAS

b. Oct. 6, 1936 Ht. 5-11 Wt. 185 Coll.—North Carolina

Yr	Team	G	FG	FT	TP	Avg.
1958-59	Syracuse	1	1	0	2	2.0

KELLER, BILL

b. Aug. 30, 1947 Ht. 5-10 Wt. 180 College—Purdue

Yr	Team	G	FG	FT	TP	Avg.
1969-70	Indiana ABA	82	210 (42)	164	710	8.7
1970-71	Indiana ABA	83	333 (84)	267	1185	14.3
1971-72	Indiana ABA	76	208 (56)	153	737	9.7
1972-73	Indiana ABA	83	350 (71)	234	1147	13.8
1973-74	Indiana ABA	75	229 (50)	107	715	9.5
1974-75	Indiana ABA	79	317 (80)	113	987	12.5
1975-76	Indiana ABA	78	287 (123)	164	1107	14.2
	Totals	556	1934 (506)	1202	6588	11.8

KELLER, GARY

b. June 13, 1944 Ht. 6-9 Wt. 220 College—Florida

Yr	Team	G	FG	FT	TP	Avg.
1967-68	Minnesota ABA	69	184 (0)	139	507	7.4
1968-69	Miami ABA	53	78 (0)	72	228	4.3
	Totals	122	262 (0)	211	735	6.0

KELLER, KENNETH

b. 1922 Ht. 6-1 Wt. 180 College—St. John's (N.Y.)

Yr	Team	G	FG	FT	TP	Avg.
1946-47	Wash.-Prov.	28	10	2	22	0.8

Yr	Team	G	FG	FT	TP	Avg.

KELLEY, GERARD (Jerry)

b. 1922 Ht. 6-2 Wt. 172 College—Marshall

Yr	Team	G	FG	FT	TP	Avg.
1946-47	Boston	43	91	74	256	6.0
1947-48	Providence	3	3	0	6	2.0
	Totals	46	94	74	262	5.7

KELLY, ARVESTA

b. Nov. 20, 1945 Ht. 6-3 Wt. 175 Coll.—Lincoln (Mo.)

Yr	Team	G	FG	FT	TP	Avg.
1967-68	Pittsburgh ABA	16	23 (3)	8	63	3.9
1968-69	Minnesota ABA	68	130 (25)	63	398	5.9
1969-70	Pittsburgh ABA	70	363 (21)	168	957	13.6
1970-71	Car.-Pitt. ABA	22	20 (0)	18	58	2.6
1971-72	Pitt.-Ind. ABA	12	12 (1)	3	30	2.5
	Totals	188	548 (50)	260	1506	8.0

KELLY, TOM

b. March 5, 1924 Ht. 6-2 Wt. 172 College—N.Y.U.

Yr	Team	G	FG	FT	TP	Avg.
1948-49	Boston	27	73	45	191	7.1

KELSO, BEN

b. April 11, 1949 Ht. 6-3 Wt. 195 Coll.—Cen. Michigan

Yr	Team	G	FG	FT	TP	Avg.
1973-74	Detroit	46	35	15	85	1.8

KENDRICK, FRANK

b. Nov. 11, 1951 Ht. 6-6 Wt. 198 College—Purdue

Yr	Team	G	FG	FT	TP	Avg.
1974-75	Golden State	24	31	18	80	3.3

KENNEDY, EUGENE

b. Aug. 23, 1949 Ht. 6-6 Wt. 205 Coll.—Texas Christian

Yr	Team	G	FG	FT	TP	Avg.
1971-72	Dallas ABA	65	234 (0)	88	556	8.6
1972-73	Dallas ABA	70	365 (0)	148	878	12.5
1973-74	San Antonio ABA	76	194 (0)	60	448	5.9
1974-75	St. Louis ABA	74	280 (1)	129	692	9.4
1975-76	Utah ABA	16	38 (0)	9	85	5.9
1976-77	Houston	32	31	3	65	2.0
	Totals	333	1142 (1)	437	2724	8.2

KENNEDY, JOE

b. Jan. 12, 1947 Ht. 6-6 Wt. 210 College—Duke

Yr	Team	G	FG	FT	TP	Avg.
1968-69	Seattle	72	174	98	446	6.2
1969-70	Seattle	14	3	2	8	0.6
	Totals	86	177	100	454	5.3

KENNEDY, WILLIAM (Pickles)

b. May 17, 1938 Ht. 5-11 Wt. 180 College—Temple

Yr	Team	G	FG	FT	TP	Avg.
1960-61	Philadelphia	7	4	4	12	1.7

KENVILLE, BILL (The Kid)

b. Dec. 1, 1930 Ht. 6-2 Wt. 190 Coll.—St. Bonaventure

Yr	Team	G	FG	FT	TP	Avg.
1953-54	Syracuse	72	149	136	434	6.0
1954-55	Syracuse	70	172	154	498	7.1
1955-56	Syracuse	72	170	195	535	7.4
1956-57	Ft. Wayne	71	204	174	582	8.2
1957-58	Detroit	35	106	46	248	7.4
1959-60	Detroit	25	47	33	127	5.1
	Totals	345	848	738	2434	7.1

KERR, JOHN (Red)

b. Aug. 17, 1932 Ht. 6-9 Wt. 230 College—Illinois

Yr	Team	G	FG	FT	TP	Avg.
1954-55	Syracuse	72	301	152	754	10.5
1955-56	Syracuse	72	377	207	961	13.3
1956-57	Syracuse	72	333	225	891	12.4
1957-58	Syracuse	72	407	280	1094	15.2
1958-59	Syracuse	72	502	281	1285	17.8
1959-60	Syracuse	75	436	233	1105	14.7
1960-61	Syracuse	79	419	218	1056	13.4
1961-62	Syracuse	80	541	222	1304	16.3
1962-63	Syracuse	80	507	241	1255	15.7
1963-64	Philadelphia	80	536	268	1340	16.8
1964-65	Philadelphia	80	264	126	654	8.2
1965-66	Baltimore	71	286	209	781	11.0
	Totals	905	4909	2662	12480	13.8

KERRIS, JACK

b. Jan. 30, 1925 Ht. 6-6 Wt. 215 Coll.—Loyola (Ill.)

Yr	Team	G	FG	FT	TP	Avg.
1949-50	Tri-Cities-Ft. Wayne	68	157	169	483	7.1
1950-51	Ft. Wayne	68	255	201	711	10.5
1951-52	Ft. Wayne	66	186	217	589	8.9
1952-53	Ft. W.-Balt.	69	93	88	274	4.0
	Totals	271	691	675	2057	7.6

KERWIN, TOM

Ht. 6-7 Wt. 210 College—Centenary

Yr	Team	G	FG	FT	TP	Avg.
1967-68	Pittsburgh ABA	13	7 (0)	0	14	1.1

KEYE, JULIUS

b. July 5, 1946 Ht. 6-10 Wt. 225 Coll.—Alcorn A & M

Yr	Team	G	FG	FT	TP	Avg.
1969-70	Denver ABA	77	245 (0)	116	606	7.9
1970-71	Denver ABA	83	505 (0)	212	1222	14.7
1971-72	Denver ABA	84	192 (0)	108	492	5.9
1972-73	Denver ABA	83	160 (3)	130	459	5.5
1973-74	Denver ABA	79	146 (1)	57	352	4.5
1974-75	Memphis ABA	12	12 (0)	36	30	2.5
	Totals	418	1260 (4)	629	3161	7.6

KILEY, JACK

b. 1930 Ht. 6-1 Wt. 170 College—Syracuse

Yr	Team	G	FG	FT	TP	Avg.
1951-52	Ft. Wayne	47	44	30	118	2.5
1952-53	Ft. Wayne	6	2	2	6	1.0
	Totals	53	46	32	124	2.3

KILLUM, ERNEST

b. June 11, 1948 Ht. 6-3 Wt. 180 College—Stetson

Yr	Team	G	FG	FT	TP	Avg.
1970-71	Los Angeles	4	0	1	1	0.3

KIMBALL, THOMAS (Toby)

b. Sept. 23, 1942 Ht. 6-8 Wt. 220 College—Connecticut

Yr	Team	G	FG	FT	TP	Avg.
1966-67	Boston	38	35	27	97	2.6

Yr	Team	G	FG	FT	TP	Avg.
1967-68	San Diego	81	354	181	889	11.0
1968-69	San Diego	76	239	117	595	7.8
1969-70	San Diego	77	218	107	543	7.1
1970-71	San Diego	80	111	51	273	3.4
1971-72	Milwaukee	74	107	44	258	3.4
	Totals	426	1064	527	2655	6.2

KING, DANIEL

b. Jan. 7, 1931 Ht. 6-6 Wt. 220 Coll.—W. Kentucky

1954-55	Baltimore	12	7	5	19	1.6

KING, GEORGE

b. Aug. 16, 1928 Ht. 6-0 Wt. 185 Coll.—Morris Harvey

1951-52	Syracuse	66	235	188	658	10.0
1952-53	Syracuse	71	255	284	794	11.2
1953-54	Syracuse	72	280	257	817	11.3
1954-55	Syracuse	67	228	140	596	8.9
1955-56	Syracuse	72	284	176	744	10.3
1957-58	Cincinnati	63	235	140	610	9.7
	Totals	411	1517	1185	4219	10.3

KING, JAMES (Country)

b. Feb. 7, 1941 Ht. 6-2 Wt. 175 College—Tulsa

1963-64	Los Angeles	60	84	66	234	3.9
1964-65	Los Angeles	77	184	118	486	6.3
1965-66	Los Angeles	76	238	94	570	7.5
1966-67	San Francisco	67	286	174	746	11.1
1967-68	San Francisco	54	340	217	897	16.6
1968-69	San Francisco	46	137	78	352	7.7
1969-70	S.F.-Cin.	34	53	33	139	4.1
1970-71	Chicago	55	100	64	264	4.8
1971-72	Chicago	73	162	89	413	5.7
	Totals	542	1584	933	4101	7.6

KING, LOYD

b. May 29, 1949 Ht. 6-2 Wt. 180 Coll.—Virginia Tech.

1971-72	Memphis ABA	74	164 (21)	96	487	6.6
1972-73	Memphis ABA	10	6 (0)	7	19	1.9
	Totals	84	170 (21)	103	506	6.0

KING, MAURICE (Maury)

b. March 12, 1935 Ht. 6-3 Wt. 195 College—Kansas

1959-60	Boston	1	5	0	10	10.0
1962-63	Chicago	37	94	28	216	5.8
	Totals	38	99	28	226	5.9

KING, RON

b. 1951 Ht. 6-4 Wt. 195 College—Florida State

1973-74	Kentucky ABA	9	22 (2)	14	64	7.1

KING, THOMAS

b. Jan. 23, 1926 Ht. 6-1 Wt. 165 College—Michigan

1946-47	Detroit	58	97	101	295	5.1

KINNEY, ROBERT (Hi-Pocket)

b. Sept. 16, 1920 Ht. 6-6½ Wt. 215 College—Rice

1945-46	Fort Wayne NL	13	16	2	34	2.6

Yr	Team	G	FG	FT	TP	Avg.
1946-47	Fort Wayne NL	44	102	42	246	5.6
1947-48	Fort Wayne NL	58	149	92	390	6.7
1948-49	Ft. W.-Boston	58	161	136	458	7.9
1949-50	Boston	60	233	201	667	11.1
	Totals	233	661	473	1795	7.7

KIRK, WALTON (Junior)

b. Sept. 3, 1924 Ht. 6-3 Wt. 173 College—Illinois

1947-48	Fort Wayne NL	45	62	44	168	3.7
1948-49	Ft. W.-Ind.	49	140	167	447	9.1
1949-50	And.-Tri-C.	58	97	155	349	6.0
1951-52	Milwaukee	11	28	55	111	10.1
	Totals	163	327	421	1075	6.6

KIRKLAND, WILBUR

Ht. 6-7 Wt. 191 College—Cheyney State

1969-70	Pittsburgh ABA	2	3 (0)	0	6	3.0

KISSANE, JIM

b. Aug. 17, 1946 Ht. 6-7 Wt. 210 Coll.—Boston Coll.

1968-69	Minnesota ABA	2	2 (0)	2	6	3.0

KISTLER, DOUGLAS

b. March 21, 1938 Ht. 6-9 Wt. 210 College—Duke

1961-62	New York	5	3	2	8	1.6

KLIER, LEO (Crystal)

b. May 21, 1923 Ht. 6-2 Wt. 170 Coll.—Notre Dame

1946-47	Indianapolis NL	44	162	93	417	9.5
1947-48	Indianapolis NL	56	227	152	606	10.8
1948-49	Ft. Wayne	47	125	97	347	7.4
1949-50	Ft. Wayne	66	157	141	455	6.9
	Totals	213	671	483	1825	8.6

KLOTZ, LOUIS HERMAN (Red)

b. Oct. 21, 1921 Ht. 5-7 Wt. 150 College—Villanova

1947-48	Baltimore	11	7	1	15	1.4

KLUEH, DUANE

b. Jan 6, 1926 Ht. 6-3 Wt. 175 Coll.—Indiana State

1949-50	Den.-Ft. W.	52	159	157	475	9.1
1950-51	Ft. Wayne	61	157	135	449	7.4
	Totals	113	316	292	924	8.2

KLUTTZ, LONNIE

b. Sept. 13, 1945 Ht. 6-7 Wt. 220 Coll.—N. Car. A & T

1970-71	Carolina ABA	3	0 (0)	0	0	0.0

KNIGHT, BOB

b. 1931 Ht. 6-2 Wt. 185

1954-55	New York	2	3	1	7	3.5

Yr	Team	G	FG	FT	TP	Avg.

KNIGHT, RON

b. Aug. 4, 1947 Ht. 6-7 Wt. 220 Coll.—Los Angeles St.

Yr	Team	G	FG	FT	TP	Avg.
1970-71	Portland	52	99	19	217	4.2
1971-72	Portland	49	112	31	255	5.2
	Totals	101	211	50	472	4.7

KNOREK, LEONARD (Lee)

b. July 15, 1921 Ht. 6-7 Wt. 215 College—Denison and Detroit

Yr	Team	G	FG	FT	TP	Avg.
1946-47	New York	22	62	47	171	7.8
1947-48	New York	48	99	61	259	5.4
1948-49	New York	60	156	131	443	7.4
1949-50	Baltimore	1	0	0	0	0.0
	Totals	131	317	239	873	6.7

KNOSTMAN, RICHARD

b. Aug. 9, 1931 Ht. 6-6 Wt. 215 Coll.—Kansas State

Yr	Team	G	FG	FT	TP	Avg.
1953-54	Syracuse	5	3	7	13	2.6

KNOWLES, RODNEY

b. Feb. 27, 1946 Ht. 6-9 Wt. 215 College—Davidson

Yr	Team	G	FG	FT	TP	Avg.
1968-69	Phoenix	8	4	1	9	1.1
1968-69	New York ABA	1	0 (0)	0	0	0.0
	Totals	9	4 (0)	1	9	1.0

KOJIS, DON

b. Jan. 15, 1939 Ht. 6-3 Wt. 215 College—Marquette

Yr	Team	G	FG	FT	TP	Avg.
1963-64	Baltimore	78	203	82	488	6.3
1964-65	Detroit	65	180	62	422	6.5
1965-66	Detroit	60	182	76	440	7.3
1966-67	Chicago	78	329	134	792	10.2
1967-68	San Diego	69	530	300	1360	19.7
1968-69	San Diego	81	687	446	1820	22.5
1969-70	San Diego	56	338	181	857	15.3
1970-71	Seattle	79	454	249	1157	14.6
1971-72	Seattle	81	322	188	832	11.4
1972-73	K.C.-Omaha	77	276	106	658	8.5
1973-74	K.C.-Omaha	77	400	210	1010	13.1
1974-75	Kansas City	77	46	20	112	5.3
	Totals	814	3947	2054	9948	12.2

KOMENICH, MILO (Miles)

b. June 23, 1920 Ht. 6-7 Wt. 220 College—Wyoming

Yr	Team	G	FG	FT	TP	Avg.
1946-47	Fort Wayne NL	36	50	23	123	3.4
1947-48	Ft. W.-And. NL	50	127	44	298	6.0
1948-49	Anderson NL	64	243	124	610	9.5
1949-50	Anderson	64	244	146	634	9.9
	Totals	214	664	337	1665	7.8

KOMIVES, HOWARD (Butch)

b. May 9, 1941 Ht. 6-1 Wt. 185 Coll.—Bowling Green

Yr	Team	G	FG	FT	TP	Avg.
1964-65	New York	80	381	212	974	12.2
1965-66	New York	80	436	241	1113	13.9
1966-67	New York	65	402	217	1021	15.7
1967-68	New York	78	233	132	598	7.7
1968-69	N.Y.-Det.	85	379	211	969	11.4
1969-70	Detroit	82	363	190	916	11.2
1970-71	Detroit	82	275	121	671	8.2
1971-72	Detroit	79	262	164	688	8.7
1972-73	Buffalo	67	163	85	411	6.1
1973-74	K.C.-Omaha	44	78	33	189	4.3
	Totals	742	2972	1606	7550	10.2

KONDLA, TOM

b. Nov. 30, 1946 Ht. 6-8 Wt. 225 College—Minnesota

Yr	Team	G	FG	FT	TP	Avg.
1968-69	Minn.-Hou. ABA	42	58 (0)	22	138	3.3

KOPER, HERBERT (Bud)

b. Aug. 9, 1942 Ht. 6-6 Wt. 210 Coll.—Oklahoma City

Yr	Team	G	FG	FT	TP	Avg.
1964-65	San Francisco	56	106	35	247	4.4

KOSKI, TONY

Ht. 6-8½ Wt. 215 College-Providence

Yr	Team	G	FG	FT	TP	Avg.
1968-69	New York ABA	5	2 (0)	2	6	1.2

KOSMALSKI, LEN

b. Nov. 29, 1951 Ht. 7-0 Wt. 245 College—Tennessee

Yr	Team	G	FG	FT	TP	Avg.
1974-75	K.C.-O.	67	33	24	90	1.3
1975-76	Kansas City	9	8	4	20	2.2
	Totals	76	41	28	110	1.4

KOSTECKA, ANDY

b. Feb. 10, 1921 Ht. 6-3 Wt. 203 College—Georgetown

Yr	Team	G	FG	FT	TP	Avg.
1948-49	Indianapolis	21	46	43	135	6.4

KOTTMAN, HAROLD

b. Aug. 22, 1922 Ht. 6-8 Wt. 220 Coll.—Cul. Stockton

Yr	Team	G	FG	FT	TP	Avg.
1946-47	Boston	53	59	47	165	3.1

KOZELKO, TOM

b. July 1, 1951 Ht. 6-8 Wt. 220 College—Toledo

Yr	Team	G	FG	FT	TP	Avg.
1973-74	Capital	49	59	23	141	2.9
1974-75	Washington	73	60	31	151	2.1
1975-76	Washington	67	48	19	115	1.7
	Totals	189	167	73	407	2.2

KOZLICKI, RON

Ht. 6-7 College—Northwestern

Yr	Team	G	FG	FT	TP	Avg.
1967-68	Indiana ABA	37	35 (6)	21	109	2.9

KRAMER, BARRY

b. Nov. 10, 1942 Ht. 6-4 Wt. 200 College—N.Y.U.

Yr	Team	G	FG	FT	TP	Avg.
1964-65	S.F.-N.Y.	52	63	60	186	3.6
1969-70	New York ABA	7	10 (0)	7	27	3.9
	Totals	59	73 (0)	67	213	3.6

KRAMER, STEVE

Ht. 6-5 Wt. 200 College—Brigham Young

Yr	Team	G	FG	FT	TP	Avg.
1967-68	Anaheim ABA	50	217 (1)	129	566	11.3
1968-69	Houston ABA	23	113 (0)	95	321	14.0
1969-70	Carolina ABA	51	49 (0)	63	161	3.3
	Totals	124	379 (1)	287	1048	8.5

KRAUS, DANIEL

Ht. 6-0 Wt. 195 College—Georgetown

Yr	Team	G	FG	FT	TP	Avg.
1948-59	Baltimore	13	5	11	21	1.6

Yr	Team	G	FG	FT	TP	Avg.

KRAUTBLATT, HERB

b. Nov. 19, 1926 Ht. 6-1 Wt. 190 College—Rider

Yr	Team	G	FG	FT	TP	Avg.
1948-49	Baltimore	10	4	5	13	1.3

KREBS, JAMES

b. Sept. 8, 1935 Ht. 6-8 Wt. 230 Coll.—S. Methodist
d. May 6, 1965

Yr	Team	G	FG	FT	TP	Avg.
1957-58	Minneapolis	68	199	135	533	7.8
1958-59	Minneapolis	72	271	92	634	8.8
1959-60	Minneapolis	75	237	98	572	7.6
1960-61	Los Angeles	75	275	79	629	8.4
1961-62	Los Angeles	78	312	156	780	10.0
1962-63	Los Angeles	79	272	115	659	8.3
1963-64	Los Angeles	68	134	65	333	4.9
	Totals	515	1700	740	4140	8.0

KRON, TOMMY

b. Feb. 28, 1943 Ht. 6-5 Wt. 200 College—Kentucky

Yr	Team	G	FG	FT	TP	Avg.
1966-67	St. Louis	33	27	13	67	2.0
1967-68	Seattle	76	277	184	738	9.7
1968-69	Seattle	76	146	96	388	5.1
1969-70	Kentucky ABA	40	48 (7)	41	158	4.0
	Totals	225	498 (7)	334	1351	6.0

KROPP, TOM

b. Feb. 12, 1953 Ht. 6-3 Wt. 205 Coll.—Kearney State

Yr	Team	G	FG	FT	TP	Avg.
1975-76	Washington	25	7	5	19	0.8
1976-77	Chicago	53	73	28	174	3.3
	Totals	78	80	33	193	2.5

KUBERSKI, STEVE

b. Nov. 6, 1947 Ht. 6-8 Wt. 215 College—Bradley

Yr	Team	G	FG	FT	TP	Avg.
1969-70	Boston	51	130	64	324	6.4
1970-71	Boston	82	313	133	759	9.3
1971-72	Boston	71	185	80	450	6.3
1972-73	Boston	78	140	65	345	4.4
1973-74	Boston	78	157	86	400	5.1
1974-75	Milwaukee	59	62	44	168	2.8
1975-76	Buf.-Bos.	70	135	71	341	4.9
1976-77	Boston	76	131	63	325	4.3
1977-78	Boston	3	1	0	2	0.7
	Totals	568	1254	606	3114	5.5

KUBIAK, LEO

b. Dec. 25, 1927 Ht. 5-11 Wt. 175 Coll.—Bowling Green

Yr	Team	G	FG	FT	TP	Avg.
1948-49	Waterloo NL	62	177	108	462	7.5
1949-50	Waterloo	62	259	192	710	11.5
	Totals	124	436	300	1172	9.5

KUDELKA, FRANK (Apples)

b. 1925 Ht. 6-2 Wt. 193 St. Mary's (Calif.)

Yr	Team	G	FG	FT	TP	Avg.
1949-50	Chicago	65	172	89	433	6.7
1950-51	Wash.-Bos.	62	179	83	441	7.1
1951-52	Baltimore	65	204	198	606	9.3
1952-53	Balt.-Phila.	36	59	44	162	4.5
	Totals	228	614	414	1642	7.2

KUKA, RAPHAEL (Ray)

b. Feb. 17, 1922 Ht. 6-3 Wt. 200 College—Montana State and Notre Dame

Yr	Team	G	FG	FT	TP	Avg.
1947-48	New York	44	89	50	228	5.2
1948-49	New York	8	10	5	25	3.1
	Totals	52	99	55	253	4.9

KUNZE, TERRY

Ht. 6-4 Wt. 210 College—Minnesota

Yr	Team	G	FG	FT	TP	Avg.
1967-68	Minnesota ABA	46	78 (5)	59	230	5.0

KUPEC, C. J.

b. Jan. 16, 1953 Ht. 6-6 Wt. 220 College—Michigan

Yr	Team	G	FG	FT	TP	Avg.
1975-76	Los Angeles	16	10	7	27	1.7
1976-77	Los Angeles	82	153	78	384	4.7
1977-78	Houston	49	84	27	195	4.0
	Totals	147	247	112	606	4.1

LACEFIELD, REGGIE

b. April 10, 1945 Ht. 6-6 Wt. 230 Coll.—W. Michigan

Yr	Team	G	FG	FT	TP	Avg.
1968-69	Kentucky ABA	8	11 (0)	2	24	3.0

LACKEY, BOB

b. April 4, 1949 Ht. 6-6 Wt. 210 College—Marquette

Yr	Team	G	FG	FT	TP	Avg.
1972-73	New York ABA	68	151 (2)	99	407	6.0
1973-74	New York ABA	3	3 (0)	0	6	2.0
	Totals	71	154 (2)	99	413	5.8

LaCOUR, FRED

b. Feb. 7, 1938 Ht. 6-5 Wt. 210 Coll.—San Francisco

Yr	Team	G	FG	FT	TP	Avg.
1960-61	St. Louis	55	123	63	309	5.6
1961-62	St. Louis	73	230	106	566	7.7
1962-63	San Francisco	16	28	9	65	4.1
	Totals	144	381	178	940	6.5

LACY, EDGAR

b. Aug. 2, 1944 Ht. 6-6 Wt. 190 College—UCLA

Yr	Team	G	FG	FT	TP	Avg.
1968-69	Los Angeles ABA	46	98 (0)	38	234	5.1

LADNER, WENDELL

b. Oct. 6, 1948 Ht. 6-5 Wt. 220 Coll.—S. Mississippi
d. June 24, 1975

Yr	Team	G	FG	FT	TP	Avg.
1970-71	Memphis ABA	77	564 (8)	154	1306	17.0
1971-72	Mem.-Car. ABA	82	430 (61)	122	1165	14.2
1972-73	Mem.-Ken. ABA	52	134 (12)	55	359	6.9
1973-74	Ken.-N.Y. ABA	64	220 (24)	29	541	8.5
1974-75	New York ABA	25	38 (7)	6	103	4.1
	Totals	300	1386 (112)	366	3474	11.6

LALICH, PETER

b. June 23, 1920 Ht. 6-2 Wt. 190 Coll.—Ohio Univ.

Yr	Team	G	FG	FT	TP	Avg.
1942-43	Sheboygan NL	1	0	0	0	0.0
1943-44	Cleveland NL	17	44	21	109	6.4
1944-45	Pittsburgh NL	9	8	4	20	2.2
1945-46	Youngstown	11	2	3	7	0.6
1946-47	Cleveland	1	0	0	0	0.0
	Totals	39	54	28	136	3.5

Yr	Team	G	FG	FT	TP	Avg.
LAMAR, DWIGHT						
b. April 7, 1951 Ht. 6-1 Wt. 180 Coll.—S.W. Louisiana						
1973-74	San Diego ABA	84	617 (69)	272	1713	20.4
1974-75	San Diego ABA	77	642 (25)	247	1606	20.9
1975-76	S.D.-Ind. ABA	41	253 (24)	79	657	16.0
1976-77	Los Angeles	71	228	46	502	7.1
	Totals	273	1740 (118)	644	4478	16.4
LANTZ, STU						
b. July 13, 1946 Ht. 6-3 Wt. 175 College—Nebraska						
1968-69	San Diego	73	220	129	569	7.8
1969-70	San Diego	82	455	278	1188	14.5
1970-71	San Diego	82	585	519	1689	20.6
1971-72	Houston	81	557	387	1501	18.5
1972-73	Detroit	51	185	120	490	9.6
1973-74	Detroit	50	154	139	447	8.9
1974-75	N.O.-L.A.	75	228	192	648	8.6
1975-76	Los Angeles	53	85	80	250	4.7
	Totals	547	2469	1844	6782	12.4
LARESE, YORK						
b. July 18, 1938 Ht. 6-4 Wt. 183 Coll.—North Carolina						
1961-62	Chi.-Phila.	59	122	58	302	5.1
LaRUSSO, RUDY						
b. Nov. 11, 1937 Ht. 6-8 Wt. 220 College-Dartmouth						
1959-60	Minneapolis	71	355	265	975	13.7
1960-61	Los Angeles	79	416	323	1155	14.6
1961-62	Los Angeles	80	516	342	1374	17.1
1962-63	Los Angeles	74	321	282	924	12.5
1963-64	Los Angeles	79	337	298	972	12.3
1964-65	Los Angeles	78	381	321	1083	13.9
1965-66	Los Angeles	77	410	350	1170	15.2
1966-67	Los Angeles	45	211	156	578	12.8
1967-68	San Francisco	79	602	522	1726	21.8
1968-69	San Francisco	75	553	444	1550	20.7
	Totals	737	4102	3303	11507	15.6
LASKOWSKI, JOHN						
b. June 7, 1953 Ht. 6-6 Wt. 190 College—Indiana						
1975-76	Chicago	71	284	87	655	9.2
1976-77	Chicago	47	75	27	177	3.8
	Totals	118	359	114	832	7.1
LATTIN, DAVID (Big Daddy)						
b. Dec. 23, 1943 Ht. 6-7 Wt. 230 Coll.—Texas Western						
1967-68	San Francisco	44	37	23	97	2.2
1968-69	Phoenix	68	150	109	419	6.2
1970-71	Pittsburgh ABA	71	177 (0)	108	462	6.5
1971-72	Pittsburgh ABA	64	329 (0)	148	806	12.6
1972-73	Memphis ABA	16	48 (0)	34	130	8.1
	Totals	263	741 (0)	422	1914	7.3
LAUREL, RICH						
b. July 11, 1954 Ht. 6-7 Wt. 195 College—Hofstra						
1977-78	Milwaukee	10	10	4	24	2.4

Yr	Team	G	FG	FT	TP	Avg.
LAURIE, HARRY						
b. Nov. 2, 1944 Ht. 6-1 Wt. 178 College—Loyola (III.) and St. Peter's						
1968-69	Pittsburgh ABA	9	3 (0)	7	13	1.4
LAUTENBACH, WALTER						
b. Nov. 17, 1922 Ht. 6-2 Wt. 190 College—Wisconsin						
1947-48	Oshkosh NL	60	159	36	354	5.9
1948-49	Oshkosh NL	61	104	26	234	3.8
1949-50	Sheboygan	55	100	38	238	4.3
	Totals	176	363	100	826	4.7
LAVELLI, TONY						
b. July 11, 1926 Ht. 6-3 Wt. 185 College—Yale						
1949-50	Boston	56	162	168	492	8.8
1950-51	Bos.-N.Y.	30	32	35	99	3.3
	Totals	86	194	203	591	6.9
LAVOY, BOB						
b. June 29, 1926 Ht. 6-7 Wt. 185 Coll.—W. Kentucky						
1950-51	Indianapolis	63	221	84	526	8.3
1951-52	Indianapolis	63	240	168	648	10.3
1952-53	Indianapolis	70	225	168	618	8.8
1953-54	Milw.-Syra.	68	135	94	364	5.4
	Totals	264	821	514	2156	8.2
LAYTON, DENNIS (Mo)						
b. Dec. 24, 1948 Ht 6-1 Wt. 180 Coll.—So. California						
1971-72	Phoenix	80	304	122	730	9.1
1972-73	Phoenix	65	187	90	464	7.1
1973-74	Portland	22	55	14	124	5.6
1973-74	Memphis ABA	3	8 (0)	3	19	6.3
1976-77	N.Y. Knicks	56	134	58	326	5.8
1977-78	San Antonio	41	85	12	182	4.4
	Totals	267	773 (0)	299	1845	6.9
LEAKS, MANNY						
b. Nov. 27, 1945 Ht. 6-8 Wt. 235 College—Niagara						
1968-69	Ky.-N.Y.-Dal. ABA	78	299 (0)	160	758	9.7
1969-70	Dallas ABA	84	636 (0)	305	1577	18.7
1970-71	Tex.-N.Y. ABA	80	510 (0)	279	1299	16.2
1971-72	N.Y.-Utah-Florida ABA	69	240 (0)	74	554	8.0
	Totals	311	1685 (0)	818	4188	13.5
LEAR, HAL (King)						
b. Jan. 31, 1935 Ht. 6-0 Wt. 163 College—Temple						
1956-57	Philadelphia	3	2	0	4	1.3

Yr	Team	G	FG	FT	TP	Avg.

LEE, CLYDE

b. March 14, 1944 Ht. 6-10 Wt. 205 College—Vanderbilt

Yr	Team	G	FG	FT	TP	Avg.
1966-67	San Francisco	74	205	105	515	7.0
1967-68	San Francisco	82	373	229	975	11.9
1968-69	San Francisco	65	268	160	696	10.7
1969-70	San Francisco	82	362	178	902	11.0
1970-71	San Francisco	82	194	111	499	6.1
1971-72	Golden State	78	256	120	632	8.1
1972-73	Golden State	66	170	74	414	6.3
1973-74	Golden State	54	129	62	320	5.9
1974-75	Atl.-Phila.	80	176	119	471	5.9
1975-76	Philadelphia	79	123	63	309	3.9
	Totals	742	2256	1221	5733	7.7

LEE, DAVE

b. March 31, 1942 Ht. 6-7½ Wt. 225 Coll.—San Fran.

Yr	Team	G	FG	FT	TP	Avg.
1967-68	Oakland ABA	54	123 (2)	120	372	6.9
1968-69	New Orleans ABA	4	1 (0)	0	2	0.6
	Totals	58	124 (2)	120	374	6.4

LEE, GEORGE

b. Nov. 23, 1936 Ht. 6-4 Wt. 200 College—Michigan

Yr	Team	G	FG	FT	TP	Avg.
1960-61	Detroit	74	310	276	896	12.1
1961-62	Detroit	75	179	213	571	7.6
1962-63	San Francisco	64	149	152	450	7.0
1963-64	San Francisco	54	64	47	175	3.2
1964-65	San Francisco	19	27	38	92	4.8
1966-67	San Francisco	1	3	6	12	12.0
1967-68	San Francisco	10	8	17	33	3.3
	Totals	297	740	749	2229	7.5

LEE, GREG

b. Dec. 12, 1951 Ht. 6-3 Wt. 190 College—UCLA

Yr	Team	G	FG	FT	TP	Avg.
1974-75	San Diego ABA	5	8 (0)	2	18	3.6
1975-76	Portland	5	2	2	6	1.2
	Totals	10	10 (0)	4	24	2.4

LEE, RUSSELL

b. Jan. 27, 1950 Ht. 6-5 Wt. 185 College—Marshall

Yr	Team	G	FG	FT	TP	Avg.
1972-73	Milwaukee	46	49	32	130	2.8
1973-74	Milwaukee	36	38	11	87	2.4
1974-75	New Orleans	15	29	7	65	4.3
	Totals	97	116	50	282	2.9

LEEDE, ED

b. July 17, 1927 Ht. 6-3 Wt. 185 College—Dartmouth

Yr	Team	G	FG	FT	TP	Avg.
1949-50	Boston	64	174	223	571	8.9
1950-51	Boston	57	119	140	378	6.6
	Totals	121	293	363	949	7.8

LEFKOWITZ, HENRY

b. Aug. 31, 1923 Ht. 6-2 Wt. 190 Coll.—West. Reserve

Yr	Team	G	FG	FT	TP	Avg.
1946-47	Cleveland	24	22	7	51	2.1

LEHMANN, GEORGE

b. May 1, 1942 Ht. 6-3 Wt. 190 College—Campbell

Yr	Team	G	FG	FT	TP	Avg.
1967-68	St. Louis	55	59	35	153	2.8
1968-69	Atl.-L.A. ABA	43	190 (48)	140	664	15.4

Yr	Team	G	FG	FT	TP	Avg.
1969-70	L.A.-N.Y.-Miami-ABA	81	226 (92)	180	908	11.2
1970-71	Carolina ABA	83	381 (154)	214	1438	17.3
1971-72	Car.-Mem. ABA	53	232 (71)	169	846	16.0
1972-73	Memphis ABA	28	69 (26)	61	277	9.9
1973-74	Memphis ABA	33	50 (18)	18	172	5.2
	Totals	376	1207 (409)	817	4458	11.9

LENTZ, LEARY

b. Feb. 23, 1945 Ht. 6-6 Wt. 200 College—Houston

Yr	Team	G	FG	FT	TP	Avg.
1967-68	Houston ABA	78	343 (0)	147	833	10.7
1968-69	Hou.-N.Y. ABA	70	135 (0)	76	346	4.9
	Totals	148	478 (0)	223	1179	8.0

LEONARD, ROBERT (Slick)

b. July 17, 1932 Ht. 6-3 Wt. 185 College—Indiana

Yr	Team	G	FG	FT	TP	Avg.
1956-57	Minneapolis	72	303	186	792	11.0
1957-58	Minneapolis	66	266	205	737	11.2
1958-59	Minneapolis	58	206	120	532	9.2
1959-60	Minneapolis	73	231	136	598	8.2
1960-61	Los Ang.	55	61	71	193	3.5
1961-62	Chicago	70	423	279	1125	16.1
1962-63	Chicago	32	84	59	227	7.1
	Totals	426	1574	1056	4204	9.9

LEVANE, ANDREW (Fuzzy)

b. April 11, 1920 Ht. 6-2 Wt. 190 Coll.—St. John's (N.Y.)

Yr	Team	G	FG	FT	TP	Avg.
1945-46	Rochester NL	22	52	8	112	5.1
1946-47	Rochester NL	39	133	49	315	8.1
1947-48	Rochester NL	54	147	45	339	6.3
1948-49	Rochester	36	55	13	123	3.4
1949-50	Syracuse	60	139	54	332	5.5
1952-53	Milwaukee	7	3	2	8	1.1
	Totals	218	529	171	1229	5.6

LEWIS, BOB

b. March 20, 1945 Ht. 6-3 Wt. 185 College—N.C.

Yr	Team	G	FG	FT	TP	Avg.
1967-68	San Francisco	41	59	61	179	4.4
1968-69	San Francisco	62	113	83	309	5.0
1969-70	San Francisco	73	213	100	526	7.2
1970-71	Cleveland	79	179	109	467	5.9
	Totals	255	564	353	1481	5.8

LEWIS, FRED

b. Jan 6, 1921 Ht. 6-2 Wt. 195 Coll.—LIU/E. Kentucky

Yr	Team	G	FG	FT	TP	Avg.
1946-47	Sheboygan NL	44	230	125	585	13.3
1947-48	Sheb.-Ind. NL	44	169	101	439	10.0
1948-49	Ind.-Balt.	61	272	138	682	11.2
1949-50	Balt.-Phila.	34	46	25	117	3.4
	Totals	183	717	389	1823	10.0

LEWIS, FRED

b. Jan. 7, 1943 Ht. 6-0 Wt. 180 Coll.—Arizona State

Yr	Team	G	FG	FT	TP	Avg.
1966-67	Cincinnati	32	60	29	149	4.7
1967-68	Indiana ABA	76	526 (16)	465	1565	20.6
1968-69	Indiana ABA	78	550 (22)	419	1585	20.3
1969-70	Indiana ABA	81	401 (47)	383	1326	16.4
1970-71	Indiana ABA	81	488 (59)	372	1525	18.8
1971-72	Indiana ABA	77	374 (31)	341	1182	15.4
1972-73	Indiana ABA	72	337 (38)	287	1075	14.9
1973-74	Indiana ABA	78	277 (13)	182	775	9.9
1974-75	Mem.-St. L. ABA	69	561 (18)	355	1531	22.2
1975-76	St. Louis ABA	74	372 (31)	259	1096	14.8
1976-77	Indiana	32	81	62	224	7.0
	Totals	750	4027 (275)	3154	12033	16.0

LEWIS, GRADY

b. March 25, 1917 Ht. 6-7 Wt. 215 College—Southwestern and Oklahoma

Yr	Team	G	FG	FT	TP	Avg.
1946-47	Detroit	60	106	75	287	4.8
1947-48	St. L.-Balt.	45	114	87	315	7.0
1948-49	St. Louis	34	53	42	148	4.4
	Totals	139	273	204	750	5.4

LEWIS, MIKE

b. March 12, 1946 Ht. 6-8 Wt. 225 College—Duke

Yr	Team	G	FG	FT	TP	Avg.
1968-69	Ind.-Minn. ABA	76	247 (0)	153	647	8.5
1969-70	Pittsburgh ABA	78	499 (0)	269	1267	16.2
1970-71	Pittsburgh ABA	83	420 (0)	235	1075	12.9
1971-72	Pittsburgh ABA	82	385 (0)	165	935	11.4
1972-73	Carolina ABA	15	59 (0)	33	151	10.1
1973-74	Carolina ABA	3	3 (0)	0	6	2.0
	Totals	337	1613 (0)	855	4081	12.1

LIEBOWITZ, BARRY

Ht. 6-2 Wt. 185 College—Long Island University

Yr	Team	G	FG	FT	TP	Avg.
1967-68	N.J.-Oak. ABA	82	323	248	894	10.9

LIGON, BILL

b. May 19, 1952 Ht. 6-4 Wt. 180 College—Vanderbilt

Yr	Team	G	FG	FT	TP	Avg.
1974-75	Detroit	38	55	16	126	3.3

LIGON, JIM (Goose)

b. Feb. 22, 1944 Ht. 6-7 Wt. 215

Yr	Team	G	FG	FT	TP	Avg.
1967-68	Kentucky ABA	78	427 (1)	405	1262	16.2
1968-69	Kentucky ABA	75	390 (1)	337	1120	14.9
1969-70	Kentucky ABA	84	507 (0)	287	1301	15.5
1970-71	Kentucky ABA	84	429 (0)	214	1072	12.8
1971-72	Ky.-Pitt. ABA	82	212 (1)	141	568	6.9
1972-73	Virginia ABA	12	58 (0)	28	144	12.0
1973-74	Virginia ABA	19	37 (0)	19	93	4.9
	Totals	434	2060 (3)	1431	5560	12.8

LITTLE, SAM

College—Delta State

Yr	Team	G	FG	FT	TP	Avg.
1969-70	Kentucky ABA	3	2 (0)	1	5	1.7

LITTLES, GENE

b. June 29, 1943 Ht. 6-1 Wt. 165 College—High Point

Yr	Team	G	FG	FT	TP	Avg.
1969-70	Carolina ABA	82	414 (0)	197	1025	12.5
1970-71	Carolina ABA	70	219 (4)	117	567	8.1
1971-72	Carolina ABA	69	273 (7)	178	745	10.8
1972-73	Carolina ABA	84	302 (8)	179	807	9.6
1973-74	Carolina ABA	84	290 (4)	115	707	8.4
1974-75	Kentucky ABA	61	83 (2)	43	215	3.5
	Totals	450	1581 (25)	829	4066	9.0

LIVINGSTONE, RONALD

b. Oct. 9, 1925 Ht. 6-10 Wt. 220 Coll.—Wyoming and St. Mary's (Calif.)

Yr	Team	G	FG	FT	TP	Avg.
1949-50	Balt.-Phila.	54	163	122	448	8.3
1950-51	Philadelphia	63	104	76	284	4.5
	Totals	117	267	198	732	6.3

LLOYD, CHUCK

Ht. 6-8 Wt. 220 College—Yankton

Yr	Team	G	FG	FT	TP	Avg.
1970-71	Carolina ABA	14	23 (0)	20	66	4.7

LLOYD, EARL (Big Cat)

b. April 3, 1928 Ht. 6-6 Wt. 220 Coll.—W. Va. State

Yr	Team	G	FG	FT	TP	Avg.
1950-51	Washington	7	16	11	43	6.1
1952-53	Syracuse	64	156	160	472	7.4
1953-54	Syracuse	72	249	156	654	9.1
1954-55	Syracuse	72	286	159	731	10.2
1955-56	Syracuse	72	213	186	612	8.5
1956-57	Syracuse	72	256	134	646	9.0
1957-58	Syracuse	61	119	79	317	5.2
1958-59	Detroit	72	234	137	605	8.4
1959-60	Detroit	68	237	128	602	8.8
	Totals	560	1766	1150	4682	8.4

LLOYD, ROBERT

b. Jan. 3, 1946 Ht. 6-2 Wt. 185 College—Rutgers

Yr	Team	G	FG	FT	TP	Avg.
1967-68	New Jersey ABA	58	144 (3)	170	467	8.1
1968-69	New York ABA	67	203 (12)	218	660	9.9
	Totals	125	347 (15)	388	1127	9.0

Yr	Team	G	FG	FT	TP	Avg.

LOCHMANN, REINHOLD D. (Riney)

b. May 26, 1944 Ht. 6-6 Wt. 215 College—Kansas

Yr	Team	G	FG	FT	TP	Avg.
1967-68	Dallas ABA	63	107 (1)	49	266	4.2
1968-69	Dallas ABA	60	114 (1)	60	291	4.9
1969-70	Dallas ABA	47	70 (3)	25	174	3.7
	Totals	170	291 (5)	134	731	4.3

LOCHMUELLER, ROBERT

b. 1928 Ht. 6-5 Wt. 185 College—Louisville

Yr	Team	G	FG	FT	TP	Avg.
1952-53	Syracuse	62	79	74	232	3.7

LOFGRAN, DON

b. Nov. 18, 1928 Ht. 6-6 Wt. 200 College—San Fran.
d. June, 1976

Yr	Team	G	FG	FT	TP	Avg.
1950-51	Syracuse-Ind.	61	79	79	237	3.9
1951-52	Indianapolis	63	149	156	454	7.2
1952-53	Philadelphia	64	173	126	472	7.4
1953-54	Milwaukee	21	35	32	102	4.9
	Totals	209	436	393	1265	6.1

LOGAN, HENRY

b. March 14, 1946 Ht. 6-0 Wt. 185 College—Western Carolina

Yr	Team	G	FG	FT	TP	Avg.
1968-69	Oakland ABA	76	338 (1)	268	947	12.5
1969-70	Washington ABA	32	110 (0)	91	311	9.7
	Totals	108	448 (1)	359	1258	11.6

LOGAN, JOHN

b. Jan. 1, 1921 Ht. 6-2 Wt. 175 College—Indiana

Yr	Team	G	FG	FT	TP	Avg.
1946-47	St. Louis	61	290	190	770	12.6
1947-48	St. Louis	48	221	202	644	13.4
1948-49	St. Louis	57	282	239	803	14.1
1949-50	St. Louis	62	251	253	755	12.2
1950-51	Tri-Cities	29	81	62	224	7.7
	Totals	257	1125	946	3196	12.4

LONG, PAUL

b. Feb. 8, 1944 Ht. 6-2 Wt. 180 College—Wake Forest

Yr	Team	G	FG	FT	TP	Avg.
1967-68	Detroit	16	23	11	57	3.6
1968-69	Kentucky ABA	9	9 (0)	17	35	3.9
1969-70	Detroit	25	28	27	83	3.3
1970-71	Buffalo	30	57	20	134	4.5
	Totals	80	117 (0)	75	309	3.9

LONG, WILLIE

b. March 1, 1950 Ht. 6-8 Wt. 235 College—New Mexico

Yr	Team	G	FG	FT	TP	Avg.
1971-72	Floridians ABA	75	336 (0)	206	878	11.7
1972-73	Denver ABA	56	183 (0)	138	504	12.6
1973-74	Denver ABA	82	383 (0)	270	1036	11.4
	Totals	213	902 (0)	614	2418	11.4

LOSCUTOFF, JAMES (Jungle Jim)

b. Feb. 4, 1930 Ht. 6-5 Wt. 230 College—Oregon

Yr	Team	G	FG	FT	TP	Avg.
1955-56	Boston	71	226	139	591	8.3
1956-57	Boston	70	306	132	744	10.6
1957-58	Boston	5	11	1	23	4.6
1958-59	Boston	66	242	62	546	8.3
1959-60	Boston	28	66	22	154	5.5
1960-61	Boston	76	154	50	358	4.7
1961-62	Boston	79	188	45	421	5.3
1962-63	Boston	64	94	22	210	3.3
1963-64	Boston	53	56	18	130	2.5
	Totals	512	1343	491	3177	6.2

LOTT, PLUMMER

b. Dec. 11, 1945 Ht. 6-5 Wt. 210 College—Seattle

Yr	Team	G	FG	FT	TP	Avg.
1967-68	Seattle	44	46	19	111	2.5
1968-69	Seattle	23	17	2	36	1.6
	Totals	67	63	21	147	2.2

LOUGHERY, KEVIN (Murph)

b. March 28, 1940 Ht. 6-3 Wt. 190 College—St. John's (N.Y.)

Yr	Team	G	FG	FT	TP	Avg.
1962-63	Detroit	57	146	71	363	6.4
1963-64	Det.-Balt.	66	236	126	598	9.1
1964-65	Baltimore	80	406	212	1024	12.8
1965-66	Baltimore	74	526	297	1349	18.2
1966-67	Baltimore	76	520	340	1380	18.2
1967-68	Baltimore	77	458	305	1221	15.9
1968-69	Baltimore	80	717	372	1806	22.6
1969-70	Baltimore	55	477	253	1207	21.9
1970-71	Baltimore	82	481	275	1237	15.1
1971-72	Balt.-Phila.	76	341	263	945	12.4
	Totals	723	4308	2514	11130	15.4

LOVE, BOB

b. Dec. 8, 1942 Ht. 6-8 Wt. 215 College—Southern U.

Yr	Team	G	FG	FT	TP	Avg.
1966-67	Cincinnati	66	173	93	439	6.7
1967-68	Cincinnati	72	193	78	464	6.4
1968-69	Mil.-Chi.	49	108	71	287	5.9
1969-70	Chicago	82	640	442	1722	21.0
1970-71	Chicago	81	765	513	2043	25.2
1971-72	Chicago	79	819	399	2037	25.8
1972-73	Chicago	82	774	347	1895	23.1
1973-74	Chicago	82	731	323	1785	21.8
1974-75	Chicago	61	539	264	1342	22.0
1975-76	Chicago	76	543	362	1448	19.1
1976-77	Chi.-NYN-Sea.	59	162	109	433	7.3
	Totals	789	5447	3001	13895	17.6

LOVE, STAN

b. April 9, 1949 Ht. 6-9 Wt. 215 College—Oregon

Yr	Team	G	FG	FT	TP	Avg.
1971-72	Baltimore	74	242	103	587	7.9
1972-73	Baltimore	72	190	79	459	6.4
1973-74	Los Angeles	51	119	49	287	5.6
1974-75	Los Angeles	30	85	47	217	7.2
	Totals	227	636	278	1550	6.8

LOVELLETTE, CLYDE

b. Sept. 7, 1929 Ht. 6-9 Wt. 235 College—Kansas

Yr	Team	G	FG	FT	TP	Avg.
1953-54	Minneapolis	72	237	114	588	8.2
1954-55	Minneapolis	70	519	273	1311	18.7
1955-56	Minneapolis	71	594	338	1526	21.5
1956-57	Minneapolis	69	574	286	1434	20.8
1957-58	Cincinnati	71	679	301	1659	23.4
1958-59	St. Louis	70	402	205	1009	14.4
1959-60	St. Louis	68	550	316	1416	20.8

Yr	Team	G	FG	FT	TP	Avg.
1960-61	St. Louis	67	599	273	1471	22.0
1961-62	St. Louis	40	341	155	837	20.9
1962-63	Boston	61	161	73	395	6.5
1963-64	Boston	45	128	45	301	6.7
	Totals	704	4784	2379	11947	17.0

LOWERY, CHARLES
b. Nov. 12, 1949 Ht. 6-3 Wt. 185 College—Puget Sound

Yr	Team	G	FG	FT	TP	Avg.
1971-72	Milwaukee	20	17	11	45	2.3

LUCAS, ALBERT (Lukey)
b. July 4, 1922 Ht. 6-3 Wt. 195 College—Fordham

Yr	Team	G	FG	FT	TP	Avg.
1944-45	Sheboygan NL	26	57	36	150	5.8
1945-46	Sheboygan NL	32	75	24	174	5.4
1946-47	Sheboygan NL	42	87	32	206	4.9
1947-48	Sheboygan NL	58	98	39	235	4.1
1948-49	Boston	2	1	0	2	1.0
	Totals	160	318	131	767	4.8

LUCAS, JERRY (Luke)
b. March 30, 1940 Ht. 6-8 Wt. 230 College—Ohio State

Yr	Team	G	FG	FT	TP	Avg.
1963-64	Cincinnati	79	545	310	1400	17.7
1964-65	Cincinnati	66	558	298	1414	21.4
1965-66	Cincinnati	79	690	317	1697	21.5
1966-67	Cincinnati	81	577	284	1438	17.8
1967-68	Cincinnati	82	707	346	1760	21.4
1968-69	Cincinnati	74	555	247	1357	18.3
1969-70	Cin.-S.F.	67	405	200	1010	15.1
1970-71	San Fran.	80	623	289	1535	19.2
1971-72	New York	77	543	197	1283	16.7
1972-73	New York	71	312	80	704	9.9
1973-74	New York	73	194	67	455	6.2
	Totals	829	5709	2635	14053	17.0

LUCKENBILL, TED
b. July 27, 1939 Ht. 6-6 Wt. 205 College—Houston

Yr	Team	G	FG	FT	TP	Avg.
1961-62	Phila.	67	43	49	135	2.0
1962-63	San Fran.	20	26	9	61	3.1
	Totals	87	69	58	196	2.3

LUISI, JAMES
b. 1930 Ht. 6-2 Wt. 180 College—St. Francis (N.Y.)

Yr	Team	G	FG	FT	TP	Avg.
1953-54	Baltimore	31	31	27	89	2.9

LUJACK, AL
b. Oct. 5, 1921 College—Georgetown

Yr	Team	G	FG	FT	TP	Avg.
1946-47	Washington	5	1	2	4	0.8

LUMPKIN, PHIL
b. Dec. 20, 1951 Ht. 6-0 Wt. 167 College—Miami (OH)

Yr	Team	G	FG	FT	TP	Avg.
1974-75	Portland	48	86	30	202	4.2
1975-76	Phoenix	34	22	26	70	2.1
	Totals	82	108	56	272	3.3

LUMPP, RAY
b. July 11, 1923 Ht. 6-1 Wt. 178 College—N.Y.U.

Yr	Team	G	FG	FT	TP	Avg.
1948-49	Ind.-N.Y.	61	279	219	777	12.7
1949-50	New York	58	91	86	268	4.6
1950-51	New York	64	153	124	430	6.7
1951-52	New York	62	184	90	458	7.4
1952-53	N.Y.-Balt.	55	188	153	529	9.6
	Totals	300	895	672	2462	8.2

LYNAM, R. B.
Ht. 6-1 Wt. 200 College—Oklahoma Baptist

Yr	Team	G	FG	FT	TP	Avg.
1967-68	Denver ABA	7	5 (0)	7	17	2.4

LYNN, LONNIE
Ht. 6-7½ Wt. 215 College—Wilberforce

Yr	Team	G	FG	FT	TP	Avg.
1969-70	Den.-Pitt. ABA	52	112 (0)	36	260	5.0

LYNN, MIKE
b. Nov. 25, 1945 Ht. 6-7 Wt. 215 College—UCLA

Yr	Team	G	FG	FT	TP	Avg.
1969-70	Los Angeles	44	44	31	119	2.7
1970-71	Buffalo	5	2	3	7	1.4
	Totals	49	46	34	126	2.6

MACALUSO, MIKE
b. July 20, 1951 Ht. 6-5 Wt. 210 College—Canisius

Yr	Team	G	FG	FT	TP	Avg.
1973-74	Buffalo	30	19	10	48	1.6

MACAULEY, EDWARD (Easy Ed)
b. March 22, 1928 Ht. 6-8 Wt. 190 College—St. Louis

Yr	Team	G	FG	FT	TP	Avg.
1949-50	St. Louis	67	351	379	1081	16.1
1950-51	Boston	68	459	466	1384	20.4
1951-52	Boston	66	384	496	1264	19.2
1952-53	Boston	69	451	500	1402	20.3
1953-54	Boston	71	462	420	1344	18.9
1954-55	Boston	71	403	442	1248	17.6
1955-56	Boston	71	420	400	1240	17.5
1956-57	St. Louis	72	414	359	1187	16.5
1957-58	St. Louis	72	376	267	1019	14.2
1958-59	St. Louis	14	22	21	65	4.6
	Totals	641	3742	3750	11234	17.5

MacGILVRAY, RONNIE
b. July 20, 1930 Ht. 6-2 Wt. 185 College—St. John's (N.Y.)

Yr	Team	G	FG	FT	TP	Avg.
1954-55	Milwaukee	6	2	4	8	1.3

MACKNOWSKI, JOHN (Whitey)
b. Jan. 7, 1923 Ht. 6-0 Wt. 185 College—Seton Hall

Yr	Team	G	FG	FT	TP	Avg.
1948-49	Syracuse NL	62	146	128	420	6.8
1949-50	Syracuse	59	154	131	439	7.4
1950-51	Syracuse	58	131	122	384	6.6
	Totals	179	431	381	1243	6.9

MADDOX, JACK
Ht. 6-3½ Wt. 190 College—West Texas

Yr	Team	G	FG	FT	TP	Avg.
1946-47	Oshkosh NL	43	102	33	237	5.5
1947-48	Oshkosh NL	60	146	59	351	5.9
1948-49	Hammond NL	17	39	18	96	5.6
1948-49	Indianapolis	1	0	0	0	0.0
	Totals	121	287	110	684	5.7

MAGER, NORM
b. March 23, 1926 Ht. 6-5 Wt. 185 College St. John's (N.Y.) and CCNY

Yr	Team	G	FG	FT	TP	Avg.
1950-51	Baltimore	22	32	37	101	4.6

Yr	Team	G	FG	FT	TP	Avg.

MAHAFFEY, RANDY

b. Sept. 28, 1945 Ht. 6-7 Wt. 210 College—Clemson

Yr	Team	G	FG	FT	TP	Avg.
1967-68	Kentucky ABA	75	373 (0)	281	1027	13.7
1968-69	Ky.-N.Y. ABA	79	351 (0)	232	934	11.8
1969-70	Carolina ABA	84	367 (0)	194	928	11.0
1970-71	Carolina ABA	83	385 (0)	156	926	11.7
	Totals	321	1476 (0)	863	3815	11.9

MAHNKEN, JOHN

b. June 16, 1922 Ht. 6-8 Wt. 220 College—Georgetown

Yr	Team	G	FG	FT	TP	Avg.
1945-46	Rochester NL	16	50	23	123	7.7
1946-47	Washington	60	223	111	557	9.3
1947-48	Washington	48	131	54	316	6.6
1948-49	Balt.-Ind.-Ft. W.	57	215	104	534	9.4
1949-50	Ft. W.—Tri-Cit.-Bos.	62	132	77	341	5.5
1950-51	Bos.-Ind.	58	111	45	267	4.6
1951-52	Boston	60	78	26	182	3.0
1952-53	Boston	69	76	39	191	2.8
	Totals	430	1016	479	2511	5.8

MAHONEY, BRIAN

b. 1948 Ht. 6-3 Wt. 175 College—Manhattan

Yr	Team	G	FG	FT	TP	Avg.
1972-73	New York ABA	19	17 (0)	24	58	3.1

MAHONEY, FRANCIS (Mo)

b. Nov. 20, 1927 Ht. 6-0 Wt. 205 College—Brown

Yr	Team	G	FG	FT	TP	Avg.
1952-53	Boston	6	4	4	12	2.0
1953-54	Baltimore	2	0	0	0	0.0
	Totals	8	4	4	12	1.5

MALAMED, LIONEL

b. Nov. 15, 1924 Ht. 5-9 Wt. 150 College—CCNY

Yr	Team	G	FG	FT	TP	Avg.
1948-49	Ind.-Rochester	44	97	64	258	5.9

MALOY, MIKE

b. May 10, 1949 Ht. 6-7 Wt. 215 College—Davidson

Yr	Team	G	FG	FT	TP	Avg.
1970-71	Virginia ABA	55	149 (0)	98	396	7.2
1971-72	Virginia ABA	7	12 (0)	2	26	3.7
1972-73	Dallas ABA	9	7 (0)	6	20	2.2
	Totals	71	168 (0)	106	442	6.2

MANAKAS, TED

b. Feb. 22, 1951 Ht. 6-2 Wt. 180 College—Princeton

Yr	Team	G	FG	FT	TP	Avg.
1973-74	K.C.-Omaha	5	4	4	12	2.4

MANDIC, JOHN

b. Oct. 3, 1919 Ht. 6-4 Wt. 205 College—Oreg. State

Yr	Team	G	FG	FT	TP	Avg.
1947-48	Rochester NL	33	32	13	77	2.3
1948-49	Indianapolis	56	97	75	269	4.8
1949-50	Wash.-Balt.	25	22	22	66	2.6
	Totals	114	151	110	412	3.6

MANGIAPANE, FRANK

b. Aug. 25, 1925 Ht. 5-10 Wt. 195 College—NYU

Yr	Team	G	FG	FT	TP	Avg.
1946-47	New York	6	2	1	5	0.8

MANNING, ED

b. Jan. 2, 1944 Ht. 6-7½ Wt. 215 Coll.—Jackson State

Yr	Team	G	FG	FT	TP	Avg.
1967-68	Baltimore	71	112	60	284	4.0
1968-69	Baltimore	63	129	35	293	4.7
1969-70	Balt.-Chi.	67	119	42	280	4.2
1970-71	Portland	79	243	75	561	7.1
1971-72	Carolina ABA	77	228 (0)	95	551	7.2
1972-73	Carolina ABA	83	263 (0)	64	590	7.1
1973-74	Carolina ABA	82	296 (1)	86	681	8.3
1974-75	New York ABA	70	103 (0)	35	241	3.4
	Totals	591	1493 (1)	492	3481	5.9

MANNING, GUY

b. Feb. 4, 1944 Ht. 6-6½ Wt. 205 Coll.—Prairie View

Yr	Team	G	FG	FT	TP	Avg.
1967-68	Houston ABA	59	204 (2)	115	529	9.0
1968-69	Houston ABA	14	27 (0)	21	75	5.4
	Totals	73	231 (2)	136	604	8.3

MANTIS, NICHOLAS

b. Dec. 7, 1935 Ht. 6-3 Wt. 190 College—Northwestern

Yr	Team	G	FG	FT	TP	Avg.
1959-60	Minneapolis	10	10	1	21	2.1
1962-63	St. L.-Chi.	42	94	27	215	5.1
	Totals	52	104	28	236	4.5

MARAVICH, PRESS

b. Aug. 20, 1920 Ht. 6-0 Wt. 185 Coll.—Davis & Elkins

Yr	Team	G	FG	FT	TP	Avg.
1945-46	Youngstown NL	31	70	34	174	5.6
1946-47	Pittsburgh	51	102	30	234	4.6
	Totals	82	172	64	408	5.0

MARIASCHIN, SAUL

b. Sept. 1, 1924 Ht. 5-11 Wt. 165 College—Harvard

Yr	Team	G	FG	FT	TP	Avg.
1947-48	Boston	43	125	83	333	7.7

MARIN, JACK

b. Oct. 12, 1944 Ht. 6-6½ Wt. 200 College—Duke

Yr	Team	G	FG	FT	TP	Avg.
1966-67	Baltimore	74	283	145	711	9.6
1967-68	Baltimore	82	429	250	1108	13.5
1968-69	Baltimore	82	505	292	1302	15.9
1969-70	Baltimore	82	666	286	1618	19.7
1970-71	Baltimore	82	626	290	1542	18.8
1971-72	Baltimore	78	690	356	1736	22.3
1972-73	Houston	81	624	248	1496	18.5
1973-74	Hou.-Buf.	74	355	153	863	11.7
1974-75	Buffalo	81	380	193	953	11.8
1975-76	Buf.-Chi.	79	343	161	847	10.7
1976-77	Chicago	54	167	31	365	6.8
	Totals	849	5068	2405	12541	14.8

Yr	Team	G	FG	FT	TP	Avg.

MARLATT, HARVEY

b. Aug. 26, 1948 Ht. 6-3 Wt. 185 Coll.—Eastern Mich.

Yr	Team	G	FG	FT	TP	Avg.
1970-71	Detroit	23	25	15	65	2.8
1971-72	Detroit	31	60	36	156	5.0
1972-73	Detroit	7	2	0	4	0.6
	Totals	61	87	51	225	3.7

MARSH, JIM

b. 1946 Ht. 6-7 Wt. 215 College—USC

Yr	Team	G	FG	FT	TP	Avg.
1971-72	Portland	39	39	41	119	3.1

MARSH, RICKY

b. March 10, 1954 Ht. 6-3 Wt. 200 College—Manhattan

Yr	Team	G	FG	FT	TP	Avg.
1977-78	Gold. St.	60	123	23	269	4.5

MARSHALL, THOMAS

b. Jan. 6, 1931 Ht. 6-4 Wt. 215 College—Western Ky.

Yr	Team	G	FG	FT	TP	Avg.
1956-57	Rochester	40	56	47	159	4.0
1957-58	Det.-Cinn.	38	52	48	152	4.0
	Totals	78	108	95	311	4.0

MARSHALL, VESTER

b. Dec. 22, 1948 Ht. 6-7 Wt. 200 College—Oklahoma

Yr	Team	G	FG	FT	TP	Avg.
1973-74	Seattle	13	7	3	17	1.3

MARTIN, DONALD

b. 1920 Ht. 6-8 Wt. 220 College—Georgetown

Yr	Team	G	FG	FT	TP	Avg.
1946-47	Providence	60	311	111	733	12.3
1947-48	Providence	32	46	9	101	3.2
	Totals	92	357	120	834	9.1

MARTIN, JAMES D.

b. May 25, 1920 Ht. 5-8 Wt. 160 College—Central Mo.

Yr	Team	G	FG	FT	TP	Avg.
1946-47	St. Louis	54	89	13	191	3.5
1947-48	St. Louis	39	35	15	85	2.2
1948-49	St. L.-Balt.	44	52	30	134	3.0
	Totals	137	176	58	410	3.0

MARTIN, LARUE

b. March 30, 1950 Ht. 6-11 Wt. 208 Coll.—Loyola (Ill.)

Yr	Team	G	FG	FT	TP	Avg.
1972-73	Portland	77	145	50	340	4.4
1973-74	Portland	50	101	42	244	4.9
1974-75	Portland	81	236	99	571	7.0
1975-76	Portland	63	109	57	275	4.4
	Totals	271	591	248	1430	5.3

MARTIN, PHIL

Ht. 6-3 Wt. 190 College—Toledo

Yr	Team	G	FG	FT	TP	Avg.
1954-55	Milwaukee	7	5	2	12	1.7

MARTIN, RONALD (Whitey)

b. April 11, 1939 Ht. 6-2 Wt. 185 College—St. Bonaventure

Yr	Team	G	FG	FT	TP	Avg.
1961-62	New York	66	95	37	227	3.4

MARTIN, SLATER (Dugie)

b. Oct. 22, 1925 Ht. 5-10 Wt. 170 College—Texas

Yr	Team	G	FG	FT	TP	Avg.
1949-50	Minneapolis	67	106	59	271	4.0
1950-51	Minneapolis	68	227	121	575	3.5
1951-52	Minneapolis	66	237	142	616	9.3
1952-53	Minneapolis	70	260	224	744	10.6
1953-54	Minneapolis	69	254	176	684	9.9
1954-55	Minneapolis	72	350	276	976	13.6
1955-56	Minneapolis	72	309	329	947	13.2
1956-57	N.Y.-St. L.	66	244	230	718	10.9
1957-58	St. Louis	60	258	206	722	12.0
1958-59	St. Louis	71	245	197	687	9.4
	Totals	681	2490	1960	6940	10.2

MASINO, AL

b. 1928 Ht. 5-11 Wt. 174 College—Canisius

Yr	Team	G	FG	FT	TP	Avg.
1952-53	Milwaukee	72	134	128	396	5.5
1953-54	Roch.-Syra.	27	26	30	82	3.0
	Totals	99	160	158	478	4.8

MAST, EDDIE

b. Oct. 3, 1948 Ht. 6-9 Wt. 220 College—Temple

Yr	Team	G	FG	FT	TP	Avg.
1970-71	New York	30	25	11	61	2.0
1971-72	New York	40	39	25	103	2.6
1972-73	Atlanta	42	50	19	119	2.8
	Totals	112	114	55	283	2.5

MATHIS, JOHN

b. July 14, 1943 Ht. 6-6½ Wt. 220 Coll.—Savannah St.

Yr	Team	G	FG	FT	TP	Avg.
1967-68	New Jersey ABA	51	69 (0)	35	173	3.4

MAUGHAN, ARIEL (Ace)

b. April 23, 1923 Ht. 6-4 Wt. 190 College—Utah State

Yr	Team	G	FG	FT	TP	Avg.
1946-47	Detroit	59	224	84	532	9.0
1947-48	Prov.-St. L.	42	76	32	184	4.4
1948-49	St. Louis	55	206	184	596	10.8
1949-50	St. Louis	68	160	157	477	7.0
1950-51	Washington	35	78	101	257	7.3
	Totals	259	744	558	2046	7.9

MAY, DON

b. Jan. 3, 1946 Ht. 6-4 Wt. 220 College—Dayton

Yr	Team	G	FG	FT	TP	Avg.
1968-69	New York	48	81	42	204	4.3
1969-70	New York	37	39	18	96	2.6
1970-71	Buffalo	76	629	277	1535	20.2
1971-72	Atlanta	75	234	126	594	7.9
1972-73	At.-Ph.	58	189	75	453	7.8
1973-74	Philadelphia	56	152	89	393	7.0
1974-75	Kansas City	29	27	10	64	2.2
	Totals	379	1351	637	3339	8.8

MAYES, CLYDE

b. March 17, 1953 Ht. 6-7 Wt. 230 College—Furman

Yr	Team	G	FG	FT	TP	Avg.
1975-76	Milwaukee	65	114	56	284	4.4
1976-77	Ind.-Buf.-Port.	9	5	3	13	1.4
	Totals	74	119	59	297	4.0

MAYFIELD, KEN

b. May 11, 1948 Ht. 6-2 Wt. 185 College—Tuskegee

Yr	Team	G	FG	FT	TP	Avg.
1975-76	New York	13	17	3	37	2.8

MAZZA, MATT

b. Sept. 23, 1923 Ht. 6-3 Wt. 210 College—Mich. State

Yr	Team	G	FG	FT	TP	Avg.
1949-50	Sheboygan	26	33	32	98	3.8

Yr	Team	G	FG	FT	TP	Avg.
McBRIDE, KEN						
Ht. 6-3 Wt. 190 College—Maryland State						
1954-55	Milwaukee	12	48	21	117	9.8
McCANN, BRENDAN						
b. July 5, 1935 Ht. 6-2 Wt. 178 College—St. Bonaventure						
1957-58	New York	36	22	25	69	1.9
1958-59	New York	1	0	0	0	0.0
1959-60	New York	4	1	4	6	1.5
	Totals	41	23	29	75	1.8
McCARRON, MICHAEL						
b. March 2, 1922 Ht. 5-11 Wt. 180 College—Seton Hall						
1946-47	Toronto	60	236	177	649	10.8
1949-50	Balt.-St. L.	8	3	3	9	1.1
	Totals	68	239	180	658	9.7
McCARTER, ANDRE						
b. Aug. 25, 1953 Ht. 6-3 Wt. 190 College—UCLA						
1976-77	Kansas City	59	119	32	270	4.6
1977-78	Kansas City	1	0	0	0	0.0
	Totals	60	119	32	270	4.5
McCARTER, WILLIE						
b. July 26, 1946 Ht. 6-3 Wt. 175 College—Drake						
1969-70	Los Angeles	40	132	43	307	7.7
1970-71	Los Angeles	76	247	46	540	7.1
1971-72	Portland	39	103	37	243	6.2
	Totals	155	482	126	1090	7.0
McCARTHY, JOHN						
b. April 25, 1934 Ht. 6-1 Wt. 185 College—Canisius						
1956-57	Rochester	72	173	130	476	6.6
1958-59	Cincinnati	47	245	116	606	12.9
1959-60	St. Louis	75	240	149	629	8.4
1960-61	St. Louis	79	266	122	654	8.3
1961-62	St. Louis	15	18	12	48	3.2
1963-64	Boston	28	16	5	37	1.3
	Totals	316	958	534	2450	7.8
McCARTY, HOWARD						
b. 1919 Ht. 6-2 Wt. 190 College—Wayne State						
1945-46	Cleveland NL	13	40	13	93	7.2
1946-47	Detroit NL	16	46	29	121	7.6
1946-47	Detroit	19	10	1	21	1.1
	Totals	48	96	43	235	4.9
McCLOSKEY, JACK						
b. 1926 Ht. 6-2 Wt. 192 College—Pennsylvania						
1952-53	Philadelphia	1	3	0	6	6.0
McCONATHY, JOHN						
b. 1930 Ht. 6-5 Wt. 195 College—Northwest Louisiana						
1951-52	Milwaukee	11	4	6	14	1.3
McCONNELL, BUCKY						
Ht. 5-10 Wt. 170 College—Marshall						
1952-53	Milwaukee	14	27	14	68	4.9

Yr	Team	G	FG	FT	TP	Avg.
McCRACKEN, PAUL						
b. Sept. 11, 1950 Ht. 6-4 Wt. 180 Coll.—Northridge St.						
1972-73	Houston	24	44	23	111	4.6
1973-74	Houston	4	1	0	2	0.5
1976-77	Chicago	9	18	11	47	5.2
	Totals	37	63	34	160	4.3
McDANIELS, JIM						
b. April 2, 1948 Ht. 7-0 Wt. 225 Coll.—W. Kentucky						
1971-72	Carolina ABA	58	659 (0)	234	1552	26.8
1971-72	Seattle	12	51	11	113	9.4
1972-73	Seattle	68	154	70	378	5.6
1973-74	Seattle	27	63	23	149	5.5
1975-76	Los Angeles	35	41	9	91	2.6
1975-76	Kentucky ABA	29	78 (0)	23	179	6.2
1977-78	Buffalo	42	100	36	236	5.6
	Totals	271	1146 (0)	406	2698	9.9
McDONALD, GLENN						
b. March 18, 1952 Ht. 6-6 Wt. 190 College—Lg. Bch. St.						
1974-75	Boston	62	70	28	168	2.7
1975-76	Boston	75	191	40	422	5.6
1976-77	Milwaukee	9	8	3	19	2.1
	Totals	146	269	71	609	4.2
McDONALD, ROD						
b. April 9, 1945 Ht. 6-6 Wt. 205 College—Whitworth						
1970-71	Utah ABA	29	48 (2)	15	117	4.0
1971-72	Utah ABA	33	34 (0)	27	95	2.9
1972-73	Utah ABA	25	26 (1)	15	70	2.8
	Totals	87	108 (3)	57	282	3.2
McFARLAND, PAT						
b. Dec. 7, 1951 Ht. 6-5 Wt. 185 College—St. Joseph's						
1973-74	Denver	67	151 (8)	35	361	5.4
1974-75	Denver	70	198 (2)	52	454	6.5
1975-76	San Diego	11	54 (1)	21	132	12.0
	Totals	148	403 (11)	108	947	6.4
McGAHA, MEL						
b. Sept. 26, 1926 Ht. 6-1 Wt. 190 College—Arkansas						
1948-49	New York	51	62	52	176	3.5
McGILL, BILL (The Hill)						
b. Sept. 16, 1939 Ht. 6-9½ Wt. 225 College—Utah						
1962-63	Chicago	61	181	80	442	7.2
1963-64	Balt.-N.Y.	74	456	204	1116	15.1
1964-65	St. L.-L.A.	24	21	13	55	2.3
1968-69	Denver ABA	78	411 (0)	180	1002	12.8
1969-70	L.A.-Dallas ABA	59	201 (0)	77	479	8.1
	Totals	296	1270 (0)	554	3094	10.5

Yr	Team	G	FG	FT	TP	Avg.

McGLOCKLIN, JON

b. June 10, 1943 Ht. 6-5 Wt. 205 College—Indiana

Yr	Team	G	FG	FT	TP	Avg.
1965-66	Cincinnati	72	153	62	368	5.1
1966-67	Cincinnati	60	217	74	508	8.5
1967-68	San Diego	65	316	156	788	12.1
1968-69	Milwaukee	80	662	246	1570	19.6
1969-70	Milwaukee	82	639	169	1447	17.6
1970-71	Milwaukee	82	574	144	1292	15.8
1971-72	Milwaukee	80	374	109	857	10.7
1972-73	Milwaukee	80	351	63	765	9.6
1973-74	Milwaukee	79	329	72	730	9.2
1974-75	Milwaukee	79	323	63	709	9.0
1975-76	Milwaukee	33	63	9	135	4.1
	Totals	792	4001	1167	9169	11.6

McGREGOR, GIL

b. June 14, 1949 Ht. 6-8 Wt. 240 College—Wake Forest

| 1971-72 | Cincinnati | 42 | 66 | 39 | 171 | 4.1 |

McGRIFF, ELTON (Mac)

b. Aug. 21, 1942 Ht. 6-9 Wt. 230 College—Creighton

1967-68	Dallas ABA	20	49 (0)	33	131	6.6
1968-69	Dal.-N.O.-Ky.	36	75 (0)	57	207	5.8
	Totals	56	124 (0)	90	338	6.0

McGUIRE, AL

b. Sept. 7, 1928 Ht. 6-2 Wt. 180 College—St. John's (N.Y.)

1951-52	New York	59	72	64	208	3.5
1952-53	New York	58	112	128	352	6.1
1953-54	New York	64	58	58	174	2.7
1954-55	Baltimore	10	9	5	23	2.3
	Totals	191	251	255	757	4.0

McGUIRE, ALLIE

b. July 10, 1951 Ht. 6-3 Wt. 175 College—Marquette

| 1973-74 | New York | 2 | 2 | 0 | 4 | 2.0 |

McGUIRE, RICHARD (Tricky Dick)

b. Jan. 25, 1926 Ht. 6-0 Wt. 180 College—St. John's (N.Y.) and Dartmouth

1949-50	New York	68	190	204	584	8.6
1950-51	New York	64	179	179	537	8.4
1951-52	New York	64	204	183	591	9.2
1952-53	New York	61	142	153	437	7.2
1953-54	New York	68	201	220	622	9.1
1954-55	New York	71	226	195	647	9.1
1955-56	New York	62	152	121	425	6.9
1956-57	New York	72	140	105	385	5.3
1957-58	Detroit	69	203	150	556	8.1
1958-59	Detroit	71	232	191	655	9.2
1959-60	Detroit	68	179	124	482	7.1
	Totals	738	2048	1825	5921	8.0

McHARTLEY, MAURICE (Mo)

b. Aug. 1, 1942 Ht. 6-3 Wt. 200 College—North Carolina A & T

| 1967-68 | Dallas ABA | 58 | 327 (3) | 225 | 888 | 15.3 |
| 1968-69 | N.Y.-Miami ABA | 76 | 384 (6) | 263 | 1049 | 13.8 |

Yr	Team	G	FG	FT	TP	Avg.
1969-70	Miami-Pitt.-Dall. ABA	55	149 (6)	98	414	7.5
	Totals	189	860 (15)	586	2351	12.4

McINTOSH, KENNEDY

b. Jan. 21, 1949 Ht. 6-7 Wt. 225 College—Eastern Mich.

| 1971-72 | Chicago | 43 | 57 | 21 | 135 | 3.1 |

McINTYRE, BOB

b. Jan. 23, 1944 Ht. 6-7 Wt. 215 College—St. John's

| 1967-68 | New Jersey ABA | 21 | 70 (0) | 34 | 174 | 8.3 |

McKEE, GERALD

b. Aug. 4, 1946 Ht. 6-3 Wt. 190 College—Ohio Univ.

| 1969-70 | Indiana ABA | 1 | 0 (0) | 0 | 0 | 0.0 |

McKENZIE, STAN

b. Oct. 6, 1944 Ht. 6-5 Wt. 210 College—NYU

1967-68	Baltimore	50	73	58	204	4.1
1968-69	Phoenix	80	264	219	747	9.3
1969-70	Phoenix	58	81	58	220	3.8
1970-71	Portland	82	398	331	1127	13.7
1971-72	Portland	82	410	315	1135	13.8
1972-73	Port.-Hou.	33	48	30	126	3.8
1973-74	Houston	11	7	6	20	1.8
	Totals	396	1281	1017	3579	9.0

McKINNEY, HORACE (Bones)

b. Jan. 1, 1919 Ht. 6-6 Wt. 187 College—North Carolina and North Carolina State

1946-47	Washington	58	275	145	695	12.0
1947-48	Washington	43	182	121	485	11.3
1948-49	Washington	57	263	197	723	12.7
1949-50	Washington	53	187	118	492	9.3
1950-51	Wash.-Bos.	44	102	58	262	6.0
1951-52	Boston	63	136	65	337	5.3
	Totals	318	1145	704	2994	9.4

McLEMORE, McCOY

b. April 3, 1942 Ht. 6-7 Wt. 230 College—Drake

1964-65	San Fran.	78	244	157	645	8.3
1965-66	San Fran.	80	225	142	592	7.4
1966-67	Chicago	79	258	210	726	9.2
1967-68	Chicago	76	374	215	963	12.7
1968-69	Pho.-Det.	81	282	169	733	9.0
1969-70	Detroit	73	233	119	585	8.0
1970-71	Cleve.-Mil.	86	303	204	810	9.4
1971-72	Mil.-Hou.	27	28	20	76	2.8
	Totals	580	1947	1236	5130	8.8

McLEOD, GEORGE

b. 1932 Ht. 6-5 Wt. 200 College—Texas Christian

| 1952-53 | Baltimore | 10 | 2 | 8 | 12 | 1.2 |

McMAHON, JACK

b. Dec. 3, 1928 Ht. 6-1 Wt. 185 College—St. John's (N.Y.)

1952-53	Rochester	70	176	155	507	7.2
1953-54	Rochester	71	250	211	711	10.0
1954-55	Rochester	72	251	143	645	9.0
1955-56	Roch.-St. L.	70	202	110	514	7.3

Yr	Team	G	FG	FT	TP	Avg.
1956-57	St. Louis	72	239	142	620	8.6
1957-58	St. Louis	72	216	134	566	7.9
1958-59	St. Louis	72	248	96	592	8.2
	Totals	499	1582	991	4155	8.3

McMILLON, SHELLIE

b. March 11, 1936 Ht. 6-5 Wt. 205 College—Bradley

Yr	Team	G	FG	FT	TP	Avg.
1958-59	Detroit	48	127	55	309	6.4
1959-60	Detroit	75	267	132	666	8.9
1960-61	Detroit	78	322	140	784	10.1
1961-62	Det.-St. L.	62	265	108	638	10.3
	Totals	263	981	435	2397	9.1

McMULLAN, MALCOLM

b. Aug. 23, 1927 Ht. 6-5 Wt. 210 Coll.—Xavier (Ohio) and Kentucky

Yr	Team	G	FG	FT	TP	Avg.
1949-50	Indianapolis	58	123	77	323	5.6
1950-51	Indianapolis	51	78	48	204	4.0
	Totals	109	201	125	527	4.8

McNABB, CHESTER

b. 1921 Ht. 6-2 Wt. 200 College—West Texas

Yr	Team	G	FG	FT	TP	Avg.
1947-48	Baltimore	2	0	0	0	0.0

McNAMEE, JOE

b. 1927 Ht. 6-6 Wt. 210 College—San Francisco

Yr	Team	G	FG	FT	TP	Avg.
1950-51	Rochester	60	48	27	123	2.1
1951-52	Roch.-Balt.	58	68	30	166	2.9
	Totals	118	116	57	289	2.4

McNEILL, ROBERT

b. Oct. 22, 1938 Ht. 6-1 Wt. 180 College—St. Joseph's (Pa.)

Yr	Team	G	FG	FT	TP	Avg.
1960-61	New York	75	166	105	437	5.8
1961-62	Phila.-L.A.	50	56	26	138	2.8
	Totals	125	222	131	575	4.6

McNULTY, CARL

b. Feb. 14, 1930 Ht. 6-3 Wt. 185 College—Purdue

Yr	Team	G	FG	FT	TP	Avg.
1954-55	Milwaukee	1	1	0	2	2.0

McPIPE, ROY

b. May 5, 1950 Ht. 6-3 Wt. 205 College—Eastern Mt.

Yr	Team	G	FG	FT	TP	Avg.
1974-75	Utah ABA	5	6 (2)	3	21	4.2

McREYNOLDS, THALES

b. June 8, 1943 Ht. 6-3 Wt. 185 College—Miles

Yr	Team	G	FG	FT	TP	Avg.
1965-66	Baltimore	5	1	1	3	0.6

McWILLIAMS, ERIC

b. April 18, 1950 Ht. 6-8 Wt. 200 College—Lg. Bch. St.

Yr	Team	G	FG	FT	TP	Avg.
1972-73	Houston	44	34	18	86	2.0

MEARNS, GEORGE

b. April 18, 1922 Ht. 6-3 Wt. 175 College—Rhode Isl.

Yr	Team	G	FG	FT	TP	Avg.
1946-47	Providence	57	128	126	382	6.7
1947-48	Providence	24	23	15	61	2.5
	Totals	81	151	141	443	5.5

MEELY, CLIFF

b. July 10, 1947 Ht. 6-8 Wt. 215 College—Colorado

Yr	Team	G	FG	FT	TP	Avg.
1971-72	Houston	77	315	133	763	9.9
1972-73	Houston	82	268	92	628	7.7
1973-74	Houston	77	330	90	750	9.7
1974-75	Houston	48	156	68	380	7.9
1975-76	Hou.-L.A.	34	52	33	137	4.0
	Totals	318	1121	416	2658	8.4

MEHEN, RICHARD

b. May 20, 1922 Ht. 6-6 Wt. 195 College—Tennessee

Yr	Team	G	FG	FT	TP	Avg.
1947-48	Toledo NL	57	151	85	387	6.8
1948-49	Waterloo NL	62	315	211	841	13.6
1949-50	Waterloo	62	347	198	892	14.4
1950-51	Balt.-Boston-Ft. W.	66	192	90	474	7.2
1951-52	Milwaukee	65	293	117	703	10.8
	Totals	312	1298	701	3297	10.6

MEINEKE, DON (Monk)

b. Oct. 30, 1930 Ht. 6-7 Wt. 210 College—Dayton

Yr	Team	G	FG	FT	TP	Avg.
1952-53	Ft. Wayne	68	240	245	725	10.7
1953-54	Ft. Wayne	71	135	136	406	5.7
1954-55	Ft. Wayne	68	136	119	391	5.8
1955-56	Rochester	69	154	181	489	7.1
1957-58	Cincinnati	67	125	77	327	4.9
	Totals	343	790	758	2338	6.8

MEINHOLD, CARL (Red)

b. 1925 Ht. 6-2 Wt. 185 College—Long Island Univ.

Yr	Team	G	FG	FT	TP	Avg.
1947-48	Baltimore	48	108	37	253	5.3
1948-49	Chi.-Prov.	50	101	61	263	5.2
	Totals	98	209	98	516	5.3

MELCHIONNI, BILL

b. Oct. 19, 1944 Ht. 6-1 Wt. 165 College—Villanova

Yr	Team	G	FG	FT	TP	Avg.
1966-67	Philadelphia	71	138	39	315	4.4
1967-68	Philadelphia	71	146	33	325	4.6
1969-70	New York ABA	80	474 (5)	255	1218	15.2
1970-71	New York ABA	81	559 (2)	301	1425	17.5
1971-72	New York ABA	80	670 (2)	336	1682	21.0
1972-73	New York ABA	61	285 (6)	163	751	12.3
1973-74	New York ABA	56	111 (5)	59	296	5.3
1974-75	New York ABA	77	193 (8)	62	472	6.1
	Totals	577	2576 (28)	1248	6484	11.2

MELCHIONNI, GARY

b. Jan. 19, 1951 Ht. 6-2 Wt. 187 College—Duke

Yr	Team	G	FG	FT	TP	Avg.
1973-74	Phoenix	69	202	92	496	7.2
1974-75	Phoenix	68	232	114	578	8.5
	Totals	137	434	206	1074	7.8

MELVIN, EDWARD

b. Feb. 13, 1916 Ht. 5-9 Wt. 170 College—Duquesne

Yr	Team	G	FG	FT	TP	Avg.
1946-47	Pittsburgh	57	99	83	281	4.9

Yr	Team	G	FG	FT	TP	Avg.

MEMINGER, DEAN

b. May 13, 1948 Ht. 6-1 Wt. 175 College—Marquette

Yr	Team	G	FG	FT	TP	Avg.
1971-72	New York	78	139	79	357	4.6
1972-73	New York	80	188	81	457	5.7
1973-74	New York	78	274	103	651	8.3
1974-75	Atlanta	80	233	168	634	7.9
1975-76	Atlanta	68	155	100	410	6.0
1976-77	N.Y. Knicks	32	15	13	43	1.3
	Totals	416	1004	544	2552	6.1

MENCEL, CHUCK

b. April 21, 1933 Ht. 6-0 Wt. 168 College—Minnesota

Yr	Team	G	FG	FT	TP	Avg.
1955-56	Minneapolis	69	120	78	318	4.6
1956-57	Minneapolis	72	243	179	665	9.2
	Totals	141	363	257	983	7.0

MENKE, KEN (Angles)

b. 1922 Ht. 6-0 Wt. 168 College—Illinois

Yr	Team	G	FG	FT	TP	Avg.
1947-48	Ft. Wayne NL	44	39	45	123	2.8
1949-50	Waterloo	6	6	3	15	2.5
	Totals	50	45	48	138	2.8

MENYARD, DEWITT

Ht. 6-10 Wt. 210 College—Utah

Yr	Team	G	FG	FT	TP	Avg.
1967-68	Houston ABA	71	256 (0)	131	643	9.1

MERIWETHER, PORTER

b. March 16, 1940 Ht. 6-2 Wt. 180 College—Tenn. St.

Yr	Team	G	FG	FT	TP	Avg.
1962-63	Syracuse	31	48	23	119	3.8

MESCHERY, TOM

b. Oct. 26, 1938 Ht. 6-6 Wt. 215 College—St. Mary's (Calif.)

Yr	Team	G	FG	FT	TP	Avg.
1961-62	Philadelphia	80	375	216	966	12.1
1962-63	San Fran.	64	397	228	1022	16.0
1963-64	San Fran.	80	436	207	1079	13.5
1964-65	San Fran.	79	361	278	1000	12.2
1965-66	San Fran.	80	401	224	1026	12.8
1966-67	San Fran.	72	293	175	761	10.6
1967-68	Seattle	82	473	244	1190	14.5
1968-69	Seattle	82	462	220	1144	14.0
1969-70	Seattle	80	394	196	984	12.3
1970-71	Seattle	79	285	162	732	9.3
	Totals	778	3877	2150	9904	12.7

MEYER, BILL

Ht. 6-3 Wt. 195 College—Hiram

Yr	Team	G	FG	FT	TP	Avg.
1967-68	Pittsburgh ABA	7	10 (0)	2	22	3.1

MIASEK, STAN

b. 1924 Ht. 6-5 Wt. 210

Yr	Team	G	FG	FT	TP	Avg.
1946-47	Detroit	60	331	233	895	14.9
1947-48	Chicago	48	263	190	716	14.9
1948-49	Chicago	58	169	113	451	7.8
1949-50	Chicago	68	176	146	498	7.3
1951-52	Baltimore	66	258	263	779	11.8
1952-53	Balt.-Milw.	65	178	156	512	7.9
	Totals	365	1375	1101	3851	10.6

MIHALIK, ZIGMUND (Red)

Ht. 6-0 Wt. 180

Yr	Team	G	FG	FT	TP	Avg.
1946-47	Pittsburgh	7	3	0	6	0.9
1946-47	Youngstown NL	31	41	12	94	3.0
	Totals	38	44	12	100	2.6

MIKAN, EDWARD

b. Oct. 20, 1925 Ht. 6-8 Wt. 230 College—DePaul

Yr	Team	G	FG	FT	TP	Avg.
1948-49	Chicago	60	229	136	594	9.9
1949-50	Chi.-Roch.	65	89	92	270	4.2
1950-51	Roch.-Wash.-Phila.	61	193	137	523	8.6
1951-52	Philadelphia	66	202	116	520	7.9
1952-53	Phila.-Ind.	62	78	79	235	3.8
1953-54	Boston	9	8	5	21	2.3
	Totals	323	799	565	2163	6.7

MIKAN, GEORGE

b. June 18, 1924 Ht. 6-10 Wt. 245 College—DePaul

Yr	Team	G	FG	FT	TP	Avg.
1946-47	Chicago NL	25	147	119	413	16.5
1947-48	Minneapolis NL	56	406	383	1195	21.3
1948-49	Minneapolis	60	583	532	1698	28.3
1949-50	Minneapolis	68	649	567	1865	27.4
1950-51	Minneapolis	68	678	576	1932	28.4
1951-52	Minneapolis	64	545	433	1523	23.8
1952-53	Minneapolis	70	500	442	1442	20.6
1953-54	Minneapolis	72	441	424	1306	18.1
1955-56	Minneapolis	37	148	94	390	10.5
	Totals	520	4097	3570	11764	22.6

MIKAN, LARRY

b. April 8, 1948 Ht. 6-7 Wt. 215 College—Minnesota

Yr	Team	G	FG	FT	TP	Avg.
1970-71	Cleveland	53	62	34	158	3.0

MIKKELSEN, VERN

b. Oct. 21, 1928 Ht. 6-7 Wt. 230 College—Hamline

Yr	Team	G	FG	FT	TP	Avg.
1949-50	Minneapolis	68	288	215	791	11.6
1950-51	Minneapolis	64	359	186	904	14.1
1951-52	Minneapolis	66	363	283	1009	15.3
1952-53	Minneapolis	70	378	291	1047	15.0
1953-54	Minneapolis	72	288	221	797	11.1
1954-55	Minneapolis	71	440	447	1327	18.7
1955-56	Minneapolis	72	317	328	962	13.4
1956-57	Minneapolis	72	322	342	986	13.7
1957-58	Minneapolis	72	439	370	1248	17.3
1958-59	Minneapolis	72	353	286	992	13.8
	Totals	699	3547	2969	10063	14.4

MIKSIS, AL

b. Feb. 2, 1928 Ht. 6-7 Wt. 210 College—Eastern Ill.

Yr	Team	G	FG	FT	TP	Avg.
1949-50	Waterloo	8	5	17	27	3.4

MILES, EDDIE

b. July 5, 1940 Ht. 6-4 Wt. 196 College—Seattle

Yr	Team	G	FG	FT	TP	Avg.
1963-64	Detroit	60	131	62	324	5.4
1964-65	Detroit	76	439	166	1044	13.7
1965-66	Detroit	80	634	298	1566	19.6
1966-67	Detroit	81	582	261	1425	17.6
1967-68	Detroit	76	561	282	1404	18.5
1968-69	Detroit	80	441	182	1064	13.3
1969-70	Det.-Balt.	47	238	133	609	13.0
1970-71	Baltimore	63	252	118	622	9.9
1971-72	New York	42	23	16	62	1.5
	Totals	605	3301	1518	8120	13.4

Yr	Team	G	FG	FT	TP	Avg.

MILITZOK, NAT

b. 1923 Ht. 6-3 Wt. 195 College—CCNY, Hofstra and Cornell

Yr	Team	G	FG	FT	TP	Avg.
1946-47	N.Y.-Toronto	56	90	64	244	4.4

MILLER, EDWIN (Ed)

b. June 18, 1931 Ht. 6-8 Wt. 225 College—Syracuse

Yr	Team	G	FG	FT	TP	Avg.
1952-53	Milw.-Balt.	70	273	187	733	10.5
1953-54	Baltimore	72	244	231	719	10.0
	Totals	142	517	418	1452	10.2

MILLER, HARRY

b. 1923 Ht. 6-4 Wt. 230 College—North Carolina

Yr	Team	G	FG	FT	TP	Avg.
1946-47	Toronto	53	58	36	152	2.9

MILLER, JAY

b. July 19, 1943 Ht. 6-5 Wt. 210 College—Notre Dame

Yr	Team	G	FG	FT	TP	Avg.
1967-68	St. Louis	8	8	4	20	2.5
1968-69	Milwaukee	3	2	5	9	3.0
1968-69	L.A.-Ind. ABA	52	147 (0)	127	421	8.1
1969-70	Indiana ABA	52	75 (0)	41	191	3.7
1970-71	Indiana ABA	2	4 (0)	0	8	4.0
	Totals	117	236 (0)	177	649	5.5

MILLER, LARRY (Mills)

b. April 4, 1946 Ht. 6-4 Wt. 210 College—N.C.

Yr	Team	G	FG	FT	TP	Avg.
1968-69	Los Angeles ABA	78	431 (42)	340	1328	17.0
1969-70	L.A.-Car. ABA	80	302 (15)	223	872	10.9
1970-71	Carolina ABA	77	351 (13)	197	938	12.2
1971-72	Carolina ABA	83	550 (12)	393	1529	18.4
1972-73	San Diego ABA	83	450 (0)	306	1206	14.5
1973-74	S.D.-Vir. ABA	80	281 (0)	151	713	8.9
1974-75	Utah ABA	5	3 (0)	3	9	1.8
	Totals	486	2368 (82)	1613	6595	13.6

MILLER, WALTER

b. July 30, 1915 Ht. 6-2 Wt. 191 College—Duquesne

Yr	Team	G	FG	FT	TP	Avg.
1937-38	Pittsburgh NL	9	18	10	46	5.1
1938-39	Pittsburgh NL	19	52	44	148	7.8
1945-46	Youngstown NL	10	4	5	13	1.3
1946-47	Pittsburgh	12	7	9	23	1.9
	Totals	50	81	68	230	4.6

MILLER, WILLIAM

b. Nov. 23, 1924 Ht. 6-3 Wt. 190 College—N.C.

Yr	Team	G	FG	FT	TP	Avg.
1948-49	Chi.-St. L.	28	21	11	53	1.9

MILLS, JOHN

b. Sept. 7, 1919 Ht. 6-8 Wt. 210 College—Western Ky.

Yr	Team	G	FG	FT	TP	Avg.
1944-45	Cleveland NL	29	29	42	100	3.4
1945-46	Cleveland NL	19	13	25	51	2.7
1946-47	Pittsburgh	47	55	71	181	3.9
	Totals	95	97	138	332	3.5

MINOR, DAVAGE (Dave)

b. Feb. 23, 1922 Ht. 6-2 Wt. 185 College—Toledo and UCLA

Yr	Team	G	FG	FT	TP	Avg.
1951-52	Baltimore	57	185	101	471	8.3
1952-53	Balt.-Milw.	59	154	98	406	6.9
	Totals	116	339	199	877	7.6

MINOR, MARK

b. May 14, 1950 Ht. 6-6 Wt. 215 College—Ohio State

Yr	Team	G	FG	FT	TP	Avg.
1972-73	Boston	4	1	3	5	1.3

MISAKA, WAT

b. Dec. 21, 1923 Ht. 5-7 Wt. 150 College—Utah

Yr	Team	G	FG	FT	TP	Avg.
1947-48	New York	3	3	1	7	2.3

MITCHELL, LELAND

b. Feb. 22, 1941 Ht. 6-4 Wt. 210 College—Miss. State

Yr	Team	G	FG	FT	TP	Avg.
1967-68	New Orleans ABA	78	101 (21)	56	321	4.1

MITCHELL, MURRAY

b. March 19, 1923 Ht. 6-6 College—Sam Houston

Yr	Team	G	FG	FT	TP	Avg.
1949-50	Anderson	2	1	0	2	1.0

MLKVY, BILL

b. Jan. 19, 1931 Ht. 6-4 Wt. 190 College—Temple

Yr	Team	G	FG	FT	TP	Avg.
1952-53	Philadelphia	31	75	31	181	5.8

MODZELEWSKI, STANLEY (Stutz)

See Stutz, Stan

MOE, DOUG

b. Sept. 21, 1938 Ht. 6-5 Wt. 220 College—N.C.

Yr	Team	G	FG	FT	TP	Avg.
1967-68	New Orleans ABA	78	662 (3)	551	1884	24.2
1968-69	Oakland ABA	75	524 (5)	360	1423	19.0
1969-70	Carolina ABA	80	527 (8)	304	1382	17.2
1970-71	Virginia ABA	78	395 (2)	221	1017	13.0
1971-72	Virginia ABA	67	174 (1)	104	455	6.8
	Totals	378	2282 (19)	1540	6161	16.3

MOFFETT, LARRY

b. Nov. 5, 1954 Ht. 6-8 Wt. 210 College—Nev.L. Vegas

Yr	Team	G	FG	FT	TP	Avg.
1977-78	Houston	20	5	6	16	0.8

Yr	Team	G	FG	FT	TP	Avg.

MOGUS, LEO

b. April 13, 1921 Ht. 6-4 Wt. 205 Coll.—Youngstown

Yr	Team	G	FG	FT	TP	Avg.
1945-46	Youngstown NL	16	61	66	188	11.8
1946-47	Cleve.-Toronto	58	259	235	753	13.0
1948-49	Balt.-Ft. W.-Ind.	52	172	177	521	10.0
1949-50	Philadelphia	64	172	218	562	8.8
1950-51	Philadelphia	57	43	53	139	2.4
	Totals	247	707	749	2163	8.8

MOLINAS, JACK

b. 1932 Ht. 6-6 Wt. 200 College—Columbia
d. Aug. 3, 1975

Yr	Team	G	FG	FT	TP	Avg.
1953-54	Ft. Wayne	29	108	134	350	12.1

MOLIS, WAYNE

b. April 17, 1943 Ht. 6-8 Wt. 230 College—Lewis

Yr	Team	G	FG	FT	TP	Avg.
1966-67	New York	13	19	7	45	3.5
1967-68	Oakland ABA	5	5 (0)	4	14	2.8
	Totals	18	24 (0)	11	59	3.3

MONTGOMERY, HOWARD

b. Aug. 22, 1940 Ht. 6-4½ Wt. 220 Coll.—Pan-American

Yr	Team	G	FG	FT	TP	Avg.
1962-63	San Fran.	20	65	14	144	7.2

MOONEY, JAMES

b. 1927 Ht. 6-5 Wt. 215 College—Villanova

Yr	Team	G	FG	FT	TP	Avg.
1952-53	Balt.-Phil.	18	54	27	135	7.5

MOORE, GENE

b. July 29, 1945 Ht. 6-9 Wt. 240 College—St. Louis U.

Yr	Team	G	FG	FT	TP	Avg.
1968-69	Kentucky ABA	76	417 (0)	204	1038	13.7
1969-70	Kentucky ABA	83	628 (2)	209	1471	17.7
1970-71	Texas ABA	84	465 (2)	189	1125	13.4
1971-72	Dal.-N.Y. ABA	77	252 (1)	89	596	7.7
1972-73	San Diego ABA	83	396 (4)	180	984	11.9
1973-74	San Diego ABA	49	153 (1)	41	350	7.1
1974-75	St. Louis ABA	13	13 (0)	4	30	2.3
	Totals	465	2324 (10)	916	5594	12.0

MOORE, JACKIE

b. Sept. 24, 1932 Ht. 6-5 Wt. 182 College—LaSalle

Yr	Team	G	FG	FT	TP	Avg.
1954-55	Syra.-Milw.-Phila.	23	44	22	110	4.8
1955-56	Philadelphia	54	50	32	132	2.4
1956-57	Philadelphia	57	43	37	123	2.2
	Totals	134	137	91	365	2.7

MOORE, LARRY

b. 1967-68 Anaheim

Yr	Team	G	FG	FT	TP	Avg.
1967-68	Anaheim ABA	12	8 (0)	11	27	2.3

MOORE, OTTO

b. Aug. 27, 1946 Ht. 6-11 Wt. 205 Coll.—Pan American

Yr	Team	G	FG	FT	TP	Avg.
1968-69	Detroit	74	241	88	570	7.7
1969-70	Detroit	81	383	194	960	11.9
1970-71	Detroit	82	310	121	741	9.0
1971-72	Phoenix	81	260	94	614	7.6
1972-73	Houston	82	418	127	963	11.7
1973-74	Hou.-K.C.-O.	78	120	39	279	3.6
1974-75	Det.-N.O.	42	118	46	282	6.7
1975-76	New Orleans	81	293	144	730	9.0
1976-77	New Orleans	81	193	91	477	5.9
	Totals	682	2336	944	5616	8.2

MOORE, RICHIE

Ht. 6-2 Wt. 190 College—Hiram Scott

Yr	Team	G	FG	FT	TP	Avg.
1967-68	Denver ABA	18	24 (0)	21	69	3.8

MORELAND, JACK

b. March 11, 1938 Ht. 6-7 Wt. 215 College—La. Tech.
d. Dec. 19, 1971

Yr	Team	G	FG	FT	TP	Avg.
1960-61	Detroit	64	191	86	468	7.3
1961-62	Detroit	74	205	139	549	7.4
1962-63	Detroit	78	271	145	687	8.8
1963-64	Detroit	78	272	164	708	9.1
1964-65	Detroit	54	103	66	272	5.0
1967-68	New Orleans ABA	76	457 (2)	192	1112	14.6
1968-69	New Orleans ABA	78	466 (2)	221	1159	14.9
1969-70	New Orleans ABA	80	315 (2)	139	775	9.2
	Totals	582	2280 (6)	1152	5730	9.8

MORGAN, REX

b. Oct. 27, 1948 Ht. 6-5 Wt. 190 College—Jacksonville

Yr	Team	G	FG	FT	TP	Avg.
1970-71	Boston	34	41	35	117	3.4
1971-72	Boston	28	16	23	55	2.0
	Totals	62	57	58	172	2.8

MORGENTHALER, ELMORE

b. 1925 Ht. 6-9 Wt. 230 College—Boston College and New Mexico State

Yr	Team	G	FG	FT	TP	Avg.
1946-47	Providence	11	4	7	15	1.4
1948-49	Philadelphia	20	15	12	42	2.1
	Totals	31	19	19	57	1.8

MORRIS, G. MAX

b. March 14, 1925 Ht. 6-2 Wt. 195 College—Northwestern

Yr	Team	G	FG	FT	TP	Avg.
1946-47	Chicago NL	33	44	33	121	3.7
1947-48	Sheboygan NL	39	132	132	396	10.2
1948-49	Sheboygan NL	41	70	68	208	5.1
1949-50	Sheboygan	62	252	277	781	12.6
	Totals	175	498	510	1506	8.6

MORRISON, DWIGHT (Red)

b. 1931 Ht. 6-8 Wt. 225 College—Idaho

Yr	Team	G	FG	FT	TP	Avg.
1954-55	Boston	71	120	72	312	4.4
1955-56	Boston	71	89	44	222	3.1
1957-58	St. Louis	13	9	3	21	1.6
	Totals	155	218	119	555	3.6

Yr	Team	G	FG	FT	TP	Avg.

MORRISON, JOHN

Ht. 6-2 Wt. 190 College—Canisius

| 1967-68 | Denver ABA | 9 | 9 (1) | 6 | 27 | 3.0 |

MOUNT, RICK

b. Jan. 5, 1947 Ht. 6-4 Wt. 185 College—Purdue

1970-71	Indiana ABA	66	126 (23)	116	437	6.6
1971-72	Indiana ABA	78	363 (57)	216	1113	14.3
1972-73	Kentucky ABA	61	360 (9)	159	906	14.9
1973-74	Ken.-Utah ABA	52	167 (12)	59	429	8.3
1974-75	Memphis ABA	26	161 (20)	63	445	17.1
	Totals	283	1177 (121)	613	3330	11.8

MRAZOVICH, CHARLES

b. Feb. 26, 1924 Ht. 6-5 Wt. 185 College—Eastern Ky.

| 1950-51 | Indianapolis | 23 | 24 | 28 | 76 | 3.3 |

MUELLER, ERWIN

b. March 12, 1944 Ht. 6-8 Wt. 230 Coll.—San Fran.

1966-67	Chicago	80	422	171	1015	12.7
1967-68	Chi.-L.A.	74	223	107	553	7.5
1968-69	Chi.-Sea.	78	144	89	377	4.8
1969-70	Sea.-Det.	78	300	189	789	10.1
1970-71	Detroit	52	126	60	312	6.0
1971-72	Detroit	42	68	43	179	4.3
1972-73	Detroit	21	9	5	23	1.1
1972-73	Virginia ABA	17	17 (0)	3	37	2.2
1973-74	Memphis ABA	3	0 (0)	2	2	0.7
	Totals	445	1309 (0)	669	3287	7.4

MULLANEY, JOE

b. Nov. 17, 1925 Ht. 6-0 Wt. 165 College—Holy Cross

| 1949-50 | Boston | 37 | 9 | 12 | 30 | 0.8 |

MULLENS, ROBERT

b. Nov. 1, 1922 Ht. 6-1 Wt. 175 College—Fordham

| 1946-47 | N.Y.-Toronto | 54 | 125 | 64 | 314 | 5.8 |

MULLINS, JEFF (Pork Chop)

b. March 18, 1942 Ht. 6-4 Wt. 190 College—Duke

1964-65	St. Louis	44	87	41	215	4.9
1965-66	St. Louis	44	113	29	255	5.8
1966-67	San Fran.	77	421	150	992	12.9
1967-68	San Fran.	79	610	273	1493	18.9
1968-69	San Fran.	78	697	381	1775	22.8
1969-70	San Fran.	74	656	320	1632	22.1
1970-71	San Fran.	75	630	302	1562	20.8
1971-72	Golden St.	80	685	350	1720	21.5
1972-73	Golden St.	81	651	143	1445	17.8
1973-74	Golden St.	77	541	168	1250	16.2
1974-75	Golden St.	66	234	71	539	8.2
1975-76	Golden St.	29	58	23	139	4.8
	Totals	804	5383	2251	13017	16.2

MUNROE, GEORGE

b. Jan. 5, 1922 Ht. 5-11½ Wt. 170 College—Dartmouth

1946-47	St. Louis	59	164	86	414	7.0
1947-48	Boston	21	27	17	71	3.4
	Totals	80	191	103	485	6.1

MURPHY, ALLEN

b. July 15, 1952 Ht. 6-5 Wt. 190 College—Louisville

| 1975-76 | Kentucky ABA | 29 | 43 | 27 | 113 | 3.9 |

MURPHY, JOHN

b. 1923 Ht. 6-2 Wt. 175 College—Manhattan and John Marshall

| 1946-47 | N.Y.-Phila. | 20 | 11 | 10 | 32 | 1.6 |

MURPHY, RICHARD

b. 1921 Ht. 6-1 Wt. 180 College—Manhattan
d. Oct. 22, 1973

| 1946-47 | N.Y.-Boston | 31 | 15 | 4 | 34 | 1.1 |

MURRAY, KEN

b. April 20, 1928 Ht. 6-2 Wt. 195 College— St. Bonaventure

1950-51	Balt.-Ft. W.	66	301	248	850	12.9
1953-54	Ft. Wayne	49	53	43	149	3.0
1954-55	Balt.-Phila.	66	187	98	472	7.2
	Totals	181	541	389	1471	8.1

MURRELL, WILLIE

b. Sept. 13, 1941 Ht. 6-6½ Wt. 225 College—Eastern Oklahoma and Kansas State

1967-68	Denver ABA	71	495 (3)	166	1165	16.4
1968-69	Miami ABA	75	472 (4)	191	1147	15.3
1969-70	Kentucky ABA	35	44 (4)	18	118	3.4
	Totals	181	1011 (11)	375	2430	13.4

MURREY, DORRIE

b. Sept. 7, 1943 Ht. 6-8 Wt. 215 College—Detroit

1966-67	Detroit	35	33	32	98	2.8
1967-68	Seattle	81	211	168	590	7.3
1968-69	Seattle	38	75	62	212	5.6
1969-70	Seattle	81	153	136	442	5.5
1970-71	Port.-Balt.	71	78	75	231	3.3
1971-72	Baltimore	51	43	24	110	2.2
	Totals	357	593	497	1683	4.7

MUSI, ANGELO

b. July 25, 1918 Ht. 5-9 Wt. 145 College—Temple

1946-47	Phila.	60	230	102	562	9.4
1947-48	Phila.	43	134	51	319	7.4
1948-49	Phila.	58	194	90	478	8.2
	Totals	161	558	243	1359	8.4

NABER, ROBERT

b. Sept. 3, 1929 Ht. 6-3 Wt. 185 College—Louisville

| 1952-53 | Indianapolis | 4 | 0 | 1 | 1 | 0.3 |

NACHAMKIN, BORIS

Ht. 6-6 Wt. 210 College—New York University

| 1954-55 | Rochester | 6 | 6 | 8 | 20 | 3.3 |

Yr	Team	G	FG	FT	TP	Avg.

NAGEL, JERRY

b. May 18, 1928 Ht. 6-0½ Wt. 190 Coll.—Loyola (Ill.)

Yr	Team	G	FG	FT	TP	Avg.
1949-50	Ft. Wayne	14	6	1	13	0.9

NAGY, FRITZ

b. Jan. 3, 1924 Ht. 6-2 Wt. 185 College—Akron

Yr	Team	G	FG	FT	TP	Avg.
1947-48	Indianapolis NL	39	42	42	126	3.2
1948-49	Indianapolis	50	94	65	253	5.1
	Totals	89	136	107	379	4.3

NAPOLITANO, PAUL

b. 1922 Ht. 6-2 Wt. 185 College—San Francisco

Yr	Team	G	FG	FT	TP	Avg.
1947-48	Minneapolis NL	52	72	11	155	3.0
1948-49	Indianapolis	1	0	0	0	0.0
	Totals	53	72	11	155	2.9

NASH, CHARLES (Cotton)

b. July 24, 1942 Ht. 6-5 Wt. 225 College—Kentucky

Yr	Team	G	FG	FT	TP	Avg.
1964-65	L.A.-San Fran.	45	47	43	137	3.0
1967-68	Kentucky ABA	39	106 (0)	121	333	8.5
	Totals	84	153 (0)	164	470	5.6

NAULLS, WILLIE

b. Oct. 7, 1934 Ht. 6-6 Wt. 225 College—UCLA

Yr	Team	G	FG	FT	TP	Avg.
1956-57	St. L.-New York	71	293	132	718	10.1
1957-58	New York	68	472	284	1228	18.1
1958-59	New York	68	405	258	1068	15.7
1959-60	New York	65	551	286	1388	21.3
1960-61	New York	79	737	372	1846	23.4
1961-62	New York	75	747	383	1877	25.0
1962-63	N.Y.-San Fran.	70	370	166	906	12.7
1963-64	Boston	78	321	125	767	9.8
1964-65	Boston	71	302	143	747	10.5
1965-66	Boston	71	328	104	760	10.7
	Totals	716	4526	2253	11305	15.8

NEAL, EBBERLE (Jim)

b. 1930 Ht. 6-11 Wt. 235 College—Wofford

Yr	Team	G	FG	FT	TP	Avg.
1953-54	Syracuse	67	117	78	312	4.7
1954-55	Baltimore	13	12	15	39	3.3
	Totals	80	129	93	351	4.4

NEGRATTI, ALBERT

b. 1922 Ht. 6-3½ Wt. 200 College—Seton Hall

Yr	Team	G	FG	FT	TP	Avg.
1945-46	Rochester NL	16	19	10	48	3.0
1946-47	Rochester NL	33	15	14	44	1.3
1946-47	Washington	11	13	5	31	2.8
	Totals	60	47	29	123	2.1

NELSON, BARRY

b. Sept. 19, 1949 Ht. 6-10 Wt. 230 Coll.—Duquesne

Yr	Team	G	FG	FT	TP	Avg.
1971-72	Milwaukee	28	15	5	35	1.3

NELSON, DON

b. May 15, 1940 Ht. 6-6 Wt. 210 College—Iowa

Yr	Team	G	FG	FT	TP	Avg.
1962-63	Chicago	63	129	161	419	6.7
1963-64	Los Angeles	80	135	149	419	5.2
1964-65	Los Angeles	39	36	20	92	2.4
1965-66	Boston	75	271	223	765	10.2
1966-67	Boston	79	227	141	595	7.5
1967-68	Boston	82	312	195	819	10.0
1968-69	Boston	82	374	201	949	11.6
1969-70	Boston	82	461	337	1259	15.4
1970-71	Boston	82	412	317	1141	13.9
1971-72	Boston	82	389	356	1134	13.8
1972-73	Boston	72	309	159	777	10.8
1973-74	Boston	82	364	215	943	11.5
1974-75	Boston	79	423	263	1109	14.0
1975-76	Boston	75	175	127	477	6.4
	Totals	1053	4017	2864	10898	10.3

NELSON, LOUIE

b. May 28, 1951 Ht. 6-3 Wt. 190 College—Washington

Yr	Team	G	FG	FT	TP	Avg.
1973-74	Capital	49	93	53	239	4.9
1974-75	New Orleans	72	307	192	806	11.2
1975-76	New Orleans	66	327	169	823	12.5
1976-77	San Antonio	4	7	4	18	4.5
1977-78	K.C.-N.J.	33	85	57	227	6.9
	Totals	224	819	475	2113	9.4

NEMELKA, DICK

Ht. 6-0 Wt. 175 College—Brigham Young

Yr	Team	G	FG	FT	TP	Avg.
1970-71	Utah ABA	39	62 (20)	32	216	5.5

NETOLICKY, BOB (Neto)

b. Aug. 2, 1942 Ht. 6-9 Wt. 225 College—Drake

Yr	Team	G	FG	FT	TP	Avg.
1967-68	Indiana ABA	71	468 (0)	220	1156	16.3
1968-69	Indiana ABA	78	583 (0)	306	1472	18.9
1969-70	Indiana ABA	82	671 (2)	343	1691	20.6
1970-71	Indiana ABA	82	649 (2)	237	1541	18.8
1971-72	Indiana ABA	83	518 (4)	202	1250	15.1
1972-73	Dallas ABA	84	650 (0)	269	1569	18.7
1973-74	S.A.-Ind. ABA	75	312 (2)	106	736	9.8
1974-75	Indiana ABA	59	187 (2)	62	442	7.5
1975-76	Indiana ABA	4	8 (0)	3	19	4.8
	Totals	618	4046 (12)	1748	9876	16.0

NEUMANN, JOHNNY

b. Sept. 11, 1951 Ht. 6-6 Wt. 200 College—Mississippi

Yr	Team	G	FG	FT	TP	Avg.
1971-72	Memphis ABA	77	519 (26)	293	1409	18.3
1972-73	Memphis ABA	79	596 (9)	329	1548	19.5
1973-74	Mem.-Utah ABA	87	464 (18)	166	1148	13.2
1974-75	Vir.-Ind. ABA	52	165 (21)	52	445	8.6
1975-76	Vir.-Ken. ABA	77	322 (71)	151	1008	13.1

Yr	Team	G	FG	FT	TP	Avg.
1976-77	Buff.-L.A.	63	161	59	381	6.0
1977-78	Indiana	20	35	13	83	4.2
	Totals	455	2262 (145)	1063	6022	13.2

NEUMANN, PAUL

b. Jan. 30, 1938 Ht. 6-1 Wt. 175 College—Stanford

Yr	Team	G	FG	FT	TP	Avg.
1961-62	Syracuse	79	172	133	477	6.0
1962-63	Syracuse	80	237	181	655	8.2
1963-64	Phila.	74	324	210	858	11.6
1964-65	Phila.-San Fran.	76	365	234	964	12.7
1965-66	San Fran.	66	343	265	951	14.4
1966-67	San Fran.	78	386	312	1084	13.9
	Totals	453	1827	1335	4989	11.0

NEWMARK, DAVE

b. Sept. 11, 1946 Ht. 7-0 Wt. 240 College—Columbia

Yr	Team	G	FG	FT	TP	Avg.
1968-69	Chicago	81	185	86	456	5.6
1969-70	Atlanta	64	127	59	313	4.9
1970-71	Carolina ABA	31	100 (0)	34	234	7.6
	Totals	176	412 (0)	179	1003	5.7

NEWTON, BILL

b. Dec. 22, 1950 Ht. 6-9 Wt. 220 College—Indiana

Yr	Team	G	FG	FT	TP	Avg.
1972-73	Indiana ABA	24	23 (1)	9	58	2.4
1973-74	Indiana ABA	11	7 (0)	1	15	1.4
	Totals	35	30 (1)	10	73	2.1

NICHOLS, JACK

b. April 9, 1926 Ht. 6-7 Wt. 230 College—Washington

Yr	Team	G	FG	FT	TP	Avg.
1948-49	Washington	34	153	92	398	11.7
1949-50	Wash.-Tri-Cities	67	310	259	879	13.1
1950-51	Tri-Cities	5	18	10	46	9.2
1952-53	Milwaukee	69	425	240	1090	15.8
1953-54	Mil.-Boston	75	163	113	439	5.9
1954-55	Boston	64	249	138	636	9.9
1955-56	Boston	60	330	200	860	14.3
1956-57	Boston	61	195	108	498	8.2
1957-58	Boston	69	170	59	399	5.8
	Totals	504	2013	1219	5245	10.4

NIEMANN, RICH

b. July 2, 1946 Ht. 7-0 Wt. 245 Coll.—St. Louis Univ.

Yr	Team	G	FG	FT	TP	Avg.
1968-69	Det.-Mil.	34	44	19	107	3.1
1969-70	Boston	6	2	2	6	1.0
1969-70	Carolina ABA	63	285 (0)	141	711	11.3
1970-71	Floridians ABA	51	121 (0)	43	285	5.6
1971-72	Dallas ABA	33	48 (0)	25	121	3.7
	Totals	187	500 (0)	230	1230	6.6

NIEMIERA, RICHARD

b. May 26, 1926 Ht. 6-1 Wt. 165 College—Notre Dame

Yr	Team	G	FG	FT	TP	Avg.
1946-47	Ft. Wayne NL	13	28	17	73	5.6
1947-48	Ft. Wayne NL	59	118	97	333	5.6
1948-49	Ft. Wayne	55	115	132	362	6.6
1949-50	Ft. W.-Anderson	60	110	104	324	5.4
	Totals	187	371	350	1092	5.8

NOBLE, CHUCK

b. July 24, 1931 Ht. 6-4 Wt. 195 College—Louisville

Yr	Team	G	FG	FT	TP	Avg.
1955-56	Ft. Wayne	72	270	146	686	9.5
1956-57	Ft. Wayne	54	200	76	476	8.8
1957-58	Detroit	61	199	56	454	7.4
1958-59	Detroit	65	189	83	461	7.1
1959-60	Detroit	58	276	101	653	11.3
1960-61	Detroit	75	196	82	474	6.3
1961-62	Detroit	26	32	8	72	2.8
	Totals	411	1362	552	3276	8.0

NOEL, PAUL

Ht. 6-4 Wt. 185 College—Kentucky

Yr	Team	G	FG	FT	TP	Avg.
1947-48	New York	29	40	19	99	3.4
1948-49	New York	47	70	37	177	3.8
1949-50	New York	65	98	53	249	3.8
1950-51	Rochester	52	49	32	130	2.5
1951-52	Rochester	8	2	2	6	0.8
	Totals	201	259	143	661	3.3

NOLAN, JIM

Ht. 6-8 Wt. 210 College—Georgia Tech.

Yr	Team	G	FG	FT	TP	Avg.
1949-50	Philadelphia	5	4	0	8	1.6

NOLEN, PAUL

b. June 9, 1927 Ht. 6-10 Wt. 215 College—Texas Tech.

Yr	Team	G	FG	FT	TP	Avg.
1953-54	Baltimore	1	0	0	0	0.0

NORDMANN, ROBERT (Bevo)

b. Dec. 11, 1939 Ht. 6-10 Wt. 225 College—St. Louis

Yr	Team	G	FG	FT	TP	Avg.
1961-62	Cincinnati	58	51	29	131	2.2
1962-63	St. L.-N.Y.	53	156	59	371	7.0
1963-64	N.Y.-St. L.	19	27	9	63	3.3
1964-65	Boston	3	3	0	6	2.2
	Totals	133	237	97	571	4.3

NORLANDER, JOHN

b. March 5, 1921 Ht. 6-3 Wt. 180 College—Hamline and Maryland State

Yr	Team	G	FG	FT	TP	Avg.
1946-47	Washington	60	223	180	626	10.4
1947-48	Washington	48	167	135	469	9.8
1948-49	Washington	60	164	116	444	7.4
1949-50	Washington	40	99	53	251	6.3
1950-51	Washington	9	6	9	21	2.3
	Totals	217	659	493	1811	8.3

NORWOOD, WILLIE

b. Aug. 8, 1947 Ht. 6-7 Wt. 220 College—Alcorn A & M

Yr	Team	G	FG	FT	TP	Avg.
1971-72	Detroit	78	222	140	584	7.5
1972-73	Detroit	79	249	154	652	8.3
1973-74	Detroit	74	247	95	589	8.0
1974-75	Detroit	24	64	31	159	6.6
1975-76	Seattle	64	146	152	444	6.9
1976-77	Seattle	76	216	151	583	7.7
1977-78	Sea.-Port.	35	74	50	198	5.7
	Totals	430	1218	773	3209	7.5

NOSTRAND, GEORGE

b. April 5, 1924 Ht. 6-8 Wt. 197 College—High Point and Wyoming

Yr	Team	G	FG	FT	TP	Avg.
1946-47	Cleve. Toronto	61	192	98	482	7.9
1947-48	Providence	45	196	129	521	11.6
1948-49	Prov.-Boston	60	212	165	589	9.8
1949-50	Bos.-Tri-C.-Chi.	55	78	56	212	3.9
	Totals	221	678	448	1804	8.2

Yr	Team	G	FG	FT	TP	Avg.

NOSZKA, STANLEY

b. Sept. 19, 1920 Ht. 6-1 Wt. 185 College—Duquesne

Yr	Team	G	FG	FT	TP	Avg.
1945-46	Youngstown NL	2	0	1	1	0.5
1946-47	Pittsburgh	48	199	109	507	8.6
1947-48	Boston	22	27	24	78	3.5
1948-49	Boston	30	30	15	75	2.5
	Totals	102	256	149	661	6.5

NOVAK, MICHAEL

b. April 23, 1915 Ht. 6-9 Wt. 220 College—Loyola (III.)

Yr	Team	G	FG	FT	TP	Avg.
1939-40	Chicago NL	28	114	65	293	10.5
1940-41	Chicago NL	23	56	34	146	6.3
1941-42	Chicago NL	19	58	31	147	7.7
1942-43	Chicago NL	18	50	35	135	7.5
1943-44	Sheboygan NL	22	39	14	92	4.2
1944-45	Sheboygan NL	27	88	57	233	8.6
1945-46	Sheboygan NL	34	111	88	310	9.1
1946-47	Syracuse NL	36	153	73	379	10.5
1947-48	Syracuse NL	60	211	124	546	9.1
1948-49	Rochester	60	124	72	320	5.3
1949-50	Roch.-Phila.	60	37	25	99	1.7
1953-54	Syracuse	5	0	1	1	0.2
	Totals	392	1041	619	2701	6.9

NOWELL, MEL

b. Dec. 27, 1939 Ht. 6-2 Wt. 174 College—Ohio State

Yr	Team	G	FG	FT	TP	Avg.
1962-63	Chicago	39	92	48	232	5.9
1967-68	New Jersey ABA	76	264 (9)	176	731	9.6
	Totals	115	356 (9)	224	963	8.4

O'BOYLE, JOHN

b. March 7, 1928 Ht. 6-2 Wt. 186 College—Colo. State

Yr	Team	G	FG	FT	TP	Avg.
1952-53	Milwaukee	5	8	5	21	4.2

O'BRIEN, JIM

b. April 9, 1950 Ht. 6-3 Wt. 170 College—Boston Coll.

Yr	Team	G	FG	FT	TP	Avg.
1971-72	Pitt.-Ky. ABA	84	166 (7)	65	418	5.0
1972-73	Kentucky ABA	68	126 (0)	68	320	4.7
1973-74	Ken.-S.D. ABA	72	204 (7)	79	508	7.1
1974-75	San Diego ABA	79	206 (4)	125	549	7.0
	Totals	302	702 (18)	337	1795	5.9

O'BRIEN, JIM

b. Nov. 7, 1951 Ht. 6-7 Wt. 200 College—Maryland

Yr	Team	G	FG	FT	TP	Avg.
1973-74	New York ABA	11	15 (0)	9	39	3.6
1974-75	Memphis ABA	47	82 (6)	47	229	4.9
	Totals	58	97 (6)	56	268	4.6

O'BRIEN, RALPH (Buckshot)

b. April 28, 1928 Ht. 5-9 Wt. 160 College—Butler

Yr	Team	G	FG	FT	TP	Avg.
1951-52	Indianapolis	64	228	122	578	9.0
1952-53	Ind.-Balt.	55	96	78	270	4.9
	Totals	119	324	200	848	7.1

O'BRIEN, ROBERT

b. Jan. 26, 1927 Ht. 6-4½ Wt. 190 College—Kansas and Pepperdine

Yr	Team	G	FG	FT	TP	Avg.
1947-48	Philadelphia	22	17	15	49	2.2
1948-49	Phila.-St. L.	24	10	12	32	1.3
	Totals	46	27	27	81	1.8

O'CONNELL, DERMOTT

b. April 13, 1928 Ht. 6-0 Wt. 174 College—Holy Cross

Yr	Team	G	FG	FT	TP	Avg.
1948-49	Boston	21	87	30	204	9.7
1949-50	Bos.-St. Louis	61	111	47	269	4.4
	Totals	82	198	77	473	5.8

O'DONNELL, ANDY

b. March 10, 1925 Ht. 6-1 Wt. 180 Coll.—Loyola (Md.)

Yr	Team	G	FG	FT	TP	Avg.
1949-50	Baltimore	25	38	14	90	3.6

OGDEN, BUD

b. Dec. 19, 1946 Ht. 6-6 Wt. 215 College—Santa Clara

Yr	Team	G	FG	FT	TP	Avg.
1969-70	Philadelphia	47	82	27	191	4.1
1970-71	Philadelphia	27	24	18	66	2.4
	Totals	74	106	45	257	3.5

OGDEN, RALPH

b. Jan. 25, 1948 Ht. 6-5 Wt. 205 College—Santa Clara

Yr	Team	G	FG	FT	TP	Avg.
1970-71	San Francisco	32	17	8	42	1.3

O'GRADY, FRANCIS

b. Jan. 19, 1920 Ht. 5-11 Wt. 160 Coll.—Georgetown

Yr	Team	G	FG	FT	TP	Avg.
1946-47	Washington	55	55	38	148	2.7
1947-48	Washington	44	67	36	170	3.9
1948-49	St. L.-Prov.	47	85	49	219	4.7
	Totals	146	207	123	537	3.7

O'HANLON, FRAN

b. 1948 Ht. 6-1 Wt. 175 College—Villanova

Yr	Team	G	FG	FT	TP	Avg.
1970-71	Floridians ABA	14	8 (0)	6	22	1.6

OHL, DON

b. April 18, 1936 Ht. 6-3 Wt. 190 College—Illinois

Yr	Team	G	FG	FT	TP	Avg.
1960-61	Detroit	79	427	200	1054	13.1
1961-62	Detroit	77	555	201	1311	17.0
1962-63	Detroit	80	636	275	1547	19.3
1963-64	Detroit	71	500	225	1225	17.3
1964-65	Baltimore	77	568	284	1420	18.4
1965-66	Baltimore	73	593	316	1502	20.6
1966-67	Baltimore	58	452	276	1180	20.3
1967-68	Balt.-St. L.	70	393	197	983	14.0
1968-69	Atlanta	76	385	147	917	12.1
1969-70	Atlanta	66	176	58	410	6.2
	Totals	727	4685	2179	11549	15.9

Yr	Team	G	FG	FT	TP	Avg.

O'KEEFE, RICHARD

b. Sept. 29, 1923 Ht. 6-2 Wt. 185 College—Santa Clara

Yr	Team	G	FG	FT	TP	Avg.
1947-48	Washington	37	63	30	156	4.2
1948-49	Washington	50	70	51	191	3.8
1949-50	Washington	68	162	150	474	7.0
1950-51	Washington	17	21	25	67	3.9
	Totals	172	316	256	888	5.2

O'KEEFE, THOMAS

b. July 16, 1926 Ht. 6-2 Wt. 185 College—Notre Dame and Georgetown

1950-51	Balt.-Wash.	6	10	3	23	3.8

OLDHAM, JOHN

b. June 22, 1923 Ht. 6-3 Wt. 185 Coll.—W. Kentucky

1949-50	Ft. Wayne	59	127	103	357	6.1
1950-51	Ft. Wayne	68	199	171	569	8.4
	Totals	127	326	274	926	7.3

OLEYNICK, FRANK

b. Feb. 20, 1955 Ht. 6-3 Wt. 190 College—Seattle

1975-76	Seattle	52	127	53	307	5.9
1976-77	Seattle	50	81	39	201	4.0
	Totals	102	208	92	508	5.0

OLLRICH, GENE

Ht. 5-11 Wt. 160 College—Drake

1949-50	Waterloo	14	17	10	44	3.1

OLSEN, ENOCH (Bud)

b. July 25, 1940 Ht. 6-8 Wt. 220 College—Louisville

1962-63	Cincinnati	52	43	27	113	2.2
1963-64	Cincinnati	49	85	32	202	4.1
1964-65	Cincinnati	79	224	144	592	7.5
1965-66	Cinn.-San. Fran.	59	81	39	201	3.4
1966-67	San Francisco	40	75	23	173	4.3
1967-68	Seattle	73	130	17	277	3.8
1968-69	Bos.-Det.	17	15	4	34	2.0
1969-70	Kentucky ABA	84	157 (1)	26	343	4.1
	Totals	453	810 (1)	312	1935	4.3

O'MALLEY, GRADY

b. April 25, 1948 Ht. 6-5 Wt. 205 College—Manhattan

1969-70	Atlanta	24	21	8	50	2.1

O'NEIL, MIKE

Ht. 6-3 Wt. 210

1952-53	Milwaukee	4	4	4	12	3.0

ORMS, BARRY

b. May 2, 1946 Ht. 6-3 Wt. 190 Coll.—St. Louis Un.

1968-69	Baltimore	64	76	29	181	2.8
1969-70	Ind.-Pitt. ABA	77	267 (5)	152	701	9.1
	Totals	141	343 (5)	181	882	6.2

ORR, JOHN

b. 1927 Ht. 6-3 College—Beloit and St. Benedict

1949-50	St. L.-Waterloo	34	40	12	92	2.7

OSBORNE, CHARLES

b. Jan. 21, 1939 Ht. 6-6 Wt. 210 Coll.—W. Kentucky

1961-62	Syracuse	4	1	3	5	1.3

O'SHEA, KEVIN

b. July 10, 1925 Ht. 6-2 Wt. 175 College—Notre Dame

1950-51	Minneapolis	63	87	97	271	4.3
1951-52	Mil.-Balt.	65	153	144	450	6.9
1952-53	Baltimore	46	71	48	190	4.1
	Totals	174	311	289	911	5.2

O'SHIELDS, GARLAND (Mule)

b. May 23, 1921 Ht. 6-1 Wt. 195 College—Tennessee

1946-47	Chicago	9	2	0	4	0.4
1947-48	Syracuse NL	5	3	3	9	1.8
	Totals	14	5	3	13	0.9

OSTERKORN, WALLY

b. July 6, 1928 Ht. 6-5 Wt. 215 College—Illinois

1951-52	Syracuse	66	145	199	489	7.4
1952-53	Syracuse	49	85	106	276	5.6
1953-54	Syracuse	70	203	209	615	8.8
1954-55	Syracuse	19	20	16	56	2.9
	Totals	204	453	530	1436	7.0

OTTEN, DON

b. April 18, 1921 Ht. 6-11 Wt. 250 College—Bowling Green

1946-47	Buf.-Tri-C. NL	44	200	169	569	12.9
1947-48	Tri-Cities NL	60	282	260	824	13.7
1948-49	Tri-Cities	64	301	297	899	14.0
1949-50	Tri-Cities-Wash.	64	242	341	825	12.9
1950-51	Wash.-Balt.-Ft. W.	67	162	246	570	8.5
1951-52	Ft. W.-Mil.	64	222	323	767	12.0
1952-53	Milwaukee	24	34	64	132	5.5
	Totals	387	1443	1700	4586	11.9

OTTEN, MAC

b. Dec. 16, 1925 Ht. 6-7 Wt. 220 College—Bowling Green

1949-50	Tri-Cities-St. L.	59	51	40	142	2.4

OVERTON, CLAUDELL (Claude)

b. Dec. 16, 1927 Ht. 6-2 Wt. 195 College—East Central Oklahoma

1952-53	Philadelphia	15	19	20	58	3.9

OWENS, EDDIE

b. Dec. 26, 1953 Ht. 6-7 Wt. 210 Coll.—Nev. L. Vegas

1977-78	Buffalo	8	9	3	21	2.6

OWENS, JAMES (Red)

b. Sept. 2, 1925 Ht. 6-3 Wt. 185 College—Baylor

1949-50	Tri-Cities-And.	61	86	68	240	3.9
1951-52	Balt.-Milwaukee	29	83	64	230	7.9
	Totals	90	169	132	470	5.2

Yr	Team	G	FG	FT	TP	Avg.
OWENS, JIM						

b. May 1, 1950 Ht. 6-5 Wt. 200 College—Arizona St.

Yr	Team	G	FG	FT	TP	Avg.
1973-74	Phoenix	17	21	11	53	3.1
1974-75	Phoenix	41	56	12	124	3.0
	Totals	58	77	23	177	3.1

PACE, JOE

b. Dec. 18, 1953 Ht. 6-10 Wt. 220 College—Coppin St.

Yr	Team	G	FG	FT	TP	Avg.
1976-77	Washington	30	24	16	64	2.1
1977-78	Washington	49	67	57	191	3.9
	Totals	79	91	73	255	3.2

PACK, WAYNE

b. July 5, 1950 Ht. 6-0 Wt. 165 Coll.—Tennessee Tech.

Yr	Team	G	FG	FT	TP	Avg.
1974-75	Indiana ABA	21	23 (5)	10	61	2.9

PAGETT, DANA

b. March 29, 1949 Ht. 6-2 Wt. 180 Coll.—So. California

Yr	Team	G	FG	FT	TP	Avg.
1971-72	Virginia ABA	5	0 (1)	2	5	1.0

PAINE, FRED

b. Dec. 7, 1925 Ht. 6-5 Wt. 210 College—Westminster (Pa.)

Yr	Team	G	FG	FT	TP	Avg.
1948-49	Providence	3	3	1	7	2.3

PALAZZI, TOGO

b. Aug. 8, 1932 Ht. 6-4 Wt. 205 College—Holy Cross

Yr	Team	G	FG	FT	TP	Avg.
1954-55	Boston	53	101	45	247	4.7
1955-56	Boston	63	145	85	375	6.0
1956-57	Bos.-Syracuse	63	210	136	556	8.8
1957-58	Syracuse	67	228	123	579	8.6
1958-59	Syracuse	71	240	115	595	8.4
1959-60	Syracuse	7	13	4	30	4.3
	Totals	324	937	508	2382	7.4

PALMER, ERROL

Ht. 6-5 Wt. 195 College—DePaul

Yr	Team	G	FG	FT	TP	Avg.
1967-68	Minnesota ABA	63	165 (0)	170	500	7.9

PALMER, JAMES

b. June 8, 1933, Ht. 6-8 Wt. 224 College—Dayton

Yr	Team	G	FG	FT	TP	Avg.
1958-59	Cincinnati	67	256	178	690	10.3
1959-60	Cin.-New York	74	246	119	611	8.3
1960-61	New York	56	125	44	294	5.3
	Totals	197	627	341	1595	8.1

PALMER, JOHN (Bud)

b. Sept. 14, 1921 Ht. 6-4 Wt. 180 College—Princeton

Yr	Team	G	FG	FT	TP	Avg.
1946-47	New York	42	160	81	401	9.5
1947-48	New York	48	224	174	622	13.0
1948-49	New York	58	240	234	714	12.3
	Totals	148	624	489	1737	11.7

PARHAM, ESTES (Easy)

b. Dec. 27, 1921 Ht. 6-3 Wt. 200 Coll.—Texas Wesleyan

Yr	Team	G	FG	FT	TP	Avg.
1948-49	St. Louis	60	124	96	344	5.7
1949-50	St. Louis	66	137	88	362	5.5
1950-51	Philadelphia	7	3	4	10	1.4
	Totals	133	264	188	716	5.4

Yr	Team	G	FG	FT	TP	Avg.
PARK, MEDFORD (Med)						

b. April 11, 1933 Ht. 6-2 Wt. 205 College—Missouri

Yr	Team	G	FG	FT	TP	Avg.
1955-56	St. Louis	40	53	44	150	3.8
1956-57	St. Louis	66	118	108	344	5.2
1957-58	St. Louis	71	133	118	384	5.4
1958-59	St. L.-Cin.	62	145	115	405	6.5
1959-60	Cincinnati	74	226	189	641	8.7
	Totals	313	675	574	1924	6.1

PARKHILL, BARRY

b. May 10, 1951 Ht. 6-4 Wt. 185 College—Virginia

Yr	Team	G	FG	FT	TP	Avg.
1973-74	Virginia ABA	60	112 (3)	50	283	4.7
1974-75	Virginia ABA	78	266 (0)	75	607	7.8
1975-76	St. Louis ABA	35	36 (1)	5	80	2.3
	Totals	173	414 (4)	130	970	5.6

PARKINSON, JACK

b. March 4, 1924 Ht. 6-0 Wt. 174 College—Kentucky

Yr	Team	G	FG	FT	TP	Avg.
1949-50	Indianapolis	4	1	1	3	0.8

PARKS, CHARLEY

Ht. 6-5 Wt. 210 College—Idaho State

Yr	Team	G	FG	FT	TP	Avg.
1968-69	Denver ABA	2	0 (0)	0	0	0.0

PARKS, RICH

b. October 26, 1943 Ht. 6-7 Wt. 235 Coll.—St. Louis Un.

Yr	Team	G	FG	FT	TP	Avg.
1967-68	Pittsburgh ABA	40	58 (1)	12	131	3.3

PARR, JACK

b. March 13, 1936 Ht. 6-9 Wt. 222 College—Kansas St.

Yr	Team	G	FG	FT	TP	Avg.
1958-59	Cincinnati	66	109	44	262	4.0

PARRACK, DOYLE

b. Dec. 6, 1921 Ht. 6-0 Wt. 165 Coll.—Oklahoma A&M

Yr	Team	G	FG	FT	TP	Avg.
1946-47	Chicago	58	110	52	272	4.7

PARSLEY, CHARLES

Ht. 6-2 Wt. 175 College—Western Kentucky

Yr	Team	G	FG	FT	TP	Avg.
1948-49	Philadelphia	9	8	6	22	2.4

PASSAGLIA, MARTIN

b. 1918 Ht. 6-1 Wt. 195 College—Santa Clara

Yr	Team	G	FG	FT	TP	Avg.
1946-47	Washington	43	51	18	120	2.8
1948-49	Indianapolis	19	14	3	31	1.6
	Totals	62	65	21	151	2.4

PASTUSHOK, GEORGE

b. 1922 Ht. 6-1 Wt. 195 College—St. John's (N.Y.)

Yr	Team	G	FG	FT	TP	Avg.
1946-47	Providence	39	48	25	121	3.1

PATRICK, STANLEY

b. May 5, 1922 Ht. 6-3 Wt. 215 College—Santa Clara and Illinois

Yr	Team	G	FG	FT	TP	Avg.
1944-45	Chicago NL	28	187	84	458	16.4
1945-46	Chicago NL	33	123	66	312	9.5
1946-47	Chicago NL	42	72	36	180	4.3

Yr	Team	G	FG	FT	TP	Avg.
1947-48	Flint NL	48	149	90	388	8.1
1948-49	Hammond NL	61	150	127	427	7.0
1949-50	Wat.-Sheboygan	53	116	89	321	6.1
	Totals	265	797	492	2086	7.9

PATTERSON, GEORGE

b. Nov. 26, 1939 Ht. 6-8 Wt. 240 College—Toledo

		G	FG	FT	TP	Avg.
1967-68	Detroit	59	44	32	120	2.0

PATTERSON, STEVE

b. June 24, 1948 Ht. 6-9 Wt. 225 College—UCLA

		G	FG	FT	TP	Avg.
1971-72	Cleveland	65	94	23	211	3.2
1972-73	Cleveland	62	71	34	176	2.8
1973-74	Cleveland	76	262	69	593	7.8
1974-75	Cleveland	81	161	48	370	4.6
1975-76	Cleve.-Chi.	66	84	34	202	3.1
	Totals	350	672	208	1552	4.4

PATTERSON, TOMMY

b. Oct. 15, 1948 Ht. 6-6 Wt. 220 College—Ouachita Baptist

		G	FG	FT	TP	Avg.
1972-73	Baltimore	23	21	13	55	2.4
1973-74	Capital	2	0	1	1	0.5
	Totals	25	21	14	56	2.2

PATTERSON, WORTHINGTON (Worthy)

b. June 17, 1931 Ht. 6-2 Wt. 175 College—Connecticut

		G	FG	FT	TP	Avg.
1957-58	St. Louis	4	3	1	7	1.8

PAULK, CHARLES

b. June 14, 1944 Ht. 6-9 Wt. 219 Coll.—Northeastern Oklahoma

		G	FG	FT	TP	Avg.
1968-69	Milwaukee	17	19	13	51	3.0
1970-71	Cincinnati	68	274	79	627	9.2
1971-72	Chi.-N.Y.	28	16	8	40	1.4
	Totals	113	309	100	718	6.4

PAULSON, GERALD (Jerry)

b. July 21, 1935 Ht. 6-2 Wt. 187 College—Manhattan

		G	FG	FT	TP	Avg.
1957-58	Cincinnati	6	8	4	20	3.3

PAXSON, JAMES

b. Dec. 19, 1932 Ht. 6-6 Wt. 200 College—Dayton

		G	FG	FT	TP	Avg.
1956-57	Minneapolis	71	138	170	446	6.3
1957-58	Cincinnati	67	225	209	659	9.8
	Totals	138	363	379	1105	8.0

PAYAK, JOHN

b. Nov. 20, 1926 Ht. 6-4 Wt. 180 Coll.—Bowling Green

		G	FG	FT	TP	Avg.
1949-50	Phila.-Waterloo	52	98	121	317	6.1
1952-53	Milwaukee	68	128	180	436	6.4
	Totals	120	226	301	753	6.3

PAYNE, TOM

b. Nov. 19, 1950 Ht. 7-2 Wt. 240 College—Kentucky

		G	FG	FT	TP	Avg.
1971-72	Atlanta	29	45	29	119	4.1

PAYTON, MEL

b. 1927 Ht. 6-4 Wt. 185 College—Tulane

		G	FG	FT	TP	Avg.
1951-52	Philadelphia	45	54	21	129	2.9
1952-53	Indianapolis	66	173	120	466	7.1
	Totals	111	227	141	595	5.4

PEARCY, GEORGE (Wig)

b. July 2, 1919 Ht. 6-1 Wt. 165 College—Indiana State

		G	FG	FT	TP	Avg.
1946-47	Detroit	37	31	32	94	2.5

PEARCY, HENRY

b. 1922 Ht. 6-1 Wt. 170 College—Indiana State

		G	FG	FT	TP	Avg.
1946-47	Detroit	29	24	25	73	2.5

PEEK, RICH

Ht. 6-11 Wt. 230 College—Louisiana Tech

		G	FG	FT	TP	Avg.
1967-68	Dallas ABA	51	101 (0)	35	237	4.6

PEEPLES, GEORGE

b. Oct. 30, 1943 Ht. 6-8 Wt. 205 College—Iowa

		G	FG	FT	TP	Avg.
1967-68	Indiana ABA	65	138 (0)	115	391	6.0
1968-69	Indiana ABA	64	122 (0)	101	345	5.4
1969-70	Carolina ABA	83	279 (0)	209	767	9.2
1970-71	Carolina ABA	82	377 (0)	202	956	11.7
1971-72	Dallas ABA	6	11 (0)	7	29	4.8
1972-73	Indiana ABA	9	4 (0)	6	14	1.6
	Totals	309	931 (0)	640	2502	8.1

PELKINGTON, JOHN

b. 1916 Ht. 6-6 Wt. 220 College—Manhattan

		G	FG	FT	TP	Avg.
1940-41	Akron NL	24	57	70	184	7.7
1942-43	Ft. Wayne NL	23	83	70	236	10.3
1943-44	Ft. Wayne NL	20	46	40	132	6.6
1944-45	Ft. Wayne NL	30	85	76	246	8.2
1945-46	Ft. Wayne NL	33	94	76	264	8.0
1946-47	Ft. Wayne NL	42	129	125	383	9.1
1947-48	Ft. Wayne NL	54	174	156	504	9.3
1948-49	Ft. Wayne-Baltimore	54	193	211	597	11.1
	Totals	280	861	824	2546	9.1

PENDER, JERRY

b. 1951 Ht. 6-3 Wt. 185 College—Fresno State

		G	FG	FT	TP	Avg.
1973-74	San Diego ABA	11	7 (1)	10	27	2.5

PERKINS, WARREN

b. Feb. 2, 1924 Ht. 6-3 Wt. 190 College—Tulane

		G	FG	FT	TP	Avg.
1949-50	Tri-Cities	60	128	115	371	6.2
1950-51	Tri-Cities	66	135	126	396	6.0
	Totals	126	263	241	767	6.1

Yr	Team	G	FG	FT	TP	Avg.

PERRY, AULCIE

b. July 3, 1950 Ht. 6-11 Wt. 215 College—Bethune Cookman

Yr	Team	G	FG	FT	TP	Avg.
1974-75	Virginia ABA	21	81 (0)	19	181	8.6

PERRY, CURTIS

b. Sept. 13, 1948 Ht. 6-7 Wt. 220 Coll.—Southwest Mo.

Yr	Team	G	FG	FT	TP	Avg.
1970-71	San Diego	18	21	11	53	2.9
1971-72	Hou.-Mil.	75	181	76	438	5.8
1972-73	Milwaukee	67	265	83	613	9.1
1973-74	Milwaukee	81	325	78	728	9.0
1974-75	Phoenix	79	437	184	1058	13.4
1975-76	Phoenix	71	386	175	947	13.3
1976-77	Phoenix	44	179	112	470	10.7
1977-78	Phoenix	45	110	51	271	6.0
	Totals	480	1904	770	4578	9.5

PERRY, RON

b. Dec. 29, 1943 Ht. 6-3 Wt. 190 Coll.—Virginia Tech

Yr	Team	G	FG	FT	TP	Avg.
1967-68	Minnesota ABA	67	277 (62)	118	858	12.8
1968-69	Miami-N.Y.-Ind. ABA	74	335 (67)	212	1083	14.6
1969-70	Car.-N.O. ABA	46	94 (10)	69	287	6.2
	Totals	187	706 (139)	399	2228	11.9

PETERSEN, LOY

b. July 26, 1945 Ht. 6-5 Wt. 205 College—Oreg. St.

Yr	Team	G	FG	FT	TP	Avg.
1968-69	Chicago	38	44	19	107	2.8
1969-70	Chicago	31	33	26	92	3.0
	Totals	69	77	45	199	2.9

PETERSON, EDWARD

b. 1925 Ht. 6-9 Wt. 230 College—Cornell

Yr	Team	G	FG	FT	TP	Avg.
1948-49	Syracuse NL	63	165	104	434	6.9
1949-50	Syracuse	62	167	111	445	7.2
1950-51	Syr.-Tri-Cities	53	130	99	359	6.8
	Totals	178	462	314	1238	7.0

PETERSON, MEL

b. March 23, 1938 Ht. 6-4½ Wt. 185 College—Wheaton

Yr	Team	G	FG	FT	TP	Avg.
1963-64	Baltimore	2	1	0	2	1.0
1967-68	Oakland ABA	77	314 (9)	76	731	9.5
1968-69	Oakland ABA	51	132 (0)	12	276	5.4
1969-70	Los Angeles ABA	4	10 (0)	3	23	5.8
	Totals	134	457 (9)	91	1032	7.7

PETERSON, ROBERT

b. 1932 Ht. 6-5 Wt. 210 College—Oregon

Yr	Team	G	FG	FT	TP	Avg.
1953-54	Balt.-Milw.	8	3	9	15	1.9
1954-55	New York	37	62	30	154	4.2
1955-56	New York	58	121	68	310	5.3
	Totals	103	186	107	479	4.7

PETRIE, GEOFFREY

b. April 17, 1948 Ht. 6-4 Wt. 190 College—Princeton

Yr	Team	G	FG	FT	TP	Avg.
1970-71	Portland	82	784	463	2031	24.8
1971-72	Portland	60	465	202	1132	18.9
1972-73	Portland	79	836	298	1970	24.9
1973-74	Portland	73	740	291	1771	24.3
1974-75	Portland	80	602	261	1465	18.3
1975-76	Portland	72	543	277	1363	18.9
1976-77	Atlanta			Injured		
	Totals	446	3970	1792	9732	21.8

PETTIT, BOB

b. Dec. 12, 1932 Ht. 6-9 Wt. 215 College—La. State

Yr	Team	G	FG	FT	TP	Avg.
1954-55	Milwaukee	72	520	426	1466	20.4
1955-56	St. Louis	72	646	557	1849	25.7
1956-57	St. Louis	71	613	529	1755	24.7
1957-58	St. Louis	70	581	557	1719	24.6
1958-59	St. Louis	72	719	667	2105	29.2
1959-60	St. Louis	72	669	544	1882	26.1
1960-61	St. Louis	76	769	582	2120	27.9
1961-62	St. Louis	78	867	695	2429	31.1
1962-63	St. Louis	79	778	685	2241	28.4
1963-64	St. Louis	80	791	608	2190	27.4
1964-65	St. Louis	50	396	332	1124	22.5
	Totals	792	7349	6182	20880	26.4

PETTWAY, JERRY

b. Feb. 13, 1944 Ht. 6-3 Wt. 185 Coll.—Nthwd (MI)

Yr	Team	G	FG	FT	TP	Avg.
1967-68	Houston ABA	76	273 (16)	119	713	9.4
1968-69	Houston ABA	11	37 (0)	5	79	7.2
	Totals	87	310 (16)	124	792	9.1

PHELAN, JACK

b. Nov. 6, 1925 Ht. 6-5 College—DePaul

Yr	Team	G	FG	FT	TP	Avg.
1949-50	Wat.-Sheboygan	55	87	52	226	4.1

PHELAN, JIM

Ht. 6-1 Wt. 175 College—LaSalle

Yr	Team	G	FG	FT	TP	Avg.
1953-54	Philadelphia	4	0	3	3	0.8

PHILLIP, ANDY

b. March 7, 1922 Ht. 6-2 Wt. 195 College—Illinois

Yr	Team	G	FG	FT	TP	Avg.
1947-48	Chicago	32	143	60	346	10.8
1948-49	Chicago	60	285	148	718	12.0
1949-50	Chicago	65	284	190	758	11.2
1950-51	Philadelphia	66	275	190	740	11.2
1951-52	Philadelphia	66	279	232	790	12.0
1952-53	Phila.-Ft. W.	70	250	222	722	10.3
1953-54	Ft. Wayne	71	255	241	751	10.6
1954-55	Ft. Wayne	64	202	213	617	9.6
1955-56	Ft. Wayne	70	148	112	408	5.8
1956-57	Boston	67	105	88	298	4.4
1957-58	Boston	70	97	42	236	3.4
	Totals	701	2323	1738	6384	9.1

PHILLIPS, GARY

b. Dec. 7, 1939 Ht. 6-3 Wt. 189 College—Houston

Yr	Team	G	FG	FT	TP	Avg.
1961-62	Boston	72	110	50	270	3.7
1962-63	San Fran.	75	256	97	609	8.1
1963-64	San Fran.	66	256	146	658	10.0
1964-65	San Fran.	73	198	120	516	7.1
1965-66	San Fran.	67	106	54	266	4.0
	Totals	353	926	467	2319	6.6

Yr	Team	G	FG	FT	TP	Avg.

PHILLIPS, GENE

b. Oct. 25, 1948 Ht. 6-4 Wt. 180 Coll.—Sthrn Methodist

Yr	Team	G	FG	FT	TP	Avg.
1971-72	Dallas ABA	28	23 (7)	11	78	2.8
1972-73	Dallas ABA	3	0 (0)	0	0	0.0
	Totals	31	23 (7)	11	78	2.5

PIATKOWSKI, WALT

b. June 11, 1945 Ht. 6-8 Wt. 225 Coll.—Bowling Green

Yr	Team	G	FG	FT	TP	Avg.
1968-69	Denver ABA	77	372 (27)	117	942	12.2
1969-70	Denver ABA	75	204 (11)	76	517	6.9
1971-72	Floridians ABA	6	3 (0)	0	6	1.0
	Totals	158	579 (38)	193	1465	9.3

PILCH, JOHN

b. July 11, 1925 Ht. 6-3 Wt. 185 College—Wyoming

Yr	Team	G	FG	FT	TP	Avg.
1951-52	Minneapolis	9	1	3	5	0.6

PIONTEK, DAVID

b. Aug. 27, 1934 Ht. 6-6 Wt. 230 College—Xavier (Ohio)

Yr	Team	G	FG	FT	TP	Avg.
1956-57	Rochester	71	257	122	636	9.0
1957-58	Cincinnati	71	150	95	395	5.6
1958-59	Cincinnati	72	305	156	766	10.6
1959-60	Cinn.-St. Lou.	77	292	129	713	9.3
1960-61	St. Louis	29	47	16	110	3.8
1961-62	Chicago	45	83	39	205	4.5
1962-63	Cincinnati	48	60	10	130	2.6
	Totals	413	1194	567	2955	7.2

POLLARD, JIM

b. July 9, 1922 Ht. 6-3½ Wt. 190 College—Stanford

Yr	Team	G	FG	FT	TP	Avg.
1947-48	Minneapolis NL	59	310	140	760	12.9
1948-49	Minneapolis	53	314	156	784	14.8
1949-50	Minneapolis	66	394	185	973	14.7
1950-51	Minneapolis	54	256	117	629	11.6
1951-52	Minneapolis	65	411	183	1005	15.5
1952-53	Minneapolis	66	333	193	859	13.0
1953-54	Minneapolis	71	326	179	831	11.7
1954-55	Minneapolis	63	265	151	681	10.8
	Totals	497	2609	1304	6522	13.1

POLSON, RALPH

b. 1930 Ht. 6-7½ Wt. 205 College—Whitworth

Yr	Team	G	FG	FT	TP	Avg.
1952-53	N.Y.-Phila.	49	65	61	191	3.9

PONDEXTER, CLIFTON

b. Sept. 15, 1954 Ht. 6-9 Wt. 235 Coll.—Lg. Beach St.

Yr	Team	G	FG	FT	TP	Avg.
1975-76	Chicago	75	156	122	434	5.8
1976-77	Chicago	78	107	42	256	3.3
1977-78	Chicago	44	37	14	88	2.0
	Totals	197	300	178	778	3.9

PORTER, HOWARD

b. Aug. 31, 1948 Ht. 6-8 Wt. 220 College—Villanova

Yr	Team	G	FG	FT	TP	Avg.
1971-72	Chicago	67	171	59	401	6.0
1972-73	Chicago	43	98	22	218	5.1
1973-74	Chicago	73	296	92	684	9.4
1974-75	N.Y.-Det.	58	201	66	468	8.1
1975-76	Detroit	75	298	73	669	8.9

Yr	Team	G	FG	FT	TP	Avg.
1976-77	Detroit	78	465	103	1033	132
1977-78	Det.-N.J.	63	309	124	742	11.8
	Totals	457	1838	539	4215	9.2

PORTER, WILLIE

b. July 3, 1942 Ht. 6-7 Wt. 205 Coll.—Tennesse State

Yr	Team	G	FG	FT	TP	Avg.
1967-68	Oak.-Pitt. ABA	56	225 (0)	199	649	11.6
1968-69	Minn.-Hou. ABA	13	28 (0)	17	73	5.6
	Totals	69	253 (0)	216	722	10.5

PORTMAN, BOB

b. March 22, 1947 Ht. 6-5 Wt. 200 College—Creighton

Yr	Team	G	FG	FT	TP	Avg.
1969-70	San Francisco	60	177	66	420	7.0
1970-71	San Francisco	69	221	77	519	7.6
1971-72	Golden State	61	89	53	231	3.9
1972-73	Golden State	32	32	20	84	2.6
	Totals	221	519	216	1254	5.7

POSTLEY, JOHN

Ht. 6-5 College—Bethune-Cookman

Yr	Team	G	FG	FT	TP	Avg.
1967-68	Pittsburgh ABA	1	1 (0)	0	2	2.0

POWELL, CINCINNATUS (Cincy)

b. Feb. 25, 1942 Ht. 6-7 Wt. 227 College—Portland

Yr	Team	G	FG	FT	TP	Avg.
1967-68	Dallas ABA	77	532 (1)	343	1410	18.3
1968-69	Dallas ABA	75	553 (2)	342	1454	19.4
1969-70	Dallas ABA	76	560 (2)	402	1528	20.1
1970-71	Kentucky ABA	81	574 (4)	302	1462	18.1
1971-72	Kentucky ABA	65	426 (4)	185	1049	16.1
1972-73	Utah ABA	83	420 (3)	167	1016	12.2
1973-74	Virginia ABA	82	518 (10)	209	1275	15.6
1974-75	Virginia ABA	60	209 (5)	119	552	9.2
	Totals	599	3792 (31)	2069	9746	16.3

PRADD, MARLBERT (Mal)

b. Nov. 17, 1944 Ht. 6-3 Wt. 170 College—Dillard

Yr	Team	G	FG	FT	TP	Avg.
1967-68	New Orleans ABA	29	27 (0)	20	74	2.6
1968-69	New Orleans ABA	50	78 (3)	93	258	5.2
	Totals	79	105 (3)	113	332	4.2

PRATT, MIKE

b. Aug. 4, 1948 Ht. 6-4 Wt. 205 College—Kentucky

Yr	Team	G	FG	FT	TP	Avg.
1970-71	Kentucky ABA	78	167 (3)	91	440	5.6
1971-72	Kentucky ABA	65	117 (16)	84	366	5.6
	Totals	143	284 (19)	175	806	5.6

PREVIS, STEVE

b. Feb. 9, 1950 Ht. 6-3 Wt. 183 Coll.—North Carolina

Yr	Team	G	FG	FT	TP	Avg.
1972-73	Carolina ABA	30	22 (1)	8	55	1.8

Yr	Team	G	FG	FT	TP	Avg.
PRICE, MIKE						
b. Sept. 11, 1948 Ht. 6-3 Wt. 200 College—Illinois						
1970-71	New York	56	30	24	84	1.5
1971-72	New York	6	5	9	19	3.2
1971-72	Indiana ABA	4	3 (0)	0	6	1.5
	Totals	66	38 (0)	33	109	1.7

PRIDDY, ROBERT

b. 1930 Ht. 6-3 Wt. 190 College—New Mexico A&M

1952-53	Baltimore	16	14	8	36	2.3

PRITCHARD, JOHN

b. 1927 Ht. 6-9 Wt. 220 College—Drake

1949-50	Waterloo	7	9	4	22	3.1

PUGH, LESLIE

b. Sept. 18, 1923 Ht. 6-7 Wt. 195 College—Ohio State

1948-49	Providence	60	168	125	461	7.7
1949-50	Baltimore	56	68	115	251	4.5
	Totals	116	236	240	712	6.1

PUGH, ROY

b. 1923 Ht. 6-6 Wt. 210 College—Southern Methodist

1947-48	Indianapolis NL	4	1	2	4	1.0
1948-49	Ft. W.-Ind. Phila.	23	13	6	32	1.4
	Totals	27	14	8	36	1.3

PUTNAM, DONALD

b. 1922 Ht. 6-1 Wt. 170 College—Colo. and Denver

1946-47	St. Louis	58	156	68	380	6.6
1947-48	St. Louis	42	105	57	267	6.4
1948-49	St. Louis	59	98	52	248	4.2
1949-50	St. Louis	57	51	33	135	2.4
	Totals	216	410	210	1030	4.8

QUICK, BOB

b. March 5, 1946 Ht. 6-5 Wt. 215 College-Xavier

1968-69	Baltimore	28	30	27	87	3.1
1969-70	Balt.-Det.	34	63	49	175	5.1
1970-71	Detroit	56	155	138	448	8.0
1971-72	Detroit	18	39	34	112	6.2
1971-72	Dallas ABA	6	8 (0)	10	26	4.3
	Totals	142	295 (0)	258	848	6.0

RACKLEY, LUTHER

b. June 11, 1946 Ht. 6-10 Wt. 220 College—Xavier

1969-70	Cincinnati	66	190	124	504	7.6
1970-71	Cleveland	74	219	121	559	7.6
1971-72	Cleve.-N.Y.	71	103	50	256	3.6
1972-73	Memphis ABA	57	170 (0)	78	418	7.3
1972-73	New York	1	0	0	0	0.0
1973-74	Philadelphia	9	5	8	18	2.0
	Totals	278	687 (0)	381	1755	6.3

RADER, HOWARD

Ht. 6-1 Wt. 190 College—Long Island University

1946-47	Buf.-Tri-C. NL	41	76	43	195	4.8
1947-48	Tri-Cities NL	45	44	29	117	2.6
1948-49	Baltimore	13	7	3	17	1.3
	Totals	99	127	75	329	3.3

RADOVICH, FRANK

b. March 3, 1938 Ht. 6-8 Wt. 235 College—Indiana

1961-62	Philadelphia	37	37	13	87	2.4

RADOVICH, GEORGE (Moe)

b. 1930 Ht. 6-0 Wt. 160 College—Wyoming

1952-53	Philadelphia	4	5	4	14	3.5

RADZISZEWSKI, RAY

b. March 1, 1935 Ht. 6-5 Wt. 210 College—St. Joseph's (Pa.)

1957-58	Philadelphia	1	0	0	0	0.0

RAGELIS, RAY

b. 1929 Ht. 6-4 Wt. 205 College—Northwestern

1951-52	Rochester	51	25	18	68	1.3

RAIKEN, SHERWIN

b. 1928 Ht. 6-2 Wt. 185 College—Villanova

1952-53	New York	6	3	3	9	1.5

RAMSEY, CAL

b. July 13, 1937 Ht. 6-4 Wt. 200 College—N.Y. Univ.

1959-60	St. L.-N.Y.	11	39	19	97	8.8
1960-61	Syracuse	2	2	2	6	3.0
	Totals	13	41	21	103	7.9

RAMSEY, FRANK

b. July 13, 1931 Ht. 6-3 Wt. 190 College—Kentucky

1954-55	Boston	64	236	243	715	11.2
1956-57	Boston	35	137	144	418	11.9
1957-58	Boston	69	377	383	1137	16.5
1958-59	Boston	72	383	341	1107	15.4
1959-60	Boston	73	422	273	1117	15.3
1960-61	Boston	79	448	295	1191	15.1
1961-62	Boston	79	436	334	1206	15.3
1962-63	Boston	77	284	271	839	10.9
1963-64	Boston	75	226	196	648	8.6
	Totals	623	2949	2480	8378	13.4

RAMSEY, RAY

b. 1921 Ht. 6-2 Wt. 166 College—Bradley

1947-48	Tri-Cities NL	2	0	0	0	0.0
1948-49	Baltimore	2	0	2	2	1.0
	Totals	4	0	2	2	0.5

RANZINO, SAM

b. June 21, 1927 Ht. 6-1 Wt. 185 Coll.—N.C. State

1951-52	Rochester	39	30	26	86	2.2

Yr	Team	G	FG	FT	TP	Avg.

RASCOE, BOBBY

b. July 22, 1940 Ht. 6-4 Wt. 205 College—Western Kentucky

Yr	Team	G	FG	FT	TP	Avg.
1967-68	Kentucky ABA	77	245 (0)	190	680	8.8
1968-69	Kentucky ABA	78	198 (3)	129	534	6.8
1969-70	Kentucky ABA	4	4 (0)	6	14	3.5
	Totals	159	447 (3)	325	1228	7.7

RATKOVICZ, GEORGE

b. Nov. 13, 1922 Ht. 6-7 Wt. 225

Yr	Team	G	FG	FT	TP	Avg.
1941-42	Chicago NL	13	9	14	32	2.5
1945-46	Chicago NL	33	80	66	226	6.8
1946-47	Chicago NL	37	43	26	112	3.0
1947-48	Rochester NL	53	79	76	234	4.4
1948-49	Tri-Cities NL	64	109	106	324	5.1
1949-50	Syracuse	62	162	211	535	8.6
1950-51	Syracuse	66	264	321	849	12.9
1951-52	Syracuse	66	165	163	493	7.5
1952-53	Balt.-Milw.	71	208	262	678	9.5
1953-54	Milwaukee	69	197	176	570	8.3
1954-55	Milwaukee	9	3	10	16	1.8
	Totals	543	1319	1431	4069	7.5

RATLEFF, ED

b. March 29, 1950 Ht. 6-6 Wt. 195 College—Lg. Bch. St.

Yr	Team	G	FG	FT	TP	Avg.
1973-74	Houston	81	254	103	611	7.5
1974-75	Houston	80	392	157	941	11.8
1975-76	Houston	72	314	168	796	11.1
1976-77	Houston	37	70	26	166	4.5
1977-78	Houston	68	130	39	299	4.4
	Totals	338	1160	493	2813	8.3

RATLIFF, MIKE

b. June 7, 1951 Ht. 6-10 Wt. 230 College—Eau Claire State

Yr	Team	G	FG	FT	TP	Avg.
1972-73	K.C.—Omaha	58	98	45	241	4.2
1973-74	K.C.—Omaha	2	0	0	0	0.0
	Totals	60	98	45	241	4.0

RAY, DON (Duck)

b. July 8, 1921 Ht. 6-6 Wt. 190 College—Western Kentucky

Yr	Team	G	FG	FT	TP	Avg.
1948-49	Tri-Cities NL	46	123	80	326	7.1
1949-50	Tri-Cities	61	130	104	364	6.0
	Totals	107	253	184	690	6.4

RAY, JAMES

b. Jan. 12, 1934 Ht. 6-1 Wt. 180 College—Toledo

Yr	Team	G	FG	FT	TP	Avg.
1956-57	Syracuse	4	2	3	7	1.8
1959-60	Syracuse	4	1	0	2	0.5
	Totals	8	3	3	9	1.1

RAYL, JIM

b. June 21, 1941 Ht. 6-2 Wt. 180 College—Indiana

Yr	Team	G	FG	FT	TP	Avg.
1967-68	Indiana ABA	74	260 (57)	195	886	12.0
1968-69	Indiana ABA	27	38 (34)	61	239	8.9
	Totals	101	298 (91)	256	1125	11.1

RAYMOND, CRAIG

b. April 5, 1945 Ht. 6-11 Wt. 235 College—Brigham Young

Yr	Team	G	FG	FT	TP	Avg.
1968-69	Philadelphia	27	22	11	55	2.0
1969-70	Pitt.-L.A. ABA	80	386 (0)	190	962	12.0
1970-71	Memphis ABA	56	142 (0)	67	351	6.3
1971-72	Mem.-Fla. ABA	64	104 (0)	48	256	4.0
1972-73	S.D.-Ind. ABA	14	12 (0)	10	34	2.4
	Totals	241	666 (0)	326	1658	6.9

REA, CONNIE

b. 1931 Ht. 6-3 Wt. 175 College—Centenary

Yr	Team	G	FG	FT	TP	Avg.
1953-54	Baltimore	20	9	5	23	1.2

REAVES, JOE

b. May 27, 1950 Ht. 6-6 Wt. 220 College—Bethel

Yr	Team	G	FG	FT	TP	Avg.
1973-74	Phoenix	7	6	4	16	2.3
1973-74	Memphis ABA	12	30 (0)	4	64	5.3
	Totals	19	36 (0)	8	80	4.2

REDDOUT, FRANK

Ht. 6-5 Wt. 195 College—Syracuse

Yr	Team	G	FG	FT	TP	Avg.
1953-54	Rochester	7	5	3	13	1.9

REED, HUBERT (Hub)

b. Oct. 4, 1936 Ht. 6-9 Wt. 220 College—Okla. City

Yr	Team	G	FG	FT	TP	Avg.
1958-59	St. Louis	65	136	53	325	5.0
1959-60	St. L.-Cinc.	71	270	134	674	9.5
1960-61	Cincinnati	75	156	85	397	5.3
1961-62	Cincinnati	80	203	60	466	5.8
1962-63	Cincinnati	80	199	74	472	5.9
1963-64	Los Angeles	46	33	10	76	1.7
1964-65	Detroit	62	84	40	208	3.4
	Totals	479	1081	456	2618	5.5

REED, RON

b. Nov. 2, 1942 Ht. 6-2 Wt. 205 College—Notre Dame

Yr	Team	G	FG	FT	TP	Avg.
1965-66	Detroit	57	186	54	426	7.5
1966-67	Detroit	62	223	79	525	8.5
	Totals	119	409	133	951	8.0

REED, WILLIS

b. June 25, 1942 Ht. 6-10 Wt. 235 College—Grambling

Yr	Team	G	FG	FT	TP	Avg.
1964-65	New York	80	629	302	1560	19.5
1965-66	New York	76	438	302	1178	15.5
1966-67	New York	78	635	358	1628	20.9
1967-68	New York	81	659	367	1685	20.8
1968-69	New York	82	704	325	1733	21.1
1969-70	New York	81	702	351	1755	21.7
1970-71	New York	73	614	299	1527	20.9
1971-72	New York	11	60	27	147	13.4
1972-73	New York	69	334	92	760	11.0
1973-74	New York	19	84	42	210	11.1
	Totals	650	4859	2465	12183	18.7

REGAN, RICHIE

b. Nov. 30, 1930 Ht. 6-2 Wt. 180 College—Seton Hall

Yr	Team	G	FG	FT	TP	Avg.
1955-56	Rochester	72	240	85	565	7.8
1956-57	Rochester	71	257	182	696	9.8
1957-58	Cincinnati	72	202	120	524	7.3
	Totals	215	699	387	1785	8.3

Yr	Team	G	FG	FT	TP	Avg.
REHFELDT, DON						

b. Jan. 7, 1927 Ht. 6-6 Wt. 210 College—Wisconsin

Yr	Team	G	FG	FT	TP	Avg.
1950-51	Baltimore	59	164	103	431	8.6
1951-52	Balt.-Milw.	39	99	63	261	6.7
	Totals	98	263	166	692	7.1

REID, JIM

b. Aug. 3, 1945 Ht. 6-6 Wt. 210 College—Winston-Salem State

Yr	Team	G	FG	FT	TP	Avg.
1967-68	Philadelphia	6	10	1	21	3.5

REISER, JOSEPH (Chick)

b. Dec. 17, 1914 Ht. 5-11 Wt. 165 Coll.—NY University

Yr	Team	G	FG	FT	TP	Avg.
1943-44	Ft. Wayne NL	22	28	25	81	3.7
1944-45	Ft. Wayne NL	30	82	53	217	7.2
1945-46	Ft. Wayne NL	34	90	53	233	6.9
1946-47	Ft. Wayne NL	44	153	104	410	9.3
1947-48	Baltimore	47	202	137	541	11.5
1948-49	Baltimore	57	219	188	626	11.0
1949-50	Washington	67	197	212	606	9.0
	Totals	301	971	772	2714	9.0

RENNICKE, JOHN

Ht. 6-2 Wt. 185 College—Drake

Yr	Team	G	FG	FT	TP	Avg.
1951-52	Milwaukee	6	4	3	11	1.8

RENSBERGER, ROBERT

b. 1920 Ht. 6-2 Wt. 170 College—Notre Dame

Yr	Team	G	FG	FT	TP	Avg.
1946-47	Chicago	3	0	0	0	0.0

REYNOLDS, GEORGE

b. Nov. 23, 1947 Ht. 6-4 Wt. 195 College—Houston

Yr	Team	G	FG	FT	TP	Avg.
1969-70	Detroit	10	8	5	21	2.1

RHINE, KENDALL

b. Feb. 13, 1943 Ht. 6-10 Wt. 240 College—Rice

Yr	Team	G	FG	FT	TP	Avg.
1967-68	Kentucky ABA	52	50 (0)	27	127	2.4
1968-69	Houston ABA	73	255 (0)	149	659	9.0
	Totals	125	305 (0)	176	786	6.3

RHODES, GENE

b. Sept. 2, 1927 Ht. 6-1 Wt. 170 Coll.—Western Ky.

Yr	Team	G	FG	FT	TP	Avg.
1952-53	Indianapolis	65	109	119	337	5.2

RICHTER, JOHN

b. March 12, 1937 Ht. 6-9 Wt. 225 Coll.—N.C. State

Yr	Team	G	FG	FT	TP	Avg.
1959-60	Boston	66	113	59	285	4.3

RICKETTS, DICK

b. Dec. 4, 1933 Ht. 6-7 Wt. 220 College—Duquesne

Yr	Team	G	FG	FT	TP	Avg.
1955-56	St. L.-Rchstr	68	235	138	608	8.9
1956-57	Rochester	72	299	206	804	11.2
1957-58	Cincinnati	72	215	132	562	7.8
	Totals	212	749	476	1974	9.3

RIDGLE, JACKIE

b. Feb. 13, 1948 Ht. 6-4 Wt. 195 College—California

Yr	Team	G	FG	FT	TP	Avg.
1971-72	Cleveland	32	19	19	57	1.8

RIEBE, MEL (Mouse)

b. July 12, 1916 Ht. 5-11½ Wt. 180

Yr	Team	G	FG	FT	TP	Avg.
1943-44	Cleveland NL	18	113	97	323	17.9
1944-45	Cleveland NL	30	223	161	607	20.2
1945-46	Cleveland NL	5	23	26	72	14.4
1946-47	Cleveland	55	276	111	663	12.1
1947-48	Boston	48	202	85	489	10.2
1948-49	Bos.-Providence	43	172	79	423	9.8
	Totals	199	1009	559	2577	12.9

RIEDY, BOB

Ht. 6-6 College—Duke

Yr	Team	G	FG	FT	TP	Avg.
1967-68	Houston ABA	23	45 (0)	41	131	5.7

RIFFEY, JAMES

b. 1924 Ht. 6-4 Wt. 200 College—Tulane

Yr	Team	G	FG	FT	TP	Avg.
1950-51	Ft. Wayne	35	65	20	150	4.3

RIKER, TOM

b. Feb. 28, 1950 Ht. 6-10 Wt. 225 Coll.—S. Carolina

Yr	Team	G	FG	FT	TP	Avg.
1972-73	New York	14	10	15	35	2.5
1973-74	New York	17	13	12	38	2.2
1974-75	New York	51	53	46	152	3.0
	Totals	82	76	73	225	2.7

RILEY, BOB

b. July 6, 1948 Ht. 6-9 Wt. 235 College—Mt. St. Mary's

Yr	Team	G	FG	FT	TP	Avg.
1970-71	Atlanta	7	4	5	13	1.9

RILEY, PAT

b. March 20, 1945 Ht. 6-4 Wt. 205 College—Kentucky

Yr	Team	G	FG	FT	TP	Avg.
1967-68	San Diego	80	250	128	628	7.9
1968-69	San Diego	56	202	90	494	8.8
1969-70	San Diego	36	75	40	190	5.3
1970-71	Los Angeles	54	105	56	266	4.9
1971-72	Los Angeles	67	197	55	449	6.7
1972-73	Los Angeles	55	167	65	339	7.3
1973-74	Los Angeles	72	287	110	684	9.5
1974-75	Los Angeles	46	219	69	507	11.0
1975-76	L.A.-Phoe.	62	117	55	289	4.7
	Totals	528	1619	668	3906	7.4

RILEY, RON

b. Nov. 11, 1950 Ht. 6-8 Wt. 200 College—USC

Yr	Team	G	FG	FT	TP	Avg.
1972-73	K.C.-O.	74	273	79	625	8.4
1973-74	K.C.-O.-Hou.	48	81	24	186	3.9
1974-75	Houston	77	196	71	463	6.0
1975-76	Houston	65	115	38	268	4.1
	Totals	264	665	212	1542	5.8

RINALDI, RICH

b. Aug. 3, 1949 Ht. 6-3 Wt. 195 College—St. Peter's

Yr	Team	G	FG	FT	TP	Avg.
1971-72	Baltimore	39	42	20	104	2.7
1972-73	Baltimore	33	116	48	280	8.5
1973-74	Capital	7	3	3	9	1.3
1973-74	New York ABA	5	4 (0)	4	12	2.4
	Totals	84	165 (0)	75	405	4.8

Yr	Team	G	FG	FT	TP	Avg.

RIORDAN, MIKE

b. July 9, 1945 Ht. 6-4 Wt. 200 College—Providence

Yr	Team	G	FG	FT	TP	Avg.
1968-69	New York	54	49	28	126	2.3
1969-70	New York	81	255	114	624	7.7
1970-71	New York	82	162	67	391	4.8
1971-72	N.Y.-Balt.	58	233	84	550	9.5
1972-73	Baltimore	82	652	179	1483	18.1
1973-74	Capital	81	577	136	1290	15.9
1974-75	Washington	74	520	98	1138	15.4
1975-76	Washington	78	291	71	653	8.4
1976-77	Washington	49	34	11	79	1.6
	Totals	639	2773	788	6334	9.9

RISEN, ARNOLD (Stilts)

b. Oct. 9, 1924 Ht. 6-9 Wt. 200 College—Ohio State

Yr	Team	G	FG	FT	TP	Avg.
1945-46	Indianapolis NL	18	77	65	219	12.2
1946-47	Indianapolis NL	44	204	174	582	13.2
1947-48	Ind.-Roch. NL	61	282	241	805	13.1
1948-49	Rochester	60	345	305	995	16.6
1949-50	Rochester	62	206	213	625	10.1
1950-51	Rochester	66	377	323	1077	16.3
1951-52	Rochester	66	365	302	1032	15.6
1952-53	Rochester	68	295	294	884	13.0
1953-54	Rochester	72	321	307	949	11.6
1954-55	Rochester	69	259	279	797	11.6
1955-56	Boston	68	189	170	548	8.1
1956-57	Boston	43	119	106	344	8.0
1957-58	Boston	63	134	114	382	6.1
	Totals	760	3173	2893	9239	12.2

RITTER, GOEBEL (Tex)

b. 1924 Ht. 6-2 Wt. 185 College—Eastern Kentucky

Yr	Team	G	FG	FT	TP	Avg.
1948-49	New York	55	123	91	337	6.1
1949-50	New York	62	100	125	325	5.2
1950-51	New York	34	39	49	127	3.7
	Totals	151	262	265	789	5.2

ROBBINS, AUSTIN (Red)

b. Sept. 30, 1944 Ht. 6-8 Wt. 200 College—Tennessee

Yr	Team	G	FG	FT	TP	Avg.
1967-68	New Orleans ABA	73	446 (2)	245	1143	15.7
1968-69	New Orleans ABA	76	449 (7)	291	1210	15.9
1969-70	New Orleans ABA	82	518 (7)	285	1342	16.4
1970-71	Utah ABA	82	385 (11)	227	1030	12.6
1971-72	Utah ABA	78	350 (29)	167	954	12.2
1972-73	San Diego ABA	58	209 (9)	131	576	9.9
1973-74	S.D.-Ken. ABA	80	275 (1)	116	669	8.4
1974-75	Ken.-Vir. ABA	57	304 (3)	162	779	13.7
	Totals	586	2936 (69)	1624	7703	13.1

ROBBINS, LEE ROY

b. 1923 Ht. 6-3 Wt. 175 College—Colorado

Yr	Team	G	FG	FT	TP	Avg.
1947-48	Providence	31	72	51	195	6.3
1948-49	Providence	16	9	11	29	1.8
	Totals	47	81	62	224	4.8

ROBERTS, JOSEPH

b. May 18, 1936 Ht. 6-6 Wt. 214 College—Ohio State

Yr	Team	G	FG	FT	TP	Avg.
1960-61	Syracuse	68	130	62	322	4.7
1961-62	Syracuse	80	243	129	615	7.7
1962-63	Syracuse	33	73	35	181	5.5
1967-68	Kentucky ABA	37	53 (1)	28	137	3.7
	Totals	218	499 (1)	254	1255	5.8

ROBERTS, MARV

b. Jan. 29, 1950 Ht. 6-8 Wt. 220 College—Utah State

Yr	Team	G	FG	FT	TP	Avg.
1971-72	Denver ABA	68	216 (1)	86	521	7.7
1972-73	Denver ABA	77	373 (1)	201	950	12.3
1973-74	Den.-Cav. ABA	74	265 (1)	129	662	9.0
1974-75	Kentucky ABA	83	201 (0)	127	529	6.4
1975-76	Ken.-Vir. ABA	72	259 (0)	107	625	8.7
1976-77	Los Angeles	28	27	4	58	2.1
	Totals	402	1341 (3)	654	3345	8.3

ROBERTS, WILLIAM

b. 1925 Ht. 6-9 Wt. 210 College—Wyoming

Yr	Team	G	FG	FT	TP	Avg.
1948-49	Chic.-Bos.-St. Louis	50	89	44	222	4.4
1949-50	St. Louis	67	77	28	182	2.7
	Totals	117	166	72	404	3.5

ROBERTSON, OSCAR (The Big O)

b. Nov. 24, 1938 Ht. 6-5 Wt. 205 College—Cincinnati

Yr	Team	G	FG	FT	TP	Avg.
1960-61	Cincinnati	71	756	653	2165	30.5
1961-62	Cincinnati	79	866	700	2432	30.8
1962-63	Cincinnati	80	825	614	2264	28.3
1963-64	Cincinnati	79	840	800	2480	31.4
1964-65	Cincinnati	75	807	665	2279	30.4
1965-66	Cincinnati	76	818	742	2378	31.3
1966-67	Cincinnati	79	838	736	2412	30.5
1967-68	Cincinnati	65	660	576	1896	29.2
1968-69	Cincinnati	79	656	643	1955	24.7
1969-70	Cincinnati	69	647	454	1748	25.3
1970-71	Milwaukee	81	592	385	1569	19.4
1971-72	Milwaukee	64	419	276	1114	17.4
1972-73	Milwaukee	73	446	238	1130	15.5
1973-74	Milwaukee	70	338	212	888	12.7
	Totals	1040	9508	7694	26710	25.7

ROBINSON, FLYNN

b. April 28, 1941 Ht. 6-1 Wt. 190 College—Wyoming

Yr	Team	G	FG	FT	TP	Avg.
1966-67	Cincinnati	76	274	120	668	8.8
1967-68	Cinn.-Chicago	75	444	288	1176	15.7
1968-69	Chi.-Mil.	83	625	412	1662	20.0
1969-70	Milwaukee	81	663	439	1765	21.8
1970-71	Cincinnati	71	374	195	943	13.3
1971-72	Los Angeles	64	262	111	635	9.9
1972-73	L.A.-Balt.	44	133	32	298	6.8
1973-74	San Diego ABA	49	177 (8)	52	430	8.8
	Totals	543	2952 (8)	1649	7577	14.0

ROBINSON, RONNIE

b. Mar. 9, 1951 Ht. 6-8 Wt. 220 Coll.—Memphis State

Yr	Team	G	FG	FT	TP	Avg.
1973-74	Utah-Mem. ABA	62	174 (0)	49	397	6.4

Yr	Team	G	FG	FT	TP	Avg.
1974-75	Memphis ABA	10	18 (0)	4	40	4.0
	Totals	72	192 (0)	53	437	6.1

ROBINSON, SAM

b. Apr. 1, 1948 Ht. 6-7 Wt. 200 Coll.—Lg Beach State

Yr	Team	G	FG	FT	TP	Avg.
1970-71	Floridians ABA	83	401 (4)	103	917	11.5
1971-72	Floridians ABA	51	126 (0)	54	306	6.0
	Totals	134	527 (4)	157	1223	9.1

ROBINSON, WILL

b. 1949 Ht. 6-2 Wt. 175 College—West Virginia

Yr	Team	G	FG	FT	TP	Avg.
1973-74	Memphis ABA	45	166 (0)	57	389	8.6

ROCHA, EPHRAIM (Red)

b. Sept. 18, 1923 Ht. 6-9 Wt. 185 College—Oreg. State

Yr	Team	G	FG	FT	TP	Avg.
1947-48	St. Louis	48	232	147	611	12.8
1948-49	St. Louis	58	223	162	608	10.5
1949-50	St. Louis	65	275	220	770	11.8
1950-51	Baltimore	64	297	242	836	13.1
1951-52	Syracuse	66	300	254	854	12.9
1952-53	Syracuse	69	268	234	770	11.2
1954-55	Syracuse	72	295	222	812	11.3
1955-56	Syracuse	72	250	220	720	10.0
1956-57	Ft. Wayne	72	136	109	381	5.3
	Totals	586	2276	1810	6362	10.9

ROCHE, JOHN

b. Sept. 29, 1949 Ht. 6-3 Wt. 170 Coll.—South Carolina

Yr	Team	G	FG	FT	TP	Avg.
1971-72	New York ABA	82	391 (12)	240	1058	12.9
1972-73	New York ABA	77	370 (34)	265	1107	14.4
1973-74	N.Y.-Ken. ABA	84	361 (36)	148	978	11.6
1974-75	Ken.-Utah ABA	58	228 (13)	85	580	10.0
1975-76	Utah ABA	16	103 (9)	31	264	16.5
1975-76	Los Angeles	15	3	2	8	0.5
	Totals	332	1456 (104)	771	3995	12.0

ROCK, GENE

b. 1922 Ht. 5-9½ Wt. 155 College—Southern California

Yr	Team	G	FG	FT	TP	Avg.
1947-48	Chicago	11	4	2	10	0.9

ROCKER, JACK

Ht. 6-5 Wt. 185 College—California

Yr	Team	G	FG	FT	TP	Avg.
1947-48	Minn. NL	5	2	0	4	0.8
1947-48	Phila.	9	8	1	17	1.9
	Totals	14	10	1	21	1.5

RODGERS, GUY

b. Sept. 1, 1935 Ht. 6-0 Wt. 185 College—Temple

Yr	Team	G	FG	FT	TP	Avg.
1958-59	Philadelphia	45	211	61	483	10.7
1959-60	Philadelphia	68	338	111	787	11.6
1960-61	Philadelphia	78	397	206	1000	12.8
1961-62	Philadelphia	80	267	121	655	8.2
1962-63	San Fran.	79	445	208	1098	14.1
1963-64	San Fran.	79	337	198	872	11.0
1964-65	San Fran.	79	465	223	1153	14.6

Yr	Team	G	FG	FT	TP	Avg.
1965-66	San Fran.	79	586	296	1468	18.6
1966-67	Chicago	81	538	383	1459	18.0
1967-68	Chi.-Cin.	78	148	107	403	5.2
1968-69	Milwaukee	81	325	184	834	10.3
1969-70	Milwaukee	64	68	67	203	3.2
	Totals	891	4125	2165	10415	11.7

ROGERS, HARRY

b. 1953 Ht. 6-7 Wt. 195 College—St. Louis

Yr	Team	G	FG	FT	TP	Avg.
1975-76	St. Louis ABA	18	60 (0)	17	137	7.6

ROGERS, MARSHALL

b. Aug. 27, 1953 Ht. 6-1 Wt. 190 Coll.—Pan American

Yr	Team	G	FG	FT	TP	Avg.
1976-77	Golden State	26	43	14	100	3.8

ROGERS, WILLIE DANIEL

b. Sept. 11, 1945 Ht. 6-3 Wt. 195 College—Oklahoma

Yr	Team	G	FG	FT	TP	Avg.
1968-69	Denver ABA	40	27 (0)	31	85	2.1

ROGES, ALBERT

b. 1931 Ht. 6-4 Wt. 200 College—Long Island Univ.

Yr	Team	G	FG	FT	TP	Avg.
1953-54	Baltimore	67	220	130	570	8.5
1954-55	Balt.-Ft. W.	17	23	15	61	3.6
	Totals	84	243	145	631	7.5

ROHLOFF, KEN

b. April 18, 1939 Ht. 6-0 Wt. 195 College—N.C. State

Yr	Team	G	FG	FT	TP	Avg.
1963-64	St. Louis	2	0	0	0	0.0

ROLLINS, KEN

b. Sept. 14, 1923 Ht. 6-0 Wt. 168 College—Kentucky

Yr	Team	G	FG	FT	TP	Avg.
1948-49	Chicago	59	144	77	365	6.2
1949-50	Chicago	66	144	66	354	5.4
1952-53	Boston	43	38	22	98	2.3
	Totals	168	326	165	817	4.9

ROLLINS, PHILIP

b. Jan. 19, 1934 Ht. 6-2 Wt. 190 College—Louisville

Yr	Team	G	FG	FT	TP	Avg.
1958-59	Phila.-Cin.	44	83	63	229	5.2
1959-60	Cincinnati	72	158	77	393	5.5
1960-61	Cin.-St. L.-N.Y.	61	105	56	266	4.4
	Totals	177	346	196	888	5.0

ROOK, JERRY

Ht. 6-5 Wt. 220 College—Arkansas State

Yr	Team	G	FG	FT	TP	Avg.
1969-70	New Orleans ABA	28	37 (0)	11	85	3.0

ROSENBERG, ALEXANDER (Petey)

b. April 7, 1918 Ht. 5-10 Wt. 165 College—St. Joseph's (Pa.)

Yr	Team	G	FG	FT	TP	Avg.
1946-47	Philadelphia	51	60	30	150	2.9

ROSENBLUTH, LEONARD

b. Jan. 22, 1933 Ht. 6-5 Wt. 200 College—N.C. State

Yr	Team	G	FG	FT	TP	Avg.
1957-58	Philadelphia	53	91	53	235	4.4
1958-59	Philadelphia	29	43	21	107	3.7
	Totals	82	134	74	342	4.2

Yr	Team	G	FG	FT	TP	Avg.

ROSENSTEIN, HENRY

b. 1920 Ht. 6-4 Wt. 185 College—CCNY

Yr	Team	G	FG	FT	TP	Avg.
1946-47	New York	31	38	57	133	4.3
1947-48	Providence	29	81	87	249	8.6
	Totals	60	119	144	382	6.4

ROSENTHAL, RICHARD

Ht. 6-5 Wt. 205 College—Notre Dame

Yr	Team	G	FG	FT	TP	Avg.
1954-55	Ft. Wayne	67	197	130	524	7.8
1956-57	Ft. Wayne	18	21	9	51	2.8
	Totals	85	218	139	575	6.8

ROTHENBERG, IRWIN (Irv)

b. Dec. 31, 1922 Ht. 6-8 Wt. 215 College—L.I.U.

Yr	Team	G	FG	FT	TP	Avg.
1946-47	Cleveland	29	36	30	102	3.5
1947-48	Balt.-St. L. Wash.	49	103	87	293	6.0
1948-49	New York	53	101	112	314	5.9
	Totals	131	240	229	709	5.4

ROTTNER, MARVIN (Mickey)

b. Mar. 23, 1919 Ht. 5-10 Wt. 185 Coll.—Loyola (Ill.)

Yr	Team	G	FG	FT	TP	Avg.
1945-46	Sheboygan NL	5	10	0	20	4.0
1946-47	Chicago	56	190	43	423	7.6
1947-48	Chicago	44	53	11	117	2.7
	Totals	105	253	54	560	5.3

ROUX, GIFFORD

b. 1923 Ht. 6-5 Wt. 195 College—Kansas

Yr	Team	G	FG	FT	TP	Avg.
1946-47	St. Louis	60	142	70	354	5.9
1947-48	St. Louis	46	68	40	176	3.8
1948-49	St. L.-Prov.	45	29	29	87	1.9
	Totals	151	239	139	617	4.1

ROYALS, REGGIE

b. Sept. 18, 1954 Ht. 6-11 Wt. 220 College—St. John's

Yr	Team	G	FG	FT	TP	Avg.
1974-75	San Diego ABA	2	2 (0)	0	4	2.0

ROYER, BOB

b. 1927 Ht. 5-10 Wt. 155 College—K.C. and Ind. State

Yr	Team	G	FG	FT	TP	Avg.
1949-50	Denver	42	78	41	197	4.7

RUDOMETKIN, JOHN

b. June 6, 1940 Ht. 6-6 Wt. 205 College—So. Calif.

Yr	Team	G	FG	FT	TP	Avg.
1962-63	New York	56	108	73	289	5.2
1963-64	New York	52	154	87	395	7.6
1964-65	N.Y. San Fran.	23	52	34	138	6.0
	Totals	131	314	194	822	6.3

RUFFNER, PAUL

b. Oct. 15, 1948 Ht. 6-10 Wt. 225 College—Brigham Young

Yr	Team	G	FG	FT	TP	Avg.
1970-71	Chicago	10	15	4	34	3.4
1971-72	Pittsburgh ABA	79	182 (0)	84	448	5.7
1973-74	Buffalo	20	11	8	30	1.5
1974-75	Buffalo	22	22	1	45	2.0
	Totals	131	230 (0)	97	557	4.3

RUKLICK, JOSEPH

b. Aug. 3, 1938 Ht. 6-9 Wt. 220 College—Northwestern

Yr	Team	G	FG	FT	TP	Avg.
1959-60	Philadelphia	39	85	26	196	5.0
1960-61	Philadelphia	29	43	8	94	3.2
1961-62	Philadelphia	46	48	12	108	1.8
	Totals	114	176	46	398	3.5

RULE, BOB

b. June 29, 1944 Ht. 6-9 Wt. 220 College—Colo. St.

Yr	Team	G	FG	FT	TP	Avg.
1967-68	Seattle	82	568	348	1484	18.1
1968-69	Seattle	82	776	413	1965	24.0
1969-70	Seattle	80	789	387	1965	24.6
1970-71	Seattle	4	47	25	119	29.8
1971-72	Sea.-Phil.	76	461	226	1148	15.1
1972-73	Phila.-Cleve.	52	60	20	140	2.7
1973-74	Cleveland	26	76	34	186	7.2
1974-75	Milwaukee	1	0	0	0	0.0
	Totals	403	2777	1453	7007	17.4

RULLO, GENEROSO (Jerry)

b. 1923 Ht. 5-10 Wt. 165 College—Temple

Yr	Team	G	FG	FT	TP	Avg.
1946-47	Philadelphia	50	52	23	127	2.5
1947-48	Baltimore	2	0	0	0	0.0
1948-49	Philadelphia	39	53	31	137	3.5
1949-50	Philadelphia	4	3	1	7	1.8
	Totals	95	108	55	271	2.9

RUSSELL, BILL

b. Feb. 12, 1934 Ht. 6-9½ Wt. 220 College—San Fran.

Yr	Team	G	FG	FT	TP	Avg.
1956-57	Boston	48	277	152	706	14.7
1957-58	Boston	69	456	230	1142	16.6
1958-59	Boston	70	456	256	1168	16.7
1959-60	Boston	74	555	240	1350	18.2
1960-61	Boston	78	532	258	1322	16.9
1961-62	Boston	76	575	286	1436	18.9
1962-63	Boston	78	511	287	1309	16.8
1963-64	Boston	78	466	236	1168	15.0
1964-65	Boston	78	429	244	1102	14.1
1965-66	Boston	78	391	223	1005	12.9
1966-67	Boston	81	395	285	1075	13.4
1967-68	Boston	78	365	247	977	12.5
1968-69	Boston	77	279	204	762	9.9
	Totals	963	5687	3148	14522	15.1

RUSSELL, CAZZIE

b. June 7, 1944 Ht. 6-5½ Wt. 218 College—Michigan

Yr	Team	G	FG	FT	TP	Avg.
1966-67	New York	77	344	179	867	11.3
1967-68	New York	82	551	282	1384	16.9
1968-69	New York	50	362	191	915	18.3
1969-70	New York	78	385	124	894	11.5
1970-71	New York	57	216	92	524	9.2
1971-72	Golden State	79	689	315	1693	21.4
1972-73	Golden State	80	541	172	1254	15.7
1973-74	Golden State	82	738	208	1684	20.5
1974-75	Los Angeles	40	264	101	629	15.7
1975-76	Los Angeles	74	371	132	874	11.8
1976-77	Los Angeles	82	578	188	1344	16.4
1977-78	Chicago	36	133	49	315	8.8
	Totals	817	5172	2033	12377	15.1

RUSSELL, FRANK

b. April 17, 1949 Ht. 6-3 Wt. 180 College—Detroit

Yr	Team	G	FG	FT	TP	Avg.
1972-73	Chicago	23	29	16	74	3.2

RUSSELL, PIERRE

b. Dec. 13, 1949 Ht. 6-4 Wt. 190 College—Kansas

Yr	Team	G	FG	FT	TP	Avg.
1971-72	Kentucky ABA	51	65 (0)	16	146	2.9

Yr	Team	G	FG	FT	TP	Avg.
1972-73	Kentucky ABA	59	117 (2)	49	289	4.9
	Totals	110	182 (2)	65	435	4.0

RUSSELL, RUBIN

Ht. 6-3 Wt. 180 College—North Texas State

Yr	Team	G	FG	FT	TP	Avg.
1967-68	Dallas-Ky. ABA	26	52 (4)	25	141	5.4

SADOWSKI, EDWARD (Big Ed)

b. July 11, 1917 Ht. 6-5 Wt. 240 College—Seton Hall

Yr	Team	G	FG	FT	TP	Avg.
1940-41	Detroit NL	24	95	66	256	10.7
1944-45	Ft. Wayne NL	1	4	2	10	10.0
1945-46	Ft. Wayne NL	34	122	82	326	9.6
1946-47	Tor.-Cleve.	53	329	219	877	16.5
1947-48	Boston	47	308	294	910	19.4
1948-49	Philadelphia	60	340	240	920	15.3
1949-50	Phila.-Balt.	69	299	274	872	12.6
	Totals	288	1497	1177	4171	14.5

SAILORS, KEN

b. Jan. 14, 1922 Ht. 5-10 Wt. 1976 College—Wyoming

Yr	Team	G	FG	FT	TP	Avg.
1946-47	Cleveland	58	229	119	577	9.9
1947-48	Chi.-Phila.-Prov.	44	207	110	524	11.9
1948-49	Providence	57	309	281	899	15.8
1949-50	Denver	57	329	329	987	17.3
1950-51	Bos.-Balt.	60	181	131	493	8.2
	Totals	276	1255	970	3480	12.6

SALVADORI, ALBERT (Al)

b. May 6, 1945 Ht. 6-9½ Wt. 220 Coll.—South Carolina

Yr	Team	G	FG	FT	TP	Avg.
1967-68	Oakland ABA	17	20 (1)	11	54	3.2

SANDERS, AL

b. 1950 Ht. 6-7 Wt. 240 College—Louisiana State

Yr	Team	G	FG	FT	TP	Avg.
1972-73	Virginia ABA	4	2 (0)	4	8	2.0

SANDERS, THOMAS (Satch)

b. Nov. 8, 1938 Ht. 6-6 Wt. 210 College—N.Y. Univ.

Yr	Team	G	FG	FT	TP	Avg.
1960-61	Boston	68	148	67	363	5.3
1961-62	Boston	80	350	197	897	11.2
1962-63	Boston	80	339	186	864	10.8
1963-64	Boston	80	349	213	911	11.4
1964-65	Boston	80	374	193	941	11.8
1965-66	Boston	72	349	211	909	12.6
1966-67	Boston	81	323	178	824	10.2
1967-68	Boston	78	296	200	792	10.2
1968-69	Boston	82	364	187	915	11.2
1969-70	Boston	57	246	161	653	11.5
1970-71	Boston	17	16	7	39	2.3
1971-72	Boston	82	215	111	541	6.6
1972-73	Boston	59	47	23	117	2.0
	Totals	916	3416	1934	8766	9.6

SANFORD, RON

b. June 11, 1946 Ht. 6-9 Wt. 215 Coll.—New Mexico

Yr	Team	G	FG	FT	TP	Avg.
1971-72	Dallas ABA	1	0 (0)	0	0	0.0

SANTINI, ROBERT

b. Feb. 17, 1935 Ht. 6-5 Wt. 190 College—Iona

Yr	Team	G	FG	FT	TP	Avg.
1955-56	New York	4	5	1	11	2.8

SAUL, FRANK (Pep)

b. Feb. 16, 1924 Ht. 6-2 Wt. 185 College—Seton Hall

Yr	Team	G	FG	FT	TP	Avg.
1949-50	Rochester	49	74	34	182	3.7
1950-51	Rochester	65	105	72	282	4.3
1951-52	Balt.-Minn.	64	157	119	433	6.8
1952-53	Minneapolis	70	187	142	516	7.4
1953-54	Minneapolis	71	162	128	452	6.4
1954-55	Milwaukee	65	96	95	287	4.4
	Totals	384	781	590	2152	5.6

SAULDSBERRY, WOODY

b. July 11, 1934 Ht. 6-7 Wt. 220 Coll.—Tex. Southern

Yr	Team	G	FG	FT	TP	Avg.
1957-58	Philadelphia	71	389	134	912	12.8
1958-59	Philadelphia	72	501	110	1112	15.4
1959-60	Philadelphia	71	325	55	705	9.9
1960-61	St. Louis	68	230	56	516	7.6
1961-62	St. L.-Chic.	63	298	79	675	10.7
1962-63	Chi.-St. L.	77	366	107	839	10.9
1965-66	Boston	39	80	11	171	4.4
	Totals	461	2189	552	4930	10.7

SAULTERS, GLYNN

b. Feb. 10, 1945 Ht. 6-2 Wt. 175 College—Western LA.

Yr	Team	G	FG	FT	TP	Avg.
1968-69	New Orleans ABA	22	22 (0)	15	59	2.7

SAUNDERS, FRED

b. June 13, 1951 Ht. 6-7 Wt. 210 College—Syracuse

Yr	Team	G	FG	FT	TP	Avg.
1974-75	Phoenix	69	176	66	418	6.1
1975-76	Phoenix	17	28	6	62	3.6
1976-77	Boston	68	184	35	403	5.9
1977-78	Bos.-N.O.	56	99	26	224	4.0
	Totals	210	487	133	1107	5.3

SAVAGE, DON

b. April 9, 1929 Ht. 6-3 Wt. 205 College—LeMoyne (N.Y.)

Yr	Team	G	FG	FT	TP	Avg.
1951-52	Syracuse	12	9	18	36	3.0
1956-57	Syracuse	5	6	6	18	3.6
	Totals	17	15	24	54	3.2

SAWYER, ALAN

b. 1928 Ht. 6-5 Wt. 195 College—UCLA

Yr	Team	G	FG	FT	TP	Avg.
1950-51	Washington	33	87	43	217	6.6

SCHADE, FRANK

b. Jan. 22, 1950 Ht. 6-1 Wt. 170 College—Eau Claire St.

Yr	Team	G	FG	FT	TP	Avg.
1972-73	K.C.-O.	9	2	6	10	1.1

SCHADLER, BERNARD (Ben)

b. March 9, 1924 Ht. 6-2 Wt. 185 Coll.—Northwestern

Yr	Team	G	FG	FT	TP	Avg.
1947-48	Chicago	37	23	10	56	1.5
1948-49	Det.-Wat. NL	53	150	58	358	6.8
	Totals	90	173	68	414	4.6

SCHAEFFER, BILLY
b. Dec. 11, 1951 Ht. 6-5 Wt. 200 College—St. John's

Yr	Team	G	FG	FT	TP	Avg.
1973-74	New York ABA	59	169 (2)	41	385	6.5
1974-75	New York ABA	27	59 (2)	15	139	5.2
1975-76	N.Y.-Vir. ABA	51	112 (2)	48	278	5.5
	Totals	137	340 (6)	104	802	5.9

SCHAEFER, HERMAN
b. 1919 Ht. 6-0 Wt. 175 College—Indiana

Yr	Team	G	FG	FT	TP	Avg.
1941-42	Ft. Wayne NL	24	85	37	207	8.6
1942-43	Ft. Wayne NL	21	36	12	84	4.0
1945-46	Ft. Wayne NL	15	10	3	23	1.5
1946-47	Indianapolis NL	44	147	65	359	8.2
1947-48	Ind.-Minn. NL	57	110	78	298	5.2
1948-49	Minneapolis	58	214	174	602	10.4
1949-50	Minneapolis	65	122	86	330	5.1
	Totals	284	724	455	1903	6.7

SCHAFER, ROBERT
Ht. 6-3 Wt. 195 College—Villanova

Yr	Team	G	FG	FT	TP	Avg.
1955-56	Phila.-St. L.	54	81	63	224	4.1
1956-57	Syracuse	11	19	11	49	4.5
	Totals	65	100	73	273	4.2

SCHARNUS, BEN (Whitey)
b. Jan. 6, 1918 Ht. 6-2 Wt. 173 College—Seton Hall

Yr	Team	G	FG	FT	TP	Avg.
1946-47	Cleveland	51	33	37	103	2.0
1948-49	Providence	1	0	0	0	0.0
	Totals	52	33	37	103	2.0

SCHATZMAN, MARVIN
b. 1926 Ht. 6-5 Wt. 200 College—St. Louis

Yr	Team	G	FG	FT	TP	Avg.
1949-50	Baltimore	34	43	29	115	3.4

SCHAUS, FRED
b. June 30, 1925 Ht. 6-5 Wt. 210 College—West Va.

Yr	Team	G	FG	FT	TP	Avg.
1949-50	Ft. Wayne	68	351	270	972	14.3
1950-51	Ft. Wayne	68	312	404	1028	15.1
1951-52	Ft. Wayne	62	281	310	872	14.1
1952-53	Ft. Wayne	69	240	243	723	10.5
1953-54	Ft. W.-N.Y.	67	161	153	475	7.1
	Totals	334	1345	1380	4070	12.2

SCHAYES, DOLPH
b. May 19, 1928 Ht. 6-8 Wt. 220 College—N.Y. Univ.

Yr	Team	G	FG	FT	TP	Avg.
1948-49	Syracuse NL	63	271	267	809	12.8
1949-50	Syracuse	64	348	376	1072	16.8
1950-51	Syracuse	66	332	457	1121	17.0
1951-52	Syracuse	63	263	342	868	13.8
1952-53	Syracuse	71	375	512	1262	17.8
1953-54	Syracuse	72	370	488	1228	17.1
1954-55	Syracuse	72	422	489	1333	18.5
1955-56	Syracuse	72	465	542	1472	20.4
1956-57	Syracuse	72	496	625	1617	22.5
1957-58	Syracuse	72	581	629	1791	24.9
1958-59	Syracuse	72	504	526	1534	21.3
1959-60	Syracuse	75	578	533	1689	22.5
1960-61	Syracuse	79	594	680	1868	23.6
1961-62	Syracuse	56	268	286	822	14.7
1962-63	Syracuse	66	223	181	627	9.5
1963-64	Phila.	24	44	46	134	5.6
	Totals	1059	6134	6979	19247	18.2

SCHECTMAN, OSCAR (Ossie)
b. 1919 Ht. 6-0½ Wt. 175 College—Long Island Univ.

Yr	Team	G	FG	FT	TP	Avg.
1946-47	New York	54	162	111	435	8.1

SCHELLHASE, DAVE
b. Oct. 14, 1944 Ht. 6-3½ Wt. 205 College—Purdue

Yr	Team	G	FG	FT	TP	Avg.
1966-67	Chicago	31	40	14	94	3.0
1967-68	Chicago	42	47	20	114	2.7
	Totals	73	87	34	208	2.8

SCHERER, HERB
b. Dec. 21, 1929 Ht. 6-9 Wt. 215 College—LIU

Yr	Team	G	FG	FT	TP	Avg.
1950-51	Tri-Cities	20	24	20	68	3.4
1951-52	New York	12	19	9	47	3.9
	Totals	32	43	29	115	3.6

SCHLUETER, DALE
b. Nov. 12, 1945 Ht. 6-10 Wt. 226 College—Col. State

Yr	Team	G	FG	FT	TP	Avg.
1968-69	San Francisco	31	68	45	181	5.8
1969-70	San Francisco	63	82	60	224	3.6
1970-71	Portland	80	257	143	657	8.2
1971-72	Portland	81	353	241	974	11.7
1972-73	Philadelphia	78	166	86	418	5.4
1973-74	Atlanta	57	63	38	164	2.9
1974-75	Buffalo	76	92	84	268	3.5
1975-76	Buffalo	71	61	54	176	2.5
1976-77	Phoenix	39	26	18	70	1.8
1977-78	Portland	10	8	9	25	2.5
	Totals	586	1176	778	3130	5.3

SCHNELLBACHER, OTTO
b. April 15, 1923 Ht. 6-5 Wt. 185 College—Kansas

Yr	Team	G	FG	FT	TP	Avg.
1948-49	Prov.-St.L.	43	93	89	275	6.4

SCHNITTKER, RICHARD
b. May 27, 1928 Ht. 6-5 Wt. 205 College—Ohio State

Yr	Team	G	FG	FT	TP	Avg.
1950-51	Washington	29	85	123	293	10.1
1953-54	Minneapolis	71	122	86	330	4.6
1954-55	Minneapolis	72	226	298	750	10.4
1955-56	Minneapolis	72	254	304	812	11.3
1956-57	Minneapolis	70	113	160	386	5.5
1957-58	Minneapolis	50	128	201	457	9.1
	Totals	364	928	1172	3028	8.3

SCHOLZ, DAVE
b. April 12, 1948 Ht. 6-8 Wt. 220 College—Illinois

Yr	Team	G	FG	FT	TP	Avg.
1969-70	Philadelphia	1	1	0	2	2.0

SCHOON, MILTON
b. Feb. 25, 1922 Ht. 6-9 Wt. 230 College—Valparaiso

Yr	Team	G	FG	FT	TP	Avg.
1946-47	Detroit	41	43	34	120	2.9
1947-48	Flint NL	55	114	120	348	6.3
1948-49	Sheboygan NL	57	81	109	271	4.8
1949-50	Sheboygan	62	150	196	496	8.0
	Totals	215	388	459	1235	5.7

Yr	Team	G	FG	FT	TP	Avg.

SCHULTZ, HOWARD (Stretch)

b. July 3, 1922 Ht. 6-8 Wt. 220 College—Hamline

Yr	Team	G	FG	FT	TP	Avg.
1946-47	Anderson NL	41	155	147	457	11.1
1947-48	Anderson NL	60	213	179	605	10.1
1948-49	Anderson NL	64	176	186	538	8.4
1949-50	And.-Ft. Wayne	67	179	196	554	8.3
1951-52	Minneapolis	66	89	90	268	4.1
1952-53	Minneapolis	40	24	43	91	2.3
	Totals	338	836	841	2513	7.4

SCHULZ, RICHARD

b. Jan. 3, 1917 Ht. 6-2 Wt. 205

Yr	Team	G	FG	FT	TP	Avg.
1942-43	Sheboygan NL	1	0	0	0	0.0
1943-44	Sheboygan NL	20	18	10	46	2.3
1944-45	Sheboygan NL	29	86	71	243	8.4
1945-46	Sheboygan NL	29	56	66	178	6.1
1946-47	Cleve.-Toronto	57	130	94	354	6.2
1947-48	Baltimore	48	133	117	383	8.0
1948-49	Washington	50	65	65	195	3.9
1949-50	Wash.-Tri-Cities-Sheb.	50	63	83	209	4.2
	Totals	284	551	506	1608	5.7

SCHURIG, ROGER

Ht. 6-3 College-Vanderbilt

Yr	Team	G	FG	FT	TP	Avg.
1967-68	Houston ABA	21	32 (3)	27	100	4.8

SCOLARI, FRED

b. March 1, 1922 Ht. 5-10 Wt. 180 Coll.—San Francisco

Yr	Team	G	FG	FT	TP	Avg.
1946-47	Washington	58	291	146	728	12.6
1947-48	Washington	47	229	131	589	12.5
1948-49	Washington	48	196	146	538	11.2
1949-50	Washington	66	312	236	860	13.0
1950-51	Wash.-Syr.	66	302	279	883	13.4
1951-52	Baltimore	64	290	353	933	14.6
1952-53	Balt.-Ft. W.	62	277	276	830	13.4
1953-54	Ft. Wayne	64	159	144	462	7.2
1954-55	Boston	59	76	39	191	3.2
	Totals	534	2132	1750	6014	11.3

SCOTT, RAY (Chink)

b. July 12, 1938 Ht. 6-9 Wt. 215 College—Portland

Yr	Team	G	FG	FT	TP	Avg.
1961-62	Detroit	75	370	255	995	13.3
1962-63	Detroit	76	460	308	1228	16.2
1963-64	Detroit	80	539	328	1406	17.6
1964-65	Detroit	66	402	220	1024	15.5
1965-66	Detroit	79	544	323	1411	17.9
1966-67	Det-Baltimore	72	458	256	1172	16.3
1967-68	Baltimore	81	490	348	1328	16.4
1968-69	Baltimore	82	386	195	967	11.8
1969-70	Baltimore	73	257	139	653	8.9
1970-71	Virginia ABA	72	419 (1)	187	1028	14.3
1971-72	Virginia ABA	55	161 (2)	89	417	7.6
	Totals	811	4486 (3)	2648	11629	14.3

SCOTT, WILLIE

Ht. 6-5 Wt. 210 College—Alabama State

Yr	Team	G	FG	FT	TP	Avg.
1969-70	Dallas ABA	8	6 (0)	1	13	1.6

SCRANTON, PAUL

Ht. 6-5 Wt. 230 College—Cal. Poly-Pomona

Yr	Team	G	FG	FT	TP	Avg.
1967-68	Anaheim ABA	5	4 (0)	1	9	1.8

SEALS, BRUCE

b. June 18, 1953 Ht. 6-9 Wt. 210 College—Xavier

Yr	Team	G	FG	FT	TP	Avg.
1973-74	Utah ABA	78	210 (19)	68	545	7.0
1974-75	Utah ABA	35	60 (0)	20	140	4.0
1975-76	Seattle	81	388	181	957	11.8
1976-77	Seattle	81	378	138	894	11.0
1977-78	Seattle	73	230	111	571	7.8
	Totals	348	1266 (19)	518	3107	8.9

SEARS, KEN (Big Cat)

b. Aug. 17, 1933 Ht. 6-9 Wt. 200 Coll.—Santa Clara

Yr	Team	G	FG	FT	TP	Avg.
1955-56	New York	70	319	258	896	12.8
1956-57	New York	72	343	383	1069	14.8
1957-58	New York	72	445	452	1342	18.6
1958-59	New York	71	491	506	1488	21.0
1959-60	New York	64	412	363	1187	18.5
1960-61	New York	52	241	268	750	14.4
1962-63	NY-San Fran.	77	161	131	453	5.9
1963-64	San Fran.	51	53	64	170	3.3
	Totals	529	2465	2425	7355	13.9

SEE, WAYNE

Ht. 6-3 College—Arizona State

Yr	Team	G	FG	FT	TP	Avg.
1949-50	Waterloo	61	113	94	320	5.2

SELBO, GLEN

b. 1926 Ht. 6-3 Wt. 195 College—Wisconsin

Yr	Team	G	FG	FT	TP	Avg.
1947-48	Oshkosh NL	59	157	62	376	6.4
1948-49	Oshkosh NL	60	119	77	315	5.3
1949-50	Sheboygan	13	10	22	42	3.2
	Totals	132	286	161	733	5.6

SELLERS, PHIL

b. Nov. 20, 1953 Ht. 6-4 Wt. 195 College—Rutgers

Yr	Team	G	FG	FT	TP	Avg.
1976-77	Detroit	44	73	52	198	4.5

SELTZ, ROLLIE

b. Jan. 25, 1924 Ht. 5-10½ Wt. 170 College—Hamline

Yr	Team	G	FG	FT	TP	Avg.
1946-47	Anderson NL	41	123	104	350	8.5
1947-48	Anderson NL	59	118	90	326	5.5
1948-49	Waterloo NL	62	188	127	503	8.1
1949-50	Anderson	34	93	80	266	7.8
	Totals	196	522	401	1445	7.4

Yr	Team	G	FG	FT	TP	Avg.

SELVAGE, LES

Ht. 6-1 Wt. 175 College—Kirksville State

Yr	Team	G	FG	FT	TP	Avg.
1967-68	Anaheim ABA	78	224 (147)	206	1095	14.0
1969-70	Los Angeles ABA	4	4 (0)	0	8	2.0
	Totals	82	228 (147)	206	1103	13.5

SELVY, FRANK

b. Nov. 9, 1932 Ht. 6-2½ Wt. 180 College—Furman

Yr	Team	G	FG	FT	TP	Avg.
1954-55	Balt.-Milw.	71	452	444	1348	19.0
1955-56	St. Louis	17	67	53	187	11.0
1957-58	St. L.-Minn.	38	44	47	135	3.6
1958-59	New York	68	233	201	667	9.8
1959-60	Syr.-Minn.	62	205	153	563	9.1
1960-61	Los Angeles	77	311	210	832	10.8
1961-62	Los Angeles	79	433	298	1164	14.7
1962-63	Los Angeles	80	317	192	826	10.3
1963-64	Los Angeles	73	160	78	398	5.5
	Totals	565	2222	1676	6120	10.8

SEMINOFF, JAMES

b. 1920 Ht. 6-2 Wt. 190 Coll.—Southern California

Yr	Team	G	FG	FT	TP	Avg.
1946-47	Chicago	60	184	71	439	7.3
1947-48	Chicago	48	113	73	299	6.3
1948-49	Boston	58	153	151	457	7.9
1949-50	Boston	65	85	142	312	4.8
	Totals	231	535	437	1507	6.5

SENESKY, GEORGE

b. April 4, 1922 Ht. 6-2 Wt. 180 Coll.—St. Joseph's (Pa.)

Yr	Team	G	FG	FT	TP	Avg.
1946-47	Philadelphia	58	142	82	366	6.3
1947-48	Philadelphia	47	158	98	414	8.8
1948-49	Philadelphia	60	138	111	387	6.4
1949-50	Philadelphia	68	227	157	611	9.0
1950-51	Philadelphia	65	249	181	679	10.4
1951-52	Philadelphia	57	164	146	474	8.3
1952-53	Philadelphia	69	160	93	413	6.0
1953-54	Philadelphia	58	41	29	111	1.9
	Totals	482	1279	897	3455	7.2

SEYMOUR, PAUL

b. Jan. 30, 1928 Ht. 6-2 Wt. 180 College—Toledo

Yr	Team	G	FG	FT	TP	Avg.
1946-47	Toledo NL	33	41	17	99	3.0
1947-48	Baltimore	22	27	22	76	3.5
1947-48	Syracuse NL	30	79	47	205	6.8
1948-49	Syracuse NL	63	120	70	310	4.9
1949-50	Syracuse	62	175	126	476	7.7
1950-51	Syracuse	51	125	117	367	7.2
1951-52	Syracuse	66	206	186	598	9.1
1952-53	Syracuse	67	306	340	952	14.2
1953-54	Syracuse	71	316	299	931	13.1
1954-55	Syracuse	72	375	300	1050	14.6
1955-56	Syracuse	57	227	188	642	11.3
1956-57	Syracuse	65	143	101	387	6.0
1957-58	Syracuse	64	107	53	267	4.2
1958-59	Syracuse	21	32	26	90	4.3
1959-60	Syracuse	4	0	0	0	0.0
	Totals	748	2279	1892	6450	8.6

SHABACK, NICHOLAS

b. 1919 Ht. 5-11 Wt. 182

Yr	Team	G	FG	FT	TP	Avg.
1946-47	Cleveland	53	102	38	242	4.6

SHACKELFORD, LYNN

b. Aug. 27, 1947 Ht. 6-5 Wt. 195 College—UCLA

Yr	Team	G	FG	FT	TP	Avg.
1969-70	Miami ABA	22	18 (4)	10	58	2.6

SHAEFFER, CARL

b. 1925 Ht. 6-3½ Wt. 185 College—Alabama

Yr	Team	G	FG	FT	TP	Avg.
1949-50	Indianapolis	43	59	32	150	3.5
1950-51	Indianapolis	10	6	3	15	1.5
	Totals	53	65	35	165	3.1

SHAFFER, LEE

b. Feb. 23, 1939 Ht. 6-7 Wt. 220 Coll.—No. Carolina

Yr	Team	G	FG	FT	TP	Avg.
1961-62	Syracuse	75	514	239	1267	16.9
1962-63	Syracuse	80	597	294	1488	18.6
1963-64	Philadelphia	41	217	102	536	13.1
	Totals	196	1328	635	3291	16.8

SHANNON, EARL

b. Nov. 23, 1921 Ht. 5-11 Wt. 170 Coll.—Rhode Island

Yr	Team	G	FG	FT	TP	Avg.
1946-47	Providence	57	245	197	687	12.1
1947-48	Providence	45	123	116	362	8.0
1948-49	Prov.-Bos.	32	34	39	107	3.3
	Totals	134	402	352	1156	8.6

SHANNON, HOWARD

b. June 10, 1923 Ht. 6-2 Wt. 175 College—Kansas State and North Texas State

Yr	Team	G	FG	FT	TP	Avg.
1948-49	Providence	55	292	152	736	13.1
1949-50	Boston	67	222	143	587	8.8
	Totals	122	514	295	1323	10.8

SHARE, CHARLIE

b. March 14, 1927 Ht. 6-11 Wt. 235 Coll.—Bowling Gr.

Yr	Team	G	FG	FT	TP	Avg.
1951-52	Ft. Wayne	63	76	96	248	3.9
1952-53	Ft. Wayne	67	91	172	354	5.3
1953-54	Ft. W.-Milw.	68	188	188	564	8.3
1954-55	Milwaukee	69	235	351	821	11.9
1955-56	St. Louis	72	315	346	976	13.6
1956-57	St. Louis	72	235	269	739	10.3
1957-58	St. Louis	72	216	190	622	8.6
1958-59	St. Louis	72	147	139	433	6.6
	Totals	555	1503	1751	4757	8.6

SHARMAN, BILL

b. May 25, 1926 Ht. 6-1 Wt. 190 Coll.—So. California

Yr	Team	G	FG	FT	TP	Avg.
1950-51	Washington	31	141	96	378	12.2
1951-52	Boston	63	244	183	671	10.7
1952-53	Boston	71	403	341	1147	16.2
1953-54	Boston	72	412	331	1155	16.0
1954-55	Boston	68	453	347	1253	18.4
1955-56	Boston	72	538	358	1434	19.9
1956-57	Boston	67	516	381	1413	21.1
1957-58	Boston	63	550	302	1402	22.3
1958-59	Boston	72	562	342	1466	20.4
1959-60	Boston	71	559	252	1370	19.3
1960-61	Boston	60	383	210	976	16.3
	Totals	710	4761	3143	12665	17.8

SHAVLIK, RON

b. Dec. 4, 1933 Ht. 6-8 Wt. 200 Coll.—No. Carolina St.

Yr	Team	G	FG	FT	TP	Avg.
1956-57	New York	7	4	2	10	1.4
1957-58	New York	1	0	0	0	0.0
	Totals	8	4	2	10	1.3

Yr	Team	G	FG	FT	TP	Avg.

SHEA, ROBERT

b. 1924 Ht. 6-2 Wt. 194 Coll.—Rhode Island

Yr	Team	G	FG	FT	TP	Avg.
1946-47	Providence	43	37	19	93	2.2

SHEFFIELD, FRED

b. Nov. 5, 1923 Ht. 6-2 Wt. 165 College—Utah

Yr	Team	G	FG	FT	TP	Avg.
1946-47	Philadelphia	22	29	16	74	3.4

SHEPHERD, BILLY

b. Nov. 18, 1949 Ht. 5-10 Wt. 165 College—Butler

Yr	Team	G	FG	FT	TP	Avg.
1972-73	Virginia ABA	16	3 (4)	9	27	1.7
1973-74	San Diego ABA	84	135 (65)	42	507	6.0
1974-75	Memphis ABA	69	101 (60)	52	434	6.3
	Totals	169	239 (129)	103	968	5.7

SHIPP, CHARLES

b. Dec. 3, 1913 Ht. 6-1 Wt. 205

Yr	Team	G	FG	FT	TP	Avg.
1937-38	Akron NL	16	38	14	90	5.6
1938-39	Akron NL	24	59	24	142	5.9
1939-40	Oshkosh NL	28	74	26	174	6.2
1940-41	Oshkosh NL	22	46	21	113	5.1
1941-42	Oshkosh NL	24	70	38	178	7.4
1942-43	Oshkosh NL	23	52	36	140	6.1
1943-44	Oshkosh NL	20	57	36	150	7.5
1944-45	Ft. Wayne NL	30	31	16	78	2.6
1945-46	Ft. Wayne NL	34	42	14	98	2.9
1946-47	Ft. W.-And. NL	44	89	58	236	5.4
1947-48	Anderson NL	55	103	63	269	4.9
1948-49	Waterloo NL	56	104	59	267	4.8
1949-50	Waterloo NL	23	35	37	107	4.7
	Totals	399	800	442	2042	5.1

SHORT, EUGENE

b. Aug. 7, 1953 Ht. 6-7 Wt. 200 Coll.—Jackson State

Yr	Team	G	FG	FT	TP	Avg.
1975-76	Sea.-N.Y.	34	32	20	84	2.5

SHRIDER, DICK

b. 1923 Ht. 6-2 Wt. 190 College—Ohio University

Yr	Team	G	FG	FT	TP	Avg.
1948-49	Detroit NL	3	3	3	9	3.0
1948-49	New York	4	0	1	1	0.3
	Totals	7	3	4	10	1.4

SHUE, GENE

b. Dec. 18, 1931 Ht. 6-2 Wt. 175 College—Maryland

Yr	Team	G	FG	FT	TP	Avg.
1954-55	Phila.-N.Y.	62	100	59	259	4.2
1955-56	New York	72	240	181	661	9.2
1956-57	Ft. Wayne	72	273	241	787	10.9
1957-58	Detroit	63	353	276	982	15.6
1958-59	Detroit	72	464	338	1266	17.6
1959-60	Detroit	75	620	472	1712	22.8
1960-61	Detroit	78	650	465	1765	22.6
1961-62	Detroit	80	580	362	1522	19.0
1962-63	New York	78	354	208	916	11.7
1963-64	Baltimore	48	81	36	198	3.1
	Totals	700	3715	2638	10068	14.4

SIBERT, SAM

b. Feb. 11, 1949 Ht. 6-7 Wt. 215 Coll.—Kentucky St.

Yr	Team	G	FG	FT	TP	Avg.
1972-73	K.C.-Omaha	5	4	4	12	2.4

SIBLEY, MARK

b. Nov. 13, 1950 Ht. 6-2 Wt. 175 Coll.—Northwestern

Yr	Team	G	FG	FT	TP	Avg.
1973-74	Portland	28	20	6	46	1.6

SIDLE, DON

b. June 21, 1946 Ht. 6-9 Wt. 215 College—Oklahoma

Yr	Team	G	FG	FT	TP	Avg.
1968-69	Miami ABA	77	304 (0)	321	929	12.1
1969-70	Miami ABA	84	638 (1)	469	1748	20.8
1970-71	Den.-Ind. ABA	84	423 (2)	241	1093	12.0
1971-72	Ind.-Mem. ABA	69	174 (1)	124	475	6.9
	Totals	314	1539 (4)	1155	4245	13.5

SIEGFRIED, LARRY

b. May 22, 1939 Ht. 6-4 Wt. 192 Coll.—Ohio State

Yr	Team	G	FG	FT	TP	Avg.
1963-64	Boston	31	35	31	101	3.3
1964-65	Boston	72	173	109	455	6.3
1965-66	Boston	71	349	274	972	13.7
1966-67	Boston	73	368	294	1030	14.1
1967-68	Boston	62	261	236	758	12.2
1968-69	Boston	79	392	336	1120	14.2
1969-70	Boston	78	382	220	984	12.6
1970-71	San Diego	53	146	130	422	8.0
1971-72	Hou.-Atl.	31	43	32	118	3.8
	Totals	550	2149	1662	5960	10.8

SIEWERT, RALPH (Sky)

Ht. 7-1 Wt. 230 College—North Dakota State

Yr	Team	G	FG	FT	TP	Avg.
1946-47	St. Louis-Tor.	21	6	8	20	1.0

SILLIMAN, MIKE

b. May 4, 1944 Ht. 6-6 Wt. 225 Coll.—U.S. Mil. Acad.

Yr	Team	G	FG	FT	TP	Avg.
1970-71	Buffalo	36	36	19	91	2.5

SIMMONS, CONNIE

b. March 15, 1925 Ht. 6-8 Wt. 225

Yr	Team	G	FG	FT	TP	Avg.
1946-47	Boston	60	246	128	620	10.3
1947-48	Bos.-Balt.	45	162	62	386	8.6
1948-49	Baltimore	60	299	181	779	13.0
1949-50	New York	60	241	198	680	11.3
1950-51	New York	66	229	146	604	9.2
1951-52	New York	66	227	175	629	9.5
1952-53	New York	65	240	249	729	11.2
1953-54	New York	72	255	210	720	10.0
1954-55	Balt.-Syra.	36	137	72	346	9.6
1955-56	Rochester	68	144	78	366	5.4
	Totals	598	2180	1499	5859	9.8

SIMMONS, GRANT

Ht. 6-3 Wt. 190 College—Nebraska

Yr	Team	G	FG	FT	TP	Avg.
1967-68	Denver ABA	78	291 (1)	208	793	10.2
1968-69	Denver ABA	17	21 (1)	20	65	3.8
	Totals	95	312 (2)	228	858	9.0

Yr	Team	G	FG	FT	TP	Avg.

SIMMONS, JOHN

b. 1922 Ht. 6-1 Wt. 184 Coll.—New York University

1946-47	Boston	60	120	78	318	5.3

SIMON, WALT

b. Dec. 1, 1941 Ht. 6-6 Wt. 200 College—Benedict

1967-68	New Jersey ABA	78	432 (1)	169	1036	13.3
1968-69	New York ABA	68	564 (6)	290	1436	21.1
1969-70	New York ABA	81	453 (1)	178	1162	14.4
1970-71	Kentucky ABA	83	273 (1)	100	649	7.8
1971-72	Kentucky ABA	67	242 (1)	109	596	8.9
1972-73	Kentucky ABA	83	429 (3)	143	1010	12.2
1973-74	Kentucky ABA	80	231 (2)	57	525	6.6
	Totals	540	2624 (15)	1121	6414	11.9

SIMS, DOUG

b. June 29, 1943 Ht. 6-7 Wt. 195 Coll.—Kent State

1968-69	Cincinnati	4	2	0	4	1.0

SIMS, ROBERT

b. Oct. 9, 1938 Ht. 6-5 Wt. 220 College—Pepperdine

1961-62	L.A.-St. Louis	65	193	123	509	7.8
1967-68	Anaheim ABA	2	2 (0)	4	8	4.0
	Totals	67	195 (0)	127	517	7.7

SIMS, SCOTT

b. April 18, 1955 Ht. 6-1 Wt. 170 College—Missouri

1977-78	San Antonio	12	10	10	30	2.5

SINICOLA, EMILIO (Zeke)

b. 1930 Ht. 5-10 Wt. 165 College—Niagara

1951-52	Ft. Wayne	3	1	0	2	0.7
1953-54	Ft. Wayne	9	4	3	11	1.2
	Totals	12	5	3	13	1.1

SKINNER, TALVIN

b. Sept. 10, 1952 Ht. 6-5 Wt. 210 Coll.—Md. East. Shore

1974-75	Seattle	73	142	63	347	4.8
1975-76	Seattle	72	132	49	313	4.3
	Totals	145	274	112	660	4.6

SKOOG, MEYER (Whitey)

b. Nov. 2, 1926 Ht. 5-11 Wt. 180 Coll.—Minnesota

1951-52	Minneapolis	35	102	30	234	6.7
1952-53	Minneapolis	68	102	46	250	3.7
1953-54	Minneapolis	71	212	72	496	7.0
1954-55	Minneapolis	72	330	125	785	10.9
1955-56	Minneapolis	72	340	155	835	11.0
1956-57	Minneapolis	23	78	44	200	8.7
	Totals	341	1164	472	2800	8.2

SLADE, JEFFREY

b. March 1, 1941 Ht. 6-6 Wt. 220 College—Kenyon

1962-63	Chicago	3	2	0	4	1.3

SLAUGHTER, JIM

b. 1928 Ht. 6-11 Wt. 212 College—South Carolina

1951-52	Baltimore	28	53	41	147	5.3

SLOAN, JERRY (Spider)

b. March 28, 1942 Ht. 6-6 Wt. 195 Coll.—Evansville

1965-66	Baltimore	59	120	98	338	5.7
1966-67	Chicago	80	525	340	1390	17.4
1967-68	Chicago	77	369	289	1027	13.3
1968-69	Chicago	78	488	333	1309	16.8
1969-70	Chicago	53	310	207	827	15.6
1970-71	Chicago	80	592	278	1462	18.3
1971-72	Chicago	82	535	258	1328	16.2
1972-73	Chicago	69	301	94	696	10.1
1973-74	Chicago	77	412	194	1018	13.2
1974-75	Chicago	78	380	193	953	12.2
1975-76	Chicago	22	84	55	223	10.1
	Totals	755	4116	2339	10571	14.0

SMAWLEY, BELUS

b. 1921 Ht. 6-1½ Wt. 195 Coll.—Appalachian State

1946-47	St. Louis	22	113	36	262	11.9
1947-48	St. Louis	48	212	111	535	11.2
1948-49	St. Louis	59	352	210	914	15.5
1949-50	St. Louis	61	287	260	834	13.7
1950-51	Syr.-Balt.	60	252	227	731	12.2
	Totals	250	1216	844	3276	13.1

SMILEY, JACK (Smiles)

b. Dec. 22, 1922 Ht. 6-3 Wt. 190 College—Illinois

1947-48	Ft. Wayne NL	60	105	90	300	5.0
1948-49	Ft. Wayne	59	141	112	394	6.7
1949-50	And.-Waterloo	59	98	136	332	5.6
	Totals	178	344	338	1026	5.8

SMITH, ADRIAN (Odie)

b. Oct. 5, 1936 Ht. 6-1 Wt. 180 College—Kentucky

1961-62	Cincinnati	80	202	172	576	7.2
1962-63	Cincinnati	79	241	223	705	8.9
1963-64	Cincinnati	66	234	154	622	9.4
1964-65	Cincinnati	80	463	284	1210	15.1
1965-66	Cincinnati	80	531	408	1470	18.4
1966-67	Cincinnati	81	502	343	1347	16.6
1967-68	Cincinnati	82	480	320	1280	15.6
1968-69	Cincinnati	73	243	217	703	9.6
1969-70	Cin.-S.F.	77	153	152	458	5.9
1970-71	San Francisco	21	38	35	111	5.3
1971-72	Virginia ABA	53	85 (2)	92	268	5.1
	Totals	772	3172 (2)	2400	8750	11.3

SMITH, ALAN

b. Jan. 15, 1947 Ht. 6-1 Wt. 185 College—Bradley

1971-72	Denver ABA	83	260 (32)	153	769	9.3
1972-73	Denver ABA	83	298 (17)	272	919	11.1
1973-74	Denver ABA	76	289 (22)	187	831	10.9
1974-75	Utah ABA	80	191 (34)	157	641	8.0
1975-76	Utah ABA	15	36 (6)	48	138	9.2
	Totals	337	1074 (111)	817	3298	9.8

Yr	Team	G	FG	FT	TP	Avg.
SMITH, BILL						
b. Feb. 14, 1949 Ht. 7-0½ Wt. 220 College—Syracuse						
1971-72	Portland	22	72	38	182	8.3
1972-73	Portland	8	9	5	23	2.9
	Totals	30	81	43	205	6.8
SMITH, DELBERT (Deb)						
b. Jan. 7, 1920 Ht. 6-3 Wt. 180 College—Utah						
1946-47	St. Louis	48	32	9	73	1.5
SMITH, DON						
b. 1920 Ht. 6-2 Wt. 190 College—Minnesota						
1942-43	Oshkosh NL	13	22	15	59	4.5
1945-46	Oshkosh NL	9	1	6	8	0.9
1946-47	Osh.-Ind. NL	12	5	5	15	1.3
1947-48	Minneapolis NL	57	69	62	200	3.5
1948-49	Minneapolis	8	2	2	6	0.8
	Totals	99	99	90	288	2.9
SMITH, DON						
b. Oct. 10, 1951 Ht. 6-0 Wt. 160 College—Dayton						
1974-75	Philadelphia	54	131	21	283	5.2
SMITH, EDWARD						
b. July 5, 1929 Ht. 6-6 Wt. 195 College—Harvard						
1953-54	New York	11	11	6	28	2.5
SMITH, GARFIELD						
b. Nov. 18, 1945 Ht. 6-9 Wt. 235 Coll.—Eastern KY						
1970-71	Boston	37	42	22	106	2.9
1971-72	Boston	26	28	6	62	2.4
1972-73	San Diego ABA	71	116 (0)	28	260	3.7
	Totals	134	186 (0)	56	428	3.2
SMITH, GREG						
b. Jan. 28, 1947 Ht. 6-5 Wt. 195 Coll.—W. Kentucky						
1968-69	Milwaukee	79	276	91	643	8.1
1969-70	Milwaukee	82	339	125	803	9.8
1970-71	Milwaukee	82	409	141	959	11.7
1971-72	Mil.-Hou.	82	309	111	729	8.9
1972-73	Hou.-Port.	76	234	75	543	7.1
1973-74	Portland	67	99	48	246	3.7
1974-75	Portland	55	71	32	174	3.2
1975-76	Portland	1	0	0	0	0.0
	Totals	524	1737	623	4097	7.8
SMITH, JOHN, JR.						
b. May 24, 1944 Ht. 7-0 Wt. 235 Coll.—Sthrn Colo.						
1968-69	Dallas ABA	77	246 (0)	116	608	7.9
1969-70	Dallas-Pitt-N.Y. ABA	70	105 (0)	56	266	3.8
	Totals	147	351 (0)	172	847	5.9
SMITH, KEN						
b. July 12, 1953 Ht. 6-7 Wt. 185 College—Tulsa						
1975-76	San Antonio ABA	19	33(1)	13	82	4.3

Yr	Team	G	FG	FT	TP	Avg.
SMITH, PETE						
b. 1950 Ht. 6-6 Wt. 205 College—Valdosta State						
1972-73	San Diego ABA	5	2	0	4	0.8
SMITH, ROBERT						
b. Aug. 20, 1937 Ht. 6-4 Wt. 190 Coll.—West Virginia						
1959-60	Minneapolis	10	13	11	37	3.7
1961-62	Los Angeles	3	0	0	0	0.0
	Totals	13	13	11	37	2.8
SMITH, SAM						
b. Jan. 27, 1944 Ht. 6-7 Wt. 230 College—Louisville and Kentucky Wesleyan						
1967-68	Minnesota ABA	77	282 (2)	185	755	9.8
1968-69	Kentucky ABA	62	172 (1)	114	461	7.4
1969-70	Kentucky ABA	81	306 (1)	163	778	9.6
1970-71	Ky.-Utah ABA	35	38 (1)	24	103	2.5
	Totals	255	798 (5)	486	2097	8.2
SMITH, THOMAS						
b. 1929 Ht. 6-1 Wt. 165 College—St. Peter's						
1951-52	New York	1	0	4	4	4.0
SMITH, WILLIAM						
b. April 26, 1939 Ht. 6-5 Wt. 190 College—St. Peter's						
1961-62	New York	9	8	7	23	2.6
SMYTH, JOSEPH						
b. 1929 Ht. 6-3½ Wt. 215 College—Niagara						
1953-54	Baltimore	40	48	35	131	3.3
SOBEK, GEORGE (Chips)						
b. Feb. 10, 1920 Ht. 6-0½ Wt. 180 Coll.—Notre Dame						
1945-46	Indianapolis NL	1	2	1	5	5.0
1946-47	Toledo	42	186	179	551	13.1
1947-48	Toledo NL	48	118	124	360	7.5
1948-49	Hammond NL	57	143	232	518	9.1
1949-50	Sheboygan	60	95	156	346	5.8
	Totals	208	544	692	1780	8.6
SOBIESZCZYK, RON (Sobie)						
b. Sept. 21, 1934 Ht. 6-3 Wt. 195 College—DePaul						
1956-57	New York	71	166	152	484	6.8
1957-58	New York	55	217	196	630	11.5
1958-59	New York	50	144	112	400	8.0
1959-60	N.Y.-Minn.	16	37	31	105	6.6
	Totals	192	564	491	1619	8.4
SOJOURNER, MIKE						
b. Oct. 16, 1953 Ht. 6-9 Wt. 225 College—Utah						
1974-75	Atlanta	73	378	95	851	11.7
1975-76	Atlanta	67	248	80	576	8.6
1976-77	Atlanta	51	95	41	231	4.5
	Totals	191	721	216	1658	8.7

Yr	Team	G	FG	FT	TP	Avg.

SOJOURNER, WILLIE

b. Sept. 10, 1948 Ht. 6-8 Wt. 225 College—Weber State

Yr	Team	G	FG	FT	TP	Avg.
1971-72	Virginia ABA	84	222 (0)	124	568	6.8
1972-73	Virginia ABA	64	199 (0)	84	482	7.5
1973-74	New York ABA	82	202 (0)	54	458	5.6
1974-75	New York ABA	79	154 (1)	49	360	4.6
	Totals	309	777 (1)	311	1868	6.0

SOMERSET, WILLARD (Willie)

b. March 17, 1942 Ht. 5-10 Wt. 190 College—Duquesne

Yr	Team	G	FG	FT	TP	Avg.
1965-66	Baltimore	8	18	9	45	5.6
1967-68	Houston ABA	61	434 (33)	359	1326	21.7
1968-69	Hou.-N.Y. ABA	74	583 (36)	484	1758	23.8
	Totals	143	1035 (69)	852	3129	21.9

SORENSON, DAVE

b. July 8, 1948 Ht. 6-8 Wt. 227 College—Ohio State

Yr	Team	G	FG	FT	TP	Avg.
1970-71	Cleveland	79	353	229	890	11.3
1971-72	Cleveland	76	213	106	532	7.0
1972-73	Cleve.-Phila.	58	124	64	312	5.4
	Totals	213	690	354	1734	8.1

SOVRAN, GINO

Ht. 6-2 Wt. 175 College—Assumption (Ont.)

Yr	Team	G	FG	FT	TP	Avg.
1946-47	Toronto	6	5	1	11	1.8

SPAIN, KEN

b. Oct. 6, 1946 Ht. 6-9 Wt. 235 College—Houston

Yr	Team	G	FG	FT	TP	Avg.
1970-71	Pittsburgh ABA	11	8 (0)	8	24	2.2

SPARKS, DAN

b. April 17, 1945 Ht. 6-8 Wt. 200 College—Vincennes and Weber State

Yr	Team	G	FG	FT	TP	Avg.
1968-69	Miami ABA	64	153 (0)	113	419	6.5
1969-70	Miami ABA	3	7 (0)	5	19	6.3
	Totals	67	160 (0)	118	438	6.5

SPARROW, GUY

b. Nov. 2, 1932 Ht. 6-6 Wt. 218 College—Detroit

Yr	Team	G	FG	FT	TP	Avg.
1957-58	New York	72	318	165	801	11.1
1958-59	N.Y.-Phila.	67	129	78	336	5.0
1959-60	Philadelphia	11	14	2	30	2.7
	Totals	150	461	245	1167	7.8

SPEARS, MARION (Odie)

b. June 26, 1925 Ht. 6-5 Wt. 205 Coll.—W. Kentucky

Yr	Team	G	FG	FT	TP	Avg.
1948-49	Chicago	57	200	131	531	9.3
1949-50	Chicago	57	227	158	712	12.5
1951-52	Rochester	66	225	116	566	8.6
1952-53	Rochester	62	198	199	595	9.6
1953-54	Rochester	72	184	183	551	7.7
1954-55	Rochester	71	226	220	672	9.5
1955-56	Ft. Wayne	72	166	159	491	6.8
1956-57	Ft. W.-St. Lou.	11	12	19	43	3.9
	Totals	468	1488	1185	4161	8.8

SPECTOR, ARTHUR (Speed)

b. Oct. 17, 1920 Ht. 6-4 Wt. 200 College—Villanova

Yr	Team	G	FG	FT	TP	Avg.
1946-47	Boston	55	123	83	329	6.0
1947-48	Boston	48	67	60	194	4.0
1948-49	Boston	59	130	64	324	5.5
1949-50	Boston	7	2	1	5	0.7
	Totals	169	322	208	852	5.0

SPICER, LOU

b. 1923 Ht. 6-2 Wt. 195 College—Syracuse

Yr	Team	G	FG	FT	TP	Avg.
1946-47	Providence	4	0	1	1	0.3

SPITZER, CRAIG

Ht. 7-0 Wt. 220 College—Tulane

Yr	Team	G	FG	FT	TP	Avg.
1967-68	Chicago	10	8	2	18	1.8

SPOELSTRA, ART

b. Sept. 11, 1932 Ht. 6-9 Wt. 220 Coll.—W. Kentucky

Yr	Team	G	FG	FT	TP	Avg.
1954-55	Rochester	70	159	108	426	6.1
1955-56	Rochester	72	226	163	615	8.5
1956-57	Rochester	69	217	88	522	7.6
1957-58	Minn.-N.Y.	67	161	127	449	6.7
	Totals	278	763	486	2012	7.2

SPRAGGINS, BRUCE

b. 1940 Ht. 6-5 Wt. 190 College—Virginia Union

Yr	Team	G	FG	FT	TP	Avg.
1967-68	New Jersey ABA	70	304 (2)	238	852	12.2

SPRINGER, JIM

b. 1924 Ht. 6-9 Wt. 235 College—Canterbury

Yr	Team	G	FG	FT	TP	Avg.
1947-48	And.-Ind NL	25	12	25	49	2.0
1948-49	Indianapolis	2	0	1	1	0.5
	Totals	27	12	26	50	1.9

SPRUILL, JIM

Ht. 6-2½ Wt. 225 College—Rice

Yr	Team	G	FG	FT	TP	Avg.
1948-49	Indianapolis	1	1	0	2	2.0

STAGGS, ERV

Ht. 6-6 Wt. 195 College—North Carolina A & T

Yr	Team	G	FG	FT	TP	Avg.
1969-70	Miami ABA	53	187 (2)	73	453	8.5

STALLWORTH, BUD

b. Jan. 18, 1950 Ht. 6-5 Wt. 190 College—Kansas

Yr	Team	G	FG	FT	TP	Avg.
1972-73	Seattle	77	198	86	482	6.3
1973-74	Seattle	67	188	48	424	6.3
1974-75	New Orleans	73	298	125	721	9.9
1975-76	New Orleans	56	211	85	507	9.1
1976-77	New Orleans	40	126	17	269	6.7
	Totals	313	1021	361	2403	7.7

STALLWORTH, DAVID (The Rave)

b. Dec. 20, 1941 Ht. 6-7 Wt. 200 Coll.—Wichita State

Yr	Team	G	FG	FT	TP	Avg.
1965-66	New York	80	373	258	1004	12.6
1966-67	New York	76	380	229	989	13.0
1969-70	New York	82	239	161	639	7.8
1970-71	New York	81	295	169	759	9.4
1971-72	N.Y.-Balt.	78	336	152	824	10.6
1972-73	Baltimore	73	180	78	438	6.0
1973-74	Capital	45	75	47	197	4.4
1974-75	New York	7	5	0	10	1.4
	Totals	522	1883	1094	4860	9.3

Yr	Team	G	FG	FT	TP	Avg.

STANCZAK, EDMUND (Moose)

b. Aug. 15, 1921 Ht. 6-1½ Wt. 205

Yr	Team	G	FG	FT	TP	Avg.
1946-47	Anderson NL	44	142	118	402	9.1
1947-48	Anderson NL	55	73	61	207	3.8
1948-49	Anderson NL	64	191	202	584	9.1
1949-50	Anderson	57	159	203	521	9.1
1950-51	Boston	17	11	35	57	3.4
	Totals	237	576	619	1771	7.5

STARR, KEITH

b. March 14, 1954 Ht. 6-7 Wt. 200 Coll.—Pittsburgh

1976-77	Chicago	17	6	2	14	0.8

STAVERMAN, LARRY

b. Oct. 11, 1936 Ht. 6-7 Wt. 205 Coll.—Villa Madonna

1958-59	Cincinnati	57	101	45	247	4.3
1959-60	Cincinnati	49	70	47	187	3.8
1960-61	Cincinnati	66	111	79	301	4.6
1962-63	Chicago	33	94	49	237	7.2
1963-64	Bt.-Det.-Cinn.	60	98	69	265	4.4
	Totals	265	474	289	1237	4.7

STEPHENS, JACK

b. May 18, 1933 Ht. 6-3 Wt. 185 Coll.—Notre Dame

1955-56	St. Louis	72	248	247	743	10.3

STEVENS, WAYNE

b. June 19, 1936 Ht. 6-3½ Wt. 185 College—Cincinnati

1959-60	Cincinnati	8	3	7	13	1.6

STEWART, DENNIS

b. April 11, 1947 Ht. 6-6 Wt. 220 College—Michigan

1970-71	Baltimore	2	1	2	4	2.0
1970-71	Floridians ABA	10	14 (0)	5	36	3.6
	Totals	12	15 (0)	7	40	3.3

STEWART, NORMAN

b. Jan. 20, 1935 Ht. 6-5 Wt. 205 College—Missouri

1956-57	St. Louis	5	4	2	10	2.0

STITH, SAM

b. July 22, 1937 Ht. 6-2 Wt. 185 Coll.—St. Bonaventure

1961-62	New York	32	59	23	141	4.4

STITH, THOMAS

b. Jan. 21, 1939 Ht. 6-5 Wt. 210 Coll.—St. Bonaventure

1962-63	New York	25	37	3	77	3.1

STIVALL, PAUL

b. Aug. 16, 1948 Ht. 6-5 Wt. 225 Coll.—Arizona State

1972-73	Phoenix	25	26	24	76	3.0
1973-74	San Diego ABA	13	36 (0)	28	100	7.7
	Totals	38	62 (0)	52	176	4.6

STOKES, MAURICE (Mo)

b. June 17, 1933 Ht. 6-7 Wt. 240 Coll.—St. Francis (Pa.)
d. Apr. 6, 1970

1955-56	Rochester	67	403	319	1125	16.8
1956-57	Rochester	72	434	256	1124	15.6
1957-58	Cincinnati	63	414	238	1066	16.9
	Totals	202	1251	813	3315	16.4

STOLKEY, ARTHUR

b. Oct. 23, 1920 Ht. 6-1 Wt. 180 College—Detroit

1946-47	Detroit	23	36	30	102	4.4

STOLL, RANDY

Ht. 6-7 Wt. 235 College—Washington State

1967-68	Anaheim ABA	25	66 (0)	10	142	5.7

STONE, GEORGE (Radar)

b. Feb. 9, 1946 Ht. 6-7 Wt. 195 College—Marshall

1968-69	Los Angeles ABA	74	409 (28)	261	1163	15.7
1969-70	Los Angeles ABA	83	447 (65)	239	1328	16.0
1970-71	Utah ABA	78	323 (50)	121	917	11.8
1971-72	Utah-Car. ABA	24	48 (1)	25	124	4.5
	Totals	259	1227 (144)	646	3532	13.6

STRAWDER, JOSEPH

b. Sept. 21, 1940 Ht. 6-10 Wt. 235 College—Bradley

1965-66	Detroit	79	250	176	676	8.6
1966-67	Detroit	79	281	188	750	9.4
1967-68	Detroit	73	206	139	551	7.5
	Totals	231	737	503	1977	8.6

STRICKER, BILL

b. Jan. 22, 1948 Ht. 6-9 Wt. 210 College—Pacific

1970-71	Portland	1	2	0	4	4.0

STRICKLAND, ROGER (The Rifle)

b. Sept. 4, 1940 Ht. 6-5 Wt. 200 College—Jacksonville

1963-64	Baltimore	1	1	0	2	2.0

STROUD, W. D. (Red)

b. May 2, 1941 Ht. 6-1 Wt. 160 Coll.—Mississippi State

1967-68	New Orleans ABA	7	4 (1)	9	20	2.9

STUMP, EUGENE

b. Nov. 13, 1923 Ht. 6-2½ Wt. 185 College—DePaul

1947-48	Boston	43	59	24	142	3.3
1948-49	Boston	56	193	92	478	8.5
1949-50	Minn.-Waterloo	49	63	37	163	3.3
	Totals	148	315	153	783	5.3

STUTZ, STAN (Stanley Modzelewski)

b. April 14, 1920 Ht. 5-11 Wt. 175 Coll.—Rhode Is.

1946-47	New York	60	172	133	477	8.0
1947-48	New York	47	109	113	331	7.0
1948-49	Baltimore	59	121	131	373	6.3
	Totals	166	402	377	1181	7.1

Yr	Team	G	FG	FT	TP	Avg.
SUITER, GARY						
b. Jan. 18, 1945 Ht. 6-9 Wt. 235 Coll.—Midwestern						
1970-71	Cleveland	30	19	4	42	1.4
SUNDERLAGE, DON						
b. Dec. 20, 1929 Ht. 6-1 Wt. 180 College—Illinois						
1953-54	Milwaukee	68	254	252	760	11.2
1954-55	Minneapolis	45	33	48	114	2.5
	Totals	113	287	300	874	7.7
SURHOFF, RICHARD						
b. 1932 Ht. 6-4 Wt. 210 Coll.—L. I. Univ. & J. Marshall						
1952-53	New York	26	13	19	45	1.7
1953-54	Milwaukee	32	43	47	133	4.2
	Totals	58	56	66	178	3.1
SUTOR, GEORGE						
b. Sept. 14, 1943 Ht. 6-8 Wt. 240 College—LaSalle						
1967-68	Kentucky ABA	1	0 (0)	0	0	0.0
1968-69	Minnesota ABA	64	139 (0)	71	349	5.5
1969-70	Car.-Mia. ABA	14	12 (0)	7	31	2.2
	Totals	79	151 (0)	78	380	4.8
SWAGERTY, KEITH						
b. Oct. 30, 1945 Ht. 6-7 Wt. 235 College—Pacific						
1968-69	Houston ABA	77	362 (0)	256	980	12.7
1969-70	Kentucky ABA	3	2 (0)	3	7	2.3
	Totals	80	364 (0)	259	987	12.3
SWAIN, BENNIE						
b. Dec. 16, 1933 Ht. 6-8 Wt. 222 Coll.—Texas Southern						
1958-59	Boston	58	99	67	265	4.6
SWANSON, NORMAN						
b. 1930 Ht. 6-6 Wt. 212 College—Detroit						
1953-54	Rochester	63	31	38	100	1.6
SWARTZ, DAN						
b. Dec. 23, 1934 Ht. 6-4 Wt. 215 Coll.—Morehead St.						
1962-63	Boston	39	57	61	175	4.5
SWIFT, HARLEY (Skeeter)						
b. June 19, 1946 Ht. 6-3 Wt. 210 Coll.—Middle Tenn.						
1969-70	New Orleans ABA	66	177 (38)	139	607	9.2
1970-71	Mem.-Pitt. ABA	80	363 (39)	206	1049	13.1
1971-72	Pittsburgh ABA	79	368 (33)	224	1059	13.4
1972-73	Dallas ABA	42	158 (19)	128	501	11.9
1973-74	San Antonio ABA	16	22 (1)	16	63	3.9
	Totals	283	1088 (130)	713	3279	11.6

Yr	Team	G	FG	FT	TP	Avg.
SYDNOR, WALLACE (Buck)						
b. Sept. 19, 1921 Ht. 5-10 Wt. 175 Coll.—W. Kentucky						
1946-47	Chicago	15	5	5	15	1.0
SZCZERBIAK, WALT						
b. Aug. 21, 1949 Ht. 6-6 Wt. 210 Coll.—Geo. Washington						
1971-72	Pittsburgh ABA	53	149 (0)	35	333	6.3
TANENBAUM, SIDNEY						
b. Oct. 8, 1925 Ht. 6-0 Wt. 160 Coll.—N.Y. University						
1947-48	New York	24	90	62	242	10.1
1948-49	N.Y.-Balt.	46	146	99	391	8.5
	Totals	70	236	161	633	9.0
TART, LEVERN DONIHUE (Doc)						
b. June 1, 1942 Ht. 6-3 Wt. 195 College—Bradley						
1967-68	Oak.-N.J. ABA	73	632 (1)	451	1718	22.5
1968-69	N.Y.-Hous.- Den. ABA	61	274 (0)	193	741	12.2
1969-70	New York ABA	80	745 (11)	412	1935	24.1
1970-71	N.Y.-Tex. ABA	60	347 (10)	198	922	15.4
	Totals	274	1998 (22)	1254	5316	19.4
TAYLOR, FRED						
b. Feb. 5, 1948 Ht. 6-5 Wt. 187 Coll.—Pan American						
1970-71	Phoenix	54	110	78	298	5.5
1971-72	Pho.-Cin.	34	36	15	87	2.6
	Totals	88	146	93	385	4.3
TAYLOR, OLLIE						
b. March 7, 1947 Ht. 6-2 Wt. 194 College—Houston						
1970-71	New York ABA	80	246 (5)	187	694	8.7
1971-72	New York ABA	82	245 (0)	218	708	8.6
1972-73	San Diego ABA	69	314 (11)	286	947	13.7
1973-74	N.Y.-Car. ABA	31	63 (2)	58	190	6.1
	Totals	262	868 (18)	749	2539	9.7
TAYLOR, ROLAND (Fatty)						
b. March 13, 1946 Ht. 6-0 Wt. 175 College—LaSalle						
1969-70	Washington ABA	83	242 (1)	178	665	8.0
1970-71	Virginia ABA	84	176 (4)	175	539	6.4
1971-72	Virginia ABA	84	305 (1)	164	777	9.3
1972-73	Virginia ABA	78	313 (3)	150	785	10.1
1973-74	Virginia ABA	80	289 (3)	185	772	9.7
1974-75	Denver ABA	76	245 (6)	129	637	8.4
1975-76	Virginia ABA	76	232 (11)	125	622	8.2
1976-77	Denver	79	132	37	301	3.8
	Totals	640	1934 (29)	1143	5098	8.0

Yr	Team	G	FG	FT	TP	Avg.
TAYLOR, RON						
b. Nov. 21, 1946 Ht. 7-1 Wt. 265 College—Sthrn Cal.						
1969-70	Wash.-N.Y. ABA	75	156 (0)	57	369	4.9
1970-71	Virginia ABA	1	1 (0)	0	2	2.0
1971-72	Pittsburgh ABA	1	0 (0)	0	0	0.0
	Totals	77	157 (0)	57	371	4.8
TEMPLE, COLLIS						
b. Nov. 8, 1952 Ht. 6-8 Wt. 220 College—LSU						
1974-75	San Antonio ABA	24	17 (0)	8	42	1.8 (0)
TERRY, CHUCK						
b. Sept. 27, 1950 Ht. 6-6 Wt. 215 Coll.—Long Beach St.						
1972-73	Milwaukee	67	55	17	127	1.9
1973-74	Milwaukee	7	4	0	8	1.1
1973-74	San Antonio ABA	61	131 (1)	36	301	4.9
1974-75	San Antonio ABA	79	145 (3)	39	338	4.3
1975-76	New York ABA	66	90 (6)	22	220	3.3
1976-77	N.Y. Nets	61	128	48	304	5.0
	Totals	341	553 (10)	162	1298	3.8
TERRY, CLAUDE						
b. Jan. 12, 1950 Ht. 6-5 Wt. 195 College—Stanford						
1972-73	Denver ABA	68	110 (10)	74	324	4.8
1973-74	Denver ABA	60	99 (14)	60	300	5.0
1974-75	Denver ABA	70	183 (10)	70	466	6.7
1975-76	Denver ABA	79	219 (13)	80	557	7.1
1976-77	Buffalo-Atl.	45	96	36	228	5.1
1977-78	Atlanta	27	25	9	59	2.2
	Totals	349	732 (47)	329	1934	5.5
THACKER, TOM (Tack)						
b. Nov. 2, 1939 Ht. 6-2 Wt. 170 College—Cincinnati						
1963-64	Cincinnati	48	53	26	132	2.8
1964-65	Cincinnati	55	56	23	135	2.5
1965-66	Cincinnati	50	84	15	183	3.7
1967-68	Boston	65	114	43	271	4.2
1968-69	Indiana ABA	18	40 (0)	18	98	5.4
1969-70	Indiana ABA	70	60 (10)	38	188	2.7
1970-71	Indiana ABA	8	6 (0)	1	13	1.6
	Totals	314	413 (10)	164	1020	3.2
THEARD, FLOYD						
b. Sept. 5, 1944 Ht. 6-1 Wt. 170 Coll.—Kentucky State						
1969-70	Denver ABA	25	39 (0)	18	96	3.8

Yr	Team	G	FG	FT	TP	Avg.
THIEBEN, WILLIAM						
Ht. 6-7 Wt. 215 College—Hofstra						
1956-57	Ft. Wayne	58	90	57	237	4.1
1957-58	Detroit	27	42	16	100	3.7
	Totals	85	132	73	337	4.0
THIGPEN, JUSTUS						
College—Weber State						
1969-70	Pittsburgh ABA	3	5 (0)	1	11	3.7
THOMAS, JOE						
b. March 9, 1948 Ht. 6-5 Wt. 205 Coll.—Marquette						
1970-71	Phoenix	39	23	9	55	1.4
THOMAS, RON						
b. Nov. 19, 1950 Ht. 6-6 Wt. 215 College—Louisville						
1972-73	Kentucky ABA	31	62 (0)	21	145	4.7
1973-74	Kentucky ABA	71	127 (1)	37	294	4.1
1974-75	Kentucky ABA	79	189 (1)	58	439	4.3
1975-76	Kentucky ABA	83	133 (1)	55	324	3.9
	Totals	264	511 (3)	171	1202	4.5
THOMAS, TERRY						
b. Aug. 20, 1953 Ht. 6-8 Wt. 220 College—Detroit						
1975-76	Detroit	28	28	21	77	2.8
THOMAS, WILLIS						
Ht. 6-2 Wt. 185 College—Harbor Junior College						
1967-68	Den.-Ana. ABA	62	243 (0)	69	555	9.0
THOMPSON, GEORGE						
b. Nov. 29, 1947 Ht. 6-2 Wt. 215 College—Marquette						
1969-70	Pittsburgh ABA	54	252 (7)	176	701	12.9
1970-71	Pittsburgh ABA	82	552 (23)	347	1520	18.5
1971-72	Pittsburgh ABA	70	655 (41)	455	1888	27.0
1972-73	Memphis ABA	80	559 (20)	549	1727	21.6
1973-74	Memphis ABA	78	529 (10)	410	1498	19.2
1974-75	Milwaukee	73	306	168	780	10.7
	Totals	437	2853 (101)	2105	8114	18.6
THOMPSON, JACK						
Ht. 6-1 Wt. 185 College—South Carolina						
1968-69	Indiana ABA	2	1 (0)	0	2	1.0
THOMPSON, JOHN						
b. Sept. 2, 1941 Ht. 6-10 Wt. 230 College—Providence						
1964-65	Boston	64	84	62	230	3.6
1965-66	Boston	10	14	4	32	3.2
	Totals	74	98	66	262	3.5

Yr	Team	G	FG	FT	TP	Avg.

THOREN, DUANE (Skip)

b. April 5, 1943 Ht. 6-10 Wt. 230 College—Illinois

Yr	Team	G	FG	FT	TP	Avg.
1967-68	Minnesota ABA	63	206 (0)	102	514	8.2
1968-69	Miami ABA	78	532 (0)	241	1305	16.7
1969-70	Miami ABA	29	164 (0)	92	420	14.5
	Totals	170	902 (0)	435	2239	13.2

THORN, ROD

b. May 23, 1941 Ht. 6-4 Wt. 195 Coll.—W. Virginia

1963-64	Baltimore	75	411	258	1080	14.4
1964-65	Detroit	74	320	176	816	11.0
1965-66	Det.-St. Lou.	73	306	168	780	10.7
1966-67	St. Louis	67	233	125	591	8.8
1967-68	Seattle	66	377	252	1006	15.2
1968-69	Seattle	29	131	71	333	11.5
1969-70	Seattle	19	20	15	55	2.9
1970-71	Seattle	63	141	69	351	5.6
	Totals	466	1939	1134	5012	10.8

THORTON, DALLAS

b. Sept. 1, 1946 Ht. 6-4 Wt. 190 College—Kentucky Wesleyan

1968-69	Miami ABA	45	106 (2)	79	297	6.6
1969-70	Miami ABA	5	15 (0)	14	44	8.8
	Totals	50	121 (2)	93	341	6.8

THURMOND, NATE

b. July 25, 1941 Ht. 6-11 Wt. 225 Coll.—Bowling Green

1963-64	San Francisco	76	219	95	533	7.0
1964-65	San Francisco	77	519	235	1273	16.5
1965-66	San Francisco	73	454	280	1188	16.3
1966-67	San Francisco	65	467	280	1214	18.7
1967-68	San Francisco	51	382	282	1046	20.5
1968-69	San Francisco	71	571	382	1524	21.5
1969-70	San Francisco	43	341	261	943	21.9
1970-71	San Francisco	82	623	395	1641	20.0
1971-72	Golden St.	78	628	417	1673	21.4
1972-73	Golden St.	79	517	315	1349	17.1
1973-74	Golden St.	62	308	191	807	13.0
1974-75	Chicago	80	250	132	632	7.9
1975-76	Chi.-Cleve.	78	142	62	346	4.4
1976-77	Cleveland	49	100	68	268	5.5
	Totals	964	5521	3395	14437	15.0

THURSTON, MEL

Ht. 6-0 Wt. 175 College—Canisius

1946-47	Buf.-Tri-C. NL	39	39	36	114	2.9
1947-48	Tri-Cities NL	34	36	38	110	3.2
1947-48	Providence	14	32	14	78	5.6
	Totals	87	107	88	302	3.5

TIDRICK, HOWARD (Hal)

b. 1919 Ht. 6-1 Wt. 190 Coll.—Washington & Jefferson

1944-45	Sheboygan NL	1	0	0	0	0.0
1946-47	Toledo NL	44	232	115	579	13.2
1947-48	Toledo NL	59	267	189	723	12.3

Yr	Team	G	FG	FT	TP	Avg.
1948-49	Indianapolis-Balt.	61	194	164	552	9.0
	Totals	165	693	468	1854	11.2

TIEMAN, DANIEL

b. Nov. 30, 1940 Ht. 6-0 Wt. 185 Coll.—Villa Madonna

1962-63	Cincinnati	29	15	4	34	1.2

TINGLE, JACK

b. 1925 Ht. 6-4 Wt. 205 College—Kentucky

1947-48	Washington	37	36	17	89	2.4
1948-49	Minneapolis	2	1	0	2	1.0
	Totals	39	37	17	91	2.3

TINSLEY, GEORGE

b. Sept. 19, 1946 Ht. 6-5 Wt. 205 College—Kentucky Wesleyan

1969-70	Wash.-Ky. ABA	77	172 (1)	159	506	6.6
1971-72	Floridians ABA	51	65 (5)	46	191	3.8
	Totals	128	237 (6)	205	697	5.4

TODOROVICH, MARKO (Mike)

b. June 11, 1923 Ht. 6-5 Wt. 229 College—Notre Dame & Wyoming

1947-48	Sheboygan NL	60	277	223	777	13.0
1948-49	Sheboygan NL	60	239	170	648	10.8
1949-50	St. L.-Tri-C.	65	263	266	792	12.2
1950-51	Tri-Cities	66	221	211	653	9.9
	Totals	251	1000	870	2870	11.4

TOLSON, DEAN

b. Nov. 25, 1951 Ht. 6-8 Wt. 190 College—Arkansas

1974-75	Seattle	19	16	11	43	2.3
1976-77	Seattle	60	137	85	359	6.0
1977-78	Seattle	1	0	0	0	0.0
	Totals	80	153	96	402	5.1

TONKOVICH, ANDY

Ht. 6-1 Wt. 185 College—Marshall

1948-49	Providence	17	19	6	44	2.6

TOOMAY, JOHN

b. 1924 Ht. 6-6 Wt. 215 Coll.—College of Pacific

1947-48	Chic.-Prov.	23	61	60	182	7.9
1948-49	Balt.-Wash.	36	32	36	100	2.8
1949-50	Denver	62	204	186	594	9.6
	Totals	121	297	282	876	7.2

TORGOFF, IRVING

b. 1917 Ht. 6-2 Wt. 192 Coll.—Long Island University

1939-40	Detroit NL	26	64	43	171	6.6
1946-47	Washington	58	187	116	490	8.4
1947-48	Washington	47	111	117	339	7.2
1948-49	Balt.-Phila.	42	59	50	168	4.0
	Totals	173	421	326	1168	6.8

Yr	Team	G	FG	FT	TP	Avg.

TORMOHLEN, EUGENE
b. May 12, 1937 Ht. 6-9 Wt. 245 Coll.—Tennessee

Yr	Team	G	FG	FT	TP	Avg.
1962-63	St. Louis	7	5	2	12	1.7
1963-64	St. Louis	51	94	22	210	4.1
1965-66	St. Louis	71	144	54	342	4.8
1966-67	St. Louis	63	172	50	394	6.3
1967-68	St. Louis	77	98	33	229	3.0
1969-70	Atlanta	2	2	0	4	2.0
	Totals	271	515	161	1191	4.4

TOSHEFF, BILL
b. June 2, 1926 Ht. 6-1 Wt. 175 College—Indiana

Yr	Team	G	FG	FT	TP	Avg.
1951-52	Indianapolis	65	213	182	608	9.4
1952-53	Indianapolis	67	253	253	759	11.3
1953-54	Milwaukee	71	168	156	492	6.9
	Totals	203	634	591	1859	9.2

TOUGH, ROBERT (Red)
b. 1920 Ht. 6-0 Wt. 185 College—St. John's (N.Y.)

Yr	Team	G	FG	FT	TP	Avg.
1945-46	Ft. Wayne NL	5	12	5	29	5.8
1946-47	Ft. Wayne NL	44	124	55	303	6.9
1947-48	Ft. Wayne NL	60	129	48	306	5.1
1948-49	Ft. Wayne NL	53	183	100	466	8.8
1949-50	Balt.-Waterloo	29	43	37	123	4.2
	Totals	191	491	245	1227	6.4

TOWE, MONTE
b. Sept. 27, 1953 Ht. 5-7 Wt. 150 College—NC State

Yr	Team	G	FG	FT	TP	Avg.
1975-76	Denver ABA	64	63 (9)	36	189	3.0
1976-77	Denver	51	56	18	130	2.5
	Totals	115	119 (9)	54	319	2.8

TOWERY, CARLISLE (Blackie)
b. June 20, 1920 Ht. 6-4½ Wt. 210 Coll.—Western KY

Yr	Team	G	FG	FT	TP	Avg.
1941-42	Ft. Wayne NL	24	64	35	163	6.8
1942-43	Ft. Wayne NL	23	53	33	139	6.0
1943-44	Ft. Wayne NL	22	48	33	129	5.9
1944-45	Ft. Wayne NL	1	0	1	1	1.0
1946-47	Ft. Wayne NL	41	100	80	280	6.8
1947-48	Ft. Wayne NL	59	139	129	407	6.9
1948-49	Ft. W.-Ind.	60	203	195	601	10.0
1949-50	Baltimore	68	222	153	597	8.8
	Totals	298	829	659	2317	7.8

TRAPP, GEORGE
b. July 11, 1948 Ht. 6-8½ Wt. 200 Coll.—Long Beach St.

Yr	Team	G	FG	FT	TP	Avg.
1971-72	Atlanta	60	144	105	393	6.6
1972-73	Atlanta	77	359	150	868	11.3
1973-74	Detroit	82	333	99	765	9.3
1974-75	Detroit	78	288	99	675	8.7
1975-76	Detroit	76	278	63	619	8.1
1976-77	Detroit	6	15	3	33	5.5
	Totals	379	1417	519	3353	8.8

TRAPP, JOHN Q.
b. Oct. 2, 1945 Ht. 6-7 Wt. 215 Coll.—Nevada Southern

Yr	Team	G	FG	FT	TP	Avg.
1968-69	San Diego	25	29	19	77	3.1
1969-70	San Diego	70	185	72	442	6.3
1970-71	San Diego	82	322	142	786	9.6
1971-72	Los Angeles	58	139	51	329	5.7
1972-73	L.A.-Phila.	44	171	90	432	9.8
1972-73	Denver ABA	25	54 (0)	19	127	5.1
	Totals	304	900 (0)	393	2193	7.2

TRESVANT, JOHN
b. Nov. 6, 1939 Ht. 6-7 Wt. 215 College—Seattle

Yr	Team	G	FG	FT	TP	Avg.
1964-65	St. Louis	4	4	6	14	3.5
1965-66	St. L.-Det.	61	171	142	484	7.9
1966-67	Detroit	68	256	164	676	9.9
1967-68	Det.-Cin.	85	396	250	1042	12.3
1968-69	Cin.-Sea.	77	380	202	962	12.5
1969-70	Sea.-L.A.	69	264	206	734	10.6
1970-71	L.A.-Balt.	75	202	146	550	7.3
1971-72	Baltimore	65	162	121	445	6.8
1972-73	Baltimore	55	85	41	211	3.8
	Totals	559	1920	1278	5118	9.2

TRIPTOW, RICHARD (Tiptoe)
b. Nov. 3, 1922 Ht. 6-0 Wt. 170 College—DePaul

Yr	Team	G	FG	FT	TP	Avg.
1944-45	Chicago NL	30	113	73	299	10.0
1945-46	Chicago NL	34	68	85	221	6.5
1946-47	Chicago NL	44	59	60	178	4.0
1947-48	Tri-C.-Ft. W. NL	57	92	87	271	4.8
1948-49	Ft. Wayne	55	116	102	334	6.1
1949-50	Baltimore	4	0	2	2	0.5
	Totals	224	448	409	1305	5.8

TRUITT, ANSLEY
b. Aug. 24, 1950 Ht. 6-9 Wt. 215 College—California

Yr	Team	G	FG	FT	TP	Avg.
1972-73	Dallas ABA	16	18 (0)	3	39	2.4

TSCHOGL, JOHN
b. April 25, 1950 Ht. 6-6 Wt. 206 Coll.—Santa Barbara

Yr	Team	G	FG	FT	TP	Avg.
1972-73	Atlanta	10	14	2	30	3.0
1973-74	Atlanta	64	59	10	128	2.0
1974-75	Philadelphia	39	53	13	119	3.1
	Totals	113	126	25	277	2.5

TSIOROPOULOS, LOUIS
b. Aug. 31, 1930 Ht. 6-5 Wt. 195 College—Kentucky

Yr	Team	G	FG	FT	TP	Avg.
1956-57	Boston	52	79	69	227	4.4
1957-58	Boston	70	198	142	538	7.7
1958-59	Boston	35	60	25	145	4.1
	Totals	157	337	236	910	5.8

TUCKER, AL
b. Feb. 24, 1943 Ht. 6-8 Wt. 190 Coll.—OK Baptist

Yr	Team	G	FG	FT	TP	Avg.
1967-68	Seattle	81	437	186	1060	13.1
1968-69	Sea.-Cin.	84	361	158	880	10.5
1969-70	Chi.-Balt.	61	146	70	362	5.9
1970-71	Baltimore	31	52	25	129	4.2
1970-71	Florida ABA	14	63 (3)	34	169	12.1
1971-72	Floridians ABA	81	347 (30)	157	941	11.6
	Totals	352	1406 (33)	630	3541	10.1

Yr	Team	G	FG	FT	TP	Avg.

TUCKER, JAMES

b. Dec. 11, 1932 Ht. 6-7½ Wt. 185 Coll.—Duquesne

Yr	Team	G	FG	FT	TP	Avg.
1954-55	Syracuse	20	39	27	105	5.3
1955-56	Syracuse	70	101	66	268	3.8
1956-57	Syracuse	9	17	0	34	3.8
	Totals	99	157	93	407	4.1

TURNER, GARY

College—Texas Christian

Yr	Team	G	FG	FT	TP	Avg.
1967-68	Houston ABA	2	2 (0)	2	6	3.0

TURNER, HERSCHELL

Ht. 6-2 Wt. 195 College—Nebraska

Yr	Team	G	FG	FT	TP	Avg.
1967-68	Pitt.-Ana. ABA	41	45 (6)	23	131	3.2

TURNER, JACK

b. June 29, 1930 Ht. 6-4 Wt. 170 Coll.—W. Kentucky

Yr	Team	G	FG	FT	TP	Avg.
1954-55	New York	65	111	60	282	4.3

TURNER, JOHN

b. June 5, 1939 Ht. 6-5 Wt. 200 College—Louisville

Yr	Team	G	FG	FT	TP	Avg.
1961-62	Chicago	42	84	32	200	4.8

TURNER, WILLIAM

b. Feb. 18, 1944 Ht. 6-7 Wt. 220 College—Akron

Yr	Team	G	FG	FT	TP	Avg.
1967-68	San Fran.	42	68	36	172	4.1
1968-69	San Fran.	79	222	175	619	7.8
1969-70	S.F.-Cin.	72	197	123	517	7.2
1970-71	San Fran.	18	26	13	65	3.6
1971-72	Golden St.	62	71	40	182	2.9
	Totals	273	584	387	1555	5.7

TWYMAN, JACK

b. May 11, 1934 Ht. 6-6 Wt. 210 College—Cincinnati

Yr	Team	G	FG	FT	TP	Avg.
1955-56	Rochester	72	417	204	1038	14.4
1956-57	Rochester	72	449	276	1174	16.3
1957-58	Cincinnati	72	465	307	1237	17.2
1958-59	Cincinnati	72	710	437	1857	25.8
1959-60	Cincinnati	75	870	598	2338	31.2
1960-61	Cincinnati	79	796	405	1997	25.3
1961-62	Cincinnati	80	739	353	1831	22.9
1962-63	Cincinnati	80	641	304	1586	19.8
1963-64	Cincinnati	68	447	189	1083	19.9
1964-65	Cincinnati	80	479	198	1156	14.5
1965-66	Cincinnati	73	224	95	543	7.4
	Totals	823	6237	3366	15840	19.2

TYRA, CHARLES

b. Aug. 16, 1935 Ht. 6-8 Wt. 235 Coll.—Louisville

Yr	Team	G	FG	FT	TP	Avg.
1957-58	New York	68	175	150	500	7.4
1958-59	New York	69	240	129	609	8.8
1959-60	New York	74	406	133	945	12.8
1960-61	New York	59	199	120	518	8.8
1961-62	Chicago	78	193	133	519	6.6
	Totals	348	1213	665	3091	8.9

UPLINGER, HAL

b. 1920 Ht. 6-4 Wt. 185 Coll.—Long Island University

Yr	Team	G	FG	FT	TP	Avg.
1953-54	Baltimore	23	33	20	86	3.7

VACENDAK, STEVE

b. Aug. 15, 1944 Ht. 6-1½ Wt. 185 College—Duke

Yr	Team	G	FG	FT	TP	Avg.
1967-68	Pittsburgh ABA	9	13 (0)	10	36	4.0

Yr	Team	G	FG	FT	TP	Avg.
1968-69	Minnesota ABA	60	286 (2)	167	745	12.4
1969-70	Pitt.-Miami ABA	14	15 (0)	13	43	3.1
	Totals	83	314 (2)	190	824	9.9

VALLELY, JOHN

b. Oct. 3, 1948 Ht. 6-3 Wt. 185 College—UCLA

Yr	Team	G	FG	FT	TP	Avg.
1970-71	Atlanta	51	73	45	191	3.7
1971-72	Atl.-Hou.	49	69	30	168	3.4
	Totals	100	142	75	359	3.6

VAN ARSDALE, RICHARD

b. Feb. 22, 1943 Ht. 6-4½ Wt. 210 Coll.—Indiana

Yr	Team	G	FG	FT	TP	Avg.
1965-66	New York	79	359	251	969	12.3
1966-67	New York	79	410	371	1191	15.1
1967-68	New York	78	316	227	859	11.0
1968-69	Phoenix	80	612	454	1678	21.0
1969-70	Phoenix	77	592	459	1643	21.3
1970-71	Phoenix	81	609	553	1771	21.9
1971-72	Phoenix	82	545	529	1619	19.7
1972-73	Phoenix	81	532	426	1490	18.4
1973-74	Phoenix	78	514	361	1389	17.8
1974-75	Phoenix	70	421	282	1124	16.1
1975-76	Phoenix	58	276	195	747	12.9
1976-77	Phoenix	78	227	145	599	7.7
	Totals	921	5413	4253	15079	16.4

VAN ARSDALE, THOMAS

b. Feb. 22, 1943 Ht. 6-5 Wt. 215 College—Indiana

Yr	Team	G	FG	FT	TP	Avg.
1965-66	Detroit	79	312	209	833	10.5
1966-67	Detroit	79	347	272	966	12.2
1967-68	Det.-Cin.	77	211	188	610	7.9
1968-69	Cincinnati	77	547	398	1492	19.4
1969-70	Cincinnati	71	620	381	1621	22.8
1970-71	Cincinnati	82	749	377	1875	22.9
1971-72	Cincinnati	73	550	299	1399	19.2
1972-73	K.C.-O.-Phila.	79	445	250	1140	14.4
1973-74	Philadelphia	78	614	298	1526	19.6
1974-75	Phil.-Atl.	82	593	322	1508	18.4
1975-76	Atlanta	75	346	126	818	10.9
1976-77	Phoenix	77	171	102	444	5.8
	Totals	929	5505	3222	14232	15.3

VAN BREDA KOLFF, WILLIAM (Butch)

b. Oct. 28, 1922 Ht. 6-3 Wt. 185 Coll.—Princeton & NYU

Yr	Team	G	FG	FT	TP	Avg.
1946-47	New York	16	7	11	25	1.6
1947-48	New York	44	53	74	180	4.1
1948-49	New York	59	127	161	415	7.0
1949-50	New York	56	55	96	206	3.7
	Totals	175	242	342	826	4.7

VANCE, ELLIS (Gene)

b. Feb. 25, 1923 Ht. 6-3 Wt. 196 Coll.—Illinois

Yr	Team	G	FG	FT	TP	Avg.
1947-48	Chicago	48	163	76	402	8.4
1948-49	Chicago	56	222	131	575	10.3
1949-50	Tri-Cities	35	110	86	306	8.7
1950-51	Tri-Cities	28	44	43	131	4.7
1951-52	Milwaukee	7	7	9	23	3.3
	Totals	174	546	345	1437	8.3

VANDEWEGHE, ERNIE

b. Sept. 12, 1928 Ht. 6-3 Wt. 195 College—Colgate

Yr	Team	G	FG	FT	TP	Avg.
1949-50	New York	42	164	93	421	10.0
1950-51	New York	44	135	68	338	7.7
1951-52	New York	57	200	124	524	9.2
1952-53	New York	61	272	187	731	12.0
1953-54	New York	15	37	25	99	6.6
1955-56	New York	5	10	2	22	4.4
	Totals	224	818	499	2135	9.5

Yr	Team	G	FG	FT	TP	Avg.

VAN ZANT, DENNIS

b. June 1, 1952 Ht. 6-9 Wt. 210 Coll.—Azuza Pacific

Yr	Team	G	FG	FT	TP	Avg.
1975-76	San Antonio	1	0	2	2	2.0

VAUGHN, CHARLES (Chico)

b. Feb. 19, 1940 Ht. 6-3 Wt. 215 Coll.—Sthrn Illinois

Yr	Team	G	FG	FT	TP	Avg.
1962-63	St. Louis	77	295	188	778	10.1
1963-64	St. Louis	68	238	107	583	8.6
1964-65	St. Louis	75	344	182	870	11.6
1965-66	St. L.-Det.	56	182	106	470	8.4
1966-67	Detroit	51	85	50	220	4.3
1967-68	Pittsburgh ABA	74	375 (137)	308	1469	19.9
1968-69	Minnesota ABA	69	270 (145)	253	1228	17.8
1969-70	Pittsburgh ABA	21	42 (24)	48	204	9.7
	Totals	491	1831 (306)	1242	5822	11.9

VAUGHN, DAVID

b. June 4, 1952 Ht. 7-0 Wt. 220 College—Oral Roberts

Yr	Team	G	FG	FT	TP	Avg.
1974-75	Virginia ABA	83	422 (0)	125	969	11.7
1975-76	Virginia ABA	10	12 (0)	5	29	2.9
	Totals	93	434 (0)	130	998	10.7

VAUGHN, VIRGIL

Ht. 6-4 Wt. 205 College—Kentucky Wesleyan

Yr	Team	G	FG	FT	TP	Avg.
1946-47	Boston	17	15	15	45	2.6
1947-48	Syracuse NL	11	29	5	63	5.7
	Totals	28	44	20	108	3.9

VERGA, ROBERT BRUCE

b. Sept. 7, 1945 Ht. 6-1 Wt. 190 College—Duke

Yr	Team	G	FG	FT	TP	Avg.
1967-68	Dallas ABA	31	267 (13)	162	735	23.7
1968-69	Den.-N.Y.-Hou. ABA	63	397 (19)	336	1187	18.8
1969-70	Carolina ABA	82	801 (66)	458	2258	27.5
1970-71	Carolina ABA	75	540 (10)	302	1412	18.8
1971-72	Car.-Pitt. ABA	70	440 (19)	285	1222	17.5
1973-74	Portland	21	42	20	104	5.0
	Totals	342	2487 (127)	1563	6915	20.2

VIRDEN, CLAUDE

b. Nov. 25, 1947 Ht. 6-6 Wt. 200 College—Murray State

Yr	Team	G	FG	FT	TP	Avg.
1972-73	Kentucky ABA	31	130 (0)	46	306	9.9

VOLKER, FLOYD

b. June 21, 1921 Ht. 6-4 Wt. 205 College—Wyoming

Yr	Team	G	FG	FT	TP	Avg.
1947-48	Oshkosh NL	57	102	31	235	4.1
1948-49	Oshkosh NL	64	166	78	410	6.4
1949-50	Ind.-Denver	54	613	71	397	7.4
	Totals	175	431	180	1042	6.0

VON NIEDA, STANLEY (Whitey)

b. 1923 Ht. 6-1 Wt. 175 College—Penn State

Yr	Team	G	FG	FT	TP	Avg.
1947-48	Tri-Cities NL	60	276	174	726	12.1
1948-49	Tri-Cities NL	64	247	147	641	10.0
1949-50	Tri-Cities Balt.	59	120	73	313	5.3
	Totals	183	643	394	1680	9.2

WAGER, CLINT

b. 1921 Ht. 6-6 Wt. 230 College—St. Mary's (Minn.)

Yr	Team	G	FG	FT	TP	Avg.
1943-44	Oshkosh NL	22	79	72	230	10.4
1944-45	Oshkosh NL	27	70	28	168	6.2
1945-46	Oshkosh NL	34	68	31	167	4.9
1946-47	Oshkosh NL	44	68	50	186	4.2
1947-48	Oshkosh NL	59	90	56	236	4.0
1948-49	Hammond NL	61	125	82	332	5.4
1949-50	Ft. Wayne	63	57	29	143	2.3
	Totals	310	557	348	1462	4.7

WAGNER, DAN

b. 1923 Ht. 6-0 Wt. 170 College—Texas

Yr	Team	G	FG	FT	TP	Avg.
1947-48	Flint NL	50	96	59	251	5.0
1948-49	Sheboygan NL	62	111	109	331	5.3
1949-50	Sheboygan NL	11	19	31	69	6.3
	Totals	123	226	199	651	5.3

WAGNER, PHIL

Ht. 6-2 Wt. 190 College—Georgia Tech

Yr	Team	G	FG	FT	TP	Avg.
1968-69	Indiana ABA	12	10 (1)	13	36	3.0

WALK, NEAL

b. July 29, 1948 Ht. 6-10 Wt. 250 College—Florida

Yr	Team	G	FG	FT	TP	Avg.
1969-70	Phoenix	82	257	155	669	8.2
1970-71	Phoenix	82	426	205	1057	12.9
1971-72	Phoenix	81	506	256	1268	15.7
1972-73	Phoenix	81	678	279	1635	20.2
1973-74	Phoenix	82	573	235	1381	16.8
1974-75	N.O.-N.Y.	67	198	86	482	7.2
1975-76	New York	82	262	79	603	7.4
1976-77	N.Y. Knicks	11	28	6	62	5.6
	Totals	568	2928	1301	7157	12.6

WALKER, ANDY

b. March 25, 1955 Ht. 6-4 Wt. 190 College—Niagara

Yr	Team	G	FG	FT	TP	Avg.
1976-77	New Orleans	40	72	36	180	4.5

WALKER, BRADY

b. March 15, 1921 Ht. 6-6 Wt. 205 Coll.—Brigham Yg.

Yr	Team	G	FG	FT	TP	Avg.
1948-49	Providence	59	202	87	491	8.3
1949-50	Boston	68	218	72	508	7.5
1950-51	Bos.-Balt.	66	164	72	400	6.1
1951-52	Baltimore	35	89	26	204	5.8
	Totals	228	673	257	1603	7.0

Yr	Team	G	FG	FT	TP	Avg.

WALKER, CHESTER (Chet)

b. Feb. 22, 1940 Ht. 6-6½ Wt. 210 College—Bradley

Yr	Team	G	FG	FT	TP	Avg.
1962-63	Syracuse	78	352	253	957	12.3
1963-64	Philadelphia	76	492	330	1314	17.3
1964-65	Philadelphia	79	377	288	1042	13.2
1965-66	Philadelphia	80	443	335	1221	15.3
1966-67	Philadelphia	81	561	445	1567	19.3
1967-68	Philadelphia	82	539	387	1465	17.9
1968-69	Philadelphia	82	554	369	1477	18.0
1969-70	Chicago	78	596	483	1675	21.5
1970-71	Chicago	81	650	480	1780	22.0
1971-72	Chicago	78	619	481	1719	22.0
1972-73	Chicago	79	597	376	1570	19.9
1973-74	Chicago	82	572	439	1583	19.3
1974-75	Chicago	76	524	413	1461	19.2
	Totals	1032	6876	5079	18831	18.2

WALKER, HORACE

b. April 17, 1938 Ht. 6-3½ Wt. 210 Coll.—Mich. St.

Yr	Team	G	FG	FT	TP	Avg.
1961-62	Chicago	64	147	139	433	6.8

WALKER, JIM

b. April 8, 1944 Ht. 6-3 Wt. 205 Coll.—Providence

Yr	Team	G	FG	FT	TP	Avg.
1967-68	Detroit	81	289	134	712	8.8
1968-69	Detroit	69	312	182	806	11.7
1969-70	Detroit	81	666	355	1687	20.8
1970-71	Detroit	79	524	344	1392	17.6
1971-72	Detroit	78	634	397	1665	21.3
1972-73	Houston	81	605	244	1454	18.0
1973-74	Hou.-K.C.-O.	75	582	273	1437	19.2
1974-75	K.C.-Omaha	81	553	247	1353	16.7
1975-76	Kansas City	73	459	231	1149	15.7
	Totals	698	4624	2407	11655	16.7

WALKER, PHIL

b. March 20, 1956 Ht. 6-3 Wt. 190 College—Millersville (Pa.)

Yr	Team	G	FG	FT	TP	Avg.
1977-78	Washington	40	57	64	178	4.5

WALLACE, MICHAEL (Red)

b. July 12, 1918 Ht. 6-1 Wt. 185 College—Scranton

Yr	Team	G	FG	FT	TP	Avg.
1946-47	Bos.-Toronto	61	225	106	556	9.1

WALLER, DWIGHT

b. Oct. 5, 1945 Ht. 6-7 Wt. 230 Coll.—Tennessee State

Yr	Team	G	FG	FT	TP	Avg.
1968-69	Atlanta	11	2	3	7	0.6
1971-72	Denver ABA	2	2 (0)	0	4	2.0
	Totals	13	4 (0)	3	11	0.8

WALSH, JAMES

b. Aug. 29, 1931 Ht. 6-4 Wt. 195 College—Stanford
d. March 4, 1976

Yr	Team	G	FG	FT	TP	Avg.
1957-58	Philadelphia	10	5	10	20	2.0

WALTHER, PAUL (Lefty)

b. 1927 Ht. 6-2 Wt. 160 College—Tennessee

Yr	Team	G	FG	FT	TP	Avg.
1949-50	Minn.-Ind.	53	114	63	291	5.5
1950-51	Indianapolis	63	213	145	571	9.1
1951-52	Indianapolis	55	220	231	671	12.2
1952-53	Indianapolis	67	227	264	718	10.7
1953-54	Philadelphia	64	138	145	421	6.6
1954-55	Ft. Wayne	68	56	54	166	2.4
	Totals	370	968	902	2838	7.7

WALTHOUR, ISAAC (Rabbit)

b. 1929 Ht. 5-11 Wt. 163

Yr	Team	G	FG	FT	TP	Avg.
1953-54	Milwaukee	4	1	0	2	0.5

WANZER, ROBERT (Bobby)

b. June 4, 1921 Ht. 6-0 Wt. 172 College—Seton Hall

Yr	Team	G	FG	FT	TP	Avg.
1947-48	Rochester NL	40	55	57	167	4.2
1948-49	Rochester	60	202	209	613	10.2
1949-50	Rochester	67	254	283	791	11.8
1950-51	Rochester	68	252	232	736	10.8
1951-52	Rochester	66	328	377	1033	15.7
1952-53	Rochester	70	318	384	1020	14.6
1953-54	Rochester	72	322	314	958	13.3
1954-55	Rochester	72	324	294	942	13.1
1955-56	Rochester	72	245	259	749	10.4
1956-57	Rochester	21	23	36	82	3.9
	Totals	608	2323	2445	7091	11.7

WARBINGTON, PERRY

b. Sept. 7, 1952 Ht. 6-2 Wt. 166 Coll.—Georgia So.

Yr	Team	G	FG	FT	TP	Avg.
1974-75	Philadelphia	5	4	2	10	2.0

WARD, GERRY

b. Sept. 6, 1941 Ht. 6-4 Wt. 200 Coll.—Boston College

Yr	Team	G	FG	FT	TP	Avg.
1963-64	St. Louis	24	16	11	43	1.8
1964-65	Boston	3	2	1	5	1.7
1965-66	Philadelphia	66	67	39	173	2.6
1966-67	Chicago	76	117	87	321	4.2
	Totals	169	202	138	542	3.2

WARD, HENRY

b. Jan. 30, 1952 Ht. 6-4 Wt. 195 Coll.—Jackson State

Yr	Team	G	FG	FT	TP	Avg.
1975-76	San Antonio ABA	61	148 (6)	16	330	5.4
1976-77	San Antonio	27	34	15	83	31
	Totals	88	182 (6)	31	413	4.7

WARE, JIM

b. May 2, 1944 Ht. 6-7½ Wt. 210 Coll.—Oklahoma City

Yr	Team	G	FG	FT	TP	Avg.
1966-67	Cincinnati	33	30	10	70	2.1
1967-68	San Diego	30	25	23	73	2.4
1968-69	Dallas ABA	1	3 (0)	1	7	7.0
	Totals	64	58 (0)	34	150	2.3

WARLEY, BEN

b. Sept. 4, 1936 Ht. 6-6 Wt. 200 Coll.—Tennessee State

Yr	Team	G	FG	FT	TP	Avg.
1962-63	Syracuse	26	50	25	125	4.8
1963-64	Philadelphia	79	215	220	650	8.2
1964-65	Philadelphia	64	94	124	312	4.8
1965-66	Phila.-Balt.	57	116	64	296	5.2
1966-67	Baltimore	62	125	134	384	6.2
1967-68	Anaheim ABA	71	383 (52)	313	1235	17.4
1968-69	Los Angeles ABA	35	141 (31)	116	491	14.0
1969-70	Denver ABA	42	45 (15)	58	193	4.6
	Totals	436	1169 (98)	1054	3686	8.5

Yr	Team	G	FG	FT	TP	Avg.

WARLICK, ROBERT

b. March 20, 1941 Ht. 6-5 Wt. 205 Coll.—Pepperdine

Yr	Team	G	FG	FT	TP	Avg.
1965-66	Detroit	10	11	2	24	2.4
1966-67	San Fran.	12	15	6	36	3.0
1967-68	San Fran.	69	257	97	611	8.9
1968-69	Mil.-Phoe.	66	213	87	513	7.8
	Totals	157	496	192	1184	7.5

WARNER, CORNELL

b. Aug. 12, 1948 Ht. 6-9 Wt. 220 Coll.—Jackson State

Yr	Team	G	FG	FT	TP	Avg.
1970-71	Buffalo	65	156	79	391	6.0
1971-72	Buffalo	62	162	58	382	6.2
1972-73	Buf.-Cleve.	72	174	59	407	5.7
1973-74	Cleve.-Mil.	72	174	85	433	6.0
1974-75	Milwaukee	79	248	106	602	7.6
1975-76	Los Angeles	81	251	89	591	7.3
1976-77	Los Angeles	14	25	4	54	3.9
	Totals	445	1190	480	2860	6.4

WARREN, BOB (Colonel)

b. July 17, 1946 Ht. 6-5 Wt. 190 College—Vanderbilt

Yr	Team	G	FG	FT	TP	Avg.
1968-69	Los Angeles ABA	76	254 (31)	297	898	11.8
1969-70	Los Angeles ABA	72	241 (25)	176	733	10.2
1970-71	Memphis ABA	46	125 (21)	107	420	9.2
1971-72	Mem.-Car. ABA	75	302 (11)	213	850	11.3
1972-73	Car.-Dal.-Ut. ABA	77	239 (5)	236	729	9.5
1973-74	Utah-S.A. ABA	59	110 (0)	63	283	4.8
1974-75	San Antonio ABA	71	125 (2)	77	333	4.7
	Totals	473	1396 (95)	1169	4246	9.0

WARREN, JOHN

b. July 7, 1947 Ht. 6-3 Wt. 180 College—St. John's

Yr	Team	G	FG	FT	TP	Avg.
1969-70	New York	44	44	24	112	2.5
1970-71	Cleveland	82	380	180	940	11.5
1971-72	Cleveland	68	144	49	337	5.0
1972-73	Cleveland	40	54	18	126	3.2
1973-74	Cleveland	69	132	35	299	4.3
	Totals	303	754	306	1814	6.0

WASHINGTON, BOBBY

b. July 11, 1947 Ht. 6-0 Wt. 175 College—Eastern KY

Yr	Team	G	FG	FT	TP	Avg.
1969-70	Kentucky ABA	2	0 (0)	0	0	0.0
1970-71	Cleveland	47	123	104	350	7.4
1971-72	Cleveland	69	123	104	350	5.1
	Totals	118	246 (0)	208	700	5.9

WASHINGTON, DON

b. April 22, 1952 Ht. 6-8 Wt. 210 College—N. Carolina

Yr	Team	G	FG	FT	TP	Avg.
1974-75	Denver ABA	50	79 (0)	38	196	3.9
1975-76	Utah ABA	6	12 (0)	0	24	4.0
	Totals	56	91 (0)	38	220	3.9

WASHINGTON, JAMES

b. July 1, 1943 Ht. 6-7 Wt. 215 College—Villanova

Yr	Team	G	FG	FT	TP	Avg.
1965-66	St. Louis	65	158	68	384	5.9
1966-67	Chicago	77	252	88	592	7.7
1967-68	Chicago	82'	418	187	1023	12.5
1968-69	Chicago	80	440	241	1121	14.0
1969-70	Philadelphia	79	401	204	1006	12.7
1970-71	Philadelphia	78	395	259	1049	13.4
1971-72	Phil.-Atl.	84	393	256	1042	12.4
1972-73	Atlanta	75	308	163	779	10.4
1973-74	Atlanta	73	297	134	728	10.0
1974-75	Atl.-Buf.	80	191	62	444	5.6
	Totals	773	3253	1662	8168	10.6

WASHINGTON, STAN

b. Jan. 23, 1952 Ht. 6-4 Wt. 190 College—San Diego

Yr	Team	G	FG	FT	TP	Avg.
1974-75	Washington	1	0	0	0	0.0

WASHINGTON, TOM

b. April 21, 1944 Ht. 6-7 Wt. 225 Coll.—Cheney State

Yr	Team	G	FG	FT	TP	Avg.
1967-68	Pittsburgh ABA	63	310 (2)	106	732	11.6
1968-69	Minnesota ABA	69	421 (0)	190	1032	15.0
1969-70	Pitt.-L.A. ABA	81	316 (4)	155	799	9.8
1970-71	Floridians ABA	57	216 (0)	102	534	9.3
1971-72	New York ABA	80	387 (0)	107	881	11.0
1972-73	New York ABA	76	229 (0)	63	521	6.9
	Totals	426	1879 (6)	723	4499	10.6

WATSON, BOB

b. March 22, 1930 Ht. 6-0 Wt. 162 College-Kentucky

Yr	Team	G	FG	FT	TP	Avg.
1954-55	Milwaukee	63	72	31	175	2.8

WATTS, RONALD

b. May 21, 1943 Ht. 6-6 Wt. 210 Coll.—Wake Forest

Yr	Team	G	FG	FT	TP	Avg.
1965-66	Boston	1	1	0	2	2.0
1966-67	Boston	27	11	16	38	1.4
	Totals	28	12	16	40	1.4

WATTS, SAM

Ht. 6-3 Wt. 185 College—Great Falls

Yr	Team	G	FG	FT	TP	Avg.
1970-71	Pittsburgh ABA	54	95 (14)	49	281	5.2

WEBB, JEFF

b. July 6, 1948 Ht. 6-4 Wt. 170 Coll.—Kansas State

Yr	Team	G	FG	FT	TP	Avg.
1970-71	Milwaukee	29	27	11	65	2.2
1971-72	Mil.-Phoe.	46	40	16	96	2.1
	Totals	75	67	27	161	2.1

WEBER, FOREST (Jake)

b. March 18, 1918 Ht. 6-6 Wt. 225 College—Purdue

Yr	Team	G	FG	FT	TP	Avg.
1945-46	Indianapolis NL	5	7	4	18	3.6
1946-47	N.Y.-Prov.	50	59	55	173	3.5
	Totals	55	66	59	191	3.5

Yr	Team	G	FG	FT	TP	Avg.

WEBSTER, ELNARDO

b. March 6, 1948 Ht. 6-5 Wt. 195 College—St. Peter's

Yr	Team	G	FG	FT	TP	Avg.
1971-72	N.Y.-Mem. ABA	19	49 (1)	21	122	6.4

WEHR, DICK

b. 1925 Ht. 6-4 Wt. 180 Coll.—Rice and Indiana

Yr	Team	G	FG	FT	TP	Avg.
1948-49	Indianapolis	9	5	2	12	1.3

WEISS, ROBERT

b. May 7, 1942 Ht. 6-2 Wt. 180 College—Penn State

Yr	Team	G	FG	FT	TP	Avg.
1965-66	Philadelphia	7	3	0	6	0.9
1966-67	Philadelphia	6	5	2	12	2.0
1967-68	Seattle	82	295	213	803	9.8
1968-69	Mil.-Chi.	77	189	128	506	6.6
1969-70	Chicago	82	365	213	943	11.5
1970-71	Chicago	82	278	226	782	9.5
1971-72	Chicago	82	358	212	928	11.3
1972-73	Chicago	82	279	159	717	8.7
1973-74	Chicago	79	263	142	668	8.5
1974-75	Buffalo	76	102	54	258	3.4
1975-76	Buffalo	66	89	35	213	3.2
1976-77	Washington	62	62	29	153	2.5
	Totals	783	2288	1413	5989	7.6

WEITZMAN, RICH

b. April 30, 1946 Ht. 6-2 Wt. 185 Coll.—Northeastern

Yr	Team	G	FG	FT	TP	Avg.
1967-68	Boston	25	12	9	33	1.3

WELLS, OWEN

b. Dec. 9, 1950 Ht. 6-7 Wt. 200 College—Detroit

Yr	Team	G	FG	FT	TP	Avg.
1974-75	Houston	33	42	15	99	3.0

WELLS, RALPH

b. Sept. 3, 1940 Ht. 6-1 Wt. 180 Coll.—Northwestern

Yr	Team	G	FG	FT	TP	Avg.
1962-63	Chicago	3	1	0	2	0.7

WERTIS, RAY

b. 1922 Ht. 5-11 Wt. 175 College—St. John's (N.Y.)

Yr	Team	G	FG	FT	TP	Avg.
1946-47	Cleve.-Tor.	61	79	56	214	3.5
1947-48	Providence	7	13	6	32	4.6
	Totals	68	92	62	246	3.6

WESLEY, WALT

b. April 25, 1945 Ht. 6-11 Wt. 230 College—Kansas

Yr	Team	G	FG	FT	TP	Avg.
1966-67	Cincinnati	64	131	52	314	4.9
1967-68	Cincinnati	66	188	76	452	6.8
1968-69	Cincinnati	82	245	134	624	7.6
1969-70	Chicago	72	270	145	685	9.5
1970-71	Cleveland	82	565	325	1455	17.7
1971-72	Cleveland	82	412	196	1020	12.4
1972-73	Cleve.-Phoe.	57	77	26	180	3.2
1973-74	Capital	39	71	26	168	4.3
1974-75	Phil.-Mil.	45	42	16	100	2.2
1975-76	Los Angeles	1	1	2	4	4.0
	Totals	590	2002	998	5002	8.5

WEST, JERRY

b. May 28, 1938 Ht. 6-3 Wt. 175 Coll.—W. Virginia

Yr	Team	G	FG	FT	TP	Avg.
1960-61	Los Angeles	79	529	331	1389	17.6
1961-62	Los Angeles	75	799	712	2310	30.8
1962-63	Los Angeles	55	559	371	1489	26.6
1963-64	Los Angeles	72	740	584	2064	28.7
1964-65	Los Angeles	74	822	648	2292	31.0
1965-66	Los Angeles	79	818	840	2476	31.4
1966-67	Los Angeles	66	645	602	1892	28.7
1967-68	Los Angeles	51	476	391	1343	26.3
1968-69	Los Angeles	61	545	490	1580	25.9
1969-70	Los Angeles	74	831	647	2309	31.2
1970-71	Los Angeles	69	667	525	1859	26.9
1971-72	Los Angeles	77	735	515	1985	25.8
1972-73	Los Angeles	69	618	339	1575	22.8
1973-74	Los Angeles	31	232	165	629	20.3
	Totals	932	9016	7160	25192	27.0

WEST, ROLAND

Ht. 6-4 Wt. 178 College—Cincinnati

Yr	Team	G	FG	FT	TP	Avg.
1967-68	Baltimore	4	2	0	4	1.0

WESTBROOK, DEXTER

b. 1943 Ht. 6-8 Wt. 190 College—Providence

Yr	Team	G	FG	FT	TP	Avg.
1967-68	N.J.-Pitt. ABA	12	19 (0)	10	48	4.0

WETZEL, JOHN

b. Oct. 22, 1944 Ht. 6-5 Wt. 185 College—VPI

Yr	Team	G	FG	FT	TP	Avg.
1967-68	Los Angeles	38	52	35	139	3.7
1970-71	Phoenix	70	124	83	331	4.7
1971-72	Phoenix	51	31	24	86	1.7
1972-73	Atlanta	28	42	14	98	3.5
1973-74	Atlanta	70	107	41	255	3.6
1974-75	Atlanta	63	87	68	242	3.8
1975-76	Phoenix	37	22	20	64	1.7
	Totals	357	465	285	1215	3.4

WHITE, HERB

b. June 15, 1948 Ht. 6-2 Wt. 195 Coll.—Georgia

Yr	Team	G	FG	FT	TP	Avg.
1970-71	Atlanta	38	34	22	90	2.4

WHITE, HUBIE

b. Jan. 26, 1940 Ht. 6-4 Wt. 205 College—Villanova

Yr	Team	G	FG	FT	TP	Avg.
1962-63	San Francisco	29	40	12	92	3.2
1963-64	Philadelphia	23	31	17	79	3.4
1969-70	Miami ABA	54	139 (7)	62	361	6.7
1970-71	Pittsburgh ABA	14	15 (2)	10	46	3.3
	Totals	120	225 (9)	101	578	4.8

WHITNEY, HENRY (Hank)

b. April 28, 1939 Ht. 6-7 Wt. 235 College—Iowa State

Yr	Team	G	FG	FT	TP	Avg.
1967-68	New Jersey ABA	37	217 (0)	157	591	16.0
1968-69	N.Y.-Hous. ABA	49	131 (0)	89	351	7.2
1969-70	Carolina ABA	59	170 (0)	57	397	6.7
	Totals	145	518 (0)	303	1339	9.2

WHITTAKER, LUCIAN (Skippy)

Ht. 6-1 Wt. 185 College—Kentucky

Yr	Team	G	FG	FT	TP	Avg.
1954-55	Boston	3	1	0	2	0.7

WIDBY, RON

Ht. 6-4 Wt. 210 College—Tennessee

Yr	Team	G	FG	FT	TP	Avg.
1967-68	New Orleans ABA	20	27 (0)	4	58	2.9

Yr	Team	G	FG	FT	TP	Avg.
WIER, MURRAY						
b. Dec. 12, 1926 Ht. 5-9 Wt. 155 College—Iowa						
1948-49	Tri-Cities NL	60	80	79	239	4.0
1949-50	Tri-Cities	56	157	115	429	7.7
	Totals	116	237	194	668	5.8
WIESENHAHN, ROBERT						
b. Dec. 22, 1938 Ht. 6-4 Wt. 215 College—Cincinnati						
1961-62	Cincinnati	60	51	17	119	2.0
WILBURN, KEN						
b. June 8, 1944 Ht. 6-6 Wt. 195 Coll.—Cen. State (OH)						
1967-68	Chicago	3	5	1	11	3.3
1968-69	Chicago	4	3	1	7	1.8
1968-69	Minn.-N.Y.-Den. ABA	47	76 (0)	38	190	4.0
	Totals	54	84 (0)	40	208	3.9
WILCUTT, D. C.						
b. March 25, 1923 Ht. 6-2 Wt. 165 College—St. Louis						
1948-49	St. Louis	22	18	15	51	2.3
1949-50	St. Louis	37	24	29	77	2.1
	Totals	59	42	44	128	2.2
WILEY, EUGENE						
b. Nov. 12, 1937 Ht. 6-10 Wt. 210 College—Wichita						
1962-63	Los Angeles	75	109	23	241	3.2
1963-64	Los Angeles	77	144	45	333	4.3
1964-65	Los Angeles	80	175	56	406	5.1
1965-66	Los Angeles	67	123	43	289	4.3
1967-68	Oak.-Dal. ABA	9	7 (0)	4	18	2.0
	Totals	308	558 (0)	171	1287	4.2
WILFONG, WIN						
b. Mar. 18, 1932 Ht. 6-2 Wt. 185 Coll.—Mem. St. & MO.						
1957-58	St. Louis	71	196	163	555	7.8
1958-59	St. Louis	63	99	62	260	4.1
1959-60	Cincinnati	72	283	161	727	10.1
1960-61	Cincinnati	62	109	75	293	4.7
	Totals	268	687	461	1835	6.8
WILKINS, LEN						
b. Oct. 28, 1937 Ht. 6-1 Wt. 185 Coll.—Providence						
1960-61	St. Louis	75	335	220	890	11.9
1961-62	St. Louis	20	140	84	364	18.2
1962-63	St. Louis	75	333	222	888	11.8
1963-64	St. Louis	78	334	270	938	12.0
1964-65	St. Louis	78	434	416	1284	16.5
1965-66	St. Louis	69	411	422	1244	18.0
1966-67	St. Louis	78	448	459	1355	17.4
1967-68	St. Louis	82	546	546	1638	20.0
1968-69	Seattle	82	644	547	1835	22.4
1969-70	Seattle	75	448	438	1334	17.8
1970-71	Seattle	71	471	461	1403	19.8
1971-72	Seattle	80	479	480	1438	18.0
1972-73	Cleveland	75	572	394	1538	20.5
1973-74	Cleveland	74	462	289	1213	16.4
1974-75	Portland	65	134	152	420	6.5
	Totals	1077	6189	5394	17772	16.5
WILLIAMS, AL						
b. 1948 Ht. 6-6 Wt. 215 College—Drake						
1970-71	Kentucky	11	19	5	43	3.9

Yr	Team	G	FG	FT	TP	Avg.
WILLIAMS, ART (Hambone)						
b. Sept. 29, 1939 Ht. 6-2 Wt. 180 Coll.—California Poly						
1967-68	San Diego	79	265	113	643	8.1
1968-69	San Diego	79	227	105	559	7.1
1969-70	San Diego	80	189	88	466	5.8
1970-71	Boston	74	150	60	360	4.9
1971-72	Boston	81	161	90	412	5.1
1972-73	Boston	81	110	43	263	3.2
1973-74	Boston	67	73	27	173	2.6
1974-75	San Diego ABA	7	8 (0)	0	16	2.3
	Totals	548	1183 (0)	526	2892	5.3
WILLIAMS, BERNIE						
b. Dec. 30, 1945 Ht. 6-3 Wt. 175 College—LaSalle						
1969-70	San Diego	72	251	96	598	8.3
1970-71	San Diego	56	112	68	292	5.2
1971-72	Virginia ABA	78	331 (18)	113	829	10.6
1972-73	Virginia ABA	71	346 (10)	166	888	12.5
1973-74	Virginia ABA	6	5 (1)	2	15	2.5
	Totals	283	1045 (29)	445	2622	9.3
WILLIAMS, CHARLES						
b. Sept. 5, 1943 Ht. 6-0 Wt. 165 College—Seattle						
1967-68	Pittsburgh ABA	78	591 (51)	290	1625	20.8
1968-69	Minnesota ABA	66	418 (66)	203	1237	18.7
1969-70	Pittsburgh ABA	26	177 (16)	104	506	19.4
1970-71	Pitt.-Mem. ABA	88	468 (33)	204	1239	14.1
1971-72	Memphis ABA	82	439 (41)	294	1295	15.8
1972-73	Mem.-Utah ABA	32	34 (3)	41	118	3.7
	Totals	372	2127 (210)	1136	6020	16.2
WILLIAMS, CHUCK						
b. June 6, 1946 Ht. 6-2 Wt. 175 College—Colorado						
1970-71	Pittsburgh ABA	83	267 (1)	249	786	9.5
1971-72	Denver ABA	84	263 (0)	205	731	8.7
1972-73	San Diego ABA	83	487 (1)	493	1470	17.7
1973-74	S.D.-Ken. ABA	90	401 (4)	299	1113	12.4
1974-75	Memphis ABA	81	466 (10)	212	1174	14.5
1975-76	Denver ABA	79	339 (0)	188	866	11.0
1976-77	Den.-Buf	65	78	68	224	3.4
1977-78	Buffalo	73	208	114	530	7.3
	Totals	638	2509 (16)	1828	6894	10.8
WILLIAMS, CHUCKIE						
b. Dec. 31, 1953 Ht. 6-3 Wt. 180 Coll.—Kansas State						
1976-77	Cleveland	22	14	9	37	1.7
WILLIAMS, CLIFF						
b. April 15, 1945 Ht. 6-3 Wt. 180 Coll.—Bowling Green						
1968-69	Detroit	3	2	0	4	1.3

Yr	Team	G	FG	FT	TP	Avg.

WILLIAMS, FLY

b. Feb. 18, 1953 Ht. 6-5 Wt. 200 College—Austin Peay

Yr	Team	G	FG	FT	TP	Avg.
1974-75	St. Louis ABA	71	295 (2)	69	665	9.4

WILLIAMS, GENE

b. April 1, 1947 Ht. 6-7 Wt. 235 College—Kansas State

Yr	Team	G	FG	FT	TP	Avg.
1969-70	Kentucky ABA	1	0 (0)	0	0	0.0

WILLIAMS, HENRY

b. April 28, 1952 Ht. 6-5 Wt. 210 College—Jacksonville

Yr	Team	G	FG	FT	TP	Avg.
1974-75	Utah ABA	40	73 (3)	18	173	4.3

WILLIAMS, MILT

b. Nov. 22, 1945 Ht. 6-2½ Wt. 185 College—Lincoln and Campbell

Yr	Team	G	FG	FT	TP	Avg.
1970-71	New York	5	1	2	4	0.8
1971-72	Atlanta	10	23	21	67	6.7
1973-74	Seattle	53	62	41	165	3.1
1974-75	St. Louis ABA	4	11 (0)	0	22	5.5
	Totals	72	97 (0)	64	258	3.6

WILLIAMS, ROBERT

b. May 12, 1931 Ht. 6-6 Wt. 230 Coll.—Florida A & M

Yr	Team	G	FG	FT	TP	Avg.
1955-56	Minneapolis	20	21	24	66	3.3
1956-57	Minneapolis	4	1	2	4	1.0
	Totals	24	22	26	70	2.9

WILLIAMS, RON (Fritz)

b. Sept. 24, 1944 Ht. 6-3 Wt. 190 Coll.—W. Virginia

Yr	Team	G	FG	FT	TP	Avg.
1968-69	San Fran.	75	238	109	585	7.8
1969-70	San Fran.	80	452	277	1181	14.8
1970-71	San Fran.	82	426	331	1183	14.4
1971-72	Golden St.	80	291	195	777	9.7
1972-73	Golden St.	73	180	75	435	6.0
1973-74	Milwaukee	71	192	60	444	6.3
1974-75	Milwaukee	46	62	24	148	3.2
1975-76	Los Angeles	9	17	10	44	4.9
	Totals	516	1858	1081	4797	9.3

WILLIAMS, SAM

b. Jan. 22, 1945 Ht. 6-3 Wt. 180 College—Iowa

Yr	Team	G	FG	FT	TP	Avg.
1968-69	Milwaukee	55	78	72	228	4.1
1969-70	Milwaukee	11	11	5	27	2.5
	Totals	66	89	77	255	3.9

WILLIAMS, WARD

b. June 26, 1923 Ht. 6-4 Wt. 195 College—Indiana

Yr	Team	G	FG	FT	TP	Avg.
1948-49	Ft. Wayne	53	61	93	215	4.1

WILLIAMS, WILLIE

b. July 28, 1946 Ht. 6-7 Wt. 198 Coll.—Florida State

Yr	Team	G	FG	FT	TP	Avg.
1970-71	Bos.-Cin.	25	10	3	23	0.9

WILLIFORD, VANN

b. Jan. 26, 1948 Ht. 6-6 Wt. 195 Coll.—N. Carolina St.

Yr	Team	G	FG	FT	TP	Avg.
1970-71	Carolina	38	59 (3)	21	148	3.9

WILLOUGHBY, BILL

b. May 20, 1957 Ht. 6-8 Wt. 205 College—None

Yr	Team	G	FG	FT	TP	Avg.
1975-76	Atlanta	62	113	66	292	4.7
1976-77	Atlanta	39	75	43	193	4.9
1977-78	Buffalo	56	156	64	376	6.7
	Totals	157	344	173	861	5.5

WILSON, BOB

b. 1927 Ht. 6-4 Wt. 185 College—West Virginia State

Yr	Team	G	FG	FT	TP	Avg.
1951-52	Milwaukee	63	79	78	236	3.7

WILSON, BOBBY

Ht. 6-8 Wt. 215 College—Kansas

Yr	Team	G	FG	FT	TP	Avg.
1967-68	Dallas ABA	69	225 (1)	163	616	8.9

WILSON, BOBBY

b. Jan. 15, 1951 Ht. 6-3 Wt. 180 College—Wichita St.

Yr	Team	G	FG	FT	TP	Avg.
1974-75	Chicago	48	115	46	276	5.8
1975-76	Chicago	58	197	43	437	7.5
1976-77	Boston	25	19	11	49	2.0
1977-78	Indiana	12	14	2	30	2.5
	Totals	143	345	102	792	5.5

WILSON, GEORGE

b. May 9, 1942 Ht. 6-8 Wt. 225 Coll.—Cincinnati

Yr	Team	G	FG	FT	TP	Avg.
1964-65	Cincinnati	39	41	9	91	2.3
1965-66	Cincinnati	47	54	27	135	2.9
1966-67	Cin.-Chicago	55	85	58	228	4.1
1967-68	Seattle	77	179	109	467	6.1
1968-69	Phoe.-Phil.	79	272	153	697	8.8
1969-70	Philadelphia	67	118	122	358	5.3
1970-71	Buffalo	46	92	56	240	5.2
	Totals	410	841	534	2216	5.4

WILSON, ISAIAH (Bunny)

b. May 31, 1948 Ht. 6-2½ Wt. 175 College—Baltimore

Yr	Team	G	FG	FT	TP	Avg.
1971-72	Detroit	48	63	41	167	3.5

WILSON, JASPER

b. July 12, 1947 Ht. 6-6 Wt. 200 Coll.—Southern Univ.

Yr	Team	G	FG	FT	TP	Avg.
1968-69	New Orleans ABA	66	123 (5)	82	343	5.2
1969-70	New Orleans ABA	4	7 (1)	6	23	5.8
	Totals	70	130 (6)	88	366	5.2

WILSON, JIM

Ht. 5-10 College—Cheney State

Yr	Team	G	FG	FT	TP	Avg.
1970-71	Pittsburgh ABA	6	1 (0)	4	6	1.0

WILSON, STEVE

b. Oct. 16, 1948 Ht. 6-5 Wt. 185 College—Hanover

Yr	Team	G	FG	FT	TP	Avg.
1970-71	Denver ABA	39	44 (8)	22	134	3.4
1971-72	Denver ABA	9	5 (0)	4	14	1.7
	Totals	48	49 (8)	26	148	3.1

Yr	Team	G	FG	FT	TP	Avg.
WINDIS, TONY						
b. 1933 Ht. 6-1 Wt. 160 College—Wyoming						
1959-60	Detroit	9	16	4	36	4.0
WINDSOR, JOHN						
b. April 3, 1940 Ht. 6-8 Wt. 215 College—Stanford						
1963-64	San Fran.	10	9	7	25	2.5
WINFIELD, LEE						
b. Feb. 4, 1947 Ht. 6-2 Wt. 175 Coll.—No. Texas St.						
1969-70	Seattle	64	138	87	363	5.7
1970-71	Seattle	79	334	162	830	10.5
1971-72	Seattle	81	343	175	861	10.6
1972-73	Seattle	53	143	62	348	6.6
1973-74	Buffalo	36	37	33	107	3.0
1974-75	Buffalo	68	164	49	377	5.5
1975-76	Kansas City	22	32	9	73	3.3
	Totals	403	1191	579	2959	7.3
WINGO, HARTHORNE						
b. Sept. 9, 1948 Ht. 6-8 Wt. 210 Coll.—Friendship J.C.						
1972-73	New York	11	9	2	20	1.5
1973-74	New York	60	82	48	212	3.5
1974-75	New York	82	233	141	607	7.4
1975-76	New York	57	72	40	184	3.2
	Totals	212	396	231	1023	4.8
WINKLER, MARV						
b. Feb. 18, 1948 Ht. 6-1 Wt. 175 Coll.—SW Louisiana						
1970-71	Milwaukee	3	3	2	8	2.7
1971-72	Indiana ABA	20	13 (2)	8	40	2.0
	Totals	23	16 (2)	10	48	2.1
WISE, SKIP						
b. July 25, 1955 Ht. 6-3 Wt. 180 College—Clemson						
1975-76	San Antonio ABA	2	2 (0)	0	4	2.0
WISE, WILLIE						
b. March 3, 1947 Ht. 6-6 Wt. 215 College—Drake						
1969-70	Los Angeles ABA	82	479 (4)	278	1248	15.2
1970-71	Utah ABA	82	486 (5)	312	1299	15.8
1971-72	Utah ABA	84	737 (6)	459	1951	23.2
1972-73	Utah ABA	83	669 (3)	476	1823	22.0
1973-74	Utah ABA	82	712 (2)	396	1826	22.3
1974-75	Virginia ABA	16	127 (1)	77	331	20.9
1975-76	Virginia ABA	46	247 (0)	135	629	13.7
1976-77	Denver	75	237	142	616	8.2
1977-78	Seattle	2	0	1	1	0.5
	Totals	552	3694 (21)	2276	9727	17.6
WITTE, LUKE						
b. Oct. 19, 1950 Ht. 7-0 Wt. 240 College—Ohio State						
1973-74	Cleveland	57	105	46	256	4.5
1974-75	Cleveland	39	33	19	85	2.2
1975-76	Cleveland	22	11	9	31	1.4
1976-77	Cleveland	0	0	0	0	0
	Totals	118	149	74	372	3.2

Yr	Team	G	FG	FT	TP	Avg.
WITTMAN, GREG						
b. May 10, 1947 Ht. 6-8 Wt. 210 Coll.—W. Carolina						
1969-70	Denver ABA	50	76 (4)	32	196	4.0
1970-71	Tex.-Fla. ABA	10	6 (0)	4	16	1.6
	Totals	60	82 (4)	36	212	3.5
WOHL, DAVE						
b. Nov. 2, 1949 Ht. 6-2 Wt. 185 College—Pennsylvania						
1971-72	Philadelphia	79	243	156	642	8.1
1972-73	Port.-Buf.	78	254	103	611	7.8
1973-74	Buf.-Hou.	67	121	75	317	4.7
1974-75	Houston	75	203	79	485	6.5
1975-76	Houston	50	66	38	170	3.1
1976-77	Hou.-NYN	51	116	61	293	5.7
1977-78	New Jersey	10	12	11	35	3.5
	Totals	410	1015	523	2553	6.2
WOODS, BOB						
b. 1927 Ht. 5-10½ College—Northern Illinois						
1949-50	Sheboygan	6	3	1	7	1.2
WOODS, TOMMY						
Ht. 6-7 Wt. 215 College—East Tennessee State						
1967-68	Kentucky ABA	18	14 (0)	14	42	2.3
WOOLLARD, BOB						
Ht. 6-10 College—Wake Forest						
1969-70	Miami ABA	20	32 (0)	20	84	4.2
WORKMAN, MARK						
b. March 10, 1930 Ht. 6-9 Wt. 217 Coll.—W. Virginia						
1952-53	Milw.-Phila.	65	130	70	330	5.1
1953-54	Baltimore	14	25	6	56	4.0
	Totals	79	155	76	386	4.9
WORKMAN, TOM						
b. Nov. 14, 1944 Ht. 6-7 Wt. 230 College—Seattle						
1967-68	St. Louis-Balt.	20	19	18	56	2.8
1968-69	Baltimore	21	22	9	53	2.5
1969-70	Detroit	2	0	0	0	0.0
1969-70	Los Angeles ABA	26	115 (1)	77	310	11.9
1970-71	Utah-Den. ABA	56	130 (3)	86	355	6.3
	Totals	125	286 (4)	190	774	6.2
WORSLEY, WILLIE						
b. Nov. 13, 1945 Ht. 5-10 Wt. 175 Coll.—Texas-El Paso						
1968-69	New York ABA	24	26 (10)	63	145	6.0
WRIGHT, HOWARD						
Ht. 6-3 Wt. 185 College—Austin Peay						
1970-71	Kentucky ABA	52	85 (9)	40	237	4.6
1971-72	Kentucky ABA	1	0 (0)	0	0	0.0
	Totals	53	85 (9)	40	237	4.5

Yr	Team	G	FG	FT	TP	Avg.

WRIGHT, JOBY

b. Sept. 5, 1950 Ht. 6-8 Wt. 222 College—Indiana

Yr	Team	G	FG	FT	TP	Avg.
1972-73	Seattle	77	133	37	303	3.9
1973-74	Memphis ABA	3	5	2	12	4.0
1975-76	S.D.-Vir. ABA	23	50	21	121	5.3
	Totals	103	188	60	436	4.2

WRIGHT, LEROY

b. May 6, 1938 Ht. 6-9 Wt. 215 College—Pacific

Yr	Team	G	FG	FT	TP	Avg.
1967-68	Pittsburgh ABA	17	24 (0)	9	57	3.4
1968-69	Minnesota ABA	10	4 (0)	0	8	0.8
	Totals	27	28 (0)	9	65	2.4

WRIGHT, LONNIE

b. Jan. 23, 1944 Ht. 6-2 Wt. 205 College—Colorado St.

Yr	Team	G	FG	FT	TP	Avg.
1967-68	Denver ABA	38	144 (2)	79	373	9.8
1968-69	Denver ABA	69	434 (19)	205	1130	16.4
1969-70	Denver ABA	79	339 (54)	121	961	12.2
1970-71	Den.-Fla. ABA	72	182 (17)	93	508	7.1
1971-72	Floridians ABA	77	233 (19)	95	618	8.0
	Totals	335	1332 (111)	593	3590	10.7

WUYCIK, DENNIS

b. Mar. 29, 1950 Ht. 6-6 Wt. 215 Coll.—North Carolina

Yr	Team	G	FG	FT	TP	Avg.
1972-73	Carolina ABA	83	151 (0)	75	377	4.5
1973-74	Carolina ABA	49	87 (1)	51	228	4.7
1974-75	St. Louis ABA	25	34 (0)	11	79	3.2
	Totals	157	272 (1)	137	684	4.4

YATES, BARRY

b. Jan. 30, 1946 Ht. 6-7 Wt. 215 College—Maryland

Yr	Team	G	FG	FT	TP	Avg.
1971-72	Philadelphia	24	31	7	69	2.9

YATES, WAYNE

b. Nov. 7, 1937 Ht. 6-8 Wt. 235 Coll.—Memphis St.

Yr	Team	G	FG	FT	TP	Avg.
1961-62	Los Angeles	37	31	10	72	1.9

YARDLEY, GEORGE

b. Nov. 3, 1928 Ht. 6-5 Wt. 195 College—Stanford

Yr	Team	G	FG	FT	TP	Avg.
1953-54	Ft. Wayne	63	209	146	564	9.0
1954-55	Ft. Wayne	60	363	310	1036	17.3
1955-56	Ft. Wayne	71	434	365	1233	17.4
1956-57	Ft. Wayne	72	522	503	1547	21.5
1957-58	Detroit	72	673	655	2001	27.8
1958-59	Det.-Syr.	61	446	317	1209	19.8
	Totals	399	2647	2296	7590	19.0

YELVERTON, CHARLIE

b. Dec. 5, 1948 Ht. 6-2 Wt. 190 College—Fordham

Yr	Team	G	FG	FT	TP	Avg.
1971-72	Portland	69	206	133	545	7.9

ZASLOFSKY, MAX (Slats)

b. Dec. 7, 1925 Ht. 6-2 Wt. 170 College—Chicago and St. John's (N.Y.)

Yr	Team	G	FG	FT	TP	Avg.
1946-47	Chicago	61	336	205	877	14.4
1947-48	Chicago	48	373	261	1007	21.0
1948-49	Chicago	58	425	347	1197	20.6
1949-50	Chicago	68	397	321	1115	16.4
1950-51	New York	66	302	231	835	12.7
1951-52	New York	66	322	287	931	14.1
1952-53	New York	29	123	98	344	11.9
1953-54	Balt.-Mil.-Ft. Wayne	65	278	255	811	12.5
1954-55	Ft. Wayne	70	269	247	785	11.2
1955-56	Ft. Wayne	9	29	30	88	9.8
	Totals	540	2854	2282	7990	14.8

ZAWOLUK, ROBERT (Zeke)

b. Dec. 13, 1930 Ht. 6-7 Wt. 215 Coll.—St. John's (N.Y.)

Yr	Team	G	FG	FT	TP	Avg.
1952-53	Indianapolis	41	55	77	187	4.6
1953-54	Philadelphia	71	203	186	592	8.3
1954-55	Philadelphia	67	138	155	431	6.4
	Totals	179	396	418	1210	6.8

ZELLER, DAVID

b. June 8, 1939 Ht. 6-1½ Wt. 175 Coll.—Miami (Ohio)

Yr	Team	G	FG	FT	TP	Avg.
1961-62	Cincinnati	61	36	18	90	1.5

ZELLER, GARY

b. Nov. 20, 1947 Ht. 6-3 Wt. 205 College—Drake

Yr	Team	G	FG	FT	TP	Avg.
1970-71	Baltimore	50	34	15	83	1.7
1971-72	Balt.-N.Y. ABA	40	90 (0)	26	206	5.2
	Totals	90	124 (0)	41	289	3.2

ZELLER, HARRY (Hank)

b. 1919 Ht. 6-4 Wt. 210 College—Pittsburgh

Yr	Team	G	FG	FT	TP	Avg.
1946-47	Pittsburgh	48	120	122	362	7.5

ZOPF, BILL

b. June 7, 1948 Ht. 6-1 Wt. 170 College—Duquesne

Yr	Team	G	FG	FT	TP	Avg.
1970-71	Milwaukee	53	49	20	118	2.2

ZUNIC, MATT

b. Sept. 12, 1919 Ht. 6-7 Wt. 195 Coll.—George Washington

Yr	Team	G	FG	FT	TP	Avg.
1947-48	Flint NL	57	123	85	331	5.8
1948-49	Washington	56	98	77	273	4.9
	Totals	113	221	162	604	5.3

Appendix A

THE RULES

Out of the confusing and often contradictory sets of rules that governed basketball in its early years, a basic uniformity was established by the National Basketball Committee of the United States and Canada, which was in existence from 1934 to 1978.

The leaders of the National Collegiate Athletic Association and the National Federation of High Schools mutually agreed to form their own rule bodies in 1978, with the understanding that both bodies would work cooperatively in maintaining a close similarity in amateur playing rules.

The only essential rule differences occur between the NCAA-High School Federation rules, and the professional and international rules.

For example, the National Basketball Association (the pros) allows six personal fouls rather than the five of college or high-school play before a player is disqualified.

The professional game is 48 minutes long and divided into four 12-minute quarters, as opposed to the 40-minute college game, divided in halves, and the 32-minute high school contest, divided into 8-minute quarters.

Except for the start of the game, the pros have eliminated the jump ball at the beginning of each period, replacing it with alternate possession of the ball for a throw-in. The colleges and high schools have been experimenting since 1976 with the elimination of all jump balls because of problems encountered when tossing the ball, but have maintained the long-established rule.

The pros adopted the use of three officials for regular-season and playoff games starting with the 1978–79 season. The NCAA initiated use of a third official in its post-season tournament in 1978–79, while leaving the use of two or three referees for regular-season games to the discretion of its member conferences.

Professional basketball rules include a shooting-time limitation of 24 seconds, during which a team must attempt a shot that makes contact with backboard or rim after gaining possession of the ball. Collegiate men have no time limit for shooting, while collegiate women, playing under rules set by the National Association of Girls and Women's Sports, have a 30-second regulation.

Professional rules outlaw any type of zone defense, while the college and high-school rules contain no such limitation.

Both the amateurs and the pros have legalized the dunk shot during the game, but the dunk is illegal during a warmup or dead-ball situation for a college or high-school player.

In the pros, team fouls in excess of four per quarter are penalized with an additional free throw. In the college and high school games, the bonus free throws (one-and-one) start with the seventh foul per half and the fifth foul per quarter, respectively.

The pros and colleges use a 94-by-50-foot court, while the high-school court dimensions are 84 feet by 50 feet. The free-throw lanes are 12 feet wide in college and high school, while the pros use a lane width of 16 feet.

The rules adopted by the International Amateur Federation (FIBA) govern international and Olympic play. The differences between NCAA and FIBA rules have been minimized to the point that the amateur game played around the world is governed by rules similar to those of the United States.

The FIBA rules include a 30-second limit for attempting a shot. The bonus situation, under FIBA rules, goes into effect after a team has committed ten player fouls (personal or technical) in a half, and all subsequent player fouls are penalized by two free throws. Under FIBA rules, if a player is fouled in the act of shooting an unsuccessful try, three shots are awarded to make two points. Only coaches may request a time-out, and a maximum of two charged time-outs may be granted per half under FIBA rules.

OFFICIAL RULES

(Reprinted by permission of the National Association of High School Athletic Associations)

THE GAME Basketball is played by two teams of five players each. The purpose of each team is to throw the ball into its own basket and to prevent the other team from scoring. The ball may be thrown, batted, rolled or dribbled in any direction, subject to restrictions laid down in the following rules.

RULE 1   Equipment

SECTION 1. The playing court shall be a rectangular surface free from obstructions and with dimensions not greater than 94 feet in length by 50 feet in width.

IDEAL MEASUREMENTS ARE:
   High School Age...................50 by 84 feet
These are the dimensions for the playing court only.

SECTION 2. The playing court shall be marked with **sidelines, end lines** and other lines as shown on the appended court diagram. There shall be at least 3 feet (and preferably 10 feet) of unobstructed space outside. If it is desirable to use contrasting colored floor areas instead of the 2-inch lines, see comments in the supplement. If, on an unofficial court, there are less than 3 feet of unobstructed space outside any sideline or end line, a narrow broken line shall be marked in the court parallel with and 3 feet inside that boundary. This **restraining line** becomes the boundary line during a throw-in as in 7-6, on that side or end. It continues to be the boundary until the ball crosses the line.

SECTION 3. The center circle is a circle 2 inches in width and having a radius of 2 feet measured to the inside. A 2-inch wide restraining circle concentric with the center circle shall be drawn with a radius of 6 feet measured to the outside. Spaces for non-jumpers around all restraining circles are 36 inches deep.

SECTION 4. A division line 2 inches wide dividing the court into two parts shall be formed by extending the center circle diameter in both directions until it intersects the sidelines. If the court is less than 74 feet long, it should be divided by two lines, each parallel to and 40 feet from the farther end line.

SECTION 5. A free throw lane, 12 feet wide measured to the outside of each lane boundary and the semicircle with the free throw line as a diameter, shall be marked at each end of the court with dimensions and markings as shown on the court diagram. All lines designating the free throw lane, but not lane space marks and neutral zone marks, are part of the lane. The color of the lane space marks and neutral zone marks shall contrast with the color of the boundary lines. The lane space marks (2 inches by 8 inches) and neutral zone marks (12 inches by 8 inches) identify areas which

BASKETBALL COURT DIAGRAM

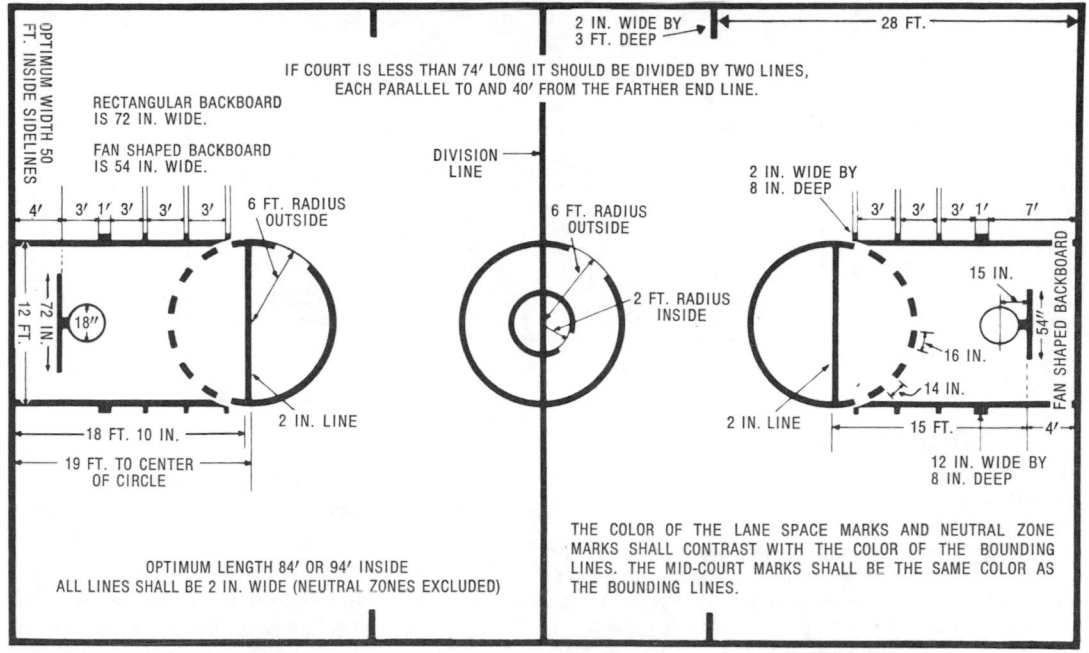

OPTIMUM WIDTH 50 FT. INSIDE SIDELINES

RECTANGULAR BACKBOARD IS 72 IN. WIDE.

FAN SHAPED BACKBOARD IS 54 IN. WIDE.

IF COURT IS LESS THAN 74' LONG IT SHOULD BE DIVIDED BY TWO LINES, EACH PARALLEL TO AND 40' FROM THE FARTHER END LINE.

2 IN. WIDE BY 3 FT. DEEP

28 FT.

DIVISION LINE

6 FT. RADIUS OUTSIDE

2 FT. RADIUS INSIDE

2 IN. WIDE BY 8 IN. DEEP

6 FT. RADIUS OUTSIDE

FAN SHAPED BACKBOARD

15 IN.

16 IN.

14 IN.

54"

18"

72 IN.

12 FT.

2 IN. LINE

18 FT. 10 IN.

19 FT. TO CENTER OF CIRCLE

OPTIMUM LENGTH 84' OR 94' INSIDE
ALL LINES SHALL BE 2 IN. WIDE (NEUTRAL ZONES EXCLUDED)

2 IN. LINE

15 FT.

12 IN. WIDE BY 8 IN. DEEP

THE COLOR OF THE LANE SPACE MARKS AND NEUTRAL ZONE MARKS SHALL CONTRAST WITH THE COLOR OF THE BOUNDING LINES. THE MID-COURT MARKS SHALL BE THE SAME COLOR AS THE BOUNDING LINES.

Left End Shows Large Backboard for College Games.

MINIMUM of 3 FT.
Preferably 10 ft. of unobstructed space outside. If impossible to provide 3 ft. a narrow broken 1 in. line should be marked inside the court parallel with and 3 ft. inside the boundary.

SEMICIRCLE BROKEN LINES
For the broken line semicircle in the free throw lane, it is recommended there be 8 marks 16 in. long and 7 spaces 14 in. long.

Right End Shows Small Backboard for High School

extend from the outer edge of the lane lines 36 inches toward the sidelines.

SECTION 6. A free throw line, two inches wide, shall be drawn across each of the circles which have an outside radius of 6 feet as shown on the court diagram. It shall be parallel to the end line and shall have its farther edge 15 feet from the plane of the face of the backboard.

SECTION 7. Each of the two backboards shall be of any rigid material. The front surface shall be flat and, unless it is transparent, it shall be white. The backboard shall be either of two types: (1) a rectangle 6 feet horizontally and 4 feet vertically, or (2) a fan-shaped backboard, 54 inches wide and with dimensions as shown on the diagram.

If the backboard is transparent, it shall be marked as follows: A rectangle shall be centered behind the ring and marked by a 2-inch white line. The rectangle shall have outside dimensions of 24 inches horizontally and 18 inches vertically. For the rectangular backboard, the top edge of the baseline shall be level with the ring. For the fan-shaped backboard, the baseline shall be omitted and the two vertical lines shall be extended to the bottom of the backboard. (The rectangular target in a bright orange color may be used on a non-

transparent backboard.) The border of the backboard shall be marked with a white line. The border shall be 3 inches in width for the rectangular backboard and 3 inches or less in width for the fan-shaped backboard.

Either type backboard in either transparent or non-transparent material is legal.

SECTION 8. Each backboard shall be midway between the sidelines, with the plane of its front face perpendicular to the floor, parallel to the end line and 4 feet from it. The upper edge of the backboard shall be: 13 feet above the floor for the rectangular and 12 feet 8 inches for the fan-shaped backboard. The bottom and each side of the all rectangular backboard shall be padded in accordance with the specifications as described in the Comments on the Rules.

SECTION 9. The backboards shall be protected from spectators to a distance of at least 3 feet at each end.

SECTION 10. Each basket shall consist of a single metal ring, 18 inches in inside diameter, its flange and braces, and a white cord 12-mesh net, 15 to 18 inches in length, suspended from beneath the ring. Each ring shall be not more than five-eighths of an inch in diameter, with the possible addition of small-gauge loops on the underedge for attaching a

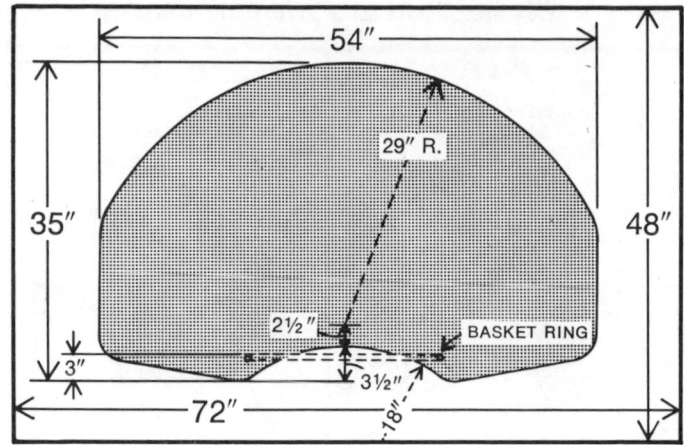

The diagram above gives specification for both types of backboards. See Rule 1, Sections 7, 8, 9. It is not legal to paint a fan-shaped board on a rectangular backboard.

NOTE—Any backboard support, all of which is not directly behind the backboard, should be at least 6 inches behind it if the support extends above the top and at least 2 feet behind it if the support extends beyond the side. Atachment of ring to backboard shall be as prescribed in standards adopted by the Committee and available on request. For the fan-shaped backboard in transparent material, the recurved cut-out at the bottom may be filled in and the ring attached to the front of the backboard.

12-mesh net. The ring and its attaching flange and braces shall be bright orange in color. The cord of the net shall be not less than 120-thread nor more than 144-thread twine, or plastic material of comparable dimensions constructed so as to check the ball momentarily as it passes through.

SECTION 11. Each basket ring shall be securely attached to the backboard. It shall have its upper edge 10 feet above and parallel to the floor and shall be equidistant from the vertical edges of the backboard. The nearest point of the inside edge of the ring shall be 6 inches from the plane of the face of the backboard.

SECTION 12. The ball shall be: spherical; of the molded type; and its color shall be the approved orange shade or natural color. If the panels are leather, they shall be cemented to the spherically molded fabric which surrounds an air-tight rubber lining. Channels and/or seams shall not exceed one-fourth inch in width. Its circumference shall be within a maximum of 30 inches and a minimum of 29½ inches for adults and within a maximum of 29½ inches and a minimum of 29 inches for players below senior high school age. Its weight shall be not less than 20 nor more than 22 ounces. It shall be inflated to an air pressure such that when it is dropped to the playing surface from a height of six feet, measured to the bottom of the ball, it will rebound to a height, measured to the top of the ball, of not less than 49 inches when it strikes on its least resilient spot nor more than 54 inches when it strikes on its most resilient spot.

NOTE—To be legal, a ball must be tested for resilience at the factory and the air pressure which will give the required reaction must be stamped on it. The pressure for game use must be such as to make the ball bounce legally.

SECTION 13. The home team shall provide a ball which meets the specifications of section 12. The referee shall be the sole judge of the legality of the ball and he or she may select for use a ball provided by the visiting team.

SECTION 14. It is recommended that the benches for players of both teams be placed along that side of the court on which the scorers' and timers' table is located.

RULE 2   Officials and Their Duties

SECTION 1. The officials shall be a referee and an umpire (or when the teams mutually agree, a referee and two umpires), who shall be assisted by two timers and by two scorers. A single timer and a single scorer may be used if they are trained personnel acceptable to the referee. The scorers and timers shall be located at the scorers' and timers' table on the side of the court.

NOTE—The officials shall wear uniforms distinct from those of either team.

SECTION 2. The referee shall inspect and approve all equipment, including court, baskets, ball, backboards, and timers' and scorers' signals. Prior to the scheduled starting time of the game, he shall designate the official timepiece, its operator, the official scorebook and official scorer. The referee shall be responsible for notifying each captain 3 minutes before each half is to begin.

The referee shall not permit any player to wear equipment which, in his or her judgment, is dangerous to other players. Elbow, hand, finger, wrist or forearm guard, cast or brace made of hard and unyielding leather, plaster, pliable (soft) plastic, metal or any other hard substance, even though covered with soft padding, shall always be declared illegal. Head decorations and/or head wear other than a non-abrasive, unadorned, single colored head band no wider than 2 inches made of cloth, elastic, fiber, soft leather, pliable plastic or rubber are illegal. Players may not wear jewelry.

Any equipment, which is unnatural and designed to increase a player's height or reach or to gain an advantage, shall not be used.

SECTION 3. The referee shall toss the ball at center to start each period. He or she shall decide whether a goal shall count if the officials disagree. He or she shall have power to forfeit a game when conditions warrant. He or she shall decide matters upon which the timers and the scorers disagree. At the end of each half he or she shall check and approve the score. His or her approval at the end of the game terminates the jurisdiction of the officials.

SECTION 4. The referee shall have power to make decisions on any points not specifically covered in the rules.

SECTION 5. The officials shall conduct the game in accordance with the rules. This includes: notifying the captains when play is about to begin at the start of the game, following an intermission or charged time-out, or after any unusual delay in putting the ball in play; putting the ball in play; determining when the ball becomes dead; prohibiting practice during a dead ball, except between halves; administering penalties; ordering time-out; beckoning substitutes to enter the court; warning a team for lack of sufficient action; signaling the point value of a goal by raising one or two fingers to face level and silently and visibly counting seconds to administer rules 4-15, 7-6, 8-4, 9-1, 9-8, and 10-2-c.

SECTION 6. The officials shall penalize unsportsmanlike conduct by any player, coach, substitute, team attendant or follower. If there is flagrant misconduct the officials shall penalize by removing any offending player from the game and banishing any offending coach, substitute, team attendant or follower from the vicinity of the court. A player who commits his or her fifth personal foul shall be removed from the game.

Ques.—Who is responsible for behavior of spectators? **Ans.**—The home management or game committee, insofar as they can reasonably be expected to control the spectators. The officials may call fouls on either team if its supporters act in such a way as to interfere with the proper conduct of the game. Discretion must be used in calling such fouls, however, lest a team be unjustly penalized.

SECTION 7. Neither official shall have authority to set aside or question decisions made by the other within the limits of his or her respective outlined duties.

Ques. (1)—Does referee's decision take precedence over umpire's in calling a foul? **Ans.**—No.

Ques. (2)—A violation, as outlined in Rule 9-2 to 10, and personal contact occur at about the same time. Both are observed by the same official or the violation is observed by one official and the contact by the other. What is the proper procedure? **Ans.**—The officials should decide which occurred first. If the violation was first, it caused the ball to become dead, hence, the contact which followed was not a foul unless unsportsmanlike. If the contact occurred first, it caused the ball to become dead and no violation occurred.

SECTION 8. The officials shall have power to make decisions for infractions of rules committed either within or outside the boundary lines. Prior to the game the officials' jurisdiction shall begin when the officials arrive on the floor. This shall be at least fifteen minutes before the scheduled starting time of the game. Their jurisdiction extends through the referee's approval of the final score. This includes the periods when the game may be momentarily stopped for any reason.

SECTION 9. (a) When a foul occurs, an official shall signal the timer to stop the clock, and shall designate the offender to the scorers and indicate with fingers the number of free throws.

NOTE—It is strongly recommended that a player when charged with a foul raise one hand only at full arm's length above the head and lower it in such a manner as not to indicate resentment.

(b) When a team is entitled to a throw-in, an official shall clearly signal the act which caused the ball to become dead, the throw-in spot unless it follows a successful goal or an awarded goal, and the player or team entitled to the throw-in. The official shall hand (not toss) the ball to the thrower-in for a throw-in unless the throw-in is from outside an endline following a successful goal.

SECTION 10. Officials may correct an error if a rule is inadvertently set aside and results in: (a) failure to award a merited free throw; or (b) awarding an unmerited free throw; or (c) permitting a wrong player to attempt a free throw; or (d) attempting a free throw at the wrong basket; or (e) erroneously counting or canceling a score.

In order to correct any of the 5 official's errors listed above, such error must be recognized by an official before the ball again becomes alive following the first dead ball after the clock has started.

If the error is a free throw by the wrong player, or at the wrong basket or the awarding of an unmerited free throw, the free throw and the activity during it, other than unsportsmanlike conduct, shall be canceled. However, other points scored, consumed time and additional activity, which may occur prior to the recognition of a mistake, shall not be nullified. Error because of free throw attempts by the wrong player or at the wrong basket shall be corrected by applying rule 8-1 and 2.

If an error is corrected, play shall be resumed from the point at which it was interrupted to rectify the error.

NOTE—Having more than five squad members participating simultaneously; or participating after having been disqualified; or wearing an identical number; or a player participating after changing his or her number without reporting it to the scorers and an official; requiring an addition to or change in the squad list or a change entered in the scorebook, are infractions which shall also be penalized if discovered during the time a provision is being violated (see penalty following Rule 10-9).

SECTION 11. The scorers shall record the field goals made, the free throws made and missed, and shall keep a running summary of the points scored. They shall record the personal and technical fouls called on each player and shall notify the referee immediately when the fifth personal foul is called on any player. They shall record the time-outs charged to each team, and shall notify a team and its coach through an official whenever that team takes a fifth charged time-out. They shall signal the nearer official each time a team is granted a charged time-out in excess of the legal number and in each half when a player commits a common foul beginning with her or his team's 5th personal foul (for a game played in quarters). The scorebook of the home team shall be the official book, unless the referee rules otherwise. The official scorebook shall remain at the scorer's table throughout the game including all intermissions. The scorers shall compare their records after each goal, each foul and each charged time-out, notifying the referee at once of any discrepancy.

If the error cannot be found, the referee shall accept the record of the official book, unless he or she has knowledge which permits her or him to decide otherwise. If the discrepancy is in the score and the error is not resolved, the referee shall accept the progressive team totals of the official scorebook.

The scorers shall keep a record of the names and numbers of players who are to start the game and of all substitutes who enter the game. When there is an infraction of the rules pertaining to submission of the roster, substitutions or numbers of players, they shall notify the nearer official.

To signal the officials, the scorers shall use a sounding device unlike that used by the referee and umpire. This may be used immediately if (or as soon as) the ball is dead, or is in control of the offending team.

NOTE—The Rules Committee strongly recommends that the official scorer wear a black and white striped garment and that his or her location be clearly marked.

Ques. (1)—What is the procedure if a player who has committed his or her 5th personal foul continues to play because the scorers have failed to notify the official? **Ans.**—As soon as scorers discover the irregularity, they should sound the horn after (or as soon as) the ball is in control of the offending team or is dead. The disqualified player must be removed immediately. Any points which may have been scored while such player was illegally in the game are counted. **If other aspects of the error are correctable, the procedure to be followed is included among the duties of the officials** (2-10).

Ques. (2)—Should scorers notify a player when he or she has committed his or her 4th personal foul? **Ans.**—No; but a captain may request an official to obtain this information when it can be done without delaying the game.

Ques. (3)—What should be done if the scorer's horn sounds while the ball is alive? **Ans.**—Players should ignore the horn since it does not make the ball dead. The scorers should not signal while the ball is in play except in certain cases such as are noted in the first question above. The officials must use their judgment in blowing the ball dead to consult the scorers.

Ques. (4)—If the scorers fail to notify a team or its coach when it takes its fifth charged time-out, should the team be penalized if it takes a sixth time-out? **Ans.**—Yes.

SECTION 12. The timers shall note when each half is to start and shall notify the referee more than three minutes before this time so that he or she may notify the teams, or cause them to be notified, at least three minutes before the half is to start. They shall signal the scorers three minutes before starting time. They shall record playing time and time of stoppages as provided in the rules.

The timers shall be provided with a clock to be used for timing periods and intermissions, and a stopwatch for timing time-outs. The clock shall be operated by one of the timers. The clock and stopwatch shall be placed so that they may be seen by both timers.

The clock shall be started as prescribed in Rule 5-10.

Fifteen seconds before the expiration of an intermission, a charged time-out or a time-out for replacing a disqualified player, the timer shall sound a warning signal immediately after which the players shall be ready to resume play.

The clock shall be stopped: at the expiration of time for each period, and when an official signals time-out, as in 5-8. For a charged time-out, the timers shall start the stopwatch and shall direct the scorers to signal the referee when it is time to resume play.

Expiration of playing time in each quarter, half, or extra period shall be indicated by the timer's signal. This signal terminates player activity. If the timer's signal fails to sound, or is not heard, the timers shall go on the court or use other means to notify the referee immediately. If, in the meantime, a goal has been made or a foul has occurred, the referee shall consult the timers. If the timers agree that time expired before the ball was in flight, the goal shall not count. If they agree that the period ended (as in 5-6-c) before the foul occurred, the foul shall be disregarded unless it was unsportsmanlike. If the timers disagree, the goal shall count or the foul shall be penalized unless the referee has knowledge which alters such ruling.

If an obvious error by the timer has occurred because of the failure to start or stop the clock at the proper moment, the referee may correct the error only when he or she has definite information relative to the time involved.

Ques.—Should timers tell players or coaches how much time remains? **Ans.**—On request, an official should give this information to both teams when the ball is dead and time is out.

RULE 3   Players and Substitutes

SECTION 1. Each team consists of 5 players, one of whom is the captain.

Ques.—May a team play with less than 5 players? **Ans.**—A team must begin with 5 players, but if it has no substitutes to replace disqualified players, it must continue with less than 5.

SECTION 2. The captain is the representative of his or her team and may address an official on matters of interpretation or to obtain essential information, if it is done in a courteous manner. Any player may address an official to request a time-out (5-8-3) or permission to leave the court.

At least 10 minutes before scheduled starting time each team shall supply the scorers with: (a) name and number of each squad member who may participate and (b) the five starting players designated.

After the time limit specified has been reached a team is charged with a technical foul for: (1) failure to comply with (a) or (b); (2) each name added to the squad list; (3) each change in a squad member's number without reporting the change to the scorers and an official; and (4) each change in the starting line-up.

SECTION 3. A substitute who desires to enter shall report to the scorers, giving his or her number and the number of the player who is being replaced. Substitutions between halves shall be made to the official scorer by the substitute(s) or a team representative prior to the signal which ends the intermission. If entry is at any time other than between halves, and a substitute, who is entitled and ready to enter, reports to the scorers before change of status of the ball is about to occur, the scorers shall use a sounding device if (or as soon as) the ball is dead and time is out. The substitute shall remain outside the boundary until an official beckons him or her, whereupon he or she shall enter immediately. If the ball is about to become alive, the beckoning signal should be withheld. The entering player shall not replace a free thrower or a jumper except as stated in 6-3-c, d, and e and 8-2 and 3. If the substitute enters to replace a player who must jump or attempt a free throw, he or she shall withdraw until the next opportunity to substitute.

A player who has been withdrawn may not re-enter before the next opportunity to substitute after the clock has started following his or her replacement.

Ques. (1)—When does a substitute become a player? **Ans.**—When he or she legally enters the court to participate or if he or she entered illegally during a dead ball, after the ball has become alive.

Ques. (2)—Following substitutions, should the official line up players to aid them in locating opponents? **Ans.**—This shall be done at the request of a captain only when three or more substitutes for the same team enter during an opportunity to substitute.

SECTION 4. (a) Team shirts shall be of the same solid color front and back. The only decorations permitted are: (1) side inserts or trim of any color centered vertically below the arm pit and not to exceed 4" in width (2" on each side of the seam), (2) piping not to exceed one inch around the neck and arm openings, (3) a waist opening band of any color(s) not to exceed 4 inches wide and at least 4 inches below the bottom of the number or name if it appears under the number. Team shirts for females may have collars and sleeves of any color(s). Shirts purchased after June 1976 with a waist opening band exceeding 4 inches in width are illegal.

NOTE—Girls' basketball teams below the varsity level may wear uniforms made illegal in 1973 by Rule 3, Section 4 (a).

(b) An identifying name may be placed horizontally or vertically on either or on both the front and back of the shirt.

(c) Each player shall be numbered on the front and back of the shirt with plain arabic numerals of solid color contrasting with the color of the shirt, and made of material not less than three-quarters inch wide. The number on the back shall be at least 6 inches high and that on the front at least 4 inches high. Neither of the single digit numbers (1) or (2) nor any digit greater than 5 shall be used nor may a number have more than two digits.

Ques. (1)—If contesting teams have uniforms of the same color, what shall be done? **Ans.**—If possible, each team should have two sets of uniforms, one of light color and the other dark. The light color is for home games. The team which violates this policy should change. If there is doubt, the officials should request the home team to change; on a neutral floor the officials decide.

Ques. (2)—What is the penalty for wearing an illegal number or a shirt with diagonal or tailed lettering? **Ans.**—The penalty is a technical foul if the player enters the game, and the infraction is discovered before the clock starts.

Ques. (3)—May the numbers on the shirt have a border? **Ans.**—Yes, but only when the border is no wider than one-quarter inch.

(d) Members of the same squad shall not wear identical numbers.

Ques.—If two or more squad members are wearing identical numbers, what is the penalty? **Ans.**—A second listed squad member (and any following members wearing an identical number) is charged with a technical foul. The penalty shall be imposed whenever the infraction is discovered. When there is duplication only one of the squad will be permitted to wear a given number. All others must change to a number not already in use before they may participate.

RULE 4   Definitions

SECTION 1. A basket is the 18-inch ring, its flange and braces, and appended net through which players attempt to throw the ball. A team's own basket is the one into which its players try to throw the ball. The visiting team shall have the irrevocable choice of baskets at which it may practice before the game and this basket shall be its choice for the 1st half. The teams shall change baskets for the 2nd half.

SECTION 2. Blocking is illegal personal contact which impedes the progress of an opponent.

SECTION 3. A bonus free throw is a second free throw which is awarded for each common foul (except a player control foul) committed by a player of a team beginning with that team's 5th personal foul in a half, provided the 1st free throw for the foul is successful.

SECTION 4. Boundary lines of the court consist of end and side lines. The inside edges of these lines define the inbounds and out of bounds areas.

SECTION 5. Change of status is the time at which a dead ball becomes alive or a live ball becomes dead. Change of status is about to occur when:

(a) A player has started to make a throw-in; or

(b) 80% of the time limit count has expired; or

(c) An official is ready to make the toss for a jump; or

(d) An official starts to place the ball at the disposal of a free thrower.

SECTION 6. A player is in control when he or she is holding a live ball or dribbling it.

A team is in control when a player of the team is in control and also while a live ball is being passed between teammates. Team control continues until: the ball is in flight during a try for goal; or an opponent secures control; or the ball becomes dead. There is no team control: during a jump ball; a throw-in; during the tapping of a rebound; or after the ball is in flight during a try for goal. In these situations team control is reestablished when a player secures control.

SECTION 7. A disqualified player is one who is barred from further participation in the game because of committing his or her fifth personal foul, or a flagrant foul, or for infraction of Rule 10-6-a or b.

SECTION 8. A dribble is ball movement caused by a player in control who bats, pushes, or taps the ball to the floor once or several times. During a dribble the ball may be batted into the air, provided it is permitted to strike the floor one or more times before the ball is touched again.

The dribble may be started by:

(a) Batting, tapping, or throwing the ball into the air; or

(b) Batting, pushing, or tapping the ball to the floor.

The dribble ends when: (a) the dribbler catches the ball with one or both hands; or (b) the dribbler touches the ball with both hands simultaneously; or (c) the dribbler is unable to immediately catch or continue to dribble the ball; or (d) an opponent bats the ball; or (e) the ball becomes dead.

Ques. (1)—Is a player dribbling while tapping the ball during a jump, or when a pass rebounds from his or her hand, or when he or she fumbles, or when he or she taps a rebound or a pass away from other players who are attempting to get it? **Ans.**—No. The player is not in control under these conditions.

Ques. (2)—Is it a dribble when a player stands still and: (a) bounces the ball; or (b) holds the ball and touches it to the floor once or more? **Ans.**—(a) Yes. (b) No.

Ques. (3)—May a dribbler alternate hands? **Ans.**—Yes.

Ques. (4)—Prior to beginning, or after completing the dribble, A1 tosses the ball, one or several times, from hand to hand. **Ans.**—Legal. The act of tossing the ball from one hand to the other is administered exactly as if A1 were holding the ball. Foot movement limitations are identical for a player holding the ball and for tossing it from one hand to the other.

SECTION 9. Dunking (or stuffing) is the driving, or forcing, or pushing, or attempting to force a ball through the basket with the hand(s).

SECTION 10. Extra period is the extension of playing time necessary to break a tie score.

SECTION 11. (a) A foul is an infraction of the rules, which is charged and penalized.

(b) A common foul is a personal foul, which is neither flagrant nor intentional nor committed against a player trying for field goal, nor a part of a double or multiple foul.

(c) A double foul is a situation in which 2 opponents commit personal fouls against each other at approximately the same time. **A false double foul** is a situation in which there are fouls by both teams, the second of which occurs before the clock is started following the first, but such that at least one of the attributes of a double foul is absent.

(d) A flagrant foul is an unsportsmanlike act and may be a personal or technical foul of a violent or savage nature, or a technical non-contact foul, which displays vulgar or abusive conduct. It may or may not be intentional.

(e) An intentional foul is a personal or technical foul, which in the judgment of the official

appears to be designed or premeditated. It is not based on the severity of the act.

(f) A multiple foul is a situation in which 2 or more teammates commit personal fouls against the same opponent at approximately the same time. **A false multiple foul** is a situation in which there are 2 or more fouls by the same team and such that the last foul is committed before the clock is started following the first, and such that at least one of the attributes of a multiple foul is absent.

(g) A personal foul (10-11) is a player foul which involves contact with an opponent while the ball is alive or after the ball is in possession of a player for a throw-in.

(h) A player control foul is a common foul commited by a player while he, she, or a teammate is in control.

(i) A technical foul (10-1 through 10) is: a foul by a non-player, or a player foul which does not involve contact with an opponent, or a player foul which involves unsportsmanlike contact with an opponent while the ball is dead, except as indicated in last clause of (g) above.

(j) An unsportsmanlike foul is a technical foul which consists of unfair, unethical or dishonorable conduct.

SECTION 12. A free throw is the privilege given a player to score one point by an unhindered try for goal from within the free throw circle and behind the free throw line. A free throw starts when the ball is given to the free thrower at the free throw line or is placed on the line. It ends when: the try is successful; or it is certain the try will not be successful; or when the try touches the floor or any player; or when the ball becomes dead.

SECTION 13 (a) A team's front court consists of that part of the court between its end line and the nearer edge of the division line and including its basket and the inbounds part of its backboard. **(b) A team's back court** consists of the rest of the court including its opponent's basket and inbounds part of the backboard and the entire division line. **(c) A team's midcourt** is that part of its front court between the division line and a parallel imaginary line 28 feet from the inside edge of the end boundary to the nearer edge of the mid-court area marker. This imaginary line is located by two 3 foot lines 2 inches wide measured from the inside edge of each side boundary and drawn at right angles to it. **(d) A team's fore-court** extends from the nearer edge of the mid-court area marker to the inside edge of the end boundary.

(e) A live ball is in the front or back court of

the team in control as follows: (1) **A ball which is in contact** with a player or with the court is in the back court if either the ball or the player (either player if the ball is touching more than one) is touching the back court. It is in the front court if neither the ball nor the player is touching the back court. (2) **A ball which is not in contact** with a player or the court retains the same status as when it was last in contact with a player or the court.

Ques.—From the front court, A passes the ball across the division line. It touches a teammate who is in the air after leaping from the back court or it touches an official in the back court. Is the ball in the back court? Ans.—Yes. See 4-19.

SECTION 14. A fumble is the accidental loss of player control by unintentionally dropping the ball or permitting it to slip from one's grasp.

SECTION 15. Held ball occurs when:

(a) Opponents have hands so firmly on the ball that control cannot be obtained without undue roughness; or

(b) A team, in its front court, controls the ball for 5 seconds in an area enclosed by screening teammates; or

(c) A closely guarded player, in his or her mid-court, dribbles, or combines dribbling and holding the ball for 5 seconds; or

(d) A closely guarded player anywhere in his or her front court holds or dribbles the ball for 5 seconds.

Exception to (c) and (d):

1. When a player dribbles from the MID-COURT into the fore-court, a new 5-second count shall begin; or

2. When a player starts a dribble in the FORE-COURT, a new 5-second count shall begin if the player ends the dribble anywhere in the front court and then holds the ball.

The player in control is closely guarded when an opponent is in a guarding stance at a distance not exceeding 6 feet from him or her.

Ques.—Is it a held ball merely because the player holding the ball is lying or sitting on the floor? Ans.—No.

SECTION 16. Holding is personal contact with an opponent which interferes with his or her freedom of movement.

SECTION 17. A jump ball is a method of putting the ball into play by tossing it up between 2 opponents in one of the 3 circles. It begins when the ball leaves the official's hand, and ends as outlined in rule 6-4.

SECTION 18. Lack of sufficient action is the failure of the responsible team to force play as required by the Comments on the Rules.

SECTION 19. The location of a player (or non-player) is determined by where he or she is touching the floor as far as being inbounds or out of bounds or being in the front court or back court is concerned. When he or she is in the air from a leap, his or her status with reference to these two factors is the same as at the time he or she was last in contact with the floor or an extension of the floor such as a bleacher. When the ball touches an official, it is the same as touching the floor at the official's location.

SECTION 20. A multiple throw is a succession of free throws attempted by the same team.

SECTION 21. A pass is movement of the ball caused by a player, who throws, bats, or rolls the ball to another player.

SECTION 22. A penalty for a foul is the charging of the offender with the foul and awarding one or more free throws, or awarding the ball to the opponents for a throw-in. The penalty for a violation is the awarding of the ball to the opponents for a throw-in or one or more points or a substitute free throw.

SECTION 23. A pivot takes place when a player who is holding the ball steps once or more than once in any direction with the same foot, the other foot, called the pivot foot, being kept at its point of contact with the floor.

SECTION 24. A rule is one of the groups of laws which govern the game. A game law (commonly called a rule) sometimes states or implies the ball is dead or a foul or violation is involved. If it does not, it is assumed the ball is alive and no foul or violation has occurred to affect the given situation. A single infraction is not complicated by a second infraction unless so stated or implied.

SECTION 25. Running with the ball (traveling) is moving a foot or the feet in any direction in excess of prescribed limits while holding the ball. The limits follow:

Item 1. A player who receives the ball while standing still may pivot, using either foot as the pivot foot.

Item 2. A player who receives the ball while his or her feet are moving or who is dribbling, may stop as follows:

(a) If he or she catches the ball while **both feet** are off the floor and:

(1) **He or she alights with both feet** touching the floor simultaneously, he or she may pivot using either foot as the pivot foot; or

(2) **He or she alights with first one foot** touching the floor followed by the other, he or she may pivot using

the first foot to touch the floor as the pivot foot; or

(3) **He or she alights on one foot,** he or she may jump off that foot and alight with both feet simultaneously but he or she may not pivot before releasing the ball.

(b) If he or she catches the ball while only **one foot** is off the floor:

(1) **He or she may step** with the foot which is off the floor and may then pivot using the other foot as the pivot foot; or

(2) **He or she may jump** with the foot which is on the floor and alight with both feet simultaneously, but he or she may not pivot before releasing the ball.

Item 3. After a player has come to a stop, he or she may pass or throw for goal under the following conditions:

(a) In Items 1, 2a(1), 2a(2), and 2b(1), he or she may **lift either foot,** but if he or she passes or throws for goal, the ball must leave his or her hand before the pivot foot again touches the floor; or if he or she has jumped before either foot touches the floor.

(b) In Items 2a(3) and 2b(2), he or she may **lift either foot or jump** before he or she passes or throws for goal. However, the ball must leave his or her hand before a foot which has left the floor retouches it.

Item 4. A player who receives the ball as in Item 1 or a player who comes to a stop after he or she receives the ball while he or she is moving his or her feet, may start a dribble under the following conditions:

(a) In Items 1, 2a(1), 2a(2), and 2b(1), the ball must leave his or her hand **before the pivot foot leaves the floor.**

(b) In Items 2a(3) and 2b(2), the ball must leave his or her hand **before either foot leaves the floor.**

Ques. (1)—Is it traveling, if a player falls to the floor while holding the ball? **Ans.**—No, unless he or she makes progress by sliding.

Ques. (2)—A1 gains control of the ball while on the floor and then rolls or slides, after which he or she passes to A2 before getting to his or her feet. **Ans.**—Legal, unless A1 gains an advantage when he or she rolls or slides.

Ques. (3)—A1 jumps to throw the ball. B1 prevents the throw by placing one or both hands firmly on the ball so that: (a) A1; or (b) A1 and B1 both return to the floor holding it. **Ans.**—Held ball. However, if A1 voluntarily drops the ball before he or she returns to the floor and he or she then touches the ball before it is touched by another player, A1 has committed a traveling violation.

SECTION 26. A screen is legal action by a player who, without causing contact, delays or prevents an opponent from reaching a desired position.

SECTION 27. A tap (tip) is the striking or batting of the ball with any part of the hand(s) while there is not player control by the tapper. The tap starts when the ball has left the player's hand(s). The tap (or tip) in flight from a player toward his or her basket ends in exactly the same manner as a try. (See 4-29a)

SECTION 28. A throw-in is a method of putting the ball in play from out of bounds in accordance with Rule 7. The throw-in begins when the ball is at the disposal of the player or team entitled to it and ends when the passed ball touches or is touched by an inbounds player other than the thrower-in.

SECTION 29. (a) A try for field goal is an attempt by a player to score 2 points by throwing the ball into his or her basket. The try starts when the player begins the motion which habitually precedes the release of the ball. The try ends when the throw is successful, or it is certain the throw is unsuccessful, or when the thrown ball touches the floor or any player, or when the ball becomes dead.

(b) The act of shooting begins simultaneously with the start of the try and ends when the ball is clearly in flight.

SECTION 30. A violation is a rule infraction of the type listed in Rule 9.

RULE 5   Scoring and Timing Regulations

SECTION 1. A goal is made when a live ball enters the basket from above and remains in or passes through.

SECTION 2. A goal from the field counts 2 points for the team into whose basket the ball is thrown. A goal from a free throw is credited to the thrower and counts 1 point for his or her team.

NOTE—A field goal in A's basket after being last touched by B is not credited to any player but is mentioned in a footnote and two points are added to A's total.

Ques.—A player throws a field goal in his or her opponents' basket. Who gets credit for the goal? **Ans.**—It is not credited to a player. It is added to the opponents' score and mentioned in a footnote.

SECTION 3. The winning team is the one which has accumulated the greater number of points when the game ends.

SECTION 4. The referee shall forfeit the game if a team refuses to play after being instructed to do so by either official. If the team to which the game is forfeited is ahead, the score at the time of forfeiture shall stand. If this team is not ahead the score shall be recorded as 2–0 in its favor.

Ques.—When the game is forfeited, are the points made by each player credited to him or her? Ans.—The league officers should decide. It is customary to include such points in the scoring records.

SECTION 5. Playing time shall be: (a) for teams of high school age, 4 quarters of 8 minutes each with intermissions of 1 minute after the 1st and 3rd quarters and 10 minutes between halves; (b) for teams younger than in (a), 4 quarters of 6 minutes each with intermissions the same as for (a).

Games involving only students below the 9th grade shall be played in 6 minute quarters. An organization sponsoring games involving teams which combine 9th grade students with students in the 8th and/or 7th grades may be played in 8 minute quarters.

A period or periods may be shortened in an emergency or at any time by mutual agreement of the opposing coaches and referee. Playing time for non-varsity game quarters may be reduced by mutual agreement of opposing coaches.

SECTION 6. Each period begins when the ball first becomes alive. **It ends** when time expires except that: (a) if the ball is in flight during a try for field goal or in flight from a tap by a player toward his or her basket, the period ends when the try or tap ends; or (b) if a held ball or violation occurs so near the expiration of time that the clock is not stopped before time expires, the period ends with the held ball or violation; or (c) if a foul occurs so near the expiration of time that the timer cannot get the clock stopped before time expires or if the foul occurs after time expires but while the ball is in flight during a try for field goal or in flight from tap by a player toward his or her basket, the period ends when the free throw or throws and all related activity have been completed.

SECTION 7. If the score is tied at the end of the second half, play shall continue without change of baskets for one or more extra periods with a one-minute intermission before each extra period. The game ends if, at the end of any extra period, the score is not tied.

The length of each extra period shall be 3 minutes. As many such periods as are necessary to break the tie shall be played. Extra periods are an extension of the 2nd half.

Ques.—With the score tied, a foul is committed near the expiration of time in the second half. If the free throw is successful, should an extra period be played? Ans.—If the foul occurs before the ball becomes dead and the period is ended as outlined in 5-6, no extra period is played. But if the foul occurs after the period has clearly ended, the extra period is played.

SECTION 8. Time-out occurs and the clock, if running, shall be stopped when an official:

Item 1. Signals: (a) a foul; (b) a held ball; or (c) a violation.

Item 2. Stops play: (a) because of an injury; (b) to confer with scorers or timers; (c) because of unusual delay in getting a dead ball alive; or (d) for any emergency.

Item 3. Grants a player's request for a time-out, such request being granted only when the ball is dead or in control of a player of his or her team and when no change of status of the ball is about to occur.

Item 4. Responds to the scorer's signal to grant a coach's request that a correctable error be prevented or rectified. The request to the scorer must be made before the ball becomes alive following the first dead ball after the clock has started. The appeal to the official shall be presented at the scorers' table when a coach of each team may be present.

NOTE—When a player is injured as in Item 2-a, the official may suspend play after the ball is dead or is in control of the injured player's team or when the opponents complete a play. A play is completed when a team loses control (including throwing for goal), or withholds the ball from play by ceasing to attempt to score or advance the ball to a scoring position. When necessary to protect an injured player, the official may suspend play immediately.

SECTION 9. A time-out shall be charged to a team for each minute or fraction of a minute consumed under Items 2-a, 3 and 4 of Section 8.

EXCEPTIONS: No time-out is charged:

(a) If in Item 2(a) an injured player is ready to play immediately or is replaced until at least the next opportunity to substitute after the clock has started following his or her replacement.

(b) If in Item 3 the player's request results from displaced eyeglasses or lens; or

(c) If in Item 4 a correctable error is prevented or rectified.

SECTION 10. After time has been out, the clock shall be started when the official signals time-in. If official neglects to signal, the timer is authorized to start the clock unless an official specifically signals continued time-out.

(a) **If play is resumed by a jump,** the clock shall be started when the tossed ball is legally tapped.

(b) **If a free throw is not successful** and ball is to remain alive, the clock shall be started when the ball is touched or touches a player on the court.

(c) **If play is resumed by a throw-in,** the clock shall be started when the ball touches or is touched by a player on the court.

Ques.—During a free throw which is not successful, a violation occurs. Should the clock be started when the ball is touched or touches a player on the court? **Ans.**—No, and official should avoid using the time-in chopping motion if the ball is not to remain alive.

SECTION 11. Each team is entitled to 5 charged time-outs during a regulation game (two halves or four quarters of play). During each extra period, each team is always entitled to at least 1 time-out. Unused time-outs accumulate and may be used at any time. Time-outs in excess of the allotted number may be requested and shall be granted during regulation playing time or any overtime period at the expense of a technical foul for each. In no case shall successive charged time-outs be granted after expiration of playing time for the fourth quarter, or after the expiration of any overtime period.

RULE 6   Live Ball and Dead Ball

SECTION 1. The game shall be started by a jump ball in the center circle. After any subsequent dead ball, play shall be resumed by a jump ball or by a throw-in or by placing it at the disposal of a free thrower. The ball becomes alive when: (a) on a jump ball, the ball leaves the official's hand; or (b) on a throw-in, the ball touches or is touched by a player who is inbounds; or (c) on a free throw, the ball is placed at the disposal of the free thrower.

SECTION 2. The ball shall be put in play in the center circle by a jump between any two opponents: (a) at the beginning of each quarter and extra period; or (b) after a double foul.

Ques.—Does a quarter, half, or extra period start with a jump ball if a foul occurs before the ball becomes alive? **Ans.**—No. Any rules statement is made on the assumption that no infraction is involved unless mentioned or implied. If such infraction occurs, the rule governing it is followed in accordance with Rule 4-24.

SECTION 3. The ball shall be put in play by a jump ball at the center of the restraining circle which is nearest the spot where: (a) a held ball occurs; or (b) the ball goes out of bounds as in 7-3; or (c) a double free throw violation occurs; or (d) a live ball lodges on a basket support; or (e) the ball becomes dead when neither team is in control and no goal or infraction or end of a period is involved. In (a) and (b), the jump shall be between the two involved players unless injury or disqualification requires substitution for a jumper, in which case his or her substitute shall jump. In (c), (d), and (e), the jump shall be between any two opponents.

SECTION 4. (a) For any jump ball, each jumper shall have one or both feet on or inside that half of the jumping circle (imaginary if in a free throw restraining circle) which is farther from his or her own basket and both feet within the restraining circle. An official shall then toss the ball upward between the jumpers in a plane at right angles to the sidelines, to a height greater than either of them can jump and so that it will drop between them. The ball must be tapped by one or both of the jumpers after it reaches its highest point. If it touches the floor without being tapped by at least one of the jumpers, the official shall toss the ball again.

(b) **Neither jumper shall:** tap the tossed ball before it reaches its highest point; nor leave the jumping circle until the ball has been tapped; nor catch the jump ball; nor touch it more than twice. The jump ball and these restrictions end when the tapped ball touches one of the eight non-jumpers, the floor, the basket or the backboard.

(c) **When the official is ready** to make the toss, a non-jumper shall not move onto the circle or change position around the circle until the ball has left the official's hand.

(d) **None of the 8 non-jumpers** shall have either foot break the plane of the restraining circle cylinder until the ball has been tapped. Teammates may not occupy adjacent positions around the restraining circle if an opponent indicates his or her desire for one of these positions before the official is ready to toss the ball; nor may any player take a position in any occupied space.

Ques.—During jump ball, is a jumper required to: (a) face his or her own basket; and (b) jump and attempt to tap the tossed ball? **Ans.**—(a) No specific facing is required. However, a jumper must be in the proper half of the jumping circle. (b) No. But if neither jumper taps the ball, it should be tossed again with both jumpers being ordered to jump.

SECTION 5. The ball shall be put in play by a throw-in under circumstances as outlined in Rules 7, 8-5, and 9-1 to 11.

SECTION 6. The ball shall be put in play by

placing it at the disposal of a free thrower before each free throw.

SECTION 7. The ball becomes dead or remains dead when:

(a) **Any goal** is made as in 5-1;

(b) **It is apparent** the free throw will not be successful: on a free throw for a technical foul or a false double foul, or a free throw which is to be followed by another throw;

(c) **Held ball** occurs or ball lodges on the basket support;

(d) **Official's whistle** is blown;

(e) **Time expires** for a quarter, half, or extra period;

(f) **A foul occurs;** or

(g) **Any floor violation** (9-2 to 10) occurs, or there is basket interference (9-11), or there is a free throw violation by the thrower's team (9-1).

EXCEPTION 1. The ball does not become dead until the try or tap ends when: (a) d, e, or f in 6-7 above occurs while a try for a field goal or a tapped ball by a player toward his or her basket are in flight; or (b) d or f in 6-7 above occurs while a try for a free throw is in flight; or (c) a foul is committed by an opponent of a player who has started a try for field goal (is in the act of shooting) before the foul occurred provided time did not expire before the ball was in flight. The trying motion must be continuous and begins after the ball comes to rest in the player's hand or hands and is completed when the ball is clearly in flight. The trying motion may include arm, foot, or body movements used by the player when throwing the ball at his or her basket; or (d) when the ball is in flight on a try for field goal or during a free throw and a defensive player excessively swings his or her arms or elbows without contacting an opponent, the ball remains alive.

Ques.—If the ball is in flight during A's try for field goal or A's tap in flight toward own basket when time for the period expires, and if the ball is subsequently touched, does the goal count if made? **Ans.**—No. The ball becomes dead when touched while in flight during the try or tap. If it is basket interference (9-11) by B, 2 points are awarded to A.

EXCEPTION 2: The ball does not become dead while it is in the air on a tap by a player toward his or her basket if: (a) time expires; or (b) a foul is committed; or (c) any opponent of the player making the tap at his or her basket swings his or her arms or elbows excessively without making contact.

RULE 7   Out of Bounds and the Throw-In

SECTION 1. A player is out of bounds when he or she touches the floor or any object other than a player on or outside a boundary. For location of a player in the air, see 4-19.

The ball is out of bounds when it touches: a player who is out of bounds; or any other person, the floor, or any object on or outside a boundary; or the supports or back of the backboard; or ceiling, overhead equipment or supports.

NOTE—When the rectangular backboard is used, the ball is out of bounds if it passes over the backboard.

Ques. (1)—Ball rebounds from the edge of backboard and across boundary line, but before it touches the floor or any obstruction out of bounds, it is caught by a player who is inbounds. Is the ball inbounds or out of bounds? **Ans.**—Inbounds.

Ques. (2)—The ball touches or rolls along the edge of the backboard without touching the supports. Is the ball dead? **Ans.**—No, unless ground rules to the contrary have been mutually agreed upon before the game.

SECTION 2. The ball is caused to go out of bounds by the last player to touch or to be touched by it before it goes out, provided it is out of bounds because of touching something other than a player.

If the ball is out of bounds because of touching or being touched by a player who is on or outside a boundary, such player causes it to go out.

Ques. (1)—Live ball is held by A. (a) The ball held by or passed by A touches B when B is on or outside the boundary; or (b) the ball is batted to out of bounds by B who is inbounds. **Ans.**—Ball awarded to A for a throw-in.

Ques. (2)—Ball passed by A touches an official and goes out of bounds. Whose ball? **Ans.**—B's ball.

SECTION 3. If the ball goes out of bounds and was last touched simultaneously by two opponents, both of whom are inbounds or out of bounds, or if the official is in doubt as to who last touched the ball, or if the officials disagree, play shall be resumed by a jump ball between the two involved players in the nearest restraining circle.

SECTION 4. The ball is awarded out of bounds after: (a) a violation as in Rule 9; or (b) a free throw for a technical foul as in Rule 8-5-b; or (c) a field goal or a successful free throw for personal foul as in 8-5-a or an awarded goal as in 9-11; or (d) the ball becomes dead while a team is in control provided no infraction or the end of a period is involved; or (e) a player control foul; or (f) a common foul until the bonus rule goes into effect.

SECTION 5. (a) When the ball is out of bounds after any violation as outlined in Rule 9-2-11, the official shall designate a nearby opponent of the player who committed the violation, and he or she shall hand the ball to this player or his or her substitute for a throw-in from the designated spot nearest the violation, except as indicated in the penalties which follow in rule 9-10 and 11.

(b) After a dead ball, as listed in section 4-d, any player of the team in control shall make the throw-in from the designated out of bounds spot nearest to the ball when it became dead.

(c) After a player control foul, or after a common foul prior to the bonus rule being in effect any player of the offended team shall make the throw-in from the designated spot nearest the foul, except that, if the ball has passed through the basket during the dead ball period immediately following the foul, no point can be scored and the ball is awarded to any player of the offended team out of bounds at either end of that free throw line extended which is nearer the goal through which the ball was thrown.

(d) If in items a, b, or c, the throw-in spot is behind a backboard, the throw-in shall be made from the nearer free throw lane line extended.

(e) After a goal as listed in section 4-c, the team not credited with the score shall make the throw-in from the end of the court where the goal was made and from any point outside the end boundary. Any player of the team may make a direct throw-in or he or she may pass the ball along the end boundary to a teammate behind the boundary line.

(f) After a technical foul, any player of the team to whom the free throw has been awarded shall make the throw-in from out of bounds at the division line on either side of the court.

(g) After a free throw violation by the throwing team as listed in Rule 9-1, any opponent of the throwing team shall make the throw-in from out of bounds at either end of the free throw line extended.

SECTION 6. The throw-in starts when the ball is at the disposal of a player entitled to the throw-in and he or she shall pass the ball directly into the court, except as provided in 7-5-e, so that, after it crosses the boundary line and before going out of bounds, it touches or is touched by another player on the court within 5 seconds from the time the throw-in starts. Until the passed ball has crossed the plane of the boundary: (a) the thrower shall not leave the designated throw-in spot; (b) no player shall have any part of his or her person over the inside plane of the boundary line; and (c) teammates shall not occupy adjacent positions near the boundary if an opponent desires one of the positions. The 3-foot restraining line is sometimes the temporary boundary as in rule 1-2.

Ques.—B has the ball out of bounds. His or her throw-in: (a) enters a basket before touching anyone; or (b) strikes ring or backboard and rebounds; or (c) touches another player and then enters basket. **Ans.**—(a) Violation by B. A's ball at either end of the nearer free throw line extended. No goal because ball is dead. (b) Ball becomes alive when touched. (c)—Legal goal for team in whose basket the ball remains or through which it passes.

RULE 8   Free Throw

SECTION 1. When a free throw is awarded, an official shall take the ball to the free throw line of the offended team. After allowing reasonable time for players to take their positions, he or she shall put the ball in play by placing it at the disposal of the free thrower. The same procedure shall be followed for each free throw of a multiple throw. During a free throw for personal foul, each of the lane spaces adjacent to the end line shall be occupied by one opponent of the free thrower. A teammate of the free thrower is entitled to the next adjacent lane space on each side and to each other alternate position along each lane line. Not more than one player may occupy any part of a designated lane space. If the ball is to become dead when the last free throw for a specific penalty is not successful, players shall not take positions along the free throw lane.

NOTE—To avoid disconcerting the free thrower, neither official should stand in the free throw lane or the lane extended.

SECTION 2. The free throw or throws awarded because of a personal foul shall be attempted by the offended player. If such player must withdraw because of an injury or disqualification, his or her substitute shall attempt the throw or throws unless no substitute is available, in which event any teammate may attempt the throw or throws. Note: See ques. (1) under 2-11.

SECTION 3. The free throw awarded because of a technical foul may be attempted by any player, including an entering substitute, of the offended team.

SECTION 4. The try for goal shall be made within 10 seconds after the ball has been placed at the disposal of the free thrower at the free throw line. This shall apply to each free throw.

SECTION 5. After a free throw which is not followed by another free throw, the ball shall be put in play by a throw-in: (a) as after a field goal (7-5) if the try is for a personal foul and is successful; or (b) by any player of the free thrower's team from out of bounds at the division line if the free throw is for a technical foul.

SECTION 6. If a free throw for a personal foul is unsuccessful, or if there is a multiple throw for a personal foul (or fouls) and last free throw is unsuccessful, ball remains alive.

If there is a multiple throw and both a personal and technical foul are involved, the tries shall be attempted in the order in which the related fouls were called, and if the last try is for a technical foul the ball shall be put in play as after any technical foul.

SECTION 7. After the last free throw following a false double foul (4-11-c), the ball shall be put in play as if the penalty for the last foul of the false double foul were the only one administered, unless one of the fouls committed is a double foul, in which case the ball will be put in play with a center jump between any two opponents.

Ques.—Two free throws are awarded to A1 and, before time is in, two free throws are awarded to B for a technical foul on the coach of team A. What is the correct procedure? **Ans.**—With no players lined up, A1 shall attempt his or her two free throws and team B shall attempt its two free throws after which ball is awarded to team B out of bounds at the division line.

RULE 9   Violations and Penalties

A player shall not—

SECTION 1. Violate the free throw provisions: (a) The try shall be attempted from within the free throw circle and behind the free throw line. (b) After the ball is placed at the disposal of a free thrower: (1) he or she shall throw within 10 seconds and in such a way that the ball enters the basket or touches the ring before the free throw ends; (2) no opponent shall disconcert the free thrower; (3) no player shall enter or leave a lane space; and (4) the free thrower shall not have either foot beyond the vertical plane of that edge of the free throw line which is farther from the basket; nor any lines which bound the semi-circle; and no other player of either team shall have either foot beyond the vertical plane or cylinder of the outside edge of any lane boundary, nor beyond the vertical plane of any edge of the space (2 inches by 36 inches) designated by a lane space mark or the space (12 inches by 36 inches) designated by a neutral zone mark. The restrictions in (3) and (4) apply until the ball touches the ring or backboard or until the free throw ends. (c) An opponent of the free thrower shall occupy each lane space adjacent to the end line during the try, and no teammate of the free thrower may occupy either of these lane spaces.

PENALTY—(1) If violation is by the free thrower or his or her teammate only, no point can be scored by that throw. Ball becomes dead when violation occurs. Ball is awarded out of bounds on the sideline to the free thrower's team opposite center circle after a technical foul, and to any opponent out of bounds at either end of the free throw line extended after a personal foul. **(2) If violation is by the free thrower's opponent only: if the try is successful, the goal counts and violation is disregarded; if it is not successful, and the ball becomes dead when the free throw ends, a substitute throw shall be attempted by the same thrower under conditions the same as for the throw for which it is substituted. (3) If there is a violation by each team, ball becomes dead when violation by the free thrower's team occurs, no point can be scored, and play shall be resumed by a jump between any two opponents in the nearest circle. The out of bounds provision in penalty item (1) and the jump ball provision in penalty item (3) do not apply if the free throw is to be followed by another free throw. In penalty item (3), if an opponent of the thrower touches the free throw before it has touched the ring, the violation for failure to touch the ring is ignored or if a violation by the free thrower follows disconcertion, a substitute free throw shall be awarded.**

Ques.—During a free throw by A1, B1 pushes A2 and B1 or B2 is in lane too soon. **Ans.**—If free throw is successful, penalize the foul. If free throw is not successful, award a substitute free throw and also penalize foul.

SECTION 2. Cause the ball to go out of bounds.

Ques.—Dribbler in control steps on or outside a boundary, but does not touch the ball while he or she is out of bounds? Is this a violation? **Ans.**—Yes.

SECTION 3. Violate provisions governing the throw-in. The thrower-in shall not: (a) leave the designated throw-in spot; (b) fail to pass the ball directly into the court so that after it crosses the boundary line it touches or is touched by another player on the court before going out of bounds; (c) consume more than 5 seconds from the time the throw-in starts until it touches or is touched by a player on the court; (d) carry the ball onto the court; (e) touch it in the court before it has touched another player; nor (f) throw the ball so that it enters the basket before touching anyone.

No player shall: (g) have any part of his or her person beyond the vertical inside plane of any end line or side line before the ball has crossed the line; nor (h) become the thrower-in or be out of bounds after an official has designated another player.

Ques.—During throw-in, A1 steps or reaches through boundary plane while holding ball. Ans.—Violation. Allowance should be made if space is limited.

SECTION 4. Run with ball, kick it, strike it with fist or cause it to enter and pass through the basket from below.

NOTE—Kicking the ball is a violation only when it is a positive act; accidentally striking the ball with the foot or leg is not a violation.
Ques.—What is kicking the ball? Ans.—Kicking the ball is striking it intentionally with knee or any part of leg or foot below the knee. It is a fundamental of basketball that the ball must be played with the hands.

SECTION 5. Dribble a second time after his or her first dribble has ended, unless it is after he or she has lost control because of: (a) a try for field goal; or (b) a bat by an opponent; or (c) a pass or fumble which has then touched or been touched by another player.

SECTION 6. Violate any provision of 6-4. If both teams simultaneously commit violations during the jump ball, or if the official makes a bad toss, the toss should be repeated.

SECTION 7. Remain for more than 3 seconds in that part of his or her free throw lane between the end boundary and the farther edge of the free throw line while the ball is in control of his or her team in his or her front court. Allowance shall be made for a player who, having been in the restricted area for less than 3 seconds, dribbles in to try for goal.

Ques.—Does the 3-second restriction apply: (a) to a player who has only one foot touching the lane boundary; or (b) while the ball is dead or is in flight during a try? Ans.—(a) Yes, the line is part of the lane. (b) No, the team is not in control.

SECTION 8. Be (and his or her team shall not be) **in continuous control of** a ball which is in his or her back court for more than 10 consecutive seconds.

SECTION 9. Be the first to touch a ball which he or she or a teammate caused to go from front court to back court by being the last to touch the ball while it was in control of his or her team and before it went to the back court.

EXCEPTION: It is not a violation when, after a jump ball at the center circle, a player is the first to secure control of the ball while both feet are off the floor, and he or she then returns to the floor with one or both feet in the back court.

Ques.—A receives pass in his or her front court and throws ball to his or her back court where ball: (a) is touched by a teammate; or (b) goes directly out of bounds; or (c) lies or bounces with all players hesitating to touch it. Ans.—Violation when touched in (a). In (b) it is a violation for going out of bounds. In (c) ball is alive so that B may secure control. If A touches the ball first, it is a violation. The ball continues to be in team control of A, and if A does not touch it the 10-second count starts when the ball arrives in the back court.

SECTION 10. Excessively swing his or her arms or elbows, even though there is no contact with an opponent.

PENALTY—(Sections 2 to 10): Ball becomes dead or remains dead when violation occurs. Ball is awarded to a nearby opponent for a throw-in at the out of bounds spot nearest the violation. If the ball passes through a basket during the dead ball period immediately following a violation, no point can be scored and the ball is awarded to an opponent out of bounds at either end of that free throw line extended nearer the goal through which the ball was thrown.

SECTION 11. (a) Touch the ball or basket when the ball is on or within either basket; or (b) touch the ball when it is touching the cylinder having the ring as its lower base; or (c) touch the ball during a field goal try while it is in its downward flight entirely above the basket ring level and has the possibility of entering the basket in flight; or (d) touch a ball which has been tapped by a player toward his or her own basket while the ball is in its downward flight entirely above the basket ring level and has the possibility of entering the basket in flight. If the ball has touched or been touched by a player before it began its downward flight or if the ball has touched the ring, the restrictions in (c) and (d) do not apply.

EXCEPTION: In (a) or (b), if a player has his or her hand legally in contact with the ball, it is not a violation if such contact with the ball continues after it enters a basket cylinder, or if, in such action, the player touches the basket.

PENALTY—If violation is at the opponent's

basket, offended team is awarded one point if during a free throw and two points in any other case. The crediting of the score and subsequent procedure is the same as if the awarded score had resulted from the ball having gone through the basket, except that the official shall hand the ball to a player of the team entitled to the throw-in.

If the violation is at a team's own basket, no points can be scored and the ball is awarded to the offended team at the out of bounds spot on the side at either end of the free throw line extended.

If the violation results from touching the ball while it is in the basket after entering from below, the ball is awarded out of bounds to the opponent and no points are scored.

If there is a violation by both teams, play shall be resumed **by a jump ball between any two opponents in the nearest circle.**

Ques.—While the ball is in flight during a try for field goal by A or is in flight toward the basket of team A following a tap by A1, a teammate of A pushes an opponent. After this personal foul, the ball is on the ring when B bats it away. Which infraction should be penalized? Ans.—Both. In each situation, award 2 points to A. Then penalize for personal foul.

RULE 10   Fouls and Penalties

A. TECHNICAL FOUL . . .

(See technical infractions in Comments on the Rules)
A team—
SECTION 1. (a) Shall be prohibited from using television monitoring or replay equipment at courtside for coaching purposes.

(b) Shall occupy the players' bench to which it is assigned.
A team shall not—
SECTION 2. Allow the game to develop into an actionless contest.

This includes the following and similar acts:

(a) When clock is not running—consuming a full minute through not being ready when it is time to start either half; or

(b) Fail to supply scorers with data as outlined in rule 3-2; or

(c) When behind in the score, or while on defense with the score tied and after a warning by an official, failing to be continuously aggressive in attempting to secure the ball if on defense, or to advance the ball beyond the mid-court if on offense and there is no opposing action in the mid-court. See "Comments" for interpretation of "reasonably active" and for procedure for administration.
SECTION 3. Change its designated starting line-up or add to its squad list (3-2-a and b).
SECTION 4. Have more than five squad members participating simultaneously.
A team is assessed a technical foul—
SECTION 5. For an excess time-out (5-11).
A player shall not—
SECTION 6. (a) Participate after changing his or her number without reporting it to the scorers and an official;

(b) Participate after having been disqualified;

(c) Wear an identical number (This item also applies to all squad members included in the names supplied to the scorers (3-4-d);

(d) Wear an illegal number;

(e) Wear an illegal shirt;

(f) Grasp either basket during the time of the official's jurisdiction or dunk or stuff, or attempt to dunk or stuff a dead ball prior to or during the game or during any intermission until jurisdiction of the officials has ended. (This item applies to all squad members);

(g) Cause the opponents' backboard to vibrate while the ball is in flight during a try or is touching the backboard or is on or in the basket or in the cylinder above the basket;

(h) Leave the court for an unauthorized reason; or

(i) Purposely delay his or her return to the court after being legally out of bounds.

(j) Attempt to gain an advantage: by interfering with ball after a goal; or by failing to immediately pass ball to nearer official if in control when a violation is called; or by repeated infractions of 9-3-g and h.

(k) Delay the game by preventing the ball from being made promptly alive.

Ques.—A player steps out of bounds to avoid contact. Ans.—This is not a foul unless he or she leaves to conceal himself or herself or to deceive in some other way. If he or she is a dribbler, the ball is out of bounds.

SECTION 7. Use unsportsmanlike tactics, such as: (a) disrespectfully addressing or contacting an official or gesturing in such a manner as to indicate resentment; (b) using profanity; (c) baiting an opponent or obstructing his or her vision by waving hands near his or her eyes; (d) climbing on a teammate to secure greater height to handle ball; (e) knowingly attempting a free throw to which the player was not entitled; or (f) causing unsportsmanlike conduct or contact as in 4-11-i.

NOTE—Contact after the ball has become dead is ignored unless it is unsportsmanlike or is during a throw-in.

A substitute shall not—
SECTION 8. Enter the court: (a) without reporting to scorers; or (b) without his or her name appearing on the pre-game squad list; or (c) (unless between halves) without being beckoned by an official.

NOTE—Substitutions between halves shall be made to the scorer prior to the signal which ends the intermission.

A coach, player, substitute, team attendant or follower shall not—
SECTION 9. (a) Disrespectfully address an official; or (b) attempt to influence his or her decisions; or (c) use profanity; or (d) disrespectfully address or bait an opponent; or (e) object to an official's decision by rising from the bench or using gestures; or (f) incite undesirable crowd reactions; or (g) enter the court unless by permission of an official to attend an injured player; or (h) fail to replace a disqualified player in one minute when a substitute is available.

Coaches shall remain seated on the bench except to—
SECTION 10. (a) rise and stand in front of his or her seat to signal players to request a time-out; (b) while the clock is stopped stand in front of his or her seat to signal or communicate to his or her squad member; (c) spontaneously react to an outstanding play by a member of his or her team; (d) confer with personnel at the scorer's table to specifically request a time-out for a correctable error as in 2-10; (e) attend an injured player when beckoned onto the court by an official; or (f) rise during a charged time-out or intermission.

PENALTY—(Section 1 to 10): If the foul is committed by a squad member, one free throw is awarded. A second free throw is awarded if the foul is flagrant or intentional. If a foul is committed by a coach, team attendant or follower, the offended team shall be awarded two free throws. The captain shall designate the free thrower.

For section 3 one free throw is awarded for each change or addition.

For sections 3, 5, and 6 (a), (b), or (c), an infraction shall be penalized if it is discovered during the time the rule is being violated.

For section 6 (a), (b) or for flagrant or persistent infraction of any item including (f), two free throws shall be awarded and the offender shall be disqualified.

The third technical foul charged to any coach, any squad member, or any bench personnel shall be considered to be flagrant. If the offender is a coach, team attendant, or a follower, he or she shall go to his or her team's locker room or leave the building until the game has ended. If the offender is a player, or a substitute, he or she shall be banished from the vicinity of the court. For failure to comply, the referee may forfeit the game.

B. PERSONAL FOUL . . .
(See personal contact comments.)
SECTION 11. A player shall not: hold, push, charge, trip; nor impede the progress of an opponent by extended arm, shoulder, hip, or knee, or by bending the body into other than a normal position; nor use any rough tactics. He or she shall not contact an opponent with his or her hand unless such contact is only with the opponent's hand while it is on the ball and is incidental to an attempt to play the ball. Contact caused by a defensive player approaching the ball holder from behind is a form of pushing, and that caused by the momentum of a player who has thrown for a goal is a form of charging.

A dribbler shall not charge into nor contact an opponent in his or her path nor attempt to dribble between two opponents or between an opponent and a boundary, unless the space is such as to provide a reasonable chance for him or her to go through without contact. If a dribbler, without contact, passes an opponent sufficiently to have head and shoulders in advance of him or her, the greater responsibility for subsequent contact is on the opponent. If a dribbler in his or her progress has established a straight line path, he or she may not be crowded out of that path but, if an opponent is able legally to establish a defensive position in that path, the dribbler must avoid contact by changing direction or ending his or her dribble.

A player who screens shall not: (a) when he or she is behind a stationary opponent, take a position closer than a normal step from him or her; (b) when he or she assumes a position at the side or in front of a stationary opponent, make contact with him or her; (c) take a position so close to a moving opponent that this opponent cannot avoid contact by stopping or changing direction. In (c), the speed of the player to be screened will determine where the screener may take his or her stationary position. This position will vary and may be one to two normal steps or strides from the opponent. (d) After assuming his or her legal screening position move to maintain it, unless he or she moves in the same direction and path of his or her opponent.

If the screener violates any of these provisions and contact results, he or she has committed a personal foul.

PENALTY—Offender is charged with one foul and if it is his or her fifth personal foul, or if it is flagrant, he or she is disqualified. The offended player is awarded free throws as follows:

1. **One free throw for:**
   a. a foul against a field goal thrower whose try is successful; or
   b. each foul which is a part of a multiple foul.
2. **Two free throws for:**

a. foul against field goal thrower whose try is unsuccessful; or
b. an intentional foul; or, c. any single flagrant foul.

3. **Bonus free throw for:**
   a. each common foul (except player control) beginning with a team's fifth personal foul during the half in a game played in quarters, provided the first attempt is successful.
4. **No free throws for:**
   a. each common foul before the bonus rule is in effect; or
   b. a double foul; or
   c. a player control foul; or
   d. a double foul, one or both fouls of which are flagrant or intentional.
5. In case of a false double or a false multiple foul, each foul carries its own penalty.

The specified number of free throws is

awarded for each foul which is a part of a false double or a false multiple foul.

NOTE—If there is any doubt as to whether there is player control during the time he or she or a teammate commits a common foul, the interpretation shall be that the ball was in player control.

Ques. (1)—A guard moves into the path of a dribbler and contact occurs. Who is responsible? **Ans.**—Either may be responsible but the greater responsibility is that of the dribbler if the guard conforms to the following principles which officials use in reaching a decision. The guard is assumed to have established a guarding position if he or she is in the dribbler's path facing him or her. No specific stance or distance is specified. It is assumed the guard may shift to maintain his or her position in the path of the dribbler provided he or she does not charge into the dribbler nor otherwise cause contact as outlined in the 2nd paragraph of 10-10. However, if he or she jumps into position, both feet must return to the floor after the jump, before he or she has established a guarding position.

The responsibility of the dribbler for contact is not shifted merely because the guard turns or ducks to absorb shock when contact caused by the dribbler is imminent. The guard may not cause contact by moving under or in front of a passer or thrower after he or she is in the air with both feet off the floor.

Ques. (2)—One or both fouls of either a multiple foul or of a double foul is flagrant. What is the procedure? **Ans.**—For a multiple foul, one free throw is awarded for each foul. For a double foul no free throws are awarded. In either case, any player who commits a flagrant foul is disqualified.

Ques. (3)—Does goal count if ball goes in the basket after a foul? **Ans.**—Yes, unless ball becomes dead (Rule 6–7) before it enters the basket.

Appendix B

BASKETBALL BOOKS IN PRINT

(Source: *Books in Print,* R. R. Bowker Company)

Athletes in Action. *One Way to Play Basketball.* (illus.). San Diego, Calif.: Beta Book Company, 1970 (Paperback, $3.95).

Auerbach, Arnold (Red). *Basketball for the Player, the Fan, and the Coach.* (illus.). New York: Simon & Schuster, 1976, $8.95. New York: Pocket Books paperback, $1.75.

Auerbach, Arnold (Red) and Fitzgerald, Joe. *Red Auerbach: An Autobiography.* New York: G. P. Putnam's Sons, 1977 ($9.95).

Bell, Marty. *The Legend of Dr. J: The Story of Julius Erving.* (illus.). New York: Coward, McCann & Geoghegan, 1975 ($7.95). New York: New American Library paperback, 1976 ($1.50).

Benagh, Jim. *Making It to Number One.* New York: Dodd, Mead, 1976 ($10.00).

Bolton, Clyde. *The Basketball Tide: A Story of Alabama Basketball.* (illus.). Huntsville, Ala.: The Strode Publishers, 1977 ($8.95).

Bradley, Bill. *Life on the Run: A Career in Basketball.* New York: Quadrangle Books, 1976 ($8.95).

Byrd, Ben. *The Basketball Vols: University of Tennessee Basketball.* (illus.). (College Sports Ser.). Orig. Title: *Tennessee Basketball.* Huntsville, Ala.: The Strode Publishers, 1974 ($7.95).

Caudle, Edwin C. *Collegiate Basketball: Facts and Figures on the Cage Sport.* Winston-Salem, N.C.: John F. Blair, 1960 ($6.95) (Supplement, $.65).

Chamberlain, Wilt and Shaw, David. *Wilt: Just Like Any Other Seven-foot Black Millionaire Who Lives Next Door.* (illus.). New York: Warner Books, 1973 (1975) (Paperback, 1975, $1.95).

Chapin, Dwight and Prugh, Jeff. *The Wizard of Westwood.* New York: Warner Books, 1973 (Paperback, $1.50).

Cohen, Stanley. *The Game They Played.* New York: Farrar, Straus & Giroux, 1977 ($8.95).

Cousy, Robert J. and Devaney, John. *The Killer Instinct.* New York: Random House, 1975 ($7.95).

Cummins, Gloria and Cummins, Jim. *Basketball by the Pros.* (illus.). New York: Van Nostrand Reinhold, 1976 ($12.50) (Paperback, $7.95).

Curran, J. *New York City High School Basketball.* Englewood Cliffs, N.J.: Prentice-Hall, 1972 ($8.95).

Educational Research Council of America. *Pro Basketball Player* (rev. ed.), ed. Theodore N. Ferris and John P. Marchak. (Real People at Work Ser.). (illus.). Washington, D.C.: *Changing Times,* 1976 (Paperback text ed., $1.65).

Fischer, Howard A. *Bible Basketball.* Chicago: Moody Press, 1970 (Paperback, $1.25).

Fitzgerald, Joe. *That Championship Feeling: The Story of the Boston Celtics.* New York: Charles Scribner's Sons, 1975 ($8.95).

Fox, Larry. *Illustrated History of Basketball* (repr.). New York: Grosset & Dunlap, 1974 ($6.95).

Frazier, Walt and Berkow, Ira. *Rockin' Steady: A Guide to Basketball and Cool.* (illus.). Englewood Cliffs, N.J.: Prentice-Hall, 1974 ($9.95). Paperback, New York: Warner Books ($1.50).

Gault, Frank and Gault, Clare. *The Harlem Globetrotters.* New York: Walker & Company, 1977 ($5.95).

Goldaper, Sam. *Great Moments in Pro Basketball.* New York: Grosset & Dunlap, 1977 (Paperback, $1.25).

Goodrich, Gail and Levin, Rich. *Winning Basketball.* (Winning Ser.). (illus.). Chicago: Contemporary Books, 1976 ($8.95) (Paperback, $4.95).

Hammel, Bob and Crewell, Larry (eds.). *NCAA Indiana All the Way.* Bloomington: Indiana University Press, 1976 ($10.00) (Paperback, $4.95).

Harris, Merv (ed.). *On the Court with the Superstars of the NBA.* New York: Pocket Books paperback, 1974 ($1.25).

————. *The Lonely Heroes: Professional Basketball's Great Centers.* (illus.). New York: The Viking Press, 1975 ($8.95).

Havlicek, John and Ryan, Bob. *Hondo: Celtic Man in Motion.* (illus.). Englewood Cliffs, N.J.: Prentice-Hall, 1977 ($8.95).

Hollander, Zander. *Basketball's Greatest Games.* (illus.). Englewood Cliffs, N.J.: Prentice-Hall, 1971 ($7.95).

————. *The Complete Handbook of Pro Basketball* (1979 ed.). New York: New American Library paperback, 1978 ($2.50).

————. (ed.). *The Pro Basketball Encyclopedia.* (illus.). Los Angeles: Corwin Books, 1977 ($20).

————. *Pro Basketball: Its Superstars and History.* New York: Scholastic Book Services paperback, 1971 ($.95).

Holzman, Red and Lewin, Leonard. *Defense! Defense!* Orig. title: *Holzman's Basketball.* New York: Warner Books paperback, 1974 ($1.50).

Isaacs, Neil D. *All the Moves: A History of College Basketball.* (illus.). Philadelphia: J. B. Lippincott Company, 1975 ($12.95).

Jackson, Phil and Rosen, Charles. *Maverick: More Than a Game.* New York: Playboy Press, 1976 ($9.95) (Paperback, $1.75).

Klein, David. *A Thinking Person's Guide to Pro Basketball.* New York: Grosset & Dunlap, 1978 ($1.95).

Libby, Bill. *The Walton Gang.* (illus.). New York: Coward, McCann & Geoghegan, 1974 ($8.95).

Libby, Bill and Haywood, Spencer. *Stand Up for Something: The Spencer Haywood Story.* (illus.). New York: Grosset & Dunlap, 1972 ($6.95).

Linehan, Don. *Soft Touch: A Sport That Lets You Touch Life.* (illus.). Washington, D.C.: Acropolis Books, 1976 ($12.50) (Paperback, $5.95).

Logan, Robert. *The Bulls and Chicago: A Stormy Affair.* (illus.). Chicago: Follett Publishing Company, 1975 ($7.95).

Maclean, Norman and Ecksl, Norb. *The Basketball Quizbook.* (illus.). New York: Drake Publishers paperback, 1976 ($4.95).

Mendell, Ronald L. *Who's Who in Basketball.* New Rochelle, N.Y.: Arlington House, 1973 ($7.95).

Meyer, Ray and Damer, Roy. *Winning College Basketball.* (Winning Ser.). (illus.). Chicago: Contemporary Books, 1977 ($8.95) (Paperback, $4.95).

Motta, Dick and Jenkins, Jerry. *Stuff It: The Story of Dick Motta, Toughest Little Coach in the NBA.* (illus.). Radnor, Pa.: Chilton Book Company, 1975 ($7.50).

Naismith, Brian and Hill, Terry. *Basketball.* North Pomfret, Vt.: David & Charles, 1978 ($15.95).

Neft, David S., et al. *The Sports Encyclopedia: Pro Basketball.* New York: Grosset & Dunlap, 1975 ($9.95).

Paige, David. *Pro Basketball: An Almanac of Facts and Records.* (illus.). (Illustrated Sports Almanac). Mankato, Minn.: Creative Educational, 1977 ($5.95).

Powers, Richie and Mulvoy, Mark. *Overtime: An Uninhibited Account of a Referee's Life in the NBA.* (illus.). New York: David McKay Co., 1975 ($7.95).

Rappaport, Ken. *Tar Heel, North Carolina Basketball.* (illus.). Huntsville, Ala.: The Strode Publishers, 1976 ($8.95).

Reed, Willis and Pepe, Phil. *View from the Rim: Willis Reed on Basketball.* (illus.). Philadelphia: J. B. Lippincott Company, 1972 ($6.25).

Rice, Russ. *Kentucky Basketball.* Huntsville, Ala.: The Strode Publishers, 1976 ($9.95).

Rupp, Adolph F. *Rupp's Championship Basketball,* 2nd ed. Englewood Cliffs, N.J.: Prentice-Hall, 1957 ($8.75).

Ryan, Bob. *Celtics' Pride: The Rebuilding of Boston's World Championship Basketball Team.* (A *Sports Illustrated* Book Ser.).

(illus.). Boston: Little, Brown, 1975 ($7.95).

Sports Illustrated Staff. Sports Illustrated *Basketball*. (illus.). Philadelphia: J. B. Lippincott Company, 1971 ($4.95) (Paperback, $1.95).

Steitz, Edward. *Illustrated Basketball Rules*. (illus.). Garden City, N.Y.: Doubleday & Company paperback, 1976 ($2.50).

Telander, Rick. *Heaven Is a Playground*. New York: St. Martin's Press, 1977 ($8.95).

White, Dan. *Play to Win: A Profile of Prince-ton Basketball Coach Pete Carril*. Englewood Cliffs, N.J.: Prentice-Hall, 1977 ($8.95).

Wilkens, Lenny. *The Lenny Wilkens Story*. Middlebury, Vt.: Paul S. Eriksson, 1974 ($6.95).

Wolf, David. *Foul: The Connie Hawkins Story*. New York: Holt, Rinehart & Winston, 1972 ($7.95).

Wooden, John, et al. *The Wooden-Sharman Method: A Guide to Winning Basketball*. (illus.). New York: Macmillan, 1975 ($9.95).

Juvenile Literature
Parentheses indicate grades

Allen, Phog, et al. *Basketball* (rev. ed.). (Athletic Institute Ser.). (illus.). (gr. 5 up). New York: Sterling Publishing Co., 1968 ($4.95). (PLB, $4.99).

Antonacci, Robert J. and Barr, Jene. *Basketball for Young Champions*. (gr. 4–7). New York: McGraw-Hill Book Company, 1960 (PLB, $5.72).

Armstrong, Robert. *The Centers* (Stars of the NBA Ser.). (illus.). (gr. 3–7). Mankato, Minn.: Creative Educational, 1977 (PLB, $5.95).

————. *The Coaches*. (Stars of the NBA Ser.). (illus.). (gr. 3–7). Mankato, Minn.: Creative Educational, 1977 (PLB, $5.95).

————. *The Forwards*. (Stars of the NBA Ser.). (illus.). (gr. 3–7). Mankato, Minn.: Creative Educational, 1977 (PLB, $5.95).

————. *George McGinnis* (Sports Superstars Ser.). (illus.). (gr. 3–9). Mankato, Minn.: Creative Educational, 1977 (PLB, $4.95).

————. *The Guards*. (Stars of the NBA Ser.). (illus.). (gr. 3–7). Mankato, Minn.: Creative Educational, 1977 (PLB, $5.95).

Baker, Eugene. *I Want to Be a Basketball Player*. (I Want to Be Books). (illus.). (gr. k–4). Chicago: Childrens Press, 1972 (PLB, $5.00).

Batson, Larry. *Bill Walton*. (Sports Superstars Ser.). (illus.). (gr. 3–9). Mankato, Minn.: Creative Educational, 1974 (PLB, $4.95).

————. *An Interview with Bobby Knight*. (Interviews Ser.). (illus.). (gr. 3–8). Mankato, Minn.: Creative Educational, 1977 (PLB, $5.95).

Bee, Clair. *Make the Team in Basketball* (rev. ed.). (illus.). (gr. 4 up). New York: Grosset & Dunlap, 1961 ($3.95).

Benagh, Jim. *Incredible Basketball Feats*. (illus., orig.). New York: Grosset & Dunlap paperback, 1974 ($1.25).

Berger, Phil. *Heroes of Pro Basketball*. (Pro Basketball Library: No. 1). (illus.). (gr. 5–9). New York: Random House, 1968 ($2.50) (PLB, $3.69).

Bortstein, Larry. *Dr. J—Dave Cowens*. (orig.). (gr. 7 up). New York: Grosset & Dunlap paperback, 1974 ($.95).

Braun, Thomas. *John Havlicek*. (Sports Superstar Ser.). (illus.). (gr. 3–9). Mankato, Minn.: Creative Educational, 1976 (PLB, $4.95).

————. *Julius Erving*. (Sports Superstars Ser.). (illus.). (gr. 3–9) Mankato, Minn.: Creative Educational, 1976 (PLB, $4.95)

Bruns, Bill & Wolf, Dave. *Great Moments in Pro Basketball*. (Pro Basketball Library: No. 2). (illus.). (gr. 5–9). New York: Random House, 1968 ($2.50) (PLB, $3.69).

Burchard, Marshall. *Sports Hero: Rick Barry* (new ed.). (Sports Hero Ser.). (illus.). (gr. 3–6). New York: G. P. Putnam's Sons, 1977 (PLB, $4.99).

————. *Sports Hero: The Story of Julius Erving* (new ed.). (Sports Hero Ser.). (illus.). (gr. 3–7). New York: G. P. Putnam's Sons, 1976 (PLB, $4.99).

Burchard, S. H. *Sports Star: Walt Frazier*. (Sports Star Ser.). (illus.). (gr. 1–5). New York: Harcourt Brace Jovanovich, 1975 ($4.95) (Paperback $1.95).

Cebulash, Mel. *Basketball Players Do Amazing Things*. (Step-up Bks.; No. 23). (illus.). (gr. 2–3). New York: Random House, 1976 ($2.95) (PLB, $3.99).

Clark, Steve. *Illustrated Basketball Dictionary for Young People* (new ed.). (Sports Dictionary Ser.). (illus.). (gr. 5 up). New York: Harvey House, 1977 (PLB, $5.89).

Cook, Joseph J. and Cook, Joseph J., Jr. *Famous Firsts in Basketball* (new ed.). (Famous Firsts Ser.). (illus.). (gr. 5–8). New York: G. P. Putnam's Sons, 1976 (PLB, $4.49).

Cooke, David C. *Better Basketball for Boys.* (illus.). (gr. 4–6). New York: Dodd, Mead, 1960 (PLB, $4.50).

Coombs, Charles. *Be a Winner in Basketball* (illus.). (gr. 4–6). New York: William Morrow & Co., 1975 (PLB, $6.01).

Deegan, Paul J. *Bill Russell* (Creative Superstars Ser.). Mankato, Minn.: Creative Educational, 1974 (PLB, $4.95).

Devaney, John. *The Story of Basketball.* (Giant Landmark Ser.; No. 26). (illus.). (gr. 5 up). New York: Random House, 1976 ($4.95) (PLB, $5.99).

———. *Tiny: The Story of Nate Archibald.* (Sports Shelf Ser.). (illus.). (gr. 4 up). New York: G. P. Putnam's Sons (PLB, $5.29).

Felser, Larry. *Pro Basketball's Super Scorers* (gr. 7–12). New York: Scholastic Book Services paperback, 1976 ($.95).

Fenner, Phyllis R. (ed.). *Quick Pivot: Stories of Basketball.* (illus.). (gr. 5 up). New York: Alfred A. Knopf, 1965 (PLB, $5.69).

Garstang, J. G. *Basketball: the Modern Way* (enl. ed.). (illus.). (gr. 7 up). New York: Sterling Publishing Co., 1967 ($4.95) (PLB, $4.99).

Gault, Clare and Gault, Frank. *How to Be a Good Basketball Player.* (gr. k–6). New York: Scholastic Book Services paperback, 1977 ($.59).

Geline, Robert & Turner, Priscilla. *Forward: Rick Barry.* (illus.). Milwaukee, Wis.: Raintree Publishers, 1976 ($6.60) (PLB, $6.60).

Gergen, Joe. *Dr. J: The Story of Julius Erving.* (illus.). (gr. 4–9). New York: Scholastic Book Services paperback, 1975 ($.95).

Goldaper, Sam. *Hot Shots.* (gr. 5 up). New York: Grosset & Dunlap paperback, 1975 ($1.25).

Gutman, Bill. *The Harlem Globetrotters: Basketball's Funniest Team.* (Sports Library). (illus.). (gr. 4). Champaign, Ill.: Garrard Publishing Company, 1977 ($4.28).

———. *Modern Basketball Superstars.* (illus.). (gr. 4–9). New York: Dodd, Mead, 1975 (PLB, $4.95).

Harris, Richard. *I Can Read About Basketball* (new ed.). (illus.). (gr. 2–5). Mahwah, N.J.: Troll Associates paperback, 1976 ($.95).

Haskins, James. *Bob McAdoo, Superstar.* (illus.). (gr. 5 up). New York: Lothrop, Lee & Shepard, 1977 ($5.95) (PLB, $5.49).

———. *Doctor J: A Biography of Julius Erving.* (illus.). (gr. 8–9). Garden City, N.Y.: Doubleday & Company, 1975 (PLB, $4.95).

———. *From Lew Alcindor to Kareem Abdul-Jabbar.* (illus.). (gr. 5–12). New York: Lothrop, Lee & Shepard, 1972 (PLB, $5.09).

———. *George McGinnis: Basketball Superstar.* (illus.). (gr. 6 up). New York: Hastings House, 1978 ($6.95).

Heuman, William. *Famous Pro Basketball Stars.* (illus.). (gr. 7 up). New York: Dodd, Mead, 1970 ($4.50).

Hill, Ray. *Pro Basketball's Little Men.* (Pro Basketball Library). (illus.). (gr. 5 up). New York: Random House, 1974 ($2.50) (PLB, $3.69).

———. *Unsung Heroes of Pro Basketball.* (illus.). (gr. 5 up). New York: Random House, 1973 ($2.50) (PLB, $3.69).

Hirshberg, Al. *Basketball's Greatest Stars.* (Sports Shelf Ser.). (illus.). (gr. 6–10). New York: G. P. Putnam's Sons, 1963 (PLB, $4.97).

———. *Basketball's Greatest Teams.* (Sports Shelf Ser.). (illus.). (gr. 5 up). New York: G. P. Putnam's Sons, 1966 (PLB, $5.69).

Hollander, Zander (ed.). *Great Rookies of Pro Basketball* (Pro Basketball Library; No. 3). (gr. 5–9). New York: Random House, 1969 ($2.50).

Jackson, Robert B. *Earl the Pearl* (rev. ed.). (illus.). (gr. 3–6). New York: Henry Z. Walck, 1974 ($5.95).

———. *Jabbar, Giant of the NBA.* (illus.). (gr. 4–7). New York: Henry Z. Walck, 1972 ($5.95).

Jacobs, Linda. *Julius Erving: Doctor J and Julius W.* (Black American Athletes Ser.). (illus.). (gr. 4–6). St. Paul, Minn.: EMC Corporation, 1976 (PLB, $4.95) (Paperback, $2.95).

Klein, Dave. *Rookie: World of the NBA.* (illus.). (gr. 7–9). New York: Grosset & Dunlap paperback, 1973 ($.95).

Lee, S. C. *Best Basketball Booster.* (Strode Superstar Ser.). (illus.). (gr. 3–6). Huntsville, Ala.: The Strode Publishers, 1974 ($3.95).

Liss, Howard. *Basketball Talk for Beginners.* (illus.). (gr. 4 up). New York: Julian Messner, 1970 (PLB, $5.29).

———. *Strange but True Basketball Stories.* (Pro Basketball Library; No. 6). (illus.).

(gr. 5 up). New York: Random House, 1972 ($2.50). (PLB, $3.69).

Masin, Herman. *How to Star in Basketball.* (illus.). (gr. 5–10). New York: Scholastic Book Services, 1966 ($3.95). (Paperback, 1975, $.95).

Miers, Earl S. *Basketball.* (illus.). (gr. 4–8). New York: Grosset & Dunlap paperback, 1974 ($2.95).

Monroe, Earl and Unseld, Wes. *Basketball Skillbook,* ed. Ray Siegener. (illus.). New York: Atheneum, 1973 ($6.95).

Morris, Greg. *Basketball Basics.* (illus.). (gr. 2–6). Englewood Cliffs, N.J.: Prentice-Hall, 1976 ($5.95).

Munford, Kerry and Wordsworth, Morris A. *Beginner's Guide to Basketball.* Levittown, N.Y.: Transatlantic Arts, 1974 ($12.50).

Olney, Ross. *Basketball.* (Golden Sports Book Ser.). (illus.). (gr. 4 up). Racine, Wis.: Western Publishing Co., 1976 (PLB, $6.77).

O'Connor, Dick. *Rick Barry: Basketball Ace.* (Putnam Sports Shelf Books). (illus.). (gr. 6–8). New York: G. P. Putnam's Sons, 1977 (PLB, $5.29).

O'Reilly, Sean. *Meet the Centers.* (Early Sports Books: Basketball). (illus.). (gr. 2–6). Mankato, Minn.: Creative Educational, 1977 ($4.95).

————. *Meet the Coaches.* (Early Sports Books: Basketball). (illus.). (gr. 2–6). Mankato, Minn.: Creative Educational, 1977 (PLB, $4.95).

————. *Meet the Forwards.* (Early Sports Books: Basketball). (illus.). (gr. 2–6). Mankato, Minn.: Creative Educational, 1977 (PLB, $4.95).

————. *Meet the Guards.* (Early Sports Books: Basketball). (illus.). (gr. 2–6). Mankato, Minn.: Creative Educational, 1977 (PLB, $4.95).

Padwe, Sandy. *Basketball Hall of Fame.* (gr. 7 up). New York: Grosset & Dunlap, paperback, 1973 ($.95).

Paulsen, Gary. *Dribbling, Shooting, and Scoring Sometimes.* (illus.). (gr. k–3). Milwaukee, Wis.: Raintree Publishers, 1976 (PLB, $6.60).

Rainbolt, Richard. *Basketball's Big Men.* (The Sports Heroes Library). (illus.). (gr. 5–11). Minneapolis, Minn.: Lerner Publications Company, 1975 (PLB, $4.95).

Rubin, Bob. *Basketball's Big Men: Super Giants and Superstars.* (illus.). (gr. 5–9). New York: Scholastic Book Services paperback, 1975 ($.95).

————. *Great Centers of Pro Basketball.* (Pro Basketball Library). (illus.). (gr. 5 up).
New York: Random House, 1975 ($2.50) (PLB, $3.69).

Rydell, Wendell. *Basketball.* (Sports Bk. Ser.). (illus.). (gr. 5 up). New York: Abelard-Schuman, 1971 ($3.95).

Sabin, Lou. *Hot Shots of Pro Basketball.* (Pro Basketball Library). (illus.). (gr. 5 up). New York: Random House, 1974 ($2.50) (PLB, $3.69).

Sabin, Lou and Sendler, Dave. *Stars of Pro Basketball.* (Pro Basketball Library; No. 4). (illus.). (gr. 5–9). New York: Random House, 1970 ($2.50) (PLB, $3.69).

————. *The Fabulous Dr. J: All-Time All-Star.* (Putnam's Sports Shelf Biographies Ser.). (illus.). (gr. 5 up). New York: G. P. Putnam's Sons, 1976 (PLB, $5.29).

————. *Pro Basketball's Greatest: Selected All-Star Offensive and Defensive Teams* (new ed.). (Sports Shelf Ser.). (gr. 5 up). New York: G. P. Putnam's Sons, 1976 (PLB, $5.29).

Sahadi, Lou. *Basketball's Fastest Hands.* (gr. 7–12). New York: Scholastic Book Services paperback, 1977 ($.95).

Schiffer, Don. *The First Book of Basketball* (rev. ed.). (First Books Ser.). (illus.). (gr. 4–6). New York: Franklin Watts, 1977 ($4.47).

Stambler, Irwin. *Bill Walton: Super Center* (new ed.). (Sports Shelf Biography Ser.). (gr. 5 up). New York: G. P. Putnam's Sons, 1976 (PLB, $5.29).

Sullivan, George. *Dave Cowens: A Biography.* Garden City, N.Y.: Doubleday & Company, 1977 ($5.95).

————. *This Is Pro Basketball.* (illus.). (gr. 5 up). New York: Dodd, Mead, 1977 ($6.50).

————. *Winning Basketball.* (illus.). (gr. 7 up). New York: David McKay Co., 1976 ($7.95).

Tuttle, Anthony. *Bob McAdoo.* (Sports Superstars Ser.). (illus.). (gr. 3–9). Mankato, Minn.: Creative Educational, 1976 ($4.95).

Van Riper, Guernsey, Jr. *Game of Basketball.* (Sports Library Ser.). (illus.). (gr. 3–6). Champaign, Ill.: Garrard Publishing Company, 1968 (PLB, $4.28).

Vecsey, George. *Harlem Globetrotters.* (gr. 4–9). New York: Scholastic Book Services paperback, 1971 ($.95).

————. *Pro Basketball Champions.* (illus.). (gr. 4–6). New York: Scholastic Book Services paperback, 1970 ($.95).

Weber, Bruce. *All-Pro Basketball Stars 1977.* (gr. 7 up.) New York: Scholastic Book Services, 1977 ($.95).

Basketball For Women

American Alliance for Health, Physical Education, and Recreation. *Basketball Selected Articles*. Paperback, 1971 ($1.00).

Barnes, Mildred. *Girl's Basketball* (rev. ed.). (Athletic Institute Ser.). (illus.). New York: Sterling Publishing Co., 1975 ($4.95) (PLB, $4.99).

———. *Women's Basketball*. (illus.). Boston: Allyn & Bacon, 1972 (text ed., $13.95).

Bell, Mary M. *Women's Basketball* (2nd ed.). Dubuque, Ia.: Wm. C. Brown Company paperback, 1973 ($3.95).

Ebert, Francis H. and Cheatum, Billye A. *Basketball* (2nd ed.). (illus.). Philadelphia: W. B. Saunders Company, 1977 (Paperback text ed., $7.95).

Lowry, Carla. *Pictorial Basketball for Women*. Sacramento, Calif.: Creative Book Company paperback, 1968 ($2.00).

Miller, Kenneth and Horky, Rita. *Modern Basketball for Women*. Columbus, O.: Charles E. Merrill Publishing Company, 1970 (Paperback text ed., $4.95).

Neal, Patsy E. *Basketball Techniques for Women*. (illus.). New York: John Wiley & Sons, 1966 ($9.95).

Rush, Cathy and Mifflin, Lawrie. *Women's Basketball*. New York: Hawthorn Books paperback, 1976 ($5.95).

Schaafsma, Frances. *Basketball for Women* (3rd ed.). (Physical Education Activities Ser.). Dubuque, Ia.: Wm. C. Brown Company, 1977 (Paperback text ed., $2.50).

Stutts, Ann. *Women's Basketball* (2nd ed.). (Phys. Ed. Ser.). Santa Monica, Calif.: Goodyear Publishing Co., 1973 (Paperback text ed., $2.95).

Warren, William E. *Team Patterns in Girl's and Women's Basketball*. (illus.). Cranbury, N.J.: A. S. Barnes & Co., 1976 ($8.95).

Index

Tabular material which is listed in the Contents, such as the NBA-ABA All-Time Register, has not been indexed, nor have box scores and team and individual standings in the collegiate and professional yearly roundups. Boldface numerals denote page references to photo captions.

Dees, Archie, 62
Dehner, Lew, 18
Dehnert, Henry "Dutch," 137, 272, **273,** 275, **276,** 277, **277,** 445
Delph, Marvin, 104
Delta State College, **227,** 228
DeMatha High School, 111
DeNike, Tommy, 121
Denton, Randy, 89
Denver, University of, 40, 64, 83, 106, 112, **112**
Denver (NBL), 279, 287, 288, 290
Denver Central Bankers, 113
Denver Nuggets, 112, 128, 129, 338, 350, 351, 353, 354, 356, 371, 374, 378, 380, 381, 382–83, 384, 385, **385,** 400
Denver Rockets, 113, 139
DePaul University, 18, 20, 22, 26, 27, 28, 29, **29,** 31, 32, 36, 49, 50, 58, 66, 68, 79, 98, 104, 106 117–18, 121, 141, 281, 283, 405
DePre, Joe, 87
DeSantis, Joe, 104
Detroit, University of, 58, 66, 68, 77, 79, 85, **85,** 104, 106
Detroit Falcons, 281, 283, 284
Detroit Pistons, 131, 279, 304, **304, 306,** 308, 309, 318–19, **318,** 322–24, **324,** 325, 329, 334, 337, 338, 345, 356, 411
Devlin, Corky, 55
Dick, John, 17
Dickerson, Ray, **277**
Dickey, Dick, 37, 40, 42
Diddle, Ed, 135, **135,** 446–47
Didrikson, Mildred "Babe," 267
Dierking, Connie, 61, 318
DiGregorio, Ernie, 89, 91, 93, 344–45
Dillon, John, 31
Dischinger, Terry, 66, 68, 70, 120, 261, 315
Dolan, Joe, **35**
Doll, Bob, 20, 24, 264
Dolph, Jack, 374
Donohue, John, 111
Dose, Tom, 72
Douglas, Bob, 278, **278,** 447
Douglas, Leon, 95, 97, 100
Dove, Sonny, 79, 81
Downey, Dave, 72
Downing, Steve, 93
Drake, Bruce, 448
Drake University, 18, 62, 68, 74, 85, 87, 89
Driesell, C. G. "Lefty," 141
Driscoll, Terry, 81, 83, 85
Drollinger, Ralph, 97, 100
Drucker, James, 427
Drucker, Norm, 431
Duerod, Terry, 106
Duffey, Ike W., 282
Duke, University of, 20, 24, 26, 28, 31, 35, 46, 48, 49, 55, 62, 66, 70, 71, 73, 74, 77, 78, 79, 81, 82, 83, 89, 101, 103, 104, **105,** 106, 116–17, **117,** 141
Dukes, Walter, 47, 50, **51**
Dunbar, Louis, 97
Dunn, T. R., 100

Duquesne University, 18, 20, 22, 24, 34, 40, 42, 50, 52, 55, **56,** 58, 70, 77, 85, 87, 89, 121, 141, 290
Durbin, Brice B., 233
Durden, Don, 26
Durham, Jarrett, 85, 87, 89
Durrett, Ken, 89
Duval, Dennis, 95
Dyer, Rich, 79

East Carolina College, 91
East District YMCA team, 7
Eastern Intercollegiate Conference, 18
Eastern Kentucky State College, 42, 50, 55, 64, 68, 77, 91, 106
Eastern League, 7, 271, 426–27, 431
Eastern Massachusetts Officials Board, 429
East Tennessee State University, 50, 83
Ebben, Bill, 58
Ebert, Paul, 53
Eddleman, Dwight, 40
Edwards, Michael, 104
Egan, Johnny, 68, 71, 131, 335
Egypt, 317
Eliot, Charles W., 429
Elliott, Bob, 100
Elliott, Pete, 37
Ellis, Alex "Boo," 60, 62
Elis, Bo, 95, 101
Ellis, Dick, 77
Ellis, Leroy, 70
Elmore, Bob, 100, 101
Elmore, Len, 91, 95
Embry, Wayne, 60, 62, 332
Endacott, Paul, 447
England, 77, 114, 325, 328
Engleman, Howard, 22
English, Alex, 93
Englund, Gene, 21, 287
Enke, Fred, 141
Enright, Jim, 431, 453
Erickson, Bill, 40
Erickson, Keith, 77
Ernst, Vinnie, 68, 71, 131
Erving, Julius, 87, 89, 91, 350–51, 377, 378, 381, **381,** 382, 383, 384, 385, 401
as a top twenty professional player, 399–400, **400**
Estes, Wayne, 73, 75, 77
Evans, Mike, 102
Evans, Ray, 26
Evansville College, 141

Fairchild, John, 77
Fairfield University, 104
Faris, Bob, 18
Farley, Dick, 53
Farmer, Mike, 60, 62, 426
Faught, Bob, 24
Faust, H. **270**
Feerick, Bob, 283, 284–85
Ferrari, Al, 50
Ferrin, Arnie, 27, **27,** 29, 34, 288

Ferry, Bob, 64
Finch, Larry, 93
Finkel, Henry, 77, 79
Finley, Charles O., 378
Fisher, Harry A., 449
Fitch, Bill, 349, 356
Fitzsimmons, Cotton, 356
Fleishman, Jerry, 26
Fleming, Ernie, 91
Fletcher, Rod, 49
Fliegel, Bernard, 17
Flint (NBL), 279, 287
Flora, Dom, 62
Florida, University of, 49, 77, 81, 83, 86, 141
Florida State University, 87, 91, 104
Floyd, Darrell, 55, 58
Flynn, Ray, 71
Fogle, Larry, 95
Foley, Jack "The Shot," 66, 68
Follmer, Clive, 49
Ford, Phil, 100, 101, 104, 252, 262, 356
Fordham University, 13, 19, 26, 50, 52, 55, 89, 141
Foreman, Earl, 400
Forman, Don, 36
Forte, Chet, 60
Fort Wayne Pistons, 277, 279, 286, 288, 292, 294, 297, 298, **298,** 299, 300, 303, 304, 408
Foster, Bud, 141
Foster, Fred, 83
Foster, Harold E., 442
Foust, Larry, 36, 294, 299, 309
France, 261
Francis, Clarence "Bevo," 219–20, **221**
Frank, Wally, 66
Franklin, Joe, 83
Frazier, Walt, 81, 329, 333, **333,** 335, 340, 345, 347, 354
Frederick, Rex, 64
Free, Lloyd, 97, 219, 351, 356
Freeman, Don, 79, 373
Freeman, James "Buck," 8
Freeman, Robin, 58
Friedman, Max, 447
Friel, Jack, 141
Friendlich, Dick, 121
Fulks, Joe, 282, 283, 284–85, 287, 294, 307, **337,** 338, 398, 408
  in the Hall of Fame, 451–52
  as a top twenty professional player, 400–1, **401**
Fuqua, Richie, 91, 93
Furey, Jim, 272–74
Furey, Tom, 272
Furlow, Terry, 100
Furnam University, 50, 52, 53, **54,** 55, 58, 98, 102

Gabor, Bill, 31
Gainer, Elmer, 22
Gale, Laddie, 17, 451
Gales, Zip, 141
Galileo High School, 121
Galis, Nick, 106
Gallagher, John "Taps," 141

Gallatin, Harry "The Horse," 297, 304, 312
Gambee, Dave, 62, 335
Gantt, Matt, 89
Gardner, Jack, 141
Gardner, Vern, 34, 112
Garmaker, Dick, 55, 305
Gary, Greg, 89
Gayda, Ed, 42
Gebert, Kirk, 22
Geib, Treva, 120
Geneva College, 141
Gensich, Hal, 26
Gent, Pete, 70
Georgetown University, 18, 19, 24–25, 34, 104, 106, 141
George Washington University, 18, 26, 35, 43, 53, 55, 58, 68, 86, 117
Georgia, University of, 83
Georgia Institute of Technology (Georgia Tech), 16, 17, 55, 66, 87, 89
Gerber, Bob, 22, 23
Gerdy, John, 106
Gerson, Rip, 9, **9**
Gervin, George "Iceman," 129, 354, 356, 401
Gettysburg College, 115
Gianelli, John, 89
Giannini, Ralph, 20
Gibbon, Joe, 60
Gibson, Bob, 60
Giermak, Chet, 40, 42
Gill, Amory "Slats," 141, 444
Gilmore, Artis, 87, **88,** 89, 229, 340, 377, 378, 379, 380, 381, 382, 383, 384, 385
Givens, Jack, 102, 104, **105**
Glamack, George, 20, 22
Glaser, Ron, 73
Glenn, Mike, 102
Gminski, Mike, 104, 106
Gola, Tom, 48, 50, 52, 55, 86, 124, 321, 403
  in the Hall of Fame, 450
  as a top twenty college player, 115–16, **115**
Golden State Warriors, 127, 339, 340, 345, **346,** 347, 348, 349, 352, 395–96
Goldsmith, Jack, 32
Goldstein, Don, 64
Goldstein, Lou, **29**
Gondrezick, Glen, 101
Gonzaga University, 34, 36, 79
Goodrich, Gail, 74, **74,** 77, 252, 339, 345
Gotkin, Hy, **28,** 29
Gottlieb, Eddie, 279, 283, 314, 400, 403, 412, 447–48
Goukas, Matt, 77
Graf, Irwin "Ike," 18
Graham, Bonnie, 17
Graham, Mal, 79, 81
Graham, Otto, 26, **26**
Grambling College, 141, 219
Grant, Steve, 104
Grant, Travis, 220
Grate, Don, 27
Gray, Wyndol, 29, 31
Greacen, Bob, 86

Johnson, Don, 49
Johnson, Earvin "Magic," 104, 105, 106, **108,** 356
Johnson, George, 100, 104
Johnson, Gus, 72, 319
Johnson, Johnny, 87, 356
Johnson, Lyndon B., 349
Johnson, Marques, 100, 101, 354
Johnson, Marvin, 104
Johnson, Ollie, 73, 74
Johnson, Phil, 347
Johnson, Rafer, 60
Johnson, Robert, 17
Johnson, William C., 451
Johnston, Neil, 295, 296, **296,** 297, 298–99, 300, 303, 306
  as a top twenty professional player, 403–4, **403**
Jones, Bobby, 95, 383
Jones, Dwight, 93
Jones, Jim, 373, 380
Jones, K. C., 57, 141, 261, **310**
Jones, Larry, 373
Jones, Nick, 79
Jones, R. William, 442–43
Jones, Sam, 130–31, 139, 311, 321, 325, 329, **337,** 338, 402
Jones, Steve, 373
Jones, Wallace "Wah Wah," 36, 39, **39**
Jones, Wally, 75
Jordan, Ed, 100
Jordan, Jim, 29, 31
Jordan, John, **14**
Joyce, Kevin, 91, 93
Jucker, Ed, 141
Judson, Paul, 58
Julian, Alvin "Doggie," 141, 444

Kaftan, George, 34, **35,** 36
Kaiser, Roger, 66, 68
Kansas, University of, 9, 16, 19, 20, 22, 24, 26, 31, 32, 42, 48, 50, 53, 59, 60, 61, **61,** 62, 66, 68, 77, 79, 81, 83, 86, 87, 89, 91, 93, 95, 98, 104, 118–19, **119,** 124, 133, 219, 264, 307, 397
Kansas City (ABL), 426
Kansas City AC, 264
Kansas City—Omaha Kings, 304, 343, 347, 349, 356
Kansas State University, 37, 42, 46, 50, 58, 60, 62, 63, 66, 68, 73, 74, 75, 83, 91, 101, 102, 119, 141
Kaplan, Bruce, 79
Kaplan, Dick, 412
Kautz, Wilbert, 17
Keaney, Frank, 9, 141, 437–38
Keller, Gary, 77
Kelley, Rich, 97, 356
Kellogg, Junius, 44
Kennedy, John F., 349
Kennedy, Matthew P. "Pat," 429, **429,** 432, 436
Kennedy, Walter, 316 **316,** 349, **349,** 431
Kenny, Art, 111
Kenny, Larry, 20
Kenon, Larry, 93, 229, 381

Kentucky, University of, 16, 18, 20, 22, 24, 26, 27–28, 29, 31, 34, 36, 39, **39,** 42, 44, 45, 46, **46,** 48, 50, 53, 55, 58, 60, 61–62, 63, 66, 68, 70, 73, 74, 78, **80,** 81, 83, 85, 87, 89, 91, 93, 97, 100, 102–4, **105,** 123, 133, 139, 141, 261, 289, 292, 338, 430
Kentucky Colonels, 371, 374, 376–77, **376,** 378, 379, 381, 382, 383, **383**
Kentucky State College, 139, 141, 219, 220
Keogan, George E., 136–37, **137,** 438–39
Kerner, Ben, 405
Kerr, Dave, **277**
Kerr, Johnny, 49, 53, 316, **316,** 321, 322
Kerris, Jack, 34, 36
Killian, George, 230
Kimball, Toby, 77
Kinch, Chad, 106
King, Albert, 106
King, Bernard, 100, 102, 354
King, Bob, 141
King, George, 298
King, Gilbert, 97
King, Jim, 77
King, Reggie, 104
King, Ron, 91
Kinney, Bob, 22, 24
Kinsbrunner, Mac, 8–9, **9**
Kirkpatrick, Hubert, 17
Klier, Leo, 31
Knight, Billy, 95, 383, 385
Knight, Bobby, 137, **137**
Knight, Danny, 95
Knight, Toby, 101
Knostman, Dick, 50
Koffenberger, Ed, 31
Kohls, Greg, 89, 91
Kojis, Don, 64, 68
Kok, George, 32, 37
Komenich, Milo, 25
Komives, Howie, 70, 74
Kondla, Tom, 82
Koper, Bud, 73, 75
Kotsores, Bill, 27, **28,** 29
Kotz, Johnny, 21–22, 24, 26
Kozelko, Tom, 93
Kraft, Jack, 141
Kramer, Barry, 70, 71–73, 75
Kramer, Ron, 60
Kramer, Steve, 78
Krause, Edward W., 450
Krebs, Jim, 55, 60
Krivacs, Jim, 104
Krovic, Jim, 100
Kruger, Lon, 93
Kuester, John, 101
Kundla, Johnny, 406
Kunnert, Kevin, 93
Kupchak, Mitch, 97, 262
Kupec, C. J., 97
Kurland, Bob "Foothills," 28, 29, **30,** 31, **32,** 129, 136, 261, 264, **265**
  in the Hall of Fame, 439
  as a top twenty college player, 117–18, **118**

Schmidt, Ernest J., 449
Schnittker, Dick, 42
Scholastic Magazine, 252
Scholz, Dave, 86
Schommer, John J., 436
Schuckman, Allie, 9, **9**
Schue, Gene, 309
Schulman, Sam, 353
Schultz, Dan, 75
Schultz, Earl, 66
Schutsky, Bill, 83
Scolari, Fred, 408
Scott, Charlie, 83, 85, 87, 338, 340, 376, 378
Scott, Ray, 345
Searcy, Tony, 104
Sears, Kenny, 48, 55, 264, 306, 308, 426
Seattle SuperSonics, 328, 335, 338, 340, 343, 344,
    345, 347, 349, 353, 354, 355–56, **357,** 376,
    378, 411
Seattle University, 47, 49, 50, 53, 55, 58, 61–62,
    64, 68, 70, 73, 75, 81, 141, 305, 396
Sedran, Barney, 272, 441
Seiden, Al, 62, 63
Sellers, Phil, 93, 97, 100
Selvy, Frank, 50, 52, 53, **54,** 110, 299
Semenova, Juliana, 262
Senesky, George, 26
Seton Hall University, **21,** 22, 24, 36, 45, 47, 49,
    50, **51,** 55, 71, 74, 101, 106, 114–15, **114,**
    124, 141
Severance, Al, 128
Sewell, Jeff, 87
Shackleford, Lynn, 83
Shaffer, Lee, 66, 318
Shank, Theresa, 228
Share, Charlie, 36
Sharman, Bill, 42, 295, 296–97, 299, 300, 303,
    304, 305, 306, **306,** 308, 310, **337,** 338, 339,
    373, 376, 395, 405
    in the Hall of Fame, 450
    as a top twenty professional player, 412–13, **413**
Sharman on Shooting (Sharman), 413
Sharrar, Lloyd, 62
Shavlik, Ronnie, 58
Sheboygan Redskins, 285, 288, 290
Shed, Neville, 78
Sheffield, Fred, 29
Shelton, Lonnie, 356
Sheppard, Steve, 101
Sherman, Maude, 6, **7**
Shields, Don, 15
Short, Arnie, 50, 53
Short, Bob, 396
Short, Purvis, 104
Shue, Gene, 50, 53, 329, 353
Shugart, Ken, 34
Shumate, John, 93, 95
Siebert, Sonny, 62
Siegfried, Larry, 66, 68, 320
Siemiontkowski, Hank, 89, 91
Siena College, 40, 50
Sikma, Jack, 101, 219, **220,** 354, 356, **357**
Silas, James, 385

Silas, Paul, 70, 72, 74, 344, 348
Silliman, Mike, 75, 79
Simmons, Connie, 300
Simpson, Ralph, 87
Skaug, Stan, 26
Skoog, Meyer "Whitey," 40
Skurnick, Red, **277**
Skyline Conference, 37, 40, 42, 46, 49, 50, 53, 55,
    58, 60, 66, 68, 70, 72, 112
Slack, Charlie, 50, 55
Sloan, Norm, 129, 141
Slott, George, **9**
Smart, Doug, 64
Smiley, Jack, 25, **25,** 35, 123, 124
Smith, Adrian, 61, 321, 322
Smith, Bill, 89
Smith, Bobby, 86
Smith, Dean, 140, **140,** 262
Smith, Elmore, 219, 220
Smith, Glenn, 49
Smith, Phil, 95
Smith, Randy, 354
Smith, Robert, 101
Smith, "Wee" Willie, 278, **278**
Smith, Willie, 100
Smith College, 6
Smoeick, Mike, 272
Snyder, Dick, 77, 79
Snyder, Paul, 351
Sobek, George, 22
Sobers, Ricky, 98, 229
Sobieszczyk, Ron, 58
Sojourner, Mike, 95
Sojourner, Willie, 85, 87, 89
Solodare, Chuck, 432
Somerset, Willie, 70, 77
Sorenson, Dave, 86, 87
South Alabama, University of, 106
South Atlantic Conference, 95
South Carolina, University of, 60, 87, 89, 91, 93,
    95, 141
Southeastern Conference, 16, 18, 20, 22, 24, 26,
    28, 29, 31, 34, 36, 39, 42, 46, 48, 50, 53, 55,
    58, 60, 62, 63, 66, 68, 70, 73, 74, 77, 78, 81,
    83, 85, 89, 91, 93, 95, 102, 106, 122
Southern California, University of, 20, 26, 37, 42,
    53, 68, 70, 81, 85, 87, 91, 97, 106, 413
Southern Conference, 18, 20, 22, 24, 26, 28, 29,
    31, 34, 37, 40, 42, 47, 48, 50, 53, 55, 58, 60,
    62, 63, 65, 66, 68, 70, 73, 74, 77, 79, 81, 83,
    85, 87, 89, 91, 98, 100, 103, 104
Southern Illinois University, 81, 95, 102, 141
Southern Methodist University, 55, 58, 60, 62, 70,
    77, 79, 81, 89, 91, 95
Southern Oregon College, 141
Southland Conference, 85, 93
South Philadelphia Hebrew Association, 279
Southwest Conference, 16, 18, 20, 22, 24, 26, 27,
    29, 31, 34, 36, 40, 42, 47, 49, 50, 53, 55, 58,
    60, 62, 64, 66, 68, 70, 73, 74, 77, 79, 81, 83,
    85, 87, 89, 91, 95, 100, 102, 104, 106
Southwestern Louisiana, University of, 91, 93, 95,
    104

Sowinski, Frank, 102
Spanarkel, Jim, 104, 106
Spence, Phil, 129
Spivey, Bill, 46
Spoelstra, Art, 49
Springfield (Mass.) Central YMCA team, 6
Springfield College, 3, 20, 134, 435
Sprowl, Forest, 24
Stagg, Amos Alonzo, 6, **6,** 437
Stallworth, Bud, 91
Stallworth, Dave, 73, 74, 77, 333
Stanford University, 15, **17,** 22, 23, 24, 29, 42, 72–73, 97, 114, 120–21, **121,** 134, 141, 408, 435
Stannich, George, 42
Stauffer, Bill, 49
Stein, Hank, 62
Steinmetz, Christian, 439
Steitz, Dr. Edward S., 429, 430
Stephens, Jack, 55
Stephenson, Art, 82
Stewart, Norm, 58
Stith, Tom, 62, 66, 68
Stokes, Maurice, 53, 55, 300, 303, 305, 414–15
  as a top twenty college player, 127–28, **127**
Stone, George, 81, 83
Storen, Mike, 381
Strawder, Joe, 74
Streit, Judge Saul B., 45
Strom, Earl, 408–9, 431
Stroud, John, 106
Stroud, W. D., 70, 73
Studebaker, Gene, **19**
Sullivan Award, 92, 114
Sun Belt Conference, 106
Sunderlage, Don, 46
Sutphin, Al, 281
Swagerty, Keith, 79
Syracuse Nationals, 279, 285, 287, 288, 289, 292, 294, 295, 296, 297–98, 299, 303, 304, 306, 307, 310, 311–12, **313,** 314, 315, 316, 340, 411–12, **432**
Syracuse University, 24, 31, 42, 60, 75, 77, 79, 80, 91, 95, 97, 101, 104, 106
Szukala, Stan, 20

Tallant, Bob, 86
Tannenbaum, Sid, 29, 31, 35
Tarkanian, Jerry, 141
Tart, Leverne, 74
Tatum, Earl, 100
Tatum, Reece "Goose," 424, **424**
Taylor, Brian, 91, 381
Taylor, Charles H., 445
Taylor, Fred, 141
Taylor, Ollie, 87, 378
Teahan, Matt, 106
Tebell, Gus, 116
Temple Junior College, 229
Temple University, 7, 15, **16,** 17, 18, **30,** 43, 46, 58, 60, 62, 74, 81, 85, 87, 91, 106, 125–26, **125,** 141
Tennessee, University of, 22, 24, 26, 29, 64, 75,

77, 81, 83, 86, 91, 100, 102, 141
Tennessee A&I State University, 219
Tennessee Polytechnic Institute (Tennessee Tech), 62, 71
Tennessee State, 95, 106, 139
Terrell, Ira, 95
Terrell, Lee, 48
Texas, University of, 18, 24, 26, 34, 40, 47, 53, 66, 73, 77, 91, 95, 104, 141
Texas A&M, 47, 68, 74, 79, 85, 100, 141
Texas Christian University, 47, 49, 50, 55, 64, 83, 89
Texas-El Paso, *see* Texas Western College
Texas Southern University, 101, 219
Texas Technological College (Texas Tech), 53, 55, 58, 68, 70, 77
Texas Wesleyan College, 79
Texas Western College, 60, 64, 75, 78, **80,** 81, 82, 87, 91
Thacker, Tom, 71
Thigpen, Justus, 85
Thomas, Joe, 87
Thomas, Steve, 74
Thomforde, Chris, 82
Thompson, David "Skywalker," 93, 94–95, **96,** 97, 351, 385, **385,** 401
  as a top twenty college player, 128–29, **128**
Thompson, Gary, 60
Thompson, George "Brute Force," 81, 83, 85
Thompson, John, 71, 75
Thompson, John A., 441
Thompson, Mychal, 101, 104
Thomson, Bobby, 413
Thoren, Skip, 77
Thorn, Rod, 68, 73, 252
Thurmond, Nate, 70, 73, 324, 331, 337, 395
Ticco, Milton, 26
Tillman, James, 106
Tison, Hack, 74
Tobey, David, 429, 440
Todorovich, Marko, 285
Tokyo Olympic Games, 114, 136, 261–62, 263
Tolbert, Ray, 106
Toledo, University of, 17, 22, 23, 25, 35, 42, 44, 47, 53, 58, 81, 91, 106, 141
Toledo (NBL), 279, 287
Tomjanovich, Rudy, 86, 87
Toney, Andrew, 104
Toone, Bernard, 106
Torgoff, Irving, 17
Tormohlen, Gene, 64
Toronto Huskies, 281, 283, 284
Torrence, Walt, 64
Towe, Monte, 95, 128
Tower, Oswald, 429, 436
Towery, Carlisle, 20
Townsend, John, 17
Townsend, Vic, 22
Transylvania College, 141
Trapp, John Q., 87
Travis, Rich, 83
Trenton, N.J., 271
Trenton YMCA, 7, 429

Washington State University, 21–22, 26, 35, 42, 141
Waterloo Hawks, 279, 287, 288, 290
Watson, Leon, 37
Watson, Lou, 42
Watts, Stan, 141
Wayland Baptist College, 228
WCAC, *see* West Coast Athletic Conference (WCAC)
Weber State College, 77, 79, 85, 86, 89, 91, 106
Webster, Elnardo, 83
Webster, Marvin, 97, 354, 355
Weir, Murray, 37
Wells, W. R. Clifford, 435, 448
Werkman, Nick, 71–72, 74
Wesley, Walt, 77, 79
West, Jerry, 62, 63, **65**, 66, 120, 261, 309, 314, **314**, 317, 318, 319, 320, 321, 324, 330, 335, 338, 339, 340, 341, 343, 346, 347, 351, 393, 396, 401
   as a top twenty professional player, 415, **415**
Westbrook, Dexter, 79
West Chester State College, 228
West Coast Athletic Conference (WCAC), 62, 64, 66, 68, 70, 73, 74, 77, 79, 81, 83, 85, 87, 89, 91, 95, 98
Western Athletic Conference, 72, 74, 77, 78, 81, 83, 85, 87, 89, 91, 98, 100, 106
Western Kentucky State College, 20, 23–24, 39, 40, 42, 49, 52–53, 55, 66, 68, 70, 79, 81, 82, 87, 89, 91, 135, 377
Western Michigan University, 26, 34, 49, 71, 100, 141
Western Pennsylvnia League, 271
West Georgia College, 95, 219
Westminster College, 13, 22
Westphal, Paul, 87, 91, 348, 351
West Point, *see* Army (West Point)
West Texas State University, 24, 26, 49, 55, 86·
West Virginia University, 23–24, 26, 29, 31, 34, 36, 40, 47, 48, 55, 58, 60, 62, 63, **65**, 66, 68, 70, 73, 81, 83, 91, 141, 309, 415
Wetzel, John, 79
White, Byron "Whizzer," 15, **16**
White, Eddie, 272
White, Hubie, 70
White, Jo Jo, 79, 83, 86, 262, 340, 344, 348
White, Sherm, 42
Whitemore, Bob, 83
Whitty, John, 272, 275
Wichita State University, 53, 68, 73, 74, 77, 79, 83, 100, 101, 114
Wicks, Sidney, 87, 89, 340
Widby, Ron, 81
Widowitz, Paul, 20
Wiesenhahn, Bob, 68
Wilcutt, D. C., 36
Wilfong, Win, 60
Wilkens, Lenny, 66, 131, 335, 338, 353, 356
Wilkerson, Bobby, 99
Wilkes, Keith, 93, 95, 347
Wilkes-Barre, Pa. (Eastern League), 427
Wilkinson, Dave, 29

Wilkinson, Herb, 27, 32
Wilkinson, Richard "Buzz," 55
William & Mary, College of, 40, 42, 68
Williams, Bernie, 86
Williams, Fly, 93, 95
Williams, Freeman, 100, 101, 104
Williams, Gus, 97, 355–56
Williams, Lee, 435
Williams, Nate, 89
Williams, Ray, 101–2, 230
Williams, Ron, 81, 83
Williams, Sly, 106
Willims College, 7
Williamson, John, 93, 381
Williford, Van, 87
Wilmore, Henry, 89
Wilson, George, 71, **72**
Windis, Tony, 64
Wingate, Marshall, 91
Winter, Tex, 141
Wintermute, Urgel "Slim," 17
Winters, Brian, 95, 349
Winton, Gary, 101, 104
Wisconsin, University of, 21, 24, 26, 34, 37, 42, 49, 83, 97, 141
Wise, Willie, 85, 377
Witte, Luke, 89
Wittenberg University, 141
Wohl, Dave, 87
Wolfe, Andy, 32, 36
Wolfe, Bob, 81
Women, 225–28, 575
   Amateur Athletic Union, 267–68
   books on, 601
   early participation by, 6, 225
   junior colleges, 229
   in Olympic Games, 228, 262, 263
   Title IX, 225, 228
Women's Invitational Basketball Tournament, 229
Wooden, John, **92**, 93, 97, **97**, 111, 131, 430
   general data on, 140, **140**
   in the Hall of Fame, 437, 448
Woolpert, Phil, 140–41, **141**
Workman, Mark, 47, 48
Worsley, Willie, 78
Wright, Lonnie, 77
Wulk, Ned, 141
Wuycik, Dennis, 91
Wynne, Clayton, 26
Wyoming, University of, 22, 24–25, **25**, 31, 32, 34, 40, 42, 48, 49, 50, 58, 64, 77, 81, 85, 401

Xavier AA, 264
Xavier University (Ohio), 36, 62, 74, 141

Yale University, 7, 28, 31, 34, 37, 40, 60, 70, 141
Yancey, Bill, 278, **278**
Yankee Conference, 34, 37, 40, 42, 47, 49, 50, 55, 60, 62, 64, 66, 68, 70, 73, 75, 77, 79, 81, 83, 85, 87, 91, 98
Yardley, George, 42, 264, 304, **304**, 305
Yates, Tony, 71, 77
Yelverton, Charlie, 89

Young, Jewell, 17
Young Men's Christian Association (YMCA), 3,
    6–7, 8, 21, 264, 271, 429
Youngstown (NBL), 279
Yugoslavia, 262, 317
Yunkus, Rich, 87, 89

Zaslofsky, Max, 283, 284–85, 287, 289, 300, 371
Zawoluk, Robert "Zeke," 42, 47, 49
Zimmer, Andy, 24
Zuber, Dallas, 35